AF861759

NEW YORK

SCHOOL LAW

36TH EDITION

Information about the New York State Education Law, Regulations and Decisions of the Commissioner of Education, and Other Laws and Legal Opinions Relating to Education for the Guidance of School Boards and School Administrators in New York State

Copyright © 1945, 1948, 1950, 1952, 1954, 1956, 1958, 1960, 1962, 1964, 1966, 1968, 1970, 1972, 1974, 1976, 1978, 1980, 1982, 1984, 1986, 1988, 1990, 1992, 1994, 1996, 1998, 2000, 2002, 2004, 2006, 2008, 2010, 2012, 2014 by The New York State School Boards Association, Inc., 24 Century Hill Drive, Suite 200, Latham, NY 12110-2125. Thirty-sixth edition, 2016. Revised biennially.

This publication is intended to provide information about general questions pertaining to various statutory and regulatory enactments and administrative and court decisions affecting public schools. It is not intended to provide the answers to specific questions. The answers to the questions are brief and are intended to call attention to the applicable law rather than provide a definitive review. Laws are changed by each session of the New York State Legislature and United States Congress, and interpretive administrative and court decisions are handed down continually. To obtain answers to specific legal questions, seek legal advice from your school board's attorney.

Printed in the United States of America

ISBN 978-1-5221-1061-3 (Print)
ISBN 978-1-5221-1064-4 (Ebook)

Product Number 3070317 (Pub. 30703)

11M-LexisNexis-11/16

Distributed by LexisNexis®

NEW YORK SCHOOL LAW

36TH EDITION

New York State School Boards Association

NEW YORK STATE SCHOOL BOARDS

Executive Staff

Timothy G. Kremer
Executive Director

Jay Worona
Deputy Executive Director and General Counsel

Robert Schneider
Associate Executive Director and Chief Operating Officer

Editors

Pilar Sokol
Deputy General Counsel

Kimberly A. Fanniff
Senior Staff Counsel

Katherine J. Gaffney
Senior Staff Counsel

Contributors

Kimberly A. Fanniff
Senior Staff Counsel

Katherine J. Gaffney
Senior Staff Counsel

Maureen Kentris-Milette
Legal Secretary

Shubh N. McTague
Staff Counsel

Jeffrey Mongelli
Senior Staff Counsel

Pilar Sokol
Deputy General Counsel

CONTENTS

Annual and Special School District Meetings

Fiscal Management

Public School Staff

Employee Constitutional, Leave and Retirement Rights

Employee Contractual Relations

Students

Instruction, Curricula and Student Achievement

Transportation

Public School Facilities

Liability and Litigation

PREFACE

For 71 years and 35 editions, *School Law* has been the key resource for legal background on the day-to-day issues that affect the operation of school districts throughout New York State. What we present here is the 36th edition of *School Law*, updated to reflect changes to laws and regulations that affect public school governance.

Here you will find hundreds of new laws, regulations and case decisions that impact the legal rights and responsibilities of school boards and their staffs. *School Law, 36th Edition* will give school boards a clearer understanding of their policy-making responsibilities and enable school administrators to make informed operational decisions. It also will help school attorneys navigate the intricacies of the practice of school law, and provide insight to those who oversee the state's public education system as well as the general public on the legal requirements affecting school districts.

As with its predecessors, *School Law, 36th Edition* is presented in an easy-to-access question-and-answer format. It is organized under 14 major subjects, with distinct chapters that clearly identify subject matters relevant to all facets of school governance. In addition to the softcover, *School Law, 36th* Edition is available in an e-book format for added convenience.

School Law, 36th Edition draws upon a variety of sources, including New York State law, the rules of the Board of Regents, regulations and decisions of the commissioner of education, opinions of the state comptroller and the attorney general, federal laws and regulations, court decisions from all levels of the judicial system, and relevant guidance materials from state and federal agencies. Woven together, these sources provide a highly-customized bank of materials used to answer questions faced by school boards and others addressing the governance and operation of public schools in New York.

Once again the New York State School Boards Association wishes to acknowledge its continued publishing partnership with LexisNexis, one of the leading publishing houses in the country.

We are confident that you will rely on *School Law, 36th Edition* for answers to your legal questions affecting education and for greater understanding of the public education system in New York State.

Timothy G. Kremer
Executive Director

ACKNOWLEDGEMENT

This handbook was originated in 1945 as an outgrowth of the doctoral thesis of the late William J. Hageny, Distinguished Service Professor Emeritus, State University of New York, College at New Paltz, New Paltz, New York. We have appreciated Dr. Hageny's work on the handbook from its inception through 1988 and his contributions to creating a ready school law reference for school board members, administrators, and attorneys alike. This handbook is an effort to make school law accessible and understandable to all.

Dr. Hageny's past contributions to education include chairman of the Department of Educational Administration and professor of education, State University of New York, College at New Paltz; executive secretary of the Mid-Hudson School Study Council; and member of the Board of Trustees, Ulster County Community College. He served as president of the New York Collegiate Association for the Development of Educational Administration, New York State Association of Secondary School Principals and Council of Administrative Leadership. He also served for many years as the chief school administrator of Haldane Central School, Cold Spring, New York. Dr. Hageny graduated from Hobart College and Syracuse University and received his doctorate from Columbia University.

SCHOOL LAW

General Information

This 36th edition of *School Law* is a compendium of information about New York State school law arranged under 14 major subheadings, with uniquely distinct chapters that more clearly identify the subject matter covered under each, in a question-and-answer format. The questions are numbered according to the chapters in which they appear and their order in those chapters. When question numbers are referred to, they are set in boldface type **(14:5)**.

There are two considerations to remember when using *School Law*. First, all legal references throughout the book are to the New York State Education Law unless noted otherwise in editor's notes or footnotes at the beginning of chapters or sections, or within the questions themselves. Second, when a specific number of days is referred to in a statute or elsewhere in the law, Saturdays, Sundays, and holidays are included when calculating such days unless otherwise stated in specific provisions of the law, or the period of time is two days or less (Gen. Constr. Law § 20) or the period of time specified ends on a Saturday, Sunday, or a public holiday. In such cases, the specified time will occur on the next succeeding business day (Gen. Constr. Law § 25-a).

Abbreviations

The following abbreviations represent sources:

Case Law Citations

United States Supreme Court

U.S.	United States Reports
S.Ct.	Supreme Court Reporter

Federal Courts of Appeals

F., F.2d, F.3d	Federal Reporter
Fed. Appx.	Federal Appendix

Federal District Courts

F.Supp., F. Supp.2d	Federal Supplement

New York State Court of Appeals

N.Y., N.Y.2d, N.Y.3d	New York Reports

New York State Supreme Court, Appellate Division

A.D., A.D.2d, A.D.3d	Appellate Division Reports

New York State Lower Courts

Misc.2d, Misc.3d	New York Miscellaneous Reports

Other Reports

Ed Dept Rep	(State) Education Department Reports
Fair Empl. Prac. Case	(BNA) Fair Employment Practice Cases

FOIL-AO	Freedom of Information Law Advisory Opinions, Committee on Open Government
IDELR	Individuals with Disabilities Education Law Reporter
OML-AO	Open Meetings Law Advisory Opinions, Committee on Open Government
Opn. Att'y Gen.	New York State Attorney General's Opinions
Opn. St. Comp.	State Comptroller's Opinions
PERB	Public Employment Relations Board Official Decisions, Opinions and Related Matters
SRO	State Review Officer Decisions
St. Dep't Rep.	State Department Report
LEXIS	LexisNexis Total Research System

Statutory Citations

Federal

USC	United States Code
Pub. Law	Public Law
CFR	United States Code of Federal Regulations

State

NYCRR	New York Code of Rules and Regulations
8 NYCRR	Regulations of the Commissioner of Education

New York State Law

Arts & Cult. Aff. Law	Arts and Cultural Affairs Law
C.P.L.R.	Civil Practice Law and Rules
Civ. Rights Law	Civil Rights Law
Civ. Serv. Law	Civil Service Law
Corrections Law	Corrections Law
Educ. Law	Education Law
Elec. Law	Election Law
Envtl. Conserv. Law	Environmental Conservation Law
EPTL	Estates, Powers & Trust Law
Exec. Law	Executive Law
Gen. Constr. Law	General Construction Law
Gen. Mun. Law.	General Municipal Law
High. Law	Highway Law
Jud. Law	Judiciary Law
Lab. Law	Labor Law
Local Fin. Law	Local Finance Law
Mil. Law	Military Law
NYS Const.	New York State Constitution
Penal Law	Penal Law
Pub. Auth. Law	Public Authorities Law
Pub. Health Law	Public Health Law
Pub. Off. Law	Public Officers Law

Real. Prop. Law	Real Property Law
Real Prop. Tax Law	Real Property Tax Law
Retire. and Soc. Sec. Law	Retirement and Social Security Law
State Fin. Law	State Finance Law
Tax Law	Tax Law
Unconsol. Laws	Unconsolidated Laws
Veh. and Traf. Law	Vehicle and Traffic Law
Work. Comp. Law	Workers' Compensation Law

INTRODUCTION[1]

A number of significant legal changes have taken place since School Law was last published in 2014. The federal government enacted into law the *Every Student Succeeds Act* (ESSA) marking the first major change in federal education law since the *No Child Left Behind Act of 2001*. Significant changes to the commissioner's regulations will be forthcoming as the state adopts a plan to implement the requirements of ESSA. The state passed the *Education Transformation Act* which lengthened probationary periods for teachers and principals, amended the terms under which tenure may be granted as well as the teacher and principal evaluation system. The law also created school district receivers empowered to govern schools identified as struggling or persistently struggling.

While most of the changes have been incorporated into the main body of this book, some have also been included in the introduction because of their significance, So that information could be included up to the last minute, the introduction also contains changes not incorporated into the main body of this book or included in the index.

This introduction is organized into two main sections: new statutory and regulatory law, including recent statutory changes approved by the state legislature but awaiting action by the governor at press time, and new case law. For the latest update on specific statutes, contact the New York State School Boards Association at 1-800-342-3360.

The information in this introduction is current through September 21, 2016.

New Statutory and Regulatory Law

Not every statute and regulation that has been enacted since the publication of School Law, 35th Edition can be summarized in this section. Only the most significant ones are included here.

State Statutes

BOCES

Chapter 56 Part J of the Laws of 2015 expanded the authority of BOCES to contract with the office of children and family services for the provision of music, art and foreign language programs, in addition to the previously authorized special education and related services and career and technical education services.

Chapter 56 Part Y of the Laws of 2015 added a new provision to the education law that requires the board of trustees of the state university of New York community colleges to consult with BOCES to identify new or existing programs offered to students that would allow a student to pursue an associate of occupational studies (AOS) degree from a community college upon high school graduation.

Chapter 58 Part KK §§ 1, 2 and 4 of the Laws of 2015 expanded the authority of BOCES to contract with the commissioner of mental health for the provision of educational services to individuals in hospitals operated by the office of mental health who are between the ages of 5 and 21 and have not received a high school diploma.

---

1. Throughout this introduction, BOCES refers to boards of cooperative educational services.

Chapter 61 of the Laws of 2016 provided that a vacancy on a BOCES board may be filled by appointment until the next regular election, provided that component boards are given notification of the vacancy and allowed 10 days to provide comments or objections to filling the vacancy by appointment.

Charter Schools

Chapter 20 Part B Subpart A of the Laws of 2015 amended the New York Charter Schools Act to clarify provisions regarding the charter school cap, define the conditions under which new charters will be issued, clarify conditions under which charter schools may operate regarding the number of uncertified teachers and enrollment preferences.

Chapter 73 Part P of the Laws of 2016 provides a window of one year for a charter school to apply to change its chartering entity; all standards and requirements of the charter will remain in effect, only the entity overseeing the charter will change.

Chapter 73 Part P of the Laws of 2016 empowered the State University Trustees Charter School Committee to promulgate regulations with respect to governance, structure and operations of charter schools for which they are the charter entity.

Child Abuse Reporting

Chapter 105 of the Laws of 2016 requires all public and charter schools beginning in January 2017 to post in English and Spanish the toll free number for reporting child abuse and neglect as well as directions for accessing the Office of Children and Family Services website.

Civil Service Exams

Chapter 404 of the Laws of 2015 extended to service members called for training the opportunity to take a make-up examination if they miss the application deadline for a scheduled competitive examination for civil service employment.

Collective Bargaining

Chapter 47 of the Laws of 2015 extended, through June 30, 2017, the availability of an expedited process under the Taylor Law for obtaining injunctive relief in improper practice cases when there is deemed to be immediate and irreparable harm.

Definition of Homeless and Transfer of Disciplinary Records

Chapter 54 Part A § 36 of the Laws of 2016 extended until June 30, 2017 provisions in the education law relating to the definition of homeless and the transfer of student disciplinary records when a student seeks to enroll elsewhere. *Provisions of the Every Student Succeeds Act amended the federal McKinney Vento Homeless Assistance Act but at the time this publication went to press, the State Legislature and the Board of Regents had yet to approve any conforming changes to state law or the commissioner's regulations.*

Educational Standards

Chapter 20 Part B Subpart C § 6 of the Laws of 2015 directed the commissioner of education to conduct a comprehensive review of the education standards administered by the State Education Department with input from education stakeholders by June 30, 2016.

Employment Discrimination

Chapter 365 of the Laws of 2015 amended the Executive Law to prohibit discrimination in employment based on familial status.

Chapter 369 of the Laws of 2015 amended the Executive Law to include in the definition of reasonable accommodation actions taken with respect to not only individuals with a disability, but also those with a pregnancy-related condition.

Chapter 56 Part O of the Laws of 2015 prohibits discrimination on the basis of an actual or perceived disability against healthcare professionals who volunteer to fight Ebola overseas.

Employee Leave

Chapter 56 Part O of the Laws of 2015 requires employers to grant healthcare professionals in their employment a leave of absence to volunteer to fight Ebola overseas.

Chapter 74 of the Laws of 2016 permits employees of the City of New York up to four hours of leave annually for breast cancer screening.

Chapter 54 Part SS of the Laws of 2016 provides for paid family leave benefits but such provisions are optional for municipalities, including school districts (Workers' Comp. Law § 212-a).

Chapter 96 of the Laws of 2016 permits employees of the city of New York to take up to four hours leave on an annual basis for screening for prostate cancer.

Financial Reporting

Chapter 73 Part O of the Laws of 2016 requires the chancellor beginning with the 2017-18 school year to provide the city council and post on the Department of Education's website a detailed statement of the total funding allocation for each community school district at the time of the release of the executive budget of the mayor and at the close of the fiscal year.

Fingerprinting

Chapter 54 Part A § 34 of the Laws of 2016 extended, until July 1, 2017, the ability of school districts and BOCES to make conditional and emergency conditional appointments of staff while awaiting an employee's criminal history report.

Lead Testing

Chapter 296 of the Laws of 2016 requires school districts and BOCES to test any water outlets (faucets, drinking fountains, etc.) for lead contamination, publicly report findings of contamination and ensure a potable water supply is available during any remediation projects.

Lobbying

Chapter 56 Part CC § 6 of the Laws of 2015 amended the Legislative Law to impose new requirements regarding individuals who engage in lobbying activities with school districts.

Lyme Disease and Tick-borne Infection Awareness

Chapter 109 of the Laws of 2016 directed the commissioner of education in conjunction with the commissioners of health and environmental conservation to develop and provide free of charge age appropriate instructional tools and materials for school districts and libraries to assist in education and awareness about Lyme disease and tick-borne infections.

Minimum Wage

Chapter 54 Part K of the Laws of 2016 amended the minimum wage provisions such that the state is divided into three geographic regions which have different hourly rates and scheduled annual increases unless a temporary suspension or delay of scheduled increases is ordered based upon annual economic analyses to be conducted beginning January 1, 2019.

New York City- Mayoral Control

Chapter 73 Part O of the Laws of 2016 extended mayoral control of the city schools in New York through June 30, 2017.

Occupational and Physical Therapy

Chapter 27 of the Laws of 2015 extended for an additional five years the ability of physical therapy assistants to provide services in public and private schools, without direct on-site supervision by a physical therapist.

Chapter 124 of the Laws of 2016 increased the educational requirements for licensed occupational therapists (baccalaureate or master program) and occupational therapy assistants (associate's degree).

Open Meetings Law

Chapter 302 of the Laws of 2016 provides that public bodies, including school districts, may electronically transmit to the media notice of meetings and if a public body live-streams its meeting over the internet to include the web address of the live stream in the public notice of the meeting.

Purchasing

Chapter 62 of the Laws of 2016 provided greater flexibility for schools to make purchases of less than $25,000 from groups of growers and producers consisting of more than 10 farms without applying for permission from the commissioner of education.

Receivership

Chapter 56 of the Laws of 2015 Part EE Subpart H added a new section 211-f to the education law establishing criteria under which schools are designated as struggling or persistently struggling and subject to receivership such that a receiver is given authority to manage and operate all aspects of the school and must develop and implement a school intervention plan.

Retirement Systems

Chapter 94 of the Laws of 2105 amended the Retirement and Social Security Law in relation to the calculation of employer contributions to the New York State and Local Employees Retirement System.

Chapter 479 of the Laws of 2015 amended the methodology for calculating lump sum payments of de minimus service and retirement allowance reductions when a loan is outstanding at the time of retirement.

School Nutrition

Chapter 54 Part A § 46 of the Laws of 2016 directed the commissioner of education to examine the process for determining the number of eligible students in the federal and state free and reduced price lunch programs and to issue a report by October 1. 2016 with recommendations to ensure a more accurate representation of this population for use in such education aid formulae.

School Safety

Chapter 54 Part B of the laws of 2016 mandated additional requirements for district wide school safety plans including but not limited to developing procedures addressing suicide threats by a student, and the designation of a chief emergency officer to ensure annual review of school safety plans is conducted.

Chapter 54 part B of the Laws of 2016 requires school districts to conduct twelve fire and emergency drills, eight of which must be conducted prior to December 31st each year.

School Taxes and Tax Exemptions

Chapter 20 Part A § 18 of the Laws of 2015 extended, through June 15, 2020, the tax levy cap law applicable to school district budgets and other municipalities.

Chapter 20 Part A Subpart C of the Laws of 2015 directed the commissioner of taxation and finance to, as appropriate, promulgate rules and regulations that may provide for adjustments to the calculation of capital local expenditures excluded from the tax levy cap and have that calculation reflect a school district's share of additional budgeted capital expenditures made by a BOCES.

Chapter 20 Part A Subpart C of the Laws of 2015 directed the commissioner of taxation and finance to, as appropriate, promulgate rules and regulations regarding the calculation of the quantity change factor to have that calculation reflect development on tax exempt land.

Chapter 20 Part A Subpart H of the Laws of 2015 made available money for municipal corporations and school districts that have suffered a reduction in tax collections and receipts from payments in lieu of taxes of at least 20% due to a fossil fuel electric generating facility located within their boundaries permanently ceasing operations, or an adverse judicial determination (tax certiorari proceeding) regarding such a facility.

Chapters 60 and 73 of the Laws of 2016 transitioned the School Tax Relief (STAR) program from a state-funded exemption to a personal income tax credit (STAR credit) such that new applicants who qualify for the STAR credit or the enhanced STAR credit will be able to claim a credit equal to the lesser of STAR tax (or enhanced STAR tax) savings applicable to the taxpayer's primary residence or the taxpayer's qualifying taxes.

Chapters 60 and 73 of the Laws of 2016 provided if taxpayers previously received the basic STAR exemption on their home and now meet the requirements for the enhanced STAR exemption may apply for the exemption rather than the credit.

Chapter 59 Part E of the Laws of 2015 and Chapter 60 Part JJ of the Laws of 2016 permits the State to recoup overpayments from taxpayers improperly granted the STAR exemption.

Chapter 60 Part F of the Laws of 2016 provided that a taxpayer who in error was not afforded the benefit of a STAR exemption in the calculation of taxes owed will be entitled to a refund of such overpayment remitted directly by the State.

Chapter 253 of the Laws of 2016 amended Real Property Tax Law § 458-b to allow school districts to adopt a resolution granting an exemption from real property taxes to veterans of the cold war.

Special Education

Chapter 35 of the Laws of 2015 extended, through June 30, 2018, the various provisions of the Education Law which serve to ensure compliance with the federal Individuals with Disabilities Education Act in relation to the provision of special education and related services to children with disabilities eligible for such services under that federal law.

Chapter 76 of the Laws of 2016 extends until June 30, 2018 the ability of multidisciplinary evaluation programs to employ a certified school psychologist to conduct a multi-disciplinary evaluation of a preschool child that has or is suspected of having a disability.

State Aid

Chapter 54 Part A § 6 of the Laws of 2016 permanently eliminated the gap elimination adjustment.

Chapter 54 Part A § 8 of the Laws of 2016 requires 225 school districts across the state that have been identified as having a struggling or persistently struggling school or otherwise as high-need to set aside a portion of a district's foundation aid to be used to support the establishment of community schools.

Chapter 54 Part B of the Laws of 2016 allows a school district that was in session for less than the required 180 days to excuse up to 5 days if the school was not in session due to a credible threat to student safety as reasonably determined by a lead school official.

Chapters 53 and 73 Part L of the laws of 2016 delayed the deadline for approved annual professional performance review plans that comply with the requirements of Education Law § 3012-d to December 31, 2016. Districts that have plans approved by December 31 will not lose their increase in state aid.

Chapter 58 Part BB of the Laws of 2016 provided that the urban development corporation may distribute up to $30,000,000, dependent upon availability of funds, to local governmental entities, including school districts, affected by the closing of an electric generating facility located within the local governmental unit on or after June 25, 2015.

Student Health

Chapter 469 of the Laws of 2015 enacted provisions to better coordinate efforts between the Department of Public Health and the State Education Department regarding strategies for curtailing asthma and other respiratory diseases, collection and analysis of information regarding childhood obesity and the establishment of school-based childhood obesity prevention and physical activity programs.

Chapter 401 of the Laws of 2015 amended the Public Health Law to add meningococcal disease to the list of school vaccination requirements.

Chapter 57 Part V of the Laws of 2015 amended various sections of the Public Health Law and added a new section to the Education Law to permit school districts and BOCES, among others, to provide and maintain on-site in each instructional facility opioid antagonists for use during emergencies where a student or staff member is suspected of having an opioid overdose, whether or not there is a previous history of opioid abuse.

Student Testing

Chapter 20 Part B Subpart C § 1 of the Laws of 2015 directed the commissioner of education to annually release test questions, answers and corresponding correct answer from the most recently administered ELA and math exams in grades 3-8 and report on the general student success rate in answering such questions correctly.

Chapter 20 Part B Subpart C § 4 of the Laws of 2015 directed the commissioner of education effective December 1, 2015, to establish a content review committee charged with reviewing all standardized test items and/or selected passages use on ELA and math state assessments for grades 3 – 8.

Chapter 20 Part B Subpart C § 4 of the Laws of 2015 amended the Education Law by adding a new provision, effective December 1, 2015, that prohibits teachers, principals and superintendents from being required to sign a confidentiality agreement with their respective school district, BOCES or the State Education Department (SED) that would prevent them from discussing the contents of any items on the ELA and math assessments in grades 3 – 8 after they have been released by SED or publicly disclosed by SED or other appropriate entity.

Chapter 20 Part B Subpart C § 5 of the Laws of 2015 required that any prior SED contracts related to standardized test items and/or passages for use on state assessments in grades 3 – 8 be amended to incorporate the ban on confidentiality agreements that prevent educators from discussing the contents of such items after their release/disclosure.

Surplus Computer Equipment

Chapter 79 of the laws of 2016 extended until July 1, 2019 the ability of municipalities to donate surplus computer equipment to school districts, libraries and other not-for-profit organizations.

Teacher and Principal Continuing Education

Chapter 20 Part B Subpart C § 2 of the Laws of 2015 amended the Education Law to impose new continuing education requirements of at least 100 hours every five years on holders of a professional certificate in the classroom teacher service, a level III teaching assistant certificate, or a professional certificate in the educational leadership service.

Teacher Discipline

Chapter 56 Part EE Subpart G of the Laws of 2015 amended sections 3020 and 3020-a of the Education Law and added a new section 3020-b regarding procedures for the discipline and termination of tenured teachers and administrators.

Teacher and Principal Evaluation

Chapter 20 Part B and Subpart C § 3 and Chapter 56 Part EE Subpart E of the Laws of 2015 added a new section 3012-d to the education law which establishes a new system of evaluation for teachers and principals.

Teacher and Principal Registration

Chapter 20 Part EE Subpart C § 1 of the Laws of 2015 required that holders of a teaching certificate in the classroom teaching service, a teaching assistant certificate or an educational leadership certificate that is valid for life, register with SED every five years commencing with the 2016-17 school year.

Teacher Tenure

Chapter 56, Part EE subpart D of the Laws of 2015 amended the education law to lengthen the probationary period for teachers and administrators appointed on or after July 1, 2015, imposed new requirements to qualify for a shortened probationary period for teacher, and changed the circumstances under which tenure may be granted.

Transportation

Chapter 49 of the Laws of 2015 extended, through June 30, 2020, the authority of the commissioner of education to continue to conduct regional transportation pilots.

Whistleblower Protection

Chapter 585 of the Laws of 2015 removed the current requirement that a public employee whistleblower make a good faith effort to first disclose information to his/her supervisor of an alleged violation of law or improper government activity.

State Statutory Changes Awaiting Action by the Governor

Autism Spectrum Disorders Advisory Board

Assembly bill 10558-A would create the Autism Spectrum Disorders Advisory Board to study and review the effectiveness of supports and services currently being provided for individuals with autism spectrum disorders and make recommendations for improvement.

Charitable Gaming

Senate bill 4413 would amend the general municipal law to allow persons age 16 and over to assist in the conduct of charitable bingo games.

Early Childhood Advisory Council

Assembly bill 9902-A would codify into statute the Early Childhood Advisory Council which assesses statewide need for child care and early childhood programs, identifies barriers to accessing such programs and makes recommendations to promote a high quality early childhood education system as well as developing and implementing strategies to engage business and civic leaders in early learning and planning and advocacy.

Emergency Anaphylaxis Treatment

Senate bill 6800 would define epinephrine auto-injector device, amend requirements related to procurement and storage of such devices and requires that a person, other than a health care practitioner, complete a recognized training course prior to administering an epinephrine auto-injector device, unless the devices is used under the direction of a health care practitioner.

Energy Efficiency

Assembly bill 5991-A would create the *School Energy Efficiency Collaborative Act of 2016* to promote the efficient implementation of public school energy projects in order to reduce the funds school districts must divert away from educational programs in order to pay ever rising utility costs.

Financial Reporting

Senate bill 5795-A would require the property tax report card to include a schedule of reserve funds and a brief explanation of any plans for their use, mandate a school board resolution to pay or transfer any monies into any reserve funds and require posting to the district website the annual external audit and any corrective action plan developed as result of such audit, any final audit report of the state comptroller as well as the final annual budget and any multi-year financial plan adopted by the board.

Freedom of Information Law

Senate bill 6865-A would expedite appeals of judicial decisions rendered regarding FOIL; an appeal will be deemed abandoned if the agency (including a school district) fails to serve and file a record and brief within 60 days after the date of service upon the other party of the notice of appeal unless the parties consent to further extension or the court orders an extension.

Health Insurance

Assembly bill 9715 would prohibit the president of the state civil service commission from implementing a rule, regulation or policy memo that limits the ability of employers who participate in the NYS Health Insurance Plan (NYSHIP) from entering into collective bargaining agreements or establishing a practice for a health insurance buy-out program if an employee's spouse is also enrolled in NYSHIP.

Senate bill 2448-A would require retirees of school districts and other municipalities to be given 90 days' written notice of any proposed change to their health insurance coverage and access to a secure website with detailed information about the coverage change.

Physical and Health Education

Senate bill 3344-B would impose new requirements for school districts to report their compliance with physical education instruction established by law and regulation with the results to be used by the commissioner of education to prepare a report by July 1, 2017 for the governor and legislature analyzing the data and recommending steps to take to ensure all schools are in compliance with physical education requirements.

Assembly bill 3387-B would require health education programs to include a component regarding mental health and the "relation of physical and mental health so as to enhance student understanding, attitudes and behaviors that promote human dignity" beginning July 1, 2018.

Public Work Contracts

Senate bill 6906 would require any contract for construction, reconstruction, demolition, alteration, repair or maintenance to contain a provision which provides that a contractor's failure to give notice under the contract within prescribed time periods shall not invalidate any claims for payment by the contractor unless the failure to provide timely notice has materially prejudiced the public owner (including a school district).

Registered Sex Offenders

Assembly bill 1819-A would require a registered sex offender to notify the Division of Criminal Justices Services if he or she maintains more than one residence.

Assembly bill 9239 would require the Division of Criminal Justice Services to notify local law enforcement within 48 hours upon receipt of a change of address from a registered sex offender.

Retirement Benefits

Senate bill 7386-A would eliminate certain restrictions regarding transfer between retirement systems such as the one year time limit for members to give notice of their intent to transfer between systems and the requirement that an employee serve at least three years in the second retirement system in order to collect the better benefit between the two systems.

Student Employment

Senate bill 6701-B would include performances by children in a not-for-profit community theater in the list of exemptions from the requirements relating to employment, use or exhibition of minors for the purpose of performing arts if certain conditions are met.

Transportation, Bus, Bus Maintenance and Portable Classroom Contracts

Assembly bill 8019-C would link allowable increases for the extension of a transportation contract above the limit defined in law to the Employment Cost Index (ECI) rather than the Consumer Price Index (CPI) and would also authorize extensions of contracts for school buses, bus maintenance, and mobile instruction units to include an increase based upon the ECI.

Assembly bill 8019-C would require transportation contracts for students in pre K-12 in New York City to include employee protection provisions that give preference in hiring of school bus workers who are laid off or furloughed due to a contract being awarded to another employer.

Tax Collection

Senate bill 4737 would permit a school district located within a town to collect its own school taxes upon notice to the town's receiver of taxes by February 1 each year.

Tax Exemptions

Assembly bill 8019-C would also exempt the purchase by private contractors of school buses, parts, equipment, lubricants and fuel used in the operation of such school buses from sales tax.

Senate bill 4842-A would expand the definition of "veteran" eligible for the alternative veteran's exemption to include those veterans who served on active duty during the postal strike of 1970 (later designated "Operation Graphic Hand" by the Department of Defense).

Amendments to Federal Regulations

Fair Labor Standards Act- Overtime Rule

The U.S. Department of Labor issued a final rule updating the overtime provisions of the Fair Labor Standards Act by raising the salary level white collar and highly compensated employees must earn in order to be considered exempt from overtime provisions.

The Board of Regents and State Regulations

Academic Intervention Services

The Board of Regents approved changes to commissioner's regulations that create a two-step identification process to be used in 2016-17 school year to determine whether to furnish academic intervention services to students in grades 3-8 and also establishes standards for the 2017-18 school year and thereafter (8 NYCRR § 100.2(ee)).

Continuing Teacher and Leader Education and Registration

The Board of Regents approved changes to commissioner's regulations establishing continuing education requirements, a timeline for registration of educators, and provisions for registration renewal including conditional registration for those who do not complete required continuing education in a timely fashion (8 NYCRR Subpart 80-6). Professional development requirements under § 80-3.6 are discontinued as of the 2016-17 school year.

Coaches

The Board of Regents approved changes to commissioner's regulations to require that individuals holding, or applying for, a temporary or a professional coaching certificate complete two hours of coursework or training for identifying and reporting child abuse and maltreatment (8 NYCRR §§ 57-.1, 135.4 and 135.7).

CPR and AED Instruction

The Board of Regents approved changes to commissioner's regulations regarding instruction in cardiopulmonary resuscitation (CPR) and the use of automated external defibrillators (AED) (8 NYCRR § 100.2(c)).

The Board of Regents approved changes to commissioner's regulations to excuse a student with a disability that physically or cognitively renders the student unable to perform the tasks required for CPR instruction and use of automated external defibrillators from such instruction as provided in the student's IEP or accommodation plan (8 NYCRR § 100.2(c)(11)(iv)).

English Language Learner's (ELL) Placement

The Board of Regents approved changes to commissioner's regulations to provide parents of ELL students 10, rather than five, school days to sign and return a statement that they either are in agreement with their child's placement in a bilingual education program, or want their child placed in an English as a New Language program, instead (8 NYCRR § 154-2.3(f)(3)).

The Board of Regents approved changes to commissioner's regulation to clarify the units of study mandated for and credits given to all ELL students for Integrated English as a New Language instruction and ELL students in Bilingual Education programs for English as a New Language and bilingual core content area instruction (8 NYCRR § 154-2.3(h)).

Graduation Requirements

The Board of Regents approved changes to the commissioner's regulations allowing English language learner (ELL) students who first enter the United States in grade 9 or above to obtain a local diploma via the appeal process if they fail to obtain a score of 65 or above on the required Regents English exam after two attempts, but are otherwise eligible to graduate in January 2015 or thereafter (8 NYCRR § 100.5(d)(7)).

The Board of Regents approved the "4 + 1" pathway to graduation which allows students who first enter grade 9 in September 2011 and thereafter or are otherwise eligible to receive a diploma in June 2015 and thereafter to meet diploma requirements by passing assessments in English, math, science and social studies and an additional fifth assessment from a designated list (8 NYCRR §§ 100.2(f), (mm) and 100.5).

The Board of Regents approved the career development and occupational studies (CDOS) pathway to graduation which allows students who first entered grade 9 in September 2012 or thereafter to meet diploma requirements by completing course requirements, the requirements for the NYS career development and occupational studies commencement credential and passing assessments in English, math, science and social studies (8 NYCRR § 100.5(d)(11)).

The Board of Regents approved changes to the commissioner's regulations establishing criteria for the approval of work-readiness assessments for earning the CDOS commencement credential (8 NYCRR § 100.6(b)(4)).

The Board of Regents approved changes to commissioner's regulations beginning June 2016 and thereafter allowing all students (not just those with a disability) to earn the career development and occupational studies commencement credential (8 NYCRR § 100.6(b)).

The Board of Regents approved changes to commissioner's regulations to allow students who entered grade 9 prior to 2013 to, in the district's discretion, meet the English requirement for graduation by passing either the Regents Comprehensive Examination in English (2005 standards) or the Regents Examination in English Language Arts (Common Core) at the January 2016 and June 2016 examination administrations (8 NYCRR § 100.5(g)(1)(i)).

The Board of Regents approved changes to commissioner's regulations allowing students who began instruction in a mathematics course aligned with common core learning standards in or after September 2013 to, in the district's discretion, take the Regents examination in algebra2/trigonometry (2005 standards) in addition to the Regents examination in algebra II (common core) and may meet the requirement for graduation by passing either examination (8 NYCRR § 100.5(g)(1)(ii)).

The Board of Regents approved changes to commissioner's regulations delaying implementation of the requirement that students pass the Regents examination in global history and geography II until the class of students first entering grade 9 in September 2017. In the interim, at the district's discretion, students may meet the requirement for graduation by taking and passing either the Regents examination in global history and geography I or global history and geography II (1750 to present) during the June 2019, August 2019, January 2020 and June 2020 administration of these assessments (8 NYCRR § 100.5(a)(5)).

The Board of Regents approved changes to commissioner's regulations implementing changes to the appeals process for examination scores by removing attendance requirements and allowing an appeal if a student scored within 5 points of the 65 passing score. Disabled students, eligible to graduate in January 2016 or thereafter may file an appeal on up to 2 examinations if they fail to attain a score of 55 provided specified conditions are met (8 NYCRR § 100.5(d)(7)).

The Board of Regents approved a new local diploma option pursuant to a superintendent determination for disabled students with an IEP who achieve a minimum score of 55 on the English and math Regents examination but who, because of their disability, fail to demonstrate proficiency even with testing accommodations, on one or more of the other three Regents examinations required for graduation. The superintendent and school principal must review whether in the subject areas where the student did not achieve a passing score on the required assessment if the student has otherwise demonstrated graduation level proficiency in the subject area (8 NYCRR § 100.5(d)(12)).

The Board of Regents approved changes to commissioner's regulations clarifying at what age and under what circumstances individuals will be entitled to a high school equivalency diploma, the instruction that must be provided in school alternative preparation programs and expanded the right to attend a school district or BOCES alternative high school equivalency preparation program through age 21. Effective September 1, 2016 students may receive an equivalency diploma if they have successfully completed the National External Diploma Program (8 NYCRR § 100.7).

Lead Testing

The Commissioner of Health adopted regulations governing the lead testing program required by Chapter 296 of the Laws of 2016. The regulations set out procedures to properly draw water samples, set a deadline for samples to be taken and tested, and provided for notification to the public, the state departments of health and education and local health departments. The regulations empowered employees of the state and local departments of health to enter schools with reasonable notice to ensure compliance with the law and to assess civil penalties for non-compliance (10 NYCRR Part 67-4).

Professional Development

The Board of Regents approved changes to various provisions of the commissioner's regulations to clarify that for any professional development period beginning on July 1, 2015, a minimum of 15% of the required professional development clock hours must be dedicated to language acquisition addressing the needs of English language learners (8 NYCRR §§ 80-3.6, 100.2(dd), 154-2.3(k)).

School Accountability

The Board of Regents approved changes to commissioner's regulations to align New York's ESEA Accountability System with the latest flexibility waiver approved by the federal government, and clarified elements of the registration review of public schools under New York's ESEA accountability system (8 NYCRR § 100.18). *The New York State Education Department is currently working on creating a state accountability plan in conformance with the Every Student Succeeds Act.*

School Receivership

The Board of Regents approved changes to commissioner's regulations clarifying that the calculation of timelines as relates to the appointment of independent receivers, submission of local stakeholder consultation plan, notice of abolition of teaching positions and collective bargaining requirements must utilize calendar days (8 NYCRR § 100.19).

The Board of Regents approved changes to commissioner's regulations establishing the process by which struggling and persistently struggling schools may apply for community school grants (8 NYCRR § 100.19(k)).

School Safety

The Board of Regents approved changes to the commissioner's regulations to require the district wide school safety plan address suicide threats by students, staff training on emergency response plans, and to designate a chief emergency officer to ensure the annual review of plans is conducted, among other items (8 NYCRR § 155.17).

Seal of Biliteracy

The Board of Regents approved the process by which a school district may set up a Seal of Biliteracy Committee and apply for program approval to be able to award the seal to qualified students (8 NYCRR § 100.5(h)).

Special Education

The Board of Regents approved changes to the commissioner's regulations to provide that, starting with the 2015-16 school year, special education itinerant services (SEIS) for preschool children with disabilities ages 3-4 will be reimbursed based on the actual attendance of children receiving SEIS services rather than on the basis of enrollment in such services (8 NYCRR § 200.9(ix)).

The Board of Regents approved changes to commissioner's regulations requiring Committees on Special Education (CSE) and Committees on Preschool Special Education (CPSE) to consider specific management needs of a child prior to assignment of a one-to-one aide such as the specific supports (e.g. hygiene) an aide could provide, extent or circumstances the student would need assistance of aide and the extent a one-to-one aide might enable a student to be educated with non-disabled peers (8 NYCRR § 200.4(d)(3)).

The Board of Regents approved changes to commissioner's regulations to require that a Committee on Preschool Special Education's recommendation, included in a student's IEP, identify the site setting where services would be delivered; specify frequency, intensity, duration and location of direct special education itinerant services (SEIS); and, for students attending a regular early childhood program, specify if any services, as well as the frequency, duration and location for provision of indirect SEIS (8 NYCRR § 200.16(i)(3)(ii)(a)).

The Board of Regents approved changes to commissioner's regulations requiring preschool approved programs employ appropriately qualified directors, adopt curricula aligned with state learning standards, including evidence based practices to support emotional-social competence and policies for the prompt make-up of missed services. Additionally, the regulations prohibit the suspension, expulsion or removal of a preschool child from a special education program/services because of behavior until the appropriate transfer of the child can be arranged by the CPSE. The regulations also require programs to conduct progress monitoring of student achievement data and to provide regular reports of students' progress to the students' parents and to CPSEs (8 NYCRR § 200.20(b)).

The Board of Regents approved changes to the commissioner's regulations providing clarification regarding the subject matter jurisdiction of the State Review Officer and revising procedural requirements during appeals of impartial hearing officer determinations for students with disabilities (8 NYCRR Part 279).

Student Enrollment

The Board of Regents approved changes to the commissioner's regulations establishing new rules applicable to student residency and age determinations (8 NYCRR § 100.2(y)).

Student Health and Safety

The Board of Regents approved changes to commissioner's regulations establishing the terms and conditions under which a school district may stock epinephrine auto-injectors and administer them in emergency situations in accordance with provisions of the Public Health Law (8 NYCRR § 136.6)).

The Board of Regents approved changes to commissioner's regulations to require that school districts and BOCES permit students diagnosed with asthma or other respiratory conditions, allergies and diabetes to carry and self-administer medications during the school day on school property and at any school function (8 NYCRR § 136.7).

The Board of Regents approved changes to commissioner's regulations to permit, among others, school districts and BOCES and any person employed by them to administer an opioid antagonist in an emergency situation, in accordance with the requirements of Public Health Law § 3309(3) (8 NYCRR § 136.8).

The Department of Social Services approved changes requiring school districts to provide access to records relevant to a child abuse investigation and to allow Child Protective Service (CPS) employees to conduct an interview of such child without parental consent or court order when CPS encounters circumstances that warrant interviewing the child apart from family or other household members or the home or household where child abuse or maltreatment allegedly occurred (18 NYCRR § 432.3(i)).

Teacher and Principal Certification

The Board of Regents approved changes to commissioner's regulations to extend for up to one year the time validity of an expired initial or transitional certificate, or a conditional initial certificate, for teachers who take one of the revised content specialty (CST) exams on or after September 2014 and do not receive a score on such exam within the timeframe prescribed by the commissioner (8 NYCRR § 80-1.6).

The Board of Regents approved amendments to various provisions of the Rules of the Board of Regents and commissioner's regulations defining the practice of the profession of applied behavior analysis (ABA), and establishing licensure requirements for behavior analysts and certification requirements for behavior analyst assistants (8 NYCRR §§ 29.2, 59.14, 52-44, 51.45 and Subparts 79-17 and 79-18).

The Board of Regents approved amendments to various sections of the commissioner's regulations extending safety nets related to the administration of the State's new teacher certification assessments (8 NYCRR §§ 52.21, 80-1.5, 80-3.3, 80-3.4, 80-5.13).

The Board of Regents approved changes to commissioner's regulations regarding endorsement requirements for out of state certificates for service as a teacher, school district leader, school district business leader and school building leader. The Board of Regents also created an endorsement pathway for school building leaders seeking to obtain an initial certificate in New York (8 NYCRR §§ 80-5.8 and 80-5.20).

The Board of Regents approved changes to commissioner's regulations establishing new pathway options for the Transitional A certificate in Career and Technical Education subjects for candidates who possess industry experience, credentials or are in the process of completing certification and for candidates who hold licenses to teach in licensed private career schools with at least two years teaching experience (8 NYCRR § 80-3.5).

Teacher Citizenship

The Board of Regents approved changes to commissioner's regulations establishing that an otherwise qualified candidate cannot be denied a certificate or registration under Part 80 by reason of his or her citizenship or immigration status. Applicants will not be entitled to a license or certificate if they are ineligible pursuant to applicable federal laws or are unlawfully present in the U.S. A specific provision relative to teachers allows non-citizens to qualify for a permit or other authorization to teach in public schools in New York in accordance with specific provisions of the education law (8 NYCRR § 80-1.3).

Teacher and Principal Evaluation (APPR)

The Board of Regents approved changes to commissioner's regulations implementing the provisions of the new teacher and principal evaluation law codified at section 3012-d of the Education Law and enacted as part of the Education Transformation Act of 2015 (8 NYCRR Subparts 30-2 and 30-3 and 8 NYCRR § 100.2(o)(i)(ii)).

The Board of Regents approved changes to the commissioner's regulations establishing a transition period from the 2015-16 school year through the 2018-19 school year with respect to calculation of Annual Professional Performance Review (APPR) scores such that state provided growth scores will continue to be calculated but only for advisory purposes and the transition composite score will be used for tenure determinations, and to determine if a teacher or principal improvement plan is required (8 NYCRR §§ 30-2.14, 30-3.17).

The Board of Regents approved changes to commissioner's regulations that clarify the measures that may be used in the student performance category of a teacher's or principal's evaluation, and the methodology by which subcomponent and overall scores must be calculated in the teacher observation and principal school visit categories (8 NYCRR §§ 30-3.4, 30-3.5). Observations must be conducted pursuant to a state approved rubric aligned with either the NYS teaching standards (teachers) or ISLLC standards (principals) and the scores for observations must incorporate all evidence collected and observed over the course of the year (e.g. information learned in pre and post observation conferences).

The Board of Regents approved changes to commissioner's regulations setting out guidelines under which a teacher or principal may challenge a state provided growth score and delineating the effect a successful appeal with have on how the employee's score is recalculated while the state examines the growth model (8 NYCRR §§ 30-2.13, 30-3.16).

The Board of Regents approved changes to commissioner's regulations whereby rural school districts and other districts that meet certain requirements may be granted a hardship waiver to excuse the use of an independent evaluator for a second observation (8 NYCRR § 30-3.4(d)(2)(i)(b)).

Teacher Preparation

The Board of Regents approved changes to commissioner's regulations establishing minimum admission standards for graduate level teacher and leader preparation programs and requirements for the suspension and/or deregistration of certain programs with completers who fail to achieve a minimum pass rate on certification examinations for three consecutive years (8 NYCRR § 52.21).

Teacher and Principal Probationary Appointments

The Board of Regents approved changes to commissioner's regulations regarding the content of school board resolutions making probationary appointments (8 NYCRR § 30-1.3).

Tenured Teacher/Administrator Disciplinary Hearings

The Board of Regents approved changes to commissioner's regulations adding a new Subpart 82-3 to implement changes to Education Law § 3020-a and the addition of a new section 3020-b enacted into law by the Education Transformation Act of 2015 (8 NYCRR Subpart 82-3).

Substitute Teachers

The Board of Regents approved changes to commissioner's regulations providing that uncertified substitute teachers may work beyond the 40-day limit for an additional 50 days if the superintendent or district superintendent certifies that a recruitment search has been conducted and there are no available certified teachers to fill the position. An extension beyond the 90 days may be granted in limited circumstances (8 NYCRR § 80-5.4).

New Case Law

Administrative Tenure Areas

The commissioner of education invalidated the excessing of two administrators that a school district failed to appropriately notify or gain the consent of prior to awarding them tenure in the "elementary assistant principal" area when their initial appointments were to the broader tenure area of "assistant principal." The commissioner ordered the school district to re-calculate their seniority in the "assistant principal" tenure area and determine if the employees should be restored to employment with back pay and benefits (*Appeal of Alexander and Gonzales*, 54 Ed Dept Rep, Dec. No. 16,731 (2015)).

Bumping Rights

The Appellate Division, Third Department, determined an employee who resigned her tenured English position to serve as a library media specialist (LMS) was nonetheless entitled to exercise bumping rights when her LMS position was abolished because she did not take affirmative steps to terminate all aspects of her employment. According to the court, her receipt of a longevity payment and carry over of sick and personal leave from her prior position meant she did not waive her tenure and seniority rights (*Matter of Kwasnik v. King*, 123 A.D.3d 1234 (3d Dep't 2014), *lv. to appeal dismissed*, 25 N.Y.3d 981 (2015)).

Elections

The commissioner of education invalidated and ordered a new election be held after determining the inspectors failed to count a write-in vote that was written in the incorrect place on the ballot, thus resulting in a tie vote. According to the commissioner, since the intent of the voter was discernable the vote should be counted (*Appeal of Reed*, 55 Ed Dept Rep, Dec. No. 16,871 (2016)).

The commissioner of education refused to invalidate a school bond vote, despite the district's failure to supply enough ballots. Although the insufficient number of ballots created long lines and inconvenience for voters while additional ballots were procured; the delays did not vitiate the fundamental fairness of the election (*Appeal of Ghezzi*, 55 Ed Dept Rep, Dec. No. 16,890 (2016)).

Employment Discrimination

The U.S. Court of Appeals for the Second Circuit reinstated an African-American teacher's employment discrimination claim based upon his principal's racial bias tainting the promotion process and resulting in the teacher not being recommended for tenure by the superintendent (*Tolbert v. Smith*, 790 F.3d 427 (2d Cir. 2015)).

New York's Court of Appeals determined it was not arbitrary and capricious for the New York City Department of Education to deny employment clearance to a school bus driver convicted of drug offenses more than twenty years previously due to the mature age of the petitioner at the time of conviction and the Department's regulation mandating special consideration when drug offenses are being evaluated. The court further found the petitioner's certificate of relief from disabilities did not create a "prima facie entitlement to the license or employment sought" (*Dempsey v. N.Y. City Dep't of Educ.*, 25 N.Y.3d 291 (2015)).

The U.S. Court of Appeals for the Second Circuit determined an employee's termination was not the result of associational discrimination under the Americans with Disability Act because she was terminated for taking too much leave to care for the medical needs of her diabetic child, rather than on the basis of distraction or inattention while at work due to her relationship with a disabled person. While she could not proceed with her ADA claims, the court found the petitioner could proceed with a retaliation claim under the Family and Medical Leave Act (*Graziadio v. Culinary Institute of America*, 817 F.3d 415 (2d Cir. 2016)).

The U.S. Court of Appeals for the Second Circuit ruled a school district violated the notice requirements under the Family and Medical Leave Act because it failed to notify a teacher who took unpaid maternity leave how such leave would impact her reinstatement rights. Under the district's policies employees accrue additional seniority only during paid leave and the employee was entitled to notice of that prior to commencing her leave (*DeOliveira v. Cairo-Durham CSD*, 634 Fed. Appx. 320 (2d Cir. 2016)).

The U.S. Court of Appeals for the Second Circuit concluded that the decision to withhold or reduce a discretionary bonus may qualify as an adverse employment action because it would be impermissible to allocate the bonus on the basis of prohibited discrimination (*Davis v. N.Y. City Dep't of Educ.*, 804 F.3d 231 (2d Cir. 2015)).

Health Insurance Buy-out

The Appellate Division, Third Department ruled that a memorandum issued by the Department of Civil Service that limited circumstances pursuant to which an employee of a participating agency may decline coverage in the New York State Health Insurance Plan in exchange for a cash payment constituted a new formal rule that must be filed with the Department of State and thus was invalid (*Plainview-Old Bethpage Congress of Teachers v. N.Y. State Health Insurance Plan*, 140 A.D.3d 1329 (3d Dep't 2016)).

Immunization

The U.S. Court of Appeals for the Second Circuit upheld the constitutionality of the State's mandatory vaccination requirements and the right of school officials to temporarily exclude exempt students from school during outbreaks of vaccine preventable diseases finding the law does not violate the right to free exercise of religion (*Phillips v. City of New York,* 775 F.3d 538 (2d Cir. 2015)).

The commissioner of education upheld a school district's refusal to grant a medical exemption from immunization because the medical certification failed to identify an appropriate contraindication to vaccination as it only listed a familial reaction to vaccine administration and nothing specific to the student. A familial reaction alone is not reason to grant a medical exemption (*Appeal of J.S. and D.S.*, 55 Ed Dept Rep, Dec. No. 16,821 (2015)).

The commissioner of education granted a religious exemption from immunization that was limited in scope to the MMR vaccine based on the petitioner's showing the vaccine was derived from the cells of aborted fetuses which conflicted with her religious belief that abortion is a sin (*Appeal of N.C.*, 55 Ed Dept Rep, Dec. No. 16,805 (2015)).

Property Tax Cap

The Appellate Division, Third Department, upheld the State's property tax levy cap finding it did not violate any federal or state constitutional provisions (*New York State United Teachers v. State of N.Y.*, 140 A.D.3d 90 (3d Dep't 2016)).

Tax *Certiorari*

The Court of Appeals has ruled that a tax *certiorari* petition that has been dismissed for failure to mail the notice to the superintendent may not be revived through proceedings commenced under the civil practice laws and rules (*Westchester Joint Waterworks v. Assessor of the City of Rye*, 27 N.Y.3d 566 (2016)).

The New York State Court of Appeals determined multiple tax *certiorari* petitions are not necessary when a taxpayer is challenging the calculation of a multiyear partial tax exemption under Real Property Tax Law § 485-b given the exemption is calculated from a single assessment roll (*Highbridge Broadway LLC v. Assessor of the City of Schenectady*, 27 N.Y.3d 450 (2016)).

Recall Rights

The Appellate Division, Second Department, determined re-employment rights cannot attach unless a teacher possesses the requisite certification thus rejecting a Spanish teacher's claim of entitlement to recall for a position split between Spanish and French because the teacher was not certified in French (*Regini v. Bd. of Educ. of Bronxville CSD*, 128 A.D.3d 1073 (2d Dep't 2015)).

Seniority Credit

The Appellate Division, Third Department, ruled that a teacher was entitled to seniority credit in the English tenure area despite teaching only computer applications classes during her 11 years of employment, because the out of tenure area assignment was made without her prior written consent (*Matter of Cronk v. King*, 130 A.D.3d 1415 (3d Dep't 2015)).

Sex Offenders

The New York Court of Appeals ruled that the State intended to pre-empt local municipalities from exercising police power to adopt residency restrictions aimed at sex offenders as the adoption of local residency restrictions encroaches upon the State's authority and hinders statewide uniformity concerning sex offender placement (*People v. Diack*, 24 N.Y.3d (2015)).

Students with Disabilities

The U.S. Court of Appeals for the Second Circuit determined a school district's dismissal of a parents' request to address bullying of their child impeded their right to participate in the development of their child's individualized education plan (IEP), potentially affected the substance of the IEP and prevented the parents from "meaningfully" evaluating the sufficiency of the student's IEP, in violation of the Individuals with Disabilities Education Act (*T.K. & S.K. v. N.Y. City Dep't of Educ.*, 810 F.3d 869 (2d Cir. 2016)).

Taylor Law

The Public Employment Relations Board determined a school district did not engage in retaliatory activity by bringing disciplinary charges against four teachers who engaged in disruptive picketing activities including parking cars to block student drop off areas and leafletting in a distracting fashion at the end of the school driveway (*East Meadow Teachers' Association v. East Meadow UFSD*, 48 PERB ¶ 3006 (2015)).

Teacher Discipline

The Appellate Division, First Department upheld the termination of an uncertified tenured teacher without a hearing pursuant to the procedures of Education Law § 3020-a reasoning his employment was terminated for "failing to maintain minimum qualifications, and not for disciplinary reasons" (*Koutros v. Dep't of Educ. of the City of N.Y.*, 129 A.D.3d 434 (1st Dep't 2015)).

Unemployment Benefits

The Appellate Division, Fourth Department ruled that a teacher suspended pursuant to a § 3020-a proceeding had committed disqualifying misconduct that would preclude the receipt of unemployment benefits and remitted the case to the Unemployment Insurance Appeals Board for further consideration. The teacher was found guilty of making sarcastic comments to students, sending unprofessional email to staff and parents and violated district procedures regarding the treatment of students, parents and fellow employees *(In Re Brown*, 133 A.D.3d 1146 (3d Dep't 2015)).

1. Public Education – Governance Framework

In General

1:1. What is the University of the State of New York?

The University of the State of New York consists of all public and private elementary and secondary schools in the state; all privately and publicly controlled institutions of higher education, including the schools in the State University of New York (SUNY) system; and all libraries, museums, and other educational and cultural institutions admitted to or incorporated by the University (§ 214). It is vested with broad regulatory powers and is governed by the Board of Regents. Its primary purpose is to encourage and promote education (§§ 201, 202; see also *Moore v. Bd. of Regents*, 44 N.Y.2d 593 (1978)).

The University of the State of New York should not be confused with SUNY, which was established in 1948 (§ 352). SUNY consists of 34 state-operated and statutory campuses and 30 community colleges. It is governed by an 18-member board of trustees: 15 of whom are appointed by the governor with the advice and consent of the senate, one of whom shall be the president of the student assembly of the state university ex-officio and voting, one of whom shall be the president of the university faculty senate, ex-officio and nonvoting, and one of whom shall be the president of the faculty council of community colleges, ex-officio and nonvoting (§ 353(1)). The board of trustees appoints a chancellor who heads SUNY (§ 353(3); see also Exec. Law § 169).

1:2. What is the general framework of New York State's public education system?

The general framework of New York State's public education system consists of several levels of authority and resembles a pyramid. The base is the federal government. Its authority resides in the U.S. Constitution, federal laws and regulations, and federal court decisions. The next level, the state, relies on the New York Constitution, state laws and regulations, including the rules of the state Board of Regents, regulations and decisions of the commissioner of education, and state court decisions.

Legal authority for and jurisdiction of school boards are at the top of the pyramid. As local entities, school boards have the narrowest band of authority and may set policy only in areas in which their jurisdiction is not superseded by federal or state authority.

1:3. What is the role of the federal government regarding the operation of school districts in New York State?

The Tenth Amendment to the U.S. Constitution leaves the function of education to the individual states by providing that "[t]he powers not delegated to the United States by the Constitution, nor prohibited by it to the States, are reserved to the States respectively, or to the people."

However, as a condition for the receipt of federal monies, states must agree to comply with federal statutes that place certain responsibilities on states and local school districts. For example, under the federal Individuals with Disabilities Education Act, districts have certain duties with regard to providing education to students with disabilities (20 USC § 1400 *et seq.*). Another example is the Every Student Succeeds Act, which constitutes the 2015 reauthorization of the Elementary and Secondary Education Act

(Pub. L. No. 114-95, 129 Stat. 1802 (2015)), which, among other things, imposes testing and accountability requirements. Federal regulations established by federal agencies also stand as the law of the land unless challenged and overturned by federal courts, or changed or overruled by the particular agency.

1:4. What is the role of the state government regarding the operation of school districts in New York State?

The basis for a free public education in New York State is contained in article 11, section 1, of the state constitution, which declares that the Legislature "shall provide for the maintenance and support of a system of free common schools, wherein all the children of this state may be educated." Article 11 provides the legal authority given to the Board of Regents and to the Legislature to provide for the maintenance and support of public schools.

Both the governor and the Legislature propose and enact numerous statutes that affect education at the state level. The following statutes in the Education Law specify the authority of the state's school boards:

- Section 1604, for trustees of common school districts.
- Section 1709, for union free school board members.
- Section 1804, for central school district boards.
- Section 1950, for boards of cooperative educational services (BOCES).
- Articles 51, 52, and 52-A, for city school district boards.

In addition, the state delegates powers to school districts as it does to municipalities. School districts are considered political subdivisions of the state government (*Burlaka v. Greece CSD*, 167 Misc.2d 281 (Sup. Ct. Monroe Cnty. 1996); *Koch v. Webster CSD*, 112 Misc.2d 10 (Sup. Ct. Monroe Cnty. 1981)).

Through the enactment of Article 56 of the Education Law, the state also provides for charter schools that operate as autonomous public schools independent of existing school districts. For further discussion on charter schools, see **chapter 3**.

1:5. What are the roles of the New York State Board of Regents and the State Education Department regarding the operation of school districts?

The New York State Board of Regents and the NYS Education Department exercise the powers and functions delegated to them through the Education Law. They also establish policy by adopting rules and regulations within the limitations of state law (see **1:6-10**). These regulations have the authority of law unless they are overruled by decisions of the state's courts or the Legislature, or until they are superseded by the promulgating agency (§§ 101, 101(a), 207; see also *Bd. of Educ. of Northport-East Northport UFSD v. Ambach*, 90 A.D.2d 227 (3d Dep't), *aff'd*, 60 N.Y.2d 748 (1982), *cert. denied*, 465 U.S. 1101 (1984); *Van Allen v. McCleary*, 27 Misc.2d 81 (Sup. Ct. Nassau Cnty. 1961)).

In addition, all public elementary, middle, and secondary schools, other than charter schools, must be registered by the Board of Regents, and all are deemed to be admitted to the University of the State of New York (8 NYCRR § 3.32).

The New York State Board of Regents

1:6. What is the New York State Board of Regents?

The New York State Board of Regents is the governing body of the University of the State of New York. It was established by the state Legislature in 1784 and is the oldest continuous state educational agency in the United States.

The Regents exercise legislative functions over the state educational system, determine its educational policies and, except as related to the judicial functions of the commissioner of education, establish rules for carrying out the state's laws and policies relating to education and the functions, powers, duties, and trusts granted to or authorized by the University of the State of New York and the NYS Education Department (§ 207).

1:7. What is the composition of the Board of Regents?

There are 17 members of the Board of Regents. Each is elected to a five-year term by a concurrent resolution of both houses of the state Legislature. One Regent is selected from each of the state's 13 judicial districts, and four Regents are chosen from the state at large (§ 202). There are no ex-officio Regents; that is, members of the Regents do not serve simply by virtue of their holding an elected or appointed position (*Id.*).

A Regent's term of office expires April 1. The Legislature's concurrent resolution electing a Regent must be adopted on or before the first Tuesday of the preceding March. Absent adoption of a concurrent resolution, both houses of the state Legislature must meet in a joint session on the second Tuesday in March to select a Regent by joint ballot (*Id.*).

1:8. What are the Board of Regents' powers and duties?

The Board of Regents have broad authority over all the state's educational institutions (*Moore v. Bd. of Regents*, 44 N.Y.2d 593 (1978)). For example, they appoint the commissioner of education, who becomes the president of the University of the State of New York (§ 302; 8 NYCRR § 3).

In the performance of these functions, the Regents are empowered to charter, register, visit, examine into, and inspect any school or institution under the educational supervision of the state (§§ 215, 216, 2851(3)(c), 2853(1)(c), (2), (2-a)), to license practitioners in over 50 major professions (§ 6504), and to certify teachers and librarians (§§ 3004, 3006).

The Regents meet monthly (except in August), usually in Albany. They serve without compensation, but are reimbursed for travel and other expenses. They elect their own chancellor and vice chancellor (§ 203).

The New York State Education Department

1:9. What is the NYS Education Department?

The NYS Education Department (SED), under the direction of the commissioner of education, is the administrative arm of the University of the State of New York. It is charged with carrying out legislative mandates and the Regents' policies (§§ 101, 207, 305). The principal functions of SED are carried out within seven major areas:

- Office of P-12 Education;
- Office of Performance Improvement and Management Services;
- Office of Cultural Education;
- Office of Higher Education;
- Office of Adult Career and Continuing Education Services;
- Officc of Counsel; and,
- Office the Professions.

For more information about SED and its offices, contact SED at 518-474-3852, or via its general website at: http://www.nysed.gov.

1:10. What is the function of the NYS Education Department?

The NYS Education Department (SED) is charged with the general management and supervision of all public schools and all the education work of the state (§ 101), from prekindergarten to graduate school, and is responsible for setting educational policy, standards and rules. SED also supervises the state's nonpublic schools, oversees the over 50 licensed professions, provides vocational and educational services to people with disabilities, guides local government records programs, and operates the State Archives, Library and Museum (see generally NYS Education Department at: www.nysed.gov/about).

The Commissioner of Education

1:11. Who is the commissioner of education?

The commissioner of education is the chief executive officer of the Board of Regents and the NYS Education Department (§§ 101, 301, 305(1); 8 NYCRR § 3.7; see **1:6-8, 1:9-10**).

1:12. What are the commissioner of education's powers and duties?

The commissioner of education's powers and duties are contained primarily in section 305 of the Education Law. They include, for example, enforcement of laws relating to the educational system, execution of all educational policies determined by the Board of Regents, issuance of regulations, general supervision of all schools and institutions subject to the provisions of the Education Law, the granting, revocation, and annulment of teaching and administrative certificates, approval of school transportation and cafeteria contracts, review of appeals and petitions pursuant to section 310, removal of school officers and withholding of state aid pursuant to section 306, and execution of such other powers and duties as determined by the Board of Regents.

1:13. What are the commissioner's regulations?

The commissioner's regulations are rules that govern how the schools, institutions, and other entities under the jurisdiction of the commissioner of education are to be operated. They have the effect of law on the schools of the state unless the courts overturn them. The NYS Department of State officially compiles and publishes commissioner's regulations, which can be found in Title VIII of the Official Compilation of Codes, Rules, and Regulations of the State of New York (8 NYCRR). They include, among other things, certification requirements for teachers, curriculum requirements, mandates on the building of schools, and standards for the various professions.

1:14. Can a school district apply for a waiver from regulation?

Yes. A school district can apply for a waiver from any regulatory mandate issued by the commissioner of education or other state agencies, provided the intent of the mandate can be achieved in a more cost-effective manner. State agencies have broad power to exempt a school district from regulatory mandates that would not compromise environmental quality, health, or safety concerns, or reduce any employee rights or benefits or violate a collective bargaining agreement (State Administrative Procedure Act § 204-a).

1:15. How is an appeal brought to the commissioner of education?

Any person believing himself or herself to be aggrieved by an official act of any officer or school authority, or by any action taken at a meeting concerning any matter under the Education Law or pertaining to the schools of the state, may appeal to the commissioner of education (§ 310). For example, that person must be aggrieved in the sense that he or she has suffered personal damage or injury to his or her rights (*Appeal of The Sea Cliff-North Shore Prop. Owners Comm.*, 54 Ed Dept Rep, Dec. No. 16,730 (2015); *Appeal of Lagrange*, 51 Ed Dept Rep, Dec. No. 16,315 (2011); *Appeal of Goldin*, 43 Ed Dept Rep 330 (2004)). However, the Education Law does not authorize an appeal to the commissioner from actions taken by members of the staff of the NYS Education Department (SED) (*Appeal of Assoc. for Bilingual Child Development, Inc.*, 51 Ed Dept Rep, Dec. No. 16,366 (2012); *Appeal of N.Y. Inst. of Massage, Inc.*, 45 Ed Dept Rep 495 (2006); *Appeal of Karpen*, 40 Ed Dept Rep 199 (2000)). Such actions can only be challenged in court in an Article 78 proceeding (*Appeal of N.Y. Inst. of Massage, Inc.*).

The commissioner has issued regulations that set forth the procedures to be followed in such appeals (8 NYCRR Parts 275, 276 and 277). For example, all appeals to the commissioner must be brought within 30 days after the decision or act complained of, or from the time knowledge of the cause of the complaint came to the person appealing the decision or act. However, the commissioner, in his or her sole discretion, may excuse a failure to commence an appeal in a timely manner for good cause (8 NYCRR § 275.16). The party against whom an appeal is filed and served must answer the appeal within 20 days of service (8 NYCRR § 275.13).

Additional procedures applicable to appeals involving homeless children and youth are found at 8 NYCRR § 100.2(x).

All applicable regulatory procedures, general instructions, and sample forms, along with a series of questions and answers to help guide individuals who are not represented by an attorney but may wish to file an appeal with the commissioner, are available from SED's Office of Counsel at: http://www.counsel.nysed.gov/appeals.

1:16. Are there any limitations on the commissioner of education's ability to review an appeal?

Yes. The commissioner of education will not determine moot or advisory questions but will determine only actual matters in controversy (*Appeal of The Sea Cliff-North Shore Prop. Owners Comm.*, 54 Ed Dept Rep, Dec. No. 16,730 (2015); *Appeal of Wait*, 51 Ed Dept Rep, Dec. No. 16,353 (2012); *Appeal of D'Orazio and Carey,* 41 Ed Dept Rep 292 (2002)).

The commissioner will not decide the constitutionality of a statute. Similarly, the commissioner will not resolve "novel questions of constitutional law" in an administrative appeal (*Appeal of W.Z. and A.Z.*, 55 Ed Dept Rep, Dec. No. 16,793 (2015); *Appeal of Murphy,* 54 Ed Dept Rep, Dec. No. 16,765 (2015); *Appeal of R.C. and D.C.*, 54 Ed Dept Rep, Dec. No. 16,674 (2014)).

In addition, the commissioner has no jurisdiction to review violations of the Open Meetings Law (*Appeal of Jaidan Indust. Inc.,* 55 Ed Dept Rep, Dec. No. 16,856 (2015); *Appeal of Ament*, 51 Ed Dept Rep, Dec. No. 16,350 (2012); *Appeal of Schumann*, 47 Ed Dept Rep 249 (2007)), the Freedom of Information Law (*Appeal of Jones,* 55 Ed Dept Rep, Dec. No. 16,823 (2015); *Appeal of Ament*; *Appeal of Razzano*, 39 Ed Dept Rep 303 (1999)), the Family Educational Rights and Privacy Act (*Appeal of a Student with a Disability,* 55 Ed Dept Rep, Dec. No. 16,814 (2015); *Appeal of Kosack*, 53 Ed Dept Rep, Dec. No. 16,611 (2014)) and Section 504 of the Rehabilitation Act of 1973 (*Appeal of the Bd. of Educ. of the City Sch. Dist. of the City of Rye,* 53 Ed Dept Rep, Dec. No. 16,513 (2013); *Appeal of a Student with a Disability*, 51 Ed Dept Rep, Dec. No. 16,258 (2011)).

Furthermore, the commissioner will not substitute his or her judgment for that of a board or school official in any decision, absent a showing that the decision is arbitrary, capricious, or contrary to law or the dictates of sound educational policy (*Appeal of Chan and Grogan*, 41 Ed Dept Rep 178 (2001)).

Once an appeal has been decided, it will not be reopened by the commissioner unless it is established that there is new and material evidence that was not available at the time of the original proceedings or that the original decision was rendered under a misapprehension of the facts (8 NYCRR § 276.8; *Application to Reopen Appeal of Fuller,* 55 Ed Dept Rep, Dec. No. 16,891 (2016); *Application to Reopen Appeal of Thomas*, 51 Ed Dept Rep, Dec. No. 16,322 (2011)).

1:17. Are the commissioner of education's decisions reviewable by the courts?

Yes. The actions of the commissioner of education are subject to court review, the same as those of other state officials. The commissioner's decisions are subject to review in the courts by means of a proceeding under Article 78 of the Civil Practice Law and Rules.

The commissioner's decisions are published in Education Department Reports (Ed Dept Rep). Ordinarily they can be found in any county courthouse law library, or they can be obtained by writing directly to the NYS Library Education Center, 310 Madison Ave., Albany, NY 12230, 518-474-5355. Currently, decisions from 1991 to the present are available through the website of the NYS Education Department's Office of Counsel at: http://www.counsel.nysed.gov. Starting with volume 50 of the Education Department Reports, decisions dated from July 2009 forward are only available online.

Public School Districts

Editor's Note: For additional information about school districts, see NYS Education Department, Guide to the Reorganization of School Districts in New York State *available at: http://www.p12.nysed.gov/mgtserv/sch_dist_org/.*

1:18. What is a common school district?

A *common school district* is a school district first created by legislative action in 1812 to operate elementary schools (kindergarten through eighth grade). Even though they lack legal authority to operate a high school, common school districts remain responsible for ensuring a secondary education for their resident children.

A common school district is administered by either a sole trustee or a school board of three trustees (§ 1602(1)). The number of members of the board of trustees of a common school district may be increased or decreased as set forth in law (§ 1602; see **5:6-8**).

1:19. What is a union free school district?

A *union free school district* is a school district generally formed from one or more common school districts to operate a high school program, which common school districts cannot do. First authorized by legislation in 1853, union free school districts are administered by a school board of between three and nine members. The number of board members of a union free school district may be increased or decreased as set forth in law (§§ 1702, 1703; see **5:6-8**).

Currently, not all union free school districts operate a secondary school program, and some have been established solely as special act school districts to serve children who reside in specified childcare institutions (see **1:23**).

1:20. What is a central school district?

A *central school district* is a school district formed by combining any number of common, union free, and central school districts. First established in 1914, the central school district is the most common form of district organization in the state. Like union free districts, central school districts may operate a high school. Their school boards may consist of five, seven, or nine members (§ 1804(1)). The number of board members may be increased or decreased as set forth in law (§ 1804(3); see **5:6-8**).

1:21. What is a central high school district?

A *central high school district* is a school district that provides only secondary education to children from two or more common or union free school districts. Only three such districts exist in the state, and the Legislature has prohibited the formation of additional such districts, except in Suffolk County.

A central high school district's governing board is composed of representatives from each of its participating districts. The number of members of such board shall be not less than five. A central high school district is part of a supervisory district (§§ 1912-1914; see § 1950(2-a)(b)).

1:22. What is a city school district?

A *city school district* is a school district whose school boundary lines are identical to that of a city. There are two types of city school districts: those with a population under 125,000 and those with a population of 125,000 or more (§§ 2501, 2550). The enlargement of a city school district by the addition of one or more union free, common, or central school districts contiguous to the city school district results in an *enlarged city school district* (§ 1526; see also **2:4**).

Article 51 of the Education Law applies to city school districts with less than 125,000 inhabitants. Their governing boards may consist of five, seven, or nine members (§ 2502(2)).

Article 52 of the Education Law applies to cities with populations of 125,000 or more. There are five in New York State, commonly referred to as the Big 5 school districts: Buffalo, New York City, Rochester, Syracuse, and Yonkers. Rochester and Syracuse have seven-member boards, chosen by the voters at either a general or municipal election (§§ 2552, 2553(2)). Yonkers has a nine-member school board, each member appointed by the mayor (§§ 2552, 2553(3)). Buffalo has a nine-member school board: one member elected by the qualified voters in each of the city's six school subdistricts, and three members elected in a city-wide, at-large election by the qualified voters (§ 2553(10)(c)).

In New York City, which is also governed by Article 52-A of the Education Law, a city-wide Panel for Educational Policy has 13 members (§ 2590-b(1)(a)). Five of them are appointed by the city's borough presidents, and eight are appointed by the city's mayor, including the chancellor, who serves as an ex-officio, non-voting member of the board (§§ 2590-b(1)(a), 2590-h). The city board elects its own chairperson from among its voting members (§ 2590-b(1)(a)).

In addition, New York City has 32 community district education councils, each composed of 11 voting members and one non-voting member (§ 2590-c(1)). Nine of the voting members are parents of children attending a public school within the district who are selected by the presidents and officers of the parents' association or parent-teacher association. They serve for a term of two years (§ 2590-c(1)(a)).

Two of the 11 voting members are appointed by the borough presidents corresponding to such district. They must be residents of, or own or operate a business within the district and have extensive business, trade, or education experience and knowledge. Such members serve for two years and may be reappointed but only for one additional two-year term (§ 2590-c(1)(b)). The non-voting member is a high school senior appointed by the superintendent from among the elected student leadership (§ 2590-c(1)(c)). The community district education councils are responsible for prekindergarten, nursery, kindergarten, elementary, intermediate, junior high schools, and related community district programs within the community district (§ 2590-e).

This statutory framework for the governance of the New York City school district is scheduled to expire on June 30, 2017.

1:23. What is a special act school district?

A *special act school district* is one of those districts created by a special act of the Legislature and enumerated in Chapter 566 of the Laws of 1967, as amended (§ 4001(8); 8 NYCRR § 105.1(d)). These districts have been established on the grounds of charitable institutions caring for children and youth and serve students who, for unique reasons, cannot be served in a traditional public school system.

They are designated by the state Legislature as public school districts authorized to receive state financial aid. Section 3602 of the Education Law outlines the details on apportionment of state aid for such districts.

Special act school districts have their own school board. The commissioner of education appoints two public members to each of these boards upon the recommendation of a regional interview team for a four year term. If a board member vacates his or her office during their term, the commissioner may appoint an eligible person for the remaining balance of the term or for a full term (L. 2004, c. 628; L. 2004, c. 629; 8 NYCRR Part 105).

School boards of special act school districts seeking to close their school district must follow the procedures specified in law (§§ 4403(21), 4405(4)(j)).

1:24. What is a board of cooperative educational services?

A *board of cooperative educational services* (BOCES) is a voluntary, cooperative association of school districts in a geographic area that have banded together to provide educational or business services more economically than each district could offer by itself. Each BOCES is governed by a board of between five and 15 members elected by the component school boards (Article 40). See **chapter 7** for more detailed information.

1:25. Who determines the official name of a school district?

The Education Law provides that school districts, other than city school districts, adopt simplified legal names subject to the approval of the commissioner of education (§ 315).

The commissioner's centralization order designates the name of a centralized school district (§ 1801(2); 8 NYCRR Part 240). However, the name of a central school district established or reorganized by such an order may be changed by the district's school board if a written request is filed with the commissioner at least 14 days before the establishment or reorganization of the district (§ 315; see **2:2** for more information on centralization).

The NYS Education Department shall issue, on request, certificates certifying the name of a school district and the names of the towns and counties in which the territory of the district is located, or in the case of school districts other than city school districts, which are wholly or partly located within a city, the names of the city, as well as the towns and counties in which the territory of the district is located (§ 315).

2. School District Reorganization

Mergers and Dissolution

2:1. What is school district reorganization?

School district reorganization is the term used to define the statutory processes by which two or more school districts are merged into a single district or a school district is dissolved. The various methods of school district reorganization include centralization, annexation, consolidation, and dissolution, each of which has a different purpose and implication. Each reorganization procedure is limited in its application to one or more of the organizational types of school districts: for example, union free, central, common, and city school districts (see **1:18-22**).

2:2. What is centralization?

Centralization is the most common form of reorganization. A new central school district is created by the merger of two or more contiguous districts, with a new school board and boundaries that encompass the area of the districts being reorganized (see **2:10**). Under the Education Law, city school districts are not eligible for centralization (§§ 1801(2), 1804(1)).

2:3. What is annexation?

Annexation is a reorganization procedure whereby any school district, other than a city school district, is dissolved and its territory annexed to a contiguous central school district (§ 1802(2); see **2:11**) or to a union free school district (§ 1705; see **2:12**). The dissolution of the annexed district is a part of the annexation process, different from the dissolution of a school district ordered by the district superintendent (§ 1505; see **2:5**, **2:15**).

Unlike in centralization, annexation does not result in the creation of a new district, nor is a new school board elected. The operation of the annexing school district remains basically the same before and after the annexation. Residents of the annexed district become eligible to vote and may be elected to the school board of the annexing district in subsequent elections (see § 1705).

2:4. What is consolidation?

Consolidation is a reorganization procedure that may involve the merger of any combination of common or union free school districts to form a new common or union free school district (§ 1510; see **2:13**). Central and city school districts may not participate in the consolidation of union free and/or common school districts.

However, consolidation may also involve the incorporation into a city school district of districts contiguous to city school districts of cities with populations of less than 125,000 residents. The resulting school district becomes known as an enlarged city school district (§§ 1524, 1526; see **1:22**, **2:14**). Similar to annexation, the district to be consolidated will cease to exist.

2:5. What is dissolution?

Dissolution is a seldom-used form of reorganization in which a district superintendent (see **10:1**), by order, dissolves one or more school districts within his or her supervisory district and forms a new district from such territory. Alternatively, the district superintendent may dissolve a district and unite the territory with an adjoining district or districts, other than a city school district (§ 1505(1)).

A district superintendent may also partition existing union free, central, central high school and enlarged city school districts, dissolve and reform the district if necessary, and form a new union free or city school district out of such territory upon certain specified conditions set forth in the Education Law section 2218 (see **11:23**).

This dissolution process is different than the dissolution of a district being annexed to another (see **2:3, 2:11-12**).

2:6. What is the Master Plan and its impact on school district reorganization?

The Master Plan, codified in 1972 in section 314 of the Education Law under the name State Plan, is an administrative and statutory effort intended to advance school district reorganization so as to provide education facilities in the most efficient and economical manner, while also serving the best interests of children. The plan was originally adopted by the NYS Education Department (SED) in 1947 and was designed to encourage consolidation, annexation, and centralization in order to improve the functioning of public schools. The result was massive reorganization of districts, a reduction in the number of school districts in the state, and the creation of larger districts.

The plan is available on the SED's website at: http://www.p12.nysed.gov/mgtserv/sch_dist_org/docs/Master_Plan_For_School_District_Reorganization_Volume1.pdf.

2:7. Is there a legal procedure whereby a school district can be broken up and divided into two or more smaller districts?

Yes. An example of this was the creation of community school districts in New York City, which was accomplished by a change in the Education Law that required enactment of a specific law by the state Legislature (see Art. 52–A).

The Education Law also allows district superintendents (see **10:1**) to partition off, dissolve, and reform and form a new union free school district from certain existing districts and under certain specified conditions (§ 2218; see **11:23**). However, the district superintendent has no such authority regarding city school districts and enlarged city school districts (*Appeal of Town of New Windsor*, 45 Ed Dept Rep 539 (2006)).

2:8. What is the role of the commissioner of education in school district reorganizations?

While the commissioner of education is not authorized to compel a reorganization of school districts without voter approval (§§ 1705(1)(a), 1801(4)), the commissioner does play a pivotal role in school district reorganization. This role includes, but is not limited to, preliminary activities conducted prior to voter consideration of district reorganization (§§ 314(2), (3), 1705(1)(b), 1801(1), (2), (3)).

In most circumstances, the process of district reorganization begins with an order issued by the commissioner. For example, the commissioner issues an order laying out the new district boundaries for a centralized school district (§ 1801). The order laying out the new school district does not constitute the establishment of a new district, but is a proposal made by the commissioner upon which the residents of the new proposed district will vote.

In an annexation, the commissioner issues an order dissolving one or more common, union free, or central school districts and annexing the territory of such district(s), or portion thereof, to one or more adjoining central or union free school districts, subject to the approval of the voters of each affected district (§§ 1705(1)(a), 1801(2)).

Furthermore, only the commissioner has authority regarding the reorganization of city school districts and enlarged city school districts (see **11:23, 2:14**), and the removal of any portion of such a district to form it into a new district or for any purpose (*Appeal of Town of New Windsor*, 45 Ed Dept Rep 539 (2006); see **11:23, 2:14**).

Although the commissioner has the statutory authority to independently issue orders concerning reorganization, the practice has been that the commissioner will not issue these orders until an adequate feasibility study has been conducted and indicates that the proposal is desirable, that the people in the district have been informed of the potential reorganization, and that there is evidence that the majority of the voters in the affected district or districts support the proposal.

Reorganization Procedures

2:9. Are there any preliminary steps school districts must take before they can reorganize?

Generally, the first step toward reorganization includes joint meetings between the affected school boards to gain information and to determine whether reorganization offers sufficient benefits to warrant formal study.

If the boards agree that reorganization might be beneficial, they then typically undertake a joint *feasibility study*, also known as an efficiency study, which is a written report commissioned by a school district considering reorganization. Its purpose is to describe how a specific combination of districts may operate if reorganization were to be implemented. The commissioner of education has ruled that the authority to order a feasibility study rests solely with the school board; district voters may not compel the board to conduct such a study (*Appeal of Leman*, 32 Ed Dept Rep 579 (1993); see also NYS Education Department, *Guide to the Reorganization of School Districts in New York State* (updated May 2015), at: http://www.p12.nysed.gov/mgtserv/sch_dist_org/GuideToReorganizationOfSchoolDistricts.htm).

A feasibility study should include:

- Current and projected student enrollments;
- Current and projected professional staffing plans;
- Current and projected housing plans;
- A plan for educational programs and curricula in the proposed district;
- A plan for transportation in the proposed district; and
- Fiscal implications of the reorganization, including changes in state aid, expenditures, and local tax effort.

Once the study has been conducted, the affected boards inform their residents of the potential reorganization and assess the public's support for the proposed reorganization. The established practice is that the commissioner will not take formal action to authorize a reorganization unless there is evidence of support in each of the districts included in the proposed reorganization. Public support may be assessed through the use of petitions or advisory referendums (straw votes) (*Guide to the Reorganization of School Districts in New York State*).

Providing residents of the affected districts accurate information and an opportunity to address significant fiscal issues prior to a referendum regarding the potential reorganization is essential. Failure to provide such information and opportunity constitutes an irregularity that would require setting aside the referendum vote (*Appeal of Wolverton*, 46 Ed Dept Rep 208 (2007)). That was the case where residents of one district in an annexation reorganization (see **2:3**) did not learn of a nearly $1 million deficit in the other district until after the reorganization vote (*Appeal of Wolverton*).

School districts proposing to reorganize through consolidation, annexation, or centralization may consider minimizing the impact on school tax rates by deferring the impact for one-year and/or phased in over 10 years subject to the conditions set out in law. For example, all school districts involved would have to adopt a resolution opting for a common phase-in period after a public hearing, conducted before the reorganization vote (§ 3613).

2:10. What are the procedures involved in centralization?

After an adequate study is performed indicating that the proposed centralization is desirable and that a majority of the voters in the affected districts support it (see **2:9**), the commissioner of education may then issue an order laying out the territory of the new central school district (§ 1801(1), (2)). The order constitutes only a proposal (§ 1801(4)).

Within 10 days of making and entering the order of consolidation, the commissioner shall transmit a certified copy to the clerk of each affected district. Within five days of receipt, the clerk of each affected district must post a certified copy of the commissioner's order in five conspicuous places within each district (§ 1801(3)).

At this point, a petition requesting the commissioner to call a special meeting may then be filed. The petition must be signed by at least 100 voters or by the number of voters equal to at least 10 percent of the student population of the combined districts, whichever is less (§ 1802(1)). The commissioner may then call a special meeting to allow the qualified voters in the affected districts to determine whether or not the new district will be created (§§ 1801(4), 1802(1)(b); see also **2:16**).

The Education Law authorizes two types of special meetings: one in which either the votes of all districts are combined, or an alternative procedure in which the votes of each district are separately tabulated to determine if voter approval exists (§§ 1803, 1803-a).

After the voters approve the creation of the new district, the commissioner will call a special meeting for the election of a new school board. Voters may approve the number of board members to be elected (five, seven, or nine), and their terms of office (three, four, or five years), either at the same time they approve the reorganization or at a separate meeting before the election (see NYS Education Department, *Guide to the Reorganization of School Districts in New York State* (updated May 2015), at: http://www.p12.nysed.gov/mgtserv/sch_dist_org/GuideToReorganizationOfSchoolDistricts.htm).

2:11. What are the procedures involved in annexation to a central school district?

After an adequate study is performed indicating that the proposed annexation is desirable and that a majority of the voters in the affected districts support it (see **2:9**), the commissioner of education may issue an order annexing an existing school district to a contiguous central school district. Within five days of receiving a certified copy of the commissioner's order, the clerk of each affected district must post a certified copy of the commissioner's order in five conspicuous places within each district (§ 1801(3)). The order becomes effective in 60 days (§ 1802(2)).

However, the voters of any school district affected by the proposed annexation to a central school district may, within 60 days after the filing of the commissioner's annexation order, submit a petition requesting a referendum, signed by at least 100 qualified voters or by a number of voters equal to at least 10 percent of the student population in the district per the last census, whichever is less (§ 1802(2)(b)). Within 30 days of receipt of such petition, the commissioner must schedule a referendum and provide notice of the referendum in each district that has requested one to determine whether or not the annexation will occur (§ 1802(2)(b)). The notice of the referendum must be posted in 10 conspicuous places at least

10 days before the meeting. It must also be published in a newspaper at least three days before the meeting (§ 1802(2)(b)).

A majority of the voters in each district must vote in favor of the annexation in order for it to be valid (§ 1803(1)). If the voters reject annexation, the question may not be presented again for one year except as otherwise provided by law. If the question of annexation is not again presented within two years, the original commissioner's order becomes null and void (§ 1803(8); see **2:16**).

The school board of the annexing school district assumes responsibility for the reorganized district, except that the qualified voters of the annexed district become qualified voters of the annexing district as of the date the commissioner's order of annexation becomes final. Voters may approve a proposition at the first annual meeting to increase the number of school board members in the annexing district to give the annexed district additional opportunity for representation on the board (see NYS Education Department, *Guide to the Reorganization of School Districts in New York State* (updated May 2015), at: http://www.p12.nysed.gov/mgtserv/sch_dist_org/GuideToReorganizationOfSchoolDistricts.htm).

2:12. What are the procedures involved in an annexation to a union free school district?

After an adequate study is performed indicating that the proposed annexation is desirable and that a majority of the voters in the affected districts support it (see **2:9**), the commissioner of education may issue and file with each affected district an order annexing an existing school district to a contiguous union free school district.

In this type of annexation, the law requires voter approval of the commissioner's order proposing the annexation in order for the reorganization to become effective (§ 1705(1)(a)). Therefore, no petition by the voters is necessary. The commissioner must fix a time and place for a special meeting for residents to vote on an annexation resolution within 30 days of the filing of the order (§ 1705(1)(b)). If the voters reject the resolution, the question may not be presented to the voters again for one year. If no meeting is called within two years after the resolution's defeat, the commissioner's order becomes null and void (§ 1705(2)(b); see **2:16**).

The rules applicable to the governance of a district annexed to a union free school district are the same as in the case of annexation to a central school district, with the school board of the annexing district assuming responsibility for the reorganized district (see NYS Education Department, *Guide to the Reorganization of School Districts in New York State* (updated May 2015), at: http://www.p12.nysed.gov/mgtserv/sch_dist_org/GuideToReorganizationOfSchoolDistricts.htm; see also **2:11**).

2:13. What are the procedures involved in the consolidation of union free and/or common school districts?

Upon receipt of a petition signed by at least 10 qualified voters of each affected school district requesting a meeting to consider the consolidation of one or more school districts, the respective school boards of the affected districts must submit a consolidation proposal to the commissioner of education. Upon the commissioner's approval, a special meeting is called in each district to gain the approval for the consolidation by the qualified voters of each district (§§ 1511, 1512; see also **2:16**). Each board must give public notice that a meeting of such districts will be held at a centrally located place in order to vote upon the consolidation. The meeting must be held not less than 20 nor more than 30 days after publication of the notice (§ 1511(1)). If the consolidation is approved, a new district is created and a new school board is elected. If consolidation is rejected, the question may not be raised again for one year (§§ 1512, 1513, 1702).

The consolidated school district must elect a new school board. Its composition and the term of the office of the new board will depend on whether the consolidation created a common or a union free school district (see NYS Education Department, *Guide to the Reorganization of School Districts in New York*

State (updated May 2015), at: http://www.p12.nysed.gov/mgtserv/sch_dist_org/GuideToReorganizationOfSchoolDistricts.htm).

2:14. What are the procedures for consolidation with a city school district?

In this form of reorganization, after an adequate study is performed indicating that the proposed consolidation is desirable and that a majority of the voters in the affected districts support the proposed consolidation (see **2:9**), it must then be approved by the school board of the city district and the qualified voters of the adjoining district (§§ 1524(1), 1526; see also **2:16**). If so approved, the adjoining district is dissolved and the territory is added to the city school district. A new district is not created, nor is a new school board elected (§ 1524(1)). The school board of the city school district assumes responsibility for the entire district, and the qualified voters of the consolidated districts become qualified voters in the enlarged city school district (see NYS Education Department, *Guide to the Reorganization of School Districts in New York State* (updated May 2015), at: http://www.p12.nysed.gov/mgtserv/sch_dist_org/GuideToReorganizationOfSchoolDistricts.htm).

2:15. What are the procedures for dissolving a district?

After an adequate study is performed indicating that the proposed dissolution is desirable and that a majority of the voters in the affected districts support the proposed dissolution (see **2:9**), the district superintendent (see **10:1**) issues an order dissolving one or more districts within his or her supervisory district and annexing the territory to an adjoining district (§ 1505(1)). If the territory of more than one district superintendent is affected by the dissolution, approval by a majority of the district superintendents is required (§ 1505(1)).

Dissolution is the only reorganization process that does not specifically provide an opportunity for the qualified voters of the affected district or districts to make the final determination as to whether or not a reorganization will be implemented. However, the Education Law establishes a process by which voters may contest the dissolution by filing their objections with the local county court judge, who then appoints a committee to determine whether the dissolution should occur (§ 1505(2)).

2:16. Is there a limit to the number of times a proposal to reorganize may be submitted to the voters within a given time period?

Yes. If a reorganization proposition is defeated by the voters, a revote on the same proposal cannot be called within one year after the original vote (§§ 1512(1), 1705(2)(b), 1803(8), 1803-a(6)). Additionally, the commissioner of education's order for reorganization is deemed null and void if a second special meeting is not called within two years of the original meeting at which the voters rejected the reorganization, or if a second meeting is held and the proposal is again defeated (§§ 1705(2)(b), 1803(8), 1803-a(6)).

Impact of Reorganization

2:17. How is the name of a newly created central school district selected?

The commissioner of education designates the name of a newly centralized district in the centralization order (§ 1801(2)). Subject to the commissioner's approval, school boards of new or reorganized central school districts may select a different name by filing a written request for a name change with the commissioner no later than 14 days before the centralization order is to become effective (§ 315).

However, reorganized districts must comply with the commissioner's regulations concerning the use of simplified names (see 8 NYCRR Part 240).

2:18. What happens to the property and debts of former school districts after a reorganization?

Under all forms of reorganization, the newly reorganized district assumes the debts of the former school district, such as bonds or notes or those relating to school building construction (§§ 1517, 1705(3), 1804(5)(b)). Any other debts of the defunct district must be paid off out of that district's assets (§§ 1518, 1705(3), 1804(5)(a)).

In a centralization or annexation, the new central school district or annexing district "shall succeed to all the property rights" of the defunct district (§§ 1705(3), 1804(5)).

In a dissolution under section 1505 of the Education Law, the dissolved school district's property must be sold and the net proceeds of the sale are apportioned to the taxpayers of the dissolved district based on the latest assessment roll (§ 1520).

Special rules apply, however, to reorganizations conducted pursuant to section 2218 of the Education Law.

2:19. How does a school district reorganization affect employment contracts?

If a teacher has an employment contract with a school district, that contract is a property right subject to the normal rules of property distribution in a reorganization (*Barringer v. Powell*, 230 N.Y. 37 (1920)). For example, in a centralization, the employment contract would be an obligation assumed by the new district.

However, one court has ruled that a collective bargaining agreement is not a contract assumed by an annexing district. In this situation, the teachers from the annexed district become covered by the collective bargaining agreement between the teachers and the annexing district, and the contract between the annexed district and its union is not enforceable against the annexing district (*Cuba-Rushford CSD v. Rushford Faculty Ass'n*, 182 A.D.2d 127 (4th Dep't 1992)).

2:20. What employment rights are provided to employees of districts that have been dissolved or reorganized pursuant to annexation to a union free school district?

The Education Law only specifies the employment rights of employees in cases of dissolution of a school district, annexation to a union free school district, and reorganization conducted pursuant to section 2218. However, a separate section applicable to annexations to a union free school district provides that the employees of the annexed district become employees of the annexing district and retain their tenure status and seniority (§ 1705(4)). If fewer teaching positions are necessary following the annexation, the teachers from both districts with the greatest seniority within each tenure area are retained in positions in the annexing district, and excessed teachers from both districts are placed on preferred eligible lists based on seniority (§ 1705(4)). To determine "salary, sick leave and any other purpose" in the annexing district, service in the annexed district will be credited as service in the annexing district (§ 1705(4)).

Other sections applicable generally to school district dissolution and reorganization further provide that where a district is dissolved and added to more than one school district, the teachers of the dissolved district are entitled to select the district in which they wish to be employed. Based on their preferences and seniority, they will be appointed to positions in the newly created district (§ 1505-a(1)). A district that employs teachers from dissolved districts is required to accept the seniority credit acquired in the dissolved district and credit such seniority as if the teacher had served in the annexing district to determine "salary, sick leave and any other purpose" (§ 1505-a(3)). If there are more teachers than positions available, the teachers of a dissolved district are entitled to be placed on the preferred eligible list of the annexing district, in order of seniority acquired in the dissolved district. The teachers would then fill any future vacancies in the annexing district at the payment schedule set by that district (§ 1505-a(2), (3)).

The local civil service commission with authority over the school district (see **39:1**, **39:7**) should be consulted to determine the employment rights of non-instructional employees appointed pursuant to New York's Civil Service Law (see NYS Education Department, *Guide to the Reorganization of School Districts in New York State* (updated May 2015), at: http://www.p12.nysed.gov/mgtserv/sch_dist_org/GuideToReorganizationOfSchoolDistricts.htm).

2:21. What employment rights exist for employees of districts that have been reorganized pursuant to centralization, consolidation, or annexation to a central school district?

Although the Education Law does not specify the employment rights of employees in school district reorganizations involving centralization, consolidation, or annexation to a central school district, the NYS Education Department (SED) has clarified those rights in its *Guide to the Reorganization of School Districts in New York State* (updated May 2015), at: http://www.p12.nysed.gov/mgtserv/sch_dist_org/GuideToReorganizationOfSchoolDistricts.htm. According to SED, in a centralization or consolidation, teachers in the former school district become employees of the newly created district. Thus, the teachers from both districts with the greatest seniority within each tenure area are retained in positions in the new district and excessed teachers from both districts are placed on preferred eligible lists based on seniority.

In an annexation to a central school district, the more senior teachers from the annexed district do not displace teachers in the annexing district. However, teachers from the annexed district are entitled to fill any vacancies in the annexing district. If no vacancies exist within the teacher's tenure area, the teacher is placed on the preferred eligible list in seniority order, based on the seniority credit earned at the annexed district, which is credited as employment time within the annexing district. According to SED, similar rights are applicable in a consolidation with a city school district.

The local civil service commission with authority over the school district (see **39:1**, **39:7**) should be consulted to determine the employment rights of non-instructional employees appointed pursuant to New York's Civil Service Law.

2:22. How are superintendents affected by reorganization?

A superintendent under contract, other than one in an annexing district, does not have employment rights in the reorganized district. However, that superintendent's employment contract is considered a property right and becomes an obligation of the reorganized school district (see *Matter of Foster*, 28 Ed Dept Rep 29 (1988)). Thus, the reorganized district must pay that superintendent's salary and benefits under his or her contract, less any income obtained from the superintendent's employment elsewhere during the term of the contract (see NYS Education Department, *Guide to the Reorganization of School Districts in New York State* (updated May 2015), at: http://www.p12.nysed.gov/mgtserv/sch_dist_org/GuideToReorganizationOfSchoolDistricts.htm).

2:23. Is a school district bound by an assurance made during the reorganization process to not close a school building?

No. In general, a school board may not bind a successor board unless expressly provided for in statute. In one case, the commissioner of education determined that assurances made to maintain an elementary school at the current site in the annexed district and to "maintain comparable elementary programs" between the two school districts was not binding on the newly formed school district when it determined to close the elementary school twelve years after the annexation vote (*Appeal of Fuller*, 54 Ed Dept Rep, Dec. No. 16,758 (2015); see **5:25-26**).

2:24. Is state aid available to school districts that reorganize?

Yes. Additional operating aid and building aid is available to certain school districts that reorganize and comply with particular requirements of the Education Law (§ 3602(14); see also NYS Education Department, *Guide to the Reorganization of School Districts in New York State* (updated May 2015), at: http://www.p12.nysed.gov/mgtserv/sch_dist_org/GuideToReorganizationOfSchoolDistricts.htm). For additional information visit http://www.p12.nysed.gov/mgtserv/sch_dist_org/.

2:25. Where can more information be obtained about reorganization?

Information about reorganization can be obtained by contacting the NYS Education Department's Office of Management Services: School District Organization, or by phone at 518-474-6541 or e-mail at emscmgts@mail.nysed.gov. See also NYS State Education Department, *Guide to the Reorganization of School Districts in New York State* (updated May 2015), at: http://www.p12.nysed.gov/mgtserv/sch_dist_org/GuideToReorganizationOfSchoolDistricts.htm.

[illegible]

3. Charter Schools

Editor's Note: For further information concerning New York State's Charter Schools, contact the Charter School Office of the NYS Education Department's Office of P-12 Education at 518-474-1762, or online at: http://www.p12.nysed.gov/psc/ or the State University of New York's Charter Schools Institute at 518-445-4250, or online at: http://www.newyorkcharters.org.

Formation of Charter Schools

3:1. What is a charter school?

Except as otherwise provided in Article 56 of the Education Law, a *charter school* is an "independent and autonomous public school" and a political subdivision having boundaries coterminous with the school district or community school district in which the charter school is located (§ 2853(1)(c)). Charter schools cannot be "easily identified as either a purely private or public entity" even though their powers involve the performance of essential public and governmental purposes. The Legislature determines what particular laws governing public entities apply to charter schools (*N.Y. Charter Sch. Ass'n v. Smith*, 15 N.Y.3d 403 (2010)).

Charter schools operate pursuant to an approved "charter" issued by the Board of Regents (§§ 2851(3); 2853(1)(b); see also **3:5**), and are eligible for funding from both private and public local, state, and federal funds (§ 2856; see **3:34**). They may be a newly created school, or the result of the conversion of a previously existing public school (see § 2851(3); see also **3:5-6**). The law expressly prohibits an existing private school from converting to a charter school (§ 2852(3)).

In addition to improving student learning and achievement, the purposes of the charter schools law include: (1) increasing learning opportunities for all students, particularly those at risk of academic failure; (2) encouraging the use of different and innovative teaching methods; (3) creating new professional opportunities for educators; (4) providing parents and students with expanded educational opportunity choices within the public school system; and (5) providing schools with a method to change from rule-based to performance-based accountability systems (§ 2850(2)).

3:2. Where may a charter school be located?

A charter school may be located in part of an existing public school building, in space provided on a private work site, in a public building, or in any other suitable location. In addition, a charter school may own, lease, or rent its space. However, before a charter school can be located in part of an existing public school building, the charter entity (see **3:5-6**) shall provide notice to the parents or guardians of the students enrolled in the existing school building and hold a public hearing for the purpose of discussing the location of the charter school (§ 2853(3)(a); see also 8 NYCRR § 3.16(b)). A school district shall permit any charter school granted approval to co-locate, to use such services and facilities without cost (§2853(4)(c)).

Special rules apply to locating or co-locating a charter school in an existing public school building in New York City (§ 2853(3)(a-3)-(a-5), (d), (e); see also 8 NYCRR § 276.11). In addition, charter schools in New York City that first commence instruction or require additional space due to an expansion of grade level approved by their charter entity starting with the 2014-2015 school year, and request co-location in a public school building must be offered a co-location site in a public school building at no cost to the charter school, or space in a privately owned or other publicly owned facility at the expense of the city school district and at no expense to the charter school (Education Law § 2853(3)(e)(1); *Appeal of Rosalyn Yalow Charter School*, 54 Ed Dept Rep, Dec. No. 16,690 (2014); *Appeal of Great Oaks Charter School*, 54 Ed Dept Rep, Dec. No. 16,692 (2014)).

At the request of a charter school or a prospective applicant, a school district must provide a list of vacant, unused school buildings and vacant, unused portions of school buildings, including private school buildings, within the district that may be suitable for the operation of a charter school (§ 2853(3)(c)).

3:3. How are charter schools viewed for purposes of local zoning, land use regulation and building code compliance?

In general, for purposes of local zoning, land use regulation, and building code compliance, charter schools established pursuant to the competitive charter application process set out in Education Law § 2852(9-a) (see **3:5**) are treated as public schools. However, a charter school established under such process and located outside of New York City may seek an exemption from the public school requirements upon a specific showing of either undue hardship or some other good cause that makes compliance extremely impracticable, and that efforts to overcome the stated obstacles have been undertaken (§ 2853(3)(a-1)(i)). If an exemption is granted, such charter school is treated for these purposes as a nonpublic school (§ 2853(3)(a-2)). Charter schools that are not established pursuant to the competitive charter application process are treated for these purposes as nonpublic schools (§ 2853(3)(a-2)).

Projects for the construction, renovation or repair of buildings for charter schools are generally not subject to Labor Law provisions regarding prevailing wages and supplements (*N.Y. Charter Sch. Ass'n v. Smith*, 15 N.Y.3d 403 (2010)). One exception might apply, for example, when consistent with Labor Law § 220(2), the charter school is acting in place of, on behalf of, and for the benefit of a public entity (*Id.*).

3:4. Who can form a charter school?

Teachers, parents, school administrators, community residents, or any combination thereof, may apply to establish a charter school. They may submit their application independently, or in conjunction with a college, university, museum, educational institution, not-for-profit corporation exempt from taxation under section 501(c)(3) of the Internal Revenue Code, or if not established through the competitive application process set out in Education Law § 2852(9-a), a for-profit business or corporate entity authorized to do business in New York State (§ 2851(1)). For-profit businesses or corporate entities are not eligible either to submit an application for a charter or to operate or manage a charter school established pursuant to the competitive charter application process set out in Education Law § 2852(9-a) (§ 2851(1); see **3:5**).

The law does not allow an existing private school to convert to a charter school (§ 2852(3)). In addition, a charter may not be issued to any school that would be wholly or in part under the control or direction of any religious denomination, or in which any denominational tenet or doctrine would be taught (§ 2854(2)(a)).

3:5. What is the process for forming a charter school?

Those wishing to form a charter school must submit an application pursuant to a competitive request for proposals process to either the Board of Regents or the Board of Trustees of the State University of the State of New York as the *charter entities* established by law for this purpose (§ 2852(9-a); see NYS Education Department, Charter School Office, *Starting a Charter School* (updated May 2016) at: http://www.p12.nysed.gov/psc/startcharter.html; State University of New York, Charter Schools Institute, *Request for Proposals Process* at: http://www.newyorkcharters.org/create/request-proposals-process/). Applications for converting an existing public school into a charter school are not subject to a competitive process (§ 2851(3)(c); see **3:6**).

Applications are evaluated in accordance with the criteria and objectives contained within the respective request for proposals (§ 2852(9-a)). The law requires that a proposal rigorously demonstrate that (1) the proposed charter school will meet or exceed prescribed enrollment and retention targets for students with disabilities, English language learners, and students who are eligible applicants for the free and reduced price lunch program; and (2) the applicant has complied with prescribed public outreach requirements (§ 2852(9-a)(b); *Matter of Norris v. Walcott*, 36 Misc.3d 711 (Sup. Ct. New York Cnty. 2012)). The law grants priority to applications that, based on a scoring rubric, best demonstrate how they will achieve certain specified and additional objectives set by the Board of Regents and the Board of Trustees of the State University of the State of New York. Some of those objectives include increasing high school graduation rates and focusing on at risk high school student populations; partnering with low performing public schools to share best educational practices and innovations, demonstrating management and leadership techniques necessary to overcome initial start-up problems; and demonstrating support from the school district where the charter school will be located and the intent to establish an ongoing relationship with that district (§ 2852(9-a)(c)).

Upon approval of an application, applicants and the charter entity enter into a proposed charter agreement which sets forth the conditions under which the charter school was approved to operate and the expectations it will have to meet to continue in operation (§ 2852(5); *Matter of the Bd. of Educ. of the Roosevelt UFSD v. Bd. of Trustees of SUNY*, 282 A.D.2d 166 (3d Dep't 2001)). A charter entity other than the Board of Regents must submit a copy of the charter agreement along with the application and supporting documentation to the Regents, for final approval (§ 2852(5); *Matter of Bd. of Educ. of the Roosevelt UFSD v. Bd. of Trustees of SUNY)*.

The Board of Regents may approve and issue the charter, or it can return the proposed charter to the charter entity for reconsideration with written comments and recommendations (§ 2852(5-a)). The charter entity can then resubmit the proposed charter with or without modifications, or abandon the proposed charter. Any modifications to the charter require an applicant's written approval. However, the charter entity can abandon the proposed charter with or without applicant approval (§ 2852(5-b)).

The Board of Regents must take action on proposed charters within the specific timelines established by law. If the Regents do not act within those timelines, the charter will be deemed approved and issued by operation of law (§§ 2852(5-a), (5-b), 2852(9-a)(f); *Matter of the Bd. of Educ. of the Roosevelt UFSD v. Bd. of Trustees of SUNY)*.

3:6. What is the process for converting an existing public school into a charter school?

Those wishing to convert an existing public school into a charter school must submit an application to the local school board which serves as the charter entity under these circumstances. In New York City, the law designates the chancellor of the New York City Board of Education as the charter entity instead of the school board (§ 2851(3)).

The minimal requirements for a public school conversion application are contained in the law and may be supplemented by any other information relevant to the issuance of a charter required by the charter entity (§ 2851(2)). In addition, the law requires that parents or guardians of a majority of the students then enrolled in the existing public school must vote in favor of converting the school to a charter school (§ 2851(3)(c)).

Upon approval of the conversion application, the applicants and the charter entity enter into a proposed charter agreement which sets forth the conditions under which the charter school was approved to operate and the expectations it will have to meet to continue in operation. A copy of the charter agreement along with the application and supporting documentation must be submitted to the Board of Regents for final approval (§ 2852(5)).

The Board of Regents may approve and issue the charter, or it can return the proposed charter to the charter entity for reconsideration with written comments and recommendations (§ 2852(5-a)). The charter entity can then resubmit the proposed charter with or without modifications, or abandon the proposed charter. Any modifications to the charter require an applicant's written approval. However, the charter entity can abandon the proposed charter with or without applicant approval (§ 2852(5-b)).

The Board of Regents must take action on proposed charters within the specific timelines established by law. If the Regents do not act within those timelines, the charter will be deemed approved and issued by operation of law (§ 2852(5-a)).

3:7. Must school districts be notified of applications for a proposed charter school submitted to other charter entities?

Yes. At each significant stage of the chartering process, the charter entity and the Board of Regents must provide appropriate notification to the school district in which the charter school is or will be located and to public and nonpublic schools in the same geographic area. The charter entity must give such notice within 30 days of its receipt of an application for the formation of a new charter school or the renewal of an existing one, and at least 45 days prior to its initial approval of the charter application (§ 2857(1)).

3:8. Are charter school applications subject to a public hearing?

Yes. Prior to the issuance, revision or renewal of a charter, the school district in which the charter school is or will be located must hold a public hearing to solicit comments from the community. In the case of an application for the revision of a charter that involves the relocation of a charter school to a different district, the proposed new district also must hold a hearing (§ 2857(1); 8 NYCRR § 119.4).

Charter entities must consider and submit any comments raised to the Board of Regents along with the application for the issuance, revision, or renewal of charter (§ 2857(1)).

If a district fails to conduct the required hearing, the commissioner of education, pursuant to authority delegated by the Board of Regents, must conduct one in order to solicit comments from the community (§ 2857(1-a); 8 NYCRR § 3.16(b)).

3:9. Are school districts entitled to comment on charter school applications submitted to other charter entities?

Yes. Separate from the requirement that there be a public hearing to solicit comments from the community (see **3:8**), school districts where a charter school is or will be located must be given the opportunity to comment on charter applications prior to the issuance, revision or renewal of a charter (§ 2857(1)).

The charter entity must consider and submit to the Board of Regents any comments raised by the district along with the charter application (*Id.*).

3:10. Can a charter entity reject a charter school application?

Yes. Furthermore, a charter entity may not approve an application unless it determines that:

1. the proposed charter school meets all applicable statutory and regulatory requirements;
2. the applicant has the ability to operate the school in an educationally and fiscally sound manner;
3. approval of the application is likely to both improve student learning and achievement, and materially further the purposes of the charter school law; and
4. in a school district where the total enrollment of resident students attending charter schools in the base year is greater than five percent of the total public school enrollment of the school district in the base year: (i) granting the application would have a significant educational benefit to the students expected to attend the proposed charter school; or (ii) the school district in which the charter school will be located consents to such application (§ 2852(2); *Matter of the Bd. of Educ. of the Roosevelt UFSD v. Bd. of Trustees of SUNY*, 287 A.D.2d 858 (3d Dep't 2001)).

In addition, the Board of Regents and the Board of Trustees of the State University of the State of New York may not consider any application submitted pursuant to the competitive charter application process set out in Education Law § 2852(9-a) (see **3:5**) that does not rigorously demonstrate (1) the proposed charter school will meet or exceed prescribed enrollment and retention targets for students with disabilities, English language learners, and students who are eligible applicants for the free and reduced price lunch program; and (2) the applicant has complied with prescribed public outreach requirements (§ 2852(9-a)(b)).

The denial of an application must be in writing and state the reasons for it (§ 2852(6)).

3:11. Can an applicant appeal the denial of a charter school application?

No. If a charter entity denies a charter school application, the denial is final and may not be appealed to any authority, including a court of law (§ 2852(3), (6); *New Covenant Charter Sch. Educ. Faculty Ass'n v. Bd. of Trustees of SUNY*, 30 Misc.3d 1205A (Sup. Ct. Albany Cnty. 2010); see also NYS Education Department, Office of Innovative School Models, *Guide to Charter Schools in New York State* (2011), at: http://www.p12.nysed.gov/psc/documents/csparentguide.PDF). However, nothing in the law prevents an applicant from submitting an application that has been rejected by one charter entity to another charter entity.

The limitation on administrative or judicial review also applies when a charter entity denies a charter school renewal application (*Fahari Academy Charter Sch. v. Bd. of Educ. of the City Sch. Dist. of City of N.Y.*, 137 A.D.3d 1127 (2d Dep't 2016); *Pinnacle Charter Sch. v. Board of Regents of the Univ. of the State of N.Y.*, 108 A.D.3d 1024 (4th Dep't), *lv. to appeal denied*, 22 N.Y.3d 951 (2013); *Appeal of Ross Global Academy Charter Sch.*, 50 Ed Dept Rep, Dec. No. 16,194 (2011)).

3:12. Can a school board challenge the approval of a charter school application?

Yes. In *Matter of the Bd. of Educ. of the Roosevelt UFSD v. Bd. of Trustees of SUNY* (282 A.D.2d 166 (3d Dep't 2001)), the Appellate Division, Third Department upheld the right of a school board to challenge a SUNY Trustees' determination to grant a charter on the grounds it was arbitrary and capricious because it failed to properly consider the fiscal impact granting the charter would have on affected school districts. While the Charter Schools Act expressly prohibits an applicant from seeking judicial or administrative review of the denial of an application, no similar prohibition exists in law to prevent a school district or school board from seeking review of a determination to grant an application and issue a charter (see also, *Bd. of Educ. of the Riverhead CSD v. Board of Regents*, 301 A.D.2d 919 (3d Dep't 2003); *Mount Vernon City Sch. Dist. v. NYS Education Dep't* (Sup. Ct. Albany Cnty. 2011)).

A school district is precluded, for lack of standing, from challenging the Charter Schools Act itself on constitutional grounds (*Matter of the Bd. of Educ. of the Roosevelt UFSD v. Bd. of Trustees of SUNY*, 282 A.D.2d 166 (3d Dep't 2001); see also, related proceeding, *Matter of the Bd. of Educ. of the Roosevelt UFSD v. Bd. of Trustees of SUNY*, 287 A.D.2d 858 (3d Dep't 2001)).

3:13. Can a charter be revised?

Yes, but only upon approval of the charter entity and the Board of Regents pursuant to the process set forth in law (§§ 2852(7)(a), 2852(5-a), (5-b); see **3:5**). The commissioner of education may also act on behalf of the Board of Regents to approve revisions to charters, within parameters set forth in the Rules of the Board of Regents (8 NYCRR § 3.16(c)). The commissioner cannot, for example, approve changes with respect to the hiring or termination of a management company, or the maximum enrollment or grades served as set forth in the current charter (*Id.*).

In addition, when the revision of a charter involves relocating the charter school to a new school district, the proposed new district must be given at least 45 days notice of the relocation. The applicant must provide an analysis of the community support for the relocation, and of the projected programmatic and financial impact of the relocation on the proposed new district and other public and nonpublic schools in the area (§ 2852(7)(b)).

3:14. Is there a limit on the number of charter schools that may be established in New York State?

Yes. Although that number was initially set at 100, subsequent amendments to the law have led to incremental increases. Under current law, the total number of charters that may be issued statewide stands at 460. However, there is no limit on the number of existing public schools that may be converted into charter schools (§ 2852(9); see **3:6**). In addition, up to twenty-two charters that were surrendered, revoked or terminated on or before July 1, 2015 may be reissued pursuant to the competitive request for proposals process and do not count toward the numerical limit of 460 (§ 2852(9)(b)).

3:15. Is there a limit on the lifetime of a charter school?

Yes. The original term of a charter school established pursuant to the competitive charter application process set out in Education Law § 2853(9-a) (see **3:5**) may not exceed five years in which instruction is provided plus the period commencing with the effective date of the charter and ending with the opening of the school for instruction (§ 2851(2)(p)). The original term of a charter school created outside the competitive application process is five years (§§ 2851(2)(p), 2853(1)(a)).

Charters may be renewed only upon application, and for time periods not to exceed five years each (§§ 2851(4), 2853(1)(a)). See 8 NYCRR § 119.7 for information on the renewal application process where the charter entity is the Board of Regents.

3:16. Can a charter be revoked or terminated?

Yes. The Board of Regents or the charter entity that approved the school can revoke or terminate a charter (1) if student achievement falls below the level that would allow the commissioner of education to revoke the registration of another public school and student achievement has not shown improvement over the preceding three years; (2) for serious violation of law; (3) for material and substantial violation of the charter, including fiscal mismanagement; (4) for violations of the Civil Service Law involving interference with or discrimination against employee rights; or (5) if there is repeated failure to meet enrollment and retention targets for students with disabilities, English Language Learners, and students who are eligible for free and reduced price lunch, unless there is demonstration of extensive efforts to do so (§ 2855(1)).

Procedures applicable to charter revocation proceedings conducted by the Board of Regents require that the charter school receive written notice of any intention to revoke its charter at least 30 days prior to the effective date of the proposed revocation, along with the reasons for the proposed revocation and an opportunity to correct the problems associated with the proposed revocation (§ 2855(2); 8 NYCRR § 3.17(a)(1)). These procedures do not apply to other charter entities (8 NYCRR § 3.17(b)(1); *Williamsburg Charter High Sch. v. N. Y. City Dep't of Educ.*, 36 Misc.3d 810 (Sup. Ct. Kings Cnty. 2012)).

In addition, the charter school must have an opportunity to submit a written response to the notice of intent to revoke and, upon request, for oral argument before a three-member panel of the Board of Regents (8 NYCRR § 3.17(a)(2), (3)).

The Board of Regents' panel is responsible for submitting a recommendation to the full board based on the charter school's written response and oral argument as to whether the charter should be revoked, placed on probationary status, or subjected to a remedial action plan or such other action as the panel deems appropriate. The full board may accept or reject, in whole or in part, the panel's recommendation. The decision of the full board is final. An order revoking a charter also revokes a charter school's certificate of incorporation (§§ 219, 2853(1), 2855(3); 8 NYCRR § 3.17(a)(4), (5)).

The above procedures do not apply to Board of Regents proceedings involving revocation of a charter school's certificate of incorporation after another charter entity revokes the school's charter (8 NYCRR § 3.17(b), (c)).

Upon dissolution and after all of its debts and obligations are paid, any remaining funds attributable to public funding in the possession of the charter school must be paid over proportionately to the school districts having resident children served by the charter school in the year the charter school was dissolved or the last year students were enrolled in the charter school. The same restriction does not apply to gifts, donations, grants, or other authorized charitable contributions (§ 2851(2)(t)).

Operation of Charter Schools

3:17. Are charter schools subject to the same laws and regulations that apply to other public schools?

Not entirely. Although they are an "independent and autonomous public school" (see **3:1**), charter schools are subject to only those laws specifically identified by the Legislature as being applicable to them (*N.Y. Charter Sch. Ass'n v. Smith*, 15 N.Y.3d 403 (2010)), and discussed in more detail throughout this chapter. For example, they are bound by the same state health and safety, civil rights, and student assessment requirements as other public schools (§ 2854(1)(b)). This includes requirements under the State's Dignity for All Students Act (DASA) (§§ 10-18) for the adoption of policies and procedures for preventing and responding to acts of discrimination and harassment of students by other students and school staff on school property, including at school-sponsored functions, as well as the adoption of guidelines for promoting a safe and supportive school climate (8 NYCRR § 119.6). For more information on DASA, including, but not limited to, *A Resource and Promising Practices Guide for School Administrators & Faculty*, visit the NYS Education Department website at: http://www.p12.nysed.gov/dignityact/.

In addition, charter schools must also comply with federal civil rights laws including Title VI, Title IX, and Section 504 of the Rehabilitation Act of 1973 (see, e.g., U.S. Department of Education, Office for Civil Rights, *Dear Colleague Letter* (May 14, 2014), at: www2.ed.gov/about/offices/list/ocr/letters/colleague-201405-charter.pdf).

Charter schools also are subject to the requirements of the compulsory education law and student performance standards adopted by the Board of Regents. They may administer and their students must take Regents exams to the same extent required of other public school students (§ 2854(1)(b), (d); 8 NYCRR § 100.2(p)).

In addition, charter schools are subject to the Open Meetings Law and the Freedom of Information Law (§ 2854(1)(e)). They must comply with commissioner's regulations regarding electrically operated partitions located in classrooms or other facilities used by students (8 NYCRR § 155.25) and automated external defibrillators (§ 917; 8 NYCRR § 136.4), and are subject to fingerprinting requirements (see **3:39**).

Furthermore, charter schools are subject to annual programmatic and independent fiscal audits comparable in scope to those required for public schools (§ 2851(2)(f)). Charter schools located in New York City are also subject to financial audits of the comptroller of the New York City School District and charter schools located outside of New York City are subject to financial audits by the state comptroller at the respective comptroller's discretion (§ 2854(1)(c)).

Charter schools are subject, as well, to those provisions of Article 18 of the General Municipal Law that specifically relate to: prohibited conflicts of interest and applicable exceptions; disclosure of interest requirements; voidance of contracts willfully entered into in which there is a prohibited interest; express prohibited interests and actions; consequences of willful and knowing violations; and codes of ethics (§ 2854(1)(f)).

Nonetheless, charter schools are generally exempt from all other state and local laws, rules, regulations, or policies governing public or private schools, other than the charter schools law (§§ 2854(1)(b), 2855(5)). For example, charter schools are not subject to the prevailing wage provisions of Labor Law Article 8 that otherwise apply to the construction, renovation, repair, and maintenance of public works projects involving the facilities in which they conduct their educational mission. That rule may be different, however, regarding a facilities contract where the charter school is acting in place of, on behalf of, and for the benefit of a public entity (see *N.Y. Charter Sch. Ass'n v. Smith*).

Charter schools that have the Board of Trustees of the State of New York as their charter entity are also subject to regulations promulgated by that entity relating to charter school governance, structure and operations (§ 355(2-a)).

3:18. Are charter schools subject to oversight and supervision?

Yes. A charter school is subject to the supervision and oversight of both the Board of Regents and the charter entity that approved the charter school (§ 2853(1)(c), (2)). In this regard, each charter school must submit to the charter entity and the Board of Regents and make available to the public, including posting on the school's website, an annual report issued no later than August 1 of each year for the preceding school year. The report must include the basic educational data and academic and fiscal performance information required by law and commissioner's regulations (§ 2857(2); 8 NYCRR § 119.3). The report includes a charter school report card that contains information that must be presented in a format that is easily comparable to similar public schools, and made accessible to the community by transmitting it to local newspapers of general circulation and making it available for distribution at board of trustee meetings (§ 2857(2)(a)).

In addition, the report also must contain a discussion of the progress made by the school towards achieving the goals set forth in its charter (§ 2857(2)(b)). It must include, as well, a certified financial statement that sets forth the preceding school year's revenues and expenditures by appropriate categories, and a copy of the most recent independent fiscal audit of the school and any audit conducted by the state comptroller (§ 2857(2)(c)).

The annual report must include, as well, the school's efforts in the existing school years, and planned efforts for the succeeding school year, to meet or exceed prescribed enrollment and retention targets for students with disabilities, English language learners, and students who are eligible applicants for the free and reduced price lunch program (§ 2857(2)(d)).

The school district where a charter school is located is not required to but may visit, examine into, and inspect a charter school approved by the Board of Regents or the Board of Trustees of the State University of New York, and forward to the Board of Regents and the charter entity any evidence of non-compliance with applicable laws, regulations, and charter provisions for possible termination or revocation of the charter (§ 2853(2-a)).

3:19. Can an established charter school relocate to another school district?

Yes. However, the relocation would require a revision to its charter (see § 2852(7)(b); 8 NYCRR § 119.4; see **3:13**). As such, the move also would be subject to the notice, public hearing, and comment requirements that apply prior to the revision of a charter (see **3:7-9**).

3:20. Where should complaints about charter schools be directed?

Complaints should first be directed to the charter school's Board of Trustees, then to the chartering entity. Subsequently, complaints about charter schools that would otherwise be presented to the Board of Regents should be directed to the commissioner of education. The Regents have delegated to the commissioner the authority to receive, investigate, and respond to complaints, issue appropriate remedial orders, place a charter school on probationary status, and develop and impose on a charter school a remedial action plan (§ 2855(4); 8 NYCRR § 3.16(a)). For more information regarding the complaint process, contact the charter entity for the particular school.

An appeal to the commissioner under Education Law § 310 is not the appropriate forum to resolve a dispute against a charter school (*Appeal of C.L.,* 51 Ed Dept Rep, Dec. No. 16,307 (2011), *petition dismissed, G. L. by C. L. v. King* (Sup. Ct. Albany Cnty. 2012)).

Student Admissions and Enrollment

3:21. Who may attend a charter school?

In general, any child who is qualified for admission to a public school under New York State laws may be admitted to a charter school (§ 2854(2)(b)). Pursuant to Education Law § 2854(2)(b), the NYS Education Department created a *New York State Charter School Uniform Application Form* along with directions regarding use of the same (see http://www.p12.nysed.gov/psc/form.html). Charter schools must make their application form available in languages predominantly spoken in the community where the charter school is located (*Id.*).

A charter school may not limit admission on the basis of intellectual ability, measures of achievement or aptitude, athletic ability, disability, race, creed, gender, national origin, religion, or ancestry. Furthermore, it must demonstrate good faith efforts to attract and retain a comparable or greater enrollment of students with disabilities, limited English language learners, and students who are eligible applicants for the free and reduced price lunch program when compared to the enrollment figures of such students in the school district where the charter school is located (§ 2854(2)(a)).

However, a charter school must restrict admission to students within the grade levels it serves (§ 2854(2)(c)). In addition, it may limit admissions to students of a single gender or who are at risk of academic failure if the charter school was formed as a single-sex school or as a school designed to serve at risk students, students with disabilities or English language learners (§ 2854(2)(a)), provided that such action would not constitute impermissible discrimination under federal law (8 NYCRR § 119.5(a)(2)).

A charter school may also deny admission to any student who has been expelled or suspended from a public school until the period of suspension or expulsion from the public school has expired (§ 2854(2)(d)).

3:22. May a charter school have student admission preferences?

Yes. A charter school, for example, may establish a single sex school and/or establish enrollment preferences for students at risk of academic failure, students with disabilities, or English language learners consistent with federal law and the school design described in its charter (8 NYCRR § 119.5(a)(2)). Otherwise, a charter school must enroll each eligible child (see **3:21**) who submits an application by April 1 each year. However, if the number of students who submit a timely application for enrollment exceeds the capacity of the grade level or building, the charter school must use a random selection process, including a lottery, to admit students. In that case, however, the charter school must provide an admission preference to students returning to that school, siblings of children already enrolled in the charter school, and children residing in the local school district in which the charter school is located. Preference may also be provided to children of employees of the charter school or charter management organization, provided that such children do not constitute more than fifteen percent of the charter school's total enrollment (§ 2854(2)(b); 8 NYCRR § 119.5(a)).

The commissioner's regulations require that the random selection admission process be conducted in a transparent and equitable manner and that the time and place of the random selection process be publicized and open to the public (8 NYCRR § 119.5). For example, notice of the date, time, and place must comply with the provisions of Public Officers Law § 104 (8 NYCRR § 119.5(b)), and the location used must be open and accessible to the public and capable of accommodating the reasonably anticipated number of attendees. To accommodate a large number of anticipated attendees, lotteries may be separated by grade level with proper notice for each separate lottery (8 NYCRR § 119.5(c)(2)).

A charter school may use a traditional lottery ball process, technology-based software, paper ticket process, or any other method which generates random results. Charter school board members or employees, parents, and other specified relatives of any applicant or pupil enrolled in the charter school may not conduct the random selection process or serve as an impartial observer (8 NYCRR § 119.5(c)(1), (4)).

3:23. Is there a minimum number of students required for a charter school?

Yes. A charter school must serve at least 50 students at a single site, unless the applicant presents a compelling justification such as the location of the charter school in a geographically remote area. In addition, the law allows a charter school to serve less than 50 students during its first year of operation (§ 2851(2)(i)).

Academic Program and Services

3:24. Must charter school students take state assessments?

Yes. Charter schools must design their educational program to meet or exceed student performance standards adopted by the Board of Regents and charter school students must take state assessments to the same extent as other public school students (§ 2854(1)(b), (d); see *International High Sch. Charter Sch. v. Mills,* 276 A.D.2d 165 (3d Dep't 2000); see **56:1, 56:8, 56:11**).

3:25. May a charter school issue a high school diploma?

Yes. A charter school offering high school instruction may grant Regents diplomas and such other certificates and honors specifically authorized by its charter (§ 2854(1)(d); 8 NYCRR § 100.5(b)(7)).

3:26. Are there any restrictions on the grade levels that a charter school can offer?

A charter school may serve one or more of the grades between 1 and 12. It may also offer a kindergarten program (§ 2854(2)(c)). However, there is no authority in the law that allows a charter school to offer only preschool instruction (see **3:27**).

In addition, education corporations operating a charter school may operate more than one school or house any grade at more than one site, provided a charter is issued for each such additional school or site. Any such additional charter counts towards the cap on the total number of charter schools authorized by the New York Charter School Act (§ 2853(1)(b-1)).

3:27. May a charter school participate in a statewide universal pre-kindergarten program?

It depends. Charter schools are not eligible to participate in the statewide universal pre-kindergarten program for school districts that is funded pursuant to Education Law § 3602-e (§ 3602-e; *Appeal of Boys Preparatory Charter Sch. of N.Y.*, 55 Ed Dept Rep, Dec. No. 16,788 (2015)).

However, charter schools may participate in the statewide universal pre-kindergarten program under Education Law § 3602-ee as part of a school district's consolidated application or as an individual applicant. The provisions of law that afford charter schools located in New York City facilities at no cost do not apply to facility costs associated with offering such a pre-kindergarten program (§ 3602-ee; *Appeal of Boys Preparatory Charter Sch. of N.Y.*). In addition, charter schools that participate in the § 3602-ee program as part of a school district's consolidated application can be required to execute a contract with the school district as a condition of payment for the program (*Appeal of De Vera*, 55 Ed Dept Rep, Dec. No. 16,882 (2016)).

3:28. What is the length of the school year and school day of charter schools?

Both are determined by the individual charter school. However, the law requires that a charter school provide at least as much instruction time during the school year as required of other public schools (§ 2851(2)(n)).

3:29. Who is responsible for developing an individualized education program (IEP) for charter school students with disabilities?

The committee or subcommittee on special education (CSE or CSE subcommittee) of the student's school district of residence is responsible for developing an IEP for a student with disabilities attending a charter school, and the charter school must arrange for the provision of special education programs and services in accordance with the IEP (§ 2853(4)).

The charter school may arrange to have such services provided by the student's school district of residence, by the charter school itself, or by contract with another provider. A charter school may not contract directly with a board of cooperative educational services (BOCES) for special education or related services, but can request that the school district of residence contract with the BOCES for such services (§ 2853(4); see NYS Education Department, Charter School Office, *Charter Schools and Special Education* (updated Oct. 2013), at: http://www.p12.nysed.gov/psc/specialed.html). If the charter school arranges to have the student's district of residence provide such services, that district must provide them in the same manner as it serves students with disabilities attending its own public schools, including the provision of supplementary and related services on site (§ 2853(4)(a)).

3:30. Who is responsible for transporting charter school students to and from school?

For purposes of transportation, the law treats charter schools the same as nonpublic schools. This means that the student's school district of residence is responsible for providing a charter school student with transportation to and from school on the same basis as nonpublic school students — in other words, subject to the applicable minimum mileage limits for transportation in the school district of residence, and the requirement of the timely filing of a request for transportation pursuant to section 3635(2) of the Education Law (§ 2853(4)(b)).

A district is responsible for transporting resident students attending charter schools even in cases when during a charter school's first year of operation, the school is not yet approved and the request for transportation is not submitted until after the April 1 deadline for transportation requests by private school students (*Appeal of New Covenant Charter Sch.*, 39 Ed Dept Rep 610 (2000); see **58:9-10**). However, subsequent requests for transportation from an established charter school are subject to the April 1 deadline even when there is an enrollment cap on the school. In such a case, nothing prohibits the school from submitting by April 1 a list of students interested, but not yet enrolled (*Appeal of New Covenant Charter Sch.*, 41 Ed Dept Rep 358 (2002)).

The charter school's charter must describe the manner in which students ineligible for transportation under the law will be transported to and from school. Any supplemental transportation provided by the charter school must comply with all transportation safety laws and regulations applicable to other public schools. A charter school may contract with a school district for the provision of supplemental transportation services to a charter school, at cost (§ 2853(4)(b)).

3:31. May charter school students participate in the athletic and extracurricular activities of their school district of residence?

Yes. However, it is at the discretion of the school district of residence to allow such children to participate in athletic and extracurricular activities of the district's schools (§ 2853(4)(e)).

3:32. Are there any services that a school district must make available to charter schools?

Yes. School districts must make available to charter schools textbooks, computer software, school library materials, and health and welfare services to the same extent as nonpublic schools (§ 2853(4)(a)).

Charter School Funding

3:33. Can charter schools levy taxes or charge tuition?

No. The charter schools law expressly denies charter schools the authority to levy taxes or charge tuition (§§ 2853(1)(e), 2854(2)(a)). Additionally, charter schools may not require the payment of fees except on the same basis and to the same extent as other public schools (§ 2854(2)(a); see also NYS

Education Department, Office of Innovative School Models, *Guide to Charter Schools in New York State* (2011), at: http://www.p12.nysed.gov/psc/documents/csparentguide.PDF).

3:34. How are charter schools funded?

Charter schools receive public funding depending on the number of students the charter school serves, the adjusted expense per pupil of the various districts of residence for those students, and state and federal aid attributable to a student with a disability attending a charter school.

The basic tuition paid to charter schools is determined in accordance with a formula set in law (§ 2856(1); 8 NYCRR § 119.1(d)(3), (4)). The school district of residence of a student who enrolls in a charter school must pay directly to the charter school the appropriate payment amounts no later than the first business day of July, September, November, January, March, and May in accordance with the payment schedule set forth in the charter school law and the commissioner's regulations (§ 2856(1); 8 NYCRR § 119.1(d)(1), (2)).

A school district must also pay directly to a charter school any federal or state aid received for a student with a disability attending the charter school, in proportion to the level of services that the charter school provides directly or indirectly to the student (§ 2856(1)(b); 8 NYCRR § 119.1(d)(3)(ii)).

The state comptroller is authorized to deduct an amount equal to the unpaid obligation from any state aid available to a school district that fails to make indicated payments to a charter school. The commissioner of education must certify to the comptroller the amount of state aid to be deducted (§ 2856(2); 8 NYCRR § 119.1(a), (e)(2); *Appeal of Niagara Charter School*, 46 Ed Dept Rep 405 (2007)).

Additionally, individuals and organizations can provide funding or other assistance to the establishment and operation of a charter school. A charter school may accept gifts, donations, or grants of any kind as long as they are not subject to conditions contrary to any provision of law or a term of the charter school's charter (§ 2856(3)).

Charter schools may issue corporate bonds (see § 2853(1)(b), (d); NYS Education Department, Office of Innovative School Models, *Guide to Charter Schools in New York State* (2011), at: http://www.p12.nysed.gov/psc/documents/csparentguide.PDF). However, liability for the debts or financial obligations of a charter school rests solely on the charter school (§ 2853(1)(g)). Charter schools may not pledge the per-pupil funding from their students' school districts of residence to pay the bonds (§ 2853(3)(b); see also *Guide to Charter Schools in New York State*). In addition, the commissioner must allocate for charter schools a portion of federal funds the state receives for Qualified School Construction Bonds, Qualified Zone Academy Bonds, and Qualified Public Educational Facility Bonds (8 NYCRR §§ 155.22, 155.26; see 26 USC §§ 54E, 54F, 142, 1397E; see also **27:1**).

A school district may not submit to the voters an advisory proposition regarding increases to the proposed district budget to fund a newly formed charter school. "Advisory propositions and referenda are discouraged because they may infer voter determination of the issue" (*Appeal of the N.Y. Charter Sch. Ass'n*, 45 Ed Dept Rep 376 (2006); *Appeal of Marshall*, 41 Ed Dept Rep 219 (2001)). They are particularly ill-advised when a district is legally obligated to provide payments to a charter school in accordance with the Education Law and fails to adequately inform the voters of this obligation (*Appeal of Marshall*).

3:35. Can charter school payments be excluded when determining a district's statutory contingency budget cap?

No. Under changes enacted by Chapter 97 of the Laws of 2011, the contingency budget cap is now calculated as a cap of the district's property tax levy, not total spending. When a district enacts a contingency budget, it cannot levy a tax greater than that levied in the prior year (§§ 2023(4)(a),

2023-a(8)). There are no exclusions from this limit when a contingency budget is adopted (see NYS Education Department, Office of Educational Management Services, *Property Tax Cap Guidance April 2015 (Revised)* at: http://www.p12.nysed.gov/mgtserv/propertytax/taxcap/docs/Property_Tax_%20 Cap_General_Guidance_and_FAQS.pdf).

3:36. Are there any restrictions on the use of moneys a charter school receives from a school district?

Yes. A charter school may not expend moneys received from a local school district (see **3:34**) for the purchase or construction, acquisition, reconstruction, rehabilitation, or improvement of a school facility (§ 2853(3)(b)). However, it may apply for assistance to the "charter school stimulus fund," which is made up of public or private donations, gifts, and grants to provide discretionary support, including grants and loans to applicants and charter schools, for start-up costs and costs associated with facilities (State Fin. Law § 97-sss).

Charter School Personnel

3:37. What is the minimum number of teachers required for a charter school?

A charter school must employ at least three teachers at the school, unless the applicant presents a compelling justification such as the location of the charter school in a geographically remote area. In addition, the charter schools law allows a charter school to employ less than three teachers during its first year of operation (§ 2851(2)(i)).

3:38. Must charter school teachers be certified by New York State?

Yes. With certain limited exceptions, a charter school must employ teachers certified in accordance with the requirements applicable to other public schools. In addition, the number of uncertified teachers employed by a charter school may not exceed 30 percent of its teaching staff or five teachers, whichever is less plus five teachers of math, science, computer science, technology, or career and technical education, plus five additional teachers (§ 2854(3)(a-1)).

3:39. Are charter school teachers subject to fingerprinting and child abuse in an educational setting reporting requirements?

Yes. The Education Law and commissioner's regulations require charter schools to fingerprint prospective employees hired after July 1, 2001, for the purposes of a criminal history background check (§ 2854(3)(a-2); 8 NYCRR § 87.1 *et seq.*).

Charter schools are also subject to child abuse in an educational setting reporting requirements (§ 1125 *et seq.*; 8 NYCRR § 100.2(hh); see NYS Education Department, Charter Schools Office, *Questions and Answers Concerning the Applicability of SAVE and the School Employee Fingerprinting and Child Abuse Reporting Legislation to Charter Schools* (Mar. 2009) at: http://www.p12.nysed.gov/psc/question.html; see **51:18-24**).

3:40. Who do charter school employees work for?

Charter school staff members are employees of the charter school. However, they may be deemed employees of the school district where the charter school is located for the purpose of providing retirement benefits, including membership in the teachers' retirement and other retirement systems open to employees of public schools (§ 2854(3)(a), (c); 8 NYCRR § 119.2)). It is up to the charter school to determine whether it will treat its employees as private or public employees for retirement purposes, and to apply for admission as a participating employer in a public retirement system. The charter school and its employees are responsible for the financial contributions for such benefits (§ 2854(3)(c); 8 NYCRR § 119.2(b), (c)).

3:41. Do charter school employees enjoy collective bargaining rights?

Yes. For purposes of collective bargaining, employees of a "converted charter school" (see **3:1**), other than "managerial" or "confidential" employees, are deemed included in the same negotiating unit containing like titles or positions for district employees. They are covered by the same collective bargaining agreement covering that school district negotiating unit, unless a majority of the charter school employees in the negotiating unit want to modify the agreement as it applies to them and negotiate changes to the agreement with the approval of the charter school's board of trustees (§ 2854(3)(b)).

Employees of a "newly created charter school" (see **3:1**) are not deemed members of any existing collective bargaining unit representing employees of the school district in which the charter school is located and are not subject to any existing collective bargaining agreement between the district and its employees. However, in general, if student enrollment at the charter school exceeds 250 on the first day the school commences instruction or the average daily student enrollment exceeds that same number at any point during the first two years of operation, all employees eligible for representation will be deemed represented in a separate negotiating unit at the charter school by the same employee organization that represents like employees in the school district in which the charter school is located (§ 2854(3)(b-1)).

In addition, charter schools must afford employees not represented by a union reasonable access to any employee organization, and remain neutral in a representation vote by employees (§ 2854(3)(c-1), (c-2)).

3:42. May teachers from a public school district teach in a charter school?

Yes. A teacher employed by a public school district may request a leave of absence to teach in a charter school. The charter school law provides that a request for a leave of up to three years may not be unreasonably withheld (§ 2854(3)(d)).

In addition, a public school teacher on leave to teach at a charter school may return to the school district during the period of the leave without the loss of any right of certification, retirement, seniority, salary status, or any other benefit provided by law or the applicable collective bargaining agreement. If an appropriate position is not available for the teacher, the teacher's name is to be placed on a preferred eligible list for appointment to a future vacancy that may occur in a position similar to the one the teacher immediately held prior to the leave of absence (§ 2854(3)(d)).

[illegible]

[illegible]

[illegible]

[illegible]

[illegible]

4. Nonpublic Schools

In General

Editor's Note: Additional information concerning Nonpublic Schools is available through the Office of Nonpublic Schools Services at the NYS Education Department by phone at 518-474-3879 or 518-474-6541, or online at: http://www.p12.nysed.gov/nonpub/.

4:1. Must a school district allow students of compulsory education age to withdraw from its public schools and attend a nonpublic school?

Yes. A school district must permit a child of compulsory education age to attend a nonpublic school (see § 3204(1)). However, parents withdrawing a child of compulsory education age from the public school must furnish proof that their child is receiving required instruction elsewhere. Failure to furnish such proof raises a presumption that the child is not receiving the required instruction, which is a violation of the Education Law, and which may result in a finding of educational neglect (§ 3212(2)(d); *Matter of Aijianna L.*, 126 A.D.3d 1353 (4th Dep't), *lv. to appeal denied*, 25 N.Y.3d 912 (2015); *Matter of Cunntrel A.*, 70 A.D.3d 1308 (4th Dep't), *lv. to appeal dismissed*, 14 N.Y.3d 866 (2010); *Appeal of Brown*, 34 Ed Dept Rep 33 (1994); *Appeal of White*, 29 Ed Dept Rep 511 (1990), citing *Matter of Christa H.*, 127 A.D.2d 997 (4th Dep't 1987); *Matter of Andrew TT.*, 122 A.D.2d 362 (3d Dep't 1986); see also Fam. Ct. Act § 1012(f)(i)(A); Soc. Serv. Law § 34-a(8)).

4:2. Do school districts owe any responsibility to resident children who attend nonpublic schools?

Yes. Public school boards must ensure that resident children attending schools other than a public school receive instruction from "competent teachers" that is "at least substantially equivalent," in terms of both "time and quality," to the instruction they would receive if they attended the public schools in the district where they reside (§§ 3204(2), 3210(2); *Matter of Adam D.*, 132 Misc.2d 797 (Fam. Ct. Schoharie Cnty. 1986); *Appeal of Brown*, 34 Ed Dept Rep 33 (1994)).

The responsibility for determining substantial equivalency rests with the local school board (*Appeal of Brown*; *Appeal of Lynn*, 29 Ed Dept Rep 128 (1989); *Formal Opn. of Counsel No. 78*, 1 Ed Dept Rep 778 (1952)). However, the board may delegate the responsibility for making any such initial determination to the superintendent of schools (see *Matter of Adam D.*; *Matter of Kilroy*, 121 Misc.2d 98 (Fam. Ct. Cayuga Cnty. 1983); *Appeal of Brown*; § 1711(3)).

4:3. How can a school district determine if a student attending a nonpublic school is receiving a substantially equivalent education?

The superintendent of schools may visit the nonpublic schools of resident children to evaluate the educational programs they are receiving outside the public schools.

With respect to secondary schools, if the nonpublic school is registered by the Board of Regents, the NYS Education Department recommends that the school board of the district where that nonpublic school is located accept the registration as evidence that the nonpublic school has an equivalent program of instruction. A nonpublic secondary school may choose not to be registered. Such a choice does not mean that the school program is inadequate.

The substantial equivalency of unregistered secondary and elementary nonpublic schools must be determined through local review (NYS Education Department, *Guidelines for Determining Equivalency of Instruction in Nonpublic Schools* (updated Aug. 2015), at: www.p12.nysed.gov/nonpub/guidelinesequivofinstruction; see also **4:6**).

4:4. What steps should be taken if the school district determines that a nonpublic school does not provide a substantially equivalent education to that provided in the public school?

The school superintendent and the nonpublic school administrator should discuss any perceived deficiencies, determine whether these deficiencies can be corrected within a reasonable period of time, and create a schedule for the corrections to be made. Where appropriate the superintendent should discuss the concerns of deficiencies with the board of cooperative educational services (BOCES) district superintendent and the Nonpublic Schools Services office at the NYS Education Department (SED).

If the nonpublic school is unable or unwilling to remedy its deficiencies, and the superintendent determines that the program does not provide a "substantially equivalent education," the superintendent should notify his or her board and the school boards of other districts in which students attending the nonpublic school live. The school superintendent may share the information with the BOCES district superintendent.

In addition, the superintendent should notify nonpublic school officials of the date upon which the school board will consider the matter of equivalency. According to guidelines established by SED, once the school board approves a resolution at a public meeting that a nonpublic school is not equivalent, the administrator of the nonpublic school and the parents of the students attending the school should be notified in writing that the children will be considered truant if they continue to attend that school. Parents should be given a reasonable time in which to transfer their children to either a public school or another nonpublic school. At that time, all transportation, textbooks, and health services should be withdrawn. If parents continue to enroll their children in a nonpublic school whose program has been determined to be not equivalent, they should be notified that petitions will be filed in Family Court by the public school authorities to the effect that their children are truant. The school board's determination may be appealed to the commissioner of education under Education Law § 310 (NYS Education Department, *Guidelines for Determining Equivalency of Instruction in Nonpublic Schools* (updated Aug. 2015), at: www.p12.nysed.gov/nonpub/guidelinesequivofinstruction).

4:5. Are nonpublic schools subject to the same legal requirements that apply to public schools?

Generally, nonpublic schools are not bound by all of the requirements that apply to public schools. For example, the law does not require that nonpublic teachers and administrators meet the state's requirements for certification (see NYS Education Department, *Manual for New Administrators of Nonpublic Schools, State Requirements and Programs* (updated Aug. 2015), at: http://www.p12.nysed.gov/nonpub/manualfornewadministratorsofnps/statereqs.html). In addition, the rights of students in private schools generally are governed by the contractual arrangement between the school and the parents or by regulations or procedures set forth in a student handbook or school catalogue. Accordingly, nonpublic schools may impose tighter restrictions on students' speech and conduct than those possible within the public schools (see **chapters 52 and 53**).

However, where nonpublic schools receive federal funds, they may become subject to various federal civil rights laws, such as:

- Title IX of the Education Amendments of 1972, which bars sexual discrimination in education programs;
- Title VI of the Civil Rights Act of 1964, which bans discrimination by race, color, or national origin in federally funded programs;
- Section 504 of the Rehabilitation Act of 1973, which prohibits discrimination against students with disabilities in such programs;
- The Family Educational Rights and Privacy Act, 20 USC § 1232g, which requires parental review of and consent to the release of student educational records.

In addition, certain state laws are applicable to nonpublic schools, such as section 807-a of the Education Law, which requires that nonpublic elementary or secondary schools enrolling 25 or more students file a fire inspection report with the state. The Education Law and commissioner's regulations also require that any registered nonpublic nursery school or kindergarten attended by six or more pupils meet certain safety standards to prevent fire, health, or other safety hazards (§ 807-a(10)(a)(b); 8 NYCRR § 125.3). Public Health Law § 2164, which requires certain immunizations, also extends to nonpublic school students.

While a public school board is not responsible for enforcing these provisions, if a fire inspection reveals "an apparently serious deficiency," the board may take appropriate steps to inform the parents of nonpublic school students (NYS Education Department, *Guidelines for Determining Equivalency of Instruction in Nonpublic Schools* (updated Aug. 2015), at: www.p12.nysed.gov/nonpub/guidelinesequivofinstruction).

In addition, the commissioner's regulations on school bus safety practices that apply to public school districts also apply to nonpublic schools. This includes the same instruction and retraining requirements that apply for school bus drivers who operate student transportation owned, leased, or contracted for by public school districts (§ 305(34); see **60:7-9**).

Registration and Oversight

4:6. Must nonpublic schools be registered with the NYS Education Department?

Nonpublic schools are not required to be registered with the NYS Education Department (see 8 NYCRR § 100.2(p)). However, the commissioner's regulations provide for the voluntary registration of nonpublic nursery schools and kindergartens (8 NYCRR Part 125). In addition, nonpublic high schools may be registered by the Board of Regents upon the recommendation of the commissioner of education. Only registered nonpublic high schools may issue diplomas and administer Regents examinations (8 NYCRR § 100.2(p)).

Inquiries concerning the requirements and procedures for the registration of nonpublic secondary schools or nursery schools and kindergartens should be addressed to the Department's Office for Nonpublic School Services at NYS Education Department, EBA, 89 Washington Avenue, Albany, N.Y. 12234, by phone at 518-474-3879 or 518-474-6541, or by e-mail at: emscmgts@nysed.gov.

4:7. Does the NYS Education Department review registered nonpublic high schools?

Yes, registered nonpublic secondary schools are reviewed on a ten-year cycle (NYS Department of Education, *Manual for New Administrators of Nonpublic Schools*, *State Requirements and Programs* (updated Aug. 2015), at: http://www.p12.nysed.gov/nonpub/manualfornewadministratorsofnps/statereqs.

html). A registered nonpublic high school shall be placed under review by the commissioner of education under the following conditions:

- whenever the school scores below the registration review criteria on one or more of the measures adopted by the Board of Regents (contained in 8 NYCRR § 100.2(p)(13)), and the student achievement on such measures or other appropriate indicators has not shown improvement over the preceding three school years; or
- when other sufficient reason exists to warrant registration review, as determined by the commissioner (8 NYCRR § 100.2(p)(12)(i)(a), (b)).

The school then develops an improvement plan with technical assistance from the commissioner if needed (8 NYCRR § 100.2(p)(12)(ii)). If the school does not show progress on the criteria in question, the commissioner notifies the school that it is at risk of having its registration revoked. If after a further period of time the school still does not show progress, the commissioner will recommend to the Board of Regents that it revoke the school's registration. If the Board of Regents revokes the school's registration, the commissioner and nonpublic school officials will develop a plan to protect the educational welfare of the students (8 NYCRR § 100.2(p)(12)(iii), (iv)).

4:8. Is there any NYS Education Department review of unregistered nonpublic schools?

Yes. The NYS Education Department (SED) may review any unregistered nonpublic school when the school scores below one or more of the review criteria on indicators of student achievement as provided in the commissioner's regulations, has not shown improvement on such indicators over the preceding three school years, and has not otherwise demonstrated satisfactory performance on other student achievement indicators determined by the commissioner of education in consultation with the appropriate nonpublic school officials (8 NYCRR § 100.2(z)).

Nonpublic schools under SED review are required to notify parents, develop a school improvement plan (with technical assistance from SED if requested), and submit the plan to SED. If, after a time period established by the commissioner in consultation with the appropriate nonpublic school officials, the school has not demonstrated progress, the commissioner will formally notify the nonpublic school officials that the school is at risk of being determined to be an "unsound educational environment." If the commissioner later determines there is still insufficient progress, he will determine that the school is an unsound educational environment. The commissioner and the nonpublic school officials must then develop a plan to ensure that the educational welfare of the students is protected (8 NYCRR § 100.2(z)).

4:9. Are there any steps a public school district should take when a new nonpublic school is established within its boundaries?

Yes. Public school officials must determine whether the new nonpublic school building is a safe place by reviewing, for example, building structure reports and fire inspection reports, whether the length of the school day and school calendar are substantially equivalent to that required for public schools, and whether the program of instruction covers essentially the same subject areas as are covered in the public schools (see §§ 807-a, 3204(2), 3210(2); NYS Education Department, *State Requirements and Programs: Manual for New Administrators of Nonpublic Schools* (updated Aug. 2015), http://www.p12.nysed.gov/nonpub/manualfornewadministratorsofnps/statereqs.html).

The superintendent of schools should ask to visit the new school prior to its opening and ask the administrator of the nonpublic school for information such as the names and grade levels of students from the district, the school calendar and a list of courses and subjects which will be taught at each grade level in the school.

If public school officials determine these all are satisfactory and that the new nonpublic school will provide a substantially equivalent education, the superintendent should notify the public school board of this in writing, forward a copy of the notification to the nonpublic school and, where appropriate, notify the board of cooperative educational services district superintendent of the findings of the review. The superintendent should contact the NYS Education Department (SED), Office for Nonpublic School Services to ensure that the new school will be placed on SED's mailing list and that its head will be invited to the annual fall conference for nonpublic school administrators (NYS Education Department, *Guidelines for Determining Equivalency of Instruction in Nonpublic Schools* (updated Aug. 2015), at: www.p12.nysed.gov/nonpub/guidelinesequivofinstruction; see also **4:2-4**).

4:10. Are nonpublic schools entitled to any state aid?

Yes. Nonpublic schools may be reimbursed for the actual costs related to complying with certain state mandates, including expenses relating to the administration of state testing and evaluation programs and participation in state programs for the reporting of basic educational data (L. 1974, cs. 507 & 508).

Although the New York Constitution provides that neither the state nor any state subdivision may provide funding or use its property or credit to assist a nonpublic school (N.Y. Const. art. 11, § 3), the authorized apportionment of state aid funds for nonpublic schools is limited to the services they are required to perform for the state in connection with the state's own responsibility to evaluate students through a system of uniform testing and reporting procedures to ensure students are being adequately educated (L. 1974, cs. 507 & 508). The U.S. Supreme Court has upheld the constitutionality of these provisions under separation of church and state principles of the Establishment Clause of the First Amendment of the U.S. Constitution (§ 3601; *Committee for Pub. Educ. & Religious Liberty v. Regan*, 444 U.S. 646 (1980)).

Public School Services for Nonpublic School Students

4:11. Are there any type of services that public school districts must provide to nonpublic school students?

Yes. As authorized by law, public school districts must provide nonpublic school students with, for instance:

- health and welfare services (§ 912; see **50:4**);
- transportation (§ 3635, see **chapter 58**);
- textbook loans (§ 701(3); see **4:15-20**);
- computer software (§ 752; see **4:23**);
- instructional computer hardware (§ 754; see **4:22**);
- library materials (§ 712; see **4:21**);

(see also NYS Education Department, *Handbook on Services to Pupils Attending Nonpublic Schools* (updated Feb. 2012), at: http://www.p12.nysed.gov/nonpub/handbookonservices/home.html).

In addition, to the extent required under section 3602-c of the Education Law (also known as the dual-enrollment law), and upon parental request, school districts must provide students attending nonpublic schools with educational services in the areas of instruction for the gifted, career education, and education for students with disabilities, and counseling, psychological and social work services related to such instruction, provided such services are offered to public school students (§ 3602-c(1)). However, nonpublic school students have no right to attend public school on a part-time basis or to receive educational services from a public school beyond those areas specified in statute (*Appeal of K.L.*, 53 Ed Dept Rep, Dec. No. 16,627 (2014): *Appeal of Sutton*, 39 Ed Dept Rep 625 (2000)).

Under federal law, including the Every Student Succeds Act, school districts may also be required to provide services to students attending nonpublic schools, such as remedial instruction, and other supplementary services (§ 1011).

For information on the rights of home-schooled students under New York's dual-enrollment law, see **48:52**.

4:12. What are the basic procedures for providing dual enrollment services to students attending nonpublic schools?

Parental requests for dual-enrollment services must be filed with the school district responsible for providing the services by June 1 preceding the school year for which services are requested (§ 3602-c(2)). Request for career education or services for gifted students must be filed with the student's district of residence. Requests for education for students with disabilities must be filed with the district of location where the nonpublic school is located (*Id.*; 8 NYCRR § 177.1). There is one exception to the June 1st deadline. A student who is first identified as disabled after June 1st and before April 1st may submit a request for services within 30 days after being identified (§ 3602-c(2)(a)).

In the case of career education and instruction for gifted students, the school district of residence shall contract for such services with the school district in which the nonpublic school is located (§ 3602-c(2)(d)). However, in the case of students with disabilities, the school district where the nonpublic school attended by a disabled student is located is responsible for providing special education services to the student (§ 3602-c(2)(a), (b); 20 USC § 1412(a)(10)(A); 34 CFR §§ 300.130-144). For more information on special education services for nonpublic school students see **54:98-105**.

In addition, transportation must be furnished for students receiving gifted or career education between the nonpublic school and the site where the program is offered if the distance is more than one-fourth of a mile. Transportation for students with disabilities must be provided in accordance with their needs. The district may claim state aid for this transportation (§ 3602-c(4)).

4:13. Are school districts required to provide dual-enrollment services on site at the nonpublic schools?

No. The dual-enrollment law indicates that the services be provided in the regular classes of the public schools, with public school students in attendance (§ 3602-c(9); but see **4:14**, regarding services for students with disabilities).

4:14. Is a school district required to provide on-site special education and related services to students with disabilities who attend private schools, including parochial schools?

According to the U.S. Supreme Court there is no federal constitutional impediment to providing services to students on site at the premises of their parochial school (*Agostini v. Felton*, 521 U.S. 203 (1997)). Furthermore, under the Individuals with Disabilities Education Act, special education services may be provided to students with disabilities on the premises of private schools, including parochial schools, to the extent consistent with law (20 USC § 1412(a)(10)(A)(i)(III); 34 CFR § 300.139(a)). However, a school district is not required under federal law to provide on-site special education services to children with disabilities voluntarily enrolled in private schools.

With respect to state law, the New York Court of Appeals has ruled that section 3602-c of the Education Law (the state's dual-enrollment law) does not mandate that districts provide such services on-site for each nonpublic school student with a disability. On the other hand, on-site special education services must be provided at a nonpublic school to students whose educational needs require on-site delivery of services (*Bd. of Educ. of Bayshore UFSD v. Thomas K.*, 14 N.Y.3d 289 (2010); see also **54:102**).

4:15. Must public school districts purchase and loan textbooks to students attending nonpublic schools?

Yes. Section 701 of the Education Law requires all school boards to purchase and to loan "upon individual request" textbooks, work books, manuals, including courseware, or other content-based instructional materials in electronic format, for example, to all children residing in the district who attend kindergarten through 12th grade in any public school and in any nonpublic school. Items such as encyclopedias, almanacs, atlases, certain audiovisual materials, and review books are not considered "textbooks" (see 8 NYCRR § 21.2(a)).

Textbooks may be purchased only for resident students (see 8 NYCRR § 21.2(a)). Children who reside outside of the district in which the nonpublic school they attend is located must have their textbooks provided by their district of residence (§ 701(3)).

Under the statute, both the power and the duty to purchase and loan textbooks depend upon individual requests to the school board for such textbooks (*Appeal of Bruning*, 48 Ed Dept Rep 84 (2008), *petition dismissed*, *Bruning v. NYSED*, (Sup. Ct. Albany Cnty. Mar. 24, 2009)). Section 701(6) of the Education Law provides that school districts receive an additional apportionment of state aid to comply with the statute. No school district is required to spend more on purchasing textbooks than the amount of state aid it receives for this purpose (§ 701(4)).

4:16. Must a nonpublic school use the same textbooks as those used by the school district?

No. The choice of textbooks to be used by students attending a nonpublice school is made by that nonpublic school's personnel. However, textbooks loaned to nonpublic school students must be "designed for use in any public schools of the state or are approved by any boards of education, trustees or other school authorities" (§701(3)).

A school district can have a policy that requires nonpublic schools to submit evidence that each textbook they have chosen is in use in one or more other school districts in the state. A nonpublic school can meet this obligation by verifying from the textbook publisher that the textbook is being used by one or more New York State school district(s) and provides a properly authenticated list of the same to the district. If a district has any doubt that a textbook has been designated for use or approved by any school board, it has the option to contact the school district(s) identified, by telephone or otherwise, or decide on its own if the textbook should be approved (*Appeal of McLoughlin and Wood*, 55 Ed Dept Rep, Dec. No. 16,886 (2016)). A school district may not insist that a nonpublic school submit a board resolution or other written statement from another school district that the textbook has been approved by its board of education for use in that district (*Id.*)

4:17. Must school districts have in place a process for the distribution of textbooks to nonpublic school students?

Yes. The commissioner of education has held that a school board must establish a procedure to ensure equitable distribution of all available textbooks, "both those on hand from prior years and those newly purchased." This "procedure must assure that in each subject area students are treated equally regardless of the school attended" (*Matter of Gross*, 25 Ed Dept Rep 382 (1986); see also *Appeal of Kelly*, 35 Ed Dept Rep 235 (1996); *Matter of Caunitz*, 30 Ed Dept Rep 396 (1991); § 701(4); 8 NYCRR § 21.2(c)).

School districts cannot require that requests come through the nonpublic school, but they can accommodate that method, as long as they also permit individual requests (*Appeal of Bruning*, 48 Ed Dept Rep 84 (2008), *petition dismissed*, *Bruning v. NYSED*, (Sup. Ct. Albany Cnty. Mar. 24, 2009); NYS Education Department, *New York State Textbook Loan Program: Recommended Procedures for Textbook Purchases, Loans and Inventory Control* (updated May 2009), at: https://stateaid.nysed.gov/tsl/html_docs/txtbk03.htm. Districts can, by policy, set forth a date by which textbook requests must be received, but the date cannot be earlier than June 1st.

Parents of students not attending a particular nonpublic school prior to June 1 of the school year may submit a written request for textbooks within 30 days of enrollment in the nonpublic school. A request made later than such deadlines cannot be denied where a reasonable explanation for the delay is given (§ 701(8)).

For more information, see *New York State Textbook Loan Program: Recommended Procedures for Textbook Purchases, Loans and Inventory Control*.

4:18. Can school districts limit the amount of funds to be spent on lending textbooks to nonpublic students?

No. A school district may not set a dollar value limit on textbooks provided to each student. If inventory is insufficient, it must purchase additional books. However, a district does not have to spend in excess of the textbook aid it receives, although it may provide for additional funds as part of its annual budget. If an appropriation is inadequate to purchase all the books required, a district must determine which categories of the textbooks may be loaned to both public and nonpublic students within the resources available (*Appeal of Hoerter*, 48 Ed Dept Rep 373 (2009); *Appeal of Bruning*, 48 Ed Dept Rep 84 (2008), *petition dismissed*, *Bruning v. NYSED* (Sup. Ct. Albany Cnty. Mar. 24, 2009); *Appeal of Gallagher*, 47 Ed Dept Rep 69 (2007)).

4:19. Can school districts reimburse nonpublic school students for textbooks they may have purchased on their own?

No. Although the Education Law requires public schools to loan textbooks upon individual request, it does not authorize school districts to reimburse individuals who have purchased textbooks on their own (*Appeal of Bruning*, 48 Ed Dept Rep 84 (2008), *petition dismissed*, *Bruning v. NYSED* (Sup. Ct. Albany Cnty. Mar. 24, 2009); *Appeal of Kelly*, 35 Ed Dept Rep 235 (1996)).

4:20. Is it constitutionally permissible for a public school district to purchase and loan textbooks to students attending parochial schools?

Yes. The U.S. Supreme Court has upheld the constitutionality of New York State's Education Law textbook provisions (*Bd. of Educ. v. Allen*, 392 U.S. 236 (1968); see also *Mitchell v. Helms*, 530 U.S. 793 (2000)). However, textbooks purchased and loaned to parochial school students must be nonsectarian and designated for use in any public elementary or secondary school of the state or approved by any school board (§ 701(3); 8 NYCRR § 21.2(a)(4)).

4:21. May nonpublic school students borrow library materials?

Yes. School library materials owned or acquired by a public school district pursuant to section 711 of the Education Law must be made available on an equitable basis to all eligible students enrolled in grades kindergarten through 12 in both public and nonpublic schools located within the public school district (§ 712; 8 NYCRR § 21.4(d)).

Such library materials must be required for use as a learning aid in a particular class or program, and loaned for individual student use only (8 NYCRR § 21.4(b)). They must be loaned free of charge upon the individual request of eligible nonpublic school students. Requests may be presented directly to the lending district, or with the consent of the district, to an appropriate official at the nonpublic school attended by the student (8 NYCRR § 21.4(c)).

School authorities must establish lending procedures consistent with the commissioner's regulations and must inform authorities at the nonpublic schools within the boundaries of the public school district of these procedures (8 NYCRR § 21.4(d)).

4:22. May school districts purchase and loan instructional computer hardware to nonpublic school students?

Yes. The law provides that school districts must loan instructional computer hardware to nonpublic school students upon individual request (§ 754; 8 NYCRR §§ 21.3, 175.25). This includes such items as mini-computers; microcomputers; peripheral devices, including printers, video display plotters, and desk storage units; telecommunications hardware, including modems; special hardware boards; cables; audio, video, touch-sensitive, and other electronic to human machine interface hardware; and other computer hardware required for a computer-based instructional program (8 NYCRR §§ 21.3(b)(1)(i), 175.25(b)). However, a school district may not purchase or loan instructional computer hardware that contains software programs that are religious in nature or content (8 NYCRR § 21.3(b)(2); see also *Mitchell v. Helms*, 530 U.S. 793 (2000); *Bd. of Educ. v. Allen*, 392 U.S. 236 (1968)).

The computer hardware must be loaned free to nonpublic school students on an equitable basis (§ 754(2); 8 NYCRR § 21.3(b)(4), (6)). School districts must have in place regulations specifying the date by which requests must be made as required by law and regulations (§ 754(3); 8 NYCRR § 21.3(b)(3)).

A district is not required to loan nonpublic students instructional computer hardware in excess of the hardware acquired under section 753 of the Education Law (§ 754(2); 8 NYCRR § 21.3(b)(4)).

For more information on the loan of instructional computer hardware, see NYS Education Department, *Requirements for the Loan of Instructional Computer Hardware to Nonpublic School Students for the 2007-2008 School Year and Thereafter Pursuant to Education Law Section 754* (updated Mar. 2009), at: http://stateaid.nysed.gov/tsl/html_docs/hw_loan_req_060607.htm.

4:23. Must school districts purchase and loan computer software programs to nonpublic school students?

Yes. The law provides that school districts may purchase computer software programs and must loan these software programs upon individual request to nonpublic school students (§§ 751-752; 8 NYCRR § 21.3(a)(3)). This software must be made available on an equitable basis to all eligible pupils, in both public and nonpublic schools (8 NYCRR § 21.3(a)(4)).

Computer software does not include microcomputers, blank diskettes, cassettes or tapes, chips, computer correction devices, consoles, cords, disk drives, or other similar items of hardware (8 NYCRR § 21.3(a)). Moreover, a public school district may purchase only computer software programs that do not contain material of a religious nature (8 NYCRR § 21.3(a)(2); see also *Mitchell v. Helms*, 530 U.S. 793 (2000); *Bd. of Educ. v. Allen*, 392 U.S. 236 (1968)).

No school district is required to purchase or otherwise acquire software programs that will cost more than the "software factor" multiplied by the sum of the public school district enrollment and the enrollment of nonpublic school students within the school district (§§ 751(3), (4), 3602(1)(n)(2), (3), (6)).

4:24. Must school districts allow nonpublic school students to participate in extracurricular activities at the public schools?

No. School boards have the authority to limit participation in extracurricular activities to those students enrolled in their district's public schools (*Appeal of Ponte*, 41 Ed Dept Rep 186 (2001)).

However, a school board may establish a policy that allows students not enrolled in its public schools to participate in school-sponsored club activities (NYS Education Department, *Home Instruction Questions and Answers* (updated Mar. 2015) at: http://www.p12.nysed.gov/sss/homeinstruction/homeschoolingqanda.html).

Nonetheless, a school board may not allow students not enrolled in its public schools to participate in the district's interscholastic sports program or intramural activities (8 NYCRR §§ 135.4(c)(7)(ii)(b)(2), 135.1(g), (m); *Home Instruction Questions and Answers*)).

5. School Boards

Composition

5:1. What is a school board?

A *school board* is a corporate body that oversees and manages a public school district's affairs, personnel, and properties (§§ 1601, 1603, 1701, 2502(1), 2551). With the exception of New York City and Yonkers, its members are elected by the residents of the school district that the board oversees (see **5:2, 5:6**).

The term *corporate body* indicates that a school board is treated as a corporation, a legal entity that has an existence distinct and apart from its members and has the capacity for continuous existence without regard to changes in its membership. As such, the legalities of a school board's contracts, as well as the validity of a board's policies and resolutions, do not depend on its individual members.

Board members do not assume any personal liability for the school district even though they may be personally liable for certain conduct (see **66:1-4, 38**). Generally, school board members take official action only by majority vote at an official meeting (see **5:19**).

5:2. What is the composition of a school board?

A school board is composed of its elected members. One member is elected by the board at its annual reorganizational meeting to serve as president (see **14:1**). At its discretion, the board also may elect a vice president, who exercises the duties of the president in case of that officer's absence or disability. If the office of president becomes vacant, the vice president acts as president until a new president is elected (§ 1701).

5:3. Is there a difference between a trustee and a school board member?

No. The term *trustee* generally refers to a member of a school board of a common school district, whereas the term *school board member* generally refers to a member of the school board of any other type of school district. These terms are sometimes used interchangeably, but the more contemporary and commonly used term is board member.

Board member is also the term used throughout this book, unless a distinction is necessary for accuracy or clarity.

5:4. Are school board members local or state officials?

School board members are local officials.

Section 2 of the Public Officers Law defines *state officers* as those who are elected by all of the state's voters (such as the governor, lieutenant governor, comptroller, and attorney general); members of the state Legislature; justices of the state Supreme Court; Regents of the University of the State of New York; and every officer, appointed by one or more state officers, or by the Legislature, and authorized to exercise his or her official functions throughout the state or without limitation to any political subdivision of the state. All others are considered to be local officers, including school board members. However, their authority and duties are defined by the state and federal constitutions and laws, as well as by rules and regulations promulgated by the Board of Regents and commissioner of education.

5:5. May a student serve as an ex-officio non-voting member of a school board?

Yes. The Education Law expressly allows union free, central, central high school and small city school districts to have a high school student serve as an ex-officio non-voting member of the school board if district voters approve having a student serve in that capacity. A district may offer voters this option once every two years (§§ 1702(3), (3-a), 1804(12), (12-a), 1901(2), (3), 2502(10), (10-a)).

If prior to August 5, 2003 a school district had a policy that allowed for a student ex-officio board member, such policy may remain in effect for the selection process. Otherwise, the student board member may be any of the following: the elected student president of the high school, a student elected by the student body, a student selected by the high school student government, a student selected by either the high school principal or superintendent of schools, or a student selected by a majority vote of the school board. However, if the district has a district-wide student government or advisory committee, the student ex-officio board member must be selected by the superintendent of schools from among the members of such entities subject to a ratification vote by the majority of the board. If a district has multiple high schools its selection process must take that into consideration. The student selected must be a senior at the high school and have attended the high school for at least two years prior to the selection (§§ 1702(3)(c), (d), 1804(12)(c), (d), 1901(2)(c), (d), 2502(10)(c), (d)). Although the student board member is not entitled to vote, he or she can sit with the board at all public meetings and participate in all board hearings and meetings, except executive sessions (§§ 1702(3)(a), (b), 1804(12)(a), (b), 1901(2)(a), (b), 2502(10)(a), (b)).

In New York City, community district education councils must have a high school senior serve as a non-voting council member. The superintendent appoints a student from among the elected student leadership (§ 2590-c(1)(c)).

Public School Governance

5:6. How many school board members serve on a school board?

It depends on the type of school district. As the voters of the district determine, a common school district may have from one or three trustees (§§ 1602(1), 2101(1)). A union free school district may have from three to nine board members (§§ 1702(1), 2101(2)). A central school district may have a board consisting of five, seven, or nine members (§ 1804(1)). The board of a central high school district is comprised of a minimum of five members, at least one from each common school district and at least two from each union free school district within the central high school district (§§ 1901, 1914). A small city school district with a population under 125,000 may have a board consisting of five, seven, or nine members (§ 2502(2)). Union free, central, central high school and small city districts may also have an ex-officio student member (see **5:5**).

Except in New York City, a large city school district's board may have between three and nine members (§ 2552). For example:

- In Yonkers, nine school board members are appointed by the mayor from the city at large (§§ 2552(d), 2553(3)).
- In both Rochester and Syracuse, seven board members are elected by the voters at large, at either a general or municipal election or both (§§ 2552(b), (c), 2553(2)).
- In Buffalo, a total of nine school board members are elected by the voters from a combination of specific districts and at large seats. Six of these board members are elected from six subdistricts of equal population created by the Buffalo Common Council. Three members are elected from the city at large (§§ 2552(a), 2553(10)).

In New York City, the Panel for Educational Policy (PEP) consists of 13 appointed members and the Chancellor. Each borough president appoints one member and the mayor appoints the remaining eight. Each borough president's appointee shall be a resident of the respective borough and shall be the parent of a student attending a public school within the district. Each mayoral appointee shall be a resident of the city and two mayoral appointees shall be parents of a child attending a public school within the district. The parent members shall be eligible to continue to serve on the panel for two years after the conclusion of their child's attendance at the public school. The Chancellor serves as an ex-officio non-voting member (§ 2590-b(1)(a)). There are also two non-voting student advisory members selected by the Chancellor's High School Advisory Council. For more information on PEPs, see NYC Department of Education, *Bylaws of the Panel for Educational Policy of the Department of Education of the City School District of the City of New York*, at: http://schools.nyc.gov/NR/rdonlyres/B432D059-6BFE-4198-8453-466FDE2B22D5/69835/PEPBylawsFinal91409.pdf). New York City also has community and citywide education councils whose membership, powers and duties are set forth in law (§§ 2590-b, 2590-c and 2590-e; see also NYC Department of Education, *Citywide and Community Education Councils*, at: http://schools.nyc.gov/Offices/CEC/default.htm).

A board of cooperative educational services (BOCES) has between five and 15 members elected by the members of the school boards of the BOCES' component school districts (§ 1950(1), (2)). A more detailed discussion of BOCES members' terms, as well as other issues related to BOCES, is provided in **chapter 7**.

5:7. May the number of members on a school board be changed?

Yes. In common school districts that have only one trustee, two-thirds of the legal voters present and voting at any annual meeting may vote to increase the size of the board to three trustees (§ 1602(3); see also *Matter of Gillison*, 70 State Dep't Rep. 60 (1949)). In common school districts that already have three trustees, a simple majority of the voters present and voting may decrease the size of the board to one trustee (§ 1602(2)). When the voters determine to decrease the number of trustees to one, the trustees in office continue in office until their terms expire, and thereafter only one trustee will be elected (*Id.*).

In union free and central school districts, the number of members of a board can be increased or decreased by a majority vote of the qualified voters present and voting at the annual meeting. A proposition to increase or decrease the size of the school board must be put before the voters upon petition of 25 voters or 5 percent of the number of people who voted in the previous annual election, whichever is greater (§§ 1703(1), (2), 1804(3); *Matter of Degioia*, 17 Ed Dept Rep 451 (1978); see also *Matter of Swanson*, 29 Ed Dept Rep 503 (1990)).

In small city school districts, the board may, on its own motion, and must, on a written petition signed by 500 qualified voters of the district, submit a proposition at the annual election to increase or decrease the number of members of the board (§ 2502(4)(a)).

Petitions to change the number of members on a school board must be submitted enough in advance, according to the procedures prescribed by the board, to allow a statement giving notice of the proposition to be included in the notice of the annual meeting (§§ 1703(2), 2035(2), 2502(4)(b); see *Matter of Presutti*, 17 Ed Dept Rep 445 (1978); see also **15:10, 15:30**).

If a board receives two conflicting propositions with respect to changing the number of board members (one to increase and one to decrease) it is not required to put both before the electorate and may accept only the first properly filed proposition (*Appeal of Devine*, 44 Ed Dept Rep 278 (2005)).

For information on changing the number of members on boards of cooperative educational services, see **7:5**.

5:8. When do changes to the number of members on a school board take effect?

When the voters determine to increase the number of board members, the additional members are elected at a special meeting to be held for that purpose, between 30 and 60 days from the annual meeting approving the increase (§§ 1703(3), 1804(3); *Matter of the Appeal of Beck*, 74 State Dep't Rep. 78 (1953); *Matter of Gillison,* 70 State Dep't Rep. 60 (1949)), except in common and small city school districts where the additional members are elected at the next annual meeting (§§ 1602(3), 2502(4)(c)). The terms of the new members must be established to ensure that as nearly as possible an equal number of terms expire each year (§§ 1602(3), 1804(3), 2105(9), 2502(3), (4)(c)(3)).

If the voters approve a decrease in the number of board members, no election may be held until the number of members on the board is equal to or less than the number to which the board has been decreased. At subsequent elections in union free, central, and small city school districts, board members are to be elected for terms aimed at ensuring that an equal number of terms expire each year (§§ 1602(2), 1804(3), 2105(10), 2502(4)(c)).

5:9. What is the term of office for board members?

It depends on the type of school district. In common school districts that have just one trustee, the trustee serves only a one-year term (§§ 1602(1), 2105(1)). However, in common school districts with three trustees, the trustees are elected for three-year terms (§§ 1602(1), 2105(2)). In union free and central school districts, board members are elected for terms of three, four, or five years (§§ 1702(1), 1804(1), 2105(3)).

Members of a central high school board must be members of the school board of a component district while they are members of the central high school board. However, the term of office on the central high school board can be shorter than the term on the school board of the component district (*Appeal of Carbonaro*, 35 Ed Dept Rep 257 (1996); see also §§ 1901, 1914).

The term of office for city board members varies among the various city school districts. In most city school districts with less than 125,000 inhabitants, the term of office of a school board member is three or five years, as determined by the district (§ 2502(3)). In the Albany City School District, a board member's term is four years (§ 2502(3)). In the Rensselaer City School District, the term is five years (§ 2502(9-a)(n)).

In city school districts with 125,000 or more inhabitants (the Big 5), the term of office of school board members is as follows:

- In Buffalo, board members elected from the city school subdistricts are elected for three-year terms, while the term of office for members of the school board who are elected at large is five years (§ 2553(10)(n)).
- In New York City, members of the Panel for Educational Policy (i.e., the central board) serve at the pleasure of the appointing authority. Community education council members hold two-year terms except for the non-voting high school senior who is appointed by the superintendent from among the elected student leadership, who holds a one-year term (§§ 2590-b(1)(a), 2590-c(1); see **5:5**).
- In both Rochester and Syracuse, board members are elected to four-year terms (§ 2553(4)).
- In Yonkers, board members are appointed to five-year terms (§ 2553(4)).

Board of cooperative educational services (BOCES) board members generally serve three-year terms (§ 1950(2)). A more detailed discussion of BOCES members' terms, as well as other issues related to BOCES, is provided in **chapter 7**.

5:10. May the term of office for a board member be changed?

Yes. In central and union free school districts, board members serve either a three-, four- or five-year term. Education Law section 2105(3) specifically authorizes the voters of such districts to decrease the full term of a board member to three or four years or increase the full term of a member to four or five years. Such changes can be accomplished only by voter approval of a proposition submitted to the voters at an annual meeting or election (§ 2105(3); *Appeal of Rockwell,* 51 Ed Dept Rep, Dec. No. 16,355 (2012); *Appeal of Atkins*, 35 Ed Dept Rep 375 (1996)).

Board members in city school districts with less than 125,000 inhabitants serve either a three- or five-year term. Education Law section 2502(3) specifically authorizes such districts to decrease the full term of a board to three years or increase it to five by adopting a proposition at any regular meeting or election to do so (§ 2502(3)).

The current term of office of incumbent board members may not be increased or decreased by any such proposition. In addition, propositions to increase or decrease the term of office must specify that vacancies during each of the three years next succeeding the adoption of such proposition will be filled for terms that ensure, as nearly as possible, that equal numbers of board members will be elected each year (§§ 2105(3), 2502(3); *Appeal of Atkins*).

5:11. Are school board members required to take an oath of office?

Yes. School board members are not able to exercise the duties of office until they take the following oath: "I do solemnly swear (or affirm) that I will support the constitution of the United States, and the constitution of the State of New York, and that I will faithfully discharge the duties of the office of . . ., according to the best of my ability" (N.Y. Const. art. 13, § 1). This oath must be filed with the district clerk. In the case of a board of cooperative educational services, each board member files an oath in the office of the clerk of the county in which that member resides (Pub. Off. Law § 10).

The refusal or neglect of a school board member to file an oath of office within 30 days after the commencement of the term of office to which the person is elected, or if appointed, within 30 days after notice of appointment or commencement of the term of office to which the person is appointed, causes the office to become vacant (Pub. Off. Law § 30(1)(h); *Appeal of Campbell*, 50 Ed Dept Rep, Dec. No. 16,246 (2011); *Appeal of Rausch*, 41 Ed Dept Rep 351 (2002)).

Usually the president of the board or the district clerk administers the oath to newly elected school board members at the board's annual reorganizational meeting, although there is no legal requirement that the oath be administered at such a meeting. The fact that the oath has been administered at such meeting should be noted in the board's minutes.

There is no requirement either that the board president know the oath is being administered and/or participate in the administration of the oath (*Appeal of Campbell*). An individual who has not properly taken and filed an oath of office has no authority to administer oaths to others (*Application of Karpen*, 39 Ed Dept Rep 98 (1999)).

Members who are reelected to the school board also must take the oath at the beginning of their new term of office, just as at the beginning of the first term they held. Board officers, such as the president, vice president, clerk and treasurer, must be administered the oath each year at the time of their appointment or reappointment.

Vacancies

5:12. How do vacancies occur on a school board?

In addition to the timely expiration of a board member's term of office, vacancies on a school board may occur due to death, incapacity, resignation, removal from office, or refusal to serve (§ 2112; *Matter of Turchiarelli*, 31 Ed Dept Rep 402 (1992); see also **5:13**).

A position also may become vacant if an incumbent board member moves to a residence outside the district (Pub. Off. Law § 30(1)(d); *Matter of Willard*, 23 Ed Dept Rep 448 (1984)). However, "an individual's residence is not lost until a new residence is established through both intent and action" (*Appeal of Lavelle*, 28 Ed Dept Rep 189 (1988)).

A vacancy also will occur if a board member is convicted of a felony or crime involving his or her oath of office, is declared incompetent; refuses or fails to timely file an oath of office; or by a judgment of a court indicating the same (see Pub. Off. Law § 30(1); *Appeal of Rausch*, 41 Ed Dept Rep 351 (2002); Opn. Att'y Gen. F 97-7, I 99-3; see also **5:11**). In an informal opinion, the New York State Attorney General indicated that a school board member who pled guilty to a misdemeanor petit larceny charge after being charged with a felony for illegally collecting unemployment insurance violated her oath of office and vacated her position as a school board member by operation of law. The crime involved "willful deceit" and a "calculated disregard for honest dealings" (Opn. Att'y Gen. I 99-3, see also F 97-7).

5:13. May a vacancy on a school board be declared if a member is absent from three successive meetings?

Yes. A vacancy based on "refusal to serve" may be declared if the record clearly shows that a board member has failed to attend three successive meetings and has no sufficient excuse for the absences (§§ 2109, 2502(8), 2553(8), 2590-b(7)(g), 2590-c(6)(a); *Appeal of McQuaid Kaplan*, 50 Ed Dept Rep, Dec. No. 16,113 (2010); *Appeal of Dupras*, 47 Ed Dept Rep 471 (2008); *Appeal of Cox*, 28 Ed Dept Rep 156 (1988)). If the board member has sufficient excuse to warrant absence from the meetings, a vacancy cannot be declared (*Appeal of Mahoney,* 53 Ed Dept Rep, Dec. No. 16,605 (2014); *Appeal of Rowe*, 31 Ed Dept Rep 280 (1992); *Application of Shader*, 31 Ed Dept Rep 252 (1992)).

5:14. Are school districts obligated to fill a vacancy when one arises?

The applicable laws impose upon union free and central school districts the power and duty to fill a vacancy (§§ 1709(17), 1804(1); see *Appeal of French*, 32 Ed Dept Rep 100 (1992)) and require common school districts to immediately call a special meeting to fill the vacancy when it occurs (§ 1607(2)).

According to the commissioner of education, small city school boards are not obligated to fill a vacancy because the statutory language governing vacancies in small city schools makes filling a vacancy optional (§ 2502(6); *Appeal of Keyrouze*, 34 Ed Dept Rep 468 (1995)). However, the Albany and Rensselaer city school districts are governed by special provisions of law not examined in the commissioner's decision above. The law applicable to those districts provides that whenever a vacancy occurs other than because of the expiration of a board member's term of office or because of an increase in the size of the board, the board "shall" appoint a qualified person to fill the vacancy (§§ 2502(9)(n), 2502(9-a)(n)). In large city school districts, different rules of law and/or exceptions apply (see §§ 2553(6), (7), (9)(e), (10)(n), 2590-b(1)(a), 2590-c(6)(b), (c), (d)).

5:15. What is the procedure to fill a vacancy on a school board?

As a general rule, any school board may call a special election to fill such a vacancy within 90 days after it occurs. If that does not happen, the district superintendent may fill it by appointment in school districts under his or her jurisdiction (§ 2113(1)).

Common school districts, however, must call a special district meeting immediately to fill a vacancy (§ 1607(2)). In addition, the commissioner of education may order a special election to fill a vacancy in a union free school district (§ 2113(2)). Moreover, the Education Law requires that the Kenmore-Town of Tonawanda UFSD school board fill a vacancy by appointment of the remaining board members to serve until the next annual election (§ 2113(4)).

Otherwise, school boards in union free, central, and small city school districts may choose instead to appoint a qualified person to fill a vacancy (§§ 1709(17), 1804(1), 2502(6)).

Consistent with the limitation on the board's authority to act as a corporate body, a vote of the majority of the whole board ordinarily is required to fill a vacancy by appointment (see **5:19**). But in small city school districts, due to a unique provision of law, only a "majority of the remaining members of the board" is needed to appoint a qualified person to fill a board vacancy (§ 2502(6), (9)(n), (9-a)(n)).

If a vacancy is filled by a special district election, the elected board member serves for the remainder of the unexpired term (§ 2113(3)). If the vacancy is filled by appointment, the new board member serves only until the next regular school district election (N.Y. Const. art. 13, § 3; §§ 1709(17), 2113(3), 2502(6)).

Special rules of law govern the appointment of board members in the Albany and Rensselaer city school districts (§§ 2502(9)(n), 2502(9-a)(n)), and in large city school districts (§§ 2553(6), (7), (9)(e), (10)(n), 2590-b(1)(a), 2590-c(6)(b), (c), (d)).

A person elected or appointed to fill a vacancy takes office immediately upon filing the oath of office (§§ 1709(17), 2502(6); see **5:11, 6:33**).

Powers and Duties

5:16. What are the powers and duties of a school board?

A school board has no inherent powers and possesses only those powers expressly delegated by statute or necessarily and reasonably implied therefrom (*Appeal of Woodarek,* 46 Ed Dept Rep 1 (2006), *petition dismissed*, (Sup. Ct. Albany Cnty. May 22, 2007); *Appeal of McKenna*, 42 Ed Dept Rep 54 (2002); *Appeal of Rosenkranz,* 37 Ed Dept Rep 330 (1998); *Appeal of Bode*, 33 Ed Dept Rep 260 (1993)).

The general powers and duties of school boards are outlined in the Education Law, which assigns different powers and duties to different types of school districts, some of which are common to various types of districts, others of which are specific to a single type of district. Figure 1 below lists the different types of school districts and the Education Law sections that govern their respective responsibilities.

Fig. 1

School Board Responsibilities

Type of school district	**Education Law section**
common school districts	1604
union free school districts	1709
central school districts	1804
central high school districts	1903
small city school districts	2503
large city school districts	2554
New York City Panel for Educational Policy (formerly, the central board)	2590-g
New York City community district educational councils	2590- e

Additional powers and duties may be found in other state laws such as the General Municipal Law, the Local Finance Law, the Real Property Tax Law and the Public Officers Law, as well as in federal law and regulations, and the state education commissioner's regulations.

However, all school boards are similar in that they are responsible for the education of the children residing in their respective districts.

Generally, school boards are responsible for the admission, instruction, discipline, grading, and, as appropriate, classification of students attending the public schools in their districts; for the employment and management of necessary professional and support staff; and for purchasing, leasing, maintaining, and insuring school buildings, properties, equipment, and supplies (see generally § 1709). With the exception of large city school districts, they also must present a detailed statement of estimated expenditures (i.e., the proposed budget) for the ensuing school year, which must be submitted to the district voters annually for approval (§§ 1608, 1716, 2022, 2601-a; see also **18:1-13, 15:1**).

In addition, school boards are the only charter entity authorized to receive and approve an application for the conversion of one of their existing public schools into a charter school (§ 2851(3)(a), (c)). For more information on charter schools, see **chapter 3**.

Consistent with law, school boards also have the authority and duty to adopt whatever policies, rules, and bylaws they deem will best meet their statutory responsibilities and secure the best educational results for the students in their charge (see, e.g., §§ 1709(1), (2), 2503(2)), including rules and regulations concerning the order and discipline of the schools (§ 1709(2); *Appeal of Anonymous*, 48 Ed Dept Rep 503 (2009); see also **5:32-35**).

Special rules govern the adoption of bylaws and regulations by the city board, the chancellor, and the individual community education councils in New York City (§§ 2590-d(1), (2), 2590-g).

5:17. What is devolution, and how does it affect the powers and duties of school boards?

Devolution is the process by which the powers and duties assigned to specific school districts at the top of the list in Figure 2 below devolve and become applicable to other types of school districts through specific provisions of the Education Law (§§ 1710, 1804(1), 1805, 1903, 2503(1), 2554(1)). As shown in this figure, districts lower on the list are granted many of the powers of districts higher on the list by reference to the powers possessed by those districts. As these powers and duties devolve down to other types of districts, they are joined by additional powers and duties that then devolve to school districts located lower on the list. The additional powers, however, do not apply to school districts located higher on the table. Powers and duties devolve down but not up.

Fig. 2

Devolution

Type of District	Ed. Law Article	Ed. Law Section(s)
Common School District	33	—
Union Free School District	35	1710
Central School District	37	1804(1), 1805
Central High School District	39	1903
Small City School District	51	2503(1)
Large City School District	52	2554(1)

Unless the powers that devolve are inconsistent with other specific provisions of the Education Law applicable to a particular type of school district, such a district has all of the powers and duties assigned specifically to it, as well as all of the powers and duties assigned to the other types of school districts located above it on the list (see *Matter of Felicio*, 19 Ed Dept Rep 414 (1980)).

The figure above indicates the order of the devolution of powers and duties of school districts. The figure also refers to the article of the Education Law that governs each type of school district, as well as the section of the Education Law that provides for such devolution.

In this publication, a general reference or citation to powers and duties of school districts refers to those of union free school districts, as set forth in section 1709, which usually apply, through devolution, to all other school districts, with the exception of common school districts.

5:18. Are school board members required to take any kind of training?

Yes. Every school board member elected or appointed is required to take six hours of training on fiscal oversight, accountability, and fiduciary responsibilities within the first year of his or her term (§ 2102-a(1)(a)). Once the training is completed it does not need to be repeated if a board member is re-elected (NYS Education Department, *Accounting and Auditing, Board Member Training* (updated Oct. 2010), at: http://www.p12.nysed.gov/mgtserv/accounting/board_train.html).

In addition, every school board member elected or appointed for a first term beginning on or after July 1, 2011, must complete within the first year of his or her term general training on the powers, functions and duties of school boards, and the powers and duties of other governing and administrative authorities affecting public education (§ 2102-a(1)(b)). School board members seated or appointed before July 1, 2011, are not required to undergo this general training (§ 2102-a(1)(c)). Both requirements do not apply to board members of the City School District of the City of New York so long as the chancellor certifies that the city has a training program that meets or exceeds the requirements of the law (§ 2102-a(4)).

The curriculum used for training on fiscal oversight, accountability and fiduciary responsibilities must be approved by the commissioner of education, in consultation with the comptroller. The curriculum for the general training must be approved by the commissioner. The required training may be taken together in a single course or separately. The training must be provided by a provider approved by the commissioner (§ 2102-a(2)). Proof of completion of the training received from the provider must be filed with the district clerk. Any expenses incurred for the training are a lawful charge upon the district (§ 2102-a(3)).

Failure to complete the mandatory training within the time period required by law can subject a board member to removal from the school board (*Appeals of Stepien & Lilly*, 47 Ed Dept Rep 388 (2008)).

5:19. Do individual members of a school board have the right to take official action on the board's behalf?

Generally, no. A school board acting in its corporate capacity is required to transact its business in the same manner as the governing body of any corporation; that is, its acts are required to be authorized by resolutions or motions duly adopted or passed by a majority of the whole board (§§ 1606, 1710, 1804(1), 2502(1), 2503(1); Gen. Constr. Law § 41; *Downey v. Onteora CSD*, 2009 U.S. Dist. LEXIS 67368 (N.D.N.Y. July 28, 2009); *Coughlan v. Cowan*, 21 Misc.2d 667 (Sup. Ct. Suffolk Cnty. 1959); *Appeal of Instone-Noonan,* 39 Ed Dept Rep 413 (1999); *Matter of Ascher*, 12 Ed Dept Rep 97 (1972)). Unless the board has taken official action to designate an individual member as the representative of the board for a particular purpose, an individual board member has no more authority than any other qualified voter of the district (see Gen. Constr. Law § 41; *Coughlan v. Cowan*; *Appeal of Silano*, 33 Ed Dept Rep 20 (1993), *petition dismissed*, Special Term (Sup. Ct. Albany Cnty.), Hughes J. (Jan. 10, 1994); *Matter of Bruno*, 4 Ed Dept Rep 14 (1964)).

However, occasionally the board may delegate authority to a board officer, such as an auditor (§§ 1604(35), 1709(20-a), 2554(2-a)). It may also delegate the power to perform ministerial acts to other district officers or employees, such as authorizing the business manager to make purchases with appropriated funds of certain items that do not require competitive bidding (8 NYCRR § 170.2(b)).

5:20. What happens if a school board fails to take official action?

A transaction has no legal effect and is not considered an official action unless made at a properly constituted meeting of the board (Gen. Constr. Law § 41). For example, a state appellate court ruled that litigation commenced on a district's behalf by the school attorney with the knowledge and tacit approval of the board was invalid and without effect because the board failed to formally vote in a public meeting to authorize such litigation. As a result, the district lost its victory before the lower court (*Gersen v. Mills,* 290 A.D.2d 839 (3d Dep't 2002)). Such a vote is required whether legal proceedings are commenced in the name of the district or the board itself (see *Barkan v. Roslyn*, 67 A.D.3d 61 (2d Dep't 2009)).

5:21. Do individual school board members have the right to visit schools?

Yes. Every board member has the same right as parents or school district residents to visit the schools in accordance with whatever district procedures apply to the public in general. However, individual board members may visit schools for official purposes, such as for building inspection, or interviewing staff, only with the authorization of the board (*Appeal of Silano*, 33 Ed Dept Rep 20 (1993), *petition dismissed*, Special Term (Sup. Ct. Albany Cnty.), Hughes J. (Jan. 10, 1994); *Matter of Bruno*, 4 Ed Dept Rep 14 (1964)).

5:22. May a school board hire a superintendent of schools?

Yes. A school board has the authority to hire a superintendent of schools and enter into employment contracts of varying duration with its superintendent as permitted by law (§§ 1604(8), 1711, 2503(5), 2554(2); see **10:1-2, 10:5-7**). A board may also agree to extend the superintendent's contract, so long as the entire term of the contract plus any extensions does not exceed the maximum term authorized by statute (*Appeal of Boyle*, 35 Ed Dept Rep 162 (1995), *petition dismissed*, Special Term (Sup. Ct. Albany Cnty.), Hughes J. (Jun. 10, 1996); see also **10:7**). For more information on superintendent contracts, see New York State School Boards Association's, *The Superintendent's Contract, A Guidebook for School Board Members, Revised 2nd Edition*, available at no cost to NYSSBA members on the Association's website at: http://www.nyssba.org/member-services/member-publications/.

5:23. May a school board remove its superintendent?

Generally, yes. The board, however, must comply with any applicable provisions set forth in law or in the superintendent's contract (see **10:14-15**).

For more information on the termination of superintendent contracts, see the New York State School Boards Association's, *The Superintendent's Contract, A Guidebook for School Board Members, Revised 2nd Edition*, available at no cost to NYSSBA members on the Association's website at: http://www.nyssba.org/member-services/member-publications/.

5:24. Do board members have a right to inspect personnel records?

Yes, but only for inspection and use in the deliberation of specific matters before the school board. There is no unconditional right to review employee records. In addition, board members may only use information garnered from examination of such records to aid in fulfilling duties related to appointments, assignments, pay, promotions, demotions, discipline or dismissal or to aid in the development of personnel policies (8 NYCRR Part 84, see also *Appeal of Meyer and Pavalow*, 46 Ed Dept Rep 43 (2006); see **13:20**).

A board member wishing to review an employee's record must provide the reason for the request with sufficient specificity to allow the board as a whole to determine if there is a proper reason to examine the files. If there is, the board must then vote to go into executive session to examine the files (8 NYCRR § 84.2). It is not enough for a board member asking to review an employee's record to simply state the review's purpose is "to enable the Board to carry out its legal responsibilities under the Education Law." He or she must specifically state how the requested records would enable that endeavor (*Appeal of Meyer and Pavalow*).

5:25. May an outgoing school board extend a superintendent's contract and thus bind successor boards?

Yes. The commissioner of education has ruled that even last-minute extensions of a superintendent's contract by an outgoing board, while not democratic, are legal and bind a successor board, because there is specific statutory authority permitting multi-year contracts with a superintendent (*Appeal of Dillon*, 33 Ed Dept Rep 544 (1994); *Appeal of Knapp*, 34 Ed Dept Rep 207 (1994); see **10:7-8**). However, an outgoing board may not tack on to an already existing contract a new obligation that would, when read together with the initial contract, exceed the statutory time limits on superintendent's contracts (*Appeal of Boyle*, 35 Ed Dept Rep 162 (1995), *petition dismissed*, Special Term (Sup. Ct. Albany Cnty.), Hughes J. (Jun. 10, 1996); see **10:7**).

5:26. May an outgoing school board bind a successor board to a contract with a school attorney?

No. It is improper for an outgoing school board to bind its successor to a contract with a school district attorney (*Harrison CSD v. Nyquist*, 59 A.D.2d 434 (3d Dep't 1977)). Outgoing boards may not enter into employment contracts for professional services that bind a successor board absent express statutory authority to do so (see *Karedes v. Colella,* 292 A.D.2d 138 (3d Dep't 2002), *rev'd on other grounds*, 100 N.Y.2d 45 (2003); see also *Morin v. Foster*, 45 N.Y.2d 287 (1978)), as in the case of a superintendent's contract (see **5:25**).

5:27. May a school board enter into a "pouring rights" contract?

Yes, a school board may enter into a contract that grants a vendor the exclusive right to supply beverages such as soft drinks and fruit juices in school buildings, vending areas, concessions, or other school property, subject to nutrition laws and regulations applicable to schools. In exchange, the vendor pays commissions or fees to the district. However, districts may not permit the use of school premises or staff to facilitate the sale of a vendor's products to fund-raising groups. Nor may a board allow a vendor to distribute beverages to students free of charge (*Appeal of American Quality Beverages LLC*, 42 Ed Dept Rep 153 (2002), *petition dismissed*, (Sup. Ct. Albany Cnty.), Connor J. (Oct. 7, 2004), *appeal dismissed* (3d Dep't Aug 17, 2006); *Appeal of American Quality Beverages LLC*, 42 Ed Dept Rep 144 (2002); *Appeal of Citizens for Responsible Fiscal & Educational Policy*, 40 Ed Dept Rep 315 (2000)).

Such contracts are not subject to competitive bidding unless the products purchased under the contract value at least $10,000 (*Appeal of American Quality Beverages LLC*, 42 Ed Dept Rep 153 (2002), *petition dismissed*, (Sup. Ct. Albany Cnty.) Connor J. (October 7, 2004), *appeal dismissed*, (3d Dep't August 17, 2006). Neither are the contracts for services by private food service companies otherwise subject to prior approval by the commissioner (*Appeals of American Quality Beverages LLC*). However, districts should not accept any advance payment that they are required to pay back in the event of early termination, so as not to bind successor boards (*Appeal of American Quality Beverages LLC*, 42 Ed Dept Rep 153 (2002), *petition dismissed*, (Sup. Ct. Albany Cnty.) Connor J. (Oct. 7, 2004), *appeal dismissed*, (3d Dep't August 17, 2006)).

In addition, the sale of presweetened beverages does not violate a district's obligation to provide physical and health education in an environment conducive to healthful living. Nonetheless, districts should consider whether the installation of vending machines in school is in the best interest of students' health, particularly at the elementary level. Although lighted vending machine panels do not violate state constitutional or regulatory provisions, districts should further consider whether promotional statements on such panels are appropriate for school environments (*Id.*).

5:28. May a school board establish a school camp?

Yes. An individual school district, or two or more school districts jointly, may establish and operate a school camp on school land or land acquired for that purpose. A city school district also may establish and operate a school camp on land provided for that purpose in state parks adjacent to the district. The camp may be used to furnish education in subjects deemed proper by the board, as well as to provide physical training, recreation, and maintenance for all children of school age whether they attend public or private school. Districts may charge a reasonable fee to cover costs of food and instructional materials, although the law requires that provision be made for children who cannot afford these fees (§§ 4501-4502).

5:29. May a school board authorize credit unions to open and maintain student branches within elementary and secondary schools?

Yes. However, use of such branches is restricted to students and excludes faculty, staff, or students' families. Approval from the school board is a prerequisite to a branch opening, and student membership expires 30 days after secondary school graduation or immediately upon transfer to another school or termination of enrollment (Banking Law § 450-b). This authority facilitates and fosters the skills necessary to fulfill learning standards requirements for mathematics and career development outlined in the commissioner's regulations (8 NYCRR § 100.1(t)(1)(ii), (vii)). According to the law's sponsor's memo, it helps students "obtain the skills, knowledge and experience necessary to manage their personal finances and obtain general financial literacy," which helps prepare them for the workforce and financial independence.

5:30. Must the school board designate a bank or trust company as an official school district depository?

Yes. The school board must designate one or more banks or trust companies as depository(ies) for district funds in accordance with section 10 of the General Municipal Law. The board resolution designating a depository must specify the maximum amount that may be kept on deposit at any time in each designated bank or trust company. These designations and monetary amounts may be changed at any time by further resolution (Gen. Mun. Law § 10(2)).

5:31. What are the school board's responsibilities with respect to a school census?

In the cities of New York, Buffalo, and Rochester, the school board must take a school census for the purpose of enforcing the provisions of the compulsory education law (§ 3240). In small city school districts, each school board also serves as a permanent census board that has a duty to maintain a continuous census of all children residing in the district from five to 18 years of age, and of children with disabilities to the age of 21. A census for pre-school children from birth to five years of age may be prepared and filed biennially on or before the 15th day of October. The census board is required, upon written request therefor, to provide information to the commissioner of education (§ 3241(1), (3)).

All other school districts are simply authorized, rather than required, to take a census of all children residing in the district from birth to 18 years of age biennially (§ 3242).

However, all school districts have an obligation to locate and identify students with disabilities residing in their district including homeless children, wards of the state, and children who attend non-public schools and establish a register of such students entitled to attend school or receive preschool services. The register should include each child's name, address, birth date, child's parents' names, address(es), native language spoken in the home, nature of such child's disability or suspected disability, the dates of referral, evaluations, recommendations of the committee on special education or committee on preschool special education, actual placement, and annual program reviews, the site where the student is currently receiving an educational program, the reason why the student is not receiving an appropriate public education (where applicable), and any other student specific data needed to comply with federal law (§§ 3242, 4402(1)(a); 8 NYCRR § 200.2(a); see also **54:13-14**).

Policies

5:32. What is a policy?

A *policy* is a statement that establishes standards and/or objectives to be attained by the district. School board policies should clearly state the mission of the school district, the objectives to be reached and the standards to be maintained. In addition, they should set out processes for the allocation of responsibilities and delegation of duties to specific staff members; and the methods to be used, the procedures to be followed and the reasoning to be applied in conducting the district's business.

5:33. What is the function of school board policies?

Policies are the means by which a school board leads and governs its school district. Policies form the bylaws and rules for the governance of the district and serve as the standards to which the board, administration, and students are held accountable (see § 1709). A board's policies ensure that the school district performs its established mission and operates in an effective, uniform manner. They are legally binding and serve as the local law of the school district that may be enforced by the district. Moreover, if a school district violates its own policies, the commissioner of education may enforce the policy against the district (*Appeal of Toure*, 54 Ed Dept Rep, Dec. No. 16,660 (2014); *Appeal of Parrino*, 53 Ed Dept Rep, Dec. No. 16,588 (2014); *Appeal of Christiano*, 50 Ed Dept Rep, Dec. No. 16,217 (2011)).

5:34. Must school boards maintain policy manuals?

No. Districts may be required to adopt policies on certain issues, but they are not required to maintain or organize them in any particular manner. However, it is a common practice to organize and number policies in a single manual for ease of reference and access for the board, district staff, and the public. Such policies may also be maintained for easy board, administrator, and public access by storing them in an on-line, fully searchable format, such as the one offered through the New York State School Boards Association and its E-Policy Plus service (see **5:36** for more information).

5:35. What is the difference between a policy and a regulation?

Policies are statements by the school board establishing standards and/or objectives to be attained by the district. Policies can only be adopted or amended by the vote of a majority of the board members at an open meeting. Regulations are generally more detailed directives developed by the administration to implement the board's policies. Policies give direction and goals for the district, while regulations give specific orders and procedures to be followed to move in that direction and to attain those goals. Unless otherwise specified by the bylaws of the school board, it is the power and duty of the superintendent to enforce all provisions of law, rules, and regulations relating to the management of the schools and other educational, social, and recreational activities under the direction of the school board (§§ 1711(2)(b), 2508(2)).

It is important that board policies be both broad enough to allow administrators to exercise discretion in dealing with day-to-day problems, yet specific enough to provide clear guidance. It is equally important that regulations be written to implement, but not modify, the board's policies.

5:36. What services does the New York State School Boards Association provide to assist local school boards in developing and maintaining up-to-date policies?

The New York State School Boards Association (NYSSBA) offers a variety of free and fee-based services to assist local school boards in developing and maintaining policy manuals for more effective governance and administration. Services include:

- Development of a customized policy manual that is tailored to meet the district's needs, is streamlined, up-to-date and well-organized (Essential Policy Manual).
- School Policy Update subscription service that provides, on a regular basis, annotated sample policies that are responsive to the latest changes in law and regulation.
- An on-line policy manual service (E-Policy) that converts the district's current policy manual into a powerful on-line format that can be instantly accessed.
- Policy workshops tailored to address issues related to a district's policy needs.
- A policy service that allows a district to design its own policy package to suit the district's needs (Policy by Design).

For more information on these services, as well as access to on-line policy resources, visit NYSSBA's website at: http://www.nyssba.org and click "Member Services" and select the "Policy Services" page or contact the Legal/Policy Services Department directly at 518-783-0200.

Shared-Decision-Making

Editor's Note: This subsection discusses the basic rules governing the shared-decision-making process found in commissioner of education regulations at 8 NYCRR § 100.11. Additional requirements applicable specifically to the City School District of the City of New York are found in the Education Law (§ 2590-h (15)(b), (15)(b-1); see also Appeal of Pollicino, *48 Ed Dept Rep 279 (2008);* Appeal of Thomas, *54 Ed Dept Rep, Dec. No. 16,669 (2014)).*

5:37. What is shared-decision-making?

The terms *shared-decision-making* and *school-based management* refer to a model for decision making in the schools that emphasizes both the involvement and meaningful participation of administrators, teachers, and parents in the process (8 NYCRR § 100.11).

Every school board and board of cooperative educational services must have in place a district plan for the participation by teachers, parents, and administrators in school-based planning and shared-decision-making (8 NYCRR § 100.11(b)). The adopted plan must be made available to the public and must be filed with the district superintendent and the commissioner of education within 30 days of adoption (8 NYCRR § 100.11(d)(1), (2)).

5:38. How is a district's shared-decision-making plan developed?

The commissioner's regulations provide that a school board must consult certain individuals when developing and amending the district's plan for school-based planning and shared-decision-making. The plan the board develops with input from the district-wide committee (also referred to as the central planning committee) must outline, among other things, both the creation of the school-based shared-decision-making teams and detail those educational issues on which the teams are to provide input (8 NYCRR § 100.11(c)). However, nothing in the regulations requires that a board obtain the approval of a school-based planning team before implementing a decision (*Appeal of Gillespie*, 34 Ed Dept Rep 240 (1994)).

5:39. What must be addressed in a school district's shared-decision-making plan?

The district plan must address the following:

- The educational issues that are subject to cooperative planning and shared-decision-making at the building level.
- The manner and the extent of involvement of each of the parties.
- The means and standards to be used in evaluating the improvement in student achievement.
- The method of holding each party accountable for the decisions they helped make.
- The process for resolving disputes on educational issues at the local level.
- The manner in which all state and federal requirements for the involvement of parents in planning and decisionmaking will be coordinated and met by the overall district plan (8 NYCRR § 100.11(c)).

5:40. Are there any limitations on which educational issues a shared-decision-making committee may address?

The commissioner's regulations do not define which educational issues the school-based committees must consider. A school board is expected to work together with its district-wide planning committee to define what issues the school-based shared-decision-making committee will examine.

School-based committees might consider a range of issues, such as mission statements, school schedules, grouping for instruction, the allocation of discretionary resources, and links with community organizations.

In working with shared-decision-making committees, board members should be aware that while some education issues may be appropriate for input, they may not be appropriate for delegation. For example, a school board is required to formulate the school district budget, and that obligation cannot be delegated to a shared-decision-making team (§§ 1608(1), 1716, 1804(1), 1906(3), 2601-a(3); *Appeal of Kastberg*, 35 Ed Dept Rep 208 (1995)). Similarly, while student performance is an appropriate issue for discussion, it is the school board that must set the course of study by which students are graded and classified (§ 1709(3); *Appeal of Orris & Kelly*, 35 Ed Dept Rep 184 (1995)). Final decisions regarding what instructional programs will be offered in a district's schools are also the school board's responsibility (*Appeal of Zaleski & Gimmi*, 36 Ed Dept Rep 284 (1997)), as are decisions regarding reorganization of a district's schools (*Appeal of Parker*, 39 Ed Dept Rep 220 (1999); *Appeal of Woodward*, 36 Ed Dept Rep 445 (1997)).

The commissioner of education has found that nothing in the shared-decision-making regulation mandates that a school board obtain the approval of a school-based planning team before implementing a decision. In one case, the commissioner determined that a board may establish a day care center at one of its school facilities, despite opposition from the building's shared-decision-making committee (*Appeal of Gillespie*, 34 Ed Dept Rep 240 (1994)).

And while there is no specific case that addresses this particular issue with regard to shared-decision-making, board members should also be aware that a school board cannot delegate its responsibility to grant or deny tenure to an employee (*Cohoes City Sch. Dist. v. Cohoes Teachers Ass'n*, 40 N.Y.2d 774 (1976)).

5:41. How often must the shared-decision-making plan be reviewed?

The plan must be reviewed biennially and amended or recertified without change, as appropriate, following the same procedures as for the original plan. The amended or recertified plan must be filed with the district superintendent and submitted to the commissioner for approval, together with a statement of the plan's success in meeting its objectives, no later than February 1 of the year in which the review occurs (8 NYCRR § 100.11(f)).

5:42. Who must be involved in the biennial review of a district's school-based planning and shared-decision-making plan?

The school board must conduct the biennial review of its district's plan in collaboration with a district-wide committee composed of the superintendent of schools, administrators selected by the administrative bargaining organization(s), teachers selected by the teachers' bargaining organization(s) and parents selected by the school-related parent organization(s) (8 NYCRR § 100.11(b), (f); *Appeal of Newburgh Teachers Ass'n*, 36 Ed Dept Rep 264 (1996); see *Appeal of Chester*, 35 Ed Dept Rep 512 (1996)).

Parents who are employed by the district or employed by a collective bargaining organization representing teachers and/or administrators in the district may not serve on the committee. In those districts in which teachers or administrators are not represented by a collective bargaining organization, or where there are no school-related parent organizations, teachers, administrators and/or parents are to be selected by their peers in a manner prescribed by the school board or board of cooperative educational services (8 NYCRR § 100.11(b); *Appeal of Greenburgh Eleven Fed'n of Teachers*, 34 Ed Dept Rep 606 (1995)).

While the board must seek the district-wide committee's endorsement of any amendments to the plan, the school board has the final say over the district plan (8 NYCRR § 100.11(d), (f); see *Appeal of Meyer*, 34 Ed Dept Rep 329 (1995); *Appeal of Newburgh Teacher's Ass'n*, 34 Ed Dept Rep 621 (1995)). It is not required that all committee members agree on all elements of the plan (*Appeal of Leet*, 42 Ed Dept Rep 253 (2003); *Appeal of St. Victor*, 33 Ed Dept Rep 679 (1994)). In addition, school boards may revisit modifications suggested in earlier years (*Appeal of Leet*).

5:43. Can a board member be a member of the district-wide committee?

No. The commissioner of education has held that the intent of the regulation is not for board members to serve on the committee itself, but to work in collaboration with the district-wide committee in developing and amending the shared-decision-making plan (*Appeal of Trombley*, 39 Ed Dept Rep 115 (1999); *Appeal of Chester*, 35 Ed Dept Rep 512 (1996)).

5:44. Who may be a member of the school-based shared-decision-making team?

According to the commissioner's regulations, school-based committees engaged in shared-decision-making at the building level are to be composed of administrators, teachers, parents, and others at the discretion of the school board or board of cooperative educational services (for example, students, support staff, or community members) (8 NYCRR § 100.11(c)(1)).

5:45. What is the process for challenging a shared-decision-making plan?

According to the commissioner's regulations, anyone who feels the school board failed to properly adopt, amend, or recertify the plan may appeal to the commissioner of education no later than 30 days after the plan was adopted, amended, or recertified, unless the delay is excused by the commissioner for good cause shown (8 NYCRR § 100.11(e)(1); *Appeal of Lawrence Teachers' Ass'n,* 39 Ed Dept Rep 119 (1999)). Anyone who participated in the plan's development and claims that the plan is deficient or fails to provide for meaningful participation in the decision-making process may also file an appeal with the commissioner (8 NYCRR § 100.11(e)(2)). The grounds for such an appeal include noncompliance with any of the six enumerated requirements of the plan (8 NYCRR § 100.11(e)(2); see **5:39**).

5:46. Must school districts negotiate with their unions over shared-decision-making?

It depends on the circumstance. The Public Employment Relations Board (PERB) has held that a school district did not violate its bargaining obligation by refusing to negotiate over teachers' participation on a shared-decision-making committee or over the alleged impact of an increased workload. PERB held that the teachers were not acting in their capacity as employees of the district but rather as volunteers, and that the terms of their participation on the committee were not a mandatory subject of bargaining (*Deer Park Teachers Ass'n v. Deer Park UFSD*, 26 PERB ¶ 4642 (1993)).

However, where a school district has developed or implemented a plan for the participation of teachers and/or administrators in school-based shared-decision-making as a result of a collective bargaining agreement, any such negotiated provisions must be incorporated into the district's shared-decision-making plan (8 NYCRR § 100.11(h)).

5:47. Is the shared-decision-making process subject to the Open Meetings Law?

Although there are no court decisions that address this issue, whenever a district-wide planning committee is required to have a quorum to conduct business and is actively involved in the process of formulating recommendations at any level, the meetings of that committee are subject to the Open Meetings Law, according to the state Committee on Open Government (NYS Department of State, Committee on Open Government, OML-AO-2204 (Apr. 1, 1993)). Therefore, advance notice of meetings must be provided (*MFY Legal Servs. Inc. v. Toia*, 93 Misc.2d 147 (Sup. Ct. New York Cnty. 1977); NYS Department of State, Committee on Open Government, OML-AO-2305 (Jan. 19, 1994)).

School-based shared-decision-making committees would be subject to the Open Meetings Law if the district's shared-decision-making plan gives them decision-making authority or requires that the board seek their input and recommendations prior to taking action, even if the board rejects their recommendations (NYS Department of State, Committee on Open Government, OML-AO-3265 (Jan. 17, 2001); OML-AO-2305 (Jan. 19, 1994)).

In addition, if the meeting is required to be open to the public, it must be accessible to people with disabilities (Pub. Off. Law § 103(b); 42 USC § 12102 *et seq.*; see also **14:21**).

3:14 Who are the members of the school-based shared decision-making teams?

According to the commissioner's regulations, school-based committees involved in shared decision-making at the building level must include the principal or administrator, teachers, parents, and others at the discretion of the school district board of cooperative educational services (for example, students, support staff, community members) (8 NYCRR § 100.11(c)).

3:15 What is the process for challenging a shared decision-making plan?

According to the commissioner's regulations, any organization representing teachers, administrators, or parents that claims it did not have the opportunity to participate in the development of the plan may appeal to the commissioner of education no later than 30 days after the plan was adopted, amended or extended. The commissioner will dismiss the appeal unless good cause is shown. Such appeals are based on the grounds that the plan was not developed with the full participation of the organization, or that the plan is deficient or does not comply with the regulations (8 NYCRR § 100.11(e)(2)). The appeal process may include a conference, and any plan is subject to the commissioner's approval (8 NYCRR § 100.11(e)(2); see 3:14).

3:16 Must a school district negotiate with the teachers' union over shared decision-making?

It depends on the circumstances. The Public Employment Relations Board (PERB) has held that a school district's adoption of a shared decision-making plan was not a mandatory subject of negotiation. However, PERB held that the district must negotiate the impact of an increased workload. PERB held that the teachers' association was not asserting any of the terms of the contract but rather was asserting that the teachers' participation on the committee was not a mandatory subject of bargaining (*Spencerport Teachers' Ass'n*, 35 PERB ¶ 3014 (2002)).

In addition, the collective bargaining agreement may contain provisions relating to shared decision-making. If it does, a district must negotiate the terms of any collective bargaining agreement that affects the shared decision-making process (8 NYCRR § 100.11(c)(1)).

3:17 Are shared decision-making teams subject to the Open Meetings Law?

Although shared decision-making teams that address issues where authority to make final decisions is vested in the committee are subject to the Open Meetings Law, teams that act in an advisory capacity and merely make recommendations are not. Committees that meet in [illegible], according to the state Committee on Open Government (NYS Department of State), are subject to the Open Meetings Law, and notice of meetings must be provided (*Matter of* [illegible], Misc. 2d [illegible] (Sup. Ct. New York Cnty. 1992); NYS Department of State, Committee on Open Government, OML-AO-2605 [illegible]).

School-based shared decision-making committees would be subject to the Open Meetings Law if their members are given the authority to make decisions on behalf of the board, but not if the board seeks their input and recommendations prior to making a decision. If the board rejects their recommendations (NYS Department of State, Committee on Open Government, OML-AO-[illegible] [illegible]).

In addition, if the meeting is open to the public, it must be accessible to people with disabilities (42 USC § 12132; see § [illegible]).

6. School Board Members

Qualifications

6:1. What are the qualifications for membership on a school board?

To qualify for membership on a school board in a common, union free, central, central high school, or small city school district, an individual:

- Must be able to read and write (§ 2102).
- Must be a qualified voter of the district; that is, a citizen of the United States, at least 18 years of age or older, and not adjudged to be an incompetent (§§ 2102, 2012, 2502(7); Elec. Law § 5-106(6)). (Note: a convicted felon is barred from running for a seat on a school board if his or her maximum prison sentence has not expired or if he or she has not been pardoned or discharged from parole (Elec. Law § 5-106(2)-(4)).
- Must be and have been a resident (but need not be a taxpayer) of the district for a continuous and uninterrupted period of at least one year (30 days in the city of Rensselaer (§ 2502(9-a)(d)) immediately before the election (§§ 2102, 2502(7), (9)(d); *Appeal of Baleno*, 30 Ed Dept Rep 358 (1991)).
- May not have been removed from any school district office within the preceding year (§ 2103(2)).
- May not reside with another member of the same school board as a member of the same family (§ 2103(3); *Rosenstock v. Scaringe*, 40 N.Y.2d 563 (1976)).
- May not be a current employee of the school board (§ 2103(4); see **6:3, 6:11**).
- May not simultaneously hold another incompatible public office (*Matter of Schoch & Betheil*, 21 Ed Dept Rep 300 (1981); see also **6:6-11**).

In large city school districts, different rules of law and/or exceptions to the above rules may govern membership on the school board (see §§ 2553(1), 2590-b(1)(a), (7)(d)).

6:2. May a school district impose additional requirements for school board membership?

No. A school district may not require candidates for a school board position to meet eligibility requirements in addition to those imposed by statute (*Matter of Guilderland CSD*, 23 Ed Dept Rep 262 (1984)).

In one case, the commissioner of education invalidated a "gentlemen's agreement" observed by a school district for more than 60 years, under which seats of elected school board members were allocated among the communities comprising the district (*Appeal of Gravink*, 37 Ed Dept Rep 393 (1998)).

6:3. May a former employee of the school district serve on the school board?

Yes, even where the school board could address a matter directly pertaining to the former employee's personal interests, such as continuing retiree health insurance benefits, because contracts with a teachers' union, which is a voluntary non-profit association, are exempt from the provisions of the conflict of interest law (*Appeal of Budich*, 48 Ed Dept Rep 383 (2009); *Application of Casazza*, 32 Ed Dept Rep 462 (1993); Gen. Mun. Law § 802(1)(f); see **12:6-13**, for more information on conflicts of interest).

6:4. May an individual be a school board member if that person's spouse is employed by the district?

Yes. There is no prohibition against the employment of spouses, children, or other relatives of board members to positions in the district. Nor are board members prohibited from being elected or appointed to the board if that person's spouse, child or other relative is employed by the district.

Furthermore, due to a specific statutory exception, a "contract of employment" between the district and a board member's relative does not create a prohibited conflicting interest for the board member (Gen. Mun. Law § 800(3)(a); *Appeal of Budich*, 48 Ed Dept Rep 383 (2009); *Appeal of Behuniak & Lattimore*, 30 Ed Dept Rep 236 (1991); see **12:6-7, 12:11**).

The Education Law, however, requires a two-thirds vote by the board to employ a teacher who is related to a board member by blood or by marriage (§ 3016; see also *Appeal of Levine*, 76 St. Dept. Rep. 41 (1955)). The two-thirds vote requirement does not apply and has no effect on the continued employment of a tenured teacher who is initially hired before his or her relative is elected or appointed to the school board (*Appeal of Heizman*, 31 Ed Dept Rep 387 (1992)).

In one decision, the commissioner of education ruled that a person who sought employment as a social worker in the district where her spouse was a member of the school board, was a teacher for the purposes of this section of law and therefore needed approval from two-thirds of the board in order to be appointed (*Appeal of McNamara*, 30 Ed Dept Rep 272 (1991)).

6:5. May a member of the clergy seek office as a member of a school board?

Yes. The U.S. Supreme Court declared unconstitutional any ban on the eligibility of members of the clergy to run for public office, provided they meet all the statutory qualifications (*McDaniel v. Paty*, 435 U.S. 618 (1978)).

Incompatibility of Office

6:6. May a school board member run for or hold an additional public office?

There is no general prohibition against holding two or more public offices at the same time (Opn. Att'y Gen. I 82-1 (1982)). However, there may be situations in which two public offices or positions of employment may be in conflict with each other. In such an instance, a school board member would be precluded from holding two such offices or positions simultaneously (*People ex rel. Ryan v. Green*, 58 N.Y. 295 (1874); see **6:7-9**).

6:7. What makes two public offices or positions of employment incompatible with one another?

Two public offices or employment positions may be incompatible with each other if a statute or the common law doctrine of compatibility precludes school board members, district officers or employees from holding such positions simultaneously. For example, one person cannot simultaneously hold two public offices or positions of employment if one office is subordinate to the other, such that the person would essentially be his or her own boss, or if the functions of the two positions are inherently inconsistent with each other, such as serving simultaneously as the district's finance officer and as the auditor responsible for the integrity of the district's finances (see *O'Malley v. Macejka*, 44 N.Y.2d 530 (1978); Opn. Att'y Gen. I 92-13). There must be a great likelihood of a division of loyalties or a conflict of duties between the offices, not merely a possibility that such complications may arise on occasion.

The doctrine of compatibility of office does not prohibit an individual from being a candidate for election to a second office where that office is incompatible with the first, if he or she intends to resign from the first office if elected to the second. However, if there is a specific provision of law that makes two offices or positions incompatible, such a provision of law may expressly disqualify a person from even being a candidate for a second incompatible office or position (Opn. Att'y Gen. I 89-62; see **6:8**). The failure of an individual to resign from an incompatible office prior to election as a school board member would require a school district to nullify the election of such individual to its school board (*Appeal of Fries*, 50 Ed Dept Rep, Dec. No. 16,182 (2010)).

Once elected and upon accepting the second office, an individual vacates the first office automatically (Opn. Att'y Gen. I 89-62; *People ex rel. Ryan v. Green*, 58 N.Y. 295 (1874)).

Even where two public offices or positions of employment are compatible, a situation may arise in which holding both offices creates a conflict of interest. If this occurs, the conflict can be avoided by declining to participate in the conflicted matter (Opn. Att'y Gen. I 92-13).

6:8. Are there any public offices or employment positions that a school board member is specifically prohibited by statute from holding?

Yes. The Education Law specifically prohibits a board member from simultaneously holding the positions of district superintendent, clerk, tax collector, treasurer, or librarian (§§ 2103(1); see also Opn. Att'y Gen. I 93-38), or from being an employee of his or her school board (§ 2103(4)). In union free and central school districts, however, a board member may be appointed clerk of the board and of the district (§§ 2130(1), 1804(1); *Matter of Hurtgam*, 22 Ed Dept Rep 219 (1982)). A board member of a board of cooperative educational services (BOCES) may not be employed by any of that BOCES' component districts (§ 1950(9); see also *Appeal of Reynolds*, 42 Ed Dept Rep 278 (2003)), even when the work is on a short-term per diem basis (Opn. Att'y Gen I 2007-2).

In small city school districts, the Education Law also provides that school board members may not hold any city office other than that of police officer or firefighter (§ 2502(7); Opns. Att'y Gen. I 90-80, I 87-6). Decisions determining whether an employee holds an office within the meaning of this provision turn on the presence of traditional indicia of office, such as the taking of an oath of office, the filing of an undertaking or bond, designation as an office holder in a city charter, significant policy-making authority and other job characteristics including duties and supervisory relationships (*Application of Washock*, 41 Ed Dept Rep 280 (2002); Opns. Att'y Gen. I 90-80, I 87-6). Thus, in a case where the titles of Water Department Director and Director of Parks and Recreation involved limited supervisory and administrative duties, were classified as civil service positions, and did not have a reporting relationship to the mayor or city council, the individuals holding these positions were not precluded from serving as school board members. Although both positions required the taking of an oath of office, all city employees were required to do so (*Application of Washock*).

Under the Town Law a town supervisor may not be a trustee of a school district (Town Law § 23(1)). But there is no prohibition against a deputy town supervisor serving as a member of a school board (Opn. Att'y Gen. I 96-29; see also **6:10**).

The Election Law prohibits a county elections commissioner from serving as a school board member in a city school district (Elec. Law § 3-200(4); *Appeal of Fries*, 50 Ed Dept Rep, Dec. No. 16,182 (2011)). However, it is permissible for a school board member to simultaneously serve as chairperson of a political party committee (Opns. Att'y Gen. I 72-132, I 71-87).

6:9. Are there any offices that have been found to be incompatible with the office of school board member even without an express statutory prohibition?

Yes. For example, counsel to the state attorney general has expressed the opinion that a public school board member may not serve simultaneously as:

- a member of the school board of a private school within the district (Opn. Att'y Gen. I 87-58);
- a director of weights and measures in small city school districts (Opn. Att'y Gen. I 90-80);
- a district attorney with jurisdiction over the school district or board of cooperative educational services (BOCES) (Opn. Att'y Gen. I 2000-13);
- a city's common council in small city school districts (Opn. Att'y Gen. I 84-61);
- a city's corporation counsel in a small city school district (Opn. Att'y Gen. I 96-2); or
- a city's board of ethics in a small city school district (Opn. Att'y Gen. I 2008-5).

Likewise, a BOCES board member may not serve simultaneously as an occasional per-diem substitute in a BOCES component school district (Opn. Att'y Gen. I 2007-2).

The state Advisory Committee on Judicial Ethics has indicated that a part-time judge may not seek election to a local school board because the Rules of the Chief Administrator of the Courts prohibit judges from campaigning for elective office (Advisory Committee on Judicial Ethics Opns. 09-90, 90-79, 89-157/90-7; 22 NYCRR § 100.5(A)(1)(c),(d)). In contrast, the same Committee has opined that a part-time judge may serve on a BOCES board because that board is not popularly elected and does not levy taxes (Advisory Committee on Judicial Ethics Opn. 03-135).

The Advisory Committee also has stated that a judge who already has been elected to a school board should resign because the "position on the school board [is] one that may involve dealing with quasi-political and highly controversial issues" that are incompatible with holding judicial office (Advisory Committee on Judicial Ethics Opns. 90-79, 90-63, 89-157/90-07; see also 22 NYCRR § 100.5). But a part-time justice may accept "appointment" to the board of trustees of a publicly-funded school district for children with disabilities (special act school district), because by virtue of the "appointment," the justice would not be required to compete in a public, political election in order to obtain a seat on the school board, and because in that particular type of school district there is no public referendum on the school district's budget (Advisory Committee on Judicial Ethics Opns. 13-166/13-166(A), 94-59; 22 NYCRR § 100.4(C)(3)).

6:10. Are there any offices that are compatible with the office of school board member?

Yes. A school board member may serve simultaneously in the following offices:

- trustee of a public library (*Matter of Schoch*, 21 Ed Dept Rep 300 (1981); Opn. Att'y Gen. I 81-110);
- town assessor (Opn. Att'y Gen. I 2000-14; Opn. St. Comp. 73-1174);
- employee of a board of cooperative educational services (*Appeal of Reynolds*, 42 Ed Dept Rep 278 (2003); *Matter of Todd*, 19 Ed Dept Rep 277 (1979));
- village mayor or village trustee (Opn. Att'y Gen. I 91-59, I 81-17; see also Village Law § 3-300);
- member of a town zoning board of appeals (Opn. Att'y Gen. I 84-68);
- member of town board of assessment review (Opn. Att'y Gen. I 92-26);
- member of a city school board and county director of real property tax services (Opn. Att'y Gen. I 93-9);
- member of a city school board and city supervisor whose only function is to represent the city on a county legislature (Opn. Att'y Gen. I 2005-16);
- county treasurer, county legislator, and county clerk (Opn. Att'y Gen. I 2002-21, I 82-1; Opn. St. Comp 55-7802);
- volunteer in an athletic department of the school, depending upon the significance of the volunteer's responsibilities (Opn. Att'y Gen. I 92-13);
- deputy town supervisor and member of town council (Opn. Att'y Gen. I 96-29; Opn. St. Comp. 67-354); and
- trustee of a not-for-profit foundation that raises money and makes gifts to the school district (Opn. St. Comp. 2008-1).

- police officer or firefighter in a municipality outside the school district or within the school district unless prohibited by the legislative body for whom they are employed (§ 2103-a; Opn. St. Comp. 78-297).

This is only a partial list of opinions on compatibility of office. For more information, contact the state Attorney General's Office.

6:11. May a school board member apply for and be appointed to a position of employment with the district in which he or she serves as a school board member?

Only if expressly authorized by law, as in the case of district clerk in certain school districts (see **6:8**). Otherwise, a school board may not appoint one of its members to a position of employment with the district (*Fishman v. Bd. of Educ. of South Country CSD*, 105 A.D.3d 842 (3d Dep't 2013)); *Wood v. Town of Whitehall*, 120 Misc. 124 (Sup. Ct. Washington Cnty.), *aff'd*, 206 A.D. 786 (3d Dep't 1923); Opn. Att'y Gen. I 87-4; *Appeal of Boeddener*, 28 Ed Dept Rep 578 (1989); see also § 2103(4)). Furthermore, an appointment following resignation from the board may or may not be proper depending upon the facts and circumstances. For example, it would not be proper for a board to decide to appoint one of its members to an employment position with the district at a future date, prior to the board member's resignation when the board member still sat on the board (*Fishman*; Opn. Att'y Gen. I 87-4; *Appeal of Boeddener*).

Nomination

6:12. How are school board candidates nominated for election?

Nominating petitions must be signed by at least 25 qualified district voters or two percent of the number of voters who voted in the previous annual election of the members of the school board, whichever is greater (§ 2018(a)). In small city school districts, nominating petitions must be signed by at least 100 qualified voters (§ 2608(1)).

Ordinarily, nominating petitions are for specific seats on the school board (§ 2018(a)). However, district voters may choose to make all seats "at large," which means that each nominee is eligible for every vacancy, rather than only for a specific seat (§ 2018(b)) and nominating petitions do not state a specific seat (see *Appeal of Martin*, 32 Ed Dept Rep 567 (1993)). A duly adopted "at large" proposition becomes effective at the next election and remains valid until repealed by the voters (§ 2018(b)).

Board members in small city school districts run "at large." The nominating petition must name the specific seat for which the board member is running only if the voters have adopted a proposition requiring candidates to run for specific seats (§ 2608(1)).

In districts where candidates run for specific seats, not only must the petition include the candidate's name and residence and the residences of the people who signed the petition, it must also identify the specific seat for which the candidate is running, including the name of the incumbent, and the length of the term of office to be filled (§§ 2018(a), 2608(1)). Candidates may be nominated for only one vacancy (§ 2018(a)).

For information about write-in candidates, please see **6:19-20, 17:9**.

6:13. Must the nominating petition of an incumbent board member running for reelection identify the incumbent as the candidate in the petition?

Yes. In one case the commissioner of education ruled that an incumbent board member who sought reelection to his own seat and wrote his name in the space on the nominating petition identifying himself as the incumbent, technically violated the Education Law because he failed to list his name in the space identifying himself as the "candidate." However, the record established that as each person was asked to sign the nominating petition, the person gathering the signatures explained who was running and described the seat for which the candidate was running. Moreover, there was no proof that any voter was confused about who was seeking the nomination. Therefore the commissioner dismissed the challenge to the election (*Appeal of Grant*, 42 Ed Dept Rep 184 (2002)).

6:14. Can a person who is not a registered voter sign a nominating petition for school board candidates?

Yes. While only qualified voters may sign a board candidate's nominating petition, a person need not be a registered voter to satisfy the legal definition of a "qualified voter" (*Appeal of Dreyer*, 18 Ed Dept Rep 235 (1978); see also *Appeal of Crowley*, 39 Ed Dept Rep 665 (2000)). If a person is a citizen of the United States, at least 18 years old, and a "resident" of the school district for at least 30 days immediately prior to the election at which he or she seeks to vote, then that person satisfies the legal definition of "qualified voter" and may sign nominating petitions, even if that person is not a registered voter and therefore would be unable to vote in a district that requires voter registration.

6:15. Can a person sign a nominating petition for more than one candidate for the same board seat?

Yes. There is no limit on the number of nominating petitions a district resident may sign.

6:16. Do nominating petitions have to be verified?

Generally, no. The Education Law does not require that nominating petitions be verified. However, a school district may impose such a requirement pursuant to school board policy (see *Appeal of Loughlin*, 35 Ed Dept Rep 432 (1996)). In addition, in city school districts that may conduct certain aspects of their school board elections pursuant to provisions of the Election Law, different rules sometimes apply (see § 2502(9)(c)).

6:17. What is the deadline for the submission of nominating petitions?

Nominating petitions must be filed in the office of the district clerk no later than 30 days (20 days in small city school districts) before the annual or special district meeting at which the school board election will occur, between 9:00 a.m. and 5:00 p.m. (§§ 2018(a), 2608(1)). Notice of the deadline for filing nominating petitions must be published in the notice of the annual or special district meeting (§§ 2003(2), 2004(2), 2007(1), 2601-a(2), 2602(2); see also **15:10**). Under certain specified circumstances, the nominating deadline may be extended (see **6:21**). However, a district must adhere to the statutory timeline requirements for the submission of nominating petitions for school board, even if the district incorrectly published or misstated the deadline (*Appeal of Geiger*, 52 Ed Dept Rep, Dec. No. 16,379 (2012); *Appeal of Crespo,* 23 Ed Dept Rep 446 (1984)).

Nothing in the Education Law specifies the earliest date that candidates may begin collecting signatures on nominating petitions. In one case, the commissioner of education ruled that it was not unreasonable for a district to accept nominating petitions that contained signatures collected prior to the posting of the notice of the annual meeting, absent evidence that this practice gave some candidates an unfair advantage over others (*Appeal of Leman*, 32 Ed Dept Rep 579 (1993)).

If the deadline for filing nominating petitions falls on "a Saturday, Sunday or public holiday, the filing may be performed on the next succeeding business day" (Gen. Constr. Law § 25-a(1); see also *Appeal of Williams*, 36 Ed Dept Rep 270 (1996)).

6:18. May the school board reject a nominating petition?

Yes. A nominating petition may be rejected, for example, if it is not signed by the required number of qualified district voters (§ 2018(a)). A nominating petition may be rejected also if the candidate is ineligible for office or has declared an unwillingness to serve (§ 2035(2)).

In addition, although nominating petitions are presented to the district clerk, the school board is authorized to determine whether a board candidate is eligible to serve and to reject a nominating petition from an ineligible candidate (*Appeal of Martin*, 31 Ed Dept Rep 441 (1992)).

A failure to include the candidate's name and address or the specific seat or term of office on each page of a multi-sheet petition does not provide sufficient grounds to reject a nominating petition absent proof that persons signing the petition did not know what they were signing (*Appeal of Taubenfeld*, 18 Ed Dept Rep 10 (1978)).

However, the failure to submit a nominating petition within statutory deadlines (see **6:17**) constitutes grounds for rejecting a nominating petition, even when a district incorrectly published or misstated the deadline (*Appeal of Geiger*, 52 Ed Dept Rep, Dec. No. 16,379 (2012)).

6:19. Must a person have filed a nominating petition in order to be elected?

No. A person need not file a nominating petition in order to be elected to serve on a school board. All ballots must have one blank space for each vacancy on the board, in which voters may write in the name of any candidate who is not listed on the ballot (§§ 2032(2)(e), 2608(2); *Appeal of Thomas,* 47 Ed Dept Rep 442 (2008); see also **17:9**).

6:20. What happens if there are no candidates or not enough candidates properly nominated for each vacancy?

If this happens, the election must still be held, and the vacancies will be filled by the individuals with the most write-in votes (§§ 2032(2)(e), 2608(2)). If there are not enough write-in candidates to fill vacancies, any remaining vacancy may be filled pursuant to the provisions of sections 1709(17), 2502(6), or 2113 of the Education Law (see **5:14-15**).

6:21. What happens if a candidate who has properly filed a nominating petition withdraws, dies, or becomes ineligible for office before the election?

If a board candidate, for whom a nominating petition has been duly filed, withdraws the petition, dies, or otherwise becomes ineligible to hold the office of school board member at a point in time later than 15 days before the last day for the filing of nominating petitions, the district is required to extend the nominating deadline by as much as 15 days; provided, however, that in no event may nominating petitions be filed later than 5:00 p.m. on the seventh day before the date of the election (§§ 2018(d), 2608(1); see also *Appeal of Schultz*, 48 Ed Dept Rep 70 (2008)).

6:22. May a candidate who withdraws from an election resubmit his or her candidacy?

Yes, but that person must file a new petition within the same time limitations applicable to other candidates (§ 2018(a)).

6:23. Are school board candidates required to file campaign expenditure statements?

Yes. If a school board candidate's campaign expenditures exceed $500, the candidate must file a sworn statement with both the district clerk and the commissioner of education itemizing their expenditures and contributions received (§§ 1528-1531). To satisfy the "sworn statement" standard, the document must be sworn to or signed before a notary public (see *Appeal of the Bd. of Educ. of the Hempstead UFSD*, 55 Ed Dept Rep, Dec. No. 16,878 (2016)). This statement must list the amounts of all money or other valuable things paid, given, expended or promised by the candidate, or incurred for or on the candidate's behalf with his or her approval (§ 1528). Any expenditure made on behalf of the candidate without his or her approval is not to be included in this statement. Unapproved expenditures are limited to $25 and those making any such expenditure must file a sworn statement with the clerk and the commissioner that the candidate did not approve it (§ 1528(1)(c)).

Contribution statements shall include the dollar amount of any donation or the fair market value of any contribution which is other than money, and the name and address of the donor. If the donor is a political committee as defined in section 14-100 of the Election Law, the statement shall include the name of and the political unit represented by the committee, the date of receipt of the donation, the dollar amount of every expenditure, the name and address of the person to whom it was made, and the date thereof (§ 1528(1)(b)).

A candidate who spends $500 or less must file a sworn statement with the district clerk indicating this to be the case (§ 1528(1)(a)). No other campaign expenditure statement is required.

Candidates for community school district education councils in New York City do not need to file these statements (§ 1528(1)(a)).

6:24. Is there a deadline for school board candidates to file their campaign expenditure statements?

Yes. An initial statement must be filed at least 30 days before the election, a second statement must be filed on or before the fifth day preceding the election and a final statement must be filed within 20 days after the election (§ 1529(1)). The statement must cover the period up to and including the day next preceding the day specified for the filing of the statement (§ 1529(2)). If any contribution in excess of $1,000 is received after the close of the period to be covered in the last statement filed before the election that contribution must be reported within 24 hours of its receipt (*Id.*).

6:25. What happens if a school board candidate fails to file a campaign expenditure statement?

In the event that the appropriate statement is not filed with the district clerk, the law provides that the candidate must promptly file a copy of such statement upon notice from the school district and/or the commissioner of education that the statement was not received (§ 1529(4)). If a candidate still fails to file the statement, then the only way the law can be enforced is for any other "candidate voted for at the election" or "any five qualified voters" to commence legal action in state Supreme Court requesting the court to order the candidate to file the required statements (§ 1530).

In other words, school officials can and should remind candidates to file the appropriate expenditure statements, but only the state Supreme Court has the authority to order candidates to file these statements (see *Appeal of Tang*, 48 Ed Dept Rep 507 (2009); *Appeal of Johnson*, 45 Ed Dept Rep 320 (2005); *Appeal of Muench*, 38 Ed Dept Rep 649 (1999)).

A candidate's failure to file a complete statement of election expenditures is an insufficient basis for setting aside the results of a school board election (*Appeal of the Bd. of Educ. of the Hempstead UFSD*, 55 Ed Dept Rep, Dec. No. 16,878 (2016); *Appeal of Johnson; Appeal of Muench*).

6:26. Must school board members file statements disclosing their personal financial status?

No. The Ethics in Government Act, which requires individuals holding or running for office to make financial disclosure statements, applies to municipalities with populations of 50,000 or more, but not to school districts (Gen. Mun. Law §§ 810(1), 811). Candidates for school boards, however, are required to file campaign expenditure and contribution statements under the Education Law (§§ 1528-1531; see **6:23-25** for more information).

Election

6:27. How are school board members elected?

School board members are elected either at an annual or special school district meeting (see **15:1, 15:16**) by a plurality of the votes cast for each vacancy (§§ 2034(7)(a), 2502(9)(n), (9-a)(n), 2610(4)). In districts with "at large" seats, if there are vacant positions of different lengths, positions are filled in decreasing order of the number of votes and length of office (§§ 2034(7)(c), 2502(9)(n), (9-a)(n), 2610(4)). Thus, the candidate with the highest number of votes is entitled to the position of the longest length.

Moreover, the law provides that where the term of office for a school board seat expires at the end of the school year, and the seat is vacant, or becomes vacant on the date of the annual meeting and election, "the person elected to fill the full term vacancy is deemed elected to fill the remainder of the term preceding the commencement of the full term" (§ 2105(14)). In other words, if the seat is vacant as of the date of the annual meeting and election, the winning candidate does not wait until the current term of office expires on June 30 to begin serving in that seat. He or she takes the oath of office and immediately begins serving in that seat. This provision of law has added significance in districts where board candidates run "at large," because the term of office for a board seat that is or becomes vacant as of the day of the election, when added to the full term of office, will be the seat with the longest term of office, and as such, must be awarded to the candidate with the highest number of votes.

In city school districts with 125,000 or more inhabitants, school board elections are conducted in accordance with section 2553 of the Education Law.

6:28. Must candidates' names appear on the ballot in any particular order?

Yes. Candidates' names must be grouped together in order, as determined by the drawing of lots, either under the specific vacancy for which they have been nominated, or all together for "at large" seats. The district clerk conducts the drawing "the day after the last possible date for candidates to file a petition. In the event that any candidate is not present in person or by a person designated in a written proxy to accomplish the drawing, the district clerk shall be authorized to act as proxy" (§§ 2032(2)(b), 2608(2); see *Koppell v. N.Y. State Bd. of Elections*, 108 F.Supp.2d 355 (S.D.N.Y. 2000)).

In one case, the commissioner of education ruled that the failure of the district clerk to draw lots for placement on the ballot by the statutory deadline was a technical error that did not affect the outcome of the election (*Appeal of Reese*, 34 Ed Dept Rep 187 (1994); see also *Appeal of Olivia*, 16 Ed Dept Rep 355 (1977)). He also dismissed an appeal from a losing candidate who failed to prove that she lost the election because a district's printer mistakenly printed the candidates' names on the ballot in the wrong order (*Appeal of Apgar*, 43 Ed Dept Rep 351 (2004)).

6:29. Are there special ballot requirements in elections where board members run for "specific seats"?

Yes. The Education Law requires that "at the top of each group" of candidates running for separate specific seats on a school board there must be a description that includes, at a minimum, "the length of the term of office and the name of the last incumbent, if any, and in addition, a direction that only one

Public School Governance

vote may be cast in each separate group" (§ 2032(2)(b); see also *Appeal of Mead*, 42 Ed Dept Rep 359 (2003); *Appeal of Kuschner & Pinto*, 39 Ed Dept Rep 770 (2000)).

6:30. Who gives official notice of school board election results?

The chairperson of the meeting at which the election takes place declares the result of each ballot, as announced by the election inspectors (§ 2034(7)(a)). If the district has been divided into election districts and voting machines are used, the election inspectors must report the results to the chief election inspector of each district, who then reports the results to the district clerk within 24 hours. The school board must then tabulate and declare the result of the ballot within 24 hours of receiving the results (§ 2034(7)(b)).

The school district clerk, in turn, must notify in writing every person elected as a school board member (§§ 2108(1), 2121(5), 2610(5)). However, the presence of a person elected to the board at the district meeting at which he or she is elected is considered sufficient legal notice to the candidate of his or her election (§ 2108(2)).

The district clerk also must report the names and post office addresses of elected board members to the town clerk of the town where the district is situated. There is a $5 penalty for failing to do so (§ 2121(5)).

6:31. What happens if an election vote is tied?

If there is a tie vote for a board seat, the district must have a run-off election within 45 days. The only candidates in a run-off election are those who tied. No new nominating petitions are required (§§ 2034(10), 2610(6)).

6:32. Must newly elected school board members officially accept their election to office?

No. Newly elected school board members are considered to have accepted the office unless they file a written refusal with the school district clerk within five days after receiving notice of their election (§ 2108(2)). However, they must take and file an oath of office prior to commencing service on the board (see **5:11, 6:33**).

6:33. When does a newly-elected board member take office?

A new board member takes office when the incumbent's term of office expires, or if the seat is vacant at the time of the election, immediately after the election (§ 2105(14)).

However, the new board member must file an oath of office (N.Y. Const. art. 13, § 1; Pub. Off. Law § 10; see **5:11**). If a new member has not filed an oath of office or is otherwise not qualified to take office when the term begins, the incumbent "holds over" in office until the new member becomes "qualified," that is, takes all the steps necessary to take office (Pub. Off. Law § 5; *Appeal of Foshee*, 38 Ed Dept Rep 346 (1998); *Matter of Waxman*, 19 Ed Dept Rep 157 (1979)).

The failure or neglect of a board member to file an oath of office within 30 days after the commencement of his or her term causes the office to become vacant (Pub. Off. Law § 30(1)(h); see, for example, *Appeal of Rausch*, 41 Ed Dept Rep 351 (2002); *Appeal of Karpen*, 39 Ed Dept Rep 98 (1999)).

6:34. What happens if there is a dispute over the results of a school board election?

All disputes over any district meeting or election must be referred to the commissioner of education (§ 2037), including when the school board itself believes the election results are in dispute (see *Appeal of the Bd. of Educ. of Beekmantown CSD*, 50 Ed Dept Rep, Dec. No. 16,253 (2011); *Appeal of the Bd. of Educ. of the Rush-Henrietta CSD*, 48 Ed Dept Rep 486 (2009); *Appeal of the Bd. of Educ. of the*

Schroon Lake CSD, 47 Ed Dept Rep 502 (2008)). "Once the results of an election are declared, there is no authority in the election officials or the voters to recanvass the results" (*Appeal of LaValley*, 12 Ed Dept Rep 33 (1972)). When the ballots are placed in a locked and sealed ballot box, the box can be opened only upon an order from the commissioner, or upon a school board resolution six months after the vote provided that there are no pending challenges regarding the vote (§ 2034(6); *Appeal of Deposit CSD*, 49 Ed Dept Rep 449 (2010)).

The commissioner may, at his or her discretion, order a recount of the ballots or a new election (§§ 2034(6)(a), 2037; *Appeal of the Bd. of Educ. of the Crown Point CSD*, 51 Ed Dept Rep, Dec. No. 16,291 (2011); *Appeal of Murtagh*, 19 Ed Dept Rep 179 (1979)). A recount is warranted when the evidence establishes a "substantial attack on the integrity of the tallies and the returns of the inspectors of election, such as a showing of fraud or improper conduct" (*Appeal of the Bd. of Educ. of the Crown Point CSD*). A new vote is required when a discrepancy in the vote count has affected the results of the election or budget vote (*Matter of Boyes v. Allen*, 32 A.D.2d 990 (3d Dep't), *aff'd*, 26 N.Y.2d 709 (1969); *Appeal of Reed*, 55 Ed Dept Rep, Dec. No. 16,871 (2016); see also *Appeal of the Bd. of Educ. of the Crown Point CSD*).

Only the commissioner has the authority to order a recount of a vote on a school board election (*Appeal of Doro*, 41 Ed Dept Rep 13 (2001); *Matter of Senecal*, 22 Ed Dept Rep 367 (1983); but see *Appeal of Ell*, 34 Ed Dept Rep 394 (1995); see also **17:31**).

Public School Governance

6:35. What impact does a successful challenge to the results of a school board election have on the actions taken by the board pending appeal?

In such cases, the commissioner of education has determined that the person initially declared the winner is a *de facto* board member during the period of time that an appeal of the election results is pending. Therefore, the actions taken by the board during the pendency of the appeal are valid (*Appeal of Reed*, 55 Ed Dept Rep, Dec. No. 16,871 (2016); *Appeal of Titus*, 36 Ed Dept Rep 407 (1997); *Appeal of Loughlin*, 35 Ed Dept Rep 432 (1996)).

Resignation and Removal

6:36. May a school board member resign from office?

Yes. Under the Education Law, a school board member or other school district officer who wishes to resign may do so at an annual or special school district meeting (see **chapter 15**), or by filing a written resignation with the district superintendent of his or her district, which becomes effective only upon the approval of the district superintendent and the district superintendent's filing of the resignation with the school district clerk (§ 2111; see also Opn. Att'y Gen. I 97-1).

Alternatively, a school board member may resign under the Public Officers Law by delivering to or filing a written resignation with the district clerk (Pub. Off. Law § 31(1)(h), (3); *Appeal of Verity*, 28 Ed Dept Rep 171 (1988); see also Opn. Att'y Gen. I 97-1). The clerk must then notify the state board of elections (Pub. Off. Law § 31(5)) and the school board. A resignation received via e-mail is acceptable absent clear evidence that the e-mail was indeed sent inadvertently by mistake (*Appeal of Dupras*, 47 Ed Dept Rep 471 (2008)).

A resignation becomes effective on the date specified in the resignation or if no effective date is specified, then immediately upon delivery to or filing with the district clerk. In no event shall the effective date be more than 30 days after its proper filing (Pub. Off. Law § 31(2)).

A successor may not be appointed or elected until after the resignation becomes effective (*Roberts v. Allen*, 54 Misc.2d 746 (Sup. Ct. Albany Cnty. 1962), *appeal dismissed*, 19 A.D.2d 690 (3d Dep't 1963)).

6:37. Once a school board member has submitted his or her resignation, may it be withdrawn?

Yes, but only with the consent of the person to whom the resignation was delivered, such as the district clerk if the resignation was submitted under the Public Officers Law or the district superintendent if submitted under the Education Law (see **6:36**). The school board has no authority to consent to a request to withdraw a resignation (Pub. Off. Law § 31(4); *Appeal of Verity*, 28 Ed Dept Rep 171 (1988)).

6:38. May a school board member be removed from office?

Yes. A board member may be removed from office in one of two ways, either by the commissioner of education or the school board. A school board's authority to remove one of its members from office is separate and distinct from the commissioner's authority to remove a board member. However, a board's decision to remove a school board member from office may be reviewed by the commissioner on appeal (§§ 306, 1709(18); *Appeal of Taber,* 42 Ed Dept Rep 251 (2003)).

A school board member removed from office may not be appointed or elected to any district office for a period of one year from the date of his or her removal (§ 2103(2)).

6:39. Under what circumstances may the commissioner of education remove a school board member from office?

The commissioner of education may remove a school board member from office for the willful violation or neglect of duty or the wilful disobedience of a law or a decision, order, or regulation of the commissioner or rule of the Board of Regents (§§ 306, 1706, 2559; *Appeal of Christiano*, 50 Ed Dept Rep, Dec. No. 16,217 (2011); see also 8 NYCRR Part 277). However, the commissioner considers removal "a drastic remedy that should be taken only in extreme circumstances" (*Application of Powell*, 50 Ed Dept Rep, Dec. No. 16,216 (2011); *Application of Carbone*, 46 Ed Dept Rep 215 (2006)).

To be considered willful, a school board member's actions must have been "intentional and with a wrongful purpose" to disregard a lawful duty or violate a legal requirement (*Appeal of Christiano; Application of Student with a Disability*, 43 Ed Dept Rep 227 (2003); *Application of Santicola*, 42 Ed Dept Rep 356 (2003)).

Generally, a board member who acts in good faith on the advice of counsel will not be found to have acted with the requisite willfulness to warrant removal from office (*Appeal of Nett and Raby*, 45 Ed Dept Rep 259 (2005); *Application of Kavitsky*, 41 Ed Dept Rep 231 (2001)). However, if the advice of counsel directly contradicts established law, reliance on such advice will "not necessarily shield a board member from removal under Education Law § 306" (*Appeal of Scarrone*, 35 Ed Dept Rep 443 (1996); see also *Matter of BOCES*, 32 Ed Dept Rep 519 (1993)).

An application for removal must be made to the commissioner within 30 days of the alleged willful violation or neglect of duty or willful disobedience of law unless the commissioner excuses a delay for good cause shown (8 NYCRR § 275.16; *Appeal of Jones,* 55 Ed Dept Rep, Dec. No. 16,823 (2015); *Appeal of Emerling*, 51 Ed Dept Rep, Dec. No. 16,352 (2012); *Application of Tang*, 48 Ed Dept Rep 507 (2009)). In addition, an application for removal may be timely commenced within 30 days of a good faith discovery of the alleged conduct even though the actual conduct may have occurred more than 30 days prior to the application for removal (*Appeal of Emerling; Application of Nett and Raby*).

The commissioner has removed a board member, for instance, for behavior that interfered with the board's ability to function in a case where that board member threatened and initiated a physical altercation with another board member during a board meeting. Such conduct breached the board member's "duty to engage in constructive discussion" on matters affecting the governance of the district (*Appeal of Kozak*,

34 Ed Dept Rep 501 (1995)). The disruptive behavior must occur during a board meeting and disrupt the meeting or interfere with the board's ability to function to warrant removal (*Application of the Bd. of Educ. of the City Sch. Dist. of the City of Gloversville*, 55 Ed Dept Rep, Dec. No. 16,857 (2015); *Application of Tang*; *Application of Gabryel*, 44 Ed Dept Rep 235 (2005); *Application of Lilly*, 43 Ed Dept Rep 459 (2004)).

6:40. May a school board remove one of its members from office?

Yes. A school board may remove any of its members for "official misconduct;" that is, conduct clearly relating to a board member's official duties. This is so when a board member engages in an unauthorized exercise of power or intentionally fails to exercise power to the detriment of the district (§ 1709(18)). That was the case when a board member disclosed confidential student individualized educational program information and refused to reveal all those who had received such information (*Appeal of Nelson*, 49 Ed Dept Rep 82 (2009)). Removal was warranted also where a board member settled employee grievances and contacted staff without board authorization, used threatening and profane language, and demanded that an acting supervisor not schedule a particular maintenance employee for overtime work (*Application of Balen*, 40 Ed Dept Rep 479 (2001)). Likewise, where a board member engaged in a pattern of behavior that included personal attacks, racial slurs and antagonistic behavior toward his fellow board members and a taxpayer (*Appeals of Gill & Burnett*, 42 Ed Dept Rep 89 (2002), *petition dismissed, Gill v. Mills*, (Sup. Ct. Albany Cnty. 2003)).

Unlike a removal hearing before the commissioner of education, the charges in a removal hearing before a school board are not limited to conduct occurring in the 30 days before the hearing. Therefore, conduct addressed in the charges may go back farther in time (*Appeal of Hoefer*, 45 Ed Dept Rep 66 (2005)). Thus, the commissioner upheld a board's removal of a member who over a period of three years improperly charged over $3,000 of personal purchases to the district (see *Appeal of Jones-White*, 44 Ed Dept Rep 347 (2005)).

It should be noted, New York City community district education council members are subject to removal by the city schools chancellor (§ 2590-l).

6:41. May a school board member be removed from office for revealing confidential information learned in executive session?

Yes. In *Appeal of Nett and Raby* (45 Ed Dept Rep 259 (2005)), the commissioner of education stated that revelation of information learned in executive session is grounds for removal from the school board. According to the commissioner, the disclosure of executive session material constitutes a violation of a board member's fiduciary duties and oath of office. In addition, such disclosure violates provisions of the General Municipal Law that prohibit board members from disclosing confidential information obtained while discharging their official duties or from using such information to further personal interests (*Appeal of Nett and Raby*; Gen. Mun. Law § 805-a(1)(b); Pub. Off. Law § 10; see also *Application of the Bd. of Educ. of the Elmont UFSD*, 48 Ed Dept Rep 29 (2008); Memo to the Field, NYS Education Department, Kathy Ahearn, Counsel and Deputy Commissioner for Legal Affairs, Dec. 9, 2005, available at: http://www.counsel.nysed.gov/memos/nett).

6:42. What is the process for removing a school board member?

The removal may take place only after a hearing on the charges either before the commissioner of education, at which the board member has a right to be represented by counsel (§§ 306(1), 1706, 2559), or before the board itself (§§ 1709(18); see **6:38-40**). A written copy of the charges must be served at least 10 days before the hearing. The board member must be afforded a "full and fair opportunity to refute such charges before removal" (*Appeal of Taber*, 42 Ed Dept Rep 251 (2003)).

6:43. May a school board member be removed as president of the board without being removed as a school board member?

Yes. Although it is unlikely that the same circumstances that would support the removal of a school board president would not also give cause for the removal of that individual from the board, both offices are separate and distinct from one another (*Appeal of Johnson*, 45 Ed Dept Rep 469 (2006); *Matter of Motoyama*, 12 Ed Dept Rep 244 (1973)). Therefore, it is possible to remove someone as president of the school board without removing that person from the board.

However, because under section 2105(6) the board president serves in that capacity for a statutory period of one year, he or she does not serve at the pleasure of the board. As such, a board member may be removed from the office of board president only for cause. In addition, the sole decision on this matter indicates that only the commissioner of education may remove an individual from office as president when that individual is not being removed from the board as well (*Matter of Motoyama*).

6:44. May a school board member be censured or reprimanded?

No. Nothing in the Education Law authorizes either a school board or the commissioner of education to censure or reprimand a school board member (*Appeal of K.M.*, 55 Ed Dept Rep, Dec. No. 16,796 (2015); *Appeal of Gonzalez*, 48 Ed Dept Rep 415 (2009); *Appeal of Silano*, 33 Ed Dept Rep 20 (1993), *petition dismissed, Silano v. Sobol*, (Sup. Ct. Albany Cnty. 1994). However, a school board may criticize the actions of a board member for exhibiting poor judgment (*Appeal of Silano*). Any criticism must be carefully worded and avoid the tone of formal disciplinary charges or it will be found invalid (*Appeal of L.S.*, 44 Ed Dept Rep 142 (2004)).

Also, there is no legal basis for ordering a school board member to apologize (*Appeal of Lloyd*, 39 Ed Dept Rep 537 (2000)).

6:45. Can school board members be paid for their service as board members?

Generally, no. Opinions of the state comptroller have consistently held that school board members may not receive compensation for their services unless expressly authorized by an act of the state Legislature (Opns. St. Comp. 72-342, 71-985; see also §§ 1702(3)(b), 1804(12)(b), 1901(2)(b), 2502(10)(b)).

However, school board members may be reimbursed for expenses actually and necessarily incurred in the performance of their official duties (§§ 2118, 2590-b(1)(a), 2590-(b)(1)).

In addition, board members, including those who have been elected but whose term has not yet commenced, may receive reimbursement to cover the costs of conferences, such as those sponsored by the New York State School Boards Association, that are related to official business. Such cost must have been authorized by a resolution approved by a majority of the board, or approved by a duly authorized designee of the board, prior to attendance at such a conference. Conference travel must be made using a cost-effective and reasonable method of travel (Gen. Mun. Law § 77-b; see **25:23-24**).

7. Boards of Cooperative Educational Services (BOCES)

Editor's Note: For additional information concerning BOCES, contact the NYS Education Department's Office of Educational Management Services at 518-474-6541, or online at: http://www.p12.nysed.gov/mgtserv/boces.

Overview

7:1. What is a board of cooperative educational services (BOCES)?

A *board of cooperative educational services* (BOCES) is a voluntary, cooperative association of school districts in a geographic area that share planning, services, and programs to provide educational and support activities more economically, efficiently, and equitably than could be provided by an individual district (§ 1950). The geographic area covered by a BOCES is known as a supervisory district (see **11:2**).

BOCES are organized under section 1950 of the Education Law. BOCES services are focused on education for students with disabilities, career education, academic and alternative programs, summer schools, staff development, computer services (managerial and instructional), educational communication, and burgeoning cooperative purchasing (see **7:27**).

A BOCES board is considered a corporate body. All BOCES property is held by the BOCES board as a corporation (§ 1950(6)). BOCES boards are also considered municipal corporations, permitting them to contract with other municipalities on a cooperative basis under sections 119-n(a) and 119-o of the General Municipal Law.

For clarity purposes, the governing body of the BOCES will be referred to as the BOCES board throughout this chapter.

7:2. How many BOCES are there?

There are 37 BOCES in New York State.

7:3. Do all school districts belong to a BOCES?

No. According to the NYS Education Department, all but nine of the 691 operating school districts in New York belong to a BOCES (see http://www.p12.nysed.gov/irs/schoolDirectory/).

BOCES membership is not available to the Big 5 school districts (Buffalo, New York City, Rochester, Syracuse, and Yonkers). However, under certain circumstances, non-component districts, including the Big 5, may participate in BOCES instructional support services (see **7:33**).

7:4. Can a school district terminate its membership in a BOCES?

No. There is no authority or process by which a school district can terminate its status as a BOCES component.

However, once a district becomes a BOCES component district, it is obligated to pay annually a proportionate share of the BOCES administrative and capital expenses whether or not it participates in any BOCES program or service (§ 1950(4)(b)(7)). On the other hand, BOCES component districts contribute only toward the costs of BOCES programs and services in which they actually participate (§ 1950(4)(d)(4); see also **7:28**).

BOCES Board Members

7:5. How many members are on a BOCES board?

A BOCES board may consist of between five and 15 members. The number of BOCES board members may be increased or decreased within that range by the commissioner of education (§ 1950(1), (2-b)).

7:6. Can two residents of the same component district sit on a BOCES board at the same time?

The law prohibits the election of more than one candidate residing in a particular component school district, unless the number of seats on the BOCES board exceeds the number of component school districts or an unrepresented district declines to make a nomination, provided that a person nominated by a special act school district, a central high school district or any component thereof shall be deemed a resident of the district that nominated him or her (§ 1950(2-a)(c)). This restriction applies, no matter which district initially nominated the person.

7:7. How long is the term of office of a BOCES board member?

BOCES board members are elected to three-year terms. BOCES board members' terms commence on the first day of July following their election (§ 1950(2), (2-b); see also **7:12** and **7:16**).

7:8. What are the qualifications for serving as a BOCES board member?

A BOCES board candidate must reside within the boundaries of a component school district (§ 1950(9-a)). Any candidate nominated by a special act school district, a central high school district, or any component thereof, shall be considered a resident of the district that nominated that person (§ 1950(2-a)(b)).

A candidate can be but is not required to be a member of a component district school board. However, no employee of a component district is eligible to be elected to a BOCES board membership (§ 1950(9)), and a BOCES board member cannot accept employment in a component district (Opn. Att'y Gen. I 2007-02). On the other hand, a BOCES employee may serve on a component school board (*Appeal of Reynolds*, 42 Ed Dept Rep 278 (2003); *Application of a BOCES*, 38 Ed Dept Rep 224 (1998); *Matter of Todd*, 19 Ed Dept Rep 277 (1979)). The commissioner of education encourages BOCES employees serving on component boards to recuse themselves from voting on issues that present a conflict (*Appeal of Reynolds*). Also, the Attorney General has stated that the position of district attorney is incompatible with membership on a BOCES board (Opn. Att'y Gen. I 2000-13).

Furthermore, no more than one candidate per component district may be elected to serve, unless the number of BOCES seats exceeds the number of component districts or an unrepresented district declines to make a nomination (§ 1950(2-a)(c); see **7:6**).

7:9. How are BOCES board members nominated for office?

Members of a BOCES board are nominated by resolution of one or more of the school boards of its component districts. The resolution must be provided to the clerk of the BOCES board at least 30 days prior to the date of the election, as designated by the BOCES president (§ 1950(2-a)(b)).

7:10. Are there any restrictions on BOCES board nominations?

Yes. The clerk of the BOCES board must reject any nomination from a component school district that has another resident serving on the BOCES board unless that member's term will expire at the end of the current year, or the number of BOCES board seats exceeds the number of component school districts, or an unrepresented district declines to make a nomination (§ 1950(2-a)(b)). The clerk must also reject a nominee who is not a resident of any component school district of the BOCES (§ 1950(9-a)), or a nominee employed by a component district within the supervisory district (§ 1950(9); *Application of a BOCES*, 38 Ed Dept Rep 224 (1998); see also *Appeal of Reynolds*, 42 Ed Dept Rep 278 (2003)).

Any person or board member nominated by a special act school district, a central high school district, or any component thereof, will be deemed a resident only of the district that nominated that person (§ 1950(2-a)(b); see also *Appeal of Stris*, 40 Ed Dept Rep 495 (2001)).

There are no limitations on the number of nominations an individual component district may make (see NYS Education Department, *Questions and Answers on the BOCES Reform Act* (Oct. 1993)).

Public School Governance

7:11. Does the BOCES have a responsibility to encourage nominations?

Yes, it is the duty of the BOCES to encourage the nomination of persons residing in districts not currently represented on the BOCES board (§ 1950(2-a)(b)).

7:12. How are the members of a BOCES board elected?

BOCES board members are elected by their component member boards. By February 1 of each year, the BOCES board president must set the date of election in each component district. It is the same day designated for the vote on the tentative administrative budget, between April 16th and 30th. All component school boards meet on that same date, except for central high school boards, which must hold their meetings the next business day (§ 1950(2-a)(b)).

The BOCES clerk then must mail an election ballot to each component district at least 14 days prior to the election. On the date designated for the election, each component board is entitled to cast one vote per vacancy, but no more than one vote per candidate. BOCES board members are elected by resolution of the component boards on the ballot prepared by the BOCES clerk (§ 1950(2-a)(c)).

Each component district must mail or deliver its completed ballot to the BOCES clerk no later than one business day after the election (§ 1950(2-a)(c)). There must be a quorum of board members voting in each component district to have a valid ballot (see NYS Education Department, *Questions and Answers on the BOCES Reform Act* (Oct. 1993)).

The candidates receiving the plurality of votes cast are elected with the candidate receiving the highest vote total elected to the position with the longest term, and the candidate with the second highest vote total elected to the position with the next longest term, and so on. If the length of term of all positions to be filled is equal, candidates are elected in order of the greatest number of votes received until all vacancies are filled (§ 1950(2-a)(c)).

7:13. What happens in the event of a tie vote?

In the event of a tie vote, the BOCES board president must call a run-off election within 20 days of the initial vote, with only the candidates who received an equal number of votes deemed nominated. If the run-off election results in a tie vote, the winning candidate is determined by drawing lots (§ 1950(2-a)(d)).

7:14. What happens if the school board of a component district is unable to obtain a quorum on the day designated for the election or fails to adopt a board resolution voting on the candidates?

If a component district fails to obtain a quorum on that date, the district's ballot is void. The candidates receiving a plurality of the votes actually cast on the day of election are elected (see NYS Education Department, *Questions and Answers on the BOCES Reform Act* (Oct. 1993)).

7:15. What happens if all of the component school districts fail to vote, so that no candidate receives a plurality?

The BOCES board position(s) will remain open until there is an election that fills the vacancy. However, each component board has a duty to elect BOCES board members, and a willful neglect of this duty may constitute grounds for removal of the school board (see NYS Education Department, *Questions and Answers on the BOCES Reform Act* (Oct. 1993)).

7:16. What is the procedure to fill a vacancy on the BOCES board?

If a vacancy occurs, the BOCES may fill the vacancy by appointment, provided that notice is given to all component boards and that they are given ten days to provide any comments/objections to filling the vacancy by appointment. The person appointed shall hold the office until the next annual election of the BOCES (§ 1950(2-a)(f)).

When two or more BOCES have been merged or reorganized, elections may not be held to fill vacancies on the new board until a sufficient number of board member terms have expired so that the board has between five and 15 members (§ 1950(7)).

BOCES Board Powers and Duties

7:17. What are the powers and duties of a BOCES board?

The powers and duties of a BOCES board are listed in section 1950(4) of the Education Law. These powers and duties must be exercised in the manner prescribed by law. They provide a BOCES board the authority to, for example:

- Appoint a district superintendent of schools, subject to approval of the commissioner of education, and, at its discretion, provide for the payment of a supplementary salary to the district BOCES superintendent of schools by the BOCES (§ 1950(4)(a)(1); NYS Education Department, *BOCES Primer* (updated Apr. 2011), at: http://www.p12.nysed.gov/mgtserv/boces/primer.html).
- Prepare separate tentative budgets of expenditures for program, capital, and administrative costs for the BOCES in accordance with the commissioner's regulations (§ 1950(4)(b)(1)).
- Adopt the final program, capital, and administrative budgets no later than May 15. After applicable state aid has been deducted, component school districts are to be charged for their proportionate shares of the budget (§ 1950(4)(b)(7)).

- Conduct surveys to determine the need for cooperative educational services in the supervisory district (§ 1950(4)(c); see **7:19**).
- Provide on a cooperative basis any of the various services specified in law (§ 1950(4)(d); see **7:27**).
- Designate a depository for funds and develop procedures for the receipt, deposit, investment, and disbursement of funds including the appointment of a claims auditor and the establishment of an internal audit function subject to the laws relating to union free school districts (§ 1950(4)(k); see **25:20**).
- Employ administrative assistants, teachers, supervisors, clerical help, and other personnel recommended by the district superintendent as may be necessary to carry out its program (§ 1950(4)(e)).
- Rent, improve, alter, equip, and furnish suitable land, classrooms, offices, or buildings as necessary to deliver services (§ 1950(4)(p)(a); see **7:24-25**).
- Provide transportation for students to and from BOCES classes (§ 1950(4)(q); see **7:32**), as well as regional transportation services (see §§ 1604(21-b), 1709(25)(g), (h)).
- Provide services to school districts outside of the supervisory district as permitted by law (§ 1950(4)(r), (w)).
- Contract with nonpublic schools to provide processing services for student and other administrative records, and the processing of fingerprints for criminal history record checks (§ 1950(4)(h)(4)).
- Contract with the federal government, the state government, community colleges, agricultural and technical colleges, or other public agencies for the provision of career education programs to such agencies (§ 1950(4)(h)(5)).
- Enter into contracts with not-for-profit corporations to participate in federal programs related to career training and experience (§ 1950(4)(h)(6)).
- Lease unneeded facilities to public or private agencies, individuals, partnerships, or corporations (§ 1950(4)(p)(b); see **7:23**).
- Contract with the state government, community colleges, agricultural and technical colleges, or other public agencies for the purpose of providing electronic data-processing services to such agencies (§ 1950(4)(h)(7)).
- Through June 30, 2018, contract with the commissioner of the Office of Children and Family Services (OCFS) for the benefit of youth in OCFS custody to provide special education, related services, career and technical education services and music, art and foreign language programs provided by the BOCES to component school districts. Such contract must be approved by the commissioner (§§ 1950(4)(h)(8), 3202(6-a)).
- Through June 30, 2018, contract with the commissioner of the Office of Mental Health (OMH) for patients in hospitals operated by OMH to provide special education, related services and any alternative education programs approved by the commissioner of education and where the BOCES provides alternative education programs to component districts. Such contract must be approved by the commissioner (§§ 1950(4)(h)(9), 3202(6-b)).
- Through July 1, 2019, contract with out-of-state school districts for a period of no more than five years for special education and/or career and technical education services or for certain services related to the implementation of common core standards as well as professional development for educators. Such contracts must be approved by the commissioner of education (§ 1950(4)(h)(10)).
- Contract with public libraries for high-speed telecommunication services (§ 1950(4)(h)(11)).

BOCES are included in the definition of "educational partnership organization" and may contract with school districts to work with schools designated as persistently low achieving or under registration review (§ 211-e(1), (5)).

7:18. Does a BOCES have the responsibility to notify students of programs that would allow a student to pursue an Associate of Occupational Studies (AOS) degree from a community college upon high school graduation?

Yes. Boards of Trustees of the State University of New York community colleges are required to consult with BOCES to identify new or existing programs offered to students that would allow a student to pursue an AOS from a community college upon high school graduation. Once identified, the BOCES, in conjunction with the community college, shall make such path, identified programs, and AOS degree options known to ensure that students are aware that such options exist. Such notification shall begin in the eighth grade. BOCES must also provide materials on AOS degree options to school counselors in each school district in their region. However, no action may be taken to suggest that a student should pursue a particular degree or pathway (§ 6306(10)).

7:19. What are the responsibilities of a BOCES when determining the cooperative educational needs within its supervisory district?

Each BOCES has the duty to survey the need for cooperative educational services in its supervisory district and present the findings of its surveys to local school authorities. Each BOCES must prepare long-range plans to meet the projected need for such services in the supervisory district for the next five years "as may be specified by the commissioner." The plans must be revised annually. The plans and annual revisions must be kept on file and made available for public inspection and review by the commissioner of education on or before December 1 of each year, provided that the plans may be incorporated into a BOCES district-wide comprehensive plan (§ 1950(4)(c)).

7:20. May a BOCES purchase, own, sell, and/or exchange sites and facilities?

Yes. A BOCES may purchase, own, sell and exchange real property, but only when authorized by the "qualified voters of the BOCES district" (§ 1950(4)(t), (x); see also § 1950(14)(d); *Bd. of Educ. of East Syracuse-Minoa CSD v. Comm'r of Educ.*, 145 A.D.2d 13 (3d Dep't), *appeal denied*, 74 N.Y.2d 890 (1989)). A qualified voter of the BOCES district is a person who is a citizen of the United States, at least 18 years of age, and a resident within the BOCES for a period of 30 days prior to the meeting at which he or she will vote (§ 1951(2)(c)).

Obligations necessary for the acquisition or construction of BOCES facilities must be issued by the component school districts (§ 1950(14)), or by the Dormitory Authority if the facilities or construction are acquired through the Authority (§ 1950(13); Pub. Auth. Law § 1689). A BOCES has no authority to issue obligations for such purpose (see Local Fin. Law § 20.00 *et seq.*).

7:21. May a BOCES acquire facilities to house its services through the New York State Dormitory Authority?

Yes. A BOCES and its component school districts may enter into an agreement with the New York State Dormitory Authority to acquire facilities designed to house services to be provided by the BOCES and to share the cost of the acquisition (§ 1950(13)). No such agreement may be for longer than is required to retire the obligations or to pay the Dormitory Authority in full (§ 1950(11)).

The Dormitory Authority is authorized to construct facilities where the BOCES may operate its program, to finance their cost, lease them to the BOCES, and to transfer the facilities back to the BOCES when the costs and liabilities incurred by the authority have been paid (Pub. Auth. Law §§ 1676(2)(d), 1678(15), 1689).

7:22. Do renovations of BOCES facilities require voter or component school district approval?

No. However, if a component school district has to obtain long-term financing for its share of the cost of the renovation, all component districts must agree to the renovation (*Bd. of Educ. of East Syracuse-Minoa CSD v. Comm'r of Educ.*, 145 A.D.2d 13 (3d Dep't), *appeal denied*, 74 N.Y.2d 890 (1989)).

7:23. May a BOCES lease its unused facilities?

Yes. A BOCES may lease its unused facilities to public or private agencies and others, with the approval of the commissioner of education, for a term of not more than five years, which is renewable with the commissioner's approval (§ 1950(4)(p)(b); 8 NYCRR § 155.14).

7:24. May a BOCES rent real property?

Yes. A BOCES's authority to rent real property, however, is limited to a maximum period of 10 years for leases entered into with public entities and, through June 30, 2019, 20 years for leases entered into with non-public entities, subject to certain specified conditions or uses that are identified in section 1950(4)(p)(a) of the Education Law.

Before executing a lease, the BOCES board must adopt a resolution that explains why this action is in the best financial interests of the supervisory district, and that the rental payment is no more than fair market value as determined by the board. No such lease is enforceable against the BOCES unless and until it has been approved in writing by the commissioner of education (§ 1950(4)(p)(a); 8 NYCRR § 155.15).

7:25. May a BOCES lease personal property?

Yes. A BOCES may lease personal property such as relocatable classrooms constructed on land owned by the BOCES or leased from a third party. Before executing the agreement, the BOCES board must adopt a resolution to determine that the agreement is "in the best financial interests" of the BOCES, and the resolution must state the basis for that determination. In addition, such agreements are subject to the bidding requirements of the General Municipal Law (§ 1950(4)(y); 8 NYCRR § 155.15).

7:26. Are there any policy requirements that are unique to a BOCES?

Yes. A BOCES board is also required to develop and adopt a formal policy on the acquisition, sale, and disposal of personal property to be approved by the commissioner of education. The policy must include procedures for the acquisition of personal property by purchase or gift, and the periodic inventory of personal property. It also must include procedures for the sale of valuable personal property to the highest bidder, except that a BOCES may give vehicles received at no cost for use in an authorized welfare-to-work program to eligible program participants (§ 1950(18)).

BOCES Services

7:27. What services are available through a BOCES?

Any of the following services are available through a BOCES on a cooperative basis: school nurse-teacher; attendance supervisor; supervisor of teachers; dental hygienist; psychologist; teachers of art, music, physical education, and career education; guidance counselors; operation of classes for students with disabilities; student and financial accounting services; and maintenance and operation of cafeteria or restaurant service for the use of students and teachers while at school and to furnish meals to senior citizens (§ 1950(4)(d)(1)).

In addition, a BOCES may provide academic and other programs and services, including summer programs and services including, but not limited to: itinerant teaching services in advanced academic courses; academic course offerings; block scheduling, satellite course offerings, distance learning courses through the use of interactive television and other technologies; and academic intervention services (§ 1950(4)(d), (4)(bb)). These services must be requested by component districts and approved by the commissioner of education (§ 1950(4)(d), (4)(bb)). Academic courses may be provided for make-up credit or online courses pursuant to commissioner's regulations (8 NYCRR § 100.5(d)(8), (10)).

A BOCES also may provide activities and services pertaining to the arts, training adults for employment, and activities and services regarding environmental education (§ 1950(4)(dd), (gg), (hh)). Examples of other services not specifically mentioned in the law that have been approved by the commissioner in specific situations include: adult education coordinator; supervisor of education for students with disabilities; shared school business manager; coordinator of language arts; coordinator of education for gifted children; cooperative purchasing; transportation service; printing services; psychiatric consultant service; coordinator of career education; clinical programs for reading and speech correction; school health coordinator; in-service workshops; and educational communications center.

When providing instructional or educational services, a BOCES may not employ an independent contractor or outside employment service for that purpose, not even on a per-diem substitute basis (*BOCES of Erie, Chautauqua & Cattaraugus Counties v. Univ. of the State Educ. Dep't*, 40 A.D.3d 1349 (3d Dep't 2007)).

7:28. How does a component school district secure educational services through a BOCES?

The annual procedure for securing such BOCES services is as follows:

- By February 1, component districts must file their non-binding requests for services with their BOCES (§ 1950(4)(d)(3)).
- By February 15, BOCES must submit proposed operating plans to the NYS Education Department (§ 1950(4)(d)(3)).
- By March 10, BOCES must notify their component school districts of the services that the commissioner of education has approved for the coming school year. This notice must include the local uniform cost for each service established in accordance with the Education Law and commissioner's regulations (§ 1950(4)(d)(3)).
- By May 1, component school districts must notify BOCES of their intent to participate in shared services and identify those services (§ 1950(4)(d)(4)).
- By June 1, BOCES must submit to the commissioner an operating plan and budget based upon component districts' requests. This must include the budgeted unit cost of programs and services calculated pursuant to the Education Law. If a BOCES receives requests for unanticipated shared services subsequent to the adoption of the budget, then it must submit an amended operating plan to the commissioner and include a statement concerning the availability of district funds to pay for the district's share of the additional services from each superintendent who has requested the services (§ 1950(4)(d)(5)).
- By August 1, BOCES must file with the commissioner a copy of each contract for services executed with component districts (§ 1950(4)(d)(4)).
- By September 1, BOCES must submit an annual program report and evaluation to the commissioner (§ 1950(4)(d)(5)).

It is up to a component's school board to decide whether to contract for particular BOCES programs (*Appeal of Williams III*, 42 Ed Dept Rep 260 (2003); *Appeal of a Student with a Disability*, 42 Ed Dept Rep 163 (2002)). When a school board determines to provide a program through BOCES, this has the same effect, legally, as providing that program in its own school. In such an instance, the BOCES is considered part of the component district (*Appeal of Kendrick & Sillato*, 32 Ed Dept Rep 464 (1993)).

7:29. May a local school board limit student enrollment in particular BOCES programs?

Yes. School boards are required to provide their high school students with access to career education programs commensurate with the interests and capabilities of those wishing or having a need to participate in such a program (§ 4602(1)). However, a board that makes available career education courses within its own curriculum does not have to contract with a BOCES for such a program, even if its own offerings are different from those provided by the BOCES (*Appeal of a Student with a Disability*, 42 Ed Dept Rep 163 (2002)). In addition, such a board also may consider its financial situation in deciding whether to permit its students to enroll in a BOCES program (*Appeal of Mento*, 48 Ed Dept Rep 396 (2009)).

A school board may limit student enrollment in a BOCES career education program to students who, for example:

- Are 11th and 12th grade students (*Appeal of Giordano*, 29 Ed Dept Rep 210 (1990); see also *Matter of Tripi*, 21 Ed Dept Rep 349 (1981)).
- Meet district prerequisites for admission to the BOCES program (*Matter of Tripi*).
- Have exhausted all available opportunities within the district (*Appeal of Baez*, 48 Ed Dept Rep 418 (2009)).

7:30. What is the maximum amount of time an itinerant teacher or worker may spend in a single component school district in order for the service to be approved as a shared BOCES service?

According to the NYS Education Department, a person whose services are to be shared may not spend any more than 60 percent or three days per week of his or her time in any one school district. A district may not expect to use most of such a person's time when engaged in a token sharing with one or two other districts (NYS Education Department, *CO-SERS 101: An Introduction to BOCES Services* (revised 2009), at: http://www.p12.nysed.gov/mgtserv/boces/CO-SERS/CO-SERS101_REVISED_2009.ppt; see also NYS Education Department, *BOCES Administrative Handbook I: General Guidelines and Procedures for CO-SER Preparation* (2002), at: www.p12.nysed.gov/mgtserv/boces/handbooks/Handbook1.htm).

7:31. What state aid is paid to districts to reimburse them for services purchased from BOCES?

Component districts are eligible to receive BOCES operating aid for approved services costs and administrative charges, BOCES facilities aid, and BOCES rental aid. BOCES operating aid is based on prior-year approved expenditures, while aid for facilities and rental are based on current-year expenditures. Approved expenditures include salaries of BOCES employees only up to $30,000 (§ 1950(5)).

The total of the three types of aids is subject to a save-harmless provision; that is, no district will receive less BOCES aid than it received in the 1967-68 school year (§ 1950(5)(f)).

7:32. May BOCES provide student transportation services?

Yes. Transportation to and from classes operated by a BOCES may be provided at the request of one or more school districts. School districts and BOCES are authorized to enter into contracts with

Public School Governance

other districts, private contractors, BOCES, and any municipal corporations or authorities to provide the transportation (§ 1950(4)(q)).

Additionally, school districts may enter into regional transportation contracts with BOCES to provide transportation between home and school, between school and special education programs or programs at other school districts, for field trips or extracurricular activities, or for cooperative school bus maintenance (§§ 1604(21-b); 1709(25)(g), (h); see **57:13**).

7:33. May a non-component district receive BOCES instructional support services?

Yes. Any non-component school district, including members of the Big 5, can, upon consent of the BOCES and with the approval of the commissioner of education, participate as a component district of the BOCES serving its geographic area or an adjoining BOCES for the sole purpose of purchasing instructional support services. The district must pay its share of the expenses of the program, including a charge for administration costs (§ 1950(8-c)).

In addition, for the 2016-17 school year, the non-component city school district of the city of Rochester, upon consent of the BOCES serving its geographical region, may purchase from the BOCES medical and health services pursuant to Article 19 of the Education Law (L. 2016, c. 54 pt. A, § 41).

7:34. Are there any services the BOCES are specifically prohibited from providing as aidable shared services?

Yes. Cooperative maintenance services other than school bus maintenance (see **7:32**), or municipal services including, but not limited to, lawn mowing services and heating, ventilation or air conditioning repair or maintenance or trash collection, or any other municipal service as defined by the commissioner of education, will not be authorized as an aidable BOCES shared service (§ 1950(4)(d)(2)).

In addition, certain technology purchases and installations may not qualify as an aidable shared service, unless the component school district demonstrates that it would be more cost-effective to go through a BOCES than otherwise (§ 1950(4)(d)(2-a)).

7:35. Are BOCES subject to financial audits?

Yes. There are two external types of audits that are to be conducted in BOCES districts:

- *State audits*. The state comptroller shall conduct a fiscal audit of each BOCES. The priority and frequency of these audits will be based on a risk assessment process conducted by the comptroller. The resulting audit report must be made available to the public, upon request, for at least five years following its issuance (§ 2116-a(3-a); Gen. Mun. Law § 33). In addition, the commissioner of education shall conduct periodic fiscal audits of the BOCES and, to the extent sufficient resources are provided to the NYS Education Department, shall assure that each BOCES is audited at least once every three years (§ 305(25)).
- *Independent audits*. The commissioner's regulations require that BOCES obtain an annual audit, in a form prescribed by the commissioner of education, of all funds by a certified public accountant or public accountant. The auditor's final report must be adopted by resolution of the BOCES board and a copy must be filed with the commissioner by October 15 of each year (8 NYCRR §§ 170.3(a), 170.12(e)).

In addition to these external audits, the BOCES must establish an internal audit function (§ 1950(4)(k); 8 NYCRR § 170.12(b)), and an audit committee (8 NYCRR § 170.12(d)). A claims auditor and deputy claims auditor may also be appointed (§§ 1709(20-a), 1950(4)(k); 8 NYCRR § 170.12(c)). For more information on financial audits, claims auditors, and other fiscal responsibilities, see **chapter 25**.

8. School District Officers

In General

8:1. Who are the school district's officers?

The school district's officers include school board members and trustees, and other individuals identified by law and appointed by the school board to help administer the district's affairs. They include:

- Superintendent of schools (§§ 2(13), 1604(8), 1711, 2503(5), 2507, 2508, 2554(2); see **10:1**), and in the case of a board of cooperative educational services, a district superintendent (§§ 2(13), 2204; see **10:1**).
- Supervisor of attendance or attendance officer (§ 2(13)).
- School district clerk (§§ 2(13), 2130(1), 2503(15)).
- Treasurer (§§ 2(13), 2101(1), 2130(4), 2503(15)).
- Tax collector (§§ 2(13), 2101(1), 2130(4), 2506; and Town Law § 38).
- Claims auditor and deputy claims auditor at the discretion of the board (§§ 1709(20-a), 2526, 2554(2-a); see **8:14**).
- Chancellor of the City School District of the City of New York (*Lawson v. N.Y. City Bd. of Educ.*, 2011 U.S. Dist. LEXIS 127789 (S.D.N.Y. Aug. 30, 2011)).

Building principals and assistant principals are not school district officers (*Lawson v. N.Y. City Bd. of Educ.*; *Carlson v. Geneva City Sch. Dist.*, 679 F.Supp.2d 355 (W.D.N.Y. 2010); see also *Appeal of Gonzalez*, 48 Ed Dept Rep 415 (2009); *Appeal of Danison*, 31 Ed Dept Rep 169 (1991); see **8:17**)).

Separate individuals must hold each of the offices of school tax collector, school district treasurer, school district clerk, and of claims auditor or deputy claims auditor if one is appointed (§ 2130; 8 NYCRR § 170.2(a)).

Community members appointed to the district's audit committee are deemed school district officers for indemnification purposes under sections 3811-3813 of the Education Law (§ 2116-c(3)).

For more information on claim audits and audit committees, see **25:9-11**.

8:2. Are all individuals serving in a superintendent's position considered school district officers?

No. A deputy superintendent is a district employee, not a school district officer (*Appeal of Berman*, 46 Ed Dept Rep 64 (2006)). The same is true of an assistant superintendent (*Appeal of Affronti*, 54 Ed Dept Rep, Dec. No. 16,756 (2015); *Appeal of Johnston*, 50 Ed Dept Rep, Dec. No. 16,184 (2010)).

8:3. Is a school board's legal counsel or school attorney a school district officer?

No. The school attorney and those in similar positions are not school district officers (*Appeal of Destino*, 52 Ed Dep Rep, Dec. No. 16,461 (2013); *Matter of McGinley*, 23 Ed Dept Rep 350 (1984), citing *Matter of Harrison CSD v. Nyquist*, 59 A.D.2d 434 (3d Dep't 1977), *appeal denied*, 44 N.Y.2d 645 (1978)). They are either an employee or an independent contractor (2 NYCRR §§ 315.2(b), (c), 315.3(c)).

Public School Governance

8:4. Must certain school district officers file a bond?

Yes. The school board must establish the limits of a bond (known in the law as an "official undertaking") and require the treasurer, tax collector, and claims auditor to file one. As an alternative, the board may include these officers in a blanket bond (§§ 2130(5), 2527; Pub. Off. Law § 11(2); 8 NYCRR § 170.2(d); see also **8:11, 8:13**).

8:5. Who determines the amount of compensation paid to a school district officer?

The school board determines the amount of compensation for the district treasurer, tax collector, superintendent of schools, and auditor. The board may also determine the amount of compensation to be provided to the district clerk if it was not decided at the annual meeting (§§ 2123, 2130(3), 2506; *Appeal of Palillo*, 6 Ed Dept Rep 117 (1967)).

8:6. May school district officers do business with the school district that employs them?

No, unless allowed by the conflict of interest law, which applies to school district officers and employees as well as school board members (Gen. Mun. Law § 800 *et seq.*; see **chapter 12**).

Qualifications of School District Officers

8:7. What are the qualifications of school district officers?

The general rule is that a school district officer must be able to read and write and must be a qualified voter of the district (§ 2102). For further information on the qualifications for school board members, see **6:1, 6:6-11**.

Residency in the school district is not a requirement for the district superintendent, superintendent of schools, district clerk, treasurer, or tax collector (§§ 2102, 2205; see *Appeal of Connor*, 48 Ed Dept Rep 113 (2008)). Therefore, these school district officers are not required to be qualified voters of the district. However, a school board may impose a residency requirement as a qualification of employment (*Matter of O'Connor v. Bd. of Educ. of the City Sch. Dist. of the City of Niagara Falls*, 48 A.D.3d 1254 (4th Dep't 2008), *lv. to appeal dismissed*, 10 N.Y.3d 928 (2010); see also *Felix v. N.Y. City Dep't of Citywide Admin. Servs.*, 3 N.Y.3d 498 (2004); *Mandelkern v. City of Buffalo*, 64 A.D.2d 279 (4th Dep't 1978); *Appeal of Connor*).

The Education Law states that a claims auditor or deputy claims auditor in a common or union free school district need not be a district resident (§§ 1604(35)(b), 1709(20-a)(b)). Although the provisions applicable to city school districts are silent regarding a claims auditor's or deputy claims auditor's residency, the same rules applicable to common and union free school districts should apply under the concept of devolution (see **5:16-17**; §§ 2526 (1-a), 2554(2-a)).

8:8. Are school district officers required to take a constitutional oath of office?

Yes. School district officers, such as board members and trustees, superintendent, clerk and treasurer, are required to take and file an oath of office with the district clerk (Pub. Off. Law § 10; *Scro v. Bd. of Educ. of the Jordan-Elbridge CSD*, 87 A.D.3d 1342 (4th Dep't 2011), *lv. to appeal denied,* 18 N.Y.3d 810 (2012); *Appeal of Sidmore*, 55 Ed Dept Rep, Dec. No. 16,904 (2016); *Appeal of Karpen*, 39 Ed Dept Rep 98 (1999)).

Usually the oath is administered at the board's annual reorganizational meeting by either the board president or the district clerk. Whoever administers the oath must have properly taken and filed an oath of office before administering the oath to others (*Application of Karpen*; for further information on the oath of office for school board members, see **5:11**). The fact that the oath has been administered should be noted in the board's minutes. The failure to take and file the oath of office within 30 days after notice of appointment or the commencement of the term of office to which the officer is appointed causes the office to become vacant (*Scro v. Bd. of Educ. of the Jordan-Elbridge CSD; Appeal of Sidmore; Application of Karpen*).

A district superintendent (see **10:1, 11:1**) also must take an oath upon the discharge of the duties of his or her office. This must be done no later than five days after the date on which his or her term of office begins (§ 2206; Pub. Off. Law § 10).

Appointment of School District Officers

8:9. May a school board member be appointed district clerk?

It depends. Generally, a school board member may not serve as a district clerk (§ 2103(1)). However, school boards in union free and central school districts may appoint either one of their members or another individual as clerk (§§ 2130(1), 1804(1); *Appeal of Aarseth*, 32 Ed Dept Rep 626 (1993); *Matter of Hurtgam*, 22 Ed Dept Rep 219 (1982); see also **6:8**).

8:10. May the school board appoint someone to fulfill the district clerk's duties if the current clerk is unavailable?

Although the Education Law does not specifically provide for the appointment of a deputy or acting clerk, certain duties of the district clerk must be carried out, notwithstanding the clerk's temporary incapacitation. For example, the notice of an annual meeting must be given whether or not the clerk is available to carry out this function (§ 2004(1)).

Therefore, by practical necessity, a school board may designate an individual to carry out the district clerk's duties when he or she is incapacitated or otherwise unavailable.

8:11. May the school board appoint a deputy treasurer?

Yes. The school board may appoint a deputy treasurer to sign checks in lieu of the treasurer or other officer required to sign such checks, in case of his or her absence or inability. The deputy treasurer must also execute and file an "official undertaking" (a bond) in the same manner and amount as required of the treasurer (§ 1720(2); see also **8:4**).

8:12. May the school board appoint a bank to act as the district's treasurer?

No. The school district's treasurer must be an individual. But a school board, by resolution, may enter into a contract to provide for the deposit of the school district's periodic payroll in a bank or trust company for district disbursal in accordance with provisions of section 96-b of the Banking Law (§§ 1719, 1720).

However, if the school district's treasurer or deputy treasurer has an interest in it, then it would be a prohibited conflict of interest for the school board to designate that bank or trust company as a depository, paying agent, registration agent, or an agent for investment of funds (Gen. Mun. Law § 801(2); see § 802(1)(a) for exception; see also **8:6**).

8:13. May the school board appoint one of its members to sign checks?

Yes. The school board may, by resolution, appoint a member to sign checks in lieu of the treasurer in case of his or her absence or inability, or in addition to the treasurer, if the board decides to require another district officer to countersign all checks. This board member must also execute and file a bond in the same manner and amount as is required of the treasurer (§ 1720(2); Opn. St. Comp. 73-1122; see **8:4**).

8:14. Must a school board appoint a claims auditor or a deputy claims auditor?

No. The position of the school district's claims auditor is a discretionary appointment of the school board. The Education Law stipulates, however, that the following people may *not* be appointed as the district's internal claims auditor: a member of the school board, the district clerk, the district treasurer, the superintendent of schools or other official responsible for the district's business management, the district's designated purchasing agent, or clerical or professional personnel directly involved in the accounting and purchasing functions of the district (§§ 1604(35), 1709(20-a), 2503(5), 2526, 2554(2-a); 8 NYCRR § 170.2(a); Opn. St. Comp. 67-290).

The claims auditor shall report directly to the school board and hold the position subject to the pleasure of the board (§§ 1604(35), 1709(20-a), 2503(5), 2526, 2554(2-a); see **25:10**).

Also, in its discretion, a school board may appoint a deputy claims auditor to act as claims auditor in the absence of the claims auditor (§§ 1604(35), 1709(20-a), 2503, 2526, 2554(2-a)). The Education Law prohibits appointing as deputy claims auditor a person who is also a member of the school board, the district clerk or treasurer, the superintendent or other official responsible for the district's business management, the district's designated purchasing agent, or clerical or other professional personnel directly involved in the accounting and purchasing functions of the district (§§ 1604(35), 1709(20-a), 2526, 2554; see **25:10**).

8:15. Must the claims auditor be an employee of the district?

No. The Education Law authorizes a school board to use independent contractors, inter-municipal cooperative agreements, and BOCES shared services to the extent authorized by section 1950, to fulfill the claims auditor function (§§ 1604(35)(b), (c), 1709(20-a), 2526, 2554; see also **25:10**).

Removal of School District Officers

8:16. Can the school board remove school district officers from their positions?

The school district treasurer and collector serve at the pleasure of the school board, which means the board has the right to dismiss them at any time without cause (§§ 2130(4), 2503(15), 2506(1); *Scro v. Bd. of Educ. of the Jordan-Elbridge CSD*, 87 A.D.3d 1342 (4th Dep't 2011), *lv. to appeal denied,* 18 N.Y.3d 810 (2012); *Appeal of Myers*, 34 Ed Dept Rep 238 (1994); *Matter of Probeck*, 58 State Dep't Rep. 470 (1937)). So does the claims auditor (§§ 1604(35)(a), 1709(20-a)(a), 1950(4)(k), 2526(1)). District clerks and other board officers, however, may only be removed for cause, except that in small city school districts the district clerk also serves at the pleasure of the board (§ 2503(15); see *Matter of*

Motoyama, 12 Ed Dept Rep 244 (1973); see also **6:38-42** for details on the removal of board members, and **11:8**, **10:14-15** on the removal of district superintendents and superintendents of schools).

8:17. Can the commissioner of education remove school district officers from their positions?

Yes. The commissioner of education may remove school district officers the same as school board members, upon a finding of willful violation or neglect of duty or the willful disobedience of a law or a decision, order or regulation of the commissioner, or rule of the Board of Regents (§ 306; see *Application of Dickinson*, 50 Ed Dept Rep, Dec. No. 16,223 (2011); *Appeal of Gonzalez*, 48 Ed Dept Rep 415 (2009); see also **6:39**). In this context, the term *school district officers* refers to clerks, collectors, treasurers, district superintendents, school superintendents, or other school officers in addition to school board members (§ 306; *Appeal of Davis*, 37 Ed Dept Rep 17 (1997); see also **8:1**). The term does not include, for example, school principals, athletic directors and coaches who, instead, are district employees (*Lawson v. N.Y. City Bd. of Educ.*, 2011 U.S. Dist. LEXIS 127789 (S.D.N.Y. Aug. 30, 2011); *Carlson v. Geneva City Sch. Dist.*, 679 F.Supp.2d 355 (W.D.N.Y. Jan. 8, 2010); *Appeal of Gonzalez*; *Appeal of Davis*).

8:18. What is the procedure for removing a district clerk who may be removed only for cause?

The commissioner of education may remove a clerk or other school officer from office after a hearing at which the officer has a right to be represented by counsel. Removal of the clerk can be for any willful violation, neglect of duty under the Education Law, or any other act pertaining to common schools or other educational institutions participating in state funds, or for willful disobedience of any decision, order, rule, or regulation of the Board of Regents or the commissioner (§ 306; see *Matter of Motoyama*, 12 Ed Dept Rep 244 (1973)).

9. School District Administrators

In General

9:1. What are the typical school administrative positions in New York State?

Every school district in New York State may appoint a superintendent of schools (§§ 1604(8), 1711(1), 2503(5), 2554(2), 2590-h(17); see **10:1**). School districts must appoint a full-time building principal for every school, unless the commissioner of education approves an alternative mode of building administration after reviewing evidence submitted by the district (8 NYCRR § 100.2(a); *Appeal of Branch & McElfresh*, 41 Ed Dept Rep 334 (2002); see **29:1**). Other common administrative positions in New York State, appointed at the option of the school board, are associate and assistant superintendents, supervisors, department chairpersons, and assistant principals.

9:2. May school districts share administrators?

Yes. Under Education Law Article 40-A, school districts may arrange to share the services of a superintendent, associate superintendent, assistant superintendent or any other employee with districtwide administrative or supervisory responsibilities with one or more other school districts (§ 1981(1)). Districts also may share the services of a director of physical education (8 NYCRR § 135.4(c)(4)(iii)).

A shared administrator who is not in a tenure-track position is considered an employee by all districts sharing his or her services. All decisions regarding the appointment or compensation of that administrator must be made with the consent of a majority of each participating school district's board. The compensation and benefits of a shared administrator are provided by each participating school district, based on an agreed-upon formula (§ 1981(2)(a)).

For a shared administrator who may be granted tenure, the participating districts must designate a participating district as the principal employing district. That administrator is considered to be employed by the principal employing district, but decisions regarding the probationary appointment and compensation package must be made with the consent of a majority of each of the school boards of each participating district (§ 1981(2)(b)).

The principal employing district makes decisions regarding the termination, discipline, or tenure of that administrator in consultation with all other participating districts. The services rendered by the shared administrator in any participating district is deemed to have been rendered in the principal employing district for all purposes, including tenure credit, seniority, and discipline (§ 1981(2)(b)).

All agreements to share personnel, such as administrators, between districts must be approved by the district superintendent (see **11:1**), or by the commissioner of education or his or her designee if there is no local district superintendent (§ 1981(4)).

9:3. May school districts transfer administrators to different positions?

Yes. An administrator may be transferred to another position or assigned to perform other duties and functions encompassed within his or her tenure area (*Appeal of Jodre,* 50 Ed Dept Rep, Dec. No. 16,162 (2010); *Matter of Monaco*, 24 Ed Dept Rep 48 (1984)).

In addition, a school board may transfer principals without the recommendation of the superintendent of schools (*Appeal of Donahue,* 52 Ed Dept Rep, Dec. No. 16,431 (2012); *Appeal of Lander*, 42 Ed Dept Rep 201 (2002)).

However, administrators may not be transferred outside their tenure area without their consent (*Cowan v. Bd. of Educ. of the Brentwood UFSD*, 99 A.D.2d 831 (2d Dep't 1984); *Appeal of Caruana*, 41 Ed Dept Rep 227 (2001); *Matter of Zamek*, 19 Ed Dept Rep 77 (1979)). Administrators challenging a transfer would have the burden of establishing they have been involuntarily transferred to a position outside their tenure area or that their tenure rights have been otherwise infringed (*Appeal of Dunshee*, 44 Ed Dept Rep 414 (2005); *Appeal of Rabeler*, 46 Ed Dept Rep 382 (2007)).

The latter would be the case if a tenured administrator is transferred involuntarily as a means of discipline in lieu of affording the administrator his or her due process rights pursuant to section 3020-a of the Education Law (*Appeal of J.S.*, 49 Ed Dept Rep 445 (2010); *Appeal of Irving*, 39 Ed Dept Rep 761 (2000); see **9:25**). In *Appeal of Irving*, a district transferred a principal to the position of assistant principal at another school. According to the commissioner of education, the sole reason for the transfer was the superintendent's conclusion that the principal engaged in misconduct, which violated her rights as a tenured administrator under section 3020-a, including the right to contest the charges.

School boards must be careful that any reorganization or restructuring of their administrative staff does not effectuate a method of transferring administrators outside their tenure areas without consent (*Appeal of Murray*, 48 Ed Dept Rep 517 (2009)).

9:4. Is a school board bound by an employment contract with an administrative employee?

Yes, if one exists. A school district can waive its statutory right to discharge a probationary administrator at any time during the probationary term by entering into a durational employment contract (*Consedine v. Portville CSD*, 12 N.Y.3d 286 (2009); see also *Averback v. Bd. of Educ. of New Paltz CSD*, 147 A.D.2d 152 (3d Dep't), *appeal denied*, 74 N.Y.2d 611 (1989); *Appeal of Charland*, 32 Ed Dept Rep 291 (1992)). However, such waiver will be enforceable only if there is explicit contract language or compelling evidence that a school district made a conscious decision to waive such right (*Consedine v. Portville CSD*).

In addition, the commissioner of education has held that an employment contract between a small city school district and a deputy superintendent of schools is statutorily authorized under the Education Law (*Appeal of Reilly*, 37 Ed Dept Rep 688 (1998); see § 2509(3)).

9:5. Are school administrators subject to New York State's fingerprinting law?

Yes. All prospective school district or board of cooperative educational services employees, including administrators, must be fingerprinted. In general, commissioner's regulations define a *prospective school employee* to mean any paid employee or contract service provider "who will reasonably be expected by [the district] to provide services which involve direct contact, meaning in person, face-to-face communication or interaction, with students under the age of 21," more than five days during the school year (8 NYCRR § 87.2(k)). A prospective employee who refuses to be fingerprinted may not be hired (§§ 305(30), 1604(39), 1709(39), 1804(9), 1950(4)(ll), 2503(18), 2554(25), 2590-h(20), 3004-b, 3035; 8 NYCRR Part 87).

For a more detailed explanation of the requirements of the fingerprinting law, see **chapter 41**.

9:6. Are school districts and boards of cooperative educational services (BOCES) required to provide school administrators with training on preventing and responding to harassment, bullying/cyberbullying and discrimination of students?

Yes. Pursuant to the *Dignity for All Students Act* (DASA), (§§ 10–18), school districts and BOCES must adopt guidelines for employee and administrator training programs to promote a positive school environment free from harassment, bullying/cyberbullying and discrimination of students by staff and other students based on, but not limited to, their actual or perceived race, color, weight, national origin, ethnic group, religion, religious practice, disability, sexual orientation, gender or sex.

The guidelines must include, but not be limited to:

- developing nondiscriminatory instructional and counseling methods;
- training administrators and instructional and non-instructional staff to raise their sensitivity to potential acts of harassment, bullying/cyberbullying and discrimination of students by other students or school staff, and
- training employees to prevent and respond to such incidents (§ 13; 8 NYCRR § 100.2(jj)(3)).

In addition, at least one DASA coordinator must be designated in every school, and he or she must be instructed in the commissioner of education's DASA regulations and trained to handle human relations in the areas of race, color, weight, national origin, ethnic group, religion, religious practice, disability, sexual orientation, gender, and sex (8 NYCRR § 100.2(jj)(4)).

The DASA training may be implemented and conducted in conjunction with existing professional development training and/or with any other training for school employees (8 NYCRR § 100.2(jj)(3)(vi)).

For more information on DASA, see **51:40-45.**

Certification Requirements

9:7. What type of certification is required to serve as an administrator in New York State?

For certification requirements, the commissioner's regulations set out three classes of certificates for school administrators (8 NYCRR § 80-3.10; see also 8 NYCRR § 80-2.4). For candidates applying for certification on or after September 2, 2006, these include:

- *School District Leader (SDL)*. The SDL class includes district superintendents, superintendents of schools, deputy, associate and assistant superintendents, and any other persons having responsibilities involving general district-wide administration, except a person serving as a school district business leader (8 NYCRR § 80-3.10(b)).
- *School District Business Leader (SDBL)*. The school district business leader certificate is required for deputy superintendents of schools for business, associate and assistant superintendents of schools for business, and any other person having professional responsibility for the business operation of the school district (8 NYCRR § 80-3.10(c)), such as a school business official or administrator.
- *School Building Leader (SBL)*. A school building leader certificate is required for principals, housemasters, assistant principals, supervisors, department chairpersons, coordinators, unit heads, and any other persons serving more than 25 percent of his or her assignment in any building level leadership position (8 NYCRR § 80 3.10(a); see also *Matter of Connor*, 22 Ed Dept Rep 313 (1982)).

Different certificate titles were issued to candidates who applied for certification as school administrators before September 2, 2006. For them, the SDL translates into a *school district administrator (SDA)* certificate, the SBL certificate translates into a *school administrator and supervisor (SAS)* certificate, and the SDBL translates into a *school business administrator* (*SBA*) certificate (8 NYCRR

§ 80-2.4). An SDA and SDL certificate constitute a "superintendent's certificate" within the meaning of section 3003 of the Education Law, which sets out the qualifications of superintendents (see *Appeal of Kippen*, 48 Ed Dept Rep 469 (2009)).

The scope of practice for each certificate is limited to the positions covered by the certificate title. For example, holders of a school district leader certificate may not serve as a school building leader or school district business leader unless they are additionally certified as such, or hold an equivalent school administrator and supervisor or school business administrator certificate issued pursuant to rules applicable prior to September 2, 2006 (8 NYCRR § 80-3.10(b)(2); see also 8 NYCRR § 80-3.10(c)(2)).

9:8. What are the requirements for a school district leader certificate?

The certificate requirements are a master's degree or higher from a regionally accredited higher education institution or equivalent as determined by the NYS Education Department (8 NYCRR § 80-3.10(b)(3)(i)(a)); successful completion of an approved program leading to a professional certificate as a school district leader in the educational leadership service, including achieving a satisfactory level of performance on the New York State Assessment for school district leadership or an equivalent assessment if attending an approved program outside New York State (8 NYCRR § 80-3.10(b)(3)(i)(a)(2)); and three years of experience in classroom teaching and/or educational leadership and/or pupil personnel service in nursery school through 12th grade (8 NYCRR § 80-3.10(b)(3)(i)(b); see **9:9** for alternative certification routes). Candidates applying for certification as a school district leader on or after May 1, 2015 shall also achieve a satisfactory level of performance on the educating all students test (8 NYCRR § 80-3.10(b)(3)(i)(c)).

A school district leader certificate is continuously valid so long as professional development requirements are met (8 NYCRR § 80-3.10(b)(1)).

9:9. Are there alternative routes for obtaining certification as a school district leader?

Yes. There are two alternative routes by which exceptionally qualified persons may qualify for a professional school district leader (SDL) certificate (see **9:7-8** for more information on certification requirements).

First, by meeting the requirements of the alternative school district leader certification program (8 NYCRR §§ 80-3.10(b)(3)(ii), 80-5.15; see also 8 NYCRR § 52.21(c)(4)). Individuals enrolled in such programs must hold a transitional D certificate (8 NYCRR § 80-5.15(a)). Candidates holding transitional D certificates will qualify for a professional SDL certificate upon completing the alternative school district leadership program and three years of educational leadership service and/or classroom teaching service and/or pupil personnel service experience with at least one year of service in a position that requires SDL certification (8 NYCRR § 80-5.15(b); see also 8 NYCRR § 80-5.15(a)(2)). Candidates applying for a professional certificate through this alternative pathway on or after May 1, 2015 must also achieve a satisfactory level of performance on the educating all students test (8 NYCRR § 80-5.15(b)(4)).

The second alternative pathway to certification is through a screening panel review process at the request of a school board or board of cooperative educational services. Under this second route, the commissioner of education may waive the requirements for the SDL certificate for a person who is exceptionally qualified but does not meet all of the graduate course or teaching requirements, and whose training and experience are the substantial equivalent of such requirements (§ 3003(3); 8 NYCRR § 80-3.10(b)(3)(iii); *Snyder v. N.Y. State Bd. of Regents,* 31 Misc.3d 556 (Sup. Ct. Albany Cnty. 2010)).

In its formal request for a waiver to the NYS Education Department (SED), the board must submit its resolution noting its approval of the request; the job description; its rationale for requesting such certification of the individual; a statement identifying the exceptional qualifications of the candidate; and the individual's completed application for certification, vitae and official transcripts of collegiate study. Such a certification, if issued, is valid only for service in the district requesting the waiver. The commissioner then refers the request to a screening panel consisting of SED representatives and appropriate educational organizations for review and advice (8 NYCRR § 80-3.10(b)(3)(iii); *Snyder v. N.Y. State Bd. of Regents*).

9:10. What are the requirements for a school district business leader certificate?

The requirements for a school district business leader (SDBL) certificate are a master's or higher degree from a regionally accredited higher education institution or equivalent as determined by the NYS Education Department and successful completion of an approved program leading to a professional certificate as a school district business leader in the educational leadership service, including achieving a satisfactory level of performance on the New York State assessment for school district business leadership or an equivalent assessment if attending an approved program outside New York State (8 NYCRR § 80-3.10(c)(3)(i), (ii)). SDBL certificates are continuously valid so long as professional development requirements are met (8 NYCRR § 80-3.10(c)(1)).

9:11. What are the requirements for a school building leader certificate?

School building leaders first must obtain an initial certificate that will be valid for five years from its effective date (8 NYCRR § 80-3.10(a)(1)(i)). A professional certificate obtained after an initial certificate will be valid continuously so long as professional development requirements are met (8 NYCRR § 80-3.10(a)(2)(i)).

The requirements for a School Building Leader (SBL) initial certificate are a master's degree or higher from a regionally accredited higher education institution or equivalent as determined by the NYS Education Department (8 NYCRR § 80-3.10(a)(1)(ii)(a)); successful completion of a program leading to the initial certificate as a school building leader; a satisfactory score on the New York State assessment for school building leadership (8 NYCRR § 80-3.10(a)(1)(ii)(b)); and three years of classroom teaching and/or pupil personnel service experience in nursery school through 12th grade (8 NYCRR § 80-3.10(a)(1)(ii)(c)). In addition, candidates applying for certification on or after May 1, 2014 and candidates who apply on or before April 30, 2014 but do not meet all requirements for an initial certificate on or before April 30, 2014, must also achieve a satisfactory level of performance on the educating all students test (8 NYCRR § 80-3.10(a)(1)(b)).

The requirements for an SBL professional certificate are an SBL initial certificate; three years of school experience in an educational leadership position with at least one of those in a school building leader position; and participation in a mentoring program as required by commissioner's regulations (8 NYCRR § 80-3.10(a)(2)(ii)).

9:12. How does military service affect the time an individual has to complete requirements for certification as an administrator?

Any certificate that would otherwise expire while an individual is on active military duty will be extended automatically for the period of active duty and for 12 months after release from active duty (Mil. Law § 308-b). Similarly, the law waives continuing education requirements for holders of certificates obtained prior to entering military service, for the period the certificate holder is engaged in active military service and pro-rates any required continuing education during a reporting period when the individual spent part of the time on active duty (Mil. Law § 308-a).

Public School Governance

9:13. May individuals with equivalent certification from other states work as school district leaders and school district business leaders in New York?

Yes, if they meet certain requirements. Individuals with certification from other states that are equivalent to a New York school district leader (SDL) or school district business leader (SDBL) certificate may apply for endorsement of their certificate, allowing them to work in New York State. To receive endorsement, an individual with a valid certificate from another state or territory or the District of Columbia equivalent to a New York SDL or SDBL certificate must hold a master's or higher degree from an appropriately accredited institution and have three years of satisfactory experience as required by regulation (8 NYCRR § 80-5.20(a)(1), (b)(1)).

The candidate must also meet the general requirements of commissioner's regulations subpart 80-1, including citizenship, study of child abuse identification and reporting, harassment, bullying and discrimination prevention and intervention and school violence prevention and intervention, as well as the criminal history record check (8 NYCRR § 80-5.20(a)(1)(ii), (b)(1)(ii); see 8 NYCRR §§ 80-1.3, 80-1.4, 80-1.11, 80-1.13)).

In addition, candidates must submit satisfactory evidence that the candidate received evaluation ratings of effective or highly effective, or the substantial equivalent of such ratings, in each of their three most recent years of experience in a public school in another state, territory or the District of Columbia in the certificate title sought as an SDL or SDBL (8 NYCRR § 80-5.20(a)(1)(iv)(b), (b)(1)(iv)(b)).

Similar requirements apply to individuals from other states seeking school building leader certification in New York (8 NYCRR § 80-20(c)).

9:14. Is there a legal procedure for decertifying a school administrator?

No, but there is a procedure, specified in Part 83 of the commissioner's regulations, regarding determinations of good moral character. This could lead to the revocation, annulment, or suspension of an administrator's certificate, or the imposition of another penalty prescribed by the commissioner's regulations (§ 305(7); 8 NYCRR §§ 83.5(c), 83.6; see *Matter of Kelly*, 20 Ed Dept Rep 503 (1981)).

In addition, the commissioner of education is authorized and required to automatically revoke and annul the certificate of:

- Any school district administrator, school administrator or supervisor, or school business administrator who is convicted of defrauding a school district of property in excess of $1,000, subject to the conditions set forth in law (§ 305(7-b)).
- Any school superintendent or school administrator or supervisor who is convicted of a sex offense for which registration as a sex offender is required (§ 305(7-a), (7-a)(b)(3); see also **31:38**).

9:15. What specialized training, if any, is required for administrators and those applying for certification as an administrator?

Any person applying for a certificate valid for service in a superintendent position must have completed two hours of coursework on or training in the identification and reporting of child abuse and maltreatment (§ 3003(4); 8 NYCRR § 80-1.4). Those applying for a certificate or license valid for service as school administrator, supervisor, or superintendent must complete two hours of training in school violence prevention and intervention (§ 3004(3); 8 NYCRR § 80-1.4).

All candidates applying for a certificate or license valid for supervisory or administrative service after December 31, 2013 must have completed at least six hours of coursework or training, of which at least three hours must be through face-to-face instruction, in harassment, bullying and discrimination prevention and intervention (§ 14(5); 8 NYCRR § 80-1.13).

In addition, school administrators and supervisors assigned to serve as a special education administrator on or after September 2, 2009, must complete enhanced training on the needs of autistic children, prior to or as soon as practicable following the assignment. Those serving as a special education administrator prior to that date had to complete the training by that date (§ 3004(4), (5)).

Probationary Appointments and Tenure Areas

9:16. How are school administrators appointed?

Starting with appointments made on or after July 1, 2015, principals, administrators, supervisors and all other members of the supervising staff of school districts and board of cooperative educational services (BOCES), must be appointed by the school board to a four-year probationary term (§§ 3012(1)(b)(ii), 3014(1)(b)). Prior to that date, such appointments were made for a three-year term (§§ 3012(1)(b)(i), 3014(1)(a)). The appointment requires the recommendation of the superintendent of schools in a school district, or the district superintendent in a BOCES. This rule does not apply to superintendents of schools, associate and assistant superintendents in small city school districts, and executive directors, associate, assistant, district, and community superintendents and examiners in Buffalo, New York City, Rochester, Syracuse, and Yonkers (§§ 2509(1)(b), 2573(1)(b)). Special rules apply to the appointment of individuals in these districts depending on the position and district involved (see §§ 2509(3), (4), 2573(3), (4)).

Unlike teachers, administrators who have received tenure in another school district in the state are not entitled to a shortened probationary period, and must serve the full probationary period, according to the NYS Education Department (Opn. of Counsel, No. 235, 15 Ed Dept Rep 538 (1975); see **33:7**, **34:12**).

In New York City, principals and other supervisory personnel are appointed by community superintendents from candidates screened by committees as prescribed by chancellor's regulations (see §§ 2590-f(1)(d), (e), 2590-h).

9:17. What tenure areas are applicable to school administrators?

There are no clearly defined guidelines for determining administrative and supervisory tenure areas (*Bell v. Bd. of Educ. of Vestal CSD*, 61 N.Y.2d 149 (1984)). Part 30 of the commissioner's regulations, which establishes teacher tenure areas, is not applicable to administrative and supervisory personnel (*Appeal of Wills*, 49 Ed Dept Rep 147 (2009); *Matter of Moore*, 15 Ed Dept Rep 475 (1976)). Instead, a school board may maintain a single district-wide "administrator" tenure area or establish more defined administrative tenure areas (see *Bell v. Bd. of Educ. of Vestal CSD*; *Appeal of Alexander*, 54 Ed Dept Rep, Dec. No. 16,731 (2015); *Appeal of Murray*, 48 Ed Dept Rep 517 (2009); *Appeal of Wills*). In either case, school boards must ensure their tenure system for administrators is coherent (*Appeal of Wills*). In addition, when establishing narrow, specific, administrative tenure areas "consciously" and "by design" they also should make sure that the employee has been sufficiently alerted to that fact (*Bell v. Bd. of Educ. of Vestal CSD; Appeal of Waite*, 55 Ed Dept Rep, Dec. No. 16,801 (2015); *Appeal of Alexander*).

The tenure area of an administrator is the area in which the original probationary appointment was made (*Schlick v. Bd. of Educ. of Mamaroneck UFSD*, 227 A.D.2d 407 (2d Dep't 1996); see also *Appeal of Murray*). School administrators may be transferred within their tenure area, but may not be transferred outside their tenure areas involuntarily (*Appeal of Murray*; see **9:3**).

Nonetheless, an administrator also can be deemed to serve simultaneously in both an administrative and teacher tenure area, and thus receive seniority credit and tenure in both. However, for that to happen the individual must perform more than 50 percent of his or her duties in the administrative tenure area and at least 40 percent of his or her duties in a teacher tenure area (*Appeal of Pearse*, 50 Ed Dept Rep, Dec. No. 16,159 (2010); see **9:18**).

9:18. How do school districts with more than one administrative tenure area determine what positions belong in a particular tenure area?

Where a school board has established more than one administrative tenure area, case law has identified factors that should be considered to determine whether certain administrative and supervisory positions must be considered to lie within the same tenure area. Among the factors to be considered are "the notice given to the individuals involved as to their tenure status, the duties of various positions, the adverse practical impact of nonrecognition of a particular area and membership in collective bargaining units" (*Matter of Plesent*, 16 Ed Dept Rep 348 (1977)).

Documentation such as an appointment letter or a board resolution that refers to an administrator's tenure area and comparisons of duties and responsibilities are important factors in determining the tenure area of administrators (see *Matter of Roloff*, 16 Ed Dept Rep 274 (1977); *Matter of Parsons*, 16 Ed Dept Rep 134 (1976)). Under the principle commonly known as the "50 percent rule," positions will generally be deemed to lie within the same administrative tenure area if a majority of the job duties are similar (*Coates v. Ambach*, 52 A.D.2d 261 (3d Dep't 1976), *aff'd*, 42 N.Y.2d 846 (1977)). Consequently, the mere fact that two positions, such as director and chairperson, are supervisory in nature does not compel the conclusion that they are within the same tenure area (see *Matter of Plesent*; *Appeal of Wills*, 49 Ed Dept Rep 147 (2009)).

However, the 50 percent rule should not be rigidly applied. Emphasis should be on the type, quality, and breadth of responsibilities associated with the positions being compared (*Cowan v. Bd. of Educ. of the Brentwood UFSD*, 99 A.D.2d 831 (2d Dep't), *appeal discontinued*, 63 N.Y.2d 702 (1984); *Matter of Plesent*; see also *Appeal of Walters*, 49 Ed Dept Rep 115 (2009); *Appeal of Elmendorf*, 36 Ed Dept Rep 308 (1997); *Matter of Abeles*, 18 Ed Dept Rep 521 (1979); *Matter of Falanga*, 17 Ed Dept Rep 267 (1978)).

The 50 percent rule has also been applied in determining whether a particular employee serves in an administrative or teacher tenure area. An employee will be deemed to serve in an administrative rather than teacher tenure area if the employee spends over 50 percent of his or her time on administrative duties (*Appeal of Klein*, 43 Ed Dept Rep 305 (2003); see also *Maine-Endwell Teachers Ass'n v. Maine-Endwell CSD*, 92 A.D.2d 1052 (3d Dep't 1983); *Matter of Funnell*, 19 Ed Dept Rep 448 (1980)). Depending on the circumstances, such an individual could be deemed to simultaneously serve in a teacher tenure area (*Appeal of Pearse*, 50 Ed Dept Rep, Dec. No. 16,159 (2010); see **9:17**).

9:19. Does service as a substitute administrator count toward an administrative probationary period?

No. Administrative employees do not receive so-called "Jarema credit" (see **34:11-19**), for time spent as substitutes for administrators who are temporarily unable to perform their duties (*McManus v. Bd. of Educ. of the Hempstead UFSD*, 87 N.Y.2d 183 (1995); see *Roberts v. Cmty. Sch. Bd. of Cmty. Dist. No. 6*, 66 N.Y.2d 652 (1985)). While teachers may apply Jarema credit for time spent as a substitute teacher towards the probationary period required before tenure (§§ 2509(1)(a), 2573(1)(a), 3012(1)(a)), administrators are not given similar rights (see §§ 2509(1)(b), 2573(1)(b), 3012(1)(b)).

9:20. Does service as an "acting" administrator in a vacant position count toward an administrative probationary period?

Yes. A board must count as service toward a probationary period time spent by an employee assigned to a vacant position in an "acting" capacity when that employee is subsequently appointed to a probationary term in that position. The employee will be deemed to have commenced the probationary term for that particular position when appointed to fill the vacant position (*McManus v. Bd. of Educ. of the Hempstead UFSD*, 87 N.Y.2d 183 (1995); see also *Appeal of Vega*, 48 Ed Dept Rep 131 (2008)). However, a summer vacation period included within a leave of absence does not count toward the probationary period (*Appeal of Vega*).

9:21. Does service rendered outside an administrative tenure area pending the outcome of criminal charges count toward an administrative probationary period?

No. In *Feldman v. Community Sch. Dist. 32*, 231 A.D.2d 632 (2d Dep't 1996), *lv. to appeal denied*, 89 N.Y.2d 811 (1997), an assistant principal who was reassigned to the central district office during his probationary period pending the outcome of criminal charges did not receive credit for the time spent in the central district office assignment because he did not perform the duties of assistant principal during that time.

Public School Governance

9:22. Does part-time service as an administrator count toward an administrative probationary period?

An individual must spend over 50 percent of his or her time performing administrative duties for such part-time service to constitute service within an administrative tenure area. As such, a lesser amount of time spent on administrative duties may not count toward an administrative probationary period (see *Appeal of Klein*, 43 Ed Dept Rep 305 (2003); *Matter of Funnell*, 19 Ed Dept Rep 448 (1980)).

Abolition of Administrative Positions

9:23. May a school board abolish an administrative position?

Yes, if the position is no longer necessary to the school system. School boards have broad latitude to abolish, reorganize, or consolidate administrative and teaching positions (*Matter of Riendeau*, 23 Ed Dept Rep 487 (1984); see *Lally v. Johnson City CSD,* 105 A.D.3d 1129 (3d Dep't 2013); *Girard v. Bd. of Educ. of City Sch. Dist. of City of Buffalo*, 168 A.D.2d 183 (4th Dep't 1991); *Ryan v. Ambach*, 71 A.D.2d 719 (3d Dep't 1979); see also **36:1-6**). However, a position may not be abolished as a pretext to circumvent an employee's tenure rights (*Matter of Riendeau*).

Whenever a board abolishes an administrative position, the administrator with the least amount of seniority in the tenure area is the first to be dismissed (§§ 2510(2), 2585(3), 2588(3)(b), 3013(2); see also *Appeal of Wills*, 49 Ed Dept Rep 147 (2009)). If a board improperly dismisses an administrator as being the least senior administrator in the tenure area but subsequently corrects its error and reappoints the administrator, that administrator is entitled to back pay and seniority credit for the period of dismissal (*Appeal of Ford,* 52 Ed Dept Rep, Dec. No. 16,443 (2012)). For more information on administrative tenure areas, see **9:17-18**.

9:24. Is an administrator whose position is abolished entitled to another position in the school district?

Yes, under certain circumstances, an administrator may be reinstated to another position in the district for which appointments on tenure may be made under the Education Law (see *Matter of Merz*, 21 Ed Dept Rep 449 (1982); *Appeal of Heath*, 37 Ed Dept Rep 544 (1998)).

First, if a school board abolishes an office or position and creates another one with similar duties, the administrator whose position is to be abolished may be entitled to be appointed to the newly created position without reduction in salary or increment (§§ 2510(1), 2585(2), 2588(2), 3013(1); see § 1981(2)(b)(ii)). To claim such entitlement, the administrator must show that:

- The newly created position is in the same tenure area as the abolished position (*Appeal of McDougall,* 53 Ed Dept Rep, Dec. No. 16,505 (2013); *Appeal of Wills*, 49 Ed Dept Rep 147 (2009); *Appeal of Heath; Appeal of Elmendorf,* 36 Ed Dept Rep 308 (1997); see also *Appeal of Pronti*, 54 Ed Dept Rep, Dec. No. 16,698 (2015).
- The newly created and abolished positions have more than 50 percent of duties in common, provided that, in comparing the duties of two positions, the degree of comparable skill, experience, training and certification required to carry out the duties and responsibilities of each position also must be considered (*Appeal of McDougall, Appeal of Wills; Appeal of Heath; Appeal of Elmendorf; Appeal of Pronti*). For example, the commissioner of education has held that the positions of building principal and assistant superintendent are not similar because of the district-wide responsibilities and the additional skill, training, and certification requirements of the position of assistant superintendent (*Appeal of McDougall; Appeal of Elmendorf*).

Public School Governance

The administrator may have the right to a pre-termination hearing before the school board where there is a possibility that the duties of the position being abolished and the duties of a newly created position are similar (*Appeal of Elmendorf*; see also *Davis v. Mills*, 98 N.Y.2d 120 (2002); *Appeal of Goldberg*, 54 Ed Dept Rep, Dec. No. 16,635 (2014)).

Second, an administrator whose position is abolished has the right to be placed on a preferred eligible list (PEL) of candidates for appointment to a similar position within his or her tenure area. The administrator may be "called back" from the PEL for reinstatement for up to seven years after the position is abolished (§§ 2510(3)(a), 2585(4), 3013(3)(a)), not just for the position the administrator held which was abolished, but also for any position similar to that one (*Appeal of Kantrowitz*, 48 Ed Dept Rep 218 (2008); see also **36:14-23**). For more information on administrative tenure areas, see **9:17-18**.

Administrator Discipline and Termination

9:25. Are there specific procedures for disciplining and/or terminating the employment of administrators or supervisors?

Yes. The probationary appointment of an administrative employee may be terminated at any time on the recommendation of the superintendent and by majority vote of the school board (§§ 2509(1)(b), 2573(1)(b), 3012(1)(b), 3014(1), provided the employee is not terminated for an illegal or unconstitutional reason, and the notice requirements of section 3019-a of the Education Law are met (*Appeal of Wint*, 33 Ed Dept Rep 9 (1993)). A failure to provide the required termination notice entitles the dismissed administrator to back pay, but not reinstatement (see *Appeal of Wint*).

Education Law section 3031 applies to the dismissal of probationary administrators and supervisors who are not recommended for tenure (*Appeal of Gold*, 34 Ed Dept Rep 372 (1995); see § 3012(2)). The procedure is similar to that applicable to teachers (see **34:31-45**).

Annual professional performance review (APPR) must be a significant factor in decisions concerning their employment, including termination and tenure determinations (§ 3012-d(1); 8 NYCRR § 30-3.1(d); see also **37:6**). An administrator in charge of an instructional program at a board of cooperative educational services is deemed a building principal for this purpose (§ 3012-d(2)(b) 8 NYCRR § 30-3.2(n); see **37:1**).

Under certain circumstances an administrator who is terminated during his or her probationary period may be entitled, to a name-clearing hearing. For example, the U.S. Court of Appeals for the Second Circuit, with jurisdiction our New York, found that an administrator who received negative evaluations and reasons for termination, which damaged the administrator's professional reputation to such a degree as to virtually preclude her from getting another job as an administrator in the future, was entitled to a name-clearing hearing (*Donato v. Plainview-Old Bethpage CSD*, 96 F.3d 623 (2d Cir. 1996), *cert. denied*, 519 U.S. 1150, *remanded*, 985 F.Supp. 316 (E.D.N.Y. 1997)).

Tenured administrative employees, like tenured teachers, are subject to the protections of section 3020-a and, as applicable, section 3020-b of the Education Law (see **chapter 38**). Accordingly, a school district improperly transferred a tenured principal to the position of assistant principal at another school based solely on a superintendent's conclusion that the principal had engaged in misconduct (*Appeal of Irving*, 39 Ed Dept Rep 761 (2000)).

In New York City, community superintendents are hired and fired by the chancellor, but they enjoy some due process protections, such as notice and pre-termination opportunity to respond (§ 2590-h; *Bd. of Educ. of N.Y. City v. Mills*, 8 A.D.3d 834 (3d Dep't 2004)).

9:26. May a school district permit an administrator accused of child abuse to tender a silent resignation?

No. A school district may not agree to withhold from law enforcement authorities the fact that an allegation of child abuse in an educational setting (see **51:18**) has been made against an administrator in exchange for the administrator's resignation or voluntary suspension. Any such agreement constitutes a class E felony and is also punishable by a civil penalty of up to $20,000 (§ 1133; see also **51:21**).

9:27. Is a wrongfully terminated probationary administrator entitled to back pay?

No. Only "tenured employees . . . are entitled to back pay during periods of . . . improper termination" because their tenured status affords them a property interest in their salary (*Okebiyi v. Crew*, 303 A.D.2d 684 (2d Dep't 2003)).

10. The Superintendent of Schools

In General

10:1. What is a superintendent of schools?

A *superintendent of schools* is the chief executive officer of a school district (§§ 1711(2)(a), 2508(1), 2566(1)). Any reference to the terms district principal, supervising principal, or principal of the district generally refer to the superintendent of schools (Gen. Constr. Law § 47-a), also commonly referred to as the school superintendent or the superintendent.

A *district superintendent*, on the other hand, is the chief executive officer of a board of cooperative educational services (BOCES) and is the general supervising officer of the supervisory district. The district superintendent has responsibilities for both the BOCES and the component districts that comprise the BOCES (see **chapter 11** for more information on the district superintendent).

For purpose of clarity, the term "superintendent" as used in this chapter refers to a superintendent of schools.

10:2. Is a superintendent a member of the school board?

No, except in city school districts, where the superintendent "shall have a seat on the board." However, in all school districts, the superintendent has the right to speak on all matters before the board, but he or she does not have the right to vote on matters before the board (§§ 1711(2)(a), 2508(1), 2566(1)).

10:3. Is a superintendent required to take an oath of office?

Although statutory law does not specifically require superintendents to take an oath of office (cf. §§ 2206 (district superintendents), 3002 (teachers); Pub. Off. Law §§ 2, 10 (board members, district clerk, treasurer); see **11:7**), the commissioner of education has held that superintendents must take an oath of office as a matter of public policy. According to the commissioner, "it is sound public policy to treat school superintendents as public officers with respect to oaths of office" (*Application of Karpen*, 39 Ed Dept Rep 98 (1999)). The oath must be administered by someone who has properly taken or filed an oath of office (*Application of Karpen*; see Pub. Off. Law § 10).

10:4. Is a school board required to evaluate its superintendent?

Yes. The commissioner's regulations require school boards to annually review the performance of their superintendent according to procedures developed by the school board in consultation with the superintendent. The evaluation procedures must be filed in the district office and available for public review no later than September 10 of each year (8 NYCRR § 100.2(o)(1)(vi)).

10:5. How do superintendents of schools acquire their positions in New York State?

A school board may appoint a superintendent of schools (§§ 1604(8), 1711(1), 2503(5), 2554(2)). These superintendents serve at the pleasure of the board, unless they and their boards have entered into employment contracts. Such contracts, however, may include procedures for terminating the superintendent's services prior to the end of the term (§ 1711(3); see **10:6–9** for more information on superintendents' contracts).

Employment Contract

10:6. Is a contract necessary to employ a superintendent?

No. However, many school boards enter into such contracts with their superintendents. This type of contract may include terms and conditions of employment such as duties, compensation, and termination of the contract (§ 1711(3); see §§ 2507(1), 2565(1); *Matter of Balen*, 20 Ed Dept Rep 304 (1980)). In the absence of a contract, resolutions concerning term appointments embodied in minutes of board meetings may be used to identify the terms and conditions of employment.

A school board may not enter into a contract with a superintendent that contains any provisions relating to an increase in salary, compensation, or other benefits which are based on or tied to the terms of any contract or collective bargaining agreement with the district's teachers or other district employees (§§ 1711(3), 2507(1), 2565(1)).

10:7. How long may a superintendent's contract last?

School districts may enter into contracts with their superintendents for terms of three to five years (§ 1711(3)).

City school districts, however, are prohibited from entering into a superintendent's contract that fixes the term or tenure of the superintendent's services. Instead, superintendents serve at the pleasure of their board unless they are appointed to a term (§§ 2507(1), 2565(1), (3); *Matter of Brewster*, 15 Ed Dept Rep 526 (1976); see *Appeal of Prattella*, 37 Ed Dept Rep 693 (1998)). If appointed to a term, the term may not exceed five years in city school districts with a population of less than 250,000, and four years in Rochester and city school districts with a population of over 250,000 (§§ 2507(1), 2565(1), (3)). However, these school boards may have contracts that fix the other terms of employment, such as duties and salaries, with their superintendents (§§ 2507(1), 2565(1); *Matter of Venezia*, 19 Ed Dept Rep 273 (1979); see *Matter of Balen*, 20 Ed Dept Rep 304 (1980)), provided that terms and provisions relating to an increase in salary, compensation, or other benefits may not be based on or tied to the terms of any district contract or collective bargaining agreement entered into with teachers or other district employees (§§ 2507(1), 2565(1)).

School boards may not circumvent the statutory limitations on the length of employment contracts for superintendents by entering into multiple contracts that, when read together, create an obligation longer than that authorized by law (*Appeal of Boyle*, 35 Ed Dept Rep 162 (1995)). For example, a five-year contract that was tacked onto an existing contract with three years remaining was invalid because these two contracts were in effect simultaneous and extended the service of the superintendent for three years beyond the statutory limit (*Appeal of Boyle*). However, school boards may extend an existing contract or supplant a prior contract with a new one, provided that the duration of the initial contract or the extension or subsequent contract does not exceed the statutory limitation (*Appeal of Knapp*, 34 Ed Dept Rep 207 (1994); *Appeal of Stephens*, 28 Ed Dept Rep 269 (1989), *aff'd sub nom. Lewiston-Porter CSD v. Sobol*, 154 A.D.2d 777 (3d Dep't 1989), *appeal dismissed*, 75 N.Y.2d 978 (1990); see *Appeal of Boyle*).

In addition, a superintendent's contract can include an extension and renewal provision that automatically extends the contract unless notice of contrary intent is given in accordance with the terms of the contract. Absent other contractual provisions, the automatic extension is dependent solely on the notice requirements in the contract irrespective of the satisfactory or unsatisfactory performance of the superintendent (*Appeal of Wilson*, 47 Ed Dept Rep 448 (2008), *aff'd on other grounds, Wilson v. Bd. of Educ. Harborfields CSD,* 65 A.D.3d 1158 (2d Dep't), *lv. to appeal denied*, 13 N.Y.3d 714 (2009)).

A superintendent's contract of five years duration, when read together with an immediately preceding interim superintendent's contract, will not be deemed to circumvent the statutory limitations where the contract as interim did not specify a time period and was terminable at will by either the school board or the interim. In such an instance, the interim superintendent's contract will not have obligated the board to employ the individual for any period of time. The only employment obligation arises from the contract as superintendent of permissible duration (*Appeal of Loschiavo*, 45 Ed Dept Rep 525 (2006)).

In New York City, the chancellor, who also sits on the city-wide Panel for Educational Policy and acts as its chairperson, serves at the pleasure of the mayor in accordance with law (§ 2590-h).

10:8. May an outgoing board extend a superintendent's contract?

Yes. The commissioner of education has ruled that, although it may be undemocratic, it is not illegal for a "lame-duck" board to extend the superintendent's contract and even award him or her a salary increase prior to the installation of the new board (*Appeal of Knapp*, 34 Ed Dept Rep 207 (1994); *Appeal of Dillon*, 33 Ed Dept Rep 544 (1994)). Because such an action taken by an outgoing board is procedurally correct, a new board may not nullify it (*Appeal of Dillon*).

10:9. Must the school board of a newly-consolidated school district honor the contract of a former superintendent of one of the merged districts?

Yes. The commissioner of education has determined that a consolidated district, which is a combination of common, central or union free school districts merged to form a new district (see **2:4, 2:13-14**), as the successor in interest of the districts that have merged, is obligated to honor the contract entered into by the former superintendent and the former board (§ 1804(5)(b); *Matter of Foster*, 28 Ed Dept Rep 29 (1988)).

However, the consolidated district need not employ the former superintendent. Instead, it may discharge its obligation by paying the former superintendent the salary that he or she would have earned pursuant to the contract, less any income the former superintendent earns from employment elsewhere during the term of the contract (*Matter of Foster*).

Powers and Duties

10:10. What are the statutory powers and duties of a superintendent of schools?

Education Law section 1711(2) states that superintendents of schools have the following powers and duties, unless otherwise specified by the bylaws of the school board:

- To be the chief executive officer of the school district and the educational system, and to have the right to speak on all matters before the board, but not to vote.
- To enforce all provisions of law, rules, and regulations relating to the management of the schools and other educational, social, and recreational activities under the direction of the board of education.
- To prepare the content of each course of study authorized by the school board. The content of each such course shall be submitted to the board for its approval and, when thus approved, the

superintendent shall cause such courses of study to be used in the grades, classes, and schools for which they are authorized.

- To recommend suitable lists of textbooks to be used in the schools.
- To have supervision and direction of associate, assistant, and other superintendents, directors, supervisors, principals, teachers, lecturers, medical inspectors, nurses, claims auditors, attendance officers, janitors, and other persons employed in the management of the schools or the other educational activities of the district authorized by [the Education Law] and under the direction and management of the school board; to transfer teachers from one school to another, or from one grade of the course of study to another grade in such course, and to report immediately such transfers to the board for its consideration and actions; to report to the board violations of regulations and cases of insubordination, and to suspend an associate, assistant, or other superintendent, director, supervisor, expert, principal, teacher, or other employee until the next regular meeting of such board, when all facts relating to the case shall be submitted to the board for its consideration and action.
- To have supervision and direction over the enforcement and observance of the courses of study, the examination and promotion of pupils, and over all other matters pertaining to playgrounds, medical inspection, recreation and social center work, libraries, lectures, and all other education activities under the management, direction, and control of the school board. (For city school districts, see §§ 2508, 2554, and 2566; see also § 2573(6)).

With regard to the transfer of teachers, the Education Law specifically provides that a collective bargaining agreement may modify the superintendent's authority (§§ 1711(4), 2508(7), 2566(9); *Bd. of Educ. of the Arlington CSD v. Arlington Teachers Ass'n*, 78 N.Y.2d 33 (1991)). Additionally, the transfer of tenured teachers from classrooms to non-classroom duties reasonably related to their tenure area does not constitute discipline under 3020-a (*McElroy v. Bd. of Educ. of the Bellmore-Merrick CHSD*, 5 Misc.3d 321 (Sup. Ct. Nassau Cnty. 2004); see also **33:24**). A superintendent may not transfer a tenured administrator to another position as a disciplinary measure (*Appeal of Irving*, 39 Ed Dept Rep 761 (2000); see also **9:3**).

In New York City, the chancellor also sits on the city-wide Panel for Educational Policy and serves as its chairperson. He or she also has the power to appoint and set salaries for employees in non-represented managerial titles in accordance with law (§§ 2590-g(2), 2590-h(17), (41)).

10:11. May a superintendent of schools grant an employee leave to serve as an emergency service volunteer?

Yes. A superintendent of schools has the authority to grant emergency service volunteer leave to district employees certified by the American Red Cross to participate in specialized disaster relief operations upon written request by the American Red Cross. Such leave from work shall be with pay and not exceed 20 days in any calendar year. The employee must be paid while on leave at the regular rate of pay for those regular work hours he or she is absent from work while participating in authorized specialized disaster relief operations. There may be no loss of seniority, sick leave, vacation leave or other overtime compensation to which the employer is otherwise entitled (Gen. Mun. Law § 92-c; for a more detailed discussion of employee leaves, see **chapter 43**).

10:12. Does a superintendent of schools need school board approval to initiate legal proceedings on behalf of the school district?

Yes. A superintendent of schools has no authority to commence legal proceedings on behalf of a school district absent school board approval, including an appeal from a commissioner of education decision. In addition, any school board vote authorizing such action must take place within the applicable period of limitations for commencing the particular legal proceeding (*Gersen v. Mills*, 290 A.D.2d 839 (3d Dep't 2002); see also *Barkan v. Roslyn UFSD*, 67 A.D.3d 61 (2d Dep't 2009)).

10:13. Does the school board have the authority to change the superintendent's duties during his or her employment contract?

Generally, yes. The board retains the authority to change the superintendent's powers and duties unless the board has given up that authority in the superintendent's employment contract (§ 1711(2), (3)). Except where that authority has been removed, a board has broad latitude in establishing work requirements (*Appeal of Fusco*, 39 Ed Dept Rep 836 (2000); *Matter of Hagen*, 17 Ed Dept Rep 400 (1978)).

Dismissal and Termination

10:14. Under what circumstances may a school board terminate a superintendent's contract?

A superintendent's contract may be terminated through non-renewal. In this context, attention must be paid to any automatic extension, "roll-over," or "evergreen" provisions contained in the contract. Procedures for providing notice of non-renewal must be carefully observed (*Appeal of Hernandez*, 29 Ed Dept Rep 508 (1990); *Matter of Northrup*, 24 Ed Dept Rep 262 (1985)).

Prior to its expiration date, a superintendent's contract may be terminated for cause in accordance with the provisions of the contract and in compliance with applicable due process requirements (§ 1711(3); *Appeal of Pinckney*, 35 Ed Dept Rep 461 (1996); *Matter of Driscoll*, 14 Ed Dept Rep 148 (1974)). The services of a superintendent appointed for a specified period of time in city school districts may also be terminated for cause as long as applicable due process requirements are observed (*Matter of Brewster*, 15 Ed Dept Rep 526 (1976); see **10:15**).

In addition, a school board may terminate the employment of a superintendent who fails to comply with residency provisions contained in the superintendent's contract. No due process requirements would apply where the contract provides that failure to comply with the residency requirement would render the contract null and void (*Appeal of Connor*, 48 Ed Dept Rep 113 (2008); see also *Beck-Nichols v. Bianco*, 20 N.Y.3d 540 (2013)). Other contractual terms providing for due process in termination for cause/misconduct situations would be inapplicable because a residency requirement constitutes an employment qualification rather than misconduct (*Id.*).

10:15. What legal restrictions apply to dismissal proceedings against school superintendents?

Dismissal of a superintendent during the term of his or her contract or appointment requires cause and adherence to the provisions of the contract and to applicable due process procedures. Due process procedures must be followed because this kind of contract gives rise to a legally founded expectation of continued employment and is a property right within the meaning of case law (see, e.g., *Appeal of Pinckney*, 35 Ed Dept Rep 461 (1996); *Matter of Driscoll*, 14 Ed Dept Rep 148 (1974)).

Due process under such circumstances involves, at minimum, the right to: receive written charges and to respond in writing to such charges; be represented by counsel; a formal hearing, with the right to produce evidence and cross-examine witnesses who testify in support of the charges; obtain a transcript of such hearing; formal written findings sustaining or dismissing the charges (*Matter of DeFreitas*, 14 Ed Dept Rep 329 (1975)); and continued pay until due process requirements are met (*Appeal of Pinckney*). The contract may modify or supplement these requirements.

It should be noted that the Education Law specifically authorizes the inclusion of procedures for termination of employment as a term of the contract between the board and the superintendent (§ 1711(3)).

11. The District (BOCES) Superintendent

11:1. What is a district superintendent and how does this position differ from that of superintendent of schools?

A *district superintendent* is the chief executive officer of a board of cooperative educational services (BOCES) and the general supervising officer of the supervisory district (see **11:2**) that comprises the BOCES. This person is responsible for both the BOCES and its component districts, performs duties assigned by the commissioner of education, and serves as the NYS Education Department's field representative in the supervisory district (§§ 1950(2), 2213, 2215). In comparison, a superintendent of schools is the chief executive officer of a single local school district (§ 1711; see **10:1**). See **chapter 7** for more information on BOCES and **chapter 10** for more information on the superintendent of schools.

11:2. What constitutes the supervisory district overseen by the district superintendent?

A *supervisory district* is made up of the total geographic area under the supervision of a district superintendent, as established under section 2201 of the Education Law.

11:3. What are the qualifications for the position of district superintendent of schools?

A district superintendent must be at least 21 years of age, a citizen of the United States, a resident of New York State, and certified or entitled to a superintendent's certificate (§ 2205; see **9:7-9** for specific certification requirements).

11:4. Is a district superintendent subject to the fingerprinting requirements of the Education Law and commissioner's regulation?

It depends. Any district superintendent candidate who applies for an administrative certificate on or after July 1, 2001, who was not provisionally certified prior to that date, is subject to the fingerprinting requirements as a condition of obtaining certification (§ 3004-b; 8 NYCRR § 87.3; see also **9:5, 30:2**).

In addition, a district superintendent appointed on or after July 1, 2001, to a board of cooperative educational services in which he or she was not continuously employed prior to that date, would also be subject to the fingerprinting requirement to the extent that in his or her capacity as district superintendent, he or she would have direct, in-person, face-to-face contact with students under age 21 for more than five days during the school year (§ 1950(4)(ll); 8 NYCRR §§ 87.2, 87.4; see also **9:5, 30:2**).

11:5. How is a district superintendent appointed?

A district superintendent is appointed by the BOCES board of a supervisory district. This appointment is subject to the commissioner of education's approval (§ 2204(1), (2)). In some instances, the commissioner may appoint an interim district superintendent until the board of cooperative educational services fills the vacancy (§ 2204(1)). See **11:10** for more information on how district superintendent vacancies are filled.

11:6. Is there a maximum length for the duration of a district superintendent's employment contract?

Yes. The duration of any employment contract between a board of cooperative educational services and a district superintendent entered after July 1, 1993 may not exceed three years. Copies of the agreement and any amendments thereto must be filed within five days of the contract's execution with the commissioner of education (§ 1950(4)(a)(1); see **11:8** for information on the removal of a district superintendent).

11:7. Must a district superintendent take an oath of office?

Yes. The district superintendent must take a constitutional oath of office before assuming his or her duties and not later than five days after the date on which the term of office is to start. The oath may be taken before a county clerk, a justice of the peace, or a notary public, and must be filed in the office of the secretary of state (§ 2206).

11:8. May a district superintendent be removed from office?

Yes. A district superintendent may be removed from office at any time by majority vote of the BOCES board, or by the commissioner of education under section 306 of the Education Law (§ 2212). A district superintendent who is removed from office is ineligible for appointment as a district superintendent in any supervisory district (see **11:2**) for five years (§ 2205(3)).

11:9. Under what circumstances does a vacancy in the office of a district superintendent occur?

Under section 2208 of the Education Law, a district superintendent's office becomes vacant when the current incumbent dies; files a written resignation with the commissioner of education and the clerk of the board of cooperative educational services; accepts the office of supervisor, town clerk, or trustee of a school district; or fails to take and file the oath of office. A vacancy will also occur if the district superintendent is removed from office by the BOCES board or the commissioner (§§ 2208, 2212; see **11:8**).

11:10. How is a vacancy in the office of district superintendent filled?

When a vacancy occurs, the commissioner of education shall direct the BOCES board to meet to appoint a new district superintendent, unless the commissioner has provided for a smaller number of supervisory districts. Each board member has one vote and the person receiving the majority of all votes cast shall be appointed, subject to the approval of the commissioner. A copy of the proceedings and the appointment certified by the BOCES board president and the BOCES board clerk must be filed in the county clerk's office and with the commissioner of education by the BOCES board clerk within five days of the appointment (§ 2204(1)–(3)).

If the vacancy is not filled at this meeting, the meeting may be adjourned to a subsequent date, and the commissioner may appoint an interim district superintendent who serves until the board fills the vacancy. A district superintendent from one supervisory district who is appointed to be a temporary or acting superintendent in another supervisory district does not receive any compensation for duties associated with the temporary or acting position (§ 2204(1), (4)).

11:11. How is a district superintendent's salary paid?

Each district superintendent receives an annual salary of $43,499 from the state, payable by the commissioner of education (§ 2209(1)). In addition, the board of cooperative educational services

(BOCES) may decide to pay the district superintendent a supplementary salary (§ 1950(4)(a)(1)). If the board decides to do so, this supplemental amount along with other supplementary benefits (see **11:12**) must be listed in the BOCES administrative budget that is provided to the trustees or board members of each component district (§ 1950(4)(b)(1)).

Additionally, the town supervisors in any supervisory district may vote to further increase the district superintendent's salary. This additional amount is paid by a tax levied on the towns comprising the supervisory district (§ 2209(2)).

11:12. Is there a limit or cap on a district superintendent's salary?

Yes. The total salary paid to district superintendents, including the amount paid by the state under section 2209 of the Education Law and the supplementary salary paid by the supervisory district (see **11:2**), may not exceed the lesser of 6 percent over the salary cap of the preceding school year, or 98 percent of the commissioner of education's 2003–04 salary which amounts to $166,762 (§ 1950(4)(a)(2)).

11:13. What items must be included in the total salary cap?

In addition to the amount paid by the state under Education Law section 2209 and the supplementary salary paid by the supervisory district (see **11:11-12**), the following items must also be included in the total salary cap:

- payments for life insurance having a cash value;
- payments for the employee contribution, co-pay, or uncovered medical expenses under a health insurance plan;
- payments for transportation or travel expenses in excess of actual documented expenses incurred in the performance of the board of cooperative educational services (BOCES) and state functions; and
- any other lump sum payments that are not specifically excluded from total salary by the Education Law (§ 1950(4)(a)(2)).

Any variation of these limitations may subject a district superintendent to penalties, including termination (§ 2212-b).

A statement describing the district superintendent's compensation must be included in the BOCES budget prior to the BOCES annual meeting (§ 1950(4)(b)(1)).

11:14. Are there limits on other benefits provided to a district superintendent?

Yes. Under the BOCES Reform Act, a district superintendent is an employee of the state (see Opn. Att'y Gen. I 2013-1; Opn. Att'y Gen. F 97-10). His or her maximum vacation time and sick leave and accrued or unused vacation or sick leave may not exceed the maximum permitted for management/confidential employees of New York State — 200 sick days and vacation without limit, except that as of January 1 each year, the amount of vacation cannot exceed 40 vacation days (4 NYCRR §§ 28-1.2, 28-1.3). This 40-day limitation on the accrual of vacation may be exceeded in a few special circumstances (see 4 NYCRR § 28-1.2(e)).

A district superintendent may be granted up to 13 days of vacation leave during his or her first year of employment and one additional vacation day on each subsequent annual anniversary date, for a total of up to 20 vacation days per year (more if the district superintendent has 20 years of continuous state service) (4 NYCRR § 28-1.2(b), (c)).

A district superintendent who was in state service on December 31, 1985 may be provided up to 13 sick days per year (4 NYCRR § 28-1.3(b)). All other district superintendents to whom the BOCES Reform Act applies are limited to a maximum of eight days sick leave per year (4 NYCRR § 28-2.1(c)).

Further, at the time of separation from service, a district superintendent may not be compensated for accrued and unused vacation credits or sick leave, or use accrued and unused sick leave for retirement service credit or to pay health insurance premiums after retirement at a rate in excess of that allowed for other management/confidential employees (§ 1950(4)(a)(2)).

Specifically, a district superintendent may not be compensated for more than 30 accrued, unused vacation days upon separation of service (4 NYCRR § 30.1).

Upon separation from service, a district superintendent may be permitted to use up to 200 days of accumulated, unused sick leave to pay for health insurance in retirement (4 NYCRR §§ 28-1.3(b), 2.1(c)).

11:15. May the supervisory district give pay raises to the district superintendent based upon increases in other collective bargaining agreements within the supervisory district?

No. The terms of a district superintendent's contract may not be tied to the terms of any collective bargaining agreements made with other employees in the supervisory district (§ 1950(4)(a)(2)).

11:16. May the commissioner of education withhold payment of the district superintendent's salary?

Yes. If the commissioner of education determines that a district superintendent has persistently neglected to perform an official duty, he or she may withhold part or all of the district superintendent's salary as it becomes due. However, the commissioner may decide to pay the withheld portion (in whole or in part) to the district superintendent at a later date (§ 2211).

Pursuant to section 2212-b of the Education Law, the commissioner must withhold from a district superintendent's state salary an amount of money equal to twice the value of any violation of the applicable salary and benefit caps (see **11:12–14**), unless the commissioner determines that the violation was inadvertent. In this case, the commissioner shall withhold the monetary value of the violation (§ 2212-b(2)).

11:17. May a district superintendent hold another job during his or her term of office?

No. A district superintendent must devote his or her full time to the office and may not "engage in any other occupation or profession" (§ 2213). Additionally, a district superintendent, once appointed, must vacate any prior position with the board of cooperative educational services (BOCES) upon appointment as district superintendent. The contract for employment as district superintendent must be the only contract the district superintendent holds with the BOCES (§ 1950(4)(a)(3)).

11:18. Are there any specific business activities in which district superintendents are prohibited from participating?

Yes. District superintendents are expressly prohibited from:

- Having a direct or indirect interest, other than as an author, in the sale, publication, or manufacture of school books, maps, charts, or school apparatus, or in the sale or manufacture of school furniture or any other school supplies or library supplies.
- Having a direct or indirect interest in any contract made by the trustees of a school district.
- Having a direct or indirect interest in any agency or bureau maintained to obtain or help obtain positions for teachers or superintendents.
- Directly or indirectly receiving any emolument, gift, pay, reward or promise of pay or reward for recommending or procuring the sale, use or adoption, or assisting in the sale, use or adoption of

any book, map, chart, school apparatus or furniture or other supplies for any school or library or for recommending a teacher or helping a teacher obtain a teaching position (§ 2214).

11:19. What are the district superintendent's responsibilities in the organization and operation of a board of cooperative educational services (BOCES)?

The district superintendent is the chief executive officer of the BOCES board. Where a BOCES is composed of two or more supervisory districts, the district superintendents, together with the president of the BOCES board, serve as an executive committee (§ 1950(2)).

11:20. What are the general powers and duties of the district superintendent?

Section 2215 of the Education Law states that a district superintendent's general powers and duties are to:

- Ascertain and maintain records in regard to school district boundaries (see also §§ 1508, 1509; *Pocantico Home & Land Co., LLC v. UFSD of the Tarrytowns*, 20 A.D.3d 458 (2d Dep't 2005); *Bd. of Educ. of Shenendehowa CSD v. Comm'r of Educ.*, 182 A.D.2d 944 (3d Dep't 1992); see also **11:23**).
- Hold teacher conferences and counsel teachers in relation to discipline, school management, and other schoolwork, as well as on matters promoting the general good of all schools of the district.
- Counsel trustees and board members and other school officers in relation to their powers and duties.
- Direct trustees and board members to "abate any nuisance" in or on school grounds, at the direction of the commissioner of education.
- Approve the amount, or the sureties on bonds, of treasurers and tax collectors of school districts.
- Condemn a schoolhouse, at the direction of the commissioner (§ 412).
- Examine and license teachers pursuant to the provisions of the Education Law and conduct other examinations as directed by the commissioner.
- Examine any charges affecting the moral character of any teacher residing or employed within the supervisory district (see **11:2**) and to revoke, if warranted, that teacher's certificate pursuant to section 3018 of the Education Law.
- Take affidavits and administer oaths in all matters pertaining to the public school system, free of charge.
- Take and report testimony in cases under appeal to the commissioner, as the commissioner directs. In such a case or in any matter to be heard or determined by the district superintendent, he or she may issue a subpoena to compel the attendance of a witness.
- Exercise at his or her discretion any of the powers and perform any of the duties of another district superintendent at the written request of that superintendent. A district superintendent must also perform such duties when directed to do so by the commissioner.
- Make an annual report to the commissioner by August 1 of each year, and submit any other reports he or she may request.
- Participate in the permanent computerized state-wide school district address match and income verification system as provided by section 171of the Tax Law and as directed by the commissioner.
- Report to the commissioner on cost-effective practices in school districts within his or her supervisory district.
- Determine the adequacy and appropriateness of facility spaces available in their supervisory district to house special education programs consistent with least restrictive environment requirements.

- Ensure the stability and continuity of program placements for students with disabilities, including procedures for ensuring that programs and services located in appropriate facilities will not be relocated without adequate consideration of the needs of participating students with disabilities.
- Fill, under certain circumstances, a vacancy on a school board by appointing a competent person (§ 2113).

Pursuant to the commissioner's regulations, the district superintendent is also responsible for coordinating the activities of the team charged with interviewing candidates for the public member seats in the school board of a special act school district (L. 2004, c. 629; 8 NYCRR § 105.3(a)).

In addition, the district superintendent or his or her designee shall represent the educational system on the interagency children's services team responsible for coordinating services for children with emotional and behavioral disorders within their county or local consortium of counties, along with appropriate local school district representatives determined by the district superintendent (Soc. Serv. Law § 483-c(3)(a)(ii), (b)(ii)).

11:21. What are the district superintendent's responsibilities in appointing teachers for probation and tenure in local districts and boards of cooperative educational services (BOCES)?

A district superintendent plays no role in appointing teachers for probation and tenure in local districts. These recommendations are made by the local superintendent of schools to the local school board (§§ 2509(1), (2), 2573, 3012(1)).

However, the district superintendent does have the power to recommend BOCES staff members to the BOCES board, including teachers, administrative assistants, and supervisors, for a probationary period of up to three years (§ 3014(1)). The district superintendent is also charged with making tenure recommendations to the BOCES board for those employees (§ 3014(2)).

11:22. May the district superintendent revoke a teacher's certificate?

Yes, although this authority is seldom invoked. The district superintendent is empowered to examine any charge affecting the moral character of any teacher residing in or employed within his or her supervisory district (see **11:2**) and to revoke such teacher's certificate (§ 2215(10)). The teacher is given reasonable notice of the charge and an opportunity to defend himself or herself. If the charge is sustained, the teacher's certificate is annulled and the individual declared unfit to teach. The district superintendent must then notify the commissioner of education immediately of such annulment and declaration (§ 3018).

11:23. What are the powers and duties of the district superintendent in relation to the formation, alteration, and dissolution of school districts?

A district superintendent may organize a new common or union free school district out of the territory of one or more districts that are wholly within the geographic area served by his or her board of cooperative educational services "whenever the educational interests of the community require it" (§ 1504(1)). The district superintendents of two or more adjoining supervisory districts may form a joint school district out of the adjoining portions of their respective districts "when public interests require it" (§ 1504(2)).

District superintendents also may dissolve one or more school districts by order and form a new district from this territory. They also may unite the territory or a portion thereof, by order, to an adjoining school district. However, the adjoining district may not be a city school district (§ 1505(1); *Appeal of the Town of New Windsor*, 45 Ed Dept Rep 539 (2006)), or a central school district (§ 1801).

In addition, a district superintendent may alter district boundaries with the written consent of all the districts to be affected (§ 1507; *Appeal of Bugbee, Sr.,* 52 Ed Dept Rep, Dec. No. 16,478 (2013); *Appeal of Spectrum Communities LLC*, 46 Ed Dept Rep 160 (2006), *aff'd sub nom. Andreou v. Mills,* Index No. 1095-07 (Sup. Ct. Albany Cnty. 2008); *Matter of Zeltmann*, 15 Ed Dept Rep 47 (1975)). Objections to altering boundaries are provided for in sections 1508 and 1509 of the Education Law (*Appeal of Roberta*, 38 Ed Dept Rep 690 (1999); see **chapter 2** on School District Reorganization). The commissioner of education will not order school districts to agree to a boundary change unless necessary to protect the best educational interests of the children involved. Parental preference is not enough (*Andreou v. Mills*).

Similarly, a district superintendent also may order the partitioning of territory from an existing union free, central high school, or enlarged city school district; the dissolution and reformation of the existing district; and the formation of a new union free or city school district out of such territory, upon approval by a majority of the qualified voters or two-thirds of the school board of each of the affected districts, and satisfaction of certain statutorily prescribed conditions (§ 2218).

However, in regards to city school districts and enlarged city school districts, only the commissioner of education may be involved in the consolidation, alteration of boundaries, or creation of such districts (*Appeal of the Town of New Windsor*). Likewise, only the commissioner is involved in the formation and changes of central school districts (§§ 1801, 1802).

11:24. Is a district superintendent entitled to the protections of Public Officers Law section 17, which governs defense and indemnification of state employees?

Yes, in certain circumstances. A district superintendent is a state employee entitled to the protections of Public Officers Law section 17 in connection with lawsuits that arise out of the performance of the district superintendent's state functions (Opn. Att'y Gen. 2013-F1, 97-F10). For further information on the issue of defense and indemnification and how such protections may be available to a district superintendent in relation to the performance of non-state functions, see **chapter 67**.

12. Ethics

Codes of Ethics

12:1. Must a school board adopt a code of ethics and operate according to its tenets?

Yes. The General Municipal Law requires all school boards to adopt a code of ethics for the guidance of its officers and employees that sets forth the standards of conduct reasonably expected of them (Gen. Mun. Law § 806).

The law requires school district codes of ethics to "provide standards for officers and employees with respect to disclosure of interest in legislation before the local governing body, holding of investments in conflict with official duties, private employment in conflict with official duties, future employment and such other standards relating to the conduct of officers and employees as may be deemed advisable" (Gen. Mun. Law § 806(1)(a); see also *Appeal of Hubbard,* 43 Ed Dept Rep 164 (2003); Opn. St. Comp. 82-189).

However, the board's code may not violate state law (*Appeal of Grinnell*, 37 Ed Dept Rep 504 (1998)). For example, the commissioner of education has held improper a board's attempt to apply a provision of its code of ethics as an additional qualification for membership on the board, eligibility for which is governed specifically by the Education Law (*Matter of Guilderland CSD*, 23 Ed Dept Rep 262 (1984)). In another case, the commissioner declared null and void a portion of a board's code of ethics that prohibited board members from voting on the employment contracts of their relatives (*Appeal of Behuniak & Lattimore*, 30 Ed Dept Rep 236 (1991)). Likewise, a board's code of ethics may not preclude a board member from voting on a contract involving a collective bargaining unit if the board member is or was a member of a similar bargaining unit while employed in another district, or regardless of current employment (*Appeal of Grinnell*).

For more information on codes of ethics, contact the Office of the State Comptroller, Division of Local Government and School Accountability, 110 State Street, 12th floor, Albany, N.Y. 12236, telephone: 866-321-8503 or 518-408-4934; e-mail: localgov@osc.state.ny.us.

12:2. Must the school district's code of ethics be distributed?

Yes. The superintendent of schools, as chief executive officer of the district, must distribute a copy of the code of ethics to every district officer and employee. The failure to distribute or receive the code will have no effect on the duty to comply with the code or with its enforcement (Gen. Mun. Law § 806(2)).

In addition, the superintendent must ensure that the district posts a copy of the provisions of the General Municipal Law regarding conflicts of interest in each public building in a place conspicuous to its officers and employees. However, failure to post the provisions will have no effect on the duty to comply with the law or with its enforcement (Gen. Mun. Law § 807).

12:3. Are there certain actions by school board members, district officers, and employees that are specifically prohibited by law?

Yes. Public officers and employees — including school board members, district officers, and employees — are specifically prohibited from:

- Soliciting or accepting any gift worth more than $75 under circumstances where it reasonably could be inferred that the gift was intended to influence or reward official action. School districts, through their own codes of ethics, can set the figure lower than $75, though not higher (Gen. Mun. Law § 805-a(1)(a); Opn. Att'y Gen. I 99-16; see also Penal Law §§ 200.00, 200.10). For information on a school board's ability to accept or make gifts on behalf of the school district as an entity, see **25:28–33**.
- Disclosing confidential information acquired during the course of their official duties or using such information to further their personal interests (Gen. Mun. Law § 805-a(1)(b); see *Appeal of Nett and Raby,* 45 Ed Dept Rep 259 (2005); *Application of Balen*, 40 Ed Dept Rep 250 (2000)).
- Representing clients for compensation before the board or district (Gen. Mun. Law § 805-a(1)(c)).
- Entering into contingency arrangements with clients for compensation in any matter before the school board or district (Gen. Mun. Law § 805-a(1)(d)).
- With certain limited exceptions, having an interest in any contract, lease, purchase, or sale over which they have any responsibility to negotiate, prepare, authorize, approve, or audit (Gen. Mun. Law §§ 800–805).

In addition to any penalty contained in any other provision of law, any person who knowingly and intentionally violates these rules of law may be fined, suspended, or removed from office or employment (Gen. Mun. Law § 805-a(2)). A school board member or district officer who is convicted of certain crimes where the victim is the school district may be required by the court to make restitution up to the full amount of the actual out-of-pocket loss suffered by the district (Penal Law § 60.27).

12:4. How far reaching is the prohibition against the acceptance or solicitation of gifts?

School board members may not accept or solicit gifts worth more than $75 either directly or indirectly. The prohibition extends to any kind of gift including money, service, loan, travel, entertainment, hospitality, thing or promise, or any other form (Gen. Mun. Law § 805-a(1); *Appeal of Dashefsky*, 46 Ed Dept Rep 219 (2006)).

Generally the gift prohibition applies if the gift:

- could reasonably be inferred as intended to influence the board member receiving the gift, or
- could reasonably be expected to influence the board member in the performance of official duties, or
- was intended as a reward for the board member's official action (*Id.*).

According to the commissioner of education, violation of the gift prohibition also occurs when "there is an appearance that a gift will influence" a board member (*Appeal of Dashefsky*).

Under these rules, the commissioner has found impermissible, for example, the attendance of board members at a reception hosted by a law firm retained by their school board and which allegedly cost between $200 and $300 per person (*Id.*). The commissioner also has admonished board members to scrupulously observe the gift prohibitions applicable to them (*Id.*).

12:5. What factors must be considered when determining whether a gift is impermissible?

The commissioner of education has advised school board members to review a 1994 advisory opinion from the State Ethics Commission that interpreted similar gift prohibitions applicable to state officials and employees (*Appeal of Dashefsky*, 46 Ed Dept Rep 219 (2006)). Based on the law in effect at that time, the commission determined that:

- A gift's value is determined generally by looking at its retail cost.
- The $75 threshold is met by multiple gifts if during any 12-month period, the aggregate value of gifts equals or exceeds $75.
- The lawfulness of a gift can depend on the identity of the donor and the donor's relationship to the recipient of the gift.
- Gifts to a public official's family or friends may be impermissible, as well as donations to a charitable organization designated by a public official.

Food and refreshment items of modest cost such as soft drinks, coffee, and doughnuts offered other than as part of a meal are permissible, even when offered at an annual event hosted by a vendor with whom a public official does business. Also permissible are unsolicited advertising or promotional material of little intrinsic value such as pens, pencils, note pads, and calendars.

A copy of the full text of Advisory Opinion 94-16 is available on line at: http://www.jcope.ny.gov/advice/finder.html.

Note: The State Ethics Commission has been replaced by the Joint Commission on Public Ethics ("JCOPE") which has issued regulations on this issue to reflect changes in law that apply to state officers and employees (www.jcope.ny.gov). However, there have not been corresponding changes to General Municipal Law § 805-a which applies to school district officers and employees.

In addition, state law imposes gift limits on those who lobby school districts under certain circumstances (Legislative Law, Article 1-A). For additional information on these requirements, contact JCOPE at 518-408-3976.

Conflicts of Interest

12:6. What is a conflict of interest?

The term *conflict of interest* describes a situation in which a school board member, district officer, or employee is in a position to benefit financially from a decision he or she may make on behalf of the district through the exercise of official authority or disposing of public funds. Financial interests that are prohibited by law include:

- Interest in a contract with the school district where a school board member, district officer, or employee has the power or may appoint someone who has the power to negotiate, authorize, approve, prepare, make payment, or audit bills or claims under the contract unless otherwise exempted under law (Gen. Mun. Law §§ 801(1), 802).
- Interest by a chief fiscal officer, treasurer, or his or her deputy or employee in a bank or other financial institution that is used by the school district he or she serves (Gen. Mun. Law § 801(2)), unless otherwise permitted under the law (Gen. Mun. Law § 802(1)(a)).

Interest is defined as a direct or indirect financial or material benefit that accrues to the officer or employee as a result of a contract with the school district (Gen. Mun. Law § 800(3)). The General Municipal Law expressly makes the provisions regarding conflicts of interest applicable to school districts (Gen. Mun. Law § 800(4)).

Contract is defined to include any claim, account, or demand against, or agreement, express or implied, as well as the designation of a depository of public funds or a newspaper for use by the school district (Gen. Mun. Law § 800(2)).

12:7. In what instances would a board member, district officer, or employee have an interest that could result in a prohibited conflict of interest?

A school board member, district officer, or employee is deemed to have an interest in a firm, partnership, or association of which he or she is a member or employee; a corporation of which he or she is an officer, director, or employee; or a corporation in which he or she owns or directly or indirectly controls any stock.

A board member, district officer or employee also is deemed to have an interest in a contract between the district and his or her spouse, minor child, or dependents, except a contract of employment as the law specifically allows a school district officer's or employee's spouse, minor child, or dependent to enter into an employment contract with the district (Gen. Mun. Law § 800(3); see also *Appeal of Lombardo,* 44 Ed Dept Rep 167 (2004); *Appeal of Lawson*, 42 Ed Dept Rep 210 (2002); *Application of Kavitsky*, 41 Ed Dept Rep 231 (2001)).

In addition, interests that are not prohibited but which nonetheless may create an appearance of impropriety may be properly restricted by the district's code of ethics, as long as the restriction is not inconsistent with other provisions of law (Opn. St. Comp. 88-77; *Appeal of Behuniak & Lattimore*, 30 Ed Dept Rep 236 (1991)).

12:8. Is a school board member, district officer or employee required to publicly disclose an interest even if it is not a prohibited interest?

Yes. Except as otherwise provided in law, such individuals are required to publicly disclose, in writing, any interest they or their spouse may have, will have, or later acquire in any actual or proposed contract; purchase agreement, lease agreement; or other agreement involving the district, including oral agreements, even if the interest is not a prohibited interest. The disclosure must be made to the school board and immediate supervisor, where applicable. It must also be made part of the official record of the district (Gen. Mun. Law § 803(1)(2); see also § 802(2); *Matter of Ackerberg*, 25 Ed Dept Rep 232 (1985); see also **12:6**).

12:9. How can a school board determine whether one of its members has a prohibited conflict of interest?

To decide whether one of its members has a prohibited conflict of interest, a board must determine:

- Whether there is a contract with the school district.
- Whether the board member in question has an interest in that contract.
- Whether the board member is authorized to exercise any of his or her powers or duties with respect to the agreement (see Gen. Mun. Law § 801(1); see **12:6**).
- Whether any exception to the conflict of interest law is applicable (Gen. Mun. Law § 802; see also Opn. St. Comp. 89-39; see **12:11–12**).

For additional information on determining whether a board member has a prohibited conflict of interest, see Office of the State Comptroller, *A Tutorial on Local Government Ethics and Transparency in New York State Module 1 – Conflict of Interest of Municipal Officers and Employees* at: www.osc.state.ny.us/localgov/training/modules/protecting/one/index.htm.

12:10. What are some examples of a prohibited conflict of interest for school board members?

A school board member had a conflict of interest, for instance, when the district purchased heating oil from the company of which the board member was president and in which he owned more than five percent of the stock (*Appeal of Golden*, 32 Ed Dept Rep 202 (1992)). Additionally, a prohibited interest may be found where a school board member, who is an attorney, is the business partner of the attorney hired to perform legal services for the school district, and the board member shares in the monies of the partnership which were derived from the contract with the school district or would otherwise benefit either directly or indirectly from the moneys paid to the law partner by the district under the contract (Opn. St. Comp. 2004-4).

In contrast, where a vice president of a corporation that both installed and continued to maintain a school telephone system was elected to a school board, there was no prohibited conflict of interest in the contracts entered into with his corporation prior to his election. However, there was the potential for a conflict of interest after he became a board member, depending upon his responsibilities as an officer of the company (if any), in connection with the contracts at issue (Opn. St. Comp. 86-58).

12:11. What are some examples of situations which do not involve a prohibited conflict of interest?

Section 802 of the General Municipal Law lists several specific exceptions. For example:

- A contract entered into by the district with a person who later is elected or appointed to the school board remains valid, except that this exception does not apply when the contract comes up for renewal (Gen. Mun. Law § 802(1)(h)).
- A school board member may enter into a contract or multiple contracts with the school district if the total consideration paid under the contract is, or contracts are, less than $750 (Gen. Mun. Law § 802(2)(e)).
- A school board member who is a bank officer at the bank's main office has no conflict of interest, where the school district has designated a branch of that bank as a depository for district funds and the bank employee would never have occasion to become involved in any school district transactions occurring at that bank branch (Gen. Mun. Law § 802(1)(a), (1)(b); Opn. St. Comp. 77-504).
- A school board member may be employed as school physician upon authorization by a two-thirds vote of the board (Gen. Mun. Law § 802(1)(i)).

Board members voting on the employment of or collective bargaining agreements pertaining to their relatives do not have a prohibited conflict of interest either (Gen. Mun. Law § 800(3); Educ. Law § 3016(2); *Appeal of Budich*, 48 Ed Dept Rep 383 (2009); *Appeal of Behuniak & Lattimore*, 30 Ed Dept Rep 236 (1991); see also **6:4**, **12:1**, **12:12**).

Additionally, there is no prohibited conflict of interest where a board member:

- Lives in the same house and splits expenses with a district employee (*Appeal of Santicola*, 42 Ed Dept Rep 356 (2003)).
- Also serves on the board of a not-for-profit foundation that raises money and makes gifts to the school district in which the school board member serves (Opn. St. Comp. 2008-1). However, the board member should not participate in school board discussions or decisions relating to the gifts from, or other matters relating to, the foundation. In addition, the school board member should disclose his or her relationship with the foundation (*Id.*).
- Has a friendship or personal relationship with an individual who contracts with the board where the board member receives no financial or material benefit as a result of the contract (*Application of Chiacchia*, 53 Ed Dep Rep, Dec. No. 16,593 (2014)).

12:12. Does an interest arising from a collective bargaining agreement constitute a prohibited conflict of interest?

No. Collective bargaining agreements fall within a statutory exception to the general rule regarding contracts with membership corporations or other voluntary, nonprofit corporations or associations.

Therefore, a personal interest arising from such a contract is not a prohibited interest under the law (Gen. Mun. Law § 802(1)(f); *Stettine v. County of Suffolk*, 66 N.Y.2d 354 (1985); see also Opn. St. Comp. 89-24; *Appeal of Budich*, 48 Ed Dept Rep 383 (2009)).

The commissioner of education, citing the *Stettine* case, has rejected petitions attacking the election of board members who are retired district employees with continuing health insurance benefits under the district's collective bargaining agreement (see *Application of Casazza*, 32 Ed Dept Rep 462 (1993); *Appeal of Samuels*, 25 Ed Dept Rep 228 (1985); see **6:3**). This, of course, does not affect the prohibition against current employees serving as board members (see **6:1**).

12:13. What are the consequences of violating the conflict of interest law?

Any contract willfully entered into by or with a school district in which there is a prohibited interest is void and unenforceable (Gen. Mun. Law § 804). Furthermore, a school board member who knowingly and willfully violates the law in this regard or fails to disclose an interest in a contract may be guilty of a misdemeanor (Gen. Mun. Law § 805) and/or subject to removal from office by the commissioner of education (see *Appeal of Golden*, 32 Ed Dept Rep 202 (1992); see also **6:39**).

13. Confidentiality of School Records

Public Access and Inspection

13:1. Are school district records subject to public access and inspection?

Yes. Each school board is required by the Education Law and the Public Officers Law to have school district records available for inspection and copying at all reasonable times (§ 2116; Pub. Off. Law § 87).

The Freedom of Information Law, which is part of the Public Officers Law and is also commonly referred to as FOIL, requires government bodies and agencies, including school districts, to allow the public access to official documents and records (Pub. Off. Law Art. 6, §§ 84–90). However, FOIL also allows districts to withhold access to certain categories of documents, including those that are required by law to be kept confidential (see Pub. Off. Law §§ 87(2), 89(7)).

While the Education Law provides that the records, books, and papers of the office of any officer of a school district are the property of the district and open for inspection and copying (§ 2116), the commissioner of education has determined that there is no broader scope of disclosure under section 2116 of the Education Law than under FOIL. In other words, a school district can refuse to disclose records requested under this section to the same extent that it could deny a FOIL request pursuant to one of the exceptions from disclosure available under FOIL (*Appeal of Martinez*, 37 Ed Dept Rep 435 (1998); see also *Appeal of Gentile*, 47 Ed Dept Rep 438 (2008)).

Additionally, school boards must make any agency records and proposed resolutions, rules, regulations, policies or amendments thereto that are scheduled for discussion at a board meeting available upon request of any member of the public, to the extent practicable, prior to or at the meeting where the records will be discussed. The board may charge a reasonable fee for copies of the records (see **13:15**). The records must also be posted on the district's website to the extent practicable prior to the meeting (Pub. Off. Law § 103(e); see NYS Department of State, Committee on Open Government, *Questions and Answers Regarding Records Discussed at Open Meetings* (Feb. 2012), at: http://www.dos.ny.gov/coog/QA-2-12.html).

For a discussion of school district records subject to public access, and those that may be withheld from public access, see **13:3, 13:5-11**.

13:2. Are there any restrictions on who may access school district records?

Not generally. Any member of the public has the right to examine and/or copy these records or documents according to procedures adopted by the district in accordance with the law (see Pub. Off. Law § 87(1)(b); see **13:12-17**). A fee may be charged for copies (see **13:15**). Although there are restrictions on the types of district records accessible under the Freedom of Information Law (FOIL) (see **13:5-11**), there is no general restriction as to who may access district records.

While section 2116 of the Education Law provides that district records are to be available for inspection to any qualified voter, FOIL has been held to broaden the category of such persons to include individuals living outside the school district as well (*Duncan v. Savino*, 90 Misc.2d 282 (Sup. Ct. Steuben Cnty. 1977)).

However, access to individual student records is limited to parents and eligible students under the Family Educational Rights and Privacy Act, also known as FERPA or the Buckley Amendment, unless they give prior consent to such access or one of the law's exceptions applies (20 USC § 1232g; see also 34 CFR Part 99; see **13:21-25**). State law also prohibits the unauthorized release of personally identifiable information about students (Educ Law § 2-d; see **13:21**).

13:3. What types of school district records are subject to public access and inspection?

The Freedom of Information Law defines a record as "any information kept, held, filed, produced or reproduced by, with or for" the school district, "in any physical form whatsoever, including, but not limited to, reports, statements, examinations, memoranda, opinions, folders, files, books, manuals, pamphlets, forms, papers, designs, drawings, maps, photos, letters, microfilms, computer tapes or discs, rules, regulations or codes" (Pub. Off. Law § 86(4)). Examples of recorded information that may be inspected by interested citizens are school contracts, statements of expenditures, and minutes of board meetings. According to the Committee on Open Government, this definition includes information sent by e-mail and text message because they are merely means of transmitting information and, "presumably," that information can be captured and retained (NYS Department of State, Committee on Open Government, FOIL-AO-18052 (Mar. 24, 2010); FOIL–AO–18052 (Mar. 24, 2010); see also NYS Department of State, Committee on Open Government, *Retention and Disposal of Electronic Communications* (Dec. 2013), at: http://www.dos.ny.gov/coog/news/dec13.html).

Records transmitted via private, personal e-mail accounts (as opposed to district-provided accounts) are not exempt from disclosure rules (see **13:5**), and should be retained in accordance with the law (NYS Department of State, Committee on Open Government, FOIL–AO–18052 (Mar. 24, 2010); FOIL-AO-16969 (Jan. 30, 2008); see Arts and Cult. Aff. Law §§ 57.17, 57.25; 8 NYCRR 185.12 (Appendix I); see also **13:1**).

13:4. Are school districts required to prepare new records in order to comply with a request for information submitted under the Freedom of Information Law?

No. Only existing records are subject to disclosure. A school district does not need to prepare a record that does not already exist solely for the purpose of responding to a request for information (Pub. Off. Law § 89(3); *Curro v. Capasso*, 209 A.D.2d 346 (1st Dep't 1994)). School districts must maintain a list of records by subject matter and update that list annually (Pub. Off. Law § 87(3)(c)).

However, districts that have the ability to do so with reasonable effort must retrieve or extract a record or data maintained in a computer storage system. Any programming necessary to retrieve such records, and to either transfer them to the medium requested by the person asking for a copy of the records or to allow them to be read or printed, does not constitute the preparation or creation of a new record (Pub. Off. Law § 89(3)(a)), provided the programming involves a simple manipulation of the computer and running programs with existing software to retrieve the requested documents (see *Matter of N.Y. Committee for Occupational Safety & Health v. Bloomberg*, 72 A.D.3d 153 (1st Dep't 2010)). The creation of new software that would not otherwise exist without the Freedom of Information Law request may constitute the creation of a new document (*Id.*).

In addition, districts that can scan records to transmit them via e-mail must do so with no charge involved, if scanning does not require any effort additional to an alternative method of responding (NYS Department of State, Committee on Open Government, FOIL-AO-16572 (May 16, 2007)).

13:5. May any district records be withheld from public access and inspection?

Yes. While the Freedom of Information Law (FOIL) generally requires access to be given to all public records, it also specifically exempts certain types of records from mandatory disclosure. Some of the exempt records more commonly involved in school district operations include:

- Those specifically exempted by a state or federal statute (see **13:8**, **13:10**, **13:21-25**).
- Certain law enforcement documents and records (see *Madeiros v. N.Y. State Educ. Dep't*, 133 A.D.3d 962 (3d Dep't 2015), *lv. to appeal granted*, 27 N.Y.3d 903 (2016)).
- Records that, if disclosed, would constitute an "unwarranted invasion of personal privacy" (see Pub. Off. Law § 89(2)).
- Records that, if disclosed, would impair current or imminent contract awards or collective bargaining negotiations.
- Interagency and intra–agency materials that are not: statistical or factual tabulations or data; instructions to staff that affect the public; final agency policy or determinations; or external audits.
- Information that, if disclosed, would endanger the life or safety of any person.
- Questions or answers to an exam that has not yet been administered.
- Computer access codes (see Pub. Off. Law § 87(2)).
- The name or home address of an applicant for appointment to public employment (Pub. Off. Law § 89(7); but see *Mothers on the Move, Inc. v. Messer*, 236 A.D.2d 408 (2d Dep't 1997); *Daily News, L.P. v. N.Y. City Office of Payroll Admin.*, 9 A.D.3d 308 (1st Dep't), *lv. to appeal denied*, 3 N.Y.3d 609 (2004)).
- The home address of a retiree. However, retirees' names are not exempt from disclosure (*Empire Center for N.Y. State Policy v. N.Y. State Teachers' Retirement System*, 23 N.Y.3d 438 (2014)).

However, FOIL is liberally construed and its exceptions are treated very narrowly to provide the public maximum access to government records (*Hamilton v. Bd. of Educ. of Jordan-Elbridge CSD*, 29 Misc.3d 1201(A) (Sup. Ct. Onondaga Cty. 2010)). For example, a budget examiner's worksheets have been determined to be subject to inspection as "statistical or factual tabulations," not exempt as internal documents (Pub. Off. Law § 87(2)(g)(i); see *Dunlea v. Goldmark*, 54 A.D.2d 446 (3d Dep't 1976), *aff'd*, 43 N.Y.2d 754 (1977); see also *Verizon N.Y. v. Bradbury*, 40 A.D.3d 1113 (2d Dep't 2007)).

In addition, FOIL does not permit exempting from public disclosure government records that do not otherwise qualify for exception pursuant to one of its specific provisions (*In re City of Newark v. Law Dep't of the City of N.Y.*, 305 A.D.2d 28 (1st Dep't 2003)). Courts may order the disclosure of documents that contain both exempt and non-exempt information after they are redacted to remove the exempt information (*Schenectady Cty. Soc. for Prevention of Cruelty to Animals v. Mills*, 18 N.Y.3d 42 (2011)). Moreover, school districts cannot bargain away the public right to access their district's records (*LaRocca v. Bd. of Educ. of Jericho UFSD*, 220 A.D.2d 424 (2d Dep't 1995); *Mulgrew v. Bd. of Educ. of the City Sch. Dist. of the City of N.Y.*, 31 Misc.3d 296 (Sup. Ct. N.Y. Cnty), *aff'd*, 87 A.D.3d 506 (1st Dep't 2011), *lv. to appeal denied*, 18 N.Y.3d 806 (2012).

13:6. What are some examples of unwarranted invasions of privacy?

The Freedom of Information Law itself provides a non-exhaustive list of examples that constitute an unwarranted invasion of privacy (§ 89(2)(b)(i) (vii)). One such example expressly prohibits the release of staff names and addresses for commercial or fund raising purposes (§ 89(2)(b)(iii)), including the release of such information to a union for purposes of expanding the membership and obtaining membership dues (*N.Y. State United Teachers v. Brighter Choice Charter Schools*, 15 N.Y.3d 560 (2010)). Another prohibits the release of e-mail addresses or social network user names collected from taxpayers who pay their real property taxes electronically pursuant to Real Property Tax Law § 104 (§ 89(2)(b)(vii)). Otherwise, what constitutes an unwarranted invasion of privacy generally is examined in terms of what would be offensive and objectionable to a reasonable person of ordinary sensibilities (*Matter of Pennington v. Clark*, 16 A.D.3d 1049 (4th Dep't 2005), *lv. to appeal denied*, 5 N.Y.3d 712 (2005)).

There is a distinction, however, in how that axiom applies to ordinary persons as opposed to public employees. Certain information regarding public employees is available through FOIL such as salaries, attendance records, and qualifications for employment (see NYS Department of State, Committee on Open Government, *FOIL and Privacy: Where Do We Draw the Line*? (Feb. 2013), at: http://www.dos.ny.gov/coog/drawtheline.html).

In addition, government agencies may not immunize documents from disclosure under FOIL by designating them as confidential, either unilaterally or by agreement with a private party, including a contract between a school district and its superintendent (see *Hamilton v. Bd. of Educ. of Jordan-Elbridge CSD*; NYS Department of State, Committee on Open Government, FOIL–AO–19175 (Sept. 4, 2014)).

13:7. Are handwritten notes taken by a school board member during an executive session accessible under the Freedom of Information Law (FOIL)?

According to the Committee on Open Government, handwritten notes taken by a board member during the course of an executive session would constitute agency records that are subject to the rights of access conferred by FOIL. In the Committee's view, while those records may be in the physical possession of the board member, they are the property and in the legal custody of the school district.

However, such notes constitute intra-agency materials. Therefore, they are subject to public process only if they consist of statistical or factual information, instructions to staff that affect the public, final agency or determinations or external audits, unless their content can be withheld under one of the other statutory exemptions (NYS Department of State, Committee on Open Government, FOIL–AO–19183 (Oct. 2, 2014); see **13:5**).

13:8. Are records pertaining to the job performance of classroom teachers and building principals accessible under the Freedom of Information Law (FOIL)?

In general, materials that are statistical or factual tabulations or data regarding the proficiency of public employees in the performance of their job duties are subject to disclosure under FOIL (*Mulgrew v. Bd. of Educ. of the City Sch. Dist. of the City of N.Y.*, 31 Misc.3d 296 (Sup. Ct. NY Cty), *aff'd,* 87 A.D.3d 506 (1st Dep't 2011), *lv. to appeal denied*, 18 N.Y.3d 806 (2012)). However, the Legislature exempted annual professional performance reviews (APPRs) from access by the general public through FOIL (§§ 3012-c(10)(c), 3012-d(15)). Instead, it restricts the disclosure of such information to limited circumstances (*Id.*; see **37:17-19**).

Lesson observation reports consisting solely of an administrator's critique and evaluation and improvement recommendations have been deemed exempt from disclosure as intra-agency material (*Matter of Elentuck v. Green*, 202 A.D.2d 425 (2d Dep't), *lv. to appeal denied*, 84 N.Y.2d 809 (1994)). Similarly, according to the Committee on Open Government, counseling memos that consist of opinions, advice, or recommendation may be withheld (NYS Department of State, Committee on Open Government, FOIL-AO-13978 (Mar. 31, 2003)).

Similarly, a state appellate court ordered the production of factual data or final agency determinations from materials related to an investigation concerning whether a school employee who gave a speech critical of education policy positions taken by mayoral candidates violated school district regulations. The court found a "significant public interest" in the materials, which could shed light into the adequacy of the investigation. Any unwarranted invasion of personal privacy could be avoided by redacting personally identifiable information from the materials (*Thomas v. Condon*, 128 A.D.3d 528 (1st Dep't 2015)).

Likewise, a school district was ordered to produce investigative records related to a complaint that school administrators had improperly influenced the re-scoring of a Regents' examination, after redaction of materials that were not factual tabulations or date, or final agency policy or determinations. The appellate court based its decision on a finding that there was a "significant public interest in the proper academic assessment of public school students and therefore in the requested materials, which may shed light on the adequacy of [the] investigation" (*Sell v. N.Y. City Dep't of Educ.*, 24 A.D.3d 594 (1st Dep't 2016)).

13:9. Are investigative reports regarding complaints about school staff misconduct subject to disclosure under the Freedom of Information Law (FOIL)?

Yes, except for those portions of the records with content that is determined to meet one of the statutory exemptions (see **13:5**). For example, in a case involving a FOIL request for a copy of an investigative report prepared in response to a complaint alleging school administrators violated federal law, a state appellate court concluded that there is "no statutory blanket exemption for investigative records, even when allegations of misconduct are "quasi criminal" in nature or not substantiated. . ." The court then ordered the lower court to inspect the document to determine if redaction "could strike an appropriate balance between personal privacy and public interests and which material could be properly disclosed" (*Matter of Thomas v. N.Y. City Educ. Dep't*, 103 A.D.3d 495 (1st Dep't 2013); see also *Yager v. Massena CSD*, 119 A.D.3d 1066 (3d Dep't 2014)).

13:10. Are students' records accessible under the Freedom of Information Law (FOIL)?

No. FOIL exempts from disclosure records that are specifically exempted by federal or state statute (Pub. Off. Law § 87(2)(a)). Access to student records is protected under the federal Family Educational Rights and Privacy Act, also known as the Buckley Amendment (see 20 USC § 1232g *et seq.*; see also 34 CFR Part 99; see **13:21-25**). State law also prohibits the unauthorized release of personally identifiable information about students (Educ. Law § 2-d; see **13:21**).

13:11. Are Education Law section 3020–a settlement agreements or decisions available to the public under FOIL?

Generally, agreements settling disciplinary charges are subject to disclosure under the Freedom of Information Law (FOIL). However, certain portions of such agreements should be reviewed and edited before disclosure to the public in order to protect privacy, including charges that were denied and charges mentioning the names of other employees or students (*LaRocca v. Bd. of Educ. of Jericho UFSD*, 220 A.D.2d 424 (2d Dep't 1995); see also *Anonymous v. Bd. of Educ. for the Mexico CSD*, 162 Misc.2d 300 (Sup. Ct. Oswego Cnty. 1994); *Buffalo Evening News, Inc. v. Bd. of Educ. of the Hamburg CSD,* unreported (Sup. Ct. Erie Cnty. 1987)).

Similarly, 3020-a panel or hearing officer decisions with a finding of guilt may be disclosed pursuant to a FOIL request (*DeMichele v. Greenburgh CSD No. 7*, 167 F.3d 784 (2d Cir. 1999)). Again, certain portions should be reviewed and edited before disclosure to the public in order to protect privacy, including charges that were dismissed and those parts of the decision mentioning the names of other employees or students (NYS Department of State, Committee on Open Government, FOIL–AO–19239 (Jan. 20, 2015)).

13:12. What are the procedures to gain access to school district records?

School districts are required under the Freedom of Information Law (FOIL) to adopt procedures by which interested citizens may review district records. These procedures must specify the times when and places where records are available, the names or titles of persons responsible for providing records, and any fees for copying records. Districts must accept FOIL requests and permit inspection of records during all hours they are regularly open for business (Pub. Off. Law § 87(1)(b); 21 NYCRR § 1401.4).

Interested persons must make their request for records in writing to the school district and must identify the desired records in sufficient detail for the request to be honored. Requests should be directed to the records access officer, the individual whom school districts must designate by law to be responsible for ensuring compliance with FOIL (Pub. Off. Law §§ 87(1)(b), 89(3)(a)).

School districts must provide a copy of the records requested in the medium requested, if they can reasonably make such a copy themselves or by engaging an outside professional service. Records provided in a computer format may not be encrypted (Pub. Off. Law § 87(5)(a)). In addition, districts may not enter into or renew a contract for the creation or maintenance of records that would impair the right of the public to inspect or copy such records (Pub. Off. Law § 87(5)(b)). Those that maintain records in a computer storage system must design their retrieval method to permit the segregation and retrieval of accessible records from those exempt from disclosure, when practicable and reasonable (Pub. Off. Law § 89(9)).

13:13. Must school districts accept and respond electronically to requests for access to school district records?

It depends. To the extent they have reasonable means available, school districts must accept requests submitted in the form of electronic mail. Unless the request seeks a response in some other form, districts also must respond to electronic mail requests electronically using, to the extent practicable, a form consistent with the one developed by the Committee on Open Government (Pub. Off. Law § 89(3)(b)). The Committee has made a form available at: http://www.dos.ny.gov/coog/emailresponse.html. It recommends the designation of a single e-mail address to be used solely to respond to e-mail requests.

Records provided in computer format may not be encrypted. School districts may not enter into or renew contracts for the creation or maintenance of records that impair the public's right to inspect or copy district records (Pub. Off. Law § 87(5)(b)).

13:14. May school districts deny "voluminous and burdensome" requests for school district records?

Not generally. Districts may not deny a request for records on the basis that it is voluminous or burdensome because of insufficient staffing, or on any other basis, if they can engage an outside professional service to provide copying, programming, or other services required to fulfill the request (Pub. Off. Law § 89(3)(a)).

13:15. May school districts charge a fee for copies of school district records?

Yes. School districts may charge copying fees up to 25 cents per page for photocopies no larger than 9 × 14 inches (Pub. Off. Law § 87(1)(b)(iii)).

In addition, they may charge for the actual cost of reproducing any other record. When determining the actual cost of such reproduction, districts can include an amount equal to the hourly salary of the lowest paid employee with the skills necessary to prepare the record, the actual cost of the storage device or media provided to the person making the request, and the actual cost of hiring an outside professional service to prepare a copy when the district's technology is inadequate to do so. However, they may not include search time or administrative costs. No reproduction fee may be charged for such other records unless at least two hours of employee time is needed to prepare a copy (Pub. Off. Law § 87(1)(b)(iii), (c)(iv)).

They also may charge 25 cents per page for the cost of preparing a photocopy needed to redact information before responding to a Freedom of Information Law request (*Brown v. Goord*, 45 A.D.3d 930 (3d Dep't 2007), *lv. to appeal dismissed*, 10 N.Y.3d 796 (2008)), including e-mail responses (NYS Department of State, Committee on Open Government, FOIL-AO-16571 (May 14, 2007)).

A school district may delay fulfillment of a subsequent FOIL request until fees owed on prior FOIL requests are paid (*Fenstermaker v. Edgemont UFSD*, 48 A.D.3d 564 (2d Dep't 2008)).

13:16. Are there procedures for appealing a school district's denial of a FOIL request?

Yes. School districts must maintain a procedure that allows for appeals regarding a denial of access to district records. The procedure must allow a person to appeal a denial within 30 days to the individual designated by the school board to receive and decide such appeals. Within 10 business days of receipt of the appeal, that person must either provide the record requested or a written explanation of the reason for the further denial. Failure to follow the outlined provisions will constitute a denial of access subject to appeal (Pub. Off. Law § 89(4)(a)).

The district must provide a "particularized and specific justification for denying access" or a "factual basis" for claiming an exemption (*Rushford v. Oneida–Herkimer Solid Waste Auth.*, 217 A.D.2d 966 (4th Dep't 1995)). The district must also file each appeal and its outcome with the Committee on Open Government (Pub. Off. Law § 89(4)(a); 21 NYCRR § 1401.7(g),(h)) at the following address: Committee on Open Government, NYS Department of State, One Commerce Plaza, 99 Washington Avenue, Suite 650, Albany, N.Y. 12231.

Anyone who is dissatisfied with the district's final decision on a request for access to records may appeal the decision to the supreme court of the appropriate county (Pub. Off. Law § 89(4)(b)). The commissioner of education does not hear appeals regarding alleged violations of FOIL (*Appeal of Jaidan Industries*, 55 Ed Dept Rep, Dec. No. 16,856 (2015); *Appeal of Ament*, 51 Ed Dept Rep, Dec. No. 16,350 (2012); *Appeal of Agee*, 50 Ed Dept Rep, Dec. No. 16,157 (2010)).

13:17. Are there time lines that apply for responding to a FOIL request?

Yes. The school district must respond within five business days of the receipt of a written request by making the record available, by issuing a written denial, or by acknowledging the request and stating approximately when the request will be granted or denied within a reasonable time based upon the circumstances of the request (Pub. Off. Law § 89(3)).

If a request cannot be granted within 20 business days from the date of acknowledgement of the request the district must state in writing both the reason the request cannot be granted within 20 business days, and a date certain within a reasonable period when it will be granted depending on the circumstances of the request (Pub. Off. Law § 89(3)).

In determining a reasonable time for granting or denying a request the district shall consider the volume of the request, the ease or difficulty in locating, retrieving or generating records, the complexity of the request, the need to review records to determine the extent to which they must be disclosed, the number of requests received by the district, and other similar factors (21 NYCRR § 1401.5(d)). The district may also contact the person seeking the records if a request is voluminous to ascertain the nature of records of primary interest and attempt to reasonably reduce the volume of the request (21 NYCRR § 1401.2(b)(3)).

13:18. What penalties may be imposed against a school district for denying access to district records?

If records are withheld without a reasonable basis under the Freedom of Information Law (FOIL), the school district may be assessed reasonable attorneys' fees and other costs of litigation reasonably incurred by a person who has sued for disclosure (Pub. Off. Law § 89(4)(c)). Such fees will be assessed if the district either had no reasonable basis for denying access, or failed to respond to a request or appeal within the applicable statutory timelines (*Id.*; *South Shore Press, Inc. v. Havemeyer,* 136 A.D.3d 929 (2d Dep't 2016); *NY Civil Liberties Union v. City of Saratoga Springs*, 87 A.D.3d 336 (3d Dep't 2011)).

A school district that denies access to requested records must justify the denial by showing the information requested "falls squarely within a FOIL exemption" (*Matter of Data Tree, LLC v. Romaine*, 9 N.Y.3d 454 (2007)). The justification for denying access under the claimed exemption must be "particularized and specific" (*Id.*).

The willful concealment or destruction of public records with the intent to prevent public inspection of such records is also a violation of section 240.65 of the Penal Law and section 89(8) of the Public Officers Law, punishable by a fine of up to $250 and/or a jail term of up to 15 days (Penal Law §§ 70.15(4), 80.05(4)).

13:19. Are there any restrictions on the destruction of school district records?

Yes. Public records must be maintained and preserved in accordance with the "Local Government Records Law," which is contained in article 57-A of New York's Arts and Cultural Affairs Law. Pursuant to this law, the commissioner of education has created a document called the "Records Retention and Disposition Schedule ED-1" with which school districts must comply (Arts & Cult. Aff. Law §§ 57.17(1), 57.23, 57.25; 8 NYCRR § 185.12; 8 NYCRR App. I; see also Pub. Off. Law § 80; Educ. Law § 2121(7)). It is available at: http://www.archives.nysed.gov/records/retention_ed-1.

Records may be destroyed only after being retained for a period specified in the Schedule ED–1 (Arts & Cult. Aff. Law § 57.25(2)). Moreover, before any records listed on the Schedule ED–1 may be disposed of, the school board must formally adopt the Schedule ED–1 by passing a resolution (8 NYCRR § 185.12 (Appendix I, p. 2418; see p. 2423 for a sample resolution)).

Documents that are not listed in the schedule may be destroyed only with the permission of the commissioner (8 NYCRR § 185.6(a)). Records of employee disciplinary matters, investigations, and evaluations may be disposed of according to the terms of a collective bargaining agreement (8 NYCRR § 185.6(d)).

Records may be preserved on microfilm and the originals disposed of, unless they date from before 1910 or have "enduring statewide significance," according to the commissioner's criteria (8 NYCRR §§ 185.6(c), 185.7), in which case they may be destroyed only with the commissioner's approval. Film reproductions are treated legally as original documents (Arts & Cult. Aff. Law § 57.29).

The destruction of canceled bonds and notes and similar obligations is governed by regulations of the state comptroller (Loc. Fin. Law § 63.10; Opn. St. Comp. 80–351).

Board Access to Personnel Records

13:20. Do school board members have access to school employees' personnel records?

Yes, under certain circumstances. The commissioner's regulations provide that any board member may request that personnel records be examined by the board in executive session, but only for inspection and use in the deliberation of specific matters before the board and if certain procedures are followed (see *Appeal of Meyer & Pavalow*, 46 Ed Dept Rep 43 (2006); 8 NYCRR Part 84). A school board that permitted a non-board member in attendance at an executive session to have access to personnel records violated the regulation (*Appeal of Whalen*, 34 Ed Dept Rep 282 (1994)).

Pursuant to commissioner's regulations, information from employees' personnel records may be accessed and used by school board members only to help make decisions on personnel matters, such as appointments, assignments, promotions, demotions, pay, discipline, or dismissal; to aid in the development and implementation of personnel policies; and to enable the board to carry out its legal responsibilities (8 NYCRR § 84.3; *Appeal of Meyer & Pavalow*). For example, a board may review personnel files to determine whether the district's legal obligations are being met by the superintendent and/or other administrative staff, such as whether or not employee evaluations are being performed (*Application of Bean*, 42 Ed Dept Rep 171 (2002)).

Any board member may request that the superintendent bring the personnel records of a designated employee or group of employees to the public board meeting. The board must then decide whether to meet in executive session to examine the records, based on a determination that the rationale for the request falls within one of the purposes set out in commissioner's regulations, even if a majority of the board does not wish to view the records (see *Gustin v. Joiner*, 95 Misc.2d 277 (Sup. Ct. Westchester Cnty. 1978), *aff'd*, 68 A.D.2d 880 (2d Dep't 1979)). Records are brought by the superintendent to the executive session and returned to the superintendent at the end of the session (8 NYCRR § 84.2). A determination that the rationale for the request satisfies regulatory requirements obligates a board to grant a request for review of the records in executive session.

Under other circumstances, an individual board member has no greater right of access to district records than any other member of the public (*Matter of Bruno*, 4 Ed Dept Rep 14 (1964)). Therefore, that individual board member would be able to access only that which is available under the Freedom of Information Law (see *Buffalo Teachers Fed'n, Inc. v. Buffalo Bd. of Educ.*, 156 A.D.2d 1027 (4th Dep't 1989), *appeal denied*, 75 N.Y.2d 708 (1990)).

Disclosure of Student Records

Editor's Note: Additional information on the Family Educational Rights and Privacy Act is available from the Family Policy Compliance Office at the U.S. Department of Education, 400 Maryland Avenue, S.W. Washington D.C. 20202; website at: http://www2.ed.gov/policy/gen/guid/fpco/index.html. The U.S. Department of Education's Privacy Technical Assistance Center has made available guidance for school districts on best practices in data transparency and communications which can be found at: http://ptac.aem-tx.com/.

13:21. Who is entitled to access student records?

Under the Family Educational Rights and Privacy Act (20 USC § 1232g *et seq.*) and its accompanying regulations (34 CFR Part 99), only parents or eligible students (meaning any student who has reached 18 years of age or is attending an institution of post–secondary education) have the right to see educational records pertaining to the student.

Parents of otherwise eligible students may still access the student's education record under certain specified circumstances, such as when the student is a dependent under the Internal Revenue Code (34 CFR § 99.31(a)(8)). Absent a custody decree or court order to the contrary, nothing prevents a non-custodial parent with no decision-making authority regarding his or her child's education from "requesting information about, keeping apprised of. . .the child's educational progress" (*Fuentes v. Bd.*

of Educ. of the City of N.Y., 12 N.Y.3d 309 (2009); *Taylor v. Vermont Dep't of Educ.*, 313 F.3d 768 (2d Cir. 2002)).

Disclosure to anyone else without the prior written consent of the parent or eligible student is limited except as provided by law (see 20 USC § 1232g *et seq.*; see also 34 CFR Part 99; *Fuentes v. Bd. of Educ. of the City of N.Y.*; *Owasso Indep. Sch. Dist. No. I–011 v. Falvo*, 534 U.S. 426 (2002); *Taylor v. Vermont Dep't of Educ.*).

In addition, state law prohibits the unauthorized release of personally identifiable information about students and imposes requirements regarding the same on school districts. For example, under state law, school districts are required to publish a parents' bill of rights regarding data privacy and security to be posted on the district website and be included with every contract between the district and a third party contractor that receives student data (see http://www.p12.nysed.gov/docs/parents-bill-of-rights.pdf). State law also requires that the commissioner of education promulgate regulations establishing standards for district data security and privacy policies and to develop one or more model policies to be used by school districts. Once the regulations are issued, school districts are required to have a policy in place that is consistent with federal and state law (Educ Law § 2-d).

13:22. Are there any exceptions to the prior consent requirement for the disclosure of student records?

Yes. There are certain exceptions to the prior consent requirement (see **13:21**). For example, districts may disclose student records without prior consent from a parent or eligible student to other school officials who have "legitimate educational interests" and certain other state and federal officials (20 USC § 1232g(b)(1)(A)). However, districts must use reasonable methods to ensure school officials are given access only to those education records in which the official has a legitimate educational interest.

Another example of when records can be subject to inspection without prior consent from a parent or eligible student is pursuant to a court order or any lawfully issued subpoena, provided that in certain cases, parents and students are notified by the school district in advance of compliance with the court order or the subpoena (*Ragusa v. Malverne UFSD*, 549 F.Supp.2d 288 (E.D.N.Y. 2008); 20 USC § 1232g(b)(2)(B); 34 CFR § 99.31(a)(9)(i)).

13:23. Can school districts transfer student records to another school without prior consent from a parent or eligible student?

Yes, but only to officials of another school where a student seeks or intends to enroll, and when the student is already enrolled in another school, if such records relate to the student's enrollment at the new school and in accordance with certain conditions (20 USC § 1232g(b)(1)(B); 34 CFR § 99.31(a)(2); see also 34 CFR § 99.34).

13:24. What is directory information and may school districts disclose such information without prior parental consent?

Directory information refers to, for example, student names and addresses, telephone numbers and e-mail addresses. It also includes student photographs, date and place of birth, grade level, dates of attendance, participation in officially recognized activities and sports, and, enrollment status. Districts may disclose such information without prior consent if they give notice of the categories of information so designated, and give parents or eligible students a reasonable period of time to inform the district that such information should not be released without their consent (20 USC § 1232g(a)(5)(A), (B); 34 CFR § 99.3).

School districts also may adopt policies that restrict disclosure of directory information to specific parties, for specific purposes or both (34 CFR § 99.37(d)). For example, districts could limit the disclosure of directory information to school publications such as the yearbook and graduation programs (U.S. Department of Education, *Revised FERPA Regulations: An Overview for SEAS and LEAS* (Dec. 2011), at: http://www2.ed.gov/policy/gen/guid/fpco/pdf/sealea_overview.pdf).

But even if a district does not otherwise release directory information, if it receives federal funds under the Elementary and Secondary Education Act of 1965, it must provide to post-secondary schools and the military, upon request, the names, addresses, and telephone numbers of all high school students, unless the parents of a student has submitted a prior consent request. It also must provide military recruiters the same access to students that it generally provides to post-secondary schools or prospective employees (20 USC § 7908).

State law prohibits the use of student social security numbers for public listing of grades, class rosters, or other lists provided to teachers, identification cards, student directories, or similar listings, except as otherwise specifically authorized or required by law (§ 2–b).

The Family Educational Rights and Privacy Act (FERPA) prohibits the release of a student's social security number as directory information. Student ID numbers can be disclosed as directory information only if they qualify as electronic identifiers (34 CFR § 99.3) used to deliver certain student services such as access to library resources. However, parents may not prevent the release of their child's name, identifier or institutional e-mail address in a class in which their child is enrolled, or from wearing a student identification badge that contains an identification number that has been properly labeled as directory information (34 CFR § 99.37(c)).

Under the McKinney-Vento Act, as reauthorized under Every Student Succeeds Act, information regarding a homeless student's living situation shall be treated as a student education record and may not be considered directory information (§ 9102(g)(3)(G)). As a result, information about a student's living situation must be provided the same protections as other non-directory, personally identifiable information contained in student education records under FERPA (http://www2.ed.gov/policy/elsec/leg/essa/160240ehcyguidance072716.pdf).

13:25. Must school districts take steps to prevent inadvertent unauthorized disclosure of student records?

Yes. School districts must use reasonable methods to identify and authenticate the identity of parents, students, school officials, and other parties to whom it discloses education records (34 CFR § 99.31(c)). Districts without physical or technological controls over access to records must ensure there is a policy for controlling access that is effective and remains in compliance with the legitimate educational interests requirement of the Family Educational Rights and Privacy Act (34 CFR § 99.31(a)(1)(ii)).

14. School Board Meetings

Editor's Note: For more information on the requirements of the Open Meetings Law see School District Obligations Under the Open Meetings Law: Fact and Fiction *available from the New York State School Boards Association website at: http://bit.ly/2b1dR4D. Additional information on both the Open Meetings Law and the Freedom of Information Law is available from the Committee on Open Government at One Commerce Plaza, 99 Washington Avenue, Suite 650, Albany, N.Y., 12231; website at: http://www.dos.ny.gov/coog/, by email at: coog@dos.ny.gov, or telephone: 518-474-2518.*

In General

14:1. What types of meetings are conducted by school boards?

School board meetings fall into the following categories:

- The annual *organizational* or *reorganizational* meeting, which is when the school board elects and appoints its officers and committees for the coming year, and board members take or renew their oaths of office. In most school districts, this meeting must be held each year in July. For specific dates and times (where applicable) that school districts must hold their annual organizational meeting, see **14:16**.
- *Regular* board meetings, which are the regularly scheduled business meetings held throughout the year (see **14:6**).
- *Special* board meetings, which are not regularly scheduled and may be called by any member of the board to address a particular item or items (see **14:7**).

"Board" meetings are distinct from school "district" meetings, such as the annual district meeting, at which a school board presents its annual budget to voters in the district and at which school board elections are held, or special district meetings, called for either by the voters or by the school board for district residents to vote on specific issues and propositions. See **chapter 15** for more information on school district meetings.

14:2. What are the requirements for holding a school board meeting?

There must be a quorum of the board and public notice of the time and place of the meeting (see **14:3-4, 14:8, 14:10-11**).

14:3. What constitutes a quorum of a school board?

A *quorum* is a simple majority (more than half) of the total number of board members (Gen. Constr. Law § 41). A quorum is required for the board to conduct any business. A majority of the entire board, not simply of those present, is required for the board to take any official action (*Id.;* Opn. of Counsel #70, 1 Ed Dept Rep 770 (1952); see also *Appeal of Greenwald*, 31 Ed Dept Rep 12 (1991)). For example, if a board has five members and three are present at a meeting, all three would have to vote in favor of a resolution for it to pass; a two–to–one vote would not be sufficient.

Generally, a school board may not adopt a policy requiring affirmative votes by more than a majority of the whole number of the board to take official action because neither the Education Law nor the General Construction Law authorizes a board to adopt requirements in excess of those already provided by statute (*Application of Grinnell*, 37 Ed Dept Rep 504 (1998); *Matter of Miller*, 17 Ed Dept Rep 275 (1978); but see *Appeal of Volpe*, 25 Ed Dept Rep 398 (1986)).

14:4. Must school districts publish notice of school board meetings?

Yes. The Education Law does not require notice of board meetings to be published (*Matter of Thomas*, 10 Ed Dept Rep 108 (1971)). However, under the Open Meetings Law, if the meeting is scheduled at least one week in advance, school boards must give public notice stating the time and place of the meeting to the news media and conspicuously post the notice in one or more designated public locations at least 72 hours before the meeting (Pub. Off. Law § 104(1)). If a school board livestreams its meetings on the internet then the web address to view the livestream must be included in the meeting notice (Pub. Off. Law § 104(5)).

If the meeting is scheduled less than a week in advance, public notice of the time and place must be given to the news media "to the extent practicable" and posted conspicuously a reasonable time before the meeting (Pub. Off. Law § 104(2); *Previdi v. Hirsch*, 138 Misc.2d 436 (Sup. Ct. Westchester Cnty. 1988)).

Any school district that has the ability to do so must also post notice of the time and place of board meetings on its website (Pub. Off. Law § 104(6); see *Rivers v. Young*, 26 Misc.3d 946 (Sup. Ct. Westchester Cnty. 2009)).

Although school boards are required to provide notice of when and where their meetings will take place, such notice does not have to include the matters to be discussed (*Appeal of Allen & Wong*, 40 Ed Dept Rep 372 (2000); *Matter of the CSD No. 1 of the Towns of Neversink, Fallsburgh & Liberty*, 10 Ed Dept Rep 203 (1971)).

However, school boards must make any agency records and proposed resolutions, rules, regulations, policies or amendments thereto that are scheduled for discussion at a board meeting available upon request of any member of the public, to the extent practicable, prior to or at the meeting where the records will be discussed. The board may charge a reasonable fee for copies of records (see **13:15**). The records must also be posted on the district's website to the extent practicable prior to the meeting (Pub. Off. Law § 103(e); see also NYS Department of State, Committee on Open Government, *Questions and Answers Regarding Records Discussed at Open Meetings* (Feb. 2012), at: http://www.dos.ny.gov/coog/QA-2-12.html).

14:5. Must school board meetings be held within the school district limits?

No (see Pub. Off. Law § 102(1); *Matter of Petersen v. Incorp. Vill. of Saltaire*, 77 A.D.3d 954 (2d Dep't 2010)). However, meeting in a location intended to avoid the public and news media may be deemed a violation of the Open Meetings Law, which may result in the annulment of any action taken at the meeting. A board would be able to reconsider the matter at a later meeting conducted in compliance with the Open Meetings Law (see Pub. Off. Law §§ 103, 107(1)).

Even when meetings are held within school district limits, any meeting that must be open to the public pursuant to the Open Meetings Law (see **14:21-25**) must be held at an appropriate facility that can adequately accommodate members of the public that would want to attend (Pub. Off. Law § 103(d)).

Regular and Special Board Meetings

14:6. Are school boards required to hold a certain number of regular meetings?

Yes. The Education Law requires school boards to meet at least once each quarter of the year (§ 1708(1)). Most boards, however, meet at least once a month. In city school districts, monthly meetings are required

(§§ 2504(2), 2563(2)), 2590–b(1)(b), 2590–e(14)), except that in New York City, community district educational councils also must meet with the community superintendent, each building principal and parent and parent–teacher associations and their elected officers as set forth in this law (§ 2590-d(2)(b)). Like in other city school districts, the New York city board must meet at least once per month with at least one regular public meeting in each borough per year (§ 2590-b(1)(b)).

14:7. Who may call a special meeting of the school board?

Any school board member has the authority to call a special meeting of the board (see *Matter of Felicio*, 19 Ed Dept Rep 414 (1980)), as long as notice of the meeting is given to the other board members at least 24 hours in advance (§ 1606(3); see also *Appeal of Campbell*, 50 Ed Dept Rep, Dec. No. 16,246 (2011); *Application of Bean*, 42 Ed Dept Rep 171 (2002)). A school board member may call a special board meeting without the prior knowledge and consent of the board president (*Appeal of Campbell*). The notice provided normally states the purpose of the meeting, although there is no specific requirement that it do so.

A majority of the board cannot decide to hold a meeting and dispense with providing notice to the remaining members. The law requires good faith efforts to give actual notice of a special or emergency meeting to each board member. Failure to do so may invalidate any action taken at the meeting (see *Matter of Colasuonno*, 22 Ed Dept Rep 215 (1982)).

However, if it is determined that one board member did not receive notice, the action taken may be sustained if the member signs an affidavit waiving notice (*Matter of Bd. of Educ. of UFSD No. 1 of the Town of Hume*, 29 State Dep't Rep. 624 (1923)). It is advisable, therefore, in situations where notice cannot be given within 24 hours, that each board member sign a waiver of notice to be entered in the minutes.

Although special meetings are ordinarily held to consider a single item of business, other items of business may be included on the agenda for that meeting by consent of the board members present. There is no requirement that the notice of a special board meeting contain any notice of a proposed agenda (*Matter of the CSD No. 1 of the Towns of Neversink, Fallsburgh & Liberty*, 10 Ed Dept Rep 203 (1971)).

Care should be taken, however, to see that the special board meeting does not usurp the place of regularly scheduled board meetings for the consideration of regular school district business.

14:8. What type of notice must school board members receive prior to a school board meeting?

School board members must receive at least 24 hours notice of any board meeting (§ 1606(3); see also *Appeal of Campbell*, 50 Ed Dept Rep, Dec. No. 16,246 (2011); *Application of Bean*, 42 Ed Dept Rep 171 (2000)). A board majority may not dispense with notice of a board meeting to other board members, but individual board members may waive this 24–hour notice requirement in case of an emergency (*Matter of Colasuonno*, 22 Ed Dept Rep 215 (1982); *Matter of Carlson*, 11 Ed Dept Rep 284 (1972)). See also **14:7**.

14:9. Is an agenda necessary for a board meeting?

No. Good business practice may indicate that an agenda of the regular session is in order. However, an agenda is not specifically required for either regular meetings or executive sessions (*Matter of Exmoor House, LLC v. Vill. of Millbrook Planning Bd.*, 82 A.D.3d 763 (2d Dep't 2011)). Moreover, the procedure to be followed at school board meetings is left to the policies adopted by the board (*Matter of Kramer*, 72 State Dep't Rep. 114 (1951); but see § 2590–c(4) regarding the application of New York City board of education policies to the preparation of an agenda for meetings of community district education councils).

14:10. Can school board members vote by telephone or e-mail?

No. According to one state appellate court, voting by phone violates the Open Meetings Law. Any such vote also could result in the nullification of board action that depended on the vote cast by phone for its formal adoption (see *Town of Eastchester v. N. Y. State Bd. of Real Prop. Servs.*, 23 A.D.3d 484 (2d Dep't 2005)). According to that same court, if the Legislature wanted to allow teleconferencing as a valid means for holding a public meeting, it would have done so when it amended the law to add the provisions that allow the use of videoconferencing (*City of White Plains v. N. Y. State Bd. of Real Prop. Servs.*, 18 A.D.3d 549 (2d Dep't 2005); see **14:11**).

In addition, the Director of the Committee on Open Government has repeatedly indicated that a series of communications between individual members or telephone calls among members that result in a collective decision, a meeting held by means of a telephone conference, or a vote taken by phone or mail would be inconsistent with the Open Meetings Law. (NYS Department of State, Committee on Open Government, OML-AO-05420 (Sept. 4, 2014), see also OML-AO-4306 (Dec. 18, 2006), OML–AO–3732 (Dec. 29, 2003)). However, a vote may be cast through the use of videoconferencing if specific criteria are met. See **14:11**.

14:11. Can school board members vote via videoconference?

Yes. The Public Officer's Law expressly allows any public body, including a school board, to meet via videoconferencing. Thus, a school board may properly conduct a meeting and vote on public matters through the use of videoconferencing. In such an instance, the public notice of the meeting must indicate that videoconferencing will be used, specify the location(s) for the meeting, and state that the public may attend at any of the locations (Pub. Off. Law §§ 102, 103, and 104).

14:12. Is the president or presiding officer of the school board entitled to vote at board meetings?

Yes. A school board member does not lose a vote while serving as presiding officer. His or her vote is expected on every matter and should not be reserved only for tie votes (Opn. of Counsel No. 70, 1 Ed Dept Rep 770 (1952)).

14:13. May a school board rescind action previously taken at a board meeting?

Generally, the courts have held that a school board may rescind an action it has taken at any time before such action becomes final. For example, the New York Court of Appeals has held that a board may not be barred from reconsidering a prior decision not to dismiss a probationary employee. Such a dismissal need not be for cause, and it would be illogical not to allow a board to reconsider its decision not to terminate a probationary employee based, for example, on changing needs and requirements of the district (*Venes v. Community Sch. Bd.*, 43 N.Y.2d 520 (1978)).

14:14. May school board members prevent action on a matter by refusing to vote on a motion?

If a majority of the school board votes in favor of a motion, it is approved, whether the remaining members of the board vote against it, abstain, or otherwise refuse to vote (see **14:3**).

When a motion is voted on, board members are expected to be counted and must be reported in the minutes either as voting for or against each motion, or as having abstained from voting (Pub. Off. Law § 87(3)(a)).

In one case, the commissioner of education ruled that school board members may not abstain from voting on whether to grant tenure to a school employee based upon philosophical objections to the state's tenure system. Board members who abstain from voting on tenure recommendations on that basis face possible removal from office for dereliction of duty (*Appeal of Craft & Dworkin*, 36 Ed Dept Rep 314 (1997); see also *Appeal of Hoefer*, 45 Ed Dept Rep 66 (2005) (voting against every tenure recommendation is a dereliction of duty); see **34:39**).

Organizational Meeting

14:15. What is the annual school board reorganizational meeting?

The annual school board *reorganizational or organizational meeting* is the school board's meeting held after the annual election of school board members. Here, the organization of the board is established, school board officers are elected, and other district officers are appointed for the upcoming year. In addition, at this meeting, boards often appoint other personnel, such as the internal auditor, school attorney, records access officer, and records management officer, and designate depositories for district funds and newspapers for required notices (§§ 1701, 2502(9)(o); see **8:1-3, 8:9-14**).

In city school districts with a population less than 125,000 inhabitants, the school board must also set the dates and times for its regular school board meetings, which are required to occur at least monthly (§ 2504(2)).

The school board's annual reorganizational meeting is different and apart from the annual district meeting, at which district voters vote on the district's annual budget and elect school board members (see **15:1**).

14:16. Is there a specific time set by law for the annual school board reorganizational meeting?

Yes. In union free and central school districts, the reorganizational meeting must be held on the first Tuesday in July. If that day is a legal holiday, then the meeting must be held on the first Wednesday in July (§ 1707(1)). Alternatively, a school board in these districts may, by resolution, decide to hold the annual reorganizational meeting at any time during the first 15 days in July (§ 1707(2)).

The annual reorganizational meeting of central high school districts in Nassau County must be held on the second Tuesday in July (§ 1904).

In city school districts with less than 125,000 inhabitants, the reorganizational meeting must be held during the first week in July, unless otherwise specified by law (§§ 2504(1), 2502(9)(o), 2502(9-a)(o)).

In large city school districts, the reorganizational meeting occurs on the second Tuesday in May, except as otherwise specified by law (§§ 2563(1), 2553(9)(f), 2553(10)(o)). In New York City, the annual meeting shall be held on the first Tuesday in July (§ 2563(1)).

14:17. Which school board officers are chosen at the annual reorganizational meeting?

A school board is required by law to elect a president and may, at its discretion, elect a vice president (§§ 1701, 2504(1)).

The board may exercise fairly broad discretion in determining its internal organization, officers, and staff. It may appoint staff assistants and a school attorney, designate board and/or advisory committees to assist in a wide variety of functions, and employ consultants as desired for the efficient management of its work.

14:18. May a school board vest in a vice president all the powers of the president of the board in the event of the president's absence or disability?

Yes. Section 1701 of the Education Law authorizes a school board to elect one of its members as vice president with the power to exercise the duties of the president in case of his or her absence or disability.

Furthermore, if there is a vacancy in the office of president, the vice president shall act as president until a new president is elected.

14:19. What happens when there is a vacancy in the office of president?

When there is a vacancy in the office of president, the vice president shall act as president until a new president is elected (§ 1701).

14:20. May a school board govern through the appointment of standing committees?

No. While there is no state law that either prohibits or requires standing committees, board committees that constitute less than a quorum of the entire board cannot take official action for the board (Gen. Constr. Law § 41; see *Appeal of Greenwald*, 31 Ed Dept Rep 12 (1991); see also **5:19**).

However, a school board may appoint advisory committees to assist in addressing specific problems or issues. Those asked to serve on these committees should understand that their role is advisory and that the final decision on all issues considered rests ultimately with the board.

Certain advisory committees are required by law or commissioner's regulations, and their composition and duties are prescribed therein. For example, the Education Law requires visitation committees to visit every school under the board's jurisdiction at least once annually (§ 1708(2)). The commissioner's regulations require each school board to establish an acquired immune deficiency syndrome (AIDS) advisory council to advise the board concerning the content, implementation, and evaluation of an AIDS instruction program (8 NYCRR § 135.3(b)(2), (c)(2)(i)).

Basic Open Meetings Law Requirements

14:21. Are school board meetings open to the public?

Yes. Because school boards are public bodies, the Open Meetings Law requires school board meetings where school district business will be discussed to be open to the public (Pub. Off. Law § 103; see also Educ. Law § 1708(3)). The public may be excluded only from properly convened executive sessions of the board and other meetings exempted under the law (Pub. Off. Law §§ 105(2), 108; Educ. Law § 1708(3); see **14:22, 14:27-29**).

Public business includes not only binding votes of the board, but also any activity that is preliminary to such a vote or involves consideration of a matter that could be the subject of board action (Pub. Off. Law § 102; *Zehner v. Bd. of Educ. of Jordan-Elbridge CSD*, 29 Misc.3d 1206(A) (Sup. Ct. Onondaga Cnty. 2010), *aff'd* 91 A.D.3d 1349 (4th Dep't 2012); *Goodson Todman Enters., Ltd. v. Kingston Common Council*, 153 A.D.2d 103 (3d Dep't 1990); but see *Hill v. Planning Bd. of Amherst*, 140 A.D.2d 967 (4th Dep't 1988)).

A school board's authority to adopt rules and regulations for the maintenance of public order on school property does not give a board the right to automatically exclude members of the public from attending a board meeting (*Matter of Goetschius v. Bd. of Educ. of Greenburgh 11 UFSD*, 244 A.D.2d 552 (2d Dep't 1997)). But a school board's use of a metal detector as a security measure at the entrance to public meetings does not necessarily constitute a violation of the Open Meetings Law (*Matter of Goetschius v. Bd. of Educ. of Greenburgh 11 UFSD,* 281 A.D.2d 416 (2d Dep't 2001)).

In addition, any meeting that must be open to the public pursuant to the Open Meetings Law must be held at an appropriate facility that can adequately accommodate members of the public who would want to attend (Pub. Off. Law § 103(d); see also **14:22-25**).

14:22. Are there any types of meeting not covered by the Open Meetings Law?

Yes. The Open Meetings Law exempts the following types of meetings:

- "judicial or quasi–judicial proceeding" and
- "any matter made confidential by federal or state law" (Pub. Off. Law § 108(3)).

A meeting where a school board reviews the transcript and evidence presented at a student disciplinary meeting when parents appeal their child's suspension would be considered a quasi–judicial proceeding. However, a school board vote to uphold or modify the suspension must take place in open session at a meeting conducted under the Open Meetings Law (see *Cheevers v. Town of Union,* unreported (Sup. Ct. Broome Cnty. Sept. 3, 1998)).

An example of an exempt meeting regarding a matter made confidential by a federal law is a meeting that would involve a discussion of student records. A federal law known as the Family Educational Rights and Privacy Act prohibits school officials from divulging, without parental consent, education records that are specifically identifiable to a particular student or students (20 USC § 1232g; see **13:10**). Therefore, a board may meet in private with parents who wish to discuss concerns that require presentation of private student records (NYS Department of State, Committee on Open Government, OML-AO-3863 (Sept. 3, 2004)).

An example of an exempt meeting regarding a matter made confidential by state law is a meeting between a school board and the board's attorney that is protected by attorney–client privilege pursuant to the New York's Civil Practice Law and Rules (C.P.L.R. § 4503; for a review of the nature and scope of the privilege itself, see *Appeal of Goldin*, 40 Ed Dept Rep 628 (2001)). However, boards should be mindful of times when the attorney-client privilege may be waived. For example, in a case where a town planning board allowed additional people into executive session when the attorney was present and providing legal advice, the board attempted to assert privilege and the court found the privilege waived. The court held that the presence of additional individuals "eliminated any reasonable expectation of confidentiality, effectively waiving any [attorney-client] privilege" (*Ballard v. N.Y. Safety Track LLC,* 126 A.D.3d 1073 (3d Dep't 2015)).

14:23. Are work sessions and planning meetings of the school board open to the public?

Yes. School board work sessions and planning meetings are deemed a school board meeting just the same as any regular or special board meeting. Pursuant to the Open Meetings Law, any meeting of at least a quorum of a public body in which public business is to be conducted must be open to the public unless it is a properly convened executive session or otherwise exempted under the law. This rule applies even if the meeting is held only for the purpose of informal discussions, with no formal vote or action taken (Pub. Off. Law §§ 102(1), 103(a), 108; *Goodson Todman Enters., Ltd., v. Kingston Common Council*, 153 A.D.2d 103 (3d Dep't 1990); see also **14:21**).

14:24. Are board committee meetings open to the public?

Meetings of a committee or subcommittee consisting solely of board members that discuss or conduct public business are subject to the Open Meetings Law (Pub. Off. Law § 102; NYS Department of State, Committee on Open Government, OML–AO–4158 (Mar. 15, 2006), OML-AO-4057 (Oct. 19, 2005); see *Syracuse United Neighbors v. City of Syracuse*, 80 A.D.2d 984 (4th Dep't 1981), *appeal dismissed*, 55 N.Y.2d 995 (1982)). In addition, according to the Committee on Open Government, if a majority of a committee consisting solely of board members meets and is joined by other board members "at the same table to discuss school district business," the committee meeting then becomes a meeting of the board if those present constitute a quorum of the board (OML-AO-4057). That would not be the case if the additional board members attended the committee meeting only as observers (*Id.*; see also OML-AO-3329 (June 26, 2001)). Additionally, meetings of a committee that consists of school board members and an equal or lesser number of district employees, are subject to the Open Meetings Law (OML-AO-5068 (Mar. 18, 2011)).

On the other hand, meetings of board advisory committees, which do not consist exclusively of board members, are created solely to advise and make recommendations to the board, without any power to take final action, generally are not subject to the requirements of the Open Meetings Law (see *Jae v. Bd. of Educ. of Pelham UFSD*, 22 A.D.3d 581 (2d Dep't 2005); *Goodson Todman Enters., Ltd. v. Town Bd. of Milan*, 151 A.D.2d 642 (2d Dep't 1989); *Poughkeepsie Newspapers v. Mayor's Intergovernmental Task Force*, 145 A.D.2d 65 (2d Dep't 1989); *Koubek v. Cnty. of Nassau*, 2012 U.S. Dist. LEXIS 46385 (E.D.N.Y. Mar. 28, 2012)). An exception would apply if the core membership of the advisory group consists of board members (OML-AO-4158).

14:25. Are shared-decision-making committee meetings open to the public?

According to the Committee on Open Government, district-wide shared-decision-making committees are subject to the Open Meetings Law because they perform a governmental function to the extent that school boards may not adopt a shared-decision-making plan without their collaboration and participation (NYS Department of State, Committee on Open Government, OML-AO-3329 (June 26, 2001), OML-AO-2456 (Jan. 31, 1995)).

On the other hand, whether school-based-shared-decision-making committees are subject to the Open Meetings Law depends on their responsibilities (OML-AO-3329). That would be the case if a district's shared-decision-making plan provides them with decision-making authority (*Id.*; OML-AO-3265 (Jan. 17, 2001)). It also would be the case if a school-based-shared-decision-making committee has authority to make recommendations and the school board must consider its recommendations before taking action, even when the board does not have to follow its recommendations (OML-AO-3329).

14:26. What penalties may be assessed against a school board that violates the Open Meetings Law?

Courts have the power to declare void, in whole or in part, any action taken in violation of the Open Meetings Law without prejudice, thus allowing for reconsideration of the invalidated action in compliance with legal requirements (Pub. Off. Law § 107(1); *Gernatt Asphalt Prods. v. Town of Sardinia*, 87 N.Y.2d 668 (1996); *Matter of MCI Telecomm. Corp. v. Pub. Serv. Comm'n of the State of N.Y.*, 231 A.D.2d 284 (3d Dep't 1997)). However, in order to invalidate action that already has been taken by a school board, the courts have held that a complaint alleging a violation of the Open Meetings Law must demonstrate the complainant was prejudiced by the board's failure to comply with the law (*Smithtown v. Illion Hous. Auth.*, 130 A.D.2d 965 (4th Dep't), *aff'd,* 72 N.Y.2d 1034 (1988); *Matter of Inner–City Press/Community on the Move v. N. Y. State Banking Bd.*, 170 Misc.2d 684 (Sup. Ct. New York Cnty. 1996)). In one case, a court invalidated a school board's appeal from an adverse decision by the commissioner of education because the board failed to take a formal vote at a public meeting to approve the litigation (*Gersen v. Mills*, 290 A.D.2d 839 (3d Dep't 2002)).

Moreover, courts may, in their discretion, award reasonable attorneys' fees to a party who sues a school district for a violation of the Open Meetings Law and prevails (Pub. Off. Law § 107(2); see also *Matter of Gordon v. Village of Monticello*, 87 N.Y.2d 124 (1995); *Zehner v. Bd. of Educ. of Jordan-Elbridge CSD*, 91 A.D.3d 1349 (4th Dep't 2012); *Matter of Orange Cnty. Pubs. Div. of Ottawa Newspapers Inc. v. Cnty. of Orange*, 120 A.D.2d 596 (2d Dep't 1986)). However, they must award such fees upon a finding that a vote was taken in material violation of the Open Meetings Law, or that substantial deliberations related to the vote were had in private prior to the vote unless it was reasonable for the school board to believe a closed session was permissible (Pub. Off. Law § 107(2)).

In addition, a court could require that members of a school board found to have acted in violation of the Open Meetings Law participate in training conducted by staff of the Committee on Open Government (Pub. Off. Law § 107(1); *Zehner v. Bd. of Educ. of Jordan-Elbridge CSD* (Sup. Ct. Onondaga Cnty. 2011)).

Executive Sessions

14:27. What is an executive session?

An executive session is a portion of the school board meeting that is not open to the public. It can take place only upon a majority vote of the total membership of the board taken at an open meeting (Pub. Off. Law § 105(1)).

Executive sessions are permitted only for the purpose of discussing one or more of the following subjects:

- Matters that will imperil the public safety if disclosed.
- Any matter that may disclose the identity of a law enforcement agent or informer.
- Information relating to current or future investigation or prosecution of a criminal offense that would imperil effective law enforcement if disclosed.
- Proposed, pending, or current litigation.
- Collective negotiations pursuant to article 14 of the Civil Service Law.
- The medical, financial, credit, or employment history of a particular person or corporation, or matters leading to the appointment, employment, promotion, demotion, discipline, suspension, dismissal, or removal of a particular person or corporation.
- The preparation, grading, or administration of exams.
- The proposed acquisition, sale, or lease of real property or the proposed acquisition, sale, or exchange of securities, but only when publicity would substantially affect the value of these things (Pub. Off. Law § 105(a)–(h)).

The motion to go into executive session should specify the subject or subjects to be discussed (*Ballard v. N. Y. Safety Track LLC*, 126 A.D.3d 1073 (3d Dep't 2015); see also NYS Department of State, Committee on Open Government, OML-AO-2748 (Apr. 22, 1997)). It is insufficient to recite verbatim the statutory language (*Zehner v. Bd. of Educ. of Jordan-Elbridge CSD*, 91 A.D.3d 1349 (4th Dep't 2012); *Gordon v. Village of Monticello*, 207 A.D.2d 55 (3d Dep't 1994), *rev'd on other grounds*, 87 N.Y.2d 124 (1995)).

14:28. Can school boards take formal action in an executive session?

With certain limited exceptions, no official action can be taken on issues discussed in executive session without first returning to open session (see § 1708; *Zehner v. Bd. of Educ. of Jordan-Elbridge CSD*, 91 A.D.3d 1349 (4th Dep't 2012)); *Matter of Crapster*, 22 Ed Dept Rep 29 (1982)).

An exception includes voting on charges against a tenured teacher (§§ 1708(3), 3020–a(2); *Sanna v. Lindenhurst Bd. of Educ.*, 85 A.D.2d 157 (2d Dep't), *aff'd*, 58 N.Y.2d 626 (1982); *United Teachers of Northport v. Northport UFSD*, 50 A.D.2d 897 (2d Dep't 1975); *Formal Opn. of Counsel No. 239*, 16 Ed Dept Rep 457 (1976)).

No public body, including a school board, may vote to appropriate money during an executive session (Pub. Off. Law § 105(1)).

14:29. Who is entitled to attend executive sessions?

All members of the school board and "any other persons authorized by" the board may attend executive sessions (Pub. Off. Law § 105(2); see also Educ. Law § 1708(3)). However, it should be noted that in both large and small city school districts, the superintendent possesses the power "to have a seat on the school board and the right to speak on all matters before the board, but not to vote" (§§ 2508(1), 2566(1)). In addition, if a board has a student board member, that student may not attend executive sessions (§§ 1702(3)(b), 1804(12)(b), 1901(2)(b), 2502(10)(b)).

Any guests which a board may invite into executive session do not need to be identified either in the motion to enter into executive session or in any minutes that may be taken (*Jae v. Bd. of Educ. of Pelham UFSD,* 22 A.D.3d 581 (2d Dep't 2005)). Nonetheless, according to the Committee on Open Government, disputes over the attendance of a person other than a board member at executive session could be resolved by voting on a motion to permit or reject the attendance of the non-member (NYS Department of State, Committee on Open Government, OML-AO-4854 (Jan. 25, 2010)).

14:30. Do confidentiality rules apply to matters properly discussed in executive session?

Yes. As a result, it is important that a school board exercise discretion in deciding whom to invite into executive session. In one case, the commissioner of education ruled that the attendance at an executive session of a former school board member, who was awaiting the results of an appeal of the election he lost, was in conflict with statutory and regulatory provisions providing for the confidentiality of personnel and student records (*Appeal of Whalen*, 34 Ed Dept Rep 282 (1994)).

Moreover, board members themselves also must be careful to maintain confidential information they acquire in executive session (*Application of the Bd. of Educ. of the Elmont UFSD*, 48 Ed Dept Rep 29 (2008); *Appeal of Nett,* 45 Ed Dept Rep 259 (2005); see Gen. Mun. Law § 805–a(1)(b); see also Opn. Att'y Gen. I 2000–2; Family Educational Rights and Privacy Act (20 USC § 1232g)). Disclosure of such information would subject a school board member to removal from the board (*Appeal of Nett*; see **6:41**).

For more information regarding attorney-client confidentiality, see **14:22**.

Public Participation

14:31. Does the public have a right to speak at school board meetings?

Although school board meetings must be open to the public (§ 1708(3); Pub. Off. Law § 103; see also **14:21**), there is no requirement that school boards allow members of the public to speak at school board meetings (*Appeal of Kushner*, 49 Ed Dept Rep 263 (2010)), except in New York City, where community district educational councils must hold monthly meetings at which the public must be allowed to speak (§ 2590–e(14)). However, the commissioner of education encourages school boards, whenever possible, to allow citizens to speak on matters under consideration (*Appeal of Wittneben*, 31 Ed Dept Rep 375 (1992)). Boards can limit the time for a person to speak (see *Matter of Kramer*, 72 State Dep't Rep. 114 (1951)).

The commissioner has ruled that a school board need not permit nonresidents to speak at public board meetings, even where the board has a policy of permitting residents to speak (*Matter of Martin*, 32 Ed Dept Rep 381 (1992)). The state Committee on Open Government concurs with the commissioner that school boards are not required to allow members of the public to speak at board meetings in the first place, but cautions that, under the Open Meetings Law, if a school board permits public participation, it may not discriminate between residents and nonresidents (NYS Department of State, Committee on Open Government, OML-AO-4141 (Feb. 24, 2006)).

Even if members of the public are not permitted to speak, any meeting that must be open to the public pursuant to the Open Meetings Law (see **14:21-25**) must be held at an appropriate facility that can adequately accommodate members of the public that would want to attend (Pub. Off. Law § 103(d)).

14:32. Does the public have a right to speak about any topic at school board meetings?

No. School boards, for example, may justifiably restrict the ability of members of the public speaking at their meetings to offer public commentary on matters involving privacy issues otherwise protected by law. That would be the case, for example, when a member of the public wants to engage in a discussion that potentially may disclose information about particular students, even when the disclosure would be made by someone other than a school official (NYS Department of State, Committee on Open Government, OML-AO-3405 (Feb. 8, 2002)). Instead, the member of the public wishing to discuss such a matter may meet with the board in private under the exemption to the Open Meetings Law that applies to matters made confidential by law (*Id.*; see **14:22**).

In addition, according to one federal district court in New York, school board meetings are a limited public forum and school boards may preclude discussion of a particular topic at board meetings. Any such exclusion must be reasonable and viewpoint neutral. That was the case, for example, where a school board precluded discussion on a girl's soccer issue to avoid short changing those not interested in soccer, particularly since the topic had been discussed at a prior board meeting and the board was aware of opinions on the issue (*Curley v. Philo*, 2009 U.S. Dist. LEXIS 59980 (N.D.N.Y July 14, 2009)).

Public School Governance

14:33. Do people attending a public school board meeting have the right to audio- or videotape the meeting?

Yes. Pursuant to the Open Meetings Law, all school board meetings that are open to the public (see **14:21-25**), are open to being photographed, broadcast, webcast, or otherwise recorded and/or transmitted by audio or video means, including the transmission of signals by cable (Pub. Off. Law § 103(d)). However, school boards may adopt rules regarding such activities to ensure the orderly conduct of meetings, consistent with recommendations of the Committee on Open Government (Pub. Off. Law § 103(2); see NYS Department of State, Committee on Open Government, *Model Rules Public Access to Meetings* at: http://www.dos.ny.gov/coog/modelregs_photo_record_broadcast.html; see **14:34**).

14:34. What rules apply to the recording and broadcasting school board meetings by people who attend such meetings?

The Open Meetings Law allows school boards to adopt rules regarding the public's ability to photograph, broadcast, webcast, audio- or videotape, or otherwise record school board meetings. However, such rules must be consistent with the recommendations of the Committee on Open Government, available at: http://www.dos.ny.gov/coog/modelregs_photo_record_broadcast.html. Furthermore, they must be conspicuously posted during board meetings and written copies made available upon request to those attending (Pub. Off. Law § 103(d)).

Prior to codification of the public's right to record and broadcast school board meetings, various court decisions, and the Committee on Open Government itself, had established general rules that are still relevant. For example, school boards were required to allow the use of unobtrusive, hand-held tape-recording devices at public meetings as long as it caused no public inconvenience, annoyance or alarm, or disturbed the meeting (*Mitchell v. Bd. of Educ. of Garden City UFSD*, 113 A.D.2d 924 (2d Dep't 1985); NYS Department of State, Committee on Open Government, OML-AO-3037 (June 18, 1999)). Similarly, school boards could regulate the use of cameras to prevent a genuine interference with the conduct of a meeting (*Csorny v. Shoreham Wading River CSD*, 305 A.D.2d 83 (2d Dep't 2003); NYS Department of State, Committee on Open Government, OML-AO-1317 (Aug. 26, 1986)), rather than based on school board member objections to appearing on television or fears of publicly airing comments at a meeting (*Csorny v. Shoreham Wading River CSD*).

Minutes

14:35. Must minutes be taken at school board meetings?

Yes. The Open Meetings Law requires that formal minutes of all actions be taken at open meetings (Pub. Off. Law § 106(1)). Similarly, the Education Law requires that school boards in union free school districts keep an accurate record of their proceedings (§ 1721), a requirement which, through the concept of devolution, applies to central, central high school, and city school districts as well (see **5:17**).

Minutes must consist of a record or summary of all motions, proposals, resolutions, and other matters formally voted upon, including the result of any vote (Pub. Off. Law § 106(1)). Bare-bone resolutions do not satisfy this requirement (*Mitzner v. Goshen CSD Bd. of Educ.* (Sup. Ct. Orange Cnty. 1993); NYS Department of State, Committee on Open Government, OML-AO-5208 (Nov. 18, 2011); OML-AO-3472 (June 18, 2002)). In addition, records of votes must include the final vote of each board member on every matter voted on (Pub. Off. Law § 87(3)(a)). Secret ballots are not allowed for any purpose (*Smithson v. Illion Hous. Auth.*, 130 A.D.2d 965 (4th Dep't), *aff'd,* 72 N.Y.2d 1034 (1988)).

There is no requirement that the minutes be a verbatim account of everything said at a meeting (NYS Department of State, Committee on Open Government, OML-AO-4801 (Aug. 25, 2009)).

14:36. Must minutes be taken of executive session?

Not generally because with limited exceptions, school boards are not authorized to take action in executive sessions (see **14:28**). However, where boards have such authority (*Id.*), minutes of an executive session must be taken.

Such minutes need only contain a record of any final determinations, the date, and the vote. They need not contain any matter that is not available to the public under the Freedom of Information Law (see Pub. Off. Law § 106(2); *Plattsburgh Pub'g Co., Div. of Ottoway Newspapers, Inc. v. City of Plattsburgh*, 185 A.D.2d 518 (3d Dep't 1992)).

14:37. Is the public entitled to access the minutes of school board meetings?

Yes. According to the provisions of the Open Meetings Law, minutes of school board meetings must be available to the public within two weeks from the date of the meeting. (Pub. Off. Law § 106(3)). Minutes taken at a properly convened executive session are not available to the public under the Open Meetings Law unless action is taken by a formal vote in the executive session as authorized by law (*Kline & Sons, Inc. v. Cnty. of Hamilton*, 235 A.D.2d 44 (3d Dep't 1997); see **14:27-28, 14:35**). Minutes taken at executive sessions recording actions taken by formal vote of the board must be available to the public within one week (Pub. Off. Law § 106(3)).

Minutes must be made available to the public even if they have not been approved by the board (NYS Department of State, Committee on Open Government, OML-AO-4845 (Dec. 21, 2009); FOIL-AO-14084 (June 18, 2003); FOIL-AO-8543 (Nov. 17, 1994)). The law also requires that the district maintain a record of the final votes of each member of the board (Pub. Off. Law §§ 87(3)(a), 106(1)). These records may not be destroyed (see **13:19**).

15. School District Meetings

The Annual School District Meeting and Election

15:1. What is the annual meeting and election?

Historically, the annual school district meeting was an actual meeting of the residents of a school district, which occurred immediately prior to or simultaneously with the vote on the proposed school district budget for the upcoming school year. However, school districts now must present the proposed budget for the ensuing school year to the voters at a public hearing held seven to 14 days prior to the date of the annual meeting and election. The public hearing replaces the annual meeting as the forum for presentation of the proposed budget to the voters (*Appeal of Hubbard*, 45 Ed Dept Rep 422 (2006); see also **19:16-21**).

Therefore, the only remaining significance of the term "annual meeting" is that the date set by law for holding the annual meeting is the date that the budget vote and school board elections must occur.

15:2. Must a school district hold an annual meeting and election?

Yes, except large city school districts (the Big 5) and special act school districts. The purpose of the annual meeting and election is to allow qualified voters residing in the school district to vote on the school district's budget for the upcoming school year and to elect candidates to fill any vacancies on the school board (Article 41 and Article 53).

For information on the annual meeting of a board of cooperative educational services, see **15:13-15**.

15:3. When is the annual meeting and election held?

Each school district must hold its annual meeting and election on the third Tuesday in May, which constitutes the state-wide day for conducting school district budget votes and annual school board elections. If, at the request of a local school board, the commissioner of education certifies no later than March 1 that the election would conflict with religious observances, the election may be held on the second Tuesday in May (§§ 1804(4), 1906(1), 2002(1), 2022(1), 2601-a(2)). In such an instance, the date would change only for the district making the request. That district must submit to the Office of Educational Management Services at the NYS Education Department a request letter and supporting documentation with sufficient time for processing and issuance of an order allowing the date change (see NYS Education Department, *2011 Voting Date Change* (updated Jan. 2011), at: http://www.p12.nysed.gov/mgtserv/districtclerks/2010StatewideVotingDateChangeUpdate.htm).

Voting on school budgets and board member elections on separate days and/or on a date other than the one set by law is not permitted. However, by specific provision of law, although the Albany City School District holds its annual budget vote on the third Tuesday in May like other school districts, its school board members are elected at a general election the first Tuesday in November conducted by the Albany County Board of Elections (§§ 2502(9)(b), (p), 2602(1)). In addition, school board elections in the Big 5 also take place at different dates and times as specified by law (§ 2553).

15:4. Is there a specific time of day that the annual meeting and election must be held?

Yes. Most school districts must hold their annual meeting and election during at least six consecutive hours after 6:00 a.m., two hours of which must be after 6:00 p.m., as determined by resolution of the trustees or school board (§ 2002(1)).

Small city school districts must hold their annual meeting and election during at least nine consecutive hours, beginning not earlier than 7:00 a.m., two hours of which must be after 6:00 p.m., as established by board resolution (§ 2602(3)).

School districts that are not divided into election districts and conduct their election or vote by a show of hands or voice vote must hold their annual meeting and election at 7:30 p.m., unless the time is changed by a vote at a previous district meeting (§ 2002(1)). In such districts, once the proposed budget has been presented, the meeting may not be adjourned or concluded until the budget has been voted on (*Appeal of Mazzurco*, 6 Ed Dept Rep 101 (1967); see also *Appeal of Kerr*, 76 St. Dep't Rep. 121 (1955)).

15:5. What happens if a district fails to hold its annual meeting and election on the required date?

If this happens, the school board or the district clerk must call a special district meeting to transact the business of the annual meeting, which must be held on the same date specified by law for conducting a school budget revote (see **19:28**). If the school board or district clerk fails to call such a special meeting, then the district superintendent of the board of cooperative educational services or the commissioner of education may order a special district meeting to conduct the business of the annual meeting.

The officers elected at such a special meeting hold their offices only until the next annual meeting, and until their elected successors have been qualified (§ 2005; see **8:7** for qualification of officers).

School District Meetings

15:6. May the annual meeting and election be postponed pending settlement of collective bargaining negotiations?

No. The date for holding the annual meeting and election is fixed by law and may not be altered to await the outcome of contract negotiations (§§ 2002(1), 1804(4), 1906(1), 2022(1), 2601-a(2); see Opn. of Counsel No. 228, 8 Ed Dept Rep 227 (1969)).

In cases where a budget must be presented and voted on before the settlement of contract negotiations, a school board may estimate the amount it will need to meet salary and other obligations under the contract. Once the contract is settled, if insufficient funds are provided for in the budget or if the budget is defeated, then the board may appropriate an additional amount to meet these obligations (see *Matter of New Paltz CSD*, 30 Ed Dept Rep 300 (1991), citing *Matter of Fagan*, 15 Ed Dept Rep 296 (1976)). The board also may issue a budget note during the last nine months of the school year, in an amount not to exceed 5 percent (more with voter approval) of the district's annual budget (Local Fin. Law § 29(3)). If a school district finds itself in this situation it should consult with the school attorney regarding any restrictions the property tax levy cap may have on the district's ability to utilize these options.

However, if the budget is defeated, the total contingency budget, including the additional amount appropriated by the board, is subject to certain caps on contingency budget expenditures (§ 2023; see also **20:4-5**).

15:7. Where is the annual meeting and election held?

The annual meeting and election is held at the school(s) designated by the school board for this purpose. If the district has no school, or if the school is not accessible or adequate, then the annual meeting and election may be held in any place suitable for the occasion (§ 2002(1)).

15:8. Who calls the annual meeting and election to order?

In common school districts, the annual meeting and election is called to order by the sole trustee, the chairperson of the board of trustees, or a person chosen by the trustee or trustees. Once the meeting is called to order, the qualified district voters present at the meeting nominate and elect a qualified voter in attendance to serve as permanent chairperson (§§ 2021(1), 2025(1)).

In union free, central, and small city school districts, a qualified voter appointed by the school board as permanent chairperson declares the polls open and closed at the appropriate time (§§ 2025(2), 2601-a(2)).

As qualified voters, members of the school board are eligible to serve as chairperson (*Appeal of Uciechowski*, 32 Ed Dept Rep 511 (1993)). However, a school board member running for reelection should avoid serving in that capacity to prevent the appearance of impropriety even though such conduct, on its own, would not warrant overturning the election results (*Appeal of O'Brien,* 54 Ed Dept Rep, Dec. No. 16,772 (2015); *Appeal of Bentley & Boll*, 51 Ed Dept Rep, Dec. No. 16,356 (2012)).

15:9. What notice must be given to the public regarding the annual meeting and election?

The district clerk must publish notice of the date, time, and place of the annual meeting and election four times during the seven weeks preceding the date of the annual meeting and election, in two newspapers having general circulation, or one newspaper of general circulation, if there is only one, with the first publication occurring at least 45 days before the date of the annual meeting and election (§§ 2003(1), 2004(1), 2121(4), 2601-a(2)).

A newspaper of general circulation is, with narrow exceptions, one that is published at least weekly; that contains news, editorials, features, advertising or other matter regarded as of current interest; and that is of paid circulation (Gen. Constr. Law § 60).

The fees that newspapers may charge for publishing the notice of annual meeting are set forth in section 8007 of the Civil Practice Law and Rules. A school district may not pay a claim for publication of a notice in a newspaper that does not meet the legal definition of a newspaper of general circulation (Opn. St. Comp. 93-33).

If no newspaper of general circulation is available, or if both newspapers having general circulation in the district refuse to publish the notice at the rates prescribed by law, the notice must be posted in at least 20 of the most public places 45 days before the meeting (§§ 2003(1), 2004(1), 2601-a(2)).

Nothing in the law prohibits districts from also posting signs in public places announcing the date, time and place of the annual election and budget vote, in addition to publication in a newspaper(s) of general circulation (*Appeal of Tillet*, 51 Ed Dept Rep, Dec. No. 16,327 (2012)).

15:10. What must be included in the notice of the annual meeting and election?

The notice must state the date, time, and place of the annual district meeting and election (§§ 2003(1), 2004(1), 2601-a(2)). It also must include the following:

- The date, time, and place of the public hearing on the budget (§§ 1608(2), 1716(2), 2601-a(2)).
- A statement that district residents may obtain a copy of the proposed budget at any district schoolhouse, during designated hours, on each day other than a Saturday, Sunday, or holiday during the 14 days preceding the date of the annual meeting and election and on the day of the election (§§ 1608(2), 1716(2), 2004(6)(d)).
- Notice of any proposed tax, together with a statement specifying both the purpose and the amount of spending for which the tax will be levied, where such tax is proposed to finance:
  (1) an addition to or change of site or purchase of a new site;
  (2) purchase of any new site or structure;
  (3) grading or improving a school site;

(4) purchase of an addition to the site of any schoolhouse;
(5) purchase of lands and buildings for agricultural, athletic, playground, or social center purposes;
(6) construction of any new schoolhouse or the erection of an addition to any schoolhouse already built; and
(7) payment or refund of any outstanding bonded indebtedness (§ 416(3)).

- Where required by statute, the substance of each specific proposition to be voted on, for example, a proposition:
  (1) To levy a tax by installments as a condition prerequisite to the adoption of a bond resolution or capital note resolution where such bonds or capital notes will be issued to finance a specific object or purpose. The notice of the meeting at which such a proposition shall be voted upon must state the estimated maximum cost of each item of such specific object or purpose and the estimated total cost of all the items (§§ 416(2), 2009; see also Local Fin. Law § 41.10). "There is no legal requirement that the notice of the election specify the term of the bonds" (*Appeal of Brousseau*, 39 Ed Dept Rep 397 (1999)), or that the notice or proposition itself include the cost of interest (*Appeal of Herloski,* 50 Ed Dept Rep, Dec. No. 16,089 (2010)).
  (2) To rescind a district vote to raise money or to reduce the amount thereof (§ 416(5)).
  (3) To establish certain reserve funds and/or to make expenditures therefrom (§ 3651(1)(b), (3)).
  (4) To increase or decrease the number of members of the school board (§§ 1703(2), 2502(4)(b); see also *Appeal of Rosenberg*, 31 Ed Dept Rep 398 (1992); *Appeal of Como*, 30 Ed Dept Rep 214 (1990), *petition dismissed, Bd. of Educ., Brentwood UFSD v. Sobol* (Sup. Ct. Albany Cnty. 1991); *Appeal of Swanson*, 29 Ed Dept Rep 503 (1990); *Appeal of Presutti*, 17 Ed Dept Rep 445 (1978)).
  (5) To increase or decrease the term of office (i.e., the number of years served) of board members in small city school districts (§ 2502(4)(b)).
- A statement that qualified voters may apply for absentee ballots at the district clerk's office and that a list of persons to whom absentee ballots have been issued will be available for inspection in the district clerk's office during each of the five days prior to the day of the election, except Sundays (§ 2004(7); cf. §§ 2018-a(6), 2018-b(7), which state that this list need only be available for public inspection in the district clerk's office "during regular office hours until the day of the election").
- The time and place that the board of registration will meet to prepare the register of the school district (where applicable), together with notice that any person who is not already registered, upon proving that he or she is entitled to vote in the district, may have his or her name placed upon the register. In addition, the notice shall state that the register containing the names of qualified voters will be available for inspection in the clerk's office during the hours determined by the district on each of the five days prior to the day of the election, except Sundays (§§ 2004(5), (6)). Additional rules regarding this particular notice apply to small city school districts (§ 2606(5), (6)).

In addition, the notice also must state that petitions for nominating candidates for office of school board member must be filed in the district clerk's office between 9:00 a.m. and 5:00 p.m. no later than 30 days (20 days in small city districts) before the election (§§ 2003(2), 2004(2), 2601-a(2), 2608(1)). If the deadline for filing petitions falls on "a Saturday, Sunday or public holiday," the filing may be performed on the "next succeeding business day" (Gen. Constr. Law § 25-a(1); see also *Appeal of Williams*, 36 Ed Dept Rep 270 (1996)). Therefore, when this situation occurs, the notice of the annual meeting and election must state that nominating petitions may be filed with the district clerk, during the hours specified by law, on the Monday following the 30th day before the election (specify date).

According to the commissioner of education, school districts must adhere to the statutory deadlines for submitting nominating petitions, even if they incorrectly published or misstated the deadline (*Appeal of Geiger*, 52 Ed Dept Rep, Dec. No. 16,379 (2012)).

15:11. What happens if the notice of the annual meeting and election does not comply with the law?

If a district fails to comply with the legal requirements for providing adequate public notice, the results of the budget vote and/or board member elections, in all likelihood, will be upheld and will not be found illegal, unless it appears that the failure to give proper notice was willful or fraudulent (§ 2010; see also *Appeals of Campbell & Coleman*, 41 Ed Dept Rep 207 (2001)). "Where the notice given is reasonably calculated to and effectively does give notice to the public of the election, a technical failure to give proper notice is not a basis for invalidating an election result" (*Appeal of Winograd*, 42 Ed Dept Rep 180 (2002)).

For example, in one case, a district provided correct information for publication in the local newspaper, indicating that it would hold its budget hearing on May 6 of that year. However, the newspaper incorrectly advertised the date of the hearing as May 5. Observing that all the other information the district provided to community residents listed the correct date, the commissioner of education found nothing willful or fraudulent about the error in the notice of the budget hearing and refused to overturn the results of the election (*Appeal of Leman*, 39 Ed Dept Rep 35 (1999)).

In another case, the commissioner refused to overturn the election results where the district had published notice in only one newspaper, not realizing until just five days before the election that the law generally requires publication in two newspapers, at which point in time it was too late to correct the error. The commissioner found that the error was not willful or fraudulent, especially since, upon discovering the error, the district mailed and hand-delivered a flyer regarding the election to district households (*Appeal of Hebel*, 34 Ed Dept Rep 319 (1994); see also *Appeal of Winograd*; *Appeal of Bartosik*, 37 Ed Dept Rep 531 (1998); and *Application of Martin*, 32 Ed Dept Rep 208 (1992)).

15:12. Are school boards required to provide a financial report for the prior school year at the annual meeting?

Only in common school districts. In such districts, the trustees must provide a financial statement at the annual meeting that accounts for all moneys received for the use of the district, or raised or collected by taxes, in the preceding year, and that indicates how they were spent (§ 1610). The trustees' willful neglect or refusal to do so will result in members forfeiting their offices (§ 1611). Other types of school districts are required by law to publish an annual financial statement instead of presenting it at the annual meeting (see **25:4**).

The Annual BOCES Meeting

15:13. When is the board of cooperative educational services (BOCES) annual meeting held?

The BOCES annual meeting must be held between April 1 and April 15 on a date and at a place and hour designated by the BOCES board president (§ 1950(4)(o)).

15:14. What is the purpose of the board of cooperative educational services (BOCES) annual meeting?

The purpose of the BOCES annual meeting is to present the tentative administrative, capital, and program budgets of the BOCES to school board members of component school districts prior to the vote on the tentative administrative budget (§ 1950(4)(o)). Other BOCES-wide business may be conducted at the meeting as well (see NYS Education Department, *Questions and Answers on the BOCES Reform Act*, (Oct. 1993)).

15:15. What notice must be given of the board of cooperative educational services (BOCES) annual meeting?

Notice of the time, date, and place of the annual meeting must be given to each of the members of the board and the clerk of each of the component districts by mail at least 14 days prior to the meeting (§ 1950(4)(o)). The BOCES must also publish the notice at least once each week within the two weeks preceding the annual meeting, the first publication to be at least 14 days before the meeting in two newspapers having general circulation, or one newspaper of general circulation if there is only one, within the BOCES (§ 1950(4)(b)(4)).

In addition to the date, time, and place of the meeting, the notice also must contain the following:

- A statement that the tentative BOCES budgets will be presented to the component school board members at the meeting;
- A summary of the tentative BOCES capital and program budgets in a form prescribed by the commissioner;
- A summary of the tentative BOCES administrative budget in a form prescribed by the commissioner that includes the salary and benefits payable to supervisory and administrative staff of the BOCES and the total compensation payable to the district superintendent of schools;
- When and where the tentative budgets will be available to the public for inspection (§ 1950(4)(b)(4)).

Special School District Meetings

15:16. What is a special school district meeting?

A *special school district meeting* is a meeting of the qualified voters of the district called for a specific purpose or purposes, such as resubmitting the district budget for a revote or conducting an election to fill a vacancy on the school board (§§ 2006–2008).

15:17. Must special school district meetings be held at a specific time?

Unlike the annual meeting and election, there is no date designated by law for holding special school district meetings, except for a special district meeting to conduct a budget revote, which must be held on the third Tuesday in June (see **19:28**). Moreover, the meeting generally need not continue for any specific period of time, so long as enough time is allowed for all voters present at the meeting to vote on the matters before them (see *Appeal of Faulkner*, 16 Ed Dept Rep 93 (1976)).

However, in small city school districts, a special district meeting must be held at least nine consecutive hours beginning not earlier than 7:00 a.m., at least two hours of which must be after 6:00 p.m. (§ 2602(3); *Appeal of Ghezzi,* 55 Ed Dept Rep, Dec. No. 16,890 (2016)).

In addition, in union free and central school districts, a special district meeting for the purpose of electing school board members must be held for at least six consecutive hours between 7:00 a.m. (as opposed to 6:00 a.m. for annual elections) and 9:00 p.m., at least two hours of which must be after 6:00 p.m. Such an election may go longer than the statutory six hours so long as proper notice is given (§ 2007(4)). In one case, the commissioner of education upheld the results of a special district meeting held until after 10:00 p.m. (*Appeal of Demos*, 34 Ed Dept Rep 54 (1994)).

15:18. How are special school district meetings called?

Generally, special district meetings are called by the school board when the board deems it necessary and proper (§§ 2006(1), 2007(1), 2602(2)), or when petitioned by 25 voters or five percent of those voting in the previous annual election, whichever is greater (§ 2008(2)). The statutory obligations related to calling a special school district meeting with respect to petition for a voter referendum are vested on the school board, not the superintendent of schools (*Appeal of Kolbmann*, 48 Ed Dept Rep 370 (2009)).

The commissioner of education and the district superintendent of the board of cooperative educational services also have authority to call special meetings under certain circumstances as set forth in law (§§ 2005, 2008(1), 2113(2)).

15:19. May a school board refuse a voter's petition to call a special school district meeting?

Yes. A school board may refuse to call a special school district meeting if its purpose is to address matters not within the power of the voters (see § 2021); if its purpose is illegal; if the petition for such a meeting was not filed within 20 days of publication of the passage of a bond or note resolution, pursuant to Local Finance Law section 81.00 (see, for example, *Appeal of Johnson*, 41 Ed Dept Rep 407 (2002)); or if the district asserts another valid reason for refusing to call the requested meeting, subject to review by the commissioner of education (§ 2008(2)(a)–(d)).

However, school boards must either accept or reject petitions for a special school district meeting within 20 days of their submission (§ 2008(2); see *Appeal of French*, 32 Ed Dept Rep 100 (1992)). If a petition is accepted, notice of the meeting must be given within 20 days of the petition's receipt (§ 2008(2)).

15:20. What notice must be given to the public regarding a special school district meeting?

School districts must include the same items of information in the notice of a special district meeting as are required in the notice of annual meeting, which are applicable to the purpose or purposes for which the special district meeting was called (§§ 2006, 2007, 2004; see **15:10**).

15:21. When must notice be given to the public regarding a special school district meeting?

In general, notice of a special school district meeting must be published or posted in the same manner and following the same timeline required for the notice of the annual meeting: 45 days ahead of the meeting, with publication once each week for four weeks in two newspapers of general circulation (§ 2007(1); see also **15:10**).

However, there are two circumstances when a full 45-day notice of a special district meeting is not required:

- when a special meeting is called to "revote" on the same budget, a modified budget; or
- when the school board rejects all bids for a contract or contracts for public work, transportation, or purchase, and the board deems it necessary and proper to call a special district meeting to take appropriate action.

Under either of these two circumstances, notice of the special district meeting is required only two weeks in advance, by publishing notice once each week during the two weeks before the vote, with the first publication being 14 days before the vote (§ 2007(3)(a)).

In common school districts, special rules apply regarding the manner for giving notice of a special district meeting. Notice must be given to each resident by the district clerk (by hand delivery to their residence) at least six days before the meeting, unless district residents have voted at a district meeting to use another method. In the alternative, notice can be published in two newspapers (or one if there is only one) having general circulation once each week during the four weeks prior to the meeting, with the first publication at least 22 days before the meeting. If no newspaper is available, notice must be posted in at least 20 public places between 22 and 28 days before the meeting (§ 2006(1), (2)).

Districts should be mindful, however, that the law requires them to hold a public hearing seven to 14 days prior to a special district meeting at which a budget vote will occur (§§ 1608(1), 1716(1), 2022(1); see **19:16, 19:18**). In addition, the law requires districts to mail a budget notice to all qualified voters in the district after the date of the public hearing, but no later than six days prior to a special district meeting at which a school budget vote will occur (§ 2022(2-a); see **19:20-21**).

15:22. How is a special school district meeting conducted?

A special school district meeting is conducted in the same way as the annual meeting and election: the chairperson of a special school district meeting is appointed in the same manner and calls the meeting to order (see **15:8**). Written records of the proceedings must be kept, and the district clerk serves as the clerk of the meeting (§ 2025).

Voter Propositions

15:23. Can voters petition their local school board to have propositions placed on the ballot at the annual meeting and election?

Yes, subject to the two-vote limit on budget propositions (see **19:29**). However, the school board may refuse to place such a proposition on the ballot if, for example, its purpose is not within the power of the voters, or if it requires an expenditure of money but fails to specify the amount for which voter approval is sought (§§ 2008(2), 2021, 2035(2); *Appeals of Ciffone & Kaufmann*, 45 Ed Dept Rep 444 (2006); *Appeal of Leman & Roujansky*, 32 Ed Dept Rep 579 (1993); *Matter of Sampson*, 14 Ed Dept Rep 162 (1974); see also **15:31**). In addition, any voter submitted proposition that requires an expenditure of money which would exceed the tax levy cap (see **18:1, 19:5-15**) for the corresponding school year must be approved by sixty percent of the voters present and voting (§§ 2008, 2023-a(9), 2035(3)).

A school board also may refuse to place a proposition on the ballot if the petition submitted to the board is ambiguous, unfeasible, would cause difficulty interpreting voting results (see **15:26**), concerns an issue previously presented to the voters (**15:25**), or fails to contain the requisite number of petition signatures set by board policy (**15:28**).

15:24. Who determines whether a particular proposition is within the power of the voters to submit for placement on the ballot?

The school board makes this determination, subject to review by the commissioner of education. This authority must be exercised with care because school boards do not have unfettered discretion to refuse propositions (*Appeal of Como*, 30 Ed Dept Rep 214 (1990), *petition dismissed, Bd. of Educ., Brentwood UFSD v. Sobol* (Sup. Ct. Albany Cnty. 1991)).

Examples of cases where the commissioner has upheld a school board's refusal to place a proposition on the ballot have involved propositions that:

- Would have asked the voters to set aside $200,000 to fund a lawsuit against school officials. The proposition was not within the power of the voters (*Appeal of Cox, Jr.*, 37 Ed Dept Rep 404 (1998)).
- Would have required the school board to submit a budget to the voters more than once before adopting a contingency budget. School boards, not the voters, have the authority to determine whether to place a budget before the voters a second time or adopt a contingency budget (*Appeal of Osten*, 35 Ed Dept Rep 160 (1995); see also **19:26**).
- Sought to direct the school board to move the district's administrative offices from leased space into the high school library, as discussed by the board itself at one time. "Decisions concerning

the use of school facilities are within the discretion of the board of education" (*Appeal of Johnson*, 44 Ed Dept Rep 382 (2005)).

- Would have required the board to schedule a vote on an alternative budget proposed by a citizens' group before adopting a contingency budget. The authority to develop a budget rests with the school board, not the voters (*Appeal of Sperl*, 33 Ed Dept Rep 388 (1994)).
- Sought to curtail the school board's authority to contract with other districts for the education of its students by limiting the choices to three neighboring districts. Although district voters approve contracts with other districts for the education of resident children, only a school board may designate the receiving district(s). Moreover, the applicable statute and regulations do not contain any geographical limitations (*Appeal of Berhalter & Conti*, 48 Ed Dept Rep 446 (2009)).

15:25. Can a school board reject a voter petition to add a proposition to the ballot on an issue previously submitted to the voters?

Yes. Once any issue has been placed before the voters in a particular year, a school board may refuse to place the issue before the voters again in the same year (*Appeal of Pace*, 47 Ed Dept Rep 515 (2008); *Appeal of Brush*, 34 Ed Dept Rep 273 (1994)). An exception would apply when the proposition seeks to abolish any library established by a public vote at the previous district meeting (§ 268; *Appeal of Pace*).

15:26. Can a school board reject a voter petition to add a ballot proposition that is ambiguous, unfeasible, or would cause difficulty interpreting voting results?

Yes. According to the commissioner of education,

> [A] board may not be compelled to place before the voters at an annual meeting all propositions submitted in conformity with §2035 and its bylaws, regardless of ambiguity, feasibility, or difficulty in interpreting election results when conflicting matters are voted on simultaneously. A board must exercise its independent judgment within the law to be certain that the will of the voters can be ascertained.

(*Appeal of Krause,* 27 Ed Dept Rep 57 (1987); see also *Appeal of Huber,* 41 Ed Dept Rep 240 (2001), *petition dismissed, Huber v. Mills,* (Sup. Ct. Albany Cnty. 2003).

For example, two conflicting propositions, one for construction, and the other for renovation, should not be placed on the same ballot (*Appeal of McDougall & Murphy*, 37 Ed Dept Rep 611 (1998); see also *Appeal of Martin*, 32 Ed Dept Rep 567 (1993); and *Appeal of Huber*; but compare with *Appeal of Kohilakis*, 33 Ed Dept Rep 513 (1994)).

In one case, the commissioner found that a school board properly rejected a proposition submitted by the voters that called for a decrease in the size of the school board, because the board already had accepted a voter proposition for placement on the ballot at the same annual meeting and election that called for an increase in the size of the board (*Appeal of Devine*, 44 Ed Dept Rep 278 (2005)).

15:27. Can a school board alter the language of an ambiguous proposition submitted by the voters?

Yes. A school board has the power to alter the language of a proposition submitted by the voters to bring the proposition into conformity with the law (*Appeal of Como*, 30 Ed Dept Rep 214 (1990), *petition dismissed, Bd. of Educ., Brentwood UFSD v. Sobol*, (Sup. Ct. Albany Cnty. 1991)). However, it may not be required to do so (*Appeal of Krause*, 27 Ed Dept Rep 57 (1987); but see *Appeal of Como*).

In addition, where it is possible for the school board to make minor modifications to two otherwise mutually inconsistent propositions, such that the voters are presented with a clear choice between alternatives, there is nothing improper about the school board submitting both propositions to the voters (*Appeals of the Bd. of Trustees of the George F. Johnson Mem. Library*, 40 Ed Dept Rep 331 (2000)). For example, according to the commissioner of education, it was perfectly acceptable for a school board to submit one proposition to the voters to eliminate the annual tax levy for a particular library, while placing a second proposition on the ballot at the same election, proposing that the tax levy for the very same library be increased in the event that the voters did not adopt the first proposition eliminating library funding (*Appeals of the Bd. of Trustees of the George F. Johnson Mem. Library*).

15:28. Is there a minimum number of signatures that a voter petition must have to place a proposition on the ballot at the annual meeting and election?

It depends upon the policy of the particular school board. The law requires each school board that uses voting machines for the conduct of its elections and referenda to adopt a rule for submitting voter-initiated propositions that can specify a reasonable minimum number of signatures required for such petitions (§ 2035(2); *Appeal of Huber,* 41 Ed Dept Rep 240 (2001), *petition dismissed, Huber v. Mills,* (Sup. Ct. Albany Cnty. 2003)). According to the commissioner of education, a rule requiring 1,000 signatures on a petition representing 27% of the total number of voters in the previous election is unreasonable (*Appeal of Como*, 30 Ed Dept Rep 214 (1990), *petition dismissed, Bd. of Educ., Brentwood UFSD v. Sobol,* (Sup. Ct. Albany Cnty. 1991)). School boards must ensure compliance with any such rule after it has been established (§ 2035(2); *Matter of Fetta*, 8 Ed Dept Rep 201 (1969)), but may amend it, in their discretion (§ 2035(2)). This rule does not apply to propositions placed on the ballot by the school board itself (§ 2035(2); *Appeals of Hendrickson & Guyer*, 28 Ed Dept Rep 354 (1989)).

15:29. Must a voter petition to add a proposition to the ballot include the addresses of those signing the petition?

No. The law does not require voters to list their addresses on a petition to add a proposition to the ballot, nor does it require that such a petition contain a sworn statement (*Appeal of Atkins*, 35 Ed Dept Rep 375 (1996)).

15:30. Is there a deadline for filing a voter petition to place a proposition on the ballot at the annual meeting and election?

Such a voter petition must be filed with the school board at least 30 days before the election date, unless the proposition is required by law to be included in the published or posted notice of the annual or special district meeting (§ 2035).

In addition, a school board may establish a rule that requires the proposition be submitted a reasonable period of time before the first publication or posting of the legal notice (*Appeal of Rosenberg*, 31 Ed Dept Rep 398 (1992); see also *Appeal of Como*, 30 Ed Dept Rep 214 (1990), *petition dismissed, Bd. of Educ., Brentwood UFSD v. Sobol,* (Sup. Ct. Albany Cnty. 1991); *Appeal of Presutti*, 17 Ed Dept Rep 445 (1978)). The commissioner of education has sustained as reasonable board policies requiring the submission of propositions to the board 90 and 60 days in advance of the annual meeting, where such propositions are of the type that must be included in the notice of annual meeting (*Appeal of Reynolds*, 42 Ed Dept Rep 231 (2003); see also *Appeal of Presutti*).

15:31. Should a school board place propositions on the ballot concerning matters that do not require voter approval?

No. Although technically not illegal, the commissioner of education consistently has advised against this practice because advisory votes may imply voter determination of the issue submitted for consideration (*Appeal of D'Orazio & Carey*, 41 Ed Dept Rep 292 (2002); *Appeal of Moonan & Richards*, 28 Ed Dept Rep 390 (1989); *Matter of Feldheim*, 8 Ed Dept Rep 136 (1969)).

In addition, although an advisory vote is not legally binding on a school board, "it can easily lead to the inference that the board is seeking to avoid its responsibility to make decisions within its legal powers, and is therefore . . . an undesirable practice and should be discouraged" (*Matter of Feldheim*; see also *Appeal of Rosenberg*, 31 Ed Dept Rep 398 (1992)). Accordingly, the commissioner has ruled that even though a school board may present the issue of a proposed school closing to its voters, the school board remains the ultimate decision making authority with respect to school building closures (*Appeal of Herrala,* 51 Ed Dept Rep, Dec. No. 16,264 (2011); *Appeal of Clyne,* 18 Ed Dept Rep 286 (1978)).

A non-binding referendum is "particularly ill-advised" when the matter can only be remedied by a change in the law, and the school board fails to inform the voters of the advisory nature of the vote (*Appeal of Marshall & Troge*, 41 Ed Dept Rep 219 (2001); see also *Appeal of Moonan & Richards*).

15:32. May a school board place a free association library funding proposition on the ballot at its annual district meeting?

Yes. A school district has the authority to levy taxes for a free association library pursuant to Education Law § 259(1) (*Appeal of Murphy*, 54 Ed Dept Rep, Dec. No. 16,765 (2015)).

Improper Advocacy

15:33. May a school district urge voters to vote in favor of a proposed school district budget or other ballot proposition?

No. School districts are prohibited from spending public money to encourage voters to vote in favor of the school budget or any proposition. District funds may not be used to express "favoritism, partisanship, partiality, approval or disapproval . . . of any issue, worthy as it may be" (*Phillips v. Maurer*, 67 N.Y.2d 672 (1986); see also *Appeal of Munoz-Feliciano*, 54 Ed Dept Rep, Dec. No. 16,773 (2015); *Appeal of Hubbard*, 39 Ed Dept Rep 363 (1999)).

This prohibition is not limited to advocating a "yes" vote. Even subtle promotional activities are prohibited (*Appeal of Meyer*, 38 Ed Dept Rep 285 (1998); *Appeal of Sotirovich*, 51 Ed Dept Rep, Dec. No. 16,360 (2012)), including the purchase of newspaper advertisements and the distribution of a newsletter by one school district attempting to sway the outcome of another school district's vote as to where to send its high school students (*Appeal of the Bd. of Educ. of the Greenwood Lake UFSD,* 47 Ed Dept Rep 446 (2008), *petition dismissed, Bd. of Educ., Greenwood Lake UFSD v. Mills,* (Sup. Ct. Albany Cnty. 2009)).

However, "it is not impermissible *per se* to state that rejection of the budget may result in the elimination of programs" (*Appeal of Julian*, 42 Ed Dept Rep 300 (2003)). Similarly, it does not constitute partisan activity to fail to disclose the effects of rejection (*Appeal of Lombardo*, 46 Ed Dept Rep 282 (2006)). In addition, there is nothing wrong with stating, as fact, in a district newsletter, that a particular proposition has the "unanimous support of the board of education" if indeed that is the case (*Appeal of Brown*, 43 Ed Dept Rep 231 (2003)).

15:34. May individual school board members acting in their personal capacity urge voters to vote in favor of a proposed school district budget or other ballot proposition?

Yes. Individual school board members and other school officials, acting in their personal capacity, have the same right as any other member of the community to express their views on public issues. They may actively support a proposed budget and other ballot propositions, as long as they do so at their own expense and on their own behalf. In other words, they cannot use district funds, facilities, or channels of communication, or claim to be speaking on behalf of the school board and must avoid giving the impression they are doing so (*Appeal of Munoz-Feliciano*, 54 Ed Dept Rep, Dec. No 16,773 (2015); *Appeal of Bentley & Boll,* 51 Ed Dept Rep, Dec. No. 16,356 (2012); *Appeal of Johnson*, 45 Ed Dept Rep 469 (2006); *Appeal of Goldin*, 40 Ed Dept Rep 628 (2001); *Matter of Wolff*, 17 Ed Dept Rep 297 (1978)).

In one case, for example, the commissioner of education found that while it would be improper for a board member to use the district's postage permit to mail partisan materials, there would be nothing improper about the same board member using his own private bulk mail permit to distribute campaign literature in support of candidates running for the school board (*Appeal of Allen*, 39 Ed Dept Rep 528 (2000)). Likewise, there is nothing improper about a board member expressing his or her personal views regarding school board candidates through the use of his or her personal email account (*Appeal of Leger-Vargas*, 54 Ed Dept Rep, Dec. No. 16,771 (2015)).

In another case, the commissioner dismissed an appeal filed against a school board where a board candidate inadvertently included a school district telephone number on a campaign flyer but did not actually use the district's telephone for campaign purposes (*Appeal of Grant*, 42 Ed Dept Rep 184 (2002)). However, individual board members who prepare and pay for flyers without the use of district resources must still take care not to mislead voters (see *Appeal of Vogel*, 46 Ed Dept Rep 481 (2007)).

Board members expressing their personal views in any format must "clearly distinguish their personal views from those of the board they represent" (*Appeal of Wallace*, 46 Ed Dept Rep 347 (2007)). A byline of an editorial that identifies the author as a board member would be inappropriate, because it gives the impression that the author was speaking in his or her official capacity (*Id.*; see also *Appeal of Koehler,* 52 Ed Dept Rep, Dec. No. 16,373 (2012)).

15:35. May school districts provide factual materials to the voters about the school budget and other ballot propositions?

Yes. Districts may provide purely factual and strictly objective materials on the school budget or other ballot propositions through means aimed at reaching the electorate as a whole in order to help them make an informed decision (*Appeal of Sotirovich*, 51 Ed Dept Rep, Dec. No. 16,360 (2012); *Appeal of Prentice*, 38 Ed Dept Rep 736 (1999); see also *Appeal of Loriz*, 27 Ed Dept Rep 376 (1988)). In fact, school boards and school superintendents have a "statutory obligation to present and publicize school budgets so as to 'promote public comprehension' " (*Gersen v. Mills* (Sup. Ct. Albany Cnty. 2000), Special Term, Sheridan, J., unreported, *rev'd on other grounds*, 290 A.D.2d 839 (3d Dep't 2002)). Such activities promote "the general public policy of this State to foster public awareness and understanding of governmental actions and to encourage participation therein" (*Gersen v. Mills*, citing Pub. Off. Law § 84).

However, if factual information distributed by a district is later found to be inaccurate, the commissioner of education may overturn the results of a vote and order a new meeting on the matter (see *Appeal of Wolverton*, 46 Ed Dept Rep 208 (2006), *petition dismissed*, *Bd. of Educ. Campbell-Savona CSD v. Mills* (Sup. Ct. Albany Cnty. 2006)). That was the case with respect to a school district annexation vote where the voters were not given accurate information regarding the financial status of one of the districts involved (*Id.*).

15:36. May a school board use a videotape to communicate budget information to the voters?

It depends. In one case, the commissioner of education admonished a district for using a promotional video to characterize as minimal the tax increase that would result from voter approval of the proposed budget. In the video, the superintendent stated, "The budget will result in a tax increase of *only* 1.9 percent." According to the commissioner, characterizing the percentage increase as "only" a given percentage sought "to persuade residents to vote in favor of the budget and propositions" (*Appeal of Hubbard,* 39 Ed Dept Rep 363 (1999)).

In another case, however, the commissioner upheld a district's decision to allow various factions within the community to videotape the condition of school facilities in connection with a proposed bond proposition asking district voters to approve a major renovation project. The "sufficiency and condition" of the facilities were "obviously relevant" for voters to decide whether to approve the proposition and the district did not restrict access to videotaping of its facilities to anyone (*Appeal of Huber,* 41 Ed Dept Rep 240 (2001), *petition dismissed, Huber v. Mills* (Sup. Ct. Albany Cnty. 2003); but compare *Appeal of Karpoff,* 40 Ed Dept Rep 459 (2000), 192 Misc.2d 487 (Sup. Ct. Albany Cnty. 2001), *aff'd,* 296 A.D.2d 691 (3d Dep't), *appeal denied,* 99 N.Y.2d 501 (2002)).

15:37. What are some examples of improper budget advocacy by a school district?

School District Meetings

Determining precisely what type of language constitutes improper advocacy can be difficult. For example, in one case, a district pamphlet included a statement indicating that a favorable vote on a bond referendum for school construction and renovation would "bring families back" to the community. The commissioner of education ruled that while the district's use of the statement "presents a close question . . . on balance . . . the statement is intended to persuade the public by promoting the positive consequences of a 'yes' vote. It does not set forth objective facts designed to educate or inform the public. Thus, this statement constitutes improper advocacy." The commissioner then admonished the district "to refrain from speculating about the effect future proposals might have on bringing families back to the city in an attempt to persuade the public to take a particular position on such propositions" (*Appeal of D'Oronzio*, 41 Ed Dept Rep 457 (2002)).

In yet another case, the commissioner admonished a district based on a letter from the superintendent that included the sentence: "*Unfortunately*, with a school budget defeat and the adoption of an austerity budget, we are not able to make these purchases or provide the services as stated above without voter authorization [emphasis added]." According to the commissioner, "[t]he use of '*unfortunately*,' in the context of the letter, could be construed as improper advocacy on behalf of the propositions and the use of such term or similar language should be avoided" (*Appeal of Schadtle*, 38 Ed Dept Rep 599 (1999); see also *Appeal of Eckert*, 40 Ed Dept Rep 433 (2000); *Appeal of Miller*, 39 Ed Dept Rep 348 (1999)).

The commissioner also has found problematic language in a letter by individual board members expressing their support for a budget proposal that stated "The BOCES board strongly believes that it is our responsibility to move forward on a plan that is mutually beneficial to all of its school districts. We encourage voters to support this proposal. . . ." Even though the letter was written by individual board members on their own behalf and at their own cost, the commissioner cautioned the language did not clearly distinguish between the personal views of the individual board members and those of the board (*Appeal of Johnson*, 45 Ed Dept Rep 469 (2006); see also *Appeal of Koehler*, 52 Ed Dept Rep, Dec. No. 16,373 (2012)).

In contrast, a court overturned a commissioner's decision, which held that a school district's use of the word "need" in informational materials describing the proposed school budget constituted improper advocacy (*Gersen v. Mills* (Sup. Ct. Albany Cnty. 2000), Special Term, Sheridan, J., unreported, *rev'd on other grounds*, 290 A.D.2d 839 (3d Dep't 2002)). According to the court, the district was simply "explaining the reasons for various provisions in the budget, [and] such relatively neutral language neither advocates a position nor 'patently exhorts' the voters to cast their ballots in favor of the proposed budget."

15:38. May school officials treat as "fact" statements about property values diminishing if the school budget is defeated at the polls?

No. Although there is a common perception in many communities that property values correspond directly with the quality of the public schools, the commissioner has directed school officials to "refrain from speculating about the effect future proposals might have on property values in an attempt to persuade the public to take a particular position" on a ballot proposition (*Appeal of Karpoff,* 40 Ed Dept Rep 459 (2000), 192 Misc.2d 487 (Sup. Ct. Albany Cnty. 2001), *aff'd,* 296 A.D.2d 691 (3d Dep't), *appeal denied,* 99 N.Y.2d 501 (2002); see also *Appeal of Eckert*, 40 Ed Dept Rep 433 (2000); but compare *Appeal of Berg*, 53 Ed Dept Rep, Dec. No. 16,616 (2014)).

15:39. What are some examples of communications by a school district that do not constitute improper budget advocacy?

General statements that a district's "extra-curricular activities in music, art, and sports have, again, been superlative" have been deemed "mere platitudes" that do "not exhort the electorate to vote in any particular way or otherwise convey favoritism, partisanship, partiality, approval or disapproval for the budget proposal or any particular candidates" (*Appeal of Carroll*, 42 Ed Dept Rep 326 (2003)).

Similarly, the commissioner of education found nothing wrong with the following factual statement included in a description of the district's long-term facilities plan: ". . . we educate children in hallways and converted closets. The overburdened cafeterias force them to have lunch at 10:40 in the morning or, at the high school, to go off campus to eat. There is not enough gym space. . ." (*Appeal of Meyer & Mittlesteadt, Jr.*, 40 Ed Dept Rep 34 (2000)).

The commissioner did not find improper, either, a statement in a district's newsletter that described budget development as a difficult task due in part to "severe cutbacks in recent years" (*Appeal of Wallace*, 46 Ed Dept Rep 347 (2007)). Similarly, a district does not engage in improper advocacy by placing signs in public places and on district property announcing the date, time and place of the annual election and budget vote (*Appeal of Tillet*, 51 Ed Dept Rep, Dec. No. 16,327 (2012)).

15:40. What happens if a district advocates on behalf of the proposed budget or other proposition?

If the commissioner of education finds that such advocacy affected the outcome of the vote, he or she may annul the results of the vote and order a new election (*Appeal of Leman*, 38 Ed Dept Rep 683 (1999); see also **17:34-35**). The commissioner also may remove from office school officials who engage in a willful violation of *Phillips v. Maurer*, 67 N.Y.2d 672 (1986) (see **15:33**) or neglect their duty to adhere to the court's ruling in that case (see § 306(1); see **6:39**). In addition, the commissioner can withhold state funding from any district that willfully advocates on behalf of the proposed budget or other proposition (see § 306(2)).

15:41. Should districts avoid creating an "appearance of impropriety" when engaging in activities that technically do not constitute partisan advocacy?

Yes. According to the commissioner of education, districts should avoid engaging in activities that create an "appearance of impropriety," even if the activity itself technically does not violate the prohibition against partisan advocacy.

For example, in one case, the commissioner found that the use of district phones by students and administrators to call potential voters to encourage them to vote creates the appearance of improper partisan activity, where selective phone lists are used (*Appeal of Boni*, 40 Ed Dept Rep 292 (2000); *Appeal of Schadtle*, 38 Ed Dept Rep 599 (1999); *Appeal of Tortorello & Bartnik*, 29 Ed Dept Rep 306 (1990)). However, in the absence of partisan phone lists, the use of district phones to remind residents to vote is not improper (*Appeal of Gang*, 32 Ed Dept Rep 337 (1992); *Appeal of Boni;* see **15:50**).

The commissioner also has frowned on rewards that parents can redeem at the polls and exchange for a book or other token for their child (*Appeal of Hiller*, 47 Ed Dept Rep 304 (2007)). The commissioner also has warned school board members that in order to avoid the appearance of impropriety they should refrain from asking, in an official capacity, merchants to post signs in support of upcoming propositions (*Appeal of Koehler*, 52 Ed Dept Rep, Dec. No. 16,373 (2012)).

15:42. Can school officials permit private individuals and organizations to use district facilities or channels of communication to encourage the electorate to vote in a particular way?

No. The commissioner of education has ruled that districts cannot do indirectly that which they cannot do directly. In general, this means that school officials can neither actively encourage nor tacitly permit anyone else to use district facilities or channels of communication to engage in promotional activities. School boards are "ultimately accountable for how district facilities and resources are used and must avoid even the appearance of impermissible partisan activity" (*Appeal of Maliha*, 41 Ed Dept Rep 367 (2002); *Appeal of McBride*, 39 Ed Dept Rep 702 (2000); see also *Appeal of Cass*, 46 Ed Dept Rep 321 (2007); *Appeal of Karpoff*, 40 Ed Dept Rep 459 (2000), 192 Misc.2d 487 (Sup. Ct. Albany Cnty. 2001), *aff'd*, 296 A.D.2d 691 (3d Dep't), *appeal denied*, 99 N.Y.2d 501 (2002)).

For example, the commissioner has ruled that a school board should not make sets of mailing labels available to outside organizations including the parent-teacher association (PTA), in the absence of safeguards to ensure that such district resources will not be used to exhort the electorate to vote in a particular way (*Appeal of Hoey & Kosowski*, 45 Ed Dept Rep 501 (2006); *Appeal of Allen*, 39 Ed Dept Rep 528 (2000); see also *Appeal of Lawson*, 38 Ed Dept Rep 713 (1999)). The commissioner also has expressed concerns over the distribution of PTA flyers urging passing the budget sent home in students' backpacks (*Appeal of Hoey & Kosowski*).

However, the commissioner has found it permissible for the PTA to give out stickers to students that say "vote yes for us" outside district schools (*Id.*). In addition, a district may allow outside organizations to videotape facilities that are the subject of an upcoming vote on a capital project proposition, if the district does not single out specific organizations and provides such access to everyone (*Appeal of Huber,* 41 Ed Dept Rep 240 (2001), *petition dismissed, Huber, v. Mills* (Sup. Ct. Albany Cnty. 2003); *Appeal of Karpoff*).

In addition, the "mere presence" of a link on a district's website to another website where partisan views are advocated does not constitute an improper use of district communication channels; however, it is recommended that the district include a disclaimer on its website "to clarify that the district is not responsible for facts or opinions contained on any linked sites" (*Appeal of Hager & Scheuerman*, 43 Ed Dept Rep 363 (2004); *Appeal of Koehler*, 52 Ed Dept Rep, Dec. No. 16,373 (2012)).

15:43. Can school officials permit employee unions or staff to use district facilities or channels of communication to encourage a particular vote?

No, not even pursuant to a collective bargaining agreement provision that otherwise allows a union "the right to use office machines and equipment for [union] business" (*Appeal of Himmelberg, Jr. & Little*, 46 Ed Dept Rep 228 (2006)). According to the commissioner of education, such an agreement cannot authorize unconstitutional partisan use of district resources (*Id.*; see also **15:42**). Therefore, it was improper for a union president to use a district's email system to disseminate a message endorsing two candidates running for the school board (*Id.*; *Appeal of Williams*, 55 Ed Dept Rep, Dec. No. 16,900 (2016)).

Similarly, it was improper for a local teachers' union to use school mailboxes to distribute flyers to union members urging them to vote for certain preferred board candidates. Although the superintendent told union leaders to desist and directed building principals to retrieve the flyers from the mailboxes upon learning of the distribution, the commissioner admonished the district to take steps to prevent other groups from taking similar action in the future (*Appeal of VanAllen*, 38 Ed Dept Rep 701 (1999); see also *Appeal of Hoefer*, 41 Ed Dept Rep 203 (2001); but compare with *Appeal of Huber*, 41 Ed Dept Rep 240 (2001), *petition dismissed*, *Huber, v. Mills,* (Sup. Ct. Albany Cnty. 2003) where school officials did not know members of the teachers' union distributed flyers through teachers mailboxes soliciting them to participate in a television commercial supporting a facilities proposition).

In contrast, a federal district court in New York enjoined a school district from enforcing a regulation that prohibited teachers from placing campaign materials related to a presidential election in their colleagues' mailboxes and from posting such materials on union bulletin boards in areas closed to students (*Weingarten v. Bd. of Educ. of the City Sch. Dist. of the City of N.Y.*, 591 F.Supp.2d 511 (S.D.N.Y. 2008); but compare *Weingarten v. Bd. of Educ. of the City Sch. Dist. of the City of N.Y.*, 680 F.Supp.2d 595 (S.D.N.Y. 2010) where the court upheld a regulation that prohibited teachers from wearing political campaign buttons in school).

15:44. Can school officials permit staff to communicate their partisan views to students while on school time?

No. According to the commissioner of education, districts must take affirmative steps to ensure that teachers and staff do not convey partisan positions to students on school time on matters pending before the voters (*Appeal of Lawson*, 36 Ed Dept Rep 450 (1997)). However, the commissioner also has ruled that there was nothing improper about a teacher explaining the meaning of a "contingency budget" to students in class because the teacher only provided factual information to the students (*Appeal of Roxbury Taxpayers Alliance*, 34 Ed Dept Rep 576 (1995)).

Likewise, a federal district court in New York upheld a school district regulation that prohibited staff from wearing political buttons in the classroom. The regulation required that all school personnel "maintain a posture of complete neutrality" and "not wear buttons, pins articles of clothing, or any other items advocating a candidate, candidates, slate of candidates or political organization/committee." The court agreed with the school district that such displays of political partisanship are inconsistent with a school district's educational mission, can improperly influence students and impinge on their right to learn in an environment free from partisan political influence, and convey a message of school district support for the view expressed by such displays (*Weingarten v. Bd. of Educ. of the City Sch. Dist. of the City of N.Y.*, 680 F.Supp.2d 595 (S.D.N.Y. 2010)).

15:45. Can school officials permit students to use district facilities or channels of communication to encourage a particular vote?

It depends. According to the commissioner of education, school officials may permit student editors of a district-funded newspaper to editorialize in support of particular school board candidates or the proposed school budget, provided that the district does not act to influence the content of such editorials. Moreover, students may distribute literature on school grounds expressing their opinions about school budget votes and elections, subject to the imposition of reasonable restrictions by the district on the time, place, and manner of distribution; provided, however, that the district does not use district personnel or funds to support such activities (*Appeal of Doro*, 40 Ed Dept Rep 281 (2000)).

15:46. May school officials allow the parent-teacher association (PTA) and other organizations and individuals to use district facilities or channels of communication to disseminate nonpartisan information about board candidates and/or budget propositions?

Yes. The commissioner of education has stated that while districts may not allow PTAs to use district facilities or established channels of communication for partisan purposes, they may do so for informational and nonpartisan purposes (*Appeal of McBride*, 39 Ed Dept Rep 702 (2000)).

In one case, the commissioner ruled that it was permissible for a school district to allow the PTA to distribute to students, on school grounds, a flyer consisting of copies of the biographies of each of the candidates running for the school board, as well as their verbatim responses to a survey containing five questions that the commissioner found objective and nonpartisan. Specifically, the commissioner found that the "questions were broad and open-ended, and each candidate's response was distributed without editing, censoring or alteration." Under the circumstances, the commissioner concluded, "the questions served to educate and inform the public about the candidate's positions and qualifications, and [did] not advocate a particular position" (*Appeal of Boni*, 41 Ed Dept Rep 214 (2001), *petition dismissed*, *Boni v. Mills* (Sup. Ct. Albany Cnty. 2003).

15:47. May a school district prohibit the distribution of anonymous literature on the school budget?

No. The U.S. Supreme Court ruled that a state statute that prohibited the distribution of anonymous literature violated the First Amendment. The literature at issue expressed opposition to a proposed school tax levy and did not identify the author, but rather purported to express the views of "concerned parents and taxpayers." The individual who distributed the literature was fined $100 after a school official filed a complaint against her with the Elections Commission for violating the state law that prohibited the distribution of campaign literature that did not contain the name and address of the person or campaign official issuing the literature (*McIntyre v. Ohio Elections Comm'n*, 514 U.S. 334 (1995)).

Since that U.S. Supreme Court ruling, New York amended its Vehicle and Traffic law to prohibit anyone from attaching handbills or other forms of advertisements to a vehicle's windshield or windshield wipers, regardless of whether such materials are distributed anonymously or by known persons. However, this prohibition extends only to the distribution of such literature on vehicles to curtail littering. It remains to be seen whether the courts would find that this law impermissibly deprives citizens of their First Amendment rights, or merely imposes a constitutionally permissible restriction on the place and manner of speech (Veh. & Traf. Law § 375(1)(b)).

Electioneering

15:48. Is electioneering permitted during school board elections or when voting on the school budget or propositions?

No. The Education Law prohibits electioneering on the day of the election within a 100-foot zone measured from the entrance to the polling place (§§ 2031-a, 2609(4-a)). District elections inspectors are required to post distance markers delineating the 100-foot zone (§§ 2031-a(1), 2609(4-a)(a); *Cullen v.*

Fliegner, 18 F.3d 96 (2d Cir. 1994)). The facial validity of a statute establishing such a zone has survived strict constitutional scrutiny (see *Burson v. Freeman*, 504 U.S. 191 (1992)).

15:49. What constitutes electioneering?

Electioneering includes, but is not limited to, such activity as distributing or displaying a candidate's campaign materials or materials in support of or in opposition to any proposition. For example, the commissioner of education determined that a school board candidate engaged in improper electioneering when she told voters within 100 feet of the polling place that because of her efforts the district's proposed budget was under the mandated tax cap and that as a result homeowners would receive a real estate tax rebate check from the state (*Appeal of Tourè,* 54 Ed Dept Rep, Dec. No. 16,600 (2014)).

It should be noted, however, that the law specifically allows a school board to display within any polling place a copy or copies of any budget or proposition to be voted upon (§§ 2031-a(2), 2609(4-a)(b)). In addition, the commissioner has ruled that districts do not engage in electioneering when they distribute purely factual materials at polling places (*Appeal of VanAllen*, 38 Ed Dept Rep 701 (1999); *Appeal of Leman*, 38 Ed Dept Rep 683 (1999); *Appeal of Hart*, 34 Ed Dept Rep 299 (1994); *Appeal of Tomkins*, 34 Ed Dept Rep 174 (1994)).

15:50. What are some examples of activities that do not constitute electioneering?

The meeting of a partisan group in a schoolhouse during the hours of an election in and of itself does not constitute electioneering (*Appeal of Giuliano*, 37 Ed Dept Rep 572 (1998)). Nor does the mere presence of partisan officials at a polling place in and of itself constitute electioneering (*Appeal of Loriz*, 35 Ed Dept Rep 231 (1995)). Similarly, it does not constitute electioneering on the part of school board candidates to speak with voters within 100 feet of the polling place, absent evidence the candidates were trying to influence voters (*Appeal of Bentley & Boll,* 51 Ed Dept Rep, Dec. No. 16,356 (2012)).

In addition, calling potential voters to encourage them to exercise their right to vote does not necessarily constitute electioneering (*Appeal of Gang*, 32 Ed Dept Rep 337 (1992)). However, it is improper for district personnel to make such calls using a selective list of voters, such as a list of district residents with children enrolled in public school (who arguably are more likely to support the district budget and/or other propositions) (*Appeal of Boni*, 40 Ed Dept Rep 292 (2000); *Appeal of Schadtle*, 38 Ed Dept Rep 599 (1999)).

Holding a barbecue fundraiser "at the same time as the election, even if the grill is within 100 feet of the voting booth, does not constitute electioneering in and of itself" (*Appeal of Santicola*, 36 Ed Dept Rep 416 (1997); see also *Appeal of McBride*, 39 Ed Dept Rep 702 (2000)). Neither does holding a school concert on the night of the budget vote, provided that the district gives notice of the concert to all district residents in the same manner and not just to those district residents whom the school board believes will be supportive of the propositions on the ballot (*Appeal of Rampello*, 37 Ed Dept Rep 153 (1997); *Appeal of Sowinski*, 34 Ed Dept Rep 184 (1994)).

15:51. What is the penalty for violating the prohibition against electioneering?

Any person who willfully violates the prohibition on electioneering may be found guilty of a misdemeanor (§§ 2031-a(3), 2609(4-a)(c)). However, absent proof that electioneering affected the outcome of an election, proof that electioneering occurred is no basis to overturn the results of the election (*Appeal of Lawson*, 38 Ed Dept Rep 713 (1999); see also *Appeal of Ponella*, 38 Ed Dept Rep 610 (1999); *Appeal of Karliner*, 36 Ed Dept Rep 30 (1996)).

16. School District Voters

Voter Qualifications

16:1. Who is a qualified voter?

A *qualified voter* is a person who is a citizen of the United States, at least 18 years old, a resident of the school district for at least 30 days prior to the meeting at which he or she offers to vote, and who is not otherwise prohibited from voting under the provisions of section 5-106 of the Election Law (for example, a person who has been adjudged to be mentally incompetent). Only qualified voters of the school district may vote on a question brought before an annual meeting and election or special school district meeting (§§ 2012, 2603).

A person need not be a registered voter to satisfy the legal definition of a "qualified voter" (*Appeal of King & Moore*, 55 Ed Dept Rep, Dec. No. 16,865 (2016); *Appeal of Dreyer*, 18 Ed Dept Rep 235 (1978); see also *Appeal of Crowley*, 39 Ed Dept Rep 665 (2000); see **6:14**). Owning a home in a school district does not necessarily make the owner a district resident for purposes of being considered a qualified voter eligible to participate in a school district annual or special school district meeting or election. "A person may have only one legal residence or domicile, and that is the place where such person intends to have his or her permanent residence or home. The residency of dual home owners is dependent on the intent and conduct of the owner" (*Appeal of Taylor*, 39 Ed Dept Rep 712 (2000); see also *Appeal of Klein*, 47 Ed Dept Rep 409 (2008)). Dual homeownership by itself does not entitle the property owner to designate residency for purposes of participating in a district's elections (*Appeal of Ryan, Starbuck, and Toomey*, 50 Ed Dept Rep, Dec. No. 16,202 (2011)).

School districts may not require voters to pay taxes or have children attending the public schools to be eligible to vote (*Kramer v. Union Free Sch. Dist. No. 15*, 395 U.S. 621 (1969)). Military personnel residing on a military base may also be qualified voters in the school district where that base is located (*Appeal of Kuleszo*, 30 Ed Dept Rep 465 (1991)).

16:2. Is a convicted felon eligible to vote at a school district meeting and election?

It depends. New York Election Law provides that a convicted felon has a right to vote, only if he or she has been pardoned, his or her maximum prison sentence has expired, or he or she has been discharged from parole (Elec. Law § 5-106(2)). The U.S. Court of Appeals for the Second Circuit has ruled that this provision of state law does not violate the federal Voting Rights Act, 42 USC § 1973 (*Hayden v. Pataki,* 449 F.3d 305 (2d Cir. 2006); *Hayden v. Paterson,* 594 F.3d 150 (2d Cir. 2010)).

16:3. What happens if an unqualified person votes or lies about his or her qualifications to vote?

The district may sue unqualified voters for a fine of $10 to be used for the benefit of the district (§ 2020(3); see also *Appeal of Lyon*, 30 Ed Dept Rep 169 (1990)). In addition, a person who willfully makes a false statement about his or her qualifications to vote may be found guilty of a misdemeanor (§ 2020(1), (2)), and may be subject to a fine of up to $1,000 and/or imprisonment for up to one year (Penal Law §§ 55.10(2)(b), 70.15(1), 80.05(1)).

If a voter is challenged in timely fashion (i.e., no later than the time the voter presents himself or herself at the polls to vote), and the voter is permitted to vote because he or she makes the declaration required by Education Law § 2019 (see **16:13-16**) stating that he or she is qualified to vote, then the burden of proof shifts to the school district to demonstrate that the voter is not qualified (*Appeal of Lyon*). The board can conduct an investigation following the election to determine if that person was indeed a qualified voter (*Appeal of Boehm,* 27 Ed Dept Rep 96 (1987)). In fact, in at least two reported decisions, the commissioner of education has ordered school boards to conduct such an investigation and to seek the penalties authorized by section 2020 if warranted (see *Appeal of Cobb*, 32 Ed Dept Rep 139 (1992); see also *Matter of Bernocco,* 20 Ed Dept Rep 343 (1980)).

If it appears that the election results were affected by votes cast by unqualified persons, the commissioner may invalidate the vote and require a special meeting or election (*Appeal of Cobb*; see **17:35**).

Voter Registration

16:4. Must qualified voters register with the district to vote in a school district meeting or election?

Not necessarily. Not all districts provide for personal registration. The law permits, but does not require, school boards in union free and central school districts to provide for personal registration of voters in their districts (§ 2014; *Appeal of King & Moore*, 55 Ed Dept Rep, Dec. No. 16,865 (2016); see also **16:5**).

School boards that adopt a resolution providing for personal registration must notify the appropriate board of elections within five days of its adoption (Elec. Law § 5-612(4)). They also must notify the board of elections at least 45 days before the date of the annual district meeting and election, and at least 14 days before the date of any special district meeting (Elec. Law § 5-612(5)).

In comparison, small city school districts are required by law to provide for personal registration of voters in their districts (§ 2606).

16:5. In districts that require personal registration, must voters be registered with the school district in order to vote?

Not necessarily. Even in school districts that require personal voter registration (§§ 2014, 2606), qualified voters who are registered with the county board of elections are eligible to vote at school district meetings without further registration (Elec. Law § 5-612(2); see also *Appeal of Crowley*, 39 Ed Dept Rep 665 (2000); *Appeal of Muench*, 38 Ed Dept Rep 649 (1999); *Appeal of Shortell*, 27 Ed Dept Rep 190 (1987)). In addition, individuals whose names do not appear on the registration list may be presented to vote, as well, if they meet certain statutorily prescribed conditions (see §§ 2015(3), (4), 2019, 2609(5); see also **16:14**).

16:6. How does a school district know if a person is registered with the county board of elections?

The county board of elections is required to provide a list of registered voters to the school district at least 30 days prior to any regularly scheduled election, and a supplemental list of voters who registered after delivery of the first registration list at least 10 days before any regular or special election (Elec. Law § 5-612(3)).

In small city school districts, the school district board of registration may require the board of elections (or other lawful authority having custody of the register(s) used in the last general election preceding the school board election) to turn over the register(s) to the board of registration on or before March 1st of each year for use in preparing the school district registers. At the same time, however, the board of elections (or other authority having lawful custody of the registers) may elect to furnish, in place of the original registers, either a duplicate of the central file registration records, or a list of registered voters, certified to be a complete and accurate copy of the names and addresses of all persons entered in such register for the preceding general election as well as the names of persons who have registered with the board of elections (or other authority) up to five days before the date of furnishing such list (§ 2606(2)). The law authorizes the school board to require the use of such registers on election day for the purpose of verifying the signature of each voter (§ 2609(2)). The registers must be returned following the day of the election (§ 2606(2)).

16:7. When and where does personal registration take place?

The time and location of voter registration is set by school board resolution. However, the last day of registration must not be more than 14 days nor less than five days before the annual district meeting and election (§ 2014(2); see also *Matter of Ferraro*, 24 Ed Dept Rep 275 (1985)). Such registration must be open for at least four consecutive hours between 7:00 a.m. and 8:00 p.m. (§ 2014(2); see also *Matter of Lortz*, 7 Ed Dept Rep 3 (1967)). In small city school districts, the last day of registration cannot be less than two weeks preceding the election (§ 2606(2)).

The school district board of registration also must conduct registration at the annual meeting and election for the purpose of registering voters to vote in *future* school district elections (§ 2014(2); see also McKinney's 1956 Session Laws of New York, Memorandum of NYS Education Department for L. 1956, c. 930, pp.1956–57). It is improper for a school district to allow any person who registers with the district on election day to vote in the election occurring on that day (*Appeal of Collins*, 39 Ed Dept Rep 226 (1999); see also *Matter of Watson,* 19 Ed Dept Rep 136 (1979)).

The last day of registration of voters prior to a special district meeting must occur not more than seven days nor less than two days before the date of the meeting (§ 2007(3)(c); for information about voter registration in small city school districts, see § 2606).

Subject to approval of the district voters, districts may have continuous registration during specified hours of the school day at the office of the district clerk or business office by the district clerk, assistant district clerk or a member of the board of registration (§ 2014(2); see also *Appeal of Pecher*, 30 Ed Dept Rep 116 (1990)). If approved by the voters, such registration "shall take place at the school or schools within the district designated in the resolution" adopted by the voters (§ 2014(2)). In such case, the board of registration, at the school board's discretion, would not be required to meet prior to the annual meeting or election or special meeting or election solely for the purpose of registering voters (§ 2014(6)).

16:8. What information is included in the voter registration list?

The registration list used for each district meeting must include the name of everyone who has registered to vote at the meeting, and may include anyone who has registered and voted in prior school district meetings in the preceding four calendar years. However, the name of anyone who has died or moved out of the school district, or who otherwise has become ineligible to vote, must be removed (§ 2014(2)). More specifically, the registration list must include the name and street address of each voter on the list, arranged alphabetically by last name. If there is no street address, some description must be included that accurately locates the place of residence. It also must have a column or columns in which to indicate whether each person listed has voted previously in any school district election or elections or at any meetings (§ 2014(2)).

The registration list is not the same thing as a poll list (see **17:13**).

16:9. Who prepares the voter registration list?

The voter registration list is prepared by the school district's board of registration (§ 2014(2)). This board consists of four qualified voters of the district appointed annually by the school board, not later than 30 days after the district's annual meeting or election, who serve until 30 days after the annual meeting or election the following year. The board of registration is entitled to compensation at a rate fixed by the school board for each day actually and necessarily spent on the duties of the office (§ 2014(1)).

16:10. May school employees provide voter registration forms to district residents and encourage their participation in district elections?

Yes. In a couple of cases, the commissioner of education dismissed complaints alleging that it was improper for teachers to participate in voter registration drives. In one case where a teacher registered high school seniors to vote in school district elections, the commissioner ruled that "[t]here is nothing inherently wrong with registering a student to vote provided the student is not directed to vote a certain way" (*Appeal of Hoefer*, 41 Ed Dept Rep 203 (2001)). In another case, the commissioner dismissed an appeal challenging a district's practice of having its social studies teachers give voter registration forms to students to take home to their parents and then forwarding to the county board of elections those registration forms that were completed by parents and returned to the district (see *Application of Bliss*, 45 Ed Dept Rep 308 (2005)).

However, it is important to distinguish between registration with the school district itself and registration through a county board of elections. If a school district has a board of registration, or permits registration in the business office or office of the clerk (as authorized by voter proposition), then only members of the board of registration or other authorized district personnel have authority to register voters on the district's behalf. However, with respect to registration with a county board of elections, it is not uncommon for third parties to distribute and collect voter registration cards and then mail or deliver them to the county board, which ultimately determines the qualifications of the registrant.

Thus, although a teacher typically would not have any authority to register voters on behalf of a school district, unless for example that teacher also was a member of the district's board of registration, nothing would prohibit a teacher from distributing to students or other persons voter registration cards obtained from the local county board of election, provided that the teacher does not engage in partisan advocacy on school grounds (*Application of Bliss*).

16:11. Must school districts make voter registration lists available for public inspection?

Yes. Voter registration lists must be filed in the office of the district clerk at least five days before any school district meeting or election and must be open to public inspection by any qualified voter at all reasonable times and days of the week, except Sunday, up to and including the day of the election (§ 2015(1)). However, in small city school districts, there is no requirement that the list of registered voters be made available on the day of the election (§ 2606; *Appeal of Fraser-McBride,* 36 Ed Dept Rep 488 (1997)).

16:12. May a school district discontinue its system of personal registration?

Yes. The school board may discontinue personal registration by a board resolution passed at least two months before the next school district meeting or election. However, personal registration may not then be re-instituted without voter approval (§ 2014(3); see *Appeal of Fitzpatrick*, 28 Ed Dept Rep 194 (1988); see also *Matter of White v. Bd. of Educ.*, 53 Misc.2d 800 (Sup. Ct. Monroe Cnty. 1967), *aff'd,* 28 A.D.2d 828 (4th Dep't 1967)).

On the other hand, school boards in small city school districts may not discontinue their system of personal registration, as they are required by law to maintain such a system (§ 2006; see **16:4**).

Challenges to Voter Qualifications

16:13. Can a person's qualifications to vote be challenged?

Yes. Any qualified voter has the right, although not the duty to challenge, either prior to or at the district meeting, the qualifications of any other voter (§§ 2015(3), (4), 2019, 2609(5); *Matter of Thompson*, 76 State Dep't Rep. 162 (1956)).

When a qualified voter challenges a person's qualification to vote, the chairperson presiding at the meeting or election in a non-city district shall require the person offering to vote to make the following declaration: "I do declare and affirm that I am, and have been, for the thirty days last past, an actual resident of this school district and that I am qualified to vote at this meeting" (§ 2019). In a city school district, the chairman of the board of inspectors must administer to those challenged the following oath: "I do solemnly swear (or affirm) that I am a citizen of the United States; that I am of the age of eighteen years or more; that I have been an inhabitant of the State for the past year, a resident of the county for the past four months and for the thirty days past an actual resident of this city school district and am therefore qualified to vote at this election" (§ 2609(5)).

If the person challenged makes this declaration, then he or she shall be permitted to vote, but if the person refuses, his or her vote must be rejected (§§ 2019, 2609(5)).

16:14. What happens if a voter's name does not appear on the registration list or registration poll ledger?

If a person's name cannot be found on the list of registered voters or in the registration poll ledger, then district elections officials shall not permit that person to vote, unless: (1) the person presents a court order requiring that he or she be permitted to vote in the manner otherwise prescribed for voters whose names are on the list of registered voters or in the registration poll ledger; or (2) the person submits an affidavit attesting to his or her qualifications to vote (§ 2019-a(1)).

If the person is permitted to vote by affidavit, he or she must print on the outside of an envelope a sworn statement indicating (1) that he or she has duly registered to vote; (2) the address at which he or she is registered; (3) that he or she remains a duly qualified voter in the election district where he or she resides; (4) that his or her poll record appears to be lost or misplaced or that his or her name has been incorrectly omitted from the list of registered voters; and (5) that he or she understands that any false statement made therein is perjury punishable according to law (§ 2019-a(1)(b)).

A person who is permitted to vote by affidavit must vote by paper ballot, which is placed inside the envelope upon which the affidavit was written and then sealed therein until the close of the election and the canvassing of ballots (*Id.*; see also *Appeal of Brown*, 38 Ed Dept Rep 816 (1999); *Appeal of Muench*, 38 Ed Dept Rep 649 (1999)). "If it is determined that a voter who cast an affidavit ballot was not registered, the ballot may not be counted" (*Appeal of Crowley*, 39 Ed Dept Rep 665 (2000); *Appeal of Vaughan*, 33 Ed Dept Rep 189 (1993)).

16:15. Is there a deadline for challenging a person's qualifications to vote?

Yes. All challenges to the qualifications of a voter must be raised no later than the time the voter goes to the polls to vote (*Appeal of Grant*, 42 Ed Dept Rep 184 (2002); see also *Appeal of Pappas*, 38 Ed

Dept Rep 582 (1999); *Appeal of Carlson,* 37 Ed Dept Rep 351 (1998); *Appeal of Fraser-McBride*, 36 Ed Dept Rep 488 (1997)).

Moreover, anyone qualified to challenge a voter (see **16:1**, **16:13**) who does not exercise such right is not allowed to object to such voter's participation (*Appeal of Crowley*, 39 Ed Dept Rep 665 (2000); see also *Appeal of Horton*, 35 Ed Dept Rep 168 (1995)).

"[I]f a person . . . has the opportunity to challenge, but does not do so . . . then he cannot be heard to complain, only after the event and only when the outcome is not according to such person's liking. . ." (*Matter of Kavanaugh*, 5 Ed Dept Rep 19 (1965); see also *Appeal of Crowley*; *Matter of Katz*, 18 Ed Dept Rep 276 (1978)).

16:16. May school districts ask for proof of residency before allowing individuals to cast their vote?

Yes. In districts without personal registration, the Education Law authorizes (but does not require) district election officials to require voters at any school district meeting or election to provide one form of proof of residency, determined by the school district, such as a driver's license, non-driver identification card, utility bill or voter registration card. In addition, district election officials also may require such persons offering to vote to provide their signature, printed name, and address (§ 2018-c; *Appeal of King & Moore*, 55 Ed Dept Rep, Dec. No. 16,865 (2016); *Appeal of Pugliese*, 40 Ed Dept Rep 499 (2001)).

In addition, in districts with personal registration, the commissioner has recognized the right of school officials to request proof of residency from a voter prior to the election, as a condition of maintaining the voter's name on the voter registration list (*Appeal of Taylor*, 39 Ed Dept Rep 712 (2000)). For example, a district may require a voter to supply a "redacted" copy of the voter's income tax return. This means that the voter can blacken out the tax information but must allow school officials to see what address the voter has declared as his or her residence for tax purposes (*Id.*).

Furthermore, in small city school districts, if the Board of Elections furnishes the school board with "certified registry lists" in place of the "original registers," the school board may require that any voter offer proof of identity before being allowed to vote, provided that the board must establish "reasonable rules and regulations governing the evidence necessary to prove the identity of each voter" no later than 10 days before the election (§ 2609(2)).

17. The Voting Process

In General

17:1. Do the provisions of the New York State Election Law apply to school districts?

The Election Law applies to school districts only as specifically provided by law (Elec. Law § 1-102; see also Educ. Law § 2609; *Appeal of Reed*, 55 Ed Dept Rep, Dec. No. 16,871 (2016); *Appeal of Pasquini,* 53 Ed Dept Rep, Dec. No. 16,500 (2013); *Appeal of Lanzilotta*, 48 Ed Dept Rep 428 (2009)). In general, the Education Law governs school district meetings and elections, not the Election Law (Educ. Law Art. 41).

17:2. Must school district polling places be handicapped accessible?

Yes. School districts must ensure that their designated polling locations have adequate access and parking for the disabled during the times the polls are opened. That was not the case where, during dismissal time, a school's driveway was open only to school buses and a school's additional parking lot was closed for construction (*Appeal of Goldstein*, 46 Ed Dept Rep 355 (2007)).

17:3. May school districts be divided into election districts?

Yes. Actually, small city school districts must be divided into election districts, except that those with a population of less than 10,000 may designate the entire city school district as a single election district (§ 2604; *Appeal of Saleh,* 51 Ed Dept Rep, Dec. No. 16,310 (2011)). Union free and central school districts, on the other hand, may be divided into election districts if they have adopted a system of personal registration (*Matter of Christie,* 1 Ed Dept Rep 5 (1958); see also *Matter of Nicoletta*, 7 Ed Dept Rep 115 (1968)).

The reason for this rule relates to the right of every qualified voter to challenge the qualifications of any other person offering to vote at a district meeting or election. No person can be physically present in more than one polling place at a time. Therefore, if a school district is divided into election districts, such that voting occurs simultaneously in multiple locations, the only way an individual can exercise his or her right to challenge the qualifications of multiple voters who may vote in different locations, is by examining the list of registered voters prior to voting day and filing a written challenge pursuant to Education Law section 2015 to the qualifications of voters whose names appear on the register (see *Matter of Christie*).

17:4. What is the process for dividing school districts into election districts?

Union free and central school districts with personal registration of voters may be divided into election districts by action of the board or by a majority vote of the qualified voters present and voting at a district meeting (§ 2017(1); see also *Matter of Clarke*, 13 Ed Dept Rep 256 (1974)). Each election district must have at least 300 qualified voters, and if possible, have a school building (§ 2017).

Once the decision is made, the school board must immediately adopt a resolution dividing the district into the number of election districts as it may determine. The election districts so formed continue in

School District Meetings

existence until modified by board resolution (§ 2017(2)). However, any such resolution must be adopted at least 30 days before the annual or special meeting or election. Voters then vote within their respective election districts (*Id.*).

School boards in small city school districts may pass a resolution modifying election districts already in existence pursuant to a prior board resolution. As with union free and central school districts, election districts in small city school districts should contain a public schoolhouse where possible, in which voting shall take place. A city school district with less than 10,000 inhabitants may, by board resolution, designate the entire school district as a single election district (§ 2604; see also *Appeal of Saleh,* 51 Ed Dept Rep, Dec. No. 16,310 (2011); see **17:3**).

17:5. Must voting booths be used at school district meetings?

Yes, in districts other than common school districts (§§ 2030(2), 2609(3)).

17:6. Must ballots be used at school district meetings?

Generally, yes. However, in school districts that prior to 1998 conducted their vote at the annual meeting, votes may be taken by recording the ayes and nays of the qualified voters attending and voting at the district meeting (§§ 2022(3), 2608, 2031, 2032).

17:7. May voting machines be used at school district meetings?

Yes. Although the use of voting machines is optional, it is considered to be in compliance with any provision of law requiring the vote to be by ballot (§§ 2035(1), 2611; *Hurd v. Nyquist*, 72 Misc.2d 213 (Sup. Ct. Albany Cnty. 1972); *Matter of Nicoletti*, 21 Ed Dept Rep 38 (1981)).

If voting machines are used, they must be examined by the election inspectors before each use to ensure all the counters are set at zero, that the ballot labels are properly placed, and that each machine is in all respects in proper condition for use (§ 2035(1); see also *Appeal of Breud, Jr.*, 38 Ed Dept Rep 748 (1999)).

A voting machine or machines may be purchased by the school district or, with the consent of the county board of elections, the school district may use voting machines belonging to the county or the town in which any part of the school district is located. Rental and other terms or conditions are set by resolutions of the board of elections (§ 2035(1); Elec. Law § 3-224).

17:8. Who provides the ballots or voting machines used at school district meetings?

Ballots are provided by the school district. When used for school board elections, ballots must contain the names of candidates who have been nominated, listed in the order determined by drawing lots (§§ 2032(2)(b), 2608(2); see also **6:28**). If paper ballots are used, a choice is indicated by an "×" or a "✓" by pencil or pen in a square before the name of the candidate (§ 2032(2)(d)). Regardless of whether paper ballots or voting machines are used, blank spaces must be provided for write-in candidates (§ 2032(2)(e); *Appeal of Thomas*, 47 Ed Dept Rep 442 (2008); see also **6:19** and **17:9**).

A voting machine or machines may be purchased by the school district or, with the consent of the county board of elections, the school district may use voting machines belonging to the county or the town in which any part of the school district is located. Rental and other terms or conditions are set by resolutions of the board of elections (§ 2035(1); Elec. Law § 3-224).

17:9. Must ballots and voting machines allow for write-in candidates?

Yes. Regardless of whether paper ballots or voting machines are used, slots for write-in votes must be provided to afford voters the opportunity to select an alternative candidate of their choice for each vacancy to be filled (§ 2032; *Appeal of Thomas*, 47 Ed Dept Rep 442 (2008); see also **6:19**). In districts where candidates run for specific seats on the board (§ 2018(a); see also **6:12**), one blank space must be provided under the name of the last candidate for each specific office for write-in candidates (§ 2032(2)(e)). Where candidates run at large for every vacancy rather than for a specific seat, slots for write-in votes equal to the number of vacancies to be filled must be provided (*Appeal of Thomas*; see also **6:12**).

If the ballot does not have an open space for write-in votes, and the outcome of the election is affected as a result of the omission, the election may be nullified by the commissioner of education (*Appeal of Bd. of Trustees of Syosset Pub. Library*, 32 Ed Dept Rep 460 (1993); see also *Appeal of Thomas*).

Where voting machines are used, it is improper to require voters to cast write-in ballots in a separate ballot box (*Appeal of Emond,* 54 Ed Dept Rep, Dec. No. 16,754 (2015); *Matter of Yost*, 21 Ed Dept Rep 140 (1981)).

17:10. Are there any special rules that school districts need to be aware of when counting write-in votes?

Yes. For example, there is no requirement in the Education Law that a voter place a check mark or an "x" or any other kind of mark next to the name of the write-in candidate (*Appeal of Titus*, 36 Ed Dept Rep 407 (1997); *Appeal of Gresty*, 31 Ed Dept Rep 90 (1991)). If the name of a qualified person is written on a write-in ballot, it must be counted.

In addition, write-in ballots with minor misspellings of a candidate's name should be credited to that candidate in the absence of a showing that there is another district resident with the same or a similar name (*Appeal of Cook*, 20 Ed Dept Rep 1 (1980)).

Furthermore, even though a candidate's name is pre-printed on a ballot, a voter is not precluded from writing in the candidate's name in the place designated on the machine for the office of board member (*Appeal of Roberts*, 33 Ed Dept Rep 601 (1994)).

Write-in ballots cast in the correct column but the wrong row should be counted because the voter's intent is apparent and should not be frustrated (*Appeal of Reed*, 55 Ed Dept Rep, Dec. No. 16,871 (2016)).

17:11. May proxy votes be cast at school district meetings?

No. There is no statutory authority permitting the use of proxy votes at school district meetings (*Appeal of Mauro*, 35 Ed Dept Rep 517 (1996); *Matter of Kirchhof*, 70 St. Dep't Rep. 33 (1949); *Matter of Dist. No. 1 of the Town of Pittstown*, 58 State Dep't Rep. 423 (1937)).

17:12. What happens if people are still in line waiting to vote at the time for closing the polls?

All qualified voters who are present at the polling place must be allowed to vote (§§ 2033, 2609(4); *Appeal of Caswell,* 48 Ed Dept Rep 472 (2009); *Appeal of Fugle*, 32 Ed Dept Rep 480 (1993)). However, a voter who signs the voting ledger but leaves without voting and returns later may be prevented from voting because there would be no way to determine whether he or she already cast a vote (*Appeal of Antaki*, 47 Ed Dept Rep 228 (2007), *petition dismissed*, *Antaki v. Mills* (Sup. Ct. Albany Cnty. 2008)).

17:13. Must a poll list be made of those voting at school district meetings?

Yes. The district clerk or assistant clerk(s) maintain a poll list that contains the names and addresses of the people who actually vote in a district meeting or election. The clerk or assistant clerk(s) must record the name and legal residences of all voters as they deposit their ballots (§§ 2029, 2609(4); see *Appeal of Gang*, 32 Ed Dept Rep 337 (1992)).

However, a school district's technical failure to maintain a complete and accurate poll list is not a basis to invalidate an election, absent proof that this irregularity affected the outcome of the election (*Appeal of Crowley*, 39 Ed Dept Rep 665 (2000); *Appeal of Diamond*, 39 Ed Dept Rep 541 (2000); *Appeal of Singer,* 34 Ed Dept Rep 355 (1995); *Matter of Kavanaugh*, 5 Ed Dept Rep 19 (1965)).

Moreover, discrepancies between the machine count and the sign-in sheets at the conclusion of an election do not necessarily require that the commissioner invalidate an election absent evidence "that the outcome of the election was affected by the apparent failure of some voters to sign a poll list" (*Appeals of Campbell & Coleman*, 41 Ed Dept Rep 207 (2001)).

Seventeen-year-old students enrolled in a public school may serve as a poll clerk provided they have parental consent. For purposes of school attendance, students serving in such a capacity while school is in session are to be recorded as in attendance (§§ 2025(6), 2607, 3207-a; see also Elec. Law § 3-400(6), (8); Lab. Law §§ 132(3)(f), 143(6)). However, the failure to appoint such a student does not, by itself, constitute grounds for invalidating the vote outcome (§ 2036).

17:14. Are poll lists subject to public inspection?

Yes. Poll lists are public documents and as such must be made available for inspection and copying by interested persons (§ 2116). On the day of the election, districts may make poll list(s) available in an evenhanded manner and without undue disruption to the electoral process (*Appeal of Walsh*, 34 Ed Dept Rep 544 (1995); *Appeal of Schneider*, 29 Ed Dept Rep 151 (1989); see also *Appeal of Crowley*, 39 Ed Dept Rep 665 (2000)).

17:15. May school districts conduct exit polls at the polling place?

There is nothing improper about conducting an "exit poll" at a polling place so long as voter access to the polls is not hampered (*Appeal of Tudor*, 38 Ed Dept Rep 591 (1999)).

17:16. May school board candidates appoint poll watchers?

Yes, but only in school districts that have adopted a system of personal registration (§ 2019-a(2)(c), (d); see also *Appeal of Morris,* 37 Ed Dept Rep 590 (1998)). There is no authority for a candidate to appoint poll watchers in districts without personal registration (*Appeal of Chaplin, Jr.*, 30 Ed Dept Rep 420 (1991)).

Even in districts without personal registration, there is nothing to prevent a qualified voter who supports a particular candidate from being present at a polling place and exercising his or her right to challenge the qualifications of other voters under the Education Law (§§ 2015, 2019, 2609(5)). However, such an individual may not interfere with the election or engage in electioneering, which of course, even a designated poll watcher cannot do. According to the commissioner of education, "the mere presence of partisan individuals or groups on school grounds during a school election is not in and of itself improper provided that no electioneering takes place" (*Appeal of Giuliano*, 37 Ed Dept Rep 572 (1998)).

17:17. Must there be election inspectors at school district meetings?

Yes. In non-city districts, there must be at least two election inspectors for each ballot box or voting machine in use (§ 2025(3)).

In common school districts, election inspectors are elected by the voters. The election inspectors choose a chief election inspector. There must be at least two inspectors per voting machine or ballot box (§ 2025(3)(a)).

In union free and central school districts, the school board appoints the election inspectors (at least two per machine or ballot box), in connection with the conduct of a district meeting and election. The board also designates a chief election inspector. Where the district is divided into election districts, the board must appoint a chief election inspector for each election district (§ 2025(3)(b)).

In small city school districts, the school board is required to appoint three election inspectors for each election district, and may appoint additional election inspectors if necessary. The inspectors themselves elect one of their number as chairperson and one as poll clerk. The chairperson may appoint one of the inspectors as assistant poll clerk (§ 2607).

The failure to appoint the required number of election inspectors can invalidate a school district election only if the error affects the outcome of the election (*Appeal of Uciechowski*, 32 Ed Dept Rep 511 (1993)). The same is true if a district removes one of the election inspectors on the day of the district meeting (*Appeal of Lanzilotta*, 48 Ed Dept Rep 428 (2009)).

17:18. Are there any restrictions on who may serve as an election inspector?

In small city school districts, the Education Law requires that election inspectors be qualified voters of the school district (§ 2607; see also **16:1**). However, the Education Law also permits the appointment of 17-year-old students enrolled in a school district to serve as an election inspector in all school districts (§§ 2025, 2607, 3207-a; see also Elec. Law § 3-400(6), (8); Lab. Law §§ 132(3)(f), 143(6)), with parental consent (§ 3207-a). Students serving as an election inspector while school is in session are to be recorded as in attendance (§ 3207-a).

The failure to appoint or elect a qualified voter or a 17 year-old student as an election inspector does not, in and of itself, constitute cause for invalidating the proceedings of an annual or special school district meeting (§ 2036).

Nothing prohibits district employees, school board members, relatives of board members or candidates from serving as election inspectors (*Appeal of Caswell,* 48 Ed Dept Rep 472 (2009); *Appeal of Marchesani*, 44 Ed Dept Rep 460 (2005); *Appeal of Crowley*, 39 Ed Dept Rep 665 (2000); *Appeal of Goldman*, 35 Ed Dept Rep 126 (1995); *Appeal of Bleier*, 32 Ed Dept Rep 63 (1992)).

There is no legal requirement that election inspectors receive training (*Appeals of Ghezzi & Farr*, 55 Ed Dept Rep, Dec. No. 16,890 (2016)).

17:19. Are election inspectors entitled to compensation?

Election inspectors in union free and central school districts are compensated at a rate set by the school board (§ 2025(5)). Election inspectors in small city school districts are compensated at a rate set by the school board, not to exceed the basic compensation paid to election inspectors at the preceding general election, as fixed by the governing body of the city in which the school district is located (§ 2607).

Absentee Ballots

17:20. Must school districts make available absentee ballots?

Yes. All school districts are required by law to make absentee ballots available to qualified voters for the election of school board members, school district public library trustees, the adoption of the annual budget, and school district public library budgets and referenda (§§ 2018-a, 2018-b, 2613).

A board of cooperative educational services (BOCES) that is holding certain referenda for submission to the voters within the BOCES supervisory district also must make absentee ballots available to qualified voters pursuant to procedures established by regulations promulgated by the commissioner of education (§ 1951(2)(s)).

17:21. Who is entitled to an absentee ballot?

In general, absentee ballots must be provided upon proper application to any qualified voter who will be unable to vote in person due to illness or physical disability, hospitalization, incarceration (unless incarcerated for conviction of a felony), travel outside the voter's county or city of residence for employment or business reasons, studies, or vacation on the day of the election (§§ 2018-a(2), 2018-b(2)).

Dual home ownership does not automatically confer entitlement to an absentee ballot, as a person may have only one legal residence or domicile for purposes of voting at a school district election or budget vote (*Appeals of Ryan, Starbuck, and Toomey*, 50 Ed Dept Rep, Dec. No. 16,202 (2011); *Appeal of Klein*, 47 Ed Dept Rep 409 (2008); see **16:1**). Absent proof of permanent residence, the owner of a home within a school district would not be entitled to an absentee ballot (*Id.*). That was the case where the owner of two homes in different counties sought to vote by absentee ballot in a district where one of the homes was located even though he claimed a State School Tax Relief exemption available only for a primary residence on the other (*Appeal of Klein*). That also was the case where various owners of homes within a school district were either registered to vote on national elections in another state, or operated a business outside the state and lived within the district "from time to time and for varying periods of time" (*Appeal of Ryan, Starbuck, and Toomey*).

17:22. Can a person request more than one absentee ballot application?

Yes. Moreover, there is no authority under the Education Law for a school district to demand a list of the voters who will use the applications from an individual seeking multiple absentee ballot applications (*Appeal of the Roxbury Taxpayers Alliance*, 34 Ed Dept Rep 576 (1995)).

17:23. What is the process for issuing absentee ballots?

In districts with personal registration, the board of registration must automatically mail an absentee ballot to each voter whose registration record on file with the county board of elections is marked "permanently disabled" (§ 2018-a(2)(g)).

In districts without personal registration, the district clerk or other designee of the school board must automatically mail an absentee ballot to voters who have previously applied for an absentee ballot and whose registration record on file with the county board of elections is marked "permanently disabled" (§ 2018-b(2)(g)).

All other voters must submit an application prior to obtaining an absentee ballot (§§ 2018-a(2)(a), 2018-b(2)(a)), except as noted below (see also **17:24, 17:28**). The information that must be included in the application is set by statute (§§ 2018-a(2)(a), 2018-b(2)(a)). The application must be received by the district clerk or designee at least seven days before the election, if the ballot is to be mailed to the voter, or the day before the election, if the ballot is to be issued to the voter in person (§§ 2018-a(2)(a), 2018-b(2)(a)).

Upon receipt of an application, either the board of registration (in districts with personal registration) or district clerk or other designee of the school board (in districts without personal registration) must review the application to determine if the applicant is a qualified voter and is otherwise entitled to vote by absentee ballot (§§ 2018-a(3), 2018-b(3)). Applications that do not specify the reasons why a voter will be unable to vote in person on the day of the election, cannot be accepted (see *Matter of Levine*, 24 Ed Dept Rep 172 (1984), *aff'd sub nom. Capobianco v. Ambach*, 112 A.D.2d 640 (3d Dep't 1985); cf. *Appeal of Frasier*, 34 Ed Dept Rep 315 (1994)).

If the application is proper in all respects, the board of registration or district clerk or other designee of the board then mails or personally issues an absentee ballot to the voter. The board of registration or district clerk must then record the name of the voter to whom the absentee ballot was issued on the district's personal registration list or poll list (§§ 2018-a(3), 2018-b(3)).

17:24. May a district issue an absentee ballot to a voter who has not submitted an application?

Yes, but only under limited circumstances. Districts with personal registration must automatically issue an absentee ballot to any voter whose registration record is marked "permanently disabled." Districts without personal registration must automatically issue an absentee ballot to any voter who has previously applied for an absentee ballot and whose registration record is marked "permanently disabled" (see **17:23**).

The only other time a district may issue a ballot prior to receiving a properly completed application is upon receipt of a request for an absentee ballot by letter signed by the voter. Moreover, this exception only applies in districts that do not use personal registration. In such districts, any qualified voter may request a ballot by signed letter, rather than by application. The letter must be received by the district clerk or designee no earlier than 30 days before the election and no later than seven days before the election. Upon receipt of the letter request, the clerk must send both an application and a ballot to the voter at the same time. The voter then completes both the application and the ballot and returns them together in the same envelope. In fact, the law specifically provides that the ballot will not be counted unless the completed application is returned with it (§ 2018-b(4)).

A word of caution is in order: this same procedure is not statutorily authorized in districts that use personal registration. In one case involving a district that used a system of personal registration, the commissioner of education invalidated the absentee ballots of two voters who returned their absentee ballot applications inside the same envelopes as their ballots. According to the commissioner, the "inclusion of the applications in the sealed ballot envelopes with the ballots was an act extrinsic to the ballot in violation of § 2034(3)(a), which voids the whole ballot" (*Appeal of McGrath*, 38 Ed Dept Rep 707 (1999)).

17:25. How far in advance of a district vote must a school district make absentee ballots available to voters?

The law is generally silent on when districts must begin making absentee ballot applications available to voters. With the exception of absentee ballots issued upon receipt of a request by letter (see **17:24**), nothing in the law specifies how far in advance of an election school districts must begin making applications for absentee ballots available (see *Appeal of Roxbury Taxpayers Alliance*, 34 Ed Dept Rep 576 (1995)).

However, since the notice of the district meeting must include a statement that qualified voters may apply for absentee ballots at the clerk's office (§ 2004(7)), as a practical matter, ballot applications should be made available at the time of the first publication of the notice of the district meeting and must be made available far enough in advance of the meeting date to permit voters to apply for and return completed ballots as required by law.

17:26. Must a school district maintain a list of individuals who have been issued absentee ballots?

Yes. The board of registration (in districts with personal registration) must make a list of all persons to whom absentee ballots have been issued, and file the list in the office of the district clerk, where it must be available for public inspection during regular office hours until the day of the election (§ 2018-a(6)).

Similarly, the district clerk or other designee of the school board (in districts without personal registration) must make a list of all persons to whom absentee ballots have been issued and make it available for public inspection during regular office hours until the day of the election (§ 2018-b(7); see also *Appeal of Laurie*, 42 Ed Dept Rep 313 (2003); but see § 2004(7)).

There is no statutorily prescribed schedule by which school districts must make the absentee voter ballot list available for public inspection (*Appeal of Williams*, 55 Ed Dept Rep, Dec. No. 16,900 (2016)). However, the list should be made available with sufficient time for a qualified voter to challenge the qualifications of someone on the list to vote by absentee ballot (see **17:29-30**).

17:27. What is the deadline for the submission of absentee ballots?

No absentee voter's ballot will be counted unless it is received in the office of the district clerk (clerk or designee of the school board in districts without personal registration) by 5:00 p.m. on the day of the election (§§ 2018-a(8), 2018-b(9); *Appeal of Touré,* 54 Ed Dept Rep, Dec. No. 16,660 (2014)).

17:28. Is absentee voting conducted differently in nursing homes and other adult care facilities?

Yes, under certain, limited circumstances. Education Law section 1501-c makes Election Law section 8-407 applicable to "all elections conducted . . . by a school district" pursuant to Title II of the Education Law. Pursuant to Election Law section 8-407, a county or city board of elections must send election inspectors between one and 13 days before a school district election to supervise the completion of absentee ballots by residents of a nursing home (or other qualifying adult care facility) for which the board of elections has received 25 or more absentee ballot applications. In its discretion, a county or city board of elections can make absentee ballots available to residents of all such facilities within its jurisdiction, without regard to the number of absentee ballot applications received from the residents of such facilities.

It is beyond a school district's authority to supervise the voting (*Appeal of Georges*, 45 Ed Dept Rep 453 (2006)).

17:29. Can an absentee ballot be challenged?

Yes. Any qualified voter may, prior to the election, file a written challenge to the qualifications of any person whose name appears on the list of absentee voters prepared for transmittal to the election inspectors on the day of the election (see **17:26**), stating the reason for such challenge (§§ 2018-a(6), 2018-b(7)). The written challenge must be transmitted by the clerk or designee to the election inspectors on the day of the election (§§ 2018-a(6), 2018-b(7)).

The commissioner of education has ruled it improper for districts with personal registration to open and/or count absentee ballots before the polls close because in those districts any qualified voter may challenge an absentee ballot during the public canvassing of such ballots after the polls close (§ 2018-a(10), (11); *Appeal of Pappas*, 38 Ed Dept Rep 582 (1999); see also **17:32**). However, there is no requirement that school board candidates or their poll watchers be present when the absentee ballots are opened (*Appeal of Bennett,* 48 Ed Dept Rep 311 (2009), *vacated on other grounds*, *Bennett v. Mills* (Sup. Ct. Albany Cnty. 2009); *Appeal of Georges*, 45 Ed Dept Rep 453 (2006)).

Preventing a qualified voter from exercising his or her right to object to a submitted absentee ballot may be grounds for invalidating the election results (*Appeal of Heller*, 34 Ed Dept Rep 220 (1994)).

17:30. Can a person wait until after the election to challenge an absentee ballot?

Not generally. The law does not permit a person to wait until after the election to challenge another person's right to vote by absentee ballot (see *Appeal of Karliner*, 36 Ed Dept Rep 30 (1996)). However, in one case, the commissioner excused a petitioner's untimely challenge, finding that the board's failure to post a list of all persons to whom absentee ballots were issued and the failure to have available a comprehensive list of such persons "prevented petitioner from having a reasonable opportunity to challenge the disputed absentee ballots at the time of the election" (*Matter of Levine*, 24 Ed Dept Rep 172 (1984), *aff'd sub nom. Capobianco v. Ambach*, 112 A.D.2d 640 (3d Dep't 1985)). In another case, the commissioner excused an untimely challenge to absentee ballots cast in a district library vote, where it was alleged that a school board member fraudulently induced several voters to file false applications, and such fraud "was undetected at the time because the board member was somehow able to circumvent the statutory requirements for the handling of absentee ballots" (see *Appeal of the Weller Library Comm'n*, 42 Ed Dept Rep 338 (2003); see also *Appeal of Touré*, 54 Ed Dept Rep, Dec. No. 16,660 (2014)).

Counting of Votes

17:31. How are votes counted?

The election inspectors count the ballots and tally the votes (§§ 2034(2), 2610(2); *Appeal of Murtagh*, 19 Ed Dept Rep 179 (1979)). For the process for districts that do not use voting machines, see § 2034(1). For additional or different procedures in small city school districts see § 2610.

The sole method of securing a recount of the vote is pursuant to an appeal to the commissioner of education (§ 2034(6)(a); *Appeal of the Bd. of Educ. of the Deposit CSD,* 49 Ed Dept Rep 449 (2010); *Appeal of Bennett*, 48 Ed Dept Rep 311 (2009), *vacated on other grounds*, *Bennett v. Mills,* (Sup. Ct. Albany Cnty. 2009); *Appeal of Ell*, 34 Ed Dept Rep 394 (1995); see also **17:34**).

School District Meetings

17:32. How are absentee ballots counted?

After the closing of the polls, the election inspectors examine absentee voters' ballots received by the district in the manner required by law. Absent any grounds for rejecting such ballot, the election inspectors will open the envelope containing the absentee ballot, withdraw the ballot and deposit it unfolded in the proper ballot box (§§ 2018-a(10), 2018-b(11); see also §§ 2018-a(6), 2018-b(7)). The election inspectors will then count or canvass the absentee ballots along with the other ballots cast or the votes recorded on voting machines (§§ 2018-a(12), 2018-b(12)).

Counting of absentee ballots with incorrect or no dates is not unlawful. Missing or inaccurate dates on the ballot envelopes are not grounds for voiding a ballot (*Appeal of Georges*, 45 Ed Dept Rep 453 (2006)).

In school districts with personal registration, the election inspectors must examine and open the absentee ballot envelopes in public so that qualified voters present in the polling place have an opportunity to object to the voting of any such ballot (§ 2018-a(11); *Appeal of Pappas*, 38 Ed Dept Rep 582 (1999)). There is no requirement, however, that the absentee ballots be opened in front of candidates running for a seat on the school board or their poll watchers (*Appeal of Ringelheim,* 49 Ed Dept Rep 378 (2010); *Appeal of Bennett*, 48 Ed Dept Rep 311 (2009), *vacated on other grounds*, *Bennett v. Mills* (Sup. Ct. Albany Cnty. 2009); *Appeal of Georges*). Neither is there a requirement that there be a public announcement as to the counting of the ballots (*Appeal of Bennett; Appeal of Pappas*), or that there be a close proximity between the counting of the absentee ballots and other votes cast (*Appeal of Bennett*).

For information on challenges to absentee ballots, see **17:29-30**.

17:33. Who announces the results of the vote count?

The chairperson of the meeting at which the election takes place declares the result of each ballot, as announced by the election inspectors (§ 2034(7)(a)).

If a district has been divided into election districts, and voting machines are used, the election inspectors must make a written report of the results, signed by all the inspectors, to the chief election inspector of each district, who then reports the results to the district clerk within 24 hours. The school board then tabulates and declares the result of the ballot within 24 hours of receiving the results (§§ 2034(7)(b), 2610(4)).

Challenges to Vote Results

17:34. What happens if an error is discovered related to the tallying of votes?

All disputes regarding the validity of any district meeting or election must be referred to the commissioner of education (§ 2037; *Appeal of the Bd. of Educ. of the Hempstead UFSD*, 55 Ed Dept Rep, Dec. No. 16,878 (2016); *Appeal of Bennett*, 48 Ed Dept Rep 311 (2009), *vacated on other grounds*, *Bennett v. Mills,* (Sup. Ct. Albany Cnty. 2009)).

Upon the filing of a petition, the commissioner may annul the vote, and in his or her discretion order a new meeting or election or a recounting of the votes (§§ 2034(6)(a), 2037; see *Appeal of the Bd. of Educ. of North Colonie CSD,* 51 Ed Dept Rep, Dec. No. 16,351 (2012); *Appeal of the Bd. of Educ. of the Crown Point CSD,* 51 Ed Dept Rep, Dec. No. 16,291 (2011); *Appeal of the Bd. of Educ. of the City Sch. Dist. of the City of Elmira*, 47 Ed Dept Rep 27 (2007)).

The petition may be filed by a district resident or a school board itself (see *Appeal of Bd. of Educ. of the Hempstead UFSD*; *Appeal of the Bd. of Educ. of the Goshen CSD*, 47 Ed Dept Rep 352 (2008); *Appeal of the Bd. of Educ. of the City Sch. Dist. of the City of Elmira*). For example, in one case, the commissioner granted a school board's petition seeking to overturn the election of school board members and install the correct candidates after the district clerk discovered a mathematical error had been made in the original tallying of the votes (*Appeal of the Bd. of Educ. of the City Sch. Dist. of the City of Elmira*). In another case, the commissioner granted a school board's petition to overturn and correct election results submitted after the school board discovered the tally for election of board members only included results from one of six voting machines (*Appeal of the Bd. of Educ. of the Hyde Park CSD,* 48 Ed Dept Rep 501 (2009)).

The commissioner's decisions in these matters are final and not subject to review (§ 2037; but see *Finch, Pruyn & Company, Inc. v. Mills*, 297 A.D.2d 406 (3d Dep't 2002)).

17:35. What happens if a school district election is found to have been improperly held in other respects?

The commissioner of education may set aside the election results and/or may order the district to conduct a new election (§ 2037). However, there is a presumption of regularity in the conduct of school district elections. The burden of proof rests on the person who challenges the results to establish all the facts based upon which he or she seeks to have the commissioner overturn the election results.

17:36. What is the basic standard used by the commissioner of education to overturn the results of a school district election?

First, the challenger must prove that an irregularity occurred, such as a violation of the Education Law or commissioner's regulations. "Mere speculation as to the possible existence of irregularities provides an insufficient basis on which to annul election results" (*Appeal of Antaki and Mosman*, 47 Ed Dept

Rep 228 (2007), *petition dismissed, Antaki v. Mills* (Sup. Ct. Albany Cnty. 2008); see also *Appeal of DeBerardinis,* 39 Ed Dept Rep 145 (1999)).

Second, the challenger must prove that the irregularity actually affected the outcome of the election. Usually, if an irregularity occurred but did not actually affect the outcome of the election, the commissioner will decline to overturn the results of the election (see *Appeal of Carey*, 53 Ed Dept Rep, Dec. No. 16,435 (2012); *Appeal of Karpoff,* 40 Ed Dept Rep 459 (2000), 192 Misc.2d 487 (Sup. Ct. Albany Cnty. 2001), *aff'd*, 296 A.D.2d 691 (3d Dep't 2002), *appeal denied*, 99 N.Y.2d 501 (2002)). Thus, in one case, the commissioner declined to overturn a bond vote even though the district failed to provide the legally required number of printed scanner ballots to the election inspectors prior to the opening of the polls. The district's use of emergency paper ballots was reasonable and that the challengers failed to prove that the outcome of the vote was affected (*Appeal of Ghezzi & Farr*, 55 Ed Dept Rep, Dec. No. 16,890 (2016)).

But, on occasion, the probability that the irregularity affected the outcome of a vote will suffice. That was the case where the commissioner invalidated certain absentee ballots and the vote on a library proposition ended in a tie. Even though there was no proof that the invalidated absentee ballots actually cast a vote on the library proposition, the commissioner found "the probability that the will of the voters was not expressed, because of illegally cast absentee votes, to be too high to allow the election results to stand" (*Appeal of the Weller Library Comm'n*, 42 Ed Dept Rep 338 (2003); see also *Appeal of Pasquini*, 53 Ed Dept Rep, Dec. No. 16,500 (2013); *Appeal of Cobb*, 32 Ed Dept Rep 139 (1992); *Matter of Boyes v. Allen*, 32 A.D.2d 990 (3d Dep't 1969), *aff'd*, 26 N.Y.2d 709 (1970); *Appeal of Crawmer*, 36 Ed Dept Rep 206 (1995), *aff'd,* 239 A.D.2d 844 (3d Dep't 1997), *appeal dismissed*, 90 N.Y.2d 934, *appeal denied*, 91 N.Y.2d 804 (1997)).

Also on occasion, the commissioner may overturn the results of a school district election under an alternative standard (see **17:37**).

17:37. Are there any alternative standards used by the commissioner of education to overturn a school district election?

Yes. The commissioner of education may overturn the results of an election also if the challenger can prove irregularities occurred that were "so pervasive that they vitiated the electoral process" or can "demonstrate a clear and convincing picture of informality to the point of laxity in adherence to the Education Law." The commissioner has made it clear, however, that "it is a rare case where errors in the conduct of the election become so pervasive that they vitiate the fundamental fairness of the election" (*Appeal of Touissant*, 53 Ed Dept Rep Dec. No. 16,494 (2013); *Appeal of Georges,* 45 Ed Dept Rep 453 (2006); *Appeal of Levine*, 24 Ed Dept Rep 172 (1984), *aff'd sub nom. Capobianco v. Ambach,* 112 A.D.2d 640 (3d Dep't 1985)).

That happened, for example, in a case where the irregularities included, but were not limited to, the failure to have a sufficient number of election inspectors, the failure to open all the absentee ballots in public, the lack of clarity as to whether paper ballots were counted in the results, and a discrepancy between the number of voters on the poll list and votes cast (*Appeal of Lanzilotta*, 48 Ed Dept Rep 428 (2009)).

Other examples involving voting machines include:

- where the voting machines malfunctioned and the number of votes registered on the machines did not match the machines' public counters showing how many voters voted (*Appeal of Bd. of Educ. of the Goshen CSD*, 47 Ed Dept Rep 352 (2008)).
- where approximately 30 percent of the votes were cast using a lever not corresponding to a candidate's name causing nearly one-third of the voters to misplace their vote (*Appeal of Bd. of Educ. of the Schroon Lake CSD,* 47 Ed Dept Rep 502 (2008)).

- where the voting machines incorrectly displayed the prior year's budget proposal (*Appeal of the Bd. of Educ. of the Rush-Henrietta CSD,* 48 Ed Dept Rep 486 (2009)), and a prior year school bus proposition (*Appeal of the Bd. of Educ. of the Beekmantown CSD,* 50 Ed Dept Rep, Dec. No. 16,253 (2011)).

In comparison, voting machine problems did not support overturning the results of an election in a case where the rear doors of the voting machines were open and unlocked, but the key on the side of the machine that locked the control to prevent tampering was in the proper position and the machines functioned properly, and where the curtain fell off a voting machine during voting but was fixed by the Board of Elections and the malfunction did not affect the vote count while the machine was in service (*Appeal of Bennett*, 48 Ed Dept Rep 311 (2009); see also *Appeal of the Bd. of Educ. of the North Colonie CSD,* 51 Ed Dept Rep, Dec. No. 16,351 (2012)).

17:38. Must school districts keep district meeting and elections records?

Yes. The "Records Retention and Disposition Schedule ED-1" (8 NYCRR § 185.12 "Appendix I"), which all school districts and boards of cooperative educational services must follow, sets forth specific periods of time that various types of school elections records must be maintained. For example, "final election results, including election inspectors' return and statement of canvass (where information is not duplicated in report of final election results) and election results report" must be *permanently* maintained.

Schedule ED-1 is available electronically at: http://www.archives.nysed.gov/records/retention_ed-1. For additional information, contact your respective Local Government Regional Advisory Officer at http://www.archives.nysed.gov/directories/rao.

In addition, in districts that use paper ballots and ballot boxes, the Education Law further requires that after the election is over and the results have been announced, the election inspectors must lock and seal the ballot boxes, and the chief election inspector must deliver them to the district clerk. Thereafter, the ballot boxes cannot be opened, except: (1) upon order of the commissioner; or (2) after the elapse of a period of six months without challenge to the election, the board passes a resolution ordering the opening of the ballot boxes and the destruction of the ballots therein (§ 2034(6)).

18. The School Budget

Overview

18:1. Are school districts required to have a budget?

Yes. The Education Law requires that school districts other than large city school districts present an annual budget to the district voters for their approval (§§ 1608, 1716, 1804(4), 2601-a; see also **5:1**). If the voters refuse to approve a budget, the school board must adopt a contingency budget (§§ 2022(4), (5), 2023(1), 2601-a(4), (5); see also **chapter 20**).

There is no limit on the level of expenditures provided for by a school budget. However, there is a *tax levy limit* on the amount of taxes school districts may levy in any given year.

Property tax levies from one year to the next can grow only by the lesser of 2% or the sum of 1 plus the inflation factor (§ 2023-a(2)). Nonetheless, the *allowable growth factor* will never be less than 1 (§ 2023-a(2)). The applicable *inflation factor* is the unadjusted monthly average change from January to December for the "All Items Consumer Price Index for All Urban Consumers" (CPI-U) in the base year, as published by the Bureau of Labor Statistics (§ 2023-a(2)(f); NYS Education Department, *Property Tax Cap Guidance* (Apr. 2015), at: http://www.p12.nysed.gov/mgtserv/propertytax/taxcap/docs/Property_Tax_%20Cap_General_Guidance_and_FAQS.pdf).

The tax levy limitation, also referred to as the tax levy cap, is applicable to common, union free, central, central high and small city school districts (§ 2023-a(2)(h)). With respect to the Big 5 school districts, New York City is not subject to the tax levy cap. The Buffalo, Rochester, Syracuse and Yonkers districts have no taxing authority and are fiscally dependent on their respective cities. However, those cities are also subject to the tax levy cap and the districts will be affected by the impact of the cap on their cities (see *Property Tax Cap Guidance*).

As a practical matter, although the property tax levy limitation does not impose a cap on school district budgets, it will impact budget planning and expenditures. This is because a school budget that meets the tax levy limitation requires only a majority vote of the school district voters present and voting to pass. However, a school budget that would result in a tax levy that exceeds the district's tax levy cap requires a supermajority vote of 60% to pass (§ 2023-a(6)(a)). An effort to challenge the tax levy cap law as unconstitutional failed in court (*N.Y. State United Teachers v. State of N.Y.*, 46 Misc.3d 250 (Sup. Ct. Albany Cnty. 2014), *aff'd*, 140 A.D.3d 90 (3d Dep't 2016)).

For information on the calculation of a school district's tax levy limitation, see **19:5–15**.

School Budget Components and Attachments

18:2. What kind of information must be included in the proposed school district budget?

School districts must present a detailed written statement of the amount of money that will be required for the coming school year for school purposes, specifying the various purposes of proposed funding and the amount of each. This statement must show the total amount necessary to pay boards of cooperative educational services in full, with no deduction of estimated state aid. It must also include the amount of state aid to be provided and its percentage relationship to total expenditures. This statement must be completed at least seven days before the budget hearing at which it is to be presented (§§ 1608(1), 1716(1), 2601-a(3); see **19:1, 19:16**).

The proposed budget must be written in plain language; in other words, easy to read and understand. It must include a complete, accurate, and detailed written statement of estimated revenues, including payments in lieu of taxes, and property tax refunds from certiorari proceedings, proposed expenditures, transfers to other funds, and the amount of fund balance to be used in support of budgetary appropriations, as well as a comparison with the prior year's data (§§ 305(26), 1608(3), 1716(3), 2601-a(3); 8 NYCRR § 170.9; see also *Appeal of Herloski*, 43 Ed Dept Rep 348 (2004)).

Districts must present their proposed budgets in three component parts: (1) a program component; (2) a capital component; and (3) an administrative component (§§ 1608(4), 1716(4), 2601-a(3); see also 8 NYCRR § 170.8(a)).

Districts also must append a number of attachments to the budget document, including a statement on administrative salaries, a school district report card, a property tax report card, a tax exemption report, and, as required by commissioner's regulations, a school leadership and school progress report card (see **18:6–12**).

18:3. What must be included in the program component of the proposed budget?

The program component must include all program expenditures of the school district, including the salaries and benefits of teachers and any school administrators and supervisors who spend the majority of their time performing teaching duties, and all transportation operating expenses (§§ 1608(4), 1716(4), 2601-a(3)). This must include appropriations for the following accounts and functions: inservice training-instruction, teaching-regular school, programs for students with disabilities, occupational education, teaching-special schools, school library and audio-visual, educational television, computer assisted instruction, attendance-regular school, guidance-regular school, health services, psychological services-regular school, social work services-regular school, personnel services-special schools, co-curricular activities-regular school, interscholastic athletics-regular school, district transportation services excluding school bus purchases, garage building, contract transportation, recreation, youth programs, civic activities, employee benefits attributable to salaries included in other accounts and functions in the program component, transfers to school lunch, school store, special aid funds, legal services relating directly to other accounts, and functions in the program component (8 NYCRR § 170.8(c)).

18:4. What must be included in the capital component of the proposed budget?

The capital component must include all transportation capital, debt service and lease expenditures and costs resulting from judgments in tax certiorari proceedings or the payment of awards from court judgments, and administrative orders or settled or compromised claims. It must also include all facilities costs of the school district, including facilities lease expenditures; the annual debt service and total debt for all facilities financed by bonds and notes of the school district; and the costs of construction, acquisition, reconstruction, rehabilitation, or improvement of school buildings. This part of the budget must include a rental, operations, and maintenance section that includes base rental costs per square foot; operation and maintenance charges per square foot and total costs per square foot for each facility leased by the school district; and any and all expenditures associated with custodial salaries and benefits, service contracts, supplies, utilities, and maintenance and repair of school facilities (§§ 1608(4), 1716(4), 2601-a(3)). This must include appropriations for the following accounts and functions: operation of plant; maintenance of plant; school bus purchases; debt service; transfers to capital and debt service funds; and employee benefits attributable to salaries included in other accounts and functions in the capital component (8 NYCRR § 170.8(d)).

In accordance with the above statutory and regulatory requirements, a school district may not place the purchase of school buses and maintenance vehicles in a separate proposition when such items are being bought with general funds. Instead, they belong in the capital component of the budget. A separate proposition is permissible only when specifically required by law as in the case of installment purchase contracts or bonding (*Appeal of Hubbard*, 45 Ed Dept Rep 496 (2006)).

18:5. What must be included in the administrative component of the proposed budget?

The administrative component must include: office and central administrative expenses; traveling expenses and all compensation, salaries and benefits of all school administrators and supervisors, including business administrators, superintendents of schools and deputy, assistant, associate or other superintendents under all existing employment contracts or collective bargaining agreements; any and all expenditures associated with the operation of the school board, the office of the superintendent of schools, general administration, and the school business office; and consulting costs not directly related to student services and programs, planning and all other administrative activities (§§ 1608(4), 1716(4), 2601-a(3)). This must include appropriations for the following accounts and functions:

- school board;
- district clerk;
- district meetings;
- chief school administrator;
- business administration;
- auditing;
- treasurer;
- tax collector;
- purchasing;
- fiscal agent fees;
- legal services except those directly relating to a function included in the program component;
- personnel services;
- records management;
- public information services;
- curriculum development and supervision;
- research;
- planning;
- evaluation;
- supervision-regular school;
- supervision-special schools;
- central data processing;
- central printing and mailing;
- central storeroom;
- special items excluding tax certiorari;
- judgments and compromised claims; and,
- employee benefits attributable to salaries included in other accounts and functions in the administrative component (8 NYCRR § 170.8(b)).

18:6. What attachments must be appended to the proposed budget?

A school board must append to its proposed budget:

- an administrative salaries statement;

- the New York State school report card;
- a property tax report card; and
- a tax exemption report (see §§ 1716(5)–(7); Real Prop. Tax Law § 495(2); see **18:7–11**).

In addition, a school board must append to its proposed budget a copy of the school leadership and school progress report cards prepared by the commissioner of education (§ 305(39); see **18:12**).

18:7. What must be included in the administrative salaries statement that must be attached to the proposed budget?

The administrative salaries statement must detail the total compensation, including salary, benefits, and any in-kind or other form of remuneration to be paid to the superintendent of schools, and assistant or associate superintendents, together with a list of any other certified administrator(s) who will earn a salary of $130,000 or more (excluding other compensation and benefits) in the upcoming year, with their position title and salary. This dollar amount increases annually. For updated information, a detailed definition of salary, fringe benefits and other remuneration go to: http://www.p12.nysed.gov/mgtserv/admincomp/.

This statement must also be submitted to the commissioner of education within five days of its preparation on a form prescribed by the commissioner. The commissioner then compiles such data into a single state-wide compilation and makes it available to the governor, the Legislature, and other interested parties upon request (§§ 1608(5), 1716(5), 2601-a(3)).

18:8. What must be included in the New York State school report card that must be attached to the proposed budget?

Each school board must append to copies of its proposed budget its New York State school report card. This report card consists of the following reports prepared by the NYS Education Department, based on data submitted by each district:

- the New York State Report Card;
- the New York State Accountability Report; and
- the Fiscal Supplement (8 NYCRR § 100.2(m)(1); see also **56:19-20**).

In addition to attaching this report card to the proposed budget, school districts also must make it available for distribution at the annual meeting, transmit it to local newspapers of general circulation, and make it available to parents (8 NYCRR § 100.2(m)(3)).

Note: The statutory provisions that authorize the commissioner of education to promulgate regulations setting forth the contents of the report card refer to it as the "School District Report Card" (see §§ 1608(6), 1716(6), 2554(24), 2590-e(8), 2601-a(7)).

18:9. What must be included in the property tax report card that must be attached to the proposed budget?

The property tax report card must contain the following information:

- The amount of total spending and the total estimated school tax levy (*Appeal of Grib*, 45 Ed Dept Rep 413 (2006)) that would result from the adoption of the proposed budget.
- The percentage increase or decrease in total spending and in the total estimated school tax levy as compared with the school district budget and tax levy for the preceding school year.
- The district's tax levy limit determined pursuant to Education Law § 2023-a.
- The estimated school tax levy excluding any levy to support: (1) expenditures resulting from court orders or judgments arising from tort actions that exceed 5% of the total tax levied in the prior year; (2) increases in employer contribution rates to state retirement systems in excess of two percentage points; and (3) capital expenditures.

- The projected enrollment growth for the school year for which the budget is prepared, and the percentage change in enrollment from the previous year (see *Appeal of Goldin*, 43 Ed Dept Rep 20 (2003)). The commissioner's regulations require use of the definition of "enrollment" as set forth in Education Law section 3602(1)(n)(2) (see 8 NYCRR § 170.11(a)(6), (7)).
- The percentage increase in the consumer price index (CPI) averaged during the 12 months preceding January 1 of the prior school year as compared with the average CPI for the 12-month period immediately preceding January 1 of the current school year (§§ 1608(7)(a), (c), 1716(7)(c); 8 NYCRR § 170.11(a)(8)).
- The projected amount of the unappropriated unreserved fund balance that will be retained if the proposed budget is adopted.
- The projected amounts of the reserved fund balance and the appropriated fund balance.
- The percentage of the proposed budget that the unappropriated unreserved fund balance represents.
- The actual unappropriated unreserved fund balance retained in the budget for the preceding school year and the percentage of the preceding school year's budget that it represents (§§ 1608(7)(a), 1716(7)(a)).

In addition to attaching this tax report card to the proposed budget, districts must make it available for distribution on the day of the budget vote and transmit it to local newspapers of general circulation.

A copy of the property tax report card format, including the revisions for the tax levy limit information, is available from the NYS Education Department at: http://www.p12.nysed.gov/mgtserv/propertytax/. Although not required by law, the form includes a breakout of the permissible exclusions to the school tax levy limit (see NYS Education Department, *Property Tax Cap Guidance* (Apr. 2015), at: http://www.p12.nysed.gov/mgtserv/propertytax/taxcap/docs/Property_Tax_%20Cap_General_Guidance_and_FAQS.pdf). The breakout helps the public's understanding of the proposed tax levy and permissible exclusions to the school tax levy limit.

At the time this publication went to press, a bill passed by both houses of the Legislature, but awaiting action by the governor, would require additional information regarding reserve funds be included in the property tax report card (2016 Assembly Bill A.7675A).

18:10. Must a school board submit to the NYS Education Department (SED) a copy of the property tax report card it attaches to its proposed budget?

Yes. A copy of the tax report card must be submitted to SED by the end of the business day immediately following its approval by the school board, but no later than 24 days prior to the date of the annual meeting and election (§§ 1608(7), 1716(7), 2601-a(3); 8 NYCRR § 170.11(e)). School boards should ensure that they pass a resolution or motion adopting the real property tax report card before transmitting it to SED (see *Appeal of Hubbard*, 47 Ed Dept Rep 287 (2007); *Appeal of Hubbard*, 44 Ed Dept Rep 375 (2005)). Otherwise, they may be subject to removal from office by the commissioner of education (*Appeal of Hubbard,* 47 Ed Dept Rep 287).

SED compiles the data from all school districts whose budgets are subject to a vote of the qualified voters and makes this compilation available electronically at least 10 days prior to the state-wide uniform voting day (§§ 1608(7), 1716(7), 2601-a(3)).

18:11. What must be included in the tax exemption report that must be attached to the proposed budget?

The tax exemption report that must be attached to the proposed budget must include the following information:

- How much of the total assessed value of the final assessment roll(s) used in the budgetary process is exempt from taxation.
- Every type of exemption granted, identified by statutory authority.
- The cumulative impact of each type of exemption.
- The cumulative amount expected to be received from recipients of each type of exemption as payment in lieu of taxes or other payments.
- The cumulative impact of all exemptions granted (Real Property Tax Law § 495(1)).

The tax exemption report, which also becomes part of the final budget, is subject to the same budget preparation notice requirements, and must be posted on any district bulletin board maintained for public notice and existing district website (Real Property Tax Law § 495(2)). In addition, it must be prepared using a form prescribed by the NYS Office of Real Property Services (ORPS) available with other tax exemption report information on ORPS' website at: http://www.tax.ny.gov/research/property/exempt/exemptionreporting.htm.

18:12. What is included in the school leadership and school progress report cards that must be attached to the proposed budget?

Both report cards include an assessment by the commissioner of education of a school's progress toward achieving standards of excellence developed by the commissioner. Those standards apply to parental involvement, curriculum, teacher quality and accountability measures (§ 305(39)). The report cards are intended to help the school board, the state, and the public assess the performance of school leaders and the schools they lead (*Id.*; see **56:19-20**).

In addition, both the school leadership and school progress report cards must be made publicly available in the same manner as a school district report card (*Id.*).

18:13. Must the proposed budget include an estimate of the tax "rate" needed to generate the estimated tax levy?

No. However, while not required to do so, school districts may provide the voters with an estimate of the tax rate that would result from voter approval of the proposed budget. Any school district supplying such information to the voters should consider including an appropriate disclaimer about the accuracy and reliability of the information (*Appeal of Russo*, 41 Ed Dept Rep 182 (2001)).

Fund Balances, Appropriations and Transfers

18:14. May a school board include a fund in its budget to cover unanticipated expenses?

No. There is no authority for a school board to include in its budget what would amount to an "unofficial reserve fund" to pay for previously unbudgeted expenses (*Appeal of Clark*, 37 Ed Dept Rep 386 (1998); see **chapter 26** for information on authorized reserve funds).

18:15. May a school board retain a fund balance from unexpended funds that remain in the general fund at the end of the fiscal year?

Yes, within certain limitations. At the end of each fiscal year, a school board may retain unexpended, unreserved funds remaining in the district's general fund in an amount equal to 4 percent of the district budget for the upcoming school year. This is known as the district's *fund balance*. The board may use these funds to pay for items that constitute ordinary contingent expenses (Real Prop. Tax Law § 1318; see also *Appeal of Silletti*, 40 Ed Dept Rep 426 (2000)).

Funds properly retained under other sections of law, such as a reserve fund established pursuant to the Education Law or the General Municipal Law, are excluded from the 4 percent limitation (Real Prop. Tax Law § 1318(1); *Appeal of Wolfley and McCauley,* 50 Ed Dept Rep, Dec. No. 16,225 (2011); *Appeal of Turner, Welk and Krzeminski,* 50 Ed Dept Rep, Dec. No. 16,224 (2011); *Appeal of Doro*, 46 Ed Dept Rep 295 (2007); see also **chapter 26**).

18:16. For what purposes may a school district use unexpended, unreserved funds that exceed four percent of its budget for the upcoming school year?

The school board must use any unexpended, unreserved funds in excess of the 4 percent limit (see **18:15**), also known as *surplus funds*, to reduce the district's tax levy for the upcoming school year (Real Prop. Tax Law § 1318; *Appeal of Affronti,* 55 Ed Dept Rep, Dec. No. 16,756 (2015); *Appeal of Doro,* 46 Ed Dept Rep 295 (2007); *Appeal of Liberatore*, 42 Ed Dept Rep 321 (2003)). The tax collector's warrant must "state the amount of unexpended surplus funds in the custody of the board" and also must state "that except as authorized or required by law, such unexpended surplus funds have been applied in determining the amount of the school tax levy" (Real Prop. Tax Law § 1318; see also *Appeal of Uy & Norden*, 44 Ed Dept Rep 368 (2005); *Appeal of Silletti*, 40 Ed Dept Rep 426 (2000)).

Moreover, when determining the amount of revenue that the district needs to raise from the tax levy, the district must calculate the amount of state aid that it is likely to receive based on the "best estimate" available at the time the tax warrant is issued. According to the commissioner of education, once the state budget has been enacted into law, the amount of state aid projected for each district in the state budget becomes the *best estimate* of state aid available, and districts must use this projection when determining how much revenue to raise through the local real property tax levy (*Appeal of Wolfley and McCauley*, 50 Ed Dept Rep, Dec. No. 16,225 (2011); *Appeal of Thurnherr, Welk and Krzeminski*, 50 Ed Dept Rep, Dec. No. 16,224 (2011); *Appeal of Muench*, 44 Ed Dept Rep 398 (2005); see also *Appeal of Cook*, 47 Ed Dept Rep 402 (2008)).

A district may deviate from state aid projections for purposes of determining the best estimate of state aid when there is a satisfactory reason for doing so that is rational, reasonable, and consistent with law (*Appeal of Cirillo,* 52 Ed Dept Rep, Dec. No. 16,463 (2013); *Appeal of Muench,* 45 Ed Dept Rep 508 (2006)). A district that excluded deferred building aid attributable to projects completed in prior years from its state aid projections acted rationally because the excluded funds were attributed to revenue for the prior school year and still subject to the calculation of any surplus funds (*Appeal of Cirillo*).

18:17. May a school district levy a tax to create a planned balance?

Yes. With voter approval, school districts may levy a tax in one fiscal year to be appropriated during the next fiscal year (*Appeal of Rabideau*, 38 Ed Dept Rep 359 (1998); see also *Matter of Gardner*, 22 Ed Dept Rep 94 (1982)). This levy of such a tax establishes a *planned balance*. The primary purpose of a planned balance is to avoid the cost of borrowing to meet expenses during the first part of the fiscal year before state aid is received (*Matter of Wozniak*, 11 Ed Dept Rep 63 (1971)).

Section 2021(21) of the Education Law provides that the planned balance of a district budget is limited to the amount necessary to meet expenses during the first 120 days of the fiscal year following the fiscal year in which such tax is collected.

School districts in Suffolk County should consult the Suffolk County Tax Act regarding different provisions in that area.

18:18. Must a school board appropriate district funds in the full amount authorized in a voter approved proposition or voter approved budget?

No. A school board is not obligated to appropriate district funds in the full amount authorized by the voters. "[L]anguage in a proposition authorizing the expenditure of funds is permissive and does not require that the approved expenditure actually be made" (*Appeal of Blizzard*, 35 Ed Dept Rep 120 (1995)). Similarly, a school board is not necessarily obligated to appropriate funds in the full amount lined out in a voter approved budget. "[T]he simple act of placing a figure in a proposed budget does not in and of itself legally bind a board of education to spend that amount" (*Appeal of Behe*, 31 Ed Dept Rep 544 (1992)).

18:19. May a school board increase the budget appropriation approved by the voters?

It depends. Generally, a school board lacks authority to increase the budget appropriations approved by the voters (see § 1718; 8 NYCRR § 170.2(k)). However, a school board may revise a voter approved budget if it receives grants in aid for specific purposes, other gifts required to be spent for particular objects, and insurance proceeds received for the loss, theft, damage or destruction of district property (§1718(2); *Appeal of Cirillo*, 46 Ed Dept Rep 388 (2007)).

18:20. May a school district legally transfer funds between budget categories without voter approval?

Yes. Section 170.2(l) of the commissioner's regulations provides that "the board of education of every union free school district shall have the power and it shall be its duty: . . . (1) to make transfers between and within functional unit appropriations for teachers' salaries and ordinary contingent expenses" (*Appeal of Leman*, 39 Ed Dept Rep 35 (1999); *Appeal of Blizzard*, 35 Ed Dept Rep 120 (1995); *Appeal of Lauterback*, 30 Ed Dept Rep 223 (1990); see also *Matter of Wozniak*, 21 Ed Dept Rep 297 (1981)). School boards may, by resolution, authorize the superintendent of schools to make transfers within limits as established by the board (8 NYCRR § 170.2(l); see also *Appeal of Gargan*, 40 Ed Dept Rep 465 (2000)).

From an accounting standpoint, this regulation allows districts to transfer funds between contingent expenditure codes and/or to transfer funds from non-contingent expenditure codes to contingent expenditure codes (*Appeal of Blizzard*). However, the regulation does not allow districts to transfer funds from contingent expenditure codes to non-contingent expenditure codes, or to transfer funds between non-contingent expenditure codes.

See section 170.1 of the commissioner's regulations for rules pertaining to financial accounting in common school districts.

19. School Budget Development and Adoption

In General

19:1. Is there a deadline by which a school board must complete the budget that it plans to submit to the voters for approval?

Yes. The school board must complete the proposed budget document at least seven days before the public hearing at which the board will present the budget to the voters. However, because the budget hearing must be held seven to 14 days before the annual meeting and election, the school board must complete the budget 14 to 21 days prior to the date of the annual meeting and election, depending upon the hearing date selected by the board (§§ 1608(2), 1716(2), 2601-a(3)). This provision also applies to a budget revote (see **19:26, 19:28**).

In addition, boards must share certain budget estimates with the NYS Education Department (SED) prior to the budget vote (§§ 1608(7), 1716(7), 2601-a(3)). These estimates must be included in the district's "Property Tax Report Card" (see **18:9**) and transmitted to SED immediately following approval by the school board, but in no event later than 24 days prior to the date of the annual meeting and election (*Id.*). Therefore, as a practical matter, since the estimates provided in the property tax report card depend upon the district's budget projections, school boards may find it necessary to complete their budgets in time to make the calculations that must be stated in this report card for timely transmittal to SED.

Furthermore, a school district authorized to issue bonds or bond anticipation notes to liquidate an operating deficit must submit its budget to the comptroller and commissioner of education 30 days prior to the date the board must adopt the proposed budget. A board subject to this requirement will need to complete its proposed budget significantly earlier than the Education Law requires (Local Fin. Law § 10.10(d), see also Local Fin. Law § 29.20; see **27:4**).

19:2. Can a school board make adjustments to a completed proposed budget?

Once a school board settles upon the final dollar amount of the district budget, it still may be possible for the board to adjust various projected budgetary expenditures without changing the total dollar amount of the budget submitted to the NYS Education Department in the district's property tax report card (see **18:9**). For example, if a board chose to delete one $300,000 expenditure and simply replace it with another $300,000 expenditure, its total spending would not be altered.

19:3. Must the school board make a copy of the proposed school district budget available to the public before the district meeting at which it is presented?

Yes. Copies of the budget, together with the attachments required by law (see **18:6-12**), must be made available to district residents, upon request, at the district offices, at any public library or free association library within the district and on the school district's website, if one exists, during the 14 days immediately preceding the date of the annual meeting and election or special district meeting at which a budget vote will occur, as well as at the budget hearing and on the day of the vote (§§ 1608(2), 1716(2), 2004(6)(d), 2601-a(3)).

There is no legal requirement that the actual text of the budget be published in a newspaper or otherwise. Nor is there a legal requirement that a school district mail copies of its proposed district budget to anyone (*Appeal of Eckel*, 46 Ed Dept Rep 279 (2006); *Appeal of Chernish & DeRidder*, 39 Ed Dept Rep 204 (1999); see also *Appeal of Herloski*, 43 Ed Dept Rep 348 (2004)).

The school board must indicate in the notice of the annual meeting and election or special district meeting at which a budget vote will occur that residents may obtain a copy of the budget at any schoolhouse in the district, during designated hours, on each day other than a Saturday, Sunday, or holiday during the 14 days immediately preceding the date of the annual meeting and election, and on the day of the vote. Furthermore, at least once during the school year, the board must include, in a district-wide mailing, notice of the availability of copies of the budget (§§ 1608(2), 1716(2), 2004(6)(d), 2601-a(3)).

19:4. Must the school board make available to the public a copy of the proposed school district budget being submitted for a revote prior to the district meeting at which it will be presented?

Yes. A school board must make available a true and correct copy of any budget being resubmitted to the voters to "provide up-to-date, accurate information to the electorate" prior to a budget revote (*Appeal of Walker*, 41 Ed Dept Rep 365 (2002)).

School Budget Tax Levy Cap

19:5. Is there a deadline by which a school district must calculate its tax levy limit?

Yes. By March 1st each year, school districts must have completed the calculation of their tax levy limit and submitted to the state comptroller, the commissioner of education and the commissioner of taxation and finance, any information necessary for the calculation of the tax levy limit (§ 2023-a(3)(b)). School districts can make their calculations using the form on the state comptroller's website and then submit the calculation electronically (http://www.osc.state.ny.us/localgov/realprop/index.htm). Instructions for how to fill out the form can be found online at: http://www.osc.state.ny.us/localgov/realprop/schools/files/instructions.pdf.

A school district's determination of the tax levy limit is subject to review by the commissioner of education and the commissioner of taxation and finance (§ 2023-a(3)(b)).

Additional guidance on filling out the form is also available from the NYS Education Department's *School District Budgeting and Implementing the Property Tax Cap* (updated Apr. 2012), at: http://www.p12.nysed.gov/mgtserv/propertytax/taxcap/docs/SED-Webinar_2-17-12.pdf.

In tax years 2016, 2017, 2018 and 2019 districts have additional reporting requirements pursuant to the property tax relief credit law adopted in 2015. Qualified taxpayers will be entitled to a credit against personal income tax if they live in a school district that adopts a budget within the levy limit and who meet other requirements of the statute (Tax Law § 606(n-1)). For qualified taxpayers to receive the property tax relief credit the superintendent must certify to the state comptroller, and the commissioners of education and taxation and finance by July 21 each year that the budget as adopted does not exceed the tax levy limit (§ 2023-b(2)(a), (b)).

Additionally, each school district subject to the tax levy cap must report both its proposed and adopted budgets to the state comptroller and the commissioner of education (§ 2023-b(2)(d)).

19:6. Are there any tax levy expenditures excluded from the calculation of the tax levy limit?

Yes. There are three categories of tax levy expenditures expressly excluded from the tax levy limit. Those include tax levies related to:

- Necessary expenditures resulting from a court order or judgment against a school district arising out of a tort action for any amount that exceeds 5% of the total tax levied in the prior school year

(§ 2023-a(2)(i)(i)). However, tax certiorari decisions and breach of contract actions are not tort actions and awards pursuant to such litigation may not be excluded from the cap (see NYS Education Department, *Property Tax Cap Guidance* (revised Apr. 2015), at: http://www.p12.nysed.gov/mgtserv/propertytax/taxcap/docs/Property_Tax_%20Cap_General_Guidance_and_FAQS.pdf).

- Necessary expenditures for payment in the coming fiscal year of school district employer contributions to the New York State and Local Employees' Retirement System (ERS) and/or the New York State Teachers' Retirement system (TRS) caused by growth in the statewide average actuarial contribution rate (ERS) or the normal contribution rate (TRS) minus two percentage points, in years when the contribution rates increase by more than two percentage points from the previous year (§ 2023-a(2)(i)(ii), (iii)). For more information on how to calculate the pension exclusion, see *Property Tax Cap Guidance*).
- Expenditures necessary to support the capital tax levy (§ 2023-a(2)(i)(iv); see **19:8**).

As a practical matter, the property tax levy limitation applies to the growth of tax levies. Expenses paid for wholly from reserve accounts do not involve a tax levy. Therefore, non-capital expenditures from reserve accounts are not relevant to the calculation of the district's tax levy limit. On the other hand, a capital expenditure made from a reserve account or fund balance, does impact the calculation of the tax levy limit (see **19:12**).

19:7. Is there a formula for calculating a school districts' tax levy limit?

School districts calculate their respective tax levy limit for each school year according to a prescribed formula (§ 2023-a(3)(a)). That formula and more detailed explanations of the steps required to calculate the tax levy limit is available from the NYS Education Department in its *Property Tax Cap Guidance* (revised Apr. 2015), at: http://www.p12.nysed.gov/mgtserv/propertytax/taxcap/docs/Property_Tax_%20Cap_General_Guidance_and_FAQS.pdf).

The formula for calculation of the tax levy limit is as follows:

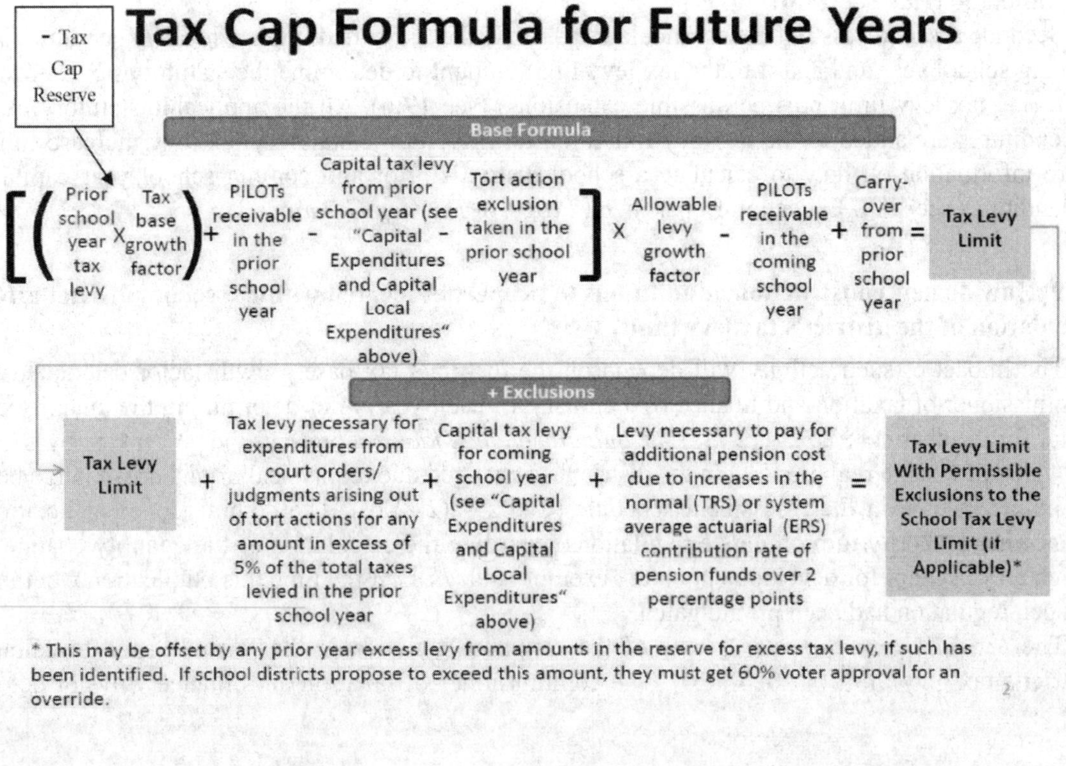

As seen above, by adding the expenditures necessary to support the statutorily excluded expenditures the district arrives at the statutory tax levy increase limit (see **19:6**). If a district proposes to exceed the statutory tax levy increase limit (tax levy limit plus permissible exclusions) the budget proposition(s) submitted to the voters must pass by 60% rather than a simple majority (§ 2023-a(6)(a); see **18:1**).

The tax levy cap formula for the 2012–2013 school year was slightly different as the tort action exclusion (see **19:6**) and available carryover allowance (see **19:11**) were not applicable.

19:8. How do capital local expenditures affect the calculation of a school district's overall tax levy limit?

Capital local expenditures are included within a school district's capital tax levy (§ 2023-a(2)(c), (d)). They include the taxes associated with budgeted expenditures resulting from the financing, refinancing, acquisition, design, construction, reconstruction, rehabilitation, improvement, furnishing and equipping of, or otherwise providing for, school district capital facilities or school district capital equipment, including debt service and lease expenditures and transportation capital debt service (§ 2023-a(2)(c)). They do not include school district expenses for a board of cooperative educational services (BOCES) capital project. As such, those BOCES capital expenditures are not excluded from the tax levy limit (NYS Education Department, *Property Tax Cap Guidance* (revised Apr. 2015), at: http://www.p12.nysed.gov/mgtserv/propertytax/taxcap/docs/Property_Tax_%20Cap_General_Guidance_and_FAQS.pdf). The commissioner of taxation and finance was given authority in 2015 to promulgate regulations which may provide for adjustment of capital local expenditures to reflect a school district's share of BOCES capital expenditures (§ 2023-a(2)(c)). At the time this publication went to press no such regulations had been promulgated.

Capital local expenditures come into play in two aspects of the tax levy limit formula (see **19:7**). First, a school district must calculate its capital local expenditures for the prior school year in order to subtract them from the prior year's total tax levy because such expenditures are excluded from the tax levy limitation (*Id.*; see **19:6**)

Second, a school district must calculate, as well, the estimated capital local expenditure for the coming school year and add it to the tax levy limit amount to determine the statutory tax levy increase limit (i.e. tax levy limit plus permissible exclusions) (see **19:6**). All the applicable statutory excluded expenditures are added to the tax levy limitation to arrive at the statutory tax levy increase limit. For more information on how to calculate a school district's prior and coming school year capital local expenditures see NYS Education Department, *Property Tax Cap Guidance*.

19:9. How do new construction or additions to properties located within a school district affect the calculation of the district's tax levy limit?

The impact of such activity will depend on the district's tax base growth factor calculated by the commissioner of taxation and finance by February 15 each year, after determining the quantity change factor for the district (§ 2023-a(2-a)). The *quantity change factor* represents the percentage by which the full value of taxable real property in the district has changed due to physical or quantity change between set points in time in the assessment schedule (§ 2023-a(2-a)(b)). The commissioner of taxation and finance has authority to promulgate regulations regarding the calculation of the quantity change factor which may account for development on tax exempt land (*Id.*). At the time this publication went to press no such regulation had been promulgated.

The *tax base growth factor* is one of the elements included in the formula used to calculate a district's tax levy limit (§ 2023-a(3)). The commissioner of taxation and finance will not determine a tax base growth factor if the quantity change factor is negative. If the quantity change factor is positive, a tax base growth factor will be determined equal to one plus the quantity change factor (§ 2023-a(2-a)(c)).

However, the tax base growth factor will never be less than one. As such, if a property becomes subject to a PILOT during the year, the tax base will be reduced by the full value of the property subject to the PILOT, but the district cannot experience a negative quantity change factor (NYS Education Department, *Property Tax Cap Guidance* (revised Apr. 2015), at: http://www.p12.nysed.gov/mgtserv/propertytax/taxcap/docs/Property_Tax_%20Cap_General_Guidance_and_FAQS.pdf).

19:10. How does the adoption of a contingency budget affect the calculation of the tax levy limit the following year?

The adoption of a contingency budget means that a school district cannot levy a tax which is greater than that levied in the prior year (i.e. a zero tax levy increase) (§§ 2023(4)(a), 2023-a(8)). A school district which adopts a contingency budget will have available carryover (see **19:11**), up to 1.5% of the tax levy limit for the previous school year at its disposal to increase the tax levy limit in the next succeeding school year (see § 2023-a(2)(b)). However, unused exclusions associated with capital expenses, growth in pension costs or tort judgments may not be carried forward (NYS Education Department, *Property Tax Cap Guidance* (revised Apr. 2015), at: http://www.p12.nysed.gov/mgtserv/propertytax/taxcap/docs/Property_Tax_%20Cap_General_Guidance_and_FAQS.pdf).

19:11. What other factors, if any, may impact the calculation of the tax levy limit?

A district's tax levy may also be affected by any *available carryover*, which refers to the amount by which the tax levy for the prior school year was below the applicable tax levy limit for such school year, if any, which cannot be more than 1.5% of the tax levy limit for such school year (§ 2023-a(2)(b)). Any available carryover must be used in the school year immediately following the school year which generated the carryover.

19:12. How do expenditures from a reserve fund impact the tax levy limit?

The tax levy limit only affects the amount a school district can levy; it does not apply a limit to district spending. Expenditures from reserve accounts that are non-capital expenditures are not relevant to the calculation of the district's tax levy limit. However, to the extent that a capital expenditure is made from a reserve account or fund balance, the amount of that expenditure does impact the calculation of the tax levy limit. Capital expenditures from reserves or fund balance are subtracted from the total amount of capital expenditures that may be excluded from a school district's tax levy limit (NYS Education Department, *Property Tax Cap Guidance* (revised Apr. 2015), at: http://www.p12.nysed.gov/mgtserv/propertytax/taxcap/docs/Property_Tax_%20Cap_General_Guidance_and_FAQS.pdf).

19:13. Can a school district's tax levy limit ever be less than the limit of the prior year?

Yes. A school district may experience such a situation when there are increases in Payments in Lieu of Taxes (PILOTS) or a reduction in capital expenditures that negatively affect levy growth.

According to the NYS Education Department, if a district has increasing or new PILOTS its tax levy limit may shrink because that amount of those PILOTS is subtracted from the total calculated by multiplying the prior year's total expenditures by the levy growth factor (NYS Education Department, *Property Tax Cap Guidance* (revised Apr. 2015), at: http://www.p12.nysed.gov/mgtserv/propertytax/taxcap/docs/Property_Tax_%20Cap_General_Guidance_and_FAQS.pdf).

Decreases in capital local expenditures may also negatively affect levy growth as those expenditures are added to the tax levy limit to arrive at a statutory tax levy increase limit (i.e. tax levy limit plus permissible exclusions). Lower capital expenditures will mean less exclusion money is being added to the tax levy limit (*Id.*).

19:14. May a school district exceed the tax levy limit?

Yes, a school district may propose a budget that will exceed the tax levy limit plus allowable exclusions. However, in order for such a budget to be approved it must be adopted by 60% of the qualified voters present and voting (§ 2023-a(6)(a)). In addition, the budget proposition(s) must be accompanied by a statutorily prescribed statement indicating that passage of the proposed budget would result in a tax levy in excess of the limitation (§ 2023-a(6)(b); see **19:25**).

Exceeding that tax levy limit in 2016, 2017, 2018, and 2019 will prevent residents from receiving a property tax relief credit (Tax Law § 606(n-1); see also §2023-b(2); see **22:3**).

19:15. What happens if a school district improperly exceeds the tax levy limit?

A school district which improperly exceeds the tax levy limit due to clerical or technical errors must place the excess amount of the excess levy in reserve in accordance with requirements prescribed by the state comptroller. The monies and any interest earned thereon must be used to reduce the tax levy for the ensuing school year (§ 2023-a(5); see also Office of the State Comptroller, Division of Local Government and School Accountability, *Reserve for Excess Tax Levy*, memorandum (Jan. 2012), at: http://www.osc.state.ny.us/localgov/pubs/releases/2011_12taxcapreserve.pdf). For more information on the tax reserve, see **chapter 26**.

In addition, when a school district improperly exceeds the property tax levy limit in one school year, the tax levy limit for the subsequent fiscal year must be based on the allowable limit for the previous fiscal year, not the total levy that included the excess amount (*Id.*).

School Budget Hearings

19:16. Are school districts required to hold a public hearing on the proposed budget prior to the budget vote?

Yes. Each school district must hold a public hearing on the budget at least seven days but not more than 14 days prior to the annual meeting and election or special district meeting at which a school budget vote will occur (§§ 1608(2), 1716(2). At the public hearing, the school board presents the proposed budget for the upcoming school year to the voters (*Appeal of Hubbard*, 45 Ed Dept Rep 422 (2006)).

Notice of the date, time, and place of the public hearing must be included in the notice of annual meeting and election or special district meeting (§§ 1608(2), 1716(2); see **15:9-10**).

19:17. Must a quorum of the board be present for the budget hearing?

Not necessarily. Many school boards conduct their budget hearing as part of a school board meeting, albeit in a location that accommodates a greater number of attendees than a typical board meeting. If the budget hearing is conducted as part of a board meeting, then a quorum of the board must approve any action taken, just as with any other board meeting (see **14:2-3**). However, if the budget hearing is not conducted as part of a board meeting, then a quorum of the board is not mandated. In one case, the commissioner of education dismissed an appeal claiming that a school board's budget hearing was improperly conducted because a quorum of the board did not attend the hearing. The commissioner found no legal requirement that a quorum of the board attend the budget hearing (see *Appeals of Campbell & Bedard & Coleman,* 41 Ed Dept Rep 207 (2001)).

19:18. Are large city school districts required to hold a public hearing on the proposed budget?

No. In large city school districts (the Big 5), school boards do not adopt a budget. Instead, they prepare an itemized estimate of the sum needed for necessary and other authorized expenses. The estimate is then filed with and acted upon by designated city officials (§§ 2576, 2590-q).

In Buffalo, it is filed with the city official authorized to receive department estimates and acted upon by such officer and the city council (§ 2576(4)).

In New York City, community district education councils submit their budget estimates to the chancellor. The chancellor then submits the estimates adopted by the city board to the mayor in the manner prescribed by the city charter (§ 2590-q). In addition, each community superintendent must prepare semi-annual and year-end reports, which include, but are not limited to, an accounting of all funds received and spent by the subject community district education council from all sources. Copies of these reports are given to the chancellor and the community district education council and must be available to the public. For specific information, see section 2590-q(17) of the Education Law.

In Rochester, Syracuse, and Yonkers, the estimate is filed with the mayor or city manager and then evaluated and dealt with in a manner similar to estimates from other city departments (§ 2576(2)).

19:19. May school district residents delete budgetary items from the board's proposed budget and call for a separate vote on the deleted items at a special meeting?

No. The Education Law provides that district residents may file a petition with the school board requesting a vote on one or more propositions regarding items that are within the powers of the voters to approve, such as capital construction and/or changes in the mileage limitations for the transportation of students. This section does not, however, include the right to delete corresponding items from the board's own proposed budget (*Matter of Amsel,* 28 Ed Dept Rep 406 (1989); see also *Appeal of Krause,* 27 Ed Dept Rep 57 (1987)).

19:20. What budget information must districts provide to residents after the public hearing on the budget?

Each school district must mail a school "Budget Notice" to all qualified voters in the district, at a point in time after the date of the public hearing on the budget, but no later than six days prior to the annual meeting and election or special district meeting at which a school budget vote will occur. It must include various comparisons and estimates specified in law and be provided in a form prescribed by the commissioner of education (§ 2022(2-a); see also **19:21**).

For a sample copy of the budget notice format prescribed by the commissioner, go to: http://www.p12.nysed.gov/mgtserv/budgeting/.

19:21. What must be included in the budget notice districts are required to provide residents after the public hearing on the budget?

The budget notice must compare the percentage increase or decrease in total spending under the proposed budget with total spending under the district budget adopted for the current school year. It also must compare the percentage increase or decrease in total spending under the proposed budget with the percentage increase or decrease in the consumer price index from January 1 of the prior school year to January 1 of the current school year (§ 2022(2-a)).

In addition, the budget notice must contain a description of how total spending and the tax levy resulting from the proposed budget would compare with a projected contingency budget, if a contingency budget were adopted on the same day as the vote on the proposed budget. This comparison must be in total, and also broken down by budget components (i.e., program, administrative, and capital). It must include a statement explaining the assumptions made in estimating the projected contingency budget (§ 2022(2-a)(a)). Projected contingency budget calculations are not subject to review and approval by the NYS Education Department (SED) (*Appeal of Russo*, 46 Ed Dept Rep 266 (2007)). Although the projected contingency budget is calculated pursuant to a state formula, the commissioner of education has cautioned districts not to refer to the estimate as being "state calculated" since the state does not in fact make this calculation for school districts (*Appeal of Rizzi*, 50 Ed Dept Rep, Dec. No. 16,160 (2010)).

The budget notice must include, as well, an estimate of the tax savings that would be available to an eligible homeowner under the basic School Tax Relief (STAR) exemption if the proposed budget was adopted (§ 2022(2-a)(b)). For more information on the STAR exemption, see **21:30-51**.

The budget notice must state the date, time, and place of the budget vote, in the same manner as in the notice of annual meeting (§ 2022(2-a)).

Finally, the budget notice must contain the district's tax levy limit, and the estimated school tax levy excluding any levy necessary to support expenditures for (1) expenditures resulting from court orders or judgments arising from tort actions that exceed 5% of the total tax levied in the prior year; (2) increases in employer contribution rates to state retirement systems in excess of two percentage points; and (3) capital expenditures (§ 2022(2-a)).

A sample budget notice is available from SED at: http://www.p12.nysed.gov/mgtserv/budgeting/. While not explicitly required by law, the sample budget notice includes a column to report the total school tax levy for permissible exclusions to the tax levy limit, which helps the public's understanding of the proposed school year tax levy (including permissible exclusions to the school tax levy limit) (see also NYS Education Department, *Property Tax Cap Guidance* (revised Apr. 2015), at: http://www.p12.nysed.gov/mgtserv/propertytax/taxcap/docs/Property_Tax_%20Cap_General_Guidance_and_FAQS.pdf).

Supplemental Budget Propositions

19:22. Can a school board submit supplemental budget propositions to the voters?

Yes. A school board has the power to submit additional items of expenditure to the voters separate and apart from those specified in the proposed budget, either on the board's own initiative or pursuant to a petition of voters (§§ 2022(2), 2035(2); see **15:23-31**). However, this authority is subject to the two-vote limit on budget propositions (see **19:29**).

Prior to the State's enactment of a property tax levy cap, the NYS Education Department had advised a board should not submit separate propositions to the voters concerning matters that are required by law to be included within one of the three budget components (see *Appeal of Hubbard*, 45 Ed Dept Rep 496 (2006); NYS Education Department, *Annual School District Budget-Presentation of Separate Propositions* Memorandum (Feb. 2006), at: http://www.p12.nysed.gov/mgtserv/budgeting/separateprop.html; see also **18:2-5**).

However, a board now may submit multiple budget propositions (§ 2023-a(9)). For example, a board may choose to put up a budget proposition with the core budget expenses and a second proposition addressing expenditures related to the additional academic programs the board would like to offer (see NYS Education Department, *Property Tax Cap Guidance* (revised Apr. 2015), at: http://www.p12.nysed.gov/mgtserv/propertytax/taxcap/docs/Property_Tax_%20Cap_General_Guidance_and_FAQS.pdf).

19:23. What types of supplemental propositions may school boards submit to the voters?

According to the NYS Education Department there are four basic types of permissible supplemental budget propositions: additional transportation service, educational programs, capital expenditure and transportation capital expenditure (see NYS Education Department, *Property Tax Cap Guidance* (revised Apr. 2015), at: http://www.p12.nysed.gov/mgtserv/propertytax/taxcap/docs/Property_Tax_%20Cap_General_Guidance_and_FAQS.pdf).

A board may combine multiple unrelated items in a single proposition or present separate propositions for each item to the voters (*Appeal of Zeller*, 45 Ed Dept Rep 337 (2006)). However, a board must be careful about combining unrelated items in a proposition. Expenditure items excluded from the tax levy limitation should not be combined with items that are subject to the tax levy limitation. Keeping the items separate will prevent items that are excluded from the cap, and otherwise would require only a simple majority vote to pass, from becoming subject to a super majority vote. Expenditure items that are subject to the cap will require a super majority of 60% to pass if a combination of the core budget proposition and supplemental propositions result in total expenditures that exceed the tax levy limitation. On the other hand, separate propositions containing only items that are excluded from the tax levy limitation will only require a simple majority to pass (see **19:25**).

Voter Approval of the School Budget

19:24. Is a minimum percentage of total eligible voters in the district required in order to approve a district's budget?

No. There is no such requirement in the law (*Appeal of Sherrill*, 43 Ed Dept Rep 312 (2003)).

Moreover, according to the commissioner of education, abstentions are irrelevant in determining the number of "qualified voters present and voting in a district wide election or referendum." For example, in one case, 2,272 voters signed the voter register. Of those, 1,109 voted "yes" for a particular proposition, while 1,076 voted "no." The commissioner ruled that the proposition was approved by a majority of the qualified voters present and voting, even though 87 of the people who signed the register did not vote on the proposition (see *Appeal of Gibeau*, 30 Ed Dept Rep 279 (1991)). The commissioner rejected the petitioner's argument in *Appeal of Gibeau* that the proposition did not pass because the abstentions when added to the "no" votes exceeded the "yes" votes (see also *Matter of Lush*, 77 St. Dep't Rep. 175 (1957), holding that "blank and void ballots are not considered in determining whether a proposition received a majority vote").

19:25. What percentage of voters must approve a budget in order for it to be adopted?

If a school board proposes a budget within the property tax levy limit, only a simple majority of qualified voters present and voting is necessary to adopt a budget. However, a budget where total expenditures exceed the property tax levy limit requires 60% of the qualified voters present and voting to approve the budget (§ 2023-a(6)(a); see *N.Y. State United Teachers v. State of N.Y.*, 46 Misc.3d 250 (Albany Cnty. 2014), *aff'd,* 140 A.D.3d 90 (3d Dep't 2016) (holding supermajority requirement is constitutional)).

The percentage of voters who must approve a budget with multiple propositions will depend on whether voter approval of a combination of the core budget proposition and the additional proposition(s) would require a district to exceed the tax levy limit. The following chart illustrates the percentage level of voter approval required in such an instance:

Proposition Type	Level of Voter Approval
Proposition for additional transportation service	**60% or more**
Proposition for additional educational programs (separate from core budget proposition)	**60% or more**
Proposition for capital expenditure	**Simple majority**
Proposition for capital transportation expenditure	**Simple majority**

Additional propositions for capital expenditures and capital transportation expenditures do not require a super majority vote because those expenses have been excluded from the tax levy limit (§ 2023-a(2)(i)(iv); see NYS Education Department, *Property Tax Cap Guidance* (revised Apr. 2015), at: http://www.p12.nysed.gov/mgtserv/propertytax/taxcap/docs/Property_Tax_%20Cap_General_Guidance_and_FAQS.pdf).

Districts that propose a budget or combination of budget propositions which exceed the tax levy limit must include in the ballot the following statement: "Adoption of this budget requires a tax levy increase of __ which exceeds the statutory tax levy increase limit of __ for this school fiscal year and therefore exceeds the state tax cap and must be approved by sixty percent of the qualified voters present and voting" (§ 2023-a(6)(b)). The first blank space is for the percent by which the total proposed tax levy for the upcoming school year (including permissible exclusions) exceeds the total tax levy for the prior school year (including permissible exclusions). The second blank space is for the percent by which the sum of the tax levy limit plus the permissible exclusions exceeds the total tax levy for the prior school year (including permissible exclusions) (*Property Tax Cap Guidance*).

A state supreme court determined this ballot statement conveys neutral facts necessary to inform a voter about the impact of his or her vote and does not violate free speech rights (*N.Y. State United Teachers v. State of N.Y.*, 46 Misc. 3d 250 (Albany Cnty. 2014) *aff'd*, 140 A.D.3d 90 (3d Dep't 2016)).

Public School Finances

19:26. What happens if the voters reject the proposed school district budget?

A school board may do one of the following:

- Prepare and adopt a contingency budget without going back to the voters, subject to the caps on contingency budgets. In this case, the board has the authority to levy a tax sufficient to pay for teachers' salaries and items that constitute ordinary contingent expenses (§§ 2022(4), (5), 2023, 2601-a(4), (5); see **chapter 20**).
- Present the original budget for a second vote, or a revised budget, at a special district meeting, within the limitations set by law (§§ 2022(4), 2601-a(4); see also **19:28, 15:20-22**).
- Adopt a contingency budget, and then present one or more propositions to the voters, giving them the opportunity to vote to fund services that cannot be provided without voter approval. A separate proposition may be presented for each such service, or several services may be included in one proposition (*Appeal of Aarseth*, 32 Ed Dept Rep 506 (1993)). Nothing in the law prohibits school districts from combining several unrelated objects and purposes in a single proposition (Local Fin. Law § 11.00; *Appeal of Friedman*, 36 Ed Dept Rep 431 (1997)). However, the additional items of expenditure must fall within the property tax levy limit for contingency budgets (see **20:4**).

A school board is under no obligation to submit a budget to the voters more than once prior to the adoption of a contingency budget, and the voters cannot compel it to do so (§ 2022(4), (5); see also *Appeal of Osten*, 35 Ed Dept Rep 160 (1995); *Appeal of Brosseau*, 31 Ed Dept Rep 155 (1991)).

For information on contingency budgets, see **chapter 20**.

19:27. What happens if the voters reject a proposed budget but adopt a supplemental proposition?

It will depend on the type of proposition (see **19:29**). Additional services required by a supplemental transportation proposition must be provided whether a district resubmits the budget for a revote or adopts a contingency budget. The expenditure for such services must be accounted for within the zero levy increase if the district adopts a contingency budget (see **20:4**). If the supplemental proposition authorized other types of expenditures, such as academic programs, capital or transportation capital expenditures, the district may decide not to make the approved expenditures (see NYS Education Department, *Property Tax Cap Guidance* (revised Apr. 2015), at: http://www.p12.nysed.gov/mgtserv/propertytax/taxcap/docs/Property_Tax_%20Cap_General_Guidance_and_FAQS.pdf; NYS Education Department, *School District Budgeting and Implementing the Property Tax Cap* (Feb. 2012), at: http://www.p12.nysed.gov/mgtserv/propertytax/taxcap/docs/SED-Webinar_2-17-12.pdf).

With respect to a supplemental academic program proposition, a school board retains its authority to prescribe the course of study by which its pupils will be graded and classified (§§ 1604(10), 1709(3), (5), (13), 1804(1), 2503(3), (4)(c), 2554(11); see *Appeal of Mishkind,* 49 Ed Dept Rep 417 (2010), *Appeal of Schildhorn,* 44 Ed Dept Rep 212 (2004); *Appeal of Reilly and Juliano,* 20 Ed Dept Rep 191 (1980), *Appeal of Talbot and Suskind,* 10 Ed Dept Rep 83 (1970)). As a practical matter, a board would not have to implement the expenditures required by a supplemental academic program proposition if it could not accommodate such expenditures within the zero levy increase for a contingency budget (see **20:1–4**), and also provide the required basic educational program.

19:28. Is there a uniform voting date for holding a budget revote?

Yes. If a school board decides to hold a budget revote, it must be held on the third Tuesday in June. The only exception is if the commissioner of education, at the request of the school district, certifies no later than March 1st that such vote would conflict with religious observances, in which case the revote must be held (if at all) on the second Tuesday in June (§ 2007(3)(b); see also **15:3**).

The law does not compel any school board to submit its district budget to the voters for approval a second time. It simply sets the date for holding a budget revote if the decision is made to do so (§§ 1804(4), 1906(1), 2005, 2006(1), 2007(3), 2601-a(2), (4), 2022(4)).

19:29. How many times can a school board submit a budget or any proposition involving the expenditure of money for a vote at a district meeting?

Two times. If the voters fail to approve a proposed budget after the second submission, or if the board elects not to put the proposed budget to a public vote a second time, the board must adopt a contingency budget (§§ 2022(4), 2601-a(4)).

In addition, school districts cannot submit to the voters more than twice during any 12-month period a proposition for the construction of a new schoolhouse or an addition to an existing schoolhouse at the same site. Moreover, districts cannot submit the second proposition to the voters within 90 days of the first vote. However, neither of these limitations applies where the voters approve a building project, but the bids that subsequently are received on the project exceed the amount approved by the voters (§ 416(6)).

20. Contingency Budgets

Overview

20:1. What is a contingency budget?

A *contingency budget* is prepared and adopted by the school board when the voters reject the board's proposed budget. The contingency budget funds only teachers' salaries and those items the board determines to be "ordinary contingent expenses" (§§ 2022(5), 2023(1), 2023-a(7), (8), 2601-a(4), (5); see **20:8-12** for more information on ordinary contingent expenses).

A school board does not have to develop a line-by-line contingency budget that identifies non-contingent expenditures. However, a contingency budget must have the same degree of specificity by both function and object that is required for budgets that are presented to the voters so that voters may have a full understanding of revenue and expenditures and be able to examine expenses that may be non-contingent, without having to resort to outside materials (*Appeal of Hubbard*, 47 Ed Dept Rep 259 (2007); *Appeal of Hubbard*, 43 Ed Dept Rep 3 (2003)).

The board is authorized to levy a tax to fund contingent expenses if the proposed budget is defeated (§§ 2022(5), 2023(1), 2023-a(7), (8), 2601-a(4), (5)). When adopting a contingency budget, the board may still submit to the voters separate propositions on specific items that require their approval, such as expanding the district's transportation mileage limitations (§§ 2022(2), 2601-a(3)). However, a board may not submit a budget proposition more than twice (§§ 2022(4), 2601-a(4); see **19:29**).

20:2. Can school district voters require their local school board to include funding in the district's contingency budget for particular programs or services, such as school sports or extracurricular activities?

No. Authority for determining what to include in the district's budget rests with the school board, not the voters (§ 1716). The voters have no authority to select the curriculum or otherwise determine which instructional programs, or other services, will be offered by the district (*Appeal of Brush*, 34 Ed Dept Rep 273 (1994)). This remains true when a district is operating on a contingency budget. The law governing the adoption of contingency budgets "does not abrogate the discretion of a board of education to determine whether to include or exclude specific items of expense or activities in the district's education program" (*Appeal of Polmanteer*, 44 Ed Dept Rep 221 (2004); see also *Polmanteer v. Bobo*, 19 A.D.3d 69 (4th Dep't 2005); *Appeal of Baisch*, 40 Ed Dept Rep 405 (2000); *Appeal of Sperl*, 33 Ed Dept Rep 388 (1994)).

20:3. When must a school board adopt a contingency budget?

A school board must adopt a contingency budget after the proposed budget has been defeated twice by the voters. A board may adopt a contingency budget after the voters defeat the proposed budget once (§§ 2022(4), (5), 2023(1), 2023-a(8), 2601-a(4), (5)).

In any event, as a practical matter, the school board either must adopt a contingency budget for the ensuing fiscal year by July 1 or must pass resolutions to approve contingency budget appropriations for specific purposes, as needed, until the board adopts the overall contingency budget. This is because all general fund appropriations and revenues close to fund balance at the end of the fiscal year on June 30.

Moreover, as an additional practical matter, the board must adopt a contingency budget prior to the issuance of the tax levy, in order to ensure the collection of taxes sufficient to fund the ordinary contingent expenditures for which the board will make appropriations during the fiscal year.

Contingency Budget Tax Levy and Spending Caps

20:4. Is there a cap on the total district tax levy during a contingency budget?

Yes. A contingency budget may not result in a tax levy greater than the tax that was levied for the prior school year (i.e. a zero levy increase) (§§ 2023(4)(a), 2023-a(8)).

Prior to the State's adoption of the limitation on increases for school district property tax levies, the law provided that a contingency budget could not result in an increase in total spending over parameters set by law. Certain expenditures such as those for tax certiorari proceedings, expenditures for emergency repairs as a result of damage or destruction of a school building and payments for charter schools, among others, were excluded from the determination of total spending. However, beginning with the 2012–2013 school year, no expenditures are excluded from a district's budget when calculating expenditures to determine if the budget falls within the zero tax levy increase for contingency budgets. Expenditures which are normally excluded from the calculation of the tax levy limit, such as the capital tax levy, may not be excluded from calculation of the tax levy when adopting a contingency budget (§§ 2023(4)(a), 2023-a(8); see NYS Education Department, *Property Tax Cap Guidance* (revised Apr. 2015), at: http://www.p12.nysed.gov/mgtserv/propertytax/taxcap/docs/Property_Tax_%20Cap_General_Guidance_and_FAQS.pdf).

The school board's contingency budget resolution must refer to a statement indicating the projected percentage increase or decrease in total spending for the school year, together with an explanation of the reasons that the board disregarded any portion of an increase in spending in formulating its contingency budget (§ 2023(4)(b)).

20:5. Are there separate caps on district spending during a contingency budget?

Yes. In addition to the cap on the tax levy during a contingency budget (see **20:4**), the administrative component of a contingency budget is capped at the lesser of (1) the percentage that the administrative component had comprised in the prior year's budget exclusive of the capital component, or (2) the percentage that the administrative component had comprised in the last defeated budget, excluding the capital component.

For example, if the program component for the current year's budget is $10 million and the administrative component is $1.5 million, then the administrative component of a contingency budget for the following year is capped at 13 percent (i.e., 1.5/11.5), or less, if the administrative component of the last proposed defeated budget comprised a smaller percentage (§§ 2023(3), 2601-a(5)).

20:6. May a school board amend and/or revise the final contingency budget after its adoption by majority vote of the board?

Yes. In fact, even an incoming board, as newly constituted at the annual organizational meeting, may make adjustments to the contingency budget adopted by the predecessor board, provided that the district continues "to maintain the educational program as required by statute and regulation" (*Appeal of Citizens for Educ.*, 36 Ed Dept Rep 12 (1996)).

However, any such amendments or revisions may not exceed the tax levy limitation or spending limitation of the contingency budget administrative component cap (§ 2023(4)(c); see **20:1-2**). The only exception allowed is appropriations for the expenditure of gifts, grants in aid for specific purposes or for general use or insurance proceeds authorized pursuant to Education Law section 1718(2) (§ 2023(4)(c)).

Ordinary Contingent Expenses

20:7. What constitutes an "ordinary contingent expense" for purposes of a school budget?

Ordinary contingent expenses have been defined under law to include: (1) legal obligations; (2) expenditures specifically authorized by statute; and (3) other items necessary to maintain the educational program, preserve property and ensure the health and safety of the students and staff (§ 2601-a(5); *Formal Opn. of Counsel No. 213*, 7 Ed Dept Rep 153 (1967)).

The school board is responsible for initially determining what items constitute ordinary contingent expenses (*Matter of Gouverneur CSD*, 15 Ed Dept Rep 468 (1976)). A school board's determination of which items to include in its contingency budget is subject to review by the commissioner of education if the board's decision is challenged (§ 2024; see also *Appeals of Gorman*, 39 Ed Dept Rep 377 (1999); *Bd. of Educ. of Freeport UFSD v. Nyquist*, 71 A.D.2d 757 (3d Dep't 1979), *aff'd,* 50 N.Y.2d 889 (1980); *Onteora CSD v. Onteora Non-Teaching Emps. Ass'n*, 79 A.D.2d 415 (3d Dep't 1981); *Matter of Raffone v. Pearsall*, 39 A.D.2d 208 (2d Dep't 1972)).

However, the commissioner will not overturn a school board's contingency budget decisions on appeal "unless there is a clear showing that the board's decision was illegal or arbitrary and unreasonable" (*Appeal of Baisch*, 40 Ed Dept Rep 405 (2000)).

20:8. What are some examples of ordinary contingent expenses?

Examples of ordinary contingent expenses include legal obligations, expenditures specifically authorized by statute and other items necessary to the maintenance of a school district's educational program, the preservation of school property, and ensuring the health and safety of students and staff (*Formal Opn. of Counsel No. 213*, 7 Ed Dept Rep 153 (1967); see **20:9-13**).

20:9. What legal obligations are considered ordinary contingent expenses?

Based on Education Law section 2601-a(5)(c) and *Formal Opn. of Counsel No. 213*, 7 Ed Dept Rep 153 (1967), legal obligations considered an ordinary contingent expense include:

- Debt service (both principal and interest payments).
- Judgments from courts and orders of the commissioner of education and other administrative bodies or officers.
- Social Security and retirement obligations, as well as other payroll taxes and assessments.
- Pre-existing contractual obligations, including collective bargaining agreements under the Taylor Law (see, for example, *Matter of Powell*, 22 Ed Dept Rep 353 (1983); see also *Appeals of Gorman*, 39 Ed Dept Rep 377 (1999), where the commissioner upheld a district's entry into a lease of photocopying machines during a contingency budget, among other reasons, because the teachers' collective bargaining agreement required the district to maintain a certain number of

photocopying machines for teachers' use; see also *Appeal of Johnson*, 38 Ed Dept Rep 327 (1998), in which the commissioner upheld as an ordinary contingent expense a district's undisputed past practice of allowing certain secretaries to take time off for emergency snow days without requiring them to charge their leave accruals).

- Payments made to a former superintendent in settlement of claims arising from a contract (*Appeal of Gallagher*, 39 Ed Dept Rep 697 (2000); see also *Matter of Rowley*, 22 Ed Dept Rep 385 (1983)).

20:10. What ordinary contingent expenditures are specifically authorized by statute?

Ordinary contingent expenditures specifically authorized by statute include:

- Teachers' salaries (§§ 2022(5), 2023(1), 2601-a(5)(a); see also *Appeal of Ambrosio*, 30 Ed Dept Rep 387 (1991)).
- Interschool athletics, field trips and other extracurricular activities (§§ 2023(1), 2601-a(5)(f)); see also *Appeal of Baisch*, 40 Ed Dept Rep 405 (2000); *Appeal of Polmanteer*, 44 Ed Dept Rep 221 (2004); *Polmanteer v. Bobo*, 19 A.D.3d 69 (4th Dep't 2005)). However, school districts may pay for all or part of the costs of a field trip only if the field trip is part of their educational program (*Appeal of Christe*, 39 Ed Dept Rep 685 (2000)).
- Transportation within the state-mandated mileage limitations (K–8 students: 2–15 miles; 9–12 students: 3–15 miles (§ 3635(1)); children with disabilities: up to 50 miles (§§ 4401(4), 4402(4)(d)).
- Transportation to and from school under the mileage limitations last approved by the voters if more generous than the minimum mileage limitations required under state law (§§ 2023(2), 2503(12), 2601-a(5)(b); see also *Appeal of Wenger*, 37 Ed Dept Rep 5 (1997)).
- Transportation related to interschool athletics, field trips, and extracurricular activities (§§ 2023(1), (2), 2601-a(5)(f)).
- The cost of providing transportation in a child safety zone (§ 3635-b(10)).
- Expenses for cafeteria or restaurant services (§§ 1604(28), 1709(22), 2023(1)), except in small city school districts (see § 2503(9)(a)).
- Textbooks (§§ 701(3), 2601-a(5)(b)).
- Expenses in connection with membership in the New York State School Boards Association, Inc. (§ 1618).
- Convention and conference expenses (Gen. Mun. Law § 77-b; see also *Matter of Cappa*, 18 Ed Dept Rep 373 (1978)).
- Admission of non-resident pupils upon payment of tuition in accordance with Part 174 of the commissioner's regulations (§ 3202(2); see also *Appeal of Bosco*, 34 Ed Dept Rep 295 (1994)).
- Under limited circumstances: youth bureaus, recreation and youth service projects, and other youth programs (Exec. Law §§ 422–423).
- The district's share of services from a board of cooperative educational services (BOCES) (§§ 1950, 2601-a(5)(b); see also *Matter of New Paltz CSD*, 30 Ed Dept Rep 300 (1991)).
- Health and welfare services (§§ 912, 2601-a(5)(b)).
- Grants in aid received from either the state or federal government, other gifts, and insurance proceeds not involving the expenditure of local money (§§ 1718(2), 2023(4)(c); see also *Appeal of Baisch*, 40 Ed Dept Rep 405 (2000)).
- Kindergarten, nursery, and night schools (§§ 1712, 2601-a(5)(b)).
- Prekindergarten, if the board chooses to offer a prekindergarten program (§ 3602-e(11)).
- Accident insurance for students (§ 1709(8-a), (8-b)).
- In-service training for teachers (§ 1709(32)).

- Eye safety devices (§ 409-a).
- Library books and other instructional materials associated with a library (§§ 2023(1), 2601-a(5)(d)).
- Energy performance contracts entered into by either a school district or a BOCES (Energy Law § 9-103(3); see also *Appeals of Gorman*, 39 Ed Dept Rep 377 (1999)).

20:11. What are some examples of necessary items deemed to constitute ordinary contingent expenses?

Based on *Formal Opn. of Counsel No. 213*, 7 Ed Dept Rep 153 (1967), as well as the specific statutes and cases noted below, the following is a partial list of other items necessary to maintain the educational program, preserve property, and assure the health and safety of students and staff that are deemed ordinary contingent expenses:

- Necessary travel expenses of board members and employees on official business (§§ 1604(27), 2118).
- Amounts needed to pay for necessary legal services (§ 2601-a(5)(e)).
- "Teacher supplies" but not "student supplies."
- Employment of security guards to ensure "safety of students and staff" (*Appeal of Loriz*, 33 Ed Dept Rep 50 (1993)).
- Salaries for necessary non-teaching employees (§ 2601-a(5)(e); see also *Appeal of Berry*, 34 Ed Dept Rep 325 (1995); *Appeal of Blizzard*, 34 Ed Dept Rep 268 (1994); *Matter of Gouverneur CSD*, 15 Ed Dept Rep 468 (1976)).
- Utilities, including fuel, water, light, power, and telephone (§ 2601-a(5)(e)).
- Use of school buildings for teachers' meetings and parent-teacher association meetings with school-connected purposes. However, this does not include programs of entertainment or of a social nature (see *Appeal of Forlani*, 23 Ed Dept Rep 325 (1984)).
- Emergency repairs of school plant (see, for example, *Appeal of Russo*, 47 Ed Dept Rep 429 (2008); and *Appeals of Gorman*, 39 Ed Dept Rep 377 (1999), upholding necessary roof repairs; see also *Matter of Mitzner*, 31 Ed Dept Rep 142 (1991), upholding replacement of lighting fixtures required for safety reasons).
- Maintenance of necessary, sanitary facilities.
- Necessary expenditures for complying with the commissioner's regulation pertaining to such items as fire alarm systems and fire escapes (see *Appeals of Gorman*; see also *Appeal of Gargan*, 40 Ed Dept Rep 465 (2000)).
- Rental of temporary classroom facilities with approval of the commissioner, in the case of an unforeseeable emergency (§§ 1726(5), 2601-a(5)(e)). But in the absence of an unforeseeable emergency, voter approval is required (*Appeal of Wiesen*, 35 Ed Dept Rep 157 (1995)).
- Required civil defense equipment.
- Certain expenses, such as for emergency repairs, or to equip a classroom or classrooms where it is essential to house additional students. This does not include equipment (but see *Appeals of Gorman* and *Matter of Mitzner*).
- Materials used in classes by students where uniformity is essential to the program or to preserve health and safety.
- Newspapers and periodical subscriptions for libraries and classroom use where essential for instruction or to preserve continuity of sets.
- Expenditures necessary to advise district voters concerning school matters (§ 2601-a(5)(e)). However, hiring a public relations firm to assist the district in promoting its image to district residents is not an ordinary contingent expense (*Appeal of Nolan*, 35 Ed Dept Rep 139 (1995); see also *Appeal of Mitzner*, where the commissioner provided guidance on what is meant by "necessary" information).

- Preliminary plans and specifications needed to submit propositions to voters.
- Options on land where the price of option is nominal.

Although equipment purchases generally do not constitute an ordinary contingent expense, in one case the commissioner ruled that it was permissible for a school board to replace obsolete computer equipment with new computers while on a contingency budget. Technology was a "significant element" of the district's curriculum, and the superintendent asserted that the purchase was "necessary to the district's educational mission and ability to meet the new learning standards required by the Board of Regents" (*Appeal of Schadtle, Jr.*, 40 Ed Dept Rep 60 (2000); see also *Matter of Mitzner*).

20:12. What are some examples of expenditures that do not constitute ordinary contingent expenses?

Examples of items that do not constitute ordinary contingent expenses include the following:

- New equipment (see *Appeal of Richenberg*, 47 Ed Dept Rep 459 (2008); *Appeals of Gorman*, 39 Ed Dept Rep 377 (1999); but see *Appeal of Schadtle, Jr.*, 40 Ed Dept Rep 60 (2000)).
- Public use of school buildings and grounds, except where there is no cost to the district (see *Appeal of Forlani*, 23 Ed Dept Rep 325 (1984)), but a district may charge a fee that meets or exceeds its actual costs (§ 414(2); see also *Appeal of Emilio*, 33 Ed Dept Rep 75 (1993)).
- Nonessential maintenance.
- Capital expenditures, except in an emergency (*Appeals of Gorman*).
- Consultant services to review district operations and make recommendations necessary for the creation of the budget (*Appeal of Shravah,* 36 Ed Dept Rep 396 (1997), *aff'd, Matter of Education Alternatives v. Mills*, 175 Misc.2d 105 (Sup. Ct. Albany Cnty. 1997); see also *Appeal of Gallagher*, 39 Ed Dept Rep 697 (2000)).

This list is based on *Formal Opn. of Counsel No. 213*, 7 Ed Dept Rep 153 (1967), as well as the specific cases cited.

Public School Finances

20:13. Can a school board increase teachers' salaries while the district is operating on a contingency budget?

Yes. Increases in teachers' salaries are authorized by the Education Law (§ 1709(16); *Matter of New Paltz CSD*, 30 Ed Dept Rep 300 (1991); *Formal Opn. of Counsel No. 213*, 7 Ed Dept Rep 153 (1967)). Moreover, Education Law section 2023 authorizes expenditures for teachers' salaries during a contingency budget. The commissioner of education has applied the definition of teacher found in Education Law section 3101(1) to include school superintendents, principals, and teaching assistants within the class of persons to whom a school board may grant salary increases during a contingency budget (see *Appeal of Berry*, 34 Ed Dept Rep 325 (1995); see also *Appeal of Reinhardt, Jr.*, 16 Ed Dept Rep 448 (1977)).

20:14. Can a school board increase non-instructional employees' salaries while the district is operating on a contingency budget?

Yes, in most cases. Increases in salaries for non-instructional employees who are subject to a collective bargaining agreement are authorized as a contractual obligation of the district (*Matter of Powell*, 22 Ed Dept Rep 353 (1983)). However, non-instructional employees who are not members of a collective bargaining unit and employees designated by the Public Employment Relations Board as management or confidential may not receive a salary increase during a contingency budget "unless it is impossible to assure qualified personnel for the minimum service, in which case these employees may also be paid necessary amounts" (*Appeal of Lauterback*, 30 Ed Dept Rep 223 (1990); *Appeal of Reinhardt, Jr.*, 16 Ed Dept Rep 448 (1977); *Matter of Gouverneur CSD*, 15 Ed Dept Rep 468 (1976)).

Additional pay to employees not covered by a collective bargaining agreement may be provided if they are assigned new duties (*Appeal of Berry*, 34 Ed Dept Rep 325; see also *Appeal of Parsons*, 32 Ed Dept Rep 444 (1993)).

The commissioner of education has recognized other exceptions as well. In one case, the commissioner ruled that a school board had the authority to grant a salary increase to the district treasurer while operating on a contingency budget, because Education Law section 2130(4) gives school boards specific authority to "fix the compensation of the treasurer" (*Appeal of Seerup*, 33 Ed Dept Rep 585 (1994)). In another case, the commissioner dismissed a challenge to a district's hiring of additional non-instructional staff for its special education programs during a contingency budget, where the district demonstrated that the staff increase was necessitated by a substantial increase in the number of special education students served by the district (*Appeal of Blizzard*, 34 Ed Dept Rep 268 (1994)).

20:15. How does the adoption of a contingency budget affect a school district's transportation requirements?

The Education Law requires that school districts that adopt a contingency budget continue the mileage limitations for the transportation of students last approved by the district voters. The mileage limits can be changed only by a special proposition passed by a majority of the district voters. In addition, transportation to and from interscholastic athletic events, field trips, and other extracurricular activities is permissible under a contingency budget (§§ 2023(1), (2), 2503(12), 2601-a(5)(b), (f); see also *Appeal of Wenger*, 37 Ed Dept Rep 5 (1997)).

21. School Tax Assessments[1]

Assessment Responsibilities

21:1. Who has oversight responsibility over the assessment of taxes?

The commissioner of taxation and finance has the majority of the oversight responsibility for the real property tax system. The commissioner assesses special franchises, establishes state equalization rates, approves assessments of taxable state lands, generally supervises the function of assessing throughout the state, and provides assessors information, instruction and training (§ 202). The Office of Real Property Tax Services within the NYS Department of Taxation and Finance, headed by the deputy commissioner for real property tax services, carries out duties delegated by the commissioner of taxation and finance (§§ 201, 203).

The NYS Board of Real Property Tax Services, which is independent from the authority of the Department of Taxation and Finance has the power to determine special franchise values and assessments, railroad ceilings, state equalization rates or other equalization products for which complaints are filed, and to hear and determine reviews relating to determinations made by county equalization agencies and reviews appeals relating to determinations of STAR eligibility made by the Department pursuant to § 425 (§ 200-a).

21:2. Who conducts property assessments for tax purposes?

Property assessments for tax purposes are made by local municipal, town, or county assessors, or boards of assessors charged with the duty of assessing real property within an assessing unit for purposes of taxation or special levies (§§ 102(3), 1302(1)).

Assessors may be appointed or elected (§§ 102(3), 310, 329). Appointed assessors serve for six years. However, they may serve an indefinite term if the office of assessor is a full-time position or has been classified in the competitive class of the civil service (§ 310(2), (7)).

Elected town assessors serve for six-year terms unless the town retains a board of assessors. In that case the term of office is four years. No more than two assessors are elected at the biennial election, except when the unexpired balance of a term is being filled, then three assessors may be elected (Town Law § 24).

All assessors must obtain state certification of successful completion of the basic course of training prescribed by the commissioner of taxation and finance (§ 310(5)(a)). In addition, all appointed assessors and elected assessors who serve a six-year term must complete a continuing training and education program (§ 310(5)(b)).

[1] *All statutory references in this chapter are to the New York State Real Property Tax Law unless otherwise noted. The material in the chapter refers chiefly to school districts other than the Big 5 city school districts. For selected legal opinions by statute (or by subject), visit the NYS Office of Real Property Tax Services (ORPTS) website at: http://www.tax.ny.gov/pubs_and_bulls/orpts/legal_opinions/index.htm.*

21:3. What is the timetable for the administration of the assessment system?

July 1 is the *valuation date*, which is the date by which the value of all real property subject to taxation must be determined in most cases. However, the valuation date for a city or town may differ under separate sections of law applicable to such cities and towns (§ 301; see *Gran Development LLC v. Town of Davenport Bd. of Assessors,* 124 A.D.3d 1042 (3d Dep't 2015)).

March 1 is the *taxable status date* for real property subject to taxation in most cities and towns. It is the date by which assessors must complete an inventory of all real property in the community. The taxable status date may differ for some cities and towns under separate sections of law applicable to such cities and towns (§ 302(1)). The taxable status date of cities, towns, and counties is controlling for school district purposes (§§ 302(2), 1302(3), (4)). The taxable status date in villages is usually January 1 (§ 1400).

Following the March 1 taxable status date, the next key date is May 1. By this date, the assessor(s) must publish the tentative assessment roll and make it available for public inspection until the fourth Tuesday in May (§§ 506, 526).

The fourth Tuesday in May (or other date established by city or county charter, county tax act, or other special law), also known as *grievance day*, is the date on which the local Board of Assessment Review must begin hearing assessment complaints (§ 512(1)). In addition, the governing body of an assessing unit that employs an assessor who is at the same time employed by another assessing unit may set another date or dates for the meeting of the board of assessment review. Such date, or the first date in cases where the board meets on more than one date, must be between the fourth Tuesday in May and the second Tuesday in June (§ 512(1-a)).

July 1 is the deadline for filing the final assessment roll (§ 516).

21:4. Who prepares a copy of the appropriate portion of the town or county assessment roll for school district tax-collection purposes?

Because municipalities usually are not contiguous with school districts, different portions of each municipality's tax roll contain properties that are attributed to different school districts. Therefore, once the assessment roll for town or county purposes has been completed, a duplicate assessment roll is prepared and the assessor delivers a copy of the appropriate portion to the clerk, trustee or other proper official of each school district within five days after the completion and certification of the assessment roll. The expense of preparing this document is charged to the city, town or county except when prepared for a city school district, which must reimburse the municipality preparing the duplicate assessment role (§ 1302(2)).

21:5. Who is responsible for the accuracy of the assessments included on the assessment roll?

The assessor of the local municipality is responsible for the accuracy of the assessments included on the assessment roll. An assessor is empowered to issue a revised assessment roll within certain statutorily prescribed time limits if he or she receives notice from the commissioner of taxation and finance with respect to changes in equalization rates and approval of assessments for taxable state lands (§ 1222(1)). If the assessor fails to provide a revised assessment roll to a school district after receiving notice of changes from the commissioner of taxation and finance a school district will only receive a judgment in its favor if the school district suffered cognizable damages (§§ 1222, 1302; but see *Ramapo CSD v. Adams*, 54 A.D.3d 324 (2d Dep't 2008), where a district was not awarded damages because the school budget for the year in which the assessor failed to issue a revised assessment roll ended with a surplus).

21:6. Who is responsible for the accuracy of the assessment roll with respect to whether the parcels included on the roll are within the district's boundaries?

Each school district is responsible for determining whether certain parcels of real property are within its boundaries (§ 1302(2); *Matter of Hudson Falls CSD v. Town of Moreau Assessor*, 202 A.D.2d 716 (3d Dep't), *appeal denied*, 83 N.Y.2d 760 (1994)). The district superintendent of a board of cooperative educational services district has the authority to determine the legal boundaries between adjoining school districts within his or her jurisdiction (Educ. Law § 2215(1); *Appeal of Bd. of Educ. of Fort Edward UFSD*, 33 Ed Dept Rep 457 (1994); see also **11:20, 11:23**).

21:7. What is the law regarding the correction of assessment rolls and tax rolls?

Title 3 (Corrections of Assessment Rolls and Tax Rolls) of the Real Property Tax Law defines and describes the procedures for correcting clerical errors, unlawful entries, errors in essential fact, the assessment of omitted property and other errors (§§ 550–559).

A school board may authorize a designated official to approve the correction of the tax roll and tax bill where the correction does not exceed $2,500 (§ 554(9)).

21:8. Who is responsible for resolving assessment complaints?

The board of assessment review is the body of officers empowered to hear and determine complaints about assessments (§ 102(4)). Members are appointed by the legislative body of the local government (§ 523(1)(b)).

21:9. What are the procedures for reviewing and changing assessments?

Complaints regarding assessments are filed with the assessor prior to a hearing of the board of assessment review, or with the board at a hearing, but cannot be filed in the first instance at an adjourned hearing conducted by the board (§ 524(1)).

Where a complaint is filed within three business days preceding the hearing, the board of assessment review must grant the assessor's request for an adjournment to permit the assessor to prepare a response to the complaint (§ 524(1)). Once the response has been considered, the board makes a determination of the final assessed valuation and prepares a verified statement showing any changes (§ 525(3), (4)).

As soon as possible after receiving the statement from the board, the assessor makes the changes in the assessment on the assessment roll (§ 526(5)).

Tax Certiorari Proceedings

21:10. What are the procedures for challenging a local assessment review board's refusal to reduce a property tax assessment?

A taxpayer (a person — corporate or otherwise) initiates a property tax *certiorari*. This is a legal proceeding whereby the taxpayer who has been denied a reduction in assessment by a local assessment review board challenges his or her property tax assessment on the grounds of excessiveness, inequality, illegality, or misclassification (§§ 700, 701, 706(1)). A presumption of validity attaches to the valuation of property. Thus a taxpayer challenging an assessment must present substantial evidence a property was overvalued (*Matter of Roth v. City of Syracuse*, 21 N.Y.3d 411 (2013); see also *Bd. of Managers of French Oaks Condominiums v. Town of Amherst,* 23 N.Y.3d 168 (2014)).

Procedural laws regarding *certiorari* actions are contained in Article 7 of the Real Property Tax Law.

If, alternatively, a taxpayer opts to pursue a remedy through the small claims assessment review procedure (§§ 729–739, Title 1-A), they waive their right to commence a tax certiorari under Article 7 title I, but may still seek judicial review pursuant to Article 78 of the Civil Practice Law and Rules (§ 736).

21:11. What happens if a taxpayer prevails in the tax *certiorari* proceeding?

If a petitioner prevails in a tax certiorari proceeding the school district must refund the amount of taxes plus applicable interest the court determines the petitioner to have overpaid (§ 726(1)(c), (2)). If a school district levies taxes on behalf of a school district public library it must also refund the portion of overpaid library taxes to the petitioner. School districts may charge back to such public library the portion of any court ordered tax certiorari refund attributable to library purposes (§ 726(1)(c)).

A judicially determined assessment is frozen for the next three assessment rolls (§ 727). Whether, in order to receive a refund, a tax payer must file continuous tax *certiorari* challenges for succeeding years during the pendency of an initial proceeding is a disputed question. Some courts require challenges to be filed each year and others do not (see *Torok Trust v. Town Bd. of Town of Alexandria,* 128 A.D.3d 97 (4th Dep't), *lv. to appeal denied,* 25 N.Y.3d 1098 (2015); *Matter of Scellen v. Assessor for City of Glens Falls,* 300 A.D.2d 979 (3d Dep't 2002)).

However, a petitioner challenging the calculation of a multiyear partial tax exemption under Real Property Tax Law § 485-b does not need to annually file challenges. The exemption is calculated from a single assessment roll therefore, multiple tax *certiorari* proceedings are not necessary (*Highbridge Broadway LLC v. Assessor of the City of Schenectady,* 27 N.Y. 3d 450 (2016)).

School districts with insufficient funds available to pay a tax *certiorari* judgment may finance the cost through a capital note and spread the cost of the judgment over several years (Local Fin. Law §§ 11.00(33-a), 28.00; see **27:4**). The ability to finance tax certiorari judgments in this way is valid through June 15, 2018 (L. 2013, c. 77).

21:12. How does a school district learn of the filing of a real property tax *certiorari* proceeding?

Under the Real Property Tax Law, when a taxpayer files a tax *certiorari* petition with the appropriate court challenging a tax assessment, the taxpayer must mail a copy of the petition and notice to the superintendent of schools of any school district in which any part of the real property at issue is located within 10 days from the date of service of the petition and notice on the clerk of the assessing unit. The taxpayer also must file proof of this mailing with the court within 10 days (§ 708(3)).

This is a two-part requirement; there must be proof of service and proof of filing with the court in order to prevent a tax *certiorari* proceeding from being dismissed. One appellate court found it was not frivolous for a school district to insist on proof of both service and filing prior to paying any refund awarded pursuant to a tax *certiorari* proceeding (*Country Estate Maint. Co., Inc. v. Bd. of Educ. of Charlotte Valley CSD,* 51 A.D.3d 1107 (3d Dep't 2008)).

In several cases where a taxpayer personally served or mailed the tax *certiorari* petition to the district clerk, the courts dismissed the petition as failing to meet the requirements of the statute (see *Orchard Heights Inc., v. Yancy,* 15 A.D.3d 854 (4th Dep't 2005); *Premier Self Storage v. Fusco,* 12 A.D.3d 1135 (4th Dep't 2004); *Majaars Realty Assoc. v. Town of Poughkeepsie*, 10 Misc.3d 1061(A) (Sup. Ct. Dutchess Cnty. 2005)). Another court, however, allowed the continuance of a petition that was personally served on a district employee other than the superintendent, at the direction of the superintendent's personal secretary (*Hansen v. Town of Redhook,* 28 Misc.3d 1236 (Sup. Ct. Dutchess Cnty. 2010)).

In yet another case, a court determined a school district received adequate notice of a tax *certiorari* proceeding challenging the assessed value of a property subject to a payment in lieu of taxes (PILOT) agreement (see **21:54**) even though the petition did not reference the PILOT agreement or payments thereunder. The school district's motion to intervene was denied since it was not timely made, and the district was required to comply with a court order to refund "excess taxes" (*Wagner & Stoll, LLC v. City of Schenectady*, 107 A.D.3d 1225 (3d Dep't), *lv. to appeal denied*, 22 N.Y.3d 853 (2013)).

21:13. May a school district become a party to a real property tax *certiorari* proceeding?

Yes, at the school board's discretion. Most requests by residential property owners for reductions in assessment are settled by local assessment review boards or in small claims courts. Generally, the minor reductions that result from these procedures are not problematic for school districts. However, the large reductions in assessment granted to businesses, industries, multiple dwellings, and other commercial property owners as a result of *certiorari* actions may present a problem for individual school districts.

21:14. How does a school district become a party to a real property tax *certiorari* proceeding?

Following the superintendent's receipt of the tax *certiorari* petition and notice by mail (§ 708(3)), a school board must take a vote to become a party to the action, and then serve a verified answer to the petition *or* a notice of appearance in the action within the time frame set by statute. If a district serves a "notice of appearance" instead of a verified answer, then all allegations set forth in the taxpayer's petition are deemed denied by the school district (§ 712(2-a)).

21:15. What are the rights of a school district that chooses to become a party to a tax *certiorari* proceeding?

According to at least one appellate court, a school district that invokes its option to become a party to a tax *certiorari* proceeding enjoys the same rights as other parties, "including the right to reject an unacceptable settlement offer" among the other parties to the proceeding (*Liberty Mgmt. of N.Y., Inc. v. Assessor of Glenville*, 284 A.D.2d 61 (3d Dep't 2001); see also *Matter of PNL Stillwater LLC v. Bd. of Assessors of the Town of Stillwater*, 94 A.D.3d 1401(3d Dep't 2012)).

21:16. What happens if a taxpayer fails to notify the affected school district(s) of the commencement of the tax *certiorari* proceeding as set forth in law?

Failure to mail a copy of the notice and petition to the superintendent of schools of each school district in which any part of the real property at issue is located, as required by law (see **21:12**), may result in dismissal of the petition, "unless excused for good cause shown" (§ 708(3); see also *Highbridge Development BRLLC v. Assessor of the Town of Niskayuna and S. Colonie CSD,* 121 A.D.3d 1324 (3d Dep't 2014)). The Court of Appeals, New York's highest court, has also ruled that a petition that has been dismissed for failure to mail the notice to the superintendent may not be revived through proceedings commenced under the civil practice laws and rules (*Westchester Joint Waterworks v. Assessor of the City of Rye*, 27 N.Y. 3d 566 (2016)).

Under the real property tax law, the mere absence of prejudice cannot be considered "good cause" to excuse a service defect (*Bd. of Managers of Copley Court Condominiums v. Town of Ossining*, 79 A.D.3d 1032 (2d Dep't 2010), *aff'd*, 19 N.Y.3d 869 (2012); *Orchard Heights Inc., v. Yancy,* 15 A.D.3d 854 (4th Dep't 2005); *Premier Self Storage v. Fusco,* 12 A.D.3d 1135 (4th Dep't 2004)). School districts may establish prejudice by showing the lack of notice precluded the school district from planning for an eventual judgment by timely depositing funds in a tax certiorari reserve fund (*Westchester Joint Waterworks v. Assessor of the City of Rye,* 37 Misc.3d 238 (Westchester Cnty. 2012), *aff'd as modified,* 120 A.D.3d 1352 (2d Dep't 2014), *aff'd,* 27 N.Y. 3d 566 (2016); see **26:5**).

Courts have found "good cause" shown to excuse a failure to serve under circumstances where a taxpayer's failure to mail the petition and notice to the correct school district resulted from misinformation the taxpayer received from the assessor's office (*Village Square of Penna, Inc. v. Semon*, 290 A.D.2d 184 (3d Dep't), *appeal denied*, 98 N.Y.2d 647 (2002)), or a factual/geographic mistake, as to which district the property at issue was located absent prejudice to the correct district (*Harris Bay Yacht Club, Inc. v. Town of Queensbury*, 46 A.D.3d 1304 (3d Dep't 2007)), and where notice was sent to superintendent at the sole address listed for district's offices on the websites of both the district and NYS Office of Real Property Services (*The Commons at Bon Aire Condos. v. Town of Ramapo,* 24 Misc.3d 1231 (Sup.Ct. Rockland Cnty. 2009)).

Similarly, another appellate court found good cause existed to excuse the late service of notice in the absence of prejudice to the school district in a case where no answers had been served, no appraisals exchanged, and no negotiations had taken place (*Bloomingdale's, Inc. v. City Assessor of White Plains*, 294 A.D.2d 570 (2d Dep't), *appeal denied*, 99 N.Y.2d 553 (2002)).

However, courts have not found "good cause" to exist in cases where taxpayers have sent notice to persons other than the superintendent even in the absence of prejudice to the school district (see *Landesman v. Whitton,* 46 A.D.3d 827 (2d Dep't 2007), where the notice was addressed to the school district; *Orchard Heights Inc., v. Yancy,* and *Premier Self Storage v. Fusco,* where the notice was sent to school district clerk). Additionally, a claim of geographical mistake regarding which district the property at issue was located did not constitute good cause where the parties had been engaged in litigation over assessments of the subject parcel for more than 25 years (*Wyeth Holdings Corp. v. Assessor of the Town of Orangetown,* 84 A.D.3d 1104 (2d Dep't 2011)).

21:17. What happens if a school district receives a tax *certiorari* notice and petition late?

According to one appellate court, if a school district simply receives the petition and notice late, then the district must intervene in the proceeding and make a motion to dismiss the petition for lateness. If the district fails to do this, then it waives its objection to late service and must comply with any court order or settlement reached in the matter (*Brookview Apts. v. Stuhlman*, 278 A.D.2d 825 (4th Dep't 2000)). But another appellate court has ruled that a *certiorari* petition should not be dismissed for lateness absent prejudice to the school district as a result of a late delivery of the notice and petition (*Bloomingdale's, Inc. v. City Assessor of White Plains*, 294 A.D.2d 570 (2d Dep't), *appeal denied*, 99 N.Y.2d 502 (2002)).

21:18. Is a school district that never receives the tax *certiorari* notice and petition in the manner set forth by law obligated to refund back taxes under a settlement or court order from the proceeding?

No. The two New York appellate courts that have squarely addressed the issue have ruled that if a school district *never* is served with the tax *certiorari* petition and notice before trial or settlement, then the district is not required to refund any back taxes pursuant a court order or settlement (*Brookview Apts. v. Stuhlman*, 278 A.D.2d 825 (4th Dep't 2000); see also *Cornwall Yacht Club v. Assessor*, 110 A.D.3d 1070 (2d Dep't 2013), *appeal denied*, 23 N.Y.3d 904 (2014); *Macy's Primary Real Estate, Inc. v. Assessor of City of White Plains*, 291 A.D.2d 73 (2d Dep't), *appeal denied*, 99 N.Y.2d 502 (2002); *Michael F.X. Ryan v. Town of Cortlandt,* 30 Misc.3d 560 (Sup. Ct. Westchester Cnty. 2010)).

Tax Exemptions

21:19. Are school districts required to prepare and make public a property tax exemption report?

Yes. School districts must prepare and include a tax exemption report with any notice of the preparation of the budget and attach the report to their tentative/preliminary budgets. The law requires the report to include every type of exemption granted and their cumulative impact, the cumulative amount expected to be received from recipients of each type of exemption through payments in lieu of taxes or other payments for municipal services and the cumulative impact of all exemptions granted (§ 495(1); see **18:6, 18:11**).

Under the law, the report becomes part of the final adopted budget. Additionally, it must be posted on any bulletin board the school board maintains for public notices and on its website (*Id.*).

21:20. What kinds of property are wholly exempt from real property taxation?

Examples of property wholly exempt from real property taxation include:

- Real property of the United States, except by permission of Congress (§ 400).
- Real property of New York State, other than property expressly subjected to taxation (§§ 404, 530 *et seq.*).
- Real property of a municipal corporation, within its corporate limits, held for public use (§ 406(1); but see **21:28**).
- Real property of a school district or a board of cooperative educational services (§ 408).
- Real property on Native American reservations (§ 454).
- Real property owned by corporations or associations organized exclusively for religious, charitable, hospital, or educational purposes, as specified by law (§ 420-a(1)). This property is exempt only to the extent of the value of the portion of the property so used (§ 420-a(2); see *Greater Jamaica Development Corp. v. N.Y. City Tax Commission,* 25 N.Y.3d 614 (2015); *Maetreum of Cybele, Magna Mater, Inc. v. McCoy,* 111 A.D.3d 1098 (3d Dep't 2013), *aff'd*, 24 N.Y.3d 1023 (2014); *Ahavas Chaverim Gemilas Chesed, Inc. v. Town of Mamkating,* 99 A.D.3d 1156 (3d Dep't 2012); *Vassar Bros. Hosp. v. City of Poughkeepsie*, 97 A.D.3d 756 (2d Dep't 2012); *Paws Unlimited Foundation, Inc. v. Maloney,* 91 A.D.3d 1173 (3d Dep't 2012); *St. Francis Hosp. v. Taber,* 76 A.D.3d 635 (2d Dep't 2010); *Lake Forest Senior Living Comm., Inc. v. Assessor of the City of Plattsburgh,* 72 A.D.3d 1302 (3d Dep't 2010)).
- Real property of an agricultural society that permanently uses it for a meeting hall or exhibition grounds (§ 450).
- Real property of a municipal corporation, not located within its corporate limits, used for fire protection services (provided that some fire protection services are available within the municipality), or used for municipal electrical generation or used as a public park, public aviation field, highway, or for flood control and soil conservation purposes, provided the school board agrees to the exemption in writing (§ 406(2), (8)).
- Real property of a corporation, association, or post composed of veterans of the Grand Army of the Republic, Veterans of Foreign Wars, Disabled American Veterans, the American Legion, and other veterans' organizations (§ 452).
- The homes of clergy owned by religious corporations (§ 462).
- Under certain conditions, improvements related to the accessibility of the property by an owner or member of the owner's household who is disabled (§§ 459, 459-b).
- Certain real property located on farms, including silos and farm feed storage bins, commodity sheds, bulk milk tanks and coolers, manure storage and handling facilities including composting and anaerobic digestion of agricultural materials (§§ 483-a, 483-e).

- Farm or food processing labor camps or commissaries, as defined in article seven of the Labor Law (§ 483-d).
- Mixed-use property used for both residential and commercial purposes, where local law adopted in accordance with procedures required by law, provides for the exemption of real property taxation (§ 485-a).

Exemptions may be granted for improvements to real property initiated on or after January 1, 2013 which exceed $10,000 and that meet certification standards for green building specified in law where a local law or board resolution adopted in accordance with procedures required by law, provides for the exemption (§ 470). The rate of exemption corresponds to the level of LEED, green globes rating system, national green building standards or similar program certification the building project meets unless the school district adopts a resolution establishing a maximum exemption amount (see § 470(2)).

For a complete overview of exemptions, see sections 400–494 of the Real Property Tax Law.

21:21. What kinds of property are partially exempt from real property taxation?

Examples of property partially exempt from real property taxation include:

- Real property of a minister, priest, or rabbi under certain circumstances, and the property of his or her unremarried surviving spouse, up to $1,500 (§ 460).
- Real property owned by an industrial development agency (IDA), including certain railroad property (§§ 412-a, 412-b).

Other property that may be partially exempt from taxation under certain conditions include, for example:

- Real property owned by a person who is 65 years old or older, if authorized by the school board (§ 467; see **21:24-25**).
- Real property constructed, altered, installed, or improved for the purpose of commercial, business, or industrial activity (§ 485-b).
- Residential real property constructed on or after dates specified in law in certain cities and school districts (§ 485-j).
- Subsequent to passage of a resolution by the local school board, some home improvements may be partially exempt from real property taxes for a limited period (§ 421-f).
- Newly constructed primary residences for first-time home buyers and improvements made to such properties, subject to limitations on household income as set forth in law (§ 457).
- Real property altered, installed, or improved subsequent to the Americans with Disabilities Act (ADA) to remove architectural barriers for persons with disabilities, if authorized by the school board (§ 459-a).
- Real property owned by one or more persons with disabilities (including taxpayers certified to receive a disability pension from the United States Department of Veterans Affairs), or real property owned by a husband, wife, or both, or by siblings, at least one of whom has a disability, with limited income, and persons 65 years of age or older, as set forth in statute, and if authorized by the school board (§ 459-c; 11 Opn. Counsel SBRPS No. 107 (2007)).
- Any increase in the value attributable to the construction or reconstruction of structures and buildings prior to January 1, 2019 essential to the operation of lands actively devoted to "agricultural or horticultural" use, which includes the raising, breeding, and boarding of livestock, including commercial horse boarding operations (§ 483).

Certain property owners are entitled to a partial tax exemption under the New York State School Tax Relief Program (STAR) (see **21:30-51**).

In addition, exemptions granted for building projects which meet green building standards are reduced from 100% to partial exemptions over a ten year period, but a school district may adopt a resolution establishing a maximum exemption amount (see § 470(2); see **21:20**).

For a complete overview of exemptions, see sections 400–494 of the Real Property Tax Law.

In instances where the assessor wholly discontinues a partial exemption, as opposed to reducing it, granted to a parcel on the preceding year's assessment role, notice must be given to the taxpayer by the assessor (§ 510-a).

21:22. Are there any special rules pertaining to a real property tax exemption for nuclear powered electric generating facilities and for solar or wind energy systems?

Yes. A nuclear powered electric generating facility may be exempt from school taxation for up to 15 years if authorized by resolution adopted by the school board in the district(s) in which the facility is located, except that such facility may be obligated to make payments in lieu of taxes (PILOTs) to the school district, as set forth in law (§§ 485, 490, 1227).

Exemptions for certain solar and wind energy systems in school districts shall be granted upon proper application for a period of 15 years unless by resolution a school district opts to prohibit such exemptions. Districts not opting out may instead require the property owner to enter into a contract for PILOTs that provides for annual payments in an amount not to exceed the amounts which would otherwise be payable but for the exemption. The Big 5 city school districts are excluded from the provisions of this section of law (§ 487(9)). School districts authorized to grant such exemptions may do so through January 1, 2025 (§ 487(5)).

21:23. Are there any special rules pertaining to a real property tax exemption for persons age 65 or over?

Currently, section 467 of the Real Property Tax Law enables school districts to grant persons age 65 or over, by board resolution, the following exemptions:

- A 50 percent exemption for those who have up to $29,000 in personal income, as defined by law (§ 467(3)).
- An exemption of between 5 and 45 percent along a sliding scale for those whose income is above the income ceiling adopted by the school district, as set forth by statute.

For example, if a district adopts the maximum income ceiling of $29,000 for the purpose of granting the 50 percent exemption, persons over age 65 whose personal income exceeds this amount, up to a maximum of $37,400, still will qualify for a 5 percent exemption if the district also adopts the sliding scale exemption.

In addition, any county, city, town, village or school district may adopt a local law, ordinance, or resolution to grant up to a 50 percent tax exemption on the assessed value of real property owned by one or more persons age 65 or over, by a husband and wife, siblings, a parent and an adult child with a disability one of whom is age 65 or over (§ 467(1)(a); see 11 Opn. Counsel SBRPS No. 107 (2007)). A school board must hold a public hearing prior to adopting such a resolution (§ 467(1)(a)). The board then must give a copy of the resolution to the assessor, who prepares the tax roll that will be affected by the tax exemption. The exemption cannot be granted under certain circumstances, such as in the case of real property where a child resides, if that child attends a public elementary or secondary school, unless the school board of the school district in which the property is located, after a public hearing, adopts a resolution providing for such exemption. The requirement for such a hearing and resolution is separate from, and in addition to, the requirement that a school board hold a public hearing before approving a resolution to offer the exemption to persons age 65 and over in the first place (§ 467(2)).

Persons in jointly owned homes where one or more owners qualify for the senior citizens exemption under § 467 and one or more owners qualify for the disability exemption under § 459-c of the Real Property Tax Law may take whichever exemption is most beneficial (§ 455).

Furthermore, certain persons 65 years of age or older may also qualify for the enhanced STAR program tax exemption (see **21:32**).

21:24. Must a school board give notice of the availability of a tax exemption for persons age 65 or over?

Yes. The school board must notify property owners of the availability of this exemption, if the board has adopted a resolution providing for the exemption. The statute provides a sample notice that districts may use (§ 467(4)). Those who wish to take advantage of the exemption must file an application with the assessor on or before the appropriate taxable status date (§ 467(5)). If the district adopts a resolution providing for extensions, late applications may be filed by the last day for payment of taxes without incurring interest or penalty along with an explanation of good cause for why the deadline was missed (§ 467(8-a)). The required notice may be sent electronically if the taxpayer has opted into a district program of electronic real property administration (§ 104(1)(h); see **22:13**).

Generally, the exemption must be renewed annually through an application (§ 467(6)(a)). However, a school board may, after holding a public hearing on the matter, adopt a resolution eliminating the requirement of filing an application annually for any person who has previously been granted the exemption on five consecutive assessment rolls, provided that the person includes a sworn statement with his or her tax payment indicating that he or she continues to be eligible for the exemption (§ 467(6)(b); see also 9 Opn. Counsel SBEA No. 36 (1990)).

21:25. Are there any special rules pertaining to real property tax exemptions for a person age 65 or over who purchase real property after the taxable status date?

Yes. A person who purchases real property after the taxable status date and qualifies for an exemption may file a late application for an exemption with the assessor within 30 days of the transfer of title (§ 467(9)(a)(i)). Upon approval of the application, the new property owner may receive a pro rata exemption credit to reduce the amount of taxes due on the property for the following year (§ 467(9)(a)(ii)). School districts that receive notice of pro rata exemption credits from the assessor must include such sums in the budget appropriations for the subsequent fiscal year (§ 467(9)(a)(iii)).

21:26. Are there any special rules pertaining to exemptions from school taxes that apply to property owned by veterans?

Yes. School districts have the authority to adopt resolutions implementing certain tax exemptions for veterans.

Pursuant to Chapter 518 of the Laws of 2013 a school district may implement the alternative veteran's exemption (§ 458-a). The alternative exemption applies to veterans who actively served during a period of war, received an expeditionary medal and under certain conditions veterans who served in the merchant marine, American Field Services or with the Pan American World Airways (§ 458-a(1)(e)). A veteran of the reserve components of the U.S. Armed Forces who received an honorable discharge or release there from under honorable conditions who is still a member of the reserve component may also be granted the exemption if all other requirements are met (§ 458-a(1)(e)(v)). Spouses of veterans and unremarried surviving spouses of veterans qualify for the exemption as well (§ 458-a(1)(c)). At the time this publication went to press, a bill passed by both houses of the Legislature, but awaiting action by the governor, would further expand the definition of veteran for purposes of the alternative veteran's exemption to include those veterans who served on active duty during the postal strike of 1970 (2016 Senate Bill S.4842-a).

Prior to adopting this exemption the school district must hold a public hearing (§ 458-a(2)(d)). A listing of acceptable military records that may be used to prove eligibility for the exemption are available on the websites of the Division of Veterans' Affairs and the Office of Real Property Tax Services (§ 458-a(9); see https://www.tax.ny.gov/pit/property/exemption/vetexemptproof.htm).

A school district may also opt to have the veteran's alternative exemption apply to property owned by a parent of a child who died in the line of duty while serving in the U.S. armed forces during a period of war (known as a "gold star parent") provided after a public hearing, separate and apart from a hearing about the alternative exemption in general, the district adopts a resolution providing for the gold star parent exemption (§ 458-a(7)). For additional information on the alternative exemption see http://www.tax.ny.gov/pdf/publications/orpts/veterans.pdf. A school district may also, after a public hearing, provide that when a veteran, veteran's spouse or unremarried surviving spouse already receiving the exemption sells said property and purchases property in the same county (or in New York City in the same city) the assessor will transfer and prorate the exemption received (§ 458-a(8)).

A school district which previously adopted the veterans exemption may repeal such exemption provided it does so no later than 90 days prior to the next taxable status date. Nothing precludes a school district from subsequently adopting a resolution to reinstate such exemption (§ 458-a(4)(b)).

In addition, school districts (other than large city school districts) may adopt an exemption which applies to persons with disabilities who earn less than $29,000 annually (§ 459-c). Individuals receiving a U.S. Department of Veterans' Affairs disability pension which is under the income limitation would qualify for this exemption (§ 459-c(2)(b)(v); see also 38 USC § 1521). A school district may adopt this exemption after a public hearing (§ 459-c(1)(a)).

This exemption cannot be granted under certain circumstances such as in the case of real property where a child resides, if the child attends a public elementary or secondary school, unless the school board of the school district in which the property is located, after a public hearing, adopts a resolution providing for such exemption. The requirement for such a hearing and resolution is separate from, and in addition to, the requirement that a school board hold a public hearing before approving a resolution to offer the exemption to disabled veterans with limited income in the first place (§ 459-c(4)). If the exemption is allowed for property where a child resides there must be sufficient proof the child was not brought into the residence in whole or in part for the purpose of attending a particular school in the district (*Id.*). For further information on this exemption see http://www.tax.ny.gov/pit/property/exemption/disablexempt.htm.

Chapter 253 of the Laws of 2016 amended Real Property Tax Law § 458-b to allow school districts to adopt a resolution granting an exemption from real property taxes to veterans of the cold war. The exemption is only valid for a period of ten years (§ 458-b(2)(a), (c)(iii)). Unlike, the alternative veteran's exemption, a public hearing is generally not required prior to adoption of the exemption for cold war veterans, with the exception of requiring a hearing prior to allowing the exemption to be applied to property owned by a cooperative apartment corporation (§ 458-b(7)(d)). A school district which adopts the exemption retains the right to repeal such resolution; any repeal must occur at least 90 days prior to the next taxable status date (§ 458-b(5)). A taxpayer who is granted an exemption pursuant to either section 458 or 458-a shall not be eligible for the cold war veteran's exemption (§ 458-b(2)(c)(ii)).

21:27. May taxpayers voluntarily renounce previously granted tax exemptions on their real property?

Yes. Taxpayers who wish to give up their claim to an exemption on one or more preceding assessment rolls may do so by filing an application with the county director of real property tax services no later than ten years after the levy of taxes upon the assessment roll on which the renounced exemption appears (§ 496(1), (2)).

Upon receipt of such application, the amount of taxes owed will be calculated by multiplying the assessed value that was exempted by the tax rate or rates that were applied to the applicable assessment roll or rolls. Interest shall then be calculated pursuant to Real Property Tax Law § 924-a (§ 496(2)(a), (b)). A $500 processing fee will be added to the sum of the taxes and interest calculated to be owed based upon the renunciation (§ 496(2)(c)).

The county director of real property tax services must return to the taxpayer the application form including the total amount of taxes due, and the taxpayer then has 15 days to pay the amount due (§ 496(3)).

A copy of the form must be provided to the assessor and in the case of the STAR exemption to the commissioner of taxation and finance. If a taxpayer renounces a STAR exemption any money collected, including interest must be paid to the state in the manner directed by the commissioner of taxation and finance (*Id.*).

21:28. Is a municipality exempt from paying school taxes on real property it acquires on a tax foreclosure sale?

No. A municipality is liable for school taxes on real property it acquires by deed, a referee's deed in a tax foreclosure, or pursuant to a deed made in lieu of a tax foreclosure (§ 406(5); *USFD No.11 of the Town of Urbana v. Steuben Cnty.*, 178 Misc. 415 (Sup. Ct. Steuben Cnty.), *aff'd*, 264 A.D. 945 (4th Dep't 1942); but see *Bd. of Educ. of Poughkeepsie City Sch. Dist. v. City of Poughkeepsie,* 113 A.D.3d 801 (2d Dep't 2014) (tax exemptions in city charter for lands acquired by tax deed were not superseded by the adoption of Real Property Tax Law § 406, so city did not have to pay school taxes on properties acquired by tax deed)).

21:29. Is school district property located outside a city and village subject to special assessments or *ad valorem* taxes from that city or village?

No. Section 490 of the Real Property Tax Law exempts school district real property from certain special assessments and *ad valorem* levies (§§ 408, 490).

State School Tax Relief Program (STAR) Exemption

21:30. What is the New York State School Tax Relief Program (STAR)?

STAR is a state-funded exemption from school property taxes for owner-occupied, primary residences. To be eligible for the exemption, the property must be a one-, two-, or three-family residence, a farm home, or a residential condominium, cooperative apartment, or dwelling owned by a limited partnership (§ 425(3)). The program has two components: the enhanced program for income-eligible senior citizens and the basic program for all other property owners (§ 425(2)(a), (3), (4)). The STAR exemption must be applied after any other applicable exemptions have been applied to the property's assessed value (§§ 425(7)(b), 467(1)(c)).

In 2016 legislation was enacted to transition the STAR program from a state-funded exemption to a personal income tax credit (school tax relief (STAR) credit). Individuals who currently receive the exemption (basic or enhanced) will continue to do so, unless they renounce the exemption in favor of the STAR credit (§§ 425(16)(b), (c), 496; Tax Law § 606(eee); see **21:27**). New applicants may only receive the exemption if the taxpayer both owned their home and applied for the STAR exemption prior to the 2015 STAR application deadline (§ 425(16)(a) but see **21:32, 38** for information about applying for the enhanced STAR exemption). The STAR application deadline is the taxable status date, which generally falls on March 1 but may be a different date in some localities (see NYS Department of Taxation and Finance, *STAR Property Tax Relief* at: https://www.tax.ny.gov/pit/property/star/; see **21:3**).

Individuals who qualify for the STAR credit or the enhanced STAR credit will be able to claim a credit equal to the lesser of STAR tax (or enhanced STAR tax) savings applicable to the taxpayer's primary residence or the taxpayer's qualifying taxes (Tax Law § 606(eee)(3)(b), (4)(b)). An option exists for the taxpayer to request an advance check rather than waiting to claim the credit on his or her income taxes (Tax Law § 606(eee)(10)). Taxpayers who exercise this option will continue to receive such advance payment in future years without reapplying as long as the taxpayer remains eligible therefor (Tax Law § 606(eee)(10)(A)(iii)). Advance payments will generally be issued by September 30 of each year (Tax Law § 606(eee)(10)(B)).

21:31. What rights does a taxpayer have if his or her STAR application is denied?

Prior to the 2016-2017 school year, if a STAR application was denied, the applicant could seek administrative and judicial review of the denial, subject to the same time constraints that apply to the review of assessments appearing on the current year's assessment roll (§ 425(6)(d)(ii)). Applications will no longer be granted beginning with the assessment rolls used to levy taxes for the 2016-17 school year (§ 425(16)(a)). New applicants may only receive the exemption if the taxpayer both owned their home and applied for the STAR exemption prior to the 2015 STAR application deadline (§ 425(16)(a)). The STAR application deadline is the taxable status date, which generally falls on March 1, but may be a different date in some localities. Assessors may mail applicants a form explaining the restriction and notifying the applicants of the right to claim the personal income tax credit (see NYS Department of Taxation and Finance, *STAR Property Tax Relief* at: https://www.tax.ny.gov/pit/property/star/; see **21:3**). An exception exists such that a surviving spouse, who did not previously hold title to the property, is entitled to apply for the exemption, provided the property served as the primary residence for the couple on the assessment roll used to levy taxes for the 2015-16 school year (§ 425(16)(d)).

For an explanation of a taxpayer's rights if a STAR exemption has been discontinued or revoked see **21:42-43**.

21:32. What is the enhanced STAR program?

The enhanced STAR program is available to eligible senior citizens (§ 425(2)(a), (4)). The enhanced STAR exemption is calculated in the manner prescribed in law (§ 425(2)(b)(vi)).

As a general rule, to be eligible for the enhanced STAR exemption, property owners must all be at least 65 years of age. However, the exemption is also available to a husband and wife, siblings, and a parent and adult child with a disability at least one of whom is 65 years of age as of December 31 (§ 425(4)(a), (6)(c); see also 11 Opn. Counsel SBRPS No. 107 (2007)). If a property is eligible for the senior citizens exemption (see **21:23**) authorized by § 467 it shall also be deemed eligible for the enhanced STAR exemption provided at least one of the applicants owned the property on the taxable status date for the assessment roll used to levy taxes in 2015-16 school year and the exemption was granted (§ 425(6)(c)).

The property must serve as the primary residence of that owner (§ 425(4)(a)(i)). In addition, the combined annual "income" of all of the owners and their spouses residing in the premises must not exceed the applicable income limits set forth in law (§ 425(4)(b)(i)). "Income" means "adjusted gross income" as reported for federal income tax purposes (§ 425(4)(b)(ii)). An enhanced exemption must be changed to a basic exemption if the combined income of the owners exceeds the income limits (§ 425(16)(b)(ii)). The enhanced exemption may be reinstated if the owners' combined income falls below the limit in the future (*Id.*).

A senior citizen whose income experiences a decrease due to the death of a spouse, such that he or she would now qualify for the enhanced exemption, if eligibility were based upon income for the income tax year immediately subsequent to the tax year that would otherwise be used to calculate eligibility, may have their eligibility determined based upon the decreased income if a copy of the income tax return reflecting the lesser income is filed with the assessor prior to the taxable status date (§ 425(4)(b)(i)(c-1)).

Beginning in 2016, the enhanced STAR exemption will be transitioned to an enhanced STAR credit for taxpayers who purchased their home after the 2015 STAR application deadline (see NYS Department of Taxation and Finance, *STAR Property Tax Relief* at: https://www.tax.ny.gov/pit/property/star/). Taxpayers already receiving the exemption will continue to do so as long as they qualify, unless the taxpayers choose to renounce the exemption in favor of the enhanced STAR credit on their personal income tax (§§ 425(16)(b), (c), 496; Tax Law § 606(eee); see **21:27**). Additionally, if taxpayers previously received the basic STAR exemption on their home and now meet the requirements for the enhanced STAR exemption they may apply for the exemption rather than the credit (§ 425(16)(b)(i); see also NYS Department of Taxation and Finance, *STAR Exemption Program* at: https://www.tax.ny.gov/pit/property/star/star-exemption-program.htm).

Taxpayers will qualify for the enhanced STAR credit if age 65 or older as of December 31 of the taxable year and meet the income requirement for the enhanced STAR exemption (Tax Law § 606(eee)(4)(A); § 425(4)(b)(i)(C)). The enhanced STAR credit will be equal to the lesser of the enhanced STAR tax savings applicable to the taxpayer's primary residence or the taxpayer's qualifying taxes (Tax Law § 606(eee)(4)(b)). If the taxes paid by the taxpayer constituted only a portion of the total school district taxes or in large city school districts (other than New York City) where the school and municipal taxes are combined, the credit will be calculated pursuant to the percentage that such portion paid represents (Tax Law § 606(eee)(4)(C)). Special rules apply for a separate school tax reduction credit for residents of New York City (Tax Law § 606(ggg)).

21:33. What is the basic STAR program?

The basic STAR program applies to all primary-residence homeowners, regardless of age or income, and provides a $30,000 base exemption (§ 425(2)(b)(vi)(B), (3)). Senior citizens whose income exceeds the applicable income limits set forth in law for the enhanced STAR exemption (see **21:31**) still may be eligible for the basic STAR exemption (§ 425(2)(b)(vi), (4)(a), (b)(i)).

On an annual basis, the commissioner of taxation and finance must verify whether properties previously receiving the basic exemption continue to qualify for such exemption and furnish a report to each assessor as to the eligibility status of each property (Tax Law § 171-u). To qualify for the basic exemption for the 2011–12 school year and thereafter, the combined income of all owners of a parcel who reside primarily thereon may not exceed $500,000 (§ 425(3)(b-1)).

Beginning in 2016, the basic STAR program will be transitioned to a STAR credit on personal income tax. Taxpayers already receiving the exemption will continue to do so as long as they qualify, unless the taxpayers choose to renounce the exemption in favor of the STAR credit on their personal income tax (§§ 425(16), 496; Tax Law § 606(eee)). To qualify for the credit the owners' income must not exceed $500,000. The credit will be equal to the lesser of STAR tax savings applicable to the taxpayer's primary residence or the taxpayer's qualifying taxes (Tax Law § 606(eee)(3)(b)). If the taxes paid by the taxpayer constituted only a portion of the total school district taxes or in large city school districts (other than New York City) where the school and municipal taxes are combined, the credit will be calculated pursuant to the percentage that such portion paid represents (Tax Law § 606(eee)(3)(C)). Special rules apply for a separate school tax reduction credit for residents of New York City (Tax Law § 606(ggg)).

21:34. What proof may be required to claim the STAR tax credit?

The commissioner may require a taxpayer to furnish the following information in support of his or her claim for the credit:

- Proof of income for all owners of the property;
- The total school district taxes levied on the property for the associated fiscal year (or combined city and school taxes in large city districts);
- The qualifying taxes paid by the taxpayer;
- Names and taxpayer identification numbers of all owners of the property and spouses who primarily reside on the property;
- The parcel identification number; and
- Any other information the commissioner may require to determine the credit (Tax Law § 606(eee)(8)).

21:35. May a husband and wife who own more than one home claim a STAR exemption on each home?

Generally no. To be eligible for the exemption, the property must serve as the "primary residence" of one or more of the owners (§ 425(3)(b)). However, if husband and wife are "living apart due to legal separation," each spouse may be eligible to claim the STAR exemption on the property that serves as his or her primary residence (§ 425(4-a)(a)).

21:36. Does the STAR exemption apply to a residence split by municipal boundaries?

Yes. When an applicant's primary residence (i.e. the actual residential structure itself) is located in two or more municipalities, each portion of the residence is eligible for the STAR exemption, provided that the eligibility requirements are otherwise satisfied. The exemption is pro-rated — just as the full value of the property is apportioned between each municipality by its assessor(s) — such that the total STAR savings does not exceed the STAR savings available if the property were located entirely within one municipality (§ 425(4-a)(c); see also **22:2**).

Similarly, special rules apply to calculating the STAR tax credit when a residence is split by municipal boundaries (Tax Law § 606(eee)(6)(C)).

21:37. Does the STAR exemption apply to library taxes levied by school districts on behalf of such libraries?

No. According to an opinion of counsel issued by New York's State Board of Real Property Services, which prior to 2010 oversaw the STAR exemption process, the STAR exemption does not apply to taxes or charges levied for library purposes (10 Opn. Counsel SBRPS No. 59 (1998); see also **21:1**).

21:38. How do district residents obtain either the enhanced STAR program exemption or the basic STAR program exemption?

For tax years prior to 2016-17 all owners of the property who primarily reside thereon must jointly file an application for the exemption with the assessor on or before the appropriate taxable status date (§ 425(6)(a); see **21:30**). However, such application may be filed after the appropriate taxable status date, but in no event later than the last date on which a petition with respect to complaints of assessment may be filed, under circumstances where the failure to file a timely application resulted from:

- death of the applicant's spouse, child, parent, brother, or sister; or
- an illness of the applicant or of the applicant's spouse, child, parent, brother, or sister, which actually prevented the applicant from filing on a timely basis, as certified by a licensed physician.

If either of these conditions is satisfied, then the assessor approves or denies the application as if it had been filed on or before the taxable status date (§ 425(6)(e)).

Where school district taxes are levied upon prior year assessment rolls, the assessing unit may adopt a local law allowing the submission of STAR applications for each school year on or before the taxable status date of the current year's assessment roll (§ 425(6)(d)(i)). When such a local law is in effect, the eligibility of property for a STAR exemption for a particular school year is based on the condition of the property as of the taxable status date of the prior year's assessment roll, and ownership of the property is determined as of the taxable status date of the current year's assessment roll (§ 425(6)(d)(ii)).

If the assessor is satisfied that the applicant(s) are entitled to an exemption, he or she will approve the application and such real property shall thereafter be partially exempt from school district taxation, without further application (§ 425(6)(b), (9-a)). Beginning with the 2016-17 school year, new applications for the basic STAR exemption will no longer be accepted (see **21:30-31**). Instead taxpayers must register for the STAR credit (§ 425(16); Tax Law § 606(eee); see also NYS Department of Taxation and Finance, *Register for the STAR Credit* at: https://www.tax.ny.gov/pit/property/star/register-for-star-credit.htm). An exception exists such that a surviving spouse, who did not previously hold title to the property, is entitled to apply for the exemption, provided the property served as the primary residence for the couple on the assessment roll used to levy taxes for the 2015-16 school year (§ 425(16)(d)).

The enhanced program exemption for eligible senior citizens only applies for one year, and a renewal application must be submitted each year, unless: (1) the taxpayer has elected to participate in the STAR income verification program (see **21:40**); or (2) the property continues to be eligible for the senior citizen exemption pursuant to Real Property Tax Law section 467, in which case the enhanced exemption continues to apply automatically (see **21:24**) (§ 425(9-b)). While the STAR exemption program was closed to new applicants beginning with the 2016-17 school year, renewal applications will continue to be accepted by assessors on an annual basis for the enhanced STAR exemption. Additionally, taxpayers who previously received a basic STAR exemption may apply for the enhanced STAR exemption when they qualify for such enhancement (§ 425(16)(b)(i); see also NYS Department of Taxation and Finance, *STAR Exemption Program* at: https://www.tax.ny.gov/pit/property/star/star-exemption-program.htm).

A taxpayer may petition the commissioner requesting an extension of the deadline to file an application for the enhanced STAR exemption, provided such request is filed by the last day for paying school taxes without incurring interest or penalty. The commissioner may grant the exemption if satisfied that there was good cause for the failure to meet the deadline and the applicant was otherwise entitled to the exemption (§ 425(6)(a-2)).

21:39. How is a taxpayer's continued eligibility for a basic STAR exemption verified?

Beginning in 2010 and continuing annually thereafter, the commissioner of taxation and finance must verify whether each parcel previously granted the basic exemption still satisfies the income eligibility requirements (Tax Law § 171-u(1)). The commissioner shall develop a report which is given to each assessor stating in each case whether the parcel satisfies the income eligibility requirement or that such eligibility was unable to be ascertained (Tax Law § 171-u(2)). Based upon this report, assessors will grant exemptions to eligible parcels, deny exemptions to ineligible parcels (with notice stating the findings of the commissioner as the reason therefore) and request further documentation in order to make appropriate determinations as to those parcels where the commissioner was unable to verify eligibility (Tax Law § 171-u(3)).

Further verification of the eligibility for the basic exemption was enabled by the adoption of the STAR Registration program. Taxpayers who received the basic STAR exemption in 2012-13 school year had to register with the NYS Department of Taxation and Finance by April 1, 2014 (§ 425(14)(a); see also http://www.tax.ny.gov/pit/property/star13/). Taxpayers applying for the STAR exemption for the first time must also register (*Id.*).

Taxpayers may petition to file a late registration if a sufficient explanation of the failure is provided and the petition is filed within one year of the missed deadline (§ 425(14)(a)(iii)). If the commissioner accepts a late registration after originally removing a BASIC star exemption from the property the commissioner may remit directly to the property owners the tax savings the exemption would have yielded had it not been removed (*Id.*). The commissioner may further direct the assessor to restore the exemption on a prospective basis without new application unless the assessor has cause to believe the property owner is no longer eligible for a STAR exemption for other reasons (*Id.*).

The commissioner will direct the removal or denial of a STAR exemption if:

- All owners of the property have not been registered by the prescribed date and no acceptable justification is presented for such failure;
- Owners of the property are improperly receiving multiple STAR exemptions;
- The property does not serve as the primary residence of any of its owners;
- The applicable income limitation has been exceeded; or
- The property is otherwise ineligible (§ 425(14)(b)).

Prior to denial or removal of a STAR exemption under the registration program, notice and an opportunity to provide documentation that the property qualified for the STAR exemption must be provided to the taxpayer. If the exemption is denied or must be removed the commissioner will direct the assessor to do so (§ 425(14)(c)). Such decision may only be challenged before the NYS Department of Taxation and Finance and the State Board of Real Property Tax Services. The final decision of the state board may be appealed to state supreme court (§ 425(14)(d)).

21:40. Can taxpayers have their income eligibility for the enhanced STAR exemption verified without having to reapply each year?

Yes. The application form for the enhanced STAR exemption must give applicants the opportunity to participate in the STAR income verification program (IVP) so that their income eligibility is verified annually by the NYS Department of Taxation and Finance, pursuant to an agreement between their assessor and the department (§ 425(4)(b)(iv)).

Thereafter, the taxpayer's income eligibility will be verified annually by the NYS Department of Taxation and Finance, and the taxpayer will not need to provide income documentation to the assessor unless the Tax Department informs the assessor that it is unable to verify the taxpayer's income eligibility, or that the taxpayer does not qualify for the enhanced exemption under the income eligibility guidelines. The assessor is required to mail notices to taxpayers based upon the information it receives from the NYS Department of Taxation and Finance (§ 425(4)(b)(iv), (v)(A), (5)). All assessing units are required to participate in this program (§ 425(4)(b)(iv)).

The assessor must send one of three types of notices to participants in the IVP program. If the taxpayer satisfies the eligibility requirements, the notice shall so state and include notice that if the property remains the taxpayer's primary residence and there has been no change in ownership he or she remains eligible for the enhanced exemption and need not contact the assessor (§ 425(5)(b)(i)).

If the taxpayer's income was unable to be verified, the assessor shall send notice to that effect and further state that the taxpayer must furnish documentation of the income eligibility on or before the applicable tax status date in order to continue to receive the enhanced exemption (§ 425(5)(b)(ii)).

A notice specifying the reasons for denial will be mailed to taxpayers who have failed to satisfy the eligibility requirements no later than 10 days prior to the date for hearing complaints in relation to assessments (§ 425(5)(b)(iii), (6)(b)).

The NYS Department of Taxation and Finance is prohibited from providing any other information about the income of the taxpayer other than that which is necessary to verify income eligibility for the enhanced STAR exemption. Moreover, the assessor and other municipal officials must keep such information confidential, and are subject to removal from office and/or other penalties authorized by law for failure to do so. Consistent with this requirement of confidentiality, the Freedom of Information Law is inapplicable to this information (§ 425(4)(b)(v)).

Income documentation still must be submitted to the assessor with

- the initial application for the enhanced exemption;
- renewal applications by taxpayers who previously have not participated in the income verification program;
- any application to resume the enhanced exemption after it has been discontinued;
- an application submitted in a new assessing jurisdiction (even if the same applicant previously qualified in another jurisdiction); and
- applications where the assessor is advised by the Department of Taxation and Finance that it is unable to determine whether participant(s) satisfy income eligibility requirements (§ 425(4)(b)(vi)).

Taxpayers who do not participate in the income verification program must file a renewal application with the assessor each year in order to continue receiving the enhanced exemption. If a taxpayer fails to file a renewal application the assessor shall discontinue the enhanced exemption but shall grant the basic exemption provided all other requirements are still met (§ 425(9-b); see also **21:38-39**).

21:41. What happens if the income of a participant in the STAR income verification program cannot be verified?

If the Department of Taxation and Finance is unable to verify the income of a participant in the income verification program it will notify the assessor who must mail the taxpayer a notice requesting documentation of income in the same manner and extent as provided in the initial enhanced STAR application (§ 425(12)(a)). If the taxpayer fails to provide documentation within 45 days or provides insufficient documentation the enhanced STAR exemption will be revoked (*Id.*; see **21:43**).

21:42. May a taxpayer's STAR exemption be discontinued?

Yes. The assessor is required to discontinue any STAR exemption if it appears that the property may not be the primary residence of the owner who applied for the exemption, title to the property has been transferred to new owners or the property is otherwise no longer eligible for the exemption (§ 425(11)(a)). The STAR exemption must be discontinued if the combined income of the owners exceeds the statutory limit, but may be reinstated if the owners' income falls below the statutory limit in future years (§ 425(16)(b)(iii)). A STAR exemption will be permanently discontinued if the owners fail to satisfy applicable residency or ownership requirements or both (§ 425(16)(b)(iv)).

When an assessor determines the exemption should be discontinued he or she must mail notice to the owners 120 days prior to the filing date for the tentative assessment roll. The taxpayers may seek administrative and judicial review of such decision (§§ 425(11)(b), 510).

21:43. May a taxpayer's STAR exemption be revoked?

Yes. In addition to discontinuing a STAR exemption on the next assessment roll, if an assessor determines that the property improperly received the exemption on one or more of the six preceding assessment rolls (provided the final assessment rolls were filed on or after April 1, 2010) or is advised by the tax department that the income standard with respect to the enhanced STAR exemption was not satisfied the assessor must remove the previously granted exemptions (§ 425(12)(a); see **21:39**). The assessor must also revoke the enhanced STAR exemption if the department in unable to verify the income of a taxpayer participating in the income verification program and the taxpayer fails to provide sufficient documentation to qualify (*Id.*; see **21:41**).

Each owner must be given notice of the proposed revocation in accordance with law and may seek administrative and judicial review of such decision (§ 425(12)(c)).

When an exemption is revoked, the assessed value attributable to each improperly granted exemption is entered separately on the next ensuing tax roll and the corresponding tax rate from those previous tax rolls is applied as well as interest calculated pursuant to § 924-a of the law (§ 425(12)(b)). A processing fee of $500 shall be added for improperly granted STAR exemptions occurring on assessment rolls filed on or after April 1, 2013 (§ 425(12)(b)(iii)).

21:44. May the state recoup monies from tax payers for improperly granted basic STAR exemptions?

Yes. If it is determined pursuant to the STAR registration program (see **21:39**) that a property improperly received the basic STAR exemption in the current school year or in one or more of the three proceeding school years, the commissioner may collect the tax savings attributable to each such improperly granted exemption together with interest pursuant to § 924-a of the law (§ 425(15)). Recoupment may not occur on assessment rolls that were filed prior to April 1, 2011 (§ 425(15)(a)).

Prior to directing recoupment, the commission must provide the owners with notice and an opportunity to prove the exemption was properly granted. Notice must be mailed no later than three years after the conclusion of the school year for which the exemption in question was granted, except that if the exemption was granted for 2012-2013 school year the notice must be mailed no later than September 30, 2016 (§ 425(15)(b)(i)). If the owners fail to respond within 45 days of the notice or their response fails to establish entitlement to the exemption the commissioner may continue with recoupment. Such decision may only be challenged before the Department of Taxation and Finance and the State Board of Real Property Tax Services. The final decision of the state board may be appealed to state supreme court (§ 425(15)(b)(ii), (iii)).

Monies are recouped pursuant to Article 22 of the Tax Law which provides for collection, levy and lien of personal income tax (§ 425(15)(b)). Recoupment procedures are not applicable in situations where prior exemptions have been revoked pursuant to § 425(12) (see **21:43**) or voluntarily renounced pursuant to § 496 (§ 425(15)(d); see **21:27**).

21:45. May a taxpayer recoup the overpayment of taxes when a STAR exemption was not applied in the calculation of taxes owed?

Yes. If the commissioner finds that property owner was eligible for the STAR exemption but the exemption was not taken into account in the calculation of the property taxes due to administrative error such that the property owner overpaid, the commissioner may remit directly to the property owner the tax savings that would have yielded if the STAR exemption had been applied (§ 425(15-a)).

21:46. May a taxpayer be assessed a penalty tax for material misstatements on STAR applications?

Yes. An assessor may enter a penalty tax on the assessment roll when a taxpayer is found to have made material misstatements on a STAR application that was filed on or after October 1, 2010 (§ 425(13)(a)). A material misstatement will be found when:

- A taxpayer claimed a property was his or her primary residence when it was not;
- A taxpayer claims to have relinquished the STAR exemption on a former primary residence when in fact the taxpayer had not; or
- A taxpayer receiving the enhanced STAR exemption misrepresented his or her age or income so as to qualify for the exemption (§ 425(13)(a)(i)-(iii)).

Notice of the potential imposition of the penalty tax must be mailed to the taxpayer in accordance with law and the assessor will enter the penalty tax on the next assessment roll in accordance with the procedures of sections 551 or 553 of the real property tax law (§ 425(13)(b)). The taxpayer may seek administrative or judicial review of the imposition of the penalty tax (*Id.*).

The penalty tax shall be $100 if the application was filed prior to October 1, 2013, provided the assessor's determination is made within three years of the filing of the application. If the application was filed after October 1, 2013, the penalty tax is the greater of $100 or 20% of the improperly received tax savings up to a maximum of $2,500, provided the assessor's determination is made within six years of the filing of the application (§ 425(13)(a)).

Additionally, taxpayers who are found to have made material misstatements will be disqualified from receiving a STAR exemption for five years if the application was filed prior to October 1, 2013 or six years if the application was filed after that date (§ 425(13)(c)).

21:47. Can a taxpayer's STAR exemption be suspended?

Yes, if the commissioner of taxation and finance develops a program to collect delinquent state taxes through the suspension of eligibility of properties for STAR exemptions where one or more of the property owners have past-due state tax liabilities (Tax Law § 171-y). Unless extended, such a program only can be in effect starting with the 2013–14 school year through the 2015–16 school year (L. 2012, c. 59 pt. B § 3).

To be affected, taxpayers must have more than $4,500 in past due state tax liabilities, including sales and income taxes (Tax Law § 171-y(2)(a)). The commissioner of taxation and finance will develop procedures to implement the STAR suspension program including notice requirements and the methodology to be used for offsetting lost STAR benefits against past due state taxes set forth in law (Tax Law § 171-y(2)). A property shall be ineligible for a basic or enhanced STAR exemption the next school year following receipt of the STAR exemption suspension notice (§ 425(3)(f)).

Although taxpayers may challenge a STAR suspension notice before the NYS Department of Taxation and Finance on grounds of mistake of fact as defined in the law, they have no right of action either before a court or administrative proceeding, or any other form of recourse regarding the suspension of a STAR exemption (§ 171-y(5)).

21:48. What are a school district's responsibilities under the STAR program?

School districts are required to provide information about the STAR exemption to each person who owns a residence in the school district. The statute provides a sample notice that districts may use (§ 425(5)(a)).

21:49. How do school districts set their tax rates under the STAR program?

The amount of taxes to be levied and the tax rate must be determined without regard to the STAR exemption (§ 1306-a(1)).

21:50. How will the state reimburse school districts for the tax shortfall attributable to the STAR exemption?

Under the law, the total tax savings from the STAR program must be incurred by the state. Each school district must submit an application to the commissioner of taxation and finance, who must approve the application and certify to the commissioner of education the amount of state aid payable to the district (§ 1306-a(3); Educ. Law § 3609-e). To comport with the property tax levy cap (see **22:3**), the tax savings applicable to a property cannot exceed the tax savings applicable to the property in the prior school year multiplied by 102 percent (§ 1306-a(2)).

21:51. Where can further information about the STAR program be obtained?

Contact your local tax assessor's office or contact the NYS Department of Taxation and Finance at 518-591-5232, or visit its website at: http://www.tax.ny.gov/pit/property/star/index.htm.

Industrial Development Agencies

21:52. What is an industrial development agency?

An *industrial development agency* (IDA) is an independent public benefit corporation created through state legislation at the request of one or more sponsoring municipalities. Article 18-A of the General Municipal Law sets forth powers, jurisdiction and requirements for IDAs. Legislation creating a specific IDA may contain provisions different from or in addition to the general legislation contained in the General Municipal Law.

21:53. May school board members serve on an industrial development agency (IDA) board?

Yes. The General Municipal Law states that school board members, municipal officials, and representatives of organized labor and business may serve on IDA governing boards (Gen. Mun. Law § 856(2)).

21:54. What is the taxable status of real property owned by industrial development agencies, bonds and notes issued for industrial development agency (IDA) projects, and purchases made for IDA projects?

All property titled to an industrial development agency, as well as any bonds or notes issued by an IDA, are exempt from taxation, except for transfer and estate taxes (§ 412-a; Gen. Mun. Law § 874(1), (2)).

However, an IDA is authorized to negotiate payments in lieu of taxes (PILOTs) with the private developers participating in IDA projects (Gen. Mun. Law § 858(15)). PILOT moneys received from an IDA are to be included in the school budget as if they were tax dollars (Opn. St. Comp. 82-174). Furthermore, PILOTs must be included as estimated in the annual preparation of the school district's budget (Educ. Law §§ 1608(3), 1716(3), 2601-a(3)). PILOTs received by the IDA must be given to the school district within 30 days of receipt (Gen. Mun. Law § 874(3)).

In addition, all IDAs must adopt a uniform tax exemption policy with input from affected tax jurisdictions, including school districts, which states what tax exemptions are available to those interested in seeking IDA assistance for commercial enterprises. This policy must include guidelines for the claiming of real property, mortgage recording, and sales tax exemptions. The policy must also indicate the extent to which a proposed project will require additional services, including educational services, and the extent to which the proposed project will provide additional sources of revenue for school districts (Gen. Mun. Law § 874(4)(a)).

21:55. Can industrial development agencies (IDAs) distribute payments in lieu of taxes (PILOT) revenues as they see fit?

No. Unless otherwise agreed to by the school board and municipal governments affected by an IDA project, PILOTs must be distributed in proportion to the amount of real property and other taxes which would have been received had the project not been tax-exempt (Gen. Mun. Law § 858(15)). Affected taxing jurisdictions may agree to accept less than their full allocation of PILOTS (*Matter of Palmateer v. Greene County Indus. Dev. Agency,* 38 A.D.3d 1087 (3d Dep't 2007); see also *Appeal of Palmateer*, 49 Ed Dept Rep 347 (2010)).

21:56. What responsibilities do industrial development agencies (IDAs) have with respect to notifying school districts about their IDA-assisted projects?

IDAs must provide written notice to the chief executive officer of each affected school district within which any pending project is located that requires more than $100,000 in IDA financial assistance of a public hearing on the proposed project, at least 10 days prior to the hearing. In addition to stating the time and place of the hearing, the notice of the hearing must include a general description of the project (including its location), the identity of the initial owner, operator or manager of the project, and a description of the financial assistance contemplated by the IDA with respect to the project (Gen. Mun. Law § 859-a).

IDAs also must notify school boards and municipalities within 15 days of an agreement reached for payments in lieu of taxes (PILOTS) on an IDA-assisted project (Gen. Mun. Law § 858(15)).

22. School Tax Collection[1]

Authority to Levy School Taxes

22:1. Do all school districts levy taxes?

Most do, but not all. Fiscally independent school districts levy taxes for school purposes. The state's common, union free, central, central high school, and small city school districts are all fiscally independent. They all submit their budgets to the voters for approval and levy school taxes for authorized purposes, with the exception that in central high school districts, such taxes are levied by the component school districts on behalf of the central high school district (Educ. Law §§ 1608, 1716, 1908, 2022).

Fiscally dependent school districts do not levy taxes. Only the Big 5 city school districts are fiscally dependent. They are Buffalo, New York, Rochester, Syracuse, and Yonkers. They are dependent on municipal tax revenue to fund education (Educ. Law § 2576). Municipal governments levy a single real property tax for school and nonschool purposes and allocate a portion of their tax revenues for education. Fiscally dependent districts also may receive income from other local taxes, such as income taxes and sales taxes (see, for example, **22:4**).

22:2. Which district levies taxes on a residential property that is split between two different school districts?

Under Education Law section 3203, when a residential property is intersected by the boundary line between two school districts, the owner may designate either school district as the district for attendance by his or her children. However, condominium owners cannot designate the school district of their choice and students must attend the district in which their dwellings are located if the boundary line intersects common property but not any individual dwellings (*Palm v. Tuckahoe UFSD*, 46 Misc.3d 358 (Westchester Cnty. 2014), *aff'd,* 2016 NY Sup Op 05558 (2d Dep't 2016)).

Once this designation is made, both school districts continue to levy school taxes based upon the assessments in their respective taxing jurisdictions (see 9 Opn. Counsel SBEA No. 22 (1987); see also **21:36**), but the district that does not provide instruction to the children must pay over the school taxes that it has collected on the property to the school district where the children receive instruction.

This is true regardless of how much of the property is located in the affected districts. In one case, the commissioner of education ordered a school district where the bulk of a particular split residential property was located to pay over more than $6,000 in school taxes to the district designated by the owners for attendance by their children, even though only one square foot of the entire property was located in the designated district (see *Bd. of Educ. of the Harborfields CSD*, 41 Ed Dept Rep 15 (2001); see also same case at 41 Ed Dept Rep 113 (2001); *Appeal of Fioretti,* 45 Ed Dept Rep 188 (2005)).

[1] *All statutory references in this chapter are to the New York State Real Property Tax Law unless otherwise noted. The material in the chapter refers chiefly to school districts other than the Big 5 city school districts. For selected legal opinions by statute (or by subject), visit the NYS Office of Real Property Tax Services (ORPTS) website at: http://www.tax.ny.gov/pubs_and_bulls/orpts/legal_opinions/index.htm*

Payment of taxes owed by the school district that does not provide instruction to the district where the children receive instruction become due at the completion of the applicable school year. Appeals to the commissioner of education concerning the collection of such tax payments must be commenced within 30 days from the end of the applicable school year. Failure to submit a timely claim for taxes owed and commence an appeal to the commissioner within the applicable time frame will result in the forfeiture of such moneys by the district actually providing instruction (*Appeal of Bd. of Educ. of Manhasset UFSD*, 49 Ed Dept Rep 428 (2010)).

22:3. Are there limits on taxes levied by school districts in New York State?

Yes. The Education Law limits the yearly growth of property tax levies in common, union free, central, central high school, and small city school districts. The Buffalo, Rochester, Syracuse, and Yonkers school districts have no taxing authority, but are affected by the tax levy cap rules applicable to the cities on which they are fiscally dependent. New York City is not subject to the tax levy cap and neither is the city's school district (NYS Education Department, *Property Tax Cap Guidance* (revised Apr. 2015), at: http://www.p12.nysed.gov/mgtserv/propertytax/taxcap/docs/Property_Tax_%20Cap_General_Guidance_and_FAQS.pdf).

The allowable growth factor under the tax levy cap is the lesser of two percent or the sum of one plus the inflation factor, but will never be less than one (Educ. Law § 2023-a(2)). The inflation factor will be the unadjusted monthly average "All Items Consumer Price Index for All Urban Consumers" (CPI-U) change from January to December of the base year, as published by the Bureau of Labor Statistics (Educ. Law § 2023-a(2)(f); *Property Tax Cap Guidance*). The tax levy cap first applied to school budgets and the school budget process for the 2012–13 school year. For more information on the calculation of the property tax levy cap, see **chapter 19.**

The state enacted a property tax relief credit as part of the 2015 budget. The credit is available for tax years 2016 through 2019 to taxpayers who receive a STAR tax exemption and reside in a district which adopts a budget within its property tax levy limit (Tax Law § 606(n-1); see **19:5**). The amount of the credit is calculated pursuant to a statutory formula (*Id.*). Previously, the state enacted a two year property tax freeze as part of the 2014 budget which similarly entitled taxpayers to a credit if their district adopted a budget within the levy limit and the district adopted an approved government efficiency plan (Educ. Law § 2023-b; Tax Law § 606(bbb)).

A prior constitutional limit on taxes levied by small city school districts was repealed in 1985 (N.Y. Const. art. 8, § 10). Corresponding sections of the Education Law (see Educ. Law § 2701 *et seq.*) that regulated the constitutional tax limits in small city schools districts were repealed by Chapter 171 of the Laws of 1996.

22:4. Are there any sources of tax revenue for school districts other than real property?

Yes. The Tax Law authorizes certain municipalities, including some school districts under certain limited circumstances (see, for example, Tax Law § 1212) to levy non-realty taxes for both education and general purposes. These can be, for example, taxes on utilities, real estate sales, food and drinks in restaurants and bars, vending machines, admissions to places of amusement, and general sales taxes (Tax Law §§ 1200–1263).

22:5. May school districts receive a portion of the county sales tax?

Yes. The Tax Law authorizes counties to allocate a portion of their sales tax revenues to school districts and other localities (Tax Law § 1262).

Counties that do allocate a portion of sales taxes to school districts may not reduce the amount to be paid to a district if the county participates in the State Medicaid Sales Tax Intercept. The sales tax intercept program allows a county to pay its Medicaid costs by authorizing the State Department of Tax and Finance to subtract the county's monthly Medicaid amount from the sales tax revenue owed to the county and pay it into the state treasury in lieu of the county making weekly payments. The sales tax intercept does not permit a county to make payments to local municipalities that are less than the net amount due to the localities *before* the intercept (Tax Law § 1261(f)(8); *Monroe Cnty. Pub. Sch. Dists. v. Zyra*, 51 A.D.3d 125 (4th Dep't), *lv. to appeal denied,* 52 A.D.3d 1293 (4th Dep't 2008)).

22:6. What are some key definitions related to the assessment and collection of school taxes?

Assessment is the determination, by assessors, of the valuation of real property, including exempt real property, as well as the determination of whether such real property is subject to taxation or special *ad valorem* levies (§ 102(2)).

The *assessment roll* is the list of each parcel of property in the municipality and its assessed value as it exists before a warrant for the collection of taxes is attached to it (§ 550(1)).

Real property is land, above and under water; buildings and other structures affixed to the land, including bridges and wharves; underground and elevated railroads and railroad structures; telephone and telegraph lines; mains, pipes and tanks; mobile homes and trailers; and other property (see § 102(12) for a complete definition).

The *state equalization rate* is the percentage of full value at which taxable real property in a county, city, town or village is assessed as determined by the commissioner of taxation and finance (§ 102(19)).

The *tax roll* is a final assessment roll to which tax amounts have been added and to which a warrant has been attached (§ 904(1)).

A *tax warrant* empowers the tax collector to collect the taxes (§ 904(4)).

Determining the Tax Rate

22:7. How is the amount of tax to be imposed on each parcel of property in the school district determined?

There are three methods of determining the tax amount.

(1) In a district that is completely within or coterminous with a single taxing jurisdiction, the amount of the tax is determined by multiplying the assessed value of the parcel by the tax rate per thousand dollars of assessed value. The school tax rate per thousand is determined by dividing the total amount of the tax levy by the total assessed value of the property in the town and multiplying that result by 1,000. For example, if the total amount of the levy is $8 million, and the total assessed value of all taxable property is $135 million, the tax rate per 1,000 is $59.25. The school tax on a parcel assessed at $50,000 is $2,962.96.

(2) In a district that embraces two or more towns or other local taxing jurisdictions, the full value of assessed real property in each jurisdiction is calculated by dividing the assessed valuation determined by each local assessor by the equalization rate established by the commissioner of taxation and finance for that locality (full value) (§ 1314).

(3) In the case of a school district located in more than one city or town where all affected municipalities opt to use the special large parcel equalization process for a "designated large property" (as that term is defined in law), the state board must notify the appropriate school district and assessing unit and provide instructions for the apportionment of the tax levy (§ 1316).

School boards proposing to reorganize through consolidation, centralization or annexation may opt to minimize the impact of reorganization upon school tax rates by either deferring the impact for one year or having it phased in over a period not to exceed 10 years (Educ. Law § 3613(1)). To exercise this option, the boards of all participating school districts after a public hearing must adopt a resolution regarding the phase in at least 45 days prior to the reorganization vote special district meeting. All districts must adopt the resolution for the common phase in period for it to apply (*Id.*). If adopted the tax rate for each portion of the school district is calculated pursuant to a formula in the statute (Educ. Law § 3613(2), (3)).

22:8. What is tax equalization, and what is its role in the process of setting tax rates?

Tax equalization, simply stated, is the ratio between the actual current market value of property and the assessed value of that property. *Full value*, or *market value*, is the price a piece of property would command if it were sold on the open market. *Assessed value* is the value of a piece of property established by taxing authorities on the basis of which the tax rate is applied. The assessed value is often a fraction of the actual market value.

Tax equalization is a method of computation used with the aim of equitably apportioning the tax burden where a district encompasses parts of two or more tax districts that assess property at different fractions of full value. The end result of the use of the state equalization rate is supposed to be the determination of the full market value of property and tax rate on full value. (The process for establishing the equalization rate is set forth in section 1314 of the Real Property Tax Law.) Whenever a state equalization rate is ordered to be revised as the result of a court action, a school district that used the former rate in the apportionment of taxes, once notified, must recalculate the levy and credit or debit as appropriate its constituent municipalities in its next tax levy (§ 1218).

22:9. Are residential and commercial properties taxed at the same rate?

Under the homestead/non-homestead property-classification system, residential and commercial properties can be taxed at different rates in approved assessing units (those that have undergone reassessment of all parcels at full market value and have been approved by the commissioner of taxation and finance). This ensures against a disproportionate tax burden for residential taxpayers by reducing tax rates on residential properties.

Article 19 of the Real Property Tax Law regulates the adoption and implementation procedures of the homestead tax system.

22:10. How are school districts affected by the homestead/non-homestead property-classification system?

If a locality elects this option, it must provide a copy of the local law establishing the homestead classification system to the authorities of each school district located wholly or partially within that locality. When adopted by an approved assessing unit (a town, village, or city), the homestead system applies to taxes levied on all real property by each school district wholly contained within the approved assessing unit (§ 1903(1)(a)(b)). However, an affected district may adopt a resolution rejecting this kind of property-classification system in its district (§ 1903(1)(a)). Once a school district opts out of this dual property classification system it may not subsequently reverse its decision and opt into that system again (11 Opn. Counsel SBRPS No. 33 (2002)).

22:11. Can the homestead/non-homestead property-classification system apply to school districts located in more than one city or town?

Yes, if one or more cities or towns within the school district has adopted a homestead/non-homestead property-classification system. A school board may, by resolution, adopt such a classification system, upon filing a notice of intent, as set forth in law (§ 1903-a(1)(a), (b)), and following a public hearing to be held at any time prior to the levy of school taxes (§ 1903-a(3)).

School districts may cancel notice of intent to adopt such a system by filing a notice of cancellation, as set forth in law (§ 1903-a(1)(c)). They may also, by board resolution and without a public hearing, rescind any prior action adopting such a system at any time prior to the levy of taxes for the fiscal year to which the resolution is applicable. Any such rescission must also be filed in accordance with law (§ 1903-a(5)).

Tax Collection Procedures

22:12. Are there specific procedures and deadlines for authorizing the collection of taxes?

Yes. After the tax roll has been prepared by applying the property tax rates against the properties assessed, the list must be confirmed by school board resolution. At the date and time at which this resolution is adopted, the school taxes become a lien on the properties (§ 1312).

The next step is to execute the warrant, which serves as a directive to the tax collector to collect taxes in accordance with the confirmed tax list and provides authorization for making collection (§ 1318(1)). In most school districts, the tax warrant must be affixed to the tax list on or before September 1 (§ 1306(1)). In small city school districts, the tax warrant must be affixed to the tax roll no later than 90 days after the start of the fiscal year, which begins July 1 (§ 1306(2); see also Educ. Law § 2515). At least a majority of the school board is required to sign the warrant for the collection of taxes (§ 1318(1)). For sample resolutions, see NYS Education Department, *School Tax Collection Procedures* at: http://www.p12.nysed.gov/mgtserv/taxation/SchlTaxProced.htm.

The state does not fix a limit on the number of times a tax warrant may be renewed. However, warrants of school tax collectors must be returnable in time for the school authorities to transmit necessary information regarding unpaid taxes to the county treasurer by November 15 (§§ 1318(3), 1330(2)).

School districts may enter into a municipal cooperative agreement with a county for the collection of taxes by the county treasurer. Subject to certain specified conditions, such an agreement can provide for the joint and concurrent collection of taxes by the county treasurer and a district's tax collecting officer, or it may delegate sole and exclusive authority for the collection of taxes to the county treasurer (§ 578(2)).

At the time this publication went to press, a bill passed by both houses of the Legislature, but awaiting action by the governor, would permit a school district located within a town to collect its own school taxes upon annual notice to the town's receiver of taxes as opposed to mutual agreement between the town and school district (2016 Senate Bill S.4737).

22:13. Can school districts bill and collect taxes electronically?

Yes. School boards may adopt a resolution authorizing electronic billing and collection of taxes after determining it is in the public interest to do so (§ 104(1), (3)(c)). In such an instance a district may, for example, issue statements of taxes and provide receipts electronically, as well as provide for the payment of taxes through the internet (§§ 104(1), 925-c; see also Gen. Mun. Law § 5-b). School districts may accept payment through their own websites or the website of a third-party vendor with whom they have contracted to receive such payments on their behalf (Gen. Mun. Law § 5-b(1)). School districts that contract with third party vendors are required to follow the guidelines issued by the State Comptroller with respect to such agreements (Gen. Mun. Law § 5-b(6)).

The taxpayer must receive a confirmation page that includes the date the internet transaction was completed, the amount paid, a unique confirmation number and notice advising the taxpayer to print out and retain the confirmation page as his or her receipt (Gen. Mun. Law § 5-b(2)).

Nonetheless, taxpayers are not required to accept notices, statement of taxes, receipts for payments of taxes, or other documents electronically (§ 104(3)(a)). Furthermore, e-mail addresses or social network user names given to the school district for electronic administration of taxes are exempt from disclosure pursuant to a freedom of information law request (§ 104(3)(d); see **13:5**).

The commissioner of taxation and finance is authorized to establish standards for electronic real property tax administration after consultation with local government officials, the office of court administration and the office of state comptroller (§ 104(1), (2)).

22:14. How are taxpayers notified of their school taxes?

Upon receipt of a warrant for the collection of taxes, the collecting officer must publish a notice in a newspaper, or two newspapers, if there are two, having general circulation in the school district, which states that the warrant has been received and all taxes due must be received within one month from the time of the first published notice (§§ 1322(1), 1324).

The notice must be published at least twice and as many additional times as the school authorities may direct (§§ 1322(1), 1324). If there is no newspaper having general circulation in the district, the notice must be posted immediately in at least 20 public places in the district (§ 1322(1)).

In addition, the collecting officer also must mail a statement of taxes to each real property owner on the tax list or electronically transmit such statement if a taxpayer has elected such option (§§ 1322(1), (2), 1324, 922(1), 104(1), (3); see also Gen. Mun. Law § 5-b). Where the school district has levied a tax for the purpose of a public library or on behalf of a library district, the amount of the taxes attributable to library purposes must be separately stated on each statement of taxes (§§ 1322(1), 1324; see also **21:37**).

The tax collector also must give a like notice by mail or personally to all nonresident taxpayers whose post offices may be known or ascertained, and to all railroads and utility corporations. The notice should bear the date of the posting of the notice. The tax collector is required to give such notice at least 20 days prior to the expiration of the one-month period of tax collection (§ 1322(2)).

In a school district where the school board has adopted a resolution authorizing the payment of taxes in installments, the notice that the collecting officer is required to give also must state that taxes may be paid by installments in the manner specified in the board resolution (§§ 1326(2), 1336(3); see also **22:17**).

22:15. May residential taxpayers who are age 65 or over, or disabled designate a third party to receive a duplicate tax statement from the tax collector?

Yes. The tax collector must enclose with each statement of taxes a notice that taxpayers who are age 65 or over, or disabled, and who are owner-occupants of residential real property consisting of no more than three family dwelling units, are eligible for the third-party notification procedure. This notice must explain the application procedure and other aspects of the provision (§ 1325(1)).

22:16. What kind of informational materials may a tax collector(s) include along with tax bills mailed or delivered to real property owners?

Section 1826 of the Tax Law makes it a misdemeanor for "[a]ny person, firm, corporation, or association, or employee thereof, who mails or delivers or causes to be mailed or delivered, any notice, circular, pamphlet, card, hand-bill, printed or written notice of any kind other than that which is *authorized or required by law* with a . . . tax bill or notification of a tax to be levied by the state of New York or any political subdivision thereof . . ." [emphasis added].

Various authorities have interpreted the phrase "authorized or required by law" to include not only general state statutes, but also local laws (see 9 Opn. Counsel SBEA No. 14 (1985); and 9 Opn. Counsel SBEA No. 98 (1993)). However, since school districts do not have the power to adopt "local laws," school districts may only include information with tax bills that is authorized or required by state law (9 Opn. Counsel SBEA No. 14 (1985), footnote 2).

A school board may, by resolution, require the collecting officer to enclose a summary of the adopted budget and an explanation of the computation of the tax rate (§§ 1322(1), 1324; see also **22:14**).

Also, subdivision 4 of section 467 of the Real Property Tax Law *requires* school districts that offer senior citizens a real property tax exemption pursuant to that section of law to notify real property owners of the availability of the exemption by means of a "notice or legend sent on or with each tax bill . . ." (see also 9 Opn. Counsel SBEA No. 14 (1985)).

22:17. May school taxes be paid in installments?

Yes, but the law is different for city and non-city school districts.

City school districts may adopt a resolution stating that school taxes may be paid in a specified number of installments, but no more than six. The installments must be as equal as possible, and the resolution must state the number of installments and the dates on which installments are due to be paid. If the resolution so provides, each installment subsequent to the first includes interest on the balance due calculated from the date the first installment was due, at the rate of interest determined pursuant to section 924-a (§ 1326(1)(b)). Otherwise, interest calculated pursuant to § 924-a is added to the amount of the unpaid installment (§ 1326(1)(c)). Alternatively, the board may adopt a resolution to assess interest on the balance due at the same rate of interest that is applicable to unpaid city taxes in the city in which the district is located (§ 1326(3)); the amount of any unpaid interest becomes part of the amount of unpaid tax (§ 1326(1)).

City districts also may limit installment payments to qualified senior citizens and persons with physical disabilities (§ 1327).

Non-city school districts may adopt a resolution by a two-thirds vote allowing school taxes greater than $50, to be collected in three installments. The minimum amount per installment and the due date for each installment must be specified in the school board's resolution (§ 1326-a(1)). In addition, the school district may choose to limit the installment program to certain types of property as provided in the law (§ 1326-a(4)).

Moreover, in a non-city school district, upon enactment of a local law by a county pursuant to section 972, the school board may pass a resolution prior to the date of the annual district meeting, which authorizes the payment of tax in installments as to any taxes in excess of $50 levied by the district on any parcel of real property located within the county that also is located within the school district (see also §§ 1338, 1340). This resolution must be certified by the district clerk to the clerk of the board of supervisors by August 1 following the annual meeting. The warrant for the collection of taxes levied while this resolution is in effect must explain that the property owner may elect to pay the taxes due, in installments, and must contain instructions regarding the payment of taxes in the manner specified by the local law enacted by the county (§§ 972, 1336, 1338(2)).

Additionally, a school district wholly or partially contained within a county which has been included in a federal disaster declaration, may provide, by board resolution, for the payment of taxes in installments as to any tax in excess of $50 levied by the district when a flood or other natural disaster occurs in the six months preceding the due date for school taxes. The board's resolution must specify the amount of installments and the dates such installments are due. Such a resolution applies for only one year, but additional resolutions authorizing installments may be adopted if subsequent disasters occur (§ 1326-b(1)).

Such districts also may refund taxpayers any portions previously paid if the school board adopts a resolution to that effect along with an installment payment schedule. In such an instance, a taxpayer would receive a refund upon entering into an agreement with the district for the payment of taxes according to the adopted schedule (§ 1326-b(5)).

22:18. Can a school board restrict the property tax installment payment option to certain taxpayers?

Yes. A school board may limit installment payments of school property taxes to senior citizens who qualify for the senior citizen exemption and/or to those taxpayers who are disabled as defined by law (§§ 1327, 1326-a(4)(b), (c)).

In addition, non-city school districts can limit installment payments of school property taxes to one-, two- and three-family residential properties (§ 1326-a(4)(a)).

22:19. May the tax collector accept payment of taxes on only part of a parcel of real property?

Yes, provided the taxpayer furnishes certain specifications, including apportionment, regarding the assessment of the parcel (§ 932). Once a written request is submitted by a party interested in an affected property, an assessor must apportion an assessment under the law (9 Opn. Counsel SBEA No. 13 (1987)).

22:20. What happens if school taxes are inadvertently paid to the wrong collector?

School taxes inadvertently paid to the collector of a district that does not include the assessed property within its boundaries, should be refunded by that district (§ 556).

22:21. What happens if a real property owner who is in military service fails to pay a property tax bill on time?

The law provides special protections to real property owners in active military service. Under both state and federal law, interest on delinquent taxes for properties owned by persons in military service is imposed at a reduced rate of 6 percent annually (i.e. one-half percent per month), or less pursuant to a resolution adopted by the local school board (Mil. Law § 314(4); see also 50 USC § 3991(d) (Servicemembers Civil Relief Act) and 9 Opn. Counsel SBEA No. 64 (1991)). Furthermore, the deadline for payment of any such interest penalties owed to a municipal corporation (including a school district) by a person who has been deployed to active military duty, or by the spouse or domestic partner of that individual, shall be extended for 90 days after the end of such deployment, provided the school board passes a resolution authorizing such an extension (§ 925-d).

Both state and federal law provide additional protections to real property owners in military service, including protections against foreclosure (see Mil. Law § 314; 50 USC § 3991).

22:22. What happens if any taxes remain unpaid at the time the collecting officer is required to return a warrant to the school authorities?

The collecting officer must return the tax roll and warrant with a statement of the unpaid taxes and a description of the property upon which taxes remain unpaid (§§ 1330(1), 1332(2)). When the school authorities receive this statement, they must compare it with the original tax roll. If it is correct, they must certify the statement as such (§§ 1330(2), 1332(3)).

The school authorities then immediately transmit the statement and certificate in time for the county treasurer to receive it no later than November 15 (§ 1330(2)). Different rules apply to the transmittal of this statement and certificate in city school districts (§ 1332(3)).

On or before April 1 of the next year, the county treasurer must pay the school district the amount of unpaid school taxes (§ 1330(4); see § 1332(5) for city school districts, § 1342 relating to taxes paid in installments).

22:23. Does the return of unpaid school taxes by the county to the school district include any interest paid to the county by delinquent taxpayers?

It depends. School districts that employ school tax collectors on a fixed salary basis are entitled to receive, in addition to the unpaid taxes, interest at a rate set by the commissioner of taxation and finance as set forth in law. If the school district's tax collector is compensated on a fee basis instead, the district receives no such interest (§§ 1328(2), 1330(5); Opn. St. Comp. 81-420; 8 Opn. Counsel SBEA No. 58 (1982); see also **22:25**).

22:24. What happens to the tax roll and warrant after they have been returned to the school authorities by the collecting officer?

The school authorities must deliver the tax roll and warrant to the school district clerk within 15 days (20 days in city school districts) of their return by the collecting officer. School districts under a district superintendent, however, deliver the tax list and warrant to the district superintendent who, in turn, delivers it to the school district clerk by July 1 (§§ 1330(3), 1332(4)).

22:25. How are tax collectors paid?

Some school districts employ tax collectors on a salary basis, with the salary determined by the school board (§ 1328(2); Educ. Law § 2130(4)). In other districts, the tax collector receives one percent of the amount of taxes collected during the first month after the publication of notice and not more than five percent of the amount collected after the first month (§ 1328(1)).

23. State Aid

The State's School Funding Responsibilities

Editor's Note: The NYS Education Department annually prepares a State Aid Handbook and State Aid to Schools: A Primer based upon each year's state budget figures. Editions of these yearly documents cited throughout this chapter are available at: https://stateaid.nysed.gov/generalinfo/ and http://www.oms.nysed.gov/faru/Primer/primer_cover.

23:1. What are the constitutional requirements for the provision of public elementary and secondary education in New York State?

In *Campaign for Fiscal Equity, Inc. v. State of N.Y.*, 187 Misc.2d 1 (Sup. Ct. New York Cnty. 2001), a state Supreme Court ruled that New York State had consistently violated the state constitution by failing to provide the opportunity for a "sound basic education" to New York City public school students because of inadequate funding.

The New York Court of Appeals, the state's highest court, upheld this decision and ordered the state to ascertain the actual cost of providing a sound basic education in New York City (*Campaign for Fiscal Equity, Inc. v. State*, 100 N.Y.2d 893 (2003)). The requirement for "adequate" funding in support of the constitutional requirement for a "sound basic education" was central to the court's ruling.

While the case focused solely on New York City, the ultimate and politically practical resolution of the case required a state-wide solution. The central elements of the agreement, including more flexibility in how aid may be spent by eliminating categorical aids to create "foundation aid" and pledging increases to foundation aid, are highlighted in "State Aid Categories" beginning at **23:10**.

A state appellate court has upheld a lower court's ruling, allowing a lawsuit claiming that children in eleven school districts outside New York City are being denied an opportunity for a sound basic education because the districts are substantially underfunded to proceed to a review on the merits (*Hussein v. State of New York,* 81 A.D.3d 132 (3d Dep't 2011), *aff'd,* 19 N.Y.3d 899 (2012)).

23:2. How much does it cost to operate the state's public elementary and secondary schools and what are the primary sources of support?

Prekindergarten through twelfth grade public education in New York state was a $61.5 billion enterprise in the 2014-15 school year (estimated) (NYS Education Department, Fiscal Analysis and Research Unit, *State Aid to Schools: A Primer Pursuant to Laws of 2015* (Aug. 2015)).

The funding to pay this cost is derived predominantly from a combination of three sources: the state, the federal government, and localities (school districts and local municipalities).

The State of New York provided an estimated 42.1 percent or $25.875 billion of the revenues required to operate the state's public schools in the 2014-15 school year. The state's share was 48.2 percent as recently as 2001–02 (*Id.*).

Pursuant to the 2011–12 enacted state budget, increases in state aid are tied to statewide increases in personal income growth, but such growth can never be negative (see § 3602(1)(aa), (bb), (dd), (ff), (gg), (18)). The growth in aid is allocated by a chapter law enacted for the state fiscal year in which such school year

Public School Finances

commences. However, if a chapter law is not enacted, foundation aid, and certain competitive grant awards are frozen to the base year (§ 3602(18); see **23:3**, **23:11-12**, **23:15**). Despite this statutory cap, the enacted budgets for 2013-14, 2014-15 and 2015-16 provided state aid to school districts in excess of the statewide growth in personal income (Office of the NYS Comptroller, Division of Local Government and School Accountability, *New York State School Aid: Two Perspectives* (March 2016), at: http://www.osc.state.ny.us/localgov/pubs/research/schoolaid2016.pdf).

The federal government provides about four percent of the revenues needed to support the state's public schools, although the amount provided falls some $2 billion short of what is authorized under both the Individuals with Disabilities Education Act and No Child Left Behind laws (*State Aid to Schools: A Primer Pursuant to the Laws of 2015*). In 2009–10 the federal government provided approximately eight percent of the revenues needed to support public schools pursuant to federal fiscal stabilization funds made available by the American Recovery and Reinvestment Act and the Education Jobs Program (NYS Education Department, Office of State Aid, *2011–12 State Aid Handbook* (Oct. 2011)).

Local revenues provided by the state's 696 school districts thus accounted for the largest share of the revenues required to operate the state's public schools in the 2012-13 school year (*State Aid to Schools: A Primer Pursuant to the Laws of 2015*).

23:3. What is the legal mechanism by which the award of state aid to local school districts is determined?

All school aid awarded to the state's 691 school districts is determined annually by an act of the state legislature, through the state budget process. Approval by the governor (pursuant to negotiations with the legislature) is generally forthcoming but is not required for school aid appropriations and other related legislation to become law (i.e. the legislature can override a veto by the governor).

The governor must annually submit proposed school aid appropriations to the legislature as part of the state's executive budget process. In so doing, the governor must comply with the constitution and statutory guidance and/or propose amendments to existing law as part of the executive budget spending proposal. The legislature then reviews and enacts school aid appropriations and other related legislation to implement the budget. For example, the agreement to resolve the Campaign for Fiscal Equity litigation during the 2007 state legislative session included both legislation detailing a new school aid formula and the appropriations necessary to implement it.

With its 2011–12 enacted budget, the state for the first time provided for two years of appropriations of school aid (§ 3602(1)(aa), (18)). Although such appropriations are authorized by the state constitution, prior to 2011–12 this had never been adopted as practice. School aid appropriations, once enacted, are subject to amendment at any time, but such mid-year "corrections" are highly unusual, given their educationally disruptive impact. In 2009–10, over $1 billion in state aid was cut pursuant to deficit reduction assessments (see § 3609-a(1)(c), (d)). Nearly $400 million of that was cut in December, but such funding was restored through federal fiscal stabilization funds and thus did not have an educationally disruptive impact. Prior to that, the last such change occurred in 1990–91 when $190 million in state aid payments were cut (NYS Education Department, Fiscal Analysis and Research Unit, *State Aid to Schools, A Primer Pursuant to the Laws of 2015* (Aug. 2015)).

The 2011–12 budget enacted requirements that school districts bear a share of the responsibility for eliminating the state budget gap. The state budget gap is the difference between budgeted state expenditures and the revenue available to support those expenditures. To address this problem, the law provided the amount of state aid districts receive each year would be reduced by a formula that calculates a *gap elimination adjustment* (§ 3602(17); see also NYS Education Department, Office of State Aid, *2011–12 State Aid Handbook* (Oct. 2011)). As part of the 2016 enacted budget the *gap elimination adjustment* was eliminated (§ 3602(17)(h)).

23:4. In general, how is elementary and secondary public education funded in New York State?

The state's funds come from two principal sources. The general fund accounts for some 88 percent of the state's share. The remaining 12 percent comes from the state lottery fund (NYS Education Department Fiscal, Analysis and Research Unit, *State Aid to Schools: A Primer Pursuant to Laws of 2015* (Aug. 2015)).

Of the state's total funds, some 73 percent consists of formula-driven aids and grants, about 14 percent is for the School Property Tax Relief (STAR) program, and the remaining 13 percent is paid from state lottery proceeds (NYS Education Department, Office of State Aid, *2015-16 State Aid Handbook* (undated)). "General Support for Public Schools" totaled more than $23 billion, and STAR accounted for the balance of the state's share.

The percentage of the state's funds that are shared with each of the state's 691 individual school districts varies widely, however. Accordingly, the amount needed to be raised locally varies considerably across the state.

The property tax provides 91 percent of the local share (*State Aid to Schools: A Primer Pursuant to Laws of 2015*). The Big 5 city school districts (New York, Buffalo, Yonkers, Syracuse, and Rochester) are fiscally dependent on their municipalities and do not independently levy taxes to support their services. Their parent municipalities impose property taxes and New York City imposes a modified local income tax as well as some other business and commercial taxes.

Eight counties share a portion of their sales tax collections with their school districts. In 2010–11, $280 million was raised for use by 159 school districts (*Id.*). In 2008, Monroe County sought to reduce its sales tax payments to school districts. However, a state appellate court ruled that the payments must continue as previously paid (*Monroe Cnty. Pub. Sch. Dists. v. Zyra*, 51 A.D.3d 125 (4th Dep't), *lv. to appeal denied*, 52 A.D. 3d 1293 (4th Dep't 2008).

About one half of the state's 57 small city school districts directly impose a utility tax (*State Aid to Schools: A Primer Pursuant to Laws of 2015*).

The state's 37 boards of cooperative educational services (BOCES) are funded by the school districts within their region, which receive state aid to partially reimburse them for costs incurred in providing services shared by at least two school districts.

Public School Finances

23:5. How does the state fund its school aid payments?

The bulk of state monies used to support public elementary and secondary education in New York (88 percent) is derived from the "big three" state tax revenues: the personal income tax, the sales (and use) tax, and various corporate taxes, all within the state's general fund (NYS Education Department, Fiscal Analysis and Research Unit, *State Aid to Schools: A Primer Pursuant to the Laws of 2015* (Aug. 2015)).

The state lottery is specifically authorized by the New York State Constitution to support public education and funds 13 percent of educational expenses (*Id.*). Under the State Finance Law, all revenues from the special state lottery fund (after prizes and the cost of administration have been accounted for) must be used for the support of education (State Fin. Law § 92-c). In practice, though, lottery proceeds are used by the state to supplant rather than supplement other state general fund spending for education.

23:6. How are state lottery proceeds allocated to the state's public school districts?

A school district's share of the lottery proceeds is computed according to an equalized formula based on each school district's taxable property wealth per pupil to support the general state aids otherwise payable to a school district. School districts receive a portion of their fall state aid payment in the form of a check directly from the lottery fund by the last business day of September (§ 3609-a(1)(a)(2)).

A portion of the lottery funds ($15 per resident pupil) is added to regular textbook aid, which is included in the check districts receive from the lottery fund. Lottery aid also includes a $10 payment for each blind and deaf student attending state-supported schools for the blind and deaf (State Fin. Law § 92-c(4)(b)).

23:7. When is state aid actually paid to local school districts?

The state aid payment schedule provides school districts with funds beginning in the fall of each year (§ 3609-a; see also **23:2**). The school district fiscal year begins July 1 and ends on June 30.

The payment schedule includes the following features:

- The state sends payments to the New York State Teachers' Retirement System (TRS) on behalf of districts in September, October, and November (§ 3609-a(1)(a)(1)). The relative amount of a district's TRS obligation does not affect monthly aid payment calculations.
- Lottery aid is paid in full by the last business day of September (§ 3609-a(1)(a)(2)).
- Fixed payments are paid in the months of October, November, and December. These payments guarantee a fixed percentage of a district's total aid, after TRS payments, by a given date: 12.5 percent by October 15, 18.75 percent by November 15, and 25 percent by December 15 (§ 3609-a(1)(a)(4)).
- Individualized payments are paid during the months of January through June. These are calculated to guarantee that each district receives 50 percent of its state and local revenues by the first business day of January, 60 percent by February, 70 percent by March, 80 percent by April, 90 percent by May and 100 percent in the June payment (§ 3609-a(1)(b)(2)). Any amount in excess of 100 percent of aid projections will be paid in September (§ 3609-a(1)(b)(3)(vii)).
- Boards of cooperative educational services (BOCES) aid is provided to school districts for services purchased from BOCES. After deducting payments due to TRS on behalf of BOCES, 25 percent of BOCES aid is paid on or before February 1, 55 percent is paid in June, and the remainder in September (§ 3609-d(1)).
- Growth aid is paid in full in June (§ 3609-a(1)(b)(3)(v)).
- Public and private excess cost aid payments for students with disabilities are separated from the general aid payment schedule. There are four guaranteed dates for reimbursement. The calculated sum of aids is apportioned according to the following schedule: 25 percent by December, 70 percent by March, 85 percent by June, 100 percent by August, and any amount in excess of 100 percent of aid projections by September (§ 3609-b(2)(a)).
- The School Tax Relief (STAR) program, created in 1997, provides homeowners with a real property tax exemption. In turn, the state reimburses school districts for the lost revenue through payments directly to school districts. STAR payments are paid in the months of October, November, December, and January (§ 3609-e(2)).
- For districts that participate in the federal Medicaid reimbursement program, for the 2009–10 school year and thereafter reimbursement for excess cost aids will be paid according to the following schedule: 25 percent by December 15, 70 percent by March 15, 85 percent by June 15, 100 percent by August 15, and any amount in excess of 100 percent of aid projections by September 15 (§ 3609-b(1)(a-1), (2)(a)).

23:8. What is the process for school districts to submit claims for state aid?

The superintendent of schools or district superintendent generally submits claims for aid to the Office of Management Services at the NYS Education Department. That office and the NYS Department of Audit and Control process claims for payment.

Prior year aid claims are subject to an amount appropriated by the legislature. Eligible claims are payable in the order the payments have been approved by the commissioner of education. No claim may receive more than 40 percent of the amount appropriated. In the event the number of prior year claims outweigh available funding, partial payments are to be made with the balance of the late aid payment to be made in the next state fiscal year (§ 3604(5)(c)).

23:9. Is state aid available to nonpublic schools in New York State?

Yes, in limited contexts. In addition to any aid appropriated in the state budget, nonpublic schools also secure state aid in the form of services and equipment, including school transportation, health services, career education, services for gifted students and children with disabilities, textbooks, computer software, and library materials (§§ 3635, 912, 3602-c, 701(3), 752, 712).

In 1980, the U.S. Supreme Court upheld the constitutionality of chapters 507 and 508 of New York State's Laws of 1974, the so-called mandated services law. This law requires payment of state financial aid to nonpublic schools for costs incurred by them in complying with certain state mandates, such as testing, pupil evaluation, achievement tests and attendance records (*Comm. for Pub. Educ. & Religious Liberty v. Regan*, 444 U.S. 646 (1980)).

In 1973, the U.S. Supreme Court struck down such statutes as violating the Establishment Clause of the First Amendment because they contained no requirement that nonpublic schools account for funds received and how they were spent (see *Levitt v. Comm. for Pub. Educ. & Religious Liberty*, 413 U.S. 472 (1973)). The present laws provide a means for auditing payments of state funds, thus ensuring that state funds are used only for secular services.

State Aid Categories

23:10. In general, what are the categories of state aid to local school districts?

There are three basic categories of state aid annually enacted into law: *foundation aid, reimbursable aids*, and *grants-in-aid.*

Foundation aid was formerly referred to as "comprehensive operating aid" which was created by the consolidation of eight former aid categories (see L. 1993, c. 57). The method for its determination is based upon the foundation aid formula (see **23:11-12**). Foundation aid is used for current school operations, is formula-based and is generally unrestricted in its application to operating purposes. It, like its predecessor comprehensive operating aid category, is spent according to a district's priorities as determined by the local school board unless the legislature mandates a set aside for specific purposes.

Reimbursable aid or *expense based aid*, on the other hand, requires a district to incur expenses in advance of subsequent reimbursement the following year or years by the state, according to a prescribed formula. Reimbursable aids are provided for transportation services, construction expenses (building aid), boards of cooperative educational services, and certain special education expenses. Since these aided purposes are specific and separately accounted for, they remain a form of reimbursable categorical aid.

Grants in aid or *bullet aid* is a third category of state aid targeted to a specific school district to address or redress a specific need or purpose. Such grants are categorical in nature and are awarded outside of any predictable formula. They may be awarded by a competitive process, by a legislative member or delegation of legislative members, or by the governor.

23:11. What is foundation aid for school districts?

In 2007, a new state aid formula was enacted as part of the 2007–08 state budget. That year the foundation aid portion of state school aid totaled about $13.640 billion, representing an increase of more than $1.1 billion over the 2006–07 school year (NYS Education Department, Fiscal Analysis and Research Unit, *State Aid to Schools: A Primer Pursuant to Laws of 2007* (Dec. 2007)). In order to comply with the *Campaign for Fiscal Equity* decision, the state announced a four-year educational investment plan to phase-in substantial annual state aid increases. Under the agreement, foundation aid will increase to an annual total of more than $18 billion. However, successive budget provisions have extended the phase-in such that it will not be complete until 2016–17. Both the 2009–10 and 2011–12 enacted state budgets froze foundation aid to 2008–09 levels, which was $14.9 billion (NYS Education Department, Fiscal Analysis and Research Unit, *State Aid to Schools: A Primer Pursuant to Laws of 2012* (June 2012)). However, in its 2011–12 enacted budget, the state adopted provisions providing for two years of state aid appropriations. Pursuant to the changes, increases in state aid are tied to statewide growth in personal income (§ 3602(1)(aa), (bb), (dd), (ff), (gg), (17), (18)). Despite this statutory cap, the enacted budgets for 2013-14, 2014-15 and 2015-16 provided state aid to school districts in excess of the statewide growth in personal income (Office of the NYS Comptroller, Division of Local Government and School Accountability, *New York State School Aid: Two Perspectives* (March 2016), at: http://www.osc.state.ny.us/localgov/pubs/research/schoolaid2016.pdf).

The new foundation operating aid formula consolidated some 30 separate aid categories in order to streamline, simplify, and make foundation aid as flexible as possible.

The 2016-17 enacted state budget created a $100 million set aside within foundation aid for community school programs. The set aside applies to 225 school districts across the state that have been identified as having struggling or persistently struggling school or otherwise as high-need (§ 3602(4)(e)). Community schools are public schools that emphasize family engagement and are characterized by strong partnership and additional supports for students and families designed to counter environmental factors that impede student achievement (NYS Education Department, Office of Student Support Services, *Guidance Document Foundation Aid: Community Schools Set Aside 2016-17 Enacted State Budget* (undated), at: http://www.p12.nysed.gov/sss/documents/CommunitySchoolsSetAsideGuidance.pdf). The law requires the funds to be used to supplement, not supplant, programs aimed at transforming school buildings into community hubs where academic, health, mental health, nutrition, counseling, legal and/or other services are provided to students and their families (§ 3602(4)(e); *Guidance Document Foundation Aid: Community Schools Set Aside 2016-17 Enacted State Budget*). The funds may also be used to provide a community school site coordinator or to support other costs to maximize student achievement (*Id.*). For more information on allowable expenditures districts should review the *Guidance Document Foundation Aid: Community Schools Set Aside 2016-17 Enacted State Budget.*

23:12. How is foundation aid calculated?

The formula is intended to distribute aid to school districts based upon the cost of providing an adequate education per pupil (the *Foundation Amount*) adjusted by factors for students needing extra help and time (the *Pupil Needs Index — PNI*) and regional costs (the *Regional Cost Index — RCI*). First, the *Foundation Amount* or basic cost of providing an adequate education is determined. An adequate education is associated with success in achieving the Regents Learning Standards. Districts deemed successful on this metric and which were also on the less expensive end of the scale were used to calculate the standard cost of an adequate education. The foundation amount for calculating the 2015-16 state foundation aid was $6,395.

Together, the three components of the formula constitute the *standard local cost of education*. The formula then deducts from the state's aid payment to each district an amount determined to constitute a fair local share of the total cost of general education (the *Expected Minimum Local Contribution*). The simplified formula is:

School District Foundation Aid per Pupil = Standard Local Cost of Education [Foundation Amount × PNI (Pupil Needs Index Factor) × RCI (Regional Cost Index Factor)] – Expected Minimum Local Contribution

The Foundation Amount increases as applicable based upon the PNI in a given school district. The PNI recognizes the added cost of providing extra time and help for students to succeed and uses weighted factors to account for those extra costs. The weighted factors include measures of poverty, English language proficiency, and geographic sparsity.

The RCI is used to make adjustments based on regional variations in purchasing power, based on wages of non-school professionals around the state. (School professionals are excluded from the index so it is not potentially skewed by the labor costs of school personnel themselves (NYS Education Department, Fiscal Analysis and Research Unit, *State Aid to Schools: A Primer Pursuant to the Laws of 2015* (Aug. 2015)). Nine labor force regions of the state make up the regional cost indices used in the foundation formula.

The *Expected Minimum Local Contribution* is determined using an "Income Wealth Index" (IWI). This index uses income and property wealth data to calculate the extent of a community's ability to contribute to the education of its children via the real property tax relative to the state average. The formula, however, sets an artificial floor on districts' ability to contribute, thus limiting the state's aid obligation. Some 300 school districts are affected by this provision.

Once the foundation aid amount per pupil is determined, it is then multiplied by the number of pupils in a district. The calculation of the number of pupils per district includes an additional weighting for students with disabilities, declassified students, and summer school students (§ 3602(1)(e), (1)(i), (2)).

The foundation formula also provides for a minimum annual state operating aid increase regardless of whether a district would otherwise qualify for aid under the formula. In 2007–08 this was set at three percent. The minimum increase in annual state aid at the conclusion of the extended phase-in 2016–17 would be 12.55 percent.

While the new foundation aid formula is relatively simple to grasp in concept, the specific calculations and optional methodologies used for modifying it to each of the state's 691 school districts can be quite complex. The information for calculating a specific school district's foundation aid is available on the NYS Division of the Budget website at: http://www.budget.ny.gov/ or the NYS Education Department, Office of State Aid website at: http://stateaid.nysed.gov. Questions can also be directed to the NYS Education Department's Office of Management Services, State Aid Workgroup, at 518-474-2977.

23:13. What are the major expense-driven reimbursable aids available to school districts?

Transportation aid pays districts between 6.5 and 90 percent of their approved transportation expenditures on a reimbursable basis using one of three aid ratios (§ 3602(7)(a)). One is derived from the foundation operating aid ratio. Another is based upon the resident weighted average daily attendance ratio, adjusted by a sparsity factor. A third ratio choice permits school districts to receive aid based on public and nonpublic enrollments and benefits districts transporting large numbers of non-public school students (§ 3602(7)(a)). Transportation aid is separated into capital expenses (which include bus purchases) and non-capital expenses (which include salaries, operating and maintenance expenses, contractual expenses, equipment, uniforms, health and life insurance, retirement benefits, and other costs of operation). Transportation expenditures for athletic and field trips are not eligible for aid. But expenditures for operating late bus trips for students who stay late for club or athletic activities are eligible for aid (NYS Education Department, Office of State Aid, *2015-16 State Aid Handbook* (undated)). A guide to transportation aid is available online at: https://stateaid.nysed.gov/trans/online_guide.htm; specific information on aidable vs. non aidable transportation expenses is found at: https://stateaid.nysed.gov/trans/aidable_nonaidable_list.htm.

Building aid is provided to districts for capital construction purposes (§ 3602(6)) on a formula-based reimbursement basis. The building aid ratio falls between 0 and 90 percent, except that, under additional incentive aid, districts that have reorganized (see **23:14**) were able to qualify for higher ratios (see § 3641(14)).

Projects without instructional space are not generally eligible for building aid. However, leases for a district-owned bus garage are eligible for building aid. Projects approved by the NYS Education Department (SED) on or after December 1, 2001, and projects for which no bonds were issued prior to that date are subject to an assumed amortization schedule of 30 years for new buildings, 20 years for additions to existing buildings, and 15 years for renovations, rehabilitation and reconstruction of existing buildings (§ 3602(6)(e)(3)(a)). School districts are required to notify the SED any time that obligations have been issued to fund the cost of capital construction. While the state share will be paid according to the assumed amortization schedule, local districts may finance their projects in any way they choose.

In calculating their aid entitlement, school districts may use a selected building aid ratio pursuant to formulas set out in law (*2015-16 State Aid Handbook*). Since 2001–02, state aid payments to reimburse school districts for their capital costs are delayed until the first payment on a bond is due for projects approved by the voters.

While projects costing less than $10,000 are not generally eligible for building aid, aid is available for stationary metal detectors, security cameras, safety devices for electronically operated partitions and room dividers, and other security devices approved by the commissioner of education through July 1, 2016 (§ 3602(6-c)(a)). After July 1, 2011, the maximum cost allowance for security cameras is $2,000 with a maximum expense claim of $35,000. Installation of comprehensive security camera systems which exceed $35,000 are subject to competitive bidding and require a building permit from SED's Office of Facilities Planning (*Id.*; see NYS Education Department, Office of Facilities Planning, *MCA for Security Cameras July 1, 2011 and later* (May 2011), at: http://www.p12.nysed.gov/facplan/SecurityCameraMCA051711.html; see also **28:11**). The maximum cost allowance for metal detectors and electronic partitions is $6,000 per unit (*2015-16 State Aid Handbook*).

The New York Secure Ammunition and Firearms Enforcement Act (NYSAFE) includes provisions for increasing the safety and security of student occupied facilities and provides a 10% funding enhancement for installation of electronic security systems and door hardening completed by the end of the 2014-15 school year (§ 3602(6-c)(b)). In order to receive the aid the purchase of these items must be included in the school district's school safety plan (see NYS Education Department, Office of State Aid, *New York Secure Ammunition and Firearms Enforcement Act (NYSAFE):Impact of School District Building Aid* (July 2013), at: https://stateaid.nysed.gov/build/html_docs/nysafe_3602.6-c.htm). The maximum cost allowance for electronic security systems is $10,000 per main entrance; a cost allowance of $5,000 is available for door hardening of a single exterior door (double doors will be the equivalent of 2 single doors or $10,000), and hardening of interior doors has a maximum cost allowance of $1,000. For further information as to acceptable electronic security systems and door hardening items see NYSED, Office of Facilities Planning, *Implementation of NYSAFE Act,* (June 2013), at: http://www.p12.nysed.gov/facplan/documents/NYSAFEActImplementation.pdf.

Public Excess High Cost Aid and *Private Excess Cost Aid* are two categories of reimbursable aid provided to school districts to partially defray the expenses of educating children with disabilities who require care in public or private settings beyond that which is provided to disabled children who are able to be integrated within the traditional school environment. The determination to spend extraordinary resources to meet a child's needs is made by the committee on special education.

- Public Excess High Cost Aid is available for the additional costs required for educating students with disabilities who must be served in resource-intensive public school or boards of cooperative educational services (BOCES) programs at annualized costs (§ 3602(5)).
- Private Excess Cost Aid (§ 4405(3)) supports programs serving public school children placed in approved private school settings or in the state's Rome and Batavia schools for the deaf and blind.

Supplemental Public Excess Cost Aid was created in conjunction with adoption of the new foundation aid formula (§ 3602(5-a)). This category of aid funds were paid to school districts that would have lost aid for expenses already incurred under the former categorical reimbursement system when funding for their special education students (integrated within the traditional school environment) were consolidated in the new foundation formula. A temporary formula permitted these districts to calculate their aid in the most favorable way so that their taxpayers were not unfairly disadvantaged while new rules were being put in place. The funding is frozen at the 2008-09 level through the 2016-17 school year (§ 3602(5-a)(h)).

Aid for BOCES is provided to help school districts pay for the services they purchase from boards of cooperative educational services (BOCES) (§ 1950(5)). The component school districts of a BOCES are eligible to receive BOCES aid for services like occupational education, teacher training, curriculum development and administrative and management services. The aid is given to the school districts on a reimbursable basis for payments previously made to BOCES for eligible services provided. For the most part, BOCES do not receive direct funding from the state.

23:14. What are some other formula based aid categories?

Universal prekindergarten aid is used for targeted expansion as well as for funding stability for school districts operating prekindergarten programs. The aid ranges and is reflective of district wealth and pupil needs (§ 3602-e; 8 NYCRR Part 151). Additional aid for the creation of or conversion to full day prekindergarten programs is available to districts who partner with non-profit, community and educational institutions (§ 3602-ee).

Full-day kindergarten conversion aid is provided to school districts that do not currently offer a full-day kindergarten program, as an incentive to do so (§ 3602(9)(a)). In order to qualify, districts must offer full-day kindergarten to all students. Typically this aid is available on a one time basis, however a school district may be granted a waiver to receive the aid in a second school year if the district can show significant economic hardship that affects the school district's ability to provide full day kindergarten for all children wishing to attend such program (§ 3609(9)(b)).

Special services aid is provided for career education programs and school computer services run by the Big 5 city school districts and other non-component districts of boards of cooperative educational services (BOCES) (§ 3602(10)).

High Tax Aid is awarded to high and average need school districts. This aid is divided into three tiers and eligibility is determined based on factors set forth in the statute which include the district's expense per pupil, real property tax levy, and adjusted gross income (§ 3602(16)).

Charter school transition aid is provided to districts that are most impacted by high concentrations of children attending charter schools (§ 3602(41)). The charter school basic tuition for school years 2014-15 through 2016-17 is the lesser of the sum of the basic tuition for the 2010-11 school year or the basic tuition computed for the current year plus the supplemental basic tuition as calculated pursuant to the statute (§ 2856(1)(a)(iv), (d)).

Reorganization operating aid is provided for both operating and building expenses incurred by those school districts scheduled for reorganization (§ 3602(14)). For qualifying districts that reorganized prior to July 1, 1983, the aid is equal to 25 percent of regular building aid. For districts qualifying after July 1, 1983, the maximum allowable aid is 30 percent. Total building and reorganization incentive aid may not exceed 95 percent of assumed annual expenses or project costs.

Textbook aid is provided to reimburse districts for the current-year costs of the purchase of textbooks and other approved instructional materials. All textbooks owned or acquired by a district must also be loaned to all resident pupils enrolled in kindergarten through twelfth grade in public and nonpublic schools on an equitable basis. Software for educational purposes and the cost of biweekly newspapers and news magazines are also eligible for reimbursement under textbook aid (§ 701). Home instruction students may not be included for purposes of textbook aid.

Computer software aid is provided for the purchase and loan of computer software. Software programs designed for use in public schools must also be loaned on an equitable basis to non-public school students (§§ 751–52); see also NYS Education Department, State Aid Unit, *Guidelines for State Aid Programs that Reimburse Districts for Computer Technology Expenses* (Revised Nov. 2013), at: https://stateaid.nysed.gov/tsl/pdf_docs/guidlines.pdf).

Instructional computer hardware and technology equipment aid is apportioned to districts for the lease, repair, or purchase of mini- and microcomputers, computer terminals or certain other technology equipment, such as lasers, robotics equipment, and solar energy equipment, for instructional purposes (§ 753). A portion of this aid as calculated by the statutory formula may be used for the repair of instructional computer hardware and technology equipment and training and staff development for instructional purposes (§ 753(1)). In order to receive such aid, a school district must develop a plan that demonstrates the instructional computer hardware needs of its students are being met and the district is loaning such equipment to non-public school students as required by law (§§ 753–54; see also *Guidelines for State Aid Programs that Reimburse Districts for Computer Technology Expenses*).

Library materials aid is allocated to districts to purchase library materials, which must also be loaned on an equitable basis to non-public school students (§§ 711(4), 712). Library books and instructional materials are ordinary contingent expenses and may be purchased even if a school district adopts a contingency budget.

Changes enacted in 2011 grant greater flexibility to school districts in the use of aid for instructional materials. Districts that spend more than their maximum allocation with respect to textbook, computer software or instructional computer hardware and technology equipment aids can designate such expenses as expenses for aid in one or more of the other categories (but not library materials expense), provided that the maximum allocation in the designated area exceeds the actual expense in that area. This is true even if a district has not actually made purchases in the other categories. Similarly, library materials expenses in excess of the maximum library materials aid allocation may be designated as textbook, computer software, or instructional computer hardware and technology equipment, provided that the maximum allocation in the designated area exceeds actual expenses in that area (§§ 701(2), 711(2), 751(2), 753(2); see also NYS Education Department, Office of State Aid, *2011–12 Amendments to Textbook, Software and Instructional Computer Hardware Aids Statutes* (June 2011), at: https://stateaid.nysed.gov/tsl/html_docs/amendments_statutes_tsl_2011_12.htm).

23:15. What are some key grant programs and additional aid categories?

Expanding Our Children's Education and Learning (EXCEL) is a state grant program enacted in 2006 to support school construction costs that are associated with increasing school capacity as a result of overcrowded classrooms and projects related to improving education technology, energy efficiency and public health and safety (§ 3641). The State Dormitory Authority issues the debt on behalf of eligible school districts and the state pays the annual debt service from the general fund. Since EXCEL is a grant, rather than using 100 percent of the grant for a specific eligible project, many districts have chosen instead to leverage the grant to undertake a more ambitious but still eligible project. They have simply applied the state's grant to supplant what would otherwise be their required local share payment under a traditional building project and the rest of the project is then fully paid for by the state.

Employment preparation education (EPE) aid is issued to fund adult education programs such as literacy, basic skills and high school equivalency programs (§ 3602(11)). Both boards of cooperative educational services (BOCES) and component district programs serving persons 21 years of age and older who have not yet received a high school or high school equivalency diploma are eligible for EPE aid. All EPE programs need prior State Education Department (SED) approval to receive aid.

Teachers of tomorrow recruitment and retention grants are awarded to districts to aid in their recruitment and retention of teachers, with consideration given to such factors as the degree of the district's teacher shortage, the number of temporarily and provisionally licensed teachers in the district, the district's fiscal capacity and geographic sparsity, and the number of new teachers the district intends to hire (§ 3612).

Teacher resource and computer training centers grants are awarded to over 130 centers state-wide that provide services to teachers in public school districts and BOCES (see § 316).

School health services grants are provided to the "Big 4" city school districts upstate to provide necessary health services to students in these districts, which include Yonkers, Syracuse, Rochester, and Buffalo. The legislature makes annual appropriations for this grant in the budget.

Bilingual education grants are provided to support regional bilingual programs at BOCES and to support two-way bilingual education programs for students whose native language is other than English. The legislature makes annual appropriations for this grant in the budget.

Education of Office of Mental Health and Office for People with Developmental Disabilities (OMH/OPWDD) pupils grants support educational services for children who are residents in, and those released from, OMH/OPWDD facilities pursuant to Chapter 66 of the Laws of 1978 and subdivision 5 of section 3202 of the Education Law. Aid is also provided for children who reside in intermediate care facilities for the mentally retarded who receive educational services pursuant to Chapter 721 of the Laws of 1979.

School district management efficiency grants are awarded to schools districts who implement one or more long term efficiencies in school district management, operations, procurement practices or other cost savings measures that have resulted or will result in significant reduction in total operating expenses in for example the administrative component of the budget, or certain transportation expenses (§ 3641(5)).

School district performance improvement grants are awarded to districts that have demonstrated the most improved academic achievement gains and student outcomes, as well as having implemented strategies that have the most potential for continued improvements in student performance, narrowing student achievement gaps and increasing academic performance in traditionally underserved student groups (§ 3641(6)).

Smart Schools grants support projects to provide access to classroom technology and high-speed internet connectivity to equalize opportunities for children to learn, add classroom space to expand high-quality pre-kindergarten programs, replace classroom trailers with permanent instructional space, and install high-tech smart security features in schools (§ 3641(16)). All districts were required to submit a Smart School Improvement Plan detailing how funds would be expended (see State Education Department, *Smart Schools Bond Act Implementation Guidance* (undated), at: http://www.p12.nysed.gov/mgtserv/documents/SSBAGuidancefordayandresidentialschools_final.pdf).

Legislative initiatives or "member items" are submitted by districts to individual members or regional delegations of members of the state legislature. If they are successful in obtaining a line item appropriation for their proposal, funds are made available pursuant to a contract with the appropriate state agency, usually the SED. More recently, funding approval comes as part of a large lump sum appropriation that is made available at the discretion of the leaders of each house of the state legislature. The amount allocated for legislative initiatives in the state budget is subject to negotiation between the legislature and governor each year.

23:16. How can districts receive allocations for "qualified zone academies" from the state?

In 2002, the commissioner's regulations were amended to include a detailed description of the procedures necessary for school districts to receive an allocation for qualified zone academies from the state. *Qualified zone academy bonds* are available to eligible schools for use in repair and rehabilitation of buildings, purchasing equipment for such facilities, developing course materials for use at schools, and training teachers and other personnel at these schools (see 26 USC §§ 1397E(d)(5), 54E(d)). School districts can qualify for the program if at least 35 percent of their students are eligible for free or reduced-price lunches under the National School Lunch Act or be located in a federally designated empowerment or enterprise community (26 USC § 1397E(d)(4)). An extension of the funding for qualified zone academy bonds was approved through 2016 (26 USC § 54E(d)). As a part of the application process, school districts must certify that the schools and bonds to be issued meet certain requirements, and provide copies of commitments from private entities to make qualified contributions and the written approval of the board and superintendent for such bond issue (8 NYCRR § 155.22(a)(4)).

The regulations also say that 50 percent of the state limitation amount allocation, which will be determined annually by the commissioner, shall be allocated to qualified zone academies in New York City (8 NYCRR § 155.22(a)(3)(i)(a)). A portion of the remaining 50 percent is allocated to charter schools in proportion to the percentage of students enrolled in charter schools statewide (vs. total public school enrollment) (8 NYCRR § 155.22(a)(3)(i)(b)). After the charter school allocation is made the remaining portion of the 50 percent not allocated to New York City shall be allocated to districts in the rest of the state. If the state does not exhaust its allocation limitation amount in any given year because school districts that have received an allocation have failed to spend it, the state can then adjust the split of funds between the three categories as needed (8 NYCRR § 155.22(a)(3)(i)(d)(4)).

Calculation and Distribution of State Aid

23:17. How relevant to the calculation of state aid is the school district code number that appears on the state income tax form?

The school district code identifies the school district to which the income of the taxpayer is attributed. Since income is a major factor in the calculation of a district's overall wealth (which includes property, too) and therefore the state aid it is entitled to, it is crucial that the school district code number be accurate so that the correct amount of total income can be assigned to each district properly and the fair aid amount calculated.

For the purposes of annual aid distribution, a computerized income verification process is used to verify the match between addresses and school district codes reported on income tax returns used to determine district wealth (§ 3602 (1)(h), (3)).

23:18. On what basis is state aid distributed?

There are a number of different bases on which state aid is distributed, depending on the type of aid. Some aid is distributed according to wealth-equalizing formulas. This means that the wealthier a district is, in terms of the property value and adjusted gross income behind each pupil, the less aid per pupil it receives. The poorer a district, the more aid per pupil it should receive.

Other aid is allocated based on a certain amount per pupil. Grants are allocated in a variety of ways. For example, the aid may cover a specific portion of the district's budgeted program costs, or lump sum amounts may be awarded to a limited number of districts. The latter method of allocation is often used when a grant is available only to certain districts, such as the Big 5 city school districts. Certain categories of aid, like transportation, boards of cooperative educational services, and building aid, reimburse districts for a portion of these costs.

The pupil count used to distribute aid is based on each district's average daily attendance (ADA) (§ 3602(1)(d)). ADA represents the average number of pupils present on each regular school day in a given period. The average is determined by dividing the total number of attendance days of all pupils by the number of days school was in session for the previous year (*Id.*).

23:19. On what basis is state aid distributed to the Big 5 city school districts?

Buffalo, New York City, Rochester, Syracuse, and Yonkers, each with populations over 125,000, are referred to as "the Big 5" city school districts (§ 2550). These city school districts do not levy taxes to raise revenues as do the rest of the state's school districts. Rather, they are dependent on the portion of the city budget devoted to education each year for the local share of their budgets (§ 2576). Each of these cities also receives state and federal aid. The categorical state aids are accounted for separately by the cities, and each aid must be used entirely for its designated categorical purpose. The same is true for nearly all federal aid, since it is also categorical.

Foundation aid becomes city revenue and is used to fund the schools; however, the cities do not necessarily allocate to the schools the exact amount of this aid received from the state. The cities differ in the extent to which state education aid is used (or must be used under "maintenance of effort" legal requirements) to supplement the municipal contribution to the schools.

23:20. Is there special financial aid for those public schools that incur increased costs because of nonpublic school closings in their district?

Yes, indirectly. This aid comes from an immediate inclusion of students who formerly attended nonpublic schools in the definitions of total wealth pupil units (TWPU) and resident weighted average daily attendance (RWADA) (§ 3602(2)(a)(6)). TWPU is a pupil count used along with other wealth variables to measure the relative wealth of a district. RWADA is a count of all resident public school pupils in a district, weighted for certain groups of pupils. Since the addition of these students is quickly recognized in pupil wealth and attendance measures, these aids are more accurately distributed.

23:21. Is a school penalized by the state aid formula for days on which it must be closed because of an emergency that results in the district providing less than 180 days of instruction?

Not necessarily. The commissioner of education is authorized to excuse a reduction of up to five days of instruction below 180 days for certain reasons, such as adverse weather, impairment of heating facilities or a credible threat to student safety as reasonably determined by a lead school official, if the days cannot be made up by using scheduled vacation days. Ordinarily, the apportionment of operating aid must be reduced by 1/180th for each day less than the required 180 days of instruction (§ 3604(7)).

23:22. Can districts receive aid for providing services required by the dual enrollment provision in the Education Law?

Yes. The dual enrollment provision requires school districts to provide instruction to gifted students, as well as in the areas of career education, education for students with disabilities, and counseling, psychological, and social work services related to such instruction to students who attend nonpublic schools, provided that such instruction is also given to students enrolled in the public school district (§ 3602-c).

Students receiving gifted or career education must be transported between the nonpublic school they legally attend and the public school where these services are offered, if the distance exceeds a quarter of a mile. Students with disabilities must receive transportation in accordance with the needs of such students. Such transportation is eligible for state aid (§ 3602-c(4)).

State aid for operating expenses is based on a formula that reflects the portion of the school day a nonpublic school student spends in a public school program (§ 3602-c(1)(e)). Districts that contract for these services with a board of cooperative education services (BOCES) receive aid based on the BOCES aid formula (§ 3602-c(3)). In addition, districts are reimbursed for 90 percent of approved transportation expenditures for dual enrollment services (§§ 3602(7), 3602-c(4)). Districts providing services to nonresident students under this provision are entitled to recover tuition from the students' home districts, according to the commissioner of education (see NYS Education Department, *Dual Enrollment Programs, Handbook on Services to Pupils Attending Nonpublic Schools* (revised Dec. 2012), at: http://www.p12.nysed.gov/nonpub/handbookonservices/dualenrollment.html).

23:23. Can errors in the amount of state aid paid to school districts be adjusted?

Yes. Whenever a school district has been apportioned less money than that to which it is entitled, the commissioner of education may allot the balance of what is owed to the district. The commissioner may also deduct overpayments to school districts from future state aid payments. A school district that has been overpaid may request that one third of the repayment be made in the first year, one third in the next succeeding school year, and the final third in the third succeeding school year.

23:24. Where can additional information about the distribution of state aid and details of aid formulas be found?

More detailed descriptions of aid, formulae, and dollar allocations can be obtained from the Education Unit of the NYS Division of the Budget.

For questions about individual districts, contact the NYS Education Department's Office of Management Services State Aid Workgroup at 518-474-2977 or at: http://stateaid.nysed.gov.

24. The BOCES Budget

Overview

24:1. How is the BOCES budget funded?

A BOCES budget is comprised of separate budgets for administrative, program, and capital costs. After state aid and federal aid are subtracted from the cost of operating a BOCES, all component districts must share in its administrative and capital costs. Each component district's share of these costs is determined either by resident weighted average daily attendance, real property valuation, or resident public school district enrollment as defined in the Education Law. Only one method can be applied in any year, unless otherwise provided by law (§ 1950(4)(b)(7)).

In addition, each component district pays tuition or a service fee for programs in which its students participate. Generally, districts not participating in BOCES services are not required to pay for costs associated with those services, such as salaries for employees, equipment, supplies or student transportation. However, the BOCES board may allocate the cost of such services to component school districts in accordance with terms agreed upon between the BOCES board and three-quarters of the component school districts participating in the service (§§ 1950(4)(d)(4), 1951(1)).

A component district's contribution to BOCES expenditures is derived from state aid and its local tax levy.

24:2. Is there a deadline by which a BOCES board must adopt its final budget?

Yes. The BOCES board must adopt its final program, capital, and administrative budgets no later than May 15 (§ 1950(4)(b)(7)).

24:3. Must a BOCES make available copies of its tentative administrative, program, and capital budgets?

Yes. The BOCES must provide copies of the tentative administrative, capital, and program budgets and attachments to the school boards of each component school district at least 10 days prior to the annual meeting. In addition, the BOCES must comply with any reasonable request for additional information made prior to the annual meeting.

Each component school board must make these budgets available to the residents of their respective school district, upon request (§ 1950(4)(b)(2) and (3); see also **24:4-5**).

Public School Finances

BOCES Budget Components

24:4. What is included in the BOCES program and capital budgets?

As a general rule, the program budget includes costs for those BOCES shared services that have been requested by and contracted for by the component districts (§§ 1950(4)(b), 1951(1); 8 NYCRR

§ 170.3(d)). These costs must be based on local and state-wide uniform unit costs calculated as set forth in the Education Law.

The capital budget includes, among other items, facility acquisition and construction costs; debt expenditures associated with repayment of indebtedness incurred for the acquisition of facilities and capital projects; and operation and maintenance costs such as rent, custodial salaries and benefits, and supplies and utilities. It also includes expenditures associated with the payment of court judgments and orders from administrative bodies and officers, and certain costs relating to employee retirement (§ 1950(4)(b); 8 NYCRR § 170.3(c); see also NYS Education Department, Office of District Superintendents and BOCES, *BOCES Administrative Handbook 3, General Requirements for the Administrative and the Capital Budgets* (2002), at: http://www.p12.nysed.gov/mgtserv/boces/handbooks/Handbook3.htm).

24:5. What is included in the administrative budget?

By law, the administrative budget must at least include office and central administrative expenses, traveling expenses, and salaries and benefits of supervisors and administrative personnel necessary to carry out the central administrative duties of the supervisory district, any and all expenditures associated with the BOCES board, the office of the district superintendent, general administration, central support services, planning, and all other administrative activities (§ 1950(4)(b)(1); 8 NYCRR § 170.3(b); see also NYS Education Department, Office of District Superintendents and BOCES, *BOCES Administrative Handbook 3, General Requirements for the Administrative and the Capital Budgets* (2002), at: http://www.p12.nysed.gov/mgtserv/boces/handbooks/Handbook3.htm).

The BOCES board also must attach to the administrative budget a detailed statement of the total compensation to be paid to the district (BOCES) superintendent of schools, delineating the salary, annualized cost of benefits, and any in-kind or other form of remuneration to be paid, plus a list of items of expense eligible for reimbursement on expense accounts in the ensuing school year and a statement of the amount of expenses paid to the district superintendent in the prior year for purposes of carrying out his or her official duties. The commissioner's regulations further specify the content of each of the tentative budgets and the circumstances under which salaries and benefits of BOCES administrators will be budgeted under program or administration (§ 1950(4)(b)(1); 8 NYCRR § 170.3).

In addition, each BOCES must prepare and append to the proposed administrative budget a report card that includes measures of academic performance of the BOCES educational services, fiscal performance of the supervisory district, as prescribed by the commissioner of education, and any other information required by the commissioner. The measures for each BOCES will be compared to the state-wide averages for all BOCES. The BOCES report card must be distributed publicly, as required by law (§ 1950(4)(kk); 8 NYCRR § 100.2(cc); see **56:21**). It must include a summary of the BOCES annual violent or disruptive incident report in a format prescribed by the commissioner (8 NYCRR § 100.2(cc)(4), (gg)).

BOCES Budget Adoption Process

24:6. What is the process for adopting the BOCES program and capital budgets?

The BOCES tentative program, capital, and administrative budgets must be provided to the component districts 10 days prior to the annual meeting (§ 1950(4)(b)(2); see **24:3**). Component districts review the tentative program, capital, and administrative budgets at the annual meeting held between April 1 and April 15, on a date, place, and time designated by the BOCES president (§ 1950(4)(o); see **15:13-14**).

The component districts do not vote on the program and capital budgets. They only vote on the administrative budget (see **24:7-8**).

The BOCES board adopts the final BOCES program and capital budgets, along with the administrative budget approved by the component districts, no later than May 15 (§ 1950(4)(b)(7)). Once adopted by the BOCES board, the administrative and capital budgets became a charge against all the component school districts within the BOCES supervisory district (*Id.*).

24:7. What is the process for adopting the BOCES administrative budget?

By February 1, the BOCES Board President designates a day, between April 16 and April 30, for component districts to vote on the BOCES administrative budget and elect BOCES Board members (§ 1950(2-a)(b)). The date for central high school districts is the next regular business day after that date (*Id.*). Ten days prior to the BOCES annual meeting, which is held on a date between April 1 and April 15, a tentative administrative budget is provided to the component districts (§ 1950(4)(b)(2), (4)(o); see **24:3**). At the BOCES annual meeting, a tentative administrative budget is available for inspection by the component districts (§ 1950(4)(o); see **15:13-14**). On the day between April 16 and April 30 previously designated by the BOCES board president, the component districts hold a public meeting, either a regular or special meeting, to adopt a resolution either to approve or disapprove the BOCES tentative administrative budget (§ 1950(2-a)(b), (4)(b)(5)). This resolution approving or disapproving the administrative budget must be transmitted to the BOCES no later than one business day following the vote (§ 1950(4)(b)(7)).

Approval of the tentative administrative budget requires the approval of a majority of the component school boards actually voting (§ 1950(4)(b)(5)).

24:8. What happens if the tentative administrative budget is not approved by the component districts?

If the majority of the total number of component school districts actually voting do not approve the tentative administrative budget, or if there is a tie vote (half the districts approve, half disapprove), the BOCES must prepare and adopt a contingency administrative budget (§ 1950(4)(b)(5)).

24:9. Are there any limitations on a BOCES contingency administrative budget?

Yes. In a contingency budget for BOCES the amount of the administrative budget may not exceed the amount in the prior year's budget, except for expenditures incurred in the supplemental retirement allowances, including health insurance benefits for retirees (§ 1950(4)(b)(5); 8 NYCRR § 170.3(b)).

25. Basic Fiscal Management Responsibilities

Overview

Editor's Note: The NYS Education Department, through its office of General Educational Management Services, makes available on its website information that school board members, superintendents, business officials and others may find helpful in meeting the legal requirements discussed in this chapter at: http://www.p12.nysed.gov/mgtserv/. School district audit reports completed by the Office of the State Comptroller may also be helpful. These are at: http://www.osc.state.ny.us/localgov/. As a matter of convenience, the terms "school district" and "school board" throughout this chapter also include supervisory districts and boards of cooperative educational services (BOCES). Specific instances where a statute or regulation applies only to school boards or only to BOCES are noted.

25:1. Who is legally responsible for the fiscal management of a school district?

The legal responsibility for managing a school district's fiscal affairs lies with the school board (§§ 1604, 1608, 1709, 1716, 1804, 1950, 1951, 2576(1), 2601-a; 8 NYCRR Part 170).

25:2. What are some of a school board's fiscal management responsibilities?

A school board's most basic fiscal responsibility is to safeguard its district's assets. This requires that a school board, for example:

- Ensure district expenditures do not exceed the budget approved by the voters (§ 1718; 8 NYCRR § 170.2(k)) except as otherwise authorized by law (see **25:16**).
- Designate at least one bank for the deposit of all district moneys (§§ 1950(4)(k), 2129; 8 NYCRR §§ 170.1(a), 170.2(c); see **25:20**).
- Adopt and implement policies and procedures that protect and properly account for school district funds and assets. Areas subject to such policies and procedures relate, but are not limited to, the process for purchasing goods and services (Gen. Mun. Law § 104-b(2)) and the appointment of an independent external auditor to conduct an annual audit (§ 2116-a(3); 8 NYCRR §§ 170.12(e), 170.3(a)). Additional information on this topic can be obtained from the Policy Services staff at the New York State School Boards Association. See also NYS Education Department, *Fiscal Fitness, A Guide to Monitoring Your School District's Budget* (updated Aug. 2010), at: http://www.p12.nysed.gov/mgtserv/FiscalFitnessGuide.htm.

Furthermore, as required by applicable law, a school board must:

- Appoint certain district officers including a treasurer and a tax collector (§§ 1950(4)(j), 2130(4); 8 NYCRR § 170.2(a); see also 8 NYCRR § 170.1(c), (d), (j); see **8:1**).
- Designate those responsible for purchasing, and for the certification of payrolls (Gen. Mun. Law § 104-b(2)(f); 8 NYCRR § 170.2(b)).

25:3. Must individual school board members undergo training concerning their board's fiscal management responsibilities?

Yes. Individual school board members must comply with mandatory training requirements regarding a board's financial oversight, accountability and fiduciary responsibilities (§ 2102-a; 8 NYCRR § 170.12(a)). The training must consist of at least six hours on the roles and responsibilities of board members, claims auditors and the audit committee; internal controls and risk assessment; revenue sources and the budget process; monitoring the district's financial condition and maintaining the district's fiscal health; and preventing fraud, waste, and abuse of district resources (8 NYCRR § 170.12(a)(1)(iii)(b)). Failure to complete the mandated training as required by law can subject school board members to removal from the board (*Appeals of Stepien and Lilly*, 47 Ed Dept Rep 388 (2008); see **6:38-40**).

For more information on board fiscal management training requirements see NYS Education Department, *Guidance on Implementing Fiscal Accountability Legislation, Board Member Training* (updated Aug. 2010), at: http://www.p12.nysed.gov/mgtserv/accounting/fiscalaccountability.html.

25:4. Are school boards required to publish an annual financial statement report?

Yes, although some of the specific requirements applicable to the publication of that report vary according to the type of school district involved.

In union free, central, and central high school districts, the school board must publish an annual financial report, during either July or August, that includes a full and detailed account of all moneys received and all items of expenditure in full. The report must be published in one public newspaper that is published in the district, except that in districts without such a newspaper the board must use a newspaper having general circulation in the district. Where there is no public newspaper published in the district, nor a newspaper having general circulation in the district, copies of the report must be posted in five public places in the district (§§ 1721, 1804(1), 1903(1); 8 NYCRR § 170.2(s); *Appeal of Maxam*, 34 Ed Dept Rep 289 (1994)).

The school board of a small city school district must publish the annual financial report within three months of the close of the fiscal year (see **25:15**). The report also must include "a full and complete statement of any bonds issued the preceding year for school purposes and the disposition made or to be made of the proceeds of such bonds." It must be published either in a newspaper (or two if available) "having general circulation in the city school district," or in pamphlet form for general distribution, in the manner required by the commissioner of education. However, if the report is published in pamphlet form, the board must give newspaper notice as to where and when the pamphlets are available (§ 2528).

In common school districts, the trustees present a financial statement at the annual meeting (see **15:12**).

When preparing annual financial statements, school districts need to be mindful of Governmental Accounting Standard Board (GASB) standards that require more detailed information than state law and regulations. For more information about GASB, school boards should consult their school business official and/or visit the GASB website at: http://www.gasb.org.

25:5. Are school districts required to prepare any other annual financial reports?

Yes. Each school district must file an annual report of its financial condition with the state comptroller within 60 days after the close of the fiscal year (Gen. Mun. Law § 30), in the form prescribed by the comptroller (Gen. Mun. Law § 31).

Districts which have established reserve funds pursuant to Education Law section 3651 must annually report to the commissioner of education about the operation and condition of such reserve funds (§ 3651(7); see **chapter 26**).

Boards of cooperative educational services are annually required to submit certain financial information including aggregate expenditure data for administrative, capital and service functions to the commissioner of education (§ 215-b). That data is used in the preparation of the commissioner's annual report to the governor and the legislature on *Financial and Statistical Outcomes of the Boards of Cooperative Educational Services*, also known as the "Annual 602 Report." A copy of these reports is available at: http://www.p12.nysed.gov/mgtserv/boces/finance_statistics/home.html).

25:6. Are school districts required to undergo financial audits?

Yes. All school districts other than those employing fewer than eight teachers, and boards of cooperative educational services must undergo an independent annual audit of their financial records conducted by an outside certified public accountant or a public accountant (§ 2116-a(3)(a); 8 NYCRR §§ 170.2(r), 170.3(a), 170.12(e)(1)). Except in New York City, the independent auditor must be selected pursuant to a competitive request for proposal (RFP) process, for a contract period not to exceed five years. Once the engagement expires the board must issue a new RFP (§ 2116-a(3)(b); 8 NYCRR §§ 170.3(a), 170.12(e)(3)). The auditor must furnish a draft audit report to the board and the district's audit committee (see **25:11**) for their review, and a final report and accompanying management letter to the board. The board must then pass a resolution accepting the final report (§§ 2116-a(3)(a), 2116-c(5)(d); 8 NYCRR § 170.12(d)(2)(d), (e)(2)).

In addition, governmental agencies may review and audit the financial records of a school district as authorized by law. For example, the state comptroller is authorized to examine the financial affairs of school districts (Gen. Mun. Law Art. 3, § 30 *et seq*.; see also *McCall v. Barrios-Paoli*, 93 N.Y.2d 99 (1999)), and audited at least once the accounts of all districts and boards of cooperative educational services as of March 31, 2010. Moving forward, the comptroller will conduct audits as indicated through a risk assessment process the comptroller conducts (§ 2116-a(3-a); Gen. Mun. Law § 33-35). Similarly, in the City of Buffalo, the city comptroller may examine the financial affairs of the city's public schools and audit any and all school district accounts (Gen. Mun. Law § 34-a).

For more information on the independent annual audit report see NYS Education Department, *Guidance on Implementing Fiscal Accountability Legislation* (updated Aug. 2009), at: http://www.p12.nysed.gov/mgtserv/accounting/fiscalaccountability.html.

25:7. Are school districts required to make audit reports available for public inspection?

Yes. Audit reports are public records open to inspection by the public. Moreover, pursuant to the General Municipal Law, school districts must give notice that any such report and accompanying management letters (see **25:6**), are available for public inspection. Such notice must be given at least once in the official newspaper or one having general circulation in the district if there is no official newspaper. In the absence of either, the notice must be posted conspicuously in ten public places within the district (Gen. Mun. Law § 35(1), (2)).

In addition, final reports of audits conducted by the state comptroller (see **25:6**) must be made available to the public on the district's website, if available, or otherwise for a period of at least five years (Gen. Mun. Law § 33(2)(e)).

25:8. What other actions must school districts undertake after receiving a final audit report?

In addition to making it available for public inspection (see **25:7**), a school district must undertake the following activities after receiving a final audit report:

- With respect to a final independent annual report, it must file a copy of that report and the school board resolution accepting the report (see **25:5**) with the commissioner of education by October 15 of each year, except in large city school districts where the filing date is January 1 (§ 2116-a(3)(a); 8 NYCRR §§ 170.3(a), 170.12(e)(2)). It also must file a copy of the report and any management letter with the state comptroller within ten days after receipt thereof (Gen. Mun. Law § 35(4)(a)).

- With respect to both a final independent annual audit report and a final state comptroller audit report (see **25:6**) a school district must prepare a corrective action plan in response to any findings contained therein within 90 days of receiving the report and any management letter. To the extent practicable, the corrective action plan must be implemented no later than the end of the next fiscal year. It must be filed with the NYS Education Department (§ 2116-a(3)(c); 8 NYCRR §§ 170.3(a), 170.12(e)(4)).

25:9. Who assists a school board with the fulfillment of its fiscal management responsibilities?

On a day-to-day basis, the superintendent of schools, as the chief executive officer of a school district (§ 1711(2)(a)), enforces all laws and regulations and school board policy relating to the fiscal management of a district (§ 1711(2)(b)). Nonetheless, for purposes allowed under the Local Finance Law, it is the school board president rather than the superintendent who is named as the chief executive officer and chief fiscal officer of a school district (Local Fin. Law § 2.00(5)(e), (5-a)(e)). Thus, it would be the board president to whom a school board may delegate certain fiscal responsibilities under that law including those related to, for example, the issuance and/or renewal of capital notes (Local Fin. Law § 30.00).

Others providing assistance to a school board in the management of its district's financial affairs include:

- The district's audit committee (§ 2116-c(4); 8 NYCRR § 170.12(d); see **25:11**).
- The independent external auditor appointed to conduct the district's annual audit (§§ 1950(4)(i), 2116-a(3)(a); 8 NYCRR §§ 170.3(a), 170.12(e); see **25:6**).
- The internal auditor designated to perform the district's internal audit function (§§ 1950(4)(k), 2116-b; 8 NYCRR § 170.12(b); see **25:12**).
- Others such as the district treasurer, deputy treasurer, purchasing agent, tax collector (§§ 1720(2), 1950(4)(j), 2130(4); 8 NYCRR §§ 170.1(c), (d), (i), (j), 170.2(a), (b)), as well as the claims auditor and deputy claims auditor who approve claims for purchases in districts where the board chooses to delegate its claims auditing authority (§§ 1604(35), 1709(20-a), 1950(4)(k), 2526, 2554(2-a); 8 NYCRR § 170.12(c); see **25:10**).

For more information on the audit committee, the external auditor, the internal audit function, and the claims auditor see the following NYS Education Department documents: *Guidance on Implementing Fiscal Accountability Legislation* (updated Aug. 2009), at: http://www.p12.nysed.gov/mgtserv/accounting/fiscalaccountability.html and *Claims Auditor, Internal Audit Function & Audit Committee* (updated Apr. 2013), at: http://www.p12.nysed.gov/mgtserv/accounting/.

25:10. Who is responsible for auditing and approving claims presented to a school district?

The statutory authority and responsibility for auditing and approving claims for payment presented to a school district lies with the school board (§§ 1724, 1950, 2523(2), 2524(1), 2525, 2580). However, a board may, by duly adopted resolution, establish the office of claims auditor and appoint a claims auditor, who serves at the pleasure of the board. A claims auditor has the exclusive authority to audit claims, and allow or reject all accounts, charges, claims or demands against the district, until and unless the board abolishes that office (§§ 1604(35)(a), 1709(20-a)(a), 1950(4)(k), 2526(1), 2554(2-a)(a); 8 NYCRR § 170.12(c)). In addition, a board may, by resolution, establish the office of deputy claims auditor, who shall act as the claims auditor in the absence of the claims auditor (§§ 1604(35)(a), 1709(20-a)(a), 2526(1), 2554(2-a)(a)).

A claims auditor or deputy claims auditor may not serve simultaneously as a school board member, the district's clerk or treasurer, superintendent of schools or other official responsible for business management, purchasing agent or other staff member directly involved in accounting and purchasing for the district, the internal auditor, or the external auditor. Neither may the claims auditor be a close or immediate family member of a district employee, officer or contractor providing services to the district (§§ 1604(35)(a), 1709(20-a)(a), 1950(4)(k), 2526(1), 2554(2-a)(a); 8 NYCRR § 170.12(c)(1)).

Rather than employ a claims auditor directly, school boards may delegate their claims audit authority through the use of inter-municipal cooperative agreements, shared services to the extent authorized by Education Law section 1950, or independent contractors subject to the requirements of applicable law and regulations (§§ 1604(35)(b), 1709(20-a)(b), 2526(2), 2554(2-a)(b); 8 NYCRR § 170.12(c)(3)). A school district which elects such delegation must audit all claims for services from the entity acting as the delegated claims auditor either directly or through delegation to a different independent entity (§§ 1604(35)(c), 1709(20-a)(c), 2526(3), 2554(2-a)(c)).

For more information on the claims auditor, see the following NYS Education Department documents: *Guidance on Implementing Fiscal Accountability Legislation* (updated Aug. 2009), at: http://www.p12.nysed.gov/mgtserv/accounting/fiscalaccountability.html and *Claims Auditor, Internal Audit Function & Audit Committee*, (updated April 2013), at: http://www.p12.nysed.gov/mgtserv/accounting/; see also Office of the State Comptroller, *Local Government Management Guide, Improving the Effectiveness of Your Claims Auditing Process* (July 2013), at: http://www.osc.state.ny.us/localgov/pubs/lgmg/claimsauditing.pdf.

25:11. What is the role of the audit committee in the fiscal management of a school district?

The *audit committee* is an advisory committee required for school districts employing eight teachers or more (except New York City), that reviews and advises the board on matters related to the district's independent annual audit and the internal audit function. It consists of at least three members specifically responsible for:

- Providing the school board with recommendations regarding the appointment of the external auditor (see **25:6**, **25:9**).
- Meeting with the external auditor prior to the start of the independent annual audit (see **25:6**) and reviewing and discussing with the external auditor the auditor's risk assessment of the district's fiscal operations.
- Reviewing the external auditor's draft audit report and accompanying management letter, and in collaboration with the external auditor assist the school board to interpret those documents.
- Providing recommendations to the school board regarding the acceptance of the external auditor's audit report and management letter.
- Reviewing a corrective action plan developed in response to an audit report and assisting with the implementation of that plan.
- Assisting in the oversight of the internal audit function (see **25:12**) as required by applicable law and regulations (§ 2116-c(5); 8 NYCRR § 170.12(d)).

All, some, or none of the audit committee members may be school board members. However, none may be employed by the district. Collectively, all audit committee members should possess knowledge in accounting, auditing, financial reporting, and school district finances (8 NYCRR § 170.12(d)(1)).

Community members serving on a district's audit committee are considered school district officers for purposes of indemnification (§§ 2116-c(3), 3811–3813; see also **chapter 67**).

For more information on audit committees, see the following NYS Education Department documents: *Guidance on Implementing Fiscal Accountability Legislation* (updated Aug. 2009), at: http://www.p12.nysed.gov/mgtserv/accounting/fiscalaccountability.html and *Claims Auditor, Internal Audit Function & Audit Committee* (updated April 2013), at: http://www.p12.nysed.gov/mgtserv/accounting/; see also NYS Comptroller, *Audit Committee Charter Guidance,* at: http://www.osc.state.ny.us/localgov/schoolsfa/accharter.pdf.

25:12. What is the role of the internal audit function in the fiscal management of a school district?

The *internal audit function* identifies and assesses risks in the district's financial operations, and helps to ensure that appropriate internal controls are in place to address those risks. At a minimum, the internal audit function must include:

- A risk assessment review of the district's financial policies, procedures and practices.
- An annual review and update of that risk assessment.
- Annual testing and evaluation of one or more areas of the district's internal controls taking into account risk, control weaknesses, size, and complexity of operations.
- The preparation of reports, at least on an annual basis, that analyze significant risk assessment findings, recommend changes for strengthening controls and reducing identified risks, and specify time frames for the implementation of those recommendations (§§ 2116-b(1), 1950(4)(k); 8 NYCRR § 170.12(b)(1)).

Those conducting the internal audit function are referred to as the internal auditor. A district may use its own employees, inter-municipal cooperative agreements, shared services to the extent authorized by Education Law section 1950, or an independent contractor to fulfill the internal audit function (§§ 1950(4)(k), 2116-b(4), (5); 8 NYCRR § 170.12(b)(2)).

School districts that employ less than eight teachers, had less than $5 million in general fund expenditures or fewer than 1500 enrolled students in the previous school year are exempt from maintaining an internal audit function, provided that they certify to the commissioner of education they meet the exemption requirements (§ 2116-b(2); 8 NYCRR § 170.12(b)(3)).

For more information on the internal audit function see the following NYS Education Department documents: *Guidance on Implementing Fiscal Accountability Legislation, Internal Audit Function* (updated March 2014), at: http://www.p12.nysed.gov/mgtserv/accounting/fiscalaccountability.html and *Claims Auditor, Internal Audit Function & Audit Committee* (updated April 2013), at: http:// www.p12.nysed.gov/mgtserv/accounting/; see also Office of the State Comptroller, Division of Local Government and School Accountability, *Getting the Most Out of Your Internal Audit Function* (2009), at: http://www.osc.state.ny.us/localgov/pubs/internalauditfunction.pdf.

25:13. How does the district treasurer assist the school board in fulfilling its fiscal management responsibilities?

The treasurer must provide the school board a budget status report, at least quarterly, and monthly if budget transfers have been made since the last report. At a minimum, the report must show the status of the district's revenue accounts and appropriation accounts required in the annual State budget form. With respect to the district's revenue accounts, the report must show estimated revenues, amounts received as of the date of the report, and estimated revenues for the balance of the fiscal year. Regarding the district's appropriation accounts, the report must show original appropriations, transfers and adjustments, revised appropriations, expenditures to date, outstanding encumbrances, and unencumbered balances (8 NYCRR § 170.2(p)).

In addition, the treasurer must further provide the school board with a monthly report for each fund that shows the cash balance on hand at the beginning and end of the month, receipts by source and total disbursements during the month, and reconciliation with bank statements (8 NYCRR § 170.2(o)).

25:14. Must a school district's treasurer, deputy treasurer, tax collector, and claims auditor be bonded?

Yes. The Education Law and commissioner's regulations require that the school district treasurer, deputy treasurer, tax collector, and claims auditor execute and deliver to the board an "official undertaking." Bonds must be received by the board within 10 days after each officer is notified of appointment and before each assumes his or her duties. In districts under the jurisdiction of a district superintendent, the district superintendent also must approve the bonds (§§ 1720(2), 1950(4)(j), 2130(5), 2527; 8 NYCRR §§ 170.2(d), 170.12(c)(1)(i)).

The bond required must be in an amount fixed and approved by the school board. There is no law that specifies the amount of each bond. Treasurers, collectors, and certain other public officers may be covered by a blanket bond (Pub. Off. Law § 11(2); see also **8:4**).

25:15. What is the fiscal year of a school district?

The fiscal year of a school district runs from July 1 to June 30 (see, for example, § 2515).

Cash Management

25:16. May a school board spend district funds in excess of the budget appropriations approved by the voters?

Yes, but only as authorized by law. Generally, school boards may not incur a district liability that exceeds the amount appropriated by district voters (§ 1718(1)). However, the law exempts from this prohibition liabilities incurred in connection with the expenditure of:

- State and federal grants in aid.
- Gifts required to be spent for particular objects or purposes.
- Insurance proceeds received for the loss, theft, damage or destruction of real or personal property when used or applied to repair or replace such property (§ 1718(2); *Appeal of Cook*, 32 Ed Dept Rep 71 (1992); *Matter of Cappa and Motomaya*, 11 Ed Dept Rep 128 (1971); see also *Appeal of Leman*, 39 Ed Dept Rep 35 (1999)).

In addition, when district voters fail to approve the proposed school district budget, a school board may appropriate and expend funds not approved by the district's voters for ordinary contingent expenses, subject to the requirements applicable to a contingency budget (§§ 2022(5), 2023, 2023-a(8); see **chapter 20**).

25:17. May a school board invest district funds that are not required for immediate expenditure?

Yes. A school board may invest moneys not required for immediate expenditure provided that the investment is temporary and made pursuant to the board's comprehensive investment policy. That policy, which is subject to annual review, must detail the district's operative policy and instructions regarding the investing, monitoring and reporting of district funds in accordance with the requirements of applicable law (§§ 1604-a, 1723-a, 1950(4)(k), 3652; Gen. Mun. Law §§ 11(2), 39).

Some permitted types of investments include:

- Time-deposit accounts and certificates of deposit issued by banks or trust companies, provided they are secured in the manner required for securing deposits of the district's funds (Gen. Mun. Law § 11(2)(a)(1)).
- Obligations of the United States or the State of New York, and obligations guaranteed by the United States (Gen. Mun. Law § 11(3)(a)(1)).
- Deposits in multiple Federal Deposit Insurance Corporation (FDIC) insured banks and trust companies within the $250,000 limit for FDIC accounts pursuant to a deposit placement program which meets the requirements of law (Gen. Mun. Law §§ 10(2)(a), 11(2)(a)(2)).

Moneys in certain specified reserve funds including, for example, a repair reserve fund, a workmen's compensation reserve fund, and an insurance reserve fund may be invested also in obligations of the school district that established the fund (Gen. Mun. Law § 11(3)(a)(1)).

Permitted investments may be made or purchased only if payable within the time that the proceeds will be needed to meet the expenditures for which the funds invested were obtained (Gen. Mun. Law § 11(2)(b), (6)).

Likewise, a school board may invest extra-classroom activity funds (see **25:18**) held in the school district's custody in the same manner as district funds not otherwise required for immediate expenditures (Opn. St. Comp. 94-15).

In comparison, gifts, grants or bequests in the form of a true trust are governed by separate provisions of law pertaining to the investment of trust funds (EPTL § 11-2.2; Opn. St. Comp. 94-15).

25:18. Is a school board responsible for safeguarding the financial affairs of student extra-classroom activities?

Yes. Commissioner's regulations require that school districts other than New York City that operate an educational program beyond grade six must make rules and regulations for the safeguarding, accounting and audit of all moneys received and derived from extra-classroom activities (8 NYCRR § 172.2; see also *Appeal of Vagnarelli*, 20 Ed Dept Rep 566 (1981); *Appeal of Keely*, 14 Ed Dept Rep 396 (1975)). Those rules and regulations must be consistent with the requirements set forth in commissioner's regulations (see 8 NYCRR § 172.3).

Extra-classroom activities include any organization within the district that is conducted by students and receives no financial support from district voters or the school board (8 NYCRR § 172.1). Any moneys received from the conduct, operation or maintenance of such an activity must be deposited with the official designated by the board as the treasurer of the extra-classroom activity fund (8 NYCRR § 172.4). Extra-classroom activity funds held in the custody of a school district treasurer must be invested pursuant to General Municipal Law section 11 (Opn. St. Comp. 94-15; see **25:17**).

For additional information, see NYS Education Department, *The Safeguarding, Accounting and Auditing of Extraclassroom Activity Funds: Finance Pamphlet 2* (Jan. 2015), at: http://www.p12.nysed.gov/mgtserv/accounting/docs/ExtraclassroomActivitiesJanuary2015.pdf.

25:19. May a school board accept payment by credit card *via the internet* of moneys owed to the district?

Yes. A school board may determine that it is in the public interest and adopt a resolution authorizing the district to accept the payment of, for example, fines, taxes, fees, charges, and other financial obligations and amounts owed to the district via the Internet, in addition to other methods of payment. Any method used for the acceptance of Internet payments either through its own website or that of a third party vendor the district contracts with to receive such payments on its behalf must comply with the requirements of applicable laws and regulations including the General Municipal Law and article 3 of the State Technology Law (Gen. Mun. Law § 5-b; see also § 1950(4)(ii), authorizing BOCES to enter into agreements with financing agencies for the acceptance of credit cards as a means to pay course fees and tuition for instructional programs).

25:20. Must a school board designate a bank for the deposit of school district funds?

Yes. School boards must designate at least one bank or trust company for the deposit of all funds received by the treasurer and collector (§§ 2129, 1950(4)(k); Gen. Mun. Law § 10(2)(a); 8 NYCRR §§ 170.1(a), 170.2(c); see **5:30**).

The designation must be made pursuant to a resolution adopted by a majority of the board. The resolution also must specify the maximum amount that may be kept on deposit in each particular bank or trust company, which may be changed at any time by further board resolution (Gen. Mun. Law § 10(2)(a)).

Deposits in excess of the amount insured under the Federal Deposit Insurance Act (FDIC) must be secured in accordance with the provisions of General Municipal Law section 10(3).

25:21. May a school board authorize the use of a facsimile signature to sign district checks?

Yes. A school board may adopt a resolution authorizing that district checks may be signed by facsimile signature of those whose signatures are required on the check (§§ 1720(2), 1950(4)(k), 2523(2); see also Gen. Constr. Law § 46; *Formal Opn. of Counsel No. 83*, 1 Ed Dept Rep 786 (1952); 8 Opn. St. Comp. 110, No. 5626 (1952); Opn. St. Comp. 79-665 (1979)).

Where a facsimile signature is used, however, it should be affixed under the supervision and control of the person whose signature it represents (25 Opn. St. Comp. 79, No. 69-118 (1969); 10 Opn. St. Comp. 326, No. 6901 (1954)).

25:22. May a school board establish a petty cash fund?

Yes. School boards may establish a petty cash fund for the payment, in advance of authorization, of properly itemized bills for materials, supplies or services calling for immediate payment upon delivery (§§ 1604(26), 1709(29)).

When establishing a petty cash fund, a school board must adopt rules and regulations that:

- Designate the person responsible for the fund.
- Specify the amount of the fund, which in a school district employing less than eight teachers may not exceed $5. In districts employing more than eight teachers, the balance on hand in the fund may not exceed $100 at any time.
- Prescribe the method of recordkeeping.
- Provide for the kinds of payment that can be made from the fund and that that payment from a petty cash fund may be made for materials, supplies or services only when payment is required upon delivery (8 NYCRR § 170.4(a), (b), (c), (d)).

Petty cash funds established for buildings, cafeterias, school stores, or other activities that do not operate during July and/or August must be closed out by June 30th (8 NYCRR § 170.4(e)).

25:23. Are school districts authorized to reimburse school board and employees' expenses?

Yes, to the extent authorized by law. For example, school district officers, including school board members, may be reimbursed for "expenses actually and necessarily incurred in the performance of their official duties" (§ 2118; see also § 1604(27)). However, school board members are not entitled to reimbursement of expenses incurred "in traveling to meetings at which the full attendance of the board is required or where the meeting convenes at the official place of duty of the board" (Opn. St. Comp. 93-31, 80-138). Similarly, school board members are not entitled to meals or refreshments during their attendance at board meetings unless they are prevented from eating by a pressing need to perform the business at hand during mealtime (*Id.*; see also Opn. St. Comp. 79-522, 77-667).

Board members may be entitled to reimbursement of meals taken while attending functions in connection with the performance of their official duties, "provided there is a reasoned determination the meeting will promote a valid municipal purpose" (Opn. St. Comp. 81-38).

In addition, a district may pay for the attendance of board members, officers and staff at conferences, including conventions or seminars, for the benefit of the school district (Gen. Mun. Law § 77-b(2); see also *Matter of Cappa*, 18 Ed Dept Rep 373 (1978)). But such attendance requires prior school board approval pursuant to board resolution entered into the board minutes, unless the board has delegated the authority to approve attendance at conferences to any executive officer (Gen. Mun. Law § 77-b(2); see also Opn. St. Comp. No. 93-12, 27 Opn. St. Comp. 74, No. 71-246 (1971)).

A school district may pay only for the actual and necessary expenses of those duly authorized to attend a conference and not those of the spouses of such individuals (Opn. St. Comp. 93-12). Neither may it pay for the cost of alcoholic beverages consumed at an otherwise authorized meeting or conference (Opn. St. Comp. 82-213). However, gratuities paid in connection with authorized travel expenses are reimbursable (Opn. St. Comp. 76-1194).

For more information on adopting policies and auditing travel and conference expenses, see Office of the State Comptroller, *Local Government Management Guide, Travel and Conference Expense Management* (June 2012), at: http://www.osc.state.ny.us/localgov/pubs/lgmg/travel_expense.pdf (see also **28:9**).

25:24. May school districts authorize cash advances for estimated expenditures associated with attendance at a conference?

Yes. The General Municipal Law expressly allows for cash advances to persons duly authorized to attend a conference for estimated expenditures including travel and meals, provided itemized vouchers showing actual expenditures are submitted after such attendance (Gen. Mun. Law § 77-b(6)). In addition, all moneys advanced and not expended must be returned. Any excess advance not returned at the time the itemized voucher is submitted or upon demand after audit of the voucher must be deducted from the salary or other money owed the officer or employee given the cash advance (*Id.*). All expenditures in excess of the cash advance must be audited and paid by the school district (*Id.*).

School boards should adopt rules and regulations governing the use of cash advances including the documentation needed to support a request for such advance and the procedure for submitting a voucher after actually incurring the expense, as well as the time frame for submitting both the advance request and the voucher (Opn. St. Comp. 89-10; see also Office of the State Comptroller, *Local Government Management Guide, Travel and Conference Expense Management* (June 2012), at: http://www.osc.state.ny.us/localgov/pubs/lgmg/travel_expense.pdf; see also **28:8**).

25:25. Is a school board authorized to pay dues to the New York State School Boards Association?

Yes, pursuant to Education Law section 1618 (see also Opn. St. Comp. 77-399, 77-721).

25:26. Are all claims for payment subject to audit and approval by the school board or claims auditor?

Yes. The law authorizes the payment of claims against a school district only after an itemized voucher of each individual claim has been presented to the school board or claims auditor for audit and approval (§§ 1604(13), 1724(1), 1950(4)(k), 2524(1); see **25:10**). The school board prescribes the form of such voucher (§§ 1724(1), 2524(1)), which may require that a voucher packet for each claim include, for example:

- A purchase order with appropriate authorization signed by the purchasing agent.
- A receiving report confirming that the work has been completed and/or materials delivered satisfactorily.
- Documentation that the purchasing agent approved the voucher packet.
- An original invoice describing the goods and services to be paid for and how they correlate to those contemplated by the purchase order.
- For utilities, evidence that payment is only for school district addresses (see NYS Education Department, *Claims Auditor, Internal Audit Function & Audit Committee* at: http://www.p12.nysed.gov/mgtserv/accounting/).

For additional information on analyzing claims and preventing the payment of fraudulent claims see the following Office of the State Comptroller documents: *Local Government Management Guide, Improving the Effectiveness of Your Claims Auditing Process* (July 2013), at: http://www.osc.state.ny.us/localgov/pubs/lgmg/claimsauditing.pdf and *Red Flags for Fraud* at: http://www.osc.state.ny.us/localgov/pubs/red_flags_fraud.pdf.

25:27. May any claims be paid prior to audit?

Yes. A school board may adopt a resolution that authorizes the payment of certain claims in advance of audit. These include claims for public utility services, postage, freight and express charges. Both the claimant and the officer incurring or approving the claim are jointly and severally liable for any amount disallowed during the audit and approval process (§§ 1724(3), 2524(2)).

In addition, payment may be made in advance of authorization from a petty cash fund established by the school board to pay for materials and supplies or services that require immediate payment upon delivery (§§ 1604(26), 1709(29); 8 NYCRR § 170.4; see **25:22**).

Acceptance and Use of Gifts

25:28. May school boards accept gifts on behalf of their district?

Yes. School boards may accept "any real estate transferred to it by gift, grant, bequest or devise, or any gift, legacy or annuity of whatever kind, given or bequeathed to the board and apply the same, or the interest or proceeds thereof, according to the instructions of the donor or testator" (§§ 1709(12), (12-a); see also § 404(1)).

However, school boards are not required to accept gifts, particularly when, in their view, the gifts would not contribute to the "overall welfare" of their district (see *Appeal of Baisch*, 40 Ed Dept Rep 405 (2000)).

25:29. May school boards accept gifts given in the form of a trust?

Yes, when given for the support and benefit of any or all of the district's public schools (§ 3701; see also § 1709(12), (12-a)).

Districts must report to the commissioner of education any trusts held for school purposes either by them or anyone else they are aware of. They also must transmit to the commissioner an "authenticated copy of every will, conveyance, instrument or paper embodying or creating the trust" and its terms (§ 3703).

Trust funds may be invested pursuant to the trust investment provisions of the Estates, Powers and Trusts Law (Opn. St. Comp. 94-15).

25:30. May school boards accept gifts of money and foundation grants for specific programs?

Yes. However, in accepting such a gift, a school board may not abdicate its authority to determine whether or not to offer or continue to offer the particular program, or the manner in which the program is to be offered (*Appeal of DeMasi*, 18 Ed Dept Rep 320 (1978)).

The same rule applies to the acceptance of foundation grants (*Appeal of Brarens,* 51 Ed Dept Rep, Dec. No. 16,317 (2011)). A condition from a grant foundation that the release of grant funding in several curriculum areas will be contingent on a showing of adequate professional resources for district staff to meet currently provided high standards does not, in and of itself, constitute the ceding of control over program offerings or the manner in which the programs are offered (*Appeal of Brarens*).

25:31. Are there any restrictions applicable to the acceptance of gifts on behalf of a school district?

Yes. A school board may not accept a gift that imposes conditions that are contrary to law or district policy. That would be the case, for example, if a gift of money for the support of interscholastic sports required the board to delegate to the donor the board's responsibility for determining whether or not to offer such a program (*Appeal of DeMasi*, 18 Ed Dept Rep 320 (1978); see also **25:30**).

Similarly, the terms of a trust that would require a district to administer scholarships for only male or female students would be contrary to Title IX of the Federal Amendments of 1972 (20 USC § 1681 *et seq.*), which prohibits school districts from engaging in practices or activities that discriminate on the basis of sex (see **55:42**), even though "gender restrictions in a private trust do not necessarily violate public policy" or the Equal Protection Clause of the U.S. Constitution in the absence of action by public officials in furtherance of the discriminatory practice (*Matter of Wilson*, 59 N.Y.2d 461 (1983)).

A gift conditioned on the naming of a facility after the donor of the gift would also be unlawful, if it requires that the board relinquish its authority to rename the facility (Opn. St. Comp. 90-6; see also *Appeal of Bonham*, 44 Ed Dept Rep 179 (2004)).

25:32. May a school district make gifts and charitable contributions using district funds?

No. Such a gift or contribution would be considered an improper gift of public funds under Article 8, Section 1 of the New York State Constitution, which prohibits the disbursement, gift, or loan of public moneys and resources for the benefit of private groups or individuals (see, e.g., *Appeal of LaLonde*, 31 Ed Dept Rep 408 (1992); 29 Opn. St. Comp. 154, No.73-921 (1973)).

Accordingly, a school district may not, for example:

- Make a donation in memory of the parent of a school district employee (*Appeal of LaLonde*).
- Purchase sweaters or jackets for students who have participated in athletic activities (11 Opn. St. Comp. 78, No. 7103 (1955)), even though extra-classroom activity funds, if duly authorized, may be used for this purpose because they are not school district moneys (*Id.*; see **25:18**).
- Purchase graduation pins and flowers for students (4 Opn. St. Comp. 579, No. 3350 (1948)).
- Pay for a dinner, picnic, or similar outing for employees and/or officers unless pursuant to a collective bargaining agreement (see Opn. St. Comp. 82-263).

25:33. Are there any exceptions to the constitutional prohibition against gifts of public funds?

Yes, when a public purpose is served. Accordingly, a school district may:

- Purchase a plaque of nominal value in recognition of service by unsalaried individuals (Opn. St. Comp. 79-882).
- Pay only for the meals of board members at a dinner held to recognize service, provided the cost of the dinner is reasonable (see Opn. St. Comp. 80-775).
- Pay only for the meal of a retiring board member at a dinner held to honor the retiring board member (Opn. St. Comp. 83-57).
- Pay only for the meals of school volunteers at a dinner held to recognize their contribution (see Opn. St. Comp. 82-66), rather than primarily as a social gathering (see Opn. St. Comp. 90-63).
- Purchase pins for employees in recognition of their years of service (Opn. St. Comp. 99-11).

26. Reserve Funds

Legal Framework

26:1. What is a reserve fund?

A *reserve fund* is a separate account established by a school district to finance various district costs. It can be thought of as a saving account for a specific purpose (see *Appeal of Kackmeister*, 40 Ed Dept Rep 577 (2001)).

Generally, school district reserve funds are authorized pursuant to either the Education Law or the General Municipal Law.

For additional information on reserve funds see NYS Comptroller, *Local Government Management Guide, Reserve Funds* (2010), at: http://www.osc.state.ny.us/localgov/pubs/lgmg/reservefunds.pdf.

26:2. What kinds of reserve funds are authorized under the Education Law?

The Education Law authorizes school districts to establish any of the following reserve funds.

- Capital Reserve Fund (§ 3651(1)).
- Liability Reserve Fund (§§ 1709(8-c), 1950(4)(cc)).
- Property Loss Fund (§§ 1709(8-c), 1950(4)(cc)).
- Tax Certiorari Reserve Fund (§ 3651(1-a)).
- Tax Reduction Reserve Fund (§§ 1604(36), 1709(37)).
- Uncollected Taxes Reserve Fund (§ 3651(1-b)).
- Career Education Instructional Equipment Reserve Fund (for BOCES only) (§ 1950(4)(ee)).

For more information on the basic characteristics of these funds, see **26:5**.

Although not in a traditional reserve fund, the Education Law also requires school districts that exceed their maximum allowable tax levy due to clerical or technical errors to place the excess amount of the levy in reserve consistent with any requirements prescribed by the State Comptroller. Such funds and any earned interest must be used to reduce the tax levy the following school year (§ 2023-a(5); see **26:5**).

School districts must annually prepare and file a detailed report with the commissioner of education with respect to the operation and condition of reserve funds established under the Education Law (§ 3651(7)).

26:3. What kinds of reserve funds are authorized for school districts under the General Municipal Law?

The General Municipal Law authorizes school districts to establish any of the following reserve funds:

- Employee Benefit Accrued Liability Reserve Fund (Gen. Mun. Law § 6-p).
- Insurance Reserve Fund (Gen. Mun. Law § 6-n).
- Mandatory Debt Service Reserve Fund (Gen. Mun. Law § 6-l).
- Repair Reserve Fund (Gen. Mun. Law § 6-d).
- Retirement Contribution Reserve Fund (Gen. Mun. Law § 6-r).

Fiscal Management

- Unemployment Insurance Payment Reserve Fund (Gen. Mun. Law § 6-m).
- Worker's Compensation Reserve Fund (Gen. Mun. Law § 6-j).

For more information on the basic characteristics of these funds, including which are available to boards of cooperative educational services, and which are not available to city school districts with a population of 125,000 or more, see **26:6**.

26:4. Are there additional reserve funds school districts may establish other than those authorized by the Education Law or the General Municipal Law?

Yes. Pursuant to Chapter 202 of the Laws of 2001, school districts in which a nuclear-powered electric generating facility is located may establish a *nuclear facility tax stabilization reserve fund.* The fund is available to lessen or prevent any projected increase in the amount of the real property tax levy needed to finance the general fund portion of the school district budget for the next succeeding school year, as disclosed in the school budget presented to district's voters for approval. It is funded with budgetary appropriations subject to limitations set forth in law.

Individual Reserve Fund Characteristics

26:5. What are the basic characteristics of the school district reserve funds authorized under the Education Law?

The basic characteristics of the various school district reserve funds authorized under the Education Law are set forth below. Except as otherwise noted, these reserve funds are not available to boards of cooperative educational services (BOCES).

Capital Reserve Fund

- Available to cover, in whole or in part, the cost of any object or purpose for which a school district may issue bonds pursuant to the Local Finance Law. Districts must maintain the separate identity of each such fund.
- May be established only with voter approval of a proposition that states the purpose of the fund, the ultimate amount thereof, its probable term, and the source from which the funds would be obtained (§ 3651(1)).
- Funds may be expended only with voter approval, and only for the specific purpose for which the fund was established (§ 3651(3)).
- Funds may be invested in accordance with section 11 of General Municipal Law (§§ 3651(2); 3652), with any interest or capital gains realized accruing to the fund (§ 3651(2)).
- Funds may be transferred with voter approval to other funds established pursuant to section 3651 of the Education Law (§ 3651(4)).
- May be liquidated if voters determine the original purpose for which the fund was established is no longer needed. Proceeds must be applied first to any outstanding bonded indebtedness, with the remaining balance, if any, applied to reduce the annual tax levy subject to certain limitations set in the law (§ 3651(5); see also *Appeal of Kackmeister*, 40 Ed Dept Rep 577 (2001); *Appeal of Goldin*, 43 Ed Dept Rep 20 (2003); see **26:7**).

Note: Voter approval is not required in a city school district with a population of at least 125,000 inhabitants either for the establishment of a capital reserve fund, expenditures from the fund, transfers to other funds as permitted by law, or the liquidation of the reserve fund (§ 3651(9)).

In addition, school districts located wholly or partly within the Adirondack Park that have within their boundaries state lands subject to taxation assessed as set in the law may not establish a capital reserve fund without the recommendation of the commissioner of education and the consent of the state comptroller (§ 3651(8)(b)).

Liability and Property Loss Reserve Funds

- Available as separate reserve funds, one to cover property loss and the other liability claims. Each of the two funds, separately, may not exceed three percent of the annual budget or $15,000, whichever is greater.
- May be established without voter approval, but once established the funds may not be reduced below the amounts estimated necessary to cover incurred but unsettled claims or suits (other than by payments for losses for which such amounts were established).
- Funds may be expended without voter approval, unless the expenditure is for a purpose other than the one for which the fund was established. Nonetheless, voter approval is not required to pay premiums for insurance policies purchased to insure losses incurred subsequent to the dissolution of a self-insurance plan.
- Funds may be invested in accordance with section 11 of General Municipal Law (§§ 1709(8-c), 1723-a), with any interest or capital gain realized accruing to the fund (§ 1709(8-c)).

Note: The law also allows BOCES to establish liability and property loss reserve funds, but if a BOCES establishes such a fund it may not exceed 3 percent of the annual budget (§ 1950(4)(cc)).

Tax Certiorari Reserve Fund

- Available to pay for judgments and claims resulting from tax *certiorari* proceedings under Article 7 of the Real Property Tax Law.
- May be established without voter approval, provided that the funds do not exceed the amount which might reasonably be deemed necessary to anticipated judgments and claims arising out of tax certiorari proceedings.
- Funds may be expended without voter approval (§ 3651(1-a), (3-a)).
- Funds may be invested in accordance with section 11 of General Municipal Law (§§ 3651(2), 3652), with any interest or capital gains realized accruing to the fund (§ 3651(2)).
- Funds must be returned to the general fund by July 1 of the fourth fiscal year after their deposit into the reserve if they are not used for tax certiorari proceedings for the tax roll in the specific year they were deposited, and/or will not reasonably be required to pay a tax certiorari refund related to such proceedings (§ 3651(1-a); see also *Appeal of Goldin*, 43 Ed Dept Rep 20 (2003); Opn. St. Comp. 89-17). They may not be used for proceedings commenced in years other than the specific year they were deposited (*Appeal of Goldin*).
- Funds will be deemed reasonably required to pay a tax certiorari judgment or claim if the proceeding or claim has not been finally determined or otherwise terminated or disposed of after the exhaustion of all appeals (§ 3651(1-a)).
- Funds may be transferred with voter approval to other funds established pursuant to section 3651 of the Education Law (§ 3651(4)).
- May be liquidated if voters determine the original purpose for which the fund was established is no longer needed. Proceeds must be applied first to any outstanding bonded indebtedness, with the remaining balance, if any, applied to reduce the annual tax levy subject to certain limitations set in the law (§ 3651(5); see also *Appeal of Kackmeister*, 40 Ed Dept Rep 577 (2001); *Appeal of Goldin*, 43 Ed Dept Rep 20 (2003); **26:7**).

Note: A tax certiorari reserve fund may not be established retroactively (*Matter of Westchester Joint Waterworks v. Assessor of the City of Rye,* 37 Misc.3d 238 (Westchester Cnty. 2012), *aff'd as modified,* 120 A.D.3d 1352 (2d Dep't 2014), *aff'd*, 27 N.Y. 3d 566 (2016); *Appeal of Giardina*, 46 Ed Dept Rep 524 (2007)).

Tax Reduction Reserve Fund

- Available to retain the proceeds from the sale of school district real property that are not needed to pay any debts, and gradually use such proceeds to reduce real property taxes over a period not to exceed ten years.
- May be established without voter approval.
- Funds may be expended without voter approval (§§ 1604(36), 1709(37)).
- Funds may be invested in accordance with section 11 of General Municipal Law (§§ 1604-a, 1723-a), and any interest obtained may also be used for tax reduction (§§ 1604(36), 1709(37)).

Note: Proceeds from the sale of school district property purchased with obligations still outstanding at the time the property is sold must be deposited into a mandatory reserve for debt (see **26:6**). Proceeds in excess of the amount needed to retire the debt may be used for any lawful purpose, including the establishment of a reserve for tax reduction (§§ 1604(36), 1709(37); Opn. St. Comp. 86-26; see also Opn. St. Comp. 73-792).

Uncollected Taxes Reserve Fund

- Available only to small city school districts to offset the amount of uncollected real property taxes due and owing to such a district in instances where the city or county is not required, pursuant to Real Property Tax Law section 1332, to pay the amount of unpaid taxes to the treasurer of the school district.
- May be established without voter approval.
- Funds may be expended without voter approval (§ 3651(1-b)).
- Funds may be invested in accordance with section 11 of General Municipal Law (§§ 3651(2), 3652), with any interest or capital gains realized accruing to the fund (§ 3651(2)).
- The amount of funds in the reserve is subject to certain limitations set forth in the law (§ 3651(1-b)).
- Funds may be transferred with voter approval to other funds established pursuant to section 3651 of the Education Law (§ 3651(4)).
- May be liquidated if voters determine the original purpose for which the fund was established is no longer needed. Proceeds must be applied first to any outstanding bonded indebtedness, with the remaining balance, if any, applied to reduce the annual tax levy subject to certain limitations set in the law (§ 3651(5); see also *Appeal of Kackmeister*, 40 Ed Dept Rep 577 (2001); *Appeal of Goldin*, 43 Ed Dept Rep 20 (2003); see **26:7**).

Career Education Instructional Equipment Reserve Fund

- Available only to BOCES for the replacement and purchase of advanced technology equipment used in instructional programs conducted by the BOCES (§ 1950(4)(ee); 8 NYCRR § 170.3(k)).
- May be established upon approval of the BOCES and of the school boards of a majority of the districts participating in the instructional programs of the BOCES.
- Funds are obtained by including depreciation expenses for the career education instructional equipment used in providing instructional services on a cooperative basis in the computation of the cost of career education instructional services pursuant to a formula prescribed by the commissioner of education and revenues from the sale of such equipment (§ 1950(4)(ee); 8 NYCRR § 170.3(k)(4), (6)).
- Funds may be invested in accordance with section 11 of General Municipal Law.
- Funds may be expended with approval of the commissioner of education (§ 1950(4)(ee); 8 NYCRR § 170.3(k)(7)).
- The amount of funds in the reserve is subject to certain limitations set forth by the commissioner of education (8 NYCRR § 170.3(k)(5)).

- May be liquidated upon approval by the BOCES. Any funds remaining in the fund at the time of liquidation shall be allocated to the school districts participating in the instructional programs of the BOCES in proportion to the value of the contributions to the fund made by the participating districts (§ 1950(4)(ee); 8 NYCRR § 170.3(k)(10)).

Excess Tax Levy Reserve

- Must be established, in accordance with any requirements prescribed by the NYS Comptroller, when a school district determines after the tax levy that it erroneously levied a tax in excess of its tax levy cap (see **26:2**) due to clerical or technical errors.
- Reserve funds consist of tax funds levied in excess of the tax levy cap.
- Reserve funds and any interest earned on such funds must be used to reduce the tax levy for the following school year (§ 2023-a(5); see also NYS Comptroller, *Reserve for Excess Tax Levy* (Jan. 2012), at: http://www.osc.state.ny.us/localgov/pubs/releases/2011_12taxcapreserve.pdf).

Note: The State Comptroller has made clear that the entire amount of the excess tax levy must be placed in the excess tax levy reserve in a separate interest-bearing bank account (*Reserve for Excess Tax Levy*).

In addition, school districts must use available cash and other future revenue sources to fully fund the reserve as soon as possible but no later than the end of the fiscal year, whenever the tax collections are insufficient to fund the full amount of the reserve or the excess tax levy is discovered after the collection of property taxes for the school year (*Id.*).

Furthermore, if it is determined that excess tax levies occurred in multiple years, school districts must place in reserve an amount equal to the total of the excess amounts levied in each fiscal year involved (*Id*; see also **19:15**).

26:6. What are the basic characteristics of the school district reserve funds authorized under the General Municipal Law?

The basic characteristics of the various school district reserve funds authorized under the General Municipal Law are set forth below. Except as otherwise noted, these reserve funds are not available to boards of cooperative educational services (BOCES). As further indicated, some of the funds are not available to city school districts with a population of 125,000 or more.

Employee Benefit Accrued Liability Reserve Fund

- Available for the cash payment of accrued and accumulated but unused sick leave, personal leave, holiday leave, vacation time, and other benefits earned by employees and payable upon termination, that are not covered by another existing reserve fund. (Such other fund may be discontinued and moneys transferred to this fund as set forth in law).
- May be established without voter approval, and funded with budgetary appropriations, transfers from other reserve funds as permitted by law, and such other funds as the school board may legally appropriate.
- Funds may be expended without voter approval. However, it is a misdemeanor to withdraw or expend funds except as permitted by law.
- Funds may be invested in accordance with section 11 of the General Municipal Law, with any interest or capital gain realized accruing to the fund.
- Funds must be accounted for separate and apart from all other school district funds in the manner set forth in law.
- Upon a determination that this fund is no longer needed, the fund may be discontinued, and uncompromised moneys remaining in the fund may be transferred to another reserve fund, as permitted by law (Gen. Mun. Law § 6-p).

- Moneys from this fund cannot be used to pay lump sum "retirement awards" calculated as prescribed percentages of an employee's final year salaries and paid upon retirement under a collective bargaining agreement (Opn. St. Comp. 2006–8).
- Moneys from this fund may be withdrawn to maintain educational programming subject to conditions and limitations prescribed by law. This option is limited to the 2015-16 school year unless extended by the Legislature (Gen. Mun. Law § 6-p(10)).

Note: The law also allows BOCES to establish an employee benefit accrued liability reserve fund. However, it expressly denies city school districts with a population of 125,000 or more the authority to establish such a fund (Gen. Mun. Law § 6-p(1)(a)).

A BOCES that is determined through either a state audit or its own annual independent audit to have funds in excess of those needed to pay liabilities must withdraw and repay such amounts in proportion to the payments school districts made (Gen. Mun. Law § 6-p(11)). A school district may choose to have such payment credited to offset the administrative and capital expenses payable by the district in the current year (Gen. Mun. Law § 6-p(11); Educ. Law § 1950(5)).

Insurance Reserve Fund

- Available for the payment of any loss, claim, action or judgment for which a school district is authorized or required to purchase insurance, except those already covered by another existing reserve fund and except as otherwise specified in law.
- May be established without voter approval, and funded with budgetary appropriations, transfers from other reserve funds as permitted by law, and such other funds as the school board may legally appropriate. Annual contributions to the fund may not exceed five percent of the total budget for that year or $33,000, whichever is greater.
- Funds may be expended without voter approval. However, judicial approval is necessary to pay settled or compromised claims exceeding $25,000. In addition, it is a misdemeanor to withdraw or expend funds except as permitted by law.
- Funds may be invested in accordance with section 11 of the General Municipal Law, with any interest or capital gain realized accruing to the fund.
- Funds must be accounted for separate and apart from all other district funds in the manner set forth in law (i.e., a separate account for each risk funded in the reserve).
- Upon a determination that this fund is no longer needed, the fund may be discontinued, and uncompromised moneys remaining in the fund may be transferred to another reserve fund, as permitted by law (Gen. Mun. Law § 6-n).

Note: The law also allows boards of cooperative educational services to establish an insurance reserve fund. However, it expressly denies city school districts with a population of 125,000 or more the authority to establish such a fund (Gen. Mun. Law § 6-n(1)(a)).

Fiscal Management

Mandatory Debt Service Reserve Fund

- Required when outstanding obligations remain at the time of the sale of school district property or capital improvement that was financed by obligations.
- May be established without voter approval, with the proceeds from the sale deposited into the fund, except that proceeds in excess of the amount needed to retire the outstanding obligations may be used for any lawful purpose.
- Funds may be expended without voter approval. However, it is a misdemeanor to withdraw or expend funds except as permitted by law.
- Funds may be invested in accordance with section 11 of the General Municipal Law, with any interest or capital gain realized accruing to the fund.
- Funds for each such fund must be accounted for separately (Gen. Mun. Law § 6-l).

Repair Reserve Fund

- Available to pay for repairs to capital improvements or equipment of a type that does not recur annually or at shorter intervals.
- May be established without voter approval, and funded with budgetary appropriations or other revenues not required by law to be paid into other funds or accounts.
- Funds may be expended without voter approval in cases of emergency pursuant to approval by two-thirds of the school board. Otherwise, a public hearing must be held in accordance with the procedures set forth in law. One-half of the funds expended in an emergency case must be repaid to the fund during the next fiscal year, and the remainder by the end of the second fiscal year following the fiscal year in which the funds were expended. In addition, it is a misdemeanor to withdraw or expend funds from a repair reserve fund except as permitted by law.
- Funds may be invested in accordance with section 11 of the General Municipal Law, with any interest or capital gain realized accruing to the fund.
- Funds must be accounted for separate and apart from all other school district funds in the matter set forth in law (Gen. Mun. Law § 6-d; see also Opn. St. Comp. 85-20; Opn. St. Comp. 84-8; 81-401; 26 Opn. St. Comp. 225).

Note: Funds in a repair reserve fund are also available for appropriation to a reserve fund established pursuant to section 3651 of the Education Law (Gen. Mun. Law § 6-d(3)(d); see **26:2**).

Retirement Contribution Reserve Fund

- Available to finance retirement contributions payable to the NY State and Local Employees' Retirement System.
- May be established without voter approval, and funded with budgetary appropriations, revenues not required by law to be paid into other funds or accounts, transfers from other reserve funds as permitted by law, and such other funds as the school board may legally appropriate.
- Funds may be expended without voter approval. However, it is a misdemeanor to withdraw or expend funds from a retirement contribution reserve fund except as permitted by law.
- Funds may be invested in accordance with section 11 of the General Municipal Law, with any interest or capital gain realized accruing to the fund.
- Funds must be accounted for separate and apart from all other school district funds in the manner set forth in law.
- A portion of the funds may be transferred to another reserve fund established pursuant to Gen. Mun. Law section 6-d or section 3651 of the Education Law following a public hearing conducted in the manner set forth in law (Gen. Mun. Law § 6-r; see **26:2**).

Note: The law also allows boards of cooperative educational services to establish an insurance reserve fund. However, it expressly denies city school districts with a population of 125,000 or more the authority to establish such a fund (Gen. Mun. Law § 6-r(1)(a)).

Unemployment Insurance Payment Reserve Fund

- Available to pay for the cost of reimbursing the State Unemployment Insurance Fund for payments made to claimants when a school district elects the benefit reimbursement method in lieu of making contributions under article 18 of the Labor Law.
- May be established without voter approval, and funded by budgetary appropriations, transfers from other reserve funds as permitted by law, and such other funds as the school may legally appropriate.
- Funds may be expended without voter approval, but only as required by law to pay the State Unemployment Insurance Fund the amount of benefits paid to claimants and charged to the district.
- Funds may be invested in accordance with section 11 of the General Municipal Law, with any interest or capital accruing to the fund.

- Funds must be accounted for with a separate identity.
- Funds available at the end of any fiscal year that exceed the amount needed to satisfy existing obligations and pending claims may, within 60 days of the end of the fiscal year, be transferred to another reserve fund as permitted by law, and/or applied to the budget appropriation of the next succeeding fiscal year.
- Funds exceeding the amount sufficient to pay all pending claims may be transferred to another reserve fund as permitted by law when a school district terminates its election to become liable for reimbursement payments in lieu of contributions (Gen. Mun. Law § 6-m).

Note: The law also allows boards of cooperative educational services to establish an unemployment insurance payment reserve fund.

Workers' Compensation Reserve

- Available to pay for compensation and benefits, and other authorized expenses when a school district elects to maintain a self-insured worker's compensation program.
- May be established without voter approval, and funded with budgetary appropriations and such other sums as the school board may legally appropriate.
- Funds may be expended without voter approval.
- Funds may be invested in accordance with section 11 of the General Municipal Law, with any interest or capital gain realized accruing to the fund.
- Funds must be accounted for separate and apart from all other school district funds in the manner set forth in law.
- Funds available at the end of any fiscal year that exceed the amount needed to satisfy existing obligations and pending claims may, within 60 days of the end of the fiscal year, be transferred to another reserve fund as permitted by law, and/or applied to the budget appropriation of the next succeeding fiscal year.
- Funds exceeding the amount sufficient to pay all accrued and contingent expenditures may be transferred to another reserve fund as permitted by law, when a school ceases to be a self-insurer after the establishment of the worker's compensation reserve fund (Gen. Mun. Law § 6-j).

Special Rules

26:7. Are there any special rules that apply to a school district's use of a capital reserve fund?

Yes. The proposition submitted for voter approval of the establishment of a capital reserve fund (see **26:2, 26:5**), must specify the purpose, ultimate amount, and probable term of the fund, as well as the source from which the moneys for the fund will be obtained (§ 3651(1)).

Regarding the ultimate amount of the fund, the commissioner has explained that term refers to the amount of money that may be paid into the fund over the entire term of the fund. It is not permissible to operate a capital reserve fund as a "rolling reserve fund" by replenishing the funds as they are expended without regard to the ultimate amount or probable term approved by the voters (*Appeal of Kackmeister*, 40 Ed Dept Rep 577 (2001); see also *Appeal of Golden*, 45 Ed Dept Rep 407 (2006); *Appeal of Goldin*, 43 Ed Dept Rep 20 (2003)). It is also improper to deposit moneys into a capital reserve fund and use them in the same fiscal year. Such a fund is intended for a future project, and not to finance a current project or needs (*Appeal of Kackmeister*; see also *Appeal of Uy & Norden*, 44 Ed Dept Rep 424 (2005)).

As to the probable term of the fund, the life of the fund is limited to the specific probable term set forth in the proposition that authorized the establishment of the fund, unless the voters approve a new proposition extending it before the expiration of the original probable term (*Appeal of Kackmeister; Appeal of Goldin*).

Once the probable term of the fund expires, the terms of the fund cannot be amended. In addition, no additional moneys may be deposited into the fund, even if the fund did not achieve its ultimate amount limit. However, accumulated moneys in the fund may continue to be expended after the expiration of the probable term until the fund is depleted, with proper voter authorizations (*Id.*).

Furthermore, according to the commissioner, voter approved propositions authorizing the funding of or expenditure from a capital reserve fund must be limited to the fiscal year for which the voters approved the proposition. They may not purportedly continue such authorization indefinitely into future fiscal years. Moreover, voter approved propositions authorizing the expenditure of moneys from a capital reserve fund must be specific and give the voters adequate notice of the particular intended use of the funds. Such use must be for the specific purpose for which the fund was established (*Appeal of Kackmeister*).

26:8. May a school district use surplus funds for a reserve fund?

Yes. Generally, surplus funds that exceed the four percent limitation currently applicable to the retention of unexpended operating funds from the current school year budget must be used to reduce the tax levy for the upcoming school year. However, surplus funds that otherwise would be earmarked for tax levy reduction do not include unexpended operating funds properly retained "under other sections of law" (Real Property Tax Law § 1318(1)). This exception applies to reserve funds specifically authorized by law (*Appeals of Gorman*, 43 Ed Dept Rep 32 (2003); *Appeal of Silletti*, 40 Ed Dept Rep 426 (2000); *Appeal of Simons*, 39 Ed Dept Rep 744 (2000); *Appeal of Molineaux*, 38 Ed Dept Rep 672 (1999)). It does not apply to unofficial reserve funds when created to pay for unbudgeted ordinary contingent expenses (*Appeal of Clark*, 37 Ed Dept Rep 386 (1998)).

Nonetheless, for the exception to apply, the reserve fund must be established before the tax levy that otherwise would be reduced by the retained funds (*Appeal of Affronti,* 54 Ed Dep't Rep, Dec. No. 16,756 (2015); *Appeals of Gorman*; *Appeal of Simons*; *Appeal of Mills*, 34 Ed Dept Rep 92 (1994); see also *Appeal of Lombardo*, 37 Ed Dept Rep 721 (1998)). A reserve fund may not be established retroactively (see, *Appeal of Giardina*, 46 Ed Dept Rep 524 (2007); *Matter of Westchester Joint Waterworks v. Assessor of the City of Rye,* 37 Misc.3d 238 (Westchester Cnty. 2012), *aff'd as modified,* 120 A.D.3d 1352 (2d Dep't 2014), *aff'd*, 27 N.Y. 3d 566 (2016). A district may not hold surplus funds indefinitely in anticipation of establishing a reserve fund (*Appeal of Simons*; *Appeal of Mills*).

Repeated failure to adhere to the above requirements may warrant removal from office (*Appeal of Simons*).

26:9. What happens if a school district discovers that it deposited moneys into a reserve fund without proper authority?

In such an instance, a district would have to return such moneys to the general fund (*Appeal of Lombardo*, 46 Ed Dept Rep 233 (2007); *Appeal of Golden*, 45 Ed Dept Rep 407 (2006); see also *Appeal of Hubbard*, 44 Ed Dept Rep 183 (2004)).

However, a school district that discovers it deposited moneys into a capital reserve fund in excess of the fund's ultimate amount limit (see **26:7**), may seek voter approval to extend and/or increase the fund (*Appeal of Lombardo*; *Appeal of Golden*). Upon voter approval, it may transfer back the subject funds into the new reserve fund (*Id.*). Otherwise, it must apply the excess moneys to reduce the tax levy for the upcoming school year (*Appeal of Lombardo*).

27. Borrowing

Editor's Note: All of the statutory references in this chapter are to the New York State Local Finance Law unless noted otherwise.

27:1. Can a school district borrow money?

Yes. School districts may issue long-term obligations, including serial bonds (§ 21.00) and statutory installment bonds (§ 62.10). They also may issue short-term obligations, including bond anticipation notes (BANs) (§ 23.00), tax anticipation notes (TANs) (§ 24.00), revenue anticipation notes (RANs) (§ 25.00), capital notes (§ 28.00), budget notes (§ 29.00) and deficiency notes (§ 29.20).

In addition, districts may issue:

- Bonds to liquidate operating deficits issued pursuant to a special or general law to incur such debt and in accordance with statutory requirements including certification of the amount of the deficit by the state comptroller (§ 10.10).
- Zero coupons (§ 57.00(e)).
- Variable rate obligations up to July 15, 2018 (§ 54.90).
- Discounted bonds at negotiated sales subject to rules and regulations promulgated by the state comptroller, as well as prior approval from the comptroller except as otherwise provided in the comptroller's rules and regulations (*Id.*).
- Qualified zone academy bonds available for the repair and rehabilitation of buildings, the purchase of equipment, the development of course materials, and teacher training at qualified schools (26 USC §§ 54E, 1397E; 8 NYCRR § 155.22(a)).
- Qualified school construction bonds available for the construction, rehabilitation or repair of a public school facility or for the acquisition of land on which such facility is to be constructed (26 USC § 54F; 8 NYCRR § 155.22(b)). These bonds must be used within three years of issuance (8 NYCRR § 155.22(b)(5)).

Tax exempt financing may be available through the use of qualified public educational facility (QPEF) bonds when, as part of the federal QPEF program, a school district enters into a public-private partnership agreement with a private for-profit corporation for the construction, rehabilitation, refurbishing, or equipment of a school facility. At the end of the agreement, the private corporation transfers the facility to the school district for no additional consideration (26 USC § 142(k)(2); 8 NYCRR § 155.26). Under certain conditions, QPEF bonds may be available also for projects that do not involve capital construction (8 NYCRR § 155.26).

The authority to issue qualified zone academy bonds, qualified school construction bonds and qualified public educational facility bonds extends to charter schools, as well (8 NYCRR §§ 155.22(a)(3)(i)(b), (b)(3)(iii)(a), (b), 155.26).

27:2. When may a school district issue long-term obligations?

Section 11.00 of the Local Finance Law describes the various purposes for which municipalities may issue long-term obligations, many of which are applicable to school districts including, for example, the purchase of school buses and, in some circumstances, retirement incentive programs and retirement contributions.

Serial bonds are used primarily to finance capital projects. Their use is subject to the conditions set forth in law (§§ 11.00, 21.00).

Statutory installment bonds are used when the full principal amount to be financed does not exceed $5 million in the aggregate, and the issue is to be sold at a private sale (§ 62.10).

27:3. Do any special rules apply to the use of long-term borrowing instruments?

Yes. Districts may not borrow for longer than the period of probable usefulness of the object or purpose as set forth in section 11.00 of the Local Finance Law. For example, the period of probable usefulness for school buses is five years (§ 11.00(a)(29)).

Districts may group and finance together dissimilar objects that have the same period of probable usefulness, as set forth in law (§ 11.00(a)(101)–(103)). When the dissimilar objects do not have the same period of probable usefulness, districts may use a "weighted average period of probable usefulness" as set forth in law, in order to finance them under the same bond (§ 11.00(a)).

27:4. When may a school district issue short-term obligations?

School districts may issue short-term obligations as follows:

Bond anticipation notes most commonly are used for temporary financing before the issuance of serial bonds (§ 23.00). This gives the district flexibility in timing the actual bond sale.

Capital notes may be issued to finance all or part of the cost of the purposes listed in section 11.00 of the Local Finance Law (§ 28.00).

Tax anticipation notes and *revenue anticipation notes* are used, respectively, to borrow in anticipation of the collection of taxes and the receipt of revenues, other than real property taxes, by the school district. Such taxes and revenues must be used to pay off the notes (§§ 24.00, 25.00; see also *Appeal of Aarseth*, 33 Ed Dept Rep 522 (1994)).

Budget notes may be issued during the last nine months of the fiscal year to finance required expenditures for which either no or insufficient provision was made in the annual budget or to provide temporary school buildings or facilities in a year when an unforeseeable public emergency, such as an epidemic, riot, or storm, prevents the use of all or part of the district's buildings and facilities (§ 29.00).

Deficiency notes may be issued to finance a deficiency in any fund or funds arising from revenue being less than the amount estimated in the budget for such current fiscal year, but may not exceed five percent of the amount of the annual budget (§ 29.20; see also NYS Comptroller, *Accounting for Deficiency Notes* (Mar. 2012), at: http://osc.state.ny.us/localgov/pubs/releases/deficiencynotes.pdf).

27:5. Do any special rules apply to the use of short-term borrowing instruments?

Yes. The use of bond anticipation notes, capital notes, tax anticipation notes, revenue anticipation notes, budget notes and deficiency notes are subject to the maturity, retirement, and renewal conditions set forth in law (§§ 23.00, 24.00, 25.00, 29.00, 29.20).

27:6. Do any special rules apply to the issuance of obligations to finance capital improvements or equipment purchases?

Yes. Generally, school districts must make a down payment from current funds of at least five percent of the estimated cost of a capital improvement or equipment purchase prior to the issuance of bonds or bond anticipation notes (§ 107.00(b)(2)). However, the down payment requirement does not apply to, for example:

- Capital improvements estimated to exceed $20 million (§ 107.00(d)(3)(g)).
- Objects or purposes that have a period of probable usefulness of five years or less as set forth in section 11.00 of the Local Finance Law (§ 107.00(d)(5)).

In addition, through July 15, 2018, the down payment requirement does not apply either to the issuance of bonds or notes for any object or purpose that has a period of probable usefulness determined by law (§ 107.00(d)(9); see also § 11.00).

27:7. Is there a limit to how much school districts may borrow?

Yes. School districts that have an aggregate assessed valuation of taxable real property of $100,000 or over, may not issue bonds or bond anticipation notes if the indebtedness will exceed 10 percent (Five percent in city school districts) of the full valuation of the district's taxable real property (§ 104.00; see also N.Y. Const. art. VIII, § 4). Additional limitations can apply to the amount districts can borrow through the issuance of budget notes (§ 29.00(a)(3)).

Furthermore, no installment of serial bonds or bond anticipation notes redeemed from a source other than the proceeds of bonds may be more than 50 percent in excess of the smallest previous installment (§ 21.00(d)). The purpose of this 50 percent rule is to prevent the ballooning of bond issue installments close to the date of maturity. However, districts may use level or declining debt financing as an alternative to the 50 percent rule for the purpose of retiring debt (*Id.*).

Nonetheless, districts may exceed their borrowing limitation if they are able to meet certain specified conditions. Common, union free, and central school districts must obtain voter approval of a proposition to exceed the limitation by at least a 60 percent vote, as well as the consent of the Board of Regents (§ 104.00(d)). Additional rules apply to districts located wholly or partly in the Adirondack Park (*Id.*).

Special rules apply also to city school districts seeking to exceed their borrowing limitation. The proposition submitted for voter approval must apprise the voters that the issuance of the obligations will exceed the constitutional debt limitation of the district. It requires not only a 60 percent voter approval, but also the consent of the State Comptroller in addition to the Board of Regents (§ 104.00(c); see also *Appeal of O'Brien*, 51 Ed Dept Rep, Dec. No. 16,316 (2011), *aff'd*, *O'Brien v. N.Y. Commr. of Educ.*, 112 A.D.3d 188 (3d Dep't 2013)).

The liability against taxpayers that results from a district's issuance of bonds or bond anticipation notes becomes fixed at the time the bonds or notes are issued (*O'Brien v. N.Y. Commr. of Educ.*, 112 A.D.3d 188 (3d Dep't 2013); *Hill v. Bd. of Educ. of Cent. Sch. Dist. No. 2 of Towns of Glenville, Amsterdam and Charlton*, 286 A.D. 332 (3d Dep't), *aff'd*, 309 N.Y. 945 (1955); see also *Appeal of O'Brien*; *Matter of Platt*, 11 Ed Dept Rep 113 (1971); *Matter of Iocovozzi*, 1 Ed Dept Rep 469 (1960)). Because there may be a lag time between the time a district's voters approve the issuance of bonds or notes and the date when a bond issue is ready for sale, a district must examine the debt limitation requirement when issuance becomes imminent. If a district determines that it will exceed its debt limit as a result of the actual issuance of the bonds or notes, it must call for another vote to get 60 percent voter approval before it proceeds (*Id.*).

27:8. Are there any limits on interest rates for school district borrowing?

In general, sections 57.00(b), 60.00(b), 60.10, and 63.00(b) of the Local Finance Law authorize the sale of bonds and notes without limitation on the rate of interest.

27:9. Must a school board adopt a resolution to authorize the issuance of bonds and notes?

Yes, according to section 31.00 of the Local Finance Law (see also § 40.10 regarding the form and content of deficiency note resolutions).

27:10. Are there any limitations on a school board's ability to authorize the issuance of bonds and notes?

Yes. Generally, school district voters must approve the levy of a tax to pay for the bonded indebtedness before a school board can adopt a resolution authorizing the issuance of bonds or capital notes (§§ 37.00, 104.00; Educ. Law § 416). The issuance of deficiency notes are subject to the limitations set forth in law (§§ 29.20, 40.10).

Districts other than city school districts also may need the consent of the Board of Regents and/or the state comptroller for the issuance of bonds or bond anticipation notes if the issuance of the bonds will exceed the school district's debt limitation (§ 104.00(d)).

Special rules apply to city school districts that would require the consent of both the Board of Regents and the state comptroller prior to the issuance of bonds, bond anticipation notes or capital notes which exceed the district's debt limitation (§ 104.00(b)(8), (c)).

27:11. Is a school district required to file any statements with the state comptroller before it actually sells bonds?

It depends. A school district must file a debt statement with the state comptroller before it sells any bonds that are required to be sold at public sale. A school district may file a debt statement in connection with the issuance of bond anticipation notes (§§ 109.00, 130 *et seq.*).

27:12. How are bonds and notes sold?

Generally, bonds must be sold at public sale, in accordance with the procedures set forth in law (§§ 57.00, 58.00, 59.00; 2 NYCRR Part 25). However, they may be sold at private sale in the following instances:

- The bonds are sold to the United States government or to the New York State Municipal Bond Bank Agency or to certain sinking funds or pension funds (§ 57.00(a)).
- The bonds are issued in an amount not to exceed $5 million. The total amount of bonds that may be sold at private sale in any one fiscal year of the school district is $5 million (§ 63.00).
- The sale is of a statutory installment bond or bonds that does not exceed $5 million in the aggregate (unless sold to the United States Government) and that may be issued for the full principal amount (§ 62.10).

27:13. May a school district sell bonds and notes to a bank where a district officer or employee is also an officer, director, or stockholder of that bank?

Yes. With limited exceptions, school district bonds and notes may be sold at private sale to a bank in which a school district officer or employee has an interest that otherwise would be prohibited by the conflict of interest provisions of section 803 of the General Municipal Law. Disclosure of that interest must be made as required by law. Willful participation in authorizing the sale of, or in selling school district obligations to a bank in which a school district officer or employee has an interest other than under the conditions set forth in law constitutes a misdemeanor (§ 60.10).

27:14. Must the money received from the sale of bonds and notes be deposited in a special bank account?

Yes. With the exception of the proceeds of capital notes issued in amounts of $100,000 or less and budget notes, all proceeds from the sale of bonds, bond anticipation notes, capital notes, and budget notes must be deposited in a special account in the bank or trust company and may not be commingled with the other district funds (§ 165.00(a), (a)(1)).

Nonetheless, proceeds from the sale of any two or more issues of bonds, bond anticipation notes, capital notes, or budget notes may be deposited into a single special account, provided that a separate accounting record is maintained for each issue, and the proceeds are not commingled with other district funds (§ 165.00(a)(2)).

27:15. May a school district temporarily invest the proceeds from the sale of bonds and notes pending actual use of the money?

Yes, but only the proceeds of bonds, bond anticipation notes, and capital notes. In addition, such proceeds may be invested only in accordance with the provisions of section 11 of the General Municipal Law (§ 165.00(b)). Commonly known as arbitrage, this ability to temporarily invest proceeds from the sale of bonds and notes affords districts the ability to earn interest at a better rate than the rate at which the funds were borrowed.

However, the Internal Revenue Code imposes rebate requirements on income from arbitrage that involve the return of investment profits to the federal government. The rebate requirements relate to the time period during which all gross proceeds must be spent on the purpose for which the funds were borrowed (§ 165.00(b)). For more information contact a bond counsel and/or consult the Internal Revenue Code.

27:16. May a school district use the proceeds from the sale of bonds and notes for a purpose other than the one for which they were issued?

No. All proceeds from the sale of bonds or notes, inclusive of premiums, that are not expended for the purpose(s) for which the funds were borrowed must be applied to the payment of the principal and interest on the obligations respectively (§§ 29.20(e), 165.00(a); see *Appeal of Goldin*, 40 Ed Dept Rep 628 (2001); *Appeal of Kirschenbaum*, 43 Ed Dept Rep 366 (2004)).

27:17. What happens if a school district fails to appropriate moneys needed to pay the principal and interest on outstanding bonds and notes?

The state constitution requires that school districts appropriate the amount of their debt service requirements annually. If a district fails to appropriate that money, upon the suit of a bondholder, the first revenues received by the district will be "applied to such purposes" (N.Y. Const. art. VIII, § 2).

28. Purchasing of Materials and Services

Purchasing Authority

Editor's Note: The acquisition of school sites and facilities is discussed in ***chapter 61****.*

28:1. May school districts enter into cooperative purchasing agreements?

Yes. School districts may enter into cooperative purchasing agreements with each other, subject to approval of the school board of each participating district, and the general laws applicable to school districts (Gen. Mun. Law §§ 119-n(a), 119-o(1), (2)(d); see also 18 Opn. St. Comp. 381, No. 62-803 (1962)). Any such agreement should also provide, for example, for periodic review of the terms and conditions of the agreement and for the adjudication of disputes or disagreements (see Gen. Mun. Law § 119-o(2)(j), (k)).

Guidance from the NYS Education Department, Office of Educational Management Services, recommends, for example, that the operation costs of the cooperative be prorated in accordance with the volume of purchases and use of the arrangement by each participating district. Also, each participating district should have a representative serving on a coordinating committee for the cooperative that addresses issues related to specifications of the bids, carrying out the bidding process, and sharing of costs. The guidance, *Cooperative Purchasing* (updated Oct. 2013), is available at: www.p12.nysed.gov/mgtserv/purchasing/coopurch.htm. See also **59:53** for information about cooperative bidding for transportation contracts.

For recommendations on setting up shared services, such as cooperative purchasing, see Office of the State Comptroller, Division of Local Government and School Accountability, *Local Government Management Guide, Shared Services in Local Government* (2009), at: http://www.osc.state.ny.us/localgov/pubs/lgmg/sharedservices.pdf.

28:2. May school districts make purchases through other state agencies?

Yes. A school district may purchase commodities, materials, equipment, technology, or supplies through the NYS Office of General Services (OGS) or any other state department or agency subject to rules promulgated pursuant Article 11 of the State Finance Law if the purchase exceeds $500 (Gen. Mun. Law § 104; see also State Fin. Law § 163). School districts may also enter into contracts with state agencies to provide or receive equipment and certain services, such as technology services (Gen. Mun. Law § 99-r).

A district also may purchase materials, equipment or supplies, or contract for services, other than those excepted by law, either through the county in which the district is located or through any county within the state. Such purchases would be subject to local rules established under section 408-a(2) of the County Law (Gen. Mun. Law § 103(3)).

In both instances, the district must accept sole responsibility for any payment due the vendor. Furthermore, the purchase will not be permissible if the district receives a lower bid for the purchase on the same terms, conditions and specifications (Gen. Mun. Law §§ 103(3), 104).

School districts must consider cost factors such as delivery charges and other miscellaneous costs to determine if using a county contract will result in cost savings prior to making a purchase through such contracts (Gen. Mun. Law § 103(3)). Districts should consider such factors also when evaluating whether to make a purchase under a State contract (see Office of the State Comptroller, Division of Local Government and School Accountability, *Local Government Management Guide, Seeking Competition in Procurement* (July 2014), at: http://www.osc.state.ny.us/localgov/pubs/lgmg/seekingcompetition.pdf).

Through July 31, 2017, districts are authorized to make purchases of apparatus, materials, equipment and supplies or for services related to the installation, maintenance, or repair of such apparatus, materials, equipment and supplies through use of a contract let by the federal government, any of the federal agencies, any state, or any other county or political subdivision or district therein if such contract was awarded to either the lowest responsible bidder or on the basis of best value in a manner consistent with state law and made available for use by other governmental entities (Gen. Mun. Law § 103(16)). Districts exercising this option must determine whether the proposed procurement from a non-New York entity meets the four fundamental elements identified by the state comptroller such that the contract is considered let in accordance with the provisions of General Municipal Law § 103. They are:

- public solicitation of bids or offers (the process to award contracts on the basis of best value is referred to as competitive offering; see **28:12**);
- submission of sealed bids or offers, or analogous procedures to preserve the integrity and confidentiality of submissions;
- preparation of specifications or similar document that provides common standards for bidders and offerers to compete fairly; and
- award to the lowest bidder who materially and substantially meets the specifications or, in the case of best value process, an award to the responsive and responsible offerer (see Office of the State Comptroller, Division of Local Government and School Accountability, *New "Piggybacking" Law- Exception to Competitive Bidding* (July 2016), at: http://osc.state.ny.us/localgov/pubs/piggybackinglaw.pdf).

28:3. May school districts make purchases through federal contracts?

Yes. School districts are authorized, through July 31, 2019, to make certain purchases through specified federal contracts. Those include the purchase of technology and telecommunication hardware, software, supplies, support equipment, and professional services through the federal general services administration schedule 70 (Gen. Mun. Law §§ 103(1-b), 104(2); see also Federal e-Government Act of 2002, Pub. L. No. 107-374 § 211). Compliance with schedule 70 ordering procedures is deemed compliance with New York's competitive bidding requirements (Gen. Mun. Law § 103(1-b)).

Similarly, districts may purchase law enforcement equipment suitable for counter drug activities through the U.S. Department of Defense (Gen. Mun. Law § 104(2); see also National Defense Authorization Act for fiscal year 1994, Pub. L. No. 103-160, § 1122). Alarm and signal systems, facility management systems, firefighting and rescue equipment, special purpose clothing and products to be used to facilitate recovery from terrorism, nuclear, biological, chemical or a radiological attack and major disasters declared by the president may also be purchased through federal channels (Gen. Mun. Law § 104(2); see also Local Preparedness Acquisition Act, Pub. L. No. 110-248 ("Schedule 84"), John Warner National Defense Authorization Act for Fiscal Year 2007, Pub. L. No. 109-364, § 833, and the Federal Supply Schedule Usage Act of 2010, Pub. L. No. 111-263).

Districts making these authorized purchases through federal contracts must consider whether the purchases will result in cost savings after all factors are considered, including charges for services, material, and delivery (Gen Mun. Law § 104(2)).

28:4. May a school district make purchases through the use of installment contracts?

Yes, but only through July 15, 2018. In addition, such contracts may be used only for the purchase of "equipment, machinery or apparatus" (Gen. Mun. Law § 109-b(1)(a), (b)). In addition, such contracts are subject to the conditions set forth in section 109-b of the General Municipal Law.

For example, installment contracts are subject to competitive bidding requirements (Gen. Mun. Law § 109-b(3)). In addition, entering into an installment contract requires voter approval if such approval is required to issue obligations to finance the purchase of any equipment, machinery or apparatus under the contract (Gen. Mun. Law § 109-b(5); see also *Appeal of Hubbard*, 45 Ed Dept Rep 496 (2006)).

28:5. May a school district purchase instructional equipment through a lease-purchase agreement?

Yes, with payments applied against the purchase price of the equipment, and subject to approval by the commissioner of education prior to execution. Such an agreement is also subject to the bidding requirements of the General Municipal Law (§ 1725-a; 8 NYCRR § 170.7(a), (b); see **28:11-19**).

Instructional equipment obtainable through a lease purchase agreement includes instruments, machines, apparatus or other types of equipment that are used directly in the instruction of students and which:

- are not consumed in use and retain their original shape and appearance with use;
- are not expendable items such as textbooks or supplies;
- are not a capital improvement as defined in section 2(9) of the Local Finance Law; and
- do not lose their identity through incorporation into a different or more complex unit (8 NYCRR § 170.7(c)).

An application form for approval of a lease-purchase agreement is available at: http://www.p12.nysed.gov/mgtserv/purchasing/s1725afm.pdf. It must be submitted to the commissioner no more than 90 days and no less than 30 days prior to the date of execution of the agreement, unless the commissioner grants a variance of the time limitations for good cause shown (8 NYCRR § 170.7(b)).

28:6. Can school districts refuse to make purchases from certain types of entities?

Yes. School districts may refuse to purchase apparel or sports equipment manufactured in a sweatshop (Gen. Mun. Law §§ 103(12), 104-b(6)). When competitive bidding requirements apply (see **28:11**), a district can determine that a bidder that manufactures such items in a sweatshop is not a responsible bidder, and thereby refuse to award a contract for the purchase of such items to that bidder (Gen. Mun. Law § 103(12)). A district also may prohibit such purchases when competitive bidding requirements do not apply, through its procurement policies and practices (Gen. Mun. Law § 104-b(6)). In both instances, a district must consider either or both of the following:

- The labor standards applicable to the manufacture of the apparel or sports equipment (including employee compensation, working conditions, employee rights to unionize, and the use of child labor).
- The potential vendor's failure to provide sufficient information regarding the labor standards applicable to the manufacture of the items (Gen. Mun. Law §§ 103(12), 104-b(6)).

Districts can obtain from the NYS Department of Labor a list of apparel manufacturers found not to be in compliance with applicable labor standards (Labor Law § 342).

28:7. Are school districts required or able to give a preference to certain vendors?

Yes. For example, school districts and boards of cooperative educational services must give preference to vendors who agree to provide instructional materials required in alternative format for students with disabilities at the same time that regular format instructional materials are made available for non-disabled students. In this context, alternative format refers to a medium or format other than a traditional print textbook including, for example, Braille, large print, open and closed captioned, audio, or an electronic file in an approved format, as defined in the regulations of the commissioner of education (§§ 1604(29-a), 1709(4-a), 1950(4-a), 2503(7-a), 2554(7-a), 3602(8)(b); 8 NYCRR § 200.2(b)(10)).

In addition, districts may give preference to vendors of recycled products, provided that certain conditions set forth in law are met. These include, for example, a requirement that the recycled product meet contract specifications and its price is reasonably competitive (Gen. Mun. Law § 104-a). A recycled product will be deemed reasonably competitive if its cost does not exceed 10 percent of the cost of a comparable non-recycled product, or 15 percent of such cost when at least 50 percent of the secondary material used to make the product was generated from the waste stream in New York State (*Id.*).

However, districts may not give preference to local contractors or vendors who are not the lowest responsible bidder (see **28:11-15**).

28:8. Must school districts purchase and use environmentally sensitive (green) cleaning and maintenance products?

Yes. Districts must use green cleaning and maintenance products in any school building or facility used for instructional purposes, surrounding grounds, and other sites used for playgrounds and/or athletics or other instructional purposes (§ 409-i; see also **63:7-9**).

As required by law, green cleaning guidelines for schools and a list of green products are available from the state's Office of General Services (OGS). A copy of the guidelines and the list of products can be accessed electronically at: https://greencleaning.ny.gov/Entry.asp (see also NYS Education Department, *Environmentally Sensitive Cleaning and Maintenance Products Questions & Answers* (Mar. 2006), at: http://www.p12.nysed.gov/facplan/HealthSafety/EnvironSafeCleaning_EdLaw409i.pdf).

Under the OGS guidelines, green product requirements apply to, for example, general purpose, bathroom, carpet, glass, window and mirror cleaners, vacuum cleaners, hand soaps, custodial paper products, and floor finishers and strippers.

28:9. Are school districts subject to state and local sales taxes?

It depends. School districts are exempt from the state's sales tax in their role as purchasers, users or consumers, as well as when they sell services or property of a kind not ordinarily sold by private persons (Tax Law § 1116).

Similarly, hotel/motel rooms and meal charges for district officials and employees who travel on official district business and have their travel expenses paid or fully reimbursed by the district are exempt from both state and local sales taxes (*Id.*).

However, "[b]ecause it is not practical to present a sales tax exemption form for individual restaurant meals and it is not a common practice for restaurants to accept exemption forms, . . . [a] school district may consider sales tax as an actual and necessary expense incidental to the meal when incurred in connection with travel on official business" (Office of the State Comptroller, Division of Local Government and School Accountability, *Local Government Management Guide, Improving Effectiveness of Your Claims Auditing Process*, p. 7 fn. 5 (July 2013), at: http://www.osc.state.ny.us/localgov/pubs/lgmg/claimsauditing.pdf).

However, although school lunch sales to students are tax-exempt, lunch sales to adults are subject to sales tax (Tax Law § 1105(d)(ii)(B)).

28:10. Are school districts subject to federal excise taxes?

Not generally. School districts are generally exempt from federal excise taxes. School districts should so advise vendors of this and furnish a tax exemption certificate, which may be duplicated.

For more information, see individual sections of the Internal Revenue Code for exemptions regarding specific excise taxes.

Competitive Bidding and Best Value Competitive Offering

28:11. Are school district purchases subject to competitive bidding or competitive offerings?

Yes. School districts must advertise for sealed bids in the manner required by law, and award to the lowest responsible bidder that furnishes the required security, contracts for public works that exceed $35,000 and purchase contracts that exceed $20,000 (Gen. Mun. Law § 103(1); Educ. Law §§ 1619, 2513, 2556(10); *Appeal of World Network Int'l Servs., Inc.*, 38 Ed Dept Rep 800 (1999); see also Gen. Mun. Law § 101(1)).

Pursuant to the Iran Divestment Act of 2012, political subdivisions of the state, including school districts and boards of cooperative educational services, are precluded from considering any person or entity engaging in investment activities in the energy sector in Iran as a responsible bidder or offeror, as prescribed by law (Gen. Mun. Law § 103-g). The list of such persons and entities compiled by the NYS Office of General Services is available at: http://www.ogs.ny.gov/about/regs/docs/ListofEntities.pdf (State Fin. Law § 165-a(3)(b); Gen. Mun. Law § 103-g(3)). Every bid or proposal made must include an affirmation that such person or company is not on the list created by the Office of General Services (Gen. Mun. Law § 103-g(4)).

Additionally, when determining the lowest responsible bidder, a district should consider the bidder's skill, judgement and integrity and may disapprove the low bid where good reason exists for rejecting it (see *Matter of AAA Carting & Rubbish Removal v. Town of Southeast*, 17 N.Y.3d 136 (2011)). However, a district may not award a contract to a higher bidder because of a belief that the higher bidder is preferable and more responsible based on a subjective assessment of criteria not specified in the bid request. Such a practice circumvents the open bidding process (*Id.*; see also **28:13**).

Contracts for public works generally concern items or projects involving labor or both materials and labor such as construction. Purchase contracts pertain to items or groups of items of commodities, services or technology (Gen. Mun. Law § 103(1); Opn. St. Comp. 91-64). When determining whether a particular purchase contract exceeds the $20,000 threshold that triggers the need for competitive bidding, school districts must consider the reasonably expected aggregate amount of all purchases of the same commodities, services or technology to be made within the 12-month period starting on the date of purchase. Purchases cannot be artificially divided for the purpose of satisfying the $20,000 threshold (Gen. Mun. Law § 103(1)). It is not permissible to make changes to or renew contract purchases that would bring the reasonably expected aggregate amount of all purchases of the same commodities, services or technology from the same provider within the 12-month period starting on the date of the first purchase to an amount that exceeds the threshold amount (*Id.*).

Additional special rules apply to competitive bidding on construction projects (see Gen. Mun. Law § 101; see also **61:23-24**).

28:12. May school districts opt to use a competitive offering process in place of competitive bidding?

Yes, in some instances. School districts may adopt a resolution to authorize the award of purchase contracts exceeding $20,000, based on best value as opposed to the lowest responsible bidder (Gen. Mun. Law § 103(1)). This option, referred to as *competitive offering*, is also available for service work contracts but not for purchase contracts necessary for completion of a public works contract (*Id.*).

Best value optimizes quality, cost and efficiency among responsive and responsible offerers. Its use should reflect objective and quantifiable analysis whenever possible. It also may identify a quantitative factor for best value offerers that are small businesses or certified minority or women-owned business enterprises as defined in the Executive Law (State Fin. Law § 163(j); Exec. Law § 310(1), (7), (15), (20)).

28:13. What is involved in the competitive bidding and competitive offering process?

Generally, school boards must advertise for bids or offers in the district's official newspaper(s), if any, or otherwise in a newspaper designated for such purpose (Gen. Mun. Law § 103(2)). Districts must be careful not to include atypical or restrictive provisions in bid specifications which have an anticompetitive effect such as "employee protection provisions" that require a successful bidder to give hiring priority according to seniority to employees of private bus companies who lost their jobs as a result of the change in contractor (*Matter of L&M Bus Corp. v. N.Y. City Dep't of Educ,* 17 N.Y.3d 149 (2011)).

The advertisement for bids or offers must state the time when and the place where all bids/offers received will be opened and read and where the identity of all offerers will be publically disclosed. At least five days must elapse between the first publication of the advertisement and the date specified for the opening and reading of bids/offers. The board may designate any officer or employee to open and read the bids/offers at the time and place specified in the advertisement and who shall present to the board a record of the bids/offers at the next regular or special board meeting (Gen. Mun. Law § 103(2)).

Through June 1, 2018, school districts are authorized to receive bids in an electronic format provided the school board has authorized such submissions. Bid advertisements must designate how the electronic bid will be received, which must comply with provisions of the state technology law. Submission of bids in electronic format may not be required as the sole transmission method of bids, unless for technology contracts (Gen. Mun. Law § 103(1); see also Office of the State Comptroller, Division of Local Government and School Accountability, *Local Government Management Guide, Seeking Competition in Procurement* (July 2014), at: http://www.osc.state.ny.us/localgov/pubs/lgmg/seekingcompetition.pdf).

School districts must reject a bid that does not substantially conform to the advertised specifications. However, bids with minor deviations that do not afford the bidder an unfair advantage over others may be accepted (*Appeal of Eastman Kodak Co.*, 32 Ed Dept Rep 575 (1993)). In this regard, a bid specification may use a brand name as a standard or example. But the bid cannot discriminate in favor of the specific brand name if there is a product that is equal to or better than the brand name available at a lower price (*Appeal of American Quality Beverages, LLC*, 43 Ed Dept Rep 402 (2004)).

A district may reject the bid of a vendor of apparel or sports equipment that manufactures such items in a sweatshop (Gen. Mun. Law § 103(12); see **28:6**).

Special rules apply regarding bid specification for public works (Gen. Mun. Law § 101(1), (5)). Pre-qualified bidders may be used for public works subject to the conditions and procedures set forth in law (Gen. Mun. Law § 103(15)).

28:14. May school districts give preference to particular vendors during the competitive bidding process?

Not generally. Favoritism, the manipulation of bid specifications to assure the award of a contract to a specific bidder, or shutting out competitive bidding are not permissible, absent a clear showing it is both rational and essential to the public interest (*Appeal of American Quality Beverages, LLC*, 43 Ed Dept Rep 402 (2004)), or unless otherwise permitted by law as in the case of vendors of instructional materials in alternative formats, and certain vendors of recycled products (see **28:7**).

It is not permissible to provide for a bid preference to local contractors or vendors who are not the lowest responsible bidder just because they are local (Opn. St. Comp. 92-50).

28:15. What happens if there is a tie for lowest responsible bidder?

Where two or more responsible bidders furnishing the required security submit identical bids as to price, the district may award the contract to any of the bidders, or it may reject all the bids and readvertise for new bids (Gen. Mun. Law § 103(1)).

28:16. Do the competitive bidding requirements apply to the lease of personal property by a school district?

Yes. School district agreements for the lease of personal property are subject to the bidding requirements of the General Municipal Law applicable to purchase contracts (Educ. Law § 1725; see **28:11**).

28:17. Are there any exceptions to the competitive bidding requirements?

Yes. There are a number of instances when the competitive bidding requirements do not apply. These include, as permitted by law:

- When there is an unforeseen public emergency requiring immediate action that cannot await competitive bidding under the conditions set forth in law (Gen. Mun. Law § 103(4); *see Civil Service Employees Ass'n, Inc. v. O'Rourke*, 173 Misc.2d 460 (Sup. Ct. Westchester Cnty. 1997), *aff'd in part,* 240 A.D.2d 572 (2d Dep't), *lv. to appeal denied,* 90 N.Y.2d 808 (1997); Opn. St. Comp. 81-267; Opn. St. Comp. 81-224; Opn. St. Comp. 71-543).
- When there is only one possible supplier or source from which to procure goods or services, such as in the case of a public utility or patented item (*Harlem Gas v. Mayor*, 33 N.Y. 309 (1865); see also *Williams v. Bryant*, 53 A.D.2d 229 (4th Dep't 1976); Opn. St. Comp. 83-124). The mere likelihood that only one company will bid on a contract is not enough to justify the exception (Opn. St. Comp. 83-124).
- The purchase of surplus and secondhand supplies, material or equipment from the federal government, the state of New York, and others set forth in law (Gen. Mun. Law § 103(6)).
- The purchase of eggs, livestock, fish, fresh fruits and vegetables, juice, grains and dairy products other than milk from producers or growers or associations of producers or growers (Gen. Mun. Law § 103(9); 8 NYCRR § 114.3).
- The purchase of milk from certain licensed milk processors (Gen. Mun. Law § 103(10); 8 NYCRR § 114.4).
- Contracts for professional services that require special skill, training and expertise, use of professional judgment or discretion, and/or a high degree of creativity in the performance of the contract, such as legal services, architectural services, medical services, property appraisals or insurance (*Trane Co. v. Broome Cnty.*, 76 A.D.2d 1015 (3d Dep't 1980); *Appeal of Leman & Sluys*, 39 Ed Dept Rep 407 (1999); *Appeal of Lombardo*, 38 Ed Dept Rep 730 (1999); Opn. St. Comp. 92-33; see also Office of the State Comptroller, Division of Local Government and School Accountability, *Local Government Management Guide, Seeking Competition in Procurement* (July 2014), at: http://www.osc.state.ny.us/localgov/pubs/lgmg/seekingcompetition.pdf).
- A competitive request for proposals process must be used by a school district when contracting for annual audit services, but such engagement is limited to no longer than five consecutive years (§ 2116-a(3)(b)).
- The extension for periods of up to five years of contracts for cafeteria and restaurant services, student transportation, school bus maintenance, and mobile instructional units subject to both certain limitations on annual cost increases and the approval of the commissioner of education (§ 305(14); 8 NYCRRR §§ 114.2(c), (d)(1), (g), 156.5(b); NYS Education Department, *Instructions for Transportation Contract Extension* (form CE) (updated June 2009), at http://www.p12.nysed.gov/schoolbus/regulations/html/section156.5_annual_extensions_of_transportation_contracts.html; see also *A.C. Transp., Inc. v. Bd. of Educ. of the City of N.Y.*, 253 A.D.2d 330 (1st Dep't), *lv. to appeal denied*, 93 N.Y.2d 808 (1999)).

At a school board's discretion, contracts for mobile instructional units and student transportation involving an annual expenditure of more than $20,000 may be awarded through either competitive bidding or an evaluation of proposals process, subject to approval by the commissioner (§ 305(14)(a), (e); 8 NYCRR §§ 155.21, 156.12; see **59:52-59**).

28:18. Are there any procedures school districts must follow when competitive bidding is not required?

Yes. School districts purchasing goods or services that are not subject to competitive bidding must take measures to ensure the "prudent and economical use of public moneys" (Gen. Mun. Law § 104-b(1)). Toward this objective, school boards must adopt internal policies and procedures that provide for the use of alternative proposals or quotations secured by written requests for proposals (RFPs), written or verbal quotations, or other appropriate methods of procurement, except as set forth in law (Gen. Mun. Law §§ 104-b(1), (2)(b); see also Office of the State Comptroller, Division of Local Government and School Accountability, *Local Government Management Guide, Seeking Competition in Procurement* (July 2014), at: http://www.osc.state.ny.us/localgov/pubs/lgmg/seekingcompetition.pdf). Such policies must identify the individual(s) responsible for purchasing and their respective titles, with said information updated biennially (Gen. Mun. Law § 104-b(2)(f)).

The policy should also address whether the school district may make purchases for amounts below the monetary thresholds laid out in General Municipal Law § 103 by "piggybacking" on contracts let by governmental entities identified in General Municipal Law § 103(16) (see Office of the State Comptroller, *New "Piggybacking" Law- Exception to Competitive Bidding* (July 2016), at: http://osc.state.ny.us/localgov/pubs/piggybackinglaw.pdf; see also **28:2**).

An RFP process may be properly used when the professional services exception applies (*Appeal of Leman & Sluys*, 39 Ed Dept Rep 407 (1999); see **28:17**).

Districts must evaluate, and school boards review, RFP responses received prior to awarding a contract, to ensure that any proposal accepted would be "in the best interest of the taxpayers" (see *Appeal of Leman & Sluys*). The RFP response evaluation and review process should include sufficient inquiry into whether the party ultimately awarded the contract is capable of performing the contract, and a review of contract documents by the school attorney prior to execution of the contract (*Id.*).

28:19. How do districts determine whether a particular purchase is subject to competitive bidding or an alternative procurement process?

School district procurement policies must prescribe the process for determining whether a particular purchase is subject to competitive bidding and the basis for concluding it is not (Gen. Mun. Law §§ 104-b(1), (2)(a); see also Appendix A- Categories of Procurement, Office of the State Comptroller, Division of Local Government and School Accountability, *Local Government Management Guide, Seeking Competition in Procurement* (July 2014), at: http://www.osc.state.ny.us/localgov/pubs/lgmg/seekingcompetition.pdf). Such policies and procedures must be developed in consultation with district officers involved in the procurement process, and reviewed at least annually (Gen. Mun. Law § 104-b(3), (4)).

29. School Building Principals[1]

29:1. Must there be a principal in each school?

Yes. The commissioner's regulations require that a full-time principal be employed and assigned to each school. The principal must hold appropriate certification (8 NYCRR § 100.2(a)). Thus, a teacher who does not have proper certification to serve as principal may not be appointed as "teacher in charge" upon the resignation of a building principal until a successor can be appointed (*Appeal of Giardina*, 43 Ed Dept Rep 172 (2003)).

If there are circumstances that do not justify the assignment of a principal to a particular school, or if another mode of building administration would be more effective, the commissioner of education may approve an alternative mode upon request for such a variance (8 NYCRR § 100.2(a); *Appeal of Henderson*, 43 Ed Dept Rep 43 (2003); *Appeal of Branch & McElfresh*, 41 Ed Dept Rep 334 (2002), *aff'd, Olean City Sch. Dist. v. N.Y. State Educ. Dep't*, 2 A.D.3d 1111 (3d Dep't 2003)). The commissioner has determined that a district may assign one principal to a school comprised of more than one building on the same site where the buildings are in close proximity to each other (*Matter of Middle Island Principals' Ass'n*, 19 Ed Dept Rep 507 (1980)). Two buildings that house different grades and are located miles apart do not constitute one unit (see *Appeal of Henderson*).

29:2. May a superintendent of schools serve simultaneously as a school principal?

No. Commissioner's regulations require that school boards employ and assign a full-time principal to each school. Any alternative form of school building administration must be approved by the commissioner of education (8 NYCRR § 100.2(a)). According to the commissioner, an individual may not serve as superintendent and a full-time principal, not even on a temporary basis until a full-time principal can be appointed (*Appeal of Giardina*, 43 Ed Dept Rep 172 (2003)).

29:3. May a school board transfer a principal without the recommendation of the superintendent of schools?

Yes. School boards have "the superintendence, management and control of the educational affairs of the school district" and "all the powers reasonably necessary to. . . discharge duties imposed expressly or by implication" by law. They also have an obligation to employ a full-time principal at each school. In contrast, nothing in the Education Law or commissioner's regulations requires the recommendation of a superintendent of schools to effectuate a transfer (*Appeal of Lander*, 42 Ed Dept Rep 201 (2002)).

29:4. Are school districts required to have assistant principals in school buildings?

No. There is no requirement that a school district employ assistant principals (*Matter of Ryan*, 17 Ed Dept Rep 338 (1978), *aff'd*, 71 A.D.2d 719 (3d Dep't 1979)).

[1] See **chapter 9** for information related to certification requirements for school building principals, their appointment and tenure areas, discipline and termination; **chapter 37** regarding evaluations of their performance; and **chapter 38** in relation to the discipline and termination of tenured school building principals.

29:5. Who establishes a salary schedule for the school principal?

There is no statutory or regulatory requirement that a school board adopt a salary schedule for school principals. If a school district's principals are represented by a recognized or certified union, the district must negotiate with the union over salaries, hours, and other terms and conditions of employment (Civ. Serv. Law § 204(2), (3); see **47:10-11**), and the salary schedules that result from negotiations would be embodied in a collective bargaining agreement. Otherwise, salary schedules for principals may be found in school board resolutions and/or within an individual employment contract with the principal (see **chapter 45**).

29:6. Can a school board legally reduce a principal's salary?

A school board must adhere to all the terms and conditions of employment, including salary, embodied in a collectively negotiated agreement or a principal's contract (Civ. Serv. Law § 209-a(1)(d), (e); see **9:4**).

Whether or not a contract exists, a board cannot reduce a tenured principal's salary so much that it amounts to disciplinary action, because section 3020-a of the Education Law provides the exclusive procedure for disciplinary action against tenured school district employees (*Matter of Trono*, 18 Ed Dept Rep 344 (1978); see also *Appeal of Soriano*, 55 Ed Dept Rep, Dec. No. 16,849 (2015)).

29:7. Can a school board, acting on its own, designate its school principals as "managerial" employees and thereby exclude them from membership in a negotiating unit?

No. This type of designation may be obtained only upon application to the Public Employment Relations Board (PERB) (4 NYCRR § 201.10).

Principals of schools or other administrative personnel who do not formulate district-wide policy, or who may not be reasonably required to assist directly in the preparation for and conduct of collective bargaining or who do not have a major role in contract or personnel administration, may not be so designated (Civ. Serv. Law § 201(7)(a); see **46:28-30** for further information about designating managerial personnel). While principals are not generally designated as "managerial" (see *Warsaw CSD*, 27 PERB ¶ 4022 (1994)), principals in small school districts might be because they are more likely to have a significant role in formulating policy and personnel administration (see *McGraw CSD*, 21 PERB ¶ 3001 (1988)).

29:8. Do any special rules apply to the evaluation of a school building principal's performance?

Yes. Principal evaluation are conducted pursuant to an annual professional performance review (APPR) plan developed and implemented pursuant to the requirements of Education Law § 3012-d, unless a district is still implementing an APPR plan developed under Education Law § 3012-c to the extent permitted by law.

Building principal APPRs must rate a principal's effectiveness using the following categories: highly effective, effective, developing or ineffective (§ 3012-d(3); 8 NYCRR § 30-3.5). For a more detailed discussion of the extensive requirements applicable to principal evaluations see **chapter 37**.

30. Teachers – Employment Qualifications and Compensation

Employment Qualifications – In General

30:1. What is the legal definition of a teacher?

No uniform definition of the term *teacher* exists. *Teacher* is most commonly understood to be any full-time member of the teaching staff of a school district. However, administrative and supervisory staff members are included within the definition in some provisions of the Education Law (see § 3101). Because the term *teacher* is defined differently within the Education Law, reference to the particular law under consideration is recommended.

30:2. What makes an individual qualified to teach in New York State?

An individual is qualified to teach in a New York State public school if he or she:

- Is a citizen of the United States,
- Is at least 18 years of age, and
- Possesses a New York State teacher's certificate (§ 3001; see **30:8**, **chapter 31**).

In addition, a teacher must subscribe to an oath to support the federal and state constitutions (§ 3002) and, applicants for certification and prospective employees of a school district or a board of cooperative educational services, including teachers, must be fingerprinted, as well (see **chapter 41**).

The U.S. Supreme Court has found the citizenship requirement to be constitutional because of the important civic function of public school teachers in our democratic government (*Ambach v. Norwick*, 441 U.S. 68 (1979)).

Furthermore, although certification is a central qualification, school boards have the discretion to prescribe additional qualifications, and this discretion may not be bargained away (*Bd. of Educ. of Valhalla UFSD v. Valhalla Teachers Ass'n*, 112 A.D.3d 620 (2d Dep't 2013)). Thus, a collective bargaining agreement may not mandate the automatic appointment of certified teachers without consideration of any additional qualifications a school board may prescribe (*Id.*; see also **34:33**).

30:3. Can a teacher's age be used as a qualification for employment and/or certification?

No, except to the extent that teachers in the public schools of New York State must be at least 18 years of age (§ 3001; see **30:2**). Otherwise, state law bars age-based employment and licensing qualifications for persons 18 years old or older (Exec. Law §§ 291, 296).

Moreover, age-related discrimination in hiring, promotion, compensation, workplace reduction, and other conditions of employment for employees 40 years old or older is prohibited by the federal Age Discrimination in Employment Act (ADEA) (29 USC § 621 *et seq.*; *Gross v. F.L.B. Fin. Servs., Inc.*, 557 U.S. 167 (2009); *Meacham v. Knolls Atomic Power Lab.*, 554 U.S. 84 (2008); *Ximines v. Wingate H.S. & N.Y.C. Dep't of Educ.*, 516 F.3d 156 (2d Cir. 2008); *Stone v. Bd. of Educ. of Saranac CSD*, 153 Fed. Appx. 44 (2d Cir. 2005)). Thus, districts may not specify an age requirement as a qualification for any teaching position.

To prevail on a claim of age discrimination brought under the ADEA, an employee or applicant must show his or her age was the "but for" cause of the employer's adverse action against him or her.

The employer does not have to show it would have taken the action regardless of age, even when there is some evidence that age was one motivating factor in the decision (*Gross v. F.L.B. Fin. Servs., Inc.*; see also *Bohnet v. Valley Stream UFSD 13*, 594 Fed. Appx. 53 (2d Cir. 2015)).

30:4. Are there any federal teacher qualification requirements?

No. The Elementary and Secondary Education Act, as reauthorized by the Every Student Succeeds Act of 2015 (ESSA), expressly prohibits the Secretary of Education or any other officer or employee of the Federal Government to mandate, direct, or control any teacher professional standards, certification or licensing (§§ 2102(e)(3); 2302(a)(4)). However, it requires that state educational agencies and school districts ensure all teachers working in a program supported by federal Title I Part A funds meet applicable State certification and licensure requirements, including any requirements for certification obtained through alternative routes to certification (§§ 1111(g)(2)(J), 1112(c)(6)).

30:5. Must districts notify parents of the qualifications of their child's teacher?

Yes. At the beginning of each school year, school districts receiving federal Title I, Part A funds must notify the parents of each student attending any school receiving such funds that the parents may request, and the district will provide in a timely manner, information regarding the professional qualifications of the student's classroom teachers. This information must include, at a minimum, whether:

- The teacher has met State qualification and licensing criteria for the grade levels and subject areas in which the teacher provides instruction.
- The teacher is teaching under an emergency or provisional status.
- The teacher is teaching in the field of discipline of his/her certification.
- The child is provided services by paraprofessionals and, if so, their qualifications (§ 1112(e)(1)(A)).

In addition, a school that receives Title I, Part A funds must provide to parents timely notice that their child has been assigned or has been taught for four or more consecutive weeks by a teacher who does not meet applicable State certification or licensure requirements at the grade level and subject area in which the teacher has been assigned (§ 1112(e)(1)(B)(ii); see **30:4**).

30:6. May a school district employ a teacher who is not legally qualified?

Generally, no. A district may not employ an unqualified teacher, nor may it pay the salary of an unqualified teacher (§§ 3001(2), 3009(1), 3010; see *In re N.Y. State Office of Children & Family Servs. (Lanterman)*, 62 A.D.3d 1109 (3d Dep't 2009), *aff'd*, 14 N.Y.3d 275 (2010); *Winter v. Bd. of Educ. for Rhinebeck CSD*, 79 N.Y.2d 1, *reconsideration denied*, 79 N.Y.2d 978 (1992); *Smith v. Bd. of Educ.*, 65 N.Y.2d 797 (1985); *Meliti v. Nyquist*, 41 N.Y.2d 183 (1976); *Sullivan v. Windham-Ashland-Jewett CSD*, 212 A.D.2d 63 (3d Dep't 1995), *appeal denied*, 89 N.Y.2d 814 (1997); see also *Koutros v. Dep't of Educ. of the City of N.Y.*, 129 A.D.3d 434 (1st Dep't 2015)).

Neither may a school district continue the employment of a teacher who fails to obtain permanent certification within the statutorily prescribed time limits (*In re N.Y. State Office of Children & Family Servs. (Lanterman)*; see **31:12**).

Nonetheless, a district may employ teachers whose certification expired while on active military duty as provided in law and commissioner's regulations. The license, certification, or registration of any professional that expires while that person is serving on active military duty is automatically extended until 12 months after the date that person is released from active duty. In addition, the commissioner of education may extend the expired certificates of individuals on active duty upon application by the certificate holder, for the time of the active service (Mil. Law § 308-b; 8 NYCRR § 80-1.6(b); see **31:17**).

In addition, teachers with an expired initial or transitional certificate who have failed to obtain professional certification can remain qualified to teach if they obtain an extension of their expired certificate from the commissioner (see **31:17**).

Any school board member "who applies, or directs, or consents to the application of, any district money to the payment of an unqualified teacher's salary" commits a misdemeanor (§ 3010). However, the commissioner may, in his or her discretion, "excuse the default" of a school board that employed and paid an unqualified teacher, and may legalize the past employment and authorize the payment of that teacher's salary (§ 3604(6)).

30:7. May a school district employ otherwise qualified teachers to teach outside of their area of certification?

Only as an *incidental teacher*. A certified teacher may instruct five classroom hours of teaching per week in an area for which that teacher is uncertified, pursuant to the commissioner's regulations on incidental teaching, provided that, despite extensive and documented recruitment efforts, there are no certified or qualified individuals available for the position and provided approval of the commissioner of education is obtained (see 8 NYCRR § 80-5.3; *Appeal of Krause*, 46 Ed Dept Rep 304 (2007); see **31:8**).

30:8. Under what circumstances may a school district employ a teacher who is not a United States citizen?

A person who is not a United States citizen is qualified to teach in New York if he or she is at least 18 years of age, possesses a New York State teacher's certificate, and has petitioned to become a U.S. citizen and will become a citizen of this country within the time prescribed by law (§ 3001(3)).

In addition, a person who is not a citizen of the United States may qualify to teach in the public schools pursuant to specific statutory and regulatory provisions which permit teachers from foreign countries to teach in New York State for up to two years as part of a teacher exchange program with the approval of the commissioner of education (§ 3005; 8 NYCRR § 80-1.3(b); see also § 3001).

Effective June 1, 2016, no otherwise qualified applicant can be denied a certificate or registration by reason of his or her citizenship or immigration status, unless the applicant is ineligible for a professional license under federal law (8 NYCRR § 80-1.3(a); see 8 USC § 1621). If an otherwise qualified individual is not unlawfully present in the United States, the individual cannot be precluded from obtaining a professional license under the regulations of the commissioner (*Id.*).

30:9. May a school district employ a relative of one of its school board members as a teacher?

Yes. A person related by blood or marriage to a school board member may be employed as a teacher by the district on the consent of a two-thirds majority of the board. In common school districts, the employment of relatives of trustees as teachers must be approved by two-thirds of the voters of the district who are present and voting on the issue at an annual or special district meeting (§ 3016(1)). The board member related to the applicant may participate in the vote (§ 3016(2); see also Opn St. Comp. 80-34; see also *Talley v. Brentwood UFSD*, 2009 U.S. Dist. LEXIS 53537 (E.D.N.Y. June 24, 2009) and related case at 728 F.Supp.2d 226 (E.D.N.Y. 2010)).

A two-thirds vote also may be required to grant tenure to that same teacher (Opn St. Comp. 80-34; see also *Application of Gmelch*, 32 Ed Dept Rep 167 (1992)), but not where a preferred eligible list (see **36:14-26**) mandates reappointment of a teacher related to a board member (*Application of Gmelch*).

In New York City, until June 30, 2017, city board members and other officers and employees under the jurisdiction of the citywide Panel for Educational Policy and chancellor must notify the chancellor in writing every year about the employment of "related" persons, as described in law, by the city board or any community district education council (§ 2590-h(39)).

There are no restrictions on the employment of relatives in non-teaching positions. For information concerning any potential conflict of interest resulting from the employment of board member relatives, see **6:4** and General Municipal Law sections 801 and 800(3)(a).

30:10. May a school district refuse to employ a qualified teacher on the basis of religion, race, sex, or other protected attributes?

No. State and federal laws prohibit discrimination against applicants or current employees on the basis of race, color, national origin, sex, sexual orientation, religion, creed, marital status, disability and other characteristics.

School districts may not disqualify a candidate for a teaching position based on any of these protected criteria (42 USC § 2000e *et seq.* (Title VII of the Civil Rights Act of 1964); 20 USC § 1681 *et seq.* (Title IX of the Education Amendments of 1972); N.Y. Exec. Law § 290 *et seq.* (Human Rights Law); Civ. Rights Law § 40 *et seq.*; see **30:3** regarding age discrimination and **30:11-12** regarding discrimination on the basis of disability; see also **chapter 68** for further discussion on employment discrimination).

For example, Title VII prohibits employment discrimination on the basis of pregnancy and protects the right to reinstatement of women on leave for reasons related to pregnancy (42 USC § 2000e(k)). State law prohibits inquiries regarding the religion or religious affiliation of a candidate for employment (Civ. Rights Law § 40-a).

Additional guidance and information on federal anti-discrimination laws and their impact on the rights and responsibilities of employers is available from the U.S. Equal Employment Opportunity Commission at: www.eeoc.gov/laws/guidance/subject.cfm. See also brochures and basic guides from the NYS Division of Human Rights at: www.dhr.ny.gov/brochures.

30:11. May a school district refuse to employ an otherwise qualified teacher who has a disability?

No. Federal and state laws prohibit discrimination against applicants or current employees on the basis of a disability (29 USC § 794 *et seq.* (Section 504 of the Rehabilitation Act of 1973); 42 USC § 12101 *et seq.* (Americans with Disabilities Act); Exec. Law § 290 *et seq.* (Human Rights Law); Civ. Rights Law § 40 *et seq.*; see **chapter 68**).

At the federal level, Section 504 of the Rehabilitation Act of 1973 (29 USC § 794 *et seq.*) prohibits discrimination based on an individual's disability by all recipients of federal financial assistance. The Americans with Disabilities Act of 1990 (ADA) (42 USC § 12101 *et seq.*) prohibits discrimination against individuals with disabilities in both private and governmental employment, public services, public accommodations, and telecommunications.

The ADA requires that employers with 15 or more employees provide reasonable accommodations to qualified individuals with a disability who can perform the essential functions of a position with or without reasonable accommodation. See **68:2** for further discussion of the ADA. However, it has been deemed to not preclude an employer from, for example:

- Refusing to hire an individual whose performance on the job would endanger his or her own health or safety (*Chevron USA Inc. v. Echazabal,* 536 U.S. 73 (2002); see also 29 C.F.R. § 1630.15(b)(2)).
- Terminating, for example, a dyslexic teacher whose disability impedes his or her ability to take or pass a state-required teacher certification exam because the exam is a valid job-related requirement (*Falchenberg v. N.Y. City Dep't of Educ.*, 375 F.Supp.2d 344 (S.D.N.Y. 2005)).

- Terminating a disabled probationary teacher unable to regularly show up for work because the excessive absences disrupt the education of his or her students (*Ramirez v. N.Y. City Bd. of Educ.*, 481 F.Supp.2d 209 (E.D.N.Y. 2007)).

At the state level, various laws also provide protections to disabled teachers in the context of employment (see, e.g., § 3004; Civ. Rights Law § 40-c(2); Exec. Law § 296; see also *Peters v. Baldwin UFSD*, 320 F.3d 164 (2d Cir. 2003); *Antonsen v. Ward*, 77 N.Y.2d 506 (1991); *In re State Div. of Human Rights*, 70 N.Y.2d 100 (1987)).

30:12. Must a school district provide a reasonable accommodation to an otherwise qualified disabled employee?

Yes, unless the school district can demonstrate that the accommodation would impose an undue hardship on the operation of its program (29 USC § 794; 42 USC § 12112(b)(5)(A); 34 CFR § 104.12(a); 45 CFR § 84.12(a); *Borkowski v. Valley CSD*, 63 F.3d 131 (2d Cir. 1995); see also *Mitchell v. Washingtonville CSD*, 190 F.3d 1 (2d Cir. 1999); *Young v. Central Square CSD,* 213 F.Supp.2d 202 (N.D.N.Y. 2002)). While the accommodation must be effective, the employer is not required to provide a perfect accommodation or the accommodation strongly preferred by the employee (*Noll v. Int'l Business Machines Corp*., 787 F.3d 89 (2d Cir. 2015); see also **68:2**).

Reasonable accommodations may include making facilities readily accessible to and usable by disabled persons, job restructuring, part-time or modified work schedules, acquisition or modification of equipment or devices, the provision of readers or interpreters, and other similar actions (42 USC § 12111(9); 34 CFR § 104.12(b); 45 CFR § 84.12(b)).

A variety of factors can affect an undue hardship determination. Some include the overall size of a district's program with respect to the number of employees, the number and type of facilities, the size of the district's budget, and the nature and cost of the accommodation needed (42 USC § 12111(10); 34 CFR § 104.12(c); 45 CFR § 84.12(c); *see Dean v. Univ. at Buffalo Sch. of Medicine,* 804 F.3d 178 (2d Cir. 2015)*; Powell v. Nat'l Bd. of Med. Exam'rs*, 364 F.3d 79 (2d Cir. 2004)).

According to one federal district court in New York, a section 3020-a hearing officer's factual determination that a teacher cannot perform the essential functions of her job with reasonable accommodation precludes a subsequent claim in federal court that the teacher's termination violated the Americans with Disabilities Act's reasonable accommodation provisions (*Page v. Liberty CSD*, 679 F.Supp.2d 448 (S.D.N.Y. 2010)).

Employment Qualifications – Physical and Mental Fitness

30:13. May a school district require that an applicant for a teaching position submit to a medical examination?

No. Such a requirement would constitute a violation of the Americans with Disabilities Act (42 USC § 12112(d)(2)) and Section 504 of the Rehabilitation Act of 1976 (29 USC § 794 *et seq*.).

However, a district may condition an "offer of employment" on a physical and/or psychological examination to ensure that a candidate has the physical and mental capacity to perform the duties of that position. This examination, if required, must be applied equally to all entering employees (42 USC § 12112(d)(3); 28 CFR §§ 35.140, 41.55, 42.513; 29 CFR §§ 1630.13, 1630.14; 34 CFR § 104.14).

In addition, teachers may be required to submit to a medical examination after they have begun working for a district, as permitted by applicable law (see **30:14-18**).

30:14. May school districts require a teacher to submit to a medical examination after the teacher has begun working for the district?

Yes, under certain circumstances. To safeguard the health of children attending the public schools, the school board, the BOCES board or, in New York City community school districts the superintendent, can require any employee to submit to a medical examination, including a psychiatric examination, to determine that person's physical or mental capacity to perform his or her duties (§§ 913, 2568; 42 USC § 12112(d)(4)(A); see also 8 NYCRR § 136.3(i); *Seraydar v. Three Village CSD,* 90 A.D.3d 936 (2d Dep't 2011); *Matter of Dobosen v. Bd. of Educ. of the City Sch. Dist. of the City of N.Y.*, 192 A.D.2d 399 (1st Dep't 1993); *Appeal of D.R.*, 48 Ed Dept Rep 358 (2009); but compare *Patchogue-Medford Congress of Teachers v. Bd. of Educ. of Patchogue-Medford UFSD*, 70 N.Y.2d 57 (1987)).

Moreover, a teacher may be required to submit to additional examinations if necessary to permit a doctor to render a final determination regarding that individual's fitness to teach (*Matter of Almeter*, 30 Ed Dept Rep 230 (1991)).

30:15. Who conducts a school district requested medical examination?

The school district may direct that the examination be conducted by its own physician or by a physician chosen by the employee (*Matter of Hirsch*, 20 Ed Dept Rep 211 (1980), *application to reopen denied,* 20 Ed Dept Rep 389 (1981); see related case *In re Claim of Hirsch,* 126 A.D.2d 782 (3d Dep't 1987); *Matter of Gargiul*, 15 Ed Dept Rep 360, *application to reopen denied*, 15 Ed Dept Rep 520, *aff'd*, 54 A.D.2d 1085 (4th Dep't 1976), *appeal denied*, 41 N.Y.2d 802 (1977), and related case 69 A.D.2d 986 (4th Dep't), *appeal denied*, 48 N.Y.2d 606 (1979); see also *Garguil v. Tompkins*, 704 F.2d 661 (2d Cir. 1983), and 790 F.2d 265 (2d Cir. 1986)).

30:16. Is a teacher entitled to be accompanied during a school-ordered medical examination?

Yes. The teacher is entitled to be accompanied by a physician or other person of his or her choice, including a union representative. Accordingly, the teacher must be given sufficient notice to arrange for the presence of his or her physician (§§ 913, 2568; *Schiffer v. Bd. of Educ., Garrison UFSD*, 112 A.D.2d 372 (2d Dep't), *appeal dismissed*, 66 N.Y.2d 915 (1985)).

In addition, a teacher may not be adjudged insubordinate for refusing to submit to a medical examination without a companion of his or her choice, absent a reason that warrants the denial of that right (see *Schiffer v. Bd. of Educ., Garrison UFSD*). Also, a violation of teacher's right to be accompanied during such examination may not require suppression of the results at a subsequent proceeding or annulment of a school board's determination heard on the proceeding (*Gardner v. Niskayuna CSD,* 42 A.D.3d 633 (3d Dep't), *lv. to appeal denied*, 9 N.Y.3d 813 (2007); see also *Schiffer v. Bd. of Educ., Garrison UFSD*). For instance, in *Gardner,* evidence was presented indicating that the presence of the petitioner's spouse would have compromised or invalidated the results of the evaluation.

30:17. What happens with the results of a teacher's school-ordered medical examination?

The determination based on the examination as to the physical or mental capacity of the teacher to perform his or her duties must be reported to the school board, the BOCES board (§ 913), or, in New York City community school districts, to the superintendent of schools (§ 2568). The determination may then be used for the performance evaluation of the employee, or for disability retirement.

Nonetheless, a school board is not entitled to independently review the teacher's medical records to "verify" a physician's determination that a teacher suffers no condition that prevents him or her from working (*O'Connor v. Pierson*, 426 F.3d 187 (2d Cir. 2005); see also related case at 568 F.3d 64 (2d Cir. 2009)).

Furthermore, the teacher has the right to determine the form or manner of treatment of any remedial care to be applied, so long as it conforms with Article 131 of the Education Law (§§ 910, 6520 *et seq.*).

30:18. What happens if a teacher refuses to submit to a school-ordered examination?

A teacher's refusal to comply with an examination ordered by the school board may constitute insubordination (but see **30:16**), and, if the teacher is tenured, may warrant the filing of formal disciplinary charges pursuant to section 3020-a (*McNamara v. Comm'r of Educ.*, 80 A.D.2d 660 (3d Dep't 1981), *appeal dismissed*, 64 N.Y.2d 1110 (1985); but see **30:16**).

In addition, "a board may suspend a teacher's pay if the teacher fails to comply with the school board's reasonable directive that he or she be examined" (*Appeal of El-Araby*, 28 Ed Dept Rep 524 (1989); see also *Appeal of Grossberg*, 33 Ed Dept Rep 64 (1993); *Appeal of McCall*, 33 Ed Dept Rep 148 (1993), and connected cases at 34 Ed Dept Rep 29 (1994); 34 Ed Dept Rep 484 (1995); 35 Ed Dept Rep 38, 81 (1995)). Such a teacher is not deemed suspended from employment but rather, precluded from teaching based upon his or her "own failure to comply with the board's reasonable directives" (*Kurzius v. Bd. of Educ.*, 81 A.D.2d 827 (2d Dep't), *appeal withdrawn*, 54 N.Y.2d 1027 (1981); *Grassel v. Bd. of Educ. of the City of N.Y.*, 301 A.D.2d 498 (2d Dep't 2003)).

Similarly, a school district may refuse to allow a teacher to return to work after an extended absence until the teacher provides medical records and submits to an examination by the board's appointed physician. Moreover, such a refusal would not violate a tenured teacher's due process rights. The refusal to allow the teacher to return to work under such circumstances is not considered a suspension or termination (*Strong v. Bd. of Educ. of Uniondale UFSD*, 902 F.2d 208 (2d Cir.), *cert. denied,* 498 U.S. 897 (1990)). In contrast, a school board was found to have violated a superintendent's contractual "just cause" due process rights when it terminated the superintendent based on a conclusion that she had abandoned her position by remaining on medical leave without providing adequate medical documentation (*Appeal of Cannie*, 43 Ed Dept Rep 474; *petition to review dismissed sub nom. Bd. of Educ., Uniondale UFSD v. Mills*, (Sup. Ct. Albany Cnty.), Kavanagh, J., (Dec. 7, 2004)).

Compensation

30:19. Are teachers guaranteed minimum salaries under state law?

No. There are no state-mandated minimum salaries for teachers. Often these are established locally by the school board after collective bargaining with the teachers' union.

However, the Education Law imposes other requirements related to the payment of teachers' salaries. For example, except as otherwise provided by law, a school district must pay extra salary to teachers who work more than the regular 10-month school year (§ 3101(3)). For each summer month a teacher works, the school district must pay that teacher at least an additional 1/10th of his or her annual salary (§ 3101(3); *Matter of Walsh*, 21 Ed Dept Rep 467 (1982)). If a teacher works additional days instead of a whole month, the extra salary is one 1/200th of the annual salary for each day (§ 3101(3)).

30:20. Are substitute teachers entitled to a minimum salary?

No. There is no state-mandated minimum salary for substitutes. Each school district establishes the salary for its own substitutes. However, if a district has given substitutes reasonable assurance of continued employment, the substitutes may be represented by a recognized or certified union that will negotiate on their behalf over terms and conditions of employment, including compensation (Civ. Serv. Law § 201(7)(d)). The compensation of substitutes represented by a union is a mandatory subject of bargaining with the district (see **46:13**).

Generally, a long-term substitute assigned to cover for a teacher who is on an extended leave for a definite period of time are placed in the regular teachers' bargaining unit (*Unatego CSD*, 15 PERB ¶ 3097 (1982); *Connetquot CSD,* 34 PERB ¶ 4001 (2001)). Itinerant substitutes who teach on an ad hoc basis generally are placed in their own bargaining unit (*Bethpage UFSD*, 15 PERB ¶ 4040, *aff'd*, 15 PERB ¶ 3094 (1982)).

30:21. What types of salary issues must be negotiated with a teachers' union?

The Taylor Law requires school districts to negotiate with recognized or certified employee organizations over salaries, wages, hours, and other terms and conditions of employment (Civ. Serv. Law §§ 201(4), 204(2), (3); see **chapter 46**). Salary related issues include increases (*Huntington UFSD, No.3,* 16 PERB ¶ 3061 (1983)) and/or decreases in salaries (*Cnty. of Monroe*, 10 PERB ¶ 3104 (1977)).

Additional salary issues that must be negotiated include longevity pay (*Triborough Bridge & Tunnel Auth.*, 27 PERB ¶ 3076 (1994)); merit pay (*Cnty. of Ulster*, 14 PERB ¶ 3008 (1981)); overtime pay (*Town of Henrietta*, 19 PERB ¶ 4565, *aff'd*, 19 PERB ¶ 3067 (1986)); pay for summer work (*Saugerties CSD*, 10 PERB ¶ 4529 (1977)); and premium pay for extra work, such as teaching large classes (*West Irondequoit Teachers Ass'n v. Helsby*, 35 N.Y.2d 46 (1974)).

Determining salaries for newly created positions that have not been filled is not a mandatory subject of bargaining and thus need not be bargained (*Churchville-Chili CSD*, 17 PERB ¶ 3055 (1984)). However, once the new positions are filled, the salaries must be negotiated upon the union's demand (*N.Y. City Sch. Dist.*, 22 PERB ¶ 3011 (1989)).

30:22. Must a school board recognize teaching experience outside the school district when determining a new teacher's placement on a salary schedule or longevity increments under a collective bargaining agreement?

A school board may choose to recognize prior teaching experience outside the district, but it is not legally required to do so (§ 3101(4)). However, the placement of new teachers on the salary schedule based on prior experience is a mandatory subject of bargaining (*Somers CSD*, 9 PERB ¶ 3014 (1976); *Bellmore UFSD*, 34 PERB ¶ 3009 (2001)).

30:23. May a school district make salary adjustments when a teacher fails to provide services under a contract?

Yes. Such salary adjustments are calculated based on section 3101(3) of the Education Law. For teachers who fail to render all required services during the school year, that law defines salary as being at least 1/10th of the annual salary for each full month of service and a daily rate of 1/200th of the salary (*Matter of Sarmiento*, 18 Ed Dept Rep 108 (1978)).

The calculation of salary adjustments under this statutory formula poses a problem of inequity when the number of workdays in one month does not equal 20 days. Therefore, the commissioner of education has adopted the "Huntington" formula (*Matter of Swaim*, 9 Ed Dept Rep 23 (1969)), which directs that salary adjustments for a teacher who has failed to serve at some time during the school year be calculated depending on whether a teacher misses less than or more than half of the working days of the month (*Bd. of Educ.of Clarkstown CSD v. Ambach*, 97 A.D.2d 188 (3d Dep't 1983), *aff'd*, 63 N.Y.2d 780 (1984); *Appeal of Zaccaro,* 51 Ed Dept Rep, Dec. No. 16,336, *vacated and remanded sub nom. Garden City UFSD, v. King*, (Sup. Ct. Albany Cnty., *underlying appeal withdrawn* Oct. 31, 2012)).

If a teacher works for more than half of the working days of the month, the district may deduct 1/200th of his or her annual salary for each day of unauthorized absence. If a teacher works for half of the working days of the month or less, the district need only pay the teacher 1/200th of the annual salary for each day of service rendered. These calculations apply regardless of the number of working days in the particular month.

30:24. Must a school district pay teachers' salaries for days a school is closed because of an emergency?

The usual practice is to pay salaries when schools are closed because of an emergency or inclement weather. However, in these cases, schools may require that teachers work additional school days, such as during vacation periods.

A district's collective bargaining agreement may cover payment of teachers' salaries for periods when school is closed (see *Orchard Park Teachers' Ass'n v. Bd. of Educ. of Orchard Park CSD*, 71 A.D.2d 1 (4th Dep't 1979)).

30:25. When are teachers entitled to be paid?

The salary of a teacher employed for a full school year must be paid in at least 10 installments (§ 3015(2); see *Matter of Schwartz*, 7 Ed Dept Rep 130 (1968)). In addition, if a school district employs a teacher after July 1 in any school year, the district must pay the teacher's salary at least once in each month during the school year in which the teacher is employed (§ 3015(2)).

Neither a school district nor a board of cooperative educational services can pay teachers in advance for service they have not yet rendered (§ 3015(3); see also Opn. St. Comp. 82-364, *Opn. of Counsel #28*, 1 Ed Dept Rep 730 (1951); *Opn. of Counsel #37,* 1 Ed Dept Rep 736 (1951); *Opn. of Counsel #88*, 1 Ed Dept Rep 796 (1954)). For example, a school district cannot pay teachers returning to duty at the beginning of the school year two weeks' salary, before they work for two weeks (*Bd. of Educ. of Ramapo CSD v. Ramapo Teachers Ass'n*, 200 A.D.2d 62 (3d Dep't), *appeal denied*, 84 N.Y.2d 806 (1994)).

30:26. May teachers be required to sign a general waiver or release as a condition of a salary payment?

No. Teachers and other employees of a school district may not be required or even requested to make a general release or waiver as a condition of any salary payment (§ 3108; but see *Chamberlin v. Bd. of Educ. of City Sch. Dist. of N.Y.*, 200 A.D.2d 529 (1st Dep't 1994) (waiver of arbitration award compensation not foreclosed)).

30:27. May a district reduce a teacher's salary to contribute to a tax-sheltered annuity plan, if the teacher so requests?

Yes. Any school district or board of cooperative educational services may include a provision in its teachers' collective bargaining agreement to reduce the annual salary of a teacher in order to invest in an annuity for that employee (§§ 3109, 3109-A). The annuity fund must meet specific requirements of the Internal Revenue Code (see 26 USC § 403(b)).

30:28. May a teacher be reimbursed by a school board for work-related traveling expenses?

Yes. A school board is authorized to reimburse a teacher for work-related expenses and to make rules and regulations concerning expenses, including the establishment of a mileage rate (§§ 1604(27), 1710). The establishment of a mileage rate for reimbursement is a mandatory subject of collective bargaining (*Cnty. of Tompkins*, 17 PERB ¶ 4575 (1984); see **47:10-11**).

School districts also are authorized to pay for actual and necessary expenses related to "a convention, conference, or school conducted for the betterment" of the school district (Gen. Mun. Law § 77-b; see also **25:23-24**).

30:29. Must a district pay cash for unused leave time to teachers who resign?

A district is not required to provide employees with a cash payment for accumulated unused vacation, sick, and other leave time. However, districts may adopt a resolution to grant cash payments for unused time (Gen. Mun. Law § 92; see also *Gratto v. Bd. of Educ. of the Ausable Valley CSD*, 271 A.D.2d 175 (3d Dep't 2000); *Karp v. North Country Cmty. Coll.*, 258 A.D.2d 775 (3d Dep't 1999)). Absent passage of a board resolution in advance, such payments would constitute a gift of public funds in violation of Article 8, § 1 of the State Constitution (*Gratto v. Bd. of Educ. of the Ausable Valley CSD; Karp v. North Country Cmty. Coll.*).

Payment for accumulated sick, vacation, and leave time is a mandatory subject of collective bargaining (*Village of Lynbrook*, 10 PERB ¶¶ 3065, 3067 (1977), *aff'd,* 64 A.D.2d 902 (2d Dep't 1978), *aff'd,* 48 N.Y.2d 398 (1979)); see **47:11**). Many collective bargaining agreements oblige the employer to pay for unused leave time.

30:30. Is a teacher entitled to continued coverage in the district's group health plan upon termination of employment?

Yes. Under most circumstances, an employee can continue coverage in a group health plan under the federal Comprehensive Omnibus Budget Reconciliation Act of 1985 (COBRA) (42 USC § 300bb-1 *et seq.*). This law requires school boards with 20 or more employees to offer participants in group health plans and their covered dependents an opportunity to buy back into continued coverage should they cease to be covered because of termination, reduced hours, retirement, resignation, and other specified reasons. This continued coverage must be offered for at least 18 months, in the case of termination or reduced hours, and up to 36 months in other instances.

An employee on leave pursuant to the Family Medical Leave Act (FMLA) is entitled to coverage under COBRA when (1) the employee (spouse or dependent) is covered under an employer's group health plan on the day before the first day of FMLA leave or becomes covered during the FMLA leave; (2) the employee does not return to employment with the employer at the end of the FMLA leave; and (3) the employee (spouse or dependent) would in the absence of COBRA continuation coverage lose coverage under the employer's group health plan before the end of what would be the maximum coverage period (see **43:1**).

In addition, the New York State Health Benefits Plan provides for continued health insurance coverage under certain circumstances provided by law (see 4 NYCRR § 73.2(a)(3); Civ. Serv. Law §§ 163, 165). In some instances, continued coverage may also be available to dependents upon the death of an employee or retiree (Civ. Serv. Law § 165-a; 4 NYCRR § 73.2(b)(1), (3)).

Furthermore, continued coverage upon retirement maybe available under the terms of a collective bargaining agreement between a school district and an employee organization. In such an instance, a district's decision to deny health insurance benefits to a staff member who retires while disciplinary charges are pending would be subject to arbitration if the terms of the agreement do not prohibit arbitration of that question (*Matter of Union-Endicott CSD and Endicott Teachers' Ass'n,* 77 A.D.3d 1236 (3d Dep't 2010)).

31. Teachers – Certification Requirements

Overview

31:1. What is a teacher's certificate?

A *teacher's certificate* is a license issued by the commissioner of education, which certifies that the holder meets all the necessary qualifications to teach in the public schools (§ 3004; see also § 3004-b; 8 NYCRR §§ 30-1.1(a), 80-1.2).

As of July 2009, all teacher certificates may be issued in electronic and/or paper format (8 NYCRR § 80-1.2(b)(1)).

31:2. Is state certification required for all public school teachers in New York State?

Yes. The law prohibits school districts from employing a person who does not have a valid teacher's certificate (§§ 2569, 3001), with one limited exception for teachers in Buffalo.

In Buffalo, members of the teaching and supervisory staff appointed prior to September 1, 2001 must meet local requirements for licenses issued by that city in lieu of state certification, but these local requirements must meet or exceed the minimums set by the state (see §§ 2573(10-a), 3008; 8 NYCRR § 80-2.2(d)). Members of the teaching and supervisory staff appointed on or after September 1, 2001 are required to hold a state teaching certificate, but not a local license (§ 2573(10-a)).

Although prior to 1991 teachers employed in New York City held local certificates, teachers employed since that date must now hold teaching certificates issued from the NYS Education Department, as well as a local license (§ 2569; 8 NYCRR § 80-2.2(d)).

31:3. Is there an application fee for a teacher's certificate?

Yes. The fee for a teacher's certificate based on completion of a teacher education program registered by the NYS Education Department (SED) is $50, and the fee for a certificate based on education or experience completed in other than an SED registered teaching program is $100 (§ 3006(2)).

However, the law requires the commissioner of education to waive fees paid by applicants for the renewal of a temporary teaching certificate or license that lapsed while the applicant was deployed by the United States Armed Forces and any of its reserve components in a combat theater or combat zone of operations at any time on or after August 2, 1990 (§ 3004(1-a)).

31:4. Do state certification requirements apply to teachers in nonpublic and independent schools of New York State?

No. They apply only to teachers in public schools (§ 3001).

31:5. What rules apply to student teachers?

Student teachers practice the skills being learned in the teacher education program in which they are enrolled, and gradually assume increased responsibility for instruction, classroom management, and other related duties in the area in which they are seeking certification.

A student teacher generally practices these skills under the direct supervision of the certified teacher who has official responsibility for the class. However, a student teacher may teach a class without the presence of a certified teacher in the classroom, provided that the classroom teacher is available at all times and retains supervision of the student teacher.

The number of certified teachers employed in the district cannot not be reduced based on the presence of student teachers (§ 3001; 8 NYCRR § 80-1.1(b)(37)).

31:6. Must candidates pass competency examinations to become certified to teach in New York State?

Yes. All candidates for a teaching certificate must achieve satisfactory levels of performance on the New York State Teacher Certification Examinations (NYSTCE) (8 NYCRR § 80-1.5(a)). For candidates applying for certification on or after May 1, 2014, the NYSTCE include the Academic Literacy Skills Test (ALST), the Educating All Students Test (EAS), the Teacher Performance Assessment (edTPA), and Content Specialty Tests (CSTs) (8 NYCRR § 80-3.3).

Previously, the NYSTCE included the Liberal Arts and Science Test (LAST), the Written Assessment of Teaching Skills (ATS-W), the Content Specialty Tests (CSTs), and the Performance Assessment of Teaching Skills (ATS-P) (8 NYCRR §§ 80-1.5, 80-2.2(b)).

31:7. May a district employ an uncertified teacher?

No. School districts are allowed to employ only teachers that hold a valid teacher certificate (§ 3001(2)). Furthermore, because lack of proper certification renders an individual legally unqualified to teach (*Id.*), school district moneys may not be used to pay a salary to an uncertified teacher (§ 3009(1)), unless otherwise approved by the commissioner of education (§ 3604(6)); see **30:6**).

Teachers returning from active military duty with a teaching certificate that expired while they were on duty would qualify for employment with a valid extension of the expired certificate (Mil. Law § 308-b; 8 NYCRR § 80-1.6(b)).

31:8. May a certified teacher employed by a public school teach outside his or her certification area in that school?

Not ordinarily. Nonetheless, a superintendent of schools, with the approval of the commissioner of education, may assign a teacher to instruct a subject outside his or her certification area. Such an assignment is limited to no more than five classroom hours a week, and only when no certified or qualified teacher is available for the position, despite extensive and documented recruitment efforts (8 NYCRR § 80-5.3; *Appeal of Krause,* 46 Ed Dept Rep 304 (2007)). This commonly is referred to as *incidental teaching*. Commissioner's regulations set out the procedures school districts must follow to obtain commissioner approval of incidental teaching assignments (see 8 NYCRR § 80-5.3).

In addition, teachers with a valid teaching certificate can apply for a supplementary certificate that would permit them to teach in another title with a documented shortage of certified teachers, while completing education requirements necessary to qualify for the new title (8 NYCRR § 80-5.18; and see **31:19** for a discussion of the requirements for supplementary certificates).

31:9. May a certified classroom teacher be assigned to provide instructional support services?

Yes. School districts and boards of cooperative educational services may appoint or assign experienced and qualified teachers to provide instructional support services to other school personnel (8 NYCRR § 80-5.21(a)).

Instructional support services means professional development, pedagogical support, technical assistance, consultation, and/or program coordination offered by teachers to other school personnel. Such services may include, but are not limited to:

- conducting workshops, study groups, and demonstration lessons;
- coaching and mentoring for instructional staff;
- training teachers in best practices in specific content areas;
- assisting teachers in analyzing student performance data and differentiating instruction to meet the needs of all students;
- coordinating the provision of special education services;
- providing curriculum and assessment resources to instructional staff;
- providing information and support on technology tools to extend and support student learning; and/or
- assessing curriculum development or professional development needs (8 NYCRR §§ 30-1.1(j), 80-1.1(b)(23)).

Furthermore, a teacher appointed or assigned to provide such services on or after May 1, 2009 must either:

- hold a valid permanent or professional teaching certificate, and have at least three years of satisfactory experience as a teacher; or
- hold a valid, initial, provisional, permanent or professional teaching certificate, and an educational degree beyond the bachelor's level that the school superintendent finds sufficiently qualifies the teacher to provide the services.

In both instances, the teacher also must meet any additional education and experience qualifications set by the employing school district or board of cooperative educational services (8 NYCRR §§ 30-1.2(b), (c), 30-1.9(b), 80-5.21(b)).

31:10. Who enforces the teacher certification law?

It is the NYS Education Department's (SED) responsibility to enforce the law and regulations concerning teacher certification.

In addition, Part 83 of the commissioner's regulations establish a process for determining whether an application for certification should be denied or a teacher certificate should be revoked or suspended when matters arise that cast doubt on the moral character of a certified teacher or an applicant for certification (8 NYCRR § 83.1 *et seq.*; see **31:37-43**). This process is conducted by SED to determine fitness for certification, and is different from a disciplinary hearing involving a tenured certificate holder that is conducted by an employing district under section 3020-a or section 3020-b of the Education Law (see **chapter 38**).

31:11. Where can additional information about teacher certification be obtained?

Additional information about teacher certification is available from the NYS Education Department, Office of Teaching Initiatives, 89 Washington Avenue 5N EB, Albany, N.Y. 12234; telephone: 518-474-3901, or via the Internet at: http://www.highered.nysed.gov/tcert/certificate.

Types of Teacher Certificates

31:12. What types of teacher certificates are issued by New York State?

The NYS Education Department (SED) issues both entry-level and advanced-level certificates for classroom teachers. In addition, both entry-level and advanced-level teacher certificates will vary depending on their issuance date.

For teachers applying for certification on or after February 2, 2004, SED issues three types of certificates: *initial certificates*, *transitional certificates*, and *professional certificates*. Initial and transitional certificates are entry-level certificates that allow an individual to teach in public schools, generally for three years, until he or she meets the requirements for a professional certificate. A professional certificate is an advanced-level certificate that is valid for the life of the teacher, unless revoked for cause, and so long as continuing teacher education requirements are met (see **chapter 35**). Each certificate is specific to the title or subject area for which it is issued (8 NYCRR §§ 80-1.1(b)(22), (27), (42-45), 80-3.1(a), 80-3.2; see **31:21**).

Prior to February 2, 2004, SED issued the following teacher certificates: *provisional certificates and permanent certificates* (8 NYCRR §§ 80-2.1(a), 80-3.1(a)(2)). As the entry-level certificate, a provisional certificate allowed an individual to teach in a public school for five years (8 NYCRR §§ 80-1.1(b)(26), (29), 80-1.6, 80-1.7, 80-2). A permanent certificate replaced a provisional certificate upon completion of the requirements set out in commissioner's regulations (8 NYCRR §§ 80-1.7(a)(2), 80-2.2(a)). Provisional certificate requirements varied depending upon the area of teaching and the time the application for the certificate was made (see 8 NYCRR Subpart 80-2). A permanent certificate is valid for the life of a teacher unless revoked for cause (8 NYCRR § 80-1.1(b)(26), Subpart 80-2). Individuals with an expired provisional teaching certificate who completed the requirements for permanent certification during the life of the provisional certificate remained eligible to apply for and be issued a permanent certificate through October 1, 2014. Thereafter, they become subject to the initial or professional certificate requirements that went into effect February 2, 2004 (8 NYCRR §§ 80-1.6, 80-2.1(a)(2)(i)-(ii)).

SED also issues other types of certificates, such as a supplementary certificate (see **31:19**) and an internship certificate (see **31:20**). A *supplementary certificate* enables a teacher certified in one classroom teaching title to teach in a different title for which there is a demonstrated shortage of certified teachers while studying to complete the requirements to qualify for the new certificate, provided other conditions prescribed in commissioner's regulations are also met (8 NYCRR § 80-5.18). An *internship certificate* is available to eligible students in a registered or approved graduate program of teacher education (8 NYCRR §§ 80-1.1(24), 80-5.9).

For detailed information on these and other types of certificates, contact the NYS Education Department, Office of Teaching Initiatives, 89 Washington Avenue 5N EB, Albany, N.Y. 12234, or visit its website at: http://www.highered.nysed.gov/tcert/.

31:13. What are the requirements for an initial certificate?

Candidates for an initial certificate (see **31:12**) must satisfy course of study and examination requirements prescribed in commissioner's regulations (8 NYCRR § 80-3.3).

Generally, candidates may satisfy the course of study requirements by completing a teacher education program that is registered by the NYS Education Department (SED) and leads to the certificate sought (8 NYCRR § 80-3.3(a)(3)). Except as otherwise provided, they must hold a baccalaureate (bachelor's) or higher degree from a regionally accredited institution of higher education, or such other type of institution deemed substantially equivalent by the commissioner of education or authorized by the New York State Board of Regents to confer degrees in programs registered by SED (8 NYCRR § 80-3.3(a)(3)(ii), (b)(1)).

As specified in commissioner's regulations, certain types of candidates may meet the course of study requirements by completing "equivalent study" as determined by "individual evaluation" and meeting other requirements also set out in the regulations (8 NYCRR §§ 80-3.3(a)(3)(iii), 80-3.7).

Examination requirements will vary depending on when the candidate meets all requirements for initial certification and applies for an initial certificate, as well as the specific title in which they seek certification (8 NYCRR § 80-3.3(b)(2), (c)(1)(ii), (c)(2)(ii); see **31:6**).

More information on these requirements is available from SED's Office of Teaching Initiatives website at: http://www.highered.nysed.gov/tcert/.

31:14. Is there an alternate route for obtaining an initial certificate?

Yes. For example, individual with a bachelor's or higher degree who holds a certificate issued by the National Board for Professional Teaching Standards, may be deemed to have met the requirements for an initial certificate, if the NYS Education Department determines the title held is equivalent to the initial certificate sought (8 NYCRR § 80-3.3(a)(2); see also **31:13**).

31:15. Is an initial certificate available to teachers who have completed programs of study outside of New York State?

Yes. Out-of-state classroom teachers would be eligible for an initial certificate if they meet the criteria set out in commissioner's regulations (8 NYCRR § 80-5.8(a)).

31:16. What rules apply to the issuance of a transitional certificate?

Transitional certificates (see **31:12**) are available only to certain types of individuals, while they complete the educational and testing requirements for professional certification:

- *Transitional "A":* those teaching a specific career and technical education subject in agriculture, health or a trade, mechanical technology 7-12, electrical-electronic technology 7-12, computer technology 7-12, and family and consumer science (including food and nutrition, textile and design, human services and family studies);
- *Transitional "B":* those who have a bachelor's degree, but lack courses in teacher's education courses and who are enrolled in an alternative teacher certification program;
- *Transitional "C":* those holding an appropriate academic or graduate professional degree and are enrolled in an intensive program leading to a professional certificate; or
- *Transitional "G":* those holding an appropriate graduate degree in science, technology, engineering or mathematics and who have two years teaching experience in a post-secondary institution.

Generally, transitional certificates are valid for three years from their effective date. To obtain the certificate the candidate must submit evidence of a commitment for three years of employment as a teacher in the area of the certificate sought (8 NYCRR §§ 52.21(b)(1)(xv)–(xvii), 80-1.1(b)(42)–(45), 80-3.3(b)(2); 80-3.5, 80-5.13–14). An exception applies to the Transitional G certificate, which requires a two year commitment for employment and is valid for two years (8 NYCRR § 80-5.22).

Different requirements will apply depending on which type of transitional certificate is being sought (8 NYCRR §§ 80-3.5, 80-5.13, 80-5.14, 80-5.22). For example, for a Transitional B certificate, a candidate must have a bachelor's degree with a major of at least 30 semester hours in the area of the subject they wish to teach, complete a 200-hour pre-service program, pass two certification tests, and work as a teacher with mentoring support, while continuing to take additional college courses in teacher education. In a certificate title that has a bilingual education extension, a Transitional B certificate may be reissued for one additional year (8 NYCRR § 80-5.13).

For more information about alternative teacher certification programs, visit the NYS Education Department's Office of Teaching Initiatives website at: http://www.highered.nysed.gov/tcert/.

31:17. Can an expired initial or transitional certificate be extended or reissued?

Sometimes. Upon application of the certificate holder, the commissioner of education may extend an expired initial or transitional certificate for not more than two years from its expiration date for the following reasons:

- leave taken for childbearing, childrearing, serious illness or extended illness;
- Peace Corps or other volunteer organization service;
- teaching service discontinued due to abolition of teaching positions in the employing school district;
- extreme hardship or certain other circumstances preventing the completion of professional certificate requirements; or
- inability to secure employment as a teacher or pursuit of a career other than teaching (8 NYCRR § 80-1.6(a)).

Furthermore, the commissioner may extend an expired initial or transitional certificate for no more than one additional year beyond the general two year limitation if, in the six months preceding the end of the two-year extension, the candidate is faced with "extreme hardship" or "other circumstances beyond the control of the individual" that prevents completion of the requirements for a professional certification (8 NYCRR § 80-1.6(c)).

Other time extensions are available to holders of initial or transitional certificates on active military duty (8 NYCRR § 80-1.6(b)), and candidates whose application for citizenship or permanent residency is pending before the U.S. Citizenship and Immigration (8 NYCRR § 80-1.6(d)).

In addition, and subject to the conditions set out in commissioner's regulations, an expired initial certificate may be reissued for five years to individuals who have not successfully completed the three years of teaching experience or equivalent that is required for a professional certificate. The reissued certificate cannot be further extended (8 NYCRR § 80-1.8).

31:18. What are the requirements for a professional certificate?

Generally, candidates for a professional certificate (see **31:12**) must have either an "initial" or a "Transitional C" certificate for the certificate title sought. In addition, they must have a master's or higher degree in the content core of the initial certificate or in a related content area, and three school years of teaching experience. They also must satisfy examination requirements prescribed in commissioner's regulations (8 NYCRR § 80-3.4).

Candidates with a master's or higher degree in a field other than the content core of the certificate title must have completed at least 12 semester hours of graduate study in the content core of the initial certificate or in a related content area. Furthermore, a candidate's teaching experience must include participation in a mentored program in the first year of employment in a New York public school, unless the candidate successfully completed two years of teaching prior to such teaching in the public schools (8 NYCRR § 80-3.4(a), (b)(1), (2)).

Special requirements apply to candidates seeking a professional certificate in Speech and Language Disabilities (all grades) (8 NYCRR § 80-3.4(b)(3)(ii)), or in a specific career and technical subject area within certain specified fields, a technical area, or a trade (8 NYCRR § 80-3.4(c)).

More information on these requirements is available from SED's Office of Teaching Initiatives website at: http://www.highered.nysed.gov/tcert/.

31:19. What are the requirements for a supplementary certificate?

A candidate seeking to qualify for a supplementary certificate (see **31:12**) must:

- Hold a valid provisional, initial, permanent, or professional certificate in a classroom teaching service certificate title;

- Be enrolled in a higher education program leading to an initial or professional certificate in the new title;
- Satisfy the educational requirements specified in commissioner's regulations;
- Achieve a satisfactory level of performance on the Content Special Test in the area of the new title, if available.

In addition, the candidate for a supplementary certificate must be currently employed or have a commitment of employment in the new title area from a school district that must certify to the commissioner of education it intends to employ the teacher in the new title area and will provide appropriate support to the teacher to ensure quality of instruction.

A supplementary certificate is limited to the employing school district. It is valid for three years and may not be renewed (8 NYCRR § 80-5.18).

31:20. What are the requirements for an internship certificate?

Internship certificates (see **31:12**) may be issued only to students enrolled in a registered or approved graduate program of teacher education that includes an internship experience and appropriate supervision, at the request of the institution. In addition, the student must have completed at least one-half of the semester hour requirements of the program.

An internship certificate is restricted for use within the particular school district in which the internship is to be served. It is valid for no more than two years from its effective date and may not be renewed. An exception applies to individuals called to active duty in the Armed Forces, in which case the internship certificate can be extended for the time of active service and an additional 12 months from the end of such service, provided that the holder is a student in a registered or approved teacher education graduate program (8 NYCRR §§ 80-1.1(b)(24), 80-5.9).

Teacher Certificate Title Areas

31:21. Are teacher certificates issued in specific title areas?

Yes. In addition, certificate titles vary depending on the date of a candidate's submission of the application for certification.

Teachers who applied for certification on or before February 1, 2004 were issued teaching certificates in the following classifications: lower and upper elementary grades pre-k–6, and 7–12 in academic subjects (8 NYCRR §§ 80-2.12, 80-2.13), which are valid for the life of the teacher, unless revoked for cause, and so long as continuing teacher education requirements are met (see **chapter 35**). Certificates were also issued in a number of special certification areas, including career occupational subjects (8 NYCRR § 80-2.5); special education, the deaf and hearing impaired, the blind and partially sighted, and students with speech and hearing disabilities (8 NYCRR § 80-2.6); reading teacher (8 NYCRR § 80-2.7); school media specialist (8 NYCRR § 80-2.8); bilingual education (8 NYCRR § 80-2.9); English as a second language (8 NYCRR § 80-2.10); teachers of adult, community, and continuing education (8 NYCRR § 80-5.19); and certification to teach in nonregistered evening schools (8 NYCRR § 80-5.7).

On the other hand, teachers applying for certification on or after February 2, 2004 are issued certificates in titles that are more closely aligned with academic subjects and grade levels than the certificate titles issued in the past. Those certificate titles include:

Early Childhood Education (Birth–Grade 2)
Childhood Education (Grades 1–6)
Generalist in Middle Childhood Education (Grades 5–9)

Specified Subjects (Grades 5–9)
- English Language Arts
- Language other than English (specified)
- Mathematics
- Biology
- Chemistry
- Earth Science
- Physics
- Social Studies

Specified Subjects (Grades 7–12)
- English Language Arts
- Language other than English (specified)
- Mathematics
- Biology
- Chemistry
- Earth Science
- Physics
- Social Studies
- Specific agricultural subject titles
- Specific family and consumer science titles
- Specific technical subject titles
- Specific trade subject titles
- Specific health occupations subject titles
- Specific business and marketing subject titles

All Grades:
- Dance
- Health Education
- Music
- Physical Education
- Theater
- Visual Arts
- Agriculture
- Family and Consumer Sciences
- Business and Marketing
- Technology Education
- English to Speakers of other Languages
- Library Media Specialist
- Educational Technology Specialist

Students with Disabilities (Birth–Grade 2)
Students with Disabilities (Grades 1–6)
Students with Disabilities (Grades 5–9)
Students with Disabilities (Grades 7–12)
Deaf and Hard of Hearing (All Grades)
Blind and Visually Impaired (All Grades)
Speech and Language Disabilities (All Grades)

Literacy (Birth–Grade 6)
Literacy (Grades 5–12) (8 NYCRR § 80-3.2(e)).

In addition, the commissioner of education is authorized to create special certification for teachers and administrators in the area of children with autistic needs (§ 3004(5)).

Certification areas are narrowly construed in accordance with commissioner's regulations (*Appeal of Dankleman*, 37 Ed Dept Rep 415 (1998); *Appeal of Krause,* 46 Ed Dept Rep 304 (2007)).

31:22. May a school district employ someone in a position for which no certificate exists?

Upon application of the superintendent of schools, the commissioner of education may grant a permit to a school district authorizing the district to employ a qualified person for a position for which no certificate currently exists. The application must describe in detail the nature of the position to be filled, the qualifications deemed necessary for the position, and a list of the eligible candidates who possess the desired qualifications for appointment to the position.

The permit is valid for a period of up to two years for employment in the district for which it was granted, unless extended by the commissioner for intervals of up to five years (8 NYCRR § 80-5.6(e)).

31:23. What certificate titles apply to middle school teachers?

Prior to February 2, 2004, commissioner's regulations on teacher certification posed problems for educators in middle schools because teacher certificates were traditionally issued either up to the sixth grade (elementary) or for grades 7–12 (secondary) (see **31:21**). Thus, grade-level organizational patterns that combine students from both traditional elementary and secondary grade levels created situations that required variances from standard certification categories.

Teaching certification extensions available since February 2, 2004 have helped to address that problem. Examples of certificate extension titles include Middle Childhood Education for Grades (5–6) or (7–9), and General Science (5–9) in addition to General Science (7–12) (8 NYCRR §§ 80-4.1, 80-4.2). Requirements for an extension certificate vary depending on the type of extension sought (8 NYCRR § 80-4.3) including an extension to teach a subject in grades 5-6 (8 NYCRR § 80-4.3(b)), a subject in grades 7-9 (8 NYCRR § 80-4.3(c)), general sciences in grades 5-9 (8 NYCRR § 80-4.3(i)), general sciences in grades 7-12 (8 NYCRR § 80-4.3(j)), among others.

Applications for approval or renewal of teaching assignments related to an experiment in organizational change that combines traditional elementary and secondary grade levels are subject to the requirements of commissioner's regulations at 8 NYCRR § 80-5.12. As a general rule, school districts cannot continue the assignment of a teacher in such an experiment for more than five school years, unless the teacher has obtained the teaching certificate extension appropriate to such assignment, or is eligible for a "statement of continued eligibility" (8 NYCRR § 80.5-12(a)(5)). A statement of continued eligibility is limited to the specific permanent or professional certificate that was extended but is valid for service in any school district (8 NYCRR § 80.5-12(c)).

31:24. Can a teacher certified in one certification title become certified in another, different certification title?

Yes. Nothing prevents an individual certified in one certification title from becoming certified in another, provided they meet the education, examination and experience requirements that might apply to qualify for the additional certification title (see 8 NYCRR §§ 80-3.3(b)(1),(2), (c), 80-3.4).

In addition, certain teachers with a valid teaching certificate may be eligible for a supplementary certificate that would allow them to teach in another title with a documented shortage of certified teachers, while completing education requirements in the new title (8 NYCRR § 80-5.18; see **31:19**).

Teacher Certificate Extensions and Annotations

31:25. Does the NYS Education Department issue annotations and extensions for teacher certificates that enable teachers to expand the scope of their teaching?

Yes. A *teaching certificate annotation* is available to recognize certified teachers who have attained voluntarily additional pedagogical knowledge, skills and experiences (8 NYCRR § 80-1.1(5); see **31:26**). A *teaching certificate extension* authorizes the holder of a valid teacher certificate to teach an additional student population, grade or subject not authorized by that certificate (8 NYCRR § 80-1.1(19); see **31:27**).

Current requirements for obtaining a certificate annotation or extension are set out in Subpart 80-4 of commissioner's regulations (8 NYCRR §§ 80-4.3, 80-4.4). Different requirements applied to candidates who qualified and applied for an annotation or extension on or before February 1, 2004 (8 NYCRR §§ 80-4.1(a)(1), 80-2.9, 80-2.12(c), (d), (e), 80-2.13(c), (d)).

31:26. What types of certificate annotations are currently issued by the NYS Education Department?

Severe or Multiple Disabilities is the only certificate annotation title currently available to certified teachers applying for an annotation on or after February 2, 2004 (8 NYCRR § 80-4.2(b)). It is available to holders of teacher certificates in special education-related titles (see **31:21**) who have completed extra coursework specifically focused on teaching learners with severe and multiple disabilities as prescribed in commissioner's regulations (8 NYCRR § 80-4.4).

31:27. What types of certificate extensions are currently issued by the NYS Education Department?

There are two categories of certificate extensions currently issued by the NYS Education Department (SED). Under the first category, SED issues certificate extensions in 26 specified extension titles set out in commissioner's regulations to certified teachers applying for a certificate extension on or after February 2, 2004 (8 NYCRR § 80-4.2(a)), provided they meet the requirements for the particular extension sought (8 NYCRR §§ 80-4.2(a), 80-4.3).

Under the second category of currently available certificate extensions, SED issues two types of *limited certificate extensions* designed to provide school districts sufficient flexibility in the assignment of teachers which will result in a more efficient operation of the district (8 NYCRR § 80-4.3(k), (m)). The first type applies to teachers currently employed and certified to teach grades 1-6 subjects and allows them to teach the same subjects in grades 7-8 within the employing district (8 NYCRR § 80-4.3(k)). The second type applies to teachers currently employed and certified to teach a certain subject in grades 7-12 and allows them to teach that subject in grades 5-6 within the employing district (8 NYCRR § 80-4.3(m)). The limited certificate extensions are valid for only two years from their effective date and are not renewable. Thereafter, however, a 7-8 grade level extension or a 5-6 grade level extension, as applicable, may be issued to the teacher upon completion of course requirements specified in commissioner's regulations (8 NYCRR § 80-4.3(k)(2), (m)(2)).

Substitute Teacher Certification Requirements

31:28. What is the definition of a substitute teacher?

In accordance with commissioner's regulations, a *substitute teacher* is someone a school district employs to take the place of a regularly appointed teacher who is absent but expected to return (8 NYCRR § 80-5.4(a)(1)).

There are three types of substitute teachers:

- Those holding a valid teaching certificate.

- Those without certification but completing collegiate study toward certification at a rate of not less than six semester hours per year.
- Those without a valid teaching certificate who are not working toward certification (8 NYCRR § 80-5.4(c)(1)).

31:29. On what basis are substitute teachers employed?

Substitutes are employed either on a long-term basis or on an itinerant basis.

Long-term substitutes are employed for more than 40 days in a school year (8 NYCRR § 80-5.4(a)(2); see also **31:30**). Generally, they are appointed to take over for a regularly appointed teacher who is scheduled to be absent for an extended period of time, but expected to return at the end of the leave.

Itinerant substitutes generally are employed for 40 days or less in a school year (8 NYCRR § 80-5.4(a)(3)). However, a school district or board of cooperative educational services may employ an itinerant substitute for up to a total of 90 days in a school year, and sometimes longer, if no one with a valid teaching certificate or working toward certification (see **31:28**) is available, and other conditions specified in commissioner's regulations are met (8 NYCRR § 80-5.4(c)(3)).

What are generally referred to as *per diem substitutes* are mostly itinerant substitutes. Generally, they are appointed on the occasional days when a regularly appointed teacher calls in sick.

Substitute teachers with a valid teaching certificate may be employed in either a long-term or itinerant capacity, for any number of days, except that if employed on a long-term basis they must be employed in an area for which they are certified (8 NYCRR § 80-5.4(c)(1)). A similar rule applies to substitutes who are not certified but working toward completing collegiate study toward certification (8 NYCRR § 80-5.4(c)(2); see also **31:28**).

31:30. Are all substitute teachers required to have a valid teaching certificate as a condition of employment?

No. Itinerant substitutes (see **31:29**) may be employed without a valid certificate, even if they are not working towards certification (8 NYCRR § 80-5.4(c)(3); see also **31:28**).

On the other hand, long-term substitutes (see **31:29**) must have proper certification for the position, unless they are completing collegiate study toward certification (8 NYCRR § 80-5.4(b), (c)(2)) in which case they must be employed in the area for which they are seeking certification (8 NYCRR § 80-5.4(c)(2)).

31:31. May school districts and boards of cooperative educational services (BOCES) contract with an outside employment service for substitute teachers?

No. School districts and BOCES have no authority to contract with an outside employment service for per diem substitutes (*Appeal of Woodarek,* 46 Ed Dept Rep 1 (2006), *petition to review dismissed sub nom. Kelly Svces, Inc. v. USNY*, (Sup. Ct. Albany Cnty. 2007); *Appeal of Sweeney,* 44 Ed Dept Rep 176 (2004), *aff'd sub nom., Matter of BOCES of Erie, Chautauqua & Cattaraugus Counties v. Univ. of State Educ. Dep't*, 40 A.D.3d 1340 (3d Dep't 2007); see also *Appeal of Boyd*, 51 Ed Dept Rep, Dec. No. 16,364 (2012); see **34:3**).

Supplemental Teaching Staff Certification Requirements (Teaching Assistants, Teacher Aides and Visiting Lecturers)

31:32. Must a teaching assistant be certified?

Yes. Furthermore, depending on the date of their application for certification, teaching assistants may hold one of six different types of certificates issued by the NYS Education Department, each of which has its own separate education, testing, and employment experience requirements (8 NYCRR § 80-5.6(c); see **31:33**).

A *teaching assistant* is someone employed to provide direct instructional service to students under the general supervision of a licensed or certified teacher (§ 3009(2)(b); 8 NYCRR § 80-5.6(c)(1)(i)), with duties prescribed in commissioner's regulations (8 NYCRR § 80-5.6(c)(1)(ii); see also *Matter of Madison-Oneida BOCES v. Mills*, 4 N.Y.3d 51 (2004); *Putnam Northern Westchester BOCES v. Mills,* 46 A.D.3d 1062 (3d Dep't 2007); *Appeal of Ginnane*, 43 Ed Dept Rep 239 (2003); *Appeal of Roff*, 41 Ed Dept Rep 346 (2002)).

31:33. What types of teaching assistant certificates are issued by New York State?

For teaching assistants applying for certification on or after February 1, 2004, the NYS Education Department (SED) issues four types of certificates:

- A *Level I teaching assistant certificate* which is valid for three years and renewable once for three years, provided the applicant submits evidence to SED that he or she has a commitment for employment as a Level I teaching assistant (8 NYCRR § 80-5.6(c)(2)(ii)(a)).
- A *Level II teaching assistant certificate* which is valid for three years but is not renewable (8 NYCRR § 80-5.6(c)(2)(ii)(b)).
- *A Level III teaching assistant certificate* which is continuously valid, provided that the continuing education requirement is met (8 NYCRR § 80-5.6(c)(2)(ii)(c); see **chapter 35**).
- A *pre-professional teaching assistant certificate* which is valid for five years from its effective date, at which time it must be renewed subject to the holder showing matriculation in a program leading to teacher certification as required in commissioner's regulations (8 NYCRR § 80-5.6(c)(2)(ii)(d)).

Prior to February 1, 2004, SED issued two types of teaching assistant certificates: a *temporary license* which was valid for one year and could be renewed once, and a *continuing certificate*, which remains valid as long as the holder remained continuously employed as a teaching assistant in a New York State public school for a period of five consecutive years (8 NYCRR § 80-5.6(c)(2)(i)).

31:34. Must teacher aides be certified?

No. A *teacher aide* is someone assigned to assist a teacher in nonteaching duties such as managing records, materials and equipment; attending to the physical needs of children; supervising students; and performing such other support duties determined and supervised by the teacher (§ 3009(2)(a); 8 NYCRR § 80-5.6(b)).

Unlike teaching assistants, a teacher aide's position is not certified by the commissioner of education as being in the teaching and supervisory staff of a school district. As such, they do not have to be certified under the Education Law to hold their position (see *Appeal of Dell and Tedesco*, 52 Ed Dept Rep, Dec. No. 16,417 (2012)). Instead, they are classified in the noncompetitive class of the civil service, and their employment is governed by civil service rules and regulations (*Appeal of Dell and Tedesco*; *Appeal of Latorre*, 27 Ed Dept Rep 366 (1988)). See **chapter 39** for more information on the Civil Service.

31:35. Must visiting lecturers be certified?

No. But they need to be licensed by the commissioner of education.

Upon application by the superintendent of schools, the commissioner of education may issue a license to a visiting lecturer who possesses unusual qualifications in a specific subject in order to authorize this person to supplement the regular program of instruction. The application for such a license must indicate the specific subject for which the license will be issued, the program to be supplemented, the educational credentials and relevant experience of the visiting lecturer, and the extent of services that he or she will render.

A license issued to a visiting lecturer is valid for one year (8 NYCRR § 80-5.6(d)).

A visiting lecturer who will reasonably be expected by a covered school to provide services for more than five days per school year is subject to fingerprinting and criminal history record check requirements (8 NYCRR § 87.2(k)(3)(iii)). For additional information on fingerprinting requirements, see **chapter 41**.

31:36. Are there other types of supplemental teaching support staff who must be certified?

Yes. The commissioner of education issues certificates for those in pupil personnel service, such as school psychologists and school counselors (8 NYCRR § 80-2.3).

School media specialists, such as school librarians, also must be certified (8 NYCRR § 80-2.8; see **31:21**, for additional certificate titles). Only fully certified persons can be employed in these areas.

In addition, school social workers must be licensed and registered by the NYS Education Department as either a "licensed master social worker" or a "clinical social worker" (Educ. Law Art. 154; § 7700 *et seq*.; 8 NYCRR § 80-2.3(f)).

Certification Revocation and Suspension

31:37. May a teacher's certificate be revoked or suspended?

Yes, based upon conviction of a crime or an act that raises a reasonable question regarding the teacher's moral character (8 NYCRR § 83.1(a)).

With respect to a criminal conviction, the commissioner of education is authorized and required to automatically revoke and annul the certificate of any teacher, teaching assistant, and pupil personnel services professional who is convicted of:

- A sex offense for which registration as a sex offender is required (§ 305(7-a); see Corrections Law, article 6-c; see also **31:38**), or
- Any other violent offense committed against a child who is the intended victim of such an offense (§ 305(7-a); see Penal Law § 70.02; see also **31:38**).

With respect to other types of criminal conviction, or lack of good moral character on other grounds, the commissioner may revoke or suspend a teacher's certification, or impose another alternative penalty (§ 305(7); 8 NYCRR § 83.6). Other than revoking a teacher's certificate, the commissioner may, for example:

- Suspend a teacher's certificate for a fixed period of time, or until the teacher completes a course of therapy or treatment.
- Limit the scope of a certificate by revoking an extension to teach additional subjects or grades.
- Impose a fine not to exceed $5000 (§ 305(7); 8 NYCRR § 83.6).

A teacher's failure to complete a contract of employment for a school year without good reason may also constitute sufficient grounds for the revocation of his or her teaching certificate (§ 3019).

31:38. Can conviction of a crime result in the automatic revocation of a teacher's certificate?

It depends. Yes, if the conviction is for a sex offense requiring registration as a sex offender or any other violent offense against a child who is the intended victim of such an offense (§ 305(7-a); see **31:37**). In such an instance, the commissioner of education must revoke and annul the teacher's certificate without a hearing, upon receipt of either a certified copy of a criminal history record showing that the teacher has been convicted of such an offense, or notice of such a conviction from the district attorney or other prosecuting authority who obtained the conviction (§ 305(7-a)(c), (d); see **31:40**).

Other types of conviction, however, only create a "rebuttable presumption" that the teacher lacks the necessary good moral character to retain a teaching certificate. That would be the case with respect to certain specified drug-related crimes, crimes involving the abuse of minors or students not constituting a sex offense for which registration as a sex offender is required, or any crimes committed while on school property or while in the performance of teaching duties (8 NYCRR § 83.4(d)).

31:39. What is the role of a school district in the teacher certification revocation or suspension process?

Part 83 of the commissioner's regulations requires school superintendents to report to the professional conduct officer of the NYS Education Department "any information indicating that a person holding a teaching certificate has been convicted of a crime, or has committed an act which raises a reasonable question as to the individual's moral character" (8 NYCRR § 83.1(a)). A superintendent's failure to do so may result in a part 83 investigation into the moral character of the superintendent himself or herself (see *Skiptunas v. Mills*, 2000 U.S. Dist. LEXIS 65 (N.D.N.Y Jan. 5, 2000)).

School officials required to file a part 83 report are entitled to qualified immunity from lawsuit, so long as the statements in the report are not false nor made maliciously (*Rizzo v. Edison, Inc. Charter Sch.*, 172 Fed. Appx. 391 (2d Cir. 2006)).

31:40. Who other than a school district can report to the NYS Education Department (SED) information that can constitute grounds for the revocation or suspension of a teacher's certificate?

Other than a school superintendent (see **31:39**), any individual may refer information of a criminal conviction or other act that raises a reasonable question as to the moral character of an individual holding a teaching certificate to the SED professional conduct officer, or to the executive director of the Office of Teaching Initiatives within SED, respectively (8 NYCRR § 83.1(c)).

However, in the case of a teacher convicted of a sex offense for which registration as a sex offender is required, the district attorney or other prosecuting authority who obtained the conviction must notify the commissioner of education of the conviction (§ 305(7-a)(d)).

In addition, SED must forward to its Office of Teaching information received from the Division of Criminal Justice Services while conducting a criminal history record check about an arrest and/or conviction of a certified teacher, for a determination of that individual's good moral character (8 NYCRR § 87.6(b)).

Furthermore, the state also must review the findings and recommendations of 3020-a hearing officers or panels to consider whether or not teachers subject to such local disciplinary charges should retain their teaching certificates (8 NYCRR § 83.1(d)).

31:41. What happens when the NYS Education Department (SED) receives information that can constitute grounds for the revocation or suspension of a teacher's certificate?

In cases other than those involving a conviction of a sex offense for which registration as a sex offender is required (see **31:38**), the professional conduct officer at SED conducts an investigation and reports the findings from the investigation and recommendations for action to the Professional Standards and Practices Board for Teaching or a subcommittee of that body (8 NYCRR § 83.2). The board or subcommittee reviews the case to determine whether a substantial question about the moral character of the certified teacher exists and notifies the teacher of its decision (8 NYCRR §§ 3.14, 83.3).

If the board or subcommittee finds that a substantial question does exist, notice of the basis for this conclusion is sent by certified mail to the teacher (8 NYCRR § 83.3). The teacher then has 30 days after receipt of the notice to request a hearing on the question of whether his or her certification should be revoked, suspended and another penalty imposed (8 NYCRR § 83.4(a)). A teacher's late request for a hearing may be granted in SED's discretion (*Matter of Pearlman v. Mills,* 24 A.D.3d 837 (3d Dep't 2005)).

31:42. What is involved in the process for revoking or suspending a teacher's certificate if it is determined as a result of an investigation that there are grounds for pursuing such action?

The procedures for determining whether to revoke or suspend a teacher's certificate depend on the type of case involved. In cases involving the automatic revocation of a teacher's certificate based on the teacher's conviction of a sex offense for which registration as a sex offender is required or any other violent offense against a child who is the intended victim of such an offense, there is no right to a hearing (§ 305(7-a)(c), (d); see **31:38**). Nonetheless, the teacher must be afforded the opportunity to establish he or she is not the same person as the individual convicted (§ 305(7-a)(c)). In addition, the commissioner of education must hold a hearing to determine whether to reinstate the teacher's certificate upon receipt of notice that the conviction resulting in the automatic revocation of the certificate has been set aside upon appeal, or otherwise reversed, vacated or annulled (§ 305(7-a)(e)).

In other types of cases, the procedures generally followed are in part 83 of the commissioner's regulations (§§ 305(7), 2215(10), 3018; 8 NYCRR § 83). Pursuant to those procedures, the NYS Education Department's Office of Teaching must prove at a hearing, commonly referred to as a *part 83 hearing*, that the teacher or applicant lacks good moral character. The teacher or applicant is entitled to be represented by an attorney at the hearing and may call witnesses and introduce other evidence of his or her good moral character. The hearing officer may issue subpoenas at the request of a party. At the end of the hearing, the hearing officer or hearing panel issues a decision on whether the teacher's certification should be revoked or suspended or whether an applicant's request for certification should be denied. The hearing officer must notify the commissioner and the teacher or applicant of the findings and recommendations (8 NYCRR § 83.4(f)). The commissioner or teacher may appeal the decision within 30 days, as permitted by law (8 NYCRR § 83.5(a), (b)).

31:43. How does a criminal conviction impact the hearing process for revoking or suspending a teacher certificate?

In cases that do not involve a conviction requiring automatic revocation (see **31:38**), proof of conviction does not by itself create a conclusive presumption that the teacher lacks good moral character (8 NYCRR § 83.4(d)). The burden of proving the teacher's lack of good moral character rests with the NYS Education Department (8 NYCRR § 83.4(c)).

Additionally, evidence of conviction is given different weight depending on the type of crime and whether the conviction occurred before or after the teacher became certified (8 NYCRR § 83.4(d), (e)).

Moreover, the hearing officer or panel must apply the standards for denial of a license or application set forth in Corrections Law section 752, taking into consideration the factors set forth in Corrections Law section 753 (8 NYCRR § 83.4(e); see also *Matter of Arrocha v. Bd. of Educ. of the City of N.Y.*, 93 N.Y.2d 361 (1999); *Application of Downing*, 40 Ed Dept Rep 396 (2000); see **41:10**). For example, an application for a license may be denied based on a finding of lack of good moral character as a result of a criminal conviction if there is a direct relationship between the criminal offense and the specific license sought, or if the issuance of a license involves an unreasonable risk to property or to the safety or welfare of specific individuals or the general public (Corrections Law § 752; see *Matter of Arrocha v. Bd. of Educ. of the City of N.Y.*).

[illegible] (N.Y. Educ. Law § [illegible]). The teacher [illegible] [illegible] to contest [illegible] whether [illegible] certificate [illegible] suspended and [illegible] [illegible] [illegible]

[illegible] What [illegible] process [illegible] revoking or suspending a teacher's certificate [illegible] determination that there are grounds for suspending or revoking [illegible]?

The [illegible] to revoke or suspend a teacher's certificate [illegible] [illegible] [illegible] [illegible] [illegible]

[illegible]

Q. 4 [illegible] How long does it take [illegible] [illegible] [illegible]?

[illegible]

[illegible]

32. Teachers – General Rights and Responsibilities

Teacher Workday

32:1. Is there a maximum length for a teacher's workday?

There are no laws that limit the hours of work a school board may establish for its teachers. However, the length of a teacher's workday is a mandatory subject of bargaining that must be negotiated with a collective bargaining unit, such as a teachers' union (Civ. Serv. Law §§ 201(4), 204(3); *Norwich Educ. Org.*, 41 PERB ¶ 4507 (2008); *Troy City Sch. Dist.*, 11 PERB ¶ 3056 (1978); see also **47:10-11**).

32:2. Are there standards that limit a teacher's daily teaching load?

Yes. Commissioner's regulations state the number of daily classroom periods of instruction for a teacher should not exceed five periods. A school district that requires teachers to instruct for more than six teaching periods a day or imposes a daily teaching load of more than 150 pupils must justify its deviation from this policy (8 NYCRR § 100.2(i); but see *Appeal of Romano*, 43 Ed Dept Rep 466 (2004)).

Such a deviation will be permitted only in unique and compelling circumstances (*Appeal of Romano*; *Appeal of Baker*, 33 Ed Dept Rep 395 (1994); *Appeal of LaForty*, 33 Ed Dept Rep 161 (1993)). For instance, the commissioner of education has held that an unanticipated increase in enrollment is sufficient to justify a deviation from the regulation (*Appeal of Panagos*, 54 Ed Dept Rep, Dec. No. 16,678 (2014)).

According to the commissioner, the class load limitations are not merely "aspirational" and districts must engage in "continual monitoring and evaluation of the effects of budget cuts in order to make good faith efforts to comply" with the class load limitations (*Appeal of Koenig*, 50 Ed Dept Rep, Dec. No. 16,145 (2010); *Appeal of Kleinman*, 34 Ed Dept Rep 1 (1994)).

Because the intent of the regulations is to maintain the quality of instruction for students, a key issue in these appeals is whether the teacher's work load precludes effective teaching (see *Appeal of Panagos*, 54 Ed Dept Rep, Dec. No. 16,678 (2014); *Appeal of Guzinski*, 54 Ed Dept Rep, Dec. No. 16,676 (2014)).

The commissioner may require districts unable to comply with these regulatory standards to make annual reports to the commissioner on the progress made toward eventual compliance (see *Matter of Simon*, 1 Ed Dept Rep 562 (1960); see also *Appeal of Lowell*, 26 Ed Dept Rep 333 (1987)).

In addition, districts must schedule teaching assignments so that no full-time teacher will be assigned to continuous duty for more than five hours (§ 3029).

Limitations on teachers' workloads are frequently included as a provision in collective bargaining agreements (see *Matter of Haessig v. Oswego City Sch. Dist.*, 90 A.D.3d 1657 (4th Dep't 2011)).

32:3. Are teachers entitled to a free period for lunch?

All school districts, except New York City, must allow each teacher who is employed for more than five hours a day at least a 30-minute period free from assigned duties and scheduled, so far as practical, during the hours normally allotted for student lunch periods (§ 3029).

A collective bargaining agreement may contain a provision extending but not reducing this duty-free period (*Matter of Gordon*, 18 Ed Dept Rep 518 (1979)).

32:4. May a school district unilaterally require its teachers to supervise or participate in extracurricular activities outside of regular school hours?

No. Hours of work and extra pay for extra work are mandatory subjects of collective bargaining under the Taylor Law. Therefore, districts must negotiate with their teachers concerning assignment of and payment for after-school duties (*Beacon CSD*, 14 PERB ¶ 3084 (1981); see also **47:10-11**).

Most school boards pay extra compensation for extracurricular supervision or participation, such as coaching athletics.

Participation in Shared-Decision-Making Committees

32:5. Do teachers have the right to participate in shared-decision-making and school-based planning?

Yes. Commissioner regulations require that school districts adopt a plan and establish shared-decision-making committees at both the district-wide and building level, and teachers must be members of any such committee, along with representatives from other specified groups (8 NYCRR § 100.11(b)). Such committees are intended to increase the level of shared decision making among teachers, administrators, parents and other members of the school community (8 NYCRR § 100.11; see *Appeal of Ayers,* 48 Ed Dept Rep 350 (2009); see also **5:37-47**).

32:6. How do teachers get selected to be members of a shared-decision-making committee?

Pursuant to commissioner's regulations, teachers serving on the district-wide committee must be selected by the teachers' collective bargaining organization (8 NYCRR § 100.11(b)).

On the other hand, commissioner's regulations are silent regarding the method of selecting teacher representatives to building-level shared-decision-making committees (*Appeal of Dello*, 46 Ed Dept Rep 329 (2007); *Appeal of Roby*, 34 Ed Dept Rep 654 (1995)). However, according to the Public Employment Relations Board (PERB), a teacher's union does not have the legal right to appoint teachers of its choosing to building-level shared-decision-making committees and subject such appointments to its own conditions, such as the rescission of a teacher's appointment if the teacher fails to represent union interests (*West Genesee CSD*, 31 PERB ¶ 3005 (1998)).

Curriculum Choices and Academic Freedom

32:7. Can teachers establish the curriculum they will teach in their classes?

No. The authority and obligation to establish the curriculum that will be taught in a district's schools rests with the school board (§ 1709(3)). As expressed by the commissioner of education, it is the responsibility of a school board to set the course of study by which students are graded and classified (see *Appeal of Orris*, 35 Ed Dept Rep 184 (1995); see also *Appeal of Zaleski*, 36 Ed Dept Rep 284 (1997)).

Thus, for example, although it may be appropriate to discuss curricular matters within the shared-decision-making process (see **5:37-47**), only a school board can make final determinations regarding curriculum related issues including changes to a district's grading policy (*Appeal of Orris*; *Appeal of Zaleski*).

32:8. Are there limitations on a teacher's ability to exercise academic freedom in a public school setting?

Yes. Teachers' claims of academic freedom to control the content of instruction in a public school must be balanced against a school board's legitimate interest in establishing instructional programs. As such, a school board may, for example:

- Prohibit a teacher from making references to religion in the delivery of the teacher's instructional program, unless the religious reference is a required element of the course and its use has been pre-approved by the teacher's supervisor (*Marchi v. BOCES*, 173 F.3d 469 (2d Cir.), *cert. denied*, 528 U.S. 869 (1999)).
- Direct a teacher to refrain from making sexual references in the classroom that are deemed inappropriate given the age and maturity of students (*Bernstein v. Norwich City Sch. Dist.*, 282 A.D.2d 70 (3d Dep't), *appeal denied*, 96 N.Y.2d 937 (2001); see also *Kirby v. Yonkers City Sch. Dist.*, 767 F.Supp.2d 452 (S.D.N.Y. 2011)).
- Take disciplinary action against a teacher who makes inappropriate remarks regarding ethnicity and heritage (*In re Watt (East Greenbush CSD)*, 85 A.D.3d 1357 (3d Dep't 2011)).

Nonetheless, a teacher's claim of academic freedom must be protected where the instructional material has educational value, is relevant to the curriculum, and is suitable to the age and maturity of the students (*Malverne UFSD v. Sobol*, 181 A.D.2d 371 (3d Dep't), *appeal withdrawn*, 80 N.Y.2d 972 (1992). For example, according to one court, the use of sexual terms in an eighth grade health class on the topic of HIV and AIDS is legitimately related to curriculum (*Kramer v. N.Y. City Bd. of Educ.*, 715 F.Supp.2d 335 (E.D.N.Y. 2010); but compare *Kirby v. Yonkers City Sch. Dist.*).

The placement of a critical letter in a teacher's personnel file regarding that teacher's use of material in the classroom deemed objectionable by a school board does not rise to the level of discipline such that any right to academic freedom retained by the teacher would be chilled (*O'Connor v. Sobol*, 173 A.D.2d 74 (3d Dep't 1991), *appeal dismissed*, 80 N.Y.2d 897 (1992)).

Ethics

32:9. Are teachers subject to a school district's code of ethics?

Yes. Each school district must adopt a code of ethics that provides guidance to its officers and employees regarding the standard of conduct reasonably expected of them (Gen. Mun. Law § 806; see also Opn. Att'y Gen. 99-16; see **chapter 12**).

This code of ethics must provide standards as may be deemed advisable, including limitations on outside employment and holding of investments in conflict with official duties. Thus, it may proscribe certain conduct by employees, including teachers, in addition to that which is specifically prohibited by law (Gen. Mun. Law § 806(1)(a)).

32:10. Are teachers subject to prohibited conflicts of interest rules?

Yes. The General Municipal Law prohibits certain conduct by school district employees, including teachers, that creates a conflict of interest (Gen. Mun. Law §§ 800, 801, 802, 805-a).

Accordingly, for example, an employee must not accept a gift worth more than $75 under circumstances in which it reasonably could be inferred that the gift was intended to or could in fact influence the employee in the performance of the employee's official duties, or was intended as a reward for any official action by the employee (Gen. Mun. Law § 805-a(1)(a); see *Appeal of Dashefsky*, 46 Ed Dept Rep 219 (2006); Opn. Att'y Gen. 95-10). A school board can set the limit at less than $75, but not above $75 (Opn. Att'y Gen. 99-16).

32:11. Are teachers subject to confidentiality rules?

Yes. It is impermissible for school employees, including teachers, to disclose confidential information acquired in the course of their official duties. Likewise, it is impermissible for them to use such confidential information for personal gain (Gen. Mun. Law § 805-a(1)(b); see also *Appeal of Nelson,* 49 Ed Dept Rep 82 (2009); *Application of Nett and Raby*, 45 Ed Dept Rep 259 (2005); *Application of Bd. of Educ. Elmont UFSD,* 48 Ed Dept Rep 29, *reopened and modified on other grounds* 48 Ed Dept Rep 135 (2008)).

32:12. Are teachers subject to financial disclosure requirements?

Until June 30 2017, employees of the New York City Board of Education and community district education councils may be required by chancellor's regulations and bylaws to submit financial disclosure statements and are required by state law to disclose certain other information (§ 2590-h(39), (40)).

Otherwise, the New York Court of Appeals has held that disclosures for background investigations beyond what is required by law are a mandatory subject of bargaining (*Bd. of Educ. of the City of New York v. New York State PERB,* 75 N.Y.2d 660 (1990); see **47:10-11**).

Strikes and Illegal Job Actions

32:13. Do teachers have the right to strike?

No. Teachers are subject to the provisions of the Taylor Law, which prohibits strikes by police officers, fire fighters, and other public employees (Civ. Serv. Law § 210). For more information on strikes and illegal job actions, see **46:38-41**).

32:14. What constitutes a strike or illegal job action?

The Taylor Law defines a strike or illegal job action as "any strike or other concerted stoppage of work or slowdown by public employees" (Civ. Serv. Law § 201(9)).

A refusal or even a threatened refusal by teachers to perform services in the usual and customary manner, including work not specified in the contract, is an illegal job action (*Haverling CSD*, 22 PERB ¶ 4554 (1989); *Horseheads Teacher Ass'n & New York State United Teachers*, 15 PERB ¶ 3110 (1982); *Penn Yan CSD*, 13 PERB ¶ 3046 (1980); *Webutuck Teachers Ass'n*, 13 PERB ¶ 3041 (1980); *Plainedge Fed'n of Teachers*, 11 PERB ¶ 3060 (1978); *Pearl River UFSD*, 11 PERB ¶ 3085, *aff'g* 11 PERB ¶ 4530 (1978)). Thus, boycotts of assignments, such as evening activities, extracurricular assignments, extra help, field trips and faculty meetings, are illegal strikes (see also **46:38**).

In addition, the threat of refusal or the actual refusal to perform volunteer duties during the period of time when collective bargaining negotiations are occurring in order to gain an advantage in those negotiations, known as work-to-rule, is a strike or threat of a strike that is prohibited by the Taylor Law (*Haverling CSD*).

32:15. Are there any legal consequences for teachers involved in a strike or illegal job action?

Yes. A school district may deduct twice a teacher's daily salary for each day he or she participates in a strike (Civ. Serv. Law § 210(2)(f)). The penalty for a strike of extracurricular duties is limited to a deduction of compensation for the extracurricular work (*Bd. of Educ. of Seaford UFSD*, 22 PERB ¶ 7533 (Sup. Ct. Nassau Cnty. 1989); see **46:38-41**).

In addition, if the Public Employment Relations Board (PERB) determines that the teachers' union has violated the strike ban, it will order forfeiture of the union's membership dues deduction and agency shop fee deduction privileges (Civ. Serv. Law § 210(3)(f); see, *e.g. Yonkers Federation of Teachers*, 32 PERB ¶ 3075 (1999), see **46:39**).

Student Discipline

32:16. May a teacher remove a student from his or her classroom for disruptive behavior?

Yes. A teacher has the authority to remove a "disruptive pupil" from the classroom. The removal must be consistent with the code of conduct adopted by the school board pursuant to section 2801 (§ 3214(3-a); 8 NYCRR § 100.2(l)(2)(ii)(d), (e); *Appeal of K.M.,* 49 Ed Dept Rep 244 (2010)). A "disruptive pupil" is an elementary or secondary school student under age 21 who substantially disrupts the educational process or substantially interferes with the teacher's authority in the classroom (§ 3214(2-a)(b)). The district must have established policies and procedures to provide for the continued education of students removed from the classroom (§ 3214(3-a)). For more information on teacher removals of students from the classroom, see **52:24, 52:37-40**.

32:17. May a teacher in New York State administer corporal punishment or aversive behavioral interventions to a student?

No. Corporal punishment is forbidden in public schools in New York State, although the use of physical force is permitted for certain limited purposes where alternatives cannot be employed reasonably (8 NYCRR §§ 19.5(a), 100.2(l)(3); for more information, see **52:17**). In general, the use of aversive interventions is forbidden also (8 NYCRR §§ 19.5(b); 200.22(e), (f); for more information, see **52:19**).

32:18. Must school districts defend legal actions against a teacher that arise out of a teacher's conduct in the discharge of employment duties?

Yes. School districts must provide an attorney and pay legal fees and expenses incurred in the defense of a teacher in any case involving a civil or criminal action that is based on the disciplinary action taken against any student of the district by the teacher while in the discharge of his/her official duties within the scope of his/her employment (§ 3028; see, *e.g. Inglis v. Dundee CSD Bd. of Educ*., 180 Misc.2d 156 (Sup. Ct. Yates Cnty. 1999); *Cromer v. City Sch. Dist. of Albany Bd. of Educ*., 2002 N.Y. Misc. LEXIS 580 (N.Y. App. Term Apr. 5, 2002)). This obligation extends even to cases where a teacher inflicts corporal punishment upon a student in violation of state rules (*Sagal-Cotler v. Bd. of Educ. of the City Sch. Dist. of the City of N.Y*., 20 N.Y.3d 671 (2013)).

In addition, school districts must provide legal assistance to employees facing claims of alleged negligence or acts resulting in accidental bodily injury to any person within or outside of a school building, provided the employee at the time of the accident or injury was acting within the scope of his or her employment and/or under the direction of the school board (§ 3023; see **67:3**). The teacher must give the school district notice of the commencement of legal proceedings against him or her and comply with other procedural requirements that may apply (see **67:6-7**).

For more information on a school district's defense and indemnification responsibilities, see **chapter 67**.

Student Discipline

33. Teachers – Tenure and Seniority Rights

Tenure Rights – In General

33:1. What is tenure?

Tenure is an employment status a teacher may earn by successfully completing a period of probationary employment and then, upon the superintendent's recommendation, being granted this status by the school board (§§ 2509, 2573, 3012, 3014). A teacher who has received tenure has earned the right to keep his or her job; in other words, to be free from discipline or dismissal, except for just cause to be proven by school officials in a due process hearing under section 3020-a of the Education Law.

33:2. Are teachers employed by a board of cooperative educational services (BOCES) eligible for tenure?

Yes. Probationary appointments and tenure at a BOCES are provided for by section 3014 of the Education Law.

33:3. Do part-time teachers enjoy tenure rights?

Not generally. Normally, part-time teachers do not receive probationary appointments or credit toward tenure (*Ceparano v. Ambach*, 53 N.Y.2d 873 (1981); *Lilley v. Mills*, 274 A.D.2d 644 (3d Dep't 2000)). A school board may, however, extend credit to a part-time teacher pursuant to either a board resolution (*Moritz v. Bd. of Educ. Gowanda CSD*, 60 A.D.2d 161 (4th Dep't 1977)), or a provision in a collective bargaining agreement (*Matter of Greenwald v. Bd. of Educ. of E. Ramapo CSD*, 62 A.D.2d 207 (2d Dep't 1978), *aff'd sub nom. Schlosser v. Bd. of Educ. of E. Ramapo CSD*, 47 N.Y.2d 811 (1979)).

The one exception to the general rule is kindergarten teaching, where the commissioner of education has construed the tenure statutes as encompassing both full-time (two sessions) and part-time (one session) positions (*Ablondi v. Comm'r of Educ.*, 54 A.D.2d 507 (3d Dep't 1976), *lv. to appeal denied*, 42 N.Y.2d 801 (1977); *Matter of Clark*, 17 Ed Dept Rep 311 (1978)). Consequently, even where a district uses a combination of full-time and part-time teachers to meet its kindergarten needs, part-time kindergarten teachers still receive credit toward tenure.

Nonetheless, teachers who earn tenure in a full-time position do not lose that tenure by subsequently accepting a part-time position with the district (*Tadken v. Bd. of Educ. Port Washington UFSD*, 65 A.D.2d 820 (2d Dep't 1978), *lv. to appeal denied*, 46 N.Y.2d 711 (1979)).

33:4. Do part-time teaching assistants enjoy tenure rights?

No, they do not (*Mazzone v. Hauppauge UFSD*, 41 A.D.2d 480 (2d Dep't 2007)).

33:5. What happens if a district mistakenly considers a teacher to be a part-time employee?

If a district fails to appoint a teacher to a tenure track probationary appointment because it considers the teacher to be a part-time employee but later determines the teacher is in fact a full-time employee, the teacher may be entitled to tenure by estoppel (see **33:8**) if the teacher has served the requisite probationary period (*Walters v. Amityville UFSD*, 251 A.D.2d 590 (2d Dep't 1998)).

On the other hand, the internship toward college credit in the same district in which an intern is also employed in a part-time position does not convert the part-time position into full-time probationary service for the purpose of acquiring tenure (*Hacker v. Questar III*, 31 A.D.3d 911 (3d Dep't), *lv. to appeal denied*, 7 N.Y.3d 715 (2006)).

33:6. Can tenure rights be lost?

Yes, upon submission of a resignation, a teacher relinquishes any tenure and seniority rights previously accrued, even if the teacher subsequently accepts a part-time position (*Matter of Middleton*, 16 Ed Dept Rep 50 (1976), *application to reopen denied*, 16 Ed Dept Rep 366 (1977); *connected case at* 16 Ed Dept Rep 368 (1977); see also *Appeal of Morehouse*, 37 Ed Dept Rep 428 (1998), *aff'd*, *Morehouse v. Mills*, 268 A.D.2d 767 (3d Dep't), *lv. to appeal denied*, 95 N.Y.2d 751 (2000); but see *Kwasnik v. King*, 123 A.D.3d 1264 (3d Dep't 2014)).

On the other hand, a teacher whose position is abolished does not relinquish recall rights to that position upon accepting a full-time position with the same district in a different tenure area and thereafter voluntarily resigning from that second position (*Appeal of Petkovsek,* 48 Ed Dept Rep 513 (2009)). See **33:3** for a discussion of the tenure status of teachers employed on a part-time basis.

Tenure rights also can be lost upon voluntary abandonment of a teaching position. A school district must establish abandonment of a teaching position through clear and convincing evidence that the teacher, by a voluntary and deliberate act, intended to relinquish his or her teaching position and forfeit tenure rights. That was the case where a tenured teacher who had been granted a leave of absence to work in another position later received a permanent appointment to yet another position upon leaving the one for which he had been granted a leave of absence, without seeking reinstatement as a teacher or an extension of the leave of absence (*Fehlhaber v. Bd. of Educ. of Utica City Sch. Dist.*, 96 A.D.3d 1633 (4th Dep't 2012)).

33:7. May a teacher transfer his or her tenure when accepting a position in a different school district or board of cooperative educational services (BOCES)?

No. Tenure is not transferable from one school district to another. Each school district is independent, and a teacher must serve a new probationary period whenever he or she moves to a different school district.

However, a teacher who has acquired tenure in one district or BOCES in New York State, or changes tenure areas within the same school district, was not dismissed from such district or BOCES as a result of charges brought pursuant to section 3020-a or section 3020-b of the Education Law (see **chapter 38**), and moves to another district or BOCES, is entitled to a shortened probationary period of three years (§ 2509(1)(a)(ii); see also §§ 2573(1)(a)(ii); 3012(1)(a)(ii), 3014(1)(b)). To qualify for the three year shortened probationary period, such a teacher would also have to demonstrate having received an annual professional performance review (APPR) rating in the final year of service in such other school district or BOCES (*Id.*). When such a teacher is seeking employment with a BOCES, the overall rating of the APPR for the final year of service in the other school district or BOCES must have been either effective or highly effective (§ 3014(1)(b)).

The reduced probationary periods would not be applied for a teacher previously tenured as a teaching assistant instead of as a teacher (*Putnam Northern Westchester BOCES v. Mills*, 46 A.D.3d 1062 (3d Dep't 2007); see **34:11**).

In comparison, teachers who are transferred to a different school within the same district do not lose any tenure rights within that district.

In addition, teachers who are transferred as a result of a BOCES takeover of services or a district takeover of BOCES services are entitled to full recognition of the tenure rights they previously held (§§ 3014-a, 3014-b; *Appeal of Valentine*, 38 Ed Dept Rep 39 (1998); *Appeal of Adler*, 37 Ed Dept Rep 95 (1997)). A comparable provision applies when teachers are transferred because a school district takes back students who were previously tuitioned out or takes in students tuitioned out from another district (§§ 3014-c, 3014-d). In *Appeal of Valentine* and *Appeal of Adler,* the commissioner of education held that a district that took over a BOCES program must credit former BOCES teachers now employed by the district with the BOCES service as well as any prior service and prior accumulated sick time credited by the BOCES.

Tenure by Estoppel

33:8. What is tenure by estoppel?

Tenure by estoppel, also referred to as tenure by acquiescence or tenure by operation of law, occurs when a district continues to accept and pays for the services of a teacher or administrator beyond the end of his or her probationary period with the full knowledge and consent of the school board, without the board having taken the action required by law to either grant or deny the teacher or administrator tenure prior to the expiration of the probationary term (*McManus v. Bd. of Educ. of Hempstead UFSD*, 87 N.Y.2d 183 (1995); *Matter of Gould v. Bd. of Educ. of Sewanhaka Cent. High Sch. Dist.*, 81 N.Y.2d 446 (1993); *Brown v. Bd. of Educ. of Mahopac CSD*, 129 A.D.3d 1067 (2d Dep't 2015); *Andrews v. Bd. of Educ. of City of N.Y.*, 92 A.D.3d 465 (1st Dep't 2012); *Lindsey v. Bd. of Educ. of Mt. Morris CSD*, 72 A.D.2d 185 (4th Dep't 1980); see also *Claudio v. Mattituck-Cutchogue UFSD*, 2014 U.S. Dist. LEXIS 103748 (E.D.N.Y. 2014)). In essence, tenure is imposed on the district because it acquiesced or consented to the employment of the teacher under conditions that are deemed to imply the granting of tenure. See **chapter 34** for more information on the tenure granting process.

The burden is on the teacher or administrator to show he or she has indeed acquired tenure by estoppel (*Matter of Dwyer v. Bd. of Educ. of Cazenovia CSD*, 61 A.D.2d 859 (3d Dep't 1978)).

33:9. What happens if someone who has acquired tenure by estoppel is improperly terminated?

Any such individual would be entitled to reinstatement, retroactive to the last date of employment, back pay, and all accrued benefits of employment (*Ricca v. Bd. of Educ. of City Sch. Dist. of City of N.Y.*, 47 N.Y.2d 385 (1979); *Brown v. Bd. of Educ. of Mahopac CSD*, 129 A.D.3d 1067 (2d Dep't 2015); *Matter of Walters v. Amityville UFSD*, 251 A.D.2d 590 (2d Dep't 1998)).

33:10. Are there any circumstances that can preclude a teacher from claiming entitlement to tenure by estoppel?

Yes, when the extension of services beyond the expiration of his or her probationary term (see **33:8**) is pursuant to what is commonly referred to as a *Juul* agreement (see **34:20-22**). The valid execution of a *Juul* agreement precludes such a claim (*Chisolm v. Hochman*, 109 A.D.3d 821 (2d Dep't 2013); see also *Claudio v. Mattituck-Cutchogue UFSD*, 2014 U.S. Dist. LEXIS 103748 (E.D.N.Y. 2014)).

33:11. Are there any circumstances under which a part-time teacher employed without a probationary appointment could acquire tenure by estoppel?

Yes. Although generally part-time teachers are not entitled to tenure or probationary appointments, a teacher deemed employed in a part-time capacity and without a probationary appointment would be entitled to tenure by estoppel if it is later determined that the teacher is in fact a full-time employee who has served the requisite probationary period (*Walters v. Amityville UFSD*, 251 A.D.2d 590 (2d Dep't 1998)). See **34:4** for information on part-time teachers who are entitled to a tenure-track probationary appointment.

33:12. Is it possible for a teacher who resigns to still be entitled to tenure by estoppel?

It depends. That was the case where the resignation was submitted under the mistaken belief that the teacher had not yet acquired and was going to be denied tenure. In fact, the teacher had already obtained tenure by estoppel because neither the teacher nor the district had noticed she was entitled to a shortened probationary period of two years rather than the usual three years, and had rendered service as a probationary teacher for three years (*Matter of Gould v. Bd. of Educ. of Sewanhaka Cent. High Sch. Dist.*, 81 N.Y.2d 446 (1993)). See **chapter 34** for more information on probationary appointments).

However, the district would not have had to allow the teacher to rescind the resignation if, for example, in her job application she had unambiguously stated she had never received tenure elsewhere in the state, notwithstanding six years of prior teaching experience (see *Appeal of Price*, 46 Ed Dept Rep 490 (2007)). According to the commissioner of education there could have been "breaks in service, leaves of absence, part-time service or any number of unknown actors . . . that would have precluded tenure in the first job" and districts do not have "a duty to ferret out the nuances of a teacher's employment history."

33:13. Is it possible to acquire tenure by estoppel as a result of a pending annual professional performance review (APPR) appeal?

No. School district and boards of cooperative educational services may terminate, or make tenure determinations, while an APPR appeal is pending (Educ. Law § 3012-d(9); 8 NYCRR 30-3.12(d); *Guidance on New York State's Annual Professional Performance Review for Teachers and Principals to Implement Education Law § 3012-d and the Commissioner's Regulations* (updated August 2015), q. K5 (c), at: https://www.engageny.org/resource/guidance-on-new-york-s-annual-professional-performance-review-law-and-regulations).

Tenure Areas

33:14. What is the difference between tenure and tenure areas?

Tenure is a classification of employment granted to teachers who have completed a probationary period of satisfactory service with a school district (see **33:1**). Tenure areas are subject areas of teaching positions that are established by the Board of Regents (see **33:15**).

Teachers are granted tenure in specific tenure areas established by the Board of Regents.

33:15. What is the legal definition of a tenure area?

A *tenure area* is defined as "the administrative subdivision within the organizational structure of a school district in which a professional educator is deemed to serve" (8 NYCRR § 30-1.1(h)). When a school board appoints a teacher to a probationary teaching position (see **chapter 34**), the teacher must be appointed to a position in one or more of the tenure areas, or subject areas, established by law (8 NYCRR §§ 30-1.2, 30-1.3, 30-1.4; see **33:16**).

Part 30 of the Rules of the Board of Regents establishes the various subject (sometimes referred to as "vertical") tenure areas that must be used for teachers hired after August 1, 1975. They include, for example, elementary education, mathematics, English, science and art.

Teachers who were hired before August 1, 1975 are governed by the old "horizontal" system of tenure areas that were established by each district before the enactment of part 30 (*Baer v. Nyquist*, 34 N.Y.2d 291 (1974); see also *Matter of Waiters v. Bd. of Educ.*, *Amityville UFSD*, 46 N.Y.2d 885 (1979); *Matter of Parcells*, 23 Ed Dept Rep 61 (1983)). Tenure areas often were established by grade level and not by subject area so that, for example, an English teacher and a science teacher teaching at the secondary grade level may be in the same tenure area.

As a result of this, a dual system of tenure areas exists, with one set of tenure area rules applying to persons appointed before August 1, 1975 and another set of rules governing those appointed after that date (*Rippe v. Bd. of Educ. of Comsewogue-Brookhaven Sch. Dist.*, 64 N.Y.2d 281 (1985); *Freeman v. Bd. of Educ. of Hempstead Sch. Dist.*, 205 A.D.2d 38 (2d Dep't 1994); *Matter of Platania,* 20 Ed Dept Rep 670 (1981)).

33:16. What are the tenure areas established by Part 30 of the Rules of the Board of Regents?

The part 30 tenure areas established by the Rules of the Board of Regents for teachers hired and appointed to probationary teaching positions on or after August 1, 1975 include elementary, middle grades, academic and special subject areas (8 NYCRR §§ 30-1.5-30-1.8).

- The *elementary tenure area* encompasses pre-kindergarten through sixth grade (8 NYCRR §§ 30-1.4, 30-1.5).
- The *middle grades tenure area* applies when the instruction of seventh and eighth grades is not departmentalized by academic area (8 NYCRR §§ 30-1.4, 30-1.6).
- The *academic tenure areas* of English, social studies, mathematics, science, and foreign languages apply to teachers at or above the seventh-grade level, where instruction in the core academic subjects is departmentalized (8 NYCRR §§ 30-1.4, 30-1.7).
- The s*pecial subject tenure areas,* encompass 15 academic areas, six vocational education subject areas, nine ancillary or supportive educational services, eight board of cooperative educational services (BOCES) instructional support services areas, and one teaching assistant area (8 NYCRR § 30-1.8; see **33:20**).

These tenure areas apply to all school districts except those in the cities of New York and Buffalo or to those employing fewer than eight teachers, except that the special subject tenure areas for instructional support services apply only to BOCES (8 NYCRR § 30-1.2; see also **33:22-23**). In addition, they apply to teachers of students who are under age 21 and eligible to receive a public education (*Appeal of Marsico*, 50 Ed Dept Rep, Dec. No. 16,158 (2010); *Appeal of Thomas*, 34 Ed Dept Rep 181 (1994)).

33:17. What are the tenure areas recognized for teachers not covered by Part 30 of the Rules of the Board of Regents?

Teachers hired before August 1, 1975 are subject to the old horizontal tenure areas plus several special subject areas (*Baer v. Nyquist*, 34 N.Y.2d 291 (1974)). Teachers who serve at a given horizontal level, such as elementary, middle school, junior high or high school, frequently serve in a single grade-level tenure area, regardless of the subject they teach (such as English, mathematics, social studies, science, and foreign languages). The courts and the commissioner of education also have recognized certain permissible special subject tenure areas for them, such as guidance counselor (*Steele v. Bd. of Educ. of City of N.Y.* 40 N.Y.2d 456 (1976); *Matter of Glowacki*, 14 Ed Dept Rep 122 (1974)) and music and physical education (*Baer v. Nyquist*).

In addition, part 30 may be used as a guideline to determine whether a particular subject may be considered a traditional special subject tenure area under horizontal tenure practices (*Steele v. Bd. of Educ. of City of N.Y.; Mitchell v. Bd. of Educ. of Great Neck Pub. Sch.* 40 N.Y.2d 904 (1976)). Where it is unclear if a teacher has served in a separate tenure area, resolution of the dispute depends on whether the district has treated the subject as being separate (*Hicksville Congress of Teachers v. Hicksville UFSD,* 118 A.D.2d 623 (2d Dep't 1986)). Separate tenure areas may have been created by school policy, board resolution or regulation (*Matter of Muzante*, 16 Ed Dept Rep 149 (1976)), as well as by tenure appointment resolutions, schedules of appointment or employment records (*Matter of Zappulla*, 25 Ed Dept Rep 54 (1985); *Matter of Platania*, 20 Ed Dept Rep 670 (1981)). Teachers and administrators must be notified that they are serving in a separate tenure area (*Waiters v. Bd. of Educ. Amityville UFSD*, 46 N.Y.2d 885 (1979); *Mitchell v. Bd. of Educ. of Great Neck Pub. Sch.*).

33:18. What happens if a school district appoints a teacher to an unauthorized tenure area?

The commissioner of education has ruled that as of August 1, 1975 districts may only appoint teachers to those tenure areas designated in part 30 and may not create new tenure areas for teaching positions, such as a gifted and talented teacher, that do not easily fit within those areas (*Appeal of Bales*, 32 Ed Dept Rep 559 (1993); see also *Appeal of Devente,* 48 Ed Dept Rep 150 (2008)).

If a district should appoint a teacher to an unauthorized tenure area, the teacher will be deemed to actually serve within the authorized tenure area which encompasses the teacher's actual duties (*Kaufman v. Fallsburg CSD Bd. of Educ.*, 91 N.Y.2d 57 (1997); *Abrantes v. Bd. of Educ. of the Norwood-Norfolk CSD*, 233 A.D.2d 718 (3d Dep't 1996), *appeal denied*, 89 N.Y.2d 812 (1997); *Herbert-Glover v. Bd. of Educ. of Wantagh UFSD*, 213 A.D.2d 404 (2d Dep't 1995); *Appeal of Lessing*, 34 Ed Dept Rep 451 (1995); see also *Appeal of Devente;* 8 NYCRR § 30-1.9).

33:19. May a teacher serve in more than one tenure area at the same time?

Yes. Under part 30 of the Rules of the Board of Regents, teachers are deemed to serve in any tenure area in which they spend a "substantial portion," defined as at least 40 percent, of their time. Teachers serving in more than one tenure area at the same time gain seniority credit under both tenure areas (8 NYCRR § 30-1.1(f), (g)), and also may acquire tenure in both tenure areas (8 NYCRR § 30-1.9(d)).

In addition, a teacher assigned to spend 40 percent or more of his or her time in a second tenure area may acquire tenure by estoppel (see **33:8**) in that area despite a district's failure to give him or her a formal probationary appointment (*Freeman v. Bd. of Educ. of Hempstead Sch. Dist.*, 205 A.D.2d 38 (2d Dep't 1994); see *Kaufman v. Fallsburg CSD Bd. of Educ.*, 91 N.Y.2d 57 (1997)).

On the other hand, teachers who do not devote at least 40 percent of their work time to classroom instruction in a part 30 tenure area cannot be deemed to be working in that tenure area (*Appeal of Devente*, 48 Ed Dept Rep 150 (2008); see also *Matter of Christian v. Bayport-Blue Point UFSD*, 129 A.D.3d 836 (2d Dep't 2015)). An exception applies under special tenure area assignment rules that apply to teachers appointed or assigned to devote a substantial portion of their time providing *instructional support services* to other school personnel (8 NYCRR §§ 30-1.1(e), (g), (j), 30-1.2, 30-1.9 (b); see **33:22**).

A teacher's Basic Educational Data System (BEDS) report is not definitive proof of the time a teacher has spent teaching in a specific area (*Appeal of Soukey*, 38 Ed Dept Rep 626 (1999); see also *Appeal of Gordon*, 53 Ed Dept Rep, Dec. No. 16,582 (2013)). Furthermore, a teacher cannot be credited with working in two tenure areas during the exact same time period with the same student(s) (*Appeal of Gordon*).

33:20. In what tenure area do teaching assistants serve?

The commissioner of education has certified to the NYS Civil Service Commission that the position of teaching assistant is among those within a school district's teaching and supervisory staff, and part 30 of the Rules of the Board of Regents designates the position as a special subject tenure area (8 NYCRR § 30-1.8(d)).

However, school districts may not classify teaching assistant tenure areas by specific subject assignment, for example, "teaching assistant — science," or "teaching assistant — heavy equipment" (*Appeal of Krason,* 41 Ed Dept Rep 305 (2002), *aff'd, Madison-Oneida BOCES v. Mills,* 2 A.D.3d 1240 (3d Dep't 2003), *aff'd,* 4 N.Y.3d 51 (2004); see *Appeal of McCollum*, 44 Ed Dept Rep 306 (2005); *Appeal of Denova,* 44 Ed Dept Rep 308 (2005); see also *Putnam Northern Westchester BOCES v. Mills*, 46 A.D.3d 1062 (3d Dep't 2007)).

In addition, school districts may not designate teaching assistants as teacher aides (*Appeal of Tedesco*, 52 Ed Dept Rep, Dec. No. 16,417 (2012)). The duties of both positions are separate and distinct and require different qualifications (8 NYCRR § 80-5.6 (a), (b)(1); *Appeal of Tedesco*). Moreover, unlike teaching assistants, teacher aides are classified in the noncompetitive class of the civil service (see **chapter 39**), and have no tenure or seniority rights under the Education Law (*Appeal of Tedesco*).

33:21. In what tenure area(s) are teachers who also perform administrative functions deemed to serve?

In determining whether particular employees serve in an administrative tenure area or a teacher tenure area, the courts and the commissioner of education have applied what is commonly known as the 50 percent rule: If *more than* 50 percent of an employee's duties are administrative in nature, he or she will be deemed to serve in an administrative tenure area (*Appeal of Klein*, 43 Ed Dept Rep 305 (2003), *petition dismissed*, Special Term (Sup. Ct. Albany Cnty.), Ceresia, J. (Dec. 6, 2004); *Coates v. Ambach,* 52 A.D.2d 261 (3d Dep't 1976), *aff'd,* 42 N.Y.2d 846 (1977); see also *Cowan v. Bd. of Educ. of Brentwood UFSD*, 99 A.D.2d 831 (2d Dep't), *appeal withdrawn*, 63 N.Y.2d 702 (1984); see **9:18**).

Prior to the enactment of part 30, an individual who served in an administrative rather than a teacher tenure area under the 50 percent rule was not eligible for seniority credit in the teacher tenure area. Subsequent to the enactment of part 30, however, teachers are deemed to serve in any tenure area in which they serve at least 40 percent of their time (see **33:19**; *Sapphire v. Bd. of Educ. Hastings UFSD*, 96 A.D.2d 1033 (2d Dep't), *appeal dismissed*, 60 N.Y.2d 1015 (1983)).

An educator who serves in both an administrative and teacher tenure area at the same time can receive seniority credit and tenure in both tenure areas, provided that the individual performs more than 50 percent of his or her duties in the administrative tenure area and at least 40 percent of his or her duties in a teacher tenure area (*Appeal of Pearse*, 50 Ed Dept Rep, Dec. No. 16,159 (2010); see **33:19, 33:32**).

33:22. In what tenure area do teachers employed by a school district to provide instructional support services serve?

It depends on the date of the teacher's appointment or assignment to provide instructional support services (see **33:23** regarding teachers employed by a board of cooperative educational services (BOCES) to provide instructional support services). Pursuant to commissioner's regulations also referred to as the "*Devente* regulations":

- Teachers who prior to May 1, 2009 were appointed to tenure or a probationary appointment in a part 30 tenure area (see **33:16**) by a school district or board of cooperative educational services (BOCES) to provide instructional support services and did not provide knowing consent to an assignment outside their previous tenure area when assigned to perform such services are deemed to have accrued tenure and seniority rights in the previous tenure area from the date of their assignment to perform duties in instructional support services. They continue to receive tenure and seniority rights in the previous tenure area for as long as they provide such services (8 NYCRR § 30-1.2(b)(1)).

- Those employed on May 1, 2009 who were previously appointed to provide instructional support services but who were appointed to tenure or a probationary period in an improper or unauthorized tenure area based on the performance of those duties are deemed to have been appointed or assigned to serve in a tenure area for which they hold proper certification, from the date of their assignment to provide such services, provided they hold the proper certification for that tenure area (8 NYCRR § 30-1.2(b)(2)).
- Teachers assigned to provide instructional support services on or after May 1, 2009 who were previously appointed to tenure or a probationary period in a tenure area authorized by part 30 are credited with tenure and seniority rights in their existing tenure area while performing instructional support services (8 NYCRR § 30-1.2(b)(4)).
- Those appointed or assigned on or after May 1, 2009 to provide instructional support services who were not previously appointed to tenure or a probationary period in a part 30 tenure area must meet certification and experience requirements set out in commissioner's regulations (see **31:9**) and be appointed to a tenure area for which they are properly certified (8 NYCRR §§ 30-1.2(b)(5), 30-1.9(b)).

To benefit from the protections afforded by the *Devente* regulations, a teacher must have actually performed duties that qualify as instructional support services under section 30-1.1(j) of commissioner's regulations. Supervising students assigned to in-school suspension and working with other staff regarding those students, for example, do not qualify as such (*Thorenz v. Bd. of Educ. of the Monticello CSD*, 101 A.D.3d 1563 (3d Dep't 2012) *lv. to appeal denied*, 21 N.Y.3d 851 (2013)).

A school district that appoints a teacher on or after May 20, 2011 to devote a substantial portion of his or her time to instructional support services as a result of the district taking over a program formerly operated by a BOCES where that teacher was serving in an instructional support services tenure area, must credit the teacher with tenure and seniority rights in a tenure area for which he or she holds the proper certification, from the initial date of his or her assignment to instructional support services in the BOCES (§ 3014-b, 8 NYCRR § 30-1.2(c)(4); see also **33:23**)).

These rules do not apply to city school districts in a city with a population of over 400,000 inhabitants or to districts employing fewer than eight teachers (8 NYCRR § 30-1.2(e)).

33:23. In what tenure area do teachers employed by a board of cooperative educational services (BOCES) who provide instructional support services serve?

It depends. A BOCES that appoints or assigns a teacher on or after May 20, 2011 to devote a substantial portion, (more than 40 percent), of his or her time to provide instructional support services must do so pursuant to Subpart 30-1.8 of the commissioner's regulations, which specifies eight different special subject tenure areas in instructional support services (8 NYCRR §§ 30-1.1(g); 30-1.2(c)(2); 30-1.8 (e)).

- Teachers employed by a BOCES to devote a substantial portion of their time to provide instructional support services on May 20, 2011, who were previously appointed to tenure or a probationary period in a part 30 tenure area, continue to accrue tenure and seniority rights in their previous tenure area. However, such teachers who provided knowing consent by June 20, 2011, to the BOCES to change their tenure area, accrue tenure and seniority rights in one of the eight special subject tenure areas in instructional support services from the date they were initially appointed to provide instructional support services (8 NYCRR § 30-1.2(c)).

- A BOCES that appoints a teacher on or after May 20, 2011 to devote a substantial portion of his time to instructional support services as a result of a BOCES taking over a program formerly operated by a school district, must credit the teacher with tenure and seniority rights in one of the special subject tenure area for instructional support services from the initial date of his or her assignment to the performance of instructional support services in the school district (§ 3014-a, 8 NYCRR § 30-1.2(c)(3)).

33:24. May a district transfer teachers in the elementary tenure area from one specific grade to another?

Yes. Staff assignments are within the discretion of the school authorities as long as the assignments are within the proper tenure area (*Mishkoff v. Nyquist*, 57 A.D.2d 649 (3d Dep't 1977), *lv. to appeal denied*, 43 N.Y.2d 641 (1977); *Appeal of Dillon,* 43 Ed Dept Rep 333 (2004); *Matter of Gould*, 17 Ed Dept Rep 283 (1978)).

33:25. May a teacher be transferred to a position in a different tenure area?

Yes, but only with the teacher's consent. Regardless of whether a teacher has tenure or still is a probationary employee, the teacher may not be assigned to devote a substantial portion of his or her time outside his or her existing tenure area without his or her prior written consent (8 NYCRR § 30-1.9(c); *Matter of Zamek*, 19 Ed Dept Rep 77 (1979)). In addition, an assignment from a teacher's current tenure area to a position in a tenure area in which the teacher previously acquired tenure is still an assignment outside of the teacher's current area that requires the teacher's consent (8 NYCRR § 30-1.9(c); *Appeal of Hutchinson,* 48 Ed Dept Rep 377 (2009); *Appeal of Pendl*, 28 Ed Dept Rep 511 (1989); *Appeal of Singer,* 19 Ed Dept Rep 297 (1979); *Matter of Adler*, 8 Ed Dept Rep 6 (1968); see also *Appeal of Shayo*, 12 Ed Dept Rep 143 (1973)).

However, a teacher who is certified in several subjects may be assigned to serve in another tenure area for less than 40 percent of the time without being deemed to work in a different tenure area (8 NYCRR §§ 30-1.1(g), 30-1.9(a); see **33:19, 34:8**).

A teacher transferred to a different tenure area does not lose any previously earned tenure or seniority in the former area.

Teachers who believe that their tenure area has been changed must claim some harm as a result of the change in order to invoke review by the commissioner of education (*Appeal of Lachler*, 47 Ed Dept Rep 455 (2008); *Appeal of Vuoto*, 44 Ed Dept Rep 251 (2005)).

33:26. What happens if a district transfers a teacher to a position in a different tenure area without the teacher's consent?

If a teacher is transferred to service in another tenure area without his or her consent, all service in that other area is deemed, as a matter of law, to constitute service for purposes of seniority in the teacher's prior tenure area (*Matter of Boron v. Sobol*, 205 A.D.2d 28 (3d Dep't 1994), *appeal denied,* 86 N.Y.2d 711 (1995); *Maine-Endwell Teachers Ass'n v. Maine-Endwell CSD*, 92 A.D.2d 1052 (3d Dep't 1983); *Appeal of Hutchinson*, 48 Ed Dept Rep 377 (2009); *Appeal of Lawrence*, 32 Ed Dept Rep 398 (1992); see 8 NYCRR § 30-1.9(c)). However, the New York Court of Appeals has ruled that a teacher who is transferred to another tenure area without his or her consent may knowingly and voluntarily waive his or her right to have his or her service in the latter tenure area credited for purposes of seniority in the teacher's prior tenure area. Under such circumstances, a district may grant seniority credit for such service to the teacher in the second tenure area (*Kaufman v. Fallsburg CSD Bd. of Educ.*, 91 N.Y.2d 57 (1997)).

In comparison, when a transfer to a new tenure area occurs with the teacher's consent, the teacher begins a new probationary period in a new tenure area (8 NYCRR § 30-1.9(e)), unless the teacher already has tenure in that other area.

Seniority Rights

33:27. What is the difference between tenure rights and seniority rights?

Tenure rights are those rights and privileges enjoyed by tenured teachers, the most important of which is the limitation pertaining to employment disciplinary proceedings (see **chapter 38**). *Seniority rights* affect job security based on appointment to a tenure area.

In addition, seniority rights apply to both tenured and probationary teachers, while tenure rights apply only to tenured teachers.

33:28. What are seniority rights?

Seniority rights are those rights to job security and priority within a school district based on length of actual paid service in a specific tenure area (*Volk v. Bd. of Educ. of City Sch. Dist. of Rochester*, 83 N.Y.2d 930 (1994); 8 NYCRR § 30-1.1(f)). They are earned by both probationary and tenured educators (*Alessi v. Bd. of Educ., Wilson CSD*, 105 A.D.3d 54 (4th Dep't 2013); *Matter of Carey*, 31 Ed Dept Rep 394 (1992)).

The Education Law does not provide a definition of the term seniority. It just requires that seniority be used in determining the order in which teachers are dismissed in the event that teaching positions are consolidated or abolished (§§ 2510(2), 2585(3), 3013(2); see *Appeal of Krason,* 41 Ed Dept Rep 305 (2002), *aff'd, Madison-Oneida BOCES v. Mills,* 2 A.D.3d 1240 (3d Dep't 2003), *aff'd,* 4 N.Y.3d 51(2004); *Seney v. Bd. of Educ. of E. Greenbush CSD*, 103 A.D.3d 1022 (3d Dep't 2013)).

However, commissioner's regulations do define seniority – in terms of the "length of service in a designated tenure area, . . ." (8 NYCRR § 30-1.1(f)). They also require that for an educator to accrue seniority within a given tenure area, his or her service within that tenure area must constitute "a substantial portion of the time of the professional educator" (*Id.*; see also **33:29**). This means 40 percent or more of the total time spent in the performance of instructional duties (8 NYCRR § 30-1.1 (f), (g)). However, according to one state appellate court, a teacher who was appointed to a three-year probationary term in the English 7-12 tenure area, but who was immediately assigned to teach computer application courses, accrued seniority within the English 7-12 tenure area even though she never served a substantial portion of her time in that tenure area (*Cronk v. King*, 130 A.D.3d 1415 (3d Dep't 2015); see 8 NYCRR § 30-1.9(c)).

Seniority is the sole criterion districts may use to decide which teacher will be excessed — tenured status may not be a consideration (*Matter of Fallick*, 18 Ed Dept Rep 586 (1979), *aff'd*, n.o.r., (Sup. Ct. Albany Cnty.), Hughes, J.S.C. (Feb. 11, 1980)). Likewise, certification may not be used as a factor in determining seniority (*Lynch v. Nyquist*, 41 A.D.2d 363 (3d Dep't 1973), *aff'd*, 34 N.Y.2d 588 (1974); *Silver v. Bd. of Educ. of W. Canada Valley CSD*, 46 A.D.2d 427 (4th Dep't 1975)).

In comparison, the order in which districts recall back to work teachers who have been excessed and placed on a preferred eligible list is determined by the length of their service with the district (see **36:17**).

33:29. How do tenure areas affect seniority rights?

The relationship between tenure areas and seniority rights stems from the legal requirement that when a school board decides to abolish a position within a given tenure area it must excess and terminate the services of the teacher with the least seniority within that tenure area (*Lynch v. Nyquist*, 41 A.D.2d 363

(3d Dep't 1973), *aff'd,* 34 N.Y.2d 588 (1974); *Matter of Daly*, 23 Ed Dept Rep 147 (1983); see also *Appeal of Dyminski*, 47 Ed Dept Rep 312 (2007); see **33:28**). For more information on the abolition of positions and excessing of teachers see **chapter 36**.

33:30. Can teachers accrue seniority in more than one tenure area?

Yes. A teacher who has several probationary or tenure appointments in separate tenure areas accrues seniority separately in each area, depending on the actual service performed. For example, if a teacher serves 50 percent of the time as a mathematics teacher and 50 percent of the time as a science teacher for five years, and then teaches only mathematics 100 percent of the time for two years, then that teacher has seven years of seniority credit in mathematics and five years of seniority credit in science. (See **33:22-23**, regarding special rules for teachers who provide instructional support services to other school personnel.)

However, should that teacher be terminated because of an abolition of positions, the order of his or her recall from a preferred eligible list depend on his of service within the district rather than in a tenure area (*Mahony v. Bd. of Educ. of Mahopac CSD*, 140 A.D.2d 33 (2d Dep't), *appeal denied*, 73 N.Y.2d 703 (1988)). Therefore, he or she would have seven years of seniority for purposes of reappointment to either a mathematics or science position.

Only individuals in tenure-track positions accrue seniority and have recall rights. Thus, a teacher who served in an adult education position, not certified by the commissioner of education to the state civil service commission as being in the teaching or supervisory staff, was deemed not to have spent at least 40 percent of her time in a tenure-bearing position. As such, her service could not be counted as service in the system for purposes of recall rights (*Appeal of Marsico*, 50 Ed Dept Rep, Dec. No. 16,158 (2010)).

For more information on the abolition of positions and the excessing of teachers see **chapter 36**.

33:31. Can seniority rights be transferred from one tenure area to another?

No. The Education Law does not authorize the accrual of "general" seniority credit. Such credit is earned within a specific tenure area. As a result, teachers who begin teaching in a new tenure area become the least senior member in the new tenure area, regardless of their prior years of service in a different tenure area (*Claudio v. Mattituck-Cutchogue UFSD*, 955 F.Supp.2d 118 (E.D.N.Y. 2014); see also **33:28-29**)).

33:32. Can seniority rights be waived or altered by a written agreement?

Seniority rights may be waived by agreement. However, to be effective the waiver must be clearly evidenced and given with knowledge and consent (*Feinerman v. Bd. of Coop. Educ. Services*, 48 N.Y.2d 491 (1979); *Ambramovich v. Bd. of Educ. of Cent. Sch. Dist. No.1 of Towns of Brookhaven and Smithtown*, 46 N.Y.2d 450 (1979), *reconsideration denied*, 46 N.Y.2d 1076 (1979), *cert. denied*, 444 U.S. 845 (1979); *Yastion v. Mills*, 229 A.D.2d 775 (3d Dep't 1996)).

On the other hand, school districts cannot enter into an agreement to extend seniority rights (*Id.*). In a case upheld by the Albany County Supreme Court, the commissioner of education ruled that a business education teacher was not entitled to continue to accrue seniority in a teaching tenure area while placed on special assignment in the district's business office, even though the district, the teachers' union, and the teacher signed a written agreement that the teacher would continue to accrue such seniority (*Appeal of Tropia*, 32 Ed Dept Rep 606 (1993), *aff'd, Matter of Camden CSD*, n.o.r., (Sup. Ct. Albany Cnty.), Keegan, J.S.C. (Jan. 11, 1994)).

33:33. Do teachers lose accrued seniority when they "voluntarily" sever service with the district?

Yes. Teachers lose their accrued seniority when they voluntarily sever service with the district that employs them, as for example, through resignation or retirement (*Appeal of Carey*, 31 Ed Dept Rep 394 (1992); see also *Kransdorf v. Bd. of Educ. of Northport-East Northport UFSD*, 81 N.Y.2d 871 (1993); *Alessi v. Bd. of Educ., Wilson CSD*, 105 A.D.3d 54 (4th Dep't 2013); *Appeal of Beauchamp* 50 Ed Dept Rep, Dec. No. 16,123 (2010); *Appeal of Morehouse*, 37 Ed Dept Rep 428 (1998), *aff'd,* 268 A.D.2d 767 (3d Dep't), *appeal denied*, 95 N.Y.2d 751 (2000); *Matter of Ducey*, 65 St. Dep't Rep. 65 (1943)).

A relinquishment must be knowing and voluntary, meaning that the employee must take "affirmative steps" to terminate all aspects of employment with the school district (*Alessi v. Bd. of Educ., Wilson CSD*; see also *Appeal of Petrovsek*, 48 Ed Dept Rep 513 (2009)). Thus, a teacher merely assenting to being assigned to a different title within the same tenure area, under the "guise" of a resignation is not deemed to have resigned for purposes of seniority credit as long as the title to which the teacher is assigned is otherwise eligible for such credit (*Alessi v. Bd. of Educ., Wilson CSD*).

The determination of whether a teacher voluntarily severs his/her employment will generally be based on an analysis of the specific facts of each case. For instance, a teacher was found not to have voluntarily severed her employment when she (i) was encouraged by the interim superintendent to take another position, (ii) expressed her reluctance to leave her position and requested a leave of absence, (iii) received a longevity pay increase, (iv) continued to accrue sick and personal leave time that had carried over from her prior position, and (v) received a severance payment that would not have been made if she voluntarily severed her employment (*Kwasnik v. King*, 123 A.D.3d 1264 (3d Dep't 2014)).

Furthermore, when a teacher's service with a district is "involuntarily" severed because the teacher's position is eliminated and the teacher is excessed, the teacher retains any accrued seniority upon returning to service with that district in the future; the seniority clock is not reset when a teacher returns to service after being excessed (*Appeal of Lamb*, 42 Ed Dept Rep 406 (2003)).

33:34. How is seniority calculated?

The courts and the commissioner of education have defined seniority in terms of length of actual paid service within a tenure area to a school district (*Alessi v. Bd. of Educ., Wilson CSD*, 105 A.D.3d 54 (4th Dep't 2013); *Dreyfuss v. Bd. of Educ. Union Free Sch. Dist. no. 3 Town of Washington,* 76 Misc.2d 479 (Sup. Ct. Nassau Cnty. 1973), *aff'd,* 45 A.D.2d 988 (2d Dep't 1974); *Matter of Halayko,* 23 Ed Dept Rep 384 (1984); *Appeal of Goldman*, 43 Ed Dept Rep 338 (2004)).

The first criterion for determining seniority is the actual full-time service rendered within the tenure area (*Alessi v. Bd. of Educ., Wilson CSD*; *Matter of Schoenfeld v. BOCES of Nassau Cnty.*, 98 A.D.2d 723 (2d Dep't 1983); *Appeal of Kulick*, 34 Ed Dept Rep 613 (1995)). This includes full-time regular substitute service in a particular tenure area preceding a probationary appointment in that same tenure area (*Kransdorf v. Bd. of Educ. of Northport E. Northport UFSD*, 81 N.Y.2d 871 (1993); *Alessi v. Bd. of Educ., Wilson CSD*; see also **33:38**), but not per-diem substitute service (*Alessi v. Bd. of Educ., Wilson CSD*). An "itinerant" or per diem substitute assigned on a temporary, as needed basis does not accumulate seniority (*Alessi v. Bd. of Educ., Wilson CSD*; *Appeal of Fitzsimmons*, 54 Ed Dept Rep, Dec. No. 16,686 (2014)).

If the full-time service of two or more teachers is equal, the teachers' respective appointment dates are to be used for determining seniority (*Matter of Ferguson*, 14 Ed Dept Rep 102 (1974); see also *Matter of Schoenfeld v. BOCES of Nassau Cnty.*; *Appeal of Kulick*). But when the teachers have equal seniority and the same appointment date, the more senior teacher is the one whose appointment occurred first (*Matter of Ducey*, 65 State Dep't Rep. 65 (1943)).

In the event that two teachers were appointed in the same resolution, a school district may use any reasonable method to establish seniority, including factors such as the dates on which an employment agreement was signed or returned, and also may consider the salaries of the employees (*Schoenfeld v. BOCES of Nassau Cnty.; Matter of Sommers,* 19 Ed Dept Rep 99 (1979); *Appeal of Kiernan*, 32 Ed Dept Rep 618 (1993); *Matter of Cesaratto*, 17 Ed Dept Rep 23 (1977); *Matter of Nicolette*, 17 Ed Dept Rep 381 (1978)). Use of last name alphabetical order as an objective means of breaking a seniority tie has also been deemed to be acceptable (*Appeal of Gale*, 53 Ed Dept Rep, Dec. No. 16,584 (2014)). However, a teacher's failure to provide notice of termination of services to his or her employing district at the time of appointment by another district is unavailing to break a seniority tie (*Appeal of Gale*).

33:35. Does service have to be continuous in order to count toward seniority?

No. School districts are required to comply with the requirements of section 30-1.1 (which is applicable to all probationary appointments made after August 1, 1975). This section mandates that seniority "need not have been consecutive but shall, during each term for which seniority credit is sought, have constituted a substantial portion of the time of the professional educator" (i.e., equaling 40 percent or more of the total time spent by the professional educator in the performance of his or her duties) (8 NYCRR § 30-1.1(f), (g)). Thus, years of regular full-time substitute teaching service, interrupted by periods of part-time substitute service prior to a probationary appointment, should count for purposes of seniority by virtue of section 30-1.1(f) (*Kransdorf v. Bd. of Educ. Northport-East Northport UFSD*, 81 N.Y.2d 871 (1993); *Appeal of Carey*, 31 Ed Dept Rep 394 (1992)).

33:36. Do unpaid leaves of absence count toward the calculation of seniority?

Days spent on unpaid leave of absence may not be included in determining seniority (*Matter of Halayko*, 23 Ed Dept Rep 384 (1984); *Appeal of Goldman,* 43 Ed Dept Rep 338 (2004)). Neither is there an entitlement to accrue seniority on days of unpaid leave under the Family Medical and Leave Act (*Appeal of Scarpinati de Oliveira*, 52 Ed Dept Rep, Dec. No. 16,411 (2012); see 29 C.F.R. § 825.215).

In addition, a district is not obliged to grant credit for interrupted service when the teacher has not obtained a leave of absence. However, a district may choose to grant credit for interrupted service pursuant to a collective bargaining agreement with its teachers (*Bd. of Educ. Lakeland CSD v. Lakeland Fed'n of Teachers,* 51 A.D.2d 1033 (2d Dep't 1976)).

33:37. Who settles disputes regarding the amount of seniority credit that should be awarded to a particular teacher?

If a school district and a teacher cannot agree on the amount of seniority credit to which the teacher is entitled, the teacher may appeal the district's determination to the commissioner of education, or in some cases, to a court.

According to one state appellate court "disputes involving the calculation of seniority fall within the purview of the Commissioner of Education, who possesses the requisite expertise to settle such matters" and therefore, the courts should decline to exercise jurisdiction over seniority disputes until after the commissioner has rendered a decision (*Devente v. Bd. of Educ. Broome-Tioga Bd. of Coop. Educ. Servs*., 15 A.D.3d 716 (3d Dep't 2005)).

The commissioner does not issue advisory opinions concerning an educator's seniority status. "A party may not maintain an appeal solely to obtain a declaration of his . . . relative seniority" (*Appeal of Lachler*, 47 Ed Dept Rep 455 (2008); *Appeal of Vuoto*, 44 Ed Dept Rep 251 (2005)).

33:38. Does service as a regular substitute teacher count towards seniority for purposes of calculating the length of service in the district generally, or in a particular tenure area?

Yes. A teacher must be given seniority credit for full-time regular substitute service rendered prior to a probationary appointment, if the teacher performed part-time services for the district in the interim (*Kransdorf v. Bd. of Educ. of Northport-East Northport UFSD*, 81 N.Y.2d 871 (1993); *Appeal of Goldman*, 43 Ed Dept Rep 338 (2004); *Appeal of Lamb*, 42 Ed Dept Rep 406 (2003); *Appeal of Carey*, 31 Ed Dept Rep 394 (1992); *Appeal of Kahn and Cruz*, 35 Ed Dept Rep 129 (1995)). Similarly, prior full-time regular substitute service counts toward seniority even if it is for less than the full semester required for *Jarema* credit (*Kaufman v. Fallsburg CSD*, 91 N.Y.2d 57 (1997); see also **34:15-18**).

Moreover, the New York Court of Appeals and the commissioner of education have ruled that if a teacher has been continuously employed by a district, the regular full-time substitute service need not immediately precede the probationary appointment to count as seniority credit (*Kransdorf v. Bd. of Educ. of Northport-East Northport UFSD; Appeal of Carey*).

33:39. Do part-time teachers receive seniority credit for part-time service?

Generally, part-time service does not qualify a teacher for any seniority rights except in the case of part-time kindergarten teachers (see **34:4**). However, part-time service rendered after a full-time probationary appointment is included in calculation of seniority if the district requests the change in position (*Matter of Oursler*, 15 Ed Dept Rep 258 (1975); *Matter of Blanchard,* 14 Ed Dept Rep 260 (1975)), but not if the reduction to part-time status is at the request of the teacher. Seniority is "frozen" at this point (*Matter of Walsh*, 17 Ed Dept Rep 434 (1978)). A collective bargaining agreement or board policy may oblige a school district to give seniority credit for part-time service (*Garcia v. Bd. of Educ. Newburgh City Sch. Dist.*, 100 A.D.2d 967 (2d Dep't 1984); *Matter of Greenwald v. Bd. of Educ. of E. Ramapo CSD*, 62 A.D.2d 207 (2d Dep't 1978), *aff'd sub nom. Schlosser v. Bd. of Educ. of E. Ramapo CSD*, 47 N.Y.2d 811 (1979)).

A teacher who has served full-time does not lose existing seniority upon accepting a part-time position with a school district (*Avila v. Bd. of Educ. of the North Babylon UFSD*, 240 A.D.2d 661 (2d Dep't 1997), *appeal denied*, 91 N.Y.2d 801 (1997); *Appeal of Stanzione,* 47 Ed Dept Rep 341 (2008); *Matter of Bellarosa*, 20 Ed Dept Rep 252 (1980)).

Seniority Rights in Board of Cooperative Educational Services (BOCES) Take Overs and Take Backs

33:40. What are the seniority rights of teachers, teaching assistants, and teacher aides when a BOCES takes over a program under which they were employed?

When a teacher, teaching assistant, or teacher aide will be excessed because a district program is contracted out to a BOCES, the BOCES taking over the district program must continue the employment of the district's teachers, teaching assistants, and teacher aides who worked in the program (§ 3014-a(1)). If the BOCES cannot employ them all, then it must hire those teachers, teaching assistants, and teacher aides with the greatest seniority to fill the teaching positions for the program (§ 3014-a(2)). However, the law cannot be used by teachers who are not excessed by the change to obtain a superior placement with the new provider (see *Buenzow v. Lewiston-Porter CSD*, 101 A.D.2d 30 (4th Dep't), *aff'd,* 64 N.Y.2d 676 (1984)).

The district must place all excessed teachers, teaching assistants, and teacher aides on its preferred eligible list for similar positions (§§ 3014-a(2), 3014-b(2); *Acinapuro v. BOCES*, 89 A.D.2d 329 (2d Dep't 1982)). A teacher whose position has been abolished by a BOCES takeover retains any preferred eligibility rights that he or she has acquired pursuant to sections 2510(3) and 3013(3) of the Education Law with the component district from which he or she was excessed and has the right to be placed on the preferred eligibility list for seven years (*Bojarczuk v. Mills*, 98 N.Y.2d 663 (2002); see also **33:42**)). See **chapter 36** for more information on preferred eligible lists.

The teacher, teaching assistant, or teacher aide maintains the same tenure and seniority status he or she enjoyed before the takeover. The teacher, teaching assistant, or teacher aide may also be entitled to retain the salary step and sick days credited to him or her prior to the takeover (§§ 3014-a(3), 3014-b(3); *Appeal of Adler*, 37 Ed Dept Rep 95 (1997), *rev'd on other grounds, Bd. of Educ. of the N. Tonawanda City Sch. Dist. v. Mills*, 263 A.D.2d 574 (3d Dep't), *lv. to appeal denied*, 94 N.Y.2d 751 (1999)).

A component school district does not have to transfer an entire tenure area to a BOCES in order for the BOCES takeover to be permissible (*Angello v. Bd. of Co-op Educ. Serv., Steuben Cnty.*, 80 Misc.2d 472 (Sup. Ct. Steuben Cnty.), Kennedy, J., (Jan. 26, 1976), *aff'd*, 55 A.D.2d 806 (4th Dep't 1976)).

33:41. Do teachers dismissed by a BOCES after a BOCES takeover retain any preferred eligibility (PEL) rights with the component district?

Yes. A teacher fired by a BOCES following a BOCES takeover does not necessarily lose his or her PEL rights with the component district. Under the law, however, a teacher only retains PEL rights with the component district if the teacher's record with that district demonstrates "faithful, competent service in the office or position" that he or she filled (§§ 2510(3)(a), 3013). Therefore, it is the teacher's record of service with the component that determines whether the teacher has PEL rights to a position of employment with that component, not the teacher's record of service with the BOCES (*Bojarczuk v. Mills*, 6 A.D.3d 802 (3d Dep't 2004)). See **chapter 36** for more information on preferred eligible list rights.

33:42. What are the seniority rights of teachers, teaching assistants and teacher aides when a school district takes back from a BOCES a program under which they were employed?

When a teacher, teaching assistant, or teacher aide is excessed from a BOCES because of a takeback by a component district, the former BOCES employee has a vested right to employment with the component district, and in fact, becomes an employee of the component district by operation of law, subject to availability of positions based on seniority (§ 3014-b(1); see **33:44**). In such cases, no vote of the component school board is necessary to hire the excessed BOCES teacher (*Appeal of Valentine*, 38 Ed Dept Rep 39 (1998)).

Such employees maintain the same tenure and seniority status they enjoyed before the takeback and may also be entitled to retain the salary step and sick days credited to them prior to the takeback (§§ 3014-a(3), 3014-b(3); *Appeal of Adler*, 37 Ed Dept Rep 95 (1997), *rev'd on other grounds*, *Bd. of Educ. of the N. Tonawanda City Sch. Dist. v. Mills*, 263 A.D.2d 574 (3d Dep't), *lv. to appeal denied*, 94 N.Y.2d 751 (1999)).

A similar law provides the same rights to teachers whose positions are excessed as a result of tuitioning out students to another district (§ 3014-d) or taking back tuitioned-out students (§ 3014-c). However, the two provisions may not be combined to require a component district to employ BOCES teachers excessed when a district takes back students from a BOCES program and tuitions the students out to another component district (*Herrman v. Bd. of Educ. of Haldane Sch. Dist.*, 194 A.D.2d 673 (2d Dep't 1993)). School counselors and social workers who lose their BOCES jobs due to a takeback of services by a component district are not entitled to these job protections (*Bd. of Educ. of the N. Tonawanda City Sch. Dist. v. Mills*).

33:43. What factors does the commissioner use to determine if there has been a takeback from a BOCES program by a component district?

If there is a dispute about whether a takeback has occurred, the commissioner will consider the following factors:

1. the reason why the component district withdrew from the BOCES program;
2. the program offered by the BOCES;
3. the new program offered by the component district;
4. whether the programs are equivalent;
5. the reasons why the component district may have hired new probationary teachers; and
6. the reasons why the BOCES teachers were excessed.

However, the burden is on the petitioner to prove the facts upon which the right to relief is claimed (*Appeal of Quattrone*, 44 Ed Dept Rep 186 (2004), *aff'd*, *Quattrone v. N.Y. State Educ. Dept.*, 37 A.D.3d 939 (3d Dep't 2007); *Cooper v. Bd. of Educ. of Shenendehowa CSD*, 206 A.D.2d 811 (3d Dep't 1994); *Sklar v. Bd. of Coop. Educ. Servs. of Nassau Cnty*., 104 A.D.2d 622 (2d Dep't 1984)).

33:44. What happens if a component district taking back a program from a BOCES does not have enough positions for everyone employed by the BOCES in the program?

If a district cannot employ all of the teachers, teaching assistants and teacher aides in the program it takes back, then it must hire those teachers, teaching assistants and teacher aides with the greatest seniority to fill the teaching positions for the program (§ 3014-b(2); *Buenzow v. Lewiston-Porter CSD*, 101 A.D.2d 30 (4th Dep't), *aff'd*, 64 N.Y.2d 676 (1984); *Acinapuro v. BOCES*, 89 A.D.2d 329 (2d Dep't 1982); *Gill v. Dutchess Cnty. BOCES*, 99 A.D.2d 836 (2d Dep't 1984)). However, the law cannot be used by teachers who are not excessed by the change to obtain a superior placement with the new provider (*Buenzow v. Lewiston-Porter CSD*). The district must place all excessed teachers, teaching assistants and teacher aides who cannot be employed on its preferred eligible list for similar positions (§ 3014-b(2); *Acinapuro v. BOCES*).

33:45. Do teachers excessed by a BOCES who accept employment with a component district retain preferred eligibility (PEL) rights with the BOCES?

They may. In *Brown v. Schuyler-Chemung-Tioga BOCES*, 5 A.D.3d 939 (3d Dep't 2004), a state appellate court held that an employee who was excessed by a BOCES and accepted employment with a component district nonetheless retained PEL rights with the BOCES. The court based its ruling on the New York Court of Appeals decision in *Bojarczuk v. Mills*, 98 N.Y.2d 663 (2002), wherein New York's highest court implicitly reversed a contrary ruling by the commissioner of education in *Appeal of Chernoff*, 37 Ed Dept Rep 709 (1998), *aff'd,* n.o.r. (Sup. Ct. Albany Cnty. 1999). See also **33:40**.

34. Teachers – Probationary Appointments and the Granting of Tenure

Probationary Appointments – In General

34:1. What is a probationary appointment?

A *probationary appointment* is an employment status granted teachers (and certain types of administrators) which allows a school district to evaluate their competency before deciding whether to grant or deny them tenure (see **33:1**). *Probationary teachers* are employed for a specified period of probation which usually lasts four years (see **34:11-14**)

34:2. Is a probationary appointment required for every teaching position?

No. But it is required when a school district employs a teacher to fill a vacant, unencumbered, full-time teaching position.

There is no legal authority for a school district to fill a vacant position with a temporary appointment. Such an action would constitute an unlawful evasion of the tenure laws (*Bd. of Educ. of Oneida CSD v. Nyquist*, 59 A.D.2d 76 (3d Dep't 1977), *rev'd*, 45 N.Y.2d 975 (1978); *see Appeal of McKenna,* 42 Ed Dept Rep 54 (2002)). Similarly, a school district may not assign a substitute teacher to temporarily fill a vacant position, even when there are ongoing negotiations over the possible transfer of the duties of the vacant positions (*DiPiazza v. Bd. of Educ. of Comsewogue UFSD*, 214 A.D.2d 729 (2d Dep't 1995)).

Even when a teacher is granted a leave of absence, the position remains encumbered and is not considered vacant (*Brewer v. Bd. of Educ. of Plainview-Old Bethpage CSD*, 51 N.Y.2d 855 (1980)). On the other hand, if a teacher on extended leave resigns during the leave, his or her position should be considered vacant and unencumbered even if the resignation is dated prospectively (*Matter of Dionisio v. Bd. of Educ. of Mahopac CSD*, 96 A.D.2d 1041 (2d Dep't 1983), *aff'd sub nom. Daul v. Bd. of Educ. of Mahopac CSD*, 63 N.Y.2d 862 (1984)).

34:3. May a school district employ an independent contractor instead of hiring a probationary teacher to provide core instructional services?

Not generally. Except as otherwise expressly provided by law, there is no authority allowing a school district to contract with an independent contractor to provide core instructional or educational services (*Appeal of Boyd*, 51 Ed Dept Rep, Dec. No. 16,364 (2012); *Appeal of Barker and Pitcher*, 45 Ed Dept Rep 430 (2006); *Appeal of McKenna,* 42 Ed Dept Rep 54 (2002); see NYS Education Department, *Frequently Asked Questions Related to Contracts for Instruction* (June 2010), at: http://www.counsel.nysed.gov/memos/q_and_a_contracts.html). Neither may a school district contract with an outside employment service for the provision of substitute teachers (*Appeal of Woodarek*, 46 Ed Dept Rep 1 (2006)).

A board of cooperative educational services (BOCES) also lacks authority to hire an independent contractor or outside employment service to provide core instructional services, including substitute teacher services (*Appeal of Woodarek*; *Appeal of Sweeney*, 44 Ed Dept Rep 176 (2004), *aff'd sub nom. Matter of BOCES of Erie, Chautauqua & Cattaraugus Cnties. v. Univ. of St. Educ. Dep't,* 40 A.D.3d 1349 (3d Dep't 2007); see **7:17**).

On the other hand, without completely foreclosing the use of an independent contractor for the provision of online courses, the commissioner of education has indicated that any such use must comply with the requirements of commissioner's regulations applicable to the provision of such services (*Appeal of Boyd*).

In addition, there are limited circumstances in which a school district may contract for the provision of special education related services, transition services for students with disabilities, instruction for suspended students, and instruction for homebound students. Before contracting for such services, however, a school district must document that it will retain supervisory control over the individuals providing the services and that, despite reasonable efforts, it has been unable to provide such services by hiring new employees or utilizing existing staff, or through contracts with other school districts or BOCES. The term of any such contract should not exceed a period of one year and should not be extended unless, despite renewed reasonable efforts, the district is unable to provide the services itself or through contracts with other districts or BOCES (see *Frequently Asked Questions Related to Contracts for Instruction*).

34:4. Are part-time teachers entitled to a probationary appointment?

As a general rule, part-time teachers do not receive probationary appointments or credit toward tenure (*Ceparano v. Ambach*, 53 N.Y.2d 873 (1981); *Lilley v. Mills*, 274 A.D.2d 644 (3d Dep't 2000)). Nor do part-time teaching assistants (*Mazzone v. Haupauge UFSD,* 41 A.D.3d 480 (2d Dep't 2007)).

An exception applies to kindergarten teachers, where the commissioner of education has construed the tenure statutes to encompass both full-time (two sessions) and part-time (one session) positions (*Ablondi v. Comm'r of Educ*., 54 A.D.2d 507 (3d Dep't 1976), *appeal denied*, 42 N.Y.2d 801 (1977); *Matter of Clark*, 17 Ed Dept Rep 311 (1978)). This exception applies even where a district uses a combination of full-time and part-time teachers to meet its kindergarten needs.

In addition, a school board may extend credit to a part-time teacher either by a board resolution (*Moritz v. Bd. of Educ. Gowanda CSD*, 60 A.D.2d 161 (4th Dep't 1977)) or by a provision in a collective bargaining agreement (*Matter of Greenwald v. Bd. of Educ. of E. Ramapo CSD*, 62 A.D.2d 207 (2d Dep't 1978), *aff'd sub nom. Schlosser v. Bd. of Educ. of E. Ramapo CSD*, 47 N.Y.2d 811 (1979)).

34:5. May prospective teachers waive their right to a probationary appointment in a tenure-bearing position?

Yes, under certain circumstances. The New York Court of Appeals has held that a teacher may waive his or her right to a probationary appointment and consideration for tenure through an agreement. However, a teacher can be held to the terms of such a waiver only as long as he or she freely, knowingly and voluntarily accepts them (*Feinerman v. BOCES*, 48 N.Y.2d 491 (1979); see also *Yastion v. Mills*, 229 A.D.2d 775 (3d Dep't 1996); *Kelland v. Comm'r of Educ*., 96 A.D.2d 979 (3d Dep't 1983); *Appeal of Thomas*, 34 Ed Dept Rep 181 (1994); *Matter of Anderson*, 22 Ed Dept Rep 59 (1982)).

In comparison, some courts have ruled that a district may not require all prospective teachers in a district to sign a waiver of their tenure rights as a condition to being hired by the district (*Costello v. Bd. of Educ. of East Islip*, 250 A.D.2d 846 (2d Dep't 1998); *Lambert v. Middle Country CSD*, 174 Misc.2d 487 (Sup. Ct. Nassau Cnty. 1997)).

34:6. Must school districts enter into individual contracts of employment with probationary teachers?

Such contracts of employment technically are not required. However, most districts enter into collective bargaining agreements with teacher unions that describe the terms and conditions of employment for all teachers, including probationary teachers (see **chapter 45**).

The Probationary Appointment Process

34:7. How are teachers employed and appointed on probation?

School districts employ and appoint teachers on probation by majority vote of the school board upon recommendation of the superintendent of schools (§§ 2509(1)(a)(i), (ii), 2573(1)(a)(i), (ii), 3012(1)(a)(i), (ii)), or in the case of a board of cooperative educational services (BOCES), by majority vote of the BOCES board upon recommendation of the district superintendent (§ 3014(1)(a), (b)).

For each probationary appointment, the board must indicate in its appointing resolution: the name of the appointee, the tenure area of the teaching position, the certification status of the teacher, and the beginning and end dates of the probationary appointment (8 NYCRR § 30-1.3).

In addition, the appointing resolution for probationary appointments made on or after July 1, 2015, must reflect that, except to the extent required by applicable law, in order to be granted tenure a classroom teacher must have received overall annual professional performance review ratings or either effective or highly effective in at least three of the four proceeding years. It also must reflect that if the classroom teacher receives an ineffective overall rating in the final year of the probationary period he/she will not be eligible for tenure at that time (8 NYCRR § 30-1.3(d)).

34:8. Does the employment of some teachers require more than one probationary appointment?

Yes. Each tenure area that makes up 40 percent or more of a teacher's total instructional course load requires a separate probationary appointment (8 NYCRR § 30-1.9(d)). Thus, a teacher hired to divide his or her time equally between mathematics and science would need two separate probationary appointments.

Likewise, a tenured teacher whose duties are reassigned to include instruction in a new tenure area for more than 40 percent of his or her work load also is entitled to a probationary appointment in the new tenure area (8 NYCRR § 30-1.9(e)).

However, even in the absence of a probationary appointment, if a teacher is serving 40 percent or more of his or her time in two separate tenure areas, the teacher is deemed as having received a probationary appointment in each such area, notwithstanding the absence of a formal probationary appointment (*Freeman v. Bd. of Educ. of Hempstead Sch. Dist.*, 205 A.D.2d 38 (2d Dep't 1994); *Appeal of Pearse*, 50 Ed Dept Rep, Dec. No. 16,159 (2010)).

34:9. How are teachers informed of their probationary appointment(s)?

Usually the district sends a letter or a notice to the teacher, which indicates the tenure area of appointment, the duration of the probationary period, and the salary. The teacher should acknowledge the receipt of the notice and accept or reject the appointment.

It is important that school districts provide clear and explicit notice to both probationary and tenured teachers of the tenure area to which they have been appointed. In addition, teachers must be alerted sufficiently when they are entering a different tenure area by board action (*Mitchell v. Bd. of Educ. of Great Neck Pub. Sch.*, 40 N.Y.2d 904 (1976); *Matter of Keeney*, 17 Ed Dept Rep 314 (1978); 8 NYCRR § 30-1.9(c)).

34:10. Is it permissible for school districts to negotiate over the probationary appointment process?

Yes. A school district may collectively negotiate the process used for appointing probationary teachers, including prior approval of candidates for teaching positions by a committee of teachers (*Mineola UFSD v. Mineola Teachers' Ass'n*, 37 A.D.3d 605 (2d Dep't 2007)).

Length of Probationary Appointments

34:11. What is the length of a teacher's probationary appointment?

The length of a teacher's probationary appointment depends on the date of the teacher's appointment. For teachers appointed before July 1, 2015, the durational period of a probationary appointment is generally three years (§§ 2509(1)(a)(i), 2573(1)(a)(i), 3012(1)(a)(i), 3014(1)(a)). For teachers appointed on or after July 1, 2015, the durational period of a probationary appointment is generally four years (§§ 2509(1)(a)(ii), 2573(1)(a)(ii), 3012(1)(a)(ii), 3014(1)(b)).

However, there are two exceptions to the general rule. One applies to teachers who have previously received tenure. The other, often referred to as the *Jarema* credit exception, applies to regular substitute teachers who meet certain conditions. (See **34:13, 15-18**).

34:12. Are shortened probationary appointments possible?

Yes. Teachers are entitled to a shortened probationary appointment if they:

- Previously have received tenure in another school district or board of cooperative educational services (BOCES), or in another tenure area within the same district or BOCES.
- Are entitled to *Jarema credit*, meaning they served as a regular substitute prior to their appointment.

However, the conditions under which teachers might be entitled to a shortened probationary appointment will depend on the date of the teacher's appointment (see **34:13-19**).

Shortened Probationary Appointments for Teachers Appointed On or After July 1, 2015

34:13. Under what circumstances are teachers appointed on or after July 1, 2015 entitled to a shortened probationary period based on prior substitute service?

Teachers appointed to a probationary period on or after July 1, 2015 will be entitled to a shortened probationary period of two years, instead of the regular four year term, if they have rendered satisfactory service as a regular substitute for a period of two years. In addition, if they were serving as a classroom teacher during the period of regular substitute service, they must have received annual professional performance reviews in each of the two years of regular substitute service (§ 2509(1)(a)(ii), see also §§ 2573(1)(a)(ii), 3012(1)(a)(ii)).

34:14. Under what circumstances are teachers appointed on or after July 1, 2015 entitled to a shortened probationary period based on a prior tenure award?

Teachers appointed to a probationary term on or after July 1, 2015, who previously acquired tenure in another school district or board of cooperative educational services (BOCES), or in another tenure area within the same district or BOCES, would be entitled to a shortened three-year probationary period, instead of the regular four year term, if the teacher demonstrates that he or she received an annual professional performance review (APPR) rating in his or her final year of service in such other school or BOCES (§ 2509(1)(a)(ii), see also §§ 2573(1)(a)(ii), 3012(1)(a)(ii)).

When such appointment is being made by a BOCES, the APPR rating must have been either effective or high effective (§ 3014(1)(b)).

Shortened Probationary Appointments for Teachers Appointed Prior to July 1, 2015

34:15. On what basis are teachers appointed before July 1, 2015 entitled to a shortened probationary period based on prior service as a substitute teacher?

Teachers appointed before July 1, 2015 are entitled to *Jarema* credit if they served as a regular substitute for at least a full semester immediately preceding an appointment to a probationary position in the same tenure area. In such an instance the teacher would be entitled to have up to two years of the prior substitute service applied toward completion of the probationary period (§§ 2509(1)(a), 2573(1)(a), 3012(1)(a); *Robins v. Blaney,* 59 N.Y.2d 393 (1983); *Appeal of Negri*, 19 Ed Dept Rep 35 (1979), *aff'd, Negri v. Ambach*, n.o.r. (Sup. Ct. Albany Cnty.), Hughes, J.S.C. (1980)).

However, a teacher appointed before July 1, 2015, who is entitled to a two-year probationary appointment because he or she previously acquired tenure (see **34:11-12**) and who also has rendered substitute service that qualifies for *Jarema* credit, cannot aggregate the two reductions in the probationary period. The two exceptions are "independent of each other, with the shorter of the two probationary periods to govern in particular cases when both are applicable" (*Carpenter v. Bd. of Educ. of Locust Valley CSD*, 71 N.Y.2d 832 (1988); see also *Appeal of Balandis*, 27 Ed Dept Rep 359 (1988)).

34:16. What is the definition of "regular substitute" applicable to teachers appointed before July 1, 2015 for purposes of acquiring *Jarema* credit?

There is no such statutory or regulatory definition. However, according to the New York Court of Appeals, the term is defined by the actual nature and continuity of the substitute service, rather than the anticipated duration of the replaced teacher's absence (*Speichler v. BOCES, Second Supervisory Dist.*, 90 N.Y.2d 110 (1997); see also *Appeal of Triana v. Bd. of Educ. of City Sch. Dist. of N.Y. City*, 47 A.D.3d 554 (1st Dep't 2008); *Appeal of Goldman*, 43 Ed Dept Rep 338 (2004); *Matter of Ducey,* 65 State Dep't Rep. 65 (1943)).

Accordingly, a teacher who served as a daily "per diem substitute" for a teacher on leave for an indefinite time period, and taught continuously every school day for at least one full semester before her formal appointment to a probationary term, was deemed entitled to *Jarema* credit (see **34:12**) for that time period (*Speichler v. BOCES, Second Supervisory Dist.*). Similarly, a "permanent" substitute who served all of the functions of a "regular" substitute also was deemed entitled to *Jarema* credit (*Hudson v. Bd. of Educ. of the Hempstead Pub. Sch. Dist.* (Sup. Ct. Nassau Cnty. 1997)).

34:17. What constitutes regular substitute service eligible for *Jarema* credit applied to teachers appointed before July 1, 2015?

A school district is only required to grant *Jarema* credit (see **34:15**) to an individual who is employed as a regular substitute for a full semester or more. Where the period of service as a regular substitute is for less than a full semester, the substitute teacher would not be entitled to any *Jarema* credit toward his or her probationary period. That would be the case where a teacher does not commence regular substitute service at the beginning of the semester or does not finish the entire semester (*Lifson v. Bd. of Educ. of the Nanuet Pub. Schs.,* 109 A.D.2d 743 (2d Dep't), *aff'd*, 66 N.Y.2d 896 (1985); *Appeal of Czajkowski*, 34 Ed Dept Rep 589 (1995)).

Depending on the circumstances, a teacher's occasional absences during an otherwise full semester of regular full-time substitute service will not defeat the teacher's entitlement to *Jarema* credit (*Appeal of Goldman*, 43 Ed Dept Rep 338 (2004)).

In addition, summer months are included in calculating *Jarema* credit, such that a teacher who serves as a regular substitute for a school year is entitled to 12 months of *Jarema* credit (*Appeal of Creswell,* 41 Ed Dept Rep 235 (2001)).

34:18. Are there any limitations on the application of *Jarema* credit for teachers appointed before July 1, 2015?

Yes. To be eligible for *Jarema* credit, the regular substitute service must have been rendered for at least one full semester and immediately precede the teacher's probationary appointment (see **34:17**). However, the acceptance of other teaching employment in between the completion of qualifying regular substitute service and a teacher's probationary appointment can disqualify the teacher from claiming entitlement to *Jarema* credit. That was the case where a court ruled that a teacher's acceptance of a part-time teaching position between the critical time period created a "gap" that made the teacher ineligible for *Jarema* credit (*Appeal of MacDonald*, 40 Ed Dept Rep 560 (2001)).

In addition, according to a ruling affirmed by a state appellate court, "*Jarema* credit is not available to a regular substitute who does not possess a valid teacher's certificate." That was the case where the substitute teacher only possessed a temporary license during her five years of employment (*Pierce v. Monroe 2-Orleans BOCES*, 195 Misc.2d 178 (Sup. Ct. Monroe Cnty. 2003), *aff'd,* 12 A.D.3d 1046 (4th Dep't 2004); *Appeal of Goldberg,* 47 Ed Dept Rep 489 (2008)).

Regular substitute service under an intern certificate does not qualify for *Jarema* credit either (*Matter of Berrios v. Bd. of Educ. of Yonkers City Sch. Dist.*, 87 A.D.3d 329 (2d Dep't 2011), *appeal denied*, 17 N.Y.3d 712 (2011)).

Furthermore, *Jarema* credit is not available to administrators (see **9:19**).

34:19. How do the shortened probationary appointment rules affect those appointed before July 1, 2015 and transitioning between teaching and teaching assistant positions?

According to one state appellate court, a teacher previously tenured as a teaching assistant, instead of as a teacher, is not entitled to a shortened probationary period (*Putnam Northern Westchester BOCES v. Mills*, 46 A.D.3d 1062 (3d Dep't 2007); *Abbott v. Barker CSD Bd. of Educ.*, n.o.r. (Sup. Ct. Niagara Cnty.), Ralph A. Boniello, III, J.S.C (May 7, 2002), *aff'd*, 305 A.D.2d 1104 (4th Dep't 2003), *appeal denied*, 100 N.Y.2d 510 (2003)).

In addition, the commissioner of education has ruled that a teaching assistant previously tenured as a teacher is not entitled to *Jarema* credit (see **34:12**). Citing the *Putnam* decision, the commissioner concluded that the duties and qualifications between teaching assistants and teachers are "drastically different" and thus, there is no justification for a reduced probationary period in such cases (*Appeal of Zalaman*, 49 Ed Dept Rep 43 (2009)).

Extension of Probationary Terms

34:20. Can the length of the probationary appointment of a teacher be extended?

Yes, but the rules are different depending on the date of a teacher's appointment. Teachers appointed to a probationary term before July 1, 2015 and their employing district may enter into an agreement to extend a probationary appointment when the teacher will not be recommended for tenure (*Juul v. Bd. of Educ. of Hempstead UFSD*, 76 A.D.2d 837 (2d Dep't 1980), *aff'd*, 55 N.Y.2d 648 (1981)). Such an agreement, commonly referred to as a *Juul* agreement, usually extends the probationary appointment for one additional year (*Id.*). However, school districts may choose to enter into more than one *Juul* agreement with the same teacher (see *In the Matter of the Arbitration of the Bd. of Educ. of Thousand Islands CSD*, 106 A.D.3d 1530 (4th Dep't 2013); see also *Douglass v. Rochester City Sch. Dist.*, 522 Fed. Appx. 5 (2d Cir. 2013)). *Juul* agreements are valid as long as they are entered into freely, with full knowledge of their consequences (*Juul v. Bd. of Educ. of Hempstead UFSD*).

In comparison, the circumstances under which a school district may extend the probationary term of a teacher appointed on or after July 1, 2015 are restricted by statute (§ 2509(2)(b); see also §§ 2573(5)(b), 6(b), 3012(2)(b), 3014(2)(b); see **34:40-41**).

34:21. Are *Juul* agreements employment contracts?

Not according to at least one state appellate court. According to a majority of that court, instead of setting terms of employment, a *Juul* agreement (see **34:20**) simply waives a right in exchange for countervailing benefits (*Marshall v. Pittsford CSD*, 100 A.D.3d 1498 (4th Dep't 2012), *lv. to appeal denied*, 20 N.Y.3d 859 (2013)).

Essentially, under a *Juul* agreement, a district waives its right to dismiss the teacher at the end of the probationary period, and the teacher waives any claim to tenure (*Juul v. Bd. of Educ. of Hempstead UFSD*, 76 A.D.2d 837 (2d Dep't 1980), *aff'd*, 55 N.Y.2d 648 (1981); *Marshall v. Pittsford CSD*; see also **33:8**). The teacher is given a second chance to prove his or her worth rather than be dismissed, and the district is free to grant or withhold tenure at the end of the fourth year (see *Appeal of Fink*, 33 Ed Dept Rep 340 (1993)).

Pursuant to the ruling of one state appellate court, a *Juul* agreement also can waive a teacher union's right to pursue a grievance and arbitration under a collective bargaining agreement (CBA) on behalf of a teacher terminated at the expiration of the *Juul* agreement, if the agreement "clearly manifest[s] an intent to exclude the subject matter of [the teacher's] termination" from the CBA's grievance and arbitration provisions (*In the Matter of the Arbitration of the Bd. of Educ. of Thousand Islands CSD,* 106 A.D.3d 1530 (4th Dep't 2014)).

34:22. Must *Juul* agreements be approved by a school board?

Yes. According to at least one state appellate court, the failure of a school board to approve a *Juul* agreement (see **34:20**) constitutes "an impermissible abdication" of school board responsibilities (*Marshall v. Pittsford CSD*, 100 A.D.3d 1498 (4th Dep't 2012), *lv. to appeal. denied*, 20 N.Y.3d 859 (2013)).

Such a failure, however, is not necessarily detrimental to the enforcement of a *Juul* agreement. That was the case where the *Juul* agreement was signed by the teacher's union president and the superintendent of schools after the superintendent had unequivocally stated her intention to recommend against tenure at the end of the teacher's probationary period, and the teacher accepted the extension of her probationary period and also agreed to waive any right to claim tenure by estoppel or otherwise. Having accepted the benefits of a fairly made *Juul* agreement, the teacher was precluded from later challenging its validity (*Id.*).

Probationary Appointment Termination[1]

34:23. Can probationary teachers be dismissed during their term of probation?

Yes. A teacher's probationary appointment may be terminated at any time on the recommendation of the superintendent, provided the dismissal is approved by a majority vote of the school board (§§ 2509(1)(a)(i), (ii), 2573(1)(a)(i), (ii), 3012(1)(i), (ii); see also *Matter of Amnawah v. Bd. of Educ. of the City of N.Y.*, 266 A.D.2d 455 (2d Dep't 1999)), or in the case of a board of cooperative educational services (BOCES), upon the recommendation of the district superintendent by majority vote of the BOCES board (§ 3014(1)(a), (b)).

There is no requirement that a school board address community concerns regarding the termination of a probationary teacher (*Appeal of Hinson*, 48 Ed Dept Rep 437 (2009)).

There is no requirement either that a district conduct a hearing to effect the termination of probationary teacher. However, the district must meet certain notice requirements in order to fire a teacher during his or her probationary period (§§ 2509(1)(a)(i), (ii), 2573(1)(a)(i), (ii), 3019-a; see also **34:26**).

34:24. On what grounds may teachers be dismissed during their term of probation?

A teacher's probationary appointment can be terminated for any reason, except in bad faith, for a constitutionally impermissible or illegal purpose, or in violation of statutory or decisional law (*Frasier v. Bd. of Educ. of City Sch. Dist. of City of N.Y.*, 71 N.Y.2d 763 (1988); *James v. Bd. of Educ. of the CSD No. 1 of the Towns of Orangetown & Clarkstown*, 37 N.Y.2d 891 (1975); *Capece v. Schultz*, 117 A.D.3d 1045 (2d Dep't 2014); *Zarinfar v. Bd. of Educ. of City of N.Y.*, 93 A.D.3d 466 (1st Dep't 2012); *Appeal of Tahir*, 46 Ed Dept Rep 16 (2006)).

The burden rests with the teacher to prove that he or she was terminated for an impermissible reason or in bad faith (*Capece v. Schultz*; see also *Appeal of Fine,* 51 Ed Dept Rep, Dec. No. 16,266 (2011); *Appeal of Christiano,* 51 Ed Dept Rep, Dec. No. 16,218 (2011); *Appeal of Bozyk*, 45 Ed Dept Rep 516 (2006); *Appeal of Scott*, 44 Ed Dept Rep 339 (2005)).

34:25. Must a teacher's annual professional performance review (APPR) be considered when the teacher is being dismissed during the course of his or her probationary appointment?

Yes. School districts and BOCES wishing to dismiss a teacher during his or her probationary period must consider the teacher's APPR as a "significant factor" (§ 3012-d(1); 8 NYCRR § 30-3.1(d)). However, this does not mean that a teacher's APPR is the sole or determinative factor in a probationary teacher's dismissal, just that it must be considered (NYS Education Department, *Guidance on New York State's Annual Professional Performance Review For Teachers and Principals to Implement Education Law*

[1] As a general rule, probationary appointments end naturally upon expiration of their term, by which time a probationary teacher is either granted or denied tenure (see **34:31-45**), unless the parties agree to extend the probationary period for an additional year (see **34:20, 34:40**). However, a probationary appointment also can end upon the dismissal of a probationary teacher during the period of probation. The questions and answers in this section address the second situation.

§ 3012-d and the Commissioner's Regulations (updated May 2016), q. I14 at: https://www.engageny.org/file/133336/download/appr-guidance-3012-d.pdf?token=oBAeajES. See also **34:31**).

Nonetheless, a school district or BOCES has an unfettered statutory right to terminate a probationary teacher without regard to the APPR if the dismissal is based on statutorily and constitutionally permissible reasons (§ 3012-d(9); 8 NYCRR § 30-3.1(d)).

For more information on the annual professional performance review of teachers, see **chapter 37**.

34:26. What notice must be given to probationary teachers being dismissed during the course of their probationary appointment?

The superintendent of schools must give the probationary teacher notice that he or she will recommend to the board that the teacher be dismissed at least 30 days prior to the board meeting at which such recommendation will be considered (§ 3031). In addition, upon the teacher's request, the superintendent of schools in school districts other than New York City also must provide the reason(s) for the proposed dismissal recommendation within seven days after the request. The teacher may file a written response with the clerk of the board seven days before the board meets to consider the recommendation for dismissal (§ 3031(b); *Appeal of Hinson*, 48 Ed Dept Rep 437 (2009)).

In addition, when a majority of the school board accepts the recommendation of the superintendent of schools and votes to dismiss, the teacher is entitled to a 30-day written notice of termination (§ 3019-a).

The two notification periods do not run concurrently (*Appeal of Madden-Lynch*, 31 Ed Dept Rep 411(1992); see also *Appeal of Slater*, 12 Ed Dept Rep 275 (1973)).

This process does not apply to probationary teachers whose employment is terminated because their positions have been properly abolished (*Appeal of Laurencon*, 45 Ed Dept Rep 514 (2006)).

34:27. What happens if a school district fails to give the required notices to a teacher being dismissed during the course of his or her probationary period?

Failure by the superintendent of schools to provide the requisite notice under section 3031 (see **34:26**) does not entitle the teacher to automatic reinstatement or back pay. The remedy is for the board to reconsider the termination recommendation with proper notice to the teacher and an opportunity for him or her to respond (*Zunic v. Nyquist*, 48 A.D. 2d 378 (3d Dep't 1975), *aff'd*, 40 N.Y.2d 962 (1976); *Appeal of Dorcely*, 45 Ed Dept Rep 383 (2006); *Appeal of Gold*, 34 Ed Dept Rep 372 (1995)).

Similarly, a failure to provide the termination notice required by section 3019-a (see **34:26**) entitles a dismissed teacher to back pay but not reinstatement (*Appeal of Madden-Lynch*, 31 Ed Dept Rep 411 (1992); see also *Matter of Mutschler v. Bd. of Educ. of the William Floyd UFSD*, 177 A.D.2d 629 (2d Dep't 1991)). Nonetheless, back pay was deemed not available to a probationary teacher who was dismissed for lack of certification without proper notice because the Education Law precludes school districts from paying a teacher who is uncertified at the time of initial hiring (*Sullivan v. Windham-Ashland-Jewett CSD*, 212 A.D.2d 63 (3d Dep't 1995), *appeal denied*, 89 N.Y.2d 814 (1997)). However, it was available to a probationary teacher who was dismissed with only two days' notice even though the other 28 days fell during summer vacation, when the teacher would not have worked and would not have been paid (*Matter of Vetter v. Bd. of Educ. of the Ravena-Coeymans-Selkirk CSD*, 14 N.Y.3d 729 (2010); see also *Matter of Tucker v. Bd. of Educ., CSD No. 10,* 82 N.Y.2d 274 (1993)).

34:28. Are teachers dismissed during the course of their probationary appointment entitled to a hearing?

Not generally. A teacher dismissed during his or her probationary period of employment would be entitled to a hearing only if he or she establishes the termination was for a constitutionally impermissible purpose or in violation of a statutory proscription (*Strax v. Rockland Cnty. BOCES*, 257 A.D.2d 578 (2d Dep't 1999); see *Appeal of Dorcely*, 45 Ed Dept Rep 383 (2006)).

For information on the right of terminated probationary teachers to a name-clearing hearing see **34:29.**

34:29. Are teachers terminated during the course of their probationary appointment entitled to a name clearing hearing?

Not generally. A terminated probationary teacher is entitled to a name-clearing hearing only if the reasons for termination "denigrate the employee's competence as a professional and impugn the employee's professional reputation in such a fashion as to effectively put a significant roadblock in that employee's continued ability to practice his or her profession" (*Donato v. Plainview-Old Bethpage CSD*, 96 F.3d 623 (2d Cir. 1996), *cert. denied*, 519 U.S. 1150 (1997), *remanded,* 985 F.Supp. 316 (E.D.N.Y. 1997); see also *Patterson v. City of Utica*, 370 F.3d 322 (2d Cir. 2004); *Swinton v. Safir*, 93 N.Y.2d 758 (1999); but see *Aquilone v. City of N.Y.*, 262 A.D.2d 13 (1st Dep't 1999), *appeal denied*, 93 N.Y.2d 819 (1999); *Wilcox v. Newark Valley CSD*, 74 A.D.3d 1558 (3d Dep't 2010); *Appeal of M.D.*, 47 Ed Dept Rep 51 (2007); **39:41**).

The right to a name-clearing hearing is triggered when the reasons for termination are placed in the discharged employee's personnel file and are likely to be disclosed to prospective employers (*Id.*). That would not be the case where the reasons for termination are kept in a separate file that would never be made available to the teacher's potential employers, and the school district's policy regarding prospective employers is to merely confirm a teacher's hiring date, position held, and length of employment without providing any additional information (*Wilcox v. Newark Valley CSD*, 107 A.D.3d 1127 (3d Dep't 2013), *lv. to appeal dismissed*, 26 N.Y.3d 1060 (2015).

During a name-clearing hearing, a school district is not required to prove the truth of the charges that formed the basis for terminating the employee. The burden of proof rests with the terminated employee to disprove the charges. "To be meaningful, the name clearing proceeding must be run by the same actor who diminished the [employee's] reputation" (*Donato v. Plainview-Old Bethpage CSD*, 985 F. Supp. 316 (E.D.N.Y. 1997); see also *Patterson v. City of Utica*; *Velez v. Levy*, 401 F.3d 75 (2d Cir. 2005); *Peres v. Oceanside UFSD*, 2008 U.S. Dist. LEXIS 7403 (E.D.N.Y. Jan. 31, 2008); **39:41**).

A post-termination name-clearing hearing that is reasonably close in time to the termination is adequate (*Segal v. City of N.Y.*, 459 F.3d 207 (2d Cir. 2006); see also *Blasi v. N.Y.C. Bd. of Educ*. 544 Fed. Appx. 10 (2d Cir. 2013)).

If a name-clearing hearing is unlikely to remedy any ill effects caused by the employer's stigmatizing actions, a terminated employee may be able to recover monetary damages (*Patterson v. City of Utica*).

34:30. Can school districts negotiate over procedures that affect the dismissal of probationary teachers?

Yes. Therefore, school officials should refer to any applicable collective bargaining agreement when taking action to dismiss a probationary teacher. For example, where a collective bargaining agreement allows a teacher's union to submit to arbitration tenure decisions it feels a school board acted upon "capriciously, arbitrarily, or discriminatorily," the union can demand to see the underlying documentation leading to the termination of a probationary teacher (*Hampton Bays UFSD v. PERB*, 62 A.D.3d 1066 (3d Dep't), *lv. to appeal denied*, 13 N.Y.3d 711 (2009)).

Provisions in a collective bargaining agreement that allow discontinued probationary teachers to seek internal review of their dismissal do not toll the statutory four-month statute of limitations for challenging a probationary teacher's dismissal (*Kahn v. N.Y. City Dep't of Educ.*, 18 N.Y.3d 457 (2012)). The four-month period starts to run from the effective date of termination (*Kahn v. N.Y. City Dep't of Educ.*; see also *Zarinfar v. Bd. of Educ. of the City Sch. Dist. of the City of N.Y.*, 93 A.D.3d 466 (1st Dep't 2012)).

The Tenure Granting Process

34:31. What are the basic procedures involved in granting a teacher tenure?

Except when a teacher acquires tenure by estoppel (see **33:8**), the granting of tenure requires an affirmative recommendation in favor of tenure from the superintendent of schools, and the school board's acceptance of that recommendation (§§ 2509(2)(a), (b), 2573(5)(a), (b), 3012(2)(a), (b), 3014(2)(a), (b); see also **34:32**).

As a general rule, on or before the end of a teacher's probationary period, the superintendent recommends for tenure those teachers who are found competent, efficient, and satisfactory. In addition, teachers appointed to a probationary term on or after July 1, 2015 will have to have received the requisite number of effective or highly effective annual professional performance reviews during their probationary period, as set forth in law (§ 2509(2)(b); see also §§ 2573(5)(b), 6(b), 3012(2)(b), 3014(2)(b)).

This recommendation is made in writing to the school board. The board may then appoint to tenure any or all of the teachers recommended (§ 2509(2); see also §§ 3014(1)(b); 2573(5), 3012(2)).

A tenure appointment must be considered separately for each tenure area that requires more than 40 percent of a teacher's instructional time (8 NYCRR § 30-1.9(c); see **33:19, 33:21, 34:7-8**). Thus, a teacher with two probationary appointments in separate tenure areas may be granted tenure in one, both, or neither (see **34:38-45** for information on the tenure denial process).

In addition, when making tenure determinations about a teacher, school officials must consider the teacher's annual professional performance review (APPR) as a significant, but not the sole or determinative factor (§ 3012-d(1); 8 NYCRR § 30-3.1(d); NYS Education Department, *Guidance on New York State's Annual Professional Performance Review For Teachers and Principals to Implement Education Law § 3012-d and the Commissioner's Regulations* (updated May 2016), q. I5, at: https://www.engageny.org/file/133336/download/appr-guidance-3012-d.pdf?token=oBAeajES**)**. For more information on the annual professional performance review of teachers, see **chapter 37.**

34:32. Who has the final authority to grant a teacher tenure?

Although a teacher may not be granted tenure without the recommendation of the superintendent of schools (*Anderson v. Bd. of Educ. of the City of Yonkers*, 46 A.D.2d 360 (2d Dep't 1974), *aff'd*, 38 N.Y.2d 897 (1976); *Matter of Burke*, 11 Ed Dept Rep 231 (1972)), it is up to a school board, by majority vote, to accept the superintendent's recommendation and grant a teacher tenure (§§ 2509(2), 3014(1)); *Appeal of Spadone,* 39 Ed Dept Rep 638 (2000)). The granting of tenure lies within the jurisdiction and discretion of the school board (see *Capece v. Schultz*, 117 A.D.3d 1045 (2d Dep't 2014)).

In addition, school boards can reject any superintendent recommendation in favor of tenure and vote to deny tenure despite that recommendation (§§ 2573(5)), (6), 3031; see **34:38-45** for information on the tenure denial process). However, a school board's vote to reject a superintendent's recommendation in favor of tenure is considered initially as advisory in nature, and the school board must reconsider the issue at a second meeting. At least 30 days before final consideration of the superintendent's recommendation, the board must notify the teacher of its intention to deny tenure and the date of the board meeting when it will take final action (§ 3031(b)).

34:33. Can a school board bargain away its authority to make tenure decisions?

No. The power to grant or deny tenure may not be impaired by a collective bargaining agreement because the Education Law vests authority to make tenure decisions in the school board (*Cohoes City Sch. Dist. v. Cohoes Teachers Ass'n,* 40 N.Y.2d 774 (1976); see **47:11** regarding prohibited subjects of bargaining).

Thus, a school district can enter into a collective bargaining agreement that permits an arbitrator to review procedural aspects of the tenure determination, but not a substantive review of the board's decision (*Vestal CSD v. Vestal Teachers Ass'n*, 60 A.D.2d 720 (3d Dep't 1977), *aff'd,* 46 N.Y.2d 746 (1978); *Bd. of Educ. of Elwood UFSD v. Elwood Teachers Alliance*, 94 A.D.2d 692 (2d Dep't 1983)). Accordingly, in a proper case, an arbitrator may direct a school district to extend the probationary period of a teacher and to re-evaluate the teacher at the end of the extended probationary period (*Cohoes City Sch. Dist.*). The Public Employment Relations Board (PERB) has imposed similar orders (see *Sag Harbor UFSD*, 8 PERB ¶ 4524, *aff'd*, 54 A.D.2d 391 (3d Dep't 1976)).

34:34. When does a school board resolution granting tenure become effective?

According to the New York Court of Appeals, tenure does not become effective, and a teacher granted tenure is not entitled to the benefits of tenure, until the effective date specified in the resolution granting tenure (*Remus v. Bd. of Educ. for Tonawanda City Sch. Dist. and Shaffer v. Schenectady Sch. Dist.* 96 N.Y.2d 271 (2001); see **34:36**).

A teacher whose position is abolished and placed on a preferred eligible list before the effective date of his or her tenure award, is not entitled to be recalled back from that list as a tenured teacher. In such an instance, tenure never took effect (*Appeal of Dickinson*, 49 Ed Dept Rep 463 (2010); 51 Ed Dept Rep, Dec. No. 16,256 (2011)). See **chapter 36** for more information on the abolition of teaching positions and preferred eligible lists.

34:35. What is the impact of a teacher's resignation before the effective date of his or her tenure?

According to one state appellate court, that teacher is tenured. In *Marcus v. Bd. of Educ. of the Cohoes City Sch. Dist.*, 64 A.D.2d 475 (3d Dep't 1978), a teacher granted tenure resigned three weeks before his tenure became effective. A few years later, he received a probationary appointment in another district and claimed tenure by estoppel (see **33:8**) on the grounds that his receipt of tenure in the prior district reduced his probationary period to two years (see **33:7, 34:11**). The court rejected the argument that since the teacher's tenure at the prior district did not become effective until after he resigned, he was not tenured when he resigned.

34:36. Can a school board rescind a prior grant of tenure?

Yes. The New York Court of Appeals addressed this question in two consolidated cases (*Remus v. Bd. of Educ. for Tonawanda City Sch. Dist. and Shaffer v. Schenectady City Sch. Dist.*, 96 N.Y.2d 271 (2001)).

In the first case, the name of a teacher whom the superintendent did not intend to recommend for tenure mistakenly appeared on a list of persons recommended to the school board for tenure due to clerical error. Unaware of the clerical error, the board passed a resolution granting tenure to every teacher on the list. Shortly thereafter, and still well before the effective date specified in the board resolution granting tenure, the board learned of its mistake and passed a subsequent resolution rescinding the prior grant of tenure. The Court of Appeals held that the teacher did not have the protection of tenure because the school district was entitled to rescind its erroneous grant of tenure prior to its effective date (*Shaffer v. Schenectady Sch. Dist.*).

In the other case, the school board passed a resolution in June conferring tenure effective in September. Shortly thereafter, but still well before the September effective date, the district learned that the teacher, while acting as a school chaperone, had consumed alcoholic beverages with students. The teacher declined the district's offer to extend her probationary period one year, and the board rescinded its grant of tenure. The Court of Appeals ruled that a school board is not prohibited from making a deferred award of tenure, and the teacher did not have the benefits of tenure before the effective date previously stated by the board (*Id.*).

34:37. What is the impact of a school board's decision to rescind a prior grant of tenure?

Where a school board rescinds a prospective grant of tenure prior to the date that tenure vests, the teacher reverts to the status of a non-tenured teacher approaching the end of the probationary period. As such, that teacher is only entitled to the same termination notices as any other probationary teacher who is being denied tenure (see **34:26** for a description of the required notices) and not to a 3020-a hearing (*Mahoney v. Mills*, 29 A.D.3d 1043 (3d Dep't 2006), *appeal denied,* 7 N.Y.3d 708 (2006) see also **chapter 38**).

The Tenure Denial Process

34:38. What are the basic procedures involved in denying tenure to a probationary teacher?

It depends. Generally, a school district's decision to deny tenure to a probationary teacher is based on the failure of a superintendent of schools to make a recommendation in favor of tenure. In such an instance, the superintendent must notify the teacher of the decision to recommend against tenure in accordance with the notice requirements set forth in law (§§ 2509(1)(a)(i), (ii), 2573(1)(a)(i), (ii), 3012(2)(a), (b), 3014(2)(a), (b), 3031; see **34:42**). Thereafter, the teacher must be afforded the opportunity to request the reason(s) for the recommendation against tenure and to submit a response (§ 3031; see **34:42**) before being dismissed.

However, on occasion, a school district's denial of tenure to a probationary teacher is based on a school board's decision to reject a superintendent's recommendation in favor of tenure (§ 3031; see **34:32**). In such an instance, the teacher is entitled to notice the same as when a superintendent recommends against tenure, but this time of the board's intention to deny tenure. Similarly, the teacher must be afforded an opportunity to request a written statement giving the board's reasons for denial and opportunity to submit a response (§ 3031(b); **34:42**). As is the case with a superintendent's non-recommendation of tenure, the board's statement in support of its decision to deny tenure, notwithstanding the superintendent's recommendation in favor of tenure, must be sufficiently specific to permit the teacher to make an "intelligent and meaningful" response (*Appeal of Dituri & Blake*, 42 Ed Dept Rep 363 (2003)). The commissioner of education has found, for example, that a board's statement that probationary employees "failed to function effectively" is insufficient to enable them to prepare meaningful responses (*Appeal of Dituri and Blake*). However, "the specificity of a bill of particulars is not required" (*Appeal of Scott,* 44 Ed Dept Rep 339 (2005); see also *Appeal of Dorcely,* 45 Ed Dept Rep 383 (2006) (sufficient specificity); *Matter of Stevens*, 13 Ed Dept Rep 64 (1973)).

34:39. For what reasons may a probationary teacher be denied tenure?

School districts may deny tenure to a probationary teacher for any reason that is not unconstitutional or in violation of the law (*James v. Bd. of Educ. of Cent. Sch. Dist. No.1 of the Towns of Orangetown & Clarkstown*, 37 N.Y.2d 891 (1975); see also NYS Education Department, *Guidance on New York State's Annual Professional Performance Review For Teachers and Principals to Implement Education Law*

§ 3012-d and the Commissioner's Regulations (updated May 2016), q. I14-17, at: https://www.engageny.org/file/133336/download/appr-guidance-3012-d.pdf?token=oBAeajES).

For example, in one case, the commissioner of education found a school district could deny tenure to a teacher who had been excessively absent, even though the absences did not exceed the number of sick days under the teachers' collective bargaining agreement (*Appeal of Toma*, 31 Ed Dept Rep 477 (1992)). On the other hand, a denial of tenure based upon a philosophical objection to the tenure system is invalid (*Conetta v. Bd. of Educ. of Patchogue-Medford UFSD*, 165 Misc.2d 329 (Sup. Ct. Nassau Cnty. 1995)). Likewise, a school board member may not consistently vote "no" on all tenure appointments, nor abstain from voting on tenure because of a philosophical objection to tenure (*Appeal of Hoefer*, 45 Ed Dept Rep 66 (2005); *Appeal of Craft & Dworkin*, 36 Ed Dept Rep 314 (1997)).

Furthermore, unless a teacher demonstrates that the reasons given for the denial of tenure lack a rational basis, the courts will not find the district acted in bad faith in denying tenure (*James v. Bd. of Educ. of Cent. Sch. Dist. No.1 of the Towns of Orangetown & Clarkstown*; *Mahoney v. Mills*, 29 A.D.3d 1043 (3d Dep't 2006); *Strax v. Rockland Cnty. BOCES*, 257 A.D.2d 578 (2d Dep't 1999); see also *Appeal of Hodge,* 49 Ed Dept Rep 6 (2009); *Appeal of Cohen,* 47 Ed Dept Rep 372 (2008); *Appeal of Hall*, 46 Ed Dept Rep 394 (2007); *Appeal of Scott*, 44 Ed Dept Rep 339 (2005)). But even upon a finding of arbitrariness on the part of a school board, a court lacks authority to grant a teacher tenure itself because the granting of tenure is an administrative function that is within the jurisdiction and discretion of the school board (*Capece v. Schultz*, 117 A.D.3d 1045 (2d Dep't 2014)).

34:40. How do annual professional performance reviews (APPR) affect the tenure denial process?

School districts and BOCES must consider the teacher's APPR as a "significant factor" in tenure determinations (§ 3012-d(1); 8 NYCRR § 30-3.1(d)). However, this does not mean that a teacher's APPR is the sole or determinative factor in determining whether to grant tenure, just that it must be considered (NYS Education Department, *Guidance on New York State's Annual Professional Performance Review For Teachers and Principals to Implement Education Law § 3012-d and the Commissioner's Regulations* (updated May 2016), q. I14, at: https://www.engageny.org/file/133336/download/appr-guidance-3012-d.pdf?token=oBAeajES see also **34:31**).

Furthermore, teachers appointed to a probationary term on or after July 1, 2015 are not eligible for tenure unless they have received an overall APPR rating of either effective or highly effective in at least three of the four years of their probationary period, exclusive of any breaks in service. In addition, the APPR rating for the final year of probation cannot be ineffective (§ 2509(2)(b), see also §§ 2573(5)(b), 6(b), 3012(2)(b), 3014(2)(b)). A school board may, in its discretion, extend the probationary period of a teacher who receives an ineffective APPR rating for the last year of the probationary term if the teacher has received a rating of effective or highly effective during each of the other years of probation (*Id.*)

34:41. Can a school board award a teacher tenure on a contingency basis?

Yes. Teachers appointed to a probationary term on or after July 1, 2015 "remain in probationary status until the end of the school year in which" they have "received such ratings of effective or highly effective for at least three of the four preceding school years exclusive of any break in service" subject to the terms set out in law. During that "extended" probationary period, a school board may confer a conditional grant of tenure contingent upon a classroom teacher's receipt of a minimum rating in the final year of the probationary period, consistent with the APPR rating requirements established in law (§ 2509(2)(b), see also §§ 2573(5)(b), 6(b), 3012(2)(b), 3014(2)(b); **34:31**). If the contingency is not met after all appeals are exhausted, the grant of tenure is void and unenforceable, unless the school board, in its discretion, extends the probationary period for an additional year (*Id.*).

For more information on the APPR system, see **chapter 37.**

34:42. What notice must be given to a probationary teacher who is being denied tenure?

The superintendent of schools must notify the teacher in writing at least 60 days prior to the expiration of the probationary period that he or she will not be making a recommendation in favor of tenure (§§ 2509(1)(a)(i), (ii), 2573(1)(a)(i), (ii), 3012(2)(a), (b); see also *Matter of Meehan*, 11 Ed Dept Rep 34 (1971)). In addition, the superintendent also must notify the teacher that the school board will review the failure to recommend tenure at a board meeting to be held in the manner required by law. Both notices may be contained within the same written statement, or transmitted separately (§ 3031).

Upon the teacher's request, the superintendent of schools in school districts other than New York City also must provide the teacher, in writing, the reason(s) for the recommendation to deny tenure within seven days after the request (§ 3031). The teacher may file a written response with the clerk seven days before the school board meets to consider the teacher's dismissal based on the superintendent's failure to recommend tenure (§ 3031; *Appeal of Hinson*, 48 Ed Dept Rep 437 (2009)). The law does not require that the teacher be given an opportunity to speak or present evidence at the board meeting.

The statement of reasons for the non-recommendation of tenure cannot be vague. It must be sufficiently specific to enable the teacher to make an intelligent and meaningful response to the stated reasons (*Brunecz v. City of Dunkirk Bd. of Educ.*, 23 A.D.3d 1126 (4th Dep't 2005); *Appeal of Rubinstein*, 45 Ed Dept Rep 299 (2005)). However, a teacher's right to such a statement is a "procedural" right, not a "substantive" one. Therefore, the remedy afforded to a teacher who does not initially receive a sufficiently specific statement is to provide one (*Matter of Liberty CSD & Liberty Faculty Ass'n*, 25 A.D.3d 908 (3d Dep't 2006), *appeal denied*, 6 N.Y.3d 714 (2006); *Farrell v. Bd. of Educ. of Carmel CSD No.2*, 64 A.D.2d 703 (2d Dep't 1978); *Rathbone v. Bd. of Educ. of Hamilton CSD*, 47 A.D.2d 172 (3d Dep't 1975), *aff'd*, 41 N.Y.2d 825 (1977)).

The above notice procedures do not apply in the case of probationary teachers who resign voluntarily to prevent any reference of dismissal in their personnel file (*Biegel v. Bd. of Educ. Ellenville CSD*, 211 A.D.2d 969 (3d Dep't 1995)), or to part-time employees not eligible for tenure (*Appeal of Longshore*, 32 Ed Dept Rep 311 (1992); see **34:4**).

34:43. What happens if a school district fails to give the required denial of tenure notices?

If a district fails to provide the required notice for denial of tenure, the teacher does not acquire tenure (*Rathbone v. Bd. of Educ. of Hamilton CSD*, 47 A.D.2d 172 (3d Dep't 1975), *aff'd*, 41 N.Y.2d 825 (1977); *Brunecz v. City of Dunkirk Bd. of Educ.*, 23 A.D.3d 1126 (4th Dep't 2005)). Neither is the teacher automatically entitled to reinstatement or salary beyond the last day he or she rendered service. Instead, the relief granted must remedy the actual harm suffered including, for example, an opportunity for the teacher to submit a response to a superintendent's recommendation and have the school board consider that response (*Appeal of Gold*, 34 Ed Dept Rep 372 (1995)). Generally, a teacher also would be entitled, for example, to one day's pay for each day a superintendent's notice of his or her intention to not recommend tenure is late (*Tucker v. Cmty. Sch. Dist. No. 10*, 82 N.Y.2d 274 (1993); *Brunecz v. City of Dunkirk Bd. of Educ.*; see also *Zarinfar v. Bd. of Educ. of the City Sch. Dist. of the City of N.Y.*, 44 Misc.3d 1215(A) (Sup. Ct. N.Y. Cnty. 2013); *appeal dismissed*, 127 A.D.3d 496 (1st Dep't. 2015)).

In a case in which a district learned of inappropriate conduct by a probationary teacher 22 days before the end of the probationary period, the New York Court of Appeals ruled the district could deny tenure to the teacher even though it was impossible for the district to comply with the notice requirements of section 2573(1) (*Tucker v. Cmty. Sch. Dist. No. 10*; see also *Appeal of Thier,* 36 Ed Dept Rep 222 (1996)). However, the court did require the district to pay back wages to the teacher for each day the notice was late (*Tucker v. Cmty. Sch. Dist. No. 10*).

34:44. When is a decision to deny tenure final?

According to the commissioner of education, notwithstanding a school board's legal obligation to review a recommendation to deny tenure (§ 3031; see **34:42**), when the superintendent of schools fails to recommend tenure "the probationary period expires as a matter of law upon the last day of the probationary period" (*Matter of Leviness*, 18 Ed Dept Rep 213 (1978)). In addition, "the refusal of the superintendent to make an affirmative recommendation that tenure be granted is not merely a recommendation, but rather a final act" (*Appeal of Clancy*, 29 Ed Dept Rep 28 (1989)). Therefore, while it is not improper for a school board to vote in concurrence with a superintendent's recommendation to deny tenure, it is unnecessary (*Matter of Egan*, 15 Ed Dept Rep 196 (1975)).

At least one state appellate court disagrees with the commissioner (*Dembovich v. Liberty CSD Bd. of Educ.*, 296 A.D.2d 794 (3d Dep't 2002); see also connected case, *In re Liberty CSD*, 25 A.D.3d 908 (3d Dep't 2006), *appeal denied*, 6 N.Y.3d 741 (2006)).

34:45. What are the rights of a teacher who resigns rather than be denied tenure?

A teacher who resigns under a mistaken belief that he or she does not already have tenure and is going to be denied tenure has a right to rescind the resignation (*Gould v. Bd. of Educ. of Sewanhaka Cent. High Sch. Dist*., 81 N.Y.2d 446 (1993); see *Ronga v. Klein*, 23 Misc.3d 1103(A), (Sup. Ct. N.Y. Cnty. 2009), *aff'd*, 81 A.D.3d 567 (1st Dep't 2011), *appeal denied*, 17 N.Y.2d 704 (2011); *Appeal of Price*, 46 Ed Dept Rep 490 (2007); see **33:8**).

In addition, a teacher who resigns rather than be denied tenure may be eligible for unemployment insurance benefits. According to a state appellate court, the teacher's "resignation" under such circumstances is not voluntary, and therefore, he or she is eligible for unemployment benefits (*In re the Claim of Harp*, 202 A.D.2d 876 (3d Dep't 1994); see **69:15-21**).

35. Teacher and School Leader Certificate Registration and Continuing Education Requirements

Certificate Registration

35:1. Are teachers and education leaders required to register their certificate with the State Education Department (SED)?

Yes. Commencing with the 2016-17 school year, all holders of a:

- Permanent or professional teaching certificate in the classroom teaching services,
- Permanent or professional leader certificate in the educational leadership services (school building leader, school district leader, school district business leader), or
- A Level III Teaching Assistant certificate

must register their certificate with SED every five years (§ 3006(3)(A)), in order to be able to practice in a public school or board of cooperative educational services (BOCES) in New York (§ 3006(3)(B); 8 NYCRR § 80-6.2; NYS Education Department, *Memo on New Law and Regulation Pertaining to Registration, Continuing Teacher and Leader Education (CTLE) and Approval of Providers of CTLE* (June 1, 2016), at: http://www.highered.nysed.gov/tcert/pdf/memo06012016.pdf).

For purposes of certificate registration requirements, the five-year *registration period* refers to both the initial registration period and each subsequent five-year period thereafter (§ 80-6.1(e)). Those with a certificate issued prior to July 1, 2016 must apply for initial registration during the 2016-17 school year during their month of birth beginning on July 1, 2016 and renew their registration in the last year of each subsequent five-year period (8 NYCRR § 80-6.2(c)). Certificates issued on or after July 1, 2016 are automatically registered, but the certificate holder must still re-register during the fifth succeeding birthday month thereafter and during each birthday month in the last year of each subsequent five-year period (8 NYCRR § 90-6.2(d)).

35:2. What does it mean to "practice" for purposes of certificate registration requirements?

Practicing in this context means that the certificate holder is employed 90 days or more during a school year by a school district or board of cooperative educational services in New York State, in a position requiring certification (§ 80-6.1(a), (d)). A day of employment includes a day actually worked in whole or in part, or a day not actually worked but paid (§ 80-6.1(d)).

35:3. What happens if a certificate holder is not practicing in New York and allows the certificate to lapse?

Any such individual must re-register their certificate before resuming practice in New York after a lapse of registration (§ 3006(3)(B); 8 NYCRR § 80-6.2(e)). Such an individual also must satisfy continuing teacher and leader education requirements before they are able to re-register (§ 3006-a(1)(D); 8 NYCRR § 80-6.8; see **35:5-9**).

35:4. Are there any special requirements that certificate holders must comply with before they are able to re-register their certificate?

Yes. They must comply with continuing teacher and leader education (CTLE) requirements but only if they hold a:

- Professional certificate in the classroom teaching services,
- Professional certificate in the educational leadership service (school building leaders, school district leaders, school district business leaders), or
- Level III teaching certificate

(§ 3006-a(1)(A), (B); 8 NYCRR §§ 80-6.1(c), 80-6.3(a)); see also 8 NYCRR § 80-6.6; **35:5 – 9**).
Figure 1 below summarizes the certificate registration and CTLE requirements.

Figure 1

Registration and CTLE Requirements			
Certificate Type	**Employment Status**	**Registration Requirements**	**Continuing Teacher and Leader Education (CTLE) Requirements**
Permanent Certificate Holders			
PERMANENT Classroom Teacher/School Leader	Practicing in a NYS school district or BOCES	Active registration is required	NOT subject to CTLE
PERMANENT Classroom Teacher/School Leader	NOT practicing in a NYS school district or BOCES	May choose "INACTIVE" status for their registration	NOT subject to CTLE
PERMANENT Pupil Personnel Services (PPS) such as School Attendance Teachers, School Counselors, School Psychologists, School Social Workers, School Dental Hygiene Teachers and School Nurse Teachers	Practicing OR NOT practicing in a NYS school district or BOCES	NOT subject to registration	NOT subject to CTLE
Professional Certificate Holders			
PROFESSIONAL Classroom Teacher/School Leader	Practicing in a NYS school district or BOCES	Active registration is required	100 hours of CTLE is required during every five year registration period
PROFESSIONAL Classroom Teacher/School Leader	NOT practicing in a NYS school district or BOCES	May choose "INACTIVE" status for their registration	NOT subject to CTLE if INACTIVE
Teaching Assistant Certificate Holders			
Level III Teaching Assistant	Practicing in a NYS school district or BOCES	Active registration is required	100 hours of CTLE is required during every five year registration period
Level III Teaching Assistant	NOT practicing in a NYS school district or BOCES	May choose "INACTIVE" status for their registration	NOT subject to CTLE if INACTIVE
Continuing Teaching Assistant	Practicing OR NOT practicing in a NYS school district or BOCES	NOT subject to registration	NOT subject to CTLE
Level I, Level I Renewal, Level II Teaching Assistants	Practicing OR NOT practicing in a NYS school district or BOCES	NOT subject to registration	NOT subject to CTLE
Other Certificate Holders			
Initial Classroom Teacher/School Leader	Practicing OR NOT practicing in a NYS school district or BOCES	NOT subject to registration	NOT subject to CTLE
Provisional Classroom Teacher or Provisional School Administrator/Supervisor	Practicing OR NOT practicing in a NYS school district or BOCES	NOT subject to registration	NOT subject to CTLE
Provisional Pupil Personnel Services (PPS)	Practicing OR NOT practicing in a NYS school district or BOCES	NOT subject to registration	NOT subject to CTLE

Continuing Teacher and Leader Education (CTLE) Requirements

35:5. What is the definition of CTLE?

CTLE means "activities designed to improve the teacher or leader's pedagogical and/or leadership skills, targeted at improving student performance, including but not limited to formal continuing teacher and leader education activities. Such activities shall promote the professionalization of teaching and be closely aligned to district goals for student performance which meet the standards prescribed by regulations of the commissioner [of education]" (§ 3006-a(2)(C)).

35:6. Who must comply with the CTLE requirements?

Only CTLE certificate holders are required to comply with the CTLE requirements (see **35:4**).

Thus, the CTLE requirements do not apply to holders of continuing teaching assistant certificates and pupil personnel services certificates such as school attendance teachers, school counselors, school psychologists, school social workers, school dental hygiene teachers and school nurse teachers (NYS Education Department, Office of Teaching Initiatives, *New Registration and Continuing Teacher and Leader Education (CTLE) Requirements for Classroom Teachers and School Leaders Holding a Permanent or Professional Certificate, and Level III Teaching Assistant Certificate Holders* (updated July 13, 2016), at: http://www.highered.nysed.gov/tcert/news/newsitem05122015.html).

35:7. What are the basic CTLE requirements?

Certificate holders subject to CTLE requirements (see **35:4**) must complete 100 clock hours of acceptable CTLE during their five-year certificate registration period (§ 3006-a(2)(A); 8 NYCRR § 80-6.3(a)(1)). However, nothing prevents a school district from agreeing, pursuant to collective bargaining, to additional hours (§ 3006-a(2)(B)).

Acceptable CTLE consists of activities that meet the definition of CTLE (see **35:5**), and are provided by a sponsor approved by the NYS Education Department, provides study in the content area of any certificate title held by the certificate holder or in pedagogy, and includes required study in language acquisition addressing the needs of English language learners (8 NYCRR §§ 80-6.3(a)(1), (2); 80-6.9).

The CTLE requirements may be completed at any time during the registration period (see **35:1**), but CTLE completed during a prior registration period may not be carried over to a subsequent registration period (8 NYCRR §§ 80-6.3(a)(3), 80-6.6(d)).

Adjustments in terms of clock hours and/or time for completion of the CTLE requirements are allowed in accordance with commissioner's regulations (§ 3006-a(1)(A),(C), (2)(A); 8 NYCRR § 80-6.3(b)).

35:8. How are the CTLE requirements applied to holders of multiple certificates?

Such individuals register once, and there is only one 100 hour CTLE requirement per person (NYS Education Department, *Frequently Asked Questions: New Registration and CTLE Requirement* (updated June 2016), at: http://www.highered.nysed.gov/tcert/pdf/CTLE%20FAQ%2006102016.pdf).

35:9. What happens if someone is unable to satisfy the CTLE requirements?

Such individuals may not practice (see **35:2**) until they have met the CTLE requirements, unless they are issued a registration or conditional registration certificate in accordance with law and commissioner's regulations (§ 3006-a(1)(B), (3)); 8 NYCRR § 80-6.5).

Anyone who continues to practice after being denied registration for failure to meet CTLE requirements shall be subject to moral character review under Education Law § 305(7) (§ 3006-a(3)).

35:10. Who may provide CTLE programming?

Only sponsors approved by the NYS Education Department (SED) can provide CTLE programming (8 NYCRR §§ 80-6.4, 80-6.10). Approved sponsors are approved for a five-year term and must reapply at the expiration of that term (8 NYCRR § 80-6.10(d)).

The list of entities that may apply to SED for approval as a CTLE sponsor include school districts and boards of cooperative educational services (BOCES) in addition to others (8 NYCRR § 80-6.10(b)).

To be approved as a CTLE sponsor, school districts and BOCES must submit their professional development plan and attest that they meet the requirements for CTLE sponsor approval. Such plans should include a list of contracted entities or individuals that will provide CTLE on behalf of the school district or BOCES (NYS Education Department, *Memo on New Law and Regulation Pertaining to Registration, Continuing Teacher and Leader (CTLE) and Approval of Providers of CTLE* (June 1, 2016), at: http://www.highered.nysed.gov/tcert/pdf/memo06012016.pdf).

Individual school district or BOCES employees providing CTLE activities do not need to be listed in the plan. However, consultants must, even if the school district or BOCES previously approved or vetted them (NYS Education Department, *Frequently Asked Questions: New Registration and CTLE Requirement* (updated June 2016), at: http://www.highered.nysed.gov/tcert/pdf/CTLE%20FAQ%2006102016.pdf).

35:11. Must school districts and boards of cooperative educational services report CTLE hours completed by their employees?

Yes, but only as it relates to their status as a CTLE sponsor. As such, they must upload, through the online TEACH system, information related to CTLE programs and activities provided to certificate holders, including participants, number of hours provided, and the type of CTLE programs and activities provided (NYS Education Department, *Frequently Asked Questions: New Registration and CTLE Requirement* (updated June 2016), at: http://www.highered.nysed.gov/tcert/pdf/CTLE%20FAQ%2006102016.pdf).

In addition, all CTLE sponsors must provide those attending their CTLE activities with a certificate of completion for purposes of record-keeping (*Id.*).

36. Teachers – Abolition of Positions and Excessing[1]

Authority to Abolish Positions

36:1. May a school board abolish positions?

Yes (§§ 2510, 2585, 3013). Furthermore, school boards have been deemed to enjoy broad latitude to abolish, reorganize, or consolidate positions (*Zurlo v. Ambach*, 53 N.Y.2d 1035 (1981); *Cohen v. Crown Point CSD*, 306 A.D.2d 732 (3d Dep't 2003); *Young v. Bd. of Educ. of Cent. Sch. Dist. No. 6 Town of Huntington*, 35 N.Y.2d 31 (1974); *Currier v. Tompkins-Seneca-Tioga BOCES*, 80 A.D.2d 979 (3d Dep't 1981)). However, there must be a bona fide reason for the abolition, reorganization, or consolidation of positions, such as when a position is no longer necessary to the school system or economic considerations require it (*Id.* see **36:7**).

A teacher or administrator alleging that his or her position was abolished in bad faith has the burden of showing that the position was not abolished for bona fide reasons. They might do so, for example, by showing that savings were not accomplished or that a replacement employee was hired, or through other evidence that establishes an improper reason such as retaliation (*Matter of Lally v. Johnson City CSD*, 105 A.D.3d 1129 (3d Dep't 2013); see also **36:7**).

In addition, the decision to abolish positions for economic reasons is inextricably intertwined with a school board's non-delegable duty to formulate its school district's budget. Therefore, a school board may not delegate this authority by adopting a policy that would require agreement from the school superintendent for the abolition of positions (*Appeal of Roberts,* 49 Ed Dept Rep 354 (2010)).

While school districts may agree to limit their authority to abolish positions pursuant to "no layoff" provisions in collective bargaining agreements, such contract provisions must be explicit, unambiguous, of reasonable duration, clearly state the scope of any such limitation on the school district's authority, and not have been negotiated between parties of unequal bargaining power during a time of declared financial emergency (*Matter of Johnson City Professional Firefighters Local 921 (Village of Johnson City)*, 18 N.Y.3d 32 (2011), *reargument denied*, 18 N.Y.3d 937 (2012); *Matter of Bd. of Educ. of Yonkers City Sch. Dist. v. Yonkers Fedn. of Teachers,* 40 N.Y.2d 268 (1976)).

Furthermore, a collective bargaining agreement may not contravene the rights of teachers under the Education Law that are associated with the abolition of positions (see *Marino v. Bd. of Educ. of the Hauppage UFSD*, 262 A.D.2d 321 (2d Dep't 1999); compare *Dietz v. Bd. of Educ. of Rochester City Sch. Dist.*, 98 A.D.3d 1251 (4th Dep't 2012)).

36:2. Are there any procedures that school boards must follow when abolishing a position?

Yes. Whenever a school board acts to abolish a teaching position, it must discontinue "the services of the teacher having the least seniority in the system within the tenure [area] of the position abolished" (§§ 2510(2), 3013(2)). For this purpose, seniority is based on actual "length of service" in a designated tenure area and need not have been consecutive (8 NYCRR § 30-1.1(f); *Claudio v. Mattituck-Cutchogue*

[1] The abolition, reorganization and consolidation of positions is governed by Education Law §§ 2510, 2585 and 3013, which apply similarly to teachers and administrators in a school district.

UFSD, 2014 U.S. Dist. LEXIS 103748 (E.D.N.Y. 2014)). But seniority within a given tenure area is accrued only if service in that area constitutes forty percent or more of the total time the teacher spends performing instructional services (8 NYCRR § 30-1.1(f), (g); *Appeal of Ciesla*, 52 Ed Dept Rep, Dec. No. 16,480 (2013); compare 8 NYCRR § 30-1.9 which applies to teachers rendering instructional support services).

For purposes of calculating seniority when identifying the least senior person subject to dismissal as a result of the abolition of a position, a state appellate court counted regular substitute service immediately following a "resignation" with no actual break in service toward this calculation (*Alessi v. Bd. of Educ., Wilson CSD*, 105 A.D.3d 54 (4th Dep't 2013)). According to the commissioner of education, however, unpaid leave days are not included in that calculation, even when the unpaid leave is taken pursuant to the federal Family and Medical Leave Act (*Appeal of Scarpinati de Oliveira*, 52 Ed Dept Rep, Dec. No. 16,411 (2012)).

In addition, a school board must adopt a formal resolution abolishing a particular position and provide notice to the teacher that his or her position is being abolished. The board's resolution must identify the tenure area in which a position is to be abolished (*Appeal of Lessing*, 34 Ed Dept Rep 451 (1995)).

School boards should review the applicable collective bargaining agreement to determine if it requires a particular method or manner of giving notice to teachers whose positions are being abolished.

36:3. Are school districts required to "shuffle" schedules before abolishing a position?

Before abolishing a position and discontinuing the services of the affected teacher (see **36:1**), school boards must consider whether it is possible to make schedule adjustments and shuffle teachers within the same tenure area to continue the services of the teacher within his or her certification *(Chambers v. Bd. of Educ. of Lisbon CSD*, 47 N.Y.2d 279 (1979); *Matter of Musorofiti v Bd. of Educ. of S. Huntington USFD*, 108 A.D.2d 863 (2nd Dep't), *aff'd*, 65 N.Y.2d 880 (1985); *Seney v. Bd. of Educ. of the East Greenbush CSD*, 103 A.D.3d 1022 (3d Dep't 2013)).

When a teacher challenges the abolition of positions in cases where schedule shuffling has not taken place, districts must demonstrate the impossibility of retaining the teacher through adjustment of schedules (*Chambers v. Bd. of Educ. of Lisbon CSD*; *Amos v. Bd. of Educ. of Cheektowaga-Sloan UFSD*, 54 A.D.2d 297 (4th Dep't 1976), *aff'd*, 43 N.Y.2d 706 (1977); *Seney v. Bd. of Educ. of the East Greenbush CSD*). A board can meet this burden by demonstrating proposed schedules are "not educationally or financially feasible" (*Chambers v. Bd. of Educ. of Lisbon CSD*; *Seney v. Bd. of Educ. of the East Greenbush CSD*).

A school district has no obligation to shuffle the schedules of teachers outside the tenure area of the particular teacher whose position is being abolished (*Appeal of Chaney*, 33 Ed Dept Rep 12 (1993); see also *Appeal of Soukey*, 38 Ed Dept Rep 626 (1999); but see *Matter of Taber v. Sherburne-Earlville CSD*, 244 A.D.2d 634 (3d Dep't 1997)).

36:4. Are teachers whose position is abolished automatically subject to termination?

No. Teachers whose position is abolished may avoid termination if they enjoy bumping rights (see **36:10-13**).

In addition, if a district creates a new position at the same time that it abolishes an existing position, the teacher or administrator who would be excessed must be hired at his or her existing salary for the new position if the duties performed under both positions are similar and the record of the person has been one of faithful, competent service in the prior position (§§ 2510(1), 2585(2), 3013(1)). The two positions are considered similar if more than 50 percent of the functions to be performed in the new position are the same as those performed under the old position (*Elmendorf v. Howell,* 962 F.Supp. 326 (N.D.N.Y. 1997); *Coates v. Ambach*, 52 A.D.2d 261 (3d Dep't 1976), *aff'd,* 42 N.Y.2d 846 (1977); *Appeal of Klein*, 43 Ed Dept Rep 305 (2003), *petition dismissed*, Special Term (Sup. Ct. Albany Cnty., Ceresia, J. (Dec. 6, 2004); see **36:14**). The 50 percent rule should not be applied rigidly, and the emphasis should be on the type of duties the employee could have been expected to perform in the old position (*Matter of Cowan v. Bd. of Educ. of Brentwood UFSD*, 99 A.D.2d 831 (2d Dep't), *appeal withdrawn*, 63 N.Y.2d 702 (1984); *Appeal of Elmendorf*, 36 Ed Dept Rep 308 (1997); see also *Sever v. Bd. of Educ. of Maine-Endwell CSD*, 2012 U.S. Dist. LEXIS 126686 (2012); *Elmendorf v. Howell*).

36:5. Must a school district conduct a pre-termination hearing prior to dismissing a teacher or administrator whose position is abolished?

No. Teachers and administrators dismissed from service pursuant to an abolition of positions are not entitled to a pre-termination hearing (*Mitchell v. Bd. of Educ. of Great Neck Pub. Schs*., 40 N.Y.2d 904 (1976); see also *Broomer v. Huntington UFSD*, 2013 U.S. Dist. LEXIS 113971 (E.D.N.Y. 2013), *aff'd,* 566 Fed. Appx 91 (2d Cir. 2014); *Quattrone v. Erie 2 Chautaqua-Cattaraugus Bd. of Coop. Educ. Servs*., 2011 U.S. Dist. LEXIS 118250 (W.D.N.Y. 2011), *aff'd,* 503 F. Appx. 12 (2d Cir. 2012); *Sever v. Bd. of Educ. of Maine-Endwell CSD*, 2012 U.S. Dist. LEXIS 126686 (2012)).

However, such a hearing may be required when a position is abolished and another one created concurrently if the teacher whose position is abolished claims entitlement to the concurrently created position and there is an issue regarding whether both positions are indeed similar to each other. In such an instance, the teacher whose position is abolished would be entitled to a pre-termination hearing to offer proof on the similarity of the positions (*Broomer v. Huntington UFSD*; *Sever v. Bd. of Educ. of Maine-Endwell CSD; DeSimone v. Bd. of Educ. S. Huntington UFSD*, 604 F.Supp. 1180 (E.D.N.Y. 1985) and 612 F.Supp. 1568 (E.D.N.Y. 1985); *Fairbairn v. Bd. of Educ. S. Country CSD*, 876 F.Supp. 432 (E.D.N.Y. 1995); compare *Appeal of Banigo,* 2009 U.S. Dist. LEXIS 19009 (E.D.N.Y. Mar. 4, 2009); *Appeal of Elmendorf*, 36 Ed Dept Rep 308 (1997); see also *Elmendorf v. Howell,* 962 F.Supp. 326 (N.D.N.Y. 1997)).

In contrast, a pre-termination hearing is not required where the abolished position is, as a matter of law, dissimilar to a newly created position (*Broomer v. Huntington UFSD*; *DeSimone v. Bd. of Educ. S. Huntington UFSD*).

36:6. What happens if a school board abolishes the position of a teacher it mistakenly appointed to a nonexistent tenure area?

In a case where a school board appointed a teacher to a nonexistent tenure area, a state appellate court ruled the board could not abolish the position and terminate the teacher without first reclassifying the teacher's tenure area. The board was ordered to determine the teacher's proper tenure area based upon the work she actually performed (*Abrantes v. Bd. of Educ. of the Norwood-Norfolk CSD*, 233 A.D.2d 718 (3d Dep't 1996), *appeal denied*, 89 N.Y.2d 812 (1997); see also *Thorenz v. Bd. of Educ. of Monticello CSD*, 101 A.D.3d 1563 (3d Dep't 2012)).

In this regard, school boards need to remember that they may appoint teachers only to the tenure areas designated in part 30 of the commissioner's regulations and may not create their own tenure areas for teaching positions (8 NYCRR Part 30). In addition, a teacher whose position is abolished is not entitled to be assigned to a tenure area outside his or her area of certification, notwithstanding a professed intent to obtain the required certification (*Appeal of Coviello,* 50 Ed Dept Rep, Dec. No. 16,200 (2011)).

Improper Abolition of Positions

36:7. May a district abolish a position rather than fire a teacher?

No. Abolishing a position may not be used as a subterfuge for terminating employees (*Weimer v. Bd. of Educ. Smithtown CSD No.1*, 74 A.D.2d 574 (2d Dep't), *appeal dismissed*, 49 N.Y.2d 1046 (1980); *Bd. of Educ. v. Niagara-Wheatfield Teachers' Ass'n*, 54 A.D.2d 281 (4th Dep't 1976), *appeal denied*, 41 N.Y.2d 801 (1977); *Appeal of Jordan*, 37 Ed Dept Rep 487 (1998), *petition dismissed*, Special Term (Sup. Ct. Albany Cnty.), Keegan, J. (Mar. 30, 1999); *Appeal of Stratton*, 33 Ed Dept Rep 373 (1993); see also *Verdon v. Dutchess Cnty. Bd. of Coop. Educ. Serv.*, 47 A.D.3d 941 (2d Dep't 2008); *CSEA, Inc. v. Rockland Cnty. BOCES*, 39 A.D.3d 641 (2d Dep't 2007)). Subterfuge would be at issue, for example, if a claim is raised that the abolition of a position was intended to avoid filing disciplinary charges against a tenured teacher or administrator, or in retaliation for their commencement of litigation against their employing district (see *Lally v. Johnson City CSD*, 105 A.D.3d 1129 (3d Dep't 2013) or engagement in other protected activity (*Razzano v. Remsenburg-Speonk UFSD*, 95 A.D.3d 1335 (2d Dep't 2012)).

However, the commissioner of education has held that in a 3020-a proceeding involving a "schedule shuffling" question (see **36:3**), a hearing panel cannot require a district to show why it abolished positions in one subject rather than another (*Rappold v. Bd. of Educ. Cleveland Hills UFSD*, 20 Ed Dept Rep 664 (1981), *aff'd*, 95 A.D.2d 890 (3d Dep't 1983)).

36:8. What are the rights of an improperly excessed teacher?

Excessed teachers and administrators claiming the abolition of their position was improper may appeal to the commissioner of education within 30 days of the effective date of the abolition (*Appeal of Gordon*, 53 Ed Dept Rep, Dec. No. 16,582 (2013); see also *Appeal of Broomer*, 53 Ed Dept Rep, Dec. No. 16,607 (2014)).

In addition, they are entitled to reinstatement with benefits and back pay less any earnings from jobs worked at during normal school hours (*Matter of Lezette v. Bd. of Educ. Hudson City Sch. Dist.*, 35 N.Y.2d 272 (1974); *Appeal of Lessing*, 34 Ed Dept Rep 451 (1995); see also *Appeal of Curtis and Newell*, 48 Ed Dept Rep 184 (2008)).

Furthermore, the district may not offset the back pay it owes a reinstated teacher by the amount of unemployment benefits the teacher received. All or part of the unemployment benefits received by the teacher might be recovered by the Labor Department (*Appeal of Lessing*, 35 Ed Dept Rep 116 (1995)).

36:9. Does an improperly excessed teacher have a duty to mitigate (lessen) any damages during the pendency of proceedings brought to review the abolition of his or her position?

Yes. The New York Court of Appeals held that an improperly excessed teacher may not collect damages from his or her former employing school district to cover periods during which he or she refuses to accept comparable work (*Gross v. Bd. of Educ. of Elmsford UFSD*, 78 N.Y.2d 13 (1991)).

Bumping Rights

36:10. Does a teacher whose position is being abolished have the right to take the job of a less senior teacher?

Yes. If a position is abolished, the teacher with the least seniority within the tenure area of that position in that school district must be the person dismissed (§§ 2510(2), 2585(3), 3013(2)). However, pursuant to commissioner's regulations, a teacher whose position is eliminated in one area may exercise *bumping rights* to claim the position of another teacher in a different tenure area if the teacher previously served in that other tenure area and has more accrued seniority in it than others currently serving there (8 NYCRR § 30-1.13).

In order to claim greater seniority than others in a given tenure area, a teacher's position within that area must have been certified as educational by the commissioner of education to the New York State Civil Service Commission. In addition, the teacher must have devoted at least 40 percent of his or her work time to classroom instruction in that tenure area (*Appeal of Marsico*, 50 Ed Dept Rep, Dec. No. 16,158 (2010); *Appeal of Devente*, 48 Ed Dept Rep 150 (2008)).

Bumping rights available pursuant to commissioner's regulations are not available to administrators (*Appeal of Wills*, 49 Ed Dept Rep 147 (2009); but see *Fehlhaber v. Bd. of Educ. of Utica City Sch. Dist.*, 96 A.D.3d 1633 (4th Dep't 2012) regarding administrator "vertical" bumping rights under the state Civil Service Law).

36:11. Do all teachers enjoy bumping rights?

No. True bumping rights are available only to teachers appointed under part 30 of the Rules of the Board of Regents. An excessed teacher cannot bump back into a pre-part 30 tenure area (*Rippe v. Bd. of Educ. of Comsewogue-Brookhaven Sch. Dist.,* 64 N.Y.2d 281 (1985)). In addition, a teacher is deemed to have waived bumping rights that otherwise might have been available within a given tenure area if he or she knowingly and freely resigned from a position in that area. The employee must have taken "affirmative steps" to terminate all aspects of his/her employment (*Matter of Alessi v. Bd. of Educ., Wilson CSD*, 105 A.D.3d 54 (4th Dep't 2013); see also *Kwasnik v. King*, 123 A.D.3d 1264 (3d Dep't 2014)).

36:12. Must a school district appoint a teacher who exercises bumping rights to a new probationary term?

No. A school district may not place on probation a teacher whose position is abolished and, because of bumping, is appointed to another tenure area in which the teacher previously served and obtained tenure (*Appeal of Suchak*, 45 Ed Dept Rep 548 (2006)).

36:13. Does a teaching assistant whose position is abolished have the right to take the job of a less senior teaching assistant?

Yes. Pursuant to the mandatory tenure areas established by the Board of Regents, all teaching assistants serve in the same tenure area (*Appeal of Krason*, 41 Ed Dept Rep 305 (2002), *aff'd*, *Madison-Oneida BOCES v. Mills*, 2 A.D.3d 1240 (3d Dep't 2003), *aff'd,* 4 N.Y.3d 51 (2004); *Appeal of Denova,* 44 Ed Dept Rep 308 (2005); see also **33:20**). Therefore, when a teaching assistant's position is abolished, the least senior teaching assistant must be excessed (*Id.*; *Appeal of McCollum*, 44 Ed Dept Rep 306 (2005); see also **33:28**).

Preferred Eligible Lists and Reappointment Rights

36:14. What rights of reappointment do excessed teachers have?

A teacher who is excessed because a teaching position has been abolished must be placed on a preferred eligible list (PEL) of candidates for appointment to a vacant similar position for seven years after the position is abolished (§§ 2510(3)(a), 3013(3)(a); *Bojarzuk v. Mills*, 98 N.Y.2d 663 (2002); *Brewer v. Bd.*

of Educ. of Plainview-Old Bethpage CSD, 51 N.Y.2d 855 (1980); *Jester v. Bd. of Educ. of Chenango Forks CSD*, 109 A.D.2d 1004 (3d Dep't 1985); *Greenspan v. Dutchess Cnty. BOCES*, 96 A.D.2d 1028 (2d Dep't 1983); *Appeal of McDougall*, 53 Ed Dept Rep, Dec. No. 16,505 (2013); *Appeal of Tucholski*, 28 Ed Dept Rep 112 (1988)), and in large city school districts, until his or her name is reached on the seniority list (§ 2585(4)). The PEL applies "not just for the position which was abolished but also for any position similar to [that] one" (*Appeal of Kantrowitz*, 48 Ed Dept Rep 218 (2008)).

Regarding the period of preferred eligibility, one state appellate court has ruled that a teacher whose PEL rights expired on June 30 of a particular year was not entitled to appointment to positions from which the incumbent teachers resigned effective that same June 30, because the court found that the vacancies created by the resignations did not occur until July "at the earliest" (*Matter of Raben v. Bd. of Educ. of Hauppauge UFSD*, 175 A.D.2d 286 (2d Dep't 1991), *appeal denied*, 79 N.Y.2d 754 (1992); see also *Matter of Lombardo v. Baldwin UFSD*, 150 A.D.2d 452 (2d Dep't 1989); *Appeal of Principio*, 39 Ed Dept Rep 11 (1998)).

As to the similarity of positions requirement, two positions will be deemed similar if more than 50 percent of the duties are same (*Appeal of Klein*, 43 Ed Dept Rep 305 (2003), *petition dismissed*, Special Term (Sup. Ct. Albany Cnty.), Ceresia, J. (Dec. 6, 2004); *Appeal of Eschmann*, 55 Ed Dept Rep, Dec. No. 16, 853 (2015); *Appeal of McDougall*; *Appeal of Allen*, 36 Ed Dept Rep 299 (1997), *petition dismissed*, Special Term (Sup. Ct. Albany Cnty.) n.o.r. (Nov. 1997); see also *Greenspan v. Dutchess Cnty. BOCES*). However, this does not mean that teachers have a right to be reappointed to a position for which they are not certified. PEL reappointment rights do not attach without proper certification (*Davis v. Mills,* 98 N.Y.2d 120 (2002)). Conversely, certification alone does not entitle an excessed teacher to an available position. That position must be similar to the one from which the teacher was excessed. That depends on an analysis of the job responsibilities of the position at issue at the time it is filled, which is when a teacher's right to an appointment from the PEL might attach (*Appeal of Eschmann*).

A teacher claiming a district has improperly failed to reappoint him or her to a vacant position from the PEL may appeal to the commissioner within 30 days of the date on which another teacher commenced service in a position to which they allege they are entitled (*Appeal of Gordon*, 53 Ed Dept Rep, Dec. No. 16,582 (2013); see also *Appeal of Broomer*, 53 Ed Dept Rep, Dec. No. 16,607 (2014); compare *Speis v.Penfield Cent. Schs.*, 114 A.D.3d 1181 (4th Dep't 2014)).

36:15. How are disputes resolved regarding the similarity of two positions requirement for purposes of reappointment?

The commissioner of education has primary jurisdiction over disputes involving issues related to similarity of positions (*In the Matter of the Arbitration Between Alden CSD and Alden Cent. Schs. Administrators Assn.*, 115 A.D.3d 1340 (4th Dep't 2014); *Donato v. Mills*, 6 A.D.3d 966 (3d Dep't 2004); *Hessney v. Bd. of Educ. of Pub. Schs. of Tarrytowns*, 228 A.D.2d 954 (3d Dep't 1996), *appeal denied*, 89 N.Y.2d 801 (1996); see *Marsico v. Armstrong*, 111 A.D.3d 736 (2d Dep't 736 (2013)). Moreover, this rule has ostensibly been adopted by the New York Court of Appeals as well, which in a case involving the similarity of positions, the court wrote: "It is for the Commissioner in the first instance, and not for the courts, to establish and apply criteria to govern the selection and retention of qualified educators and staff" (*Davis v. Mills*, 98 N.Y.2d 120 (2002); see also **36:14**).

A teacher or administrator on a preferred eligible list claiming entitlement to a vacant position has the burden of proving that a majority of the duties of that position are similar to those of his or her former position (*Appeal of Eschmann*, 55 Ed Dept Rep, Dec. No. 16,853 (2015); *Appeal of McDougall*, 53 Ed Dept Rep, Dec. No. 16,505 (2013); *Appeal of Jordan*, 37 Ed Dept Rep 487 (1998), *petition dismissed*,

Special Term (Sup. Ct. Albany Cnty.), Keegan, J. (Mar. 30, 1999); see also *Matter of Coates v. Ambach*, 52 A.D.2d 261 (3d Dep't 1976), *aff'd*, 42 N.Y.2d 846 (1977)).

36:16. How do tenure areas affect the similarity of positions requirement for purposes of reappointment from a preferred eligible list (PEL)?

According to the commissioner of education and one state appellate court, two positions will not be deemed "similar" if they are in different tenure areas (*Davis v. Mills,* 285 A.D.2d 703 (3d Dep't 2001), *aff'd on other grounds,* 98 N.Y.2d 120 (2002); *Appeal of Donato*, 41 Ed Dept Rep 246 (2001), *aff'd on other grounds*, 6 A.D.3d 966 (3d Dep't 2004); *Brown v. Bd. of Educ. Morrisville-Eaton CSD*, 211 A.D.2d 887 (3d Dep't 1995)).

However, another state appellate court has ruled that there is no provision in the Education Law which requires that to be "similar," the vacant position exist within the excessed teacher's tenure area (*Levy v. Bd. of Educ. of Freeport UFSD,* 275 A.D.2d 459 (2d Dep't 2000), *appeal denied*, 95 N.Y.2d 769 (2000); *Leggio v. Oglesby*, 69 A.D.2d 446 (2d Dep't 1979), *appeal dismissed*, 53 N.Y.2d 704 (1981)). Nonetheless, that same court has since ruled that the commissioner of education should be afforded primary jurisdiction to determine questions regarding the similarity of positions (see *Moraitis v. Bd. of Educ. Deer Park UFSD*, 84 A.D.3d 1090 (2d Dep't 2011); *Matter of Ferencik v. Bd. of Educ. of Amityville UFSD,* 69 A.D.3d 938 (2d Dep't 2010); *Markow-Brown v. Bd. of Educ. Port Jefferson Pub. Schs.,* 301 A.D.2d 653 (2d Dep't 2003), *appeal denied*, 100 N.Y.2d 512 (2003); *Donato v. Bd. of Educ. of Plainview-Old Bethpage CSD*, 286 A.D.2d 388 (2d Dep't 2001)). Inasmuch as the commissioner treats tenure area as a mandatory common denominator when evaluating the similarity of positions, and the commissioner's interpretation is entitled to considerable deference by a reviewing court, the continued validity of that court's prior decisions in *Levy v. Bd. of Educ. of Freeport UFSD* and *Leggio v. Oglesby* would appear tenuous.

36:17. Is there any particular order for recalling excessed teachers?

Yes. When several different teachers have been excessed, they must be offered reappointment in order of seniority (§§ 2510(3)(a), 2585(4), 3013(3)(a)). For purposes of determining recall rights of teachers on preferred eligible lists, the length of service in the system is used, not the length of service within a particular tenure area (*Mahony v. Bd. of Educ. of Mahopac CSD*, 140 A.D.2 33 (2d Dep't), *appeal denied*, 73 N.Y.2d 703 (1988)).

36:18. Are excessed teachers entitled to notice of positions that might come available while they are on the preferred eligtble list (PEL)?

Yes. School districts are required to make a reasonable effort to notify eligible persons of vacancies so that such persons may be afforded the opportunity to accept or decline a position. It is not enough for a district to publicize a vacancy (*Appeal of Dickinson*, 49 Ed Dept Rep 463 (2010), *petition granted in part*, (Sup. Ct. Albany Cnty., Feb. 22, 2011), *on remand* 51 Ed Dept Rep, Dec. No. 16,256 (2011)).

36:19. Are there any limitations that affect an excessed teacher's right to reappointment?

Yes. For example, teachers are only entitled to reappointment within the tenure area in which they served, even if they hold certification for positions in other tenure areas (*Bd. of Educ. v. Barker Teachers Union,* 209 A.D.2d 945 (4th Dep't 1994), *appeal denied*, 85 N.Y.2d 807 (1995); *Appeal of Allen,* 36 Ed Dept Rep 299 (1997), *petition dismissed*, Special Term (Sup. Ct. Albany Cnty.) n.o.r. (Nov. 1997); *Appeal of Moravus*, 32 Ed Dept Rep 419 (1992)). In addition, they must be certified for the position to which they are reappointed (*Davis v. Mills*, 98 N.Y.2d 120 (2002), see **36:14**; see also **31:7**).

In the event that a district mistakenly reappoints a tenured teacher from the PEL to teach a subject within that teacher's tenure area but outside his or her certification, it must continue to pay the teacher's full salary during the pendency of section 3020-a charges brought to remove that teacher for lack of certification (*Winter v. Bd. of Educ. for Rhinebeck CSD,* 79 N.Y.2d 1, *reargument denied,* 79 N.Y.2d 978 (1992); see **38:42**). This is because teachers certified on the day they are initially hired by the district are deemed qualified under the Education Law for purposes of receiving a salary even if they are not specifically certified to teach in the position for which they are later mistakenly recalled to from the PEL (*Winter v. Bd. of Educ. of Rhinebeck CSD*).

In addition, a collective bargaining agreement may not require that a teacher whose position has been abolished be appointed to any job opening in his or her tenure area (*Bd. of Educ. v. Barker Teachers Union*), or any position that becomes available for which the teacher is certified (*Bd. of Educ. of Valhalla UFSD v. Valhalla Teachers Ass'n*, 112 A.D.3d 620 (2d Dep't 2013); *Bd. of Educ. v. Barker Teachers Union*).

36:20. Do teachers lose their right to remain on the preferred eligible list (PEL) if they accept a position in a different tenure area or refuse a particular offer of reemployment?

No. A teacher does not waive any right to reappointment within his or her tenure area by accepting a position in another tenure area in the district (*Matter of Mead*, 23 Ed Dept Rep 101 (1983)); or acceptance of other employment (see *Donato v. Mills*, 6 A.D.3d 966 (3d Dep't 2004)). Moreover, a teacher who accepts a subsequent position in another tenure area in the district, and who thereafter voluntarily resigns from that subsequent position does not waive his or her recall rights to the initial position (*Appeal of Petkovsek*, 48 Ed Dept Rep 513 (2009)).

A teacher does not waive any right to reappointment from the PEL for refusing an offer of reemployment (*Appeal of Stanzione*, 47 Ed Dept Rep 341 (2008)). A teacher who refuses an offer of reemployment because of a short-term commitment to another employer does not necessarily waive his or her reinstatement rights (*Lewis v. Cleveland Hill UFSD*, 119 A.D.2d 263 (4th Dep't 1986)).

However, the decision to decline a position may have lasting consequences. In one case, a school social worker who had been excessed declined a half-time social worker position offered to her by the district in recognition of her PEL rights. When the district subsequently combined the half-time social worker position with a half-time drug and alcohol counselor's position in the classified civil service, creating a single full-time position, the excessed social worker claimed she was entitled to the new full-time position. The commissioner disagreed, finding that once the excessed social worker waived her right to the half-time social worker position, the district was free to appoint someone else to fill it, which it did. Moreover the commissioner found that she had no entitlement to the civil service position, because a social worker's PEL rights as a certified educator do not extend to positions in the classified civil service that do not require educational certification (*Appeal of Markow-Brown*, 45 Ed Dept Rep 315 (2005); see also connected case, *Markow-Brown v. Bd. of Educ. Port Jefferson Pub. Schs*., 301 A.D.2d 653 (2d Dep't), *appeal denied*, 100 N.Y.2d 512 (2003)).

36:21. How does retirement affect an excessed teacher's right to reappointment from a preferred eligible list (PEL)?

A teacher's retirement terminates the teacher's PEL rights (*Appeal of Donato*, 41 Ed Dept Rep 246 (2001), *aff'd, Donato v. Mills*, 6 A.D.3d 966 (3d Dep't 2004); *Morehouse v. Mills*, 37 Ed Dept Rep 428 (1998), *aff'd,* 268 A.D.2d 767 (3d Dep't 2000), *appeal denied*, 95 N.Y.2d 751 (2000); *Matter of Girard v. Bd. of*

Educ. of City Sch. Dist. of Buffalo, 168 A.D.2d 183 (4th Dep't 1991)), unless the decision to retire was involuntarily made because of fraud, coercion, or duress (*Gould v. Bd. of Educ. of Sewanhaka Cent. High Sch. Dist.*, 81 N.Y.2d 446 (1993)). A teacher who retires after his or her position is abolished may be entitled to back pay and benefits for the period of time from the date the position was abolished to the effective date of retirement, if abolition of the teacher's position or the assignment of another teacher to teach classes previously encompassed within the abolished position was improper (*Appeal of Curtis and Newell*, 48 Ed Dept Rep 184 (2008)).

Acceptance of termination benefits also terminates a teacher's PEL rights (*Morehouse v. Mills; Matter of Gerson v. Bd. of Educ. of Comsewogue UFSD*, 214 A.D.2d 732 (2d Dep't 1995)). However, a teacher who retires under the disability retirement provisions of the Education Law and then later has such disability retirement allowance rescinded, is entitled to be placed on the PEL as of the date of the disability retirement (§ 2510(3)(a)).

36:22. Must teachers on a preferred eligible list (PEL) be offered substitute and/or part-time positions?

Yes. Teachers on the PEL also must be offered regular substitute positions of at least a five-month duration. Declining an offer of reinstatement to such a position does not extinguish the teacher's preferred eligibility rights (§§ 2510(3)(b), 3013(3)(b)).

In addition, teachers on the PEL must be offered a part-time teaching position of shorter duration if one becomes available (*Abrams v. Ambach*, 43 A.D.2d 883 (3d Dep't 1974)). In fact, a teacher recalled from the PEL and placed in a part-time position after being excessed from a full-time position is entitled to a new seven-year period on the PEL from the date the school district abolishes his or her part-time position (*Avila v. Bd. of Educ. of the North Babylon UFSD*, 240 A.D.2d 661 (2d Dep't), *appeal denied*, 91 N.Y.2d 801 (1997); *Appeal of Stanzione*, 47 Ed Dept Rep 341 (2008)).

36:23. How does reappointment from a preferred eligible list (PEL) affect a teacher's salary and other benefits?

A teacher who is reappointed to a similar position within the district is entitled to appointment without reduction in salary or increment (§§ 2510(3)(a), 2585(4), 3013(3)(a)).

However, a teacher who is granted tenure but is subsequently excessed and placed on a PEL prior to the effective date of the tenure award is not entitled to be reappointed as a tenured teacher (*Appeal of Dickinson*, 49 Ed Dept Rep 463 (2010), *petition granted in part*, (Sup. Ct. Albany Cnty., Feb. 22, 2011), *on remand*, 51 Ed Dept Rep, Dec. No. 16,256 (2011); see also *Appeal of Delanson*, 51 Ed Dept Rep, Dec. No. 16,256 (2011)).

36:24. Do excessed educators have a right to be appointed to a non-tenure-bearing position?

No. Excessed educators (instructional employees and administrators) only qualify for preferred eligibility (PEL) rights (see **36:14**) if both the position from which they are excessed and the position to which they seek appointment are tenure-bearing. The employee need not have acquired tenure; rather, both positions must be tenure-track positions. For example, an instructional employee who is excessed from a tenure-bearing position may have PEL rights only to another tenure-bearing position (*Appeal of Strong,* 41 Ed Dept Rep 425 (2002); see also *Appeal of Krause*, 46 Ed Dept Rep 304 (2007); *Matter of Merz*, 21 Ed Dept Rep 449 (1982)). Conversely, assistant superintendents in small city school districts do not receive appointments to tenure-bearing positions in the first place and therefore do not have PEL rights (§ 2509(1)(b); *Appeal of Strong*).

36:25. Does an educator excessed from a position in the unclassified civil service have a preferred eligibility (PEL) right to be appointed to a position in the classified civil service?

No. Educators who are excessed from a position in the unclassified civil service do not have PEL rights (see **36:14**) to positions in the classified civil service. Thus, where a school board abolishes an educational or instructional position in the unclassified civil service (i.e., one that requires educational certification) and creates in its place a non-educational position in the classified civil service (i.e., one that does not require educational certification) "the former incumbent of the educational position has no claim on the newly created noninstructional position" (*Appeal of Markow-Brown*, 45 Ed Dept Rep 315 (2005), and connected case, *Markow-Brown v. Bd. of Educ. Port Jefferson Pub. Schs.*, 301 A.D.2d 653 (2d Dep't), *appeal denied*, 100 N.Y.2d 512 (2003); see also *Smith v. Bd. of Educ. of E. Ramapo CSD,* 97 A.D.2d 795 (2d Dep't 1983); *Ryan v. Ambach*, 71 A.D.2d 719 (3d Dep't 1979); *Bork v. City Sch. Dist. of City of N. Tonawanda*, 60 A.D.2d 13 (4th Dep't 1977), *appeal denied*, 44 N.Y.2d 747 (1978); compare *CSEA, Inc. v. Rockland Cnty. BOCES*, 39 A.D.3d 641 (2d Dep't 2007)).

36:26. Do excessed teaching assistants have reappointment rights?

Yes. They enjoy the same reappointment rights as teachers (*Appeal of Krason,* 41 Ed Dept Rep 305 (2002), *aff'd, Madison-Oneida BOCES v. Mills,* 2 A.D.3d 1240 (3d Dep't 2003), *aff'd,* 4 N.Y.3d 51 (2004); see **36:14**).

37. Teacher and Principal Performance Evaluations[1]

Editor's Note: This chapter highlights the more prominent aspects of the annual professional performance review requirements that apply to classroom teachers and principals who are subject to evaluation under Section 3012-d of the Education Law.[2]

For the most up-to-date information on this topic, including guidance and other related documents, readers should visit the NYS Education Department websites at: www.nysed.gov and http://engageny.org.

The NYS Education Department's Guidance on New York State's Annual Professional Performance Review for Teachers and Principals to Implement Education Law §3012-d and the Commissioner's Regulations (updated May 31, 2016), *and repeatedly cited throughout this chapter, is available at: https://www.engageny.org/resource/appr-3012-d.*

Overview

37:1. Are school districts and boards of cooperative educational services (BOCES) required to evaluate the performance of the classroom teachers and principals they employ?

Yes. Each school board and BOCES must provide for the annual professional performance review (APPR) of all classroom teachers of record and principals (§ 3012-d(1); 8 NYCRR § 30-3.1(a)), based on multiple measures of effectiveness (§ 3012-d(4); 8 NYCRR § 30-3.4(a)). This includes classroom teachers and principals who plan on retiring during the school year (*Guidance on New York State's Annual Professional Performance Review for Teachers and Principals to Implement Education Law § 3012-d and the Commissioner's Regulations,* q. B14).

In this context, commissioner's regulations define the term *classroom teacher* to mean a teacher in the classroom teaching service who is certified pursuant to Part 80.1 of the commissioner's regulations, except an evening adult education teacher and supplemental school personnel (8 NYCRR §§ 30-3.2(c), 80.1). Subject to change by the commissioner of education, the term *teacher of record* refers to a classroom teacher who is "primarily and directly responsible for a student's learning activities that are aligned to the performance measures for a course" (8 NYCRR § 30-3.2(w); *Guidance on New York State's Annual Professional Performance Review for Teachers and Principals to Implement Education Law § 3012-d and the Commissioner's Regulations*, q. B2).

---

[1] At the time this publication went to press, school districts and boards of cooperative educational services had until December 31, 2016 to come into full compliance with Education Law §3012-d or risk the loss of state aid funds.

[2] The 2016-17 through 2018-19 school years constitute a period of transition to higher learning standards, as a result of which school districts will be calculating transition scores and ratings for the various subcomponents of the annual professional performance review (APPR) categories (see **37:7**) under special regulatory rules. During that period, scores and ratings will continue to be calculated pursuant to the original provisions of section 3012-d, but for advisory purposes only (8 NYCRR § 30-3.17; see **37:12**).

Principal refers to a building principal or an administrator in charge of an instructional program of a school district or BOCES (§ 3012-d(2)(b); 8 NYCRR § 30-3.2(n)). This includes a *co-principal* who is defined as a certified administrator with equal leadership responsibility for all or a portion of a school or BOCES operated program (*Guidance on New York State's Annual Professional Performance Review for Teachers and Principals to Implement Education Law § 3012-d and the Commissioner's Regulations,* q. B4). A *principal of record* means an individual who meets the definition of building principal and is a principal or co-principal in a school or instructional program (*Id.,* q. B13).

Teachers who also perform administrative functions for less than 50 percent of their time are not included in the definition of principal (*Id.,*q. B4).

37:2. Are there teachers and principals who are not subject to an annual professional performance review (APPR) under Section 3012-d of the Education Law?

Yes. Teachers and administrators who do not meet the definition of classroom teacher or building principal (see **37:1**) are evaluated, instead, pursuant to the provisions of section 100.2(o) of commissioner's regulations.

For example, pupil personnel service providers like school psychologists and school social workers, and teachers of adult, community, and continuing education are not subject to an APPR evaluation because commissioner's regulations exclude both groups from the definition of classroom teacher (8 NYCRR § 30-3.2(c); *Guidance on New York State's Annual Professional Performance Review for Teachers and Principals to Implement Education Law § 3012-d and the Commissioner's Regulations*, q. B3; see also **37:1**).

Likewise, assistant principals and associate principals are not subject to an APPR evaluation unless they also serve as a classroom teacher or otherwise meet the definition of building principal (*Guidance on New York State's Annual Professional Performance Review for Teachers and Principals to Implement Education Law § 3012-d and the Commissioner's Regulations*, q. B5).

37:3. Are there teachers who meet the definition of classroom teacher but who might not be subject to an annual professional performance review (APPR) under Section 3012-d of the Education Law?

Yes. A classroom teacher (see **37:1**) is subject to an APPR evaluation only if he or she is also a teacher of record (*Id.*). Therefore, it is possible for a teacher to meet the definition of classroom teacher and still not be subject to an APPR evaluation. For example, school librarians who are certified as a library media or school media specialist and career and technical teachers meet the definition of classroom teacher but would be subject to an APPR evaluation only if they are a teacher of record (*Guidance on New York State's Annual Professional Performance Review for Teachers and Principals to Implement Education Law § 3012-d and the Commissioner's Regulations*, qq. B2, B3, B12).

Similarly, certified speech teachers who provide instructional services would be subject to an APPR evaluation if they are a teacher of record (*Id.*, q. B11). However, certified speech teachers who only provide related services would not be considered a classroom teacher subject to an APPR evaluation (*Id.*, q. B10).

On the other hand, "push-in" and "pull-out" teachers, including providers of academic intervention services, are subject to an APPR evaluation even if they are not the sole teacher primarily responsible for the learning of a group of students (*Guidance on New York State's Annual Professional Performance Review for Teachers and Principals to Implement Education Law § 3012-d and the Commissioner's Regulations*, q. B8). So are special education teachers who team-teach (*Id.*, q. B7).

37:4. Is there a timeline for the completion of an annual professional performance review (APPR) for classroom teachers and principals?

Yes. The entire APPR of a classroom teacher or principal must be completed and provided to the teacher or principal as soon as practicable but no later than September 1 of the next school year.

However, the teacher's or principal's score and rating on the observation/school visit category and in the student performance category, if available, must be computed and provided to the teacher or principal, in writing, by no later than the last day of the school year for which he or she is being measured, but in no case later than September 1 of the next school year.

Classroom teachers and building principals may not appeal their APPR prior to receipt of their overall rating (8 NYCRR § 30-3.3(c); see also **37:13-14**).

37:5. How are classroom teachers and principals subject to an annual professional performance review (APPR) under Section 3012-d of the Education Law rated?

Upon completion of their respective APPR evaluation, such teachers and principals are rated either as highly effective, effective, developing or ineffective, commonly referred to as the HEDI categories. The overall rating is based on multiple measures in each of two statutorily prescribed categories related to student performance and teacher observation/principal school visits (§ 3012-d(4); 8 NYCRR §§ 30-3.4(b), (d)(2), 30-3.5(b), (d); see also § 3012(15); **37:7**). It is determined pursuant to a statutory methodology for the placement of teachers and principals within a HEDI matrix that integrates a teacher's scores under the two APPR categories (§ 3012-d(5); 8 NYCRR § 30-3.6(a); see **37:8-9**, **37:11**; see also § 3012-d(15)).

The figure below illustrates the correlation between the scores and ratings for each of the two APPR categories and the overall HEDI ratings.

		Observation/School Visit			
		Highly Effective (H)	Effective (E)	Developing (D)	Ineffective (I)
Student Performance	Highly Effective (H)	H	H	E	D
	Effective (E)	H	E	E	D
	Developing (D)	E	E	D	I
	Ineffective (I)	D*	D*	I	I

The asterisks in the matrix above indicate that if a classroom teacher or principal is rated ineffective on the student performance category and a state-designed supplemental assessment was included as an optional subcomponent of the student performance category, the teacher or principal can be rated no higher than ineffective overall.

(§ 3012-d(5); 8 NYCRR §§ 30-3.6; *Guidance on New York State's Annual Professional Performance Review for Teachers and Principals to Implement Education Law § 3012-d and the Commissioner's Regulations*, q. I2; see also q. F2 for information on state-designed supplemental assessments).

See **37:9** for additional information on the scoring of the APPR subcomponents.

37:6. How do annual professional performance reviews (APPR) affect the ability of school districts and boards of cooperative educational services to make employment decisions regarding classroom teachers and principals?

The APPR of a classroom teacher and principal must constitute a "significant factor" in decisions concerning his or her employment including, but not limited to, promotion, retention, tenure determination, termination, and supplemental compensation. APPRs must also be a significant factor in decisions regarding teacher and principal development, including coaching, induction support, and differentiated professional development (§ 3012-d(1); 8 NYCRR § 30-3.1(d)).

However, nothing affects the unfettered statutory right of a district to terminate or deny tenure to a probationary teacher or principal for any statutorily or constitutionally permissible reason (§ 3012-d(9); 8 NYCRR § 30-3.1(d)), including the teacher's or principal's performance that is the subject of an APPR appeal (8 NYCRR § 30-3.12(d); see also § 3012-d(15)).

Performance Review Subcomponents

37:7. What are the components of an annual professional performance review (APPR) for a classroom teacher or principal?

Pursuant to section 3012-d and related commissioner's regulations, APPRs for classroom teachers and principals must consist of multiple measures in the following statutorily prescribed categories:

- student performance, and
- teacher observation/principal school visit (§ 3012-d(2)(a); 8 NYCRR §§ 30-3.4(a), 30-3.5(a); see also § 3012-d(15)).

For more information on both the student performance and teacher observation/principal school visit categories, see *Guidance on New York State's Annual Professional Performance Review For Teachers and Principals to Implement Education Law § 3012-d and the Commissioner's Regulations*, sections D and H.

37:8. What measures (subcomponents) are included in each of the two categories of an annual professional performance review (APPR) for classroom teachers?

It depends. First, the student performance and teacher observation categories (see **37:7**) can include both mandatory and non-mandatory subcomponents. Second, there are varying measures for each of those subcomponents (§ 3012-d(4); 8 NYCRR §§ 30-3.4(b), (d)(2)).

Classroom Teachers - Student Performance Category

For classroom teachers, the mandatory subcomponent in the student performance category depends on whether the teacher's course ends in a state-created or administered test for which there is a state-provided growth model. If it does and at least 50 percent of the teacher's students are covered under the growth model, the teacher receives a state-provided growth score. Otherwise, the teacher receives a growth score based on a student learning objective (SLO) developed in accordance with the process set by the commissioner (§ 3012-d(a)(1); 8 NYCRR §30-3.4(b)(1)). For more information on SLOs, see NYS Education Department, *Guidance on New York State Student Learning Objectives (SLOs) for Use in the Required Subcomponent of the Student Performance Category of Teacher and Principal Annual*

Professional Performance Reviews (APPR) Under Education Law §3012-d (updated May 24, 2016), https://www.engageny.org/resource/appr-3012-d.

The optional subcomponent for classroom teachers in the student performance category consists of a second measure that is selected locally and applied, to the extent practicable, in a consistent manner districtwide. Subject to the conditions set out in statute and commissioner's regulations, this optional measure could consist of either a second state-provided growth score on a state-created or administered assessment; or a growth score based on a state-designed supplemental assessment that is calculated using a state-provided or approved growth model (§ 3012-d(4)(a)(2); 8 NYCRR § 30-3.4(b)(2)). Use of an optional subcomponent is subject to collective bargaining, including which measure to use from among those authorized by statute (§ 3012-d(10)(a)).

Classroom Teachers – Teacher Observation Category

For classroom teachers, the mandatory subcomponent in the teacher observation category consists of at least two teacher observations, one of which must be unannounced. One of those must be conducted by a principal or other trained administrator, and the other by one or more impartial independent trained evaluator(s) trained and selected by the school district. subject to the conditions set out in statute and commissioner's regulations (§ 3012-d(4)(b); 8 NYCRR § 30-3.4(d)(2)(i), (vi)). Commencing with the 2016-17 school year, a school district may request from the commissioner of education a waiver from the independent evaluator requirement if it believes that compliance would create an undue burden as set out in commissioner's regulations (8 NYCRR § 30-3.4(d)(2)(i)(b)).

The optional subcomponent for classroom teachers in the teacher observation category consists of observations conducted by a trained peer teacher who was rated effective or highly effective in his/her overall rating in the prior school year, and is from the same school or another school within the school district (§ 3012-d(4)(b); 8 NYCRR § 30-3.4(d)(2)(i), (ii), (vi)).

The teacher observation category must be based on a state-approved teacher practice rubric (§ 3012-d(4)(b); 8 NYCRR § 30-3.4(d)(2)(iv)), unless the school district has an approved variance from the commissioner of education (8 NYCRR § 30-3.4(d)(2)(iv)(b)). In addition, all observations for a teacher for the school year must use the same approved rubric, provided that districts may locally determine whether to use different rubrics for teachers who teach different grades and/or subjects during the school year (8 NYCRR § 30-3.4(d)(2)(v)).

37:9. What measures are included in each of the two categories of an annual professional performance review (APPR) for principals?

It depends. First, the student performance and school visit categories (see **37:7**) can include both mandatory and non-mandatory subcomponents. Second, there are varying measures for each of those subcomponents (§ 3012-d(4); 8 NYCRR §§ 30-3.5(b), (d)(2)).

Principals – Student Performance Category

For principals, the mandatory subcomponent in the student performance category depends on whether at least 30 percent of the principal's students are covered under the state-provided growth measure. If that is the case, the principal will receive a state-provided growth score based on such model. Otherwise, the principal will receive a growth score based on a student learning objective (SLO) developed in accordance with the process set by the commissioner (8 NYCRR §30-3.5(b)(1)); see also § 3012-d(15)). For more information on SLOs, see NYS Education Department, *Guidance on New York State Student Learning Objectives (SLOs) for Use in the Required Subcomponent of the Student Performance Category of Teacher and Principal Annual Professional Performance Reviews (APPR) Under Education Law § 3012-d* (updated May 24, 2016), at: http://www.engageny.org/resource/apppr-3012-d.

The optional subcomponent for principals in the student performance category consists of one or more measures selected by the school district and applied, to the extent practicable, in a consistent manner districtwide. Subject to the conditions set out in commissioner's regulations, any such optional measure could consist of either a second state-provided growth score on a state-created or administered assessment; or a growth score based on a state-designed supplemental assessment that is calculated using a state-provided or approved growth model. (8 NYCRR § 30-3.5(b)(2); see also § 3012-d(15)).

Principals – School Visit Category

For principals, the mandatory subcomponent in the school visit category consists of two school visits. One of those must be conducted by the principal's supervisor or other trained administrator, and the other by either one or more impartial independent trained evaluator(s) selected and trained by the school district, subject to the conditions set out in commissioner's regulations (8 NYCRR § 30-3.5(d)(1); see also § 3012-d(15)). Commencing with the 2016-17 school year, a school district may request from the commissioner of education a waiver from the independent evaluator requirement if it believes that compliance would create an undue burden as set out in commissioner's regulations (8 NYCRR § 30-3.5(d)(1)(ii)).

The optional subcomponent for principals in the school visit category consists of school visits conducted by a trained peer administrator who was rated effective or highly effective in his/her overall rating in the prior school year, and is from the same school or another school within the school district (8 NYCRR § 30-3.5(d)(2); see also § 3012-d(15)).

All school visits must be conducted using a principal practice rubric approved by the commissioner of education, unless the district has an approved variance from the commissioner (8 NYCRR § 30-3.5(d)(4)). In addition, all school visits for a principal for the year, must use the same approved rubric, provided that school districts may locally determine to use different rubrics for a principal assigned to different grade level configurations or building types (8 NYCRR § 30-3.5(d)(5)).

37:10. Are there any elements that may not be used in any of the subcomponents of the two categories of an annual professional performance review (APPR)?

Yes. Those include:

- Evidence of student development and performance derived from lesson plans, other artifacts of teacher practice, and student portfolios, except for student portfolios measured by a state-approved rubric were permitted by the NYS Education Department (SED);
- Parent/student feedback instruments;
- Use of professional goal-setting as evidence of teacher or principal effectiveness;
- District or regionally developed assessments not approved by SED;
- Growth/achievement targets that do not meet minimum regulatory standards set forth in commissioner's regulations (§ 3012-d(6); 8 NYCRR § 30-3.7).

Points may not be allocated based on any artifact, unless it constitutes evidence of an otherwise observable rubric subcomponent. For example, a lesson plan viewed during the course of an observation may constitute evidence of professional planning (8 NYCRR § 30-3.4(d)(2)(xi)).

37:11. How are each of the categories of an annual professional performance review (APPR) rated and scored?

Subject to special rules in effect through the 2018-19 school year (see **37:12**), the student performance and teacher observation/principal school visit categories of an APPR (see **37:7**) are rated and scored based on weights assigned to the various subcomponents (see **37:8-9**) of those two categories.

The weights assigned to the student performance category depend on whether a school district selects to use the optional subcomponent under this category. If it does not, the mandatory subcomponent is weighted at 100 percent. If it does, the mandatory subcomponent is weighted at a minimum of 50 percent, and the optional subcomponent at a maximum of 50 percent (§ 3012-d(4)(a)(2); 8 NYCRR §§ 30-3.4(c)(1), (2), 30-3.5(c)(1), (2)).

Each mandatory and optional measure used in the student performance category must result in a score between 0 and 20. Those results are then combined using a weighted average to produce an overall student performance category score. Based on such score, an overall student performance category rating is derived from the following table:

Overall Student Performance Category Score and Rating

	Minimum	Maximum
Highly Effective	18	20
Effective	15	17
Developing	13	14
Ineffective	0	12

(§ 3012-d(4)(a)(2); 8 NYCRR §§ 30-3.4(c)(3), (d)(1), 30-3.5(c)(3), (4); see also § 3012(15)).

With respect to the teacher observation category (see **37:8**), observations conducted by a principal or other trained administrator are weighted at a minimum of 80 percent, with observations by independent impartial observers weighted at a minimum of 10 percent. The weight assigned to observations by a peer observer is established locally within the minimum weighting constraints required for principal/other trained administrator and independent impartial observers (§ 3012-d(4)(b); 8 NYCRR §§ 30-3.4(d)(2)(xiii)).

Likewise, the weights assigned to the principal school visit category for principals (see **37:9**) depend on who conducts the school visit. Visits conducted by a superintendent or other trained administrator must be weighted at a minimum of 80 percent, with visits conducted by independent impartial trained administrators weighted at a minimum of 10 percent. The weight assigned to observations by trained peer administrators is established locally within the minimum weighting constraints required for the superintendent/other trained administrator and independent impartial trained evaluators (8 NYCRR § 30-3.5(d)(13)(i-iii)).

Each teacher observation and principal school visit is evaluated on a 1-4 scaled based on a state-approved rubric. Multiple observations/school visits are combined using a weighted average to produce an overall observation/school visit score. That score is then converted into an overall rating within the permissible ranges identified in the following table.

Overall Observation/School Visit Category Score and Rating

	Minimum	Maximum
Highly Effective	3.5 to 3.75	4.0
Effective	2.5 to 2.75	3.49 to 3.74
Developing	1.5 to 1.75	2.49 to 2.74
Ineffective	0	1.49 to 1.74

(§ 3012-d(4)(a)(2); 8 NYCRR §§ 30-3.4(d)(2)(xii), (xiv), 30-3.5(d)(13-15); see also § 3012-d(15)).

37:12. Are there any special rules that apply to the scoring and rating of each of the categories of an annual professional performance review (APPR)?

Yes. Through the 2018-19 school year, special rules apply for determining transition scores and ratings for classroom teachers and principals whose APPRs are based, in whole or in part, on state assessments and/or state-provided growth scores on Regents examinations, while the State completes the transition to higher learning standards through new state assessments aligned to higher learning standards, and a revised state-provided growth model (8 NYCRR § 30-3.17(b)).

During the transition period, a transition score on the student performance category and a transition rating that incorporates the student performance category rating will be generated based on:

- The scores/ratings in the subcomponents of the student performance category that are not based on state assessments and/or state-provided growth score on Regents assessments, and
- In instances where no scores/ratings in the subcomponents of the student performance category can be generated, a student learning objective will be developed by the district/board of cooperative educational services consistent with guidelines prescribed by the commissioner of education using assessments approved by the New York State Education Department that are not state assessments (8 NYCRR § 30-3.17(b)(3)).

In addition, through the 2018-19 school year, the overall transition rating will constitute a classroom teacher's or principal's final overall APPR rating under section 3012-d for purposes of tenure determinations, individual employment records, and other employment decisions and proceedings pursuant to Education Law § 3020-b (8 NYCRR § 30-3.17(c)).

For more information on the transition scores and ratings, see NYS Education Department, *Frequently Asked Questions: Sections 30-2.14 and 30-3.17 of the Rules of the Board of Regents* (updated May 2016), qq. 17-31, at: https://www.engageny.org/resource/guidance-on-new-york-s-annual-professional-performance-review-law-and-regulations.

Performance Review Appeals

37:13. May classroom teachers and principals appeal their annual professional performance review (APPR)?

Yes. School districts and boards of cooperative educational services must establish appeal procedures that allow classroom teachers and principals to challenge:

- the substance of the APPR including instances when the classroom teacher or principal is rated ineffective on the student performance category, but highly effective on the teacher observation/principal school visit category based on an anomaly as determined locally;
- adherence to the standards and methodologies required for such reviews pursuant to law;
- adherence to commissioner's regulations;
- compliance with applicable locally negotiated procedures;
- issuance and/or implementation of the terms of an improvement plan (§ 3012-d(15); 8 NYCRR §§ 30-3.12(a), 30-3.15(a)), and
- a state provided growth score pursuant to the procedures and timelines set out in commissioner's regulations at 8 NYCRR § 30-3.16.

Appeal procedures must provide for the timely and expeditious resolution of any appeal (§ 3012-d(15); 8 NYCRR §§ 30-3.12(b), 30-3.15(a)), except that appeals involving a state-provided growth score are subject to specific timelines set out in commissioner's regulations (8 NYCRR § 30-3.16).

APPRs that are the subject of an appeal may not be offered or placed in evidence in disciplinary proceedings conducted pursuant to Education Law sections 3020-a and 3020-b, or any locally negotiated alternate disciplinary procedure until the appeal process is completed (§ 3012-d(15); 8 NYCRR §§ 30-3.12(c), 30-3.15(a), 30-3.16(e)).

Nothing alters or diminishes the authority of a school board, during the pendency of an APPR appeal, to grant or deny tenure or to terminate probationary classroom teachers and principals for statutorily and constitutionally permissible reasons, including the teacher's or principal's performance that is the subject of the appeal (§ 3012-d(15); 8 NYCRR §§ 30-3.12(d), 30-3.15(a)).

37:14. Are there limitations as to when classroom teachers and principals can commence an APPR appeal?

Yes. Classroom teachers and principals must wait until they receive their overall APPR rating (see **37:5, 37:8-9**), before they can initiate an APPR appeal (§ 3012-d(15); 8 NYCRR §§ 30-3.12(e), 30-3.15(a)). Classroom teachers and principals must receive their composite score no later than September 1 of the school year next following the school year for which their performance is being measured (see **37:4**). Therefore, the appeal process cannot be initiated before that date.

Improvement Plans

37:15. Must school districts and boards of cooperative educational services (BOCES) develop and implement improvement plans for classroom teachers and principals based on their annual professional performance review (APPR) rating?

Yes. School districts and BOCES rating classroom teachers and principals as either "developing" or "ineffective" must formulate and implement a teacher improvement plan (TIP) or principal improvement plan (PIP) by October 1st in the school year following the school year for which the teachers' or principal's performance is being measured, or as soon as practicable thereafter (§ 3012-d(15); 8 NYCRR §§ 30-3.11(a), 30-3.15(a)).

Nonetheless, the NYS Education Department recommends that school districts and BOCES work collaboratively with each of their educators to develop an individualized personal professional development plan (PPDP) for them to support their continuous improvement, regardless of their rating (*Guidance on New York State's Annual Professional Performance Review For Teachers and Principals to Implement Education Law § 3012-d and the Commissioner's Regulations*, qq. I9-11; see also *Appeal of Reis*, 53 Ed Dept Rep, Dec. No. 16,510 (2013)).

Through the 2018-19 school year, the need for a classroom teacher to get a TIP and a principal to get a PIP will be based on the final overall transition rating calculated under special rules while the state transitions to higher learning standards (8 NYCRR § 30-3.17(c); see **37:12**).

37:16. Who develops the improvement plans required for classroom teachers and principals who receive a developing or ineffective annual professional performance review rating?

Such improvement plans are developed by the school superintendent or his or her designee in the exercise of their pedagogical judgment.

At a minimum, such plans must include:

- Identification of the needed areas of improvement,
- A timeline for achieving improvement,

- The manner in which improvement will be assessed, and
- Where appropriate, differentiated activities to support the teacher's or principal's performance in the areas identified in need of improvement (§ 3012-d(15); 8 NYCRR §§ 30-3.11(b), 30-3.15(a)).

Public Disclosure of Annual Professional Performance Review Data

37:17. Are the annual professional performance reviews (APPR) of classroom teachers and building principals subject to public disclosure?

Only as permitted by law. For example, APPRs of individual teachers and principals are not subject to public disclosure under the Freedom of Information Law (§ 3012-d(15); 8 NYCRR § 30-3.15(d); see § 3012-c(10)(c); Pub. Off. Law § 86 *et seq.*), which precludes members of the public from accessing such information (*Guidance on New York State's Annual Professional Performance Review for Teachers and Principals to Implement Education Law § 3012-d and the Commissioner's Regulations*, qq. P6-7).

However, school districts and boards of cooperative educational services (BOCES) must, upon parental request, provide a student's parents and legal guardians the final overall APPR rating of any classroom teacher and for the principal of the school to which their student is assigned for the current school year (§ 3012-d(15); 8 NYCRR § 30-3.15(d); see § 3012-c(10)(b)). Parents are not entitled to receive from their district or BOCES any other type of APPR data (*Guidance on New York State's Annual Professional Performance Review for Teachers and Principals to Implement Education Law § 3012-d and the Commissioner's Regulations*, q. P1-2). Through the 2018-19 school year, parents are entitled to receive the final overall transition rating of their classroom teachers and principal calculated under special rules applicable while the State transitions to higher learning standards, as well as the final overall rating calculated pursuant to the provisions of Education Law § 3012-d, along with an explanation of the overall transition rating (8 NYCRR § 30-3.17(d); see **37:12**).

Similarly, the NYS Education Department must provide the public similar information at the school district and building level with additional data such as subject and grade, district wealth, student enrollment, the percentage of teachers and principals in each final rating category, data on tenure grants and denials based on final rating categories, and other specified factors (§ 3012-d(15); 8 NYCRR § 30-3.15(d); see § 3012-c(10)(a); *Guidance on New York State's Annual Professional Performance Review for Teachers and Principals to Implement Education Law § 3012-d and the Commissioner's Regulations*, q. P6).

37:18. What are a school district's responsibilities regarding the authorized disclosure of APPR data to parents?

School districts and boards of cooperative educational services (BOCES) must provide conspicuous notice to parents of their right to obtain statutorily specified APPR information (§ 3012-d(15); 8 NYCRR § 30-3.15(d); see § 3012-c(10)(b); *Guidance on New York State's Annual Professional Performance Review for Teachers and Principals to Implement Education Law § 3012-d and the Commissioner's Regulations*, q. P1).

In addition, school districts and BOCES must make reasonable efforts to verify that parental requests are bona fide and parents making the request are indeed entitled to review and receive the APPR information they are legally allowed to request (§ 3012-d(15); 8 NYCRR § 30-3.15(d); see § 3012-c(10)(b); *Guidance on New York State's Annual Professional Performance Review for Teachers and Principals to Implement Education Law § 3012-d and the Commissioner's Regulations*, q. P1).

Furthermore, districts, BOCES and the NYS Education Department must ensure that any release of APPR data or any data used as a component of such reviews, does not include personally identifying information for any teacher or principal (§ 3012-d(15); 8 NYCRR § 30-3.15(d); see § 3012-c(10)(c)); *Guidance on New York State's Annual Professional Performance Review for Teachers and Principals to Implement Education Law § 3012-d and the Commissioner's Regulations*, q. P5).

37:19. Are there any restrictions on the manner in which parents may receive authorized APPR information?

No. Parents requesting from their school district or boards of cooperative educational services authorized APPR information may receive such data in any manner, including by phone or in person, along with an oral or written explanation of the final overall APPR ratings.

In addition, parents must be offered opportunities that will enable them to understand the scores in the context of teacher evaluation and student performance (§ 3012-d(15); 8 NYCRR § 30-3.15(d); see § 3012-c(10)(b); *Guidance on New York State's Annual Professional Performance Review for Teachers and Principals to Implement Education Law § 3012-d and the Commissioner's Regulations*, q. P3).

Evaluator Training Requirements

37:20. Is there mandated training for individuals who conduct annual professional performance review (APPR) evaluations under Section 3012-d?

Yes. School districts and boards of cooperative educational services must ensure they certify lead evaluators as qualified lead evaluators before such individuals can conduct and/or complete APPR evaluations of classroom teachers and principals (§ 3012-d(15); 8 NYCRR § 30-3.10(a), (b)).

In addition, they must describe in their APPR plan the duration and nature of the training they provide to all evaluators, and their processes both for certifying and periodically recertifying lead evaluators and for ensuring all evaluators maintain inter-rater reliability over time (§ 3012-d(15); 8 NYCRR § 30-3.10(d), (e)). Those who fail to receive certification or re-certification may not conduct or complete evaluations (§ 3012-d(15); 8 NYCRR § 30-3.10(f)).

For more information on evaluators, see *Guidance on New York State's Annual Professional Performance Review for Teachers and Principals to Implement Education Law § 3012-d and the Commissioner's Regulations*, section J).

37:21. Who is considered a lead evaluator for purposes of conducting an annual professional performance review (APPR) evaluation?

Lead evaluators are the primary individuals responsible for conducting and completing an evaluation of classroom teachers or principals (§ 3012-d(15); 8 NYCRR § 30-3.2(l); see § 3012-c(2)(d)). Typically, they are the ones who complete and sign the summative APPR (*Guidance on New York State's Annual Professional Performance Review for Teachers and Principals to Implement Education Law § 3012-d and the Commissioner's Regulations*, q. J1).

To the extent practicable, a principal or a trained administrator acting as the principal's designee must be the lead evaluator of classroom teachers. For principals, the lead evaluator should be the school or BOCES superintendent or a trained supervisor acting as their designee (*Id.*).

37:22. Can individuals other than lead evaluators conduct annual professional performance review (APPR) evaluations?

Yes, provided they receive appropriate training before conducting an evaluation (§ 3012-d(15); 8 NYCRR § 30-3.10(a); see § 3-12-c(2)(d)). *Evaluators* other than lead evaluators include any individual who conducts an evaluation of a classroom teacher or principal, including an observation or assessment that is part of the APPR evaluation (§ 3012-d(15); 8 NYCRR § 30-3.2(i)); *Guidance on New York State's Annual Professional Performance Review for Teachers and Principals to Implement Education Law § 3012-d and the Commissioner's Regulations*, q. J1).

For classroom teachers, evaluators must be a principal, other trained administrator, a trained in-school peer teacher, or other trained independent evaluator. For principals, evaluators must be the principal's supervisor, a trained independent evaluator, a trained peer principal, or other trained administrator (*Guidance on New York State's Annual Professional Performance Review for Teachers and Principals to Implement Education Law § 3012-d and the Commissioner's Regulations*, q. J1).

37:23. Are there any exceptions to the requirement that lead evaluators and evaluators complete their training before conducting an annual professional performance review (APPR) evaluation?

Yes. School superintendents and certified school administrators may conduct classroom observations or principal school visits before completing their training, provided they finish the training successfully before the evaluation is completed (§ 3012-d(15); 8 NYCRR § 30-3.10(a)).

State Monitoring

37:24. Does the NYS Education Department (SED) monitor school district and board of cooperative educational services compliance with annual professional performance review (APPR) requirements?

Yes. SED is required to annually monitor and analyze trends and patterns in teacher and principal evaluation results and data. As part of that process, SED will identify school districts and/or schools where evidence suggests that a more rigorous evaluation system is needed to improve educator effectiveness and student learning outcomes.

In particular, SED will identify school districts and schools with:

- An unacceptably low correlation between student growth on the student performance and teacher observation/principal school visit categories (see **37:7**), and/or
- Teacher and principal overall ratings and subcomponent scores and/or ratings (see **37:8-9**) that show little differentiation across educators, and/or the lack of differentiation is not justified by equivalently consistent student achievement results, and/or
- A pattern of anomalous results in the student performance and teacher observation/principal school visit categories (§ 3012-d(15); 8 NYCRR § 30-3.13(a); see § 3012-c(9)(a)).

37:25. What are the consequences of non-compliance with annual professional performance review (APPR) requirements?

Any school district so identified may be highlighted in public reports. In addition, the commissioner of education could require such a district to develop and implement a corrective action plan, that may include but is not limited to, a timeframe for the district to address any deficiencies or the commissioner may reject the district's APPR plan, changes to the district's target setting process, and a requirement that the district arrange for additional professional development, provide additional in-service training, or use independent trained evaluators to review the efficacy of the evaluation system; (§ 3012-d(15); 8 NYCRR § 30-3.13(b); see § 3012-c(9)(b)).

A corrective action plan may require changes to a collective bargaining agreement (8 NYCRR § 30-3.13(c)).

Annual Professional Performance Review Plans

37:26. Are school districts and boards of cooperative educational services required to adopt and submit for approval annual professional performance review (APPR) plans for evaluating the performance of classroom teachers and principals?

Yes. The APPR plan must include the information prescribed in commissioner's regulations (§ 3012-d(15); 8 NYCRR §§ 30-3.3(a)(1),(3), (b); see § 3012-c(2)(k)). Material changes to an approved APPR plan also must be submitted to the commissioner for approval (§ 3012-d(15); 8 NYCRR § 30-3.3(a)(1); see § 3012-c(2)(k)).

For more information on APPR plans and the plan approval process, see *Guidance on New York State's Annual Professional Performance Review for Teachers and Principals to Implement Education Law § 3012-d and the Commissioner's Regulations*, section C.

37:27. Must school districts and boards of cooperative educational services (BOCES) submit changes to their annual professional performance review plan to the commissioner of education for approval of the changes?

Yes. School districts and BOCES must submit to the commissioner of education for approval any material changes made to their APPR plan. Absent a finding of extraordinary circumstances by the commissioner, such changes must be submitted for approval by March 1 of each school year, on a form prescribed by the commissioner (§ 3012-d(15); 8 NYCRR § 30-3.3(a)(1); see § 3012-c(2)(k)).

Some examples of material changes include changes in the selection of a rubric and the number of observations to be conducted (see *Guidance on New York State's Annual Professional Performance Review for Teachers and Principals to Implement Education Law § 3012-d and the Commissioner's Regulations*, q. C8).

37:28. Must school districts post their annual professional performance review plans?

Yes. The APPR plan must be filed in the district office, and made available to the public on the district's website no later than September 10th of each school year, or within ten days after its approval by the commissioner, whichever occurs later (8 NYCRR § 30-3.3(a)(2)).

Public School Staff

38. Discipline and Termination of Tenured Teachers and Administrators[1]

In General

38:1. May a school district discipline or terminate a tenured teacher?

Yes. However, a tenured teacher may not be disciplined or terminated unless the school district follows certain rules under sections 3020-a or 3020-b of the Education Law, or at the written election of the teacher, rules specified in the collective bargaining agreement between the teachers union and the district (§§ 3020, 3020-a; 8 NYCRR Part 82). In New York City alone, only the alternative procedures specified in the collective bargaining agreement between the teachers union and the New York City Department of Education may be used (§§ 2590-f(1)(c), 3020(4); *Hickey v. New York City Dept. of Educ.*, 17 N.Y.3d 729 (2011)).

In comparison, a probationary teacher may be dismissed at any time, on the recommendation of the superintendent of schools, by a majority vote of the school board (§§ 2509(1)(a), 2573(1)(a), 3012(1)(a)), and subject to certain restrictions (see **37:6**).

38:2. Under what circumstances may a school district discipline or terminate a tenured teacher?

Tenured teachers have the right to retain their teaching positions as long as they exhibit good behavior and competent and efficient service (§§ 2509(2), 2573(5), 3012(2)). Therefore, a tenured teacher may only be disciplined or discharged for "just cause" (§ 3020(1)). Although the Education Law does not define just cause, it does provide that tenured teachers can be removed only for the following grounds: insubordination, immoral character, conduct unbecoming a teacher, inefficiency, incompetence, physical or mental disability, neglect of duty, and/or failure to maintain certification (§ 3012(2)).

Before a tenured teacher is disciplined or fired, that teacher is entitled to a hearing under either section 3020-a or section 3020-b as applicable, on the charges brought by the district, except as otherwise provided under alternative procedures contained within a negotiated collective bargaining agreement (§§ 3012(2), 3020(1); cf. *Koutros v. Dep't of Educ. of the City of N.Y.*, 129 A.D.3d 434 (1st Dep't 2015); see **38:4, 38:7**)). A limited exception to a tenured teacher's right to a disciplinary hearing exists for teachers convicted of certain sex offenses (see **38:6**).

The New York Court of Appeals has ruled that section 3020-a is constitutional (*Bd. of Educ. v. Gootnick*, 49 N.Y.2d 683 (1980)).

38:3. What is the statutory process for disciplining or firing tenured teachers?

The statutory process for removing or otherwise disciplining tenured teachers is mandated by sections 3020-a and 3020-b of the Education Law. In certain instances, section 3020-a provides for expedited proceedings, such as in cases involving misconduct constituting physical or sexual abuse of a

[1] As a general rule, the same rules that apply to the discipline and termination of tenured teachers apply to the discipline and termination of administrators who enjoy the benefits of tenure under New York's Education Law (§ 3020-a(1); 8 NYCRR § 82-3.2(a)).

student (§ 3020-a(3)(c)(i-a)). Section 3020-b sets out a streamlined process for the removal of teachers with two or more consecutive ineffective annual professional performance review ratings (§ 3020-b; 8 NYCRR Part 82; see **38-46-53**).

Pursuant to section 3020-a any person, but usually the superintendent, files written charges, and the school board (except in New York City (see **38:1**)) votes to prefer charges against the teacher (*Matter of Van Dame*, 15 Ed Dept Rep 63 (1975); *Matter of Arcuri*, 20 Ed Dept Rep 178 (1980)). Pursuant to section 3020-b, the school district or employing board brings the charges (§ 3020-b(2)(a)).

Under both sections 3020-a and 3020-b, the teacher is notified of the charges and is entitled to request a hearing on the charges (§§ 3020-a(2)(a), (c); 3020-b(2)(a), (c); 8 NYCRR §§ 82-3.3(d), 82-3.4). A pre-hearing conference must be held (§§ 3020-a(3)(c)(ii); 3020-b(3)(c)(i); 8 NYCRR § 82-3.7; see also **38:21, 38:51**).

All 3020-a hearings commenced by the filing of charges on or after July 1, 2015 and 3020-b hearings must be heard by a single hearing officer who determines the guilt or innocence of the teacher and orders any penalty to be imposed (§§ 3020-a(e)(i), (ii), 3020-b(3)(a)). With respect to section 3020-a charges filed before that date, the teacher was able to choose a single hearing officer or a three-member panel, often called a 3020-a panel, in cases concerning pedagogical incompetence or issues involving pedagogical judgement (§§ 3020-a(2)(e)(i); 8 NYCRR §§ 82-1.3(d), 82-1.4).

Except as otherwise permitted by law, districts must continue to pay the salary of teachers suspended while section 3020-a and 3020-b charges are pending (§§ 3020-a(2)(b), 3020-b(2)(b); see **38:41-43**).

A teacher's resignation after the conclusion of a hearing but prior to the hearing officer's decision does not preclude a school district from continuing the disciplinary proceedings and placing a record of the final determination in the teacher's personnel file (*Folta v. Sobol*, 210 A.D.2d 857 (3d Dep't 1994)).

38:4. What alternatives are there to the section 3020-a statutory process for disciplining or firing tenured teachers?

Districts and their bargaining units may implement alternatives to the 3020-a process. However, except for certain collective bargaining agreements covering teachers in New York City, any alternatives negotiated after September 1, 1994, must allow an employee to choose either those alternatives or the 3020-a process (§ 3020(1), (4)). It is up to the teacher to decide which set of procedures to follow – the statutory 3020-a process or the negotiated alternatives (*Kilduff v. Rochester City Sch. Dist.*, 24 N.Y.3d 505 (2014)).

In addition, a school board has the authority to negotiate the settlement of disciplinary proceedings brought against a teacher (*Matter of Cooke v. Bd. of Educ. Lawrence Sch. Dist.*, 140 A.D.2d 439 (2d Dep't 1988); *Matter of Cedar v. Comm'r of Educ.*, 53 Misc.2d 702 (Sup. Ct. Albany Cnty. 1967), *aff'd*, 30 A.D.2d 882 (3d Dep't 1968)). According to the commissioner of education, there is nothing improper about a district offering a teacher a cash incentive to resign or retire in lieu of prosecuting 3020-a charges against the teacher. Moreover, according to the commissioner, payment of such an incentive does not constitute an improper gift of public funds in violation of Article 8, § 1 of the New York State Constitution, but rather, "a proper exercise of the board's authority to negotiate a settlement of a potential claim to avoid expensive, time-consuming and uncertain litigation" (*Appeal of Allard*, 43 Ed Dept Rep 167 (2003); see also *Matter of Cooke v. Bd. of Educ. Lawrence Sch. Dist.*; *Matter of Cedar v. Comm'r of Educ.*; but see **38:33**).

If a section 3020-a disciplinary proceeding is resolved prior to a decision by the hearing officer, the board must send a copy of such resolution to the commissioner within ten days of the resolution (8 NYCRR § 82-3.4(g)).

38:5. Are there any special requirements that apply to the negotiation of alternative procedures to the statutory section 3020-a process for disciplining or firing tenured teachers?

Yes. Negotiated alternative procedures that become effective on or after July 1, 2015 must provide that all hearings pursuant to both sections 3020-a and 3020-b shall be conducted by a single hearing officer. They also must provide that two consecutive ineffective ratings obtained pursuant to annual professional performance reviews conducted under sections 3012-c or 3012-d constitute *prima facie* evidence of incompetence and just cause for removal. The same rule applies in instances involving three such consecutive ratings, except that different rules apply regarding the manner in which the prima facie evidence in each instance can be overcome (§ 3020(3), (4)(a))). For more information on section 3020-b see **38:46-53**).

38:6. Under what circumstances may a school district terminate a tenured teacher without a section 3020-a or other disciplinary hearing?

School districts may terminate without a section 3020-a or other disciplinary hearing teachers convicted of a sex offense for which registration as a sex offender is required (§ 3020-a(2)(d); see also § 305(7-a)(b); Corrections Law Article 6-C; Crim. Proc. Law § 380.95; Penal Law § 195.20). However, they would have to reinstate such a teacher with full back pay and benefits if the termination was based solely on the conviction and subsequently:

- the conviction is either set aside on appeal or otherwise reversed, vacated, or annulled and the commissioner of education reinstates the teacher's certificate; or
- it is determined that the teacher is not the same person as the convicted offender (§ 305(7-a)(f)).

The outcome would be different for teachers terminated following a section 3020-a or other disciplinary hearing on one or more grounds other than conviction of a sex offense, or certificate revocation based on the conviction (§ 305(7-a)(g)).

38:7. May a tenured teacher waive his or her right to a disciplinary hearing under section 3020-a?

Yes. A teacher may waive his or her right to a hearing under the law as part of a stipulation of settlement in a 3020-a case, provided the waiver is made knowingly and freely (*Abramovich v. Bd. of Educ.*, 46 N.Y.2d 450, *reconsideration denied*, 46 N.Y.2d 1076, *cert. denied*, 444 U.S. 845 (1979); see also *Matter of Pollock v. Kiryas Joel UFSD*, 52 A.D.3d 722 (2d Dep't 2008); *Pagan v. Bd. of Educ. of City Sch. Dist. of City of N.Y.*, 56 A.D.3d 330 (1st Dep't 2008)).

A teacher also may choose, under the law, to proceed under alternative disciplinary procedures contained within a negotiated collective bargaining agreement. Such a negotiated alternative must also result in a disposition of the charges within the same time frames established under section 3020-a (§ 3020(1); see **38.23**).

The teacher must be allowed to choose whether to proceed pursuant to the statutory procedures of section 3020-a or pursuant to negotiated alternative disciplinary procedures (*Kilduff v. Rochester City Sch. Dist.*, 24 N.Y.3d 505 (2014)).

Separate rules for negotiated alternative disciplinary procedures apply in New York City (§ 3020(3), (4)).

38:8. Are there any circumstances under which teachers can be deemed to have waived their right to a 3020-a hearing?

Yes. A teacher's unexcused failure to request a hearing within 10 days of receiving the charges is deemed a waiver of his or her right to a hearing (§ 3020-a(2)(d); 8 NYCRR § 82-3.4(c); *Matter of Gagnon v. Wappingers CSD,* 268 A.D.2d 472 (2d Dep't 2000)). Where a teacher is validly deemed to have waived a hearing, the board must proceed, within 15 days by a majority vote of the board, to determine the case and fix the penalty, if any, to be imposed (§ 3020-a (2)(d); 8 NYCRR § 82-3.4(f)).

However, a teacher with a valid excuse may be entitled to a hearing notwithstanding the failure to timely demand one (*Matter of Gagnon v. Wappingers CSD*). A district rejecting a teacher's belated request for a hearing must state its rationale for rejecting the teacher's excuse. Simply noting that a teacher has failed to file a timely request is insufficient (*Matter of Weill v. N.Y. City Dep't of Educ*., 61 A.D.3d 407 (1st Dep't 2009)). In one case, a teacher was not deemed to have waived a hearing where a school district had not sufficiently notified him of his right to a hearing (*Norgrove v. Bd. of Educ. of the City Sch. Dist. of City of N.Y*., 23 Misc.3d 684 (Sup. Ct. N.Y. Cnty. 2009); but compare *Siegel v Bd. of Educ. of City Sch. Dist. of City of N.Y.,* 58 A.D.3d 474 (1st Dep't 2009)).

A tenured teacher who initially requests a 3020-a hearing but subsequently fails to appear at the scheduled hearing also is deemed to waive the right to a hearing on the merits of his or her case. The school board then is free to vote on the charges and determine the penalty or punishment as if the teacher had never requested a hearing (*Matter of Syracuse City Sch. Dist*., 21 Ed Dept Rep 461 (1982)).

A district's decision to proceed without a hearing is not appealable to the commissioner of education. A teacher challenging any such decision must initiate proceedings in State Supreme Court (*Appeal of Frajer*, 41 Ed Dept Rep 403 (2002)), and must do so within four months after the determination to be reviewed becomes final and binding (C.P.L.R. § 7801 *et seq*.; see also *Matter of Novillo v. Bd. of Educ. of Madison CSD*, 17 A.D.3d 907 (3d Dep't), *lv. to appeal denied,* 5 N.Y.3d 714 (2005)).

38:9. May a school district proceed with a section 3020-a hearing against a tenured teacher who resigns or retires?

According to one state appellate court, there is "no cogent reason, in the absence of an irrevocable resignation or voluntary settlement, to compel a school board to terminate a... § 3020-a hearing upon the resignation of the teacher who is the subject thereof" (*Folta v. Sobol,* 210 A.D.2d 857 (3d Dep't 1994)). In that court's view, "a resignation that is not irrevocable is tantamount to a waiver under section 3020-a(2) of the Education Law and a school board may proceed accordingly" (*Id.*). Similarly, the New York Court of Appeals ruled that a school district's appeal from a § 3020-a hearing officer's decision to merely suspend a teacher was not moot just because the teacher allowed her certification to lapse while the district's appeal was pending (*City Sch. Dist. of the City of N.Y. v. McGraham*, 17 N.Y.3d 917 (2012)).

According to one section 3020-a hearing officer, where the teacher has "voluntarily, unconditionally and finally severed her employment... no valid reason remains for the [school district] to pursue 3020-a charges against her" or him (SED File No. 8431 (Sheila Cole) (2008)). In a related decision, a state appellate court ruled that the school district's decision to delay processing a teacher's retirement pending resolution of the 3020-a charges against her was not arbitrable because it did not violate any express right in the collective bargaining agreement in question (*Matter of Union-Endicott CSD v. Endicott Teachers' Ass'n,* 59 A.D.3d 799 (3d Dep't 2009); related case, *Peters v. Union-Endicott CSD*, 77 A.D.3d 12236 (3d Dep't 2011)).

38:10. Does every type of employer action that is deemed disciplinary in nature trigger a tenured teacher's right to formal due process under section 3020-a?

Yes. For example, in one case, the commissioner of education ruled that a superintendent's involuntary transfer of a principal to the position of assistant principal at another school based on the superintendent's conclusion that the principal had engaged in misconduct was a disciplinary action in violation of section 3020-a of the Education Law (*Appeal of Irving*, 39 Ed Dept Rep 761 (2000)). However, in such cases, the evidence must establish that a transfer was made to discipline the teacher and that the teacher was deprived of his or her rights (see *Appeal of Rabeler*, 46 Ed Dept Rep 382 (2007)). Thus, a school board's decision to reassign a tenured employee based on the district's educational needs will not constitute discipline for which procedural due process must be provided under section 3020-a, as long as the employee's rights are not infringed (*Appeal of Jodre*, 50 Ed Dept Rep, Dec. No. 16,162 (2010); *Appeal of Dillon*, 43 Ed Dept Rep 333 (2004); *Appeal of Gaul*, 40 Ed Dept Rep 105 (2000); see also *Appeal of Dunshee*, 44 Ed Dept Rep 414 (2005); *McElroy v. Bd. of Educ. of Bellmore Merrick CSD*, 5 Misc.3d 321 (Sup. Ct. Nassau Cnty. 2004)).

On the other hand, section 3020-a and its protections do not apply when tenured teachers are terminated for noncompliance with their employing school district's staff residency policy (*Beck-Nichols v. Bianco*, 20 N.Y.3d 540 (2013) or a residency requirement in their employment contract (*Matter of O'Connor v. Bd. of Educ. of City Sch. Dist. of Niagara Falls*, 48 A.D.3d 1254 (4th Dep't), *lv. to appeal dismissed*, 10 N.Y.3d 928 (2008); *Adrian v. City Sch. Dist. of City of Niagara Falls*, 92 A.D.3d 1272 (4th Dep't 2012), *lv. to appeal granted*, 19 N.Y.3d 804 (2012); see also *Matter of Felix v. N.Y. City Dep't of Citywide Admin. Servs*., 3 N.Y.3d 498 (2004)). According to New York's highest court, a residency requirement "defines eligibility for employment." As such it is " 'unrelated to job performance, misconduct or competency' " and, thus, outside the scope of section 3020-a (*Beck-Nichols v. Bianco*).

In comparison, a tenured alien teacher was entitled to back pay when a school district aborted section 3020-a proceedings against him after learning his H-1B visa was revoked. The district had a policy that teachers holding such a visa maintain a satisfactory rating to keep the visa. When the teacher received an unsatisfactory rating, the district notified federal authorities that the visa should be revoked, even though it had no obligation to do so. According to a state supreme court, once the teacher acquired tenure, he could be dismissed only pursuant to section 3020-a or as otherwise required by federal law and regulation (*Matter of Phillip v. Bd. of Educ. of the City Sch. Dist. of N.Y.,* 2009 N.Y. Slip Op. 32565 (Sup. Ct. New York Cnty. 2009)). On the other hand, it was rational for another district to seek visa revocation because the district's obligation to implement an unpaid suspension after a 3020-a hearing conflicted with federal visa regulations (*Brown v. Bd. of Educ. of the City Sch. Dist. of N.Y.,* 2009 N.Y. Slip Op. 31687 (Sup. Ct. New York Cnty. 2009)).

38:11. May a district counsel a teacher to refrain from particular conduct without having to initiate the 3020-a process?

Yes. A district may place a counseling letter (known as a "*Holt*" letter) critical of a tenured teacher's performance in the teacher's personnel file (*Holt v. Bd. of Educ*., 52 N.Y.2d 625 (1981); see also *Matter of Richardson*, 24 Ed Dept Rep 104 (1984)). A *Holt* letter, however, may not be used as a reprimand, which is one of the statutory penalties under section 3020-a and, as such, requires a hearing (*Appeal of Irving*, 39 Ed Dept Rep 761 (2000); see *Appeal of Fusco*, 39 Ed Dept Rep 836 (2000); see also *Matter of Grinins v. N.Y. City Dep't of Educ*., 23 Misc.3d 1117 (Sup. Ct. New York Cnty. 2009); *Gutman v. Bd. of Educ. of City Sch. Dist. of City of N.Y.*, 18 Misc.3d 609 (Sup. Ct. New York Cnty. 2007)).

In addition, a district can pursue section 3020-a charges against a teacher who has been issued counseling letters previously for the same underlying misconduct. Citing the *Holt* decision, a state appellate court determined that so long as the 3020-a charges are filed within the statute of limitations (see **38:16**), the conduct addressed in a nondisciplinary counseling memorandum may be used to support formal disciplinary charges at a later date. It is within the discretion of a school district to subsequently re-consider the same incident (*Bd. of Educ. of the Dundee CSD v. Coleman,* 96 A.D.3d 1536 (4th Dep't 2012)).

According to one federal district court in New York, a teacher improvement plan does not constitute a written reprimand subject to section 3020-a procedural safeguards, even if it infers deficiencies in pedagogical competence and judgment. Instead, it is an evaluation tool which is directed at improving performance, and which does not castigate for misconduct (*Marino v. Shoreham-Wading River CSD*, 2008 U.S. Dist. LEXIS 95178 (E.D.N.Y. Nov. 20, 2008)).

38:12. May a tenured teacher be disciplined for off-campus, off-duty conduct?

It depends. Generally, a teacher may be disciplined for off-campus, off-duty conduct only if it can be established that there is a connection, or nexus, between the off-campus conduct and the teacher's performance of his or her duties. According to the New York Court of Appeals, there is such a nexus "if the off-campus conduct in question directly affects the performance of the professional responsibilities of the teacher or if, without contribution on the part of school officials, the conduct has become the subject of such public notoriety that it significantly and reasonably impairs his or her ability to discharge the responsibilities of the position" (*Matter of Jerry v. Bd. of Educ. of City Sch. Dist. of City of Syracuse*, 35 N.Y.2d 534 (1974)).

Noting the important role that a teacher serves as a role model, one state appellate court upheld the two-year suspension without pay of a teacher convicted of criminally negligent homicide for a "hit and run" accident that caused the death of a teenager. According to the court, the nature of the crime coupled with the widespread publicity of the case were sufficient grounds for discipline under section 3020-a (*Ellis v. Ambach*, 124 A.D.2d 854 (3d Dep't 1986), *appeal denied*, 69 N.Y.2d 606 (1989)).

In *Melzer v. Bd. of Educ. of the City Sch. Dist. of the City of N.Y.*, 336 F.3d 185 (2d Cir. 2003), *cert. denied*, 540 U.S. 1183 (2004), the U.S. Court of Appeals for the Second Circuit, with jurisdiction over New York, upheld the dismissal of a tenured teacher for his active participation in a group that advocates for the release of all convicted pedophiles as well as the abolition of child pornography laws and all laws preventing consensual sexual relations between men and boys (see **42:6**).

In other cases, 3020-a hearing officers have disciplined teachers for off-campus misconduct such as the sale of drugs (SED File No. 4915, Hearing Officer Martin Scheinman (2004)); business record falsification (SED File No. 4892, Hearing Officer Howard Edelman (2004)); misdemeanor driving while intoxicated with related conduct unbecoming a teacher (SED File No. 5075, Hearing Officer Robert Douglas (2006); SED File No. 10,954 Hearing Officer Thomas Rinaldo (2008)).

A teacher who posted inappropriate comments about her students on her Facebook webpage was deemed subject to 3020-a discipline (*Rubino v. City of N.Y.*, 34 Misc.3d 1220 (Sup. Ct. New York Cnty. 2012); SED File No. 17,116, Hearing Officer Lowitt (2011)). However, termination was not warranted because she was otherwise a satisfactory teacher and posted the comments outside of school after school hours. In addition, there was no finding that she intended to nor, in fact, harmed any students nor her ability to teach (*Id.*). On the other hand, online postings about a student have been used as evidence in a 3020-a hearing to show a teacher's state of mind while making inappropriate comments and texts to a student (*City Sch. Dist. of the City of N.Y. v. McGraham*, 17 N.Y.3d 917 (2011)).

When a dean of students plead guilty to off-duty, off-campus felony drug possession and only was suspended after a 3020-a hearing, a state appellate court opined it defied common sense to reinstate him as administrator of the school's anti-drug program, and remanded the case on the question of penalty (*City Sch. Dist. of City of N.Y. v. Campbell*, 20 A.D.3d 313 (1st Dep't 2005); compare *City Sch. Dist. of City of N.Y. v. Lorber*, 50 A.D.3d 301 (1st Dep't 2008)).

38:13. Can school districts require that tenured teachers speak to investigators regarding their own possible misconduct?

No. A teacher cannot be required to speak to persons investigating allegations of misconduct for which he or she could be subjected to discipline under section 3020-a of the Education Law, because any statements he or she made during the course of such an investigation would be admissible against the teacher at the 3020-a hearing. Therefore, requiring the teacher to cooperate with investigators would violate that teacher's right against self-incrimination under 3020-a (*Bd. of Educ. of the City of N.Y. v. Mills*, 250 A.D.2d 122 (3d Dep't 1998), *appeal denied*, 93 N.Y.2d 803 (1999)).

The Filing of Charges

38:14. What is the process for filing section 3020-a disciplinary charges against a tenured teacher?

Detailed charges specifying the grounds for discipline must be filed in writing with the school district clerk or the secretary of the district or employing board (§ 3020-a(1)). The superintendent of schools usually files the charges, although any individual may file them (see **38:3**).

Upon receiving the charges, the school board must vote to determine whether there is probable cause to bring a 3020-a disciplinary hearing. The vote must be conducted in executive session within five days of submission of the charges and must be carried by a majority of the membership of the board (§ 3020-a(2)(a); 8 NYCRR § 82-3.3(c)).

After the board has voted that there is probable cause, the teacher must be immediately notified by certified or registered mail, return receipt requested, or personal service. A school district may have a duty to take additional steps to inform the teacher if it has reason to believe the teacher has not received mailed notices, such as when notices are returned unclaimed (*Norgrove v. Bd. of Educ. of the City Sch. Dist. of City of N.Y.*, 23 Misc.3d 684 (Sup. Ct. New York Cnty. 2009)). A copy of the charges must also be forwarded to the commissioner of education (§ 3020-a (2)(a); 8 NYCRR § 82-3.3(d), (f)).

The teacher has 10 days to request a hearing (§§ 3020-a(2)(c), 3012-c(6), 3020(1); 8 NYCRR § 82-3.4(a); *Chawki v. N.Y. City Dep't of Educ.*, 39 A.D.3d 321 (1st Dep't 2007); see also *Jacobs v. Mostow,* 271 Fed. Appx. 85 (2d Cir. 2008); see also **38:8**).

If the teacher requests a hearing, the district must notify the commissioner of the need for a hearing within three business days of receipt of the request, and send a copy to the employee (§ 3020-a(2)(d); see also 8 NYCRR § 82-3.4(d)).

38:15. What must be included in the notice of charges provided to the teacher?

The notice to the teacher must specify in detail the charges filed against him or her, the maximum penalty that would be imposed by the school board if a hearing is not requested or that will be sought by the board if the teacher is found guilty of the charges after a hearing, and the teacher's rights under the law (§ 3020-a(2)(a); 8 NYCRR § 82-3.3(d); *Norgrove v. Bd. of Educ. of City Sch. Dist. of City of N.Y.*, 23 Misc.3d 684 (Sup. Ct. New York Cnty. 2009)).

38:16. Is there a time limitation for the filing of section 3020-a charges?

Yes. Charges may not be brought more than three years after the occurrence of the alleged misconduct, unless it constitutes a crime when committed (§§ 3020-a(1), 2590-j(7)(c); 8 NYCRR § 82-3.3(a)). The U.S. Court of Appeals for the Second Circuit, with jurisdiction over New York, upheld the termination of a teacher found guilty of engaging in illegal sexual misconduct with two of his former students over 20 years earlier (*DeMichele v. Greenburgh CSD 7 & Arnold B. Green*, 167 F.3d 784 (2d Cir. 1999); see also *Tasch v. Bd. of Educ. of City of N.Y.*, 3 A.D.3d 502 (2d Dep't 2004); SED File No. 3698 Hearing Officer Ben Falcigno (2000)).

However, in large city school districts, charges may not be brought more than three years after the occurrence of the alleged misconduct, unless the charge is of misconduct that resulted in conviction of a crime (§ 2573(8); 8 NYCRR § 82-3.3(a); SED File No. 3650 Hearing Officer Richard Adelman (1999)).

The burden is on a school district to establish that it met the three year time requirement or that the crime exception applies (*Matter of Aronsky v. Bd. of Educ., Community Sch. Dist. No. 22 of City of N.Y.*, 75 N.Y.2d 997 (1990); *Suker v. N.Y. City Bd./Dep't of Educ.*, 129 A.D.3d 502 (1st Dep't 2015)).

Furthermore, charges must be filed during the school year during which the employee is normally required to serve (§ 3020-a(1)). Failure to do so may result in the dismissal of charges against the teacher. A motion to dismiss for failure to file charges within the school year must be made before the hearing officer designated to hear the charges (see *Appeal of Fauvell*, 47 Ed Dept Rep 350 (2008)).

Hearing Officers

38:17. Who conducts a section 3020-a hearing?

A labor arbitrator appointed as hearing officer and selected from a list provided by the American Arbitration Association (AAA) conducts a section 3020-a hearing (§ 3020-a(3)).

The hearing officer may not be a resident of the school district, except in New York City, and may not currently be serving as a mediator or fact finder in the school district. Additionally, the hearing officer may not be an agent or employee of the school board or of the teachers' union, or have served as an agent or employee in the last two years (§ 3020-a(3)(b)(i)).

38:18. What is the process for the selection of section 3020-a hearing officers?

Once a teacher requests a hearing and the charges have been forwarded to the commissioner of education, the commissioner contacts AAA to obtain a list of eligible labor arbitrators to conduct the hearing and the commissioner then mails the list of potential hearing officers and their biographies to the school district and the employee. Within fifteen days of receipt of the list, the district and the employee must each notify the commissioner of their agreed upon hearing officer selection. If there is no agreement on a hearing officer, or the district and the employee fail to notify the commissioner of their selection within 15 days, the commissioner must appoint a hearing officer from the list. These provisions do not apply to the New York City school district which has alternative procedures (§ 3020-a(3)(b)(iii); 8 NYCRR § 82-3.5).

The commissioner also must give the parties notice of each potential hearing officer's record, in his or her last five cases, in commencing and completing hearings within prescribed time periods (§ 3020-a(3)(a)). A hearing officer's compliance with section 3020-a timelines is subject to monitoring by the NYS Education Department, and a record of continued failure to commence and complete hearings within the prescribed time periods will be considered grounds for the commissioner to exclude the hearing officer from the list of potential hearing officers (§ 3020-a(3)(c)(i), (i-a)(C); 8 NYCRR 82-3.11).

38:19. Are section 3020-a hearing officers entitled to compensation?

Yes. A hearing officer's compensation is based on customary and reasonable arbitrator fees, subject to maximum rates established by the commissioner. In addition, travel and other expenses incurred in the performance of his or her duties are subject to limitations set by the commissioner (§ 3020-a(3)(b)(i); 8 NYCRR § 82-3.12). For additional information on the compensation of section 3020-a hearing officers, see

NYS Education Department, *Education Law § 3020-a Hearing Officer Rates* memorandum (Sept. 2015), at: http://www.highered.nysed.gov/tsei/ospra/memo090215.html.

Conducting a 3020-a Hearing

38:20. Is there more than one type of a section 3020-a hearing?

Yes. There is a standard section 3020-a hearing and expedited section 3020-a hearings. Expedited section 3020-a hearings include those:

- Due to revocation of the employee's certification (§ 3020-a(3)(c)(v); 8 NYCRR § 82-3.4(d)(5)(ii)).
- Due to misconduct constituting physical or sexual abuse of a student (§ 3020-a(3)(c)(i-a); 8 NYCRR § 82-3.4(d)(5)(iii)).
- Regarding the existence of probable cause to suspend without pay a teacher charged with misconduct constituting physical or sexual abuse of a student (§ 3020-a(2)(c); 8 NYCRR §§ 82-3.4(d)(5)(vi), 82-3.10).

Except as otherwise provided in statute or commissioner's regulations, standard and expedited section 3020-a hearings share common requirements such as those related to notice of charges, hearing requests, appointment of hearing officers, and pre-hearing conference (see 8 NYCRR §§ 82-3.3, 82-3.4, 82-3.5, 82-3.7). However, some special hearing procedures apply to the conduct of section 3020-a expedited hearings that affect start and completion timelines depending on the type of expedited hearing involved (8 NYCRR § 82-3.9), and probable cause hearings for suspensions without pay related to charges of misconduct constituting physical or sexual abuse of a student (8 NYCRR § 83-3.10)).

Special requirements apply, as well, to section 3020-b proceedings (see **38:46-53**).

38:21. Must the section 3020-a hearing officer conduct a pre-hearing conference?

Yes. The pre-hearing conference must take place within 10 to 15 days of the hearing officer's agreement to serve (§ 3020-a(3)(c)(ii); 8 NYCRR § 82-3.7(a)).

At the pre-hearing conference, the hearing officer:

- Issues subpoenas;
- Rules on all motions by the district and the teacher, including motions to dismiss, amend or consolidate the charges; and
- Sets a schedule for full and fair disclosure of witnesses and evidence for both parties including, but not limited to, bills of particulars or requests for production of relevant and material evidence and information such as witness statements, investigatory statements or notes, exculpatory evidence, or any other evidence (§ 3020-a(3)(c)(i)(C), (iii), (iv); 8 NYCRR § 82-3.7(c)).

At the pre-hearing conference, the hearing officer also must set a schedule for the hearing, including the location, time(s) and date(s) for the final hearing (§ 3020-a(3)(c)(vi); 8 NYCRR § 82-3.7(c)(4)). The final hearing must be completed no later than 60 days after the pre-hearing conference has concluded, unless the hearing officer determines that extraordinary circumstances warrant a limited extension (§ 3020-a(3)(c)(vi); 8 NYCRR §§ 82-3.8(a), 82-3.9), or a different timeline applies as in the case of expedited section 3020-a hearings (see **38:20**) based on revocation of certification (§ 3020-a(3)(c)(v); 8 NYCRR §§ 82-3.4(d)(5)(ii), 82-3.9(b)), charges constituting physical or sexual abuse of a student (§ 3020-a(3)(c)(i-a); 8 NYCRR §§ 82-3.4(d)(5)(iii), 82-3.9(c)), or a suspension without pay probable cause hearing (§ 3020-a(2)(c); 8 NYCRR §§ 82-3.4(d)(5)(vi), 82-3.10).

If the school district presents evidence at the pre-hearing conference that the teacher's certification has been revoked and all appeals have been exhausted, the hearing officer must conduct an expedited hearing within seven days (§ 3020-a(3)(c)(v)). Special rules apply for certificate revocation for specified sex offenses (see **38:6**).

A teacher facing criminal charges does not have the right to stay a section 3020-a hearing pending the outcome of the criminal matter (*Chaplin v. N.Y. City Dep't of Educ.*, 48 A.D.3d 226 (1st Dep't 2008)).

Regarding the production of relevant and material evidence and information, according to one state appellate court, it would be error for a court to grant a party's petition for a subpoena for records after a hearing officer at the pre-hearing conference has granted that party's request for records material and relevant to its case, unless the party shows both how the records to be produced under the subpoena are relevant and a factual basis establishing their relevance (*Watertown City Sch. Dist. v. Anonymous*, 120 A.D.3d 1587 (4th Dep't (2014)).

38:22. Must the school district and the teacher disclose to each other the evidence they will use during the section 3020-a hearing?

Yes. A school board must fully and fairly disclose the nature of its case and the evidence it will use against a teacher (§ 3020-a(3)(c)(i)). According to one section 3020-a hearing officer, the teacher also has a right to disclosure of the investigatory notes of the school district attorney (SED File No. 5951, Hearing Officer John Watson (2007)). Similarly, the teacher must disclose the witnesses and evidence he or she will offer in his or her defense during the hearing (§ 3020-a(3)(c)(i)(C)).

Indeed, at the pre-hearing conference (see **38:21**), the hearing officer must set a schedule for the full and fair disclosure of witnesses and evidence for both parties (§ 3020-a(3)(c)(i)(C), (iii), (iv); 8 NYCRR § 82-3.7(c)).

All evidence must be submitted by both parties within 125 days of the filing of the charges, unless there are extraordinary circumstances beyond the control of the parties (§ 3020-a(3)(vii); 8 NYCRR § 82-3.8(b)). The hearing officer's authority to regulate the course of the hearing helps to ensure that no party is unduly prejudiced by the 125 day limit on evidence submission (see 8 NYCRR § 82-3.8(c)).

38:23. How is a section 3020-a hearing conducted?

A hearing officer presides over the hearing (see **38:17**). The district and the teacher have the right to call witnesses to testify, to cross-examine witnesses, and to have an attorney present at the hearing. Accordingly, a teacher may not be excluded from a hearing during the testimony of a child witness, except under limited circumstances (*Stergiou v. N.Y. City Dep't of Educ.*, 106 A.D.3d 511 (1st Dep't 2013); see **38:25**).

In presenting its evidence, a school district may not access court records of a teacher who has been acquitted of misdemeanor charges even if the disciplinary hearing charges the teacher with the same conduct (*In re Joseph M.*, 82 N.Y.2d 128 (1993)).

The teacher must be given an opportunity to testify but cannot be required to do so (§ 3020-a(3)(c)(i); 8 NYCRR § 82-3.8(e). In addition, a teacher cannot be prevented from discussing the case with his or her attorney during adjournments of a 3020-a hearing even if the adjournment occurs during cross-examination of the teacher (*Matter of Elmore v. Plainview-Old Bethpage CSD*, 273 A.D.2d 307 (2d Dep't 2000); see connected cases at 296 A.D.2d 704 (3d Dep't 2002); and 299 A.D.2d 545 (2d Dep't 2002), *appeal denied*, 99 N.Y.2d 509 (2003)).

An accurate record of the proceedings must be kept at the expense of the NYS Education Department (SED) and a copy provided free of charge to the teacher and the board, upon request. SED may use any new technology or other appropriate means to transcribe or record hearings in an accurate, reliable, efficient and cost-effective manner (§ 3020-a(3)(c)(i)(C); 8 NYCRR § 82-1.12(c)).

Within 30 days of the last day of the hearing, or within 10 days of an expedited hearing of a teacher charged with a revoked certification, the hearing officer must issue a written decision (§ 3020-a(4)(a); 8 NYCRR § 82-3.8(k)). However, according to at least one court in an unreported opinion, a hearing officer's late issuance of a decision does not constitute grounds for vacating the decision (*Abreu v. N.Y. City. Dep't of Educ.*, 43 Misc.3d 1215(A) (Sup. Ct. New York Cnty. 2014)). A 3020-a hearing officer's decision must include whether the teacher is guilty or innocent of each charge, the hearing officer's finding of fact on each charge, and what penalty (see **38:28**), or other action, if any, should be taken by the board (§ 3020-a(4)(a); 8 NYCRR § 82-3(k)(2)).

38:24. What rules of procedure and evidence apply in a section 3020-a hearing?

The rules of procedure and evidence used in a section 3020-a hearing are not as strict as those followed in a court (8 NYCRR § 80-3.8(f); *Jerry v. Bd. of Educ. of City of Syracuse*, 50 A.D.2d 149, (4th Dep't), *appeal dismissed*, 39 N.Y.2d 1057 (1975); *Austin v. Bd. of Educ. of City Sch. Dist. of N.Y.*, 280 A.D.2d 365 (1st Dep't 2001); *Soucy v. Bd. of Educ. of North Colonie CSD*, 51 A.D.2d 628 (3d Dep't 1976)). Consequently, admissible evidence in a section 3020-a hearing has included, for example, hearsay evidence (*Austin v. Bd. of Educ. of City Sch. Dist. of N.Y.; Soucy v. Bd. of Educ. of North Colonie CSD*), the testimony of children (*Jerry v. Bd. of Educ. of City of Syracuse*), an employee's own statements and school records (*Giles v. Schulyer Chemung Tioga BOCES*, 199 A.D.2d 613 (3d Dep't 1993)). Such evidence can be the sole support for a 3020-a hearing officer's findings, so as long as it is "believable, relevant and probative" (*Gisor v. N.Y. City Dep't of Educ*, 94 A.D.3d 584 (1st Dep't 2012); *Giles v. Schulyer Chemung Tioga BOCES*).

Taped telephone conversations between a student and a teacher charged with maintaining an inappropriately close relationship with the student also have been ruled admissible by the commissioner if the tape is authentic and unaltered (*Appeal of Malone CSD*, 33 Ed Dept Rep 108 (1993)). However, a hearing officer did not err in refusing to give substantial weight to a tape recording because it is the hearing officer's discretion to determine what, if any, weight should be given to evidence (*Bd. of Educ. of Byram Hills CSD v. Carlson*, 72 A.D.3d 815 (2d Dep't 2011)). Nor is a 3020-a hearing officer obligated to accept polygraph test evidence offered by the teacher (*Powell v. Bd. of Educ. of Westbury UFSD*, 91 A.D.3d 955 (2d Dep't 2012)).

38:25. Are there any special rules that apply to child witnesses in a section 3020-a hearing?

Yes. Hearing officers may exclude from a public section 3020-a hearing (see **38:26**) any person other than parties, witnesses, and their attorneys where warranted to protect the privacy or reputation of a child under the age of 18 (8 NYCRR § 82-3.8(i)).

In addition, according to one appellate court, an employee may be excluded during the testimony of a child witness if a compelling interest warrants the exclusion, such as when the employee's presence would traumatize the child or interfere substantially with the child's ability to testify (*Stergiou v. NYC Dep't of Educ.*, 106 A.D.3d 511 (1st Dep't 2013)).

Furthermore, section 3020-a expressly authorizes a hearing officer to permit a child under the age of 14 to testify through the use of live, two-way closed-circuit television, as defined in statute, upon certain specified conditions. First, the hearing officer must afford the employee an opportunity to be heard. Second, the hearing officer must determine, based on clear and convincing evidence, that the child would suffer serious mental or emotional harm that would substantially impair the child's ability to communicate if:

- The child is required to testify without the use of live, two-way closed-circuit television, and
- Use of that method will diminish the likelihood or extent of such harm.

In making such determination, the hearing officer must consider any of applicable factors set out in Criminal Procedure Law § 65.20(10)). The child's testimony using live, two-way closed-circuit television must be taken in a manner consistent with Criminal Procedure Law section 65.30 (§ 3020-a(3)(c)(i)(C); see also 8 NYCRR § 82-3.8(h)).

38:26. Is a section 3020-a hearing held in public or private?

Unless the employee notifies the hearing officer at least 24 hours before the first day of the hearing that he or she demands a public hearing, the hearing will be in private. However, the pre-hearing conference must be in private (8 NYCRR §§ 82-3.7(b), 82-3.8(e)).

Portions of an otherwise public hearing during which a student will appear as a witness can become closed to the public and the media to protect the privacy of the student (*Bd. of Educ. of the Middletown Enlarged City Sch. Dist. v. Douglas*, 2006 N.Y. Slip Op. 30657(U) (Sup. Ct. Orange Cnty., Lubbell, J., 2006); see also 8 NYCRR § 82-3.8(h), (i); see also **38:23** and **38:25**)).

38:27. What happens if a teacher is acquitted of the section 3020-a charges?

If acquitted, the teacher must be restored to his or her teaching position, with full pay for any period of suspension without pay, and the charges must be removed from the teacher's employment record (§ 3020-a(4)(b); but see *Olivares v. Bd. of Educ. of City Sch. Dist. of City of N.Y.*, 39 A.D.3d 230 (1st Dep't 2007) (files kept by the administrative trials unit within the New York City School District were not deemed employment records and expungement was not required).

If the hearing officer finds that any or all charges filed against the teacher were frivolous, he or she must order the school board to reimburse the State Education Department for all or a portion of the costs of the hearing, and to reimburse the teacher for all or a portion of the reasonable costs incurred in defending the charges (§ 3020-a(4)(c); see, e.g., *Bd. of Educ. of Florida UFSD v. De Pace*, 301 A.D.2d 521 (2d Dep't), *appeal denied*, 99 N.Y.2d 511 (2003); SED File No. 4165, Hearing Officer Harold Richman (2002)).

Penalties

38:28. What types of penalties may be imposed on a tenured teacher found guilty of section 3020-a charges?

The penalties authorized by the Education Law include a written reprimand, a fine, a suspension without pay for a specified period, or dismissal. In addition, the hearing officer can order remedial action, such as continuing education, counseling or medical treatment, or leaves of absence with or without pay (§ 3020-a(4)(a)). The hearing officer may not impose more than one penalty at the same time (*Matter of Arbitration between Bernstein & Norwich City Sch. Dist.*, n.o.r. (Sup. Ct. Chenango Cnty., Dowd, J., 2000) (error to impose fine and written reprimand), *aff'd on other grounds,* 282 A.D.2d 70 (3d Dep't), *appeal denied*, 96 N.Y.2d 937 (2001)), or an unauthorized penalty (*Adrian v. Bd. of Educ. of the Ramapo CSD*, 60 A.D.2d 840 (2d Dep't 1978) (error to impose suspension without pay and fine)), although the law permits combinations of remedial actions to be imposed (§ 3020-a(4)(a)). Demotion is not one of the penalties specified in section 3020-a (*Garcia v. Dep't of Educ. of City of N.Y.*, 18 Misc.3d 503 (Sup. Ct. New York Cnty. 2007)).

In addition, a hearing officer cannot direct a school district to pay for a teacher's health insurance benefits during a suspension imposed after a 3020-a hearing. Such payments are a form of compensation, and section 3020-a only authorizes unpaid suspensions (*Bd. of Educ. of the Dundee CSD v. Coleman,* 96 A.D.3d 1536 (4th Dep't 2012)).

The "propriety of ever awarding unemployment insurance benefits to a worker who has been suspended without pay following [a 3020-a hearing]" is an open issue, but the level and scope of misconduct warranting such a suspension can rise to the level of disqualifying misconduct and unprofessional behavior that is detrimental to the interests of the employer so as to preclude the teacher from receiving unemployment benefits (*In the Matter of the Claim of Parke R. Brown (Erie 2 Chautauqua-Cattaraugus BOCES*), 133 A.D.3d 1146 (3d Dep't 2015)). That was the case where a teacher made inappropriate, demeaning and sarcastic comments to students, sent unprofessional emails to staff and parents, and confiscated a student's cell phone and impersonated that student to learn what another student thought of his teaching abilities. In addition, the teacher violated the employer's policy regarding the use of multimedia tools in the classroom and elected to show a violent movie to his students without obtaining prior parental consent (*Id*).

Public policy prohibits a section 3020-a penalty that fails to adequately protect students from the teacher in the future (*Matter of Binghamton City Sch. Dist. v. Peacock*, 46 A.D.3d 1042 (3d Dep't), *appeal dismissed*, 8 N.Y.3d 840 (2007); see also *Matter of Binghamton City Sch. Dist. v. Peacock*, 33 A.D.3d 1074 (3d Dep't 2006)). That happened, according to one state appellate court, when a teacher, who engaged in an ongoing and "grossly inappropriate" relationship with a minor student, disobeyed administrative directives to cease the relationship, and showed no remorse for his conduct, was initially suspended without pay for one year and subsequently for two years. However, the court stopped short of recommending termination as the only penalty that would sufficiently protect students (*Id.*). According to the New York Court of Appeals, the state's broad public policy of protecting students does not preclude a penalty short of termination where it is found a teacher is unlikely to repeat misconduct (*City Sch. Dist. of the City of N.Y. v. McGraham*, 17 N.Y.3d 917 (2011)).

38:29. How is the penalty determined when a teacher is found guilty of misconduct?

The hearing officer decides the appropriate penalty to be imposed if a teacher is found guilty of charges following a 3020-a hearing (§ 3020-a (4)(a)). Such a penalty, however, may not be "shockingly disproportionate" to the misconduct (*Matter of Pell v. Bd. of Educ. of Union Free Sch. Dist. No. 1 of Towns of Scarsdale & Mamaroneck, Westchester Cnty*., 34 N.Y.2d 222 (1974)).

At the request of the teacher, the hearing officer must consider the extent to which the school board has made efforts to correct the teacher's behavior, including remediation, peer intervention, or an employee assistance program (§ 3020-a(4)(a); see also *In re Carroll (Pirkle*), 296 A.D.2d 755 (3d Dep't), *appeal denied*, 98 N.Y.2d 764 (2002)).

Furthermore, the hearing officer must give serious consideration to the penalty recommended by the employing school board. Moreover, the hearing officer must base the rejection of a school board's recommended penalty on reasons based upon the record as expressed in a written determination (§ 3020-a(4)(a)).

Within 15 days of receipt of the hearing officer's decision, the employing board must implement the decision (§ 3020-a(4)(b); 8 NYCRR § 82-3.8(k)(2)).

38:30. Is a school board member automatically disqualified from voting to implement a disciplinary hearing officer's recommendation because the board member testified at the disciplinary hearing?

Not necessarily. According to New York State's highest court, disqualification is necessary only "where the testimony of the official directly supports or negates the establishment of the charges preferred... [s] uch testimony renders the decision-maker personally involved in the disciplinary process and partial"

(*Baker v. Poughkeepsie City Sch.Dist.*, 18 N.Y.3d 714, *reargument denied*, 2012 N.Y. Slip Op. 77168 (2012)). Explicitly refusing to endorse a *per se* (or automatic) disqualification rule, the New York Court of Appeals said recusal is not required in all cases, and disqualification is "inappropriate where such a person is necessary to effectuate a decision" (*Id.*; see also *Morgenthau v. Cooke,* 56 N.Y.2d 24 (1982); *Matter of McComb v. Reasoner*, 29 A.D.3d 795 (2d Dep't 2006); *Matter of Martin v. Platt,* 191 A.D.2d 758 (3d Dep't), *lv. to appeal denied*, 82 N.Y.2d 652 (1993) regarding the rule of necessity, where even if there is a reason for a board member's recusal, his or her participation is required if necessary to effectuate a responsibility of the board).

However, in *Baker v. Poughkeepsie City Sch. Dist.,* the court ruled that two school board members erred when they failed to disqualify themselves from voting to terminate a school employee after giving testimony at the employee's disciplinary hearing. Given the number of members on the board, neither of their votes were needed to take disciplinary action. Thus, disqualification was appropriate, and the court remanded the case for a re-vote without the two disqualified board members. While the employee was not restored to his position, the Court of Appeals ruled that he was entitled to back pay until the date of the revote.

38:31. Must a school district implement the penalty imposed by a section 3020-a hearing officer?

Yes. The school board must implement the penalty imposed by the section 3020-a hearing officer within 15 days of receipt of the decision (§ 3020-a(4)(b)). However, if a teacher who is suspended from employment is incarcerated, the period of suspension does not begin to run until the date of the teacher's release from incarceration (*Appeal of Manning,* 38 Ed Dept Rep 458 (1999)).

When the board disagrees with the penalty imposed by the hearing officer, its sole recourse is to appeal the decision (§ 3020-a(5); see also **38:35–36, 38:38**).

38:32. What happens if a teacher fails to comply with a section 3020-a hearing officer's order of remedial action?

In one case, a school district did not have to conduct a second section 3020-a hearing before terminating a teacher who was suspended after a section 3020-a hearing and then disregarded the hearing officer's unequivocal requirement that he complete remedial training before being reinstated. The teacher had been given a full hearing, and 10 months later, still had not completed the training (*Harris v. Dep't of Educ. of N.Y. City,* 67 A.D.3d 492 (1st Dep't 2009)).

However, in another case, a teacher who disputed a district's allegation that he had not satisfactorily completed remedial measures was entitled to a second 3020-a hearing on that issue (*Mirante v. Bd. of Educ. Utica City Sch. Dist.*, 300 A.D.2d 1000 (4th Dep't 2002)).

38:33. May a school district permit a silent resignation or secret suspension from teachers facing section 3020-a disciplinary charges?

Permitting a silent resignation or secret suspension generally is ill advised, and under some circumstances, may even subject school officials to criminal liability. School districts may not enter into any agreement to withhold from law enforcement authorities, the superintendent nor the commissioner of education the fact that an allegation of child abuse in an educational setting (see **51:21**) has been made against a school volunteer or employee (including teachers) in exchange for that individual's resignation or voluntary suspension (§ 1133(1)). Any such agreement is a class E felony and is punishable by a civil penalty of up to $20,000 (§ 1133(2)).

38:34. Are section 3020-a decisions or settlement agreements available to the public under the Freedom of Information Law (FOIL)?

Yes. Generally, agreements settling disciplinary charges are subject to disclosure under FOIL. However, certain portions of such agreements should be reviewed and edited before disclosure to the public in order to protect privacy, including charges that were denied and charges mentioning the names of other employees or students (*Western Suffolk BOCES v. Bay Shore UFSD,* 250 A.D.2d 772 (2d Dep't 1998); *LaRocca v. Bd. of Educ. of Jericho UFSD*, 220 A.D.2d 424 (2d Dep't 1995); *Buffalo Evening News, Inc. v. Bd. of Educ. of the Hamburg CSD*, n.o.r. (Sup. Ct. Erie Cnty. 1987); but see *Anonymous v. Bd. of Educ. for the Mexico CSD*, 162 Misc.2d 300 (Sup. Ct. Oswego Cnty. 1994), *aff'd*, 221 A.D.2d 1028 (4th Dep't 1995)).

A 3020-a hearing officer decision with a finding of guilt is not exempt from FOIL as part of an employee's "employment history" and as such, may be disclosed pursuant to a FOIL request (*DeMichele v. Greenburgh CSD No. 7,* 167 F.3d 784 (2d Cir. 1999); see **13:1–5, 13:11**). Again, certain portions of the decision should be reviewed and edited before redisclosure to the public in order to protect privacy, including charges that were dismissed and those parts of the decision mentioning the names of other employees or students.

According to one state appellate court, "teacher disciplinary records and/or records pertaining to allegations of teacher misconduct cannot be equated with student disciplinary records and do not contain 'information directly related to a student' such that disclosure is proscribed under the Family Education Rights and Privacy Act (FERPA)" (*Hampton Bays UFSD v. PERB*, 62 A.D.3d 1066 (3d Dep't), *appeal denied*, 13 N.Y.2d 711(2009); see also 20 USC § 1232g(a)(4)(A); **13:21–25**).

Appeals

38:35. Can either party appeal a section 3020-a hearing officer's decision?

Yes. Both the teacher and the school district have a right to appeal to the courts a 3020-a hearing officer's decision within 10 days of receipt of the hearing officer's decision (§ 3020-a(5)). That 10 day period is not subject to extension, and failure to comply with it requires dismissal of the appeal as time-barred (*Myers v. City of N.Y.*, 99 A.D.3d 415 (1st Dep't 2012); *Watkins v. Bd. of Educ. of Port Jefferson UFSD*, 26 A.D.3d 336 (2d Dep't 2006)). A court has no authority to extend the 10-day statute of limitations for the filing of an appeal (*Myers v. City of N.Y.*, 99 A.D.3d 415 (1st Dep't 2012)).

A teacher's failure to advise the district of a change in address after the start of a section 3020-a hearing, bars a claim the teacher was not properly served with notice of the district's appeal (*Bd. of Educ. of City Sch. Dist. of City of N.Y. v. Grullon,* 65 A.D.3d 934 (1st Dep't 2009)).

38:36. On what basis may a teacher or school district appeal a 3020-a hearing officer's decision?

Section 3020-a decisions may be appealed pursuant to Article 75 of the Civil Practice Law and Rules (§ 3020-a(5)), which governs review of arbitration decisions. Under this type of court review, the decision of the hearing officer can only be reversed on very narrow grounds, namely, if it were proven that there was corruption, fraud or misconduct in obtaining the hearing officer's decision, the hearing officer was not impartial, or he or she exceeded his or her statutory power (C.P.L.R. § 7511(b)(1)). According to the New York Court of Appeals, the determination of a section 3020-a hearing officer can be vacated only if "it violates a strong public policy, is irrational, or clearly exceeds a specifically enumerated limitation on the arbitrator's power" (*Santer v. Bd. of Educ. of East Meadow UFSD*, 23

N.Y.3d 251 (2014)). Reversal may also be granted if the hearing officer was not impartial (C.P.L.R. § 7511(b)(1)(ii); *Zrake v. N.Y. City Dep't of Educ.*, 41 A.D.3d 118 (1st Dep't), *appeal dismissed*, 9 N.Y.3d 1001 (2007)). Bias must be proven by clear and convincing evidence (*Zrake v. N.Y. City Dep't of Educ.*).

Since it is unusual for a court to reverse a decision under these standards, the decision of the hearing officer is likely to be final in most cases (see, e.g., *Matter of Schwartz v. N.Y. City Dep't of Educ.*, 22 A.D.3d 672 (1st Dep't 2005)). One example of a reversal includes a case where a teacher was terminated after participating in a teachers' union picketing demonstration under circumstances that created a health and safety risk to students and disrupted school operations. The balance between a strong public policy protecting speech related to collective bargaining and a strong public policy in favor of ensuring the safety of school children tipped in favor of the school district (*Santer v. Bd. of Educ. of East Meadow UFSD*).

Nonetheless, the state's highest court has ruled, as well, that section 3020-a establishes compulsory arbitration and, as such, judicial review under C.P.L.R. Article 75 requires that the award have evidentiary support and not be arbitrary and capricious (*Santer v. Bd. of Educ. of East Meadow UFSD*; see also, *City Sch. Dist. of the City of N.Y. v. McGraham,*, 17 N.Y.3d 917 (2011)).

Generally, courts lack authority to review a section 3020-a hearing officer's procedural decisions. However, according to one state appellate court, that would not be the case when a hearing officer dismisses the most serious of charges and the only one alleging misconduct. To allow such a decision to stand would deprive a school district of the opportunity to present evidence of the alleged misconduct (*Bd. of Educ. of Hauppauge UFSD v. Hogan*, 109 A.D.3d 817 (2d Dep't 2013)).

38:37. Are the factual findings of a section 3020-a hearing officer subject to judicial review?

A section 3020-a hearing officer's findings of fact are largely unreviewable because he or she observes the witnesses, and is best able to perceive candor or deception and ascertain a witness' credibility (see, e.g., *Brito v. Walcott*, 115 A.D.3d 544 (1st Dep't 2014); *In re Watt (East Greenbush CSD),* 85 A.D.3d 1357 (3d Dep't 2012); see also *Smith v. N.Y. City Dep't of Educ.*, 67 A.D.3d 555 (1st Dep't 2009), *lv. to appeal denied,* 14 N.Y.3d 705 (2010)).

38:38. Can a court adjudicating a section 3020-a appeal change the hearing officer's penalty?

No. An appellate court does not have the authority to impose a new penalty. Rather, it must remand the matter to the hearing officer, or a different hearing officer (*Solis v. Dep't of Educ. of City of N.Y.*, 30 A.D.3d 532 (1st Dep't 2006); see also *Matter of Binghamton City Sch. Dist. v. Peacock*, 46 A.D.3d 1042 (3d Dep't), *appeal dismissed*, 8 N.Y.3d 840 (2007); *Matter of Binghamton City Sch. Dist. v. Peacock*, 33 A.D.3d 1074 (3d Dep't 2006)).

38:39. Can a teacher reargue in a court action the same facts previously decided against him or her in a 3020-a proceeding?

No, because 3020-a disciplinary hearings are quasi-judicial state administrative proceedings that provide disciplined employees with a full and fair opportunity to litigate charges against them in accordance with procedures set by statute and commissioner's regulations (*Burkybile v. Bd. of Educ. of Hastings-on-Hudson UFSD*, 411 F.3d 306 (2d Cir.), *cert. denied*, 546 U.S. 1062 (2005); see also *Locurto v. Giuliani*, 447 F.3d 159 (2d Cir. 2006); *Locurto v. Safir*, 264 F.3d 154 (2d Cir. 2001); *In re Czosek*, 71 A.D.3d 1359 (3d Dep't 2010); *Kelly v. Huntington UFSD,* 2012 U.S. Dist. LEXIS 45725 (E.D.N.Y. Mar. 30, 2012); but see *Morey v. Somers CSD*, 2007 U.S. Dist. LEXIS 20265 (S.D.N.Y. Mar. 21, 2007)).

Accordingly, in one case, a section 3020-a hearing officer's findings precluded an employee's subsequent claim in federal court that her termination violated the reasonable accommodation provisions of the Americans with Disabilities Act (see **68:2**), because the section 3020-a hearing officer had already fully considered whether the employee could perform the essential functions of her job with or without reasonable accommodation, and had concluded she could not (*Page v. Liberty CSD*, 679 F.Supp.2d 448 (S.D.N.Y. 2010)).

Preclusive effect was given also to the findings in a section 3020-a hearing notwithstanding that the teacher charged did not participate in that hearing, after informing the hearing officer he did not wish to contest the proceedings. In his absence, the teacher was found guilty, and terminated. He was precluded from arguing in federal court that he had been subjected to an improper adverse employment action because he had not taken advantage of the full and fair opportunity he had available to litigate the issue in the 3020-a proceeding (*Hunt v. Klein*, 476 Fed.Appx. 889 (2d Cir. 2012)).

38:40. Can either party commence an interlocutory appeal of a section 3020-a hearing officer's procedural decision prior to the end of the hearing?

It depends. Courts lack authority to review hearing officer decisions rendered during the course of ongoing 3020-a proceedings when such decisions involve only limited procedural questions (*Bd. of Educ. of Hauppauge UFSD*, 109 A.D.3d 817 (2d Dep't 2013); *Jordan-Elbridge CSD v. Anonymous*, 37 Misc.3d 1217(A) (unreported), (Sup. Ct. Onondaga Cnty. 2012)). That would be the case, for example with respect to interlocutory orders involving discovery issues (*Jordan-Elbridge CSD v. Anonymous*), and the denial of a motion at a pre-hearing conference (see **38:21**) to preclude the introduction of evidence (*Harris v. Bd. of Educ. of City of N.Y.*, 46 Misc.3d 835, (Sup. Ct. Kings Cnty. 2014)).

The situation is different if the interlocutory decision can be deemed to be a final determination subject to appeal (*Id.*). That was the case where a section 3020-a hearing officer granted a teacher's motion to dismiss one of the charges against him. The dismissal of the charge was deemed a final determination subject to appeal because, if allowed to stand, the dismissal of that charge would have prevented the school district from adducing evidence in support of the alleged misconduct at the hearing (*Bd. of Educ. of Hauppauge UFSD*).

Suspensions While Charges are Pending

38:41. May a teacher be suspended with pay while a 3020-a charge is pending?

Yes. A school superintendent may suspend a tenured teacher with pay prior to the actual filing of charges until the next regular meeting of the board (§§ 1711(2)(e), 2508(5), 2566(6); *Appeal of Williams*, 37 Ed Dept Rep 643 (1998)). After the board votes to charge the teacher with misconduct under 3020-a, it may suspend the teacher until the case is resolved (§ 3020-a(2)(b); *Matter of Almeter*, 30 Ed Dept Rep 439 (1991)).

Generally, the teacher must be given full pay and benefits during suspension (§ 3020-a(2)(b); *Matter of Jerry v. Bd. of Educ. of the City Sch. Dist. of the City of Syracuse*, 35 N.Y.2d 534 (1974)). According to one court, such payments are not an unconstitutional gift of public funds (*Brady v. A Certain Teacher*, 166 Misc.2d 566 (Sup. Ct. Suffolk Cnty. 1995)).

A school district can reduce a teacher's pay during the pre-hearing suspension period by the amount of income the employee has earned in another job (*Matter of Jerry v. Bd. of Educ. of the City Sch. Dist. of the City of Syracuse*; see also *Matter of Caravello v. Bd. of Educ. of Norwich CSD*, 48 A.D.2d 967 (3d Dep't 1975); *Matter of Wolfson v. Bd. of Educ. of Wappinger CSD*, 47 A.D.2d 748 (2d Dep't 1975)). However, a tenured teacher is not required to mitigate or reduce damages by seeking other employment (*Hawley v. South Orangetown CSD*, 67 N.Y.2d 796 (1986)).

A district may not unilaterally impose a sign-in, sign-out procedure on a suspended employee during the pendency of a section 3020-a hearing. According to the New York Public Employment Relations

Board, such a requirement affects a condition of employment and, as such, is subject to collective bargaining (*Port Jefferson UFSD*, 33 PERB ¶ 3047 (2000)).

In one case, a teacher was not entitled to back pay for the period of time between the imposition of a one-year suspension without pay (later overturned on appeal) and his subsequent termination after a second section 3020-a hearing conducted on remand by the court. The case had been remanded solely on the question of penalty even though the hearing officer mistakenly proceeded to redetermine the merits of the charges against the teacher. The final order terminating his employment was harsher than the original one-year suspension (*N.Y. City Dep't of Educ. v. Hershkowitz,* 51 A.D.3d 560 (1st Dep't 2008)).

38:42. Can a teacher be suspended without pay while 3020-a charges are pending?

Yes, under certain circumstances. For example, a district need not pay a suspended teacher where a collective bargaining agreement provides for suspension without pay (*Romano v. Canuteson*, 11 F.3d 1140 (2d Cir. 1993); *Bd. of Educ. v. Nyquist*, 48 N.Y.2d 97 (1979); *Elmore v. Plainview-Old Bethpage CSD*, 299 A.D.2d 545 (2d Dep't 2002), *appeal denied*, 99 N.Y.2d 509 (2003)); or where the teacher faces charges for lack of certification for the course he or she has been hired to teach (*Meliti v. Nyquist*, 41 N.Y.2d 183 (1976); *Matter of Cutler v. Bd. of Educ. of Poughkeepsie City Sch. Dist.*, 104 A.D.2d 988 (2d Dep't 1984), *aff'd*, 65 N.Y.2d 797 (1985); see also *Smith v. Andrews*, 122 A.D.2d 310 (3d Dep't 1986); **30:6**, **36:19**, but see **38:43**). In addition, a district is not required to pay a suspended teacher who has plead guilty to or been found guilty of a felony drug crime or a felony crime involving the physical abuse of a minor or student pending a hearing on the charges (§ 3020-a (2)(b)).

Neither is a district required to pay a suspended teacher when charges brought on or after July 1, 2015 involve misconduct constituting physical or sexual abuse of students. In such an instance, however, the district's decision to suspend without pay is subject to an expedited probable cause hearing to determine whether that decision should be continued or reversed. In this type of case, the suspension without pay may not last longer than 120 days from the district's decision, and a prevailing teacher may recuperate any lost pay subject to the conditions set forth in statute and commissioner's regulations (§ 3020-a(2)(c); 8 NYCRR § 82-3.10)). These limitations do not affect negotiated agreements in effect in New York City as of April 1, 2015, which may be extended (*Id.*).

38:43. Are there any limitations on the authority of school districts to suspend a teacher without pay while 3020-a charges are pending?

Yes. For example, a district cannot withhold a teacher's pay during the pendency of 3020-a charges when delays are caused by the teacher's good faith request for adjournments (*Derle v. North Bellmore UFSD*, 77 N.Y.2d 483 (1991); see also *McCreery v. Babylon UFSD*, 827 F.Supp. 136 (E.D.N.Y. 1993)). Delays based on documented medical excuses, scheduling conflicts rendering the teacher's attorney unavailable or unavailability of essential witnesses are examples of good faith grounds for an adjournment (*Marconi v. Bd. of Educ. of the Seaford UFSD*, 215 A.D.2d 659 (2d Dep't 1995), *appeal denied*, 90 N.Y.2d 811 (1997)).

Similarly, a district cannot withhold a teacher's pay during the pendency of a 3020-a proceeding to terminate a teacher for lack of certification when the district itself reassigns a teacher a course he or she is not certified to teach (*Winter v. Bd. of Educ. for Rhinebeck CSD*, 79 N.Y.2d 1, *reconsideration denied*, 79 N.Y.2d 978 (1992); *Matter of Diggins v. Honeoye Falls-Lima CSD,* 50 A.D.3d 1473 (4th Dep't 2008); see also **30:6, 36:19**).

But a district did not violate section 3020-a when it stopped paying several stipends to a principal on paid suspension during the pendency of 3020-a charges (*Bauman v. Bd. of Educ. of Watkins Glen CSD,* 21 A.D.3d 630 (3d Dep't 2005)). In addition to her base pay, the principal received stipends for several program coordinator positions she held. During her suspension, she was not re-hired for the stipend positions and the superintendent eliminated the stipends from her pay. The court held that she had no contractual nor property right to the positions and section 3020-a is not violated when an employee's pay is reduced by the amount of stipends that expire during the suspension.

38:44. May a teacher who has been suspended with pay be given nonteaching assignments pending the outcome of a 3020-a proceeding?

Yes. A teacher suspended pending the outcome of a section 3020-a case may be given a nonteaching assignment provided the duties assigned "bear reasonable relationship to the suspended teacher's competence and training, and are consistent with the dignity of the profession" (*Matter of Adlerstein v. Bd. of Educ. of the City of N.Y.*, 64 N.Y.2d 90 (1984); *Hawley v. South Orangetown CSD,* 67 N.Y.2d 796 (1986)). It is permissible for a school district to assign a suspended teacher to perform such duties at a board of cooperative educational services office, which is an educational facility with a professional relationship to the district (*Leibowitz v. Bd. of Educ. of Long Beach City Sch. Dist.*, 2008 N.Y. Slip Op. 31143 (Sup. Ct. Nassau Cnty. 2008)).

A teacher who refuses to accept reassignment forfeits the right to payment of salary during the remainder of the suspension (*Adlerstein v. Bd. of Educ. of the City of N.Y.*; *Brady v. A Certain Teacher*, 166 Misc.2d 566 (Sup. Ct. Suffolk Cnty. 1995)). Moreover, the school board may prefer an additional charge against the teacher for insubordination. The same is true if a teacher accepts reassignment, but fails to adequately perform the reassigned duties (*Brady v. A Certain Teacher*).

38:45. Can a teacher facing 3020-a charges be banned from school events held off campus while the 3020-a action is pending against him or her?

Yes, but the school's ability to ban the teacher from certain off campus locations will depend on the activities sought to be restricted and the nature of the charges pending against him or her. For example, in *Appeal of Anonymous,* 44 Ed Dept Rep 260 (2005), the commissioner of education held that, during the pendency of a section 3020-a disciplinary hearing, a district had the authority to direct a tenured teacher and former track coach to not attend "any home or away track meets including [off campus] events where district students were participating." Since the section 3020-a charges in that case alleged that the teacher had an improper relationship with a student track team member, and, as track coach, she tried to fix the outcome of various track events, the commissioner found that the district's directive was reasonable and narrowly limited in scope to restrict contact with certain student athletes.

In comparison, the commissioner found unreasonably broad in scope a ban that prevented a teacher facing disciplinary charges from being on school grounds for any reason including to vote and to attend school conferences for her own children. There also was no indication as to when the ban would be lifted and, according to the commissioner, the ban bore no relation to the pending charges (*Appeal of Anonymous*, 48 Ed Dept Rep 266 (2008)). On the other hand, the commissioner upheld a subsequent modified ban on the same teacher because it considered the nature of the pending charges of berating, harassing, and threatening behavior toward district employees and denied the teacher access only to the district's home games where she would be in the presence of the complainants against her without supervision (*Appeal of Anonymous II*, 48 Ed Dept Rep 503 (2009)).

Streamlined Removal Procedures for Teachers Rated Ineffective[2]

38:46. Are tenured teachers rated ineffective pursuant to an annual professional performance review subject to removal proceedings separate from those conducted under section 3020-a?

Yes. Teachers who receive two or more consecutive ineffective annual professional performance review ratings in accordance with the provisions of section 3012-c or 3012-d are subject to streamlined removal procedures set out in section 3020-b (§ 3020-b(1), (2)).

Those consecutive ineffective ratings form the basis of incompetence charges to be heard in expedited proceedings conducted under section 3020-b. School boards *may* bring such charges against those who receive two consecutive ineffective ratings, but are *mandated* do so against those who receive three consecutive ineffective ratings (§ 3020-b(2)(a); 8 NYCRR § 82-3.9(d)(1), (e)(1)).

However, nothing in section 3020-b prevents the use of any evidence of performance to support charges of incompetence brought pursuant to section 3020-a (§ 3020-b(6)).

38:47. What is the process for filing incompetence charges under section 3020-b?

The process for the filing of incompetence charges under section 3020-b is very similar to the filing of charges process under section 3020-a (see **38:14-16**). For example, the charges must be filed in writing with the clerk or secretary of the school district or employing board, and no section 3020-b incompetence charges may be brought more than three years after the occurrence of the alleged incompetency (§ 3020-b(2)(a); see 8 NYCRR § 82-3.3).

The teacher must be immediately notified by certified or registered mail, return receipt requested, or personal service (*Id.*), and request a hearing within 10 days of the receipt of the statement of charges (§ 3020-b(2)(c); see see 8 NYCRR § 82-3.4). The failure to request a hearing within that time period will be deemed a waiver of the right to a hearing (*Id.*).

In a hearing waiver situation, the board must proceed within 15 days, by a majority vote of the board to determine the case and fix the penalty (§ 3020-b(2)(c); see 8 NYCRR § 82-3.4(f)).

If the teacher requests a hearing, the district must notify the commissioner of the need for a hearing within three working days (§ 3020-b(2)(c); see 8 NYCRR § 82-3.4(d)).

38:48. What must be included in the notice of section 3020-b incompetence charges provided to the teacher?

The statement of charges must specify the charges in detail, that dismissal is the penalty the board would impose if a hearing is not requested or that will be sought by the board after a hearing, and the employee's rights under the law, and the district must forward the charges to the employee in the manner set out in statute (§ 3020-b(2)(a); see 8 NYCRR § 82-3.4(d)).

In addition, when section 3020-b incompetence charges are brought based on two consecutive ineffective ratings (see **38:46**), the statement of charges also must allege that the employing board developed and substantially implemented a teacher improvement plan in accordance with law, following the first evaluation in which the teacher was rated ineffective, and the immediately preceding evaluation if the teacher was rated developing (§ 3020-b(2)(d); 8 NYCRR § 82-3.9(d)(2); see also §§ 3012-c(4), 3012-d(15)).

---

[2] The questions and answers in this section highlight key areas of difference between proceedings under section 3020-a and section 3020-b. As used in this section, the term teacher refers to both classroom teachers and building principals who are subject to annual professional performance reviews under sections 3012-c or 3012-d.

38:49. Who conducts a section 3020-b hearing?

A single hearing officer selected from a list provided by the American Arbitration Association (AAA) conducts a section 3020-b hearing (§ 3020-b(3)(a), (b); 8 NYCRR § 82-3.6).

Similar to section 3020-a hearing officers (see **38:17**), section 3020-b hearing officers may not be a resident of the school district, except in New York City, and may not currently be serving as a mediator or fact finder in the school district. Additionally, the hearing officer may not be an agent, employee or representative of the school board or of the teachers' union, or have served in such capacity in the last two years (§ 3020-b(3)(b)).

38:50. What is the process for the selection of a section 3020-b hearing officer?

The process for the selection of a section 3020-b hearing officer depends on whether the section 3020-b hearing is based on two or three consecutive ineffective annual professional performance review ratings (see **38:46**).

Except as otherwise provided in law and commissioner's regulations, if the section 3020-b hearing is based on two such consecutive ratings, the parties have seven days to agree on a hearing officer from the list of potential hearing officers provided by the commissioner (§ 3020-b(3)(a), (b); 8 NYCRR § 82-3.6(b)(1)). Otherwise, the commissioner will appoint a hearing officer from the list (8 NYCRR §§ 82-3.6(b)(2), (5), 82-3.9(e)(2)).

If the section 3020-b hearing is based on three consecutive ineffective ratings, the commissioner appoints the hearing officer upon receipt of the list of potential hearing officers from the American Arbitration Association (8 NYCRR § 82-3.6(c)).

38:51. Must a section 3020-b hearing officer conduct a pre-hearing conference?

Yes, but the timing of the pre-hearing conference depends on whether the section 3020-b proceeding is based on two or three consecutive ineffective annual professional performance review ratings (see **38:46**).

If the proceeding is based on two such ratings, the hearing officer must hold the pre-conference within seven days after his or her appointment. If the proceeding is based on three consecutive ineffective ratings, the hearing officer must hold the pre-hearing conference within five days of his or her appointment (8 NYCRR §§ 82-3.7(c), 82-3.9(d)(3), (e)(3); see § 3020-b(3)(c)(i)).

At the pre-hearing conference, the hearing officer must establish a hearing schedule to ensure that the required timeframes are met and an equitable distribution of days between the school district and the teacher (§ 3020-b(3)(c)(i); 8 NYCRR § 82-3.9(d)(4), (e)(4)).

38:52. How is a section 3020-b hearing conducted?

A hearing officer presides over the hearing (§ 3020-b(3)(b)).

If the section 3020-b proceeding is based on two consecutive ineffective annual professional performance review ratings (see **38:46**), the hearing must start within seven days of the pre-hearing conference and be completed no longer than 90 days after the teacher requested a hearing (§ 3020-b(3)(c)(i); 8 NYCRR § 82-3.9(d)(5)-(6)).

If the section 3020-b proceeding is based on three consecutive ineffective ratings (see **38:46**), the hearing must start within five days of the pre-hearing officer and be completed within 30 days from when the teacher asked for a hearing (§ 3020-b(3)(c)(i); 8 NYCRR § 82-3.9(e)(5)-(6)).

Except as otherwise authorized by law and commissioner's regulations, a hearing officer may not grant adjournments that would extend the hearing beyond the applicable completion timeline (§ 3020-b(3)(c)(i); 8 NYCRR § 82-3.9(d)(7), (e)(7)).

The hearing officer must issue a written decision within 10 days of the last day of the hearing. The decision must include the hearing officer's findings of fact and conclusions based on such findings, and indicate whether the penalty of removal shall be imposed (§ 3020-b(4)(a); 8 NYCRR § 82-3.9(d)(8), (e)(8)).

38:53. What rules of evidence apply in a section 3020-b hearing?

Although technical rules of evidence do not apply in a section 3020-b hearing (§ 3020-b(3)(c)(iii); 8 NYCRR § 82-3.8(f)), the hearing officer must apply the legal standards expressly set out in section 3020-b (§ 3020-b(3)(c)(v)).

Pursuant to statute, consecutive ineffective ratings shall constitute *prima facie* evidence of incompetence in section 3020-b proceedings (§ 3020-b(3)(c)(v)(A), (B)). Nonetheless, a teacher can overcome such evidence by presenting clear and convincing evidence that with respect to:

- Charges based on two consecutive ineffective ratings, he or she is not incompetent in light of all surrounding circumstances (§ 3020-b(3)(c)(v)(A)).
- Charges based on three consecutive ineffective ratings, the calculation of one or more of the underlying components on his or her annual professional performance reviews was fraudulent (mistaken identity) (§ 3020-b(3)(c)(v)(B)).

In each instance, absent extraordinary circumstance, the failure to successfully overcome the *prima facie* evidence shall be just cause for removal (§ 3020-b(3)(c)(v)(A),(B)).

39. Non-Instructional Employees

The Civil Service[1]

39:1. What is the civil service?

The civil service includes all offices and positions in the service of the state or any of its civil divisions, including school districts (*Palmer v. Bd. of Educ.*, 276 N.Y. 222 (1937), *motion to amend denied*, 276 N.Y. 682 (1938); *In re Holt*, 26 Misc.2d 247 (Sup. Ct. Kings Cnty. 1953), *aff'd*, *Holt v. Jansen*, 283 A.D. 796 (2d Dep't), *appeal denied*, 283 A.D. 815 (2d Dep't), *motion for lv. to appeal denied*, 307 N.Y. 939 (1954); see §§ 2(4)–(8), 17(1)–(2), 35(g)), except offices or positions in the military departments (§ 2(5)). The civil service is divided into two broad categories: the unclassified service (§ 35) and the classified service (§§ 40–44; see figure below).

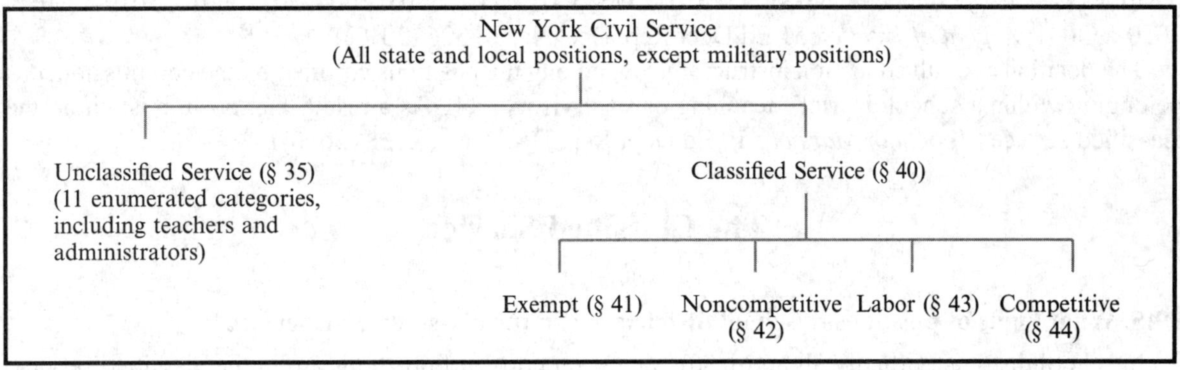

39:2. What is the unclassified service?

The *unclassified* service comprises all positions in 11 categories listed in the Civil Service Law, including teachers and supervisory personnel in school districts and boards of cooperative educational services, the State University and certain community colleges, elective offices, legislative officers and employees, and members and employees of boards of election (§ 35). If a position is not included in one of the enumerated categories of positions in the unclassified service, the position is, by definition, in the classified service (§ 40; see *Wheeler v. Parker*, 546 F.Supp.2d 7 (N.D.N.Y. 2008); *Ficken v. Vocational Educ. and Extension Bd. of the Cnty. of Suffolk*, 201 A.D.2d 481 (2d Dep't 1994), *appeal dismissed*, 238 A.D.2d 589 (2d Dep't), *appeal denied*, 90 N.Y.2d 809 (1997)).

39:3. What is the classified service?

The *classified* service comprises all offices and positions not included in the unclassified service (§ 40). The classified service is further divided into four subcategories or "jurisdictional" classes: the competitive class, the noncompetitive class, the labor class and the exempt class (§ 40; see **39:6**). Unless otherwise

[1] *All statutory references in this chapter are to the New York State Civil Service Law unless noted otherwise.*

specifically designated by law or administrative action of the local civil service agency, all positions are automatically in the competitive class (§ 44).

Article 5, section 6, of the New York Constitution provides that appointments and promotions in the classified civil service must be made according to merit and fitness to be determined by examination, which, as far as practicable, must be competitive. The New York Civil Service Law was enacted to carry out this purpose.

39:4. Are teachers and school administrators governed by the Civil Service Law?

No. Public employees whose principal functions are teaching or the supervision of teaching in a school district or board of cooperative educational services are in the unclassified service (§ 35(g), (j); see **39:1**). This includes employees such as superintendents, principals, teachers, teaching assistants, and other positions that have been certified by the commissioner of education to the NYS Civil Service Commission. The Education Law, not the Civil Service Law, governs the employment of persons in these unclassified positions (see, e.g., Educ. Law §§ 2509, 2510, 2573, 3001, 3002, 3003, 3004, 3012, 3013, 3019-a, 3020, 3020-a, 3031; *Appeal of Troeller,* 51 Ed Dept Rep, Dec. No. 16,326 (2012)).

The position of adult education instructor is not among the positions certified by the commissioner as belonging within a school district's teaching or supervisory staff. As a result, that positon is within the classified service (*Appeal of Marsico*, 50 Ed Dept Rep, Dec. No. 16,158 (2010)).

The Classified Service

39:5. What kinds of positions in school districts are in the classified civil service?

In school districts, virtually all non-instructional support staff positions are in the classified service. Thus, non-teaching administrative positions such as school tax collector, district treasurer, internal auditor, business manager, and labor relations director are generally in the classified service. So, too, are all clerical and non-instructional student-related positions, such as teacher aide and school monitor, as well as positions related to building maintenance, school security, school bus operation and the school lunch program. All local civil service agencies maintain an appendix to their local rules setting forth all positions under their jurisdiction that have been classified in other than the competitive class (see **39:9**).

39:6. How do the four classes (exempt, labor, noncompetitive, and competitive) within the classified service differ?

The *exempt* class includes all positions for which competitive or noncompetitive examination to determine the merit and fitness of applicants is found to be not practicable (§ 41(1)(e); N.Y. Const. art 5, § 6). Exempt class positions are so named because they are exempt from virtually all civil service limitations and restrictions. School boards have complete discretion in filling such positions.

An important factor to consider in determining whether a civil service position should be classified as exempt is whether the position involves highly confidential duties. However, the need for confidentiality, by itself, does not compel the classification of a particular position as exempt (*Dillon v. Nassau Cnty. Civil Serv. Comm'n*, 43 N.Y.2d 574 (1978)). School district positions typically placed in the exempt class include the secretary to the superintendent of schools, school tax collector, school district treasurer, and school district attorney (i.e., where the attorney is an "employee" and not an independent contractor). The positions of school district claims auditor and deputy claims auditor are explicitly classified by statute in the exempt class of the civil service (Educ. Law §§ 1604(35), 1709(20-a), 2526(1-a), 2554(2-a)).

There are no examinations or set minimum qualifications for exempt class positions. Instead, the person or body having the power to make the appointment, including a school board, determines the qualifications for the position and which person possesses such qualifications.

The *labor* class includes unskilled positions, with no minimum qualifications, although applicants may be required to demonstrate their ability to do the job (§ 43). Typically, appointments to labor class positions simply require notification to the local civil service agency of the employment, unless the local civil service agency decides to impose additional requirements such as physical fitness examinations (§ 43(2); see **39:9**). School district positions typically placed in the labor class include school monitor, cleaner, and food service helper.

The *noncompetitive* class includes all positions that are not in the exempt class or the labor class for which it is not practicable to ascertain the merit and fitness of applicants by competitive examination (§ 42(1); *Condell v. Jorling*, 151 A.D.2d 88 (3d Dep't 1989)). In the noncompetitive class, candidates' abilities are simply assessed against established qualifications for the position rather than being placed in competition with other candidates for the highest test score.

The noncompetitive class consists primarily of skilled trade positions. It also includes certain positions of a high-level administrative, scientific, or technical character involving a confidential relationship between the incumbent and the employer or which may require the performance of functions influencing policy (see § 42(2-a)).

Candidates for appointment to positions in the noncompetitive class need only meet the minimum qualifications for the position set by the local civil service agency. Generally, no written or oral examination is required. Instead, the local civil service agency compares the candidate's qualifications to the qualifications that it has issued for the position. If the agency determines that the candidate meets those qualifications, the employer is free to make the appointment. School district positions typically placed in the noncompetitive class include school nurse, school bus driver, teacher aide, custodial worker, building maintenance mechanic, groundskeeper, automotive mechanic, cook, and baker.

The *competitive* class includes all positions not in the exempt, labor, or noncompetitive classes (§ 44). Candidates for competitive class positions must meet minimum qualifications established by the local civil service agency and are subject to competitive (ranked) examination to show their merit and fitness for the position (§ 50(1), (4)(a); *Prof'l, Clerical, Tech. Employees Ass'n* (*Buffalo Bd. of Educ.*), 90 N.Y.2d 364 (1997)). Unless otherwise specifically designated by law or administrative action of the local civil service agency, all positions are automatically in the competitive class (§ 44). School district positions typically found in the competitive class include director of facilities, business manager, safety officer, secretary, keyboard specialist, clerk, custodian, supervisor of building maintenance, director of transportation, head bus driver, bus dispatcher, and school lunch manager.

No position shall be deemed to be in the exempt or noncompetitive class unless it appears under that class in the rules of the local civil service agency (§§ 41(2), 42(1); *Wheeler v. Parker*, 546 F.Supp.2d 7 (N.D.N.Y. 2008); see **39:9**). The rules must also specify which positions in the noncompetitive class are confidential or involve functions influencing policy (§ 42(2-a)).

39:7. Who administers and enforces the Civil Service Law with respect to school district staff employed in the classified civil service?

The administration and enforcement of the civil service system for local governments in New York State is decentralized and is primarily the responsibility of local civil service agencies (§§ 15, 17). Every county, some cities, and a few towns in the state have either a local or regional civil service commission or a personnel officer (§ 15). The county civil service commission or personnel officer is responsible for civil service administration with respect to all positions in the classified service of the county and all the local governments within the county, including school districts, except for cities that have elected to operate their own local civil service agency (§ 17(1)). A regional civil service commission or personnel officer administers the civil service for classified service positions in counties and cities under its jurisdiction (§ 17(3)). Currently, there is only one regional civil service commission in the state: it administers the civil service for classified service positions in Chemung County and the city of Elmira.

For purposes of this chapter, the term *local civil service agency* encompasses the appropriate local or regional civil service commission or personnel officer.

39:8. Who administers and enforces the Civil Service Law with respect to staff employed in the classified civil service by a board of cooperative educational services (BOCES) or multi-county district?

With respect to a BOCES or any school district that operates in more than one county, the provisions of Civil Service Law section 19 govern. As a general rule, the BOCES board or multi-county school board is responsible for deciding which county civil service agency will have jurisdiction over its employees. The board must make the decision within 90 days after the BOCES or multi-county district is established. If it fails to do so, the BOCES or district will be subject to the jurisdiction of the local civil service agency in which the greatest territorial area of the BOCES or district is located. Once the designation is made, it is final (§ 19).

39:9. What rules govern the administration of the classified civil service?

Each local civil service agency is responsible for adopting rules that govern the administration of civil service (§ 20). The local rules cover matters such as how positions will be classified, examinations, appointments, promotions, transfers, resignations, and reinstatements (§ 20(1); see also *Wheeler v. Parker*, 546 F.Supp.2d 7 (N.D.N.Y 2008)). These rules frequently reflect issues and concerns unique to that area. Since they are not uniform, they should always be reviewed in connection with any civil service question involving a position under the jurisdiction of the local civil service agency.

The local rules also contain appendices that list all positions under the local civil service agency's jurisdiction that have been classified in other than the competitive class (see *Wheeler v. Parker*). Therefore, it is necessary to look at the local county or regional civil service agency (see **39:7**) to determine the classification of a particular position (see **39:6**).

The adoption or modification of any local rules, except a modification required because of a change in statute, may occur only after a public hearing. Local rules, including those dealing with placing positions in other than the competitive class, are not effective until approved by the NYS Civil Service Commission and filed with the secretary of state (§ 20(2); see also *Matter of Trager v. Kampe*, 99 N.Y.2d 361 (2003), *appeal after remand*, 16 A.D.3d 426 (2d Dep't 2005)).

The rules and regulations duly adopted by a local civil service agency have the force and effect of law (§ 20(2); *Albano v. Kirby*, 36 N.Y.2d 526 (1975); see also *Lutz v. Krokoff*, 102 A.D.3d 146 (3d Dep't 2012); *Gramando v. Putnam Cnty. Pers. Dep't*, 58 A.D.3d 842 (2d Dep't 2009)).

39:10. What is the school board's role in making appointments to positions in the classified service?

The school board is legally responsible for making appointments to all school district positions, including positions in the classified service, except in New York City where the chancellor has the power to appoint and set salaries for staff in non-represented managerial titles (Educ. Law §§ 1604(8), 1709(15), (16), 1711(1), 1804(1), 1903, 1950(4)(e), 2503(5), 2554(2), 2573(3), 2590-g(2), 2590-h(17), (41), 3011, 3012(1)(b); *Appeal of Brown*, 32 Ed Dept Rep 212 (1992)). As the appointing authority, the board is required to notify the local civil service agency of all classified service appointments on a form prescribed by the local agency (§ 97(1); see **39:9**).

In addition, the school board is required to comply with all provisions of the Civil Service Law when making appointments to classified service positions. If the board fails to select or appoint classified service employees in accordance with the law, the board members may be personally responsible for paying that employee's salary (§ 95).

The school board must also ensure that prospective classified service employees, like all other prospective district employees, undergo a criminal background check (Educ. Law §§ 305(30), 1604(39), (40), 1709(39), (40), 1804(9), (10), 1950(4)(ll), (mm), 2503(18), (19), 2554(25), (26), 3035) See **chapter 41** for information on the fingerprinting procedures required for compliance with the criminal background check process.

39:11. May a school district assign an employee hired to perform services in one title of the classified service to the duties of another position?

Generally, no. Except in cases of temporary emergency, it is improper for an employer to assign out-of-title work to an employee, hired to perform services in one position, to the duties appropriate to another position (§ 61(2); *Kuppinger v. Governor's Office of Employee Relations*, 203 A.D.2d 664 (3d Dep't 1994)).

For example, requiring a school nurse to be responsible for monitoring security monitors and/or allowing persons into the school on an on-going basis has been found not to fall within the general statement of duties of a registered professional school nurse and therefore a violation of the Civil Service Law prohibition against out-of-title work (*CSEA v. New Hyde Park/Garden City Park UFSD*, 230 A.D.2d 702 (2d Dep't 1996)). On the other hand, requiring secretaries and typists to grant visitors access to the school by "buzzing" them in and to provide identification badges to contractors performing work in the school did not constitute out-of-title work because those duties were a reasonable outgrowth of their regular work. The job specifications of typists included, for example, receiving visitors, and secretaries were expected to have "a considerable amount of contact with the public" (*Scarsdale Ass'n of Educ. Secretaries v. Bd. of Educ. of Scarsdale UFSD,* 53 A.D.3d 572 (2d Dep't), *lv. to appeal denied*, 11 N.Y.3d 710 (2008)).

Assigning an employee duties beyond the inherent nature of the position is a mandatory subject of negotiations (*Village of Scarsdale*, 8 PERB ¶ 3075 (1975); see **31:8-9, 47:11**).

39:12. Can a school board create a new civil service position or reclassify an existing position for its school district?

Yes. A school board may create new positions in existing titles. However, the district must submit a proposal for reclassification, including a statement of the duties of the position, to the local civil service agency. The local civil service agency must furnish a certificate stating the appropriate civil service title for the position. Any new position in a reclassified title may be created only if the reclassified title was approved and certified by the local civil service agency (§ 22). The requirement that a school board get the approval of the local civil service agency before any new position is created is mandatory and non-negotiable. Failure to comply is fatal to the creation of the position (*CSEA v. Town of Harrison*, 48 N.Y.2d 66, *reargument denied*, 48 N.Y.2d 882 (1979)).

39:13. Are non-instructional employees in the classified service required to file a constitutional oath of office?

Yes. Every person employed by a school district, except employees in the labor class, must take an oath of affirmation in support of the federal and New York constitutions before he or she starts work.

This oath need only be taken once, at the time of the original appointment, provided that the employee remains continuously employed by the same employer; if there is an interruption in employment, followed by a new appointment, then the employee must take the oath again (Opn. Att'y Gen. I 84-2).

However, a Native American Indian enrolled in or affiliated with an Indian nation recognized by the United States or State of New York may choose to affirm that he or she will perform his or her duties in a manner consistent with the federal and New York constitutions, rather than declaring his or her support of these constitutions (§ 62).

The Competitive Class

39:14. How are appointments or promotions to positions in the competitive class made?

An appointment or promotion to a position in the competitive class of the classified civil service can be made only by selection of one of the three persons certified by the local civil service agency as standing highest on the appropriate eligible list who is willing to accept such an appointment or promotion (§ 61(1); *Cassidy v. Mun. Civil Serv. Comm'n of the City of New Rochelle*, 37 N.Y.2d 526 (1975)). An eligible list is a list prepared by the local civil service agency (or in some cases by the NYS Civil Service Department), which lists in rank order the names of all persons who have passed the required civil service examination for the position to which an appointment is to be made (see *Deas v. Levitt*, 73 N.Y.2d 525, *cert. denied,* 493 U.S. 933 (1989)). "Appointments and promotions [are] made from the eligible list most nearly appropriate for the position to be filled" (§ 61(1)), based on the qualifications of the position (*Gramando v. Putnam Cnty. Personnel Dep't*, 58 A.D.3d 842 (2d Dep't 2009); *Samboy v. N.Y. State Liquor Auth.*, 52 A.D.2d 1016 (3d Dep't 1976)). These determinations are made by the local civil service agency and will not be disturbed by the courts unless they are irrational and arbitrary (*Gramando v. Putnam Cnty. Personnel Dep't*).

If there are fewer than three candidates on an eligible list, a school board cannot be compelled by the Civil Service Law to make an appointment from that list. Instead, the board may make a provisional appointment from outside the list (see § 65(1); *Valentin v. N.Y. State Dep't of Tax. & Fin.*, 992 F.Supp. 536 (E.D.N.Y. 1997), *aff'd*, 175 F.3d 1009 (2d Cir. 1999); *Heslin v. City of Cohoes*, 74 A.D.2d 393 (3d Dep't 1980), *rev'd*, 53 N.Y.2d 903 (1981); see **39:16**).

However, a collective bargaining agreement may contain a provision that requires a school board to make a provisional appointment from a list of fewer than three candidates (see *Heslin v. City of Cohoes*). In addition, notwithstanding the provisions of § 61 of the Civil Service Law, a school district may agree through collective negotiations "on the manner in which it will select one of the top three qualified candidates from an eligible list for promotion." Thus, such an agreement may provide that only the top ranking candidate is eligible for a promotion (*Prof'l, Clerical, Technical Employees Ass'n (Buffalo Bd. of Educ.)*, 90 N.Y.2d 364 (1997); see **39:15**).

39:15. May a collective bargaining agreement provide alternative procedures for the appointment or promotion of competitive class staff?

Yes. The Civil Service Law gives public employers the flexibility to appoint any one of the three highest scoring individuals on an eligible list (*Cassidy v. Mun. Civil Serv. Comm'n of the City of New Rochelle*, 37 N.Y.2d 526 (1975)). Nonetheless, public employers may, through collective bargaining, agree to appoint the highest scoring individual, even though they are not required to enter into such negotiations (*Town of West Seneca*, 29 PERB ¶ 3024 (1996)).

In *Prof'l, Clerical, Technical Employees Ass'n* (*Buffalo Bd. of Educ.*), 90 N.Y.2d 364 (1997), the New York Court of Appeals held that "there is nothing in our State's Constitution, the Civil Service Law or decisional law that prohibits an appointing authority from agreeing through collective bargaining negotiations on the manner in which it will select one of the top three qualified candidates from an eligible list for promotion." The court noted that the appointment of the highest scoring candidate, where compelled by a collective bargaining agreement, does not violate public policy, since appointees are required to serve a probationary term before their appointments become permanent, during which time the appointing authority has the ability to assess other traits not measurable by competitive examination.

39:16. May a school district appoint someone to a competitive class position if there is no appropriate eligible list of candidates?

Yes. A school district may make a provisional appointment to a competitive class position when there is no eligible list available (§ 65(1)), either because an examination has not been given, the eligible list expired (*Davey v. Dep't of Civil Serv.*, 60 A.D.2d 998 (4th Dep't 1978)), or the existing eligible list contains fewer than three names (*Valentin v. N.Y. State Dep't of Tax. & Fin.*, 992 F.Supp. 536 (E.D.N.Y. 1997), *aff'd*, 175 F.3d 1009 (2d Cir. 1999)). A provisional appointment, which is typically made to an unencumbered position (i.e., one to which no one is returning or has a superior claim), is only a stop-gap that, for example, can serve to allow the provisional employee to hold a position while he or she is awaiting the opportunity to take a competitive exam or the results of an exam.

As a general rule, provisional appointments do not ripen into permanent appointments, no matter how long they exist (*Snyder v. Civil Serv. Comm'n of State of N.Y.*, 72 N.Y.2d 981 (1988); *Becker v. N.Y. State Civil Serv. Comm'n*, 61 N.Y.2d 252 (1984); *Haynes v. Cnty. of Chautauqua*, 55 N.Y.2d 814 (1981)), and the appointee can be terminated at any time for any lawful reason (*Preddice v. Callanan*, 69 N.Y.2d 812 (1987); see also *City of Long Beach v. CSEA-Long Beach Unit*, 8 N.Y.3d 465 (2007); *Matter of Lee v. Albany-Schoharie-Schenectady-Saratoga BOCES*, 69 A.D.3d 1289 (3d Dep't 2010); *Mahinda v. Bd. of Collective Bargaining*, 91 A.D.3d 564 (1st Dep't 2012)). In addition, provisional appointees must be terminated within two months after the establishment of an appropriate eligible list, unless there are a large number of people in a particular title serving on a provisional basis. In this case, the appointment can continue, with the approval of the local civil service agency, for a maximum of four months after the establishment of the eligible list to avoid programmatic disruption (§ 65(3); see also **39:17**).

39:17. What rules govern provisional appointments within the competitive class?

To be appointed provisionally to a competitive class position, the candidate must demonstrate to the local civil service agency, by way of a noncompetitive examination, that he or she is qualified for the position. The noncompetitive examination may consist of a review and evaluation of the candidate's training, experience, and other qualifications, without written, oral, or other performance tests (§ 65(1)).

The duration of a provisional appointment is limited to nine months (§ 65(2)). However, under extenuating circumstances it may be extended, provided there is no valid eligible list available (§ 65(4)). Once a provisional appointment is made, the local civil service agency must order a competitive examination within one month or as soon as practicable to ensure that the provisional appointment does not exceed nine months (§ 65(2)).

Notwithstanding the specific statutory mandate, provisional appointments regularly exceed nine months. Nonetheless, provisional appointments that exceed the nine-month limitation do not ripen into a permanent position as a result of such statutory violation or the passage of time. Provisional appointments carry no expectation nor right of tenure. Provisional positions can become permanent appointments only as a result of passing a civil service examination and eligibility (*City of Long Beach v. CSEA-Long Beach Unit*, 8 N.Y.3d 465 (2007); *Matter of Lee v. Albany-Schoharie-Schenectady-Saratoga BOCES*, 69 A.D.3d 1289 (3d Dep't 2010); see also **39:24**). However, an employer has no authority to afford through a collective bargaining agreement superior rights, such as tenure, to provisional employees serving in excess of nine months (*City of Long Beach v. CSEA-Long Beach Unit*).

A school district cannot make successive provisional appointments to circumvent the Civil Service Law (§ 65(4); *Riggi v. Blessing*, 9 A.D.2d 423 (3d Dep't 1959), *aff'd*, 10 N.Y.2d 917 (1961)). If, however, an examination for a position or group of positions fails to produce a list adequate to fill all positions being held on a provisional basis, or if the eligible list is immediately exhausted following its establishment, a new provisional appointment may be made to any such position that has not been filled by permanent appointment. In such a case, a school district may appoint a current or former provisional appointee to the position. If the current or former provisional appointee eventually becomes eligible for permanent appointment (i.e., he or she becomes one of the three highest scoring individuals on the then current eligible list willing to accept appointment), and the district wants to continue that employee in the position, the district must give the employee a permanent appointment (§ 65(4); *Becker v. N. Y. State Civ. Serv. Comm'n*, 61 N.Y.2d 252 (1984); *Haynes v. Cnty. of Chautauqua*, 55 N.Y.2d 814 (1981)).

39:18. May a school district appoint someone to a competitive class position on a temporary basis?

Yes. A temporary employee is essentially a substitute in a position that is encumbered (i.e., one to which someone else is returning or may have a superior claim). A school district may make a temporary appointment to a competitive class position (1) on an emergency basis for a period not exceeding three months; (2) to replace a permanent appointee who is on leave of absence for the duration of the leave; or (3) for up to six months when a position is not expected to exist for a longer period. If a position that is not expected to last more than six months does indeed remain in existence beyond the six-month period, the local civil service agency may authorize an extension for a period not to exceed an additional six months (§ 64(1)).

If the appointment is to be for three months or less, use of an eligible list is not required. However, if the appointment is to last between three and six months, the appointment must be made from the appropriate eligible list, but the appointee does not have to be among the top three on the list (see **39:14**). On the other hand, a temporary appointment for a duration of six months or longer does require that the appointee be among the three highest scoring candidates on the list willing to accept the appointment (§ 64(2)).

In addition, a local civil service agency can authorize a temporary appointment, without examination, when the person appointed will render professional, scientific, technical, or other expert services on either an occasional basis or on a full-time or regular part-time basis in a temporary position established to conduct a special study or project for not longer than 18 months (§ 64(3)).

Irrespective of the duration of the position to which a temporary appointment is made, the candidate must meet the stated minimum qualifications for the position and file an application with the local civil service agency.

39:19. May a school board establish a preference for residents of the school district when hiring competitive class employees?

Yes. Although a school board may not absolutely require that the candidates for a competitive class position be residents of the local school district, it may require that district residents be certified for hiring from an eligible list before nonresidents. However, this residency preference may not be applied to candidates for the position of director of facilities I, II, and III at a school district (§ 23(4-a); see also *Matter of Altamore v. Barrios-Paoli*, 90 N.Y.2d 378 (1997)). In addition, no preference for residents may be given on appointments from promotional lists (§ 23(4-a)). Establishing such a residency preference is a non-mandatory subject of bargaining under the Taylor Law (*Rensselaer City Sch. Dist.*, 13 PERB ¶ 3051, *aff'd*, 87 A.D.2d 718 (3d Dep't 1982); see **47:10-11**).

Once the district makes an appointment from among certified residents, it must continue to do so until the list of residents is exhausted. After exhausting the list of district residents, selection must be made from the entire eligible list without regard to residency (§ 23(4-a)).

On the other hand, a local civil service agency may establish a residency requirement for competitive and noncompetitive class employees, even over the objection of a local school board (§ 23(4-a); see *Buffet v. Municipal Civil Serv. Comm'n of City of Plattsburgh*, 58 A.D.2d 362 (3d Dep't 1977), *aff'd*, 45 N.Y.2d 1003 (1978)). However, a local civil service commission cannot establish a residency rule simply by listing such a requirement in the examination announcement. The local commission first must publish notice of the proposed residency rule and then conduct a public hearing. Thereafter, the rule becomes valid only upon approval by the NYS Civil Service Commission (§ 20; see also *Matter of Trager v. Kampe*, 99 N.Y.2d 361 (2003); *appeal after remand*, 16 A.D.3d 426 (2d Dep't 2005); see **39:9**).

39:20. Are military personnel, members of the organized militia, and military reservists entitled to take a make-up exam if their duties prevent them from competing for a scheduled competitive exam?

Yes. Any member of the armed forces of the United States who has duly filed an application to take a scheduled competitive examination for a civil service appointment, and who due to active military duty is deprived of the opportunity to compete in the examination, must be provided with an opportunity to compete in a special military make-up exam. This right also extends to members of the organized militia (e.g., the Army National Guard, the Air National Guard, the New York Naval Militia, and the New York Guard) and to members of the reserve armed forces (e.g., U.S. Army Reserve, U.S. Naval Reserve, U.S. Marine Corps Reserve, U.S. Air Force Reserve, and U.S. Coast Guard Reserve) (Mil. Law § 243-b).

39:21. Are veterans entitled to preference regarding appointment, promotion, or retention in a competitive class position?

Yes. The New York Constitution authorizes a preference for veterans as an exception to the rule that appointments and promotions be made on the basis of merit and fitness (N.Y. Const. art 5, § 6; Civ. Serv. Law § 85). Disabled veterans, as defined by the Civil Service Law (§ 85(1)(b)), are entitled to 10 additional points on competitive examinations for original appointment and five additional points for promotion. Veterans who are not disabled are entitled to five additional points on a competitive examination for original appointment and two-and-one-half additional points for promotion (§ 85(2)(a)). Veterans are entitled, as well, to preference in retention upon the abolition of positions (§ 85(7)).

To be eligible for the preference, the veteran must have been a member of the armed forces of the United States who served in time of war and was honorably discharged or released under honorable circumstances from such service. He or she also must be a citizen of the United States or an alien lawfully admitted for permanent residence in the United States and a resident of New York State when applying for preference (§ 85(1)(a)).

Before additional credits can be added to a veteran's grade, the veteran must have obtained a passing grade on the examination. In other words, additional credits may not be used to change a veteran's rating from failing to passing (§ 85(2)(b)).

Veteran's credit may be used only once to obtain an appointment or promotion (*Marlow v. Tully*, 63 N.Y.2d 918, *reh'g denied*, 64 N.Y.2d 775 (1984), *cert. denied*, 472 U.S. 1010, *reh'g denied,* 473 U.S. 924 (1985)). Thus, if a veteran has been permanently appointed or promoted to a position by means of additional credits that affected his or her position on the appropriate eligible list, he or she is not entitled to receive any additional credit in future examinations (§ 85(4)(a)).

39:22. Can a competitive class employee in one school district transfer to a similar position in another school district without further examination?

Yes. Local civil service agencies have rules that permit transfers to similar positions in other school districts or other units of government (§ 70(1)). Requests for transfer should be referred to the local civil service agency for approval.

As a general rule, an employee cannot be transferred without his or her consent (§ 70(1)). Exceptions to this general rule apply when there has been a "transfer of functions" (§ 70(2)) and in any city with a population of one million or more where the city and the authorized union have negotiated an agreement under the Taylor Law providing for involuntary transfers (§ 70(6)).

39:23. Is a board of cooperative educational services (BOCES) takeover situation considered a transfer under the Civil Service Law?

Yes. A BOCES' takeover of a program or service formerly provided by a school district or by a county vocational education and extension board is considered a transfer under Civil Service Law § 70. Classified service employees employed by a school district or county vocational educational extension board at the time of the takeover are considered BOCES employees entitled to protection under the Civil Service Law (Educ. Law § 3014-a(5); *Vestal Employees Ass'n v. PERB*, 94 N.Y.2d 409 (2000); *Hellner v. Bd. of Educ. of Wilson CSD*, 78 A.D.3d 1649 (3d Dep't 2010)).

39:24. Does a person appointed to a competitive class position from an eligible list automatically attain permanent status?

No. Permanent appointments to positions in the competitive class require satisfactory completion of a probationary term. The probationary term is established by the local civil service agency and is included in the local civil service rules (§ 63(2); see, e.g., *Matter of Block v. Franklin Square UFSD*, 72 A.D.2d 602 (2d Dep't 1979)). Because the length of the term may vary from one jurisdiction to another, the local civil service agency should be contacted for specific information.

Once a probationary competitive class employee attains permanent status, he or she can be terminated only for cause, after a hearing held in accordance with section 75 (see **39:30-33**) or with collectively bargained disciplinary procedures that supplement, modify or replace section 75 (see **39:39**).

In general, a probationary employee whose conduct or performance is not satisfactory may be terminated at any time after completion of the minimum period and before completion of the maximum period without a hearing so long as the decision is not made in bad faith, or for unconstitutional or illegal reasons (see *Albano v. Kirby*, 36 N.Y.2d 526 (1975); *Williams v. Comm'r of Office of Mental Health* (*State of N.Y.*), 259 A.D.2d 623 (2d Dep't 1999); *Tomlinson v. Ward*, 110 A.D.2d 537 (1st Dep't), *aff'd*, 66 N.Y.2d 771 (1985); *Macklin v. Powell*, 107 A.D.2d 964 (3d Dep't 1985)). However, local civil service rules may impose certain requirements, such as minimum notice and the opportunity to be heard (see *Albano v. Kirby*; *Saulpaugh v. Diehl*, 148 A.D.2d 928 (4th Dep't 1989)).

A person who fails to satisfactorily complete a probationary term for a promotional position may retreat back to his or her former position, which the employer cannot fill except on a temporary basis pending completion of the probationary period (§ 63(1); *Montes v. Harrison CSD*, 112 A.D.3d 633 (2d Dep't 2013)).

39:25. May "applicants" for a competitive class position be required to submit to fingerprinting and a criminal history record check?

Yes. Municipal civil service commissions have the authority to promulgate rules that require applicants for examination and competitive class positions to submit fingerprints for state and national criminal history records check to be conducted by the NYS Division of Criminal Justice Services and the Federal Bureau of Investigation. Adequate notice must be provided to applicants informing them that such criminal history records checks may be required, and the procedures involved.

Such fingerprinting requirements may not be applied to current employees or to any person who is considered an "applicant" because he or she is transferring pursuant to section 70 to a position not involving essential tests or qualifications different from or higher than those required in the position held by the employee). They may not be applied either to any person who is on a section 81 preferred list of persons suspended or demoted from either competitive class or noncompetitive class positions because their position was abolished or reduced but who have a right to reinstatement to the same or a similar position in the same jurisdictional class if one becomes available. Also exempt from the fingerprinting requirement is any person on a section 56 eligible list (which provides preferred eligibility rights for a period of one to four years) who has successfully completed a promotion exam pursuant to section 52 of the Civil Service Law (§ 50(4)).

For more information on the procedures applicable to the submission of fingerprints, see **chapter 41**.

Compensation and Work Hours

39:26. Are school district non-instructional employees entitled to minimum wage and overtime?

School district employees are covered by the federal minimum wage and overtime standards in the federal Fair Labor Standards Act (FLSA), even though exemptions from the overtime standards may apply to certain executive, administrative, and professional employees (29 USC §§ 206(a)(1), 213(a)(1); *Garcia v. San Antonio Metro. Transit Auth.*, 469 U.S. 528 (1985)). They are also covered by the New York State Minimum Wage Act (Lab. Law Art. 19). While the minimum wage under federal law is $7.25 per hour, in New York, the minimum wage is $9.00 until December 31, 2016 (Lab. Law § 652(1); 29 USC § 206(a)(1)). Thereafter, the minimum wage in New York will vary according to the location where the employee works and, in New York City, the size of the employer.

Figure 1 below illustrates the schedule of increases to minimum wages in New York starting December 31, 2016. It was prepared by the NYS Department of Labor and is available along with other related information at: http://www.labor.ny.gov/workerprotection/laborstandards/workprot/minwage.shtm.

Fig. 1	**General Minimum Wage Rate Schedule**					
Location	**12/31/16**	**12/31/17**	**12/31/18**	**12/31/19**	**12/31/20**	**2021***
NYC – Large Employers (of 11 or more)	$11.00	$13.00	$15.00			
NYC – Small Employers (10 or less)	$10.50	$12.00	$13.50	$15.00		
Long Island and Westchester	$10.00	$11.00	$12.00	$13.00	$14.00	$15.00
Greater New York State	$9.70	$10.40	$11.10	$11.80	$12.50	*

*Annual increases for the rest of the state will continue until the rate reaches $15 minimum wage (and $10 tipped wage). Starting 2021, the annual increases will be published by the Commissioner of Labor on or before October 1. They will be based on percentage increases determined by the Director of the Division of Budget, based on economic indices, including the Consumer Price Index.

FLSA requires employers to pay their non-exempt employees overtime wages of one-and-one-half times the employees' regular rates of compensation for each hour they work in excess of 40 hours per week (29 USC § 207(a)(1)).

However, public employers may provide for paid leave or "compensatory time" in lieu of overtime compensation, so long as the benefit is equal to one-and-one-half hours off for each hour over 40 worked in a week (29 USC § 207(o)(1), (7)(B)), provided there is an agreement or understanding to do so prior to the performance of work (29 USC § 207(o)(2)(A); 29 CFR § 553.23(b)(1)). When the employees have collective bargaining representation, such agreement or understanding must be between the collective bargaining representative and the employer through either a collective bargaining agreement, memorandum of understanding or other type of oral or written agreement (29 CFR § 553.23(b)(1); *Saunders v. City of N.Y.*, 594 F.Supp.2d 346 (S.D.N.Y. 2008)). When there is no collective bargaining representative, the required agreement or understanding must be between the employer and the individual employee (29 CFR § 553.23(c)(1)). Generally, no more than 240 hours of compensatory time off may be accrued (29 USC § 207(o)(3)(A)). If an employee has accrued 240 hours of compensatory time, any additional overtime must be paid at one-and-one-half times the employee's regular rate of compensation (29 USC § 207(o)(3)(A)).

Employees must be allowed to use compensatory time off on request within a reasonable period, as long as the employer's operations will not be unduly disrupted (29 USC § 207(o)(5)). Satisfaction of the reasonable period requirement will be determined by considering the customary work practices of the employer, based on each case's facts and circumstances. An undue disruption means more than a mere inconvenience and must impose an unreasonable burden on the employer's ability to provide services (*Saunders v. City of N.Y.*). An employee may be required to take compensatory leave unless the school district has agreed to the contrary (*Christensen v. Harris Cnty.*, 529 U.S. 576 (2000)).

Districts that fail to comply with FLSA may come under investigation by the U.S. Department of Labor (29 USC § 211). Both the U.S. Department of Labor and individual employees can sue school districts for back pay, overtime back payments, interest, liquidated damages (i.e., double the amount of unpaid wages), and equitable relief (29 USC §§ 216–17). Civil penalties of up to $1,100 per employee may be assessed against the employing school district for repeated or willful violations of FLSA (29 USC § 216(e)). Moreover, repeated or willful violations may also result in criminal penalties of up to six months in prison and/or fines up to $10,000 (29 USC § 216). A school district also may be required to pay attorneys' fees for a litigant who prevails in a lawsuit against it (29 USC § 216).

In one case, the U.S. Court of Appeals for the Second Circuit, with jurisdiction over New York, rejected a petitioner's suit under FLSA seeking back pay and damages from a school district. The petitioner, who worked with a high school's "intervention team" with duties including lunchtime supervision, detention and parent contact an average of 40 hours a week was found to be a volunteer rather than an employee entitled to statutory minimum and overtime wages. According to the court, the petitioner did not qualify for any paid position, any money he received was nominal and did not rise to the level of compensation, there had been no promises or expectations regarding compensation and no coercion or pressure from the district for performance of his volunteer service (*Brown v. N.Y. City Dep't of Educ.*, 755 F.3d 154 (2d Cir. 2014)).

Employers may not discriminate against employees who complain about alleged FLSA violations. According to the U.S. Supreme Court, FLSA's anti-retaliation provisions extend as well to employees who orally complain about such violations, if their complaint is clear and detailed enough for a reasonable employer to understand it, in light of both content and context, as an assertion of protected FLSA rights and a call for their protection (*Kasten v. Saint-Gobain Performance Plastics Corp.*, 536 U.S. 1 (2001); see also *Greathouse v. JHS Security Inc.*, 784 F.3d 105 (2d Cir. 2015)).

39:27. What type of school district employees are not entitled to minimum wage and overtime protections?

Although school district employees generally are covered by the federal Fair Labor Standards Act (FLSA) minimum wage and overtime provisions, there are some who are not. For example, teachers are exempt from the FLSA's overtime provisions and are therefore ineligible for overtime, irrespective of their salary levels (29 U.S.C. 213(a)(1)). In addition, school district employees considered to be a "white collar" salaried employee also are ineligible for overtime (29 C.F.R. § 541.600). So are "highly compensated" employees (29 C.F.R. § 541.601).

The white collar and highly compensated exemptions apply only to those who meet the criteria specified in federal regulations.

For more information on the FLSA overtime rules see, U.S. Department of Labor, Wage and Hour Division, *Question and Answers*, at: https://www.dol.gov/WHD/overtime/final2016/faq.htm

39:28. Must school districts submit employee payrolls to the local civil service agency?

Yes, for employees in the classified civil service. The local civil service agency with jurisdiction (see **39:7-9**) must certify at least annually that each person on the payroll list has been employed in accordance with law (§ 100(1)(a), (2)(a)). Such certification remains in effect until the next certification. However, with certain limited exceptions, the names of new or reinstated employees whose payroll status changed after the last certification must be submitted for certification on their first payroll (§ 100(2)(a)).

It is a misdemeanor for any school officer to willfully pay or authorize the payment of salary to any person in the classified service, if he or she knows that the local civil service agency has refused to certify the payroll because the individual in question has been appointed, employed, transferred, assigned to perform duties, or reinstated in violation of the Civil Service Law (§ 101; see also *Eldridge v. Carmel CSD*, 82 A.D.3d 1147 (2d Dep't 2011); *Matter of Gillen v. Smithtown Lib. Bd. of Trustees*, 94 N.Y.2d 776 (1999); see **39:10**).

39:29. Are non-instructional school employees entitled to a set time period for lunch?

Yes. A non-instructional employee working more than six hours in a shift that extends over the time from 11 a.m. to 2 p.m. must receive at least 30 minutes for a lunch period (Lab. Law § 162(2)). Those working a shift shortly before 11:00 a.m. and continuing later than 7:00 p.m. are entitled to an additional meal period of at least 20 minutes between 5:00 and 7:00 p.m. (Lab. Law § 162(3)). Non-instructional employees who work more than six hours in a shift between 1 p.m. and 6 a.m. must be given a 45-minute meal period midway in the shift (Lab. Law § 162(4)). However, the state commissioner of labor may permit a shorter meal period to be fixed (Lab. Law § 162(5)). Moreover, while school districts and their employees cannot completely bargain away the lunch or meal period, it may be modified in a collective bargaining agreement (see *Am. Broad. Cos. v. Roberts*, 61 N.Y.2d 244 (1984)). However, school districts may not unilaterally change the duration of meal breaks for unionized employees (*Cnty. of Nassau*, 24 ¶ PERB 3029 (1991)).

Discipline and Termination

39:30. Are classified service employees entitled to due process protection prior to being terminated or disciplined?

Only certain employees in the classified service are entitled to such protection and may be terminated or disciplined only pursuant to the provisions of section 75 of the Civil Service Law. All others may be disciplined or discharged without a hearing for any legal, non-discriminatory reason, not made in bad faith (see *Tyson v. Hess*, 109 A.D.2d 1068 (4th Dep't), *aff'd*, 66 N.Y.2d 943 (1985)).

The following types of classified service employees are entitled to protection under section 75 of the Civil Service Law:

- Persons holding a position by permanent appointment (as opposed to provisional or temporary appointment) in the competitive class (§ 75(1)(a)).
- Honorably discharged or honorably released veterans and exempt volunteer firefighters (as defined in the General Municipal Law) employed permanently in the classified service, regardless of the employee's jurisdictional classification, except for persons holding the positions of private secretary, cashier, or deputy of any official or department (§ 75(1)(b); see *Wamsley v. E. Ramapo CSD Bd. of Educ.*, 281 A.D.2d 633 (2d Dep't 2001)).
- Employees holding positions in the noncompetitive class who have completed at least five years of continuous service in that class, provided that the local civil service agency has specifically named the position as being in the noncompetitive class (*Wheeler v. Parker,* 546 F.Supp.2d 7 (N.D.N.Y. 2008)), and further provided the employee's position has not been designated as confidential or policy-making by the local civil service agency (§ 75(1)(c); *Wamsley v. E. Ramapo CSD Bd. of Educ.*).

The failure of a local civil service agency to identify the class for a particular position (see **39:7**), cannot deprive the holder of the due process protections of section 75 until a classification is made (*Wheeler v. Parker*).

A collective bargaining agreement may afford employees alternative disciplinary protections and procedures (*Auburn Police Local 195 v. Helsby*, 62 A.D.2d 12 (3d Dep't 1978), *aff'd*, 46 N.Y.2d 1034 (1979); see **39:39-40**). However, such an agreement may not extend any such alternate protection to individuals not otherwise entitled to the protection of section 75 of the Civil Service Law (see *City of Long Beach v. CSEA-Long Beach Unit*, 8 N.Y.3d 465 (2007); see also **39:39**).

39:31. Is there any time limit for bringing disciplinary charges against an employee under section 75?

Yes. No removal or disciplinary proceeding may be commenced more than 18 months after the occurrence of the misconduct or incompetency alleged in the charge. However, this limitation does not apply where the charges would, if proved in the appropriate court, constitute a crime (§ 75(4); see *McKinney v. Bennett*, 31 A.D.3d 860 (3d Dep't 2006); *Wojewodzic v. O'Neill*, 295 A.D.2d 670 (3d Dep't 2002); see also *De Guzman v. State of N.Y. Civil Service Comm'n*, 129 A.D.3d 1189 (3d Dep't), *lv. to appeal denied*, 26 N.Y.3d 913 (2015)).

39:32. Are there any special procedures a district must observe when investigating incidents of possible misconduct that involve non-instructional employees?

Yes. A non-instructional employee with section 75 protection (see **39:30**) is entitled to union representation when questioned, if at the time of questioning it reasonably appears that the employee may be the subject of disciplinary action. The affected employee must be notified in advance, in writing, of that right. The employee is entitled to a reasonable period of time to obtain a representative. If the employee is unable to obtain a representative within a reasonable period of time, the district has the right to then question the employee without representation (§§ 75(2), 209-a(1)(g)).

The right to union representation during questioning applies also to non-instructional probationary, provisional or temporary employees appointed under the Civil Service Law, even though they are not entitled to section 75 protection (*N.Y. State Corr. Officers and Police Benevolent Ass'n Inc.*, 43 PERB ¶ 3031 (2010)), including time to obtain representation (*Id.*; § 209-a(1)(g)).

39:33. How is a non-instructional employee covered by section 75 terminated or disciplined?

Persons entitled to protection under section 75 of the Civil Service Law (holding the types of positions identified in **39:30**) have the right to notice of any charges against them and a hearing prior to discipline (§ 75(1), (2)). They also are entitled to at least eight days to respond to the charges in writing (§ 75(2)). The law does not specify who may prefer those charges, but according to one state appellate court, a school superintendent has such authority (*Matter of Stafford v. Bd. of Educ. of Mohonasen CSD*, 61 A.D.3d 1259 (3d Dep't), *lv. to appeal denied*, 13 N.Y.3d 704 (2009)).

At the hearing, the employee may be represented by counsel or by a representative of a recognized or certified employee organization and may present witnesses on his or her behalf. The burden of proving incompetency or misconduct by the employee is on the district (§ 75(2)). A finding of guilt must be supported by "substantial evidence" (*Cassiliano v. Steisel*, 64 N.Y.2d 674 (1984)) which consists of proof that is "[m]ore than seeming or imaginary [but] less than a preponderance of the evidence, overwhelming evidence or evidence beyond a reasonable doubt" (*People ex rel. Vega v. Smith*, 66 N.Y.2d 130 (1985)), and a "reasonable mind may accept as adequate to support a conclusion or ultimate fact" (*WEOK Broad. Corp. v. Planning Bd. of Lloyd*, 79 N.Y.2d 373 (1992); *300 Gramatan Ave. Assoc. v. State Div. of Human Rights*, 45 N.Y.2d 176 (1978); *Stewart v. Bd. of Educ. of Saratoga Springs City Sch. Dist.*, 238 A.D.2d 838 (3d Dep't 1997)).

The required hearing is conducted by the school board or a designated hearing officer who makes a recommendation to the school board as to the guilt or innocence of the person against whom the charges are lodged and as to the penalty, if any (§ 75(2)). If the school board decides to designate a hearing officer, the board must make that designation in writing (§ 75(2)). Only the school board can make such a designation (*Melendez v. Bd. of Educ. of Yonkers City Sch. Dist.*, 34 A.D.3d 814 (2d Dep't 2006)). If a school board fails to officially designate the hearing officer who conducts the hearing, a court may annul the hearing officer's determination and direct the district to reinstate the employee with back pay (*Gardner v. Coxsackie-Athens CSD Bd. of Educ.*, 92 A.D.3d 1093 (3d Dep't), *appeal dismissed*, 19 N.Y.3d 917 (2012); *Payton v. Buffalo City Sch. Dist.*, 299 A.D.2d 825 (4th Dep't 2002)), even when the employee fails to object to the district's non-compliance with the official designation requirement (*Gardner v. Coxsackie-Athens CSD Bd. of Educ.*). Although a school superintendent has no authority to designate the hearing officer (*Melendez v. Bd. of Educ. of Yonkers City Sch. Dist.*), a school superintendent's letter on school district letterhead informing a hearing officer that he or she was designated by the school board at a board meeting to conduct the hearing satisfies this requirement (*McKensie v. Bd. of Educ. of City Sch. Dist. of Albany,* 100 A.D.3d 1096 (3d Dep't 2012); *Matter of Stafford v. Bd. of Educ. of Mohanasen CSD)*.

The hearing officer or the school board making the final determination of guilt or innocence and setting the penalty must be unbiased. They should have no personal knowledge of the events surrounding the charge and should not have brought or prosecuted the charges (see *Memmelaar v. Straub*, 181 A.D.2d 980 (3d Dep't 1992)). A departure from this standard violates the employee's right to due process. It also can result in the annulment of a termination determination and an award of back pay and benefits, as when two school board members who testified at the hearing failed to recuse themselves from voting when the board adopted the hearing officer's findings and recommendations (*Matter of Baker v. Poughkeepsie City Sch. Dist.*, 73 A.D.3d 916 (2d Dep't 2010), *aff'd,* 18 N.Y.3d 714 (2012); see also *Zlotnick v. City of Saratoga Springs*, 122 A.D.3d 1210 (3d Dep't 2014)).

A school administrator may not make an agreement to withhold from the commissioner of education or law enforcement authorities the fact that an allegation of child abuse in an educational setting has been made against a district employee in exchange for a resignation or voluntary suspension. Any such agreement is subject to both criminal and civil penalties (Educ. Law § 1133(1); see **9:26, 38:33**).

39:34. Does a change in an employee's work assignment constitute discipline that requires a section 75 hearing?

It may, depending on the facts and circumstances. In one case, where a bus driver worked a second job that made her unavailable for her regularly assigned bus route, the district unilaterally demoted her from a permanent position of "assigned driver" (which entitled her to enhanced benefits) to that of an "unassigned driver." According to an appellate court, the reassignment resulted in a diminution of benefits and, therefore, was a form of demotion or discipline that required compliance with section 75, even though the district provided the driver the new assignment as an accommodation designed to enable her to work both jobs (*Matter of Bailey v. Susquehanna Valley CSD. Bd. of Educ.*, 276 A.D.2d 963 (3d Dep't 2000)).

In a different case, due to concerns about alleged misconduct by a bus driver, a district decided not to reassign him to an additional bus run that was not part of his regular duties, but would have enabled him to earn additional income. The same appellate court that decided *Matter of Bailey* determined that this did not constitute discipline. Even though the district's decision to deprive the driver of the additional assignment was based on the driver's alleged misconduct, the district's action was not disciplinary in nature, because the driver did not have a protected property interest in the additional bus run, and the driver "did not suffer a reduction in title, grade, regular annual salary or benefits" (*Nydam v. Franklin CSD*, 303 A.D.2d 828 (3d Dep't 2003)).

39:35. Does the placement of a critical letter in the file of a non-instructional employee who is entitled to section 75 protection constitute discipline that would require a hearing as described in 39:33?

No. Civil Service Law section 75 does not insulate non-instructional school district personnel from all written critical comments from their supervisors. Documents such as critical administrative evaluations or admonitions that are intended to warn or instruct a given employee may be placed in an employee's file without resort to a formal hearing (*Tomaka v. Evans-Brant CSD*, 107 A.D.2d 1078 (4th Dep't), *aff'd*, 65 N.Y.2d 1048 (1985); see *Cassone v. Westchester Cnty. Health Care Corp.*, 5 A.D.3d 764 (2d Dep't 2004); *CSEA v. Southold UFSD*, 204 A.D.2d 445 (2d Dep't 1994)).

However, a letter that addresses more serious allegations may be treated as a disciplinary reprimand, requiring a hearing conducted under section 75. In deciding whether a particular written communication constitutes a reprimand that will require a hearing, no single factor will be determinative. A court will likely consider a number of factors, including the identity of the author, the subject matter of the document, the tenor of the document, the employer's characterization of the document, and whether the document's focus is on punishment or warning and instruction (*CSEA v. Southold UFSD*).

39:36. May an employee facing discipline under section 75 be suspended without pay pending the outcome of the hearing?

Yes. The Civil Service Law allows for the suspension without pay of an employee for up to 30 days pending the hearing and determination of charges (§ 75(3); *Troeller v. Dep't of Educ. of the City Sch. Dist. of the City of N.Y.*, 118 A.D.3d 640 (1st Dep't 2014)). If the employee is acquitted at the hearing or later reinstated after appeal to the local civil service agency or to the courts (see **39:38**), that employee is entitled to back pay for the period during which he or she was off the payroll, less the amount of any unemployment benefits he or she may have received during such period (§§ 75(3), 76(3), 77; see *Matter of CSEA, Local 1000 v. Brookhaven-Comsewogue UFSD*, 87 N.Y.2d 868 (1995)).

39:37. What penalty or punishment may be imposed after a section 75 hearing?

The penalty or punishment imposed after a section 75 hearing may consist of: (1) a reprimand; (2) a fine not to exceed $100 to be deducted from the employee's wages; (3) suspension without pay for a period not exceeding two months; (4) demotion in grade and title; or (5) dismissal. Any time period during which an employee was suspended without pay prior to the outcome of the hearing (see **39:36**) may become part of the penalty (§ 75(3)).

39:38. May an employee who has been disciplined under section 75 file an appeal?

Yes. An employee may appeal to the local civil service agency or to the courts any penalty, except an official reprimand that is accompanied by a remittance of compensation lost during suspension (§ 76(1)). The commissioner of education has no jurisdiction over this type of case (*Appeal of McGregor*, 35 Ed Dept Rep 363 (1996)).

If the employee chooses to appeal to the local civil service agency, the agency's decision is final and conclusive and not subject to further review in any court (§ 76(3)). However, even though the Civil Service Law proscribes judicial review of a local agency's decision, the courts still have the power and the duty to review the decision to determine if it was unconstitutional, illegal, or outside the agency's jurisdiction (*N.Y. City Dep't of Envtl. Protection v. N.Y. City Civil Serv. Comm'n*, 78 N.Y.2d 318 (1991); *De Guzman v. State of N.Y. Civil Serv. Comm'n*, 129 A.D.3d 1189 (3d Dep't 2015)).

An employee wishing to appeal his or her discipline or discharge to the courts in an Article 78 proceeding must serve a notice of claim upon the school district within three months of the imposition of the discipline (*Harder v. Bd. of Educ., Binghamton City Sch. Dist.*, 188 A.D.2d 783 (3d Dep't 1992), citing Educ. Law § 3813(1)). The four-month statute of limitations generally applicable to Article 78 proceedings is extended 30 days when a notice of claim is filed under Education Law § 3813(1) (see *Perlin v. South Orangetown CSD*, 216 A.D.2d 397 (2d Dep't 1995), *lv. to appeal dismissed,* 86 N.Y.2d 886 (1995); *Brown v. Schuyler-Chemung-Tioga BOCES*, 5 A.D.3d 939 (3d Dep't 2004); *Vail v. BOCES*, 115 A.D.2d 231 (4th Dep't 1985), *lv. to appeal denied,* 67 N.Y.2d 606 (1986)).

The courts will review the findings of fact from a hearing by determining whether there is "substantial evidence" to support the charges (*Cassilano v. Steisel*, 64 N.Y.2d 674 (1984); see **39:33** for a definition of substantial evidence).

The courts may also review the disciplinary penalty imposed, but the penalty may not be set aside unless it is "so disproportionate to the offense, in the light of all the circumstances, as to be shocking to one's sense of fairness" (*Pell v. Bd. of Educ. Union Free Sch. Dist. No. 1 of the Towns of Scarsdale & Mamaroneck*, 34 N.Y.2d 222 (1974); see also *Dempsey v. N.Y. City Dep't of Educ.*, 108 A.D.3d 454 (1st Dep't 2013); *Scahill v. Greece* CSD, 2 N.Y.3d 754 (2004); *Winters v. Bd. of Educ. of Lakeland CSD*, 99 N.Y.2d 549 (2002); *Will v. Frontier CSD Bd. of Educ.*, 97 N.Y.2d 690 (2002)). For example, it was not shocking to terminate a teacher's aide with no disciplinary history who was absent without leave for two days in defiance of the school's express directive to report to work (*Castel v. Maine-Endwell CSD*, 111 A.D.3d 1221 (3d Dep't 2013)).

39:39. Is Civil Service Law section 75 the only source of due process protection available to employees in the classified service?

No. While school districts must comply with the procedures specified in this section to discipline or discharge employees covered by the law, they also may collectively negotiate alternative disciplinary procedures with the union representing employees in recognized bargaining units (see *Barrera v. Frontier CSD*, 249 A.D.2d 927 (4th Dep't 1998)). If separate contractual procedures exist, they should be consulted prior to the discipline of any employee in the bargaining unit.

A collective bargaining agreement, however, may not extend disciplinary and termination protections to those not otherwise entitled to the protection of section 75 of the Civil Service Law (see *City of Long Beach v. CSEA-Long Beach Unit*, 8 N.Y.3d 465 (2007)).

39:40. What due process protection is available to non-instructional employees not covered by section 75?

Such employees may have job protections under a collective bargaining agreement. However, employees who do not have section 75 or collective bargaining agreement protections are "at will" employees, meaning that they can be discharged without cause and without a hearing. Simply stated, such employees can be disciplined or discharged for any reason, except an illegal reason such as because of race, religion, sex, disability (see *Tyson v. Hess*, 109 A.D.2d 1068 (4th Dep't), *aff'd*, 66 N.Y.2d 943 (1985); see also *City of Long Beach v. CSEA-Long Beach Unit*, 8 N.Y.3d 465 (2007)). Nonetheless, the holder of a position not otherwise covered by section 75 would be entitled to due process under that section of law if at the time of discipline or termination the local civil service agency had failed to identify in its rules the class for that position (*Wheeler v. Parker*, 546 F.Supp.2d 7 (N.D.N.Y. 2008); see also **39:7, 39:30**).

Unionized non-instructional employees who do not have section 75 or collective bargaining agreement protections are entitled to union representation during questioning by an employer under the conditions prescribed in law, regardless of whether the employee holds a permanent, probationary, provisional or temporary position (§ 209-a(1)(g); *N.Y. State Corr. Officers & Police Benevolent Ass'n, Inc.*, 43 PERB ¶ 3031 (2010); see **39:32, 46:5**).

39:41. Are non-instructional employees entitled to a name-clearing hearing?

Any public employee, regardless of whether the employee is entitled to the protection of Civil Service Law section 75, is entitled to a hearing to clear his or her name if the alleged reason for the employee's dismissal puts the employee's good name, reputation, honor, or integrity in question (*Bd. of Regents v. Roth*, 408 U.S. 564 (1972); see *Wisconsin v. Constantineau*, 400 U.S. 433 (1971)). Such a hearing is referred to as a "name-clearing" hearing (see *Lentlie v. Egan*, 61 N.Y.2d 874 (1984)). The right to a name-clearing hearing is available to both tenured and non-tenured employees (*Goetz v. Windsor CSD*, 698 F.2d 606 (2d Cir. 1983), *remanded*, 593 F.Supp. 526 (N.D.N.Y. 1984); *Lutwin v. Alleyne*, 86 A.D.2d 670 (2d Dep't 1982), *modified on other grounds*, 58 N.Y.2d 889 (1983); *Salvatore v. Nasser*, 81 A.D.2d 1012 (4th Dep't 1981)).

Courts have applied this rule of law, for example, where a teacher was charged with engaging in sexual conduct with autistic children (*Brandt v. BOCES III, Suffolk Cnty.*, 820 F.2d 41 (2d Cir. 1987), *appeal after remand, Brandt v. BOCES*, 845 F.2d 416 (2nd Cir. 1988)), and where a school district submitted to the NYS Education Department a complaint that could result in the revocation of a teacher's license (*VanDine v. Greece CSD*, 75 A.D.3d 1166 (4th Dep't 2010)).

In order to be entitled to a name-clearing hearing, the employee must establish that the stigmatizing statements made by the public employer have been publicly disclosed (*Bishop v. Wood*, 426 U.S. 341 (1976); *Lentlie v. Egan*). The disclosure requirement can be satisfied where the stigmatizing charges are placed in the discharged employee's personnel file and are likely to be disclosed to prospective employers (*Brandt v. BOCES III, Suffolk Cnty.*; *Wilcox v. Newark Valley CSD,* 107 A.D.3d 1127 (3d Dep't 2013); *Browne v. City of N.Y.*, 45 A.D.3d 590 (2d Dep't 2007); *Donato v. Plainview-Old Bethpage CSD*, 96 F.3d 623 (2d Cir. 1996), *cert. denied*, 519 U.S. 1150, *remanded*, 985 F.Supp. 316 (E.D.N.Y. 1997); see also *Matter of Swinton v. Safir*, 93 N.Y.2d 758 (1999); *Knox v. N.Y. City Dep't of Educ.*, 85 A.D.3d 439 (1st Dep't 2011); *Matter of Chang v. Dep't. of Educ. of the City of N.Y.*, 137 A.D.3d 597 (1st Dep't 2016)).

Allegations of professional incompetence will support a right to a name-clearing hearing only when they "stigmatize" and denigrate the employee's competence as a professional and impugn his or her reputation to the point of significantly hampering the employee's continued ability to practice his or her profession (*Bd. of Regents v. Roth; Donato v. Plainview-Old Bethpage CSD*). There must be a "temporal link" between the time when the alleged stigmatizing statements are made and the employee's dismissal (*Martz v. Incorporated Vill. of Valley Stream*, 22 F.3d 26 (2d Cir. 1994); *Kirby v. Yonkers Sch. Dist.*, 767 F.Supp.2d 452 (2011)). If a name-clearing hearing is unlikely to remedy any ill effects caused by the employer's stigmatizing actions, a terminated employee may be able to recover monetary damages (*Patterson v. City of Utica,* 370 F.3d 322 (2d Cir. 2004)).

However, statements to the press announcing personnel decisions, even when a reader might infer something unfavorable about an employee, or true public statements that an employee is under investigation, generally are not considered stigmatizing (*Wiese v. Kelly*, 2009 U.S. Dist. LEXIS 82307 (S.D.N.Y. Sept. 10, 2009); see also *Kirby v. Yonkers Sch. Dist.*; compare *Van Dine v. Greece CSD*).

39:42. What is the procedure in a name-clearing hearing?

The right to a meaningful opportunity to refute charges in a name-clearing hearing does not require a full, formal proceeding. However, a school district must offer the employee notice of the charges and a fair hearing to refute the charge before school district officials, which includes the right to counsel, to call witnesses on the employee's behalf, and to confront and cross examine witnesses supporting the allegations (*Bd. of Regents v. Roth*, 408 U.S. 564 (1972); *Donato v. Plainview-Old Bethpage CSD*, 96 F.3d 623 (2d Cir. 1996), *cert. denied*, 519 U.S. 1150, *remanded*, 985 F.Supp. 316 (E.D.N.Y. 1997); see also *Goldberg v. Kelly*, 397 U.S. 254 (1970)).

At the hearing, the employee has the burden of proving that the charges are false (*Marzullo v. Suffolk Cnty*., 97 A.D.2d 789 (2d Dep't 1983)).

Following the hearing, the employer need not rehire the employee even if the employee can prove the inaccuracy of the stigmatizing allegations. If the charges are proven false, however, the employer may be liable to the employee for damages (*Donato v. Plainview-Old Bethpage CSD*).

An Article 78 proceeding provides sufficient procedural protection as post-deprivation name-clearing hearing (*Guerra v. Jones,* 421 Fed. Appx. 15 (2d Cir. 2011); *Sprang v. Katonah-Lewisboro UFSD*, 626 F.Supp.2d 389 (S.D.N.Y. 2009); *Sheffield v. Roslyn UFSD*, 2014 U.S. Dist. LEXIS 135585 (E.D.N.Y. 2014)).

39:43. What is the so-called "whistle-blower law"?

Section 75-b of the Civil Service Law, the so-called "whistle-blower law," prohibits public employers, including a school district, from taking retaliatory personnel action against an employee who discloses to a governmental body information concerning either a violation of law, rule, or regulation, which creates a substantial and specific danger to the public health or safety, or which the employee reasonably believes to be true and reasonably believes constitutes an improper governmental action (§ 75-b(2)(a)).

If disciplinary action is brought under an applicable statute (such as section 75 of the Civil Service Law) or under a collective bargaining agreement against an employee who reveals such information, the employee may assert a defense based on this statute in the disciplinary proceedings, which must be addressed by the hearing officer or arbitrator (§ 75-b(3)). The failure of a hearing officer or arbitrator to address or consider this defense may result in his or her decision being vacated (*Matter of Kowaleski (N.Y. State Dep't of Corr. Servs.)*, 16 N.Y.3d 85 (2010)). Employees who do not have the right to such procedures may instead bring an action in court within one year after the alleged retaliatory action using the procedures set forth in section 740 of the Labor Law (§ 75-b(3)(c); see *Hanley v. N.Y. State Exec.*

Dep't, Div. for Youth, 182 A.D.2d 317 (3d Dep't 1992); see also *Tipaldo v. Lynn*, 26 N.Y.3d 204 (2015); *Dobson v. Loos*, 277 A.D.2d 1013 (4th Dep't 2000)).

The protection afforded by the "whistle-blower" law is not available where the employer has "a separate and independent basis" for alleged adverse actions taken against the employee (see *Matter of Brey v. Bd. of Educ. of Jefferson-Youngsville CSD*, 245 A.D.2d 613 (3d Dep't 1997)).

An employee does not have to provide his/her employer the information he or she intends to disclose prior to doing so (L. 2015, c. 585 § 1).

Abolition of Positions

39:44. May a school board abolish a non-instructional position?

Yes. School boards may abolish non-instructional positions for reasons of economy, consolidation, abolition of functions, or curtailment of activities (§ 80(1); see *Aldazabal v. Carey*, 44 N.Y.2d 787 (1978); *CSEA v. Rockland Cnty. BOCES*, 39 A.D.3d 641 (2d Dep't 2007); *Della Vecchia v. Town of North Hempstead*, 207 A.D.2d 484 (2d Dep't 1994), *lv. to appeal denied*, 84 N.Y.2d 812 (1995)).

School boards must act in good faith when such positions are abolished. These positions may not be abolished to circumvent the Civil Service Law (*Aldazabal v. Carey*; *James v. Broadnax*, 182 A.D.2d 887 (3d Dep't 1992)). The burden of proving that a position was abolished in bad faith rests with the employee, who must show that the employer had no bona fide reason for eliminating the position, achieved no costs savings, hired someone else as a replacement, or that the abolition was otherwise motivated by bad faith (*Cutler v. Town of Mamakating*, 137 A.D. 3d 1373 (3d Dep't 2016); *Matter of Mucci v. Binghamton*, 245 A.D.2d 678 (3d Dep't 1997), *appeal dismissed*, 91 N.Y.2d 921, *appeal denied*, 92 N.Y.2d 802 (1998); *Matter of Chandler v. Village of Spring Valley*, 104 A.D.3d 847 (2d Dep't 2013); *Linney v. City of Plattsburgh*, 49 A.D.3d 1020 (3d Dep't 2008)). Conversion of a full-time position to a part-time position may be considered abolition of the full-time position but local civil service rules should be consulted to determine the definition of "part-time employment" in that jurisdiction (*Linney v. City of Plattsburgh*; *Schoonmaker v. Capital Region BOCES*, 80 A.D.3d 965 (3d Dep't 2011)).

Generally, non-instructional employees' positions are abolished in inverse order of original permanent appointment in the classified civil service in positions the employer has chosen to eliminate (§ 80(1); *N.Y. City Transit Auth. v. Transp. Workers Union of Am., Local 100*, 88 A.D.3d 887 (2d Dep't 2011)). Employees who are blind, veterans, or spouses of disabled veterans are given preference in layoff situations (§ 85(7)).

In a layoff situation, competitive class employees may have an opportunity to "bump" other less senior employees in the same direct line of promotion or "retreat" back to a position in which the employee last served on a permanent basis (§ 80(6)).

A collective bargaining agreement which allows employees subject to layoff to displace employees in other departments is only permissible if the second department is within the same layoff unit as the originating department. If the second department is within a different layoff unit such a provision violates the Civil Service Law (*Cnty. of Chautauqua v. CSEA*, 8 N.Y.3d 513 (2007)).

After a layoff has occurred, it is the superintendent's responsibility to provide the name, title or position, date of appointment, and the date of and reason for the layoff to the local civil service agency. Laid-off or "excessed" non-instructional employees are placed on a preferred list and given preference over others in reinstatement to positions within their jurisdictional class (i.e., competitive, noncompetitive, labor, and exempt classes; see **39:6**). Employees on the preferred eligible list may be offered full-time, part-time, permanent contingent, permanent or temporary types of appointment. If an employee declines a certain type of appointment, such as temporary or part-time, he or she will no longer be eligible for any future appointments of that type (§ 81(5); *Kubicek v. Westchester Co.*, 2013 U.S. Dist. LEXIS 139552 (S.D.N.Y. 2013)).

Excessed employees remain on the preferred list for four years (§ 81(1)). An employee who is on active duty with the United States armed forces at the time of placement on the preferred list remains eligible for reinstatement for four years after the date military duty terminates (*Id.*).

39:45. Is an employee covered by section 75 entitled to notice and a hearing before his or her position is abolished?

As a general rule, no. A school district can lay off an employee entitled to the protection of section 75 without giving that employee notice and a hearing. An exception may apply if a district seeks to abolish a single employee's position and there is no indication that the employer acted for reasons of economy or efficiency, but rather it is alleged that the district targeted the employee for termination to avoid the requirements of section 75. In that case, the district has an obligation under the due process clause of the U.S. Constitution to provide the employee a hearing prior to removing the employee from his or her position, provided the employee requests such a hearing (*Dwyer v. Regan*, 777 F.2d 825 (2d Cir. 1985), *modified*, 793 F.2d 457 (2d Cir. 1986); see also *Bailey v. Village of Pittsford,* 2013 U.S. Dist. Lexis 125524 (W.D.N.Y. 2013); *Cifarelli v. Village of Babylon*, 93 F.3d 47 (2d Cir. 1996)). Such a hearing must be held before a neutral fact finder, not the employer (*Dwyer v. Regan*). The burden is on the employee to prove that the abolition was done in bad faith (*CSEA v. Rockland Cnty. BOCES*, 39 A.D.3d 641 (2d Dep't 2007); *Bianco v. Pitts*, 200 A.D.2d 741 (2d Dep't 1994); see *Cifarelli v. Village of Babylon*).

39:46. Where may additional information about civil service matters affecting schools be obtained?

Contact the city or county civil service commission or personnel officer in the city or county in which your school district is located. A complete listing of all local civil service agencies, as well as other technical assistance about the Civil Service Law, is available through the NYS Department of Civil Service website at: http://www.cs.ny.gov/. Click on "Employees" and then "Local Government Employees" and then select "Municipal Civil Service Agencies."

Medical Examinations

39:47. May a school district require that non-instructional employees submit to a medical examination after they have begun working for the district?

Yes. Both the Civil Service Law and the Education Law authorize school districts and boards of cooperative educational services to require that a non-instructional employee undergo a medical examination to determine their fitness for duty (§ 72(1); Educ. Law § 913; see also *Seraydar v. Three Village CSD*, 90 A.D.3d 936 (2d Dep't 2011); *Gardner v. Niskayuna CSD*, 42 A.D.3d 633 (3d Dep't 2010); *Appeal of D.R.*, 48 Ed Dept Rep 358 (2009)).

Pursuant to the Civil Service Law, school districts may require such an examination if they determine the non-instructional employee is unable to perform the duties of his or her position by reason of a disability (§ 72(a)). Pursuant to the Education Law, districts may require both teachers and non-teaching personnel to submit to such an examination to "safeguard the health of children attending the public schools . . . to determine the physical or mental capacity of such person to perform his or her duties" (Educ. Law § 913; *Seraydar v. Three Village CSD*; *Gardner v. Niskayuna CSD*; *Appeal of D.R.*).

This section focuses on medical examinations of non-instructional employees under the Civil Service Law. For more information on medical examinations of teachers, see **30:13-18**.

39:48. Are there any procedures school districts must follow when deciding to require that a non-instructional employee submit to a medical examination under Section 72 of the Civil Service Law?

Yes. In such an instance, school districts must:

Arrange for the medical examination to be conducted by a medical officer selected by the civil service department or civil service commission having jurisdiction over the employee's position.

Provide the employee, and the civil service department or commissioner with jurisdiction, written notice of the facts supporting its determination that a medical examination is necessary (§ 72(1); *McShane v. State of N.Y.*, 43 Misc.3d 320 (Sup. Ct. New York Cnty. 2014)).

39:49. What happens with the results of a Section 72 medical examination?

A school district may place on an involuntary leave of absence an employee certified unfit for duty by a medical officer who conducts the examination. In such an instance, the district must provide the employee with written notice of the reasons for the proposed leave, the date upon which the leave is scheduled to start, and the employee's procedural rights (§ 72(1)). The notice must be served on the employee in person or by first class, registered or certified mail, return receipt requested (*Id.*).

Non-instructional employees facing an involuntary leave of absence may object to the proposed leave and request a hearing within prescribed timelines (*Id.*). A request for a hearing holds in abeyance the district's ability to impose the leave, unless there is probable cause to believe that the employee's continued presence in the workplace creates a potential danger or will severely interfere with school operations, in which case the employee may be placed on an immediate involuntary leave of absence (§ 72(5); see *Ingram v. Nassau Cnty.*, 85 A.D.3d 1175 (2d Dep't 2011); see also *Pastore v. City of Troy*, 126 Misc.2d 113 (Sup. Ct. Rensselaer Cnty. 1984)). Following the hearing, a district may uphold, withdraw or modify the originally proposed leave, subject to the employees further right to appeal (§ 72(1)), or be reinstated in accordance with law (§ 72(2)).

While on leave, the employee is entitled to draw on all accumulated, unused sick leave, vacation, overtime and other time allowance in his or her credit (§ 72(1)). However, an employee placed on involuntary leave of absence who is not reinstated to his or her position within one year after the start of the leave may be terminated in accordance with applicable statutory provisions (§ 72(4); see also § 73).

Employees finally determined to be fit for duty must be restored to their position. In addition, the employee is entitled to back pay and the restoration of benefits but only for the period of leave during which he or she was not deemed unfit to perform the duties of the position, less any compensation they may have earned in other employment or occupation, and any unemployment benefits they may have received during the leave period (§ 72(5); *Ingram v. Nassau Cnty.*; *Petix v. N.Y. State Office of Mental Health*, 291 A.D.2d 846 (4th Dep't 2002)).

School districts must adhere strictly to the Civil Service Law provisions governing the imposition of an involuntary leave of absence. Failure to do so may result in a court order annulling the district's decision to impose such leave and reinstating the employee with back pay and other employment benefits (§ 77; *Lazzari v. Town of Eastchester*, 20 N.Y.3d 214 (2012); *Williams v. Troiano*, 129 A.D.3d 1601 (4th Dep't 2015); *Breen v. Gunn*, 137 A.D.2d 685 (2d Dep't 1988); *McShane v. State of N.Y.*, 43 Misc.3d 320 (Sup. Ct. New York Cnty. 2014)).

39:50. May an employee removed due to a disability apply for reinstatement if the disability ends?

Yes. An employee may within one year after termination of a disability resulting from occupational injury or disease apply to the local civil service commission for a medical exam to be conducted (§ 71; Work. Comp. Law § 2). If a medical officer certifies that such person is mentally and physically fit to perform the duties of his or her former position he or she must be immediately reinstated by the employer (§ 71; *Lazzari v. Town of Eastchester*, 20 N.Y.3d 214 (2012)). If there is no appropriate vacancy for the employee to fill he or she will be placed on a preferred eligible list (§ 71, see also **39:44**).

Security Guards

39:51. Is a school district required to comply with the requirements of the Security Guard Act of 1992?

Yes. If a school district employs at least one security guard, then the district is subject to the Security Guard Act of 1992 (Gen. Bus. Law § 89-f(5), (7)). Under section 89-o of the General Business Law, the secretary of state is empowered to adopt rules and regulations implementing the provisions of the act.

Any security guard employed by a school district must be registered by the NYS Department of State (Gen. Bus. Law § 89-g(1)(b); see § 89-h). Registration for a security guard is effective for two years (Gen. Bus. Law § 89-m(1)).

A district employing a security guard must provide proof of self-insurance or liability insurance coverage to the NYS Department of State. The insurance must cover death, personal injury, false arrest, false imprisonment, malicious prosecution, libel, slander, and violation of the right of privacy in the amount of $100,000 per occurrence and $300,000 in the aggregate (Gen. Bus. Law § 89-g(6)).

39:52. Whom should a school district contact for additional information or with questions regarding the Security Guard Act of 1992?

Questions about the Security Guard Act of 1992 should be directed to the NYS Department of State at 518-474-4429. Information can also be found through the NYS Department of State's website at: http://www.dos.ny.gov/licensing/securityguard/sguard.html.

40. Coaches and Athletic Trainers

Coaches

40:1. Must a teacher who coaches interscholastic sports be certified as a physical education teacher?

No. A certified physical education teacher may coach any sport in any school. However, a teacher certified in an area other than physical education also may coach any sport in any school, provided he or she has been trained in first aid, including cardiopulmonary resuscitation, and completes an education program for coaches within five years of appointment. That educational program must include an approved course in philosophy, principles, and organization of athletics to be completed within the first two years of appointment, and courses in health sciences applied to coaching and sport-specific coaching theory and techniques to be completed within five years of appointment. They must also complete a course relating to concussions (§ 3001-b; 8 NYCRR §§ 135.4(c)(7)(i)(c)(2), 135.5; see **40:9**).

The commissioner of education may grant an extension of the time period in which to complete such training to no more than seven years after such appointment. Coach training programs can be either a department-approved college program, in-service education program, or an equivalent approved by the commissioner. Coaches who have a lapse in service due to maternity leave, military leave, or other extenuating circumstances may apply for an additional extension of no more than two years. The availability of this additional extension offers the specified individuals the possibility of up to nine years from appointment to complete required coursework (8 NYCRR § 135.4(c)(7)(i)(c)(2)).

Where two or more certified teachers with coaching qualifications and experience apply for one available position, a district may appoint any one of the qualified applicants to the position (*Appeal of Chichester*, 39 Ed Dept Rep 470 (1999)). However, a district may have an obligation, based on the teachers' collective bargaining agreement or past practice, to offer available coaching positions to certified teachers who are members of the bargaining unit in that district before making such positions available to other certified teachers. Notably, the Public Employment Relations Board (PERB) has ruled that a single documented instance of offering the right of first refusal for available coaching positions to teachers in a district's collective bargaining unit does not establish a past practice that the district is obligated to follow in the future (*Canastota CSD*, 32 PERB ¶ 3003 (1999)).

40:2. May a person uncertified as a teacher coach interscholastic sports?

Yes, if he or she holds a temporary coaching license or a professional coaching certificate (8 NYCRR § 135.4(c)(7)(i)(c)(3), (4)(i)(A), (B)). An application for either must be submitted on-line through the NYS Education Department TEACH system at: http://www.highered.nysed.gov/tcert.

In addition, although fingerprinting and a criminal history record check are not a prerequisite for such a license or certificate, all prospective employees of a covered school must satisfy NYS Education Department fingerprinting requirements (8 NYCRR §§ 80-1.11, 87.2(k), 87.3(a); NYS Education Department, *Guidelines for the Coaching Requirements* (revised May 2014), at: http://www.p12.nysed.gov/ciai/pe/toolkitdocs/coaching-guidelinesRev5_14.pdf; see **chapter 41**).

40:3. Are there any limitations on the employment of an uncertified interscholastic sports coach on a temporary basis?

Yes. A school district may employ such an individual only if it has been unable to obtain the services of a certified teacher with coaching qualifications and experience or a coach with a professional coaching certificate (8 NYCRR § 135.4(c)(7)(i)(c)(3); *Appeal of Folsom*, 37 Ed Dept Rep 343 (1998); see also *Appeal of Gilbert*, 40 Ed Dept Rep 350 (2000); *Appeal of Cracchiolo*, 36 Ed Dept Rep 230 (1996)).

In addition, school districts may not hire uncertified coaches in lieu of certified applicants based on subjective determinations that the certified applicant was "not qualified" (*Appeal of Haas*, 46 Ed Dept Rep 430 (2007); *Appeal of Folsom*; *Appeal of Feiss*, 37 Ed Dept Rep 339 (1998); compare *Appeal of Brown*, 39 Ed Dept Rep 343 (1999), where a district passed over a certified coach because during the previous year he had been ejected from two games for unsportsmanlike conduct). Where no certified candidate applies for a particular coaching position for a particular season by the announced application deadline, and the district appoints an uncertified person with a temporary coaching license and coaching qualifications and experience to the position, a certified teacher who comes forward for the first time after the application deadline has no claim to that coaching position for that season (*Appeal of Folsom*).

40:4. What requirements must a person uncertified as a teacher meet to serve as a temporary coach?

Whether appointed in a paid or volunteer capacity, temporary coaches must first obtain a sport-specific *temporary coaching license*. Such a license is valid for one year, except that it may be renewed subject to the requirements specified in commissioner's regulations (8 NYCRR § 135.4(c)(7)(i)(c)(3)).

In addition, pursuant to commissioner's regulations, a temporary coaching license will be issued only if the school district seeking to employ the temporary coach has been unable to obtain the services of a certified teacher with coaching qualifications and experience, and the candidate for the license has completed the following coursework or training requirements:

- first aid training, including cardiopulmonary resuscitation training, prior to the first day of coaching;
- at least two hours of coursework or training for identifying and reporting child abuse and maltreatment (§ 3036; 8 NYCRR § 135.4(c)(7)(i)(c)(3)(ii); see also 8 NYCRR §§ 135.5, 135.7). Those already holding a temporary coaching license as of August 6, 2014 had until July 1, 2015 to meet this requirement (8 NYCRR § 135.7(b)); and
- on a biennial basis, a course of instruction related to mild traumatic brain injuries (8 NYCRR § 135.4(c)(7)(i)(c)(3)(v); see also 8 NYCRR § 136.5(b); see **40:9**)).

An uncertified non-teacher appointed to a coaching position by a school district may not undertake coaching responsibilities until he or she actually has received a temporary coaching license (*Appeal of Kimball*, 36 Ed Dept Rep 508 (1997)).

Applications for a temporary coaching license must be submitted online through SED's TEACH system and reviewed at a local level by board of cooperative educational services (BOCES) Regional Certification Offices (RCO) (see NYS Education Department, *Credentialing of Athletic Coaches Memo* (June 2009), at: http://www.highered.nysed.gov/tcert/resteachers/memos/memo06112009.html).

40:5. What are the requirements for a professional coaching certificate?

To qualify for such a certificate, the uncertified non-teacher must have completed all the requirements for a *temporary coaching license* (see **40:4**), and a minimum of three years coaching experience in a specific sport in a New York State interschool athletic program (8 NYCRR § 135.4(c)(7)(i)(c)(4)(i)(B); see also § 3001-b; 8 NYCRR § 135.5).

Each professional coaching certificate is sport specific (i.e., football, field hockey, soccer, basketball, softball, track, etc.) and is valid for a three-year period. However, it is renewable for additional three-year periods upon application to the commissioner, and satisfactory evaluations for each of the preceding three years for the specific sport for which the certificate is sought that are conducted in accordance with regulatory requirements (8 NYCRR § 135.4(c)(7)(i)(c)(4)(ii)(B), (iii)).

The commissioner's regulations place an applicant for a coaching position who possesses a professional coaching certificate on "equal footing" with certified teachers seeking appointment to the same position (*Appeal of Parisi*, 42 Ed Dept Rep 271 (2003)).

40:6. Must a school district evaluate the performance of a certified professional coach?

Yes. A school district that employs an individual as a coach pursuant to a professional coaching certificate must ensure that the principal or athletic director responsible for supervision of that individual conducts an evaluation during each year in which the non-teacher coach is employed (8 NYCRR § 135.4 (c)(7)(i)(c)(4)(iii)). While not specifically required by statute or the commissioner's regulations, school districts may consider having this review take place at the end of the season for that particular sport.

40:7. Are there any special certification requirements applicable to all coaches?

Yes. All coaches must hold valid certification in first aid or meet equivalent requirements of the commissioner of education. This must include instruction in the administration of adult cardiopulmonary resuscitation (CPR). In addition, prior to the beginning of each sports season, coaches must provide valid evidence to the superintendent that their first aid and adult CPR knowledge and skills are current under the requirements established by the American Red Cross or equivalent requirements certified by the commissioner (§§ 3001-b, 3001-c; 8 NYCRR § 135.5).

Athletic Trainers

40:8. What are the licensing requirements applicable to school district athletic trainers?

Commissioner's regulations require athletic trainers employed by school districts to possess a valid license as a "Certified Athletic Trainer" pursuant to the professional licensing standards contained in Article 162 of the Education Law.

Athletic trainers must hold a valid license as a certified athletic trainer from the State of New York and have completed training pursuant to Public Health Law section 3000-b(3)(a) in the operation and use of an automatic external defibrillator (8 NYCRR § 135.4(c)(7)(i)(d)(1); see also NYS Education Department, *License Requirements* (updated Apr. 2014), at: http://www.op.nysed.gov/prof/at/athletlic. htm).

40:9. Must coaches, physical education teachers and athletic trainers receive training on concussions?

Yes. As of July 1, 2012, all school coaches, physical education teachers, nurses and athletic trainers must complete a course on recognizing the symptoms of concussions, also referred to as mild traumatic brain injuries (MTBI), and must do so on a biennial basis. The course must include, at minimum, the definition of a "concussion," signs and symptoms of mild traumatic brain injuries, how such injuries may occur, practices regarding prevention, and the guidelines for the return to school and to certain school activities after a pupil has suffered a mild traumatic brain injury regardless of whether such injury occurred outside of school. Such training may be completed online and by teleconference approved by the NYS Education Department (§ 305(42)(a)(i); 8 NYCRR §§ 135.4(c)(7)(i)(c)(2)(iii), (3)(v), (4)(i)(A); 136.5(b); see also NYS Education Department, Office of Student Support Services, *Guidelines for Concussion Management in the Schools* (June 2012), at: http://www.p12.nysed.gov/sss/schoolhealth/schoolhealthservices/ConcussionManageGuidelines.pdf).

41. Fingerprinting Requirements

41:1. What are the fingerprinting requirements for school district employees?

The Education Law and commissioner's regulations generally require fingerprinting and a criminal history background check for applicants for certification, as well as prospective employees of school districts, charter schools, and boards of cooperative educational services (hereinafter referred to as "covered schools").

Applicants for Certification: All individuals who apply for certification as a superintendent of schools, teacher, administrator or supervisor, teaching assistant, or in any other title for which a teaching or administrative license or certificate is required pursuant to Part 80 of the commissioner's regulations, must submit their fingerprints to the NYS Education Department (SED) for a criminal history record check (§ 3004-b). However, until July 1, 2017, applicants for permanent certification who held a valid provisional certificate as of July 1, 2001, in the same title for which permanent certification is sought, are not subject to the fingerprinting requirements (§ 3004-b(1); 8 NYCRR §§ 80-1.11, 87.3). Also, until July 1, 2017, teachers applying for a temporary license for employment by the New York City School District are not subject to the fingerprinting requirements if that district had cleared them for licensure and/or employment after fingerprinting and a criminal history record check (§§ 2590-h(20), 3004-b(1); 8 NYCRR §§ 80-1.11, 87.3; see **41:5-6**).

Prospective Employees: The fingerprinting requirements also apply to prospective school employees appointed by the school board on or after July 1, 2001, who are reasonably expected by a covered school to provide services involving direct, in person, face-to-face communication or interaction with students under the age of 21 for more than five days per school year. This applies to individuals seeking a compensated position with a covered school, employees placed in the school by a contractual service provider, and employees placed directly or through contract in a covered school under a public assistance employment program (8 NYCRR § 87.2(k); see also Soc. Serv. Law Art. V, Title 9-B). An employee who worked for a covered school in the previous year is not considered a prospective employee (8 NYCRR § 87.2(k)(3)(ii)).

For more information about the fingerprinting and criminal history record check requirements, contact the NYS Education Department's Office of School Personnel Review and Accountability (OSPRA) by phone at: 518-473-2998, or email: at OSPRA@nysed.gov., or visit the OSPRA website at: http://www.highered.nysed.gov/tsei/ospra/.

41:2. Are there any school employees who are exempt from the fingerprinting requirements?

Yes. Employees appointed prior to July 1, 2001, are exempt so long as they remain at the same place of employment. If such individuals seek new employment at another covered school, they then become subject to fingerprinting and criminal history background check requirements (8 NYCRR §§ 87.2(k), 87.4).

In addition, an individual who the covered school expects will provide services for no more than five days per school year does not have to be fingerprinted if the covered school provides in-person supervision while that individual is providing services. Such individuals may include, for example, visiting artists, guest lecturers and speakers, and sports officials (8 NYCRR § 87.2(k)(3)(iii)).

For more information on who is exempt from the fingerprinting requirements and who must be fingerprinted, see NYS Education Department, *Who Must Be Fingerprinted Charts* (updated Jan. 2013), at: http://www.highered.nysed.gov/tsei/ospra/fingerprintingcharts.html.

41:3. Are nonpublic or private school employees subject to the fingerprinting requirements?

It depends. Prospective employees of a nonpublic or private school who commence providing services on or after July 1, 2007 also may be subject to the fingerprinting requirements if the school elects to fingerprint and seek clearance for employment from the NYS Education Department (§ 305(30); 8 NYCRR §§ 87.2(e), (i), 87.4).

41:4. What is the procedure to have a prospective employee fingerprinted and a criminal history record check conducted?

If a prospective employee is not already in the NYS Education Department's (SED's) criminal history record file, then he or she must be fingerprinted and consent to an investigation into his or her criminal history record (§ 3035; 8 NYCRR § 87.4(b)). The state Division of Criminal Justice Services (DCJS) and the Federal Bureau of Investigation (FBI) will process the fingerprints and provide a record of all convictions of crimes and any pending criminal charges to the commissioner of education. All criminal history records processed by the DCJS and the FBI and sent to the commissioner are confidential. These records may not be published or in any way disclosed to persons other than the commissioner, unless otherwise authorized by law (§ 3035(1); 8 NYCRR §§ 87.4, 87.5(a)). As of August 3, 2015, the capture, transmission of fingerprint applications, fee, and digital fingerprint images are processed through the Statewide Vendor Managed System operated by Morpho Trust in conjunction with DCJS. For the most up-to-date information on this topic, visit the NYS Education Department website at: http://www.highered.nysed.gov/tsei/ospra/.

On the other hand, if the prospective employee is already in the SED criminal history file, then he or she must notify the covered school of this fact, and the covered school must request a clearance for employment from SED. There is no department fee for this request (8 NYCRR § 87.4(a)(4), (b)(3)). If the criminal history record check by SED reveals that a prospective employee has no criminal convictions or pending criminal charges, SED will issue a clearance for employment to the school and notify the prospective employee (§ 3035(3); 8 NYCRR § 87.5(a)(1)).

41:5. Must a teacher previously fingerprinted and cleared for employment undergo a criminal history record check again when seeking employment in the New York City School District?

No, provided that the teacher authorizes the city school district to request that the NYS Education Department (SED) forward the contents of his or her criminal history record to officials of the city school district. In such instances, SED will also send summary information to the city school district concerning any subsequent criminal history notifications that SED receives from the Division of Criminal Justice Services concerning that person. When that employee separates from service with the city school district, the district must notify SED (8 NYCRR § 87.9).

41:6. Must a teacher previously fingerprinted and cleared for certification or employment by the New York City School District undergo a criminal history record check by the NYS Education Department (SED)?

Not if the applicant for certification or employment is also in the criminal history file maintained by SED (see **41:4**), or was previously cleared by the New York City School District and has met the following conditions:

- requested and authorized the city school district to forward to SED a copy of his or her criminal history record and any subsequent criminal history received from Division of Criminal Justice Services (DCJS); and
- was fingerprinted by the city school district on or after July 1, 1990, and those fingerprints are still on file with DCJS.

In addition, SED must be satisfied that the criminal history record received from the city school district is complete and sufficient for determining clearance, and the city school district must agree to provide SED any subsequent criminal history notifications that it receives from DCJS concerning that person.

If these conditions are met, SED's review will consist of examining the criminal history transmitted by the city school district (§§ 3004-b(1); 3035(3-a); 8 NYCRR § 87.9; see also NYS Education Department, *Fingerprinting, Special Information Relating to NYC* (updated Jan. 2013), at: http://www.highered.nysed.gov/tsei/ospra/nycprovisions.html).

41:7. Can a district hire a covered prospective employee who has not been cleared by the NYS Education Department (SED)?

A school board may, upon the recommendation of the superintendent of schools, conditionally appoint a covered prospective employee before he or she has final clearance from SED but only if SED grants that person conditional clearance for employment (see **41:8**). In addition, under certain circumstances, a board also may make an emergency conditional appointment for 20 days or less (see **41:9**).

The availability of a conditional or emergency conditional clearance is scheduled to expire July 1, 2017. Thereafter, without legislative action a covered school cannot employ or utilize a prospective school employee without full clearance for employment from SED (§§ 1604(39), 1709(39), 1804(9), 1950(4)(ll), 2503(18), 2554(25), 2854(3)(a-2), 3035(3); 8 NYCRR §§ 87.2, 87.4(a)).

41:8. What are the requirements for a conditional clearance appointment?

Conditional clearance for employment requires a determination by the NYS Education Department (SED), based upon its review of a prospective school employee's criminal history record obtained from the Division of Criminal Justice Services, that such an individual may be temporarily employed by the covered school, provided all other requirements for employment are met (8 NYCRR § 87.2(d); see also **41:7**). The process involves a number of steps.

A district must obtain from the prospective employee a signed statement indicating whether, to the best of his or her knowledge, he or she has any pending criminal charges or convictions in any jurisdiction outside of New York State (§§ 1604(39)(b), 1709(39)(b), 1804(9)(b), 1950(4)(ll)(b), 2503(18)(b), 2554(25)(b), 2854(3)(a-2)(ii); 8 NYCRR § 87.4(a)(3), (4), (b)(2), (3)). Either the district or the prospective employee may then request conditional clearance from SED. In either case, the prospective employee must sign and complete a request form (8 NYCRR § 87.4(a)(3), (4), (b)(2)).

Within 15 business days after the commissioner of education receives the prospective employee's fingerprints, the commissioner must grant or deny conditional clearance or provide the employee and school with a good faith estimate of how much additional time is necessary to make a determination (§ 3035(3)(b); 8 NYCRR § 87.5(a)(2), (3)).

A conditional appointment cannot commence until notification by the commissioner that the prospective employee has been conditionally cleared for appointment and must terminate when the prospective employer is notified of a determination by the commissioner to grant or deny clearance. If clearance is granted, the appointment continues and the conditional status is removed. Otherwise, a conditional appointment expires after 45 days, and may not be extended or renewed unless the commissioner finds there was good cause for failing to obtain clearance and issues a new conditional clearance (§§ 1604(39)(b), 1709(39)(b), 1804(9)(b), 1950(4)(ll)(b), 2503(18)(b), 2554(25)(b), 2854(3)(a-2)(ii)).

A school board cannot conditionally appoint employees unless it has developed a policy for the safety of the children who have contact with an employee holding a conditional appointment or emergency conditional appointment (§§ 1604(39)(d), 1709(39)(d), 1804(9)(d), 1950(4)(ll)(d), 2503(18)(d), 2554(25)(d), 2854(3)(a-2)(iv)).

A sample conditional appointment policy is available from the New York State School Boards Association.

41:9. What are the requirements for an emergency conditional appointment?

Until July 1, 2017, (see **41:7**) a school board may make an emergency conditional appointment only when an unforeseen emergency vacancy has occurred. An *unforeseen emergency vacancy* must meet the following criteria:

- it occurs less than 10 business days before the start of or during any school session, including summer school, without sufficient notice to allow for clearance; or when the board determines that the covered school has been unable to fill the vacancy with sufficient time for clearance or conditional clearance despite good faith efforts to do so; and
- there is no other qualified person to fill the vacancy and it is necessary to maintain services the covered school is legally required to provide or necessary to protect the health, education, or safety of students or staff (§§ 1604(39)(c), 1709(39)(c), 1804(9)(c), 1950(4)(ll)(c), 2503(18)(c), 2554(25)(c), 2854(3)(a-2)(iii); 8 NYCRR § 87.2(j)).

In addition, the school board must obtain from the prospective employee a signed statement indicating whether, to the best of his or her knowledge, he or she has a pending criminal charge or conviction in any jurisdiction. It also must initiate the process for conditional appointment discussed at **41:8** (§§ 1604(39)(c), 1709(39)(c), 1804(9)(c), 1950(4)(ll)(c), 2503(18)(c), 2554(25)(c), 2854(3)(a-2)(iii); 8 NYCRR § 87.2(j)).

An emergency conditional appointment may commence prior to notification from the commissioner of education on conditional clearance, but must terminate 20 business days from the date it starts, or upon notification by the commissioner regarding conditional clearance, whichever occurs first. If conditional clearance is granted, the appointment continues as a conditional appointment (*Id.*).

However, as in the case of a conditional clearance appointment, a board cannot make an emergency conditional appointment unless it has developed a policy for the safety of the children who have contact with an employee holding a conditional appointment or emergency conditional appointment (§§ 1604(39)(d), 1709(39)(d), 1804(9)(d), 1950(4)(ll)(d), 2503(18)(d), 2554(25)(d), 2854(3)(a-2)(iv); 8 NYCRR § 87.2(c)).

A sample policy on emergency conditional appointment is available from the New York State School Boards Association.

41:10. If a criminal history record check reveals that a prospective employee has a record of convictions and/or pending charges, does that mean that he or she will be automatically denied clearance?

No. If the prospective employee has a record of criminal conviction(s) or pending criminal charge(s), the NYS Education Department (SED) must conduct a review in accordance with standards set forth in New York's Corrections Law and Executive Law (see **31:38**). SED must assess factors such as whether there is a direct relationship between the criminal offense(s) and the employment sought, and whether employment of such individual will present an unreasonable risk to the safety, welfare, or property of the public or specific individuals (§ 3035(3); Corrections Law §§ 752, 753; Exec. Law § 296(15), (16); 8 NYCRR § 87.5(a)(4)(i), (iii); see *Dempsey v. N.Y. City Dep't of Educ.*, 25 N.Y.3d 291 (2015); *Acosta v. N.Y. City Dep't of Educ.*, 16 N.Y.3d 309 (2011); *Boatman v. NYS Dep't of Educ.*, 72 A.D.3d 1467 (3d Dep't 2010)).

Thus, in a case where a school district had not considered information provided by the employee to show her rehabilitation and good conduct, the state's highest court determined the district's refusal to grant her employment clearance to be arbitrary (*Acosta v. N.Y. City Dep't of Educ.*). However, in another case, that same court determined that a school district did not act arbitrarily when it gave greater weight to the severity and timing of the criminal offenses involved than to other factors it also was required to consider (*Dempsey v. N.Y. City Dep't of Educ.*).

41:11. What happens if the NYS Education Department (SED) denies clearance for employment to a covered prospective employee?

If SED determines that there is a basis to deny clearance for employment, it must notify the prospective employee of a possible denial of clearance and state the basis for this determination, including but not limited to a description of the criminal charge(s) or conviction(s) involved. The notification must state that a clearance for employment will be denied unless the prospective employee submits a response, demonstrating to SED's satisfaction, that clearance should be granted. The prospective employee must respond within 25 calendar days (or, if conditional clearance for employment has been requested or already granted, within 10 calendar days) from the date the notification was mailed (§ 3035(3); 8 NYCRR § 87.5(a)(4)(v); see also NYS Education Department, *Fingerprinting, Due Process and Procedure Rights* (updated Jan. 2013), at: http://www.highered.nysed.gov/tsei/ospra/dueprocess.html).

The prospective employee's response may include any affidavits or other relevant written information which he or she wishes SED to consider, including, where applicable, information in regard to his or her good conduct and rehabilitation. SED must review the response and determine (subject to the criteria set forth in the Corrections and Executive Laws) whether the information submitted by the prospective employee warrants granting clearance for employment (8 NYCRR § 87.5(a)(4)(vi), (viii); see *Dempsey v. N.Y. City Dep't of Educ.*, 25 N.Y.3d 291 (2015); *Acosta v. N.Y. City Dep't of Educ.*, 16 N.Y.3d 309 (2011); see also *Fingerprinting, Due Process and Procedure Rights*).

If the prospective employee does not submit a response within the timeframe prescribed, or if after reviewing his or her response, SED determines that clearance must be denied, SED must cancel any conditional clearance previously granted and notify the prospective employee of such denial, along with the basis for its determination and instructions for an appeal. SED must also notify the covered school (8 NYCRR § 87.5(a)(4)(vii), (viii); see also *Fingerprinting, Due Process and Procedure Rights*).

If clearance for employment is denied by SED prior to its receipt of information from the Federal Bureau of Investigation (FBI) which forms an additional basis to deny clearance for employment, and the prospective school employee has already appealed the department's determination, then SED must notify the prospective school employee of this additional information. The prospective school employee has 25 calendar days after the mailing of the notification to respond. After a review of the information provided by the FBI and the response of the prospective school employee, if any, SED must either notify the prospective employee that no change in the original denial of clearance determination will be made, or issue modified determinations denying clearance for employment including the FBI information. The modified determinations will not affect the validity of the original determinations (8 NYCRR § 87.5(a)(4)(ix)).

41:12. Can an applicant for certification or a prospective employee appeal a determination by the NYS Education Department to deny clearance?

Yes. If the NYS Education Department (SED) denies clearance to an applicant or prospective employee (hereinafter "appellant"), he or she may appeal that determination to a designee of the commissioner of education who did not participate in SED's determination within 25 calendar days of the date clearance denial was mailed (8 NYCRR § 87.5(a)(5); see also NYS Education Department, *Fingerprinting, Due Process and Procedure Rights* (updated Jan. 2013), at: http://www.highered.nysed.gov/tsei/ospra/dueprocess.html).

The appellant may submit any affidavits or other relevant written information that he or she wants considered, including, where applicable, information regarding his or her good conduct and rehabilitation (8 NYCRR § 87.5(a)(5)(iii); see also *Fingerprinting, Due Process and Procedure Rights*).

The commissioner's designee must make a determination on the appeal based on a review of the appellant's criminal history record and the written information and arguments timely submitted by him or her. The review must apply the standards for granting or denying a license or employment application set forth in the Corrections Law and Executive Law (see **31:38**). If the appeal is denied, the decision must include the findings of fact and conclusions of law upon which the determination is based. A copy of the decision must be sent to the appellant, and the covered school must be notified of the denial or grant of clearance (Corrections Law §§ 752, 753; Exec. Law § 296(16); 8 NYCRR § 87.5(a)(5)(iv); see also *Fingerprinting, Due Process and Procedure Rights*).

41:13. What are the responsibilities of a school that hires a fingerprinted employee when the employee separates from employment or ceases providing services?

Covered schools must notify the NYS Education Department of the name and other identifying information of any covered school employee who was fingerprinted as required by the Education Law and has been separated from employment or ceased providing services and the date the employee left the employment of the school (8 NYCRR § 87.4(a)(5)).

41:14. What if there is a change in an employee's criminal history record file after he or she has been employed by a covered school?

The NYS Education Department (SED) must notify a covered school if SED receives subsequent information regarding a covered employee's criminal history record and SED records show the individual is employed by the covered school. Upon receipt of such information from the Division of Criminal Justice Services, SED must notify the covered school of the date of any subsequent arrest of the covered employee and the court of jurisdiction (8 NYCRR § 87.6(a)). For applicants for, or holders of, certification as a superintendent of schools, teacher, administrator or supervisor, teaching assistant, or any other title for which a teaching or administrative license or certificate is required pursuant to part 80 of the commissioner's regulations, SED will also forward the arrest information to its Office of Teaching Initiatives for a determination of good moral character under part 83 of the commissioner's regulations (8 NYCRR § 87.6(b); see **31:37-43**).

41:15. Once an employee leaves the employment of a covered school, what becomes of their fingerprints on file at the Division of Criminal Justice Services (DCJS) and their criminal history file at the NYS Education Department (SED)?

SED will notify the DCJS to destroy the fingerprints of any individual separated from employment at a covered school who has not become employed at the same or another covered school within 12 months of separation. Any such individual may request that his or her fingerprints be destroyed prior to the expiration of this 12-month period. Individuals whose fingerprints are destroyed will be removed from SED's criminal history file (8 NYCRR § 87.7).

41:16. Who pays the fee for the NYS Education Department's (SED) criminal history record check?

Applicants for certification or licensure are responsible for the fee for clearance for certification (§ 3004-b(2); 8 NYCRR § 87.8(b)). Prospective school employees must pay the fee for SED's clearance for employment, unless the covered school agrees to pay the fee (8 NYCRR § 87.8(c)). However, prospective school employees participating in a public assistance employment program under the provisions of the Social Services Law, or receiving employment services through the Federal Temporary Assistance for Needy Families Block Grant, are exempt from paying the fee. In such cases, the Social Services District pays the fee (Soc. Serv. Law Art. V, Title 9-B; Educ. Law § 3035(4); 8 NYCRR § 87.8(d)(1)).

A prospective school employee may submit a request to the school board that the fees be waived and paid by the board instead. The board may grant such a request and pay the fee if it determines that payment of such a fee would impose an unreasonable financial hardship on the prospective employee or his or her family (§ 3035(4); 8 NYCRR § 87.8(d)(2)).

Payment of such fees may be a negotiated item in a collective bargaining agreement (§ 3035(6); see **47:15**). However, reimbursement of fingerprinting costs for new hires is not a mandatory subject of bargaining (see *Matter of Newark Valley Cardinal Bus Drivers*, 35 PERB ¶ 3006 (2002), *aff'd,* 36 PERB ¶ 7005, *aff'd, Newark Valley Cardinal Bus Driver, Local 4360, NYSUT, AFT, AFL-CIO*, 303 A.D.2d 888 (3d Dep't), *appeal denied*, 100 N.Y.2d 504 (2003)).

42. Employee Constitutional Rights

Free Speech

Editor's Note: Public school employees enjoy rights protected by various federal and state constitutional provisions such as those providing for equal protection, due process, the free exercise of religion, free speech, and protection against unreasonable searches and seizures. This chapter focuses mainly on the latter two. For information on religion in the public schools, see ***chapter 65****. Due process issues associated with the termination and discipline of teachers and non-instructional staff are addressed in* ***chapters 38 through 39****.*

42:1. Do school district employees enjoy freedom of expression rights?

Yes. The First Amendment to the United States Constitution provides, in part, that governmental entities may not abridge an individual's freedom of speech (U.S. Const. Amend. I). However, the scope of constitutional protection available to public employees, including school district staff, is limited. In the past, public employees enjoyed free speech protection under the First Amendment when they spoke on matters of public concern (*Pickering v. Bd. of Township High Sch. Dist. 205*, 391 U.S. 563 (1968)). Current judicial interpretations have narrowed that protection to situations where a public employee is speaking on a matter of public concern, as a private citizen (*Garcetti v. Ceballos*, 547 U.S. 410 (2006); *Matthews v. City of New York,* 779 F.3d 167 (2d Cir. 2015); *Smith v. County of Suffolk,* 776 F.3d 114 (2d Cir. 2015); *Almontaser v. N.Y. City Dep't of Educ.*, 519 F.3d 505 (2d Cir. 2008); *Ruotolo v. City of N.Y.*, 514 F.3d 184 (2d Cir. 2008); see also *Borough of Duryea v. Guarnieri,* 131 S.Ct. 2488 (2011)).

Accordingly, district employees may be subject to discipline and dismissal for:

- Speech that is not a matter of public concern.
- Speech that addresses a matter of public concern, but is made pursuant to the discharge of official responsibilities rather than as a citizen (*Garcetti v. Ceballos;* see also *Ross v. Breslin*, 693 F.3d 300 (2d Cir. 2012); *Storman v. Klein,* 395 Fed. Appx. 790 (2d Cir. 2010); *Woodlock v. Orange-Ulster BOCES*, 281 Fed. Appx. 66 (2d Cir. 2008)).

In the latter case, however, protection may nonetheless be available under the state's whistleblower law (Civ. Serv. Law § 75-b; see also *Ross v. Breslin;* see **39:43**). Furthermore, according to the U.S. Court of Appeals for the Second Circuit, with jurisdiction over New York, First Amendment protection would be available to a public employee who refuses to comply with a supervisor's demand to retract a truthful report written as part of the employee's official duties or to report falsely about a matter of public concern (*Jackler v. Byrne*, 658 F.3d 225 (2d Cir. 2010), *cert denied*, 132 S.Ct. 1634 (2012)).

42:2. Under what circumstances will employee speech be deemed to be spoken as a private citizen?

Whether speech is spoken as a citizen, and possibly entitled to protection under the First Amendment (see **42:1**), generally will depend on whether it is expressed outside the scope of an employee's employment duties.

For example, the United States Supreme Court ruled that a public employee who provides truthful sworn testimony pursuant to a subpoena, which is outside the course of his ordinary job responsibilities, is entitled to First Amendment protection (*Lane v. Franks*, 134 S.Ct. 2369 (2014)).

Additionally, the U.S. Court of Appeals for the Second Circuit has ruled that "when an employee whose duties do not involve formulating, implementing or providing feedback on a policy that implicates a matter of public concern engages in speech concerning that policy, and does so in a manner in which ordinary citizens would be expected to engage, he speaks as a citizen, not as a public employee" (*Matthews v. City of N.Y.*, 779 F.3d 167, 174 (2d Cir. 2015)). That was the case when a policeman reported to precinct commanders, rather than the internal affairs bureau, that a quota system imposed upon patrolmen was causing unjustified stops, arrests and summonses and having an adverse effect on the precinct's relationship with the community (*Id.*).

42:3. Under what circumstances will employee speech be deemed a part of an employee's official responsibilities?

The U.S. Court of Appeals for the Second Circuit, which has jurisdiction over New York, has ruled that speech can be deemed spoken pursuant to a public employee's official duties even if it is "not required by, or included in, the employee's job description, or in response to a request by the employer" (*Weintraub v. Bd. of Educ. of City of N.Y.*, 593 F.3d 196 (2d Cir.), *cert. denied* 131 S.Ct. 444 (2010); see also *Massaro v. N.Y. City Dep't of Educ.*, 481 Fed. Appx. 653 (2d Cir. 2012)).

That was the case where a teacher filed a grievance over the failure of school administrators to discipline a student who threw books at him in class on two occasions, even though the teacher was not required to initiate the grievance. The teacher claimed his subsequent termination constituted unlawful retaliation in violation of his First Amendment rights. However, according to the Second Circuit, the teacher's grievance was "'part-and-parcel of his concerns' about his ability to 'properly execute his duties' . . . to maintain classroom discipline, . . . an indispensible prerequisite to effective teaching and classroom learning" (*Weintraub v. Bd. of Educ. of City of N.Y*).

42:4. What are some examples of speech that was deemed to be part of an employee's official responsibilities?

Courts have consistently found that teachers' communications made through internal school channels about working conditions or the treatment of students are pursuant to a teacher's official duties. Under this rule, the following speech was not protected:

- internal reports about classroom sanitary conditions (*Massaro v. N.Y. City Dep't of Educ.*, 481 Fed Appx. 653 (2d Cir. 2012));
- reports to principal regarding over-enrollment of physical education classes (*Smith v. City of New York*, 130 F.Supp.3d 819 (S.D.N.Y. 2015));
- statements about the lack of certain classes (*Woodlock v. Orange-Ulster BOCES,* 281 Fed. Appx. 66 (2d Cir. 2008));
- statements about the adequacy of the curriculum or materials (*Felton v. Katonah Lewisboro Sch. Dist.*, 2009 U.S. Dist. LEXIS 64660 (S.D.N.Y. July 24, 2009));
- statements about special education staffing needs and provision of special education related services (*Jerram v. Cornwall CSD,* 464 Fed. Appx. 13 (2d Cir. 2012); *White v. City of New York,* 2014 U.S. Dist. LEXIS 123255 (S.D.N.Y. Sept. 3, 2014));
- reporting potential grading irregularities on state exams to school administrators (*O'Connor v. Huntington UFSD*, 2014 U.S. Dist. LEXIS 39596 (E.D.N.Y. 2014)); and
- reporting co-teacher's aggressive and frightening behavior towards students (*Anglisano v. New York City Dep't of Educ.,* 2015 U.S. Dist. LEXIS 136259 (E.D.N.Y. Sept. 30, 2015)).

In certain situations even reports to outside agencies have been found to fall within an employee's responsibilities (*Ross v. N.Y. City Dep't of Educ.*, 935 F.Supp.2d 508 (E.D.N.Y. 2013) (filing OSHA complaint regarding safety of building concerned teacher's ability to execute duties); *Kilduff v. Rochester City School Dist.,* 53 F.Supp.3d 610 (W.D.N.Y. 2014) (homeless coordinator's reports to the State Education Department was not protected speech)).

On the other hand, speech that is required by, or included in, the employee's job description, or in response to an employer's request may, nonetheless, be entitled to First Amendment protection. That was the case, for example, where a police officer was asked to retract a truthful report about an arrest (*Jackler v. Byrne*, 658 F.3d 225 (2d Cir. 2010)). Similarly, a teacher's advocacy on behalf of union and other teachers in his or her capacity as union representative is protected speech (*Pekowsky v. Yonkers Bd. of Educ*., 2014 U.S. Dist. LEXIS 73465 (S.D.N.Y. 2014)).

42:5. May a district adopt a policy or protocol for reporting school related concerns?

Districts must be careful that the adoption and implementation of a policy that establishes a protocol for staff to communicate their school related concerns does not have the effect of restricting avenues of communication as a prior restraint (*Price v. Saugerties CSD*, 2006 U.S. Dist. LEXIS 8329 (N.D.N.Y. Feb. 9, 2006); see also *Price v. Saugerties CSD*, 2007 U.S. Dist. LEXIS 67519 (N.D.N.Y Sept. 12, 2007), *aff'd*, 305 Fed. Appx. 715 (2d Cir. 2009)). An employee's failure to follow such protocols, however, may constitute grounds for disciplinary action (*Nagle v. Marron,* 663 F.3d 100 (2d Cir. 2011)).

42:6. Can a school district employee be subjected to discipline and dismissal for speech a district deems to be disruptive?

Yes, if the school district reasonably believes the speech is disruptive. A district is entitled to make that determination based on the facts surrounding the speech as the district reasonably believes them to be (*Waters v. Churchill*, 511 U.S. 661 (1994); *Connick v. Myers*, 461 U.S. 138 (1983); *Singh v. City of N.Y.*, 524 F.3d 361 (2d Cir. 2008); see also *Delano v. City of Buffalo,* 628 Fed. Appx. 23 (2d Cir. 2015); *Locurto v. Giuliani*, 447 F.3d 159 (2d Cir. 2006)). It does not have to demonstrate that an employee's speech actually caused disruption to the district's operation; rather the district's burden is to show that the speech threatened to interfere with its operations (*Locurto v. Safir*, 264 F.3d 154 (2d Cir. 2001); *Jeffries v. Harleston*, 52 F.3d 9 (2d Cir.), *cert. denied*, 516 U.S. 862 (1995); see also *Marchi v. BOCES*, 173 F.3d 469 (2d Cir.), *cert. denied*, 528 U.S. 869 (1999); *Locurto v. Giuliani*).

Accordingly, a teacher was properly terminated for his much publicized active participation in the North American Man Boy Love Association (NAMBLA), which advocates legalizing sexual relationships between men and underage boys. The potential disruptiveness of returning him to the classroom outweighed his free speech rights (*Melzer v. Bd. of Educ. of the City Sch. Dist. of City of N.Y.*, 336 F.3d 185 (2d Cir. 2003)). Similarly, two teachers were properly disciplined for participating in a union parking demonstration that created a health and safety hazard for students and disrupted school operations by causing a traffic jam that resulted in sixteen teachers reporting late (*Santer v. Bd. of Educ. of East Meadow UFSD*, 23 N.Y.3d 251 (2014); see also *East Meadow Teachers Assoc. v. East Meadow UFSD,* 48 PERB ¶ 3006 (2015)). On the other hand, a school district was precluded from taking disciplinary action against a faculty advisor to an extracurricular student newspaper who allowed the publication of a cartoon depicting board members and an administrator unfavorably. There was no evidence of "substantial disruption or material interference with school activities" (*Appeal of Bd. of Educ. of Wappingers CSD*, 34 Ed Dept Rep 323 (1994)).

42:7. Can a school district discipline an employee based upon postings an employee made on internet blogs, Facebook or other social media platforms?

It depends. Generally, social media postings may form the basis for discipline only if such postings were not in the context of a private citizen commenting on a matter of public concern. Accordingly, a teacher's free speech rights were not violated by his termination for mental unfitness after he expressed a desire to kill people, to shoot down a plane and delusional theories regarding government conspiracies in private messages he exchanged through an online game with friend. At the time he made the statements, the employee concurrently purchased several firearms (*Heller v. Bedford CSD*., 144 F. Supp. 3d 596 (S.D.N.Y. Nov. 17, 2015)).

Similarly, a school district did not improperly terminate a teaching assistant who posted a counseling memorandum he received to two internet discussion groups seeking advice as to how he should deal with a school policy he did not approve of or how to deal with the counseling memorandum he felt was undeserved. The court determined even if a discussion of the circumstances surrounding the counseling memorandum constituted protected speech, the posting of the actual memorandum was not given the memorandum addressed a parental concern about the plaintiff's behavior (*Mustafa v. Syracuse City Sch. Dist.*, 2010 U.S. Dist. LEXIS 115657 (N.D.N.Y. Nov. 1, 2010)).

However, even postings that are considered to be on matters of public concern may result in discipline if they cause a disruption to school operations. In the *Heller* case, the court stated that even if the teacher's online communications constituted protected speech his termination did not violate the First Amendment based upon the potential disruption his speech would have generated among parents and students (*Heller v. Bedford CSD*., see **42:6**). A federal appellate court with jurisdiction outside New York ruled similarly after a teacher was terminated based upon blog postings regarding her students whom she characterized as "rude, disengaged, lazy whiners" and "insolent, unappreciative, selfish brats." The postings resulted in protests and more than 200 requests from parents not to assign their child to the teacher (*Munroe v. Centr. Bucks Sch. Dist.*, 805 F.3d 454 (3d Cir. Sept. 4, 2015)).

42:8. Are there any restrictions on a school district's ability to impose a dress code on its faculty?

Yes. A school district may not unilaterally impose a dress code on its faculty. The imposition of a specific dress code for faculty is a mandatory subject of collective bargaining (*Catskill CSD*, 18 PERB ¶ 4612 (1985); see also *State of N.Y. (Dep't of Taxation & Finance)*, 30 PERB ¶ 3028 (1997); **47:10–11**).

Nonetheless, according to a Public Employment Relations Board (PERB) administrative law judge, a school district may require its staff to wear photo identification cards without first negotiating the issue with the union, where the identification system relates to the employer's mission to promote safety and accountability (*Middle Country CSD*, 30 PERB ¶ 4556 (1997)).

In addition, the U.S. Court of Appeals for the Second Circuit, which has jurisdiction over New York, has held that a dress code that requires a teacher to wear a necktie does not infringe on First Amendment rights to free expression or the right to privacy (*East Hartford Educ. Ass'n v. Bd. of Educ.*, 562 F.2d 838 (2d Cir. 1977)).

However, in a noteworthy case arising outside the school context, a New York appellate court ordered reinstatement and back pay where a Native American corrections officer was dismissed for refusing to cut his hair, as required by regulation, because of his religious beliefs. According to the court, there was no legitimate state interest shown which outweighed the employee's right to the free exercise of his religion (*Rourke v. N.Y. State Dep't of Correctional Servs.*, 201 A.D.2d 179 (3d Dep't 1994)).

42:9. May a school district bar staff from wearing political campaign buttons and pins while on duty?

Yes. In a case where a teachers' union challenged a school district's ban on the wearing of such items while on duty or in contact with students, a federal district court for the Southern District of New York ruled that school boards may, "within reason . . . regulate the speech of teachers in the classroom for legitimate pedagogical reasons." The district argued successfully that its actions were triggered by concerns that "displays of political partisanship in the schools" were inconsistent with its educational mission. The ban was necessary to avoid improperly influencing students and impinging on their "rights . . . to learn in an environment free of partisan political influence" (*Weingarten v. Bd. of Educ. of the City Sch. Dist. of the City of N.Y.,* 680 F.Supp.2d 595 (S.D.N.Y. 2010)).

However, off school grounds the right to freedom of expression guarantees an employee the ability to express his or her political beliefs (*see Elrod v. Burns*, 427 U.S. 347 (1976)). Recently, the U.S. Supreme Court has held that a public employee is entitled to free speech protection when an employer takes an adverse employment action against the employee based upon a mistaken belief regarding the employee's political activity. Accordingly, it was impermissible for a police detective to be demoted because officials incorrectly believed the detective supported a particular candidate for mayor (*Heffernan v. City of Paterson, New Jersey,* 136 S.Ct. 1412 (2016)).

Search and Seizure

42:10. Do school district employees enjoy protection against unreasonable searches and seizures by district officials?

Yes. The Fourth Amendment to the United States Constitution prohibits government officials, including school officials, from conducting unreasonable searches and seizures (U.S. Const. Amend. IV; *New Jersey v. T.L.O.*, 469 U.S. 325 (1985)).

Generally, a search will violate the Fourth Amendment unless it is based on probable cause to believe that a violation of law has occurred. But while school staff, as public employees, are constitutionally protected against an unreasonable search and seizure, school district officials may "dispense with probable cause and warrant requirements when conducting workplace searches related to investigations of work-related misconduct" (*Levanthal v. Knapek*, 266 F.3d 64 (2d Cir. 2001)).

42:11. Are there any restrictions on the ability of school officials to conduct a search of a school employee's work area?

The nature and extent of a constitutionally permissible search of a public employee's work space and items within that work space (including a computer) will depend on the employee's "expectation of privacy." Any such expectation must be based not only on the law, but also on the district's policies and practices. For example, an expectation of privacy in private possessions kept in the workplace may be diminished by workplace realities such as work related visits by fellow employees and others (*Shaul v. Cherry Valley-Springfield CSD*, 363 F.3d 177 (2d Cir. 2004)).

Nonetheless, school officials may search an area or materials in which an employee has a justifiable expectation of privacy if the search is reasonable. To be reasonable, a search must be "justified at its inception and appropriate in scope" (*Levanthal v. Knapek*, 266 F.3d 64 (2d Cir. 2001)). It will be deemed appropriate in scope if the search methods used are "reasonably related to the objective of the search and not excessively intrusive "in view of the purpose of the search" (*Id.*). In this regard, it was not improper for a public employer to search an employee's computer based on allegations that he was using the equipment to conduct work unrelated to his position with the employer (*Shanahan v. State of N.Y.*, 2011 U.S. Dist. LEXIS 6384 (S.D.N.Y. Jan. 24, 2011)).

In addition, school officials may search an employee's work area for appropriate, non-investigatory, work-related purposes, such as cleaning and preparing a teacher's classroom for use by a substitute (*Shaul*). In such an instance, a teacher who fails to take advantage of a reasonable opportunity to remove personal items from the classroom may lose all expectation of privacy in the contents of the classroom (*Id.*).

A public employer did not conduct an unlawful search when it audited an employee's government-issued pager to determine whether text messages on it were within the limit under the plan with an outside vendor and, if there were overages, whether they were attributed to personal text messages (*City of Ontario, California v. Quon*, 560 U.S. 746 (2010)). According to the U.S. Supreme Court, the employer had a reasonable work-related purpose and reviewing message transcripts was an efficient and expedient way to identify the cause of the overages. In addition, the search was not overly intrusive because the audit covered only a two-month period of usage, and messages sent while off duty were redacted.

42:12. Are there any restrictions on the ability of school officials to use video surveillance in a school employee's work area?

Yes. A school district may not video record any employee in a restroom, locker room, or room it designates for employees to change their clothes, unless authorized by court order. A violation of this prohibition may result in an award of damages and attorneys' fees and costs to an employee (Lab. Law § 203-c)).

Furthermore, as a general rule, videotape surveillance for monitoring and investigating employees is mandatorily negotiable because it bears directly and significantly on working conditions, requires employees to be participants in it, and intrudes on employees' interests such as job security, privacy, and reputation (*Matter of CSEA Local 1000, AFSCME, AFL-CIO and Nanuet UFSD*, 45 PERB ¶ 3007 (2012)).

Where videotape surveillance is not "integral" to the employer's core mission, the interests of the employer and employee must be balanced to determine if videotaping significantly or unnecessarily intrudes on employees' protected interests. Such balancing must consider the scope and length of videotaping, and the availability of images to third parties (*Id.*). For example, in *Matter of Custodian Ass'n of Elmont and Elmont UFSD*, 28 PERB ¶ 4693 (1995), an administrative law judge for the NYS Public Employment Relations Board (PERB) ruled that video footage of a school bus driver on her route over the course of two days to investigate parental complaints about unsafe driving was not mandatorily negotiable. To hold otherwise would "interfere with an employer's ability to inquire into employee conduct and frustrate investigatory activity, which is an essential aspect of managerial prerogative and which overrides the duty to negotiate." In contrast, the PERB board determined in *Matter of CSEA Local 1000,* 45 PERB ¶ 3007 (2012), that using a hidden camera to investigate an employee's job performance over the course of six months was far broader and more intrusive upon employee interests. Moreover, without deciding whether the use of video surveillance violated the Taylor Law, PERB said the union was not precluded from requesting impact negotiations concerning the issue (*Id.*).

42:13. May school officials place a GPS device on an employee's personal vehicle to track the employee's movements during the work day?

Yes. The placement of a GPS device on an employee's personal vehicle constitutes a search within the meaning of both the federal and state constitutions (*United States v. Jones*, 132 S.Ct. 945 (2012);

People v. Weaver, 12 N.Y.3d 433 (2009)), but a GPS search may occur in the absence of a warrant as part of an investigation of employee misconduct under the "workplace exception" (*Cunningham v. N.Y. State Dep't of Labor*, 21 N.Y.3d 515 (2013)). According to the court, the location of an employee's car used during working hours is not any more private than personal photographs on a desk (*Id.*).

School officials must however, ensure that the scope of the search using the GPS device is reasonable (see **42:11**). A search will not be deemed reasonable if there is no effort to avoid tracking an employee outside of business hours and all evidence gathered pursuant to such a search may be suppressed at a disciplinary hearing. Such was the case where the State Inspector General in the course of an investigation for time and attendance fraud, tracked a labor department employee's vehicle at all times for an entire month, including a period when the employee was on vacation (*Cunningham v. N.Y. State Dep't of Labor*).

43. Employee Statutory Leave Rights

Editor's Note: The acronym FMLA used throughout this chapter refers to the federal Family and Medical Leave Act. The acronym USERRA refers to the federal Uniformed Services Employment and Reemployment Rights Act.

Family and Medical Leave

Editor's Note: Fact Sheets *and* Administrator's Interpretations *cited throughout this section were issued by the U.S. Department of Labor, Wage and Hour Division.*

43:1. What is the Family and Medical Leave Act?

The *Family and Medical Leave Act* (FMLA) is a federal law that requires school districts, and other covered employers (see 29 USC §§ 2611(4)(A), 2618(a)(1); 29 CFR §§ 825.104(a), see also 20 USC § 7801, Fact Sheet #28 (Dec. 2012), at http://www.dol.gov/whd/regs/compliance/whdfs28.pdf) to provide up to 12 weeks of unpaid leave to eligible employees for medical or child-care purposes (see **43:2-3**) during a designated 12-month period (see 29 USC § 2612(a)(1), (c), (d)(1)). The 12-week period also applies to qualifying exigency leave (29 USC § 2612(a)(1)(E); 29 CFR § 825.126); see **43:4**).

FMLA leave may be taken in periods of whole weeks, single days, hours or less than an hour in certain situations. The district must allow employees to use FMLA leave in the smallest increment of time the district allows for the use of other forms of leave (29 CFR § 825.205(a)(1); *Fact Sheet #28I* (Feb. 2013), at: http://www.dol.gov/whd/regs/compliance/whdfs28i.pdf).

The 12-month period during which the 12 weeks of leave may be taken is measured either against the calendar year, any fixed 12-month "leave year" (such as a fiscal year), or a rolling 12-month period measured either forward from the date of an employee's first FMLA leave or backwards from the date an employee uses FMLA leave (29 CFR § 825.200(b); see also *Fact Sheet #28H* (Feb. 2013), at: http://www.dol.gov/whd/regs/compliance/whdfs28h.pdf). Failure by a district to select any one of these methods allows employees to use the most beneficial method for them until the district designates the appropriate measure (see 29 CFR § 825.200(e)).

In addition, eligible employees are entitled to up to 26 weeks of military caregiver leave during a single 12-month period (29 USC § 2612(a)(3); 29 CFR § 825.127(e); see **43:5**). That 12-month period encompasses the 12 work weeks of FMLA leave otherwise available for medical, child care, and/or qualifying exigency leave. School districts must determine the single 12 month period during which the 26 weeks leave may be taken by measuring forward from the date an employee's first FMLA leave to care for the covered service member begins (29 CFR §§ 825.127(e)(1), 825.200(f)).

Absences of one or more weeks when school is closed and employees are not expected to report to work do not count against FMLA leave entitlements. However, when a particular holiday falls during a week taken as FMLA leave, the entire week is counted as FMLA leave (see 29 CFR § 825.200(h); see also *Fact Sheet #28I* (Feb. 2013), at: http://www.dol.gov/whd/regs/compliance/whdfs28i.pdf).

43:2. For what purposes may an employee take family leave?

Family leave is available for the birth and care of an infant, adoption and care of a child, and the placement with the employee of a child in foster care (29 USC § 2612(a)(1)(A), (B); 29 CFR § 825.112(a)(1), (2)). An employee may only take family leave during the 12-month period beginning with the date of birth or placement of a child (29 USC § 2612(a)(2); 29 CFR §§ 825.120(a)(2), 825.121(a)(2)).

43:3. When is an employee entitled to take medical leave?

Medical leave is available to an employee who has a serious health condition that prevents the employee from performing his or her job or to care for a spouse, dependent child, or parent who has a serious health condition (29 USC §§ 2611(7), (11)-(13), 2612(a)(1)(C), (D); 29 CFR §§ 825.112(a)(3), (4), 825.113(a), (b)). A *serious health condition* is defined generally by FMLA as "an illness, injury, impairment, or physical or mental condition" that involves hospitalization or other inpatient care or continuing treatment by a health care provider (29 USC § 2611(11)), and in more detail in FMLA's implementing regulations (see 29 CFR §§ 825.113(c), (d), 825.114, 825.115, 825.600). A *spouse* includes a husband or wife as defined or recognized under state law for purposes of marriage in the state where the employee was married, including "common law" marriage and same sex marriage. Additionally, spouse includes individuals in marriages that were lawfully entered into outside the United States provided the marriage could have been entered into in at least one state (29 CFR §§825.102, 825.122(b); *Fact Sheet #28F* (July 2015), at: http://www.dol.gov/whd/regs/compliance/whdfs28f.pdf).

Medical leave may also be taken for a child age 18 or over who is incapable of self-care due to a physical or mental disability (29 USC §§ 2611(12)(b), 2612(a)(1)(C); 29 CFR §§ 825.112(a)(3), 825.113, 825.122). An employee may only take leave to care for an adult child when four conditions are met: the child has a disability as defined by the Americans with Disabilities Act, is incapable of self-care due to that disability, has a serious health condition and is in need of care due to the serious health condition (29 CFR § 825.122(d); *Administrator's Interpretation No. 2013-1*, (Jan. 14, 2013) at: http://www.dol.gov/WHD/opinion/adminIntrprtn/FMLA/2013/FMLAAI2013_1.pdf). An individual's disability may simultaneously comprise a serious health condition (*Administrator's Interpretation No. 2013-1*). A person is incapable of self-care if the individual requires active assistance or supervision to provide daily self-care in three or more "activities of daily living" (grooming, hygiene, eating, etc) or instrumental activities of daily living (cooking, cleaning, shopping, etc.) (29 CFR § 825.122(d)(1), *Administrator's Interpretation No. 2013-1*, see also *Fact Sheet #28K* (Jan. 2013), at: http://www.dol.gov/whd/regs/compliance/whdfs28k.pdf).

43:4. When may an employee take qualifying exigency leave?

Qualifying exigency leave is available when an employee's spouse, son or daughter of any age, or parent is on, or has been notified of an impending call to covered active duty in the United States Armed Forces (29 USC § 2612(a)(1)(E); 29 CFR § 825.126). What constitutes covered active duty depends on whether the service member is a member of the regular Armed Forces, national guard or reserve components of the Armed Forces (29 USC § 2611(14), (15); 29 CFR § 825.126). Qualifying exigencies can include short-notice deployment, military events and related activities, childcare and school activities, financial and legal arrangements, counseling, rest and recuperation, post-deployment activities, care of the military member's parent and additional activities related to the service member's duty or call to active duty status, provided the district and the employee agree the leave qualifies as an exigency (29 CFR § 825.126(b); see also *Fact Sheet #28M(c)*, (Feb. 2013) at: http://www.dol.gov/whd/regs/compliance/whdfs28mc.pdf).

Editor's Note: New York's Labor Law also entitles an employee whose spouse is in the U.S. Armed Forces, national guard or reserves and is deployed to a combat theater or combat zone of operations during a period of military conflict to up to 10 days unpaid leave when his or her spouse is on leave from the Armed Forces. (Lab. Law § 202-i). Leave under the state's Labor Law is independent of any applicable FMLA leave.

43:5. When is an employee entitled to take military care giver leave?

Military caregiver leave is available to care for a spouse, parent, son or daughter, or next of kin who is a covered service member and incurred a serious injury or illness "in line of duty on active duty in the Armed Forces that may render the member medically unfit to perform the duties of the member's office, grade, rank, or rating (29 USC §§ 2611(15)(a), 2612(a)(3), (4); 29 CFR §§ 825.122(a)(1), 825.127), or a veteran discharged under conditions other than dishonorable who served at any time during the five-year period preceding the date on which he or she undergoes medical treatment, recuperation or therapy for a serious injury or illness (29 USC § 2611(15)(B); 29 CFR §§ 825.122(a)(2), 825.127(a)). A serious injury or illness for a veteran includes a continuation of a serious injury or illness incurred or aggravated when the veteran was a member of the armed forces, a physical or mental condition for which the veteran received a U.S. Department of Veterans Affairs Service Related Disability Rating of 50% or more, a physical or mental condition that substantially impairs the veteran's ability to work because of a disability related to military service or an injury that is the basis for enrollment in the Department of Veterans Affair Program of Comprehensive Assistance for Family Caregivers (29 CFR § 825.127(c)(2)).

43:6. May an employee take FMLA covered leave on the basis of an in *loco parentis* relationship?

Only for purposes of both family and medical leave, a child also includes one to whom the employee stands in *loco parentis* (29 USC § 2611(12); 29 CFR § 825.122(c)), which refers to a person who takes on the role of a parent by assuming and discharging the obligations of a parent to care for a child on a day-to-day basis (*Administrator's Interpretation No. 2010-3* (June 22, 2010), at: http://www.dol.gov/WHD/opinion/adminIntrprtn/FMLA/2010/FMLAAI2010_3.pdf; and *Fact Sheet #28B* (July 2015) at: http://www.dol.gov/whd/regs/compliance/whdfs28B.pdf). The existence of such a relationship must be determined based on the specific facts of each situation. *Loco parentis* employees may include grandparents and other relatives, as well as someone co-parenting with a same-sex partner (*Id.*).

Similarly, an employee may be entitled to medical leave to care for someone who stood in *loco parentis* to the employee when the employee was a child (*Fact Sheet #28C* (July 2015), at: http://www.dol.gov/whd/regs/compliance/whdfs28C.pdf).

43:7. What makes a *school district* employee eligible for FMLA leave?

A school district employee is eligible under the law to take family and medical leave if he or she has been employed for at least 12 months and has worked at least 1,250 hours in the 12 months immediately preceding commencement of leave and is employed at a worksite where at least 50 employees are employed within 75 miles (see 29 USC § 2611(2)(A), (B)(ii); 29 CFR § 825.110(a), 825.600(a), (b); *Smith v. Westchester Cnty.*, 769 F.Supp.2d 448 (S.D.N.Y. 2011)). Therefore, employees of a rural or small school district who do not employ at least 50 people in a 75 mile radius from a particular worksite will not be eligible to take leave under the FMLA.

Under certain circumstances set out in the FMLA regulations, however, the required 12 months of employment need not necessarily be continuous (29 CFR § 825.110(b)). When issues arise, employers have the burden of establishing that an employee does not meet the eligibility criteria for FMLA leave

(*Donnelly v. Greenburgh CSD No.7*, 691 F.3d 134 (2d Cir. 2012)). The determination as to whether the employee meets the hours of service requirement and has been employed for at least 12 months must be made from the date leave is to start (29 CFR § 825.110(d); *Brown v. Omega Moulding Co.*, 2014 U.S. Dist. LEXIS 126324 (E.D.N.Y. Sept. 9, 2014)).

43:8. Are there any special rules that apply to the use of FMLA leave if spouses work for the same employer?

Yes. Spouses who work for the same employer are limited to a combined total of 12 workweeks of leave in a 12 month period for the following FMLA qualifying reasons:

- The birth of a child and bonding with the newborn child;
- The placement of a child with the employee for adoption or foster care and bonding with the newly-placed child; and
- The care of a parent with a serious health condition (29 USC § 2612(f)(1); 29 CFR §§ 825.121(a)(3), 825.201(b); see Fact Sheet #28L (July 2015), at: http://www.dol.gov/whd/regs/compliance/whdfs28l.pdf).

Similarly, eligible spouses who work for the same employer are also limited to a combined total of 26 workweeks of leave in a single 12 month period to provide military caregiver leave (29 USC § 2612(f)(2); 29 CFR § 825.127(f); see Fact Sheet #28L; see **43:5**).

This combined limitation does not apply to leave for the care of a spouse or child with a serious health condition, the employee's own serious health condition and any qualifying exigency arising out of the fact that the employee's spouse, son, daughter or parent is a military member on covered active duty (29 CFR §§ 825.121(a)(3), 825.127(f), 825.201(b); see Fact Sheet #28L; see **43:2-4**). As such, if married employees both use 6 weeks of combined leave after birth of a child (for a total of 12 weeks combined leave), each employee would be able to take another six weeks of leave for reasons not subject to the combined limitation (for example, his or her own serious health condition).

43:9. May employees take FMLA leave on an intermittent basis?

It depends. Employees may take intermittent leave for family leaves only if the school district agrees to permit intermittent leave. Otherwise, they are not entitled to intermittent family leave (29 USC § 2612(b)(1); 29 CFR §§ 825.202(a), (c), 825.203; *Kim v. Goldberg, Weprin, Finkel, Goldstein, LLP*, 862 F.Supp.2d 311 (S.D.N.Y. 2012)). Exceptions to the need for the school district's agreement for intermittent leave include an expectant mother's serious health condition in connection with birth of her child or if a newborn child has a serious health condition (29 CFR § 825.202(c)).

Unlike family leave, medical leave may be taken on an intermittent basis when "medically necessary" (29 USC § 2612(b)(1); 29 CFR §§ 825.202(b), 825.203, 825.302(f)). The district may temporarily transfer the employee to a position with equal pay and benefits if the intermittent leave is foreseeable and the position better accommodates recurring periods of leave (29 USC § 2612(b)(2); 29 CFR § 825.204). Additionally, for instructional employees whose absences due to foreseeable medical treatment will exceed 20 percent of the working days of the period over which that leave will occur, the district can require the employee either to take a block leave (take the time all at once) or accept a temporary transfer to another position with equal pay and benefits which better accommodates recurring periods of leave and for which the employee is qualified (29 USC § 2618(c); 29 CFR § 825.601).

Qualifying exigency leave may be taken on an intermittent or reduced leave schedule subject to notice and district certification requirements set forth in the law (29 USC §§ 2612(b)(1), (e)(3), 2613(f); 29 CFR §§ 825.202(d), 825.309; see **43:11**).

Military caregiver leave may be taken on an intermittent or reduced leave schedule when "medically necessary" (29 USC § 2612(b)(1)).

In addition, special rules affect the ability of instructional employees to take intermittent leave (as well as leave near the end of a semester). These rules apply to teachers but not to teaching assistants or aides whose principal job is not actually to teach, or to other personnel such as counselors, psychologists and curriculum specialists (29 USC § 2618(c), (d); 29 CFR §§ 825.600(b), (c), 825.601-603).

43:10. Must employees provide school districts notice of their intent to take FMLA leave?

Yes. As a general rule, when leave is foreseeable, employees must give their employer 30 days notice of their intent to take family, medical, or military caregiver leave (see **43:2-5**) under FMLA (29 USC § 2612(e); 29 CFR § 825.302(a), (e)). However, when such leave is not foreseeable and employees must give less than 30 days notice, they must do so as soon as practicable (29 USC § 2612(e); 29 CFR §§ 825.302(b), 825.303(a); see also *Millea v. Metro-North Railroad Co.*, 658 F.3d 154 (2d Cir. 2011); *Golden v. N.Y. City Dep't of Envtl. Prot.*, 354 Fed. Appx. 577 (2d Cir. 2009); *Nally v. New York*, 2013 U.S. Dist. LEXIS 75722 (N.D.N.Y. May 30, 2013)). When leave is due to a qualifying exigency (see **43:4**), employees must provide notice of their intent to take such leave as soon as practicable (29 USC § 2612(e)(3); 29 CFR § 825.302(a)).

In addition, when leave is foreseeable, employees must provide at least verbal notice sufficient to make the employer aware that the employee needs FMLA leave, and the anticipated timing and duration of the leave (29 CFR § 825.302(d); see also *Fact Sheet #28E* (Feb. 2013), at: http://www.dol.gov/whd/regs/compliance/whdfs28e.pdf). To comply with the as soon as practicable notice requirement applicable to unforeseeable FMLA leave, employees must give such notice either the same day or next business day, taking into account the particular facts and circumstances involved. They must give notice within the time prescribed by the district's usual requirements for taking leave (29 CFR § 825.303(a)-(c)). Notice content requirements apply that are similar to those applicable in a foreseeable leave situation, including the need to provide at least sufficient information for the district to determine if the leave is FMLA-qualifying (29 CFR § 825.303(b)). If an employee is unable to give notice his or her spokesperson may do so (29 CFR § 825.303(a)).

Although an employer "is not required to be clairvoyant," (*Slaughter v. American Building Maint. Co.*, 64 F.Supp.2d 319 (S.D.N.Y. 1999)), the particular circumstances of a situation may be sufficient to put the employer on notice of an employee's need for FMLA leave without the employee having to request FMLA leave by name (see *Debell v. Maimonides Medical Ctr.*, 2011 U.S. Dist. LEXIS 115094 (E.D.N.Y. Sept. 30, 2011); *Tambash v. St. Bonaventure Univ.*, 2004 U.S. Dist. LEXIS 19914 (W.D.N.Y. Sept. 24, 2004)). Furthermore, employers unable to make such a determination have an obligation to ask the employee for any needed additional information (29 CFR §§ 825.301(a), 825.302(c); *Debell v. Maimonides Medical Ctr.*; *Tambash v. St. Bonaventure Univ.*; *Cinelli v. Oppenheim-Ephratah CSD*, 2009 U.S. Dist. LEXIS 111766 (N.D.N.Y. Dec. 1, 2009)). Employee failure to provide such information may result in denial or delay of FMLA protection if the district cannot determine if the leave is FMLA-qualifying (29 CFR §§ 825.302(c), (d), 825.304).

School districts may require that employees comply with normal requirements for leave requests (29 CFR § 825.302(d)). However, such leave request policies must be consistent with, and may not impose requirements that are more stringent than, the FMLA. That was the case where an employer's internal leave policy required employees to notify their supervisor directly when taking FMLA leave even though the FMLA itself excuses direct notification when FMLA leave is unforeseen (*Millea v. Metro-North Railroad Co.*).

43:11. Can a school district require that employees requesting medical leave, military caregiver leave, or qualifying exigency leave provide certification in support of their request for such leave?

Yes. School districts may require that, in support of a request for medical leave (see **43:3**), an employee's or family member's health provider complete a certification specifying the date when the serious health condition commenced, the probable duration of the condition, a statement that the employee is needed to care for the family member, or other information authorized by law (29 USC § 2613(a), (b); 29 CFR §§ 825.305-310, see also *Fact Sheet #28G* (Feb. 2013), at: http://www.dol.gov/whd/regs/compliance/whdfs28g.pdf). Districts also may require subsequent re-certifications on a reasonable basis (29 USC § 2613(e); 29 CFR § 825.308).

Districts that doubt the validity of a certification submitted in support of a request for medical leave may obtain a second opinion from a health care provider designated by them for this purpose, at their expense (29 USC § 2613(c); 29 CFR § 825.307(b)). If the second doctor renders a conflicting opinion to the original medical opinion, the school district may at its own expense obtain the opinion of a third health care provider mutually agreed upon by the district and the employee. This opinion is final and binding (29 USC § 2613(d); 29 CFR § 825.307(c)).

Districts may require that employees seeking qualifying exigency leave or military caregiver leave (see **43:4-5**) submit certifications that conform to regulations promulgated by the U.S. Secretary of Labor (29 USC § 2613(f); 29 CFR §§ 825.309, 825.310; see also *Fact Sheet #28M(c)* (Feb. 2013), at: http://www.dol.gov/whd/regs/compliance/whdfs28mc.pdf).

Employees that fail to provide certification or a necessary recertification in a timely manner may have FMLA leave denied until the required certification is provided (29 CFR § 825.313; *Porter v. Donahoe*, 484 Fed. Appx. 589 (2d Cir. 2012); *Washington v. Acorda Therapeutics, Inc.*, 2014 U.S. Dist. LEXIS 129595 (S.D.N.Y. Aug. 28, 2014)).

43:12. Can a school district require employees returning from leave taken for a serious health condition or injury to provide a fitness for duty certification?

A school district may have a policy or practice that requires all similarly situated employees (same occupation, same serious health condition) returning from leave taken for a serious health condition or injury to provide a fitness for duty certification from his or her health care provider that the employee is able to perform the essential functions of his or her job (29 USC § 2614(a)(4); 29 CFR § 825.312(a); *Nichik v. N.Y. City Transit Auth.*, 2013 U.S. Dist. LEXIS 4692 (E.D.N.Y. Jan. 11, 2013) see also *Fact Sheet #28G* (Feb. 2013), at: http://www.dol.gov/whd/regs/compliance/whdfs28g.pdf). A request for a fitness for duty certification including the list of essential functions must be requested by the district at the time the leave is designated as FMLA leave (29 CFR § 825.312(b); *Powell v. Metro One Loss Prevention Servs. Group (Guard Division NY) Inc.*, 2013 U.S. Dist. LEXIS 111601 (S.D.N.Y. July 26, 2013)). An employer may only delay or deny reinstatement for failure to provide a fitness for duty certification if the employer requested such certification when it designated the leave as FMLA leave (*Id.*). An employee who fails to provide such certification is no longer entitled to reinstatement under the FMLA and may be terminated (29 CFR §§ 825.312(e), 825.313(d); *Nichik v. N.Y. City Transit Auth.*).

43:13. Can a school district require an employee to use accrued paid leave time under a collective bargaining agreement rather than take an unpaid FMLA leave?

Yes. Unless otherwise agreed to in a collective bargaining agreement, an employee may choose or a school district may require an employee to use accrued paid vacation, personal or family leave for purposes of a family leave, a medical leave to care for a spouse, dependent child, or parent with a serious health condition, or qualifying exigency leave (29 USC § 2612(d)(2)(A); 29 CFR § 825.207(a)). If the school district requires use of paid leave, it must inform the employee of same at the time the leave is designated as FMLA leave (29 CFR §§ 825.300(d), 825.207; see *Smith v. Westchester Cnty.*, 769 F.Supp.2d 448 (S.D.N.Y. 2011)). However, although leave under a disability plan may count as FMLA leave, paid leave may not be substituted if the employee is receiving workers' compensation (see 29 CFR § 825.207(d), (e)). Similarly, an employee may choose or a school district may require substitution of accrued paid vacation, personal, family, or medical/sick leave for any part of the 26 weeks an employee may take for military caregiver leave (29 USC § 2612(d)(2)(B)).

In addition, an employee may choose or a district can require an employee to use accrued paid vacation, personal, or medical/sick leave for purposes of his or her own medical leave (29 USC § 2612(d)(2)(B); 29 CFR § 825.207(a)).

Furthermore, under FMLA, an employee cannot use accrued family or sick leave when he or she would not otherwise be able to use such leave under the terms of a collective bargaining agreement or board policy (see 29 USC § 2612(d)(2)(B); 29 CFR § 825.207(b), (c)).

43:14. Is an employee entitled to their regular health benefits during a period of FMLA leave?

Although the family and medical leave is generally unpaid (see 29 USC § 2612(c), (d); 29 CFR § 825.207(a); see **43:13**), school districts must continue normal health insurance benefits during the leave except as otherwise provided by law and regulations, such as when the employee fails to return after his or her leave has ended (see 29 USC § 2614(c)(1); 29 CFR § 825.209).

If an employee regularly makes a contribution for any health plan premiums he or she must continue to do so during the period of FMLA leave (29 CFR § 825.210(a)). The district must provide the employee with written notice of the terms and conditions under which these payments must be made (29 CFR §§ 825.210(d); 825.300(c)(1)(iv); *Rodriguez v. Atria Sr. Living Group, Inc.* 887 F.Supp.2d 503 (S.D.N.Y. 2012)). If FMLA leave is substituted paid leave, the employee's share of premiums must be paid by the usual method used during paid leave (i.e. payroll deduction). But if not substituted paid leave, the employee must make payments as required by the regulations (29 CFR § 825.210(b), (c); *Rodriguez v. Atria Sr. Living Group, Inc.*).

43:15. Do employees who take FMLA leave have the right to return to their job after the leave is over?

Yes. At the end of the leave, the employee is entitled to return to the position he or she held when the leave commenced or to an equivalent position (see 29 USC § 2614(a)(1); 29 CFR §§ 825.214, 825.215). For school district employees, the determination of how an employee will be restored to an equivalent position must be made on the basis of established school board policies and practices and any applicable collective bargaining agreement (29 USC § 2618(e); 29 CFR § 825.604). For example, school districts are free under the law to assign a returning elementary teacher to a different grade from the class he or she taught prior to the leave consistent with any applicable district policy or collective bargaining agreement.

Generally, districts may not require employees to take more FMLA leave than necessary, and employees may return to work earlier than anticipated (29 CFR § 825.311(c)). However, special limitations apply with respect to instructional employees returning from leave near the conclusion of an academic term (see 29 USC § 2618(d); 29 CFR § 825.602). Depending on the duration of the leave and the length of time remaining until the end of the school term, the district can require the employee to wait until the next term to return. The additional time is not counted as FMLA leave (see 29 CFR § 825.603(b)).

An employee does not lose any previously accrued employment benefits as a result of the leave. He or she may, but is not entitled to, accrue seniority or additional benefits for the period of the leave (29 USC § 2614(a)(2), (3); 29 CFR § 825.215(d)(2); see *DeOliveira v. Cairo-Durham CSD,* 2014 U.S. Dist. LEXIS 137593 (N.D.N.Y. Sept. 30, 2014), *aff'd in part,* 634 Fed. Appx. 320 (2d Cir. 2016)).

How an instructional employee is restored to an equivalent position must be made on the basis of established school policies and procedures and collective bargaining agreements (29 CFR § 825.604). Districts have a duty to inform instructional employees in writing of any provisions relevant to restoration to the same or equivalent position prior to such employee taking leave (29 CFR §§ 825.300(c)(1)(vi), 825.604; see *DeOliveira v. Cairo-Durham CSD,* 634 Fed. Appx. 320 (2d Cir. 2016); see **43:16**).

43:16. Are school districts required to give employees notice of their rights under FMLA?

Yes. All school districts, regardless of the number of people they employ, are required to post general notices on FMLA (29 USC § 2619; 29 CFR § 825.300(a); see *LeClair v. Berkshire UFSD,* 2010 U.S. Dist. LEXIS 114835 (N.D.N.Y. Oct. 28, 2010)). Electronic postings are permitted, as long as they meet the requirements for paper notices (29 CFR § 825.300(a)). School districts that have employees who are eligible for FMLA leave must include information on FMLA in any handbook that provides information on employee benefits (29 CFR § 825.300(a)(3)). In addition to posting general notices, school districts must provide specific notices to employees as set forth in law. Failure to provide required notices may constitute an unlawful interference with an employee's FMLA rights (29 CFR §§ 825.300(e); see also *DeOliveira v. Cairo-Durham CSD,* 2014 U.S. Dist. LEXIS 137593 (N.D.N.Y. Sept. 30, 2014), *aff'd in part,* 634 Fed. Appx. 320 (2d Cir. 2016)).

Eligibility Notice

Districts must provide an eligibility notice within five business days, whenever an employee requests a FMLA-qualified leave, whether or not the employee actually requests FMLA leave, (29 CFR § 825.300(b)(1)). If an employee is not eligible for FMLA leave the notice must state at least one reason why the employee is not eligible. The eligibility notice may be oral or in writing (29 CFR § 825.300(b)(2)).

Rights and Responsibilities Notice

Districts also must provide a written rights and responsibilities notice, detailing specific expectations and obligations of the employee and explaining any consequences for failure to meet these obligations as set forth in the law, each time it distributes an eligibility notice (29 CFR § 825.300(c)). The notice must also include information regarding an employee's restoration rights to a same or equivalent job, among other items (29 CFR § 825.300(c)(vi); see 29 CFR § 825.604 for special notice to be given to instructional employees regarding restoration rights; see also *DeOliveira v. Cairo-Durham CSD,* 634 Fed. Appx. 320 (2d Cir. 2016); see **43:15**).

Designation Notice

Within five business days of designating leave as FMLA leave, the district must notify the employee, in writing, of such designation (29 CFR §§ 825.300(d), 825.301).The notice must include information regarding the substitution of paid leave and/or fitness for duty requirements, as well as the amount of leave counted against the employee's FMLA entitlement (if known) (29 CFR § 825.300(d)(1), (3); see also *Fact Sheet #28D* (undated), at: http://www.dol.gov/whd/regs/compliance/whdfs28d.pdf). Sample notices deemed acceptable by the U.S. Department of Labor are available at: www.dol.gov/whd.

43:17. May an employee sue a school district for alleged violations of FMLA?

Yes. An employee may sue a school district in state or federal court, or file a complaint in an administrative proceeding for violations of the law based on the district's alleged interference with his or her FMLA rights, or retaliation for either the employee's exercise of such rights or his or her opposition to unlawful FMLA practices (29 USC § 2617(a)(2), (b)(1); 29 CFR § 825.400(a); see *Millea v. Metro-North Railroad Co.*, 658 F.3d 154 (2d Cir. 2011); *Graziadio v. Culinary Institute of America*, 817 F. 3d 415 (2d Cir. 2016); *Smith v. Westchester Cnty.*, 769 F.Supp.2d 448 (S.D.N.Y. 2011); *Potenza v. City of N.Y.*, 365 F.3d 165 (2d Cir. 2001); *Serby v. N.Y.C. Dep't of Educ.*, 2012 U.S. Dist. LEXIS 36841 (E.D.N.Y. Mar. 19, 2012); *aff'd*, 526 Fed. Appx. 132 (2d Cir. 2013); *Powell v. Dep't of Educ. of the City of New York*, 2015 U.S. Dist. LEXIS 133255 (E.D.N.Y. Sept. 30, 2015); *Matye v. City of New York*, 2015 U.S. Dist. LEXIS 42960 (E.D.N.Y. Mar. 31, 2015)). If the court rules in favor of the employee, that employee may recover wages, salary and benefits, compensation for actual monetary loss (as for example the cost of providing care), job reinstatement or promotion, as well as attorneys' fees and costs (29 USC § 2617(a)(1), (3); 29 CFR § 825.400(c); see *Millea v. Metro-North Railroad Co.*; compare *Coleman v. Court of Appeals of Maryland*, 132 S.Ct. 1327 (2012)).

Claims of FMLA violations must be brought within two years of the date of the last alleged violation. Where an allegation is made of willful violation of FMLA's prohibition on interference with an employee's FMLA rights, the time limit is three years (29 USC § 2617(c); 29 CFR § 825.400(b); see *Riddle v. Citigroup*, 449 Fed. Appx. 66 (2d Cir. 2011)). A violation is willful if an employer knew or recklessly disregarded whether its conduct violated FMLA (*Riddle v. Citigroup; Smith v. Westchester Cnty.*; *Macklin v. American Building Maintenance,* 2016 U.S. Dist. LEXIS 2513 (S.D.N.Y. Jan. 7, 2016)).

Federal appellate courts are divided on the issue of whether public employees may be subjected to individual liability under the FMLA. The U.S. Court of Appeals for the Second Circuit, with jurisdiction over New York, has not addressed the issue. However, two federal district courts in New York have ruled they can if they control, in whole or in part, the FMLA rights of the employees suing them (*Smith v. Westchester Cnty.*; *Corrado v. New York Unified Court System,* 2016 U.S. Dist. LEXIS 19628 (E.D.N.Y. Feb. 16, 2016)).

Employee Rights

43:18. What are the collective bargaining implications of FMLA?

The leave entitlements established by FMLA do not diminish any employee benefits established in a collective bargaining agreement (29 USC § 2652(a)). Thus, if a contract provides greater leave benefits, the provisions of the contract apply.

Conversely, no collective bargaining agreement may diminish the benefits provided by FMLA (29 USC § 2652(b)). Thus, FMLA provides a minimum floor of benefits for all eligible employees, even if a collective bargaining agreement provides lesser benefits.

Any proposal for negotiations on FMLA leave is a mandatory subject of bargaining under the Taylor Law (see *Rome Hosp.*, 27 PERB ¶ 4575 (1994)), even if it duplicates the benefits promised by statute (see generally *City of Cohoes*, 31 PERB ¶ 3020 (1998), *conf'd sub nom. Uniformed Firefighters of Cohoes v. Cuevas*, 32 PERB ¶ 7026 (Sup. Ct. Albany Cnty. 1999), *aff'd,* 276 A.D.2d 184, 33 PERB ¶ 7019 (3d Dep't 2000), *lv. app. denied*, 96 N.Y.2d 711, 34 PERB ¶ 7018 (2001)).

Federal Military Service Leave

Editor's Note: An employee's federal rights to military service leave are governed by the Uniformed Services Employment and Reemployment Rights Act (USERRA). For additional information on USERRA, visit the U.S. Department of Labor's website at: http://www.dol.gov/elaws/userra.htm and http://www.dol.gov/vets/programs/userra/compliance.htm

43:19. Are school district employees entitled to leaves of absence for military service under federal law?

Yes. Under the federal Uniformed Services Employment and Reemployment Rights Act (USERRA), public employees who perform voluntary or involuntary service, whether in time of peace or war, in the uniformed services are entitled to a leave of absence from work for the duration of military duty (38 USC § 4311(a); 20 CFR §§ 1002.6, 1002.18, 1002.149). In addition, such individuals may not be discriminated against on the basis of their military status (38 USC § 4301(a)(3)), including, for example, with respect to reemployment, retention, or other employment benefits (38 USC § 4311(a); 20 CFR §§ 1002.18, 1002.19; see *Straub v. Proctor Hosp.*, 562 U.S. 411 (2011); *Hunt v. Klein,* 476 Fed. Appx. 889 (2d Cir. 2012); *Mock v. City of Rome*, 851 F.Supp.2d 428 (N.D.N.Y. 2012)). No state law or collective bargaining agreement or school board policy may reduce or limit an employee's rights in this regard, including establishing additional prerequisites for obtaining military leave (38 USC § 4302(b)).

USERRA is liberally construed to benefit those who leave their private lives to serve their country (*Fishgold v. Sullivan Dry Dock & Repair Co.*, 328 U.S. 275 (1946); *Serricchio v. Wachovia Securities LLC*, 658 F.3d 169 (2d Cir. 2011); *Mock v. City of Rome*).

43:20. What are the uniformed services under USERRA?

The *uniformed services* include the United States Armed Forces, the army national guard and air national guard (when engaged in active duty for training, inactive duty training, or full-time national guard duty); the commissioned corps of the Public Health Service and any other service designated by the President in time of war or national emergency (38 USC § 4303(13), (16); 20 CFR § 1002.5(o)).

43:21. Are school district employees on military service leave entitled to reinstatement upon completion of such service under USERRA?

Yes. USERRA protects the reemployment rights of public employees who voluntarily or involuntarily leave employment to undertake military service (38 USC §§ 4312(a), (c), 4316(b); 20 CFR §§ 1002.32, 1002.34(a), 1002.39; see *Serriccio v. Wachovia Securities LLC*, 658 F.3d 169 (2d Cir. 2011); *LaPaix v. City of N.Y.*, 2014 U.S. Dist. LEXIS 112265 (S.D.N.Y. 2014)). To be entitled to reemployment, the employee must give advance written or verbal notice of military service to the employer. The cumulative length of the current absence and all previous absences for reasons of military service cannot exceed five years (subject to certain statutory exceptions), the employee must report to or submit an application for reemployment to that employer within the time periods set forth in law, and the employee cannot have received other than honorable discharge from military service (38 USC §§ 4312(a), (e); 20 CFR §§ 1002.32(a), 1002.85-88, 1002.99-103, 1002.115-123). No notice is required if the employee is precluded from doing so by military necessity, or it is otherwise impossible or unreasonable to do so, as determined by the U.S. Secretary of Defense (38 USC § 4312(b); 20 CFR § 1002.86).

In addition, employees are entitled to be reinstated to their former position, as long as they remain qualified for the position, or in a position of like seniority, status and pay as soon as practicable under the circumstances of each case (38 USC § 4313(a); 20 CFR §§ 1002.181, 1002.193-194; *Serricchio v. Wachovia Securities LLC*).

43:22. Are there any circumstances under which USERRA excuses the obligation of school districts to reemploy employees on military service leave?

Yes. Pursuant to USERRA, a school district would not have to reemploy employees on military service leave if circumstances make such reemployment impossible or unreasonable, reemployment would cause an undue hardship on the district, or the original employment was for a brief, non-recurrent period and there was no reasonable expectation that employment would have continued indefinitely (38 USC § 4312(d)(1)).

An aggrieved employee may not file a section 1983 federal civil rights lawsuit to enforce his or her rights (*Morris-Hayes v. Bd. of Educ. of Chester UFSD*, 423 F.3d 153 (2d Cir. 2005), *rev'd on other grounds*, 211 Fed. Appx. 28 (2d Cir. 2007)).

43:23. Does USERRA protect the seniority and other rights and benefits of school district employees on military service leave?

Yes. Employees on military service leave are entitled to the seniority and other rights and benefits determined by seniority that the employee had on the date of commencement of military service, plus additional seniority, rights and benefits the employee would have retained if not for the employee's absence due to military service (38 USC § 4316(a); 20 CFR §§ 1002.193, 1002.236; see *Serricchio v. Wachovia Securities LLC*, 658 F.3d 169 (2d Cir. 2011); *Croft v. Village of Newark*, 35 F.Supp.3d 359 (W.D.N.Y. 2015); Evans *v. MassMutual Financial Group*, 856 F.Supp.2d 606 (W.D.N.Y. 2012)).

43:24. Are school district employees on military service leave entitled to continued health insurance under USERRA?

Yes. Pursuant to USERRA, school district employees on military service leave must be allowed to elect to continue coverage under a health plan, including a group health plan, for the employee and his/her dependents, for maximum periods of time as set forth in the law (38 USC § 4317(a); 20 CFR § 1002.164).

Employees who elect continued coverage cannot be required to pay more than 102% of the full premium under the plan. Those who perform military service for less than 31 days cannot be required to pay more than the employee share, if any, for the health coverage (38 USC § 4317(a)(2)). Special rules apply for multi-employer health plans (38 USC § 4317(a)(3); 20 CFR § 1002.170-171).

43:25. Must school districts provide employees on military service leave notice of their rights under USERRA?

Yes. USERRA requires that all employers give USERRA-eligible employees notice of employer and employee rights, obligations, and benefits under the law (38 USC § 4334(a)).

43:26. May an employee sue a school district for alleged violations of USERRA?

Yes. An employee may sue a school district in federal court, or file a complaint in an administrative proceeding for violations of the law based on the district's alleged discrimination of an employee based upon the employee's obligations to the uniformed services or retaliation for either the employee's exercise of such USERRA rights or his or her opposition to unlawful USERRA practices (38 USC §§ 4322, 4323; 20 CFR §§ 1002.18-1002.20, 1002.277-314). If the court rules in favor of the employee, that employee may be reinstated to his or her job pursuant to the law, recover wages, salary and benefits, as well as attorneys' fees and costs (38 USC § 4323(d), (e), (h); 20 CFR § 1002.312). If the school district's failure to comply with the law is found to be willful the court may require the school district to pay additional liquidated damages to the employee in the amount equal to the lost wages and benefits (38 USC § 4323(d)(1)(C); 20 CFR § 1002.312(c)). A violation will be considered willful if the school district either knew or showed reckless disregard for whether its conduct was prohibited by the Act (20 CFR § 1002.312(c)).

USERRA was amended in 2008 to bar the applicability of any statute of limitations (38 USC § 4327(b); see also *Mock v. City of Rome*, 851 F.Supp.2d 428 (N.D.N.Y. 2012)). Claims that arose prior to October 10, 2008 remained subject to the four year federal statute of limitations (see 28 USC § 1658,

Tully v. County of Nassau, 2012 U.S. Dist. LEXIS 18414 (E.D.N.Y. Feb. 14, 2012); *Goodman v. City of New York*, 161 Lab. Cas. (CCH) P10,413 (S.D.N.Y. Sept. 26, 2011)).

State Military Service Leave

43:27. Are school district employees entitled to leaves of absence for military service under state law?

Yes. Under New York's Military Law, employees on ordered military duty are entitled to, and are deemed to be on, a leave of absence from work while performing such service (Mil. Law §§ 242(2), 243(2)(a), (19)).

Ordered military duty includes any military duty performed for the state or the United States as a member of the organized militia or any reserve force or reserve component of the United States Armed Forces, pursuant to orders issued by the state or federal government (Mil. Law § 242(1)(b)). It also includes attendance at service school, but not participation in routine reserve officer training except when performing advanced training duty as a member of a reserve component of the Armed Forces (*Id.*). A military reservist on non-active status is not entitled to take a leave under Military Law for voluntary attendance at funerals of retired military personnel and veterans because the law only provides leave for ordered military duty (Opn. Att'y Gen. I 2003-7).

For additional information, visit the NYS Civil Service Department's website at: http://www.cs.ny.gov/pio/summaryofcslaw/summofcsl-veterans-rights.cfm.

43:28. Does state law require the reinstatement of school district employees on military service leave upon completion of such service?

Yes. New York's Military Law requires that public employees be returned to their position as soon as possible following their application for reinstatement (Mil. Law §§ 242(4), 243(2)). In addition, reinstated employees are entitled to be paid at the rate they would have received had they remained continuously employed without loss of vacation, holiday, pension, retirement or other benefits (Mil. Law §§ 242(4), (6), 243(4), (5)).

Civil service employees are entitled to protection under the law regarding promotional examinations and placement on eligible lists for appointment to another position (Mil. Law §§ 243(5)-(7-b), 243-b; *Matter of Woods v. N.Y.C. Dep't of Citywide Admin. Srvs.*, 16 N.Y.3d 505 (2011); see also *Mock v. City of Rome,* 910 F.Supp.2d 429 (N.D.N.Y. 2012)).

43:29. Does military service leave constitute paid leave under state law?

Yes. Employees on military service leave are entitled to be paid their usual pay for 30 calendar days, or 22 working days, whichever is greater, per calendar year and in any one continuous period of such absence (Mil. Law §§ 242(5), 243(1)(a), (2)(a), (19); see also Opn. St. Comp. 91-40; Opn. Att'y Gen. F 90-13; but see Mil. Law §§ 242(5-a), 243(20) for different rules applicable to employees in New York City).

43:30. May school districts provide employees on military service leave with paid leaves of absence that exceed the requirements of state law?

Yes, upon passage of a school board resolution. However, such leave must be offered equally to all employees who are similarly situated. In addition, to avoid a gift of public funds violation under Art. VIII, section 1 of the New York State Constitution, the board resolution providing for such additional paid leave must be approved prior to the time such leave is taken. When authorized in advance, such additional paid leave does not constitute a gift, but rather is deemed compensation for employment, the purpose of which is to "induce continued, faithful and competent service" (Opn. St. Comp. I 90-56; see also Gen. Mun. Law § 92(1)).

43:31. Are the rights and benefits of school district employees on military service leave protected under state law?

Yes. All protected service, even if beyond the period of mandated paid leave, is to be treated as regular service with the school district. As such, for example, it is counted as time served towards completion of a probationary period (Mil. Law §§ 242(4), 243(9), (9-a)). However, a teacher's probationary period may be extended under certain circumstances (Mil. Law § 243(9-a)).

In addition, employees on military service leave may not suffer any loss of vacation, holiday, pension or retirement rights, or any other right or privilege or be prejudiced regarding their employment status, including retention, reappointment, reemployment, reinstatement, transfer, or promotion (Mil. Law §§ 242(4), (6), 243(4)).

For additional information on pension and retirement credits for military service, visit the Office of the State Comptroller's website at: http://www.osc.state.ny.us/retire/members/military-service-credit.php.

43:32. Is military service leave subject to collective bargaining under state law?

Yes. Military service leave is a mandatory subject of bargaining under state law (*City of Albany*, 7 PERB ¶ 3078 (1974), *aff'd*, 48 A.D.2d 998 (3d Dep't), *aff'd*, 38 N.Y.2d 778 (1975)), even if the bargaining proposal duplicates the benefits provided by statute (*City of Cohoes*, 31 PERB ¶ 3020 (1998), *aff'd sub nom. Uniform Firefighters of Cohoes, Local 2562 v. Cuevas*, 276 A.D.2d 184 (3d Dep't 2000), *appeal denied*, 96 N.Y.2d 711 (2001)).

Other

43:33. Are school district employees entitled to paid family leave?

It depends. The provisions of New York's paid family leave act are optional for municipalities (Workers' Comp. Law § 212-a). If a school district elects to provide paid family leave it will need to collectively bargain the provision of those benefits for represented employees (Workers' Comp. Law § 212-b(3)(a)). For employees not represented by a union the school district may opt in to paid family leave with 90 days' notice to the employees (Workers' Comp. Law § 212-b(3)(b)).

Family leave will be available to employees to provide care for a family member with a serious health condition, to bond with a child within the first 12 months of birth, adoption or placement or for a qualifying exigency pursuant to the federal Family Medical Leave Act (Workers' Comp. Law § 200(15); see also 29 USC § 2612(a)(1)(e); 29 CFR § 825.126(a); see **43:4** regarding qualifying exigency leave). The leave must be used concurrently with an employee's federal family medical leave (Workers' Comp. Law § 205(2)(c)).

Benefits begin in 2018 and phase in through 2021. Initially employees will be entitled to eight weeks paid leave at 50% of his or her weekly wage, not to exceed the state-wide average weekly wage and will culminate in 12 weeks paid leave at 67% of an employee's weekly wage, not to exceed the state-wide average (Workers' Comp. Law § 204(2)(a)). An employee may elect to substitute vacation or personal leave for part of the family leave and receive his or her full salary or the employee can receive the benefit as defined by law (Workers' Comp. Law § 205(2)(c)).

43:34. Are school district employees who serve as volunteers in disaster relief operations entitled to paid leave?

Yes. All public officers and employees who work for a school district and who are certified by the American Red Cross as disaster volunteers may be granted a leave of absence from work of up to 20 days per year, with pay, to participate in specialized disaster relief operations, upon written request from the American Red Cross, and upon approval of the school superintendent. Upon such approval, the officer or employee is entitled to compensation at his or her regular rate of pay during those work hours that the volunteer participates in authorized disaster relief operations. Moreover, no such volunteer shall lose seniority, sick leave, vacation, or overtime compensation to which he or she is otherwise entitled during the period of approved leave (Gen. Mun. Law § 92-c).

43:35. Are school district employees entitled to leave for breast and prostate cancer screening?

Yes. Employees of school districts and boards of cooperative educational services are entitled to take up to four hours leave annually to undertake screenings for breast and prostate cancer. This leave will not be charged against any other accumulated leave of the employee (Civ. Serv. Law §§ 159-b, 159-c).

Leave taken for breast and prostate cancer screening is paid leave (Civ. Serv. Law §§ 159-b(1), 159-c(1)).

43:36. Are school district employees entitled to leave in order to donate blood?

Yes. Any employee who works an average of 20 or more hours per week is entitled to three hours of unpaid leave each year to donate blood off premises. However, an employer may choose to offer an alternative blood donation opportunity such as hosting a blood drive on campus or designating a convenient time and place for blood donation at least two times per year.

An alternative blood donation option must be offered during regular working hours, and employees who participate must be given sufficient time to donate blood and partake of nourishment to recover after the donation.

Leave for blood donation under an employer's alternative option is paid and may not require an employee to utilize any accrued paid leave (Labor Law § 202-j; see also NYS Department of Labor Guidelines at: https://www.labor.ny.gov/formsdocs/wp/LS703.pdf).

43:37. Are school district employees entitled to leave in order to vote?

Yes. Registered voters with insufficient time outside of work hours to vote in any election, may take up to two hours of paid leave if such time, when added to their non-working time, is necessary to enable them to vote (Elec. Law § 3-110(1)). Employees are deemed to have sufficient time outside of work to vote if they have four consecutive hours between the opening of polls and the beginning of a shift, or between the closing of polls and the end of a shift, when they are not required to be at work (Elec. Law § 3-110(2)).

Employees who request working time off to vote must notify their employer between two and 10 days prior to the day of the election (Elec. Law § 3-110(3)).

Employers, including school districts, must post a notice informing employees of their right to leave in order to vote not less than 10 working days before an election, and until polls close on election day (Elec. Law § 3-110(4)).

43:38. Are school district employees entitled to leave to serve on a jury?

Yes. Employers, including school districts, must grant employees leave for jury duty (Jud. Law § 519). However, employees denied such leave do not have a right to sue their employer (*Matter of*

Arnold v. N.Y.S. Div. of Human Rights, 70 A.D.3d 605 (1st Dep't 2010); *In re Eigner,* 39 Misc.3d 1214 (Bronx Cnty. 2013)).

Employers, with 10 or more employees may withhold the employee's normal wages. Such employers are required to pay the employee only $40 (the daily jury service pay), or the employee's wage, whichever is less, each day for the first three days of jury duty (Jud. Law § 519). After three days, New York State pays the employee's jury service pay until service is complete unless the employer voluntarily provides such pay. Nonetheless, collective bargaining agreements may require an employer to provide employees with full pay service as a juror. Procedures for taking jury duty leave are mandatorily negotiable under the Civil Service Law (*Matter of County of Ulster*, 16 PERB ¶ 4646 (1983)).

Employers may not charge employees on jury duty with vacation, personal, sick or any other accumulated paid leave. Employers are encouraged, but not required, to provide employees on jury duty with their full daily wage.

For more information, see NYS Unified Court System, *Jury Information for Employers* at: http://www.nyjuror.gov/pdfs/hb_EE.pdf or call 1-800-NY-JUROR.

43:39. May school district employees take leave to fight Ebola overseas?

Through December 1, 2018, healthcare professionals, including but not limited to physicians, physicians assistants, nurse practitioners, and registered professional nurses who work for school districts may request an unpaid leave of absence to serve as a healthcare professional in a country classified as having widespread transmission of the Ebola virus (Lab. Law § 202-m(3), (4)). An employer does not have to grant such a request if the employee's absence would create an undue hardship requiring significant expense or difficulty, including the safe or efficient operation of the workplace or a violation of a bona fide seniority system (Lab. Law § 202-a(3)(f), (4)). Employees seeking such leave must make the request at least 21 days in advance of the proposed start date of the leave (Lab. Law § 202-m(6)).

The duration of such leave shall be the full period requested by the employee which includes travel time and a period of rest and recovery upon return, including any quarantine period which may be imposed, unless the length of such leave presents an undue hardship (Lab. Law § 202-m(5)). If the length of the leave presents an undue hardship the employer and employee should work together to determine if a shorter period would be acceptable (*Id.*).

Upon return an employee must be restored to the same or comparable position without loss of seniority and allowed to participate in insurance or other employer provided benefits in effect at the time of the Ebola leave request (Lab. Law § 202-m(8)). Similarly, the employee may not be subject to any retaliation for requesting or obtaining such leave (Lab. Law § 202-m(9)).

44. Retirement Rights and Benefits[1]

In General

44:1. Is there a mandatory retirement age for school district employees?

No. There is no mandatory retirement age for most public employees in New York State (§ 530; Exec. Law § 296(3-a)(a); see Age Discrimination in Employment Act (ADEA), 29 USC §§ 621(b), 623(a)(1); *Johnson v. State of N.Y.*, 49 F.3d 75 (2d Cir. 1995)). In addition, any such requirement would violate state law, except where age is a "bona fide occupational qualification" (Exec. Law § 296(3-a)).

44:2. Are early retirement incentives permissible?

It depends. The federal Age Discrimination in Employment Act (ADEA) broadly prohibits age-based discrimination in the workplace (see 29 USC § 623(a)). However, it also specifically allows voluntary early retirement incentives that do not arbitrarily discriminate on the basis of age (29 USC § 623(f)(2)(B)(ii); see 29 USC § 621(b)).

Applying these principles, a federal appeals court with jurisdiction over New York upheld an early retirement incentive contained in a teachers' collective bargaining agreement. Participation in the program, which offered teachers additional benefits if they retired when they first became eligible to retire, was triggered by years of service, not age, and therefore did not arbitrarily discriminate on the basis of age. In addition, it was truly voluntary, and was made available for a reasonable amount of time. The court also ruled that the ADEA does not require that employers offer identical early retirement incentives for employees of different ages (*Auerbach v. Bd. of Educ. of the Harborfields CSD of Greenlawn*, 136 F.3d 104 (2d Cir. 1998); see also *Abramson v. Bd. of Educ. of Middle Country Sch. Dist.*, 2012 U.S. Dist. LEXIS 89410 (E.D.N.Y. 2012), *aff'd* 522 Fed. Appx. 57 (2d Cir. 2013)).

On the other hand, one federal district court with jurisdiction over part of New York found that an early retirement incentive which required that teachers retire at the end of the school year in which they first became eligible to retire or suffer a reduction in payments for already accumulated sick leave benefits violated the ADEA because it diminished their accrued benefits as they got older (*O'Brien v. Bd. of Educ. of Deer Park UFSD*, 127 F.Supp.2d 342 (E.D.N.Y. 2001)).

In order for a retirement incentive to be permitted under the ADEA's "Safe Harbor" provision, it must actually induce the employees to whom it is offered to retire. A plan that increases salaries for a targeted group of workers based on their age, without inducing them to retire, may be found to discriminate on the basis of age (*Abrahamson v. Bd. of Educ. of the Wappinger's Falls CSD*, 374 F.3d 66 (2d Cir. 2004)).

44:3. Can a school district deduct from an employee's salary the cost of participating in a tax-sheltered annuity plan to increase his or her retirement income?

Yes. The local school board must approve a tax-sheltered annuity plan, pursuant to a written agreement (usually the collective bargaining agreement between the employee's union and the district) by which the

[1] *All statutory references in this chapter are to the Retirement and Social Security Law unless otherwise noted.*

Employee Rights

district reduces the employee's annual salary for the purpose of purchasing the annuity (Educ. Law §§ 3109, 3109-A; 26 USC § 403(b)). Districts should have a clear and unambiguous hold harmless provision contained in the salary reduction agreement that employees sign to participate in the plan. Such a provision would protect a district from liability for financial losses suffered by employees as a result of the employees' own election of investment options (*Meirowitz v. Bayport-Bluepoint UFSD*, 57 A.D.3d 858 (2d Dep't 2008)).

44:4. Can the benefits of a member of a state retirement plan be changed to the member's disadvantage?

Generally, no. The state constitution makes membership in any pension or retirement system of the state or a municipality a contractual relationship and, thus, the system's benefits may not be diminished or impaired (N.Y. Const. art. 5, § 7; but see **44:5**). This constitutional provision guarantees statutory benefits in place on the date of an individual's employment (*Kleinfeldt v. N.Y. City Emps.' Ret. Sys.*, 36 N.Y.2d 95 (1975); *Birnbaum v. N.Y. State Teachers' Ret. Sys.*, 5 N.Y.2d 1 (1958)).

For example, the New York Court of Appeals invalidated any reductions in Tier III benefits that purportedly were made by Chapter 414 of the Laws of 1983. The 1983 law attempted to alter previous benefits by reducing the system's death benefit and by preventing members from withdrawing their contributions to the system until age 62, even if they left service earlier (*Public Employees Fed'n v. Cuomo*, 62 N.Y.2d 450 (1984)).

This constitutional provision also has been held to require that the mortality table in effect on the date a member joins the Teachers' Retirement System is guaranteed to the member in the calculation of her or his benefits and may not be changed (*Birnbaum v. N.Y. State Teachers' Ret. Sys.*).

44:5. Can members of a state retirement plan forfeit their pension benefits?

Yes. Pursuant to Article 3-B of the Retirement and Social Security Law, school district officers and employees who join a public retirement system on or after September 3, 2011 and who are convicted of a crime related to public office are subject to a reduction or revocation of the pension to which they are otherwise entitled (§ 157).

Actions initiated to effectuate such a reduction or revocation of benefits must proceed in accordance with the specific notice and hearing procedures set out in law. Pension benefits must be retroactively restored if the underlying conviction of a crime related to public office is reversed, vacated, or reduced to a violation, misdemeanor, or other criminal act that is not related to public office, upon application to the court who exercised jurisdiction over the pension forfeiture action (§ 157).

A crime related to public office includes:

- a felony for committing, aiding or abetting a larceny of public funds from the state or a municipality;
- a felony committed in direct connection with service as a public official; or
- a felony committed by such person who, with the intent to defraud, realizes or obtains, or attempts to realize or obtain, a profit, gain or advantage for himself or herself or for some other person, through the use or attempted use of the power, rights, privileges or duties of his or her position as a public official (§ 156(1)).

44:6. Can members of a state retirement plan retire on disability?

Yes. To be considered for an ordinary disability allowance, members must be credited with 10 years of service within New York State, except for members in Tier III, who need only five years of service if they are eligible for a primary Social Security disability benefit (§§ 62(aa)(1), 506(a), 605(b)(1); Educ. Law § 511(3)). Members who become disabled through job-related accidents may be eligible, under certain conditions, for accidental disability benefits (§§ 63, 507, 605(b)(3)).

Members of the NYC Teachers' Retirement System who are not eligible for workers' compensation will receive a disability benefit equal to two-thirds of their final average salary (§ 605(f)). Such disability benefits are considered payment in lieu of a workers' compensation benefit (§ 605(g)).

The TRS Board may approve the disability retirement application of an eligible member who would have been entitled to retire for disability, but died before the application could become effective. The eligible member's death must be as a result of the disability (Educ. Law § 511(8)(b)).

44:7. Are some retired employees entitled to supplemental pensions or cost of living adjustments (COLAs)?

Yes. Noninstructional employees who retired before 1961 are entitled to the more generous of two supplemental pensions provided by law (articles 4 and 6). Teachers who retired before July 1, 1970 receive the supplemental pension available to noninstructional employees or a supplemental pension provided under the Education Law, whichever is greater (Educ. Law § 532(e), (g)).

However, in lieu of these supplemental pensions, a retired employee who is (1) age 62 and retired for five years; or (2) age 55 and retired for 10 years; or (3) on disability retirement for five years (regardless of age) may receive an annual COLA (§ 78-a(a)(i), (ii), (iii), (h); Educ. Law § 532-a(a)(i), (ii), (iii), (h)). The COLA is 50 percent of the consumer price index and applies to the first $18,000 of a retiree's pension (§ 78-a(b)-(d); Educ. Law § 532-a(b)-(d)). The minimum annual increase is one percent and the maximum increase is three percent (§ 78-a(d); Educ. Law § 532-a(d)).

44:8. Is the retirement allowance of a retired school district employee subject to federal and New York State income tax?

There is no New York State income tax on any part of the retirement allowance (§ 110(1)). There is federal income tax on the retirement allowance (26 USC § 61(a)(11)). When the employee retires, a statement is furnished giving the necessary data for income tax purposes. In January of each year, a 1099-R statement is sent to each retiree (see 26 USC § 6041(a), (d)). The 1099-R gives the taxable portion of the allowance received during the previous year (see Instructions to 1099-R form and IRS Publication 575, Pension and Annuity Income). Check with the U.S. Internal Revenue Service for information about other changes. The website address is http://www.irs.gov. For information on taxation of member contributions to the state retirement systems, see **44:43**.

44:9. Can retired school district employees authorize automatic deductions from their retirement allowance?

Yes. Retired school district employees may have the cost of participating in union employee benefit plans and the cost of membership dues automatically deducted from their retirement allowance (§ 110-c; Educ. Law § 536(1)). Retirees participating in the NYS Health Insurance Plan may also have the cost of contributions deducted from their retirement allowance (Civ. Serv. Law § 167(3)). In addition, retired employees may authorize voluntary contributions from their retirement allowance to the political action committee of their union (Educ. Law § 536(2); NYC Administrative Code § 13-561).

44:10. Is an in-service death benefit available to retirement system members?

Yes. The retirement systems provide ordinary and accidental death benefits. The benefit depends on a number of factors including the member's date of membership, salary and length of service (see §§ 60, 60-b, 61, 448, 508, 509, 606, 607; Educ. Law § 512(b)(5)).

In addition, a pre-retirement death benefit is available with respect to members of the state retirement systems who are out of public service and who die on or after January 1, 1997 but prior to retirement, having at least 10 years of credited service at the time of death (§§ 60-c(a), 448-a(a), 508-a(a), 606-a(a); Educ. Law § 512(e); L. 1998, c. 388, § 8). The death benefit is equal to one-half of the benefit payable if the member had died in active service on the last date of employment (§§ 60-c(c), 448-a(c), 508-a(c), 606-a(c); Educ. Law § 512(e)).

A public employee who dies while on active military duty with the armed forces of the United States (other than for training purposes) is entitled to the same death benefit that would be payable had the employee died in active service to the employer. If the employee has not met the minimum service requirement, he or she will be considered to have met the requirement (L.2005, c. 105).

The New York State Teachers' Retirement System

44:11. Who is covered by the Teachers' Retirement System?

The Teachers' Retirement System (TRS) includes teachers in the public and charter schools of New York State, except New York City teachers, and some members of the State University of New York teaching staff (Educ. Law Art. 8-B; §§ 501(4), 503(4), 2854(3)(c)). New York City teachers are covered by the NYC Teachers' Retirement System (NYC Admin. Code §§ 13-501(7)(a), 13-503).

The term *teacher* is defined broadly in the law to include regular teachers, special teachers, superintendents, principals, school librarians and other members of the teaching and professional staff of public schools (Educ. Law § 501(4)). Nonetheless, in determining whether an individual is eligible for retirement service credit, TRS is obligated to "look beyond the labels" used by employers to define an employment relationship and "examine its substance." Accordingly, in one case, TRS properly denied retirement service credit to a teacher who offered a program through a board of cooperative educational services (BOCES). Although there was no contract between the teacher and the private corporation, her work involved promoting and facilitating participation in the program in school districts across the state, and the corporation reimbursed the BOCES the cost of the teacher's salary and benefits, plus overhead for her office. Thus, her work was not "teaching service" for an "employer" for purposes of participating in TRS (*Jensen-Dooling v. N.Y. State Teachers' Ret. Sys.*, 68 A.D.3d 1264 (3d Dep't 2009), *lv. to appeal denied*, 14 N.Y.3d 705 (2010)).

Although the New York Charter Schools Act of 1998 states that charter school teachers are deemed to be employees of the local school district for the purpose of membership in TRS (Educ. Law § 2854(3)(c)), TRS regulations provide for admission of individual charter schools as participating employers in the retirement system. Following admission to the retirement system, a charter school may not withdraw as a participating employer (21 NYCRR §§ 5026.1, 5026.2).

44:12. May substitute or other part-time teachers join the Teachers' Retirement System (TRS)?

Yes. Membership for substitute or other part-time teachers is at the individual employee's option (Educ. Law § 503(2); 21 NYCRR § 5000.1(d)). Employers must notify part-time teachers in writing of their right to membership in the system, and teachers must acknowledge receipt of such notice in writing (Educ. Law § 520(2)(b)). Substitute teachers must have at least 20 days of credit before they can join the system, but the credit can be from multiple districts (21 NYCRR § 5001.2(a)).

44:13. Who is responsible for operating the Teachers' Retirement System (TRS)?

Primary responsibility for the proper operation of the TRS rests with its board and staff (Educ. Law §§ 504(1), 507(1)). Additional supervision is provided by the New York State Department of Insurance (Educ. Law § 523). TRS funds may be invested only in accordance with statutory specifications (see § 177; Educ. Law § 508). An actuarial valuation is made periodically to determine whether the system has the resources to meet its obligations (see Educ. Law §§ 508(5), 517(2)(a)). Any deficiency must be made up by increasing the contributions made by school districts (Educ. Law §§ 517(2), 521(2)).

44:14. How many members are on the Teachers' Retirement System's (TRS) board, and how are they chosen?

The TRS board has 10 members (Educ. Law § 504(2)). Three of them are elected by the New York State Board of Regents. One of those members must be or have been an executive officer of a bank authorized to do business in the state and may not be an employee of the state (Educ. Law § 504(2)(a)). The other two members must be current or former school board members who have experience in finance and investment. Neither may be an employee of the state. One of those members must also be or have been an executive officer of an insurance company. These two members are chosen from a list of five presented to the Board of Regents by the New York State School Boards Association (Educ. Law § 504(2)(b)).

Two school administrators are chosen by the commissioner of education (Educ. Law § 504(2)(c)). The state comptroller or his or her appointee also sits on the board (Educ. Law § 504(2)(d)). Three active teachers are elected from among TRS's members (Educ. Law §§ 504(2)(e), 505), and one retired teacher is elected from among the retired members of the retirement system (Educ. Law §§ 504(2)(f), 505-a). The affirmative vote of a majority of the board and the concurrence of one of the active teacher members of the board is required to adopt, amend, or repeal any rule or regulation relating to member benefits (Educ. Law § 506(5)).

All members, with the exception of the comptroller or his appointee, serve for a term of three years (Educ. Law § 504(2)).

44:15. How is the Teachers' Retirement System (TRS) funded?

The TRS is funded through members' contributions (§§ 517(a), 613(a)), school district employers' contributions (Educ. Law §§ 517(2), 519(2), 521(2)) and investment income (Educ. Law § 508(2)).

44:16. How much do school districts contribute to the Teachers' Retirement System (TRS)?

The amount a school district contributes to the TRS varies from year-to-year, depending on actuarial analysis (Educ. Law §§ 517(2), 521(2)). The employer's contribution rate (ECR) payable by school districts has increased considerably in recent years from. 36 percent of a member district's payroll for the 2002–03 school year to 13.26 percent of the 2015-16 school year payroll, payable in the fall of 2016.

At the time this publication went to press, the TRS board had adopted an ECR of 11.72 percent for the 2016-17 school year, payable in the fall of 2017. The TRS board sets the rate annually, based on the recommendations of the system's actuary (for rates, see the TRS website: http://www.nystrs.org/; see also **44:13**). School districts and BOCES were given the option to choose to pay either the ECR or elect to participate in the Stable Contribution Option (SCO) established by Chapter 57 of the Laws of 2013. The SCO option allows districts to pay a stable rate for up to seven years and defer payment of the difference between the SCO and the ECR. Districts and BOCES had to choose the SCO option by June 30, 2014. More information about the SCO option is available on the TRS website.

44:17. When are school districts' contribution payments to the Teachers' Retirement System (TRS) due?

School districts' payments to the TRS are made in the fall for salaries paid during the previous school year (Educ. Law § 521(2)(h)).

44:18. How are payments made to the Teachers' Retirement System (TRS)?

Payments are credited directly to TRS by the state comptroller from each district's state aid apportionment in three equal installments due on September 15, October 15, and November 15 of each fiscal year (Educ. Law §§ 521(2)(b)-(d), (h), 3609-a(1)(a)(1)). Employers who receive no state aid or whose state aid payments are insufficient to pay the amount due the system are billed directly by the system (Educ. Law § 521(2)(h); see also **44:19**).

44:19. What happens if an employer underpays its obligation to the Teachers' Retirement System (TRS)?

The amount of the underpayment is deducted from the employer's state aid apportionment for the following year, on April 15. Employers whose payments from such appropriation are insufficient to pay the amount due, or who do not receive such payments, will be billed by the system for the underpayment (Educ. Law § 521(h)). Payments that are not made within 30 days will accrue interest (Educ. Law § 521(f)).

44:20. May a member of the Teachers' Retirement System (TRS) receive a lump sum retirement payment?

Yes. A member of TRS who is entitled to receive a retirement allowance, other than for disability, may elect at retirement to receive, in lieu of a retirement allowance, a lump sum payment which is of actuarial equivalent value to the retirement allowance if the allowance is less than $2,400 per year. Payment of the lump sum would complete the retirement system's obligation to the member (Educ. Law § 537).

44:21. What happens with unclaimed funds?

The Teachers' Retirement System (TRS) is authorized to distribute unclaimed funds in the amount of $1,000 or less (Educ. Law § 531(5)). TRS sends a notice advising of unclaimed amounts in excess of $1,000, and such funds are deemed abandoned and transferred to TRS if not claimed within one year after the date of the notice (Educ. Law § 531).

44:22. May members of the Teachers' Retirement System (TRS) change their retirement option selections after their retirement date?

Yes. TRS members as well as members of the NYC Teachers' Retirement System and the Board of Education Retirement System of the City of New York may change retirement options up to 30 days after the date of their retirement (§§ 514(d), 610(f); Educ. Law §§ 539(6), 2575(17)(q); NYC Administrative Code § 13-558(e)).

44:23. Where can further information about the Teachers' Retirement System (TRS) be obtained?

For more information about the TRS, contact TRS' offices at 10 Corporate Woods Drive, Albany, N.Y. 12211-2395; telephone 518-447-2900 or 1-800-348-7298; website at: http://www.nystrs.org/.

State and Local Employees' Retirement System

44:24. What school district employees are covered by the State and Local Employees' Retirement System?

The New York State and Local Employees' Retirement System (ERS) includes noninstructional employees in districts where a school board elects to provide retirement coverage to such employees by participating in ERS. There is no law that requires a district to do so; however, participation by an employer, once made, may not be revoked (§ 30(a)). The law likewise precludes the establishment of any retirement system for a civil service employee other than the ERS (§ 113(a)).

Any noninstructional employee in the service of the district on the date the system is adopted may or may not elect to become a member (§ 40(c)(1)). All persons appointed to full-time noninstructional positions on and after the date of adoption must become members of the ERS as of their dates of appointment (§ 600(b)(3)).

44:25. May part-time noninstructional employees join the State and Local Employees' Retirement System (ERS)?

Yes. However, membership for part-time employees is optional (§ 600(b)(3)(a)). Employers must notify part-time employees in writing of their right to membership in the system, and employees must acknowledge receipt of such notice in writing (§ 45).

44:26. May independent contractors working for school districts join the State and Local Employees' Retirement System (ERS)?

No. Consultants and independent contractors engaged by a school district are not employees and may not be reported as such to ERS (Educ. Law § 2051; comptroller's regulations §§ 315.2, 315.3; see also **44:46**).

School districts that engage the services of an attorney, physician, engineer, architect, accountant, or auditor on or after April 1, 2008 must submit to ERS a Form RS 2414 and supporting documentation for every one of those individuals they determine is an employee rather than an independent contractor. That form is due at the time when a district first starts reporting any such individual to ERS, as an employee. In addition, at the request of ERS, they must submit Form RS 2415 to verify the status of individuals hired prior to April 1, 2008 and the employee/independent contractor status of services providers other than attorneys, accountants, physicians, engineers, architects or auditors. Both forms are available at: http://www.osc.state.ny.us/retire/forms under the heading Employer Forms.

The comptroller's regulations and both RS 2414 and RS 2415 list the various factors that must be considered in determining whether someone is in actuality an employee or an independent contractor.

44:27. Who is responsible for operating the State and Local Employees' Retirement System (ERS)?

The state comptroller serves as the sole trustee and administrative head of the ERS (§§ 11(a), 13(b)).

44:28. How is the State and Local Employees' Retirement System (ERS) funded?

The ERS is funded through member and employer contributions, as determined by the Retirement and Social Security Law (see §§ 17, 21–24, 517(a), 613(a)), and investment income (§ 13(b), (c)).

44:29. How much do school districts contribute to the State and Local Employees' Retirement System (ERS)?

Each September, employers are provided with information for estimating the employer contribution for the next fiscal year. Final employer contribution rates must be based on the value of the ERS fund as of the previous April 1 (L. 2003, c. 49). Current law requires a minimum employer contribution of 4.5 percent of salaries (§§ 23-a, 323-a). More information on contribution rates may be found on the ERS website (see **44:33**).

44:30. How are payments made to the State and Local Employees' Retirement System (ERS)?

Employees' contributions are paid into ERS by payroll deductions each payroll period (§§ 517(f), 613(d)).

Employers' contributions to ERS are paid once each year following receipt of a bill from the state comptroller (§ 17(a)). Payment cannot be required before February 1 of the calendar year following the calendar year in which the statement is received (§ 17(c)).

44:31. What happens if an employer underpays its obligation to the State and Local Employees' Retirement System (ERS)?

If payment is not made within the time frame set in law interest is added to the amount beginning the first day after the date that the payment is required to be paid (§ 17(c), (d)). The state comptroller has the authority to bring suit in a state supreme court against any participating employer to recover any sum due the system (§ 17(e)).

44:32. Can members of the State and Local Employees' Retirement System (ERS) change their retirement option selections after their retirement date?

Yes. ERS members may change retirement options up to 30 days after the date of their retirement (§§ 90(e), 390(e), 447(c), 514(d), 610(f)).

44:33. Where can more information about the State and Local Employees' Retirement System (ERS) be obtained?

More information about the ERS can be obtained by contacting the New York State and Local Employees' Retirement System, 110 State Street, Albany, N.Y. 12244-0001, telephone 518-474-7736 or 866-805-0990. The general fax number is 518-402-4433. Retirement-related information may also be found at the Office of the State Comptroller's homepage at: http://www.osc.state.ny.us/retire.

State Retirement Plans — Eligibility, Benefits and Obligations

44:34. What state retirement plans are available for school district employees?

Outside New York City, noninstructional employees participate in the New York State and Local Employees' Retirement System (ERS) (§§ 40(b), (c), 500(b)(4), 600(b)(3)), while teachers participate in the New York State Teachers' Retirement System (TRS) (§§ 40(e), 500(b)(2), 600(b)(2); Educ. Law §§ 501(4), 503(1)). Public school employees in New York City are covered by the NYC Teachers' Retirement System or the Board of Education Retirement System of the City of New York (BERS) (Educ. Law § 2575(1)(a); NYC Admin. Code §§ 13-501(7)(a), 13-503).

44:35. Are any of New York State's public employee retirement plans defined contribution plans?

Yes. Tier VI provides a defined contribution plan for certain non-unionized public employees hired on or after July 1, 2013, at a salary of $75,000 or higher. Employers contribute 8 percent of wages for employees who opt for this plan, and employees contribute on the same schedule as other Tier VI employees (Educ. Law §§ 390(3-a), (8-a), 392(1-a), (2)(d)).

44:36. Do all members of state retirement plans have the same obligations and benefits?

No. The obligations and benefits of members of the New York State Teachers' Retirement System and the New York State and Local Employees' Retirement System vary, depending on the tier in which an employee belongs. For convenience, the systems use a tier concept to distinguish these groups. The same tier structure is used for members in all state retirement plans. Tiers are established to ensure that members' benefits are not reduced or impaired, since the New York Constitution prohibits diminishment of benefits (see **44:4**). Participation in a particular tier is based on the date the employee joined the system.

Members in *Tier I* include employees with a date of system membership before July 1, 1973 (see § 440(a); 2 NYCRR § 325.2(a)).

Tier II members include those employees with a date of system membership between July 1, 1973 and July 26, 1976 (2 NYCRR § 325.2(b)). Although Tier II expired on June 30, 1976 (see § 440(a)), anyone with a date of system membership between July 1 and July 27, 1976, became a member in Tier II, because Chapter 890 of the Laws of 1976, which created Tier III, was not signed into law until July 27, 1976 (*Oliver v. County of Broome*, 113 A.D.2d 239 (3d Dep't 1985), *lv. to appeal denied*, 67 N.Y.2d 607, *appeal on constitutional grounds dismissed*, 67 N.Y.2d 1027 (1986); 2 NYCRR § 325.1).

Members in *Tier III* include those employees with a date of system membership between July 27, 1976, and before September 1, 1983 (§§ 500(a), 520; 2 NYCRR § 325.2(c)).

Members in *Tier IV* generally include those employees with a date of system membership on or after September 1, 1983 (2 NYCRR § 325.2(d)) and before January 1, 2010.

Members in *Tier V* include those employees with a date of system membership on or after January 1, 2010 (L. 2009, c. 504) and before April 1, 2012.

Members in *Tier VI* include those employees with a date of system membership on or after April 1, 2012 (L. 2012, c. 18).

44:37. What retirement plans are available to Tier I and II members?

The retirement plans available to Tier I and II members depends on the type of plan the member's employer elected.

There are four noncontributory retirement plans available to members in Tiers I and II of the New York State and Local Employees' Retirement System (see **44:38**). Employees enrolled in any one of these plans are not required to contribute to it (§ 75-b(a)). If an employer does not elect a noncontributory plan, Tier I and II members have a choice of two plans, both of which require employee contributions (see **44:39**).

44:38. What are the noncontributory retirement plans available to Tier I and Tier II members?

Tier I and II members of the New York State and Local Employees' Retirement System have a choice of four noncontributory plans.

The Noncontributory Plan (1/60th Plan). At retirement, a member will receive a pension equal to 1/60th of his or her final average salary for each year of service rendered as a member on and after April 1, 1960 (§ 75-c(a)(1)(a)), plus 1/120th of final average salary for each year of service rendered as a member before April 1, 1960 (§ 75-c(a)(1)(b)), plus an annuity from any accumulated contributions left on deposit with the system (§ 75-c(a)(5)). Each year of prior service (up to a maximum of 35 years) will increase the pension by 1/60th of the member's final average salary (§§ 2(24), 75-c(a)(1)(b)).

The Noncontributory Plan with Guaranteed Benefits (Improved 1/60th Plan). At retirement, a member will receive a pension equal to 1/60th of his or her final average salary for each year of service since April 1, 1960 (see §§ 75-c(a)(1)(a), 75-e(b)(1)), plus a pension that will produce, when added to the annuity purchasable by required member contributions, a retirement allowance of 1/60th of his or her final average salary for each year of service between April 1, 1938 and April 1, 1960 (§ 75-e(b)(1)). All members' contributions in excess of the contributions required under this plan will, if left in the system, increase the member's retirement allowance (§ 75-e(b)(3)). Each year of prior service (to a maximum of 35 years) will increase the pension portion of the retirement allowance by 1/60th of final average salary (§§ 75-c(a)(1)(b), 75-e(b)(1), see § 2(24)).

The Career Plan (25 years). A member retiring with at least 25 years of total service will receive a retirement allowance of 1/50th of final average salary for each of the first 25 years of service, plus 1/60th of final average salary for each year in excess of 25 (§ 75-g(a)(1), see § 75-c(a)(1)).

The Improved Career Plan. The employer may elect to reduce the number of years of total service required for career retirement benefits to 20, and the employee will receive a retirement allowance of 1/50th of the member's final average salary for each year of service, provided that the maximum pension payable does not exceed three-quarters of final average salary (§ 75-i(a)).

In contrast, there is only one noncontributory plan available to members of Tiers I and II of the Teachers' Retirement System (TRS), the *TRS Career Plan*. At retirement, a member will receive a pension equal to 1.8 percent of final average salary for each year of New York State service rendered prior to July 1, 1959, and 2 percent of final average salary for each year of New York State service rendered after June 30, 1959, and 1 percent of final average salary for each year of out-of-state service (Educ. Law § 535(5)(a)). The out-of-state service is limited to the number of years necessary to equal 35 total years of service credit (Educ. Law § 535(5)(a)(3)). A member who retires with less than 20 years of full-time New York State service will have their pension reduced by 5 percent for every year less than the 20-year requirement, but this amount cannot be less than half of what the full pension would be (Educ. Law § 535(5)(b)). In addition to the pension benefit, a member will also receive an annuity based on his or her accumulated contributions at retirement (Educ. Law § 535(8)).

44:39. What contributory retirement plans are available to Tier I and II members?

If a member's employer has not elected a noncontributory plan (see § 75-b(a)), the employee has a choice between the Age 55 Plan and the Age 60 Plan.

The Age 60 Plan. A member in Tier I may retire at or after age 60, regardless of length of service, with a pension of 1/140th of final average salary for each year of his or her service as a member, plus 1/70th of final average salary for each year of prior service (to a maximum of 35 years), plus an annuity purchased by his or her contributions (§ 75(a), see § 2(24)). The same benefit formula applies to members in Tier II, but those members must meet the criteria described in **44:54**.

The Age 55 Plan. A member in Tier I may retire at or after age 55, regardless of length of service, with a pension of 1/120th of final average salary for each year of service as a member, plus 1/60th of final average salary for each year of prior service (to a maximum of 35 years), plus an annuity purchased by member contributions (§ 75(d), see § 2(24)). The same benefit formula applies to members in Tier II, but those members must meet the criteria described in **44:54**.

See question **44:54** for a discussion of the reduction of pension benefits applicable to members in Tier II.

44:40. What are the retirement plans available to Tiers III and IV members?

The availability of retirement plans depends on a member's tier. Tier III members may opt for benefits under the Coordinated-Escalator Retirement Plan — CO-ESC (Article 14), or under the Coordinated Retirement Plan (Article 15) (see §§ 500(a), 600(a)). Tier IV members are only entitled to the benefits under the Coordinated Retirement Plan (Article 15, see § 600(a)).

The Coordinated-Escalator Retirement Plan — CO-ESC (Article 14). Normal retirement age is 62 years (§ 501(17)). A member at normal retirement age will receive a pension equal to 1/50th of final average salary times years of credited service if the member is credited with 20 or more years of service. No more than 30 years may be applied to a pension (§ 504(a)). A member at normal retirement age with less than 20 years of credited service will receive a pension equal to 1/60th of final average salary times years of credited service (§ 504(b)). Members who retire between the ages of 55 and 62 with less than 30 years of credited service will have their pensions reduced based on their age at retirement (§ 504(c)). Regardless of the number of years of service rendered, a member's pension will be reduced by 50 percent of the member's Social Security benefit at age 62 (§§ 504(a)-(c), 511). Once retired, a member's benefits are increased annually at a rate equal to 3 percent or the amount computed on a cost-of-living index, whichever is less. In the event of a decrease in the cost-of-living index, the annual benefit will also decrease, but not below the initial benefit level (§ 510(c)).

The Coordinated Retirement Plan (Article 15). Normal retirement age is 62 years with five years of service (§§ 601(h), 602). A member at normal retirement age will receive a pension equal to 1/50th of final average salary times years of credited service if the member is credited with 20 to 30 years of service. Any years in excess of 30 years shall provide an additional retirement allowance equal to 3/200th of final average salary times years of credited service (§ 604(b)). A member at normal retirement age with less than 20 years of credited service will receive a pension equal to 1/60th of final average salary times years of credited service (§ 604(a)). Members who retire between the ages of 55 and 62 with less than 30 years of credited service will have their pensions reduced based on their age at retirement (§ 603(i)).

44:41. What retirement plan is available to Tier V members?

Normal retirement age for Tier V members is 62 years with 10 years of service (§§ 502(a), (b), 503(a), 601(h), 602(a), (b)). A member of the New York State and Local Employees' Retirement System (ERS) at normal retirement age will receive a pension equal to 1/50th of final average salary times years of credited service if the member is credited with 20 to 30 years of service. A member of the New York State Teachers' Retirement System (TRS) at normal retirement age will receive a pension equal to 1/50th of final average salary times years of credited service if the member is credited with 25 to 30 years of service. Any years in excess of 30 years shall provide an additional retirement allowance equal to 3/200th of final average salary times years of credited service (§ 604(b)).

A member of ERS at normal retirement age with less than 20 years of credited service, and a member of TRS with less than 25 years of service, will receive a pension equal to 1/60th of final average salary times years of credited service (§ 604(a)).

Members of TRS who retire between the ages of 57 and 62 with less than 30 years of credited service will have their pensions reduced based on their age at retirement. Members of ERS who retire before age 62 will have their pensions reduced based on their age at retirement (§ 603(i)).

Tier V employees are subject to an overtime ceiling. For purposes of calculating wages that are reported to the retirement systems and used to calculate an employee's final average salary, overtime is capped at $15,000 per year in 2010, increasing by three percent each year (§§ 501(24), 601(1)).

44:42. What retirement plan is available to Tier VI members?

Normal retirement age for Tier VI members is 63 years with 10 years of service (§§ 503(a), 602(b-1)(2), 603(a-1), 604(a)). A member of the New York State and Local Employees' Retirement System (ERS) or the New York State Teachers' Retirement System (TRS) at normal retirement age will receive a pension equal to 1/60th (1.66 percent) of final average salary times years of credited service if the member is credited with less than 20 years of service. A member credited with 20 to 30 years of service will receive a pension equal to 1.75 percent of final average salary for the first 20 years of service and 1/50th (2 percent) of final average salary for each year in excess of 20, but not in excess of 30 years of service (§§ 504(a), 516(d), 604(b-1)).

Members of ERS or TRS who retire between the ages of 55 and 63 will have their pensions reduced by 6.5% per year for each year before reaching age 63 (§§ 504(c), 603(i)(3)).

For Tier VI members, there is a statutory overtime ceiling of $15,000 per year beginning on April 1, 2012, with an annual increase tied to the consumer price index as determined the prior December 31 (§§ 501(24), 601(1)).

44:43. Are member contributions subject to taxation?

Under 26 USC section 414(h) of the Internal Revenue Code, as implemented by sections 517(f) and 613(d) of the state Retirement and Social Security Law, the 3 percent contribution made by Tier III, Tier IV and Tier V members, the 3.5 percent contribution made by Tier V members of the New York State Teachers Retirement System, and the contributions made by Tier VI members, are not subject to federal income tax. Those contributions are still subject to New York State taxation (Tax Law § 612(b)(26)). The contributions are included in gross income for federal income tax purposes when they are distributed at retirement or upon withdrawal from a retirement system (26 USC §§ 61(a)(11), 72, 402(a)). For information regarding taxation of retirement allowances, see **44:8**.

44:44. May members remove their contributions from the Teachers' Retirement System (TRS) or the State and Local Employees' Retirement System (ERS)?

Yes, in some cases. Tier I and II members may withdraw their voluntary contributions at any time with interest (§ 51(c); see Educ. Law § 512(a)).

Tier III, IV, V and VI members may only withdraw their contributions after they have left public employment, if they have less than 10 years of service credit, and are ineligible to receive other benefits (§§ 517(b), (c), 613(c)). Upon withdrawal of Tier III, IV, V and VI contributions, membership in the retirement system ceases (§§ 517(c), 517-a(4), 613(c); Educ. Law § 503(3)). Tier III, IV, V and VI members with 10 or more years of service credit may not withdraw their contributions (§§ 517(c), 613(c)).

Except in limited circumstances, any member who has less than five years of credited service, has left public employment for at least seven years, and has not withdrawn his or her contributions will have his or her membership in TRS or ERS cancelled (§§ 40(f)(1), 517-a(1); Educ. Law § 503(3); see also Educ. Law § 512-a(1); 21 NYCRR § 5006.2(a)). After the required notice has been given, any contributions left unclaimed may be declared abandoned (§ 109(a), (b); Educ. Law § 531(1)). However, TRS is authorized to distribute unclaimed funds of $1,000 or less (Educ. Law § 531(5); see **44:21**).

Unclaimed contributions may be reclaimed upon presentation of a valid claim by the former member or his or her estate (§ 109(c); Educ. Law § 531(4); see **44:45** in reference to a member borrowing against his or her contributions).

44:45. May a member borrow from his or her accumulated deposits in the Teachers' Retirement System (TRS) or the State and Local Employees' Retirement System (ERS)?

Any member who has credit for at least one year of service may borrow from their contributions (§§ 50(a)(1), 517-b(a), 517-c(b), 613-a(a), 613-b(b); Educ. Law § 512-b(1)). The loan for members in Tiers I and II may not be less than $25 for ERS members or $300 for TRS members, or exceed three-fourths of the member's accumulated contributions. TRS members must not have received a loan within the previous six months (§ 50(a)(1); Educ. Law § 512-b(1); 2 NYCRR § 351.2; 21 NYCRR § 5004.2). Members who are in Tiers III, IV, V and VI may borrow an amount no less than $1,000 and up to 75 percent of their accumulated contributions (§§ 517-b(a), 517-c(b), 613-a(a), 613-b(b); see also New York State and Local Retirement System, *Employer Guide* at: http://www.osc.state.ny.us/retire/word_and_pdf_documents/employers_files/employer_guide.pdf and the New York State Teachers' Retirement System, *Employer Manual* at: http://nystrs.org/main/employers/manual.htm).

In addition, the Legislature has authorized TRS to adopt rules and regulations permitting a loan at any time prior to retirement to a teacher who is not in active service or on a leave of absence (Educ. Law § 512-b(8)).

A loan must be repaid in equal installments that are at least 2 percent of the member's contract salary, and sufficient to repay the total amount due together with interest paid on the unpaid balance within five years (§§ 517-b(b), 517-c(c), 613-a(b), 613-b(c); Educ. Law § 512-b(2); 2 NYCRR § 351.6(a); 21 NYCRR § 5004.4(d)).

44:46. Are school attorneys eligible for membership in one of the state retirement plans?

Only if the school attorney is an employee of a school district or board of cooperative educational services (BOCES). A school attorney may not simultaneously be an independent contractor and an employee of a school district or BOCES. Attorneys who are not district or BOCES employees may not seek to be treated as an employee for purposes of pension benefits. Lawyers who violate this law are subject to civil penalties, and anyone who makes a false statement or falsifies records in an attempt to defraud the retirement system for the purpose of obtaining a credit toward pension benefits, or a benefit or payment in excess of $1,000 will be subject to a felony charge (Educ. Law §§ 2051, 2052; see **44:26**). School districts and BOCES must file reports with the NYS Education Department, the Comptroller, and the Attorney General specifying all lawyers who provide legal services to the district or BOCES, whether the lawyers were hired as employees, and all compensation paid for legal services (Educ. Law § 2053).

Purchase and Transfer of Service Credit

44:47. Can a member of a retirement system buy credit for prior public service?

Yes. An active member of a retirement system who previously was a member of a public retirement system, and whose earlier membership ceased because of insufficient service credit (see **44:57**), withdrawal of accumulated contributions (see **44:44**), or withdrawal of membership (see **44:51**), may be deemed to be a member of his or her current retirement system beginning with the original date of membership in the previous retirement system. If the date of earlier membership would place the member in a different tier, the member would then be deemed to be a member of that tier (§ 645(2)).

To be eligible for such prior service credit, the member must apply for such credit and repay, with interest at the rate of 5 percent compounded annually, any amount refunded to the member when he or she left the previous retirement system (§ 645(2)). Otherwise, the prior service is provided to the member without need of repayment. Any active member or retiree who became a member of Tiers I or II by paying for such credit is entitled to a refund of those payments with interest at the rate of five percent compounded annually (§ 645(3)). Any amount paid by a member or retiree for service within Tiers III, IV, and V are not entitled to a refund for such payment (§ 645(2)); *Price v. NYS & Local Employees' Retirement Sys.* 107 A.D.3d 1212 (3d Dep't 2013)).

Members in Tier I can buy prior in-state public service for time that they were not previously members, under certain circumstances (§ 41(c), see § 2(17); Educ. Law § 509(2)(a)(5)).

Members in Tiers II, III, IV, V and VI can buy credit for service that pre-dated their entry into a retirement system. The interest rate payable to the retirement system varies by membership tier (§§ 446(b), 513(b), 609(b), (b)(2)).

44:48. Can a member of a retirement system buy credit for prior public service performed out of state?

In many cases members of the New York State Teachers' Retirement System (TRS) Tier I can buy up to 10 years of out-of-state service in a public school on a matching basis with their credited New York State service (Educ. Law § 509(5)). Teachers in Tier II may receive credit for out-of-state service if it had been credited under a previous Tier I TRS membership. Teachers in Tiers III, IV, V, and VI may not receive credit for out-of-state service (Educ. Law § 509(8)(a)).

44:49. Can a member of a retirement system buy credit for military service?

Yes. Members of New York State's public retirement systems may be eligible for up to three years of additional credit for military service rendered during periods of military conflict (§ 1000). Members should contact the appropriate retirement system for detailed eligibility requirements (see **44:23, 44:33**).

In the event of death prior to retirement, the amount paid by the member for the purchase of military service credit will be refunded with interest if the military service purchased does not result in a larger death benefit or retirement allowance than would have been payable had the member not purchased the additional credit (§ 1000(9)). Tier VI members would pay an amount equal to the sum of the number of years of military service being claimed multiplied by six percent of the members' contributions in the 12 months of credited service preceding the date that the member applied for credit (§ 1000(10)).

44:50. Can a member of a retirement system who is called to active military duty receive retirement service credit without making member contributions for such credit?

Yes. Members of New York State's public retirement systems who were called to active military duty between September 11, 2001 and December 31, 2005 and who did not receive their full salary from a participating employer and were otherwise eligible to receive retirement service credit in the retirement system for active military duty, are not required to make member contributions in order to receive such credit (Mil. Law § 243-d).

44:51. Can a member of a public retirement system transfer membership between retirement systems?

Yes. An individual who joins a new state retirement system may transfer his or her active membership in another state retirement system within a designated period of time after joining the new system, usually within one year (§ 43(a), (b), (k); Educ. Law § 522(2)). Nonetheless, individuals who fail to make timely transfer can obtain credit for service under the prior retirement system if they meet certain statutorily prescribed conditions concerning the termination of their membership in the prior system (Educ. Law § 509(11)).

44:52. Can a member be reinstated to an earlier date of membership after leaving one of the public retirement systems and subsequently rejoining?

Yes. The Retirement and Social Security Law allows a member to obtain prior credit, even though that person may have had the right to transfer and failed to do so. The granting of previous service credit will alter the individual's date of membership and possibly his or her tier status. To be eligible, a member must apply for such prior service credit with the administrative head of his or her current retirement system. The member must also repay, with interest at the rate of five percent compounded annually, the amount refunded, if any, when he or she left the previous retirement system (§ 645(2); see **44:47**).

Qualifying Requirements for Service Retirement and Benefits

44:53. What are the requirements for service retirement and benefits for members in Tier I?

Tier I members of the New York State Teachers' Retirement System (TRS) may retire at any age with 35 years of total credited service (Educ. Law § 535(1)(a)). Tier I members of TRS and of the New York State and Local Employees' Retirement System may retire after age 55 with the equivalent of five or more years of credited service (§§ 75-c(a)(1)(b), 75-g(c), 75-i(a), 76(a); Educ. Law § 535(1)(b), (c)).

44:54. What are the requirements for service retirement and benefits for members in Tier II?

The normal retirement age for members in Tier II is 62 years (§ 442(a)).

Retirement is permitted between the ages of 55 and 62, but with a reduction in benefits according to the following formula:

- One half of 1 percent per month for each of the first 24 full months by which retirement predates age 62 (§ 442(a)(1)).
- One quarter of 1 percent per month for each full month by which retirement predates age 60. In no event is retirement allowed before age 55 (§ 442(a)(2)).

A Tier II member, however, may retire without reduction in benefits if he or she is at least 55 years old and has completed 30 or more years of service (§ 442(b)(1)).

44:55. What are the requirements for service retirement and benefits available to members in Tier III?

Members in Tier III are covered by the provisions of the Coordinated-Escalator Retirement Plan, as set forth in Article 14 of the Retirement and Social Security Law, or the Coordinated Retirement Plan, as set forth in Article 15 (§§ 500(a), 600(a); see **44:40**). The Article 14 plan integrates Social Security benefits with service retirement. Members must contribute three percent of their wages until they have 10 years of membership or 10 years of service credited with the retirement system (§§ 517(a), 613(a), 902(b)(1)). Members must render at least five years of credited service and attain age 62 to be eligible for normal retirement (§§ 503(a), 516(a), 603(a), 612(a)).

Members who retire between the ages of 55 and 62 with less than 30 years of credited service have their benefits reduced based on their age at retirement (§§ 504(a)-(c), 603(i), 604(a), (b)). In addition to these reductions, if a member elects to retire under Article 14, his or her retirement benefits commencing at age 62 will be reduced by 50 percent of the primary Social Security benefit (§§ 504(a)-(c), 511(a)). However, a member may retire under Article 15 at age 55 and 30 years of service with no reduction in benefits (§ 603(a)).

44:56. What are the requirements for service retirement and benefits available to members in Tier IV?

Members in Tier IV are covered by the provisions of the Coordinated Retirement Plan, as set forth in Article 15 of the Retirement and Social Security Law (see **44:40**). Members in Tier IV must contribute three percent of their wages until they have 10 years of membership or 10 years of service credited with the retirement system (§§ 613(a), 902(b)(1)). Members will be eligible for a normal retirement benefit at age 62, if they have a minimum of five years of credited New York State service, or at age 55, if credited with 30 years of service (§§ 603(a), 612(a)).

Members may retire between the ages of 55 and 62 with less than 30 years of service, with a reduced retirement allowance (§§ 603(i), 604(a), (b)).

44:57. What are the requirements for service retirement and benefits available to members in Tier V?

Members in Tier V are covered by the provisions of the Coordinated Retirement Plan (see **44:40**), as set forth in Article 15 of the Retirement and Social Security Law. Tier V members in the New York State Teachers' Retirement System (TRS) must contribute 3.5 percent of their wages (§ 613(g)). Tier V members in the New York State and Local Employees' Retirement System (ERS) must contribute three percent of their wages (§ 613(a)(1)). Tier V members in both TRS and ERS will be eligible for a normal retirement benefit at age 62, if they have a minimum of ten years of credited New York State service.

TRS Tier V members also can retire without reduction at age 57 if credited with 30 years of service (§§ 502(a), (b), 503(a), 601(h), 602(a), (b), 603(a), (t); see also § 612(a)). This option is not available to ERS Tier V members.

Both TRS and ERS Tier V members may retire between the ages of 55 and 62 with less than 30 years of service, but with a reduced retirement allowance (§§ 603(i), 604(a), (b)).

44:58. What are the requirements for service retirement and benefits available to members in Tier VI?

Members in Tier VI are covered by the provisions of the Coordinated Retirement Plan (see **44:40**), as set forth in Article 15 of the Retirement and Social Security Law. Through April 1, 2013, Tier VI members must contribute three percent of their wages. Thereafter, their contributions will be determined by their wages. Those who earn:

- $45,000 or less will contribute 3 percent of annual wages;
- More than $45,000 and up to $55,000 will contribute 3.5 percent of annual wages;
- More than $55,000 and up to $75,000 will contribute 4.5 percent of annual wages;
- More than $75,000 and up to $100,000 will contribute 5.75 percent of annual wages;
- More than $100,000 will contribute 6 percent of annual wages (§§ 517(a), 613(a)(1), (g)).

Earnings in excess of the governor of the State of New York are not included in the definition of wages (§§ 501(24), 601(1)).

Tier VI members in both the New York State Teachers' Retirement System (TRS) and the New York State and Local Employees' Retirement System (ERS) are eligible for a normal retirement benefit at age 63 if they have a minimum of ten years of credited New York State service (§ 503(a)).

Both TRS and ERS Tier VI members may retire between the ages of 55 and 63 if they have a minimum of ten years of service, but with a reduced retirement allowance (§§ 504(c), 602(b-1)(2), 603(i)(3), 604(a)). Tier VI members may be eligible for early age retirement starting at age 57 with 30 or more years of creditable service, when petitioned by their union and approved by the governor (Articles 23, 24, 25).

Additional information on Tier VI for TRS members is available from TRS at: http://www.nystrs.org/main/benefits/service.htm, and for ERS members from the Office of State Comptroller at: http://www.osc.state.ny.us/retire/members/tier-6/index.php.

44:59. What is meant by vesting?

Vesting occurs when an employee is legally entitled to receive retirement benefits without the need to render additional service. Generally, in Tiers I through IV, employees become vested after five years of service in one of the retirement systems (§§ 76(a)(1), 502(a), 516(a), 602(a), 612(a); Educ. Law §§ 503(3), 535(1)(b)). Employees in Tier V become vested after 10 years of service in one of the retirement systems (§§ 502(a), (b), 516(a), 602(a), (b), 612(a)). Employees in Tier VI become vested after 10 years of service (§ 602(b-1)). Once vested, an employee may receive benefits under one of the retirement systems upon retiring at the statutorily specified age, depending on the tier to which he or she belongs. However, retirement after five years in Tiers I through IV, or after 10 years in Tiers V and VI, but less than the statutorily required number of service years, will result in a reduced retirement benefit (see **44:53–58**).

44:60. What is meant by final average salary and how does it affect a member's retirement benefit?

Final average salary for Tiers I through V is the highest average annual compensation earned during any three consecutive years of credited service (§§ 2(9), 443(a), 512(a), 608(a); Educ. Law § 501(11)(b)). Final average salary for Tier VI members is the highest average annual compensation earned during any five consecutive years of credited service (§§ 512(a), 608(a), (b)). The retirement systems use the concept of final average salary as one factor in computing pensions for retiring members (see **44:37–42**).

The calculation of final average salary may be limited in some cases. Depending on a member's tier and date of membership, earnings for any 12-month period that exceeds certain amounts may be excluded from a member's calculation of final average salary. The limitations are set forth below:

- For Tier I members who joined on or after June 17, 1971, any amount of salary in a particular 12-month period that exceeds the salary base of the previous 12 months by more than 20 percent (§ 431(4); see *Kleinfeldt v. N.Y. City Employees' Ret. Sys.*, 36 N.Y.2d 95 (1975)).
- For Tier II members, salary earned in any one year that exceeds the average of the previous two years by more than 20 percent (§ 443(a)).
- For Tiers III, IV and V members, salary earned in any one year that exceeds the average of the previous two years by more than 10 percent (§§ 512(a), 608(a)).
- For Tier VI members, salary earned in any one year that exceeds the average of the previous four years by more than 10 percent (§§ 512(a), 608(a), (b)).

In addition, overtime compensation paid in any year to Tier V members does not count towards the calculation of final average salary if it exceeds the statutory overtime ceiling of $15,000 per year on January 1, 2010, with a three percent increase each year thereafter. For Tier VI members, there is also a statutory overtime ceiling of $15,000 per year beginning on April 1, 2012, with an annual increase tied to the consumer price index as determined the prior December 31 (§§ 501(24), 601(1)).

For Tier I members, lump sum payments for unused sick leave or vacation, and any other form of termination payments or retirement bonuses or incentives, are included in the computation of final average salary only if the member joined a retirement system before June 17, 1971, and such payments are not intended to inflate a member's final average salary or induce his or her resignation. For Tier I members who joined after June 17, 1971, and for the members of all the other tiers, final average salary does not include these payments (§§ 431, 443(a); *Kleinfeldt v. N.Y. City Employees' Ret. Sys.*; see also *Thompson v. N.Y. State Teachers' Ret. Sys.*, 78 A.D.3d 1456 (3d Dep't 2010); *Curra v. N.Y. State Teachers' Ret. Sys.* 30 A.D.3d 666 (3d Dep't 2006)). Therefore, they may not be included in any three-year final average salary calculation for any member of the New York State Teachers' Retirement System (TRS). However, payments genuinely made to delay someone's retirement that represent the value of services actually rendered constitute compensation earned that must be included in the calculation of final average salary (*Curra v. N.Y. State Teachers' Ret. Sys.*). Tier VI also excludes lump sum payments for deferred compensation, compensation paid in anticipation of retirement and, in the case of employees who receive wages from three or more employers in a 12-month period, the wages paid by the third and each successive employer (§§ 501(24), 601(l)).

Retirement benefits for Tier I TRS members who joined before June 17, 1971, may be based, in the alternative, on a five-year final average salary, including termination pay, if it constitutes compensation earned as a teacher (21 NYCRR §§ 5003.1, 5003.2; see also *Van Haneghan v. N.Y. State Teachers' Ret. Sys.*, 6 A.D.3d 1019 (3d Dep't 2004)). In addition, a contribution made by an employer on behalf of such TRS members to a defined contribution plan under § 401(a) of the Internal Revenue Code may be treated as compensation for the purpose of determining a five-year final average salary (Educ. Law § 501(11)(a)).

44:61. How do early retirement incentives offered by the state affect the age requirements for retirements in the various tiers?

Periodically, the state offers early retirement incentive plans that allow public employees to retire at an earlier age than that at which they would normally be allowed to retire. For example, a 2010 early retirement incentive eliminated the early retirement reductions for Tier II, III and IV members of the New York State and Local Employees' Retirement System (ERS) and the New York State Teachers' Retirement System (TRS) school district employees holding positions within a collective bargaining unit affiliated with the New York State United Teachers organization. The incentive allowed eligible members to retire at age 55 with 25 years of service. The state incentive had no impact on contractually negotiated retirement incentives that were agreed to prior to enactment of the state retirement incentive (L. 2010, c. 45).

Tier VI TRS and ERS members may be eligible for early age retirement starting at age 57 with 30 or more years of creditable service when petitioned by their union and approved by the governor (Articles 23, 24, 25; see **44:58**).

Employees who submit their resignations prior to a school board's decision to participate in a state early retirement incentive program are not entitled to participate in the program (*Dodge v. Bd. of Educ. for the Schodack CSD*, 237 A.D.2d 806 (3d Dep't 1997)).

44:62. Under what circumstances are school district employees entitled to health benefits when they retire?

Generally, the entitlement of school district employees to health benefits when they retire derives from either contractual provisions in an applicable collective bargaining agreement or school district policy. Nonetheless, a school district may be relieved of its contractual obligation to provide health, dental, and life insurance premiums upon retirement to an employee who engages in repeated acts of disloyalty. That was the case, under the "faithless servant doctrine," when a former treasurer and a former assistant superintendent for business pled guilty to stealing money from a district for a period of years (*William Floyd UFSD v. Wright*, 61 A.D.3d 856 (2d Dep't 2009)).

The contributions made by a school district to its retired teachers' health insurance premiums are not constitutionally protected pension benefits (*Lippman v. Bd. of Educ. of Sewanhaka Cent. High Sch. Dist.*, 104 A.D.2d 123 (3d Dep't 1984), *aff'd,* 66 N.Y.2d 313 (1985)).

However, as a general rule, if a school district provides health insurance benefits to employees after they retire, those retirees will be entitled to those benefits at the same contribution rate until the district negotiates a decrease in benefits or an increase in contribution rate from its active employees (L. 2009, c. 504, pt. B, § 14; *Kolbe v. Tibbets*, 22 N.Y.3d 344 (2013); *Matter of Anderson, Jr. v. Niagara Falls City Sch. Dist.*, 125 A.D.3d 1407 (4th Dep't 2015), *lv. to appeal denied*, 25 N.Y.3d 908 (2015)). An exception could apply if the retiree benefits derive from a contractual right that has vested (*Kolbe v. Tibbets; Guerrucci v. Sch. Dist. of City of Niagara Falls*, 126 A.D.3d 1498 (4th Dep't 2015), *lv. to appeal denied,* 25 N.Y.3d 1194 (2015)*; Non-Instructional Administrators and Supervisors Retirees Ass'n v. Sch. Dist. of the City of Niagara Falls,* 118 A.D.3d 1280 (4th Dep't 2014); *Agor v. Bd. of Educ., Northeastern Clinton CSD,* 115 A.D.3d 1047 (3d Dep't 2014); *Warner v. Bd. of Educ., Cobleskill-Richmondville CSD*, 108 A.D.3d 835 (3d Dep't 2013)).

According to one state Supreme Court the above diminishment of retiree health benefits rule even prevents school districts from eliminating reimbursement to Social Security-eligible retirees for their Medicare B premiums. The court rejected the school district's argument that the rule did not apply because no active employees were receiving reimbursement of Medicare Part B premiums, and therefore it could not make a corresponding reduction for active employees. According to the court, the law does not require that the "exact same benefit be taken from both groups (retirees and active employees), but only that there be a 'corresponding diminution of benefits....'" (*Bryant v. Bd. of Educ. of Chenango Forks CSD*, 4 Misc. 3d 423 (Sup. Ct. Broome Cnty. 2004), *rev'd on other grounds*, 21 A.D.3d 1134 (3d Dep't 2005), *on remand,* 29 Misc. 3d 706 (N.Y. Sup. Ct. 2010), *appeal dismissed as moot*, 107 A.D.3d 1170 (3d Dep't 2013); see also *Baker v. Bd. of Educ. Wappingers CSD*, 29 A.D.3d 574 (2d Dep't 2006), *lv. to appeal denied*, 7 N.Y.3d 708 (2006)).

Another state Supreme Court judge ruled that the law only allows the reduction for retirees to be made at the same time as a reduction is made for current employees (*Jones v. Bd. of Educ. of Watertown CSD*, 6 Misc.3d 1035(A) (Sup. Ct. Jefferson Cnty. 2005), *aff'd and modified*, 30 A.D.3d 967 (4th Dep't 2006)). However, on appeal by the school district, a state appellate court ruled that the prohibition against the diminishment of retiree health care coverage applies throughout the entire period the statutory prohibition remains in effect (*Jones v. Bd. of Educ. of Watertown CSD*, 30 A.D.3d 967 (4th Dep't 2006)).

Once employees have retired, they may not be able to make changes to their health insurance coverage, if that right is only extended to active employees in a district benefit plan (*Odorizzi v. Otsego Northern Catskill BOCES,* 307 A.D.2d 490 (3d Dep't 2003)).

Post Retirement Employment

44:63. Can a school district employee who is retired from service return to public employment without the loss of his or her retirement allowance?

Generally, a retiree's allowance is suspended when he or she returns to work for the state or a local government (§ 101(a); Civ. Serv. Law § 150; Educ. Law § 503(5)).

However, under specified conditions, a retiree may return to public employment without loss of retirement allowance. Commencing with the calendar year in which he or she reaches age 65, a member retired from service is not subject to restrictions on his or her earnings (§ 212(1)). Any retiree under 65 can earn up to $30,000 without prior approval from the appropriate state official and without loss, suspension, or diminution of his or her retirement allowance (§ 212(2)).

A retiree may be hired to perform duties that are essential to public health and safety without a suspension or diminution of his or her retirement allowance if the retired member is being hired to fill a vacancy caused when an employee of the local government is called into active military service of the state militia or the United States Armed Forces. An employer seeking to use this provision must certify to the retirement system in which the retiree belongs that the retired member is qualified, competent, and physically fit for the position; that there is a need for his or her services; and that his or her employment is in the best interests of government service (L. 2004, c. 418, § 13).

Except as provided above, if the retiree is a retired teacher employed in a regular position in public service, the retiree's allowance will be suspended unless the employer obtains the approval of the appropriate state official (§ 211(2); Educ. Law § 503(5); 21 NYCRR § 5023.1(a); see **44:64**). If a retired teacher's compensation for a temporary or occasional position exceeds the salary limitation above, then his or her retirement allowance will be suspended for the period an excess amount is earned (21 NYCRR § 5023.1(b), (c)).

Additional information on returning to work after retirement is available for teachers from the New York State Teachers Retirement System at: http://www.nystrs.org/NYSTRS/media/PDF/working.pdf. Similar information for participants in the New York State Employee Retirement System is available from the Office of the State Comptroller at: http://www.osc.state.ny.us/retire/publications/vo1648.php.

44:64. Is a waiver available for retirees wishing to return to public service at a salary that exceeds the limitation applicable to avoid loss of a retirement allowance?

Yes. If a retiree will earn more than the applicable amount (see **44:63**), the employer must obtain approval from the commissioner of education for a retiree to work as a teacher or administrator, or from the state civil service commission for a retiree to work as a noninstructional employee (§ 211(2)(a), (b); 8 NYCRR § 80-5.5).

The commissioner will not approve a waiver for the employment of a retired school district teacher or administrator to return to work in the same or similar position they retired from for a period of one year following the date of retirement (§ 211(2)(b)(5)(ii); 8 NYCRR § 80-5.5(b)(2)). Waivers granted are limited to a one year duration, except that they may be renewed once for up to an additional year in case of demonstrated extreme hardship or other unexpected and unforeseen circumstance beyond the school district's control (8 NYCRR § 80-5.5(d)(1)).

The commissioner will not extend a previously renewed waiver for a retiree seeking to remain employed in the same position in the same district, unless:

- the retiree is a certified teacher needed in a teacher shortage area, or
- there are extreme circumstances where a district is prohibited from hiring a permanent replacement, and such employment has been approved under these regulations (8 NYCRR § 80-5.5(d)(2)).

In addition, a prospective employer seeking approval from the commissioner must include with its waiver request satisfactory documentation that:

- the district undertook an extensive and good faith recruitment search and determined there are no available nonretired persons qualified to perform the duties of the position, or
- there is an urgent need for the retired person's services as a result of an unplanned, unpredictable and unexpected vacancy requiring an immediate temporary interim appointment, precluding an extensive recruitment search (§ 211(2)(b)(5)(i), (ii); 8 NYCRR § 80-5.5(c)(2)).

The request also must be accompanied by a copy of the board resolution approving employment subject to the commissioner's approval; a detailed recruitment plan; and a certification that a retired person employed as a superintendent under a waiver may participate in, but will not lead, the review and selection process for a permanent candidate for that position (8 NYCRR § 80-5.5(c)(3)(iii)).

The request also must certify: (1) that the retired person is duly qualified and competent, physically fit to perform the duties assigned, and properly certified as a teacher where such certification is required (§ 211(2)(b)(1)); (2) the specific reasons why there is a need for the services of the particular retiree, and why the employment of that person is in the best educational interests of the district; and (3) there are no readily available non-retired persons qualified to perform the duties to be assigned (8 NYCRR § 80-5.5(c)(1)).

School districts must notify resident taxpayers of the employment of retired persons pursuant to a commissioner's waiver, and the retired person's compensation package and right to receive a pension while employed (8 NYCRR § 80-5.5(e)). School districts and boards of cooperative educational services must report all money earned by a retiree in their employ that exceeds the earnings limitation to the retirement system from which the retiree is collecting a pension (§ 217(1)) and send a report to the retirement system and the state comptroller containing the reemployed retiree's name, date of birth, place of employment, current position, and earnings (§ 217(2)).

New York's waiver process is designed to prevent a retiree from collecting a pension from one job while accruing additional pension benefits from a second job, known as "double dipping." Thus, the waiver system has a rational basis, and does not violate equal protection principles. Moreover, since a claimant is not legally entitled under state law to a second set of benefits, the waiver system does not violate the right to substantive due process (*Connolly v. McCall*, 254 F.3d 36 (2d Cir. 2001)).

Additional information on returning to work after retirement is available for teachers from the New York State Teachers' Retirement System at: http://www.nystrs.org/NYSTRS/media/PDF/working.pdf. Similar information for participants in the New York State Employees' Retirement System is available from the Office of the State Comptroller at: http://www.osc.state.ny.us/retire/publications/vo1648.php.

Employee Rights

44:65. Can a retired school district employee who returns to public employment rejoin a state retirement system?

Yes. If a formerly retired employee has not received the approval of the appropriate state official for a waiver and/or earns a salary above the applicable earnings limitation (see §§ 211, 212; **44:63**), the retirement allowance is suspended (§ 101(a); Civ. Serv. Law § 150; Educ. Law § 503(5)) and membership in the state retirement system resumes (§ 101(a); Educ. Law § 503(11)(a)).

44:66. What happens if a retiree returns to work for a private employer?

Work for a private employer, an out-of-state employer (public or private) or the federal government does not affect a service retiree's retirement allowance (see §§ 101, 210(e), 211, 212).

Additional information on returning to work after retirement is available for teachers from the New York State Teachers' Retirement System at: http://www.nystrs.org/NYSTRS/media/PDF/working.pdf. Similar information for participants in the New York State and Local Employees' Retirement System is available from the Office of the State Comptroller at: http://www.osc.state.ny.us/retire/publications/vo1648.php.

Social Security

44:67. Are teachers in New York State covered by Social Security?

Yes. Almost all teachers in New York State now have Social Security coverage. The few exceptions are:

- Teachers who were members of the New York State Teachers' Retirement System before the Social Security referendum on December 12, 1957, and who rejected coverage or who did not sign a declaration accepting coverage before the referendum, and who did not accept Social Security during the 1959 or 1961–1962 reopenings.

- Teachers whose employment began after December 31, 1957, who are eligible to become retirement system members and who have not done so.

All newly employed teachers must participate (§ 138-a).

44:68. Are non-instructional employees of school districts covered by Social Security?

Yes. Almost all noninstructional employees of school districts are covered by Social Security. Exceptions are:

- Employees who were members of the Employees' Retirement System before the Social Security referendum on December 2, 1957, and either rejected coverage or failed to accept it before the referendum and did not accept Social Security during the 1959 or 1961–62 reopenings.
- Employees whose employment began after December 31, 1957, other than those in positions that exclude them from membership in a retirement system and who are provided with Social Security as the result of action completed before December 1957, who are eligible to become members of ERS, but whose positions do not require membership and who have not filed a membership application.

44:69. Can a school district withdraw entirely from the Social Security system?

No. The federal Social Security Act prohibits the state or any of its political subdivisions from discontinuing coverage of its employees by the Social Security system (42 USC § 418(f)).

44:70. At what age can an employee retire and receive a Social Security benefit?

An employee can retire as early as age 62 and receive a Social Security benefit (42 USC § 402(a)(2)). However, that benefit will be reduced by as much as 30 percent unless the employee delays retirement until full retirement age (42 USC § 402(q)(1), (9)). Conversely, an employee may receive a credit worth up to eight percent of the normal benefit if he or she defers collecting a benefit past full retirement age (42 USC § 402(w)).

Full retirement age is increasing from 65 in 2000 to 67 in 2022. From 2000 to 2005, the full retirement age was increased by two months per year until it reached 66 years of age. The full retirement age will remain 66 from 2005 until 2016. In 2017, it will again be increased for two months per year until 2022 when the full retirement age will be 67 (42 USC § 416(l)).

44:71. Are there limits on earnings, after retirement, for Social Security benefits?

Yes, for Social Security beneficiaries who are less than full retirement age (see **44:70**). If an individual is less than full retirement age, his or her benefits are reduced by one dollar for every two dollars earned above an annual earnings limitation set by the Social Security Administration (42 USC § 403(f)(3), (8)(A), (B)). The earnings limitation applicable to those under full retirement age in 2014 is $15,480 (http://www.ssa.gov/).

In the year an individual reaches full retirement age, one dollar in benefits will be deducted for every three dollars earned over an annual earnings limitation set by Congress. In 2014, the limitation is $41,400 (42 USC § 403(f)(3), (8)(D); see also http://www.ssa.gov/).

There is no reduction of benefits for earnings beginning with the month that a person reaches full retirement age (42 USC § 403(f)(3), (8)(E), (9)).

44:72. Should employees who intend to work beyond age 65 contact the Social Security Administration?

Yes. To enroll in Medicare, these individuals should contact the Social Security Administration, even though no retirement benefits will be paid until actual retirement (see 42 USC §§ 426, 1395c; 42 CFR §§ 406.6(c)(4), 406.10(a)(3)).

44:73. Where can further information about Social Security be obtained?

More information about Social Security can be obtained by calling the Social Security Administration at 1-800-772-1213, or at 1-800-325-0778 (for TTY users), or at: http://www.ssa.gov.

14:72 Should employees who intend to work beyond age 65 contact the Social Security Administration?

Yes. To enroll in Medicare, these individuals should contact the Social Security Administration even though no retirement benefits will be paid until actual retirement.

14:73 Where can further information about Social Security be obtained?

More information about Social Security can be obtained by calling the Social Security Administration at 1-800-772-1213 or by visiting its website at www.ssa.gov.

Employee Rights

45. Contracts of Employment[1]

45:1. What is an individual contract of employment?

An *individual contract of employment* is an agreement between a school district and an individual employee that contains a set of legally enforceable promises. Contracts of employment typically set forth terms of employment, duties of the position, salary, and employment benefits such as health insurance, retirement benefits, paid vacation and sick leave. A typical individual contract of employment is the employment contract between a school district and its superintendent of schools (see **10:5-9** and **10:14**).

45:2. How are individual contracts of employment formed?

Following a period of negotiation during which an agreement is reached, a contract usually is executed or formed when both parties sign the written document. As a matter of law, the school board is the entity that appoints all district personnel, except in New York City where the chancellor enjoys certain appointment authority, and in Buffalo and Rochester, where the superintendent makes certain appointments (see, for example, Educ. Law §§ 1604(8), 1709(16), 1950(4)(e), 2503(5), 2509(3), 2554(2), 2573(3), 2590-g(2), 2590-h(17), (41); see also **10:5-6**)). However, a common practice in many districts is for the board to approve the contract by resolution and to specify in that resolution the individual authorized to sign the contract on the board's behalf, such as the board president or the superintendent.

45:3. Do school employees typically have individual contracts of employment?

Most school district employees do not have individual contracts of employment with the district but are covered by a collective bargaining agreement. However, some employees, such as the superintendent of schools, have an individual employment contract specifying their terms and conditions of employment (see **10:5-9**). Employees designated as either "managerial" or "confidential" under the Taylor Law are precluded from being members of a bargaining unit and therefore are not covered by a collective bargaining agreement (see §§ 201(7)(a), 202, 203, 214; see **46:27-30**).

45:4. What is a collective bargaining agreement?

A *collective bargaining agreement* is a binding contract between the school district, executed by the superintendent acting as the chief executive officer of the school district, and an employee organization (or union) that represents a group of employees included within a bargaining unit (see § 201(12); **46:10**).

Employees who are covered by the terms of a collective bargaining agreement are appointed to their positions by resolution of the board, and the agreement serves to describe the terms and conditions of that employment. However, employees covered by an individual contract of employment derive their terms and conditions of employment from that contract itself (see **45:1**).

[1] *All statutory references in this chapter are to the New York State Civil Service Law unless noted otherwise. The acronym PERB used throughout this chapter refers to the New York State Public Employment Relations Board.*

Employee Contractual Relations

Board policies, as well as employee manuals or handbooks, may give employees, who are not covered by an individual contract of employment or a collective bargaining agreement, protections and assurances regarding their terms and conditions of employment, including rights regarding discipline and discharge. These policies, manuals, and handbooks may also supplement the benefits or rights of employees covered by individual contracts of employment or collective bargaining agreements. Such rights may be enforceable as contracts or create other grounds for challenging an employment decision in court (see *Weiner v. McGraw-Hill, Inc.*, 57 N.Y.2d 458 (1982)). However, these rights may be limited or extinguished through the use of a disclaimer of a contractual relationship (*Lobosco v. N.Y. Tel. Co./ NYNEX*, 96 N.Y.2d 312 (2001)). Districts should exercise care and consult with their school attorneys to avoid unintentionally creating such rights.

For more information on collective bargaining, see Chapters **46-47**.

45:5. Can changes be made in the terms of a contract of employment or a collective bargaining agreement during the period of the contract or agreement?

Generally, the parties to a contract of employment or a collective bargaining agreement must adhere to all the specifications contained therein for the duration of the contract or agreement, unless the parties agree mutually to changes in such terms (see **47:3**). A board may change the terms of a contract of employment or a collective bargaining agreement only with the consent of the employee or the employee organization, respectively, that is, by renegotiating the terms of the contract or agreement (see generally, *Town of Greece*, 32 PERB ¶ 3059 (1999), *aff'd*, 280 A.D.2d 967, 34 PERB ¶ 7006 (4th Dep't 2001)).

Additionally, all the terms of an expired collective bargaining agreement, except those that sunset on or before the expiration of the agreement pursuant to the terms of that agreement, must be continued until a new agreement is negotiated pursuant to the *Triborough* Amendment to the Taylor Law (§ 209-a(1)(e); see **47:29**; see also **46:1**).

45:6. What powers do school boards have in connection with collective bargaining agreements?

Under the Taylor Law (see **46:1**), a school board's role regarding collective bargaining agreements is limited. It is the superintendent, as chief executive officer of the school district (§ 201(10)), and not the board, as the district's legislative body, who is technically responsible for negotiating and executing collective bargaining agreements (§ 201(12)). However, as a practical matter, given the employment relationship between the board and the superintendent (a relationship that does not exist between most chief executives and legislative bodies), school boards frequently play an active role in the negotiations process.

On the other hand, the school board plays two distinct roles at the conclusion of the negotiations process. First, the board may ratify a tentative agreement reached by the district and the union before execution of the agreement (provided the right has been reserved to the board by the district's negotiator) (*Town of Dresden*, 17 PERB ¶ 3096 (1984)). Second, a board has the right to legislatively approve certain provisions of the executed agreement (§§ 201(12), 204-a(1); *Buffalo Teachers Fed'n*, 24 PERB ¶ 3033 (1991), *conf'd sub nom., Bd. of Educ. for City Sch. Dist. of City of Buffalo v. Buffalo Teachers Fed'n*, 191 A.D.2d 985, 26 PERB ¶ 7002 (4th Dep't 1993), *appeal denied*, 82 N.Y.2d 656, 26 PERB ¶ 7013 (1993); see **47:32**).

However, where a board adopted a resolution directing its superintendent to execute an agreement, as ordered by PERB, the resolution constituted legislative approval, notwithstanding a statement to the contrary (*Bd. of Educ. for the City Sch. Dist. of the City of Buffalo v. Buffalo Teachers Fed'n Inc.*, 89 N.Y.2d 370 (1996), *reh'g denied*, 89 N.Y.2d 983 (1997); see **47:37**).

46. Collective Bargaining – The Taylor Law[1]

Overview

46:1. What is the Taylor Law?

The Taylor Law, officially entitled the Public Employees' Fair Employment Act, is codified as Article 14 of the Civil Service Law. Enacted in 1967, the Taylor Law governs labor relations between public employers and public employees in New York State. The law is named after Prof. George W. Taylor of the University of Pennsylvania, chairman of Gov. Nelson Rockefeller's Committee on Public Employee Relations (also known as the Taylor Committee), whose report and recommendations formed the basis for the law. A copy of this report is appended to Chapter 1 of *Public Sector Labor and Employment Law*, 3d ed. Revised, published by the New York State Bar Ass'n (2009).

The Taylor Law's purpose is to promote harmonious and cooperative labor relations in the public sector and to avoid strikes (§ 200; *City of Newburgh v. Newman*, 69 N.Y.2d 166, 20 PERB ¶ 7008 (1987)).

46:2. What are the rights of a school district as a public employer under the Taylor Law?

As a public employer, a school district has the right to recognize (or withhold recognition of) employee organizations for the purpose of negotiating collectively and the right to enter into collective bargaining agreements (§§ 204(1), 207(3); *Town of Clay v. Helsby*, 45 A.D.2d 292, 7 PERB ¶ 7012 (4th Dep't 1974); *appeal after remand*, 51 A.D.2d 200, 9 PERB ¶ 7001 (4th Dep't 1976); see **46:15**).

In addition, while a school district is required to negotiate collectively with a certified or recognized employee organization (see **46:14**, **47:2**), the district has the right to insist that the employee organization participate in good faith bargaining with the district (§§ 204(2), (3), 209-a(2)(b)). Although a school district must engage in negotiations over mandatory subjects of bargaining, it may not be compelled to negotiate over permissive or non-mandatory subjects (*Bd. of Educ. of the City Sch. Dist. of the City of N.Y. v. PERB*, 75 N.Y.2d 660 (1990); *Webster CSD v. PERB*, 75 N.Y.2d 619, 23 PERB ¶ 7013 (1990)).

A district also has the right to negotiate free from strike activities, such as concerted stoppage of work or slowdown, or threats of strikes, and the right and the obligation to invoke the Taylor Law's procedures concerning strikes if a strike or strike activity occurs (§§ 201(9), 210; see **46:36**, **46:38-40**).

46:3. What rights are given to public employees under the Taylor Law?

Public employees are guaranteed the rights of self-organization and representation for collective negotiations (§§ 202, 203). *Self-organization rights* enable public employees to form, join and participate in, or refrain from forming, joining or participating in unions (referred to in the Taylor Law as "employee organizations") of their choice (§ 202). It is an improper practice (see **46:31**) for employers to interfere with, restrain, or coerce public employees in the exercise of these rights (§ 209-a(1)(a)). *Representation rights* enable employees to designate an employee organization as their representative in

[1] *All statutory references in this chapter are to the New York State Civil Service Law unless noted otherwise. The acronym PERB used throughout this chapter refers to the New York State Public Employment Relations Board. The Taylor Law (§§ 200-214) regulates the employee relations of public employers and employees in New York State, including school districts.*

Employee Contractual Relations

collective negotiations with their public employer over terms and conditions of employment, and in the administration of grievances arising from their negotiated agreements (§ 203).

The rights given to employees under the Taylor Law do not extend to all persons employed by a public employer. Classes of employees to whom the law does not extend include managerial or confidential employees (§ 201(7)(a)), and "casual" employees (*BOCES III, Suffolk Cnty.,* 15 PERB ¶ 3015 (1982), *aff'd, BOCES III Faculty Assoc. v. PERB*, 92 A.D.2d 937, 16 PERB ¶ 7015 (2d Dep't 1983); § 201(7)(f); see **46:27**). The law, however, extends to per diem substitute teachers who receive a reasonable assurance of continuing employment sufficient to disqualify them from receiving unemployment insurance benefits (§ 201(7)(d); see **46:13**).

46:4. What penalties may be imposed on public employers that use state funds either to encourage or discourage employees from unionizing?

New York's Labor Law provides for monetary sanctions against public employers that use state funds to engage in certain specified activities for the purpose of encouraging or discouraging employers from unionizing (Lab. Law § 211-a; see *Healthcare Ass'n of N.Y. State, Inc. v. Pataki*, 388 F.Supp.2d 6 (N.D.N.Y. 2005), *rev'd,* 471 F.3d 87 (2d Cir. 2006)).

46:5. Does an employee's right to representation under the Taylor Law include the right to union representation during questioning by an employer?

Yes. It is an improper practice (see **46:31**, **46:34**) under the Taylor Law, for a public employer to deliberately fail to permit or refuse to afford an employee the right, upon the employee's demand, to representation by a representative of the employee organization, or the organization's designee, when at the time of questioning by the employer it reasonably appears that the employee may be the subject of a potential disciplinary action. If representation is requested, and the employee is a potential target of disciplinary action at the time of questioning, the employee must be afforded reasonable time to obtain representation (§ 209-a(1)(g)). In any improper practice charge alleging a violation of this right, it shall be an affirmative defense that the employee has the right, pursuant to a negotiated agreement, policy, practice, statute or arbitration award to present to the hearing officer evidence of the failure of the employer to provide representation and obtain exclusion of the resulting evidence (*Id.*; see also *Tarrytown PBA*, 40 PERB ¶ 3024 (2007)).

This right to representation, also referred to as a *Weingarten* right, after a 1975 U.S. Supreme Court decision in *NLRB v. Weingarten* (420 U.S. 251 (1975)), is also codified in section 75 of the Civil Service Law, making it applicable to school employees who enjoy section 75 job protections (see **39:30**, **39:32**). However, its codification in section 209-a(1)(g) of the Civil Service Law uniformly extends the right to unionized employees who do not have section 75 protections. In addition, PERB has extended *Weingarten* rights to probationary employees (*N.Y. State Correctional Officers & PBA, Inc*, 43 PERB ¶ 3031 (2010)).

PERB has refused to extend *Weingarten* rights to staff asked to submit to a medical exam by their employer, finding such an exam does not constitute an investigatory interview (*N.Y. City Transit Auth.*, 36 PERB ¶ 3049 (2003)). *Weingarten* rights do not apply either to questioning during a criminal investigation (§ 209-a(1)(g); see also *City of Rochester v. PERB*, 15 A.D.3d 922 (4th Dep't 2004), *appeal denied*, 4 N.Y.3d 710 (2005)).

46:6. Who administers the Taylor Law?

The Taylor Law is administered by the Public Employment Relations Board (PERB) (see § 205). PERB consists of three members appointed by the governor and confirmed by the New York State

Senate, one of whom serves as the chairperson of the board (§ 205(1)). In addition, PERB has a staff that includes administrators, attorneys, administrative law judges (ALJs), and mediators (see § 205(4)(a), (5)(i)). It also designates fact finders and arbitrators on an *ad hoc* basis.

To help administer the Taylor Law, PERB employs ALJs to consider charges of improper practices by employee organizations or employers, to certify bargaining units, and to enforce other provisions of the Taylor Law (see § 205(4)(a); 4 NYCRR Part 212). PERB hears appeals (called "exceptions") from the decisions of the ALJs (4 NYCRR Part 213).

46:7. What are PERB's powers and duties under the Taylor Law?

PERB's powers and duties include establishing bargaining units, certifying employee organizations as the exclusive representatives of such units, remedying improper practices by employers and employee organizations, administering some strike penalty provisions, presiding over hearings, assigning mediators and fact finders to help resolve negotiation impasses, conducting research, and establishing a staff to assist in all of these powers and duties (§§ 205(4), (5), 207, 209(3), 209-a, 210(3)).

PERB, however, generally has no authority to enforce a school district's collective bargaining agreement or to exercise jurisdiction over an alleged violation of such an agreement, unless an alleged contract violation would also constitute an improper practice (§ 205(5)(d); see also *Matter of Roma v. Ruffo*, 92 N.Y.2d 489, 31 PERB ¶ 7504 (1998)). Consistent with this limitation on its jurisdiction, PERB has declined to enforce a settlement agreement reached regarding an alleged improper practice, finding that a "settlement agreement" is an agreement within the meaning of its jurisdictional limitation outlined in the Taylor Law (*State of N.Y. (Dep't of Correctional Servs.)*, 36 PERB ¶ 3040 (2003), *conf'd CSEA, Local 1000 v. PERB*, 16 A.D.3d 819, 38 PERB ¶ 7006 (3d Dep't 2005)). PERB also has found that disputes regarding an alleged breach of an oral agreement or an agreement ancillary to the main contract are beyond its jurisdiction (*State of N.Y. (Dep't of Tax. & Fin.)*, 24 PERB ¶ 3034 (1991)).

46:8. Does PERB have the authority to issue "declaratory" rulings?

Yes. PERB, however, has conferred this authority on its Director of Employment Practices and Representation who may issue such rulings when doing so "would be in the public interest," in furtherance of the policies fostered by the Taylor Law (4 NYCRR § 210.2(a)).

According to the Director, "[t]he purpose of a declaratory ruling proceeding is to provide a less adversarial means than an improper practice proceeding for resolving an existing justiciable issue between parties in two areas: whether an employee, an employer or an employee organization is covered by the [law], or whether . . . a matter is a subject of mandatory negotiations. . . ." (*Town of Henrietta*, 24 PERB ¶ 6604 (1991), *aff'd*, 25 PERB ¶ 6501 (1992); 4 NYCRR § 210.2(a)).

There must be a genuine and not merely hypothetical dispute between the parties concerning a subject for which declaratory relief may be granted (*City of Hornell and N.Y. State Conference of Mayors and Municipal Officials*, 36 PERB ¶ 3033 (2003)).

46:9. Are PERB decisions subject to court review?

Yes. PERB's decisions are reviewable pursuant to Article 78 of the Civil Practice Law and Rules (C.P.L.R.), which authorizes judicial review of determinations by administrative boards. Final orders of PERB are enforceable by the state supreme court upon petition by PERB in a special proceeding. An order by PERB that determines whether an employer or employee is subject to the Taylor Law may be deemed final when made (§ 213(a); C.P.L.R. § 7803). An Article 78 proceeding to challenge a PERB order must be filed within 30 days after service of the order by registered or certified mail (§ 213(a); *PERB v. Bd. of Educ. of City of Buffalo*, 39 N.Y.2d 86, 9 PERB ¶ 7004 (1976)).

Employee Representation Rights

46:10. What is a bargaining unit?

As it pertains to school districts, a *bargaining unit*, or *negotiating unit*, is a group of employees organized for the purpose of collective negotiations and typically represented by an employee organization (union) (see **46:14**). Three typical bargaining units in schools would be administrators and supervisors, teachers and other instructional staff, and non-instructional staff. Employees in such a unit need not be members of the union representing members of their bargaining unit (§ 202), but the union has the same duty of fair representation towards them as it has towards its members (§§ 204(2), 209-a(2)(c); see **46:22**).

46:11. How is the composition of a bargaining unit determined?

When defining a bargaining unit, the positions to be included in the unit must have a sufficient "community of interest" based on a variety of factors such as similarity of the terms and conditions of employment, shared duties and responsibilities, qualifications, common work location, common supervision, and actual or potential conflict of interest between the employees of the proposed unit (*Civil Serv. Employees Ass'n,* 46 PERB ¶ 3030 (2013); *St. Paul Boulevard Prof'l Firefighters Assn*, 42 PERB ¶ 3009 (2009); see **46:12**). Disparity in benefits is not a basis for excluding a group of unrepresented employees from an existing unit where the inclusion is otherwise most appropriate (*Unatego CSD*, 15 PERB ¶ 3097 (1982)).

Accordingly, PERB has ruled, for example, that teaching assistants are most appropriately placed in the same unit that represents teachers. According to PERB, inasmuch as teaching assistants are certified under Part 30 of the Regents Rules and have direct teaching responsibilities (albeit under the supervision of a certified teacher), they are professionals who share a unique community of interest with teachers (see *Newburgh Enlarged City Sch. Dist.*, 37 PERB ¶ 3027 (2004); see also *Southern Cayuga Sch. Dist.*, 37 PERB ¶ 3028 (2004)). Additionally, the requirements of Education Law § 3012-c for annual professional performance reviews of principals and assistant principals do not create a unique community of interest such that a bargaining unit separate and apart from other supervisory and administrative titles is necessary (*Greater Southern Tier BOCES Administrators Ass'n,* 46 PERB ¶ 4015 (2013)).

The law also requires that the appropriate unit be defined or drawn along lines that permit public officials at the level of the unit to agree or to make effective recommendations with regard to the terms and conditions of employment to be negotiated (§ 207(1)(b)). Moreover, the unit must be compatible with the joint responsibilities of the public employer and the public employees to serve the public (§ 207(1)(c); see **46:15**).

46:12. May the same bargaining unit include supervisory and non-supervisory staff?

PERB has declined to automatically place supervisors and rank-and-file employees into separate bargaining units (*Dutchess Cnty. BOCES*, 25 PERB ¶ 3048 (1992)).

Instead, PERB will consider factors, such as, whether members of the same unit have significant supervisory responsibilities over others, the nature and size of the existing and proposed unit, the nature of the services performed by the unit members, any special working relationship between them, the employer's administrative convenience, evidence of subversion of supervisory responsibilities, evidence of inadequate representation and evidence as to whether there are other existing or potential conflicts of interest among members of the unit (*Dutchess Cnty. BOCES*; *Uniondale UFSD*, 21 PERB ¶ 3060 (1988)). According to PERB, functions such as the imposition of discipline, effective initiation of disciplinary procedures or the evaluation of a subordinate may indicate a conflict of interest (*Civil Serv. Employees Ass'n,* 46 PERB ¶ 3030 (2013)). For example, in one PERB case, a BOCES teachers' bargaining unit included teaching assistants. The teachers in that bargaining unit evaluated the teaching assistants. PERB found that a bargaining unit composed of teachers and teaching assistants in this case did not pose a conflict of interest because the teachers did not make any employment decisions concerning the teaching assistants (*Dutchess Cnty. BOCES*). Similarly, a petition to create a unit solely of principals and assistant principals based partially on the argument that including other supervisory titles who evaluated principals and assistant principals under Education Law § 3012-c created a conflict was rejected (*Greater Southern Tier BOCES Administrators Ass'n,* 46 PERB ¶ 4015 (2013)). Presently, PERB administrative law judges have declined to recognize that the implementation of annual professional performance review procedures necessarily warrants the establishments of separate units (see *Poughkeepsie City Sch. Dist.*, 46 PERB ¶ 4013 (2013); *Greater Southern Tier BOCES Administrators Ass'n,* 46 PERB ¶ 4015 (2013)).

46:13. May substitute teachers be included in a bargaining unit under the Taylor Law?

Yes, if they are the type of substitutes considered to be public employees within the meaning of the Taylor Law. Specifically, the Taylor Law covers substitute teachers who have received a "reasonable assurance of continued employment" so as to be disqualified from receiving unemployment insurance benefits during summer vacation periods (§ 201(7)(d)). Substitutes who have not been given a reasonable assurance of continued employment from a district are not eligible for inclusion in a collective bargaining unit in that district (§ 201(7)(d)).

Long-term substitutes are generally placed in the same bargaining unit as teachers (*Unatego CSD*, 15 PERB ¶ 3097 (1982); *Broome-Tioga BOCES*, 31 PERB ¶ 4016 (1998)). Per diem substitutes are generally placed in their own bargaining unit (*Bethpage UFSD*, 15 PERB ¶ 4040, *aff'd*, 15 PERB ¶ 3094 (1982); *Wellsville CSD*, 30 PERB ¶ 4011 (1997)).

46:14. What is an employee organization and how does an employee organization become the authorized representative of public employees?

An *employee organization* is a union. The Taylor Law, however, does not use the term "union" to refer to the entity authorized to represent a group of public employees in collective negotiations; instead, it uses the term "employee organization" (§ 201(5)).

There are basically two procedures by which an employee organization can become the authorized representative of a group of public employees: *recognition* by the employer upon agreement with the union over a unit definition, or *certification* by PERB after determining the most appropriate unit (§§ 204(1), 207; see **46:15-17**).

Following either recognition or certification, an employer must negotiate with the employee organization with respect to terms and conditions of employment (§ 204(2)).

46:15. How does the process of employer recognition work?

Recognition is the voluntary designation by the legislative body of a public employer of an employee organization as the negotiating representative of employees in an appropriate unit (§ 204(1); 4 NYCRR

§ 200.8). But if an employee organization requests recognition and that request is denied, the employee organization may seek certification from PERB (4 NYCRR § 201.3(b); see **46:17**). Inasmuch as the rights and obligations of recognized and certified employee organizations are identical, both terms are used interchangeably in this chapter.

The recognition process begins with a request for recognition by an employee organization to the public employer. Once an employer receives a request for recognition, it must determine the appropriateness of the bargaining unit proposed by the employee organization (§ 207(1); see **46:11**). There is no steadfast rule for the definition of an appropriate bargaining unit, although public policy is in favor of the largest possible unit which permits effective negotiations and avoids fragmented bargaining units (see *N.Y. City Sch. Dist.*, 27 PERB ¶ 3067 (1994)). PERB favors "the most appropriate unit" rather than "an appropriate unit" analysis (*Inc. Village of Lake Success*, 38 PERB ¶ 3013 (2005), *conf'd sub nom. Inc. Village of Lake Success v. PERB,* 41 A.D.3d 599, 40 PERB ¶ 7004 (2d Dep't 2007)). It is important to examine the professional status of the employees to be included in the bargaining unit, the employer's organizational hierarchy, conflicting interests among the positions to be included, and the employer's administrative convenience (see *N.Y. City Sch. Dist.*, 27 PERB ¶¶ 3026, 3067 (1994)). PERB has ruled, for instance, that registered nurses may split off from a bargaining unit of non-instructional employees because the professional status of nurses is incompatible with the status of non-professional employees in the same bargaining unit, even though the nurses' association was unable to prove inadequate representation by the original bargaining unit (*Ichabod Crane CSD*, 33 PERB ¶ 3042 (2000), *conf'd sub nom. Civil Serv. Employees Ass'n v. PERB*, 300 A.D.2d 929, 35 PERB ¶ 7020 (3d Dep't 2002)).

After the unit has been defined, the employer must be satisfied that a majority of the employees in that bargaining unit have selected the employee organization (a union) which seeks recognition as their representative. Selection may be evidenced a number of different ways, including by employees' individual authorizations for the deduction of dues from their paychecks (called dues check off), or an election (§ 207(2); see *Mohawk Valley Nursing Home, Inc.*, 25 PERB ¶ 7006 (Sup. Ct. Albany Cnty. 1992); *Town of Clay v. Helsby*, 45 A.D.2d 292, 7 PERB ¶ 7012 (4th Dep't 1974), *appeal after remand*, 51 A.D.2d 200, 9 PERB ¶ 7001 (4th Dep't 1976)).

Once the employer has determined that the union represents the group of public employees it claims to represent and the union affirms that it does not assert the right to strike against any government, to assist or participate in any strike, or to impose an obligation on employees to conduct, assist or participate in a strike, the union is then designated by the employer as the exclusive negotiating representative of the employees in the unit (§§ 207(3), 204(2)).

46:16. Are there any specific procedures that districts must follow when recognizing a union?

PERB has issued regulations that set forth the procedures that an employer must comply with to voluntarily recognize a union (4 NYCRR § 201.6). An employer must:

1. Post a written notice of recognition in a conspicuous place at suitable offices of the public employer for at least five working days.
2. Include the notice in a public advertisement of a newspaper of general circulation in the employer's area for at least one day.
3. Send notification to any employee organizations that have, in a written communication within a year preceding the recognition, claimed to represent any of the employees in the unit (4 NYCRR § 201.6(a)).

The information published must include the name of the union that has been recognized, the job titles included in the recognized unit, and the date of recognition (4 NYCRR § 201.6(b)).

46:17. How does the process of certification work?

If an employer refuses a request for recognition or does not respond to such a request, an employee organization (union) may file a "petition for certification" with PERB within the time frame prescribed in PERB's regulations (4 NYCRR § 201.3(a), (b)). A petition for certification must be supported by a showing of interest of at least 30 percent of the employees within the unit alleged to be appropriate (4 NYCRR § 201.3(a)–(e)). An employee organization can establish a showing of interest with evidence of dues deduction authorizations from employees that have not been revoked, or evidence of current membership, original designation cards or petitions that were signed and dated within six months of submission, or a combination of the three (4 NYCRR § 201.4(b)). PERB may conduct an election (see § 207(2)). If necessary, PERB's Director of Employment Practices and Representation may order an investigation and/or a hearing on the petition for certification (4 NYCRR §§ 201.4(e), 201.9(a)(1), (2)).

An election will be held whenever more than one employee organization is seeking certification of the same bargaining unit or where an employee organization seeking certification is unable to show majority support of the employees in the unit (4 NYCRR § 201.9(g)(2)).

An employee organization may be certified without an election if the organization is the only organization seeking certification and it establishes that a majority of the employees within the unit choose to be represented by the organization (4 NYCRR § 201.9(g)(1)). Although PERB's regulations describe only two types of evidence that may be used in support of certification without an election, the director may also consider other types of evidence, such as a current employee organization membership list (*Beaver River CSD*, 35 PERB ¶ 3003 (2002); see 4 NYCRR § 201.9(g)(1)).

Certification will not be issued to a union that already has been "recognized" (see **46:15-16**), because the same rights are acquired by either process (see *Village of Sloatsburg*, 20 PERB ¶ 3014 (1987)).

46:18. Are employees who are hired after the recognition or certification of an employee organization included within the bargaining unit?

Generally, all employees whose positions fall within the unit's definition are considered members of the unit, regardless of when they are hired (see *State of N.Y. (Dep't of Audit & Control)*, 24 PERB ¶ 3019 (1991)). The school district must negotiate the terms and conditions of employment of all such employees with the appropriate employee organization (§ 204(2)).

However, a new position may be created that does not fall within the definition of the bargaining unit. In this case, the district is not required to negotiate the terms and conditions of employment with respect to that position (see *North Shore UFSD*, 11 PERB ¶ 3011 (1978)). In such cases, the employee organization may request the district to add the new position to the unit by recognition or file a unit placement petition with PERB seeking an order to add the new position to its existing bargaining unit (4 NYCRR § 201.2(b)).

46:19. What happens if there is a dispute regarding the representation of a particular job title by an employee organization?

Either one or both of the competing employee organizations may file a unit clarification petition and/or a unit placement petition with PERB, asking PERB to determine which bargaining unit a particular title belongs to (see, *e.g.*, *Harrison CSD*, 36 PERB ¶ 3046 (2003)). The school district then has an opportunity to respond to the petition by indicating which unit it believes properly represents the job title at issue.

A *unit placement petition* seeks a determination as to whether unrepresented positions should be added to a pre-existing unit (*United Public Serv. Employees Union*, 48 PERB ¶ 3025 (2015)) based on whether a community of interest exists between the at-issue positons and the positions in the represented unit (*City of Buffalo*, 46 PERB ¶ 3023 (2013); *Sachem CSD*, 42 PERB ¶ 3030 (2009)).

A *unit clarification petition* seeks a factual determination as to whether existing personnel are actually encompassed within the scope of the existing unit (*Monroe-Woodbury CSD*, 33 PERB ¶ 3007 (2000) based on a review of the recognition clause in the applicable collective bargaining agreement and other relevant contractual language (*Manhasset Educ. Support Personnel Assoc.*, 41 PERB ¶ 3005 (2008)).

PERB's analysis begins with a review of the collective bargaining agreement between the district and the employee organization that claims to represent the job title(s) at issue (*Clinton Cmty. Coll.*, 31 PERB ¶ 3070 (1998)). If the "unit recognition clause" (the language in the collective bargaining agreement that defines the bargaining unit) specifically includes the job title at issue, PERB will grant that employee organization's unit clarification petition without further inquiry (*Monroe-Woodbury CSD*, 33 PERB ¶ 3007 (2000)). However, if the unit recognition clause does not expressly include the job title(s) at issue, or if the unit recognition clause is ambiguous, PERB will examine the evidence regarding the parties' intent with respect to the composition of the unit (*Newburgh Enlarged CSD*, 37 PERB ¶ 3027 (2004), and their practices regarding representation of the title(s) at issue (*Cnty. of Niagara*, 21 PERB ¶ 3030 (1988)).

If PERB finds that a particular title has not been included in any bargaining unit, then upon a proper petition, PERB may order placement of that title in the appropriate bargaining unit (see **46:18**). Conversely, PERB may dismiss a unit placement petition if it finds that there is no appropriate, existing bargaining unit in which to place a particular job title (*Manhattan & Bronx Surface Transit Operating Auth.*, 37 PERB ¶ 3009 (2004)).

Furthermore, school districts may not negotiate with an incumbent employee organization while a bona fide question concerning representation is pending (*Cnty. of Rockland*, 10 PERB ¶ 3098 (1977)). Where such a question involves only some of the unit employees, the preclusion of negotiations covers only those employees (*Deer Park UFSD,* 22 PERB ¶ 3014 (1989)).

46:20. What are the rights of a recognized or certified employee organization?

A recognized or certified employee organization is guaranteed the exclusive right to represent in collective bargaining the employees in the bargaining unit that it is designated to represent (§§ 204(2), 208(1)(a)). The organization also has the right to represent those employees in grievance proceedings (§§ 204(2), 208(1)(a)); to dues checkoff for those employees who authorize the dues checkoff (§ 208(1)(b)); to agency shop fees from those employees who are included within the bargaining unit but who are not members of the union (§ 208(3)(b); see **46:24**); and the right not to be challenged by a rival union until thirty days before seven months prior to the expiration of a negotiated collective bargaining agreement (§ 208(2); 4 NYCRR § 201.3(d)). Thus, for example, where a collective bargaining agreement expires on June 30th, the preceding November is the challenge period.

A recognized or certified employee organization also has a general right to request and thereafter receive from an employer documents and information that are reasonable, relevant and necessary for use in collective negotiations (see **chapter 47**), the resolution of negotiation impasses (see **47:26-28**), and the administration of negotiated agreements including, but not limited to, for use of investigating a potential grievance and/or the processing of a pending grievance (see **46:42-48**). However, any such request may not impose an unreasonable burden on the employer (*Hampton Bays Teachers' Ass'n*, 41 PERB ¶ 3008 (2008), *conf'd, Hampton Bays UFSD v. PERB,* 62 A.D.3d 1066, 42 PERB ¶ 7005 (3d Dep't), *lv. to appeal denied*, 13 N.Y.3d 711, 42 PERB ¶ 7006, 42 PERB ¶ 7009 (2009); see also *N.Y. State Nurses Ass'n*, 45 PERB ¶ 3036 (2012)). In addition, employers may refuse to comply with such requests if production of the documents and information is prohibited by law, including a specific statute or regulation, or common law. But in such an instance, employers must still make a good faith effort at accommodating the need for the information (*Id.*).

46:21. May employees be forced to join an employee organization?

No. Section 202 of the Taylor Law guarantees public employees the right to join or refrain from joining employee organizations. However, amendments to the Taylor Law and the General Municipal Law give all public employee organizations the right to require all bargaining unit members who are not dues-paying members of that organization to pay agency shop fees (see **46:24**) in the amount of such dues (§§ 201(2)(b), 208(3)(b); Gen. Mun. Law § 93-b(3)). The employee, however, may demand the return of any part of an agency shop fee deduction that represents the employee's share of expenditures by the organization in aid of activities or causes of a political or ideological nature (*Id.*).

46:22. May employees who are not members of the employee organization be excluded from the bargaining unit?

No. Nonmembership in the employee organization is not a basis for exclusion from the bargaining unit, or for non-representation by the employee organization. Employees covered by the unit's definition who are not members of the union are still bound by and enjoy the benefits of the collective bargaining agreement (see §§ 203, 204(2), 209-a(2)(c)) and are required to pay an agency shop fee to the employee organization (see § 208(3)(b); see **46:21, 46:24**).

46:23. Is a recognized or certified employee organization entitled to dues deductions?

Yes. A public employer must deduct employee organization dues from employees' salaries upon the presentation of cards authorizing deduction of dues signed by the individual employees (§§ 201(2)(a), 208(1)(b)).

Once the employer has received these cards, authorization to deduct dues may remain effective until withdrawn or changed by the member employee in a written document presented to the employer (see Gen. Mun. Law § 93-b; *Erie Cnty.*, 5 PERB ¶ 3021 (1972)). This member employee right of revocation cannot be restricted by a collective bargaining agreement (see *Rochester City Sch. Dist.*, 10 PERB ¶ 3097 (1977)).

Failure to deduct membership dues and transmit them to the union is a per se violation of the Taylor Law (*City of Troy*, 28 PERB ¶ 3027 (1995)). Moreover, it is improper for a school district faced with competing claims from different employee organizations for dues money to hold such dues in escrow pending a resolution of the dispute. An employer may not refuse to remit dues to a certified employee organization unless that employee organization has been decertified (*Bd. of Educ. of City Sch. Dist. of City of Long Beach*, 35 PERB ¶ 3020 (2002)).

However, an employee organization may lose the right to dues checkoff if it is determined to have violated the Taylor Law's prohibition against strikes (§ 210(3)(a), (f); see **46:36, 46:38**).

46:24. May employees whose positions are included within a bargaining unit, but who choose not to join an employee organization, be required to pay fees to the organization?

Yes. Employees who choose not to join the employee organization whose positions are included in its bargaining unit are required to pay agency shop fees to the organization (§§ 201(2)(b), 208(3)(b); Gen. Mun. Law § 93-b(3)).

Agency shop fees are representation fees deducted from the pay of nonunion members in an amount equivalent to the membership dues paid by members of the employee organization. The employer must collect the agency shop fees and pay them to the employee organization (§§ 201(2)(b), 208(3)(b)).

However, agency shop fee payers who object to any portion of their fees being spent "in aid of activities or causes of a political or ideological nature only incidentally related to terms and conditions of employment" are entitled to be refunded that portion of such fees (§ 208(3)(b)). The employee organization must maintain a refund procedure, and at the request of such employees, it must provide them with financial information sufficient to determine whether a refund may be sought, and in what amount; if the employee organization fails to establish and maintain such a refund procedure, it has no authority to collect agency shop fees (§ 208(3)(b); *Civil Serv. Emps. Ass'n (Hartog)*, 32 PERB ¶ 3080 (1999); see *Hampton Bays Teachers Ass'n (Sullivan)*, 14 PERB ¶ 3018 (1981)). If the employee organization fails or refuses to provide this disclosure, the fee payer may be entitled to a full refund of all agency shop fees he or she has paid (see *St. Lawrence-Lewis Cnty. BOCES Teachers Ass'n (Baker)*, 15 PERB ¶ 3113 (1982); see **46:21**).

According to the U.S. Supreme Court, a union cannot collect a special assessment fee or dues increase for lobbying or other political activities from a non-member without receiving the affirmative consent of the non-member *(Knox v. Serv. Employees Int'l Union, Local 1000*, 132 S.Ct. 2277 (2012); see also **46:25**).

46:25. Are there any limitations on the use of agency shop fees?

Yes. Agency shop fees (see **46:24**) cannot be used over the objection of the fee payer for purposes other than the collective bargaining rights afforded to unions by the Taylor Law such as grievance adjustment and contract administration. According to the U.S. Supreme Court, non-union members may not be compelled to allow use of their agency shop fee contributions to subsidize union activities such as lobbying or other political activity or for public relations efforts to promote the teaching profession and public unionism in general (see *Lehnert v. Ferris Faculty Ass'n*, 500 U.S. 507, *reh'g denied*, 501 U.S. 1244, *remanded*, 937 F.2d 608 (6th Cir. 1991); *Abood v. Detroit Bd. of Educ.*, 431 U.S. 209, *reh'g denied*, 433 U.S. 915 (1977); see also *Seidemann v. Bowen*, 584 F.3d 104 (2d Cir. 2009)). However, such fees may be applied to the cost of social activities, conventions, publications, and a local union's affiliation with state and national union organizations, other than the pro rata share of the political or ideological expenditures of such affiliate, even over the objections of nonunion members of the bargaining unit (*Ellis v. Bhd. of Ry., Airline & Steamship Clerks*, 466 U.S. 435, *remanded*, 736 F.2d 1340 (9th Cir. 1984); *Lehnert v. Ferris Faculty Ass'n; see also Seidemann v. Bowen*).

Employee Contractual Relations

46:26. Do former employees or retirees enjoy representation rights under the Taylor Law?

Not generally. The law affords representational rights to public employees (§ 209-a(2)(c)). In rare cases, PERB has ruled that an employee organization may have a continuing duty to represent former employees under circumstances where their "severance from employment is contested or there is some other basis upon which to conclude that there is a continuing nexus to employment. . . ." (*Westchester Cnty. Correction Officers' Benevolent Ass'n, Inc.*, 30 PERB ¶ 3075 (1997)).

PERB has never extended this right to retirees (*Greece CSD*, 28 PERB ¶ 3048 (1995), *aff'd, Lanzillo v. PERB*, 29 PERB ¶ 7003 (Sup. Ct. Albany Cnty. 1996)). However, one appellate court has found that a "continuing nexus" to employment warranted an extension of the "duty of fair representation" to retirees who were excluded from receiving retroactive pay increases for a period when they were actively employed (see *Baker v. Bd. of Educ. Hoosick Falls CSD*, 3 A.D.3d 678, 37 PERB ¶ 7502 (3d Dep't 2004)).

46:27. Are there any employees excluded from coverage under the Taylor Law?

Yes. An employee may be excluded from a bargaining unit and excluded from coverage under the Taylor Law if he or she is properly designated as a "managerial" or "confidential" employee under the Taylor Law. Such a designation must be requested by the employer and have been granted by PERB (§ 201(7)(a); 4 NYCRR § 201.10; see **46:28-30**).

In addition, some district employees, such as continuing education teachers, may not be entitled to representation under the Taylor Law because they are considered "casual employees" who lack the regular and continuing employment relationship required for covered public employee status under the Taylor Law (see *BOCES III, Suffolk Cnty.*, 15 PERB ¶ 3015 (1982), *aff'd sub nom. BOCES III Faculty Assoc. v. PERB*, 92 A.D.2d 937, 16 PERB ¶ 7015 (2d Dep't 1983)). However, "casual" employment cannot be based upon a school employee providing services only during the school year (§ 201(7)(f)).

Unrepresented Employees (Managerial and Confidential)

46:28. How are employees designated as managerial or confidential under the Taylor Law?

Employers, including school boards, must file an application with PERB, pursuant to PERB's rules of practice, for designation of an employee as managerial or confidential (§ 201(7)(a); 4 NYCRR § 201.10). A school board may not unilaterally make this designation (*Wappingers CSD*, 16 PERB ¶ 3029 (1983)).

Applications may be filed at any time except for employees represented by a recognized or certified employee organization (4 NYCRR § 201.10(b)). For these employees, only one application may be made during an employee organization's period of unchallenged representation, which lasts until seven months prior to the expiration of the contract between the district and the union (§ 208(2); 4 NYCRR § 201.10(b)).

Even after the designation is made, it does not take effect with respect to employees covered by a negotiated agreement until the termination of the period of unchallenged representation enjoyed by the employee organization (§ 201(7)(a); see *Wappingers CSD*).

46:29. What are the criteria for designating someone as a managerial employee?

Pursuant to statute, a *managerial employee* is someone who either (1) formulates policy on behalf of an employer, or (2) may reasonably be required to assist directly in preparing for and conducting collective negotiations or have a major role in the administration of collective bargaining agreements or in personnel administration, provided that such role is not routine or clerical and requires the exercise of independent judgment (§ 201(7)(a)). According to PERB, this criteria should be applied strictly, with all uncertainties resolved in favor of coverage (*Fashion Inst. of Tech.*, 42 PERB ¶ 3018 (2009)).

Employees can be deemed to formulate policy if they "participate with regularity in the essential process involving the determination of the goals and objectives of the [employer], and of the methods for accomplishing those goals and objectives that have a substantial impact upon the affairs and the constituency of the [employer]. The formulation of policy does not extend to the determination of methods of operation that are merely of a technical nature" (*Id.*, citing *City of Binghamton*, 12 PERB ¶ 3099 (1977)). A prior standard that allowed the designation of an employee as managerial based on an employer's adoption of alternative forms of work organization that provide for greater employee participation in decision making (see *Dormitory Auth.*, 38 PERB ¶ 3029 (2005), *conf'd sub nom. CSEA, Inc. Local 1000, AFSCME, AFL-CIO v. PERB*, 34 A.D.3d 884 (3d Dep't 2006)) has been overruled by PERB (*Fashion Inst. of Tech.*).

Also, regarding the formulation of policy, PERB draws a distinction between individuals with supervisory duties and responsibilities, who are covered by the Taylor Law, and those with "broad powers to develop 'particular objectives of [the employer] in the fulfillment of its mission and the method, means and extent of achieving such objectives'" (*Id.*; *State of N.Y.*, 5 PERB ¶ 3001 (1972); *Bd. of Educ., Copiague Pub. Schs., UFSD No. 5*, 6 PERB ¶ 3001 (1973), *conf'd sub nom. Bd. of Educ. of Sch. Dist.*

No. 1 v. Helsby, 42 A.D.2d 1056, 6 PERB ¶ 7012 (2d Dep't 1973), *aff'd*, 35 N.Y.2d 877 (1974); *State of N.Y. Unified Ct. Sys.*, 30 PERB ¶ 3067 (1997), *conf'd sub nom. Lippman v. PERB*, 263 A.D.2d 891, 32 PERB ¶ 7017 (3d Dep't 1999)).

Regarding an employee's role in the administration of a contract, PERB similarly distinguishes between employees with duties related to personnel and contract administration such as the processing of grievances, and employees with a major role in implementing the agreement such as those with the authority to change the employer's operation procedures and methods (*Fashion Inst. of Tech.*; *State of N.Y.*, 5 PERB ¶ 3001 (1972); *Metro. Suburban Bus. Auth.*, 7 PERB ¶ 3025 (1974), *conf'd sub nom. Metro. Suburban Bus Auth. v. PERB*, 48 A.D.2d 206, 8 PERB ¶ 7009 (3d Dep't 1975), *lv. to appeal denied*, 37 N.Y.2d 712 (1975); *Bd. of Educ. of the City Sch. Dist. of the City of N.Y.*, 15 PERB ¶ 3031 (1982)).

In the past, building principals generally have not been designated as managerial (*N.Y. City Sch. Dist.*, 6 PERB ¶ 3040 (1973), but see *McGraw CSD*, 21 PERB ¶ 3001 (1988), where two principals were designated managerial because of their policy-making functions and personnel administration responsibilities; *Ellenville CSD*, 16 PERB ¶ 3066 (1983), where two principals also were designated as managerial due to the negotiating responsibilities given to them; and *Mount Morris CSD*, 41 PERB ¶ 3020 (2008), where two principals and an assistant principal were designated as managerial due to their duties, which included mandatory attendance at public board meetings and executive sessions, and filling in for the superintendent during her absences approximately two days each week).

46:30. What are the criteria for designating someone as a confidential employee?

An employee may be designated *confidential* only if he or she serves in a confidential relationship to a managerial employee who directly assists in collective bargaining or has a major role in contract or personnel administration (§ 201(7)(a)).

According to PERB case law, "an employee is confidential . . . only when in the course of assisting a managerial employee who exercises labor relations responsibilities, that employee has access or is privy to information related to collective bargaining, contract administration, or other aspects of labor-management relations on a regular basis which is not appropriate for the eyes and ears of rank and file personnel or their negotiating representative" (*Wappingers CSD*, 19 PERB ¶ 3059 (1986); *Penfield CSD*, 14 PERB ¶ 4044, *aff'd*, 14 PERB ¶ 3082 (1981)), and has a confidential relationship with a managerial employee (*Town of DeWitt*, 32 PERB ¶ 3001 (1999); *North Rose-Wolcott CSD*, 33 PERB ¶ 3002 (2000); see also *Rockland Cnty. BOCES*, 34 PERB ¶ 3032 (2001)).

Improper Practices – In General

46:31. What is an improper practice?

An *improper practice* is an action of either an employee organization or a public employer that is prohibited by section 209-a of the Civil Service Law (see **46:34-36**). Most improper practices infringe on another party's ability to exercise rights granted by law.

Until June 30, 2017, a party who files an improper practice charge also may petition PERB for injunctive relief pending a decision on the merits. That party must show reasonable cause to believe that an improper practice has occurred, and that immediate and irreparable injury, loss, or damage will result that would render a subsequent judgment on the merits ineffectual. Upon such a showing, PERB could issue an order permitting the charging party to seek injunctive relief from a state Supreme Court, but, in practice PERB itself petitions the court for such injunctive relief on behalf of the charging party (§ 209-a(4)).

46:32. Is there a deadline for filing improper practice charges?

Yes. For an improper practice charge to be timely, it must be filed within four months of either the date when the decision to take the action complained of is announced or the date when the action is implemented (4 NYCRR § 204.1(a)(1); *City of Oswego*, 23 PERB ¶ 3007 (1990)). In determining whether the filing of an improper practice charge alleging that the employer refused to negotiate in good faith is timely, PERB will consider when the employee organization had actual or constructive knowledge of the act or acts that form the basis of the charge (*N.Y. State Thruway*, 40 PERB ¶ 3014 (2007)).

It is noteworthy that even though courts have ruled that if the relief sought is fundamentally private and the issue does not have significant public policy implications, the employee organization must serve the school district a notice of claim within three months after the basis for the improper practice charge arose (Educ. Law § 3813(1); *Bd. of Educ. of the Union-Endicott CSD v. PERB*, 197 A.D.2d 276, 27 PERB ¶ 7005 (3d Dep't), *appeal denied*, 84 N.Y.2d 803, 27 PERB ¶ 7013 (1994); *Deposit CSD v. PERB*, 214 A.D.2d 288, 28 PERB ¶ 7013 (3d Dep't 1995), *appeal denied*, 88 N.Y.2d 866, 29 PERB ¶ 7007 (1996); see **66:5**), PERB has determined that the notice of claim requirement is not a prerequisite to the filing of an improper practice charge (*Manhasset UFSD*, 41 PERB ¶ 3005 (2008), *conf'd sub nom. and modified, in part*, *Manhasset UFSD v. PERB*, 61 A.D.3d 1231, 42 PERB ¶ 7004 (3d Dep't 2009), *on remittitur,* 42 PERB ¶ 3016 (2009)).

46:33. What happens if PERB agrees that an improper practice was committed?

PERB is authorized to order the offending party to cease and desist from that improper practice and to "take such affirmative action as will effectuate the policies" of the Taylor Law, including ordering payment of lost wages with interest, and reinstatement of employees with or without back pay. Under "exceptional circumstances," attorneys' fees may be awarded (§ 205(5)(d); see *City of Troy*, 28 PERB ¶ 3027 (1995); *Town of Henrietta*, 28 PERB ¶ 3079 (1995)).

PERB also has the authority, in its discretion, to make employees whole for the loss of pay and/or benefits resulting from an employer's violation of a cease and desist order and the underlying unfair labor practice, by:

1. providing that any remedy between the parties be given retroactive effect to the date on which the unfair labor practice was found to have commenced; and
2. providing for appropriate interest from that date, calculated using the short-term federal rate for the underpayment of taxes as set out in 26 USC § 6621. However, PERB might not order payment of such interest when the employee organization is also found to have refused to bargain in good faith (see § 205(5)(d); see *Manhasset UFSD*, 41 PERB ¶ 3005 (2008), *conf'd sub nom. and modified, in part, Manhasset UFSD v. PERB*, 61 A.D.3d 1231, 42 PERB ¶ 7004 (3d Dep't), *on remittitur*, 42 PERB ¶ 3016 (2009)).

46:34. What are some examples of possible improper practices by a public employer?

An employer commits an improper practice when it:

- Fails to negotiate collectively in good faith (§ 209-a(1)(d); see § 204(2), (3); see **47:4**).
- Fails to continue all the terms of an expired agreement until a new one is negotiated, unless the employee organization has engaged in, caused, instigated, encouraged, or condoned a strike (§ 209-a(1)(e); see § 210(1); see **46:36, 46:38**).
- Deliberately interferes with the rights of public employees to participate in or refrain from participating in employee organizations of their own choosing (§ 209-a(1)(a); see § 202; *East Meadow Teachers Ass'n, NYSUT, AFT, NEA, AFL-CIO,* 43 PERB ¶ 4530 (2010); *East Meadow*

Teachers Ass'n NYSUT, AFT, AFL-CIO, 48 PERB ¶ 3006 (2015); *Greenburgh 11 UFSD*, 33 PERB ¶ 3018 (2000); see also *City of Syracuse*, 36 PERB ¶ 3047 (2003), *aff'd,* 24 A.D.3d 913, 38 PERB ¶ 7017 (3d Dep't 2005); see **46:3, 46:14**).

- Dominates or interferes with the formation or administration of employee organizations (§ 209-a(1)(b); see also **46:14-17**).
- Discriminates against any employee for the purpose of encouraging or discouraging membership or participation in an employee organization (§ 209-a(1)(c)).
- Uses state funds appropriated for any purpose to train supervisors or other administrators in methods to discourage union organization or to discourage an employee from participating in a union-organizing drive (§ 209-a(1)(f); see also **46:4**).
- Fails to permit or refuses to afford an employee the right to representation by a representative of the employee organization, or the organization's designee, when at the time of questioning by the employer it reasonably appears that the employee may be the subject of a potential disciplinary action (§ 209-a(1)(g)).

In one case, a school district did not commit an improper practice when the building principal discussed grievance issues during a faculty in-service meeting, ordered the union president to leave the meeting when she became disruptive and insubordinate, and counseled her verbally and in writing for her behavior. The principal was entitled to offer his position on pending grievances and his statements were not intended to coerce any employees into relinquishing any Taylor Law rights. In addition, unions have no statutory right to use work time or the employer's facilities for conducting union activity, and employees may not break work rules to engage in protected union activity. The contract was clear as to use of the work-day faculty meeting for purposes solely designated by the district. Therefore, the principal had a right to limit the union president's comments and discipline her for her behavior (*Glen Cove City Sch. Dist.*, 42 PERB ¶ 4546 (2009)).

A public employer also commits an improper practice when it favors one union over another. That was the case where the New York City Department of Education eliminated the automatic grant of parking permits for custodian engineers but continued to issue permits to teachers pursuant to an agreement between the teachers' union and the mayor's office (*City of N.Y. v. PERB*, 103 A.D.3d 145 (3d Dep't 2012), *lv. to appeal denied,* 21 N.Y.3d 855 (2013)).

46:35. Does an employer's refusal to provide an employee with information for use in preparation for grievance arbitration constitute an improper practice?

It may. Both employers and employee organizations have a reciprocal obligation, as part of the duty to bargain in good faith, to provide each other with information that is necessary and relevant to collective bargaining (*Bd. of Educ. of the City Sch. Dist. of the City of Buffalo*, 36 PERB ¶ 3034 (2003), *conf'd*, 9 A.D.3d 851 (4th Dep't), *reargument granted*, 11 A.D.3d 1046 (4th Dep't 2004); see **47:4**)). The failure to do so may constitute an improper practice.

This employer obligation to provide information extends to "information relevant and material to the investigation or prosecution of a potential grievance" (*Hampton Bays Teachers' Ass'n*, 41 PERB ¶ 3008 (2008) *conf'd sub nom. Hampton Bays UFSD v. PERB,* 62 A.D.3d 1066, 42 PERB ¶ 7005 (3d Dep't), *lv. to appeal denied,* 13 N.Y.3d 711, 42 PERB ¶¶ 7006, 7009 (2009); see also *Bd. of Educ., City Sch. Dist. of the City of Albany*, 6 PERB ¶ 3012 (1973)). It continues after a demand for arbitration has been filed, even though the same information also may be available by way of subpoena from an arbitrator (*Greenburgh No. 11 UFSD*, 33 PERB ¶ 3059 (2000); see also **46:42-48** for a discussion on grievances).

In *Cnty. of Erie & Erie Cnty. Sheriff* (36 PERB ¶ 3021 (2003), *conf'd sub nom. Cnty. of Erie v. State*, 14 A.D.3d 14, 37 PERB ¶ 7008 (3d Dep't 2004), *amended by* 789 N.Y.S.2d 453, 38 PERB ¶ 7004

(3d Dep't 2005)), a New York appellate court upheld PERB's determination that a union was entitled to information about an employer's investigation into complaints of sexual harassment (including a list of the people interviewed and the investigator's interview summaries, findings, etc.) allegedly committed by a union member. Although acknowledging the employer's sensitivity to the rights of the alleged victims, PERB found that the union had a legitimate need for the information so that it could defend its member.

However, PERB also has ruled that under appropriate circumstances, an *in camera* inspection by the grievance arbitrator may be warranted to determine whether the employer must share otherwise privileged or confidential information with the union in furtherance of its grievance (see *State of N.Y. (OMRDD)*, 38 PERB ¶ 3036, *aff'd sub nom. In the Matter of CSEA v. PERB*, 14 Misc.3d 199, 39 PERB ¶ 7009 (Sup. Ct. Albany Cnty. 2006), *aff'd,* 46 A.D.3d 1037, 40 PERB ¶ 7009 (3d Dep't 2007); see also *Town of Evans*, 37 PERB ¶ 3016 (2004)).

46:36. What are some examples of possible improper practices by an employee organization?

An employee organization (union) commits an improper practice when it interferes with the right of public employees to participate in or refrain from participating in employee organizations of their own choosing (§§ 209-a(2)(a), 202; see also Lab. Law § 211-a), when it refuses to negotiate collectively in good faith with a public employer as it is required to do (§§ 209-a(2)(b), 204(2), (3)), or when it breaches its duty of fair representation to public employees under the Taylor Law (§ 209-a(2)(c)). To establish a breach of the duty of fair representation, the party must demonstrate that the union's conduct or actions were arbitrary, discriminatory or founded in bad faith (*Civil Serv. Employees Ass'n (Munroe)* 46 PERB ¶ 4529 (2014); see also *DeOliveria v. PERB*, (3d Cir. 2015)). A public employee's sole remedy for breaches of representation by a union is to bring an improper practice charge under the Taylor Law (*Palladino v. CNY Centro, Inc.*, 23 N.Y.3d 140 (2014)).

It also is an improper practice for an employee organization to make a credible threat of a strike in order to create pressure in negotiations (see *East Meadow UFSD*, 16 PERB ¶ 3086 (1983)), or to threaten to *work to rule*, which is a concerted refusal to participate in "voluntary" activities, such as escorting students on field trips, writing recommendation letters for students or attending faculty meetings, where the school district has a reasonable expectation of participation (see *Haverling CSD*, 22 PERB ¶ 4554 (1989); see **46:38**).

It is also an improper practice for an employee organization to fail or refuse to provide to an agency shop fee payer an independently audited statement of its expenses and those of its affiliates, upon refund of a portion of such fees, along with an explanation of how the refund amount was determined, to allow an individual to object to the amount refunded (*Pub. Employees Fed'n (Raterman)*, 15 PERB ¶ 3024 (1982), *aff'd*, *Pub. Employees Fed'n v. PERB*, 93 A.D.2d 910, 16 PERB ¶ 7016 (3d Dep't 1983); *United Univ. Professions v. Newman*, 146 A.D.2d 273, 22 PERB ¶ 7012 (3d Dep't), *appeal denied*, 74 N.Y.2d 614, 22 PERB ¶ 7033 (1989); *Civil Serv. Employees Ass'n (Hartog)*, 32 PERB ¶ 3080 (1999); see **46:24**).

46:37. Does a union commit an improper practice in violation of its duty of fair representation if it does not obtain the exact same benefits for every member of the bargaining unit?

No. The duty of fair representation does not require an employee organization to obtain the same treatment for everyone it represents. "Where a union undertakes a good faith balancing of the divergent interests of its membership and chooses to forego benefits which may be gained for one class of employees in exchange for benefits to other employees, such accommodation does not, of necessity, violate the Union's duty of fair representation" (*Civil Serv. Bar Ass'n, Local 237 v. City of N.Y.*, 64 N.Y.2d 188, 17 PERB ¶ 7503 (1984); but see *Baker v. Thompson* 194 Misc.2d 116, 36 PERB ¶ 7501 (Sup. Ct. Rensselaer Cnty. 2002), *aff'd sub nom. Baker v. Bd. of Educ.*, 3 A.D.3d 678, 37 PERB ¶ 7502 (3d Dep't 2004)).

Improper Practice –Strikes and Pressure Tactics

46:38. What types of activities constitute a prohibited strike?

Any strike activity is prohibited activity. Specifically, the Taylor Law defines prohibited *strike activity* as "any strike or other concerted stoppage of work or slowdown by public employees" (§ 201(9)). It also states that "an employee who is absent from work without permission, or who abstains wholly or in part from the full performance of his duties in his normal manner without permission, on the date or dates when a strike occurs, shall be presumed to have engaged in such strike on such date or dates" (§ 210(2)(b)). For instance, an abnormally high absentee rate among employees may be deemed a strike (*Orleans-Niagara BOCES Teachers Ass'n*, 28 PERB ¶ 3050 (1995); *CSEA of Yonkers*, 13 PERB ¶ 3026, *aff'd*, 78 A.D.2d 1016, 13 PERB ¶ 7018 (2d Dep't 1980)).

A violation of this prohibition can be found in many forms of conduct, including a boycott of voluntary assignments or other work, such as field trips (*Pearl River UFSD*, 11 PERB ¶ 4530, *aff'd*, 11 PERB ¶ 3085 (1978)) and parent orientation sessions (see *Horseheads Teachers Ass'n and N.Y. State United Teachers*, 15 PERB ¶ 3110 (1982)); a boycott of faculty meetings (see *Webutuck Teachers Ass'n*, 13 PERB ¶ 3041 (1980)); refusal to help students or volunteer for extracurricular assignments (see *Baylis v. Seaford UFSD*, 22 PERB ¶ 7533 (Sup. Ct. Nassau Cnty. 1989)); or even to threaten to "work to rule," which is a boycott of "voluntary" activities (see *Haverling CSD*, 22 PERB ¶ 4554 (1989)).

A union's responsibility for an unlawful strike can be established through circumstantial evidence (*Orleans-Niagara BOCES Teachers Ass'n*).

46:39. What types of sanctions and penalties may be imposed against employees and employee organizations in the event of a strike?

There are court-imposed, PERB-administered, and school district-imposed sanctions and penalties against striking employees and their employee organizations.

- A court may issue an injunction against a strike, and if the injunction is violated, impose penalties for contempt (§ 211; Jud. Law §§ 750–751).
- PERB may determine that the employee organization will lose its automatic dues checkoff and any agency shop fee deduction privileges (§ 210(3)(a), (f); see § 208(1)(b), (3)(b); see, *e.g.*, *Yonkers Fed'n of Teachers*, 32 PERB ¶ 3075; see also *Buffalo City Sch. Dist.*, 34 PERB ¶ 3012 (2001)).
- School districts are required to make certain deductions from the pay of each employee found in violation (§ 210(2)(f); see also **46:38**). Specifically, employees who strike are to be penalized twice their daily rate of pay for each day they are engaged in the strike (§ 210(2)(f)), as well as being subject to removal or other disciplinary action and penalties for misconduct (§ 210(2)(a)).

Furthermore, when an employee organization engages in prohibited strike activities, the district is no longer obligated to comply with the *Triborough* Amendment, which otherwise requires the continuation of the terms of an expired agreement until a new agreement is reached (§ 209-a(1)(e); see also **47:31**). The employee organization also may lose its right to charge an employer with an improper practice for making unilateral changes in mandatory subjects of bargaining (see *Somers CSD*, 9 PERB ¶ 3061 (1976)).

46:40. What are a school district's responsibilities in the event of a strike by school district employees?

Section 211 of the Civil Service Law provides that when it appears that public employees are threatening to strike, are about to strike, or have gone out on strike, the public employer, through its chief legal officer, must immediately apply to the New York State Supreme Court for an injunction against the strike. A temporary restraining order forbidding the strike may be issued by the court immediately (C.P.L.R. §§ 6301, 6313). Those who continue to strike despite the restraining order are in contempt of court and subject to penalties of up to $1,000 and/or 30 days' imprisonment, at the discretion of the court (Jud. Law § 751(1)).

Furthermore, school officials must impose the "two-for-one" payroll penalty on strikers. This penalty is a loss of twice the daily rate of pay for every day the employee strikes (§ 210(2)(f)). If the strike involved only limited activities, such as extracurricular and coaching activities, the district may be limited to withholding compensation for those activities only (see *Baylis v. Seaford UFSD*, 22 PERB ¶ 7533 (Sup. Ct. Nassau Cnty. 1989); see **46:38**). These deductions must be made between 30 and 90 days after a determination that employees have violated the law prohibiting strikes, and cannot be made outside this statutory time period (§ 210(2)(f); see *King v. Carey*, 57 N.Y.2d 505, 15 PERB ¶ 7545 (1982)). Measurement of the 30 to 90-day time period does not start until the affected employees have been notified individually of the determination that they have committed a violation (*Plainview-Old Bethpage Congress of Teachers v. Bd. of Educ.*, 100 A.D.2d 849, 17 PERB ¶ 7507 (2d Dep't), *aff'd*, 63 N.Y.2d 921, 17 PERB ¶ 7533, *reh'g denied*, 64 N.Y.2d 755 (1984)).

Separate from the imposition of the payroll penalty, the Taylor Law prohibits the payment by the employer of any compensation to a public employee for any day or any part of a day in which he or she engages in such prohibited activities (§ 210(3)(h)).

Finally, the school district is responsible for notifying and providing information to PERB concerning the strike violations (§ 210(3)(b)). School officials also should give PERB's Office of Counsel sufficient information so that it may begin proceedings to revoke the offending employee organization's dues and agency shop fee deduction privileges (see § 210(3)(a), (f); see **46:39**).

46:41. What are pressure tactics and are they permissible?

The term *pressure tactics* refers to activities by the parties during the collective bargaining process to try and influence the outcome of negotiations. Some are permissible under the law. Others, including a strike or the threat of a strike (§ 201(9)), are not (see *East Meadow UFSD*, 16 PERB ¶ 3086 (1983); see also **46:38**).

For example, a cartoon in a union newsletter depicting board members and an administrator as clowns and circus animals was found to not violate the Taylor Law (*Wappingers CSD*, 27 PERB ¶ 3033 (1994)). So was a letter from a union president to the board president's employer implying that the board president was dishonest (*Carmel CSD*, 31 PERB ¶ 3073 (1998)).

Regarding the wearing of union t-shirts, black garb, or other signs of union solidarity on a given day, there are no cases on whether this type of conduct is permissible under the Taylor Law. However, teachers, like students, do not "shed their constitutional rights to freedom of speech or expression at the schoolhouse gate" (*Tinker v. Des Moines Indep. Cmty. Sch. Dist.*, 393 U.S. 503 (1969); see also *Melzer v. Bd. of Educ. of the City Sch. Dist. of the City of N.Y.*, 336 F.3d 185 (2d Cir. 2003)). Therefore, from a constitutional perspective, districts must allow the wearing of such items unless a significant governmental interest (such as preventing a substantial likelihood of disruption of the educational process) justifies a prohibition (see *Appeal of Moessinger,* 33 Ed Dept Rep 487 (1994); *Scott v. Myers*, 191 F.3d 82 (2d Cir. 1999)).

Engaging in "informational picketing" and distributing leaflets on public property, just outside school property, has been deemed protected activity unless a district can show a safety hazard to students and staff (*East Meadow Teachers Ass'n, NYSUT, AFT, AFL-CIO*, 43 PERB ¶ 4530 (2010); *East Meadow Teachers Ass'n, NYSUT, AFT, AFL-CIO*, 48 PERB ¶ 3006 (2015); see also *Santer v. Bd. of Educ. of East Meadow UFSD*, 23 N.Y.3d 251 (2014)). Such a hazard existed where a teacher parked his car in front of a school with protest signs in the windows, students could not safely reach the curb, and the resulting traffic congestion caused 16 teachers to be late to work (*East Meadow Teachers' Ass'n; Santer v. Bd. Of Educ. of East Meadow UFSD*).

A common pressure tactic is for union members to attend school board meetings. As members of the public, union members have a right to attend open portions of school board meetings under the Open Meetings Law (*Goetschius v. Bd. of Educ. of the Greenburgh 11 UFSD*, 244 A.D.2d 552 (2d Dep't 1997)). However, under the Taylor Law they do not have a right to use school district property for communicating with the public regarding negotiation disputes (*Matter of Chateaugay CSD*, 19 PERB ¶ 3076 (1986)).

Contractual Grievances

46:42. What is a grievance?

Generally, a *grievance* is a claim that a specific provision (or provisions) of a collective bargaining agreement has been violated. However, contractual grievance procedures may be extended by mutual agreement to apply to a broad range of actions and decisions outside the contract, such as the application of district policies (see, e.g., *City of Schenectady*, 21 PERB ¶ 3022 (1988); *Pearl River UFSD*, 11 PERB ¶ 3085 (1978)).

The grievant, the party bringing the grievance, seeks a determination that the other party has violated the contract and that specific remedial action should be taken.

A school district's use of intimidating and coercive measures, such as installing metal detectors at grievance hearings or changing the location of grievance hearings or other grievance procedures, without union agreement, may violate an employee's rights under the Taylor Law to have grievances heard (*Greenburgh 11 UFSD*, 33 PERB ¶ 3018 (2000)).

46:43. How are grievances resolved?

In most cases, procedures for resolutions of grievances, or grievance procedures, are negotiated as a part of school district collective bargaining agreements. The Taylor Law provides that a certified or recognized employee organization (see **46:14-17**) has the right to represent employees in the settlement of grievances (§§ 203–204, 208(1)(a)).

Most grievance procedures involve several different levels or steps that are progressively invoked to satisfy both parties. If a grievance cannot be resolved internally between the parties, such agreements usually provide for a final settlement by either advisory or binding arbitration (see **46:46-48**).

In addition, Article 15-C of the General Municipal Law (which predates the Taylor Law) specifies rules regarding grievance procedures. Specifically, any political subdivision of the state, including school districts, that has 100 or more full-time employees, except the city of New York, must establish certain minimal grievance procedures (Gen. Mun. Law §§ 682(1), 684(1)). These mandated grievance procedures must consist of at least two stages and cover any grievance relating to employees' health or safety, physical facilities, materials or equipment furnished to employees or supervision of employees. The law does not require that grievance procedures address issues of an employee's rate of compensation, retirement benefits, disciplinary proceedings or other matters that can be appealed to the commissioner of education or through a contractual grievance procedure (see Gen. Mun. Law § 682(4)).

If a school district does not adopt a grievance procedure, the procedures established by the General Municipal Law, which consist of two stages and an appellate stage, go into effect automatically under that law's requirement (Gen. Mun. Law § 684(1)). That law also calls for final resolution of grievances by advisory arbitration by a grievance board appointed by the superintendent (Gen. Mun. Law § 684(4), (7)).

Because the arbitration is advisory, the school board either may accept or reject the grievance board's recommendations.

46:44. May a school board agree to voluntary arbitration for the resolution of grievances?

Yes. But a claimed grievance will be arbitrable only if the arbitration claim with respect to the particular subject matter is authorized by the Taylor Law, and whether the parties indeed agreed by the terms of the arbitration clause in the operable collective bargaining agreement to refer their differences in the specific area to arbitration (*Bd. of Educ. of Watertown City Sch. Dist. v. Watertown Educ. Ass'n*, 93 N.Y.2d 132, 32 PERB ¶ 7502 (1999)).

Thus, where there is an agreement to arbitrate grievances arising under a collective bargaining agreement, a particular grievance would not be mandatorily arbitrable if it falls outside of the agreement to arbitrate (*Matter of Massena CSD (Massena Confederated Sch. Employees' Assn., NYSUT, AFL-CIO)*, 64 A.D.3d 859 (3d Dep't 2009) and 82 A.D.3d 1312 (3d Dep't 2011); *Pocantico Hills CSD v. Pocantico Hills Teachers Ass'n*, 264 A.D.2d 397 (2d Dep't 1999), *appeal denied*, 94 N.Y.2d 759 (2000)). In such an instance, once an arbitrator determines a collective bargaining agreement is silent on the subject of the grievance, the arbitrator would be bound by the limiting language of the agreement. That was the case where the agreement limited the arbitrator's authority to "interpret[ing] the provisions of the [agreement] and to decide cases of alleged violations of such provisions. The arbitrator shall not supplement, enlarge, diminish, or alter the scope of meaning of the [agreement] . . . not entertain jurisdiction of any subject matter not covered [by the agreement]. . . ." (*Matter of Massena CSD (Massena Confederated Sch. Emps. Ass'n NYSUT, AFL-CIO)*).

46:45. Are there some subjects that cannot be negotiated and submitted to arbitration?

Yes. Some duties or responsibilities are so important that a school district will not be permitted to delegate them or to bargain them away. For example, a school board cannot surrender its statutory authority and allow an arbitrator to determine whether a teacher is to be granted tenure (see *Cohoes City Sch. Dist. v. Cohoes Teachers Ass'n*, 40 N.Y.2d 774, 9 PERB ¶ 7529 (1976)). Similarly, requiring a school district to arbitrate the termination of a teacher who failed to obtain or maintain proper teacher certification mandated by law violates public policy because school districts are not legally permitted to employ teachers who lack proper certification (*N.Y. State Office of Children & Family Servs. v. Lanterman*, 62 A.D.3d 1109 (3d Dep't 2009), *aff'd*, 14 N.Y.3d 275 (2010)).

In addition, a collective bargaining agreement cannot afford superior rights to employees who hold a provisional position beyond the statutorily allowable time period (*City of Long Beach v. CSEA, Inc.Long Beach Unit*, 8 N.Y.3d 465, 40 PERB ¶ 7521 (2007)). Furthermore, a school board cannot be divested of its right to inspect teacher personnel files (*Bd. of Educ., Great Neck UFSD v. Areman*, 41 N.Y.2d 527, 10 PERB ¶ 7512 (1977)); or be bound by contractual provisions that interfere with a school board's responsibility to maintain adequate classroom standards (see *Honeoye Falls-Lima CSD v. Honeoye Falls-Lima Educ. Ass'n*, 49 N.Y.2d 732, 13 PERB ¶ 7524 (1980)).

Likewise, a collective bargaining agreement cannot divest a school board of its authority to decide which positions to eliminate and determine staffing and budgetary needs to ensure the delivery of uninterrupted services (see *Cnty. of Chautauqua v. CSEA, Local 1000*, 8 N.Y.3d 513, 40 PERB ¶ 7522 (2007)). In contrast, a school board may voluntarily agree to a so called "job security" provision and to submit to arbitration disputes over job security (*Bd. of Educ. of the Yonkers City Sch. Dist. v. Yonkers Fed'n of Teachers*, 40 N.Y.2d 268 (1976)). But to be valid and enforceable, any such provision must be explicit, unambiguous and comprehensive, and of relative brief duration (*Id.*; see also *Johnson City Prof'l Firefighters Local 921 v. Village of Johnson City*, 18 N.Y.3d 32 (2011)). That was the case where a district agreed that "[d]uring the life of this contract no person in [the teacher's] bargain unit shall be terminated due to budgetary reasons or abolition of programs but only for unsatisfactory job performance as provided for under the Tenure Law" (*Bd. of Educ. of the Yonkers City Sch. Dist. v. Yonkers Fed'n of Teachers*). But it was not in a case where the provision merely stated "[p]resent members may be removed for cause but will not be removed as a result of Post elimination" (*Yonkers Sch. Crossing Guard Union of Westchester Ch., CSEA v. City of Yonkers*, 39 N.Y.2d 964 (1976)). Furthermore, to be valid and enforceable, a job security provision must not have been negotiated during a legislatively declared period of financial emergency between parties of unequal bargaining power (*Burke v. Bowen*, 40 N.Y.2d 264 (1976); see also *Johnson City Prof'l Firefighters Local 921 v. Village of Johnson City*).

Although ill advised, it does not offend public policy for a district to bargain away the right to choose between qualified applicants for a particular teaching assignment (*United Fed'n of Teachers, Local 2 v. Bd. of Educ. of the City Sch. Dist. of the City of N.Y.*, 1 N.Y.3d 72, 37 PERB ¶ 7503 (2003)). In contrast, a school board cannot be bound to appoint a certified teacher whose position has been abolished to any other vacant position in the teacher's area of certification because the board would be divested of its discretion to prescribe additional qualifications to a teaching position (*Bd. of Educ. of Valhalla UFSD v. Valhalla Teachers Ass'n,* 112 A.D.3d 620 (2d Dep't 2013)). Arbitration over hiring procedures in a collective bargaining agreement that require all candidates for teaching positions to be interviewed and approved by a teacher committee has been allowed (*Mineola UFSD v. Mineola Teachers' Ass'n*, 37 A.D.3d 605, 40 PERB ¶ 7506 (2d Dep't 2007)).

46:46. Is arbitration of a grievance dispute binding or advisory?

The parties involved in a grievance may agree that arbitration either will be advisory, where the arbitrator's decision has limited legal effect, or binding, where the arbitrator's decision will be final and binding and can be appealed only under certain limited circumstances (see **46:47**).

46:47. May grievance decisions rendered after binding arbitration be appealed in court?

Yes. Pursuant to New York's civil practice laws and rules, an arbitrator's award may be challenged in court (C.P.L.R. Art. 75). However, the standard by which a court will overturn or reject a decision rendered after arbitration is difficult to meet.

In a review of a binding arbitration decision, errors of law or fact are generally not grounds to vacate the arbitrator's award (*Falzone v. N.Y. Central Mutual Fire Ins. Co.*, 15 N.Y.3d 530 (2010)), and courts will grant a petition to vacate the award only in cases where:

- There was corruption, fraud, or misconduct in procuring the award.
- The arbitrator was biased.
- The arbitrator exceeded his or her power or so imperfectly executed that power that a final and definite award was not made (see *Bd. of Educ. v. Amityville Teacher's Ass'n*, 62 A.D.3d 992 (2d Dep't 2009); see also *Matter of Civil Serv. Employees Ass'n, Inc. Local 1000, AFSCME, AFL-CIO, Onondaga Local 834, Syracuse City Sch. Dist. Unit 6* (*Bd. of Educ. of Syracuse City Sch. Dist.*), 133 A.D.3d 1349 (4th Dep't 2015)).
- The arbitrator failed to follow procedure (C.P.L.R. § 7511(b)(1)).

An arbitrator exceeds his or her power if an award violates a strong public policy, is "totally" or "completely" irrational, or exceeds a specifically enumerated limitation on his or her power (*Silverman v. Benmor Coats, Inc.*, 61 N.Y.2d 299 (1984); *Rochester City Sch. Dist. v. Rochester Teachers Ass'n*, 41 N.Y.2d 578, 10 PERB ¶ 7513 (1977); *Peterson v. Katonah-Lewisboro UFSD*, 134 A.D.3d 1125 (2d Dep't 2015)). For example, in a case challenging the reduced salary of a former elementary school principal whose position was abolished but was later recalled as a middle school assistant principal, on the basis that both positions warranted the same level of pay, a state appellate court ruled that the commissioner of education has primary jurisdiction to determine whether two positions are similar and that arbitration over such a dispute is barred by public policy (*Alden CSD v. Alden Cent. Schs. Administrators' Ass'n.*, 115 A.D.3d 1340 (4th Dep't 2014)).

46:48. May grievance decisions rendered after advisory arbitration be appealed in court?

Advisory arbitration awards themselves usually may not be appealed. As a general rule, a court will not confirm an award issued following advisory arbitration (*Benjamin Rush Emps. United v. McCarthy*, 76 N.Y.2d 781, 23 PERB ¶ 7530 (1990)). However, in certain circumstances, the parties may, by their conduct, convert an arbitration award issued pursuant to an agreement providing for advisory arbitration into a binding determination (*Bd. of Educ. v. Yonkers Fed'n of Teachers*, 46 N.Y.2d 727 (1978); *Hempstead Classroom Teachers Ass'n v. Bd. of Educ.*, 79 A.D.2d 709, 14 PERB ¶ 7521 (2d Dep't 1980); compare with *Plainedge Fed'n of Teachers v. Plainedge UFSD*, 58 N.Y.2d 902 (1983)).

On the other hand, once a school board has made a final decision on an advisory arbitration award, that determination may be overturned by a court if the board acted in an "arbitrary" or "capricious" manner when accepting or rejecting the award (C.P.L.R. § 7803; *Pell v. Bd. of Educ. of UFSD No. 1 of the Towns of Scarsdale & Mamaroneck*, 34 N.Y.2d 222 (1974)).

46:49. How are arbitrators selected?

Arbitration clauses usually designate one of a number of organizations, usually the American Arbitration Association (AAA) or PERB, as the administrator of an arbitration agreement. Thereafter, the organization may do most of the selection and scheduling work, including sending the parties one or more lists of names of arbitrators for each party to rank or veto, and appointing the highest-ranking arbitrator who was not vetoed by either party (see, e.g., 4 NYCRR § 207.7; AAA Labor Arbitration Rule 12). Arbitrators may also be named in a collective bargaining agreement, selected from a panel created by the parties, or agreed upon by the parties *ad hoc*.

47. The Collective Bargaining Process[1]

Basic Requirements

47:1. What is collective bargaining?

According to the Taylor Law (see **46:1**), *collective bargaining*, also known as *collective negotiations*, is the process for fulfilling the mutual obligation of an employer and an employee organization to meet at reasonable times and confer in good faith over the wages, hours and other terms and conditions of employment of public employees, or the negotiation of an agreement, or any question arising thereunder, and the execution of a reached agreement (§ 204(3)).

47:2. Are public employers required to engage in collective bargaining?

Yes. The Taylor Law requires public employers to negotiate in "good faith" (see **47:4**) with an employee organization that has been recognized or certified as the exclusive representative of a bargaining unit of its public employees (§ 204(2), (3); see **46:14-17**).

An employer's refusal to negotiate in good faith is an "improper practice" (§ 209-a(1)(d); see **46:31**, **46:34**).

Nonetheless, while a bona fide question concerning representation is pending before PERB, a public employer may not negotiate with the incumbent employee organization with respect to employees affected by that question (*Deer Park UFSD*, 22 PERB ¶ 3014 (1989); *Cnty. of Rockland*, 10 PERB ¶ 3098 (1977)).

47:3. Do public employers have to continue bargaining once an agreement is reached?

Not generally. Once a collective bargaining agreement (CBA) is reached, unless the CBA contains a "re-opener clause" that unambiguously provides for a full re-opening of negotiations on a particular subject or subjects, the parties no longer have an obligation to negotiate during the duration of the CBA concerning any subject that is expressly covered by the CBA (*Matter of Roma v. Ruffo*, 92 N.Y.2d 489, 31 PERB ¶ 7504 (1998); see also *Cnty. of Nassau*, 31 PERB ¶ 3064 (1998)).

However, a newly certified or recognized employee organization has the "immediate right to negotiate for employees in the unit even though there may still be in existence an unexpired agreement entered into with the former representative." (*CSEA Local 1000, AFSCME, AFL-CIO (Avon CSD)*, 36 PERB ¶ 3032 (2003); *City of Newburgh*, 20 PERB ¶ 3017 (1987); see also § 208(1)(a)).

In addition, public employers must negotiate over the impact of managerial decisions that affect terms and conditions of employment (see **47:16-17**).

[1] *All statutory references in this chapter are to the New York State Civil Service Law unless noted otherwise. The acronym PERB used throughout this chapter refers to the New York State Public Employment Relations Board. The Taylor Law (§§ 200-214) regulates the employee relations of public employers and employees in New York State, including school districts*

47:4. What does it mean to negotiate in "good faith"?

PERB has stated that *good faith* requires a party to "approach the negotiating table with a sincere desire to reach agreement." Determination of good faith effort should be based on the totality of a party's conduct (*Town of Southampton*, 2 PERB ¶ 3011 (1969)). Good faith also requires a party to actively participate in negotiations indicating a "present intent to find a basis for agreement" (*Deposit CSD*, 27 PERB ¶ 3020 (1994), *aff'd*, 214 A.D.2d 288, 28 PERB ¶ 7013 (3d Dep't 1995), *reconsideration denied*, 29 PERB ¶ 7001 (3d Dep't), *appeal denied*, 88 N.Y.2d 866, 29 PERB ¶ 7007 (1996)).

However, the obligation to bargain in good faith under the Taylor Law does not compel either party to agree to a proposal or require the making of a concession (§ 204(3)). What is required is "a continuing willingness to submit one's demands to the consideration of the bargaining table where argument, persuasion and the free interchange of views can take place" (*East Meadow UFSD*, 16 PERB ¶ 3086 (1983)).

PERB has held the good faith requirement, for example, to prohibit misrepresentations at the bargaining table (*Cnty. of Rockland*, 29 PERB ¶ 3009 (1996)) and withholding information as to the economic consequences of a party's health insurance proposal (*Cnty. of Greene*, 42 PERB 3031 (2009)). According to PERB, the good faith requirement also requires each party to listen to and respond promptly to the other party's proposals (*City of Mount Vernon*, 11 PERB ¶ 3095 (1978); *City of Yonkers*, 7 PERB ¶ 3006 (1974)); upon request, to supply the other party with information that the other party needs to evaluate its bargaining demands (*N.Y. State Nurses Ass'n*, 45 PERB ¶ 3036 (2012); *Bd. of Educ. of the City Sch. Dist. of the City of Buffalo*, 36 PERB ¶ 3034 (2003), *conf'd*, 9 A.D.3d 851, 37 PERB ¶ 7004 (4th Dep't), *reargument granted*, 11 A.D.3d 1046, 37 PERB ¶ 7006 (4th Dep't 2004); *Serv. Employees Int'l Union*, 48 PERB ¶ 3008 (2015); and to give its negotiator sufficient authority to reach agreement on open issues (*Cnty. of Niagara*, 23 PERB ¶ 3003 (1990); see also *Sachem CSD No. 5*, 6 PERB ¶ 3014 (1973)).

Employee Contractual Relations

The duty to negotiate in good faith also encompasses the obligation of negotiators to support a tentative agreement reached at the bargaining table unless they explicitly give notice to their adversaries that they do not agree with certain proposals and do not intend to support those proposals at a ratification vote (*Copiague UFSD*, 23 PERB ¶ 3046 (1990); see also **47:33, 47:35**).

47:5. Does the "good faith" requirement impose an obligation to negotiate issues in a particular order?

No. Good faith negotiations do not require the parties to discuss issues in any particular order of priority or to negotiate any particular issue, such as wages, to the point of agreement before resolving other issues, but it does require them to be willing to discuss all issues (*Town of Haverstraw*, 9 PERB ¶ 3063, *rev. on procedural grounds*, 9 PERB ¶ 3082 (1976)).

47:6. Who participates in collective bargaining?

Generally, a negotiating team for the school district and a team for the employee organization engage in collective bargaining. The school district's negotiating team typically consists of a chief spokesperson, a recorder to take notes, an individual who is familiar with the district's educational program, and an individual who is familiar with the financial needs and resources of the district. The chief spokesperson, for example, could be an attorney, a board of cooperative educational services negotiator, or an administrator.

Given that the school superintendent is statutorily responsible for the collective bargaining agreement (see **47:7**), the school board should designate the individuals who will serve on the negotiating team, with the advice of the superintendent.

47:7. May a school board choose anyone it wishes to serve on its negotiating team?

Yes. Although the superintendent, as chief executive officer of the school district, is responsible for the collective bargaining agreement with the employee organization (§ 201(10), (12); *Utica City Sch. Dist.*, 27 PERB ¶ 3023 (1994)), a school board may generally choose whomever it pleases to serve on its negotiating team, so long as the selection is not intended to frustrate bargaining, either because of ill will or conflicting interest (*Erie Cnty. Water Auth.*, 25 PERB ¶ 3030 (1992); *City of Newburgh*, 16 PERB ¶ 4590, *aff'd*, 16 PERB ¶ 3081 (1983)).

47:8. What are ground rules and negotiation procedures?

Although not specifically mentioned in the Taylor Law, *ground rules and negotiation procedures* are agreements between a school district and a union on how negotiations will be conducted. PERB has held that negotiation procedures and ground rules are non-mandatory subjects, that they are preliminary and subordinate to substantive negotiations, and that they should not interfere with the commencement or progress of negotiations (*Marcellus CSD*, 21 PERB ¶ 3035 (1988)). See **47:10-11** for a discussion on mandatory and non-mandatory subjects.

Examples of the issues that may be agreed to by the parties are the time and place for negotiating sessions, the length of sessions, the procedures for ratification of the agreement by one or both parties, and the authority of the parties to reach an agreement. Reserving the right of ratification may be important if a school board considers such final approval important before the contract becomes binding (see **47:32-37** for a detailed discussion of ratification).

Although ground rules and negotiation procedures can be very helpful in guiding the parties through the negotiations process, PERB will consider it an improper practice if a party insists on any ground rule at the expense of commencement or progress of substantive negotiations (see *Madison CSD*, 22 PERB ¶ 3057 (1989)). Violation of a ground rule is not an improper practice as long as the two parties are able to continue negotiating in good faith (*Bd. of Educ., CSD No. 1*, 6 PERB ¶ 3049 (1973), *aff'd* 6 PERB ¶ 4526 at p. 4591 (1973); see also *Addison CSD*, 19 PERB ¶ 4559, *aff'd*, 19 PERB ¶ 3062 (1986)).

47:9. Can a school district set a deadline for an employee organization's submission of items to be negotiated?

No public employer has the power to unilaterally set a deadline for submission of the items to be negotiated. However, the employee organization and the district may agree in the collective bargaining agreement to establish a submission date for demands for future agreements. Such agreements are enforceable, and parties may waive their rights to submit demands for negotiation if the demands are submitted after the date agreed upon (*Heuvelton CSD*, 12 PERB ¶ 3007 (1979)).

On the other hand, even absent such an agreement, it may be an improper practice for either party to submit new or previously withdrawn demands after impasse (see, e.g., *Schenectady Cnty. Cmty. Coll.*, 6 PERB ¶ 3027 (1973); see also **47:26**).

Subjects of Collective Bargaining

47:10. What subjects usually are negotiated in collective bargaining?

Subjects of collective bargaining negotiations may include salary and other compensation issues, hours of employment, health insurance and other benefits, leaves of absence, grievance procedures, and other terms and conditions of employment (see §§ 201(4), 204(3)). However, it is possible that a provision in a collective bargaining agreement may waive the right to negotiate certain subjects. Furthermore, such a waiver cannot be deemed to expire at the conclusion of the agreement absent contractual language to that effect (*Prof'l Staff Congress-CUNY v. PERB*, 7 N.Y.3d 458, 39 PERB ¶ 7010 (2006)).

Issues that may arise during collective bargaining can be categorized into three groups:

- *mandatory subjects*, over which both the employer and the union have an obligation to bargain in good faith until agreement is reached or until the party that demanded negotiations withdraws the issue from the table;
- *permissive, or non-mandatory subjects*, over which either party may, but is not obligated to negotiate; and
- *prohibited subjects*, about which neither party may lawfully negotiate (*Bd. of Educ. of the City Sch. Dist. of the City of N.Y. v. PERB*, 75 N.Y.2d 660, 23 PERB ¶ 7012 (1990)).

Each party must negotiate with respect to mandatory subjects upon demand by the other party (*Bd. of Educ. of the City Sch. Dist. of the City of N.Y. v. PERB*). Any change relating to mandatory subjects of bargaining must be negotiated prior to the adoption of any such change. A willingness to negotiate after the change is immaterial (*Great Neck Water Pollution Control Dist.*, 28 PERB ¶ 3030 (1995)). It is permissible, however, for an employee organization to waive the right to demand negotiations over changes to a mandatory subject of bargaining by agreeing to specific language in a "management rights" clause. The intent to waive must be sufficiently plain and clear (*Town of Greece*, 28 PERB ¶ 3078 (1995); *Cnty. of Livingston*, 26 PERB ¶ 3074 (1993); see also *Orchard Park Sch. Related Prof'ls Ass'n*, 47 PERB ¶ 3029 (2014)).

The Taylor Law itself does not clearly delineate most mandatory, non-mandatory, or prohibited subjects of collective bargaining. PERB and the courts resolve disputes about the "scope of bargaining" or whether a particular subject is a mandatory, non-mandatory, or prohibited subject of bargaining (§§ 205(5)(d), 213(a); see **47:11**).

47:11. How are mandatory, prohibited, and non-mandatory (permissive) subjects of bargaining distinguished from one another?

A *mandatory* subject of bargaining is one which falls within section 201(4) of the Taylor Law that defines terms and conditions of employment as "salaries, wages, hours and other terms and conditions of employment." Examples of mandatory subjects of bargaining, other than those listed in section 201(4), include benefits, leave provisions, procedures for pre-approval of paid time off (provided that the procedures do not interfere with the employer's predetermined staffing requirements), workload, disciplinary procedures, and other related issues, such as the implementation of drug testing procedures and the consequences thereof (see, respectively, *City of Cohoes*, 31 PERB ¶ 3020 (1998), *conf'd sub nom. Uniformed Firefighters of Cohoes v. Cuevas*, 32 PERB ¶ 7026 (Sup. Ct. Albany Cnty. 1999), *aff'd,* 276 A.D.2d 184, 33 PERB ¶ 7019 (3d Dep't 2000), *lv. to appeal denied,* 96 N.Y.2d 711, 34 PERB ¶ 7018 (2001); *City of Albany*, 7 PERB ¶ 3078 (1974), *aff'd, Albany v. Helsby,* 48 A.D.2d 998, 8 PERB ¶ 7012 (3d Dep't), *aff'd*, 38 N.Y.2d 778, 9 PERB ¶ 7005 (1975); *Watertown Prof'l Firefighters Ass'n*, 47 PERB ¶ 3015 (2014); *Cnty. of Rockland & Rockland Cnty. Sheriff*, 31 PERB ¶ 3062 (1998); *Patchogue-Medford UFSD*, 30 PERB ¶ 3041 (1997); *Cnty. of Nassau*, 27 PERB ¶ 3054 (1994)). In general, a school district's decision to use surveillance cameras in the workplace to monitor and investigate school employees is mandatorily negotiable. However, whether a particular decision to use video surveillance is subject to mandatory negotiations depends on fact-specific examinations of employer and employee interests (*CSEA Local 1000, AFSCME, AFL-CIO (Nanuet UFSD)*, 45 PERB ¶ 3007 (2012)). Mandatory subjects of bargaining may also include work place benefits that affect employees comfort and convenience, such as listening to music (*Civil Serv. Employees Ass'n,* 46 PERB ¶ 3029 (2013)).

In addition, under the so-called *conversion theory of negotiability*, previously non-mandatory terms incorporated into a collective bargaining agreement become mandatory subjects for purposes of negotiating the next agreement (*City of Cohoes*; *Greenburgh No. 11 UFSD*, 32 PERB ¶ 3024 (1999)), or any time negotiations on a current contract are reopened (*City of Troy*, 33 PERB ¶ 4589 (2000)). However, non-mandatory subjects not already contained in an agreement are not converted into mandatory subjects (*City of N.Y.*, 40 PERB ¶ 3017 (2007), *aff'd*, 41 PERB ¶ 7001 (Sup. Ct., Albany Cnty.), *appeal dismissed,* 54 A.D.3d 480, 41 PERB ¶ 7004 (3d Dep't 2008), *lv. to appeal denied,* 12 N.Y.3d 701, 42 PERB ¶ 7001 (2009)). Furthermore, the parties can provide by contract that an agreement upon a non-mandatory subject of bargaining will not convert the non-mandatory subject of bargaining into a mandatory subject by including a "sunset" provision in the agreement that nullifies the previously non-mandatory subject at, or before the time of the expiration of the collective bargaining agreement (*Suffolk Cnty*. 18 PERB ¶ 3030 (1985), *aff'd*, 125 A.D.2d 307 (2d Dep't 1986); *Port Washington Police Dist*., 42 PERB ¶ 4506 (2009); see **47:31**). Therefore, if an issue comes up as to whether a proposal is sufficiently related to current contract terms to be deemed a mandatory subject, the answer will depend on whether the proposal seeks to include, alter, or delete a topic or category addressed specifically or at least generally in the collective bargaining agreement (*Town of Fishkill v. Town of Fishkill Police Fraternity, Inc*., 39 PERB ¶ 3035 (2006)).

A bargaining proposal that duplicates some or all of a statute that relates to a term and condition of employment is a mandatory subject of bargaining. An exception would apply if sufficiently significant policy considerations would render the statutory reiteration non-mandatory or prohibited (*City of Cohoes*).

Prohibited subjects of bargaining include subjects that are expressly prohibited by law or reserved to management by public policy. For instance, the Taylor Law specifically prohibits bargaining over retirement benefits provided, or to be provided, by a public retirement system (§ 201(4); *City of Yonkers v. Yonkers Firefighters,* 20 N.Y.3d 651 (2013); see also **46:26**). Also, New York State courts have held that law and/or public policy prohibit school districts from agreeing to delegate the board's power to grant or deny tenure (*Cohoes City Sch. Dist. v. Cohoes Teachers Ass'n*, 40 N.Y.2d 774, 9 PERB ¶ 7529 (1976)); to preclude a board from inspecting teacher personnel files (*Bd. of Educ., Great Neck UFSD v. Areman*, 41 N.Y.2d 527, 10 PERB ¶ 7512 (1977)); or to prepay the salaries of teachers on return to work in the fall because the Education Law prohibits the payment of teacher salaries in advance of the performance of services (*Bd. of Educ. v. Ramapo Teachers' Ass'n*, 200 A.D.2d 62 (3d Dep't), *appeal denied*, 84 N.Y.2d 806 (1994); see also **46:45**). On the other hand, according to the commissioner of education in *Appeal of Totolis & Richard*, 36 Ed Dept Rep 476 (1997), the payment of health insurance benefits for July and August to teachers retiring at the beginning of September does not constitute prepayment for services during the upcoming school year, but rather, payment for services rendered during the preceding school year.

Permissive or *non-mandatory* subjects of negotiation include matters that are not terms and conditions of employment but do not violate a statute or strong public policy (*Bd. of Educ. of the City Sch. Dist. of the City of N.Y. v. PERB*, 75 N.Y.2d 660, 23 PERB ¶ 7012 (1990)). Examples include hiring of substitutes (see *Somers CSD*, 9 PERB ¶ 3014 (1976)), class size (see *Queensbury UFSD*, 9 PERB ¶ 3057 (1976)), as well as services and staffing levels (*Dist. Council 72, AFSCME (Bd. of Educ. of the City Sch. Dist. of the City of N.Y.)*, 45 PERB ¶ 3004 (2012)), including staff reductions (*Somers CSD*).

47:12. Can certain issues involve more than one subject of collective bargaining?

Yes. Some general subjects may fall into more than one category. However, any single proposal that has both mandatory and non-mandatory aspects is considered a non-mandatory subject of bargaining in its entirety (see *City of White Plains*, 33 PERB ¶ 3051 (2000)). This is different from otherwise non-mandatory subjects of bargaining previously incorporated into a collective bargaining agreement which become mandatory subjects of bargaining during negotiations of a subsequent agreement (*Greenburgh No. 11 UFSD*, 32 PERB ¶ 3024 (1999)), or reopened negotiations on a current agreement (*City of Troy*, 33 PERB ¶ 4589 (2000)).

47:13. Must a school district negotiate a reduction in the length of a work year and compensation?

Not necessarily. As a general rule, workload and employee compensation are mandatory subjects of bargaining, including expansion of a teacher's work year (*North Colonie CSD*, 41 PERB 3028 (2008); see also **47:11**). However, it is within an employer's managerial prerogative to determine the time span within which work is to be performed (*Vestal CSD*, 15 PERB ¶ 3006 (1982), *conf'd sub nom. Vestal Teachers Ass'n v. Newman*, 95 A.D.2d 940 (3d Dep't 1983); *Lackawanna City Sch. Dist*., 13 PERB ¶ 3085 (1980)). Thus, for example, a board of cooperative educationl services (BOCES) did not commit an improper practice when "for good business reasons" it unilaterally shortened the work year for certain BOCES employees from 12 months to 10 months and made a commensurate reduction in their compensation (*OCM BOCES*, 37 PERB ¶ 3025 (2004)). In comparison, without a reduction in the level of services provided, or evidence that the same work can be completed in fewer hours, it would not be permissible to unilaterally convert full-time positions to part-time (*Cnty. of Erie*, 43 PERB ¶ 3016 (2010)).

Employee Contractual Relations

47:14. Must a school district negotiate rules that restrict employee use of non-working time?

Yes, as a general rule. Restrictions on employee use of non-working time, including the ability to hold additional employment, is a term and condition of employment and a mandatory subject of bargaining. Therefore, employers may not unilaterally impose work rules and policies regarding the use of such time (*City of Albany*, 42 PERB ¶ 3005 (2009); *Village of Catskill*, 43 PERB ¶ 3001 (2010); see also **47:11**).

Nonetheless, the imposition of such restrictions might be permissible, depending on whether the employer's need for such a rule outweighs the effect the rule would have on employee terms and conditions of employment. A unilaterally imposed restriction on employee use of non-working time must be related to the employer's mission and may not intrude significantly or unnecessarily on the protected interests of the employees (*Id*.). That was not the case where a village police department adopted a policy that reversed a long-standing practice that allowed employees to also hold an employment position with other law enforcement agencies. There was no evidence of problems or conflicts related to the practice (*Village of Catskill*); see also *CSEA Local 1000, AFSCME, AFL-CIO* (*State of N.Y.*), 43 PERB ¶ 3011 (2010)).

47:15. Are fingerprinting costs for job applicants a mandatory subject of bargaining?

No. The fingerprinting costs that school districts generally require job applicants to assume before employment are not a mandatory subject of bargaining because they are applicable to all job applicants and not directed at current employees (*Newark Valley Cardinal Bus Drivers*, 35 PERB ¶ 3006 (2002), *aff'd,* 35 PERB ¶ 7015 (Sup. Ct. Albany Cnty. 2002), *aff'd sub nom. Newark Valley Cardinal Bus Drivers, Local 4360 v. PERB,* 303 A.D.2d 888, 36 PERB ¶ 7005 (3d Dep't), *appeal denied*, 100 N.Y.2d 504 (2003)).

Impact Negotiations

47:16. What are impact negotiations?

Although school districts need not bargain over managerial decisions involving permissive/non-mandatory subjects of bargaining (see **47:10–11**), they are required to negotiate over the impact of such decisions on the terms and conditions of employment (*Cnty. of Nassau*, 27 PERB ¶ 3054 (1994); see *West Irondequoit Teachers Ass'n v. Helsby*, 35 N.Y.2d 46, 7 PERB ¶ 7014 (1974); *Uniformed Fire Fighters Ass'n*, 48 PERB ¶ 4509 (2015)). This requirement most often is triggered when an employer takes unilateral action that indirectly affects terms or conditions of employment, such as elimination of positions (see *New Rochelle City Sch. Dist.*, 4 PERB ¶ 3060 (1970)).

PERB has stated: "A demand for impact bargaining permits negotiation about those mandatorily negotiable effects which are inevitably or necessarily caused by an employer's exercise of a managerial prerogative" (*Cnty. of Nassau*). For example, where a board of cooperative educational services (BOCES) unilaterally assigned its teachers additional teaching duties during previously unassigned portions of their workday, PERB ruled that the BOCES had properly exercised a "management prerogative" but that the BOCES had an obligation to engage in impact bargaining upon demand, which would involve "other mandatory subjects of negotiations" (*Capital Region BOCES*, 36 PERB ¶ 3004 (2003)).

47:17. When are public employers and unions required to engage in impact negotiations?

A public employer, including a school district, is obligated to engage in impact bargaining only if the union makes a demand that it do so. A union's demand to negotiate impact must be "clearly made, and cannot be inferred from a demand to negotiate a decision" (*Lackawanna City Sch. Dist.*, 28 PERB ¶ 3023 (1995)).

The requirement that a school district negotiate impact does not mean that the district is prevented from initiating its decision unless and until an agreement is reached on the terms and conditions of employment actually or potentially affected by those decisions. A district may implement the decision before it negotiates with the union over the impact (*Niagara Frontier Transit Metro Sys., Inc.*, 36 PERB ¶ 3036 (2003); see also *State of N.Y. (SUNY Binghamton)*, 27 PERB ¶ 3018 (1994)).

Subcontracting

47:18. Must a school board negotiate its decision to subcontract bargaining unit work to a private firm or individual or to assign unit work to non-unit personnel?

The decision to transfer work from a bargaining unit to individuals outside the bargaining unit or to subcontract work to outside employers generally is considered a mandatory subject of bargaining if the work had been performed by unit members exclusively and continued uninterrupted for a period of time so that employees had a reasonable expectation that the practice would continue (*Chenango Forks Teachers Ass'n, NYSUT, AFL-CIO, Local 2561,* 40 PERB ¶ 3012 (2007); *Manhasset UFSD*, 41 PERB ¶ 3005 (2008), *conf'd sub nom and modified in part*, *Manhasset UFSD v. PERB*, 61 A.D.3d 1231, 42 PERB ¶ 7004 (3d Dep't), *on remittitur* 42 PERB ¶ 3016 (2009)), and the reassigned tasks are substantially similar, unless the qualifications for the job have been changed significantly. If there has been a significant change in the job qualifications, then a balancing test is applied, whereby it must be determined whether the interests of the employer outweigh the interests of the unit employees, individually and collectively (see *Niagara Frontier Transp. Auth.*, 18 PERB ¶ 3083 (1985); see also *Cnty. of Erie*, 39 PERB ¶ 3005 (2006)). PERB has not adopted a specific period that is required to establish exclusivity. The sufficiency of the duration depends upon the facts of each circumstance (*City of New Rochelle,* 44 PERB ¶ 3002 (2011)).

PERB can order reinstatement of employees who were terminated as a result of a unilateral decision (as opposed to a negotiated agreement) (§ 205(5)(d); see *Saratoga Springs City Sch. Dist.*, 12 PERB ¶ 3037 (1978), *aff'd*, *Saratoga Springs City Sch. Dist. v. PERB,* 68 A.D.2d 202, 12 PERB ¶ 7008 (3d Dep't), *lv. to appeal denied,* 47 N.Y.2d 711, 12 PERB ¶ 7012 (1979)) and restoration of work to the bargaining unit (see *Cnty. of Onondaga*, 27 PERB ¶ 3048 (1994)). For instance, where PERB found a district had improperly transferred unit work involving transportation of students to a subcontractor and ordered the district to cease transferring the work to non-unit employees, an appellate court found that enforcement of PERB's order was unreasonable since the district had sold its buses and leased its bus garage. PERB revised its remedial order and required the district to make comparable work available to displaced unit members and pay all back wages and benefits until comparable work became available (*Manhasset UFSD*).

However, if the work at issue was not previously performed exclusively by members of the bargaining unit that claims entitlement to perform the work, then it is not deemed "unit" work and may be performed by other personnel (see *East Meadow UFSD*, 37 PERB ¶ 3031 (2004); see also **47:19**). For example, a district did not unlawfully transfer unit work belonging to the teachers' bargaining unit when it unilaterally assigned "literacy through the arts" instruction to intervention assistants. The literacy program was new, and the work performed was not "teaching," but rather was "instructional support" which was deemed an inherent part of the intervention assistants' job responsibilities (*East Meadow UFSD*).

47:19. Are there any exceptions to the duty to negotiate subcontracting decisions?

Yes. A school district may not be required to negotiate a decision to transfer work under certain circumstances, such as where the decision to transfer unit work is directly related to a decision to alter the level of services provided by the employer to its constituency (see *New Rochelle City Sch. Dist.*, 4 PERB ¶ 3060 (1971)); where there is a substantial change in the nature of the duties actually performed by the non-unit workers (see *Hewlett-Woodmere UFSD*, 28 PERB ¶ 3039 (1995), *aff'd*, *Hewlett-Woodmere UFSD v. PERB*, 232 A.D.2d 560, 29 PERB ¶ 7019 (2d Dep't 1996); *Hyde Park CSD*, 21 PERB ¶ 3011 (1988)); and where there are significant changes in the qualifications of the workers necessary to perform the work (see *Cnty. of Erie*, 29 PERB ¶ 3045 (1996); *West Hempstead UFSD*, 14 PERB ¶ 3096 (1981)).

Subcontracting may also be permitted without negotiation where the action is authorized by law. For example, a school district's decision to have a board of cooperative educational services (BOCES) take over academic programs pursuant to section 1950(4)(bb) of the Education Law is not a mandatory subject of bargaining (*Webster CSD v. PERB*, 75 N.Y.2d 619, 23 PERB ¶ 7013 (1990)). Similarly, a district's transfer of printing services pursuant to a contract with the local BOCES has been found to be a non-mandatory subject of negotiation (*Vestal Employees. Ass'n v. PERB*, 94 N.Y.2d 409, 33 PERB ¶ 7005 (2000)). Because the legislative intent of the statute was not to require bargaining over the decision to subcontract work to the BOCES, districts need only negotiate over the impact of the decision and not the decision itself (see **47:16–17**).

On the other hand, notwithstanding two prior PERB decisions to the contrary (*Civil Serv. Employees Ass'n*, 45 PERB ¶ 3040 (2012); *Lawrence Teachers' Ass'n*, 48 PERB ¶ 3007 (2015)), a state supreme court has ruled that school districts must negotiate the transfer of pre-kindergarten services to an out-of-district entity (*Lawrence Teachers' Ass'n v. NYS PERB* (Sup. Ct. Albany Cnty. Nov. 20, 2015)).

Also, a school district does not have to negotiate a decision to transfer work where the work at issue has been performed by non-unit employees in the past (see *Hammondsport CSD*, 28 PERB ¶ 3059 (1995)); where the work was previously performed for such a limited time, and with such infrequency, that it cannot be established as "exclusive" unit work (see *Dryden CSD*, 36 PERB ¶ 3005 (2003)); or where the employee organization has agreed, in a management rights clause, to the district subcontracting unit work (see *Garden City UFSD*, 27 PERB ¶ 3029 (1994)).

A union will be deemed to have lost exclusivity over subcontracted work unless a "discernible boundary" exists that allows it to retain exclusivity over the work when, at times, it has been performed by non-unit workers. To determine the existence of such a boundary, PERB will analyze the "nature and frequency of the work performed by unit members, the geographic location where the work is performed, the employer's rationale for the practice, an explicit or implicit recognition that the at-issue work is distinct, and other facts that have set the claimed unit work apart from work performed by nonunit personnel" (*Manhasset UFSD*, 41 PERB ¶ 3005 (2008), *conf'd sub nom. and modified in part*, *Manhasset UFSD v. PERB*, 61 A.D.3d 1231, 42 PERB ¶ 7004 (3d Dep't), *on remittitur* 42 PERB ¶ 3016 (2009); see also *United Teachers of Seaford*, 47 PERB ¶ 3034 (2014)).

47:20. Does an unlawful transfer of unit work occur if the employer neither expressly consents to the transfer nor implicitly condones it?

No. In one case, a school district assigned two teaching assistants to provide academic intervention services (AIS) under the supervision of teachers. In practice, the teaching assistants provided AIS without teacher supervision. However, the evidence failed to demonstrate that the district deliberately assigned the teaching assistants to work without teacher supervision or that it was aware that this was occurring. Therefore, PERB dismissed the improper practice charge that alleged an unlawful, unilateral transfer of unit work by the employer (*Cold Spring Harbor CSD*, 36 PERB ¶ 3016 (2003), *conf'd,* 12 A.D.3d 442, 37 PERB ¶ 7009 (2d Dep't 2004)).

47:21. Can a school district contract out its cafeteria and restaurant services without engaging in collective bargaining?

The answer depends on whether the district is a city or non-city district.

In the past, school cafeteria and restaurant services were not an "ordinary contingent expense," (see **20:10–11**), which meant that these services had to be self-sustaining through state and federal aid and meal fees unless the voters approved the expenditure as part of the district's budget. Therefore, if a district's budget was defeated by the voters, the district could continue to operate cafeteria and restaurant services only if the district could finance these operations without using local taxpayer dollars.

Accordingly, in one case, a school district that was forced to end its cafeteria program after a budget defeat by the voters caused the board to adopt a contingency budget, hired a contractor to provide lunches on a self-sustaining financial basis, without district funding. An appellate court ruled that subcontracting was permissible without negotiations because the budget defeat had caused the loss of union members' jobs, not the decision to hire a contractor. In so ruling, the court reversed a prior PERB decision to the contrary (see *Germantown CSD v. PERB*, 205 A.D.2d 961, 27 PERB ¶ 7009 (3d Dep't 1994)).

However, subsequent amendments to the Education Law have made school cafeteria and restaurant services an "ordinary contingent expense" in non-city school districts (see Educ. Law §§ 1604(28), 1709(22), 2023(1)), casting doubt on the continued viability of the *Germantown* decision in such districts.

Conversely, the law pertaining to small city school districts still continues to provide that school cafeteria and restaurant service is not an ordinary contingent expense in such districts (see Educ. Law § 2503(9)(a)). Thus, the court's rationale in the *Germantown* decision would appear to remain applicable in small city school districts.

Past Practices

47:22. What is a past practice and how does it affect collective bargaining?

A *past practice* involves a mandatory subject of bargaining which has not been included in a written agreement, but which is unequivocal and has continued uninterrupted for a period of time sufficient under the circumstances for affected employees to reasonably expect it to continue without change (*Chenango Forks CSD*, 40 PERB ¶ 3012 (2007)).

For a practice to be "unequivocal" it must be "clear and unambiguous; expressed in full and definite terms; carrying no implications for future change" (*Sherburne-Earlville CSD*, 36 PERB ¶ 3011 (2003)). Therefore, even if a practice has continued for a significant period of time, if it is not unequivocal, the parties can have no reasonable expectation that it will continue. Thus, in *Sherburne-Earlville CSD,* PERB ruled that a supervisor's unauthorized practice of allowing a select few senior custodians to borrow school district equipment and tools did not establish an unequivocal practice evincing mutual agreement between the district and the employee organization. The reasonableness of an expectation of continuation can be presumed from the duration of the practice and the specific circumstances under which it has existed (*Fashion Inst. of Tech.*, 41 PERB ¶ 3010 (2008), *conf'd*, 68 A.D.3d 605, 42 PERB ¶ 7011 (1st Dep't 2009)). In another case, a union could not demonstrate that there was a past practice of limiting the number of teacher workdays to under 186 days where the district produced evidence that the collective bargaining agreement did not define the length of the school year for teachers and the district consistently applied objective factors in setting the school calendar that resulted in a varying number of workdays from year to year (*North Colonie CSD*, 41 PERB ¶ 3028 (2008)).

A proposed change in an established past practice relating to a mandatory subject of bargaining must be negotiated with the employee organization representing the affected employees before that change is decided upon by the district (see *Cnty. of Genesee*, 18 PERB ¶ 3016 (1985), *aff'd sub nom. Bork v. Newman*, 122 A.D.2d 329, 19 PERB ¶ 7016 (3d Dep't 1986)).

In one case, PERB ordered a district to continue a past practice of allowing employees to take up to eight hours to participate in blood drives after it unilaterally implemented a policy change limiting blood donation leave time to three hours (*Bd. of Educ. of the City Sch. Dist. of the City of N.Y.*, 42 PERB ¶ 3019 (2009)).

47:23. Are there any circumstances under which a school district would not be bound by a past practice?

A school district can refute that it is bound by a past practice through evidence that establishes it lacked either actual or constructive knowledge (*Chenango Forks CSD*, 40 PERB ¶ 3012 (2007). However, constructive knowledge will be deemed to exist when the past practice is reasonably subject to the employer's managerial and/or supervisory oversight, responsibilities and obligations (*Fashion Inst. of Tech.* 41 PERB ¶ 3010 (2008), *conf'd* 68 A.D. 3d 605, 42 PERB ¶ 7011 (1st Dep't 2009); *Chenango Forks CSD v. PERB*, 21 N.Y.3d 255 (2013)). This would include situations where an employer delegates such duties and responsibilities to a department head (*City of Oswego Firefighters Ass'n*, 41 PERB ¶ 3011 (2008)).

47:24. What are some examples of an improper unilateral discontinuation of a past practice?

In one instance, PERB ruled that a district was obligated to continue a past practice of allowing department chairs to continue tutoring students for compensation outside the school day, including students taught by teachers supervised by those same department chairs. PERB rejected the district's assertion that its interest in avoiding an appearance of impropriety outweighed the employees' right to earn money outside of school hours and held that the district committed an improper practice when it unilaterally discontinued the past practice (*Hewlett-Woodmere UFSD*, 38 PERB ¶ 3006 (2005)).

Similarly, a town had to negotiate over the elimination of providing take-home vehicles to certain employees despite its argument that the practice violated the town's code of ethics prohibiting use of town vehicles for personal convenience. According to the New York Court of Appeals, use of the town owned vehicle for purposes of traveling to and from work amounted to commuting benefits which are neither illegal nor unethical (*Town of Islip v. N.Y. State Public Employment Relations Bd.*, 23 N.Y. 3d 482.

47:25. May school districts alter a past practice that is inconsistent with the terms of a collective bargaining agreement?

Yes. A school district has the right to revert to contract language that contravenes a past practice (such as allowing employees a grace period for late arrivals, or allowing coffee breaks in excess of the amount of breaks provided under the contract) since actions taken pursuant to a contract cannot be labeled unilateral in violation of the Taylor Law (*Abbott Sch. Teachers Ass'n v. Abbott UFSD*, 39 PERB ¶ 4627 (2006); see *Florida UFSD*, 31 PERB ¶ 3056 (1998); see also *State of N.Y.-Unified Court Sys.*, 26 PERB ¶ 3013 (1993)). The district would have to prove there is a specific provision in a collective bargaining agreement that is reasonably clear on the subject and that the district's action constitutes a reversion to that provision from an inconsistent past practice (*Bd. of Educ. of the City Sch. Dist. of the City of N.Y.*, 42 PERB 3019 (2009)).

Similarly, a unilateral change concerning a practice unrelated to a union's right to access employer facilities for representation activities under the Taylor Law has been deemed a non-mandatory subject of bargaining. That was the case when a district unilaterally installed vending machines in a bus garage, replacing the union's longstanding operation of a profit-making coffee club. (*Pittsford Cent. Sch. Bus Drivers' & Attendants' Ass'n v. Pittsford CSD*, 40 PERB ¶ 4514 (2007)).

Bargaining Impasses

47:26. What is an impasse?

Impasse is a stalemate or deadlock in collective bargaining. It is the point at which either or both parties to the negotiation determine that there is no reasonable expectation that further negotiations would be fruitful without third-party assistance (see *City of Newburgh*, 15 PERB ¶ 3116 (1982), *aff'd*, *Newburgh v. PERB*, 97 A.D.2d 258, 16 PERB ¶ 7030 (3d Dep't 1983), *aff'd*, 63 N.Y.2d 793, 17 PERB ¶ 7017 (1984)). Under the Taylor Law, an impasse may be deemed to exist if, despite efforts to bargain in good faith, the parties fail to reach an agreement at least 120 days prior to the end of the school district's fiscal year (§ 209(1)), which is commonly the final effective date of a collective bargaining agreement. However, the courts and PERB have recognized that impasse may be declared by either party at any time before, during, or after the 120-day period, so long as negotiations are truly deadlocked (§ 209(3); *City of Mount Vernon*, 11 PERB ¶ 3095 (1978); see *N.Y. City Sch. Dist.*, 34 PERB ¶ 3016 (2001); *City of Schenectady v. Helsby*, 57 Misc.2d 91, 1 PERB ¶ 704 (Sup. Ct. Schenectady Cnty. 1968)). Impasse cannot be declared before the opposing parties' proposals have had an opportunity to be considered (*Village of Johnson City*, 12 PERB ¶ 3020 (1979)).

47:27. What happens when a school district and an employee organization reach an impasse?

Districts and employee organizations may agree to procedures on resolution of impasses, such as submission of open issues to impartial arbitration (§ 209(2); see *Newburgh v. Newman*, 69 N.Y.2d 166, 20 PERB ¶ 7008 (1987)). Such procedures may include a provision on how the costs of a mediator or arbitrator will be shared and, once agreed upon, must be followed.

In the absence of such agreed-upon impasse procedures or in the event that these procedures are unsuccessful, either party may request assistance from PERB, or PERB may render such assistance on its own (§ 209(2), (3); see **46:7**, **47:28**).

Employee Contractual Relations

The obligation to negotiate in good faith (see **47:4**) includes participation in mediation and fact-finding. As such, refusal to participate in the mediation or fact-finding process constitutes an improper practice (*Poughkeepsie City Sch. Dist.*, 27 PERB ¶ 3079 (1994); *City of Mount Vernon*, 11 PERB ¶ 3095 (1978)).

47:28. What role does PERB have in settling an impasse?

If there is no agreement on procedures to resolve an impasse in collective bargaining, or these procedures fail, either party may formally request PERB, or PERB on its own may determine to assist in resolving the impasse (§ 209(2), (3)). Such assistance may include the services of a mediator, and if mediation fails, the services of a fact finder (§ 209(3)(a), (b)). The fact finder's report of recommendations must be released to the public five days after the report is given to the school superintendent and employee organization (§ 209(3)(c)). Either party may accept or reject any or all of the fact finder's recommendations. If the impasse continues, additional mediation, called *conciliation*, may be provided (§ 209(3)(d)). This step is sometimes referred to as *superconciliation*.

There are no charges to either the employer or the employee organization for these PERB services.

47:29. What happens if the current collective bargaining agreement expires before a successor agreement is negotiated?

In such situations, by statute, all the provisions of the expired agreement continue in full force and effect until the parties agree to a new agreement. This is because section 209-a(1)(e) of the Civil Service Law, commonly referred to as the *Triborough* Amendment, makes it an improper practice for an employer to refuse to continue all the terms of an expired agreement until a new agreement is negotiated.

This obligation ends, however, if the employee organization has violated section 210(1) of the Civil Service Law by striking or by causing, instigating, encouraging, or condoning a strike. In case of such a violation, the district may be able to unilaterally change certain policies and practices (see **46:38–40**).

The New York Court of Appeals has found that the *Triborough* Amendment has the effect of extending the obligations of the agreement until a new agreement is reached (*Ass'n of Surrogates & Supreme Court Reporters v. State of N.Y.*, 79 N.Y.2d 39, 25 PERB ¶ 7502 (1992); see also *Prof'l Staff Congress-CUNY v. PERB*, 7 N.Y.3d 458, 39 PERB ¶ 7010 (2006)). However, PERB has ruled that this is a statutory obligation, and collective bargaining agreements actually do expire for purposes of the Taylor Law, since to conclude otherwise would make it impossible for any union to ever establish the element of an "expired contract," which is necessary to state a claim for relief under the *Triborough* Amendment, and thus, would effectively repeal the *Triborough* Amendment (*State of N.Y. (Office of Parks & Recreation)*, 27 PERB ¶ 3001 (1994)).

47:30. What happens if the union party to a collective bargaining agreement ceases to exist?

According to PERB, in a case where the union members voted to disband and their union became defunct:

- There was no prohibition against another bargaining unit petitioning to represent the members of the old unit.
- Upon certification, the school district then became obligated to negotiate with the new employee organization.
- Technically, the old agreement terminated, inasmuch as one of the parties to the agreement no longer existed.

- But as a practical matter, the termination of the old agreement was irrelevant, because PERB found that the district had a duty to maintain the status quo as to the terms and conditions of employment until it reached a new collective bargaining agreement with the newly certified employee organization. (See *Avon CSD*, 36 PERB ¶ 3032 (2003)).

47:31. Do all provisions in an expired agreement have to continue in effect during negotiations for a successor contract?

No. Certain obligations contained in a collective bargaining agreement may be made to end with the contract's expiration even under the *Triborough* Amendment by use of what is known as a *sunset clause* (see *Waterford-Halfmoon UFSD*, 27 PERB ¶ 3070 (1994)). Such a clause consists of a mutually agreed-upon durational restriction on a district's obligation to continue the terms of an expired agreement. It simply attaches a final effective date to a specific provision in the contract, such as one which determines the conditions upon which salary increments or step advances are to take place (see *Cortland Enlarged City Sch. Dist.*, 45 PERB ¶ 3022 (2012); *Schuylerville CSD*, 29 PERB ¶ 3029 (1996)). The effectiveness of these clauses is based on the idea that the *Triborough* Amendment requires only that the contract, as written, continue in effect until a new contract is negotiated (§ 209-a(1)(e); *Waterford-Halfmoon*).

Contract Ratification and Legislative Approval

47:32. What is the difference between a school board's contract ratification and legislative approval powers?

Legislative approval and contract ratification are two related concepts that are often confused (*City of Saratoga Springs*, 20 PERB ¶ 3031 (1987)).

Contract ratification is a voluntary process under which a tentative agreement is submitted to a school board and/or union membership for a vote to accept or reject the tentative agreement. School boards do not have an inherent or automatic right of ratification (see *Town of Dresden,* 17 PERB ¶ 3096 (1984)). The right of ratification is created by agreement or through understanding between the parties' negotiators. It is not a right that a school board or any other party may unilaterally reserve to itself (see, e.g., *Town of Dresden*; *Falconer CSD*, 6 PERB ¶ 3029 (1973); *Jamestown City Sch. Dist.*, 6 PERB ¶ 3075 (1973)). It may be waived by a board's failure to conduct a ratification vote (*Utica City Sch. Dist.*, 27 PERB ¶ 3023 (1994); *Jamesville-DeWitt CSD*, 22 PERB ¶ 3048 (1989); see **47:35**).

Legislative approval is a right and duty of the board created by statute (§§ 201(12), 204-a(1)). Unlike the negotiated right of ratification, which allows the board to approve or reject the entire tentative agreement, the statutory right of legislative approval only allows the board to act on those contract provisions that require an amendment of board policy having the force of law or require additional funding (§ 204-a(1)). As a general rule, those provisions of an executed agreement do not become binding on the school district until the board has given its approval (§ 201(12)). However, a school board's prior actions may result in a waiver of the right of legislative approval (see **47:37**).

Legislative approval of a multi-year agreement may not be conditioned upon or subject to annual appropriations. Once legislative approval has been given, the school district is bound by the agreement for its full, specified term (*Ass'n of Surrogates & Supreme Court Reporters v. State of N.Y.*, 78 N.Y.2d 143 (1991)).

47:33. What is involved in the ratification process?

The ratification process involves at least the following elements: First, the ratifying body (that is, the school board or the union membership) must be aware that negotiations have been completed and that its negotiators have reached an agreement subject only to ratification. Second, while the members of the ratifying body may differ on reasons for ratifying or rejecting the agreement, the agreement must be ratified or rejected as a whole and not on a piecemeal basis. Third, the negotiators must affirmatively support ratification, unless they have made the other party aware of their opposition to the tentative agreement. Otherwise, they must not only support the agreement, but cannot even remain neutral or take no position with respect to ratification. Finally, a decision to ratify must be clearly and unequivocally made and communicated (*Jamesville-DeWitt CSD*, 22 PERB ¶ 3048 (1989); see *Copiague UFSD*, 23 PERB ¶ 3046 (1990); *Town of Putnam Valley,* 17 PERB ¶ 3041 (1984)).

47:34. What happens if district negotiators fail to reserve at the bargaining table the school board's right to ratify a negotiated agreement?

A school board has no automatic or inherent right to ratify a negotiated agreement, although it is common for district and employee organization negotiators to agree to require ratification by the school board and/or union membership in the ground rules established for negotiation of a collective bargaining agreement or within the collective bargaining agreement itself (see **47:8, 47:32**).

According to PERB, it is an improper practice for either a school board or an employee organization to attempt to reject an agreement after their respective negotiator has given assent, unless the parties have agreed that the board and/or union membership have reserved the right to ratify or reject the terms of a tentative agreement (see *Town of Greece*, 32 PERB ¶ 3059 (1999), *aff'd*, 280 A.D.2d 967, 34 PERB ¶ 7006 (4th Dep't 2001); *Town of Dresden*, 17 PERB ¶ 3096 (1984); *Falconer CSD*, 6 PERB ¶ 3029 (1973)).

47:35. Can a school board lose its properly reserved right to ratify an agreement?

Yes. The right of a school board to ratify an agreement, even though properly reserved (see **47:32**), can nonetheless be lost by the conduct of the district's negotiators. For example, all members of the district's negotiating team have a duty to support and affirmatively seek ratification of a tentative agreement, unless a team member has explicitly given advance notice to the union that he or she does not intend to support it (*Copiague UFSD*, 23 PERB ¶ 3046 (1990)). This is considered an indication of good faith at the bargaining table. Failure to perform this duty, which may be breached simply by silence on the part of a negotiator in the face of board opposition to the tentative agreement or by neutrality during the ratification process (see *Copiague UFSD*; see also *Town of Putnam Valley,* 17 PERB ¶ 3041 (1984)), will result in the loss of an employer's right to ratify the agreement (*City of Saratoga Springs*, 20 PERB ¶ 3031 (1987)). The duty of all members of the negotiating team to support the agreement at the ratification vote is not compromised if one or more members of the team are delegated to speak for the other members of the team, and they all urge ratification (*Town of Putnam Valley*).

The right to ratify an agreement also may be lost if the negotiators fail to provide the school board with the agreement (see *Town of Greece*, 32 PERB ¶ 3059 (1999), *aff'd*, 280 A.D.2d 967, 34 PERB ¶ 7006 (4th Dep't 2001)). In addition, a school board can lose its right to ratify an agreement if it fails to conduct a ratification vote "with reasonable expedition," which is also a violation of the district's duty to negotiate in good faith (*Utica City Sch. Dist.,* 27 PERB ¶ 3023 (1994)).

47:36. What happens if a school board loses or otherwise waives its right to ratify an agreement?

If PERB finds a waiver of the right to ratify, then it can direct a district to execute the agreement (*Utica City Sch. Dist.*, 27 PERB ¶ 3023 (1994); see **46:6–9** in regard to the powers and duties of

PERB). For example, when a board loses its right of ratification because a negotiator improperly fails to affirmatively support ratification of an agreement (see **47:35**), the school superintendent can be required to execute that agreement. This occurred where one of the district's negotiators distributed material to certain members of the school board in opposition to a tentatively reached agreement on the settlement of a new contract. PERB considered this evidence of failure to negotiate in good faith, which is an improper practice (see **46:31**, **46:34**), and directed the superintendent to execute the agreement without the board's ratification (*Buffalo City Sch. Dist.*, 24 PERB ¶ 3033 (1991), *aff'd*, 191 A.D.2d 985, 26 PERB ¶ 7002 (4th Dep't), *appeal denied*, 82 N.Y.2d 656, 26 PERB ¶ 7013 (1993). See **46:33** for a discussion on PERB's authority when an improper practice is committed.

47:37. Can a school board lose its statutory right to legislatively approve a contract?

Yes. For example, in one case, PERB determined that a school board had exercised its right of legislative approval when all the members of the board served on the negotiating team that came to an agreement with the union (*Sylvan-Verona Beach Common Sch. Dist.*, 15 PERB ¶ 3067 (1982), *appeal dismissed*, 16 PERB ¶ 7004 (Sup. Ct. Oneida Cnty.), *aff'd*, 97 A.D.2d 959, 16 PERB ¶ 7029 (4th Dep't 1983)). In another case, the New York Court of Appeals ruled that a school board that had lost its right to ratify a contract because one of its negotiators failed to support ratification, did not, because of particular circumstances, have a separate right to legislatively approve the funding provisions of the contract (*Bd. of Educ. for the City Sch. Dist. of the City of Buffalo v. Buffalo Teachers Fed'n Inc.*, 89 N.Y.2d 370, 29 PERB ¶ 7506 (1996), *reh'g denied*, 89 N.Y.2d 983 (1997). See **47:32** for a discussion on the difference between ratification and legislative approval of a contract.

PERB. For example, when [illegible] ultimately [illegible] [illegible]

§ [illegible] [illegible]

For example, [illegible] [illegible]

Employee Contractual Relations

48. Students–School Attendance

Compulsory Attendance Rules

48:1. Must children in New York State attend school?

Yes. Under New York's compulsory education law, minors who turn six years old on or before December 1 in any school year must receive full-time instruction from the first day school is in session in September of such school year. Minors who turn six years old after December 1 of a school year must receive full-time instruction from the first day of school in the following September. All children must remain in attendance until the last day of the school year in which they reach the age of 16 (§ 3205(1); *In the Matter of Kiesha BB,* 30 A.D.3d 704 (3d Dep't 2006)). In this context, school year refers to the official school year commencing July 1 each year and ending June 30th of the following year (§ 2(15); *In the Matter of Kiesha BB*) rather than the instructional year, which runs from September through June (see **55:1**).

However, a school board may require minors from ages 16 through 17 who are not employed to attend school until the last day of the school year in which they become 17 years of age (§ 3205(3)).

Generally, persons over 5 and under 21 may attend the public schools of the school district in which they reside even if they are not of compulsory education age (§ 3202(1); see **48:5-7**). Students over the age of compulsory school attendance may be dropped from enrollment only if they are absent 20 consecutive school days and the school district complies with certain required procedures, including, for example, the scheduling of an informal conference with the student and the student's parents, and notification of the right to re-enroll (§ 3202(1-a)).

48:2. Are there any exemptions from the compulsory education requirements?

Yes, one. Children of compulsory education age (see **48:1**) who have completed a four-year high school course of study do not have to attend school (§ 3205(2)(a)).

Otherwise, there is no exception, not even for students under the ages of 16 or 17 who are married. Similarly, although 16 or 17-year-old students who have a certificate of full-time employment do not have to attend full-time, they still must attend school for at least 20 hours per week (§ 3205(2)(b); for more detail on employment of students see **50:46-55**).

In *Wisconsin v. Yoder*, 406 U.S. 205 (1972), the U. S. Supreme Court permitted Amish children to be exempt from compulsory school attendance after the eighth-grade level. However, the exemption was based exclusively on the recognition that the preservation of Amish society depended on its children learning how to maintain an agrarian way of life free from modern technology. According to the court, the exemption did not contravene the principles of public education; rather, it allowed Amish children to be educated in the ways necessary to preserve the Amish way of life.

48:3. Are there any exemptions that excuse attendance from an entire curriculum program?

No. According to the U.S. Court of Appeals for the Second Circuit, which has jurisdiction over New York, the claim made by the Amish (see **48:2**) is one that few other religious groups or sects

Students

can make. A parent does not have a right "to tell a public school what his or her child will and will not be taught." Although school districts may allow students to opt out from portions of a curriculum that are related to, for example, family-life instruction and AIDS education (see **55:43-44**), there are no exemptions that would excuse a child from attending a health curriculum program in its entirety (*Leebaert v. Harrington*, 332 F.3d 134 (2d Cir. 2003)).

48:4. Must children of compulsory education age attend public school?

No. Children who are required to receive full-time instruction (see **48:1**) may receive such instruction either in a public, private, or parochial school, or at home (§§ 3202, 3204(1), (2), 3205(1)(a), 3210(2), 3212(2)(d); 8 NYCRR § 100.10; *Appeal of Brown*, 34 Ed Dept Rep 33 (1994)).

However, the compulsory attendance law requires that instruction given to a minor elsewhere than a public school be "at least substantially equivalent to the instruction given to minors of like age and attainments at the public schools of the city or district where the minor resides" (§§ 3204(1), (2); *Appeal of Pope*, 40 Ed Dept Rep 473 (2001); *Appeal of Brown*; see **4:2-4**).

For more information on nonpublic school students, see **chapter 4**.

For more information on home instruction of students, see **48:38-55**.

48:5. Is a child under the compulsory education age entitled to attend public school?

Yes. The law provides that a person over 5 and under 21 years of age who does not possess a high school diploma is entitled to attend the public schools maintained in the district where he or she resides (§ 3202(1); *Appeal of C.S.*, 54 Ed Dept Rep, Dec. No. 16,697 (2015); *Appeal of Botros*, 46 Ed Dept Rep 142 (2006); see **48:1** for compulsory age requirements). Furthermore, a child over the age of five is entitled to attend public school regardless of whether the district maintains a kindergarten program. Districts without a kindergarten program must admit such a child to the first grade (*Appeal of Carney*, 15 Ed Dept Rep 325 (1976); *Formal Opn. of Counsel No. 75*, 1 Ed Dept Rep 775 (1952)).

However, when admitting a child who is under the compulsory education age, a school district can require that the child become five years old on or before December 1 of the school year he or she begins school (§ 3202(1); *Appeal of S.H.*, 40 Ed Dept Rep 527 (2001); *Appeal of Tomassetti*, 39 Ed Dept Rep 513 (2000); *Appeal of Sollitto*, 31 Ed Dept Rep 138 (1991)). Additionally, a district that maintains a policy delaying the admission of children who become five after December 1, is not required to alter the policy on an individual basis for particular students (*Frost v. Yerazunis*, 53 A.D.2d 15 (3d Dep't 1976); *Appeal of L.T.*, 47 Ed Dept Rep 23 (2007); *Appeal of S.H.*; *Appeal of Tomassetti*; *Appeal of Sollitto*). In contrast, a district may not establish an earlier admission cutoff date and require, for example, that a child become five years old by the start of the school year for which he or she seeks admission (*Matter of Benjamin*, 26 Ed Dept Rep 533 (1987)).

48:6. Are high school graduates entitled to attend public school?

Yes. The law provides that individuals under 21 years of age who have received a high school diploma must be permitted to attend classes in the district in which they reside or in a school of a board of cooperative educational services (§ 3202(1); *Matter of Brown*, 15 Ed Dept Rep 79 (1975)). However, any such person who is not a veteran must pay tuition unless the school board waives payment of such tuition (§ 3202(1)). A high school diploma earned under standards that might be different than those in New York State does not entitle an individual to attend public school tuition free (*Appeal of Botros*, 46 Ed Dept Rep 142 (2006)).

A non-veteran who has received a high school diploma may not be counted for any state aid purposes (§ 3202(1); 8 NYCRR § 174.3).

48:7. May individuals who have obtained a high school equivalency diploma, but not a high school diploma, attend public school?

Yes. According to the NYS Education Department, an otherwise qualified individual who has received a high school equivalency diploma, but not a high school diploma, may still attend the public schools in his or her district of residence, without paying tuition, until the age of 21, or until that person has obtained a high school diploma (see NYS Education Department, Office of Elementary, Middle and Secondary Education, *School Executive's Bulletin* (June 1989)).

48:8. Must public school students attend kindergarten?

No. However, a school district may require any child entering public school under the compulsory education age (see **48:1** and **48:5**) to attend and complete a year of kindergarten, unless the child has already attended a substantially equivalent nonpublic kindergarten program. In addition, with few exceptions, the Syracuse, Rochester, Buffalo, Utica and New York City school districts may require children who turn five years old on or before December 1 to attend kindergarten (§ 3205(2)(c)).

A nonpublic kindergarten program will be deemed to be substantially equivalent to that of the public schools if it is registered by the NYS Education Department. Otherwise, the district must determine its equivalency by either evaluating the program or testing the child to establish his or her ability to do first grade work. If the testing indicates that the child is able to perform at a first grade level, the district must admit the child into the first grade (*Matter of Bruce A.M.*, 32 Ed Dept Rep 335 (1992); *Matter of Pleener*, 30 Ed Dept Rep 55 (1990); *Matter of Lazar*, 6 Ed Dept Rep 7 (1966)).

A nonpublic kindergarten program may not admit children who are younger than the age of entrance into public school established by the district in which the child resides (8 NYCRR § 125.9).

48:9. Must public school students attend a prekindergarten program?

No. Under the universal prekindergarten legislation, school boards may, but are not required to, adopt a plan to provide prekindergarten services to resident children (§ 3602-e(5)). If such a plan is adopted by the school board and approved by the commissioner of education, resident children who are four years old on or before December 1 of the year in which they are enrolled or who will otherwise be first eligible to enter public school kindergarten commencing with the following year will be eligible to receive prekindergarten services (§ 3602-e(1)(c); see also *Appeal of I.A.*, 41 Ed Dept Rep 413 (2002)).

For a summer only universal prekindergarten program, resident children who are five years old on or after December 1 of the year in which they are enrolled or who will otherwise be first eligible to enter kindergarten within the current school year are eligible to participate (8 NYCRR § 151-1.2(c); see also **55:8**).

Once a child is enrolled in a prekindergarten program, an attendance policy must be applied to the child (8 NYCRR § 151-1.2(c)).

48:10. Can students attend public school part-time and receive instruction elsewhere for the balance of the school day?

Only as permitted under section 3602-c of the Education Law, more commonly known as the dual-enrollment law. Under this section, students attending nonpublic schools may receive instruction in the areas of career education, gifted and talented, and education for students with disabilities, as well as counseling, psychological, and social work services related to such instruction. Except for the provisions of the dual-enrollment law, the Legislature has not authorized partial attendance at a public school.

Accordingly, nonpublic school students do not have a right to participate in a public school's credit bearing programs other than those authorized by the dual-enrollment law (*Appeal of Pope,* 40 Ed Dept Rep 473 (2001); *Appeal of Sutton*, 39 Ed Dept Rep 625 (2000); *Matter of Mayshark*, 17 Ed Dept Rep 82 (1977)). These students also do not have a right to participate in the non-credit bearing extra-curricular activities of a public school (*Appeal of Ponte*, 41 Ed Dept Rep 186 (2001)).

Aside from nonpublic school students, the dual-enrollment law does not apply to home-schooled students. Therefore, such students may not be instructed at home for part of the day, and attend classes at a public school for part of the school day (*Id.*), or participate in board of cooperative educationl services programs (*Appeal of Ando*, 45 Ed Dept Rep 523 (2006)). The only exception applies to students with disabilities who are home-schooled (§ 3602-c(2-c)).

For more information on nonpublic and home-schooled students, see **chapter 4, 48:38-55**.

48:11. How may individuals over 21 years of age secure a high school diploma?

Section 100.7 of the commissioner's regulations provides that an adult may secure a high school equivalency diploma by achieving an acceptable score on the comprehensive examinations required under the New York State Equivalency Diploma program (see **55:17**). The individual must have lived in New York State at least one month before the examination, and meet other age and instruction-related requirements (8 NYCRR § 100.7(a)(1)).

Additionally, as an alternative to the comprehensive examinations, candidates may qualify by completion of 24 college credits (semester hours) or their equivalent at an approved institution of higher education. The 24 credits must be distributed in the areas of English language arts, mathematics, natural science, social science humanities and other elective courses, as indicated in commissioner's regulations (8 NYCRR § 100.7(a)(2)(i)(c)).

World War II, Korean conflict and Vietnam War veterans who did not obtain a high school education may be awarded a local diploma based on knowledge and experience gained while in service, under a program developed by the commissioner (§ 305(29), (29-a), (29-b)). To receive a local diploma, candidates must submit evidence of service in one of the conflicts and receipt of an honorable discharge, a statement affirming New York residency, and that the candidate does not possess a high school diploma. Next of kin of a deceased veteran eligible for a local diploma under these rules may submit the required documentation along with proof of death and kinship. No fee may be charged to issue such diplomas (8 NYCRR §§ 100.5(b)(7)(e)(xi)(a)-(c)).

48:12. Must school districts provide educational services to youths who are incarcerated in county correctional facilities or youth shelters?

Yes. The Education Law and the commissioner's regulations require school districts to provide educational services to youths under age 21 who do not have a high school diploma and who are incarcerated in county correctional facilities or youth shelters located within their districts. Such instruction must be provided under a plan approved by the commissioner of education and within the limits of funds allocated by the commissioner for such purposes. School districts may contract with a board of cooperative educational services or another school district for the provision of such services (see § 3202(7)(a); 8 NYCRR Part 118; *see generally Handberry v. Thompson*, 446 F.3d 335 (2d Cir. 2006)). The school district where the child resided at the time he or she was taken into custody is financially responsible for the cost of instructional services (§ 3202(7)(b)). State aid is available for the school district. (§ 3602(13)).

48:13. May school districts exclude pregnant students from public school programs?

No. Public schools may not discriminate against students based on their parental and/or marital status. Pregnant students must be provided with educational opportunities equal to those provided to students who are not pregnant (Title IX of the Educ. Amendments of 1972, 20 USC § 1681; 45 CFR § 86.40). In addition, pregnant students should be encouraged to remain in school and to participate in programs designed especially for them. All programs for pregnant students should be developed in cooperation with the school physician and student personnel staff to best provide for each individual. Homebound instruction (see **48:56-60**) should be made available to pregnant students when necessary.

48:14. Must school districts facilitate the enrollment of students released from residential facilities?

Yes. Districts of residence are required to promptly enroll any student released or conditionally released from a residential facility operated by the NYS Office of Children and Family Services, the NYS Office of Mental Health, the NYS Office for People with Developmental Disabilities or a local department of social services. Moreover, school districts must designate at least one employee to facilitate the prompt enrollment of these students, receive student records, and serve as the district contact person with residential facilities and state and local agencies. Districts must also implement the education plan for any such student's release as submitted to Family Court (8 NYCRR § 100.2(ff)).

48:15. May students be charged fees as a condition of attendance and participation in school programs?

No. As a general rule, no fee or charge may be required as a condition of school attendance or credit in a required course (*Appeal of Gordon*, 14 Ed Dept Rep 358 (1975)). Most judicial and administrative decisions regarding this issue date back to the 1970s. However, they establish that a school district:

- May not charge for instructional materials that are essential to the maintenance of the educational curriculum (*UFSD of the Tarrytowns v. Jackson*, 93 Misc.2d 53 (2d Dep't 1978); *Appeal of Levittown*, 17 Ed Dept Rep 142 (1977); *Appeal of Hasslacher*, 16 Ed Dept Rep 434 (1977); *Appeal of Gordon*).
- May not allow private instructors to use school facilities and charge students for non-credit bearing instruction such as private music lessons (*Appeal of Gordon*).
- May not require payment of a fee as a condition for participation in sports activities, or a donation to support such activities (*Appeal of Ambrosio*, 30 Ed Dept Rep 387 (1991); but see *Appeal of Posman*, 12 Ed Dept Rep 51 (1972)).
- May rent, sell, or loan supplies to students attending its public schools on such terms and under such rules and regulations as may be prescribed by the school board (§ 701(5); *Sodus CSD v. Rhine*, 63 A.D.2d 820 (4th Dep't 1978); *Reiss v. Abramowitz*, 39 A.D.2d 916 (2d Dep't 1972)).
- May not force parents to purchase supplies through the district (*UFSD of the Tarrytowns v. Jackson*; *Sodus CSD v. Rhine*).
- May not charge a fee to parents who do not want to purchase supplies through the district (*Sodus CSD v. Rhine*; *Appeal of Levittown*; *Appeal of Hasslacher*).

According to one court, the forced sale of supplies to parents and the imposition of a fee on parents unwilling to purchase supplies from a school district violates state constitutional provisions requiring the maintenance and support of free common schools (*UFSD of the Tarrytowns v. Jackson*).

In contrast, school districts may use district funds to pay for part or all of the costs of a field trip only if the trip is part of its educational program. Whether a field trip is part of a district's educational program will depend on factors such as whether the trip:

- has been approved as part of the school's educational program;

- occurs during the regular academic school day and year;
- is recognized for academic credit;
- is open to all students;
- provides that participating students are subject to the district's disciplinary code; and
- reflects district input into its content, planning, and how the knowledge obtained by students attending will be used in the class curriculum after the trip (*Appeal of Clark*, 45 Ed Dept Rep 340 (2006); *Appeals of Giardina & Carbone*, 43 Ed Dept Rep 395 (2004); *Appeal of Christe*, 39 Ed Dept Rep 685 (2000)).

Student Absences

Editor's Note: Additional guidance on minimum attendance standards, attendance policies, record keeping, and use of attendance data is available in the NYS Education Department's Attendance Questions and Answers at: http://www.p12.nysed.gov/sss/pps/attendance/attendanceQ-A.html.

48:16. What is the standard of attendance required of students who must attend school?

Students of compulsory education age (see **48:1**) must attend school regularly, as prescribed by the school board where the student resides or is employed, for the entire time the appropriate public schools or classes are in session. Absences are permitted only as allowed by the general rules and procedures of the public schools (§ 3210(1)(a), (2)(b); see *In the Matter of Sheena S.S.*, 263 A.D.2d 809 (3d Dep't 1999)).

In addition, school boards must adopt a comprehensive attendance policy that establishes record keeping procedures and intervention strategies to ensure sufficient attendance by all students to permit them to succeed at meeting the state learning standards (8 NYCRR § 104.1(i); *Appeal of a Student with a Disability*, 41 Ed Dept Rep 380 (2002); see **55:25**).

Students

48:17. What is truancy?

Truancy is the unlawful absence or irregular attendance upon instruction by a student of compulsory education age (see § 3213(2)(a); see also *Matter of Blackman v. Brown*, 100 Misc.2d 566 (Sup. Ct. Ulster Cnty. 1978); *DeLease v. Nolan*, 185 A.D. 82 (3d Dep't 1918)).

A significant, unexcused absentee rate that has a detrimental effect on the child's education can serve as the basis for a finding of educational neglect against a parent (*In the Matter of Jalesa P.*, 75 A.D.3d 730 (3d Dep't 2010); *In the Matter of Ashley X*, 50 A.D.3d 1194 (3d Dep't 2008); *In the Matter of Shawndalaya II*, 31 A.D.3d 823 (3d Dep't), *lv. to appeal denied*, 7 N.Y.3d 714 (2006); see **48:19-20**).

48:18. What are a school district's responsibilities regarding truant students?

Section 3213(2)(c), (d) of the Education Law requires an attendance officer or other person authorized by the school district to notify the parent of an elementary-grade student of his or her child's absence from school, if the parent so requests. The obligation to notify a parent arises only after a parent has submitted a request to be notified. (See also **48:19-23**).

School districts may establish special classes or schools for students with truancy problems provided they observe the protections applicable to cases involving the involuntary transfer of students from one school to another (§ 3214(2); *Appeal of Ackert*, 30 Ed Dept Rep 31 (1990)).

Districts may not suspend or expel students from school for truancy (*King v. Farmer*, 102 Misc.2d 610 (Sup. Ct. Westchester Cnty. 1979); *Appeal of Khan,* 35 Ed Dept Rep 322 (1996); *Appeal of Hynds*, 34 Ed Dept Rep 553 (1995); *Appeal of Strada*, 34 Ed Dept Rep 629 (1995); *Appeal of Ackert*; see **52:23**). Neither may they be dropped from attendance, except as authorized by law (see **48:1**). On the other hand, an in-school suspension is acceptable if the alternative education provided is adequate (*Appeal of Kainz*, 38 Ed Dept Rep 339 (1998); *Appeal of Miller*, 35 Ed Dept Rep 451 (1996); see **52:54**).

In addition, habitual truancy constitutes grounds for filing a person in need of supervision (PINS) petition in family court (Family Court Act §§ 712(a), 732; see also *Matter of Samantha K.*, 61 A.D.3d 1322 (3d Dep't 2009)). However, the filing of a PINS petition involving a child classified as a student with a disability may effect a change in educational placement subject to the procedural safeguards of the federal Individuals with Disabilities Education Act if the PINS petition contemplates a change in the child's educational placement (*Matter of Beau II*, 95 N.Y.2d 234 (2000)).

48:19. What is educational neglect?

Educational neglect consists of parental failure to ensure a child's prompt and regular attendance in school as required by the state's compulsory education laws, or parental actions that keep a child out of school for impermissible reasons resulting in an adverse effect on the child's educational progress or imminent danger of such an adverse effect (Family Court Act § 1012(f); NYS Office of Children and Family Services, *Model Policy on Educational Neglect* (Oct. 2008), at: http://www.ocfs.state.ny.us/main/prevention/EducationalNeglectModelPolicy.pdf; see also **48:1-2, 48:4**).

48:20. What are a school district's responsibilities regarding an educationally neglected student?

Section 34-a(8) of the Social Services Law requires that school districts work with local social services districts in the development of written policies for the reporting and investigation of educational neglect. Such policies and procedures, and any substantive changes to them, must be reviewed and approved by the Office of Children and Family Services (OCFS). In addition, they must be based on model practices and procedures developed by OCFS in conjunction with the NYS Education Department (see NYS Office of Children and Family Services, *Model Policy on Educational Neglect* (Oct. 2008), at: http://www.ocfs.state.ny.us/main/prevention/EducationalNeglectModelPolicy.pdf.).

Pursuant to the OCFS model policy, the local policies and procedures must include, at least, a process for reporting and investigation, and opportunities for timely intervention involving students, parents, school officials and Child Protective Services (CPS) staff. Reporting is primarily a school-based responsibility. The investigation process falls on CPS (*Id.*).

School districts must inform all school staff of the policy and procedure for reporting and investigating educational neglect. Mandated reporters must submit a report to the Statewide Central Register for Child Abuse and Maltreatment (SCR) whenever a student is excessively absent from school and they have reasonable cause to suspect:

- the parent is or should have been aware of the absenteeism, has contributed to or is failing to effectively address the problem, and
- educational impairment or harm to the child or imminent danger of either (*Id.*).

Mandated reporters include, but are not limited to, teachers, administrators, guidance counselors, school psychologists, school social workers, school nurses, and other school personnel required to hold a teaching or administrative license or certificate. Retaliatory action against mandated reporters who make a report to SCR is prohibited. School officials may not impose conditions, including prior approval or notification, on mandated reporters (Soc. Serv. Law § 413(1); *Model Policy on Educational Neglect*).

48:21. Must a school district have a policy regarding attendance?

Yes. Every school district is required to have in place a comprehensive attendance policy. The policy must serve to provide for the maintenance of an adequate record verifying the attendance of all children upon instruction and establish a mechanism for examining patterns of pupil absence to develop effective intervention strategies to improve school attendance (8 NYCRR § 104.1(i)). It must:

- state the policy's overall objectives and describe the specific strategies that will be used to achieve those objectives;
- specify the type of absences, tardiness, and early departures that will be deemed excused or unexcused, and the coding system that will be used to identify the reason for such absences, tardiness, and early departures;
- establish a minimum standard of attendance if the district opts to have a policy regarding attendance and eligibility for course credit (see **48:24**). In such an instance, the policy must also describe the notice to be given to parents and specific intervention strategies to be used prior to the denial of course credit;
- describe incentives to encourage attendance and discourage absences, tardiness, and early departures;
- describe the notice to be given to parents of students who are absent, tardy, or leave school early without excuses;
- describe the process to develop specific intervention strategies to address identified patterns of unexcused absences, tardiness, and early departures; and
- identify the individual(s) at each school building responsible for reviewing attendance records and initiating intervention strategies (8 NYCRR § 104.1(i)(2)).

The NYS Office of Children and Family Services recommends that a district's policy on excused and unexcused absences should be incorporated into the school district's policy on reporting and investigation of educational neglect (see **48:19–20**) developed in conjunction with the local social services district (Soc. Serv. Law § 34-a(8); NYS Office of Children and Family Services, *Model Policy on Educational Neglect* (Oct. 2008), at: http://www.ocfs.state.ny.us/main/prevention/EducationalNeglectModelPolicy.pdf).

Additionally, a school board must review student attendance records annually and revise the policy as necessary to improve attendance if the attendance records show a decline in student attendance (8 NYCRR § 104.1(i)(3)).

To promote community awareness of the policy, districts must:

- provide a plain language summary of the policy to parents before each school year and take other steps necessary to help them understand the policy;
- provide each teacher with a copy of the policy and any amendments thereto; and
- make copies of the policy available to other members of the community upon request (8 NYCRR § 104.1(i)(4)).

48:22. Must school districts maintain student attendance records?

Yes. School attendance records must be kept for use in the enforcement of the Education Law (§§ 3024, 3211(1)), and as the source for the average daily attendance used to help determine a district's state aid allocation (§ 3025(1)).

A school must maintain a register of attendance for each pupil which includes the child's name; date of birth; home address; names of parents/guardians; phone numbers to contact parents/guardians; date of enrollment; record of pupil's attendance on days of instruction; a record of each scheduled day of instruction during which the school is closed for all or part of the day because of extraordinary circumstances; and the date of withdrawal or date dropped from enrollment (8 NYCRR § 104.1(d)).

The commissioner of education can prescribe the form and manner of keeping such records (§§ 3024, 3025(1), 3211(1)).

48:23. Who is responsible for maintaining student attendance records?

A teacher, supervisory staff, or other suitable employee designated by the school board shall make entries into a register of attendance and verify the entries by oath or affirmation (§ 3211(1); 8 NYCRR § 104.1(b)(4), (5), (f), (g)). Entries will include all excused and unexcused absences, tardiness, and early departures (8 NYCRR § 104.1(d)(7)).

Each building principal and the staff member designated to initiate intervention strategies to improve attendance must review the attendance records for the purpose of taking any indicated action (8 NYCRR § 104.1(h)).

In non-departmentalized K–8 schools, attendance shall be taken once per day and if students are dismissed for lunch, again upon their return (8 NYCRR § 104.1(d)(7)(i)). In grades 9–12 and departmentalized schools at any grade level, attendance shall be taken in each period of instruction. However, if students do not change classrooms between periods, then attendance shall be taken the same as for non-departmentalized grades K–8 above (8 NYCRR § 104.1(d)(7)(ii)).

48:24. Can a school district's policy condition a student's receipt of academic credit on compliance with minimum attendance standards?

Yes. A school board may opt to adopt a policy that establishes a minimum attendance standard for course credit eligibility (8 NYCRR § 104.1(i)(2)(v); *Appeal of Hansen*, 34 Ed Dept Rep 235 (1994); *Matter of Hegarty*, 31 Ed Dept Rep 232 (1992)). However, such a policy must be applied in a neutral and consistent manner (*Appeal of Adriatico*, 39 Ed Dept Rep 248 (2000); *Appeal of Ehnot*, 37 Ed Dept Rep 648 (1998)).

A minimum attendance policy may distinguish between excused and unexcused absences so that a properly excused absence for which the student has performed any assigned make up work does not count toward possible denial of course credit (8 NYCRR § 104.1(i)(2)(v); *Appeal of a Student with a Disability*, 41 Ed Dept Rep 380 (2002)). But it may not deny course credit to a student who has exceeded the allowable number of absences but taken all tests, completed missed class work, and secured a passing grade (*Appeal of Adriatico*; *Appeal of Pasquale*, 36 Ed Dept Rep 290 (1997); *Appeal of Shepard*, 31 Ed Dept Rep 315 (1992); *Appeal of Burns*, 29 Ed Dept Rep 103 (1989)).

Although not required, a minimum attendance policy may contain an appeal process which is available to challenge the number of absences on record to ensure that no violation of the federal Individuals with Disabilities Education Act or section 504 of the Rehabilitation Act has occurred, and to provide an opportunity to waive the maximum allowable absence limit for "extenuating circumstances" without regard to whether the absences were excused or unexcused. Such an appeal process must be administered in a neutral manner and comply with applicable law (*Appeal of Ehnot*).

48:25. Can a student's unexcused absence from school with parental consent violate a district's attendance policy?

Yes. A school board can establish rules concerning the order and discipline of the schools, as it may deem necessary (§ 1709(2)), including minimum student attendance standards that also distinguish between excused and unexcused absences (8 NYCRR § 104.1(i); see **48:21**). These rules are not subject to parental consent (*Matter of Auch*, 33 Ed Dept Rep 84 (1993)). Therefore, in a case involving a parent's consent to a child's absence from school to go skiing, the commissioner of education upheld the district's enforcement of its attendance policy against the student (*Id.*).

A student's repeated unexcused absences from school with parental consent may result in educational neglect and require mandated reporting to the Statewide Central Register for Child Abuse and Maltreatment (see **48:19-20**).

48:26. May a student be absent from school for observance of religious occasions?

Yes. The Education Law recognizes school days missed for religious observance as "absences" (§ 3210(1)(b)). A student's absence from school during school hours for religious observance outside the school building and grounds will be excused upon a written request signed by his or her parent or guardian (8 NYCRR § 109.2(a)).

However, an absence for observance of a religious occasion does not exempt a student from complying with a school district policy that requires completion of compensatory work when a student exceeds a specified number of absences in any quarter (*Matter of Hegarty*, 31 Ed Dept Rep 232 (1992)).

48:27. May a student be released from school for religious instruction?

Yes. A student may be released during school hours for religious instruction upon a written request by his or her parent or guardian (§ 3210(2)(b); 8 NYCRR § 109.2(a); *Pierce v. Sullivan West CSD*, 379 F.3d 56 (2d Cir. 2004)). The courses in religious education must be maintained and operated by or under the control of duly constituted religious bodies (8 NYCRR § 109.2(b)). Students must be registered for the courses and a copy of the registration must be filed with the local public school authorities (8 NYCRR § 109.2(c)). The attendance of students enrolled in such religious classes must be reported to the public school principal at the end of each semester (8 NYCRR § 109.2(d)).

48:28. Are there any restrictions on the number of hours students can be released for religious instruction?

Absence for release-time programs for kindergarten through 12th grade cannot be for more than one hour each week at the close of either the morning or afternoon session, or both, at a time to be fixed by the local school authorities. The time designated for each separate unit — the primary grades (kindergarten-grade 3), intermediate grades (grades 4–6), junior high school grades (grades 7–9), and senior high school grades (grades 10–12) — must be the same for all students in that unit in each separate school (8 NYCRR § 109.2(e)).

If there is more than one school offering religious education within the district, the hours for absence from each particular public elementary or secondary school in that district must be the same for all such religious schools (8 NYCRR § 109.2(e)).

In addition, a school board may establish an optional program for high school students in grades 9 through 12, permitting them to enroll in a course in religion in a registered nonpublic high school, with the written approval of the student's parent or guardian. This is subject to prior approval of the public high school principal with respect to course schedule, student attendance, and reporting of student achievement. Absence to attend such a course may be excused for the number of periods per week that the course is scheduled in the nonpublic school, provided that the excused absences must be at the beginning or close of the public school session and are mutually agreed upon by the school officials (8 NYCRR § 109.2(f)).

48:29. Must school districts transport students to and from released time religious instruction?

No. School districts have no authority to transport students released for religious instruction to and from a church or parochial school where the religious instruction program is held (*Appeal of Fitch*, 2 Ed

Dept Rep 394 (1963); see also *Appeal of Santicola*, 37 Ed Dept Rep 79 (1997)). However, a district may lease school buses to a not-for-profit released time instruction provider to transport public school students to and from released time religious instruction facilities (*St. James Church v. Bd. of Educ. of the Cazenovia CSD*, 163 Misc.2d 471 (Sup. Ct. Madison Cnty. 1994)).

48:30. Do days when a student is suspended from school count as absences?

No. A school may not count days when a student is suspended from school as absences, unless the student is offered alternative instruction and fails to attend such instruction (*Appeal of Shepard*, 31 Ed Dept Rep 315 (1992)).

48:31. What can be done for children who are absent from school because of lack of suitable clothing, food, and other necessities?

Public welfare officials, except as otherwise provided by law, must furnish indigent children with suitable clothing, shoes, books, food, transportation and other necessities to enable them to attend upon instruction required by law (§ 3209(6)).

School Assignments

48:32. How are students assigned to the school they will attend?

Generally, the location of a child's residence within a school district determines the particular school a child will attend. However, school boards have broad discretion in assigning students to a particular school, including the authority to establish attendance zones and exceptions to attendance zone limitations (§ 1709(3), (33); *Matter of Older v. Bd. of Educ. of UFSD No. 1, Town of Mamaroneck*, 27 N.Y.2d 333 (1971); *Matter of Addabbo v. Donovan*, 22 A.D.2d 383 (2d Dep't), *aff'd,* 16 N.Y.2d 619, *cert. denied,* 382 U.S. 905 (1965); *Appeal of Roy*, 51 Ed Dept Rep, Dec. No. 16,279 (2011); *Appeal of Strade*, 48 Ed Dept Rep 73 (2008); *Appeal of Knoer*, 47 Ed Dept Rep 102 (2007)), such as open enrollment allowances (see *Appeal of Knoer*). A school board's decision to reorganize its schools will be upheld unless it is arbitrary, capricious, or contrary to sound educational policy (*Appeal of Strade*).

A school board's decision regarding school assignments will be overturned only if it is found to be arbitrary, capricious, or contrary to sound educational policy (*Matter of Older*; *Appeal of Araneo*, 45 Ed Dept Rep 325 (2005); *Appeal of Alves*, 44 Ed Dept Rep 334 (2005); *Appeal of Jones*, 52 Ed. Dept. Rep, Dec. No. 16,456 (2013)), or based on impermissible race classifications (*Parents Involved in Cmty. Schs. v. Seattle Sch. Dist. No. 1*, 127 S.Ct. 2738 (2007); *Grutter v. Bollinger*, 539 U.S. 306 (2003)).

48:33. Are school districts required to assign siblings to the same school?

No. Pursuant to Education Law § 1709(3) and (33), a school board has the authority and responsibility to manage and administer the affairs of the school district, including the assignment of pupils to schools therein (*Older v. Bd. of Educ. of UFSD No. 1, Town of Mamaroneck*, 27 N.Y.2d 333 (1971)). In one case, the commissioner of education upheld a school district's decision to assign one student to an elementary school outside of his attendance zone due to his special education needs, but his younger brother to his neighborhood school. The district's practice was not to place students in a non-neighborhood school simply to follow their special education sibling because a special education student's placement can change based on a recommendation of the committee on special education (see **54:25**). Placing a special education student's general education sibling in his or her neighborhood school guarantees continuity for the general education student, according to the district (*Appeal of Y.M.*, 55 Ed Dept Rep, Dec. No. 16,862 (2016)).

48:34. May students attend school outside of their attendance zone?

Generally, students are not entitled to attend school outside the attendance zone in which they reside, unless they qualify for an exception. However, exceptions allowing students to attend school outside their attendance zone may be set by school district policy.

Some of those exceptions may be based on educational necessity or a change in residence during the last quarter of a school year (see *Appeal of Hallenback*, 47 Ed Dept Rep 481 (2008)). A student's difficulty adapting to a new school, by itself, is not a sufficient basis for reassigning a student to a school outside his or her attendance zone. Neither does a student's difficulties with other students where school officials offer the opportunity to transfer out of any classes in which those other students are assigned and the offer is declined (*Appeal of P.C.*, 45 Ed Dept Rep 476 (2006)).

Nonetheless, and consistent with the federal Every Student Succeeds Act (ESSA), school districts must offer students attending a school identified as persistently dangerous the choice to transfer to another school at the same grade level within the district that has not been identified, or designated as such (8 NYCRR § 120.3(a)). However, this right is subject to health and safety code requirements regarding facility capacity (8 NYCRR §§ 100.2(p)(6)(vi), 120.3). It does not automatically entitle students to transfer to a magnet school or special focus schools (i.e., math or science schools or other similar school that has entrance requirements based on academic or other skills) (8 NYCRR § 120.3(a)). ESSA does not otherwise require school districts to provide public school choice, except that districts may choose to do so with respect to students attending a school identified for comprehensive support and improvement (§ 1111(d)(1)(D)).

In addition, students attending a school designated as persistently dangerous or who become victims of a violent criminal offense that occurs at the public school they attend have the right to transfer to a safe public school at the same grade level within the district (N.Y. Educ. Law § 2802(7); 8 NYCRR § 120.5). That designation is based on data submitted by school districts and boards of cooperative educational services annually to the commissioner of education pursuant to the state-wide Uniform Violent Incident Reporting System (§ 2802; 8 NYCRR § 100.2(gg)). That data includes information concerning violent and disruptive incidents that occurred in the prior school year including, for example, the type and location of such incidents, the nature, age and grade of the victim, and school action taken in response to the incidents (§ 2802(3)). Offenses are ranked in accordance with commissioner's regulations (8 NYCRR § 100.2(gg)(2)). The level of violence in a school is measured pursuant to a school violence index that is based on a formula established by the commissioner (8 NYCRR § 100.2(gg)(8)). More information on the Uniform Violent Incident Reporting System is available from the NYS Education Department's website at: http://www.p12.nysed.gov/sss/ssae/schoolsafety/vadir.

48:35. Can students be transferred involuntarily from one school to another in the same district?

Generally, yes. The school board, the superintendent of schools, or the district superintendent may transfer a student from regular classroom instruction to an appropriate educational setting in another school on the written recommendation of the school principal and following an independent review (§ 3214(5)(a); *Appeal of a Student Suspected of Having a Disability*, 40 Ed Dept Rep 212 (2000); see **48:37**).

However, students with disabilities may not be involuntarily transferred without the participation of the committee on special education (*Appeal of Wanda D.*, 34 Ed Dept Rep 556 (1995)). Furthermore, involuntary transfers for disciplining purposes are not permitted (see **48:36-37**).

Involuntary transfers, for purposes of this question, do not include transfers made due to changes in attendance zones, geographical boundaries, or as part of a plan to reduce racial imbalance (§ 3214(5)(a)).

48:36. May a school district transfer students involuntarily for violations of the district's code of conduct?

No. Involuntary transfers are not an authorized disciplinary penalty under the Education Law. Therefore, they are invalid as a form of discipline for violations of a district's code of conduct (*Appeal of T.C.*, 44 Ed Dept Rep 316 (2005); *Appeal of K.B.*, 41 Ed Dept Rep 431 (2002); see also **52:16**).

48:37. What process must districts follow before transferring a student involuntarily to another school?

Before a school principal may initiate an involuntary transfer, he or she must provide the student and his or her parents with written notification of the consideration of transfer recommendation. The notice must set forth the time and place for an informal conference with the principal, and specify their right to be accompanied by an attorney or an individual of their choice (§ 3214(5)(b)).

After the conference is held, and if the principal believes the student would benefit from the transfer or receive an adequate and appropriate education in another school program or facility, the principal may recommend that course of action to the superintendent. These transfers are usually recommended because of behavior or academic problems. The recommendation must include reasons indicating the need for transfer and other supporting information. A copy must be sent to the parent and the student (§ 3214(5)(c)).

Once the superintendent receives the recommendation, he or she must notify the parents and the student of the proposed transfer, their right to a fair hearing on the issue, and other procedural rights. The written notice must include a statement that the student or parents have 10 days to request a hearing (§ 3214(5)(d)).

A hearing to determine whether a student should be transferred is not the same as a hearing for disciplinary reasons. While the purpose of a disciplinary hearing is to punish a student for wrongdoing, the purpose of a transfer hearing is to determine whether the proposed transfer would be beneficial for the student (§ 3214(5); *Appeal of K.B.*, 41 Ed Dept Rep 431 (2002); *Appeal of a Student Suspected of Having a Disability*, 40 Ed Dept Rep 212 (2000), *petition dismissed*, (Sup. Ct. Albany Cnty. Jan. 18, 2001), *aff'd* 293 A.D.2d 37 (2002); *Appeal of Reeves*, 37 Ed Dept Rep 271 (1998)). Unless the parents consent to the transfer, the proposed transfer may not take place until the 10-day period to request a hearing has elapsed, or a formal decision is rendered following a hearing, whichever is later (§ 3214(5)(d)). Ultimate responsibility for the assignment of students rests with the school board (§ 1709(3)).

Home Instruction

Editor's Note: The NYS Education Department's Questions and Answers on Home Instruction, revised March 2015 and cited throughout this section, are available at: http://www.p12.nysed.gov/sss/homeinstruction/homeschoolingqanda.html.

48:38. Are parents permitted to educate their children at home?

Yes. The Education Law permits the education of children at home, provided that children of compulsory education age receive full-time instruction, and are taught by competent teachers and receive instruction that is substantially equivalent to that provided at the public schools of the student's district of residence (§§ 3204(2), 3210(2), 3212(2); 8 NYCRR § 100.10; see *In the Matter of Andrew T.T.*, 122 A.D.2d 362 (3d Dep't 1986); *In re Franz*, 55 A.D.2d 424 (2d Dep't 1977); *People v. Turner*, 277 A.D. 317 (4th Dep't 1950)). A school superintendent can certify that four years of high school instruction pursuant to approved individualized home instruction plans (see **48:42-43**) constitute the substantial equivalent of a four-year high school course of study (*Appeal of Federman*, 45 Ed Dept Rep 554 (2006)).

State law does not require any specific credentials for the person providing home instruction (NYS Education Department, *Questions and Answers on Home Instruction* (updated Mar. 2015), question 9).

A home-schooled student may satisfy compulsory education requirements through enrollment at a college, provided the student takes at least 12 credit hours. In addition, prior to enrolling in the college, the student must submit a valid individualized home instruction plan (see **48:42-43**) to the institution verifying that the compulsory education requirements will be met through full-time college study. (8 NYCRR §§ 3.47(b), 100.10(d); see also NYS Education Department, *Guidelines on Revised Rules and Regulations Relating to The Home Instruction of Students of Compulsory School Age and Full-Time College Study* (Feb. 2012), at: http://www.p12.nysed.gov/sss/homeinstruction/homeinstruct.html).

48:39. Must parents educating their children at home adhere to laws and regulations regarding home instruction?

Yes. The Education Law imposes upon parents a duty to ensure that their children receive appropriate instruction (§ 3212(2); *Appeal of Brown*, 34 Ed Dept Rep 33 (1994); *Matter of White*, 29 Ed Dept Rep 511 (1990); *Matter of Thomas H.*, 78 Misc.2d 412 (Fam. Ct. Yates Cnty. 1974)). Further, the state has a legitimate and compelling interest in ensuring that its children receive an education that will prepare them to be productive members of society (*Blackwelder v. Safnauer*, 689 F.Supp. 106 (N.D.N.Y. 1988), *appeal dismissed*, 866 F.2d 548 (2d Cir. 1989)).

When a school district is unable to obtain information from parents regarding home instruction and has insufficient evidence that appropriate instruction is taking place, it is obligated to report the case to the Statewide Central Register for Child Abuse and Maltreatment as a case of suspected educational neglect pursuant to Social Services Law section 413 (*Appeal of the Bd. of Educ. of the Lynbrook UFSD*, 41 Ed Dept Rep 174 (2001); see also **48:20**). The commissioner of education has no authority to review appeals by school districts against parents.

48:40. What specific provisions govern home instruction?

Sections 3204(2), 3210(2)(d), and 3212(2) of the Education Law, and section 100.10 of the commissioner's regulations, set forth the requirements that must be met by parents who wish to educate their children at home. Parents must, for instance, develop an individualized home instruction plan (IHIP) (8 NYCRR § 100.10(c), (d); *Appeal of Brown*, 34 Ed Dept Rep 33 (1994); *Matter of White*, 29 Ed Dept Rep 511 (1990)); submit quarterly reports (8 NYCRR § 100.10(g)); and file an annual assessment indicating the student's progress (8 NYCRR § 100.10(h)). The regulations also provide detailed requirements for courses to be taught, required attendance, and student evaluation (8 NYCRR § 100.10(e)–(h)).

48:41. What are the responsibilities of parents who educate their children at home?

The parents or other persons in parental relation to students of compulsory education age wishing to educate their children at home must do the following:

- Notify the superintendent of schools in writing each year by July 1 of their intention to educate their child at home. If they move into the district or decide to educate their child at home after the start of the school year, they must provide notice within 14 days of commencing home instruction (8 NYCRR § 100.10(b)).
- Submit an individualized home instruction plan (IHIP) for each child of compulsory attendance age to be instructed at home within four weeks of receipt of the form provided by the district or by August 15, whichever is later (8 NYCRR § 100.10(c)(2)). The plan must contain, among other items, a list of the syllabi, curriculum materials, textbooks, or plan of instruction to be used in each of the required subjects noted in the regulations, and the names of the person(s) to provide instruction or a statement that the child will be enrolled for a minimum of 12 credit hours at a degree granting institution (8 NYCRR § 100.10(d); see **48:38**; see also 8 NYCRR § 100.10(e) for a list of required courses). The school district will provide assistance in developing the IHIP, if the parent so requests (8 NYCRR § 100.10(c)(2)).
- Submit quarterly reports for each child to the school district on the dates specified in the IHIP. Each report must contain the number of hours of instruction; a description of the material covered in each subject; either a grade for the child in each subject or a written narrative evaluating the child's progress; and a written explanation if less than 80 percent of the course material set out in the IHIP was covered in any subject (8 NYCRR § 100.10(g)).
- File an annual assessment of the student at the same time as the fourth quarterly report. The assessment must be based on the results of a commercially published norm-referenced achievement test, such as the Iowa or California Test, or an alternative form of evaluation that meets the regulatory requirements. The test must be administered by the professional staff at a public or nonpublic school or at the child's home by a certified teacher or other qualified person, including the child's parent. The superintendent's consent is required when such a test is administered at a nonregistered nonpublic school or at the child's home (8 NYCRR § 100.10(h); see NYS Education Department, *Questions and Answers on Home Instruction* (updated Mar. 2015), question 59). The commissioner of education has ruled that a student must take a commercially prepared achievement test in a case where parents objected that the test "conflicted with their personal philosophy" (*Appeal of Abookire*, 33 Ed Dept Rep 473 (1994)).

48:42. What are the school district's responsibilities with respect to the individualized home instruction plan (IHIP) developed by parents educating their children at home?

Within 10 business days of receiving notice from a child's parents of their intention to educate their child at home, the school district must send to the parents a copy of the home instruction regulations, along with a form on which the parents must submit an IHIP for any child educated at home (8 NYCRR § 100.10(c)(1)).

Within 10 business days of receipt of the IHIP or by August 31, whichever is later, the school district must either notify the parents that the IHIP is satisfactory or give the parents written notice of any deficiencies (8 NYCRR § 100.10(c)(3)).

The superintendent of schools is responsible for ensuring the home-schooled student's IHIP complies with the commissioner's regulations, subject to review on an appeal to the board (8 NYCRR § 100.10(c)). If there are deficiencies, the parent must, within 15 days of receipt of such notice or by September 15, whichever is later, submit a revised IHIP that corrects the deficiencies (8 NYCRR § 100.10(c)(4)). The superintendent then reviews the revised IHIP. If he or she determines the indicated deficiencies have not been corrected, he or she will issue a notice of noncompliance within 15 days of receipt of the revised IHIP or by September 30, whichever is later (8 NYCRR § 100.10(c)(5)).

48:43. What happens if a school district determines that the individualized home instruction plan (IHIP) of a home-schooled student is deficient?

If the parents disagree with the school superintendent's determination of noncompliance (see **48:42**), they have a right to appeal to the school board (8 NYCRR § 100.10(c)(5)). If the board upholds the superintendent's determination, the parents may appeal to the commissioner of education within 30 days of receipt of notice of the board's decision (8 NYCRR § 100.10(c)(6)).

If parents lose their appeal or fail to contest the determination that their child's IHIP is deficient, they must "immediately provide for the instruction of their children at a public school or elsewhere in compliance with the Education Law sections 3204 and 3210." Further, the parents must provide to the superintendent written notice of the arrangements they have made within 10 days after administrative review of the determination of noncompliance is completed, unless they have enrolled their child in the public school (8 NYCRR § 100.10(c)(7), (8)).

48:44. May home-schooled students receive instruction at a location outside their parents' primary residence?

Yes. Instruction for students educated at home may be provided outside the parents' primary residence, provided the building where instruction takes place is in compliance with the local building code (8 NYCRR § 100.10(f)(5)).

48:45. May parents engage a tutor to provide home instruction?

Yes. Parents may engage the services of a tutor to provide instruction for all or part of the home instruction program. Moreover, parents providing home instruction to their children also can arrange to have their children receive group instruction in particular subjects. But where parents organize to have a "majority" of their children's education provided by a tutor in a group setting, they will be deemed to be operating a nonpublic school and no longer providing home instruction. As such, they will have to satisfy state law and regulations ensuring the substantial equivalency of instruction provided by nonpublic schools (NYS Education Department, *Questions and Answers on Home Instruction* (updated Mar. 2015), questions 5-6).

48:46. Are there any attendance requirements for home-schooled students?

Yes. Children in grades 1–6 must receive 900 hours of instruction and those in grades 7–12 must receive 990 hours, with attendance substantially equivalent to 180 days per school year. Absences are allowed on the same basis as prescribed by the school district for students attending the public schools. Parents must maintain records of attendance to be provided to the district upon request (8 NYCRR § 100.10(f)).

Instruction at home is usually given within the general timeframe of the normal school day, but greater flexibility in scheduling is possible. For example, parents may choose to provide instruction on weekends or in the evening. However, the total amount of instructional time per week should be generally comparable to that of the public school (NYS Education Department, *Questions and Answers on Home Instruction* (updated Mar. 2015), question 8).

48:47. Are there any courses home-schooled students are required to take?

Yes. The commissioner's regulations set forth the courses that children in grades K–12 educated at home must study (8 NYCRR § 100.10(e)). In addition to courses in specific academic areas such as English, math, science, history, arts, physical education, and others, home instruction must also cover patriotism and citizenship; health education regarding alcohol, drug and tobacco misuse; highway safety and traffic regulation, including bicycle safety; and fire and arson prevention and safety (8 NYCRR § 100.10(e)(2)(v)). Although every student must have a physical education program, activities may differ provided that the outcomes are similar to those established for students in the public school.

48:48. Are home-schooled students required to take mandated state assessments?

No. However, such tests may be used to satisfy annual assessment requirements applicable to home-schooled students (8 NYCRR § 100.10(h); NYS Education Department, *Questions and Answers on Home Instruction* (updated Mar. 2015), question 58; see also **56:4**).

In addition, if a request is made, school officials are encouraged to admit a student receiving home instruction to a Regents examination. If a Regents examination has a lab requirement, the student may be admitted to the examination if there is evidence that the student has met the lab requirement. The student's individualized home instruction plan (IHIP), quarterly reports, and/or verification from the student's teacher can provide such evidence. However, Regents examinations may only be administered at the public school or registered nonpublic school because they are secure examinations. The test results can be helpful to the student and also to public school officials (*Questions and Answers on Home Instruction*, question 57).

48:49. What happens if a home-schooled student does not perform adequately on the annual assessment?

If a student does not receive an adequate score on an annual assessment, the home instruction program will be placed on probation for a period of up to two years. The parent must submit a plan of remediation to be reviewed by the school district (8 NYCRR § 100.10(i)(1)). To be adequate, a student's annual assessment must reflect a composite score above the 33rd percentile on national norms, or indicate one academic year of growth as compared to a test administered during or subsequent to the prior school year (8 NYCRR § 100.10(h)(1)(v)).

If the objectives of the remediation plan are not met, the superintendent of schools will issue a notice of noncompliance, subject to school board review (8 NYCRR § 100.10(i)(2)), and ultimately require that the parent enroll the child in a public or other school that meets the requirements of the Education Law (8 NYCRR § 100.10(c)(7)).

During the probation period, the superintendent may require one or more home visits, if he or she has reasonable grounds to believe that the home instruction program does not comply with the regulations. The superintendent may include members of a home instruction peer review panel in the home visit team (8 NYCRR § 100.10(i)(3)). If the home instruction program is not on probation, school officials may request a home visit, but the parents are not required to consent to the request (NYS Education Department, *Questions and Answers on Home Instruction* (updated Mar. 2015), question 30).

48:50. May a home-schooled student be awarded a local or Regents diploma?

No. A high school diploma may only be awarded to a student enrolled in a registered secondary school who has completed all program requirements set by the Regents, the school, or the district (8 NYCRR § 100.2(p); see also NYS Education Department, *Questions and Answers on Home Instruction* (updated Mar. 2015), question 25).

However, where a home-schooled student has completed four years of high school instruction pursuant to approved individualized home instruction plans (see **48:42-43**), a superintendent of schools may certify that the student has complied with commissioner's regulations in completing the substantial equivalent of a four-year high school course of study (*Appeal of Federman*, 45 Ed Dept Rep 554 (2006)).

48:51. Are home-schooled students granted the same right to borrow public school textbooks, computer software, and library materials as students enrolled in nonpublic schools?

No. The state law that requires districts to loan these items to nonpublic school students does not apply to students who receive home instruction because such students are not enrolled in a nonpublic school. However, school districts may voluntarily loan such items to home-schooled students, subject to availability after the district has satisfied its legal obligations (NYS Education Department, *Questions and Answers on Home Instruction* (updated Mar. 2015), questions 16-17; see also **4:15-22**).

48:52. Do home-schooled students have the same right to dual enrollment services as students enrolled in nonpublic schools?

It depends. The dual-enrollment provisions that authorize partial attendance at a public school by nonpublic school students for the purpose of obtaining instruction in the areas of occupational and vocational education, and gifted education do not apply to home-schooled students (*Appeal of Ando*, 45 Ed Dept Rep 523 (2006); *Appeal of Pope*, 40 Ed Dept Rep 473 (2001)). A school district that may have erroneously permitted home-schooled students to participate in a public school educational program may not be required to continue an action that is contrary to law (*Appeal of Ando*).

The reason why home-schooled students are not entitled to dual-enrollment services is because the dual-enrollment law applies only to students attending nonpublic schools recognized under state law as a private elementary or secondary school. Home-schooled students do not fall into that category (*Appeal of Ando*; *Appeal of Pope*).

The only exception applies to home-schooled students with disabilities who are entitled to attend public school tuition free and have an individualized home instruction plan (see **48:42-43**) that complies with commissioner's regulations (§ 3602-c(2-c)). Such children are to be treated the same as nonpublic school students solely for the purpose of receiving special education services, as well as the computation of state aid (*Id.*; see also NYS Education Department, *New Requirements for the Provision of Special Education Services to Home-Instructed ("Home-Schooled") Students* (updated Feb. 2012), at: http://www.p12.nysed.gov/sss/homeinstruction/homeinstructionguidance708.html; see generally **54:98-105**).

48:53. Must school districts allow home-schooled students to participate in extracurricular activities at the public schools?

No. School boards have the authority to limit participation in extracurricular activities to those students enrolled in the district (*Appeal of Ponte*, 41 Ed Dept Rep 186 (2001)).

Guidance from the state education department indicates that a school board may establish a policy that allows students not enrolled in the public schools to participate in school-sponsored club activities (NYS Education Department, *Home Instruction Questions and Answers* (updated Mar. 2015), at: questions 12-13).

However, under the commissioner's regulations and state education department guidance, a school board may not allow students who are not enrolled in the district to participate in the district's interscholastic sports program or intramural activities (8 NYCRR § 135.4(c)(7)(ii)(b)(2); 8 NYCRR § 135.1(g), (m); *Bradstreet v. Sobol,* 165 Misc.2d 931 (Sup. Ct. Albany Cnty. 1995), *aff'd*, 225 A.D.2d 175 (3d Dep't 1996); *Home Instruction Questions and Answers*, question 12).

48:54. Are home-schooled students subject to the same immunization requirements as students attending school?

No. The provisions of Public Health Law section 2164, which require parents to submit proof of immunization prior to admission of their children to a school (see **50:13–23**), do not apply to students being educated at home. However, if the commissioner of health notifies school officials of the outbreak of a disease for which immunization is required, parents of home-schooled children who seek to participate in testing or other activities on the premises of a public or nonpublic school must produce proof of immunization or be denied access to the school building (NYS Education Department, *Questions and Answers on Home Instruction* (updated Mar. 2015), question 15).

48:55. Are school districts entitled to state aid for home-schooled students?

A school district cannot claim state aid for students instructed at home by their parents (NYS Education Department, *Questions and Answers on Home Instruction* (updated Mar. 2015), question 22), except for home-schooled students with disabilities receiving special education services from the district (§ 3602-c(2-c); see **48:52**).

Homebound Instruction

Editor's Note: The NYS Education Department's Handbook on Services to Pupils Attending Nonpublic Schools, updated Oct. 2013 and cited throughout this section, is available at: http://www.p12.nysed.gov/nonpub/handbookonservices/homeboundinstruction.html.

48:56. Is homebound instruction the same thing as home instruction?

No. *Homebound instruction* is provided on a temporary basis by the public school district when a student is unable to attend school because of short-term disability or discipline (see *Appeal of a Student Suspected of Having a Disability (Fayetteville-Manlius CSD)*, 40 Ed Dept Rep 75 (2001); *Appeal of Douglas & Barbara K.*, 34 Ed Dept Rep 214 (1994); *Appeal of Anthony M.*, 30 Ed Dept Rep 269 (1991)). *Home instruction* is typically provided by parents who exercise the right to instruct their child(ren) at home instead of at a public or nonpublic school (see 8 NYCRR § 100.10(a), (b); see also **48:38**, **4:1**).

48:57. Under what circumstances is a student entitled to homebound instruction?

If a prolonged absence due to a short-term physical, mental, or emotional illness is anticipated, the administrator of the student's school should talk with the student's parents about arranging for homebound instruction. According to the NYS Education Department, an absence of at least two weeks is considered a prolonged absence. The student's physician should verify any such absence due to illness (see NYS Education Department, *Handbook on Services to Pupils Attending Nonpublic Schools* (updated Oct. 2013)).

However, in one case, the commissioner of education excused a school district's obligation to provide homebound instruction where parents failed to respond to the district's initial offer for homebound instruction, and contributed to their children's absence from school by failing to follow a recommended course of treatment for lice (*Appeal of Douglas & Barbara K.*, 34 Ed Dept Rep 214 (1994)).

48:58. Who is responsible for providing homebound instruction?

The district in which the student resides is responsible for providing an appropriately certified teacher to tutor the homebound student. However, the district of residence may contract with another district to provide this service (see NYS Education Department, *Handbook on Services to Pupils Attending Nonpublic Schools* (updated Oct. 2013)).

48:59. Is a school district required to provide homebound instruction to nonpublic school students?

Yes. A nonpublic school student requiring homebound instruction should enroll in the public school during the time he or she receives homebound instruction from the public school, so that the district may count the student in its attendance report for state aid purposes (see NYS Education Department, *Handbook on Services to Pupils Attending Nonpublic Schools* (updated Oct. 2013)).

However, school districts are not required or authorized to provide part-time instruction to a student who is actively enrolled in a nonpublic school, even if the student is only permitted to attend nonpublic school for 2 hours each day (*Appeal of K.L.*, 53 Ed Dept Rep, Dec. No. 16,627 (2014)). When a district is providing homebound instruction to a nonpublic school student, the district will not be required to replicate the nonpublic schools curriculum, but should take into consideration all relevant factors when determining what curriculum will be provided (*Appeal of K.L.*).

48:60. Is there a minimum amount of instruction districts must offer homebound students?

Elementary school students on homebound instruction must receive at least five hours of instruction per week and secondary school students 10 hours per week. To the extent possible, homebound instruction should be staggered proportionately throughout the week (8 NYCRR § 175.21; see also NYS Education Department, *Handbook on Services to Pupils Attending Nonpublic Schools* (updated Oct. 2013)).

The U.S. Department of Education Office of Civil Rights has determined, however, that a school policy that provided only four hours of instruction per week to homebound students and which failed to provide for makeup sessions when teachers were unable to provide the services during a particular week violated the Americans with Disabilities Act and section 504 of the Rehabilitation Act of 1973 (*Boston Pub. Sch.*, OCR Decision, 21 IDELR 170 (1994)).

49. Student Enrollment Rules

Enrollment Procedures

49:1. Is a school district required to adopt procedures for the enrollment of students?

Yes. In addition, a school district must post such procedures, enrollment forms and instructions on its website. It also must provide individuals requesting enrollment with these materials. Such information must include a non-exhaustive list of forms of documentation that may be submitted to establish a child's residency and age (8 NYCRR § 100.2(y)(2)).

49:2. Is there a schedule that a school district must follow to enroll a child?

No. A school district must enroll a child when the parent, person in a parental relationship or the child himself requests enrollment. The child shall begin attendance the next school day or as soon as practicable (8 NYCRR § 100.2(y)(3)).

No later than three days after enrollment the parent, person in parental relation or the child must submit documentation or information to support the child's residency in the district (8 NYCRR § 100.2(y)(3); see **49:14-22**). If such documentation is submitted on the third day the decision may be rendered by the school district on the fourth day (8 NYCRR § 100.2(y)(3)). If a determination of non-residency is made on the date of the request for enrollment the district will not be required to enroll a child (*Id.*).

Age Requirements

49:3. How old must a child be to enroll in a public school?

In order to attend a public school a child must turn 5 years of age on or before December 1 of the year in which the child seeks to enroll (§ 3202(1); *Appeal of Tomassetti,* 39 Ed Dept Rep 513 (2000); *Appeal of Sollitto*, 31 Ed Dept Rep 138 (1991)). See **Chapter 48** for rules regarding compulsory attendance.

If a school district sponsors a pre-kindergarten program a child must turn 4 years of age on or before December 1 of the year in which he or she seeks to enroll or be otherwise eligible to enter public school kindergarten commencing with the following school year (§ 3602-e(1)(c); *Appeal of I.A.*, 41 Ed Dept Rep 413 (2002)).

49:4. What documentation must be provided to the school district as proof of age of a child for enrollment purposes?

A parent or guardian has a responsibility to submit evidence of age at the time a child begins to attend upon instruction (§ 3212(2)(a); *Appeal of R.L.,* 49 Ed Dept Rep 9 (2009)). Where a certified transcript of a birth certificate or record of baptism (including a certified transcript of a foreign birth certificate or record of baptism) giving the date of birth is available, no other form of evidence may be used to determine age. If neither exists, a passport (US or foreign) may be used. If the above documentation is unavailable, the district may consider other documentary or recorded evidence in existence for 2 or more years, except for an affidavit of age. This may include, but is not limited to:

- official driver's license;
- state or other government issued identification;
- school photo identification with date of birth;
- consulate identification card;
- hospital or health records;
- military dependent ID card;
- documents issued by federal, state, or local agencies (e.g. local social service agency, federal Office of Refugee Resettlement);
- court orders or other court-issued documents;
- native American tribal document; or
- records from non-profit international aid agencies and voluntary agencies (§ 3218; 8 NYCRR § 100.2(y)(3)(ii)(a)-(c)).

If the other documentary or recorded evidence of age originates from a foreign country, the district may request verification of the evidence from the appropriate foreign government or agency, consistent with the requirements of the federal Family Educational Rights and Privacy Act (FERPA). However, enrollment cannot be delayed while attempting to obtain such verification (8 NYCRR § 100.2(y)(3)(ii)(d)).

49:5. Can a school district require that a child be toilet trained to enroll in or attend a prekindergarten or kindergarten program?

No. According to guidance from the NYS Education Department, a child that meets the age and residency requirements of the law may not be excluded from a state-funded prekindergarten or kindergarten program. A district does not have authority to apply additional criteria, such as being toilet trained, as a condition of enrollment or attendance. Instead, the guidance states that the district should work with parents to develop a plan that supports the child to use the toilet independently (NYS Education Department, *Guidelines for Supporting Toilet Training* (Mar. 11, 2016), at: http://www.p12.nysed.gov/sss/documents/GuidelinesforSupportingToiletLearning_March2016.pdf).

Residency Requirements

49:6. What constitutes residency for purposes of attending the schools of a particular school district?

Residency in this context means domicile. It requires both one's physical presence as an inhabitant and the intention to reside within the district (*J.S. v. Scarsdale UFSD*, 826 F. Supp.2d 635 (S.D.N.Y. 2011); *Longwood CSD v. Springs UFSD*, 1 N.Y.3d 385 (2004); *Appeal of Perry*, 49 Ed Dept Rep 190 (2009); *Appeal of Lin*, 48 Ed Dept Rep 166 (2009)). Physical presence alone is insufficient to establish residence for purposes of attending the school in that district on a tuition-free basis (*Appeal of Reifler*, 31 Ed Dept Rep 235 (1992)), including presence in a homeless shelter at the time social services takes over a child's maintenance and support (*Longwood CSD*). Similarly, mere ownership of property within a district does not establish physical presence of the type required to confer residency status (*Appeal of C.B-M.,* 55 Ed Dept Rep, Dec. No. 16,844 (2015); *Appeal of D.D.*, 48 Ed Dept Rep 320 (2009); *Appeal of Seefried*, 46 Ed Dept Rep 311 (2007)). Neither does the mere renting of property or the actual payment of taxes (*Appeal of Alvarez,* 54 Ed Dept Rep, Dec. No. 16,661 (2014); *Appeal of D.D.*; *Appeal of T.B.*,

48 Ed Dept Rep 4 (2008); compare *Appeal of Three Students*, 48 Ed Dept Rep 40 (2008)). Pending home construction in and of itself also is insufficient to establish residency (*Appeal of Zhang,* 54 Ed Dept Rep, Dec. No. 16,733 (2015); *Appeal of Lin*)). Nonetheless, the amount of school taxes paid on property not constituting a person's legal residence must be deducted from the tuition charged to a nonresident student if the student attends school in that district instead of his legal district of residence (§ 3202(3); see **49:26**).

Intent to reside within a district is determined based on factors such as continuing ties to the community and the nature of the efforts to return (*Appeal of Macchia*, 51 Ed Dept Rep, Dec. No. 16,299 (2011); *Appeal of Lin*; *Appeal of Smith*, 48 Ed Dept Rep 125 (2008)), including a concrete and realistic plan to do so (*Appeal of Yuen*, 49 Ed Dept Rep 175 (2009); *Appeal of T.F.*, 49 Ed Dept Rep 70 (2009)).

Each school district must post to its website its enrollment forms, instructions and procedures, including how it determines residency. The documents must contain examples of documentation accepted in order to establish residency (8 NYCRR § 100.2(y)(2); see **49:1**).

49:7. Can a person have more than one residence for purposes of attending school within a particular district?

No. A person can have only one legal residence (*Catlin v. Sobol*, 155 A.D.2d 24 (3d Dep't 1990), *rev'd on other grounds*, 77 N.Y.2d 552 (1991); *Appeal of a Student with a Disability*, 51 Ed Dept Rep, Dec. No. 16,318 (2011); *Appeals of Moore*, 49 Ed Dept Rep 158 (2009); *Appeal of W.D. & P. Z-D.*, 44 Ed Dept Rep 77 (2004)). Therefore, where someone owns or rents property both within and outside a school district, only one of the properties can be considered his or her legal residence for purposes of attending school within a particular district (*Appeal of Elkareh,* 45 Ed Dept Rep 177 (2005); *Appeal of W.D. & P. Z-D*).

When a person claims legal residency in a place where he or she does not remain all year, it becomes necessary to look for some overt act that indicates the individual has made a choice to consider this his or her domicile, such as whether or not he or she registers and votes from that place, or whether he or she uses it as his or her residence for income tax purposes (see **49:6**).

Furthermore, a person does not lose his or her domicile until another one is established (*Longwood CSD v. Springs UFSD*, 1 N.Y.3d 385 (2004); *Appeal of Mullins*, 50 Ed Dept Rep, Dec. No. 16,096 (2010); *Appeal of Lockwood*, 42 Ed Dept Rep 25 (2002)). Thus, a temporary absence does not constitute the abandonment of a permanent residence, or establishment of residence in the district of temporary location, where actions reflect intent to return to the district (*Appeal of Mullins*; *Appeal of Yuen*, 49 Ed Dept Rep 175 (2009); *Appeal of J.V.*, 44 Ed Dept Rep 421 (2005); *Appeal of Weisberg*, 39 Ed Dept Rep 737, *judgment granted dismissing petition to review Weisberg v. Mills,* (Sup. Ct. Alb. Cnty. Nov. 27, 2000)). However, a bare assertion of an intention to return is insufficient to establish legal residence. Such an assertion must be supported by a concrete and realistic plan to do so (*Appeal of Cabrera*, 54 Ed Dept Rep, Dec. No. 16,645 (2014); *Appeal of Yuen*; *Appeal of Batiz,* 53 Ed Dept Rep, Dec. No. 16,498 (2013)).

Returned mail and/or absence of a name on a mailbox does not automatically establish a person's absence from a district (*Appeal of Simreen*, 47 Ed Dept Rep 172 (2007)).

49:8. Is a student's legal school district of residence presumed to be the same as his or her parents?

Generally, a student's legal school district of residence is presumed to be the district in which the student's parents or legal guardians reside (*Longwood CSD v. Springs UFSD*, 1 N.Y.3d 385 (2004); *Catlin v. Sobol,* 155 A.D.2d 24 (3d Dep't 1990), *rev'd on other grounds*, 77 N.Y.2d 552 (1991); *Appeal of Smith*, 48 Ed Dept Rep 125 (2008); *Appeal of Crawford*, 47 Ed Dept Rep 148 (2007); see **49:6** for information on the definition of residency). A parent's residence may determine a student's school district of residence even where the student lives with someone else, depending on the particular set of circumstances (see **49:21**).

However, the residency presumption can be rebutted, for example, by evidence of total and permanent transfer of custody and control to a resident of the district in which a student attends school (*Appeal of Murillo*, 55 Ed Dept Rep, Dec. No. 16,806 (2015); *Appeal of Capozzi*, 51 Ed Dept Rep, Dec. No. 16,305 (2011); *Appeal of Smith*); except when such a transfer is made solely to take advantage of the schools of a particular district (*Appeal of Begum,* 55 Ed Dept Rep, Dec. No. 16,799 (2015); *Appeal of L.B.,* 54 Ed Dept Rep, Dec. No. 16,672 (2014); *Appeal of Rea,* 51 Ed Dept Rep, Dec. No. 16,271 (2011); *Appeal of Capozzi*)). That was not the case where a student's parents moved to Florida and the student stayed behind not only to continue attending his prior school but also to help care for a grandparent with cancer (*Appeal of D.D.*, 48 Ed Dept Rep 320 (2009)).

Where the transfer of custody is made pursuant to a court proceeding, it is up to the court to determine whether the transfer is being made solely for purposes of school attendance (*Appeal of D.R.*, 45 Ed Dept Rep 550 (2006), *citing Matter of Proios*, 111 Misc.2d 252 (Sup. Ct. Nassau Cnty. 1981)).

The residency presumption can be rebutted, as well, by evidence that a student is an emancipated minor or resides apart from his or her parents for other bona fide reasons (see **49:10-11**).

49:9. What is the legal school district of residence for students of divorced parents?

Where a child's parents live apart, a child can have only one legal school district of residence (*Appeal of Students Suspected of Having Disabilities,* 54 Ed Dept Rep, Dec. No. 16,725 (2015); *Appeal of R.G.,* 54 Ed Dept Rep, Dec. No. 16,682 (2014); *Appeal of Dennis*, 51 Ed Dept Rep, Dec. No. 16,298 (2011)). In the case of divorce where a court awards custody to one parent, the child's residence is presumed to be that of the custodial parent (*Appeal of Plesko*, 37 Ed Dept Rep 238 (1997); *Appeal of Cortes*, 37 Ed Dept Rep 114 (1997); *Appeal of Juracka*, 31 Ed Dept Rep 282 (1992); *Appeal of Forde*, 29 Ed Dept Rep 359 (1990)). However, this presumption is rebuttable (*Appeal of Plesko*).

A custodial parent may designate a child's residence to be that of the non-custodial parent. Although preferable, such designation does not require legal modification of the divorce decree. But there must be compelling evidence that the custodial parent consents to the child's legal residence being that of the non-custodial parent. Absent such a designation, a child could also rebut the presumption that his or her residence is that of the custodial parent by establishing his or her status as an emancipated minor (*Appeal of Petrie*, 37 Ed Dept Rep 200 (1997); *Appeal of Barron*, 31 Ed Dept Rep 1 (1991); *Appeal of Forde*; see **49:10**).

Otherwise, in determining the residency of a child not living with his or her custodial parent, a school district must consider several factors, including the extent of the time the child actually lives in the district. In cases where parents have joint custody, where a child's time is essentially divided between the households of the divorced parents, with both parties assuming day-to-day responsibility for the child, the determination of the child's residence ultimately rests with the family, though the child's time need not be equally divided (*Appeal of Franklin-Boyd*, 45 Ed Dept Rep 33 (2005); *Appeal of T.K.*, 43 Ed Dept Rep 103 (2003); *Appeal of Seger*, 42 Ed Dept Rep 266 (2003); *Appeal of Cortes*)). Parents unable to decide may ask a family court to make the decision, and a school district must honor the court's order designating the district of school attendance (*Appeal of T.K.*). Absent proof that the child's time is essentially divided between both households, the residency of a child of divorced parents will be deemed to be that of the primary custodial parent, determined by the traditional test of physical presence and intent to remain (*Appeal of Franklin-Boyd*; *Appeal of T.K.*; *Appeal of Williams*, 42 Ed Dept Rep 8 (2002); see **49:6-7**).

Where a child's parents simply live apart but still claim joint custody, the child's residency is determined by the traditional test of physical presence and intent to remain there (see **49:6-7**) if the parents do not produce proof of the child's time being divided between both households (*Appeal of Students Suspected of Having Disabilities*; *Appeal of W.B.*, 54 Ed Dept Rep, Dec. No. 16,662 (2014); *Appeal of Rousseau*, 45 Ed Dept Rep 567 (2006)).

49:10. What evidence is required to establish that a student's residence is not the same as the student's parents because the student is an emancipated minor?

Students can rebut the presumption that their residence is with their parents if they can establish themselves as emancipated minors. A student is considered emancipated if he or she is beyond the compulsory school age, is living separate and apart from his or her parents in a manner inconsistent with parental custody and control, is not receiving financial support from his or her parents, and has no intent to return home (see *Appeal of a Student with a Disability*, 50 Ed Dept Rep, Dec. No. 16,190 (2011); *Appeal of Kehoe*, 37 Ed Dept Rep 14 (1997)).

49:11. What "other bona fide reasons" are sufficient to rebut the presumption that a student's residence is the same as the student's parents?

In the absence of a permanent transfer of custody and control (see **49:8**), or evidence that a student is an emancipated minor (see **49:10**), students can establish residence apart from their parents for other bona fide reasons such as family conflict (*Appeal of Palmieri*, 45 Ed Dept Rep 173 (2005); *Appeal of T.C.*, 43 Ed Dept Rep 44 (2003); *Appeal of Y.R.*, 42 Ed Dept Rep 376 (2003)), or the hardships of single parenting (*Appeal of I.M.*, 43 Ed Dept Rep 500 (2004); *Appeal of Taylor & Wilson*, 43 Ed Dept Rep 89 (2003)). However, the temporary transfer of custody and control of a student during a parent's illness has been deemed insufficient to overcome the presumption that a child resides with his parents (*Appeal of Mario D.*, 41 Ed Dept Rep 24 (2001)).

49:12. What is the legal school district of residence for students placed by social services?

In the case of a nonresident student placed in a family home by a social services district or a state department or agency, the cost of instruction must be paid by the district in which the student resided at the time the agency assumed responsibility for the student's support. Short-term physical presence in a homeless shelter at the time of placement by social services does not suffice to establish residency which requires physical presence plus an intent to remain (§ 3202(4)(a); see also *Longwood CSD v. Springs UFSD*, 1 N.Y.3d 385 (2004); **49:6**). However, when the home is the actual and only residence of the student and the student is not supported and maintained by the agency, the student is considered a resident of the district in which the family home is located and no tuition may be charged (§ 3202(4)(b)).

Disputes over the calculation of foster care tuition, and the respective liability therefor are reviewable in an appeal to the commissioner of education (*Appeal of the Bd. of Educ. of the Canastota CSD*, 48 Ed Dept Rep 235 (2008)). Claims for foster care tuition become due at the conclusion of the school year for which the claim is made (*Id.*).

Children who are privately placed in child care institutions are not entitled to attend school tuition free in the school district where the institution is located if the children are non-residents. Children living in such child care institutions are not deemed residents of the school district in which such institution is located purely by reason of their presence in the institution (§§ 3202(6), 4002; *Bd. of Educ. of the Garrison UFSD v. Greek Archdiocese Inst. of St. Basil,* 18 N.Y.3d 355 (2012)).

49:13. Can foreign students qualify as district residents for purposes of receiving a public education on a tuition-free basis?

Yes. The commissioner of education has ruled federal immigration status alone does not preclude a nonimmigrant from establishing residency for the purpose of attending public school on a tuition-free basis. (*Appeal of Plata*, 40 Ed Dept Rep 552 (2001); see also *Appeal of Plata-Morales*, 42 Ed Dept Rep 131 (2002); NYS Education Department, *Student Registration Guidance* (Aug. 2010), at: http://www.p12.

nysed.gov/sss/pps/residency/studentregistrationguidance082610.pdf; see also NYS Education Department, *Educational Services for Recently Arrived Unaccompanied Children* (Sept. 2014), at: http://www.p12.nysed.gov/sss/documents/EducationalServicesforRecentlyArrivedUnaccompaniedChildren.pdf; U.S. Department of Education, *Resource Guide: Supporting Undocumented Youth* (Oct. 2015), at: http://www2.ed.gov/about/overview/focus/supporting-undocumented-youth.pdf).

Unaccompanied youth recently arrived from another country are entitled to be enrolled in the public school as long as they meet the age and residency requirements (see **49:3-8**). Such children should be enrolled in the district where their sponsor resides, if the sponsor's home is the child's permanent residence and the sponsor has full authority and responsibility for the child (*Educational Services for Recently Arrived Unaccompanied Children*). A sponsor may be a parent, relative or family member or other adult sponsor. The sponsor is not required to establish custody and control through a formal guardianship proceeding (*Id.*). A child who lives with a sponsor may potentially qualify as homeless under the McKinney-Vento Act. School districts should refer students who they believe may qualify as homeless to the district's liaison (U.S. Department of Education, *Educational Services for Immigrant Children and Those Recently Arrived to the United States* (undated), at: http://www2.ed.gov/policy/rights/guid/unaccompanied-children.pdf; see **49:28-44**).

A school district is precluded from asking for documentation at the time of or as a condition of enrollment which would reveal the immigration status of a child, child's parents or person(s) in parental relation (8 NYCRR § 100.2(y)(3)(i)(a); see **49:17**).

However, a foreign student who attends a public secondary school under an F-1 visa must reimburse the school district for the full unsubsidized per capita cost of providing education at the school during the student's attendance (8 USC § 1184(m)(1)(B)(ii)).

School districts should also be aware that the USA Patriot Act (see Pub. Law 107-56), primarily applicable to institutions of higher education, requires the monitoring of nonimmigrant foreign students, including students attending public schools under an exchange program authorized to issue type J visas (Pub. Law 107-56; 8 USC § 1372(a)(1), (h)(2)). The Act also establishes that the Family Educational Rights and Privacy Act (8 USC § 1372(c)(2); 20 USC § 1232g; see **13:21-25**) does not apply to aliens to the extent the U.S. Attorney General determines necessary to carry out the monitoring program. The prohibition against asking for documentation relating to immigration status is not deemed to interfere with a school district's or a non-immigrant student's obligations regarding record keeping and reporting under federal law (8 NYCRR § 100.2(y)(3)(iii)(c)).

Residency Determinations

49:14. How is proof of parental relationship established upon enrollment?

Proof of parental relationship may be provided by an affidavit from the parent indicating that they are the parent(s) with whom the child lawfully resides (8 NYCRR § 100.2(y)(3)(i)(c)).

49:15. What evidence is required to establish that a student resides with someone other than his or her parent upon enrollment in the district?

A person in parental relationship to a child may submit an affidavit to the school district describing how they obtained total and permanent custody and control, whether through guardianship or otherwise (8 NYCRR § 100.2(y)(3)(i)(c)). A district may also accept other proof such as documentation indicating a child has been placed with a sponsor by a federal agency. A district may not require submission of a judicial custody order or and order of guardianship as a condition of enrollment (*Id.*; see **49:21**).

49:16. What documentation or information is required to support a claim of physical presence in the district?

A parent, person in parental relation or child, as appropriate, may submit a copy of a lease, mortgage statement, deed, pay stub, income tax form, utility or other bills, membership documents issued based upon residency (e.g., library cards), voter registration documents, driver's license, non-driver identification or other governmental issued identification or documents to establish physical presence in the district (8 NYCRR § 100.2(y)(3)(i)(b), (d)).

Other documentation that may prove a child's physical presence include a statement from a third party from whom the parent or person in parental relation leases or shares property or a statement by a third party relating to the parent(s)' or person(s) in parental relation's physical presence in the district (8 NYCRR § 100.2(y)(3)(i)(b)(2)-(3)).

49:17. Are there any documents a school district is prohibited from asking for at the time of enrollment?

Yes. A school district is prohibited from asking for a social security card or number or any information regarding, or which would tend to reveal, the immigration status of the child, or the child's parent or person in parental relation. This includes for example, copies of information concerning visas or other documentation indicating immigration status (8 NYCRR § 100.2(y)(3)(i)(a); see **49:13**).

49:18. Who determines whether a child is a resident entitled to attend the schools of a particular district?

The school board or its designee determines whether a child is a resident entitled to attend the schools of its district. Any determination made by a school official, other than the board or its designee, that a child is not entitled to attend the schools of the district must include notification of the procedures to obtain review of the decision within the district (8 NYCRR § 100.2(y)(6)).

49:19. Must school districts involve parents when making student residency determinations?

Yes. Prior to reaching such a determination, the board or its designee must allow the parent or guardian the opportunity to submit information concerning the child's right to attend school in the district (8 NYCRR § 100.2(y)(6); *Appeal of Cortez,* 54 Ed Dept Rep, Dec. No. 16,658 (2014)). Such an opportunity must be adequate and meaningful but does not require a face to face meeting, formal hearing or representation by counsel (*Appeal of Compass*, 53 Ed Dept Rep, Dec. No. 16,586 (2014); *Appeal of Finnell,* 51 Ed Dept Rep, Dec. No. 16,295 (2011); *Appeal of Kahnauth*, 51 Ed Dept Rep, Dec. No. 16,278 (2011)). However, a school board may adopt a policy that grants the right to an evidentiary due process hearing. In such an instance, the district would be bound by the policy, and obligated to ensure that hearing procedures comport with due process, including that the hearing be conducted by a neutral fact finder (*Appeal of Dashe*, 31 Ed Dept Rep 195 (1991)).

Students

49:20. What evidence is necessary to show a child is <u>not</u> a resident of a district?

A determination that a child is a nonresident must be supported by sufficient evidence to establish non-residence. Surveillances conducted as part of an investigation must be of sufficient duration and include both residences involved (*Appeal of Cortez,* 54 Ed Dept Rep, Dec. No. 16,658 (2014); *Appeal of Roy*, 51 Ed Dept Rep, Dec. No. 16,279 (2011); *Appeal of Stagno*, 51 Ed Dept Rep, Dec. No. 16,304 (2011); *Appeal of Salerno*, 45 Ed Dept Rep 106 (2005)). A home visit without any additional surveillance of both parents' homes was insufficient to prove students were not residents, when at the time of the visit the children were present at the in-district home (*Appeal of Cortez*). Similarly, surveillance on two dates showing children's physical presence outside a district does not rebut the presumption that the children reside with their parent, who is a district resident (*Appeal of Jackson*, 54 Ed Dept Rep, Dec. No. 16,640 (2014)). In another case, the commissioner sustained a petitioner's appeal that his son resided with him in the district based upon W-2's from multiple employers and the petitioner's explanation that the demands of his construction job meant that his son sometimes needed to stay with relatives at an out of district address (*Appeal of Gannon*, 55 Ed Dept Rep, Dec. No. 16,809 (2015)).

Information collected via the Internet (e.g., blog postings) may warrant the initiation of an investigation, and may be used to support a determination, but absent proof of reliability should not be used as the primary form of evidence of non-residency (*Appeal of Gaynor*, 51 Ed Dept Rep, Dec. No. 16,293 (2011)).

49:21. If questions arise after enrollment, what evidence is required to establish that a student's residence is not the same as the student's parents because there has been a permanent transfer of custody and control to someone else?

At times other than initial enrollment, whether a permanent transfer of custody and control has occurred will be examined based upon factors established through case law. A formal guardianship proceeding is still not required to establish a parental transfer of custody and control. However, there must be evidence that a particular location is a child's permanent residence and that the individual exercising control has full authority and responsibility with respect to the child's support and custody (*Appeal of Kendall*, 50 Ed Dept Rep, Dec. No. 16,149 (2010); *Appeal of Smith*, 48 Ed Dept Rep 125 (2008); *Appeal of Palmieri,* 45 Ed Dept Rep 174 (2005); *Appeal of Sloley-Raymond*, 44 Ed Dept Rep 27 (2004)).

Generally, if a parent continues to provide financial support for room, board, clothing and other necessities, custody and control is not deemed relinquished (*Catlin v. Sobol*, 155 A.D.2d 24 (3d Dep't 1990), *rev'd on other grounds*, 77 N.Y.2d 552 (1991); *Appeal of Cook*, 45 Ed Dept Rep 115 (2005)). Similarly, where parents retain control over important issues such as medical and educational decisions, total control is not deemed relinquished either (*Appeal of Students Suspected of Having a Disability*, 51 Ed Dept Rep, Dec. No. 16,283 (2011); *Appeal of Cook*; *Appeal of Sloley-Raymond*; *Appeal of Nelson*, 44 Ed Dept Rep 20 (2004)). That was the case where a mother signed consents and referrals for evaluation of her children with disabilities, despite claiming a transfer of custody to the children's grandmother (*Appeal of Students Suspected of Having a Disability*). Nonetheless, a continued relationship between a child and a parent who has otherwise relinquished custody and control, or continued coverage under a parent's health insurance policy, are not necessarily dispositive in resolving the question of a child's residency (*Appeal of Palmieri*; *Appeal of I.M.*, 43 Ed Dept Rep 500 (2004); *Appeal of Taylor & Wilson*, 43 Ed Dept Rep 89 (2003)).

In comparison, where a court of competent jurisdiction legally transfers custody of a child by court order or issuance of letters of guardianship, the court order will be deemed determinative for residency purposes, provided the child actually resides with the court-appointed guardian (*Appeal of Foskey*, 56 Ed Dept Rep, Dec. No. 16,933 (2016); *Appeal of D.R.*, 45 Ed Dept Rep 550 (2006); *Appeal of Johnson*, 45 Ed Dept Rep 559 (2006)). Such will be the case even if the child's parent continues a relationship with the child through "parenting time" or involvement in the child's schooling, or visitation (*Appeal of Foskey*; *Appeal of Perry*, 49 Ed Dept Rep 190 (2009); *Appeal of D.R.*). Any objection to the legitimacy of the transfer of custody would need to be made before the court issuing the order rather than in a subsequent appeal before the commissioner of education (*Id.*; see also *Appeal of Crawford*, 48 Ed Dept Rep 92 (2008)).

49:22. What notice must a school district give when it determines a child is not a resident?

If a board or its designee determines that the child is not entitled to attend its schools, the board or its designee must, within two business days, provide written notice of its decision to the child's parent, person in parental relation, or to the child as appropriate (8 NYCRR § 100.2(y)(6); *Appeal of Crowley*, 44 Ed Dept Rep 71 (2004); *Appeal of Gurka*, 43 Ed Dept Rep 521 (2004)). The written notice must state:

- That the child is not entitled to attend the public schools of the district.
- The specific basis for the determination that the child is not a resident of the district including but not limited to a description of documentary or other evidence upon which the decision is based.
- The date as of which the child will be excluded from school.
- That the board's determination may be appealed to the commissioner of education, in accordance with section 310 of the Education Law, within 30 days of the date of the determination, and that the instructions, forms and procedures for taking such an appeal (including translated version of said materials) may be obtained from the Office of Counsel, NYS Education Department, State Education Building, Albany, N.Y., 12234, or by calling 518-474-8927 (8 NYCRR § 100.2(y)(6)).

A school board that delegates the authority to make residency determinations to a designee has no obligation to hear appeals regarding its designee's determinations. Any such appeals can be filed directly with the commissioner of education (8 NYCRR § 100.2(y)(6); *Appeal of Sobel*, 43 Ed Dept Rep 93 (2003)).

For information on the process that school districts must follow when making determinations regarding a student's homeless status, see **49:37**.

Admission of Nonresident Students

49:23. May a school district admit nonresident students?

Yes. A school district may accept nonresidents upon consent of and on terms prescribed by the school board, including the payment of tuition (§§ 1709(3), (13), 3202(2); *Appeal of P.M.*, 48 Ed Dept Rep 348 (2009); *Appeal of Akiwowo*, 48 Ed Dept Rep 34 (2008)), in accordance with a formula set forth in commissioner regulations (8 NYCRR Part 174; *Appeal of Baronti,* 42 Ed Dept Rep 140 (2002); see **49:18**).

A school district may adopt a policy that allows resident students who become nonresidents to complete the school year in which they become nonresidents without payment of tuition (*Appeal of Akiwowo*; *Appeal of Bushway*, 44 Ed Dept Rep 453 (2005)).

In addition, a district may condition a nonresident student's attendance without the payment of tuition on conduct that is in the best interests of the district during their period of enrollment (*Appeal of L.V.*, 45 Ed Dept Rep 561 (2006)). The student would be entitled only to minimal due process such as notice and an opportunity to respond prior to termination of enrollment (*Id.*).

A school district that admits a nonresident student on a tuition-free basis because of confusion over the student's address has no obligation to continue allowing the student to attend its school without the payment of tuition (*Appeal of Gutierrez*, 46 Ed Dept Rep 222 (2006)).

49:24. May districts that admit nonresident students deny admission to nonresident students with disabilities?

No. School districts that admit nonresident students may not exclude students with disabilities or charge nonresident students with disabilities a different tuition rate. Such an action would be a violation of section 504 of the Rehabilitation Act (29 USC § 794) and the Americans with Disabilities Act (42 USC § 12132), which prohibit discrimination on the basis of disability (*Letter to Norlander,* from Norma Cantu,

Assistant Secretary for Civil Rights, U. S. Department of Education, Office for Civil Rights (Aug. 10, 1994); see also *Appeal of a Student with a Disability,* 46 Ed Dept Rep 18 (2006); *Appeal of Taylor*, 43 Ed Dept Rep 1 (2003)).

49:25. May a school district refuse to admit nonresident students?

It depends. In general, school districts are required to admit only district residents who are over five and under 21 years of age who have not received a high school diploma (§ 3202(1)).

However, if a student is forced to temporarily relocate outside the district due to a parent or guardian being called to active military duty, the student may continue to attend school in their original district without the payment of tuition. In such circumstances, the district is not required to provide transportation to the relocated student (§ 3202(1)).

In addition, under the non-residence attendance provisions of sections 2040 and 2045 of the Education Law, a school district may, with voter approval, contract for a period of between two and five years with another district for the education of some or all of its resident students. Districts which do not engage in multi-year contracts pursuant to Education Law § 2040 are not required to have a written contract and may secure voter approval for tuition payments simply through the approval of a school budget with allocations for such tuition payments (§ 2040(1)(d); *Appeal of the Bd. of Educ. of the Greenport UFSD*, 50 Ed Dept Rep, Dec. No. 16,251 (2011)). The district designated to receive such students may not refuse to admit them, or limit the number it will accept without demonstrating valid and sufficient reasons, such as overcrowding and voter refusal to approve expansion of school facilities (*Appeal of Bd. of Educ. of the East Quogue UFSD*, 43 Ed Dept Rep 385 (2004); *Appeal of the Bd. of Educ. of the Eastport/South Manor CHSD,* 40 Ed Dept Rep 695 (2001); *Matter of Bd. of Educ. of South Manor UFSD*, 14 Ed Dept Rep 412 (1975); *Matter of Brunswick CSD*, 14 Ed Dept Rep 33 (1974)). Only the board of education may designate by resolution the districts of attendance (*Appeal of Sabarese,* 55 Ed Dept Rep, Dec. No. 16,820 (2015)).

49:26. How is tuition determined for the instruction of nonresident students when a district has a policy that allows nonresident students to be admitted?

Tuition for nonresident students is computed according to a formula established by the commissioner of education (8 NYCRR Part 174; see also *Appeal of the Bd. of Educ. of the East Quogue UFSD*, 43 Ed Dept Rep 385 (2004); *Appeal of the Bd. of Educ. of the Garrison UFSD*, 43 Ed Dept Rep 355 (2004)). The Education Law also provides that the school tax payments of nonresidents who own assessable property in the school district must be deducted from any tuition charges levied against any such nonresident (§ 3202(3)).

Districts that seek to recover tuition payment from nonresident parents must seek such relief in a court of competent jurisdiction (*Appeal of Ciampa,* 55 Ed Dept Rep, Dec. No. 16,825 (2015); *Appeal of Azatyan*, 49 Ed Dept Rep 65 (2009); *Appeal of Vangilder*, 49 Ed Dept Rep 6 (2009)). The commissioner will not award such relief in the context of a residency appeal (*Appeal of Sitaras*, 44 Ed Dept Rep 320 (2005); *Appeal of Upstate Home for Children*, 43 Ed Dept Rep 505 (2004)). However, where the commissioner has already determined that a child is not entitled to attend a district's schools, that issue may not be re-litigated in an action to recover tuition payment (*Blind Brook-Rye UFSD v. Baronti*, 6 Misc.3d 38 (Sup. Ct. App. Term, 2d Dep't 2004)).

49:27. How is tuition determined when a district receives students pursuant to the non-resident attendance provisions of the Education Law?

Districts receiving nonresident students under the non-residence attendance provisions of the Education Law (see **49:25**) are entitled to recover tuition in accordance with the commissioner's regulations (8 NYCRR Part 174) or pursuant to the terms of a negotiated contract. Under the regulations, a district may calculate tuition as the amount of the net cost of educating each nonresident student (8 NYCRR § 174.2). If a district does not maintain its records in such a way as to calculate the net cost of educating each nonresident student it may then recover tuition costs in accordance with a formula set forth in the regulations, also referred to as the "Seneca Falls formula" (see 8 NYCRR § 174.2(a)(5); *Appeal of Bd. of Educ. of the East Quogue UFSD*, 43 Ed Dept Rep 385 (2004); *Appeal of Bd. of Educ. of the East Moriches UFSD*, 41 Ed Dept Rep 45 (2001)).

A receiving district which does not have a valid written contract establishing the tuition rate because the district of residence failed to gain voter approval may only recover the tuition costs calculated pursuant to the regulatory formula, rather than the amount agreed to in a contract (*Appeal of the Bd. of Educ. of the Greenport UFSD*, 50 Ed Dept Rep, Dec. No. 16,251 (2011); *Appeal of Bd. of Educ. of the East Quogue UFSD*).

Tuition payment from districts that contract with another for the education of some of their students becomes due according to the terms set in the contract (*Appeal of the Bd. of Educ. of the Tuxedo UFSD,* 55 Ed Dept Rep, Dec. No. 16,885 (2016)). Tuition payments in situations not governed by a contract become due at the completion of each school year (*Appeal of the Bd. of Educ. of the East Hampton UFSD*, 50 Ed Dept Rep, Dec. No. 16,128 (2010); *Appeal of Sitaras*, 44 Ed Dept Rep 320 (2005); *Appeal of Upstate Home for Children*, 43 Ed Dept Rep 505 (2004); *Appeal of the Bd. of Educ. of the East Quogue UFSD*). In a case of nonpayment, a district seeking such payment must seek relief in a court of competent jurisdiction (*Appeal of Sitaras; Appeal of Upstate Home for Children*). However, a school district which sends its students to another district will not be required to reimburse the receiving district for a settlement which the nonresident district entered into as a remedy for allegedly failing to provide a free appropriate public education under the Individuals with Disabilities Education Act (IDEA). Such settlement amount is not subject to reimbursement through the IDEA or state aid and thus is not a reimbursable educational cost for which the resident district would be liable (*Appeal of the Bd. of Educ. of the East Hampton UFSD*).

Homeless Students

Editor's Note: For additional information on the McKinney-Vento Homeless Education Assistance Act (the McKinney-Vento Act), as amended pursuant to the Every Student Succeeds Act (ESSA) of 2015, see the U.S. Department of Education Notice regarding McKinney Vento Education for Homeless Children & Youths Program *(Mar. 17, 2016), at: https://www.federalregister.gov/articles/2016/03/17/2016-06073/mckinney-vento-education-for-homeless-children-and-youths-program#h-29). See also* Education for Homeless Children and Youths Non-Regulatory Guidance *(July 2016), at: http://www2.ed.gov/policy/elsec/leg/essa/160240ehcyguidance072716.pdf. Also visit the NYS Education Department's Technical and Education Assistance Center for Homeless Students at: http://www.nysteachs.org and the Board of Regents webpage at: https://www.regents.nysed.gov/. The McKinney-Vento Act is implemented in New York State through the provisions of section 3209 of the Education Law and commissioner's regulations at 8 NYCRR § 100.2(x).*

49:28. Who is a homeless child?

Except as otherwise provided by law, a *homeless child* is a child or youth who does not have a fixed, regular, and adequate nighttime residence, or whose primary nighttime location is in a public or private shelter designed to provide temporary living accommodations, or a place not designed for, or ordinarily used as, regular sleeping accommodation for human beings. Consistent with the provisions of the McKinney-Vento Act, a child lacks a fixed, regular and adequate residence if he or she is:

- Sharing the housing of other persons due to a loss of housing, economic hardship or a similar reason.
- Living in motels, hotels, trailer parks, or camping grounds due to the lack of alternative adequate accommodations.
- Living in a car park, public space, abandoned building, substandard housing, bus or train station or similar setting.
- Abandoned in a hospital or awaiting foster care placement.
- A migratory child who qualifies as homeless.

(42 USC § 11434a(a)(2); § 3209(1)(a); 8 NYCRR § 100.2(x)(1)).

Although children awaiting foster care placement fall under the definition of homeless, children already placed in foster care do not (§ 3209(1)(a-1); 8 NYCRR § 100.2(x)(1)(i)(c)). However, "awaiting foster care placement" is deleted from the federal definition of homeless as of December 10, 2016 (Every Student Succeeds Act, P.L. 114-95 Title IX, § 9105(b)).

An inadequate nighttime residence includes a motel room with no kitchen accommodation (*Appeal of R.G.*, 41 Ed Dept Rep 428 (2002)).

An undocumented child who lives with a sponsor may qualify as homeless under the McKinney-Vento Act, school districts should refer students who they believe may qualify as homeless to the district's liaison (U.S. Department of Education, *Educational Services for Immigrant Children and Those Recently Arrived to the United States* (undated), at: http://www2.ed.gov/policy/rights/guid/unaccompanied-children.pdf). Similarly, a child removed from his or her home by child welfare workers based on a determination of immediate danger to the child and directly placed with a relative may also qualify as homeless. If such directly placed child is not under the care and custody of a child welfare agency while staying with the relative, the child may be considered to have housing that is not "regular" and the liaison should make an eligibility determination (NYS Education Department, NYS Field Memo, NCLB McKinney-Vento #07-2015 (Oct. 21, 2015), at: http://www.p12.nysed.gov/accountability/homeless/docs/fm_directplacementguidance.pdf).

School districts should review their policies on homeless children and unaccompanied youth periodically to ensure they incorporate current definitions and legal requirements (*Appeal of a Student with a Disability*, 49 Ed Dept Rep 77 (2009)).

49:29. Under what circumstances have children been found not to be homeless?

The commissioner of education has found children had a fixed, regular, and adequate night time residence and, therefore, were not homeless when they lived in:

- An apartment subsidized by a federal program that provided rental assistance grants and did not require that grant recipients leave their home when the grant expired (*Appeal of R.E.W.,* 55 Ed Dept Rep, Dec. No. 16,808 (2015); *Appeal of D.R.*, 43 Ed Dept Rep 133 (2003)).
- Rental housing on a month-to-month basis (*Appeal of M.W.*, 46 Ed Dept Rep 151 (2006)).
- A church-owned apartment absent evidence of a need to vacate such premises (*Appeal of S.D.*, 46 Ed Dept Rep 116 (2006)).
- A two-bedroom apartment a family rented from a friend even though the student slept on the couch (*Appeal of K.W.*, 48 Ed Dept Rep 451 (2009)).

Similarly, the commissioner found children were not homeless because their living arrangements were not temporary or transitional when they lived:

- In an out of district apartment after leaving a shelter with an intention to move into another district (*Appeal of S.W.*, 49 Ed Dept Rep 231 (2010)).

- In an apartment with intention to regain the home they were evicted from (*Appeal of N.W.*, 47 Ed Dept Rep 87 (2007)).
- With grandparents absent evidence that the living arrangements are temporary or transitional or that their residence was inadequate (*Appeal of J.L.*, 55 Ed Dept Rep, Dec. No. 16,811 (2015); *Appeal of R.E.W.,* 55 Ed Dept Rep, Dec. No. 16,808 (2015); *Appeal of a Student with a Disability*, 52 Ed Dept Rep, Dec. No. 16,404 (2012)).

In addition, in one case, the Commissioner rejected a claim of homelessness due to economic hardship when a family moved in with a relative outside the district after a salary decrease from $180,000 to $140,000 and a decision to incur the cost to pay for one child's private college tuition (*Appeal of E.M.F.*, 53 Ed Dept Rep, Dec. No. 16,538 (2013)).

According to the commissioner, just an expectation of eviction or foreclosure does not make housing automatically temporary or transitional (*Appeal of A.N.*, 55 Ed Dept Rep, Dec. No. 16,852 (2015); *Appeal of M.S.,* 55 Ed Dept Rep, Dec. No. 16,792 (2015); *Appeal of S.B.*, 48 Ed Dept Rep 36 (2008)).

However, moving in with a friend because of domestic violence rendered those forced out of their home homeless because the living arrangements were not only temporary but also inadequate, requiring some to sleep on the floor or couch (*Appeal of R.W.*, 49 Ed Dept Rep 73 (2009)). Similarly, a home in severe disrepair lacking appropriate insulation that did not have electricity in every room or potable water was determined by the commissioner to be "patently inadequate" and could not be considered a fixed regular nighttime residence merely because of the duration a family lived there (*Appeal of R.M.,* 54 Ed Dept Rep, Dec. No. 16,643 (2014)).

49:30. Who is a homeless unaccompanied youth?

An *unaccompanied youth* is a homeless child or youth who is not in the physical custody of a parent or legal guardian. The term does not include those living with someone other than a parent or guardian solely to take advantage of a district's schools (8 NYCRR § 100.2(x)(1)(vi); see also *Appeal of L.P.*, 50 Ed Dept Rep, Dec. No. 16,107 (2010); *Appeal of D.R.*, 48 Ed Dept Rep 60 (2008)).

Homeless unaccompanied youth include, for example, students living in runaway shelters, on the streets, or in other inadequate housing, and throwaway and abandoned students (NYS Education Department Technical and Education Assistance Center, *Unaccompanied Youth Issue Brief* (undated), at: http://www.nysteachs.org/info-topic/unaccompanied.html).

The definition of unaccompanied youth does not include automatically a child who leaves his or her parents' home, particularly when the child has a choice to return home (*Appeal of G.D.*, 45 Ed Dept Rep 191 (2005)).

49:31. In what school district may homeless students attend school?

A homeless student may attend school within the school district of his or her current location, the school district of origin, or a school district participating in a regional placement plan (8 NYCRR § 100.2(x)(2)(i)).

The school *district of origin* is the district within New York State where the homeless student was attending a public school on a tuition-free basis or was entitled to attend when circumstances arose that caused the student to become homeless (§ 3209(1)(c); 8 NYCRR § 100.2(x)(1)(iii)). Amendments to the federal McKinney-Vento Act expand the definition of school of origin to include a preschool and a designated receiving school at the next grade level for all feeder schools (42 USC § 11432(g)(3)(I)). At the time this publication went to press, New York had not yet addressed this expansion of the definition in any statutory or regulatory amendments.

The school *district of current location* is the district within New York State where the temporary housing arrangement or the residential program for a homeless or runaway student is located, which may be different from the school district of origin (§ 3209(1)(d); 8 NYCRR § 100.2(x)(1)(iv)).

A *regional placement plan* is a comprehensive regional approach to the provision of educational placements for homeless students, which must be approved by the commissioner of education (§ 3209(1)(e); 8 NYCRR § 100.2(x)(1)(v)).

Homeless students may attend school in the district they were entitled to attend before becoming homeless for the duration of homelessness (42 USC § 11432(g)(3)(A); 8 NYCRR § 100.2(x)(2)(ii)).

49:32. What school buildings are homeless students entitled to attend within their designated school district?

When the school district of origin is designated as the district of attendance, consistent with a parent's wishes and to the extent feasible, a homeless student is entitled to return to the school where previously enrolled (8 NYCRR § 100.2(x)(7)(i)(b)). Amendments to the federal law expand the definition of school of origin to include a preschool and a designated receiving school at the next grade level for all feeder schools (42 USC § 11432(g)(3)(I)). At the time this publication went to press, New York had not yet addressed this expansion of the definition in any statutory or regulatory amendments.

Homeless students who are temporarily located within the same district they attended when they became homeless may attend either the school building in the attendance zone where they are temporarily located, or the school building they previously attended until the end of the school year and one additional year if that year constitutes the student's last year in such a building (§ 3209(1)(c), (2)(b)(1); 8 NYCRR § 100.2(x)(2)(ii), (v)).

If a homeless student attends school in the district of current location, that student may attend the school building in the attendance zone of temporary location or any other school that non-homeless students who live in that same attendance zone may attend (§ 3209(1)(d); 8 NYCRR § 100.2(x)(2)(v)).

School districts cannot segregate homeless students based on their status as homeless, unless necessary for a short period of time because of health and safety emergencies or the need to provide temporary, special, and supplementary services that meet the unique needs of the child (42 USC §§ 11432(e)(3), 11433(a)(2)(B)(ii); 8 NYCRR § 100.2(x)(7)(i)(a)).

49:33. Can homeless parents or students change a previously designated school district of attendance?

Yes, if the person who made the designation (see **49:35**) finds that the original designation is educationally unsound. The change must be made before the end of the first semester of attendance or within 60 days after commencing attendance at a school, whichever occurs later (8 NYCRR § 100.2(x)(2)(vi)).

49:34. What happens if homeless students attending school in a district of location relocate to other temporary housing located outside the district or in a different attendance zone within the district?

Such students may continue to attend the same school building until the end of the school year and for one additional year if that year constitutes the child's last year in such building (§ 3209(2)(c); 8 NYCRR § 100.2(x)(2)(iii)).

49:35. Who designates which school district a homeless student will attend?

The designation as to where a homeless student will attend school is made by the student's parent or guardian, the homeless student together with the homeless liaison designated by the school district if no parent or guardian is available, or the director of a residential program for runaway and homeless youth, where applicable, in consultation with the homeless student (§ 3209(1)(b); 8 NYCRR § 100.2(x)(1)(ii)).

A parent who disagrees with a school district's recommended placement must be notified of the right to appeal the placement decision through the district's dispute resolution procedures (42 USC § 11432(g)(3)(B); 8 NYCRR § 100.2(x)(7)(ii)). However, districts must enroll homeless students in the school requested by the parent while resolving any dispute regarding school selection or enrollment (42 USC § 11432(g)(3)(E)).

49:36. What procedures must be followed to admit homeless students?

All school districts must provide a district of attendance designation form to any homeless student who seeks admission to school, or to a parent or person in parental relation who seeks to enroll such a child in school (§ 3209(2)(d); 8 NYCRR § 100.2(x)(3)).

Upon receipt of a designation form, a district designated as a homeless student's school district of attendance must immediately review the designation form to assure that it has been completed, admit the homeless student, and provide the student with access to all of its programs, activities, and services to the same extent available to resident students. A designated district also must forward a copy of the designation form to the commissioner of education, and the school district of origin where applicable (§ 3209(2)(e); 8 NYCRR § 100.2(x)(4)).

Designated school districts must admit homeless students even if they are unable to produce records normally required for enrollment, such as academic records, medical records, proof of residency, or other documentation (8 NYCRR § 100.2(x)(4)(ii)). They must immediately contact the district where the records are located to obtain a copy (§ 3209(2)(e); 8 NYCRR § 100.2(x)(4)(iv)), and the district where the student's records are located must forward a complete copy of the homeless student's records within five days of receiving a written request (§ 3209(2)(f); 8 NYCRR § 100.2(x)(5)).

Information about a homeless student's living situation must be treated as an education record and disclosed only in accordance with law. None of this information may be classified as directory information under the Family Educational Rights and Privacy Act (FERPA). Generally, under FERPA, directory information may be disclosed without parental consent, unless a parent opts out of such disclosure (42 USC § 11432(g)(3)(G); see 20 USC §1232g(a)(5)(A), (B), 34 CFR § 99.3; see also **13:21-25**).

49:37. What happens if a school district disagrees that a student is homeless?

A district designated as the school district of attendance must immediately admit a homeless student (§ 3209(e); 8 NYCRR § 100.2(x)(4)(ii)). It then must follow the procedures it has established to resolve disputes, including providing the student's parent an opportunity to submit information before it makes a final determination regarding the student's homeless status (8 NYCRR § 100.2(x)(7)(ii)(a)).

If a district determines that a student is not homeless, it must provide the student's parent written notice stating that the student is not entitled to attend its schools, the basis for its determination, and the date as of which the student will be excluded from school. The notice must state also that the district's determination may be appealed to the commissioner of education and the name and other information pertaining to the school district's homeless liaison responsible for assisting the parent in filing such an appeal, along with the form petition to be filled out by the parent with the liaison's help (8 NYCRR § 100.2(x)(7)(ii)(b); *Appeal of L.P.*, 50 Ed Dept Rep, Dec. No. 16,107 (2010); see also **49:38**).

The student remains enrolled until the district makes a final determination and for a minimum of 30 days after that determination to give the parent the opportunity to appeal to the commissioner (8 NYCRR § 100.2(x)(7)(ii)(c)).

Homeless students may sue a school district for violations of their rights under the McKinney-Vento Homeless Education Assistance Improvement Act (*National Law Ctr. on Homelessness & Poverty v. New York State*, 224 F.R.D. 314 (E.D.N.Y. 2004)).

49:38. Who at a school district is responsible for providing assistance to homeless students and parents?

School districts must appoint a liaison for homeless children and youth to serve as a primary contact between homeless families and school staff, district personnel and local social services agencies and other programs providing services to homeless students (42 USC § 11432(g)(6); § 3209(2-a); 8 NYCRR § 100.2(x)(7)(iii)).

The homeless liaison is responsible for ensuring, in part, that homeless students are identified by school personnel and through coordinated activities and outreach with other entities and agencies; enroll in and have a full and equal opportunity to succeed in school; receive educational services for which they are eligible including Head Start programs, early intervention services under the Individual with Disabilities Education Act and other preschool programs administered by the district; and are referred to health, mental health, substances abuse, dental, housing and other appropriate services. The liaison also must ensure that parents of homeless children and youth are informed of the educational and related opportunities, including transportation, available to their children, and provided with meaningful opportunities to participate in the education of their children (42 USC § 11432(g)(6)).

In addition, the liaison must assist parents in the resolution of disputes regarding enrollment, transportation, and placement (*Id.*; see **49:37**). With respect to dispute resolution, the commissioner declined to dismiss an appeal regarding a student's homeless status as untimely when the liaison failed to provide a form petition and only belatedly helped the parents draft and file the appeal (*Appeal of D.W.*, 55 Ed Dept Rep, Dec. No. 16,812 (2015)).

The liaison must also provide public notice of the educational rights of homeless children in locations frequented by parents or guardians including schools, shelters, public libraries and soup kitchens (42 USC § 11432(g)(6)(A)(vi)). Liaisons must collect and transmit data to the State Coordinator to comply with federal reporting requirements and must also ensure that school personnel providing services under the McKinney-Vento Act receive professional development and other support (42 USC § 11432(g)(6)(A)(ix), (C); see 42 USC §11432(f)(1), (3)).

49:39. Who at a school district is responsible for providing assistance to unaccompanied youth?

The liaison for homeless children and youth also must ensure that unaccompanied youth are enrolled in school and have opportunities to meet the same challenging state academic standards as other children (42 USC § 11432(g)(6)(A)(x)). Additionally, the liaison must inform unaccompanied youth of their status as independent students under the Higher Education Act and that such youths may obtain assistance from the liaison to receive verification of such status for purposes of the Free Application for Federal Student Aid (*Id.*).

49:40. Who is responsible for the payment of tuition costs incurred in educating a homeless student?

When the parents of a homeless student, or a homeless unaccompanied youth (see **49:30**) designates as the school district of attendance a district other than that of the student's last residence (see **49:31** and **49:35**), the district providing instruction will be eligible for reimbursement by the

NYS Education Department (SED) (§ 3209(3)(a)). The district where the student last attended school must, in turn, reimburse SED for its expenditure on behalf of that child. Reimbursement will be equal to the school district's basic contribution, pro-rated for the period of time for which the services are provided by a school district other than the one in which the student last attended school (§ 3209(3)(b)).

49:41. Are homeless students entitled to school transportation services?

Yes. A social services district must provide transportation for homeless students who are eligible for benefits under section 350-j of the Social Services Law and are placed in temporary housing arrangements outside their designated school district of attendance. To the extent funds are available, the NYS Office of Children and Family Services must provide transportation for homeless students in a residential program for runaway and homeless youth located outside the designated district. The social services district or the Office of Children and Family Services may contract with a school district or board of cooperative educational services (BOCES) to provide such transportation services (§ 3209(4)(a), (b)).

However, the designated school district (see **49:31** and **49:35**) must provide transportation services to homeless students who are not eligible for transportation from the social services district or the Office of Children and Family Services (§ 3209(4)(c)–(e); 8 NYCRR § 100.2(x)(6)). A district's duty to provide such transportation is triggered when it receives notice of their homeless status (§ 3209(2)(e)(1), (2); 8 NYCRR § 100.2(x)(4)(ii), (iii); *Appeal of D.U.*, 47 Ed Dept Rep 213 (2007)). Leaving blank the address section in an "Emergency/health information" form and listing a post office box as a mailing address does not constitute sufficient notice (*Appeal of D.U.*).

Homeless students who designate the district of current location to attend school are entitled to transportation services on the same basis as resident students (§ 3209(4)(d); 8 NYCRR § 100.2(x)(6)(iii)).

Disputes regarding transportation of homeless students are subject to the same dispute resolution process applicable to disputes concerning the homeless status of a child or youth (8 NYCRR § 100.2(x)(7)(ii); see **49:37**).

49:42. Are there any mileage limitations that apply to the provision of transportation to homeless students?

Yes. A designated school district that must provide transportation to a homeless student may not provide transportation in excess of 50 miles one way, unless the commissioner of education determines that it is in the best interest of the student (§ 3209(4)(c); 8 NYCRR § 100.2(x)(6)(ii)).

49:43. Is state aid available for districts that provide transportation to homeless students?

Yes. A school district may receive state aid to offset expenditures incurred by the district for the transportation of homeless students under certain circumstances (§ 3209(4)(c)).

49:44. Are students who lived outside New York State when they became homeless entitled to enroll in a public school within New York on a tuition-free basis?

Yes. Such students are deemed to be residents of the district where they are currently located and entitled to attend public school on a tuition-free basis as other resident students (§ 3209(2)(b)(2); 8 NYCRR § 100.2(x)(2)(iv)).

Students in Foster Care

49:45. Where are students in foster care entitled to attend school?

Generally, students in foster care may continue to attend school at the school they attended prior to being placed in foster care (42 USC § 675(1)(G); 18 NYCRR § 430.11(c)(1)(i); see also U.S. Department of Education, U.S. Department of Health & Human Services, *Non Regulatory Guidance: Ensuring Educational Stability for Children in Foster Care* (June 2016), at: http://www2.ed.gov/policy/elsec/leg/essa/edhhsfostercarenonregulatorguide.pdf). If it is determined that it is not in the child's best interest to continue to attend school where the student is currently enrolled, the child will be immediately enrolled in a new school (18 NYCRR § 430.11(c)(1)(i); see also NYS Education Department, Field Memo #01-2012, *Education Stability Guidance* at: http://nysteachs.org/media/INF_SED_EdStabilityGuidance2012.pdf). The child welfare agency is entitled to access to child's education records in order to aid in the determination of whether it is in the child's best interest to remain in the school of origin (20 USC § 1232g(b)(1)(L); see also NYS Education Department, NYS Field Memo #02-2013 (Sept. 12, 2013), at: http://www.p12.nysed.gov/accountability/homeless/docs/ChildWelfareandFERPA9-12-13_1_3.pdf).

When the child enrolls in a new school, the enrolling school must immediately contact the school last attended to obtain relevant academic and other records (20 USC § 6311(g)(1)(E)(iii)). Under FERPA, such records may be shared without parental consent (20 USC § 1232g(b)(1)(b); see also **13:21-25**).

49:46. What transportation are students in foster care entitled to?

Amendments to federal law made by the Every Student Succeeds Act require school districts to develop and implement clear written procedures governing how transportation to maintain foster care children in their school of origin will be provided, arranged and funded for the duration of the time the child is in foster care (20 USC §§ 6311(g)(1)(E), 6312(c)(5); see also U.S. Department of Education and U.S. Department of Health & Human Services, *Non Regulatory Guidance: Ensuring Educational Stability for Children in Foster Care* (June 2016), at: http://www2.ed.gov/policy/elsec/leg/essa/edhhsfostercarenonregulatorguide.pdf). Such written procedures must be adopted by December 10, 2016 (20 USC § 6312(c)(5)).

The procedures must ensure children in foster care needing transportation to the school of origin will promptly receive such transportation in a cost effective manner. If additional costs are incurred in providing transportation the school district will provide transportation to the school of origin if the local child welfare agency agrees to reimburse the district, the school district agrees to pay the cost or the school district and local child welfare agency agree to share costs (*Id.*).

50. Student Health and Welfare

School Health Services

50:1. Must school districts employ a school physician or school nurse?

School districts must employ either a qualified physician, or a nurse practitioner to the extent authorized by the nurse practice act, to perform the duties of the director of school health services (§ 902(2)(a); 8 NYCRR § 136.2(c)). Such duties include any conferred on the school physician or school medical inspector under any provision of law, the provision and coordination of school health services, and health appraisals of students attending the public schools (§ 902(2)(a); 8 NYCRR § 136.1(d)).

A school district may employ one or more school nurses who must be a registered professional nurse, and other health professionals, as may be necessary (§ 902(2)(b)). The term health professional refers to individuals who are duly licensed or otherwise authorized to practice a health profession including, but not limited to physicians, registered professional nurses, nurse practitioners, physician assistants, optometrists, dentists, dental hygienists, dieticians and nutritionists, and audiologists (§ 902(1); 8 NYCRR § 136.1(b)). Such individuals must aid the director of school health services and perform their duties, including health instruction, in compliance with their respective practice act (§ 902(2)(b)).

Two or more school districts may jointly employ health professionals under a sharing agreement entered into in accordance with the provisions of section 119-o of the General Municipal Law. They also may contract with a board of cooperative educational services for the provision of services of one or more registered professional nurses and other health professionals to perform school health services, including health instruction (§ 902(3)).

A school district is not required to employ a school nurse solely for the purpose of taking custody of spare inhalers, epinephrine auto injectors, insulin or blood glucose testing supplies for students with medical conditions necessitating such medication and supplies. In addition, a school nurse does not have to be available at all times in a school building for such purposes (§§ 916, 916-a, 916-b).

50:2. Must school districts employ a school nurse-teacher?

No. A school nurse-teacher is a registered nurse who also is a certified teacher or teaching assistant, qualified and trained to perform, in addition to nursing services, other educational services in the classroom. There is no state requirement that a school district employ the services of such individuals (*Bork v. North Tonawanda City Sch. Dist.*, 60 A.D.2d 13 (4th Dep't 1977), *appeal denied*, 44 N.Y.2d 647 (1978); *Matter of Festa*, 21 Ed Dept Rep 374 (1982)).

Districts may employ health professionals on their own or jointly with another district, or they can arrange through a board of cooperative educational services for the provision of services by health service professionals (§ 902(2)(b), (c)).

50:3. Are school districts required to provide school health services to students attending their public schools?

Yes. All school districts except the city school districts of New York, Rochester and Buffalo must provide students attending their public schools with school health services. *School health services* include the services of a registered professional nurse, if one is employed (§§ 901(1), 1604(25), 1709(21); 8 NYCRR § 136.2(b)), and medical examinations, dental inspection and/or screening, scoliosis screening, vision screening, audiometer tests, and other such services as may be rendered in examining students for the existence of disease or disability and in testing the eyes and ears of students (§ 901(1), (2); 8 NYCRR § 136.2(b)).

The procedures used in rendering such services must be designed to determine the health status of a child; inform parents, students and teachers of the individual child's health condition subject to federal and state confidentiality laws; guide parents, children and teachers in procedures for preventing and correcting defects and diseases; instruct school personnel in procedures to take in case of accident or illness; and to survey and make necessary recommendations concerning the health and safety aspects of school facilities and the provision of health information (§ 901(2); 8 NYCRR § 136.1(e); see also NYS Education Department, Office of Student Support Services, *Parent Guardian Notification of Student Illness or Injury* (Oct. 2013), at: http://www.p12.nysed.gov/sss/schoolhealth/schoolhealthservices/ParentGuardianNotificationReStudentIllnessInjuryMemo.pdf).

However, the obligation to provide school health services is not intended to supplant the affirmative duty of parents to provide adequate medical care for their children (see *Matter of Hofbauer*, 47 N.Y.2d 648 (1979); *Matter of Christine M.*, 157 Misc.2d 4 (Fam. Ct. Kings Cnty. 1992); *Opn. of Counsel No. 98*, 1 Ed Dept Rep 824 (1961); *Opn. of Counsel No. 67*, 1 Ed Dept Rep 766 (1952)). Moreover, school districts need to obtain parental consent before providing health care services to determine the health status of a student (*D.F. v. Bd. of Educ. of Syosset CSD*, 386 F. Supp.2d 119 (E.D.N.Y. 2005), *aff'd*, 180 Fed.Appx. 232 (2d Cir. 2006), *cert. denied,* 549 U.S. 1179 (2007)).

The NYS Education Department developed the *Parent/Guardian Notification* website page in order to strengthen, promote and sustain communication between schools and parents regarding student illness and injury that occur at school. The website includes template notification letters (http://www.schoolhealthservicesny.com/tool_kit.cfm?subpage=257).

50:4. Must school districts provide school health services to students attending private schools?

Yes. At the request of a private school, a school district must provide to resident students attending a nonpublic school health and welfare services and facilities equivalent to those available to resident students attending the district's public schools (§ 912; *Cornelia v. Bd. of Educ. of CSD No. 1, Town of Greece*, 36 A.D.2d 576 (4th Dep't), *aff'd*, 29 N.Y.2d 586 (1971); *Appeal of W.T.B. and M.B.*, 44 Ed Dept Rep 152 (2004); *Appeal of Burke*, 34 Ed Dept Rep 3 (1994)). Such services must be provided in "essentially the same manner and to the same extent" they are offered to public school students. Thus, a school district would have to ensure that a resident student who attends private school and is diabetic receives needed daily insulin testing the same as if the student attended public school (*Richard K. v. Petrone*, 31 A.D.3d 181 (2d Dep't 2006)).When students attend private school outside their district of residence, the district of residence must contract with the district where the private school is located for the provision of such services. Such an expenditure must be included in the annual budget of the school district of residence (§ 912).

Health services available to private school students may include those performed by a physician, physician assistant, dentist, dental hygienist, registered professional nurse, nurse practitioner, school psychologist, school social worker or school speech therapist. They may also include dental prophylaxis, vision and hearing tests, the taking of medical histories, and the administration of health screening tests, the maintenance of cumulative health records, and the administration of emergency care programs for ill or injured students (*Id.*).

The obligation to provide resident private school students with health services that are equivalent to those provided to resident public school students does not require that districts provide full-time nursing services to a private school (*Appeal of a Student with a Disability,* 51 Ed Dept Rep, Dec. No. 16,258 (2011); *Appeal of W.T.B. & M.B.*; *Appeal of Burke*).

Health Examinations

50:5. Are public school students required to have a medical examination before entering school?

Yes. Except in the cities of New York, Buffalo and Rochester, and unless a religious exemption applies (see **50:8**), school districts must require that students enrolled in public school have a satisfactory health examination conducted by their family physician, physician assistant or nurse practitioner, upon first entering their school at any grade level, and upon entering prekindergarten, kindergarten, and the second, fourth, seventh, and 10th grades (8 NYCRR § 136.3(b)(1)). To be acceptable, the examination must have been conducted no more than 12 months before the first day of the school year in question (8 NYCRR § 136.3(b); see 8 NYCRR § 136.1(g)).

Furthermore, a school district may require an examination and health history of any student at any time in its discretion to promote the educational interests of the student (§ 903(1); 8 NYCRR § 136.3(b)(2)).

In all school districts, the physician, physician assistant, or nurse practitioner conducting the examination must determine whether a one-time test for sickle cell anemia is necessary or desirable, and include the results of any such test in the health certificate students must submit to attend school (8 NYCRR § 136.3(b)(3); see also **50:6-7**).

50:6. Must public school students provide their school with a health certificate?

Yes. Every public school student must submit a health certificate to their school's principal or the principal's designee that indicates the student is in a fit condition to attend school. Students must submit the required health certificate within 30 calendar days after entering their school, and upon entering the second, fourth, seventh and 10th grades (§ 903(1); 8 NYCRR § 136.3(c)(1); see 8 NYCRR § 136.1(h)).

A student's health certificate, to be filed in the student's cumulative health record, must be signed by a duly licensed physician, physician assistant, or nurse practitioner, and must be based upon an examination of the student conducted not more than 12 months before the start of the school year in which it is required. Each certificate must also state the student's body mass index (BMI) and weight status category. The licensed physician, physician assistant, or nurse practitioner must determine whether a one-time test for sickle cell anemia is necessary or desirable and state in the health certificate the results of any such test (§ 903(1); 8 NYCRR § 136.3(c)(1)(i), (ii)).

School districts chosen to participate in surveys by the commissioner of health in relation to students' BMI and weight status categories must share that information in the aggregate. A parent may refuse to share their child's information in such survey (§ 903(3)(a)). Each school district shall provide the commissioner of health with any information, records and reports he or she may require for such audit (§§ 903(3)(a), 904(1); see also Pub. Health Law § 2599-b).

50:7. What happens if a student does not provide a required health certificate?

If a student does not present a required health certificate (see **50:6**), and he or she is not exempt from such requirement on religious grounds (see **50:8**), the school principal or his or her designee must notify the student's parents that if the certificate is not provided within 30 calendar days from the date of the notice, the director of school health services will conduct an examination by health appraisal of the student (§ 903(3)(a); 8 NYCRR § 136.3(c)(1)(iii); see 8 NYCRR § 136.1(h); see also NYS Education Department, Office of School Innovation, *School Health Examination Guidelines* (revised June 2015), at: http://www.p12.nysed.gov/sss/documents/SchoolHealthExaminationJune2015Rev9-15.pdf).

Each school principal or his or her designee must report to the director of health services the names of all students who have not furnished a health certificate, or who are students with disabilities. The director of health services will then arrange to have such students examined and tested to determine whether they have defective sight or hearing, or any other physical disability that might prevent them from doing well in school, or which may require a modification of their school work to prevent injury to them. The physician, physician assistant, or nurse practitioner administering the examination also must determine whether a one-time test for sickle cell anemia is necessary or desirable and, if so, conduct the test and report the results in the student's health certificate (§ 904(1); 8 NYCRR § 136.3(d)(1)–(3); see also *School Health Examination Guidelines*).

The principal or his or her designee must notify a student's parents of the existence of any uncovered sight or hearing defect, or other physical disability or condition, including sickle cell anemia. If a student's parents are unable or unwilling to provide necessary relief and treatment, the principal, or his or her designee, must report this to the director of school health services, who must then provide the relief needed (§ 904(1); 8 NYCRR § 136.3(d)(4); see also 8 NYCRR § 136.3(a)(3); see also *School Health Examination Guidelines*). Treatment means the correction of physical defects or other health problems in need of attention where the student, for the most part, is a passive recipient (8 NYCRR § 136.1(f)).

50:8. Are there any exemptions from the health examination and health certificate requirements?

Yes. School districts may not require that students submit to a health examination by their family physician, or present a health history (see **50:5**), submit a health certificate or be examined by the district's director of school health services (see **50:6-7**), or undergo a sickle cell anemia examination (see **50:5, 50:7**), if they or their parents object claiming a conflict with their genuine and sincere religious beliefs (§§ 903(4), 904(2); 8 NYCRR § 136.3(c)(1)(iii), (f); see also NYS Education Department, Office of School Innovation, *School Health Examination Guidelines* (revised June 2015), at: http://www.p12.nysed.gov/sss/documents/SchoolHealthExaminationJune2015Rev9-15.pdf).

Such an exemption must be requested in writing to the school principal or his or her designee. The principal or his or her designee may require documents supporting the request (8 NYCRR § 136.3(f)).

50:9. Must school districts request that students furnish their school a dental health certificate?

Yes. School districts must request that students furnish a dental health certificate at the same time that health certificates are required (§ 903(2)(a); 8 NYCRR § 136.3(k); see **50:6**). At their discretion, districts also may request at any time an examination and dental health history of any child to promote the educational interests of the child (§ 903(2)(a)). While a school district must request dental certificates, parents are encouraged but not required to submit a completed certificate (NYS Education Department, Office of School Innovation, *School Health Examination Guidelines* (revised June 2015), at: http://www.p12.nysed.gov/sss/documents/SchoolHealthExaminationJune2015Rev9-15.pdf).

A dental health certificate must indicate whether the student is in fit dental health condition to attend school. It must be signed by a duly licensed dentist or registered dental hygienist, and must be based on a dental examination of the student conducted not more than 12 months prior to the start of the school year in which it is requested (*Id.*).

Districts must make available to parents, upon request, a list compiled by the NYS Education Department of dentists and registered dental hygienists who will conduct dental examinations on a free or reduced cost basis (§ 903(2)(b); 8 NYCRR § 136.3(k)(3)).

50:10. Are there any exemptions from the dental health certificate and dental examination request requirements?

Yes. School districts may not request a dental health certificate from a student when the student or the student's parents object based on a conflict with their genuine sincere religious beliefs (§ 903(4); 8 NYCRR § 136.3(k)(1)).

50:11. Must school districts conduct any health screenings other than the examination of students who do not submit a health certificate?

Yes. A school district's director of school health services must ensure that all students undergo the following screening examinations:

- Scoliosis screening at least once each school year for students in grades five through nine. The commissioner of education may waive this requirement for a district that shows it does not have the capability to comply and that such compliance would place an undue financial burden upon it.
- Vision screening for students who enroll in school, within six months of their admission. Such screening must include, at a minimum, color perception, distance acuity and near vision.
- Vision screening for distance acuity for students in kindergarten, and the first, second, third, fifth, seventh, and 10th grades, and any other time deemed necessary.
- Hearing screening for students who enroll in school, within six months of their admission, and for students in grades kindergarten, first, third, fifth, seventh, and 10th, and any other time deemed necessary. Such screening shall include, but not be limited to, pure tone and threshold air conduction screening (§ 905; 8 NYCRR § 136.3(e)).

However, students may be exempt from such health screenings if they or their parents object on the grounds that they conflict with their genuine and sincere religious beliefs (§ 905(5); 8 NYCRR § 136.3(f)). As in the case of exemptions from health examinations (see **50:5-7**), students or their parents must request such an exemption in writing to the school principal or his or her designee who may require documents supporting the request (8 NYCRR § 136.3(f); see also NYS Education Department, Office of School Innovation, *School Health Examination Guidelines* (revised June 2015), at: http://www.p12.nysed.gov/sss/documents/SchoolHealthExaminationJune2015Rev9-15.pdf).

The results of any such health screening must be recorded on appropriate forms and kept on file in the school. Parents must receive written notice of the results of vision and hearing examinations and the positive results of scoliosis screenings (§ 905; 8 NYCRR § 136.3(e)(1), (2)).

50:12. What happens if a school district fails to provide required health services, or to conduct required health examinations or screenings?

In a case involving a school district's failure to screen a student for scoliosis, it was ruled that students and their parents cannot sue the district for money damages for such failure (*Uhr v. East Greenbush CSD*, 94 N.Y.2d 32 (1999)).

However, the Education Law authorizes the commissioner of education to withhold public funding from districts that willfully refuse or neglect to comply with the provision of health services requirements (§ 911(2); see also *Uhr v. East Greenbush CSD*).

Immunizations

Editor's Note: Additional guidance on Recommended School District Procedures for Implementing Requests for Religious Exemption to Immunization *is available from the NYS Education Department at: http://www.p12.nysed.gov/sss/documents/modelproceduresMarch2016.pdf.*

50:13. Are students required to submit proof of immunization to attend school?

Yes. Every student entering or attending public school must be immunized, as required by section 2164 of the Public Health Law (§ 914). In accordance with that law, public school students must be immunized against poliomyelitis, mumps, measles, diphtheria, rubella, varicella, Haemophilus influenzae type b (Hib), pertussis, tetanus, pneumococcal disease, and hepatitis B (Pub. Health Law § 2164(2)(a); 10 NYCRR §§ 66-1.1, 66-1.3; 8 NYCRR § 136.3(c)(2); see http://www.nyhealth.gov/publications/2370.pdf for a chart of current immunization requirements).

Furthermore, children born on or after January 1, 1994, and entering sixth grade or comparable age special education program on or after September 1, 2007, must receive a booster immunization containing a vaccine for diphtheria, tetanus, and acellular pertussis (Pub. Health Law § 2164(2)(b)). Beginning September 1, 2016, children entering seventh and twelfth grades must be administered vaccines against meningococcal disease (Pub. Health Law § 2164(2)(c); see also NYS Department of Health, *Frequently Asked Questions for Public Health Law §§ 2164 and 2168* (Apr. 2016), at: http://www.health.ny.gov/prevention/immunization/schools/docs/faq_immunization_regulations.pdf).

A child who has not completed all the necessary vaccinations may be admitted to school if there is proof the child is "in process" to complete the vaccinations (10 NYCRR § 66-1.3(b)). "In process" means that a child has received at least the first dose in each immunization series and has age appropriate appointments to complete the series, the child is obtaining serologic tests for proof of immunity within 30 days of notification to the parent that such testing is requested, or a child's serologic tests were negative and the child has appointments to be immunized based on the catch up schedule of the Advisory Commission on Immunization Practices (10 NYCRR § 66-1.1(f)(2), (j); see also NYS Education Department, Office of Student Support Services, *Immunization Guidelines for Schools* (revised Mar. 2016), at: http://www.p12.nysed.gov/sss/documents/IMMUNIZATIONGUIDELINESFORSCHOOLS3_16.pdf).

Homeless students are not required to present proof of immunity or immunization prior to being admitted to school. Rather, the student must be admitted and the district's homeless liaison should request the immunization records from the child's former school (§ 3209(2)(e); 8 NYCRR § 100.2(x)(4)(ii); see also *Immunization Guidelines for Schools*; see **49:36**). Similarly, refugee students are not required to have vaccinations before arrival in the United States and it is recommended these children be afforded 30 days of school attendance under the exception in public health law, if there is evidence of good faith effort to obtain immunizations or proof of past immunization via serologic testing (Pub. Health Law § 2164(7)(a); NYS Education Department, *Vaccinations in Refugee Children* (Jan. 2012), at: http://www.p12.nysed.gov/sss/schoolhealth/schoolhealthservices/VaccinationsInRefugeeChildren.pdf; see also *Immunization Guidelines for Schools*; see **50:14**).

In addition, school districts must participate in surveys and audits directed by the state commissioner of health regarding the immunization level of children entering and attending school, and provide any records or reports required for that purpose (§ 914(3); Pub. Health Law §§ 613(2), 2168; 10 NYCRR § 66-1.7; *Immunization Guidelines for Schools*). They must post educational materials on influenza and the benefits of influenza immunization in plain view in anticipation of times of highest risk for contraction of influenza as determined by the commissioner of health

(Public Health Law § 613(1)(b)). Districts may obtain such information from the NYS Department of Health's website at: http://www.health.ny.gov/diseases/communicable/influenza/seasonal/child_care_and_schools/.

50:14. What happens if a student fails to submit proof of immunization?

If a student fails to submit proof of immunization, the school principal must inform the student's parents of the necessity to have the student immunized, that the required immunizations may be administered by any health practitioner, or at no cost by the county health officer upon parental consent. The student's parents also must be informed that, as a pre-requisite for their child's admission to, or continued attendance at school, they must either choose a health practitioner to administer the immunization, or provide consent for the county health officer, or a school physician or nurse to administer the immunization, unless they state a valid reason for withholding such consent (Pub. Health Law § 2164(6); 10 NYCRR § 66-1.8(a)).

No child may be admitted to, or allowed to attend, school for more than 14 days without an appropriate immunization certificate or other acceptable evidence of immunization. A school principal may extend this period to 30 days on a case-by-case basis when a student has transferred from another state or country and can show a good faith effort to get the necessary certificate or other evidence of immunization (Pub. Health Law § 2164(7)(a); 10 NYCRR § 66-1.4; see also NYS Education Department, Office of Student Support Services, *Immunization Guidelines for Schools* (revised Mar. 2016) at: http://www.p12.nysed.gov/sss/documents/IMMUNIZATIONGUIDELINESFORSCHOOLS3_16.pdf).

In addition, a school principal must report to the local health authority the name and address of any student refused admission or continued attendance for lack of proof of immunizations. The principal also must notify the student's parents of any such exclusion, provide them with an immunization consent form, and cooperate with the local health authority in scheduling a time and place for immunizing a child for whom consent has been obtained (Pub. Health Law § 2164(8-a)(a); 10 NYCRR § 66-1.8(b), (c); see also *Immunization Guidelines for Schools*).

A student may appeal a denial of admission to, or continued attendance at, school to the commissioner of education (Pub. Health Law § 2164(7)(b)).

Editor's Note: The NYS Department of Health maintains a state-wide web-based immunization information system, a registry that allows school districts to access information on the immunization status of children. For additional information on this registry visit the NYS Immunization Information System (NYSIIS) website at: http://www.health.state.ny.us/prevention/immunization/information_system/ or contact NYSIIS by phone at 518-473-2839 or by e-mail at nysiis@health.ny.gov.

50:15. Are there any exemptions from the immunization requirements?

Yes. Students may be admitted to school or continue attendance without a certificate or proof of immunization if:

- A physician will testify or certify that administering a vaccine to a specific student will be detrimental to that student's health (Pub. Health Law § 2164(8)); or
- In the case of varicella, either a health care provider documents the child has already had varicella, or there is serologic evidence the child has immunity to varicella (10 NYCRR § 66-1.1(h), 66-1.6); or
- The student's parents claim an exemption based on genuine and sincerely held religious beliefs that are contrary to the practice of immunization (Pub. Health Law § 2164(9); see *Phillips v. City of N.Y.*, 775 F.3d 538 (2d Cir.), *cert. denied,* 136 S.Ct. 104 (2015)).

50:16. Under what circumstances is a medical exemption granted?

A medical exemption certificate must indicate why immunization would be detrimental to the student seeking the exemption and indicate a time at which such immunization would no longer be detrimental (*Appeal of L.W.*, 52 Ed Dept Rep, Dec. No. 16,416 (2012); *Appeal of N.C.*, 50 Ed Dept Rep, Dec. No. 16,172 (2010); *Appeal of D.F.*, 50 Ed Dept Rep, Dec. No. 16,132 (2010). A student may seek a medical exemption from any or all of the required vaccinations (*Appeal of M.E.F.*, 43 Ed Dept Rep 248 (2003); *Appeal of McGann*, 32 Ed Dept Rep 187 (1992)).

Such certificate must contain a specific explanation of the harmful effects (*Appeal of J.S. and D.S.*, 55 Ed Dept Rep, Dec. No. 16,821 (2015)). School officials may engage in further investigation of a doctor's note excusing a student from immunization (*Lynch v. Clarkstown CSD,* 155 Misc.2d 846 (Rockland Cnty. 1992); *Appeal of J.S. and D.S.; Appeal of a Student with a Disability,* 54 Ed Dept Rep, Dec. No. 16,667 (2014)).

Medical exemptions must be reissued annually as determinations of exemptions may change year to year based on the changing health status of students (10 NYCRR § 66-1.3(c); *Appeal of C.H.*, 52 Ed Dept Rep, Dec. No. 16,465 (2013); NYS Education Department, Office of Student Support Services, *Immunization Guidelines for Schools* (revised Mar. 2016), at: http://www.p12.nysed.gov/sss/documents/IMMUNIZATIONGUIDELINESFORSCHOOLS3_16.pdf).

50:17. How do parents request a religious exemption from immunizations?

Parents seeking a religious exemption from immunizations must submit to their school district a written and signed statement declaring their objection to immunizations due to sincere and genuine religious beliefs that prohibit the immunization of their child (10 NYCRR § 66-1.3(d); *Appeal of D.M. and K.M.*, 55 Ed Dept Rep, Dec. No. 16,863 (2016); *Appeal of C.S.*, 49 Ed Dept Rep 106 (2009); *Appeal of H.K. and T.K.*, 49 Ed Dept Rep 56 (2009)). A form made available by the NYS Education Department can be found at: http://www.p12.nysed.gov/sss/documents/modelreligousexemptionformMarch2016.pdf.

A school principal may request supporting documentation if, following review of the parental statement, questions remain about the existence of a sincerely held religious belief (10 NYCRR § 66-1.3(d); *Appeal of C.S.; Appeal of H.K. and T.K.*; see also *Appeal of R.R.*, 54 Ed Dept Rep, Dec. No 16,663 (2014)). The burden is on the parents to establish their right to the exemption (see *Appeal of C.S.*; *Appeal of H.K. and T.K.*).

50:18. Who determines if a student is entitled to a religious exemption from immunizations?

Whether a student is exempt from immunization because of religious reasons is determined, in the first instance, by school district officials (*Appeal of C.S.*, 49 Ed Dept Rep 106 (2009); *Appeal of H.K. and T.K.*, 49 Ed Dept Rep 56 (2009); *Appeal of S.B.*, 48 Ed Dept Rep 332 (2009)). The school official charged with making the decision is the principal (10 NYCRR § 66-1.3(d); *Appeal of A.C.,* 50 Ed Dept Rep, Dec. No. 16,175 (2010)).

Specifically, school officials must determine whether the purported beliefs that support the opposition to immunizations are religious in nature and, only if they are, whether they are genuine and sincerely held (*Farina v. Bd. of Educ. of the City of N.Y.*, 116 F.Supp.2d 503 (S.D.N.Y. 2000); *Sherr v. Northport-East Northport*, 672 F.Supp. 81 (E.D.N.Y. 1987); see **50:21-22**).

When determining whether a parent's religious beliefs are genuine, school district officials do not have to simply accept a statement of religious belief without some examination. Similarly, they should not simply reject a statement either without further examination (*Appeal of C.S.; Appeal of H.K. and T.K.*; *Appeal of S.B.*). The school district should evidence that the application was fully examined (*Appeal of*

L.S., 48 Ed Dept Rep 227 (2008); see also *Appeal of O.M. and R.M.*, 51 Ed Dept Rep, Dec. No. 16,267 (2011); and provide an explanation in writing for the rejection (*Appeal of L.S.*, 50 Ed Dept Rep, Dec. No. 16,180 (2010)). Such explanation must articulate the specific reasons for a denial (*Appeal of N.C.*, 55 Ed Dept Rep, Dec. No. 16,805 (2015)).

A school district may be held financially liable if it denies a religious exemption in violation of a parent's constitutional rights to the free exercise of religion under the First Amendment (*Lewis v. Sobol*, 710 F.Supp. 506 (S.D.N.Y. 1989)).

50:19. Are school districts bound by previous grants of a religious exemption from immunization?

No. Accordingly, a middle school principal, for example, can deny a religious exemption from immunization to a student previously granted such an exemption by the elementary school principal in the same school district. The middle school principal may conduct a separate inquiry to ensure compliance with statutory immunization requirements (*Appeal of K.E.*, 48 Ed Dept Rep 54 (2008)).

Similarly, a religious exemption granted by school officials in another school district previously attended by a student is not binding on school officials of the district of current attendance. Actually, district officials of the new district are obligated to make their own determination whether any one of their students qualifies for a religious exemption (*Appeal of S.B.*, 48 Ed Dept Rep 332 (2009)).

In addition, a previous denial does not preclude the possibility that a subsequent request for religious exemption can be granted based on the evolution and growth of the parent's religious belief (*Appeal of O.M. and R.M.*, 51 Ed Dept Rep, Dec. No. 16,267 (2011)).

50:20. Must parents be a member of a religion opposed to immunization to qualify for a religious exemption?

No. Parents may claim a religious exemption even if they are not members of a recognized religious organization whose doctrines oppose vaccination (*Farina v. Bd. of Educ. of the City of N.Y.*, 116 F.Supp.2d 503 (S.D.N.Y. 2000); *Lewis v. Sobol*, 710 F.Supp. 506 (S.D.N.Y. 1989); *Sherr v. Northport-East Northport UFSD*, 672 F.Supp. 81 (E.D.N.Y 1987); *Matter of Christine M.*, 157 Misc.2d 4 (Fam. Ct. Kings Cnty. 1992); *Appeal of N.C.*, 55 Ed Dept Rep, Dec. No. 16,805 (2015); *Appeal of B.R. and M.R.*, 50 Ed Dept Rep, Dec. No. 16,250 (2011), *Appeal of D.W. and N.W.*, 50 Ed Dept Rep, Dec. No. 16,144 (2010)).

Nonetheless, a religiously based opposition to immunizations must be founded on sincerely held religious beliefs rather than medical or purely moral considerations, scientific and secular theories, or philosophical and personal beliefs (*Mason v. General Brown CSD*, 851 F.2d 47 (2d Cir. 1988); *Caviezel v. Great Neck Public Sch.*, 500 Fed.Appx. 16 (2d Cir. 2012); *N.M. v. Hebrew Academy Long Beach*, 155 F.Supp.3d 247 (E.D.N.Y. 2016); *Farina v. Bd. of Educ. of the City of N.Y.*; *Sherr v. Northport-East Northport UFSD*; *Matter of Christine M.*; *Check v. N.Y. City Dep't of Educ.* 2013 U.S. Dist LEXIS 186100 (E.D.N.Y. May 20, 2013); *Appeal of D.M. and K.M.*, 55 Ed Dept Rep, Dec. No. 16,863 (2016), *Appeal of L.L.*, 54 Ed Dept Rep, Dec. No. 16,670 (2014); *Appeal of B.R. and M.R.*). This includes personalized interpretations of concepts and practices found in various religions (*Appeal of J.W.R. and E.R.*, 55 Ed Dept Rep, Dec. No. 16,899 (2016); *Appeal of N.C.*; *Appeal of B.O-G.*, 51 Ed Dept Rep, Dec. No. 16,294 (2011)).

Opposition to immunization may not be framed in terms of religious beliefs merely to gain the exemption (*Sherr v. Northport-East Northport UFSD*; *Matter of Christine M.*).

A religious exemption from immunization requirements to attend school might also apply to participation in extracurricular activities (see *Hadley v. Rush Henrietta CSD*, 409 F.Supp.2d 164 (W.D.N.Y. 2006); *case dismissed on other grounds*, 2007 U.S. Dist. LEXIS 30586 (W.D.N.Y. April 25, 2007)).

50:21. How can school district officials determine whether a parent's opposition to immunizations is based on a genuine religious belief?

Certainly school district officials do not have to accept a parents' mere statement that they have a sincere and genuine belief contrary to the practice of immunization, or that God provides an immune system as proof that a student's parents hold such beliefs. Instead, parents must articulate a description of the religious basis or origin of their beliefs (*Farina v. Bd. of Educ. of the City of N.Y.*, 116 F.Supp.2d 503 (S.D.N.Y. 2000); *Appeal of R.P.*, 47 Ed Dept Rep 124 (2007); *Appeal of J.F.,* 45 Ed Dept Rep 241 (2005); *Appeal of Quigley*, 41 Ed Dept Rep 399 (2002)). Reliance on Bible passages while at the same time being a member of a church that leaves decisions on the use of immunizations to the individual is insufficient to establish a sincerely held religious belief (*Appeal of N.C.*, 55 Ed Dept Rep, Dec. No. 16,805 (2015); *Appeal of K.N.N.M. and EAY,* 52 Ed Dept Rep, Dec. No. 16,410 (2012); *Appeal of K.E.*, 48 Ed Dept Rep 54 (2008)).

However, a parent's religious beliefs can be personal. They do not have to be consistent with the dogma of any organized religion (*Farina v. Bd. of Educ. of the City of N.Y.; Appeal of B.O-G.*, 51 Ed Dept Rep, Dec. No. 16,294 (2011); *Appeal of L.P.,* 46 Ed Dept Rep 341 (2007)), or founded upon a belief in the fundamental premise of a God as commonly understood in western philosophy (*U.S. v. Seeger*, 380 U.S. 163 (1965); *Int'l Soc'y for Krishna Consciousness, Inc. v. Barker*, 650 F.2d 430 (2d Cir. 1981); *Mason v. General Brown CSD,* 851 F.2d 47 (2d Cir. 1988); *Sherr v. Northport-East Northport UFSD*, 672 F.Supp.2d 81 (E.D.N.Y. 1989); *Matter of Christine M.*, 157 Misc.2d 4 (Fam. Ct. Kings Cnty. 1992); *Appeal of L.P.*). Therefore, parents may not be asked about their religious affiliation, or that they provide a letter from their church regarding their religious beliefs, just the nature of their beliefs (*Farina v. Bd. of Educ. of the City of N.Y.*).

What is required is that a parent's personal religious belief occupies a place in the parent's life that is parallel to that filled by the orthodox belief in God (*U.S. v. Seeger*; *Int'l Soc'y for Krishna Consciousness, Inc. v. Barker*; *Mason v. General Brown CSD*; *Sherr v. Northport-East Northport; Matter of Christine M.*), and that the parent will categorically disregard elementary self-interest rather than transgressing religious tenets (*U.S. v. Allen*, 760 F.2d 447 (2d Cir. 1985); *Int'l Soc'y for Krishna Consciousness, Inc. v. Barker*; *Lewis v. Sobol*, 710 F.Supp. 506 (S.D.N.Y. 1989); *Matter of Christine M.*).

50:22. How can school district officials determine whether a parent's religious beliefs prohibiting immunizations are sincerely held?

When determining whether a parent's religious beliefs are sincerely held, school district officials must make a good faith effort to assess the credibility of the parent's sentiments and sincerity (*Matter of Christine M.,* 157 Misc.2d 4 (Fam. Ct. Kings Cnty. 1992); *Appeal of D.W. and N.W.,* 50 Ed Dept Rep, Dec. No. 16,144 (2010); *Appeal of C.S.*, 49 Ed Dept Rep 106 (2009); *Appeal of J.F.,* 45 Ed Dept Rep 241 (2005)). They may draw inferences from the parent's words and actions (*Farina v. Bd. of Educ. of the City of N.Y.*, 116 F.Supp.2d 503 (S.D.N.Y. 2000)), including a parent's attitudes toward sickness and health, and whether the parent joined a particular organized group in order to gain an exemption from immunization (*Sherr v. Northport-East Northport UFSD*, 672 F.Supp.2d 81 (E.D.N.Y. 1989)). School district officials can also rely on their observation of the parents' demeanor and forthrightness (*Matter of Christine M.*; *Appeal of J.W.R. and E.R.*, 55 Ed Dept Rep, Dec. No. 16,899 (2016); *Appeal of H.K. and T.K.*, 49 Ed Dept Rep 56 (2009)).

Certainly, a religious belief would not be sincerely held if, for instance, the person adhering to the belief acts in a manner inconsistent with that belief, or gains by fraudulently hiding secular interests behind religious doctrine (*Int'l Soc'y for Krishna Consciousness, Inc. v. Barker*, 650 F.2d 430 (2d Cir. 1981)); *N.M. v. Hebrew Academy Long Beach*, 155 F.Supp.3d 247 (E.D.N.Y. 2016); *Lewis v. Sobol*, 710 F.Supp.

506 (S.D.N.Y. 1989); *Sherr v. Northport-East Northport UFSD*; *Matter of Christine M.*). However, an occasional or past departure from one's religious practices does not necessarily negate the sincerity of religious beliefs (*Lewis v. Sobol; Appeal of C.D.*, 46 Ed Dept Rep 317 (2007)). Accordingly, the fact that a child has been previously immunized is not dispositive in determining the parent's genuine and sincere religious beliefs against immunization (*Appeal of C.S.*; *Appeal of C.D.*).

A parent with children who have been immunized may still hold genuine and sincere religious beliefs that are contrary toward immunizations. So might parents who accept medical treatment when an illness occurs, if what they oppose is proactive rather than reactive medical treatment (*Lewis v. Sobol; Appeal of J.W.R. and E.R.*; *Appeal of D.M. and K.M.*, 55 Ed Dept Rep, Dec. No. 16,863 (2016)).

50:23. Are schools required to keep a list of susceptible students who should be temporarily excluded in the event of an outbreak of a vaccine preventable disease?

Yes. Schools must maintain a list of students, who have been excused from immunization for medical or religious reasons and those students who are "in process" for completing immunization series or serologic testing for immunity (see **50:13**). The list shall be updated each time a new student enrolls or a student's immunization status changes (10 NYCRR § 66-1.10(c)). In the event that the commissioner of health determines that there is an outbreak of vaccine preventable disease listed in Public Health Law § 2164, the commissioner may order school officials to exclude those susceptible students until it is determined the danger of transmission has passed (10 NYCRR § 66-1.10(a), (b); see also NYS Education Department, Office of Student Support Services, *Immunization Guidelines for Schools* (revised Mar. 2016), at: http://www.p12.nysed.gov/sss/documents/IMMUNIZATIONGUIDELINESFORSCHOOLS3_16.pdf). The requirement for temporary exclusion has been upheld as constitutional (*Phillips v. City of N.Y.*, 775 F.3d 538 (2d Cir.), *cert. denied*, 136 S.Ct. 104 (2015)).

School districts should consult with their attorneys regarding obligations they may have to provide alternate or homebound instruction to students excluded during an outbreak of vaccine preventable disease (U.S. Department of Education, Office of Civil Rights, *Fact Sheet Addressing the Risk of Measles in Schools While Protecting the Civil Rights of Students with Disabilities* (Mar. 2015), at: https://rems.ed.gov/docs/ED_Measles_OCR_fact_sheet_2015-3-6_Clean_508.pdf; see also **50:29**)

Communicable Diseases

50:24. Can school districts exclude from school students who show symptoms of a communicable or infectious disease?

Yes. A school district must exclude from school, and send home immediately, any student who shows symptoms of any communicable or infectious disease that is reportable under the Public Health Law and imposes a significant risk of infection of others in the school. The director of school health services must immediately notify a local public health agency of the disease (§ 906(1); 8 NYCRR § 136.3(h); see also NYS Education Department, Office of Student Support Services, *Immunization Guidelines for Schools* (revised Mar. 2016), at: http://www.p12.nysed.gov/sss/documents/IMMUNIZATIONGUIDELINESFORSCHOOLS3_16.pdf); see **50:25** for information on the exclusion of students with AIDS or HIV). Such exclusions from school do not constitute discrimination under federal law because a school is not required to permit an individual to participate in or benefit from its programs and services when that individual poses a direct threat to the health or safety of others (28 CFR § 35.139). Individuals may be considered to pose a direct threat only after individualized assessment based on a reasonable judgment which relies on current medical knowledge or the best available objective information regarding the nature, duration and severity of the risk, the probability of potential injury and whether reasonable steps may be taken to mitigate the risk (*Id.*). For example, the U.S. Centers for Disease Control and Prevention has advised that students and staff with travel related Zika virus exposure or confirmed Zika virus infection do not need to be removed from school as isolation or quarantine of exposed individuals is neither recommended nor appropriate (U.S. Centers for Disease Control and Prevention, *Zika Virus Response Planning: Interim Guidance for District and School Administrators in the Continental United States and Hawaii* at: http://www.cdc.gov/zika/schools.html).

A student returning to school after an absence on account of illness or from unknown cause may be examined by the director of school health services if the student returns to school without a certificate from a local public health officer, a duly licensed physician, physician assistant, or nurse practitioner (§ 906(2); 8 NYCRR § 136.3(h); see also *Immunization Guidelines for Schools*).

In addition, the director of school health services, or other health professionals under his direction or upon his referral, may conduct evaluations of teachers and any other school employees, and school buildings and premises, as they deem necessary to protect students and staff from communicable diseases (§ 906(3); 8 NYCRR § 136.3(i); see also *Immunization Guidelines for Schools*).

50:25. Can school districts automatically exclude from school students with acquired immunodeficiency syndrome (AIDS) or any other human immunodeficiency virus (HIV)-related illness?

No. The automatic exclusion from school or school-related activities of students solely because they have been diagnosed with AIDS or become infected with HIV would violate those students' rights under section 504 of the federal Rehabilitation Act of 1973, which prohibits discrimination on the basis of disability (*District 27 Cmty. Sch. Bd. v. Bd. of Educ.*, 130 Misc.2d 398 (Sup. Ct. Queens Cnty. 1986); see 29 USC § 794; see also *Martinez v. Sch. Bd. of Hillsborough Cnty.*, 861 F.2d 1502 (11th Cir. 1988); *Thomas v. Atascadero Unified Sch. Dist.*, 662 F.Supp. 376 (C.D. Cal. 1987)).

In addition, federal regulations implementing the Americans with Disabilities Act (ADA), which also prohibits discrimination on the basis of disability (42 USC § 12132), include HIV, whether symptomatic or asymptomatic, in the definition of "disability" (28 CFR § 35.104), and prohibit discrimination in the provision of educational and other services against individuals infected with HIV (see 28 CFR § 35.130(a)). The U. S. Supreme Court has ruled that asymptomatic HIV infection indeed is a disability under the ADA (*Bragdon v. Abbott*, 524 U.S. 624 (1998)).

Furthermore, the NYS Department of Health does not consider AIDS a communicable disease (see **50:24**) and its exclusion from this category has been upheld by the New York Court of Appeals (*N.Y. State Soc'y of Surgeons v. Axelrod*, 77 N.Y.2d 677 (1991)).

50:26. Can school districts disclose information about students with human immunodeficiency virus (HIV) and/or acquired immunodeficiency syndrome (AIDS)?

Not generally. Current law and regulations strictly limit the disclosure of confidential information about HIV or AIDS (Pub. Health Law Article 27-F; 10 NYCRR Part 63).

In most circumstances, disclosure of such information concerning a student requires an authorization for release form signed by the student, or if the student lacks the "capacity to consent," by a person legally authorized to consent on behalf of the student (Pub. Health Law § 2782; 10 NYCRR § 63.5(a)).

However, a court may issue an order requiring its release based on the presence of a clear and imminent danger to another person who unknowingly may be at significant risk as a result of contact with the student (Pub. Health Law § 2785(2)(b); 10 NYCRR § 63.6(a)(12), (b)(4)). In such an instance, the information can be given only to persons identified in the court order, only for the reasons provided in the court order (Pub. Health Law § 2785(6)).

50:27. Are there any precautions school districts must observe to prevent the spread of human immunodeficiency virus (HIV) and other diseases communicable through contact with blood and other bodily fluids?

Yes. School districts must have a written "exposure control plan." The plan must provide for employee training on how to deal with body fluids and other materials, and the keeping of accurate medical and training records. The plan must also identify positions, such as nurses, coaches, and custodians, and tasks likely to come into contact with blood and other bodily fluids. In addition, it must set forth the procedures to be followed, including "universal precautions," which require, for instance, that all bodily fluids and material be treated as infectious, and the wearing of protective equipment (29 CFR § 1910.1030(c)(1); see also NYS Education Department, Office of Student Support Services, *Blood Borne Pathogens in Classrooms* (Mar. 2014), at: http://www.p12.nysed.gov/sss/documents/bloodbornepathogenlettereducatorskhfinal.pdf; U.S. Centers for Disease Control and Prevention, *Zika Virus Response Planning: Interim Guidance for District and School Administrators in the Continental United States and Hawaii* at: http://www.cdc.gov/zika/schools.html).

50:28. Can school districts make condoms available to students?

Yes. School districts can elect to make condoms available to students as part of its program of school health services. However, they must have parental consent to actually distribute condoms to individual students (*Alfonso v. Fernandez*, 195 A.D.2d 46 (2d Dep't 1993), *appeal dismissed without opinion*, 83 N.Y.2d 906 (1994)). In addition, districts must assure that adequate personal health guidance is provided to each pupil receiving condoms in the manner prescribed by commissioner's regulations (8 NYCRR § 136.3(j); see 8 NYCRR § 135.3(c)(2)(ii); see also **55:50**).

50:29. Must school districts provide home instruction to students absent on account of illness?

It depends. A district may be obligated to provide temporary home instruction for a student suffering from a short-term physical disability (§ 1709(24); *Appeal of a Student Suspected of Having a Disability*, 40 Ed Dept Rep 75 (2000); *Appeal of Douglas & Barbara K.*, 34 Ed Dept Rep 214 (1994); *Appeal of Anthony M. & D. M.*, 30 Ed Dept Rep 269 (1991)). However, in a case where students with head lice missed one and a half months of school, the commissioner of education ruled the district was not required to provide them with home instruction during their absence. The prolonged absence was due to the parents' failure to follow the recommended course of treatment for a condition that could have been alleviated in one or two days (*Appeal of Douglas & Barbara K.*).

Medication, Drug Testing, and Other Safety Precautions

50:30. May school district staff administer medication to students?

Generally, only health care practitioners licensed or certified in New York, including, for example, physicians, nurse practitioners, physicians assistants, registered professional nurses and licensed practical nurses may administer medication to students in a school setting (§§ 902-a, 902-b; Education Law Title VIII; 8 NYCRR § 136.7(e); see also NYS Education Department, Office of Student Support Services, *Guidelines for Medication Management in Schools* (Sept. 2015), at: http://www.p12.nysed.gov/sss/documents/MedicationManagement-final2015.pdf).

A physician or other duly authorized licensed health care practitioners may train unlicensed school staff to administer glucagon or epinephrine auto injectors in emergency situations when a licensed health care practitioner is not available (§ 921; 8 NYCRR § 136.7(f)). Under provisions of the public health law, trained unlicensed individuals may administer epinephrine both to students with specific provider orders and to students and staff with symptoms of anaphylaxis regardless of previous history of severe allergic reaction (§921; Pub. Health Law § 3000-c; see **50:37**). Unlicensed staff may also administer opioid antagonists if the school district participates in an opioid overdose prevention program and they have been trained to do so pursuant to provisions of the public health law (§ 922(2), Pub. Health Law § 3309 see **50:33**).

Additionally, trained unlicensed staff may assist supervised students with self-administering medication at the direction of the student. Such assistance may include for example opening a bottle, assembling nebulizer tubing, or verifying that a student entered the number he or she intended into an insulin pump. If at any time the student cannot direct the unlicensed trained staff then the unlicensed staff may not proceed but must request a licensed school health professional to assist the student and report such incident pursuant to school policy (*Guidelines for Medication Management in Schools*).

However, only licensed health professionals can calculate insulin dosages, administer insulin, program an insulin pump, refill the reservoir, and change the infusion site for students with diabetes who use an insulin pump (§ 902-a; 8 NYCRR § 136.7(d)(6); see also *Guidelines for Medication Management in Schools*; NYS Education Department, Office of Student Support Services, *Clarification on Insulin Pumps* (Mar. 2012), at: http:www.p12.nysed.gov/sss/schoolhealth/schoolhealthservices/insulinpump.pdf).

School boards should establish a medication management policy in collaboration with school administrators and school health services personnel. Such policy should address for example written medication administration protocols and procedures including storage of medication, training of personnel and protocols for communication with students and parents (*Guidelines for Medication Management in Schools*).

50:31. Who is responsible for administering medication to students during school-sponsored events?

If a student is not independent and capable of self-administering medication and a school nurse or the student's parents are not available to do so, the parent may designate and authorize another adult such as a family member, household member, or friend to do so (§ 6908). Such designation should be in writing and kept by the school district in an easily accessible place (NYS Education Department, *Administration of Medication to Students During School-Sponsored Events by Parent/Guardian Designee* (Sept. 10, 2009), available with a sample designation form at: http://www.p12.nysed.gov/sss/schoolhealth/schoolhealthservices/fieldtrips.pdf; see also NYS Education Department, Office of Student Support Services, *Guidelines for Medication Management in Schools* (Sept. 2015), at: http://www.p12.nysed.gov/sss/documents/MedicationManagement-final2015.pdf).

A written order from a duly licensed prescriber, and written parental permission to administer medication (including nonprescription drugs) are required.

50:32. May a school district keep its own stock of prescribed medication in the health office?

School districts may maintain epinephrine auto injectors on site for use during emergencies in accordance with Public Health Law § 3000-c (§ 921; 8 NYCRR § 136.6(b)). In order to do so, a school district must have a collaborative agreement with an emergency health care provider and file such agreement with the regional emergency medical council (§ 921; 8 NYCRR § 136.6; Pub. Health Law §§ 3000-c, 3003). Districts which choose to maintain epinephrine auto injectors must have a sufficient amount available to ensure ready and appropriate access in emergencies taking into consideration the number of students, staff and other individuals expected to be within a facility, and the facility's physical layout (8 NYCRR § 136.6(b)).

School districts may also stock albuterol metered dose inhalers (MDIs) and/or liquid albuterol for use in a nebulizer for students diagnosed with asthma whose personal albuterol prescription is empty. Such stock may be maintained only pursuant to a written policy developed in collaboration with school health personnel that is approved by both the school district's medical director and school board and must be procured from a licensed pharmacy. However, students must have a patient-specific order for an albuterol MDI or for nebulized albuterol from their private health provider that includes an order permitting the student to use the school's stock in the event their prescription is empty, as well as written parental permission. Each student must have his or her own labeled spacer or tubing and face mask for delivery of the medication (see NYS Education Department, *New Policy for Stocking Albuterol Metered Dose Inhalers* (Aug. 2011), at: http://www.p12.nysed.gov/sss/schoolhealth/schoolhealthservices/Albuterol2011memo.pdf; see also NYS Education Department, Office of Student Support Services, *Guidelines for Medication Management in Schools* (Sept. 2015), at: http://www.p12.nysed.gov/sss/documents/MedicationManagement-final2015.pdf). Questions may be directed to the Office of Student Support Services at 518-486-6090.

School buildings located within the ten mile emergency planning zones of nuclear power plants are permitted to stock potassium iodide to protect the thyroid gland from injury related to the release of radioactive iodine in the environment. Administration of potassium iodide takes place only upon the direction of the local department of health during a declared state of emergency. Schools should annually provide written communication to parents regarding a potassium iodide program and provide the parent an opportunity to opt his or her child out of receiving potassium iodide during a radiological emergency (*Guidelines for Medication Management in Schools*; NYS Department of Health, *Potassium Iodide and Radiation Emergencies Fact Sheet* (revised Apr. 2011), at: https://www.health.ny.gov/environmental/radiological/potassium_iodide/fact_sheet.htm

50:33. May a school district stock and administer opioid antagonists to individuals exhibiting symptoms of an opioid overdose?

Yes, two options exist for stocking opioid antagonists. A school district's medical director may issue a non-patient specific order and protocol to authorize nurses to administer opioid-related overdose treatment (§§ 6527, 6909; NYS Department of Education, Office of Student Support Services, *Guidelines for Implementing Opioid Overdose Programs in Schools* (Aug. 2015), at: http://www.schoolhealthny.com/files/filesystem/guidance%20on%20opioid%20overdose%20prevention%20in%20the%20schools%20final.pdf and *Guidelines for Medication Management in Schools* (Sept. 2015), at: http://www.p12.nysed.gov/sss/documents/MedicationManagement-final2015.pdf). In such cases, the medical director in collaboration with the school administrators will acquire the naloxone (*Guidelines for Medication Management in Schools*).

School districts may elect to become a registered opioid overdose prevention program with the NYS Department of Health (§ 922; Pub. Health Law § 3309; 8 NYCRR 136.8; 10 NYCRR § 80.138; *Guidelines for Implementing Opioid Overdose Programs in Schools*; see also *Guidelines for Medication Management in Schools*). School districts choosing to participate in the opioid overdose prevention program must comply with the requirements of Public Health Law § 3309 including but not limited to appropriate clinical oversight, record keeping and reporting (8 NYCRR § 136.8(c)). For guidance on registering for the program, adopting appropriate policies and procedures, including amending district safety plans please refer to *Guidelines for Implementing Opioid Overdose Programs in Schools* and the NYS Department of Health website at: http://www.health.ny.gov/diseases/aids/general/opioid_overdose_prevention/schools.htm.

In determining quantities and placement of opioid antagonist to be maintained on site, consideration must be given to the number of students, staff and other individuals customarily within such facility and the physical layout of the facility (8 NYCRR § 136.8(d)). Districts with registered programs will receive a supply of naloxone from the NYS Department of Health (*Guidelines for Implementing Opioid Overdose Programs in Schools*).

50:34. May school districts keep a stock of over the counter medication in the health office to administer to students?

Schools that choose to purchase and stock over the counter medication must receive parental permission prior to administering any stock medication to a student (NYS Education Department, Office of Student Support Services, *Guidelines for Medication Management in Schools* (Sept. 2015), at: http://www.p12.nysed.gov/sss/documents/MedicationManagement-final2015.pdf).

50:35. Is sunscreen considered a medication that requires a medical provider order for use?

No. Education Law section 907 provides that students may carry and apply over the counter sunscreen to prevent over exposure to the sun while at school, provided a parent or guardian has provided written permission. If a child needs assistance applying the sunscreen, school staff may assist the child upon request if permitted by the parent or guardian and authorized by the school. A record of the written parental permission shall be maintained by the school (§ 907).

50:36. What are a school district's responsibilities regarding students with asthma and other respiratory diseases?

School districts and boards of cooperative educational services (BOCES) must permit students who have been diagnosed by a physician or a duly authorized health care provider with a severe asthmatic condition or other respiratory disease to carry and use a prescribed inhaler during the school day, with the written permission of a physician or a duly authorized health care provider and parental consent. The written permission must include an attestation from the physician or health care provider that:

- the pupil has been diagnosed with asthma or another respiratory disease for which inhaled rescue medications are prescribed to alleviate symptoms or to prevent the onset of exercise induced asthmatic symptoms;
- the pupil has demonstrated the ability to self-administer the medication effectively;
- name of the prescribed medication, the dose, and the time when medication is to be taken;
- explain the circumstances which may warrant the use of the medication; and
- the length of time for which the inhaler is prescribed (§ 916; 8 NYCRR § 136.7(b)).

The written permission should be maintained as part of the student's cumulative health record (*Id.*). Each student with asthma or another respiratory disease, who is permitted to self-administer inhaled rescue medication should have an emergency action plan on file with the school district (8 NYCRR § 136.7(a)(9), (b)(4)).

Upon parental request, such children also must be allowed to maintain an extra inhaler in the care and custody of a registered professional nurse employed by the district or BOCES. A record of this permission must be maintained in the school office (§ 916; 8 NYCRR § 136.7(b)(3)). A school district is not required to retain a licensed health professional solely for the purposes of taking custody of an extra inhaler or require that such staff be available at all times in school building for the purpose of taking custody of said supplies (*Id.*).

In addition, contingent upon a state budget appropriation for reimbursement of the associated costs, school districts must make available a nebulizer on site in every public or private school building where it provides nurse services for use by students with a patient-specific order who require inhaled medication administered by a nebulizer. The nebulizer must be administered by a school nurse or physician in accordance with the student's patient-specific order (§ 919). BOCES have the same responsibility with respect to programs under their jurisdiction (*Id.*).

50:37. What in general are a school district's responsibilities regarding allergy and anaphylaxis management and treatment?

School districts are required to consider and take action in response to the anaphylactic policy for school districts established by the NYS Department of Public Health in consultation with the NYS Education Department concerning the prevention of, and medical emergencies resulting from, anaphylaxis (Pub. Health Law § 2500-h; NYS Department of Health and NYS Education Department, *Making the Difference Caring for Students with Life Threatening Allergies* (2007), at: https://www.health.ny.gov/professionals/protocols_and_guidelines/docs/caring_for_students_with_life_threatening_allergies.pdf).

That policy includes, for instance, a procedure and treatment plan; a training course for appropriate school personnel; procedure and guidelines for the development of an individualized emergency health care plan for children with a food or other allergy which could result in anaphylaxis; and strategies for reducing the risk of exposure to anaphylactic causative agents, including food and other allergens (*Id.*).

Registered nurses may administer anaphylactic treatment agents (such as epinephrine) if there is a non-patient specific standing order and protocol authorized by a physician or a certified nurse practitioner in place as well as to a person with a patient specific order (§§ 902-b, 6527(6), 6909(4)(b), (5); see also NYS Education Department, Office of Student Support Services, *Guidelines for Medication Management in Schools* (Sept. 2015), at: http://www.p12.nysed.gov/sss/documents/MedicationManagement-final2015.pdf; NYS Education Department, Office of the Professions, *Non-Patient Specific Standing Order and Protocol Guidelines* (Jun. 2009), at: www.op.nysed.gov/prof/nurse/immunguide.htm). School districts may also choose to stock epinephrine auto injectors for use in emergency situations and train voluntary unlicensed personnel regarding administration of epinephrine to students and staff exhibiting symptoms of anaphylaxis regardless of whether or not there is a previous history of severe allergic reaction (§ 921; Pub. Health Law § 3000-c; 8 NYCRR § 136.6; *Guidelines for Medication Management in Schools*; see **50:30**). At the time this publication went to press, a bill passed by both houses of the Legislature, but awaiting action by the governor, would amend the public health law to define an epinephrine auto-injector device and require unlicensed volunteers to undergo a training course conducted by an organization approved by the commissioner of health (2016 Senate Bill S.6800).

50:38. May a student with an allergy carry his or her own epinephrine?

Yes, provided certain legal requirements are met. School districts and boards of cooperative educational services (BOCES) must permit students who have been diagnosed by a physician or a duly authorized health care provider with an allergy to carry and use prescribed epinephrine for emergency treatment of allergic reactions during the school day on school property and at any school functions with the written permission of a physician or a duly authorized health care provider and parental consent (§ 916-a(1); 8 NYCRR § 136.7(c)). The written permission must include an attestation from the physician or health care provider that:

- the pupil has been diagnosed with an allergy for which an epinephrine auto injector is needed for the emergency treatment of allergic reactions;
- the pupil has demonstrated the ability to self-administer the medication effectively;

- name of the prescribed medication, the dose, and the time when medication is to be taken;
- explain the circumstances which may warrant the use of the medication; and
- the expiration date of the order (§ 916-a(1); 8 NYCRR § 136.7(c)(1)).

The written permission should be maintained as part of the student's cumulative health record (§ 916-a(1); 8 NYCRR § 136.7(c)(2)). Each student with an allergy who is permitted to self-administer epinephrine should have an emergency action plan on file with the school district (8 NYCRR § 136.7(a)(9), (c)(4)).

Upon parental request, such children also must be allowed to maintain an extra epinephrine auto injector in the care and custody of a registered professional nurse employed by the district or BOCES. A record of this permission must be maintained in the school office (§ 916-a(1); 8 NYCRR § 136.7(c)(3)). A school district is not required to retain a licensed health professional solely for the purposes of taking custody of extra epinephrine auto injectors or require that such staff be available at all times in school building for the purpose of taking custody of said supplies (*Id.*).

50:39. What are a school district's responsibilities to students with diabetes?

School districts and boards of cooperative educational services (BOCES) must permit students who have been diagnosed by a physician or a duly authorized health care provider with diabetes to carry and use prescribed insulin through an appropriate medication delivery device, carry glucagon and carry and use equipment and supplies necessary to check blood glucose and/or ketone levels during the school day on school property and at any school functions with the written permission of a physician or a duly authorized health care provider and parental consent (§ 916-b(1), 8 NYCRR § 136.7(d)). The written permission must include an attestation from the physician or health care provider that:

- the pupil has been diagnosed with diabetes for which insulin and glucagon through appropriate medication delivery devices, and the use of equipment and supplies to check blood glucose and/or ketone levels are necessary;
- the pupil has demonstrated the ability to self-administer the medication effectively, can self-check glucose or ketone levels independently and can independently follow prescribed treatment orders;
- the prescribed blood glucose and/or ketone test and times testing is to be done;
- name of the prescribed medication, the dose or dose range of insulin the student is to self-administer and, the type of insulin delivery system and the times when insulin is to be administered and, the dose of glucagon that is to be administered;
- explain the circumstances which may warrant the use of the insulin or glucagon; and
- the expiration date of the order (§ 916-b(1); 8 NYCRR § 136.7(d)(1)).

Students

The written permission should be maintained as part of the student's cumulative health record (§ 916-b(1); 8 NYCRR § 136.7(c)(2)).

Each student with diabetes shall have a written diabetes management plan and an emergency action plan on file with the school district (8 NYCRR § 136.7(a)(9), (10), (d)(2), (5)). Students who cannot carry out the above activities independently will require assistance from the school nurse. In order to protect students from exposure to blood borne pathogens, school districts should ensure glucometers and other diabetes care equipment is not shared between people (NYS Education Department, Office of Student Support Services, *Blood Borne Pathogens in Classrooms* (Mar. 2014), at: http://www.p12.nysed.gov/sss/documents/bloodbornepathogenlettereducatorskhfinal.pdf).

Upon parental request, such children also must be allowed to maintain extra insulin, insulin delivery system, glucagon, blood glucose meter and related supplies in the care and custody of a registered professional nurse employed by the district or BOCES. Such medication and testing materials shall be readily accessible to the student as needed in accordance with school policy and the orders prescribed by the health care provider (§ 916-b(1); 8 NYCRR § 136.7(d)(3)). However, a school district is not required to retain a licensed health professional solely for the purposes of taking custody of extra insulin or diabetes supplies or require that such staff be available at all times in school building for the purpose of taking custody of said supplies (*Id.*).

Students with diabetes may also carry food, oral glucose and other substances necessary to treat hypoglycemia pursuant to district policy. District policies may not unreasonably interfere with a student's ability to treat hypoglycemia (§ 916-b(1); 8 NYCRR § 136.7(d)(4)).

50:40. May school districts test students for the use of illegal drugs?

Yes, but only upon the written request or consent of the child's parent or person in parental relation (§ 912-a(2); *Appeal of Studley*, 38 Ed Dept Rep 258 (1998); see also **53:31**). If parental authorization is obtained, the Education Law permits urine testing of students in grades 7–12 for detection of drug use (§ 912-a(1)). These tests must be conducted without notice to the student (§ 912-a(2)). If the test result indicates that the student is using drugs, the district must report such information to the local social services department and to the parent or person in parental relation, including a statement as to available programs and facilities to combat dangerous drug usage (*Id.*).

The test results may not be used for law enforcement purposes and must be kept confidential (§ 912-a(3)). The law also contains an exemption from testing based on religious considerations (§ 912-a(4)).

50:41. May school districts test students for the use of alcohol?

Although the commissioner of education has not answered this question directly, he has upheld the discipline of a student who attended a school-sponsored Senior Ball, was suspected of having consumed alcohol and was tested with an "Alco-sensor" (breathalyzer). In that case, the commissioner noted that the device had been borrowed from the town police on the day of the dance. In addition, the school official who administered the test had been trained in the use of the device, and had consulted with police officers before administering the test to make sure it was performed properly. Upon its return, the police checked the calibration of the device and found it to be accurate (*Appeal of James L.*, 39 Ed Dept Rep 482 (2000)). The commissioner similarly, upheld the discipline of another student who registered a .014 on a breathalyzer (*Appeal of E.B. and F.B.*, 53 Ed Dep Rep, Dec. No. 16,545 (2013)).

50:42. Are safety glasses required in school shops or lab courses?

Yes. School boards must provide that students and teachers participating in certain vocational, shop, and laboratory courses wear eye safety devices (§ 409-a(1); 8 NYCRR § 141.10(a)). This requirement also extends to visitors to such courses (§ 409-a(3); 8 NYCRR § 141.10(a)). School boards must also ensure eye safety devices are properly cleaned, repaired and stored (8 NYCRR § 141.10(d)).

50:43. Are school districts required to have automated external defibrillator (AED) equipment in their schools?

Yes. There must be AED equipment on site at each instructional school facility to ensure ready and appropriate access for use during emergencies (§ 917(1)). In addition, school districts must post a sign or notice at the main entrance to each facility or building where AED equipment is stored indicating their regular location (§ 917(3); Pub. Health Law § 3000-b(3)).

Each AED device must be approved by the Food and Drug Administration and be used according to the manufacturer's instructions (Pub. Health Law § 3000-b(3)(b); 8 NYCRR § 136.4(e)).

When determining the number of devices a school needs and where they should be placed, consideration shall be given to the number and ages of individuals in the building, the size and physical layout of the facility, types and locations of athletic, curricular, and extracurricular events and any unique design features of the building (§ 917(1); 8 NYCRR § 136.4(b)).

At least one staff member trained in the operation and use of an AED must be present whenever school facilities are used for school-sponsored or school-approved curricular or extracurricular events or activities and whenever a school-sponsored athletic contest is held at any location. School officials must ensure that AED equipment and a trained staff person are provided on-site whenever a school-sponsored competitive athletic event is held at a site other than a public school facility (§ 917(2); 8 NYCRR § 136.4(c), (d)).

In addition, certain school districts must instruct students on the correct use of an AED, as part of their high school health education curriculum (§ 804-d; see **55:36**).

50:44. What are a school district's responsibilities regarding a student who sustains a concussion while engaged in a school-sponsored athletic activity?

Any student who sustains, or is believed to have sustained, a mild traumatic brain injury (concussion), during such an activity must be removed immediately from the activity (§ 305(42)(a)(iii); 8 NYCRR § 136.5(d)(1)).

In addition, such a student may not resume athletic activity until he or she has been symptom free for a minimum of 24 hours and has been evaluated and received written authorization from a licensed physician, whether the injury was received in or out of school (§ 305(42)(a)(iiii); 8 NYCRR § 136.5(d)(2)). For renewed participation in extra class athletics the student must also receive clearance from the school district's medical director (8 NYCRR § 136.5(d)(2)). Such authorizations must be kept on file in the student's permanent health record. The district must follow any instructions received from the student's treating physician regarding limitations and restrictions on school attendance and activities (§ 305(42)(a)(iii); 8 NYCRR § 136.5(d)(2)(i), (ii)). Parental consent forms or permission slips for participation in interscholastic athletics must contain the definition of mild traumatic brain injury and how such injuries occur, information on the signs and symptoms of such injuries, and the state guidelines for return to activity after such an injury (§ 305(42)(a)(ii); 8 NYCRR § 136.5(c)(2)).

The NYS Department of Education (SED) and the NYS Department of Health (DOH) are required to post basic information regarding mild traumatic brain injuries on their respective websites (§ 305(42)(a)(ii); Pub. Health Law § 206(28)). Districts must post on their websites the same information or a reference on how to obtain such information from SED and DOH (8 NYCRR § 136.5(c)(3)).

50:45. Must school districts provide their staff with training on concussions?

Yes. School district and charter school coaches, physical education teachers, nurses, certified athletic trainers, who work with and/or provide instruction to students engaged in school-sponsored athletic activities must complete, on a biennial basis, a course of instruction relating to recognizing the signs and symptoms of concussion and seeking proper treatment for injuries (§ 305(42)(a)(i); 8 NYCRR § 136.5(b)(1); see also 8 NYCRR § 135.4(c)(7)(i)(c)(2)(iii), (c)(7)(i)(c)(3)(v); (c)(7)(i)(d)(2)(xi)(E)). The commissioner of education prescribes the content of such course, which must include the definition of mild traumatic brain injury, signs and symptoms of such injuries, how they occur, practices for prevention, and guidelines for the return to school and athletic activities by students who have suffered mild traumatic injury. Such instruction may be provided online or through a teleconference (§ 305(42)(a)(i); 8 NYCRR § 136.5(b)(2), (3)).

In addition, districts may establish a concussion management team composed of the athletic director, school nurse, school physician, a coach of an interscholastic team, an athletic trainer, or other appropriate personnel designated by the district (§ 305(42)(a)(iv); 8 NYCRR § 136.5(e)(1)-(2)). Such a team would be responsible for implementing the district's concussion management program. It also could establish a program for disseminating information on concussions to parents and persons in parental relation throughout each school year (§ 305(42)(a)(iv); 8 NYCRR § 136.5(e)(3)).

Student Employment

50:46. May students work while they attend school?

Yes. Students may work while they attend school, provided they obtain a valid employment certificate and do not work in excess of the number of hours prescribed by law (see §§ 3215–3228; Lab. Law § 132).

However, students may not work during the hours they are required to attend school (§ 3215(2), (3)), except that they may work in the school cafeteria during the school lunch period at the school they attend (§ 3215(4)(c)).

50:47. Are there any age restrictions that limit the ability of students to work while they attend school?

Yes. Students who work while they attend school must meet minimum age requirements prescribed for particular types of jobs and employment certificates. For example, students must be at least 11 to work as a newspaper carrier (§ 3228(1)). They must be at least 14 to work on a farm (§ 3226(1)), except that a student age 12 can work on a farm operated by his parents or guardians (§§ 3215(4)(e), 3226(2)).

50:48. How many hours may students work while they attend school?

The number of hours that students may work while they attend school varies depending on a student's age. For example, 14- and 15-year-old minors may not work:

- more than three hours on any school day;
- more than eight hours on any day when school is not in session;
- more than 18 hours per week, or no more than six days per week;
- after 7:00 p.m. or before 7:00 a.m. (Lab. Law § 142(1), (2)).

In comparison, 16- and 17-year-old minors may not work:

- more than four hours on any day preceding a school day other than on a Sunday or a holiday;
- more than eight hours on a Friday, Saturday, Sunday or holiday;
- more than 28 hours per week;
- more than six days a week and before 6:00 a.m. (Lab. Law § 143(1)).

However, a 17-year-old employed as a counselor, junior counselor, or counselor-in-training at a camp for children during the months of June, July and August is not limited in the number or hours they may work (Lab. Law § 143(4)).

Furthermore, employers who schedule minors who are 16 or 17 years old to work between 10:00 p.m. and midnight on any day preceding a school day must obtain written permission from the student's parent or guardian and a certificate from the school at the end of each marking period that indicates the student's academic performance is satisfactory, as measured by district standards (Lab. Law § 143(1)(e)). Those employing 16- and 17-year-olds between 10:00 p.m. and midnight on any day preceding a non-school day need only secure written permission from the student's parent or guardian (Lab. Law § 143(1)(f)).

50:49. Who is responsible for issuing student employment certificates?

Except in the case of child performers (see **50:53**), employment certificates and work permits are issued by the superintendent of schools, or his or her designee, or in New York City by the chancellor or his or her designee. In addition, a district superintendent or his or her designee may issue employment certificates to students attending classes operated by a board of cooperative educational services. In registered nonpublic secondary schools, the principal may issue an employment certificate (§ 3215-a(1)).

50:50. What must students do to obtain an employment certificate?

Students must apply for an employment certificate on a form prescribed by the commissioner of education (§ 3217(1)). Along with the application, they must submit:

- proof of age;
- written consent from their parent or guardian; and
- certification of physical fitness.

Students beyond compulsory education age also must submit their schooling record if they are applying for full-time employment. Similarly, in city school districts that require unemployed 16- and 17-year old students to remain in school, students must submit not only their school record but also a pledge of employment (§ 3217(2); see also §§ 3218–3222).

50:51. Does a student need a new employment certificate for each new job?

No, as long as the student continues employed in work permitted by the particular type of employment certificate he or she was issued (§ 3216(6)).

50:52. Can a student's employment certificate be revoked?

Yes. The school official who issued a student's employment certificate (see **50:49**) can revoke it for good cause, and if the student fails four or more courses in one semester (§ 3215-a(2)).

Such a determination should be based upon consideration of a student's overall academic performance and past academic record; attendance record, and the economic need of the student's family for the student's income. It also should be based on further consideration of the student's willingness to participate in work-study, school to work, or other structured programs that offer students the opportunity to earn income while earning academic credit, as well as other factors and materials submitted by the student (*Id.*).

However, nothing prevents a student from obtaining an employment certificate or permit to work during the months of July and August (*Id.*).

50:53. Are there any special rules that apply to employment certificates for child performers?

Yes. They are issued by the NYS Department of Labor and are valid for only one year from their date of issuance (Lab. Law § 151(1)(b); Arts and Cult. Affairs Law § 35.01(3)).

To renew an employment certificate, a child performer must show proof that he or she is receiving the required educational instruction and maintaining satisfactory academic performance (Lab. Law §§ 151, 152). A child performer must either attend full day instruction at school or be tutored by a certified teacher if his or her work schedule prevents regular school attendance (Lab. Law § 152(2)(a)). No child performer shall be declared absent from school while working with a permit in accordance with legal requirements. A child performer who is required by law to attend school shall not be without educational instruction and unemployed for a period of more than 10 consecutive days while the school where the child is enrolled is in session (Lab. Law § 152(3)).

50:54. Is it illegal to employ a student without a valid employment certificate?

Yes (§ 3215(2), (3); see *Provoncha v. Anytime Home Care, Inc.*, 15 A.D.3d 770 (3d Dep't), *lv. to app. denied,* 4 N.Y.3d 882 (2005); *Robles v. Mossgood Theatre-Saunders Realty*, 53 A.D.2d 972 (3d Dep't 1976)). However, students do not require an employment certificate for babysitting, caddying, shoveling snow, or other so-called casual employment (§ 3215(4); Lab. Law § 131(3)(a); 8 NYCRR § 191.1).

50:55. Are students employed without an employment certificate entitled to workers' compensation?

Yes. Section 14-a of the Workers' Compensation Law provides double compensation and death benefits for illegally employed minors and their beneficiaries. The employer alone, not the insurance carrier, is liable for the increased compensation or increased death benefits provided for by this section (see also *Provoncha v. Anytime Homecare Inc.*, 15 A.D.3d 770 (3d Dep't 2005)).

School Food Service Programs

Editor's Note: Pursuant to Section 305(41) of the Education Law, the commissioner of education is required to disseminate information on best practices that simplify access to free or reduced price meal programs and eliminate the distinction between students participating in these programs and students paying full prices so as to operate such programs more effectively.

50:56. May school districts operate and maintain a cafeteria?

Yes. School districts can provide, maintain, and operate a cafeteria or restaurant for the use of students and teachers while they are at school (§ 1709(22)). Expenses for cafeteria or restaurant services are ordinary contingent expenses (§ 2023(1)).

50:57. Are school districts required to operate a school breakfast program?

Some are. Under the federal Child Nutrition Act (42 USC § 1771 *et seq.*), school districts may apply for financial assistance to provide free and reduced price breakfast to children who meet eligibility requirements based on their family's income. But under New York Law and regulations certain school districts must operate a school breakfast program (L. 1976 c. 537; L. 1980 c. 798; L. 1993 c. 615 § 4; 8 NYCRR Part 114).

A city school district in a city with 125,000 inhabitants or more must participate in the school breakfast program. But it may apply to the commissioner of education to suspend the participation of a school in the program (8 NYCRR § 114.1(h)).

School districts with a severe need school also must provide students attending such facility the opportunity to receive a free, reduced and full paid breakfast (8 NYCRR § 114.1(i)(1)). A severe need school is one where 40 percent or more of the lunches served to students at the school in the second preceding school year were served free or at a reduced price, and in which the reimbursement rate per meal established by the U.S. Secretary of Agriculture is insufficient to cover the cost of a school breakfast program (8 NYCRR § 114.1(a)(2)).

Finally, all school districts must establish a school breakfast program for students attending grades kindergarten through six in an elementary school, or students in a comparable age range in an ungraded school, that participates in the National School Lunch Program (8 NYCRR § 114.1(a)(3), (4), (i)(2)).

At least three times a year, schools that participate in the National School Lunch, School Breakfast, Summer Food Services or Special Milk Programs with a free milk option must access information provided by the commissioner of education that helps identify students eligible to receive free meals and milk without further application based on their participation in certain federal financial assistance programs. Districts must notify the parents of students so identified and provide them the opportunity to opt out (Soc. Serv. Law § 95(7)(a)).

50:58. Can school districts be exempt from or terminate a school breakfast program?

Yes. School districts required to operate a school breakfast program (see **50:57**) may request an exemption from the commissioner of education based on lack of need for a breakfast program, economic hardship, or other good cause that makes operation of a breakfast program impractical. Parents and taxpayers must be made aware of a district's intent to request an exemption (8 NYCRR § 114.1(i)(3)–(8)).

In addition, no school district is required to operate a school breakfast program if the state terminates it own participation in the National School Breakfast Program, that program ceases to exist, or federal funding for the program is withdrawn for any reason whatsoever (L. 1976, c. 537 § 1(g)).

50:59. May school districts operate a school lunch program?

Yes, pursuant to a school board's authority to operate a school cafeteria for the use of students and teachers while at school (§ 1709(22)). In addition, all school districts can participate in the National School Lunch Program (42 USC § 1751 *et seq.*), which provides for free or reduced price lunches for children who meet eligibility requirements based on their family's income. However, certain children automatically qualify for a free lunch including, for example, children whose family receives food stamps or temporary assistance for needy families, or who are homeless, runaway or migrant children (see 42 USC § 1758(b)(2)(B)).

At least three times a year, schools that participate in the National School Lunch, School Breakfast, Summer Food Services or Special Milk Programs with a free milk option must access information provided by the commissioner of education that helps identify students eligible to receive free meals and milk without further application based on their participation in certain federal financial assistance programs. Districts must notify the parents of students so identified and provide them the opportunity to opt out (Soc. Serv. Law § 95(7)(a)).

School districts that operate a national school lunch or school breakfast program must ensure school nutrition program directors, managers and staff complete annual training/continuing education requirements (7 CFR § 210.31(e); see also U.S. Department of Agriculture, *Questions and Answers on Final Rule Professional Standards for State and Local School Nutrition Program Personnel as required by the Healthy Hunger Free Kids Act of 2010* (May 2016), at: http://www.fns.usda.gov/sites/default/files/cn/SP38-2016os.pdf; *Professional Standards for School Nutrition Program Employees Summary of Final Rule* (May 2015), at: http://www.fns.usda.gov/sites/default/files/cn/profstandards_flyer.pdf). Additionally, new school nutrition program directors hired after July 1, 2015 must meet certain education requirements which vary based upon school enrollment size (7 CFR § 210.31(b)).

50:60. Are school districts operating a school breakfast and/or lunch program required to adopt and implement a wellness policy?

Yes. School districts participating in the National School Lunch Program, School Breakfast Program, Special Milk Program and Summer Food Service Program must establish a local wellness policy for their schools (42 USC § 1758b).

At a minimum, the wellness policy must contain:

- Specific goals for nutrition promotion, education, physical activity, and other school-based activities designed to promote student wellness created after review and consideration of evidence based strategies and techniques.
- Standards for foods both available and sold in district schools during the school day. The standards for food sold must be consistent with regulatory requirements and promote student health and reduce childhood obesity.
- A plan for measuring implementation and effectiveness of the policy at least triennially, including the designation of at least one staff member charged with ensuring compliance with the policy.
- A description of how parents, students, representatives of the school food authority, the school board, school administrators, physical education teachers, school health professionals and the public will be given an opportunity to participate in the development, implementation and periodic review of the wellness policy (42 USC § 1758b(b); 7 CFR § 210.30).

A district must retain records to document its compliance with the requirements for establishing, implementing and assessing the local wellness policy (7 CFR § 210.30(f)). For further information on the wellness policy requirements, see U.S. Department of Agriculture's website at: www.fns.usda.gov/tn/local-school-wellness-policy, or contact the New York State School Boards Association Policy Services Department at 518-783-0200.

A school-based childhood obesity education program that emphasizes instruction on nutrition and physical activity is available from the NYS Department of Health as well as school based childhood obesity prevention and physical activity programs that promote health school environment and parent involvement (Pub. Health Law §§ 2599-b(2), 2599-c). That Department also is charged with the responsibility for periodically collecting and analyzing data from schools to determine the success of the program (Pub. Health Law § 2599-b(3)).

50:61. Are school districts required to establish a nutrition advisory committee?

No. However, they are encouraged to do so (§ 918). The committee may include, but not be limited to, a representative of the school board, food preparation and physical education department staff, the school nurse or health staff, a registered dietitian, if available, district faculty, parent-teacher associations, students, and students' parents (§ 918(c)).

The nutrition advisory committee could study all facets of the current nutritional policies of the district (§ 918(4)). It also would report to the school board on an annual basis regarding the status of the implementation of district programs to improve student nutritional awareness and healthy diet (§ 918(6)). In addition, the committee could report periodically on practices that will educate teachers, parents or guardians and children about healthy nutrition and raise awareness of the dangers of obesity (§ 918(5)).

50:62. Are school meals subject to sales tax?

Sale of food and drink to students on school premises are exempt from taxation. However, sale of food and drink to adults is subject to sales tax (Tax Law § 1105(d)(ii)(B)).

50:63. May a school district employ students to work in its food-service program?

Yes. Children at least 14 years old may be employed in a school's food-service program if the student presents a valid employment certificate (Lab. Law §§ 131(3)(g), 132(3)(c); see **50:46-55**).

50:64. May school districts employ a food-service management company to operate their breakfast and lunch programs?

Yes. School districts may contract with a private food-service management company for the purpose of managing and operating, in whole or in part, its food-service program (7 CFR § 210.16(a); 8 NYCRR § 114.2). But the food-service program remains the legal responsibility of the school district (7 CFR § 210.9; 8 NYCRR § 114.2(a)).

Employees of the food service management company are subject to federal training and continuing education requirements for all workers employed to work in programs participating in the national school lunch program and school breakfast program. The school district must request documentation that the employees are receiving appropriate training. If the current contract between the school district and the food-service management company does not provide for such monitoring a contract amendment will be necessary (7 CFR § 210.31(e); U.S. Department of Agriculture, *Questions and Answers on Final Rule Professional Standards for State and Local School Nutrition Program Personnel as required by the Healthy Hunger Free Kids Act of 2010* (May 2016), at: http://www.fns.usda.gov/sites/default/files/cn/SP38-2016os.pdf).

Any contract with a food-service management company may not exceed one year and must conform to the commissioner's regulations (8 NYCRR § 114.2(c), (d)). In addition, the contract must be awarded to the lowest responsible bidder. Under certain circumstances, the competitive bidding requirement does not apply to certain extensions of a contract (§ 305(14)(a); 8 NYCRR § 114.2(c), (g)). Furthermore, all food-service management company contracts must be reviewed and approved by the commissioner of education, including annual extensions of contracts (§ 305(14)(a); 8 NYCRR § 114.2(d)(1), (g)).

If contracting is being considered and the school district is subject to the terms of a collective bargaining agreement, the proposal may have to be negotiated with the bargaining unit (see **47:18**).

50:65. Do school districts contracting with a food-service management company remain eligible for reimbursement of funds expended in their breakfast and lunch programs?

Yes. Where a school district contracts with a private food-service management company, it nonetheless remains eligible to receive both federal and state reimbursement and food, in the same way it does for school-operated programs, provided the requirements in the commissioner's regulations are observed (8 NYCRR § 114.2).

50:66. Are school districts eligible to receive federally donated surplus foods and price-support commodities for their breakfast and lunch programs?

Yes. Schools participating in the National School Lunch and Breakfast programs are eligible to receive such food available for distribution (42 USC § 1777; 7 USC § 1431). However, schools must pay the transportation costs for trucking the goods from the district warehouse to the school. In addition, the cost of warehousing is prorated on the basis of the number of case lots allocated to the school. This charge is made once a year and deducted from the claim for reimbursement. The NYS Office of General Services, Bureau of Government Donated Foods, handles the operation of the Commodity Distribution Program.

50:67. Can school districts be reimbursed for meals served to preschool students?

Yes. School districts are eligible to be reimbursed for meals that meet the standards of the lunch meal pattern served to preschool children in school-sponsored classes, just as they are for meals provided to other school children, provided funds are not available from other sources to meet this need (see L. 1976, c. 537 § 1(a), (d)).

50:68. May a school district make its cafeteria facilities available for meals to community groups such as parent-teacher associations?

Yes, if permission is granted by the school board. Section 1709(22) of the Education Law permits use of the cafeteria by the community for school related functions and activities and to furnish meals to the elderly residents of the district who are 60 years of age and older.

It is recommended that a school cafeteria employee be available to ensure that facilities and equipment are used properly. The agency or group using the facilities should compensate this employee.

School districts should establish rules and regulations concerning, for example, the personnel to be involved, the number of activities during the year it is permissible for personnel to be involved in, and other pertinent matters (§ 414).

50:69. Are school district cafeteria and food-service programs subject to sanitation rules and regulations and food safety inspections?

Yes. Federal regulations require all schools to abide by all state and local laws and regulations for proper sanitation and health (7 CFR § 210.13(a); see 10 NYCRR Subpart 14-1).

Furthermore, schools participating in the National School Lunch or School Breakfast Programs must obtain at least two food safety inspections each school year (42 USC § 1758(h)(1)). The inspections must be conducted by a State or local government agency responsible for food safety inspections. Schools must post, in a publicly visible location, a report on the most recent food safety inspection. They also must provide a copy of that report to members of the public upon request (*Id.*).

In addition, during the preparation and service of meals, school food authorities must comply with Hazard Analysis and Critical Control Point (HACCP) principles established by the U.S. Secretary of Education (42 USC § 1758(h)(5)).

50:70. Are school districts required to provide information about the hazards of food choking?

Yes. School districts are required to provide parents educational materials on food choking hazards, precautions, and life-saving procedures, but only to the extent such materials are made available to districts by the NYS Department of Health, contingent on appropriations made for this purpose (Pub. Health Law § 2500-i).

51. Student Safety

Release from School

51:1. May school districts release students from school to someone other than the student's parent?

Yes, if the identity of the person requesting the release is verified against a list of names provided by the student's parent or person in parental relation at the time of the child's enrollment in the school. A school district may adopt procedures for submitting such a list at a later date or updating a list previously provided (§ 3210(1)(c)).

If someone whose name is not on the list attempts to obtain the release of a student, that student may not be released, except in the case of an emergency as determined in the sole discretion of the principal or his or her designee (*Id.*; see **51:2**).

According to the commissioner of education, the unauthorized release of a student "involves serious issues of health and safety." It may constitute grounds for termination (*Appeal of Greene*, 45 Ed Dept Rep 519 (2006); see also *Chalen v. Glen Cove Sch. Dist.*, 29 A.D.3d 508 (2d Dep't), *lv. to app. denied*, 7 N.Y.3d 709 (2006); *Heberling v. Brewster CSD*, 2012 NY Misc. Lexis 2168 (N.Y. Sup. Ct. 2012)).

51:2. Under what circumstances can a school release a student to someone whose name is not on a list previously provided by the student's parent?

A school can release a student to someone whose name is not on a list previously provided by the student's parent or person in parental relation only in case of an emergency. No situation will be deemed an emergency until the principal or his or her designee verifies the facts of the situation, contacts the student's parent or person in parental relation, and the student's parent or person in parental relation agrees to the release. This procedure, however, does not apply to the release of a student under the protective custody provisions of the Social Services Law and the Family Court Act (§ 3210(1)(c)).

51:3. May a school district release a student from school to a non-custodial parent if the student's parents are separated or divorced?

It depends. A school district may presume that either parent of a student has authority to obtain the child's release. However, a student may not be released to a non-custodial parent if the district has been provided with a certified copy of a legally binding instrument, such as a court order or decree of divorce, separation, or custody, that indicates the non-custodial parent does not have the right to obtain such release (§ 3210(1)(c)).

Missing Children

51:4. What are a school district's responsibilities toward missing children?

A school district with notice that the Division of Criminal Justice Services (CJS) has listed as missing in the statewide register for missing children a child currently or previously enrolled in one of its schools must take the following steps:

- Flag the school records of that child, in a manner that alerts a person authorized to provide access to such records that the child has been reported as a missing child, and remove such flag upon notice from CJS that the child has been recovered.
- Immediately report to the local law enforcement authority and CJS any requests concerning such records or knowledge as to the whereabouts of any missing child (§ 3222(4)).
- Immediately notify CJS if it discovers that the child is currently enrolled in one of its schools (§ 3222(5)).

51:5. How are school districts notified that a child is officially listed as missing?

The commissioner of the Division of Criminal Justice Services (CJS) is required to regularly give the NYS Education Department (SED) a bulletin with information about the children listed in the statewide register for missing children. SED, in turn, forwards the bulletin to every public and private school where parents, guardians, or others legally responsible for such missing children have given consent (Exec. Law § 837-f(10); see also Exec. Law § 837-e).

The CJS commissioner also must cooperate with public and private schools to develop education and prevention programs for communities, parents and children on child safety; operate a toll-free, 24-hour hotline for the public to use to relay information concerning missing children; and provide assistance to local agencies in the investigation of these cases (Exec. Law § 837-f(5), (8), (11)).

51:6. Must school districts provide instruction designed to prevent the abduction of children?

Yes. All students in kindergarten through eighth grade must receive instruction designed to prevent the abduction of children. Such instruction must be provided by, or under the direct supervision of, a regular classroom teacher unless it is provided by another public or private agency (§ 803-a(1)).

School districts must provide appropriate training and curriculum materials for those teachers who provide the instruction (§ 803-a(4)).

51:7. Is there a state curriculum for abduction prevention courses?

No. However, abduction prevention courses must be age appropriate and developed according to the needs and abilities of students at successive grade levels. They must provide awareness skills, information, self-confidence, and support to aid in the prevention of child abduction (§ 803-a(2)).

When developing an abduction prevention curriculum, school districts may establish a local advisory council, or use the school-based shared decision-making and planning committee, to obtain recommendations concerning the content and implementation of such course of study. A local advisory council must include, at least, parents, school board members, appropriate school personnel, business and community representatives, and law enforcement personnel having experience in the prevention of child abduction (§ 803-a(3)).

Alternately, school districts may use courses of instruction developed by other school districts, boards of cooperative educational services, or any other public or private agency (*Id.*).

Abused and Maltreated Children

51:8. Are school districts required to report cases of suspected child abuse or maltreatment ?

Yes. School officials including, but not limited to teachers, guidance counselors, school psychologists and social workers, school nurses, administrators, or other school personnel required to hold a teaching or administrative license or certificate and an employee required to hold a temporary coaching license or professional coaching certificate, are *mandated reporters* required to make a report to child protective services when they have reasonable cause to suspect a student is abused or maltreated (Soc. Serv. Law § 413(1); *Matter of Kimberly S.M. v. Bradford Cent. Sch.*, 226 A.D.2d 85 (4th Dep't 1996); *Diana G-D v. Bedford CSD*, 33 Misc.3d 970 (Sup. Ct. Westchester Cnty. 2011), *aff'd*, 104 A.D.3d 805 (2d Dep't 2013)). However, a mandated reporter is not required to report a case of suspected child abuse or maltreatment, if the reporter knows that the alleged abuser cannot be the subject of a report under the law. The law requires reports regarding only parents or other persons legally responsible for a child who commit or allow to be committed an act of abuse against the child (*Appeal of Catherine G. v. Essex County*, 3 N.Y.3d 175 (2004)). Nonetheless, when in doubt, mandated reporters should err on the side of caution and make a report (*Id.*).

Additionally, persons who are not mandated reporters also may make such a report if they have reasonable cause to suspect child abuse or maltreatment (Soc. Serv. Law § 414).

The identity of persons making a report is confidential and may not be disclosed (*Deleon v. Putnam Valley Bd. of Educ.*, 228 F.R.D. 213 (2005)).

51:9. Are mandated reporters protected from liability for reporting cases of suspected child abuse or maltreatment?

It depends. The law provides immunity from liability for mandated reporters who make such a report in good faith (Soc. Serv. Law § 419; see also *Cox v. Warwick Valley CSD*, 654 F.3d 267 (2d Cir. 2011); *Biondo v. Ossining UFSD*, 66 A.D.3d 725 (2d Dep't 2009)).

However, it is a crime to knowingly report a false claim of child abuse or maltreatment to the State Central Register (Penal Law § 240.50(4)(a)). It is also a crime to knowingly report a false claim of child abuse or maltreatment to a mandated reporter knowing that person is required to report such cases and intending that such a report be made (Penal Law § 240.50(4)(b)).

51:10. When must cases of suspected child abuse or maltreatment be reported?

Mandated reporters (see **51:8**) must report immediately cases of suspected child abuse or maltreatment whenever a child, or the child's parent, guardian or other person responsible for the child appears before the mandated reporter in the reporter's professional or official capacity and provides the reporter with information from personal knowledge that, if correct, would render the child an abused or maltreated child (Soc. Serv. Law § 413(1)).

A mandated reporter with reasonable cause to suspect child abuse must make the required report even if the identity of the person legally responsible for the child's care or the identity of the abuser is unknown. The obligation to report is based upon facts and circumstances within the knowledge of the reporter at the time the abuse is suspected (*Matter of Kimberly S.M. v. Bradford Cent. Sch.*, 226 A.D.2d 85 (4th Dep't 1996)).

51:11. What procedures must school staff follow when reporting cases of suspected child abuse or maltreatment?

Mandated reporters (see **51:8**) must first make the report to the Statewide Central Register for Child Abuse and Maltreatment and then immediately notify the head of the school (Soc. Serv. Law §§ 413(1)(b); 415). The report must include the name, title, and contact information for every staff member believed to have direct knowledge of the allegation (*Id.*).

Upon receiving notice that a mandated report has been made, the head of the school, or a designated agent, will become responsible for all subsequent administration required by the report (*Id.*). The head of the school also shall take or cause to be taken, at public expense, color photographs of visible trauma and, if medically indicated, cause to be performed an X-ray examination of the child (Soc. Serv. Law § 416).

Reports of suspected child abuse or maltreatment must be made by telephone or fax on a form supplied by the commissioner of the NYS Office of Children and Family Services. Oral reports must be made to the statewide central register of child abuse and maltreatment, unless an appropriate local plan provides these reports should be made to the local child protective service. The local child protective service would then make a report to the statewide central register. An oral report must be followed by a written report within 48 hours (Soc. Serv. Law § 415).

The hotline telephone number to report a case of suspected abuse or maltreatment is 800-342-3720. An additional hotline telephone number for school administrators and teachers to report suspected abuse or maltreatment is 800-635-1522.

51:12. What obligations does a school district have to assist child protective workers investigating a report of child abuse or maltreatment?

School districts have a responsibility to provide assistance and data to enable local child protective service (CPS) employees to carry out their investigations (Soc. Serv. Law § 425(1)). This includes providing access to records relevant to the investigation and allowing CPS to conduct an interview of such child without parent consent or court order when CPS encounters circumstances that warrant interviewing the child apart from family or other household members or the home or household where child abuse or maltreatment allegedly occurred (18 NYCRR § 432.3(i); see also **53:38**). School personnel may observe the interview (*Id.*).

School districts may require CPS workers and those who accompany them to comply with reasonable visitor policies and procedures of the school and to present appropriate identification (*Id.*).

51:13. Can school districts impose conditions on mandated reporters regarding the making of a child abuse and maltreatment report?

No. Schools and school officials may not impose any conditions, including prior approval or prior notification, upon a member of their staff who is a mandated reporter (see **51:8**) specifically required to report suspected child abuse and maltreatment (Soc. Serv. Law § 413(1)(c)).

Similarly, schools may not take any adverse employment action against employees who believe they have reasonable cause to suspect that a child is abused or maltreated and make a report in accordance with the child abuse or maltreatment reporting law (*Id.*).

51:14. What happens if school officials fail to report cases of suspected child abuse or maltreatment?

The Social Services Law provides legal penalties for failure to report cases of suspected child abuse, including liability for damages proximately caused by such failure (Soc. Serv. Law § 420).

51:15. Are school districts required to maintain policies regarding mandatory reporting of suspected child abuse or maltreatment?

Yes. School districts must develop, maintain, and disseminate written policies and procedures on mandatory reporting of child abuse or neglect; reporting procedures and obligations of persons required to report; provisions for taking a child into protective custody; mandatory reporting of deaths; immunity from liability; penalties for failure to report; and obligations for providing services and procedures necessary to safeguard the life or health of a child (§ 3209-a).

Additionally, beginning in January 2017 all public and charter schools must post in English and Spanish the toll free number for reporting child abuse and neglect as well as directions for accessing the Office of Children and Family Services website (§ 409-l). The commissioner of education must adopt regulations relating to this posting requirement (*Id.*).

51:16. Must school districts train staff on child abuse and maltreatment reporting requirements?

Yes. Every district must establish and maintain a training program for all current and new school employees regarding its policies and procedures on mandatory reporting of cases of suspected child abuse or maltreatment (§ 3209-a). Failure to provide adequate training would subject a school district to liability (see *Biondo v. Ossining UFSD*, 66 A.D.3d 725 (2d Dep't 2009)).

Districts employing mandated reporters (see **51:8**) must provide all such current and new employees with written information explaining the reporting requirements (Soc. Serv. Law § 413(2)).

Training materials on *Identifying and Reporting Child Abuse and Maltreatment/Neglect* are available from the NYS Office of Children and Family Services at: www.nysmandatedreporter.org. Information on training is also available by calling 1-800-836-0903 ext. 218.

51:17. What responsibilities do school districts employing mandated reporters of suspected child abuse or maltreatment have regarding the identification of methamphetamine laboratories?

School districts that employ mandated reporters of suspected child abuse or maltreatment (see **51:8**) who, in the normal course of their employment, visit children's homes must provide all such current and new employees information on recognizing the signs of an unlawful methamphetamine laboratory (Soc. Serv. Law § 413(4)). Therefore, school districts should identify staff members who routinely visit children's homes as part of their responsibility. They also should develop reporting procedures for instances that are required to be reported.

A brochure entitled *How to Recognize the Signs of a Clandestine Methamphetamine Laboratory* issued by the NYS Office of Alcoholism and Substance Abuse Services (OASAS) is at: http://www.ocfs.state.ny.us/main/publications/Pub5076.pdf. OASAS is the agency responsible for making available statewide information about the dangers of methamphetamine production and how to report suspected methamphetamine laboratories (Soc. Serv. Law § 413(4)).

Additional staff development is available from the staff development coordinator at the local Department of Social Services, and from the NYS Office of Children and Family Services, which can be reached at 518-473-7793.

Child Abuse in an Educational Setting

51:18. Are school districts required to report cases of suspected child abuse in an educational setting?

Yes. The Education Law requires that school districts report to law enforcement authorities allegations of child abuse in an educational setting by a district employee or volunteer (Article 23-B).

The term *child abuse* refers to the intentional or reckless infliction of physical injury, serious physical injury, or death, as well as conduct that creates a substantial risk of such injuries or death. It also includes any child sexual abuse as defined under sections 130 or 263 of the Penal Law, and the dissemination of or attempts to disseminate obscene materials to minors under article 235 of the Penal Law (§ 1125(1), (9)).

The term *educational setting* means the buildings and grounds of a public school district, vehicles used to transport students to and from school, and field trips, co-curricular and extracurricular activities, as well as sites where those activities take place. It also includes any other location where direct contact occurs between students and employees or volunteers (§ 1125(5)).

The law provides immunity from civil liability to school personnel who reasonably and in good faith comply with their responsibilities under the child abuse in an educational setting reporting requirements (§§ 1126(3), 1128(4), 1133(3)).

Special act school districts, state supported and state operated schools have additional responsibilities to protect the students with disabilities they serve pursuant to the Protection of People with Special Needs Act (Chapter 501 of the Laws of 2012; 8 NYCRR § 200.15 see also www.justicecenter.ny.gov).

51:19. What are the specific reporting duties of school personnel regarding allegations of child abuse in an educational setting?

Teachers, school nurses, guidance counselors, school psychologists and social workers, administrators, school board members, or other school personnel required to hold a teaching or administrative license must promptly file a written report with the school principal upon receipt of any oral or written allegation of child abuse in a educational setting (§ 1126(1)). The law does not define what is meant by promptly. However, the commissioner of education has indicated that the word promptly reflects legislative intent that "expedited action" occur regarding these reports. Thus actions must occur within hours or days and not months after the incidents (*Appeal of a Student with a Disability*, 49 Ed Dept Rep 93 (2009)).

If it is determined that there is reasonable suspicion to believe that an act of child abuse has occurred, the school principal must take additional steps which differ depending on who has made the allegation, and who it was made to. For example, parents must be notified of the allegation if it comes from someone other than them. In cases where reasonable suspicion exists, parents must be provided a written statement that sets forth parental rights, responsibilities and procedures to be followed. Appropriate law enforcement officials must be notified without delay (§ 1128; 8 NYCRR § 100.2(hh)(1); *Appeal of S.S.*, 42 Ed Dept Rep 273 (2003)). If, following an investigation, it is determined that there is no reasonable suspicion to believe that an act of child abuse had occurred, there is no obligation to notify law enforcement authorities, or to provide parents with a written statement setting forth parental rights, responsibilities and procedures (§ 1128; *Appeal of S.S.*).

Where the alleged child abuse occurred outside the district of attendance, the report must be submitted to the superintendent of both the district of attendance and the district where the abuse allegedly occurred. In this case, both superintendents are responsible for contacting law enforcement authorities without delay and for taking other actions required by law (§§ 1126(2), 1128).

In addition, a school superintendent must refer to the commissioner of education any report of child abuse in an educational setting forwarded to law enforcement authorities, when an employee or volunteer alleged to have committed such act holds a certification or license issued by the NYS Education Department (§ 1128-a(1)).

51:20. Are there any penalties for failure to comply with the child abuse in an educational setting reporting requirements?

Yes. Willful failure to comply with the child abuse in an educational setting reporting requirements constitutes a class A misdemeanor. The failure to contact law enforcement authorities is also punishable by a civil penalty of up to $5,000 (§ 1129).

51:21. Are school districts excused from reporting to law enforcement authorities allegations of child abuse in an educational setting if the employee or volunteer involved agrees to resign?

No. The law expressly prohibits school districts from agreeing to withhold from law enforcement authorities the fact that an allegation of child abuse in an educational setting has been made in exchange for the resignation or voluntary suspension of the employee or volunteer against whom the allegation is made (§ 1133(1)).

Such an agreement constitutes a Class E felony that is also punishable by a civil penalty of up to $20,000 (§ 1131(2)).

51:22. Are reports concerning allegations of child abuse in an educational setting confidential?

Yes. Such reports and other written materials submitted, as well as any photos taken in connection with allegations of child abuse in an educational setting, that are held by a person authorized to receive such information is confidential. They can be re-disclosed only to law enforcement authorities investigating the allegations, or pursuant to a court-ordered subpoena, or as otherwise expressly authorized by law (§ 1127), as in the case of the employee or volunteer who is the subject of a child abuse in an educational setting report (§ 1131(4)).

Such reports must be expunged from district records five years after the date of its making if, after investigation, they do not result in a criminal conviction. They may be expunged earlier, in the district's discretion (§ 1128-a(2)).

The willful re-disclosure of such materials to persons not authorized to receive or review them constitutes a Class A misdemeanor (§ 1127).

51:23. Must law enforcement officials notify school districts of the results of investigations regarding allegations of child abuse in an educational setting?

Yes. The district attorney must notify school districts of any indictment or filing of an accusatory instrument against an employee or volunteer involved in a child abuse in an educational setting report. The district attorney also must inform school districts as to the disposition of a criminal case, or the suspension or termination of an investigation (§ 1130).

In addition, the district attorney must notify the commissioner of education of any criminal conviction. Upon receipt of such information, the commissioner must conduct an investigation into the good moral character of the individual (§ 1131).

51:24. Must school districts train employees and board members on their duties regarding child abuse in an educational setting?

Yes. School districts must establish and implement on an ongoing basis a training program regarding the law on child abuse in an educational setting for all current and new teachers, school nurses, school counselors, school psychologists, school social workers, school administrators, other personnel required to hold a teaching or administrative certificate or license and school board members (§ 1132(2); 8 NYCRR § 100.2(hh)(2); see also *Application of the Bd. of Educ. of the City School Dist. of the City of Elmira*, 49 Ed Dept Rep 363 (2010)).

The program must include, at a minimum, training on the duties of all school personnel; confidentiality of records; penalties for failure to comply with the law; notification by the district attorney of the results of investigations; action taken upon conviction of a licensed or certified employee; and the prohibition against silent resignations (8 NYCRR § 100.2(hh)(2)).

In addition, school districts must provide, annually, to each teacher and all other school officials a written explanation of the reporting requirements including the immunity provisions (8 NYCRR § 100.2(hh)(3)).

Sex Offender Registration Act ("Megan's Law")

51:25. What is the Sex Offender Registration Act?

The Sex Offender Registration Act (commonly referred to as "Megan's Law") is a law that requires convicted sex offenders to register with the Division of Criminal Justice Services (CJS) upon discharge, parole, or release (Corrections Law § 168 *et seq.*). Based on the recommendations of a Board of Examiners of Sex Offenders, convicted sex offenders will be designated either as "sex predators," "sexually violent offenders" or "predicate sex offenders" and assigned to one of three risk classifications, depending on the level of risk of repeat offenses. A level one designation means the risk of repeat offense is deemed low, a level two a moderate risk, and a level three a high risk (Corrections Law § 168-l(6)). The risk level designation determines the extent of public notification of their return to the community (Corrections Law §§ 168-a(7), 168-l(6)).

51:26. Are school districts automatically notified of the release of a sex offender into their school community?

No. However, local law enforcement agencies are, and they may release relevant information about a level one, level two, or level three sex offender (see **51:25**) to any entity, including a school district, that has vulnerable populations related to the nature of the offense committed by such sex offender (Corrections Law § 168-l(6)).

Information on level two and level three sex offenders is also available to school districts on the website of the Division of Criminal Justice Services at: http://criminaljustice.ny.gov/.

The U.S. Court of Appeals for the Second Circuit with jurisdiction over New York has upheld the community notification provisions of the state's Sex Offender Registration Act (*Doe v. Pataki*, 120 F.3d 1263 (2d Cir. 1997), *cert. denied*, 522 U.S. 1122 (1998)).

Students

51:27. What kind of information can law enforcement agencies release about sex offenders re-entering a community?

Law enforcement agencies may disseminate to the public, and school districts, the following information about level two and level three sex offenders (see **51:25**):

- a photograph and description of the offender, including the exact name and any aliases used by the sex offender;
- address;
- background information including the sex offender's crime of conviction, modus of operation, type of victim targeted;
- the name and address of any institution of higher education at which the sex offender is enrolled, attends, is employed or resides; and
- a description of any special conditions imposed on the offender (Corrections Law § 168-l(6)(b), (c)).

Current law requires sex offenders to list only their primary address. At the time this publication went to press, a bill passed by both houses of the Legislature, but awaiting action by the governor, would require registered sex offenders to notify the Division of Criminal Justice Services (DCJS) if they maintain more than one residence (2016 Assembly Bill A.1819). Another bill, also awaiting action by the governor, would require DCJS to notify local law enforcement within 48 hours upon receipt of a change of address from a registered sex offender (2016 Assembly Bill A.9239).

51:28. Can school districts redisclose information they receive under the Sex Offender Registration Act?

Yes. Under the law, any entity, including a school district, that receives information on a sex offender may disclose or further disseminate such information at its discretion (Corrections Law § 168-l(6)(b), (c)).

In addition, any agency and agency officials and employees have immunity from civil or criminal liability for any decision on their part to release what they believe to be relevant and necessary information about sex offenders, unless they act with gross negligence or in bad faith. They also enjoy immunity for any failure to release such information, unless they acted with gross negligence or in bad faith (Corrections Law § 168-r). However, the knowing simulation or dissemination of a purportedly official notice that falsely suggests an individual is a registered sex offender constitutes a class A misdemeanor (Penal Law § 240.48).

51:29. Are there any restrictions on the ability of sex offenders to enter school grounds?

Yes. Level three sex offenders and persons convicted of enumerated sex offenses where the victim was under age 18 (see **51:25**) placed on conditional release or parole are prohibited from knowingly entering upon school grounds or other facilities where children are cared for, while one or more persons under the age of 18 are present. The prohibition is a mandatory condition of release (Penal Law § 65.10(4-a); Exec. Law § 259-c(14)). School grounds is defined to include any building, structure, athletic field or land contained within the boundaries of a school and any area accessible to the public within 1000 feet of the boundary line, including any parked motor vehicle (Penal Law § 220.00(14); Exec. Law § 259-c(14)). The law has the effect of prohibiting sex offender parolees from living within 1000 feet of a school (*People v. Diack*, 24 N.Y.3d 674 (2015); *Williams v. Dep't of Corrections and Community Supervision*, 136 A.D.3d 147 (1st Dep't 2016); see also **64:16**).

However, the prohibition does not extend automatically to, for example, a sentenced offender who is a registered student or has a family member enrolled in a school, if the sex offender's parole officer and the superintendent of schools agree in writing to permit entry upon school grounds for the limited purposes authorized by the parole officer and the superintendent (Penal Law § 65.10(4-a); Exec. Law § 259-c(14)).

Similarly, level two and level three offenders will be found guilty of criminal trespass in the second degree if they knowingly enter the school attended or formerly attended by the victim of the offense for which they are registered as a sex offender. Exceptions apply, however, if the registered level two or level three offender is a lawfully registered student at the school, a lawful participant in a school-sponsored event, or the parent or legal guardian of a student lawfully registered at the school and enters the school to attend that student's event or activity. Other exceptions apply if the school is the offender's designated polling place and he or she enters solely to vote, or the offender enters the school for limited purposes authorized by the superintendent of schools or chief school administrator (Penal Law § 140.15(2)).

Harassment of Students[1]

51:30. What responsibilities does a school district have to protect students from harassment and bullying under federal law?

Federal law requires school districts as recipients of federal funds to protect students from harassment and bullying on the basis of race, color, national origin, ethnic group, religion, disability, gender, sex, and sexual orientation (42 USC § 2000d et seq.; 29 USC § 794; 34 CFR Pt. 104; 20 USC §§ 1681-1688; 34 CFR Pt. 106; 28 CFR Pt. 54). Additionally, the Americans with Disabilities Act prohibits disability discrimination by public entities regardless of whether they receive federal financial assistance (42 USC § 12131-12134; 28 CFR Pt. 35; see also U.S. Department of Education, Office of Civil Rights, *Dear Colleague Letter* (Oct. 21, 2014), at: http://www2.ed.gov/about/offices/list/ocr/letters/colleague-bullying-201410.pdf).

School districts that do not adequately address harassment based on race, color, national origin, ethnic group, religion, disability, gender, sex and sexual orientation such that a hostile environment is created will be in violation of these civil right statutes and regulations. Harassment creates a hostile environment when the conduct is sufficiently severe, pervasive, or persistent so as to interfere with or limit a student's ability to participate in or benefit from the services, activities, or opportunities offered by a school (U.S. Department of Education, Office of Civil Rights, *Dear Colleague Letter* (Oct. 26, 2010), at: http://www2.ed.gov/about/offices/list/ocr/letters/colleague-201010.pdf).

51:31. Can school districts be liable for the racial harassment of students by other students?

Yes, under Title VI of the Civil Rights Act of 1964, which prohibits discrimination on the basis of race, color or national origin in programs and activities operated by recipients of federal funds, including school districts (42 USC § 2000d; *Zeno v. Pine Plains Cent. Sch. Dist.*, 702 F.3d 655 (2012); see also *T.E. v. Pine Bush CSD*, 58 F.Supp.3d 332 (2014)).

That was the case where a high school student was repeatedly harassed at school for over four years, including being called a "nigger" in hallways, death threats in class and bathrooms and an attempted assault with a chair in the cafeteria. Repeated reports to district administrators regarding these types of incidents were made by the student, his mother as well as district staff. The student graduated with an IEP diploma instead of staying in school to try to satisfy the requirements for a Regents diploma because of the harassment. According to the court, despite disciplining the many students who had harassed the student, the district failed to timely implement any non-disciplinary remedial action, for example, including racial sensitivity training for students. According to the court, responses that are not reasonably calculated to end the harassment are inadequate and that it was reasonable to conclude the district ignored the signals that greater, more directed action was necessary (*Zeno v. Pine Plains Cent. Sch. Dist.*).

Under Title VI anti-Semitic harassment and discrimination has been found to amount to racial discrimination (*T.E. v. Pine Bush CSD*; see also Office of Civil Rights, *Dear Colleague Letter* (Oct. 26, 2010), at: http://www2.ed.gov/about/offices/list/ocr/letters/colleague-201010.pdf). A federal court refused to dismiss a case against a school district where Jewish students allegedly suffered such harassment including name calling (e.g. "dirty Jew," "filthy Jew," and "ashes"), students chanting white

Students

[1] *School districts should be aware of their obligation to adopt and implement policies and code of conduct provisions that prohibit discrimination and harassment of students, including bullying and cyberbullying, by school employees or other students on school property or at a school function on the basis of race, color, weight, national origin, ethnic group, religion, religious practice, disability, gender, sex or sexual orientation, in conformity with New York's Dignity for All Students Act and commissioner's regulations (§§ 10-15; 8 NYCRR § 100.2(l); see also* **51:40-45***).*

power songs and performing Hitler salutes, and witnessed swastika graffiti throughout the school and in textbooks (*T.E. v. Pine Bush CSD*).

51:32. What responsibilities do school districts have to guard against harassment and bullying based on disability?

Section 504 of the Rehabilitation Act of 1973 (29 USC § 7904; 34 CFR § Pt. 104) and Title II of the Americans with Disabilities Act (42 USC § 12131-12134; 28 CFR Pt. 35) both prohibit discrimination on the basis of disability. Therefore, school districts have a responsibility to ensure students with disabilities are not subjected to a hostile environment such that their ability to participate in or benefit from the services, activities or opportunities offered by a school is negatively affected.

The bullying of a student with a disability on any basis, not just his or her disability, can result in a denial of a free appropriate public education (FAPE) and must be remedied (U.S. Department of Education, Office of Civil Rights, *Dear Colleague Letter* (Oct. 21, 2014), at: http://www2.ed.gov/about/offices/list/ocr/letters/colleague-bullying-201410.pdf; see also *T.K. v. New York City Dep't of Educ.*, 779 F.Supp.2d 289 (E.D.N.Y. 2011), 32 F.Supp.3d 405 (E.D.N.Y. 2014), *aff'd*, 810 F.3d 869 (2d Cir. 2016); see **54:22**).

51:33. What responsibilities do school districts have to prevent harassment and bullying based on sex, gender and sexual orientation?

Title IX of the 1972 Educational Amendments broadly provides that no person shall be excluded from participation in, be denied the benefits of, or be subjected to discrimination under any education program or activity receiving federal financial assistance (20 USC § 1681 et seq.). In the context of harassment, Title IX prohibits sex-based harassment by peers, employees, or third parties that is sufficiently serious to deny or limit a student's ability to participate in or benefit from a district's education programs and activities. Such harassment creates a hostile environment. Title IX prohibits several types of sex based harassment including sexual harassment, sexual violence and gender based harassment. Sexual harassment is unwelcome conduct of a sexual nature such as sexual advances. Sexual violence refers to physical sexual acts perpetrated against a person's will or where a person lacks capacity to give consent. Lastly, gender based harassment refers to unwelcome conduct based on an individual's actual or perceived sex, including harassment based on gender identity or nonconformity with sex stereotypes (U.S. Department of Education, Office for Civil Rights, *Title IX Resource Guide* (April 2015), at: http://www2.ed.gov/about/offices/list/ocr/docs/dcl-title-ix-coordinators-guide-201504.pdf).

For additional information on school district responsibilities to prevent and remedy instances of sexual harassment in schools under Title IX of the 1972 Educational Amendments, see U.S. Department of Education, Office for Civil Rights Dear Colleague letters and fact sheets at: http://www2.ed.gov/about/offices/list/ocr/letters/colleague-201104.html (Apr. 4, 2011) and http://www2.ed.gov/about/offices/list/ocr/letters/colleague-201010.html (Oct. 26, 2010).

51:34. Must school districts adopt policies and designate a person to oversee its compliance with Title IX?

Yes. School districts must designate at least one employee as Title IX coordinator (34 CFR § 106.8(a); see also U.S. Dep't of Education, Office of Civil Rights, *Dear Colleague Letter*, (April 24, 2015), at: http://www2.ed.gov/about/offices/list/ocr/letters/colleague-201504-title-ix-coordinators.pdf). The coordinator must investigate any complaint filed alleging violations of Title IX. A school district must notify all students and staff of the name, office address, and telephone number of the Title IX coordinator (*Id.*). The school district must also adopt and publish grievance procedures students and staff may utilize to file complaints regarding violations of Title IX (34 CFR § 106.8(b)).

Additionally, school districts must notify students and parents of elementary and secondary students that it does not discriminate on the basis of sex in the educational programs or activities which it operates, and that it is required by Title IX not to discriminate in such a manner. The notification must also state that the prohibition against discrimination based on sex extends to employment and admission into the district as well and that inquiries should be referred to the Title IX coordinator (34 CFR § 106.9).

51:35. Does Title IX protect transgender students from harassment and bullying?

The Office for Civil Rights at the U.S. Department of Education has issued a *Dear Colleague* letter explaining that Title IX prohibits discrimination based on a student's gender identity, which includes a student's transgender status (U.S. Dep't of Education, Office of Civil Rights, *Dear Colleague Letter* (May 13, 2016), at: http://www2.ed.gov/about/offices/list/ocr/letters/colleague-201605-title-ix-transgender.pdf). Along with the *Dear Colleague Letter*, the department released a guidance outlining policies and practices for supporting transgender students (see U.S. Department of Education, Office of Safe and Healthy Schools, *Examples of Policies and Emerging Practices for Supporting Transgender Students* (May 2016), at: http://www2.ed.gov/about/offices/list/oese/oshs/emergingpractices.pdf).

Additional protection is provided to transgender students under New York's Dignity for All Students Act (N.Y. Education Law Art. 2; see also **51:40**).

51:36. Can a school district be held liable for the sexual harassment of students by teachers?

Yes, under Title IX of the 1972 Educational Amendments, which prohibit discrimination on the basis of sex in all education programs and activities operated by recipients of federal funds, including school districts (20 USC § 1681 *et seq.*; *Franklin v. Gwinnett Cnty. Pub. Sch.*, 503 U.S. 60 (1992); *Papelino v. Albany Coll. of Pharmacy of Union Univ.*, 633 F.3d 81 (2d Cir. 2011)).

However, damages may not be recovered unless an official of the district who has authority to institute corrective measures on the district's behalf has actual notice of, and is deliberately indifferent to, the teacher's misconduct (*Fitzgerald v. Barnstable Sch. Comm.*, 555 U.S. 246 (2009); *Gebser v. Lago Vista Indep. Sch. Dist.*, 524 U.S. 274 (1998); see also *Baynard v. Malone*, 268 F.3d 228 (4th Cir. 2001), *cert. denied, Baynard v. Alexandria City Sch. Bd.*, 122 S. Ct. 1357 (2002); *Doe v. Sch. Bd. of Broward Cnty.*, 604 F.3d 1248 (11th Cir. 2011); *Doe v. Flaherty*, 623 F.3d 577 (8th Cir. 2010)). Accordingly, in one case, a school district was deemed not liable under Title IX for a teacher's sexual relationship with a student because the student and teacher went to extensive and elaborate lengths to hide the relationship from school officials, family and friends. Although a few rumors among students existed concerning the relationship, rumors alone did not constitute actual knowledge sufficient to impose liability (*Romero v. City of N.Y.*, 839 F. Supp.2d 588 (E.D.N.Y. 2012)).

51:37. Can a school district be held liable for the sexual harassment of students by other students?

Yes, under Title IX of the 1972 Educational Amendments, which prohibit discrimination on the basis of sex in all education programs and activities operated by recipients of federal funds, including school districts (20 USC § 1681 *et seq.*; *Davis v. Monroe Cnty. Bd. of Educ.*, 526 U.S. 629 (1999)). However, the harassment must have occurred at a location under the school district's control (*Davis v. Monroe Cnty. Bd. of Educ.*; see also *T.Z. v. City of N.Y.*, 634 F. Supp.2d 263 (E.D.N.Y. 2009)). In addition, such liability also depends on whether the harassment was "so severe, pervasive and objectively offensive" that it denied the victim equal access to education; an appropriate person at the district had "actual knowledge" of the discrimination or harassment; and the district, which has the authority to take remedial action against the harasser, acted in a deliberately indifferent manner (*Davis v. Monroe Cnty. Bd. of Educ.*; *T.Z. v. City of N.Y.*; *K.F. v. Monroe-Woodbury CSD*, 2012 U.S. Dist. LEXIS 60341 (S.D.N.Y. Apr. 30,

2012); *Tyrell v. Seaford UFSD*, 792 F. Supp.2d 601 (E.D.N.Y. 2011); *Pratt v. Indian River CSD*, 803 F. Supp.2d 135 (N.D.N.Y. 2011)).

A school acts with deliberate indifference where it fails to act in a timely and reasonable way to end harassment, or acts in a way which could not have reasonably been expected to remedy the situation (*Davis v. Monroe Cnty. Bd. of Educ.*; see also *K.F. v. Monroe-Woodbury CSD*; *Tesoriero v. Syosset CSD*, 382 F. Supp.2d 387 (E.D.N.Y. 2005)). That was the case when a fifth-grade female student alleged she was repeatedly sexually harassed by a 10-year-old male student in her class over a five-month period; she and her parents made repeated reports of the harassment to her teacher and school administrators; her grades dropped as a result of the harassment; and the school district never once disciplined the male student harasser even though he pled guilty to sexual battery for his misconduct (*Davis v. Monroe Cnty. Bd. of Educ.*; compare *Sauerhaft v. Bd. of Educ.*, 2009 U.S. Dist. LEXIS 46196 (S.D.N.Y. June 1, 2009), *aff'd*, 371 Fed. Appx 231 (2d Cir. 2010)).

Furthermore, a single incident of physical sexual assault could be sufficient to support a Title IX student on a student sexual harassment claim if it has the effect of denying the victim access to educational benefits and opportunities (*T.Z. v. City of N.Y.*; see also *M. v. Stamford Bd. of Educ.*, 2008 U.S. Dist. LEXIS 51933 (D. Conn. July 7, 2008), *decision vacated in part on reconsideration on other grounds*, 2008 U.S. Dist. LEXIS 67988 (D. Conn. Sept. 9, 2008)).

Moreover, according to one federal appellate court outside New York, a school district can be held liable for student-on-student sexual harassment under Title IX even if it has addressed each individual incident of harassment brought to its attention. That was the case where the harassment went on for a period of four years and even though at some point the district's standard response became clearly ineffective and unreasonable, the district did not change those methods (*Patterson v. Hudson Area Sch.*, 551 F.3d 438 (6th Cir.), *cert denied*, 558 U.S. 880 (2009); see also **68:13**).

51:38. Is Title IX of the 1972 Educational amendments the only source of potential school district liability for the sexual harassment of students?

No. School districts may also face liability for student-on-student sexual harassment pursuant to an action brought under section 1983 of the Civil Rights Act of 1876 (42 USC § 1983; see **29:29-41**). Such an action also could include a claim alleging a violation of Title IX and/or a violation of the Equal Protection Clause of the Fourteenth Amendment to the U.S. Constitution which prohibits, among other things, gender discrimination. According to the United States Supreme Court, the enforcement procedures contained within Title IX were not meant to be the exclusive remedies for Title IX violations (*Fitzgerald v. Barnstable Sch. Comm.*, 555 U.S. 246 (2009)).

51:39. Can school districts be held liable for harassment against students under the New York State Human Rights Law?

No. The NYS Division of Human Rights responsible for enforcing New York's Human Rights Law lacks jurisdiction to investigate complaints brought by students against school districts based on alleged discriminatory harassment arising under that law (*Matter of North Syracuse CSD v. NYS Div. of Human Rights*, 19 N.Y.3d 481 (2012)).

Dignity For All Students Act (DASA)

51:40. How does DASA affect student safety in school?

DASA seeks to "afford all students in public schools an environment free of discrimination and harassment," to "foster civility" and "prevent and prohibit conduct inconsistent with a school's educational mission" (§ 10). The Act protects all students attending public schools in New York state, including charter schools, by prohibiting harassment and bullying by employees or students on school property or at a school function (§ 12). It further bars discrimination based on actual or perceived race, color, weight, national origin, ethnic group, religion, religious practice, disability, sexual orientation, gender or sex (§ 12; 8 NYCRR § 100.2(kk)(1)(vii)). Gender is defined as "a person's actual or perceived sex and includes a person's gender identity or expression" (§ 11(6)). As such DASA affords transgender students protection from harassment and discrimination. The State Education Department has issued guidance for school districts to assist in creating safe and supportive school environments for transgender and gender nonconforming students (see NYS Education Department, *Guidance to School Districts for Creating Safe and Supportive Environment for Transgender and Gender Nonconforming Students* (July 2015), at: http://www.p12.nysed.gov/dignityact/documents/Transg_GNCGuidanceFINAL.pdf).

For purposes of DASA, school property includes any building, structure, athletic playing field, playgrounds, parking lot or land contained within the real property boundary line of a public elementary or secondary school or in or on a school bus (§ 11(1); 8 NYCRR § 100.2(kk)(1)(i); see also Veh. and Traf. Law § 142). A school function is a school-sponsored extracurricular event or activity (§ 11(2); 8 NYCRR § 100.2(kk)(1)(ii)).

According to one state supreme court, DASA also imposes on school districts a responsibility to take action when public school students engage in cyberbullying a student attending a private school (*Simon v. Bellmore-Merrick Central High Sch. Dist.*, slip opinion J. Feinman (Nassau Cnty. May 14, 2014) *rev'd on the grounds*, 133 A.D.3d 557 (1st Dep't 2015)).

51:41. How are harassment, bullying and discrimination defined under DASA?

Harassment and bullying are defined as the creation of a hostile environment by conduct or by threats, intimidation, or abuse, including cyberbullying, that:

- Has or would have the effect of unreasonably and substantially interfering with a student's educational performance, opportunities or benefits, or mental, emotional or physical well-being; or
- Reasonably causes or would reasonably be expected to cause a student to fear for his or her physical safety; or
- Reasonably causes or would reasonably be expected to cause physical injury or emotional harm to a student; or
- Occurs off school property and creates or would foreseeably create a risk of substantial disruption within the school environment, where it is foreseeable that the conduct, threats, intimidation or abuse might reach school property (§ 11(7); 8 NYCRR § 100.2(kk)(1)(viii)).

Threats, intimidation and abuse include verbal and non-verbal actions (§ 11(7); 8 NYCRR § 100.2(kk)(1)(viii)(d)). Acts of harassment and bullying include but are not limited to, acts based on a person's actual or perceived race, color, weight, national origin, ethnic group, religion, religious practice, disability, sexual orientation, gender or sex (8 NYCRR § 100.2(kk)(1)(viii)(d)).

51:42. What are a school district's obligations under DASA?

School boards and boards of cooperative educational services (BOCES) must adopt policies and procedures intended to create a school environment free from harassment, bullying and discrimination. As part of the policies and procedures the district or BOCES must:

- designate an employee to receive and investigate reports of harassment, bullying and discrimination,
- require all school employees who witness or receive reports of bullying, harassment or discrimination to orally notify the designee within one school day and file a written report within two school days,

- enable students and parents to make oral or written reports of prohibited conduct to teachers, administrators and other school personnel deemed appropriate,
- prohibit retaliation against any individual who, in good faith, reports or assists in the investigation of harassment, bullying or discrimination,
- take appropriate corrective action when a report is verified,
- include a strategy to prevent harassment, bullying and discrimination,
- require school personnel to promptly notify the appropriate law enforcement agency when any harassment, bullying or discrimination constitutes criminal conduct (§§ 13(1), 16; 8 NYCRR § 100.2(kk)(2), (4)).

At least one staff member at each school must be appointed as the DASA coordinator, who shall be provided with specialized training in harassment, bullying and discrimination as required by DASA (§ 13(3); 8 NYCRR § 100.2(jj)(4)). Additionally, the school district is responsible for developing guidelines to be used in employee training programs that raise awareness and sensitivity to potential harassment, bullying and discrimination and enable employees to prevent and respond to these behaviors (§ 13(2); 8 NYCRR § 100.2(jj); see also NYS Education Department, Office of School Innovation, *Dignity for all Students Act Guidance for Local Implementation* (Updated July 2013), at: http://www.p12.nysed.gov/dignityact/documents/DASAGuidanceLocalImplementation.pdf; *Guidance to School Districts for Creating a Safe and Supportive School Environment for Transgender and Gender Nonconforming Students* (July 2015), at: http://www.p12.nysed.gov/dignityact/documents/Transg_GNCGuidanceFINAL.pdf).

The district must also amend its code of conduct to be in conformance with the act, distribute to all school employees, students and parents either a written or electronic copy of the policies created or amended under the act and maintain current versions of the policy or policies on the school district's website (§ 13(1)(k), (l); see **52:2** and **52:6**; see also *Dignity for all Students Act Guidance for Local Implementation*).

For additional guidance on reporting incidents under DASA and model training materials see NYS Office of the Attorney General and NYS Education Department, *Dignity for All Students Act: Results of Statewide School District Survey and Guidance on Implementation* (Aug. 2016) at: https://ag.ny.gov/sites/default/files/dasa_-_dear_colleague_letter_oag-sed_guidance_document.pdf and *Dignity for All Students Act Requirements for Schools* (*Tool for Training School Employees*) at: https://ag.ny.gov/sites/default/files/dasa_training_materials_final_-_8.30.16.pdf.

51:43. What actions must a school district or board of cooperative educational services (BOCES) take upon receiving a complaint of bullying, harassment or discrimination?

A thorough investigation of all reports of conduct prohibited under the act must be promptly completed after a complaint is received. If the investigation verifies the occurrence of harassment, bullying or discrimination the district must promptly take actions reasonably calculated to end the behavior, create a more positive school culture and climate, prevent recurrence of the behavior and ensure the safety of students subjected to such conduct (§ 13(1)(d), (e); 8 NYCRR § 100.2(kk)(2); see also NYS Office of the Attorney General and NYS Education Department, *Dignity for All Students Act: Results of Statewide School District Survey and Guidance on Implementation* (Aug. 2016) at: https://ag.ny.gov/sites/default/files/dasa_-_dear_colleague_letter_oag-sed_guidance_document.pdf; NYS Education Department, Office of School Innovation, *Dignity for all Students Act Guidance for Local Implementation* (Updated July 2013), at: http://www.p12.nysed.gov/dignityact/documents/DASAGuidanceLocalImplementation.pdf).

However, the commissioner found a school district that leased space to a BOCES was not required to initiate an independent or parallel investigation regarding a complaint of sexual assault lodged by a student attending the BOCES program. The alleged incident occurred in a leased classroom staffed exclusively by BOCES personnel and serving students in a BOCES program (*Appeal of a Student with a Disability*, 54 Ed Dept Rep, Dec. No. 16,780 (2015)).

Actions to ensure the safety of a student may include the assignment of a monitor to accompany a student in the hallways between classes and to sit with the student in classrooms and on the bus. The commissioner of education found this to be a valid method of addressing bullying, and upheld the discipline of a student who refused to cooperate with the monitor assigned to ensure the student's safety (*Appeal of A.V and S.A-V.*, 53 Ed Dept Rep, Dec. No. 16,528 (2013)).

51:44. What reporting requirements does DASA impose on school districts and BOCES?

The law imposes two reporting requirements. All material incidents of harassment, bullying, and/or discrimination must be reported to the commissioner on an annual basis (§ 15; 8 NYCRR § 100.2(kk)(3)). A material incident is a single verified incident or series of verified incidents where a student is subjected to harassment, bullying, and/or discrimination by a student or employee on school property or at a school function or such conduct that occurs off school property but creates or foreseeably creates a substantial disruption within the school environment and it is foreseeable that the conduct, threats or intimidation might reach school property (§ 15; 8 NYCRR § 100.2(kk)(1)(ix)).

The following information must be reported with respect to each material incident:

- the type of bias involved,
- whether the incident resulted from student and/or employee conduct,
- whether the incident involved physical contact and/or threats, intimidation or abuse, including cyberbullying and,
- the location where the incident occurred (8 NYCRR § 100.2(kk)(3)(iii)).

Additionally, the principal must provide a regular report on data and trends related to harassment, bullying, and/or discrimination to the superintendent, at least once a year, in a manner prescribed by district policy (8 NYCRR § 100.2(kk)(2)(vi)).

51:45. Are school districts subject to liability for violations of DASA?

Students

DASA itself only states that it does not "[p]reclude or limit any right or cause of action provided under any local, state or federal ordinance, law or regulation including but, not limited to any remedies or rights available under the Individuals with Disabilities Education Act, Title VII of the Civil Rights Law or 1964, section 504 of the Rehabilitation Act of 1973 or the Americans with Disabilities Act of 1990." In addition, the Record of Proceedings involving the adoption of DASA include a statement by one legislator that "[t]he bill does not address any remedy beyond internally to the school" (N.Y. Bill Jacket, 2010 A.B. 3661, Ch. 482).

However, a decision by one state supreme court suggests that school districts may be subject to liability for violations of DASA. In that decision, the court relied on DASA's broadly worded intent to "afford all students in public schools an environment free of discrimination and harassment," to "foster civility" and "prevent and prohibit conduct inconsistent with a school's educational mission" (§ 10), to determine that DASA protections extend to private school students who are subject to cyber bullying by public school students (*Simon v. Bellmore-Merrick Central High School Dist.*, 2014 WL 11189280 (Sup. Ct. Nassan Cnty., May 14, 2014) Feinman J; *rev'd on other grounds*, 133 A.D.3d 557 (1st Dep't 2015)).

In contrast, a federal district court has found that DASA does not establish a private right of action citing the bill's legislative history that DASA's intent is preventative rather than punitive. Moreover, the federal court found the holding in *Simon* to be a narrow one requiring a school district to make efforts to protect a private school student from cyberbullying by public school students and further noted that the parties in *Simon* did not brief the issue of a private right of action (*Terrill v. Windham-Ashland-Jewett CSD*, 2016 U.S. Dist. LEXIS 42904 (N.D.N.Y. Mar. 31, 2016)). Similarly, a state appellate court determined that DASA does not explicitly grant a private right of action and to imply such a right would not further the legislative purpose or comport with the statutory scheme (*Motta v. Eldred CSD*, slip opinion, (3d Dep't July 7, 2016)).

52. Student Discipline

Codes of Conduct

Editor's Notes: For information on special rules applicable to the discipline of students with disabilities, see **chapter 54**. *For information on a school district's obligation to administer student discipline without discriminating on the basis of race, color, or national origin, see the U.S. Department of Education and the U.S. Department of Justice* Dear Colleague Letter, *dated Jan. 8, 2014, at: www2.ed.gov/about/offices/list/ocr/letters/colleague-201401-title-vi.html.*

52:1. Must a school district adopt a code of conduct?

Yes. All school districts, boards of cooperative educational services, and county vocational extension boards must adopt and enforce a code of conduct for the maintenance of order on school property and at school functions. The code must govern the conduct of students, teachers, other school personnel, and visitors (§ 2801(2); 8 NYCRR § 100.2(l)(2)(i)).

The code must be reviewed annually and updated if necessary, taking into consideration the effectiveness of the code, and the fairness and consistency of its administration (§ 2801(5); 8 NYCRR § 100.2(l)(2)(iii)(a)). It also must be filed with the commissioner of education, in a manner prescribed by the commissioner, no later than 30 days after adoption of the code or revisions to the code (*Id.*).

For purposes of a code of conduct, the term *school property* means in or within any building, structure, athletic playing field, playground, parking lot or land contained within the real property boundary line of a public school (§ 2801(1)). It also means in or on a school bus, whether owned and operated by a district or by a carrier a district contracts with for the transportation of its students (*Id.*; Veh. & Traf. Law § 142; *Appeal of M.H.*, 43 Ed Dept Rep 210 (2003)).

In connection with a code of conduct, the term *school function* refers to a school-sponsored or school-authorized extra-curricular event or activity regardless of where such event or activity takes place, including any event or activity that may take place in another state (§ 2801(1)).

Commissioner's regulations applicable to the development and adoption of a code of conduct (8 NYCRR § 100.2) incorporate relevant requirements imposed on school districts by New York's Dignity for all Students Act (DASA) (§§ 10-18) that are also integrated within pertinent portions of this chapter. For additional information, see NYS Education Department, *Amended Dignity for all Students Act Student Discrimination, Harassment and Bullying Prevention and Intervention Guidance for Updating Codes of Conduct* (June 2013), at: http://www.p12.nysed.gov/dignityact/documents/DASACodeofConductGuidance.pdf.

Further guidance on the implementation of other components of DASA is available at: http://www.p12.nysed.gov/dignityact/.

52:2. Are there any specific requirements regarding the contents of a district's code of conduct?

Yes. At a minimum, a code of conduct must include the following (8 NYCRR § 100.2(l)(2)(ii)):

- Provisions regarding conduct, dress and language that is deemed both appropriate and acceptable, and inappropriate and unacceptable, on school property and at school functions; and acceptable civil and respectful treatment of teachers, school administrators, other school personnel, students and visitors on school property and at school functions; as well as the appropriate range of disciplinary measures which may be imposed for code violations, and the roles of teachers, administrators, other school personnel, the school board and parents.

- Provisions prohibiting harassment, bullying and/or discrimination by staff or students against any student on school property, at a school function or off school property under certain circumstances as described in the commissioner's regulations that creates a hostile environment by conduct or by threats, intimidation or abuse, including cyberbullying, that rises to the level of severeness identified in commissioner's regulations.
- Standards and procedures to assure the security and safety of students and school personnel.
- Provisions for the removal of students and other persons who violate the code from the classroom, school property, and school functions.
- The period for which a disruptive student may be removed from a classroom for each incident, subject to the provisions of § 3214(3-a)(c) of the Education Law.
- Disciplinary measures for incidents on school property or at school functions involving the possession or use of illegal substances or weapons, the use of physical force, vandalism, violation of another student's civil rights and threats of violence.
- Disciplinary measures to be taken for incidents on school property or at school functions involving harassment, bullying, and/or discrimination.
- Provisions for responding to acts of discrimination and harassment by staff or students against students on school property or at a school function that incorporates a progressive model of student discipline as described in the commissioner's regulations.
- Provisions for the detention, suspension, and removal of students from the classroom, and the establishment of policies and procedures to ensure the provision of continued educational programming and activities for such students including alternative educational programs appropriate to individual student needs.
- Procedures for reporting and determining violations of the code and for imposing and carrying out disciplinary measures.
- Provisions for ensuring the code and enforcement of the code comply with state and federal laws relating to students with disabilities.
- Procedures for notifying parents of code violations, and local law enforcement agencies of code violations that may constitute a crime.
- The circumstances and procedures for filing a complaint in criminal court, and a juvenile delinquency or person in need of supervision petition in family court; and for making referrals to appropriate human service agencies.
- A student bill of rights and responsibilities that focuses on positive student behavior and a safe and supportive school climate that must be written in plain language, publicized and explained in an age-appropriate manner to all students annually.
- Guidelines and programs for in-service education programs for all district staff to ensure effective implementation of the code, including, but not limited to, guidelines on promoting a safe and supportive school climate while discouraging, among other things, harassment, bullying and/or discrimination against students by staff or other students, and including safe and supportive school climate concepts in the curriculum and classroom management.
- The minimum suspension period for violent students and students who repeatedly are substantially disruptive of the educational process or substantially interfere with the teacher's authority over

the classroom. This minimum suspension period may be reduced on a case-by-case basis to be consistent with any other state and federal law.

- A provision prohibiting retaliation against any individual who, in good faith, reports or assists in the investigation of harassment, bullying, and/or discrimination.

52:3. Who must be deemed a student who repeatedly is substantially disruptive of the educational process or substantially interferes with a teacher's authority over the classroom under a district's code of conduct?

For purposes of a school district's code of conduct, a student who *repeatedly is substantially disruptive of the educational process or substantially interferes with the teacher's authority over the classroom* is one who engages in conduct that results in the removal of the student from the classroom by a teacher on four or more occasions during a semester, or three or more occasions during a trimester, as applicable (§ 2801(2)(l); 8 NYCRR § 100.2(l)(2)(ii)(p)).

52:4. Who must be deemed a violent pupil under a district's code of conduct?

For purposes of a school district's code of conduct, a *violent pupil* refers to an elementary or secondary school student under age 21 who:

- commits an act of violence upon a teacher, administrator, or other school employee; or who while on school property does so upon another student or any other person lawfully there;
- while on school property possesses a gun, knife, explosive or incendiary bomb, or other dangerous instrument capable of causing physical injury or death, or displays what appears to be the same;
- while on school property threatens to use any instrument that appears capable of causing physical injury or death; or
- knowingly and intentionally damages or destroys district property or the personal property of a teacher, administrator, other school district employee or any person lawfully on school property (§§ 2801(2)(m), 3214(2-a)(a)).

52:5. Is there a process school districts must follow to adopt or revise their code of conduct?

Yes. The code must be developed in collaboration with student, teacher, administrator, and parent organizations; and school safety and other school personnel (§ 2801(3); 8 NYCRR § 100.2(l)(2)(i)). In addition, the code must be reviewed annually and updated if necessary, taking into consideration the effectiveness of code provisions and the fairness and consistency of its administration (§ 2801(5); 8 NYCRR §100.2(l)(2)(iii)(a)). Districts may establish a committee comprised of similar individuals to facilitate review of the code (§ 2801(5)(a); 8 NYCRR § 100.2(l)(2)(iii)(a)).

School boards and boards of cooperative educational services may adopt the code or revisions to the code of conduct only after at least one public hearing that provides for the participation of school personnel, parents, students, and other interested parties (§ 2801(3), (5); 8 NYCRR § 100.2(l)(2)(i), (iii)(a)). Districts must file their code of conduct and any revisions thereto with the commissioner of education within 30 days of adoption (§ 2801(5)(a); 8 NYCRR § 100.2(l)(2)(iii)(a)).

In New York City, the chancellor of the city school district approves a city-wide code of conduct and any revisions thereto. Community district education councils may adopt and implement additional policies consistent with the city-wide code of conduct, subject to approval by the chancellor (§ 2801(3), (5); 8 NYCRR § 100.2(l)(2)(i), (iii)(a)).

52:6. Must school districts make public their code of conduct?

Yes. School districts must ensure community awareness of their code of conduct by:

- posting the complete code on their website, if any, including any annual updates or other amendments;
- providing copies of a summary of the code to all students, in an age-appropriate version written in plain language, at a school assembly to be held at the beginning of each school year;
- mailing a plain language summary of the code to students' parents before the beginning of each school year, and making such summary available thereafter upon request;
- providing each teacher with a complete copy of the code and any amendments thereto as soon as practicable following adoption and to new teachers upon employment; and
- making complete copies available for review by students, parents or other persons in parental relation to students, non-teaching staff, and other community members (§ 2801(4); 8 NYCRR § 100.2(l)(2)(iii)(b)).

52:7. Can a school district's code of conduct provide for the automatic suspension of students who engage in certain types of behavior?

Yes, in some cases. Generally, a school district's code of conduct may not provide for the automatic suspension of students who engage in certain types of behavior without regard to the circumstances giving rise to the code violation (8 NYCRR § 100.2(l)(1)(i)(f); *Appeal of a Student with a Disability*, 33 Ed Dept Rep 101 (1993); *Appeal of Nuttall*, 30 Ed Dept Rep 351 (1991)).

However, a code of conduct must include a minimum period of suspension for violent students (see **52:2**), and students who repeatedly are substantially disruptive of the educational process, or substantially interfere with a teacher's authority over the classroom (*Id.*). That minimum period may be reduced on a case-by-case basis (§§ 2801(2)(l), (m), 3214(2-a)(a); 8 NYCRR § 100.2(l)(2)(ii)(p), (q)).

In addition, pursuant to federal and state law, students deemed to have brought or possessed a firearm at school, must be suspended for a minimum period of one calendar year, subject to modification on a case-by-case basis by the school superintendent (20 USC § 7961(b)(1); § 3214(3)(d); see **52:64-71**).

52:8. May a school district discipline students for off-campus misconduct?

Yes, if for example, the conduct endangers the health or safety of students, substantially disrupts school operations or otherwise adversely affects the educational process. Examples of cases where a district's decision to discipline a student for off-campus conduct has been upheld include students who:

- stole another student's cell phone and book bag after disembarking the school bus at the end of the school day (*Appeal of W.T.*, 46 Ed Dept Rep 363 (2007)).
- fired a BB pistol at other students off-campus and brought a BB pistol to a dinner for football players and their families (*Appeal of Orman*, 39 Ed Dept Rep 811 (2000)).
- possessed a handgun off-campus (*Appeal of R.C.*, 41 Ed Dept Rep 446 (2002)).
- e-mailed an offensive, threatening message from his home computer to other students' home computers (*Appeal of Ravick*, 40 Ed Dept Rep 262 (2000); see also **53:16**).
- agreed to meet to fight another student a few blocks from school (*Appeal of K.S.*, 43 Ed Dept Rep 492 (2004)).
- assaulted another student's mother at her home (*Pollow v. Glennon*, 594 F.Supp. 220 (S.D.N.Y. 1984), *aff'd*, 757 F.2d 496 (2d Cir. 1985)).
- posted a derogatory blog on an independent website critical of the district administration's cancellation of an event (*Doninger v. Niehoff*, 642 F.3d 334 (2d Cir. 2011)).

- shared with classmates via the internet using his home computer a picture suggesting that a teacher should be shot and killed (*Wisniewski v. Bd. of Educ. of Weedsport CSD*, 494 F.3d 34 (2d Cir. 2007), *cert. denied,* 522 U.S. 1296 (2008)).

The authority to discipline students for off-campus misconduct is not limited to incidents occurring during the school year. For example, in one case the commissioner of education upheld the suspension of students who threw eggs at a teacher's home and car during the summer recess (*Appeal of T.W. & P.K.*, 46 Ed Dept Rep 154 (2006)).

52:9. Can a school district discipline students for the unintentional consequences of their actions?

Yes, if the unintentional consequence is the direct result of an action that violates the code of conduct. That was the case, for example where a teacher who intervened in an altercation between two students was pushed into a desk and fell on her back. The student unsuccessfully argued that he was not guilty of pushing the teacher because it was not intentional (*Appeal of A.W.*, 46 Ed Dept Rep 367 (2007)).

Disciplinary Penalties

52:10. What types of disciplinary penalties may school districts impose on students who violate their code of conduct?

The following are among the types of discipline school districts may impose for violations of their student disciplinary code:

- Verbal warning.
- Written warning.
- Written notification to parents or guardians.
- Probation.
- Reprimand.
- Detention.
- Suspension from transportation.
- Suspension from participation in athletic events.
- Suspension from social or extracurricular activities.
- Suspension from other privileges.
- Exclusion from a particular class.
- In-school suspension.
- Suspension from school not in excess of five days.
- Suspension from school in excess of five days.

School districts that allow the use of a time out room as part of their behavior management approach must make sure their policies and procedures on the use of a time out room comply with commissioner's regulations regarding physical and monitoring requirements, parental rights and individualized education program (IEP) requirements for students with disabilities (8 NYCRR § 200.22(c)). For example, the physical space used as a time out room must be unlocked, able to be opened from the inside, and provide a means for continuous visual and auditory monitoring of the student at all times (8 NYCRR § 200.22(c)(5), (6)). In addition, staff must be assigned to continuously monitor students in a time out room (8 NYCRR § 200.22(c)(7)). Furthermore, school districts must specify in a student's IEP when the student's behavioral intervention plan (BIP) (see **54:91**) includes the use of a time out room. Parents must be informed prior to the initiation of a BIP that incorporates such use, be given the opportunity to see the physical space that will be used as a time out room, and be provided with a copy of the school's policy on the use of time out rooms (8 NYCRR § 200.22(c)(2), (4)).

52:11. What constitutes an appropriate disciplinary penalty?

A disciplinary penalty is appropriate as long as it is proportionate to the severity of the offense involved (*Appeal of M.W. & K.W.*, 55 Ed Dept Rep, Dec. No. 16,903 (2016); *Appeal of A.V. and S.A.*, 53 Ed Dept Rep, Dec. No. 16,528 (2013); *Appeal of K.M.*, 51 Ed Dept Rep, Dec. No. 16,320 (2011)). It would not be appropriate if it is so excessive as to warrant substitution of the commissioner's judgment for that of school officials (*Appeal of K.M.; Appeal of F.W.*, 48 Ed Dept Rep 399 (2009); *Appeal of L.O. & D.O.*, 47 Ed Dept Rep 194 (2007)).

In addition, districts may not impose a harsher penalty on a student merely because the student does not cooperate with their investigation of an incident and does not admit guilt (*Appeal of Kier*, 39 Ed Dept Rep 210 (1999)). However, districts may impose a harsher penalty for certain types of misconduct than others, such as a greater penalty for drugs than for tobacco or alcohol misconduct (see *Appeal of J.P.*, 44 Ed Dept Rep 204 (2004)).

Furthermore, a penalty may not be based on conclusions unrelated to the actual charges preferred against a student (*Appeal of A.Q.*, 41 Ed Dept Rep 331 (2002)).

52:12. What rules apply to the use of detention as a disciplinary penalty?

A district may use detention as a penalty for misconduct for which suspension would be inappropriate. However, teachers and administrators may keep a student for after school detention only if there is no parental objection and the student has appropriate transportation home (NYS Education Department, *After School Detention Memorandum to School Administrators and Pupil Service Personnel* (Mar. 1996), at: http://www.p12.nysed.gov/sss/lawsregs/afterschooldetention1996.html).

Students who fail to attend detention may be kept from participating in school activities such as field trips (*Matter of Kubinski*, 26 Ed Dept Rep 348 (1987)). Failure to attend detention also may result in the imposition of an in-school suspension (*Appeal of G.H.L.*, 46 Ed Dept Rep 571 (2007); see **52:54**).

52:13. What rules apply to the suspension of students from school transportation?

A suspension from transportation services does not require a full, formal hearing as required in school suspension cases (see **52:42-63**) because a suspension from transportation, in and of itself, does not affect a student's right to attend school. Instead, all that is required is an opportunity to informally discuss the facts underlying the suspension (*Appeal of R.D.*, 42 Ed Dept Rep 237 (2003); *Appeal of Hale*, 30 Ed Dept Rep 26 (1990)). Districts must be reasonably certain that the student being suspended from transportation services was involved in the misconduct supporting the suspension (*Appeal of Hale*; see **57:17**).

However, where suspending a student from school transportation amounts to a suspension from school attendance because of the distance between home and school and the unavailability of an alternative public or private means of transportation, a district must make "appropriate arrangements" to provide for the student's education (*Matter of Stewart*, 21 Ed Dept Rep 654 (1982)).

Special rules that apply to the discipline of students with disabilities may impact a school's ability to suspend such students' transportation (see **chapter 54**).

52:14. Under what circumstances may school districts suspend or exclude students from extracurricular activities?

School districts may suspend or exclude students from extracurricular activities pursuant to a school board's authority to establish both reasonable standards of conduct for participation in such activities (*Appeal of J.P.*, 44 Ed Dept Rep 204 (2004); *Appeal of G.M.D.*, 43 Ed Dept Rep 289 (2003)), and academic standards as prerequisites for eligibility for extracurricular activities (§ 1709(2), (3); *Matter of Clark*, 21 Ed Dept Rep 542 (1982)). Moreover, a suspension from extracurricular activities does not require a full, formal hearing. All that is required is that the student and his or her parents be given an opportunity to discuss the factual situation informally with the district official authorized to impose the discipline (*Appeal of M.W. & K.W.*, 55 Ed Dept Rep, Dec. No. 16,903 (2016); *Appeal of P.P.*, 50 Ed Dept Rep, Dec. No. 16,161 (2010); *Sala v. Warwick Valley CSD*, 2009 U.S. Dist. LEXIS 67353 (S.D.N.Y. July 29, 2009); *Mazevski v. Horseheads CSD*, 950 F.Supp. 69 (W.D.N.Y. 1997)).

A school district may reduce the period of duration of such a suspension conditioned on a student's agreement to adhere to the school district code of conduct for students (*Sala v. Warwick Valley CSD*; see also **52:33**). Such an agreement would not insulate the student from future suspensions from extracurricular activities based on additional violations of the code of conduct (*Id.*).

The commissioner of education has upheld a board policy that required attendance at 10 "insight classes" for students who consumed alcohol during an extracurricular activity, in lieu of suspending such students from the extracurricular activity (*Appeal of Douglas & Judy H.*, 36 Ed Dept Rep 224 (1996)).

The commissioner also has upheld the imposition of a more severe penalty on athletes than on non-athletes involved in the same disciplinary incident, which consisted of the athlete's suspension from the team pursuant to school policy in addition to a one-day school suspension (*Appeal of Wright*, 38 Ed Dept Rep 756 (1999); see also *Appeal of Shramek*, 39 Ed Dept Rep 577 (2000)).

52:15. Can school districts lower a student's grade as a form of discipline?

No, unless the student's misconduct is related to his or her academic performance. That would be the case where a student cheats on an examination or is illegally absent to avoid taking a test (*Appeal of Pappas,* 39 Ed Dept Rep 310 (1999); *Matter of Augustine*, 30 Ed Dept Rep 13 (1990); *Matter of Caskey*, 21 Ed Dept Rep 138 (1981); *Matter of MacWhinnie*, 20 Ed Dept Rep 145 (1980)).

The assignment of a grade of zero as a penalty for cheating will not be deemed arbitrary or capricious where a student is found to have compromised the integrity of even one portion of an examination, after a full investigation and opportunity for the student to present his version of the incident. However, a full evidentiary hearing is not required (*Appeal of D.F.*, 53 Ed Dept Rep, Dec. No. 16,624 (2014); *Appeal of a Student with a Disability*, 48 Ed Dept Rep 94 (2008)).

52:16. Can school districts involuntarily transfer students from one school to another as a penalty for student misconduct?

No. Involuntary transfers are not an authorized penalty for student misconduct (*Appeal of a Student with a Disability*, 48 Ed Dept Rep 79 (2008)). Moreover, such a transfer requires a separate procedure the purpose of which is to determine whether the proposed transfer would be beneficial to the student (*Matter of Reeves*, 37 Ed Dept Rep 271 (1998); see also *Appeal of a Student Suspected of Having a Disability,* 40 Ed Dept Rep 212 (2000), *petition dismissed, Bd. of Educ., City Sch. Dist., City of N.Y. v. Mills,* (Sup. Ct. Albany Cnty. 2001); *Appeal of Mangaroo*, 37 Ed Dept Rep 578 (1998); see § 3214(5); see **48:35-37**).

Accordingly, it would be inappropriate to require that, after completion of a long term suspension (see **52:46**), a student transfer to a board of cooperative educational services program (*Appeal of T.C.*, 44 Ed Dept Rep 316 (2005)).

52:17. Can districts use corporal punishment to address student behavior?

No. The Rules of the Board of Regents specify that no teacher, administrator, officer, employee, or agent of a school district or board of cooperative educational services may use corporal punishment against a student (8 NYCRR § 19.5(a); see *Appeal of City Sch. Dist. of the City of Elmira*, 30 Ed Dept

Rep 68 (1990)). *Corporal punishment* consists of any act of physical force upon a student for the purpose of punishing that student (8 NYCRR §§ 19.5(a)(2), 100.2(l)(3)(i)).

However, in situations where alternative procedures and methods not involving the use of physical force cannot reasonably be employed, the use of reasonable physical force is permissible to:

- Protect oneself, another student, teacher, or any person(s) from physical injury.
- Protect the property of the school or others.
- Restrain or remove a student whose behavior interferes with the orderly exercise and performance of school or school district functions, powers and duties, if that student has refused to refrain from further disruptive acts (8 NYCRR §§ 19.5(a)(3), 100.2(l)(3)(i); see *Appeal of Taber*, 32 Ed Dept Rep 346 (1992)).

School districts must submit to the commissioner of education a written report on corporal punishment complaints, by January 15 and July 15 each year. The report must include the substance of each complaint about the use of corporal punishment received by local school authorities during the reporting period, the results of each investigation, and the action, if any, taken by the school authorities in each case (8 NYCRR § 100.2(l)(3)(ii)).

52:18. Can districts use physical restraints to address student behavior?

The use of physical restraints may be used only when no other methods of controlling a student's behavior would be effective. The use of physical force to restrain a student from engaging in problem behaviors cannot be used as a substitute for systematic behavioral interventions that are designed to change, replace, modify, or eliminate a targeted behavior. Staff implementing the use of physical restraints must be appropriately trained in the safe and effective use of such intervention (8 NYCRR § 200.22(d)).

52:19. Can districts use aversive interventions to address student behavior?

Not generally. The Rules of the Board of Regents and commissioner's regulations prohibit the use of *aversive interventions,* defined as interventions intended to induce pain or discomfort to a student for the purpose of eliminating or reducing maladaptive behavior. They include, for example, any form of noxious, painful or intrusive spray, inhalant or tastes; the denial or delay of meals; and movement limitations used as punishment. They do not include such interventions as voice control, limited to loud, firm commands; time-limited ignoring of a specific behavior; token fines as part of a token economy system; brief physical prompts to interrupt or prevent a specific behavior; interventions medically necessary for the treatment or protection of the student; or other similar interventions (8 NYCRR §§ 19.5(b)(2), 200.1(lll)).

The only exception to the prohibition against the use of aversive interventions applies to child-specific cases involving school-age students with disabilities, subject to compliance with the procedures established in section 200.22(e) of the commissioner's regulations (see also *Alleyne v. NYS Educ. Dep't*, 516 F.3d 96 (2d Cir. 2008), *on remand,* 691 F.Supp.2d 322 (N.D.N.Y. 2010); *Bryant v. NYS Educ. Dep't*, 2010 U.S. Dist. LEXIS 88652 (N.D.N.Y. Aug. 26, 2010), *aff'd*, 692 F.3d 202 (2d Cir. 2012), *cert. denied*, 133 S.Ct. 2022 (2013)).

The NYS Education Department's Memorandum on *Requirements Relating to the Use of Behavioral Interventions and Supports* (Sept. 2009), provides guidance on the use of aversive interventions and time out rooms at: http://www.p12.nysed.gov/specialed/publications/policy/BImemo-909.htm.

52:20. May districts impose community service as a penalty for student misconduct?

No. A school district has no authority to impose a community service requirement as a penalty under section 3214 of the Education Law (*Appeal of L.H.*, 43 Ed Dept Rep 315 (2003); *Appeal of R.M & L.M*, 43 Ed Dept Rep 155 (2003); *Appeal of Cynthia & Robert W.*, 37 Ed Dept Rep 437 (1998); see **52:10**).

52:21. May districts require counseling as part of a penalty for student misconduct?

No. A school district has no authority to condition a student's school attendance on participation in counseling services (*Appeal of L.H.*, 43 Ed Dept Rep 315 (2003); *Appeal of R.M. & L.M.*, 43 Ed Dept Rep 155 (2003); *Appeal of Jayme K.*, 40 Ed Dept Rep 114 (2000)). However, a school district may recommend counseling in circumstances where a student may benefit from such services (*Appeal of Alexander*, 36 Ed Dept Rep 160 (1996)). In addition, it may condition a suspension revocation (see **52:30**) or a student's early return from suspension (see **52:33**) on the student's voluntary participation in counseling or specialized classes, including anger management or dispute resolution, where applicable (§ 3214(3)(e); *Appeal of B.L.G.*, 50 Ed Dept Rep, Dec. No. 16,101 (2010)).

52:22. May school districts require a psychological or psychiatric examination as part of a penalty for student misconduct?

No, a school district is not permitted to order a psychological or psychiatric examination as part of a penalty. If the district determines that such an examination is warranted, the proper avenue is to refer the student to the district's committee on special education (*Appeal of Pinckney*, 37 Ed Dept Rep 284 (1998)).

52:23. Is a school suspension a permissible penalty for truant students?

No. School districts may not suspend from school a student for truancy, as such a penalty is inconsistent with the educational goal of encouraging children to regularly attend and participate fully in school (*Appeal of Ackert*, 30 Ed Dept Rep 31 (1990)). On the other hand, an in-school suspension for truancy is acceptable if the alternative education provided is adequate (*Appeal of Kainz*, 38 Ed Dept Rep 339 (1998); *Appeal of Miller*, 35 Ed Dept Rep 451 (1996); see **52:10, 52:54**).

Classroom Removals and School Suspensions

52:24. Can students be removed from a classroom?

Yes, if they are disruptive. For classroom removal purposes, a *disruptive student* is an elementary or secondary school student under age 21 who substantially disrupts the educational process or interferes with the teacher's authority in the classroom (§ 3214(2-a)(b)). For procedures relating to classroom removals, see **52:37-40**.

52:25. Can students be suspended from school?

Yes. School districts may suspend from school students who are insubordinate, disorderly, violent, or disruptive, or whose conduct otherwise endangers the safety, morals, health or welfare of others (§ 3214(3)(a)). Furthermore, districts may suspend students from school for infractions of school rules even when a teacher has addressed the behavior problem in the classroom (*Appeal of H.B.*, 46 Ed Dept Rep 369 (2007)).

However, school officials lack authority to suspend a student who permanently withdraws from school before the imposition of a suspension penalty because there is no longer any relationship between the former student and the school district (*Appeal of Rosenkranz*, 37 Ed Dept Rep 330 (1998)).

For procedures relating to the short-term suspension of students, see **52:41-45**. Procedures relating to long-term suspension are discussed at **52:46-53**.

52:26. Can students be suspended from a particular class, as opposed to suspended from school or removed from a classroom?

Yes. Accordingly, a district may suspend from English class a student who is insubordinate during an English class field trip (*Appeal of Trombly*, 26 Ed Dept Rep 214 (1986)).

According to at least one federal court in New York, the exclusion of a student from a particular course does not involve the same constitutional due process rights applicable to school suspensions (*Mazevski v. Horseheads CSD*, 950 F.Supp. 69 (W.D.N.Y. 1997)). But the commissioner of education has determined that students suspended from a particular class enjoy the same statutory rights available under section 3214 of New York's Education Law for a school suspension of the same duration (*Appeal of Trombly*; see **52:41-63**).

52:27. Who may suspend or remove a student from a classroom?

The school board, the superintendent of schools, the board of cooperative educational services (BOCES) district superintendent of schools, or a building principal may suspend a student from attendance upon instruction (§ 3214(3)(a); see also *Appeal of V.R. & C.R.*, 43 Ed Dept Rep 99 (2003)). However, in no case may a principal suspend a student for a period exceeding five school days (§ 3214(3)(b)(1), (c)(1)).

Teachers may not suspend students. However, they may remove disruptive students from their classrooms (§ 3214(3-a); see **52:24, 52:37**).

52:28. Can a school district carry over a suspension from one school year to the next?

Yes. A school district may carry over a suspension to the following school year when misconduct occurs at the end of the school year and the suspension can be meaningfully implemented only at the beginning of the following school year. That would be the case, for example, when the misconduct occurs on the last day of classes (*Appeal of R.D.*, 42 Ed Dept Rep 237 (2003)).

52:29. Can a new school district enforce on a transfer student a suspension imposed by the student's prior school district?

No. According to the commissioner of education, there is no authority that would allow a new school district to automatically enforce a suspension imposed on a transfer student by the student's prior district. In addition, student codes of conduct vary among districts and a determination of guilt and appropriate penalty in one will not necessarily be identical in another (*Appeal of a Student with a Disability*, 49 Ed Dept Rep 204 (2009)). The new district, however, may make its own determination that the behavior supporting the suspension in the prior district also violates its own code of conduct. Based on that determination, the new district would also be able to impose an appropriate penalty under its own code. The commissioner has not specified the extent to which the new district would be able to rely on conclusions of fact made by the prior district's superintendent (*Id.*).

52:30. Can a student's suspension be revoked?

Yes. Where a student has been suspended for cause, the suspension may be revoked by the school board whenever it appears to be in the best interests of the school and the student to do so. A school board may condition a suspension revocation on the student's voluntary participation in counseling or specialized classes, including anger management or dispute resolution, where applicable (§ 3214(3)(e)).

52:31. May a student appeal a long-term suspension?

Yes. Students may appeal long-term suspensions (see **52:46**). If they do so, they must first appeal to their local school board, and thereafter to the commissioner of education (§ 3214(3)(c)); *Appeal of T.W.*, 55 Ed Dept Rep, Dec. No. 16,728 (2015); *Appeal of a Student with a* Disability, 52 Ed Dept Rep, Dec. No. 16,464 (2013); *Appeal of R.A.*, 48 Ed Dept Rep 426 (2009)). A school board may not refuse to hear an appeal from a superintendent's decision imposing a long-term suspension nor may the board impose rigid and short deadlines by when appeals must be presented to it (*Appeal of M.T.*, 48 Ed Dept Rep 263 (2008); *Appeal of J.A.*, 48 Ed Dept Rep 118 (2008); see **52:32**). The time for filing an appeal with the commissioner begins when a student's parents receive the final decision of the school board, not when their attorney receives a copy of the decision (*Appeal of R.A. & D.A.*, 43 Ed Dept Rep 281 (2003)).

In contrast, students may appeal a short-term suspension (see **52:41**) directly to the commissioner, unless a school district policy requires that students appeal a short-term suspension to the school board first (*Appeals of F.L. & D.L.*, 55 Ed Dept Rep, Dec. No. 16,888 (2016); *Appeal of L.L.*, 51 Ed Dept Rep, Dec. No. 16,334 (2012); *Appeal of F.R.*, 51 Ed Dept Rep, Dec. No. 16,263 (2011)). Such a requirement must be stated in express, rather than permissive, language. It is not enough to say that parents may appeal to the school board a superintendent's decision that upholds a short-term suspension (*Appeal of F.R.*). In addition, school districts need to give notice of such a requirement along with the notice of suspension (*Appeal of D.O.*, 53 Ed Dept Rep, Dec. No. 16,543 (2013); *Appeal of L.L*; *Appeal of F.M.*, 48 Ed Dept Rep 244 (2008)). It would be insufficient to generally refer parents to the student code of conduct for information on rights and responsibilities regarding suspension (*Id.*).

However, students may not appeal to the commissioner any issue they failed to raise on a prior appeal to their local school board (*Appeal of L.B. and R.S.*, 50 Ed Dept Rep, Dec. No. 16,133 (2010); *Appeal of Ravick*, 40 Ed Dept Rep 262 (2002)). Thus, a student may not ask the commissioner to address the issue of guilt if the only issue raised before the local school board was the appropriateness of the penalty. That would also be the case when school officials do not pass on the student's guilt because the student admitted guilt (*Appeal of D.V.*, 44 Ed Dept Rep 263 (2005)). Neither the commissioner nor a school board can consider on an appeal related to a student's long-term suspension, issues or evidence that were not raised or presented at the student disciplinary hearing underlying the suspension (*Appeal of T.B.*, 52 Ed Dept Rep, Dec. No. 16,385 (2012)).

School boards reviewing parental appeals regarding a student's suspension are not statutorily required to allow the parents to present arguments in person before the board considers their appeal in executive session. There also is no requirement that the parents attend such executive session (*Appeal of R.F. and D.F.*, 52 Ed Dept Rep, Dec. No. 16,369 (2012)).

52:32. Is there a time frame for students to appeal a long-term suspension to the school board?

Neither the Education Law nor commissioner's regulations establish such a time frame, but school boards may adopt a process for the orderly and efficient review of suspension that sets such a time frame. However, the commissioner of education has found "a rigid 10-day time frame," with "no discretion for excusing delays in an appropriate case" unacceptable (*Appeal of M.T.*, 48 Ed Dept Rep 263 (2008); see also *Appeal of B.L.G.*, 50 Ed Dept Rep, Dec. No. 16,101 (2010)). While not specifying what might be an appropriate time frame, the commissioner has noted that the regulations allow 30 days from the decision or action complained of for individuals to file an appeal to the commissioner. The regulations also allow the commissioner to excuse a delay for good cause shown (*Appeal of M.T.*).

52:33. May a student avoid suspension by signing a probation agreement?

Yes. A school district may offer a student facing a long-term suspension (see **52:46**) the option of signing a "contract of conduct" under which the district agrees to stay the suspension in return for the student's promise to strictly abide by all school disciplinary rules. If the student violates the contract of conduct, the district would reinstate the original suspension after a conference with the superintendent (*Appeal of Spensieri*, 40 Ed Dept Rep 51 (2000)). In addition, a school board may condition a student's early return from suspension on the student's voluntary participation in counseling or specialized classes, including anger management or dispute resolution, where applicable (§ 3214(3)(e); see **52:21**).

A contract of conduct must serve to stay an original suspension and allow a student to return immediately. It may not extend an initial suspension period effectively resulting in a suspension of indefinite duration (*Appeal of R.M. & L.M.*, 43 Ed Dept Rep 155 (2003)). Neither may it extend an original suspension for new misbehavior without the benefit of a superintendent's hearing or require parents to waive their child's right to due process as a condition of attending public school (*Appeal of a Student with a Disability*, 42 Ed Dept Rep 192 (2002)).

Based on *Appeal of Spensieri*, the commissioner of education would uphold a contract of conduct that provides for:

- The student's readmission to school upon condition that the student (1) diligently complete his courses, (2) abide by all school rules and regulations including the rules of conduct in the student handbook, and (3) not engage in the particular types of conduct that caused the suspension.
- Written parental notice of any violation by the student of the conditions of the agreement, and re-imposition of the original period of suspension upon any such violation.
- An opportunity for the student to request a conference with the superintendent to contest any alleged violation, after which the superintendent would issue a written determination on whether the suspension should continue to be stayed or re-imposed.

Prior to executing a contract of conduct, a district must still conduct a student disciplinary hearing, which after a finding of guilt, authorizes a district to suspend a student long-term in the first place. Before revoking a contractual probation a district must provide a minimal amount of due process including written notice, the right to request a conference, and an opportunity to contest a determination that the student violated the conditions of probation (*Appeal of Spensieri*).

52:34. What are a school district's responsibilities after a student has been suspended or removed from a classroom?

The Education Law provides that after suspending a student, school districts must take immediate steps to provide that student with alternative instruction if the student is of compulsory education age (§ 3214(3)(e); *Turner v. Kowalski*, 49 A.D.2d 943 (2d Dep't 1975); *Appeal of McMahon*, 38 Ed Dept Rep 22 (1998)). They are not required to provide alternative instruction to a suspended student over such age (*Matter of Reid v. Nyquist*, 65 Misc.2d 718 (Sup. Ct. Albany Cnty. 1971); *Matter of Chipman*, 10 Ed Dept Rep 224 (1971)). The amount of alternative instruction to be provided must be determined on a case-by-case basis. Two hours per day of alternative instruction may be sufficient to meet this responsibility (*Appeal of C.B. and B.R.*, 50 Ed Dept Rep, Dec. No. 16,192 (2011); *Appeal of V.E.*, 43 Ed Dept Rep 244 (2003)). What is required is that the alternative instruction be substantially equivalent to that received by the student prior to the suspension (*Appeal of C.B. and B.R.; Appeal of R.S.*, 48 Ed Dept Rep 215 (2008)).

However, regardless of age, a suspended student has a right to receive academic intervention services (AIS) (see **55:29-35**) during a period of suspension unless and until the students' performance indicates he or she is no longer eligible for such services (*Appeal of J.C.*, 46 Ed Dept Rep 562 (2007);

see **55:29**, **55:33**). The AIS provided to a suspended student do not have to be identical, but must be of a comparable nature and extent to that predating the suspension (*Appeal of J.C.*).

School districts also must ensure the continued educational programming of students removed from the classroom by their teacher for disruptive behavior (§ 2801(2)(e); see **52:24**, **52:26-27**).

52:35. Are there any rules regarding the contents of the alternative instruction school districts must provide to suspended students?

Alternative instruction does not have to match every aspect of the instructional program the student received in school prior to the suspension. However, it must be substantially equivalent thereto (*Appeal of C.B. and B.R.*, 50 Ed Dept Rep, Dec. No. 16,192 (2011); *Matter of W.H.*, 45 Ed Dept Rep 96 (2005)) so that the student can complete the required courses in all of his or her academic subjects (*Matter of Lee D.*, 38 Ed Dept Rep 262 (1998); *Appeal of Camille S.*, 39 Ed Dept Rep 574 (2000); *Matter of Malpica*, 20 Ed Dept Rep 365 (1981); *Matter of Gesner*, 20 Ed Dept Rep 326 (1980)).

52:36. How soon after suspension must school districts provide alternative instruction to suspended students?

School districts are required to take immediate steps to provide alternative instruction to suspended students (§ 3214(3)(e)). The term immediate does not mean instantaneously. However, school districts must act promptly, with due regard for the nature and circumstances of the particular case (*Turner v. Kowalski*, 49 A.D.2d 943 (2d Dep't 1975); *Appeal of W.H.*, 45 Ed Dept Rep 96 (2005); *Appeal of Benkelman*, 34 Ed Dept Rep 250 (1994)). For example, a school policy that stated the district would not provide alternative instruction to students suspended for less than three days was deemed inappropriate by the commissioner of education (*Appeal of Bridges*, 34 Ed Dept Rep 232 (1994); see also *Appeal of R.F.*, 43 Ed Dept Rep 206 (2003), *petition dismissed*, *Fitch v. Mills*, (Sup. Ct. Albany Cnty. 2004)). Accordingly, school districts must start providing alternative instruction to students within one or two days of their suspension.

52:37. What procedures must teachers follow when removing a disruptive student from their classroom?

A teacher removing a disruptive student (see **52:24**, **52:26**) from the classroom must inform the student and the principal or the principal's designee of the reasons for the removal (§ 3214(3-a)(a), (d)). The teacher must provide the student with an explanation of the basis for the removal and an opportunity to informally present the student's version of relevant events prior to the removal. However, if the teacher finds that the student's presence in the classroom poses a continuing danger to persons or property or an ongoing threat of disruption to the academic process, the teacher has 24 hours from the student's removal to provide the student the requisite explanation of the basis for removal and informal opportunity to be heard (§ 3214(3-a)(a); see **32:16**).

52:38. What are a school principal's responsibilities when teachers remove a disruptive student from their classroom?

The principal or the principal's designee must inform the student's parents of the removal and the reasons therefore within 24 hours of the removal and, on request, give the student and the student's parents an opportunity for an informal conference with the principal or principal's designee to discuss the reason for the removal. If the student denies the charges, the principal or the principal's designee must provide an explanation of the basis for the removal and an opportunity for the student and/or the student's parents to present the student's version at an informal hearing to be held within 48 hours of the student's removal (§ 3214(3-a)(b), (d); *Appeal of K.M.*, 49 Ed Dept Rep 244 (2010)). The responsibilities of the principal or principal's designee are not excused by a teacher's letter informing the student's parents of the removal and offering the parents and the student an opportunity to meet with the teacher (*Appeal of K.M.*).

52:39. May a school principal set aside a teacher's removal of a disruptive student from a classroom?

Yes. The principal or the principal's designee may set aside the teacher's disciplinary action upon a finding that the charges against the student are unsupported by substantial evidence; or that the removal constitutes a violation of law; or that the conduct warrants suspension from school and a suspension will be imposed. The principal must make this determination by the close of business on the day after the 48-hour period for an informal hearing (§ 3214(3-a)(c), (d); see also **52:38**).

52:40. How soon after their removal can students return to the classroom they were removed from?

Students removed from a classroom by their teacher can return to the classroom only after the principal or the principal's designee determines whether or not to set aside the removal (see **52:39**), or the period of removal expires, whichever is less (§ 3214(3-a)(d)).

Short-Term Suspension Procedures

52:41. What is a short-term suspension?

A *short-term suspension* is the term often used to refer to the suspension of a student from school for five days or less in accordance with the provisions of section 3214 of the Education Law.

52:42. What procedures apply to the short-term suspension of students from school?

Prior to suspension, the suspending authority (see **52:27**) must give the student notice of the charged misconduct. If the student denies the misconduct, the student must be provided with an explanation of the basis for the suspension (§ 3214(3)(b)(1)).

Also prior to suspension, school officials must give parents and the student:

- Immediate written notice of the proposed suspension in the parents' dominant language or mode of communication, a description of the incident underlying the proposed suspension, and their right to request an informal conference with the building principal (8 NYCRR § 100.2(1)(4)).
- The opportunity for them and the student to participate in such an informal conference with the building principal (§ 3214(3)(b)(1); 8 NYCRR § 100.2(1)(4)).

At the informal conference, the student and/or the student's parents are entitled to present the student's version of the incident and, in most cases, question the complaining witnesses against the student in the presence of the principal (*Id.*; *Appeals of F.L & D.L.*, 55 Ed Dept Rep, Dec. No. 16,888 (2016); *Appeal of R.T. and S.T.*, 53 Ed Dept Rep, Dec. No. 16,581 (2013); *Appeal of F.M.*, 48 Ed Dept Rep 244 (2008); see **52:43**). The principal may consider whether the original decision to suspend was correct or should be modified (*Appeals of F.L. & D.L.*; *Appeal of F.M.*; *Appeal of a Student Suspected of Having a Disability*, 45 Ed Dept Rep 483 (2006); see **52:45**).

Accordingly, the notice to parents must expressly inform them of their right to question complaining witnesses (*Appeal of a Student with a Disability*, 55 Ed Dept Rep, Dec. No. 16,836 (2015); *Appeal of J.R-B*, 46 Ed Dept Rep 509 (2007); *Appeal of M.S.*, 44 Ed Dept Rep 478 (2005)).

Failure to give proper notice or comply with the procedures set in law and regulations may result in the annulment and expungement of the suspension from the student's record (*Appeal of M.I.*, 55 Ed Dept Rep, Dec. No. 16,840 (2015); *Appeal of J.V.O.*, 50 Ed Dept Rep, Dec. No. 16,234 (2011); *Appeal of J.R-B*)). Parental admissions of a students' engagement in misconduct does not excuse the written notice requirements. Neither does the holding of an informal conference between the parents of the student being suspended and the principal who imposed the suspension (*Appeal of G.F. & T.F.*, 51 Ed Dept Rep, Dec. No. 16,348 (2012)).

52:43. Are there any circumstances when a student and/or the student's parents may not be entitled to question complaining witnesses at the informal conference?

Yes, where a district's interest in protecting the identity of a student outweighs the interest of the student alleged to have engaged in misconduct to question the student. For example, in one case, a student was alleged to have participated in "Kick a Jew Day" at her high school. The principal became aware that the school's small Jewish population was concerned about retaliation if they worked with the administration to identify the students who participated in the incident. During the investigation several student victims received telephone calls from families of the students asking them not to implicate their children of education and one student who witnessed the conduct agreed to speak to the principal only in confidence.

On appeal, the commissioner of education concluded that the principal reasonably believed at the time of the informal conference that her actions were necessary to protect the identities of student witnesses and victims to keep them safe from retaliation involving further acts of bullying, harassment or/and discrimination (*Appeal of C.M.*, 53 Ed Dept Rep, Dec. No. 16,583 (2014); see also *Vestal Cent. Sch. Dist. v. King,* (Sup. Ct. Albany Cnty. 2013); *D.F. v. Syosset Cent. Sch. Dist.*, 386 F.Supp.2d 119 (E.D.N.Y. 2005), *aff'd*, 180 Fed Appx 232 (2d Cir 2006), *cert. denied*, 549 US 1179 (2007)).

52:44. Are there any rules regarding the manner in which districts must provide parents the notices applicable to short-term suspension?

Yes. School districts must give parents written notice of a proposed short-term suspension and their rights (see **52:42**) prior to the actual suspension (§ 3214(3)(b)(1); 8 NYCRR § 100.2(l)(4); *Appeals of F.L. & D.L.*, 55 Ed Dept Rep, Dec. No. 16,888 (2016); *Appeal of G.F. & T.F.*, 51 Ed Dept Rep, Dec. No. 16,348 (2012); *Appeal of F.W.*, 48 Ed Dept Rep 399 (2009)). The only exception applies when the student's presence in school is a continuing danger to persons or property or an ongoing threat of disruption to the academic process. In such an instance, the requisite notice and opportunity for an informal conference must take place, instead, as soon after the suspension as is reasonably practicable (*Appeals of F.L. & D.L.; Appeal of L.O. & D.O*, 47 Ed Dept Rep 194 (2007); *Appeal of a Student Suspected of Having a Disability*, 45 Ed Dept Rep 483 (2006)). A student found in possession of marijuana on school grounds did not pose such danger or threat of disruption because he cooperated with and followed the directives of school officials during and after the search resulting in the discovery of the marijuana (*Appeal of F.W.*). In another case, however, the commissioner of education sustained a principal's reasoned determination that a student's continued presence in the school after being caught with marijuana posed a threat of disruption based on the student's emotional state and the likely disruptive impact on other students in the classroom (*Appeal of a Student with a Disability*, 50 Ed Dept Rep, Dec. No. 16,186 (2011)).

In addition, the written notice must be delivered by personal messenger, express mail, or an "equivalent means reasonably calculated to assure receipt" within 24 hours of the decision to propose suspension. Where possible, notification also must be provided by telephone (8 NYCRR § 100.2(1)(4)). However, oral notification is not a substitute for the required written notification (*Appeal of a Student with a Disability,* 55 Ed Dept Rep, Dec. No. 16,814 (2015); *Appeal of G.F. & T.F.; Appeal of a Student with a Disability*, 48 Ed Dept Rep 79 (2008)). In addition, notification by regular mail does not constitute sufficient notice (*Appeal of a Student with a Disability*, 47 Ed Dept Rep 19 (2007)), even when it follows oral notification the same day (*Appeal of G.P.*, 50 Ed Dept Rep, Dec. No. 16,218 (2011); *Appeal of R.F.*, 43 Ed Dept Rep 206 (2003), *petition dismissed, Fitch v. Mills,* (Sup. Ct. Albany Cnty. 2004)). But oral communication and hand delivery of a written notice on the same day does (*Appeal of L.O. & D.O.*). Notice sent by registered mail return receipt requested is not sufficient notice either (*Appeal of V.R. & C.R.*, 43 Ed Dept Rep 99 (2003)).

Furthermore, the notice must be in the parent's dominant language or mode of communication (8 NYCRR § 100.2(l)(4)).

52:45. Are there any rules regarding the manner in which school districts must conduct a short-term suspension informal conference?

Yes. The informal conference must take place prior to the suspension, unless the student's presence in the school poses a continuing danger or an ongoing threat of disruption to the academic process, in which case it must take place as soon after the suspension as reasonably practicable (§ 3214(3)(b)(1); 8 NYCRR § 100.2(1)(4); *Appeals of F.L. & D.L.*, 55 Ed Dept Rep, Dec. No. 16,888 (2016); *Appeal of a Student with a Disability*, 50 Ed. Dept Rep, Dec. No. 16,186 (2011); *Appeal of L.O. & D.O.*, 47 Ed Dept Rep 194 (2007)). In such an instance, the notice of suspension (see **52:44**) should indicate that the student's continued presence in the school posed a continuing danger or ongoing threat of disruption (see *Appeal of L.L.*, 51 Ed Dept Rep, Dec. No. 16,334 (2012)).

In addition, the Education Law intends for the student and the student's parents to question complaining witnesses (see **52:42**) in front of the principal (§ 3214(3)(b)(1); 8 NYCRR § 100.2(1)(4)) so that the principal, who also has the authority to terminate or reduce the suspension, can decide whether the original decision to suspend was correct or should be modified (*Appeals of F.L. & D.L.*; *Appeal of G.P.*, 50 Ed Dept Rep, Dec. No. 16,218 (2011); *Appeal of a Student with a Disability*, 47 Ed Dept Rep 19 (2007)). Therefore, in general, it is insufficient to only provide an opportunity for the parent to speak with the principal without the complaining witness present or to speak with the complaining witness without the principal present (*Appeal of B.B.*, 49 Ed Dept Rep 253 (2010); *Appeal of L.F. & J.F.*, 46 Ed Dept Rep 414 (2007)). See **52:43** for an exception to this general rule.

Long-Term Suspension Procedures

52:46. What is a long-term suspension?

A *long-term suspension* is the term often used to refer to the suspension of a student from school in excess of five days in accordance with the provisions of section 3214 of the Education Law.

52:47. What procedures apply to the long term suspension of students from school?

New York's Education Law provides that no student may be suspended in excess of five school days unless the student and the student's parents have had an opportunity for a hearing on reasonable notice (§ 3214(3)(c); see **52:55**). At such hearing, students may bring their parents, and also have the right to be represented by an attorney or other counsel, to testify on their own behalf and present witnesses and other evidence on their own behalf, and in most cases, to cross-examine witnesses against them (§ 3214(3)(c);

Appeal of M.A., 47 Ed Dept Rep 188 (2007); *Appeal of K.D.*, 37 Ed Dept Rep 702 (1998); *Appeal of Johnson*, 34 Ed Dept Rep 62 (1994); see **52:48**).

A school district may not unilaterally postpone the required hearing and keep a student out of school beyond the initial short-term suspension (see **52:41**) pending the hearing. If a district is forced to postpone a hearing and the initial short-term suspension has expired, the student must be allowed to return to school in the interim, unless the student's parents have consented to the delay (*Appeal of R.T. and S.T.*, 53 Ed Dept Rep, Dec. No. 16,581 (2013); *Appeal of a Student Suspected of Having a Disability*, 46 Ed Dept Rep 453 (2007); *Appeal of N.S.*, 42 Ed Dept Rep 190 (2002)). On the other hand, if a hearing is timely scheduled but adjourned at the parent's request, a school district can require that the student remain out of school beyond five days (*Appeal of F.W.*, 48 Ed Dept Rep 399 (2009)).

52:48. Are there limited circumstances when a student or the student's representative is not entitled to cross examine student witnesses at a disciplinary hearing?

Yes, where the district's interest in protecting the identity of the student witness outweighs the charged student's interest in cross-examination. In one case, a sixth grade student was assigned to keep a journal "expressing thoughts, concerns, or feelings." He wrote about a boy who was bullied by other children at school and desired revenge. The story described in graphic detail how the boy went on a killing spree and some of the characters in the story were named after the student's classmates. The student read the story to classmates at school. At the disciplinary hearing, the district was permitted to submit student statements describing their reaction to hearing the student's story. The students who made the statements were not identified and the student's attorney was not permitted to question them. According to the court, "the School's interest in protecting the identities of the students outweighed any interest in cross-examination" that the student had. The court further concluded that the school district "had a keen interest in keeping the identity of the students confidential" given that the district reasonably considered the student to be potentially violent, and by not disclosing the names of the students, the district was protecting them from possible retaliation (*D.F. v. Bd of Educ. of Syosset Cent. Sch. Dist.,* 386 F.Supp.2d 119 (E.D.N.Y. 2005), *aff'd,* 180 Fed Appx 232 (2d Cir. 2006), *cert. denied,* 549 US 1179 (2007)).

52:49. What type of notice must school districts give students and their parents prior to a hearing on a proposed long-term suspension?

Students and their parents have the right to a hearing on reasonable notice prior to the imposition of a long-term suspension (§ 3214(3)(c); see **52:55**). The law itself does not define "reasonable notice" and it will vary depending on the circumstances of each case. In essence, a student and the student's parents are entitled to fair notice of the charges against the student so that they can prepare and present an adequate defense (*Bd. of Educ. of Monticello CSD v. Comm'r of Educ.*, 91 N.Y.2d 133 (1997); see **52:50**). The notice must also include the date when the hearing will take place, allowing sufficient time for the student and/or parents to obtain counsel if desired (*Matter of Carey v. Savino*, 91 Misc.2d 50 (Sup. Ct. Allegany Cnty. 1977); see **52:51**). In addition, notice should be given in the dominant language of a person in parental relation to the student (*Appeal of R.A.*, 50 Ed Dept Rep, Dec. No. 16,131 (2010)).

52:50. What constitutes reasonable notice of the charges against a student facing a long-term suspension?

Notice that merely repeats the statutory grounds that form the bases upon which the student may be suspended (see **52:25**) or just states that a student violated school rules or disrupted school activities is not reasonable because it fails to provide enough information to prepare an effective defense (*Bd. of Educ. of Monticello CSD v. Comm'r of Educ.*, 91 N.Y.2d 133 (1997)). However, students in a suspension hearing are not entitled to the same protections available in a criminal proceeding. Therefore, the notice of the charges does not need to particularize every single charge against a student (*Id.; Appeal of A.B.*, 50 Ed Dept Rep, Dec. No. 16,147 (2010)). For example, in one case the commissioner of education concluded that the notice did not have to name the complaining students or list the time and location of where the alleged misconduct occurred (*Appeal of H.B.*, 46 Ed Dept Rep 369 (2007)). Neither does it need to cite the specific provisions of the code of conduct which a student allegedly violated (*Appeal of L.L.*, 45 Ed Dept Rep 217 (2005)).

What is required is that the notice give a student and the student's parents sufficient information to advise the student and the student's counsel of the activities or proceedings giving rise to the proceeding and forming the basis for the hearing and gives the student enough information to prepare an effective defense (*Appeals of F.L. & D.L.*, 55 Ed Dept Rep, Dec. No. 16,888 (2016); *Appeal of S.Z.*, 52 Ed Dept Rep, Dec. No. 16,384 (2012); *Bd. of Educ. of Monticello CSD v. Comm'r of Educ.*).

52:51. What constitutes reasonable notice of the date on which a long-term suspension hearing will be held?

As with the notice of charges against a student (see **52:50**), the law does not define what constitutes reasonable notice of the date of a long-term suspension hearing (see **52:55**). However, what constitutes reasonable notice of the hearing will vary on the circumstances of each case (*Appeal of M.A.*, 45 Ed Dept Rep 206 (2005); *Appeal of a Student with a Disability*, 41 Ed Dept Rep 253 (2002); *Appeal of J.D.*, 39 Ed Dept Rep 593 (2000)).

A single day's notice of a long-term suspension hearing is insufficient (*Matter of Carey v. Savino*, 91 Misc.2d 50 (Sup. Ct. Allegany Cnty. 1977); *Appeal of Eisenhauer*, 33 Ed Dept Rep 604 (1994)). But a three days' notice has been deemed sufficient (*Appeal of M.A*), even when the notice was given verbally and subsequently followed by written notice (*Appeal of Lago*, 38 Ed Dept Rep 723 (1999); *Appeal of DeRosa*, 36 Ed Dept Rep 336 (1997)). Two days' written notice in addition to verbal notice several days prior to the hearing would be deemed sufficient (*Appeal of K.M.*, 50 Ed Dept Rep, Dec. No. 16,178 (2010)).

In addition, the reasonableness of the notice of a hearing may be subject to evidence that the student and the student's parent might need more time to obtain counsel (*Appeal of M.A.; Appeal of J.D.; Appeal of DeRosa*).

52:52. What happens if a student is made to serve a long-term suspension without a hearing?

Students who are suspended more than five days without a hearing (see **52:55**) and parental consent may request an order of the commissioner of education directing reinstatement, pending a hearing and a determination of the charges (*Appeal of Knispel*, 35 Ed Dept Rep 145 (1995)).

In addition, they can collect damages from school officials for the violation of their constitutional rights (*Carey v. Piphus*, 435 U.S. 247 (1978)). Even if school officials can demonstrate that the suspension was justified, students deprived of their due process rights are entitled to recover nominal damages not to exceed one dollar without proof of actual injury. They may recover other damages upon proof of actual injury derived from the denial of due process (*Id.*).

52:53. Are there any limitations on the duration of a student's long-term suspension from school?

No. However, permanent suspensions/expulsions are an extreme penalty that, according to the commissioner of education, are generally educationally unsound. Therefore, it should be reserved for extraordinary circumstances, such as where a student exhibits an alarming disregard to the safety of others, and where it is necessary to safeguard the well-being of other students (*Appeal of N.V.*, 46 Ed Dept Rep 138 (2006), *petition dismissed, Bd. of Educ., No. Rockland CSD v. Mills*, (Sup. Ct. Albany Cnty. 2007); *Appeal of L.T.*, 44 Ed Dept Rep 89 (2004); *Appeal of Y.M.*, 43 Ed Dept Rep 193 (2003); *Appeal of Coleman*, 41 Ed Dept Rep 101 (2001)).

A student's sustained use of profanity against a principal, although not to be tolerated, did not meet the extraordinary circumstances standard notwithstanding the student's record of over 40 disciplinary incidents, including threats to blow up the school and murder a teacher for which the student received out-of-school suspension and was allowed to return to school (*Appeal of K.G.*, 51 Ed Dept Rep, Dec. No. 16,262 (2011)). A single fight, without more, also is an insufficient basis to permanently suspend a student from school (*Appeal of Khan*, 35 Ed Dept Rep 322 (1996)). That was the case also where a student brought an ounce of marijuana to school (*Appeal of N.V.*) and where a student accused of smoking marijuana on school grounds had over 80 previous disciplinary incidents, but not one of the prior suspensions exceeded five days (*Appeal of Y.M*). Similarly, a permanent suspension was deemed unwarranted where a student engaged in a sexual act on school grounds, but there was no evidence of physical force or coercion (*Appeal of F.M.*, 48 Ed Dept Rep 244 (2008)).

In comparison, the commissioner upheld the permanent suspension of a 17-year-old high school senior who dropped a lit piece of paper in a recycle bin that started a fire, forced evacuation of the school, and caused property damage in excess of $100,000. The student also made no effort to mitigate the potential damage. Instead he ran down the stairs and caught up with his friends (*Appeal of D.C.*, 40 Ed Dept Rep 70 (2000); see also *Appeal of McNamara*, 37 Ed Dept Rep 326 (1998); *Appeal of Sole*, 34 Ed Dept Rep 270 (1994)).

Although a student may be permanently suspended under certain circumstances, there is no authority under the Education Law to permanently banish a student from school grounds (*Appeal of McNamara*). Similarly, the commissioner has deemed unreasonable a permanent ban from school property of a student from another school district who engaged in misconduct during a game (*Appeal of M.S.*, 47 Ed Dept Rep 396 (2008)).

52:54. What is an in-school suspension, and how does it differ from out-of-school suspensions?

An *in-school suspension* is the temporary removal of a student from the classroom and his or her placement in another area in the school building designated for such a suspension where that student will receive substantially equivalent alternative education. A study hall does not satisfy the obligation to provide alternative instruction (*Appeal of Forster*, 31 Ed Dept Rep 443 (1992); *Appeal of Ackert*, 30 Ed Dept Rep 31 (1990)).

In-school suspensions also differ from out-of-school suspensions in that, unlike out-of-school suspensions, they can be imposed by someone other than the building principal or superintendent (*Appeal of M.C.,* 43 Ed Dept Rep 276 (2003)). Furthermore, they are not subject to the more formal procedures applicable to out-of-school suspensions, except that the student and the student's parents must be provided a reasonable opportunity for an informal conference with the individual who imposed the suspension to discuss the student's misconduct and the penalty involved (*Appeal of G.I.*, 50 Ed Dept Rep, Dec. No. 16,121 (2010); *Appeal of G.H.L.*, 46 Ed Dept Rep 571 (2007); *Appeal of J.D.*, 46 Ed Dept Rep 244 (2007); *Appeal of M.C.*; *Appeal of Denis,* 40 Ed Dept Rep 306 (2000)). Phone calls, letters, voice and e-mail messages inviting parents to discuss the issues provide sufficient notice of such opportunity (*Appeal of G.H.L.*).

Student Disciplinary Hearings

52:55. What is a student disciplinary hearing?

A *student disciplinary hearing*, often also referred to as a 3214 hearing or a long-term suspension hearing, is an administrative proceeding conducted in accordance with section 3214 of the Education

Law to determine whether a student is guilty of misconduct that warrants a long-term suspension from school in excess of five days and, if so, to impose such a penalty (see **52:46-53** for more information on long-term suspensions).

School districts must maintain a record of each student disciplinary hearing (§ 3214(3)(c)(1)). A stenographic transcript is not required, however, and tape recording is permissible (*Id.*). But tape recordings must be sufficiently audible to permit a meaningful review (*Appeal of P.D.*, 46 Ed Dept Rep 50 (2006)). Therefore, school districts must ensure that electronic recording devices are operating properly before commencing a hearing (*Appeal of C.Q. & J.Q.*, 41 Ed Dept Rep 294 (2002)). The failure to maintain an intelligible record of a hearing may result in the commissioner of education annulling and expunging from a student's record any suspension imposed based on the hearing (*Appeal of a Student with a Disability,* 52 Ed Dept Rep, 16,434 (2012); *Appeal of a Student with a Disability,* 50 Ed Dept Rep, 16,170 (2010); *Appeal of C.Q. & J.Q*). In the event that the record of a student disciplinary proceeding is unintelligible, a school district should consider holding a re-hearing (*Appeal of C.Q. & J.Q.).*

Although districts do not have an affirmative obligation to provide parents a copy of the record, parents may request such a copy (*Appeal of V.P.*, 42 Ed Dept Rep 3 (2002)).

52:56. May students waive the right to a long-term suspension hearing?

Yes. Students, together with their parents, may elect to either proceed to a long-term suspension hearing (see **52:55**) or waive their right to a hearing and accept a district's proposed long-term suspension. However, any waiver of the right to a hearing must be made knowingly and voluntarily and intelligently (*Appeal of a Student with a Disability*, 51 Ed Dept Rep, Dec. No. 16,343 (2012); *Appeal of McMahon*, 38 Ed Dept Rep 22 (1998)). For a waiver to be voluntary, knowing, and intelligent, the student and the student's parents must be fully, clearly, and concisely informed, in writing, of all the rights being waived and the consequences of waiving those rights (*Appeal of C.L.*, 44 Ed Dept Rep 370 (2005); *Appeal of V.L.*, 44 Ed Dept Rep 160 (2004); *Appeal of J.G.,* 39 Ed Dept Rep 393 (1999)). A settlement stipulation entered into orally by a student's attorney, on the record and before a hearing officer waiving the student's due process rights, can constitute evidence of such a waiver. That can be the case even if the stipulation is not memorialized in writing, particularly when it is followed by actions consistent with its terms (*Appeal of a Student with a Disability*).

Districts are limited in the penalty they may impose under such a waiver to those that would have been available if a hearing was actually held (*Appeal of McMahon*). Therefore, the range of possible penalties must be identified in any waiver letter provided to students and their parents (*Id.;* see also *Appeal of L.H.*, 43 Ed Dept Rep 315 (2003)).

In addition, districts may not interpret a parent's failure to request a hearing as a waiver of the right to a hearing. Absent a binding and written waiver, districts must schedule a hearing and notify students and their parents of the hearing (*Appeal of McMahon*).

52:57. Who conducts a student disciplinary hearing?

Generally, it is the superintendent of schools who conducts a student disciplinary hearing. However, both the superintendent and the school board are authorized to appoint a hearing officer to conduct student disciplinary hearings. The hearing officer's report is advisory only, and the superintendent or board may accept or reject all or any part of it (§ 3214(3)(c)).

The attorney for a school district or a board of cooperative educational services (BOCES) who provides professional services to the district or BOCES is not *per se* excluded from acting as a student discipline hearing officer (*Appeal of J.H. & T.H.,* 54 Ed Dept Rep, Dec. No. 16,687 (2014); *Appeal of*

F.W., 48 Ed Dept Rep 399 (2009)). According to the commissioner of education there is a presumption of honesty and integrity and those challenging the appointment of the hearing officer have the burden of rebutting that presumption. Moreover, the performance of multiple functions by individuals or groups is not a violation of due process *per se*. Whether such a violation occurs is a factual determination to be made in light of the circumstances surrounding the procedure. Factors to be considered include whether the hearing officer was aware of any of the facts of the case prior to the hearing or whether there is any evidence of bias or personal involvement on the hearing officer's part (*Id.*).

Hearing officers are required by statute to make findings of fact and recommendations to the superintendent regarding the appropriate measure of discipline. Although a general recommendation that an additional suspension be imposed satisfies the statutory requirements, the commissioner recommends that hearing officers include a specific recommendation regarding the duration of any recommended additional suspension (*Appeal of G.B.*, 52 Ed Dept Rep, Dec. No. 16,383 (2012)).

52:58. Who bears the burden of proof in a student disciplinary hearing?

As in a court of law, the burden of proof rests on the person making a charge of misconduct against the student, namely the school district. The student is entitled to a presumption of innocence of wrongdoing until proven otherwise (*Matter of Montero*, 10 Ed Dept Rep 49 (1970)).

The commissioner of education will not substitute his judgment for that of a superintendent or hearing officer conducting a student disciplinary hearing (see **52:57**) regarding the credibility of witnesses absent clear and convincing evidence that a determination of credibility is inconsistent with the facts (*Appeal of J.H. & T.H.*, 54 Ed Dept Rep, Dec. No. 16,687 (2014); *Appeal of J.S.*, 50 Ed Dept Rep, Dec. No. 16,091 (2010); *Appeal of L.F. & J.F.*, 46 Ed Dept Rep 414 (2007)). Such was the case where the record on an appeal to the commissioner did not include a copy of a video surveillance that was key to credit the credibility of the district's witnesses (*Appeal of a Student with a Disability*, 50 Ed Dept Rep, Dec. No. 16,176 (2010)).

52:59. What type of evidence must school districts present at a student disciplinary hearing to support a long-term suspension?

The decision to impose a long-term suspension following a student disciplinary hearing must be based on competent and substantial evidence that the student participated in the misconduct charged (*Bd. of Educ. of Monticello CSD v. Comm'r of Educ.*, 91 N.Y.2d 133 (1997); *Matter of the Bd. of Educ. of the City Sch. Dist. of the City of N.Y. v. Mills*, 293 A.D.2d 37 (3d Dep't 2002); *Appeal of J.H. & T.H.*, 54 Ed Dept Rep, Dec. No. 16,687(2014)). This standard is a lesser standard than that required in a formal trial (*Bd. of Educ. of Monticello CSD v. Comm'r of Educ.*) or criminal proceeding (*Appeal of D.B.*, 45 Ed Dept Rep 197 (2005)). Instead, districts must prove a student's guilt by presenting substantial evidence of such "quality and quantity" as to allow a "fair and detached fact finder" to "reasonably-probatively and logically" conclude the student engaged in the alleged misconduct (*Matter of the Bd. of Educ. of the City Sch. Dist. of the City of N.Y. v. Mills*). The evidence must be unequivocal (*Appeal of J.J.*, 46 Ed Dept Rep 270 (2006); *Appeal of P.D.*, 46 Ed Dept Rep 50 (2006)).

Competent and substantial evidence may consist of a student's admission of guilt (*Appeal of J.H. & T.H.; Appeal of a Student with a Disability,* 50 Ed Dept Rep, Dec. No. 16,106 (2010), *aff'd, Student with a Disability v. Steiner*, 101 A.D.3d 73 (3d Dep't 2012), *appeal denied*, 20 N.Y.3d 1032 (2013); *Appeal of M.H.*, 45 Ed Dept Rep 42 (2005)), including a knowing and voluntary "no contest" plea (*Appeal of T.B.*, 52 Ed Dept Rep, Dec. No. 16,385 (2012)), unrefuted testimony (*Appeal of D.B.*), or corroborated testimony (*Id.; Appeal of L.T.*, 44 Ed Dept Rep 89 (2004)). It also may consist of a videotape depicting

Students

a student's involvement in misconduct (*Appeal of C.R.*, 48 Ed Dept Rep 195 (2008)), as well as hearsay and reasonable inferences drawn therefrom (*Bd. of Educ. of Monticello CSD v. Comm'r of Educ.*; see also **52:60**).

A dispute over a translation of testimony during a student disciplinary hearing will be insufficient grounds on its own to overturn a student suspension following the hearing where the student is given the opportunity to question the witnesses with the assistance of his or her own translator and school officials (*Appeal of L.Z.*, 46 Ed Dept Rep 518 (2007)).

52:60. Is hearsay evidence admissible in a student disciplinary hearing?

Yes. At a student disciplinary hearing, persons having personal knowledge of the facts should be called to testify. However, hearsay evidence is admissible (*Bd. of Educ. of Monticello CSD v. Comm'r of Educ.*, 91 N.Y.2d 133 (1997); *Appeal of T.A.*, 50 Ed Dept Rep, Dec. No. 16,148 (2010); *Appeal of J.A.*, 48 Ed Dept Rep 118 (2008)).

Furthermore, hearsay alone may constitute competent and substantial evidence (see **52:59**) to support imposition of a long-term suspension. That was the case where two school officials testified at a student disciplinary hearing that the student admitted to them he was under the influence of alcohol while attending a school football game (*Appeal of M.S.*, 44 Ed Dept Rep 478 (2005); *Appeal of S.C.*, 43 Ed Dept Rep 222 (2003)).

In general, a superintendent or hearing officer conducting a student disciplinary hearing may not consider a witness' written statement unless that witness is made available for cross-examination. To do otherwise would deny the student charged with misconduct of the right to cross-examine witnesses (*Appeal of M.A.*, 47 Ed Dept Rep 188 (2007); *Appeal of D.C.*, 41 Ed Dept Rep 277 (2002)). One exception to this rule is where the district's interest in protecting the identity of a student witness outweighs any interest the charged student has in cross-examination, for example when the charged student could be potentially violent (*D.F. v. Bd. of Educ. of Syosset CSD,* 386 F.Supp.2d 119 (E.D.N.Y. 2005), *aff'd*, 180 Fed Appx 232 (2d Cir 2006), *cert. den.*, 549 US 1179 (2007); see **52:48**).

52:61. May witnesses testify via telephone at a student disciplinary hearing?

Without deciding whether telephone testimony is permissible in a student disciplinary hearing, the commissioner of education has stated that such a practice raises "serious questions" given a student's statutory right to a fair hearing and to question witnesses presented by the district (*Appeal of K.D.*, 37 Ed Dept Rep 702 (1998)).

52:62. May a student's anecdotal record be submitted into evidence at a student disciplinary hearing?

Yes. However, a student's anecdotal record may be received into evidence and considered only when fixing a penalty, and only after a finding of guilt already has been made (*Appeal of K.M.*, 51 Ed Dept Rep, Dec. No. 16,320 (2011)). A student and his parents must be given notice of its contents in advance whenever the student's anecdotal record will be considered in setting the penalty (*Appeal of L.F. & J.F.*, 46 Ed Dept Rep 414 (2007); *Appeal of a Student Suspected of Having a Disability (Somers CSD)*, 41 Ed Dept Rep 253 (2002)).

52:63. Is evidence suppressed by a court in another action or proceeding admissible in a student disciplinary hearing on a proposed long-term school suspension?

Yes. In one case, the New York Court of Appeals ruled a judge's determination that certain evidence could not be used against a student in a family court proceeding because it was obtained as a result of an illegal search was not binding in a student disciplinary proceeding (*Matter of Juan C. v. Cortines*, 89 N.Y.2d 659 (1997)). Subsequent to this decision, amendments to the Education Law now provide that if a student is being suspended, in whole or in part, for the possession on school grounds or property of any firearm, rifle, shotgun, dagger, dangerous knife, dirk, razor, stiletto, or any weapon, instrument, or appliance set forth in section 265.01 of the Penal Law, the superintendent or hearing officer may consider the admissibility of such evidence even if a court in a criminal or juvenile delinquency proceeding previously has determined that the evidence was obtained as a result of an unlawful search or seizure (§ 3214(3)(c)(1)).

Gun-Free Schools Act

Editor's Note: U.S. Department of Education Non-regulatory Guidance on Implementation of the Gun-Free Schools Act *is available at: http://www2.ed.gov/about/offices/list/osdfs/gfsa.html.*

52:64. What is the Gun-Free Schools Act?

The Gun-Free Schools Act is a federal law which requires that all states receiving federal financial assistance under the Elementary and Secondary Education Act (ESEA), have in effect a law requiring that school districts suspend students who bring to or possess a firearm at school for at least one calendar year (20 USC § 7961(b)(1)). However, a superintendent of schools or district superintendent may modify, in writing, the one year suspension on a case by case basis (*Id.*; § 3214(3)(d); see *Appeal of R.S.*, 38 Ed Dept Rep 419 (1998)). A superintendent's determination may be appealed to the school board and the commissioner of education (§ 3214(3)(d)).

Provisions in section 3214(3)(d) of the Education Law serve to implement the Gun-Free Schools Act's requirements in New York.

For purposes of the Gun-Free Schools Act, the term *school* means any setting under the control and supervision of a school district for student activities approved and authorized by the district (20 USC § 7961(f)). The term *firearm* means the same as such term is defined by federal law (18 USC § 921(a)(3); 20 USC § 7961(b)(3); see **52:65**).

52:65. What is the definition of a firearm under the Gun-Free Schools Act?

For the purposes of compliance with the Gun-Free Schools Act, a firearm means the same as that term is defined in section 921 of Title 18 of the United States Code (20 USC § 7961(b)(3)). The following are included within the definition:

- Any weapon (including a starter gun) which will or is designed to or may readily be converted to expel a projectile by the action of an explosive.
- The frame or receiver of any weapon described above.
- Any firearm muffler or firearm silencer.
- Any destructive device, which is defined as any explosive, incendiary, or poison gas, such as a bomb, grenade, rocket having a propellant charge of more than four ounces, a missile having an explosive or incendiary charge of more than one-quarter ounce, a mine, or other similar device.
- Any weapon which will, or which may be readily converted to, expel a projectile by the action of an explosive or other propellant, and that has any barrel with a bore of more than one-half inch in diameter.
- Any combination of parts either designed or intended for use in converting any device into any destructive device described in the two immediately preceding examples, and from which a destructive device may be readily assembled.

The definition does not apply to a firearm lawfully stored inside a locked vehicle on school property, or if it is for activities that are school approved and authorized and the district has appropriate safeguards to ensure student safety (20 USC § 7961(g)).

According to the commissioner of education, a BB gun is not a firearm within the meaning of the Gun-Free Schools Act because the gun uses a spring mechanism to propel the projectile instead of an explosive charge (*Appeal of Eddy*, 36 Ed Dept Rep 359 (1997)). Nonetheless, in a case where a school policy included BB guns within the definition of "weapons," the commissioner upheld the one-year suspension of a student who brought such a gun to school and fired it at a school bus as students were boarding (*Appeal of C.D.*, 43 Ed Dept Rep 425 (2004)).

52:66. What are a school district's responsibilities under the Gun-Free Schools Act and New York's Education Law implementing provisions?

In addition to providing for the suspension of students who bring to or possess a firearm at school for at least one calendar year (20 USC § 7961(b)), school districts must have a policy requiring that the superintendent refer students under the age of 16 determined to have brought a weapon or firearm to school to the county attorney for a juvenile delinquency proceeding, and students 16 years of age or older, or 14 or 15 years old who qualify for juvenile offender status, to appropriate law enforcement officials (20 USC § 7961(h)(1); § 3214(3)(d)). A weapon in this context means any device, instrument, material, or substance that is used for or is readily capable of causing death or serious bodily injury. Pocketknives with a blade of less than two-and-one-half inches in length are excluded from the definition (§ 3214(3)(d)(3)(ii); 18 USC § 930(g)(2)).

In addition, school districts receiving federal financial assistance under the federal Elementary and Secondary Education Act (ESEA) must provide an assurance in their application for such assistance that they are in compliance with Gun-Free Schools Act and implementing New York Education Law provisions (20 USC § 7961(d)(1)). The application also must include a description of the circumstances surrounding any suspension imposed under state law implementing the Gun-Free Schools Act, including the name of the school concerned, the number of students suspended from school, and the types of firearms concerned (20 USC § 7961(d)(2)).

52:67. Do the suspension requirements of the Gun-Free Schools Act apply only to violations occurring within school buildings?

No. They apply to students who bring or possess a firearm in any setting that is under the control and supervision of the school district for student activities approved and authorized by the district (20 USC § 7961(f)).

52:68. Does the Gun-Free Schools Act apply to students with disabilities?

Yes. However, the Gun-Free Schools Act must be construed to be consistent with the Individuals with Disabilities Education Act (20 USC § 7961(c); 20 USC § 1400 *et seq.*), Article 89 of New York's Education Law applicable to the education of students with disabilities (§ 3214(3)(d)), and section 504 of the Rehabilitation Act (U.S. Department of Education, *Guidance Concerning State and Local Responsibilities Under the Gun-Free Schools Act* (Jan. 2004), at: http://www.ed.gov/about/offices/list/osdfs/gfsa.html). See **54:75-94** for further information on the discipline of students with disabilities.

52:69. Does the Gun-Free Schools Act apply to private school students?

Yes, but only with respect to their participation in public school programs or activities that use federal funds available under the Elementary and Secondary Education Act. This would include, for example, a Title I program as reauthorized by the No Child Left Behind Act of 2001 (§ 3214(3)(d); U.S. Department of Education, *Guidance Concerning State and Local Responsibilities Under the Gun-Free Schools Act* (Jan. 2004), at: http://www2.ed.gov/about/offices/list/osdfs/gfsa.html).

52:70. What are the rights of students who are subject to a one-year suspension under the Gun-Free Schools Act?

A student charged with bringing or possessing a firearm at school in violation of the Gun-Free Schools Act or who brings a weapon to school in violation of New York's Education Law implementing provisions (see **52:65-66**) is entitled to the same rights and procedures applicable to long-term suspensions including, but not limited to, the right to a hearing (§ 3214(3)(d); *Appeal of J.D.*, 39 Ed Dept Rep 593 (2000); see **52:31**, **52:34-36**, **52:46-53**, **52:55-63**).

52:71. Are school districts required to provide alternative instruction to students suspended for bringing a weapon to school?

Yes. The Gun-Free Schools Act neither requires nor prohibits the provision of alternative educational services to students suspended for violating the Act. However, New York's Education Law requires that school districts provide alternative instruction to students of compulsory school age (20 USC § 7961(b)(2); § 3214(3)(e); see **52:34-36**).

[illegible]

[illegible]

[illegible]

[illegible]

Students

53. Student Constitutional Rights

Free Speech – In General

Editor's Note: Public school students enjoy rights protected by various federal and state constitutional provisions such as those providing for equal protection, due process, the free exercise of religion, free speech, and protection against unreasonable searches and seizures. This chapter focuses mainly on the latter two. For information on religion in the public schools, see ***chapter 65****. Due process issues associated with student discipline are addressed in* ***chapter 52****.*

53:1. Do First Amendment free speech protections prohibit school districts from imposing restrictions on student speech?

It depends. The First Amendment to the U.S. Constitution provides, in part, that governmental entities may not abridge an individual's freedom of speech (U.S. Const. amend. I). In addition, the U.S. Supreme Court has ruled that students do not shed their "constitutional rights to freedom of speech or expression at the schoolhouse gate" (*Tinker v. Des Moines Indep. Cmty. Sch. Dist.* 393 U.S. 503(1969)).

However, according to the U.S. Supreme Court, student free speech rights "are not automatically coextensive with the rights of adults in other settings" (*Bethel Sch. Dist. v. Fraser*, 478 U.S. 675 (1986); see also *Morse v. Frederick*, 551 U.S. 393 (2007); *Peck v. Baldwinsville CSD,* 426 F.3d 617 (2d Cir. 2005), *cert. denied,* 547 U.S. 1097 (2006)). Instead, they must be "applied in light of the special characteristics of the school environment" (*Tinker v. Des Moines Indep. Cmty. Sch. Dist.*; see also *Morse v. Frederick*; *Hazelwood Sch. Dist. v. Kuhlmeier*, 484 U.S. 260 (1988); *Peck v. Baldwinsville CSD; Bethel Sch. Dist. v. Fraser*).

53:2. Under what circumstances can school districts impose restrictions on student speech?

In general, school officials cannot prevent students from expressing their personal political or religious views or opinions on school premises, or discipline students for doing so. Instead, they may take such an action only if they reasonably believe a student's expression of such views will "materially and substantially interfere with the requirements of appropriate discipline in the operation of the school" or "impinge upon the rights of other students" or actually does (*Tinker v. Des Moines Indep. Cmty. Sch. Dist.*, 393 U.S. 503 (1969); *Guiles v. Marineau*, 461 F.3d 320 (2d Cir. 2006), *cert. denied,* 551 U.S. 1162 (2007); see also **53:7**).

For example, in one case, a fifth grade student wrote in a class assignment that his wish was to "blow up the school with the teachers in it" and shared it with other students. Regardless as to whether his wish was a joke or the student lacked the capacity to carry it out, it caused concern among staff and students and it was reasonable for school officials to conclude that, if permitted, other students would try to copy or escalate the conduct, thereby causing a substantial decrease in discipline and disruption of the educational process (*Cuff v. Valley CSD*, 677 F.3d 109 (2d Cir. 2012)).

Nonetheless, the U. S. Supreme Court has adopted certain exceptions that permit restrictions on student speech, even in the absence of any evidence of material or substantial disruption. Pursuant to those exceptions, school districts can:

- Prohibit speech that is vulgar, lewd, or indecent (*Bethel Sch. Dist. v. Fraser*, 478 U.S. 675 (1986); *R.O. v. Ithaca City Sch. Dist.*, 645 F.3d 533 (2d Cir.), *cert. denied,* 132 S. Ct. 422 (2011)). Such would be the case, for example, when students engage in sexually explicit speech that is not legally obscene at an official school assembly (*Bethel Sch. Dist. v. Fraser*) or profanity (see *Guiles v. Marineau*), or when they seek to publish in a school newspaper, or otherwise distribute on school grounds, a student-created sexually explicit cartoon (*R.O. v. Ithaca City Sch. Dist.*). In contrast, the U.S. Supreme Court has refused to rule that school districts may censor any speech that could "fit under some definition of offensive" (*Morse v. Frederick,* 551 U.S. 393 (2007); see also **53:8**), and one federal appellate court with jurisdiction over New York, just because it is inconsistent with the basic educational mission of their schools (*R.O. v. Ithaca City Sch. Dist.*).
- Exercise editorial control over the style and content of student speech that is "school-sponsored" as long as the school's actions are reasonably related to legitimate pedagogical concerns (*Hazelwood Sch. Dist. v. Kuhlmeier*, 484 U.S. 260 (1988); see also *R.O. v. Ithaca City Sch. Dist.*), and do not amount to viewpoint discrimination (*Peck v. Baldwinsville CSD*, 426 F.3d 617 (2d Cir. 2005), *cert. denied*, 547 U.S. 1097 (2006)). This authority extends to "school-sponsored publications, theatrical productions and other expressive activities that students, parents, and members of the public might reasonably perceive to bear the imprimatur of the school" (*Hazelwood Sch. Dist. v. Kuhlmeier;* see also *Peck v. Baldwinsville CSD*), including student speeches at school-sponsored "moving up" and graduation ceremonies (*A.M. v. Taconic Hills CSD,* 510 Fed. Appx. 3 (2d Cir.), *cert. denied*, 134 S. Ct. 196 (2013)). Within this context, actions taken by school officials to avoid the perception of endorsement of religion do not constitute evidence of intent to inhibit religion or viewpoint discrimination (*Peck v. Baldwinsville CSD;* see also *A.M. v. Taconic Hills CSD*).
- Restrict student speech that they reasonably regard as promoting illegal drug use (*Morse v. Frederick*). According to the U.S. Supreme Court, this restriction is warranted by the special characteristics of the school environment and the compelling government interest in stopping drug abuse (*Id.*). It should be noted that federal appellate courts outside New York have used this same standard in cases that have not involved illegal drug use. One of those cases concerned the threat of mass school violence (*Ponce v. Secorro Indep. Sch. Dist.*, 508 F.3d 765 (5th Cir. 2007); see also *Jacobs v. Clark Cnty. Sch. Dist.*, 526 F.3d 419 (9th Cir. 2008); *Blau v. Ft. Thomas Pub. Sch. Dist.*, 401 F.3d 381 (6th Cir. 2005); *Canady v. Bossier Parrish Sch. Bd.*, 240 F.3d 437 (5th Cir. 2001) involving restrictions on student dress that were unrelated to the suppression of free expression and did not substantially burden more speech than necessary to further the governmental interest involved).

The U.S. Court of Appeals for the Second Circuit, with jurisdiction over New York, has not decided yet whether the standard articulated by the U.S. Supreme Court in *Tinker v. Des Moines Indep. Cnty. Sch. Dist.*, discussed above, applies to all other student speech that does not fit within the above exceptions (see *R.O. v. Ithaca City Sch. Dist.*; *Doninger v. Niehoff*, 642 F.3d 334 (2d Cir.), *cert. denied*, 132 S. Ct. 499 (2011)).

53:3. Can school districts offer students more free speech protection than is constitutionally required?

Yes. That might be the case, for example, where school board policy limits a district's authority to exercise editorial control over school-sponsored publications (see **53:2**) to situations where there is an imminent threat of disruption to the education process or where the contents are libelous or obscene, or by establishing a process for settling disagreements over the contents of such publications (*Matter of Brenner*, 28 Ed Dept Rep 402 (1989)). Such a policy, like any other policy, must be adhered to even though it is more restrictive of a school's authority than constitutional standards (*Id.*; see also *Appeal of Adriatico*, 39 Ed Dept Rep 248 (1999)), and it must be applied consistently (see *Appeal of Joannides,* 32 Ed Dept Rep 278 (1992)).

53:4. Are the free speech rights of elementary school students more limited than those of high school students?

This issue is not firmly settled, as most litigation regarding student free speech rights has centered on children of high school age.

Several federal appellate courts outside of New York have considered student age a factor in assessing the extent of a student's free speech rights and in some cases have found that greater restrictions are permissible in an elementary school setting (*S.G. v. Sayreville Bd. of Educ.*, 333 F.3d 417 (3d Cir. 2003), *cert. denied*, 540 U.S. 1104 (2004); see also *Morgan v. Swanson*, 659 F.3d 359 (5th Cir. 2011), *cert. denied*, 132 S. Ct. 2740 (2012); *Walker-Serrano v. Leonard*, 168 F.Supp.2d 332 (M.D. Pa. 2001), *aff'd*, 325 F.3d 412 (3d Cir. 2003); *Morgan v. Plano Indep. Sch. Dist.*, 589 F.3d 740 (5th Cir. 2009), *cert. denied*, 130 S. Ct. 3503 (2010); *Baxter v. Vigo*, 26 F.3d 728 (7th Cir. 1994)). One of those courts, for example, upheld restrictions on the right of elementary school students to distribute materials in the school cafeteria during lunch time that were imposed to ensure younger, less mature students take lunch quickly and efficiently in a limited period of time (*Morgan v. Plano Indep. Sch. Dist.*).

On the other hand, according to a federal district court in New York, it was unlawful for a school district to prevent an elementary school student from distributing flyers with a religious message during non-instructional hours, in the absence of a reasonable belief that such distribution would cause disruption (*M.B. v. Liverpool CSD,* 487 F.Supp.2d 117 (N.D.N.Y. 2007); see also *Morgan v. Swanson*).

53:5. What forms of student speech might be entitled to constitutional protection?

As reflected in the questions that follow, possible violations of student First Amendment free speech rights can involve a broad range of issues related to, for example, student spoken statements or symbolic acts, distribution of written materials, dress restrictions, class work, and the use of computer technology. However, the First Amendment protects only student conduct that expresses a political or religious viewpoint in the absence of actual or potential material and substantial disruption, and that is not vulgar, lewd, indecent, or promote illegal drugs (see **53:1-2**).

Thus, it was appropriate in one case for a school district to take disciplinary action against a student who made a sexually suggestive speech at a school assembly (*Bethel Sch. Dist. v. Fraser*, 478 U.S. 675 (1986)), but not in another where a student wore a t-shirt critical of President George W. Bush that contained images of drugs and alcohol as part of a political message the student wished to convey (*Guiles v. Marineau*, 461 F.3d 320 (2d Cir. 2006), *cert. denied*, 551 U.S. 1162 (2007)). In the latter case, the images were not lewd, vulgar, or indecent on their own and there was no evidence of disruption to the educational process (*Id.*).

Similarly, a school district violated the free speech rights of an elementary school student who wanted to distribute flyers with a religious message during non-instructional hours, without a reasonable belief that it would cause disruption (*M.B. v. Liverpool CSD,* 487 F.Supp.2d 117 (N.D.N.Y. 2007); see also *Morgan v. Swanson*, 659 F.3d 359 (5th Cir. 2011), *cert. denied,* 132 S. Ct. 2740 (2012)).

53:6. What forms of student speech are not entitled to constitutional protection?

The First Amendment does not protect true threats of violence (*Appeal of Ravick*, 40 Ed Dept Rep 262 (2000), citing *Watts v. United States*, 394 U.S. 705 (1969); *People v. Deitze*, 75 N.Y.2d 47 (1989)), even if the speaker of the threat does not intend to carry it out (*D.F. v. Bd. of Educ. of Syosset CSD*, 386 F.Supp.2d 119 (E.D.N.Y. 2005), *aff'd*, 180 Fed. Appx. 232 (2d Cir. 2006), *cert. denied*, 549 U.S. 1179 (2007), citing *Virginia v. Black*, 538 U.S. 343 (2003)). It suffices that a reasonable person would foresee the statement would be interpreted by those receiving it as a serious expression of intent to harm or assault (*Lovell v. Poway Unified Sch. Dist.*, 90 F.3d 367 (9th Cir. 1996); see, e.g., *Appeal of Ravick*; *D.J.M. v. Hannibal Pub. Sch. Dist.*, 647 F.3d 754 (8th Cir. 2011)).

However, according to the U.S. Court of Appeals for the Second Circuit, with jurisdiction over New York, "school officials' have significantly broader authority to sanction student speech than the [true threat] standard allows" (*Wisniewski v. Bd. of Educ. of Weedsport CSD*, 494 F.3d 34 (2d Cir. 2007), *cert. denied,* 128 S. Ct. 1741 (2008)). The appropriate standard by which to assess a school district's ability to discipline students for statements "reasonably understood as urging violent conduct" is whether school officials reasonably conclude the statements will "materially and substantially disrupt the work and discipline of the school" (*Id.*). That was the case where a student made a drawing suggesting that one of his teachers should be shot and killed and transmitted the drawing to friends via instant messaging from a home computer. According to the court, it made no difference that the student created and transmitted the drawing away from school. "[O]ff-campus conduct can create a foreseeable risk of substantial disruption within a school" (*Id.*). It also was irrelevant whether the student intended for school officials to find out about the drawing or to cause a substantial disruption if found out (*Id.*).

Applying its own standard, the Second Circuit also upheld the six-day suspension of a 10-year-old student who wrote on a drawing that was part of an in-class assignment that it was his wish to "[b]low up the school with the teachers in it" that other students saw. The student had a history of prior similar drawings, which had raised concerns for the student by school officials. The Second Circuit agreed that it was reasonable to conclude that, if permitted, the student's action would cause a chain of events that would result in substantial disruption (*Cuff v. Valley CSD*, 677 F.3d 109 (2d Cir. 2012); see also *Cox v. Warwick Valley CSD*, 654 F.3d 267 (2d Cir. 2011)).

Similarly, the commissioner of education upheld the suspension of a student who took a picture of a substitute teacher with his camera phone and posted it on Instagram with a caption which read "I'm going to kill this bitch" (*Appeal of R.T. and S.T.*, 53 Ed Dept Rep, Dec. No. 16,581 (2013)).

53:7. Can school districts prevent students from expressing their opinion on controversial issues while on school premises?

Not generally. According to the U.S. Supreme Court, it is inevitable that during the course of a school day students will engage in personal intercommunication with others. Such communications "may not be confined to the expression of those sentiments that are officially approved" be it in the classroom, the school cafeteria or other school campus areas (*Tinker v. Des Moines Indep. Cmty. Sch. Dist.,* 393 U.S. 503 (1969)).

To justify any action prohibiting a student's expression of a particular opinion, school districts must show that the expression would result in a material and substantial interference with the work of the school or impinge on the rights of other students. An "undifferentiated fear or apprehension of disturbance" does not suffice to overcome a student's right to freedom of expression. Neither is "a mere desire" to avoid controversy and the discomfort and unpleasantness that could result from the expression (*Id.*; see *M.B. v. Liverpool CSD*, 487 F.Supp.2d 117 (N.D.N.Y 2007); *K.D. v. Fillmore CSD*, 2005 U.S. Dist. LEXIS 33871 (W.D.N.Y. Sept. 2005)).

On that basis, a school district did not violate a student's First Amendment rights when it refused him permission to use the school's loudspeaker or an assembly and to distribute a statement to deny having made racially disparaging remarks after a Latino student's death. Evidence showed other students had made threats against his life, including threats to bomb his home, and police had escorted him from school. Given the highly tense atmosphere, the district could predict a likely disruption if it allowed the student a platform to speak (*DeFabio v. E. Hampton UFSD*, 658 F.Supp.2d 461 (E.D.N.Y. 2009), *aff'd*, 623 F.3d 71 (2d Cir. 2010), *cert. denied*, 131 S. Ct. 1578 (2011)).

53:8. Can school districts prohibit student speech they deem to be offensive?

There is an open issue regarding the standard that would be applicable to deciding such a case. Based on a 1986 decision from the U.S. Supreme Court (*Bethel Sch. Dist. v. Fraser*, 478 U.S. 675 (1986)), there had been an understanding that school districts could impose restrictions on student speech that was offensive. But since then, the U.S. Court of Appeals for the Second Circuit, with jurisdiction over New York, has ruled that the term "offensive" in this context refers to speech that is lewd, vulgar, or indecent (*Guiles v. Marineau*, 461 F.3d 320 (2d Cir. 2006), *cert. denied,* 551 U.S. 1162 (2007)). In addition, the U.S. Supreme Court has refused to rule that districts may restrict all manner of offensive speech (*Morse v. Frederick*, 551 U.S. 393 (2007)).

Nonetheless, it is possible that given a particular set of facts, a court may carve an exception to the "offensive" standard, as occurred under different circumstances when the U.S. Supreme Court considered the special characteristics of the school environment and the compelling governmental interest in stopping drug abuse to uphold disciplinary action taken by school officials against a student who displayed a "Bong Hits 4 Jesus" banner during an off-campus, school-sanctioned event (*Morse v. Frederick*). It also is possible that disciplinary action for offensive speech would be upheld where there is evidence of substantial disruption to the educational process (see generally *Wisniewski v. Bd. of Educ. of Weedsport CSD*, 494 F.3d 34 (2d Cir. 2007), *cert. denied*, 552 U.S. 1296 (2008)). Similarly, districts may exercise editorial control over offensive speech in school-sponsored publications and other expressive activities (see *Hazelwood Sch. Dist. v. Kuhlmeier*, 484 U.S. 260 (1988); *R.O. v. Ithaca City Sch. Dist.*, 645 F.3d 533 (2d Cir.), *cert. denied,* 132 S. Ct. 422 (2011); see also **53:2, 53:5-6, 53:11**).

According to a federal appellate court outside New York, the suspension of a student who created a webpage to launch "verbal attacks" on a classmate, including calling her a "whore," and alleging the student had herpes did not violate the student's free speech rights. Citing *Bethel Sch. Dist. v. Fraser,* that court ruled "this is not the conduct and speech that our educational system is required to tolerate." It further determined that the school also had met the substantial disruption standard of *Tinker v. Des Moines Indep. Cnty. Sch. Dist.*, 393 U.S. 503 (1969) (*Kowalski v. Berkeley Cnty. Schools*, 652 F.3d 565 (4th Cir. 2011), *cert. denied*, 132 S. Ct. 1095 (2012); see also **53:2**).

53:9. Do students have a free speech right to advocate for passage of a school district budget or a particular school board candidate on school grounds?

It depends. According to the commissioner of education, schools may allow students to post signs on school corridors urging a yes vote on a school budget if school district policy or practice allows students to post messages containing political speech in exercise of their free speech rights. Subject to time, place and manner restrictions (see **53:13**) the commissioner also has upheld the right of students to distribute literature on school grounds that expresses an opinion on a school budget or election provided the distribution is not conducted on behalf of or at the request or direction of school officials or personnel, and district funds are not used to produce or post the literature (*Appeal of Miller*, 39 Ed Dept Rep 348 (1999)). Similarly, student editors of a school-sponsored student newspaper may write editorials related to school budgets and elections if district officials and staff do not act to influence the content of the editorials (*Appeal of Doro*, 40 Ed Dept Rep 281 (2000); *Appeal of Beil & Scariati*, 26 Ed Dept Rep 109 (1986)).

53:10. Can a student whose speech raises safety concerns be temporarily removed and isolated while school officials investigate the matter?

Yes. Free speech protections do not prevent school officials from temporarily removing and isolating in a separate room a student whose ambiguous speech raises safety concerns, in order to investigate and determine whether the student's speech represents a real threat to school safety and student learning. Even if such an investigation results in discipline, the investigation itself is not to be deemed disciplinary, but rather precautionary and protective, and entitled to "unusual deference" (*Cox v. Warwick Valley CSD*, 654 F.3d 267 (2d Cir. 2011)). That was the case where a student with a history of violent tendencies and ideations handed in an essay assignment on what he would do if he had only hours to live that concluded with him taking cyanide and shooting himself in the head in front of his friends (*Id.*). For similar reasons, the court also found the actions of school officials in making a report of suspected child abuse or neglect to the NYS Department of Child and Family Services did not constitute retaliation in violation of the student's free speech rights (*Id.*).

Free Speech – Student Publications

53:11. Can school districts regulate the content of school-sponsored student publications?

Yes, if they have a valid educational purpose and do so in a reasonable manner (*Hazelwood Sch. Dist. v. Kuhlmeier*, 484 U.S. 260 (1988); see also **53:2**). For example, school districts may establish standards for school-sponsored publications that are higher than those of "'real world' publications and refuse to disseminate student speech that does not meet those standards" (*Hazelwood Sch. Dist. v. Kuhlmeier*). They also can consider the emotional maturity of the publication's audience relative to potentially sensitive topics, and can refuse to sponsor student speech that might reasonably be perceived as advocating conduct that is unlawful or otherwise inconsistent with "the shared values of a civilized social order" or "to associate the school with any position other than neutrality on matters of political controversy" (*Id.)*. In addition, school districts seeking to regulate the content of school-sponsored student publications must make sure that they have not, through policy or practice, transformed the publication into a forum opened for indiscriminate use by student reporters and editors or others. Where a school-sponsored publication is reserved for its intended purpose, such as providing a supervised learning experience for journalism students, school officials may regulate its content in any reasonable manner (*Id.*; see also *R.O. v. Ithaca City Sch. Dist*., 645 F.3d 533 (2d Cir.), *cert. denied,* 132 S. Ct. 422 (2011)).

The U.S. Court of Appeals for the Second Circuit, with jurisdiction over New York, also has upheld use of the "vulgar, lewd and indecent" standard of *Bethel Sch. Dist. v. Fraser*, 478 U.S. 675 (1986) (see **53:2**) as an alternative basis for sustaining the validity of school actions regulating the content of school-sponsored publications (*R. O. v. Ithaca City Sch. Dist.*). That was the case where a student tried to include in a school newspaper a cartoon with drawings of stick figures in various sexual positions found to be "unquestionably" lewd. According to the Second Circuit, districts may prohibit speech in school-sponsored publications that is "less than obscene," but "vulgar, lewd and indecent, or plainly offensive" (*Id.*).

53:12. May school districts regulate the contents of advertisements in school-sponsored student publications?

Yes, if they have reserved the publication for an intended purpose and have not otherwise opened it for indiscriminate use by the general public (*Hazelwood Sch. Dist. v. Kuhlmeier*, 484 U.S. 260 (1988); see also **53:11**). Thus, one federal appellate court outside of New York ruled that a school district could reject an advertisement from a family-planning group in school district newspapers, yearbooks, and programs for athletic events (*Planned Parenthood of Southern Nevada, Inc. v. Clark Cnty. Sch. Dist.*, 941 F.2d 817 (9th Cir. 1991)).

53:13. Do students have a right to distribute on school grounds literature that is written and produced off school premises?

Yes. However, school authorities may regulate the content of such literature to the extent necessary to avoid material and substantial interference with the requirements of order and discipline in the operation of schools (*Eisner v. Stamford Bd. of Educ.*, 440 F.2d 803 (2d Cir. 1971); *Appeal of Rampello*, 37 Ed Dept Rep 153 (1997); see also **53:14-15**). They also may prevent the distribution of any such literature that is vulgar, lewd, obscene, and plainly offensive (*R.O. v. Ithaca City Sch. Dist.*, 645 F.3d 533 (2d Cir.), *cert. denied,* 132 S. Ct. 422 (2011)).

In addition, school authorities may regulate the time, manner, place, and duration of the distribution to avoid interference with normal school operations (*Eisner v. Stamford Bd. of Educ.*; *Appeal of Doro*, 40 Ed Dept Rep 281 (2000); see also *M.A.L. v. Kinsland*, 543 F.3d 841 (6th Cir. 2008), *reh'g and reh'g en banc denied*, 2009 U.S. App. LEXIS 24176 (6th Cir. 2009)). Guidelines regarding the time, manner, place and duration of distribution should be specific including, for example, the areas of school property where it would be appropriate to distribute approved materials, and requirements that those distributing the literature not block pedestrian traffic or school building entrances, and remove any litter they create. They also may provide for sanctions against those who violate the prescribed procedures.

Furthermore, guidelines for the submission of literature for pre-distribution review and approval must identify to whom the literature must be submitted for clearance, and objective criteria by which distribution may be approved or prevented. They also must set an expedited time period for school officials to decide whether or not to permit distribution (*Eisner v. Stamford Bd. of Educ.; M.B. v. Liverpool CSD,* 487 F.Supp.2d 117 (N.D.N.Y. 2007)). Such guidelines may not afford school officials unfettered discretion to suppress disfavored speech or disliked speakers (*M.B. v. Liverpool CSD*).

Pre-distribution submission requirements would apply only to a substantial distribution of written material where it can reasonably be anticipated there would be a likely disruption of school operations. They would not apply to those instances where one student passes his or her copy of a magazine or other materials to another student (*Eisner v. Stamford Bd. of Educ.)*.

The same constitutional standards would apply to student distribution of religious and nonreligious literature (see *M.B. v. Liverpool CSD*; see also *Morgan v. Swanson*, 659 F.3d 359 (5th Cir. 2011), *cert. denied,* 132 S. Ct. 2740 (2012); *Hedges v. Wauconda Cmty. Unit Sch. Dist. No. 118*, 9 F.3d 1295 (7th Cir. 1993)).

53:14. Can school officials take disciplinary action against students who produce and distribute publications off school premises?

It depends. Generally, school officials have no authority to discipline students for the publication and distribution of student magazines or papers produced and distributed off school property (*Thomas v. Bd. of Educ.*, 607 F.2d 1043 (2d Cir. 1979), *cert. denied*, 444 U.S. 1081 (1980)).

However, school officials may take disciplinary action against a student where a document produced and distributed off-campus creates a foreseeable risk of a material and substantial disruption within the school. This was the case where a student transmitted a drawing depicting the shooting of a teacher to classmates using his home computer via the internet. Under those circumstances, the court upheld a one semester suspension of the student (*Wisniewski v. Bd. of Ed. of the Weedsport CSD*, 494 F.3d 34 (2d Cir. 2007), *cert. denied*, 552 U.S. 1296 (2008); see also *Doninger v. Niehoff*, 642 F.3d 334 (2d Cir.), *cert. denied*, 132 S. Ct. 499 (2011)).

53:15. Can school officials take disciplinary action against a student who produces a publication off-campus but distributes it on school premises?

Yes. School authorities may punish both on-campus and off-campus student speech and conduct that threatens to substantially interfere with the work of the school. Thus, a school district rightfully took disciplinary action against a student who produced materials at home that called for the destruction of school property and acts of insubordination and distributed copies to other students at school (*Bd. of Educ. of Monticello CSD v. Comm'r of Educ.*, 91 N.Y.2d 133 (1997); see also *Wisniewski v. Bd. of Educ. of Weedsport CSD*, 494 F.3d 34 (2d Cir. 2007), *cert denied*, 552 U.S. 1296 (2008)).

53:16. What free speech principles apply to student expressions communicated through computer technology?

The U.S. Supreme Court has not yet addressed this question directly. As with other forms of student expressive activities, school authorities have been allowed to regulate and punish student communications through the use of computer technology that have threatened harm or been disruptive to the work of the school and impinged on the rights of other students. For example, courts and the commissioner of education have upheld disciplinary action taken by school officials against a student, or group of students, found to have engaged in the following behavior:

- Called the administration "douchebags" on her publicly accessible blog, inaccurately stated the administration had canceled a school event, and urged others to call and e-mail the administration to protest this action and to "piss [them] off" (*Doninger v. Niehoff,* 642 F.3d 334 (2d Cir.), *cert. denied*, 132 S. Ct. 499 (2011)).
- "Instant messaged" friends a drawing created on his home computer that threatened the life of a teacher and caused the district to transfer the teacher out of the student's class (*Wisniewski v. Bd. of Educ. of Weedsport CSD*, 494 F.3d 34 (2d Cir. 2007), *cert. denied*, 522 U.S. 1296 (2008)), and a student who instant messaged a classmate about getting a gun and shooting other students at school (*D.J.M. v. Hannibal Pub. Sch. Dist.*, 647 F.3d 754 (8th Cir. 2011); see **53:6**).
- Issued or posted a message about bomb threats either from their home computers (*Appeal of T.N.*, 42 Ed Dept Rep 235 (2003); *Appeal of B.B.*, 38 Ed Dept Rep 666 (1999)), or from a school computer terminal (*Appeal of David and Cynthia L.*, 40 Ed Dept Rep 297 (2000)), causing student absences and cancellation of classes.
- Sent an anti-semitic e-mail from his home computer to other students at their home threatening that the "Trench Coat Mafia" was coming to school, forcing police involvement and causing students to stay at home (*Appeal of Ravick*, 40 Ed Dept Rep 262 (2000)).
- Used a school-issued laptop computer to try and gain unauthorized access to various servers across the country, including the server of his school district, and to load programs capable of sabotaging a server (*Appeal of J.C.*, 41 Ed Dept Rep 395 (2002)).
- Used his home computer to access and alter a teacher's website at school by adding sexually explicit comments about the teacher and her husband (*Appeal of D.V.*, 44 Ed Dept Rep 263

(2005); compare *Layshock v. Hermitage Sch. Dist.*, 650 F.3d 205 (3d Cir. 2011), *cert. denied, Blue Mountain Sch. Dist. v. J.S.*, 132 S. Ct. 1097 (2012)).

- Used her home computer to create and post to MySpace.com a webpage that targeted a particular classmate, labeling her a "whore," alleging she had herpes, and inviting classmates to join the online group (*Kowalski v. Berkeley Cnty. Schools*, 652 F.3d 565 (4th Cir. 2011), *cert. denied*, 132 S. Ct. 1095 (2012); see also **53:8**).
- Took a picture of a substitute teacher with his camera phone and posted it on Instagram with the caption "I'm going to kill this bitch" (*Appeal of R.T. and S.T.*, 53 Ed Dept Rep, Dec. No. 16,581 (2013)).
- Out-of-school-text-message conversation with another student containing threats and descriptions of violent acts against a third student (*Bradford v. Norwich CSD,* 54 F.Supp.3d 177 (N.D.N.Y. 2014)).

In upholding student discipline in these types of cases, the U.S. Court of Appeals for the Second Circuit, with jurisdiction over New York, and the commissioner have looked at the foreseeable or actual impact of the speech at issue on the school environment (*Wisniewski v. Bd. of Educ. of Weedsport CSD; Appeal of Ravick*). Key to their decisions have been findings of reasonable foreseeability that, although occurring off school grounds, the home computer communications would reach the school campus and cause material and substantial disruption within the school (*Id.*).

For more information on a school district's ability to discipline students for behavior occurring off school grounds, see **52:8**.

Free Speech – Student Dress

53:17. Do free speech protections extend to the way students dress while they attend school?

Yes, in some circumstances. The clothing must constitute symbolic speech representing a student's statement of either political or religious expression (see *Tinker v. Des Moines Indep. Cmty. Sch. Dist.*, 393 U.S. 503 (1969); *Appeal of Conley*, 34 Ed Dept Rep 376 (1995); *Appeal of Mangaroo*, 33 Ed Dept Rep 286 (1993); *Appeal of Pintka*, 33 Ed Dept Rep 228 (1993); see also **53:2, 53:18-22**).

Thus, in one case, the U.S. Court of Appeals for the Second Circuit, with jurisdiction over New York, determined that school officials acted unlawfully when they took disciplinary action against a student who wore a t-shirt to school that criticized President George W. Bush and depicted images of drugs and alcohol. According to the Second Circuit, while the images may be considered in poor taste, they were not vulgar, lewd, indecent or plainly offensive, particularly because they were part of an anti-drug political message. Moreover, the parties agreed that the t-shirt did not cause any disruption or confrontation in the school and district officials did not contend that they had a reasonable belief that it would in the future (*Guiles v. Marineau,* 461 F.3d 320 (2d Cir. 2006), *cert. denied,* 551 U.S. 1162 (2007)).

Similarly, a student who wore breast cancer awareness bracelets bearing the slogan "I ♥ boobies! (KEEP A BREAST)" prevailed against her school district after a federal appellate court outside New York determined that the bracelets were not plainly lewd, commented on a social issue and the district failed to show how the bracelets threatened to substantially disrupt the school (*B.H. v. Easton Area Sch. Dist.*, 725 F.3d 293 (3d Cir. 2013), *cert denied*, 134 S. Ct. 1515 (2014)).

Likewise, in a case where school officials ordered a student not to wear a pro-life t-shirt that stated "Abortion is Homicide" a court awarded the student preliminary injunctive relief preventing enforcement of the district's dress code against him, on the basis that the school officials objected to the contents of the t-shirt and there was insufficient evidence of disruption or interference with the rights of other students. Furthermore, complaints by three female students was insufficient to meet the material disruption standard

Students

and, in the court's view, "students do not have the right not to be 'upset' when confronted with a viewpoint with which they disagree" (*K.D. v. Fillmore CSD*, 2005 U.S. Dist. LEXIS 33871 (W.D.N.Y. Sept. 2005); see also *C.H. v. Bridgeton Bd. of Educ.*, 2010 U.S. Dist. LEXIS 40038 (D.N.J. Apr. 22, 2010)).

Additionally, in a case involving the right of a male student to wear female clothes and accessories while attending school, one federal district court determined that such conduct constituted speech entitled to protection because the student was trying to express her gender identity as a female. According to the court, the female clothing was "a necessary symbol of her very identity" (*Doe v. Yunits*, 2000 Mass. Super. LEXIS 491 (Mass. Super. Ct. Oct. 11, 2000) (unreported), *petition denied, Doe v. Brockton Sch. Comm.*, 2000 Mass. App. LEXIS 1128 (Mass. App. Ct. Nov. 30, 2000); see also *McMillen v. Itawamba Cnty. Sch. Dist.,* 702 F.Supp.2d 699 (N.D. Miss. 2010)).

In contrast, however, courts have upheld the authority of schools to ban students from wearing clothing depicting controversial symbols, such as the confederate flag, that can be reasonably forecast to cause substantial disruption in the school environment (see, e.g. *Hardwick v. Heyward*, 711 F.3d 426 (4th Cir.), *cert. denied*, 134 S. Ct. 201 (2013); *Defoe v. Spiva*, 625 F.3d 324 (6th Cir. 2010), *cert denied*, 132 S. Ct. 399 (2011); *B.W.A. v. Farmington R-7 Sch. Dist.*, 554 F.3d 734 (2009); *Scott v. Sch. Bd. of Alachua Cnty.*, 324 F.3d 1246 (11th Cir.), *cert. denied*, 540 U.S. 824 (2003); see also **53:20-22**). Thus, in one case, a federal appellate court outside New York upheld a school district that told students to take off or turn inside out shirts with the American flag during a Cinco de Mayo event to honor the pride and community strength of the Mexican people. The court concluded that school officials were reasonably concerned about student safety in light of ongoing racial tensions at the school, and after receiving threats of impending violence between caucasian and Mexican students (*Dariano v. Morgan Hill Unified School District*, 767 F.3d 764 (9th Cir. 2014)).

53:18. What types of free speech restrictions apply to a school district's adoption of a student dress code?

Student dress codes may not suppress expressions that are entitled to free speech protections (see **53:17**). However, according to at least one federal appellate court outside of New York, a student dress code that bans all shirts with printed messages, except those related to district-sponsored curricular clubs, organizations, athletic teams or school spirit approved by a school principal, that is viewpoint and content neutral can be deemed to be constitutionally permissible (*Palmer v. Waxahachie Indep. Sch. Dist.*, 579 F.3d 502 (5th Cir. 2009), *cert. denied*, 558 U.S. 1111 (2010)).

In addition, student dress codes may not be vague, subjective, or overly broad (*Appeal of Parsons,* 32 Ed Dept Rep 672 (1993); see also *Newsom v. Albemarle Cnty. Sch. Bd.*, 354 F.3d 249 (4th Cir. 2003); *Sypniewski v. Warren Hills Reg'l Bd. of Educ.*, 307 F.3d 243 (3d Cir.), *cert. denied*, 538 U.S. 1033 (2003)). A student dress code might be overly broad and therefore unconstitutional if, for example, it simply bans all clothing with weapons-related messages. Such a ban also would prohibit lawful non-violent and non-threatening symbols such as the fighting insignia of military units in overseas operations in which student family members might serve (*Newsom v. Albemarle Cnty. Sch. Bd.*). However, a student dress code provision stating "no tolerance for clothing or accessories that have inappropriate symbolism, especially that which discriminates against other students based on race, religion or sex" and a specific rule banning displays of the confederate flag was found not to be unconstitutionally over broad or vague (*A.M. v. Cash,* 585 F.3d 214 (5th Cir. 2009)).

53:19. Are there restrictions other than free speech considerations that limit the ability of school districts to regulate student dress at school?

Yes. The commissioner of education has indicated that school districts may not regulate the way students dress while in school based solely on fashion or taste considerations (*Appeal of Pintka,*

33 Ed Dept Rep 228 (1993)). Instead, student dress codes must address legitimate educational concerns, such as teaching socially appropriate behavior, eliminating potential health or safety hazards, ensuring the integrity of the educational process, or avoiding school violence (*Id.*). Such would be the case if a student refuses to wear long pants in a lab area (*Appeal of Bartlett*, 33 Ed Dept Rep 234 (1993)), or remove his hat during a class exercise on demonstrating personal appearance as part of learning how to present one's self in a competitive job market and during a job interview (*Appeal of Conley*, 34 Ed Dept Rep 376 (1995)). Similarly, a federal appellate court outside New York upheld a student dress code that prohibited the wearing of pierced jewelry other than in the ear at school, based on a legitimate safety concern (*Bar-Navon v. Brevard Cnty. Sch. Bd.*, 290 Fed.Appx. 273 (11th Cir. 2008)).

In addition, school districts must develop their student dress code in consultation with teachers, administrators, other school services professionals, students, and parents (8 NYCRR § 100.2(l)(2)(i), (ii)(a)) to ensure it reflects "current community standards" on "proper decorum and deportment" (*Appeal of Pintka*; see also *Appeal of Phillips*, 38 Ed Dept Rep 297 (1998)).

53:20. Can school districts prohibit students from wearing symbols of political or controversial significance?

Not generally. As in the case of spoken statements (see **53:5**), students have a right to wear or display buttons, armbands, flags, decals, or other badges that are symbolic of personal expression. However, the wearing of such symbols may not materially and substantially interfere with the orderly process of the school or the rights of others (*Tinker v. Des Moines Indep. Cmty. Sch. Dist.*, 393 U.S. 503 (1969)). Accordingly, courts have upheld bans on displays of the confederate flag on school grounds in districts with documented hostile racial relations among students (*Hardwick v. Heyward*, 711 F.3d 426 (4th Cir.), *cert. denied*, 134 S. Ct. 201 (2013); *Defoe v. Spiva*, 625 F.3d 324 (6th Cir. 2010), *cert. denied*, 132 S.Ct. 399 (2011); *A.M. v. Cash,* 585 F.3d 214 (5th Cir. 2009); *B.W.A. v. Farmington R-7 Sch. Dist.*, 554 F.3d 734 (8th Cir. 2009); *Barr v. Lafon,* 538 F.3d 554 (6th Cir. 2008), *cert. denied*, 558 U.S. 817 (2009)). For example, one federal appellate court outside New York upheld a ban prohibiting students from wearing or displaying the American flag on Cinco de Mayo based on a history of ongoing racial tension and gang violence between white and Latino students (*Dariano v. Morgan Hill Unified Sch. Dist.*,745 F.3d 354 (9th Cir. 2014); see also **53:17**).

In addition, such symbols may not contain lewd, vulgar, or indecent material (see *Bethel Sch. Dist. v. Fraser*, 478 U.S. 675 (1986)). Thus, a school district may take disciplinary action against a student who wears clothing displaying a phallic symbol and sexual metaphors without violating the student's free speech rights (*Appeal of Parsons*, 32 Ed Dept Rep 672 (1993)).

Neither may such symbols advocate illegal drug use (see *Morse v. Frederick*, 551 U.S. 393 (2007)).

53:21. Can school districts prohibit students from wearing "gang-related" clothing and accessories from school premises?

It depends. School districts may ban such items if there is evidence of gang presence, activity, and violence in the schools that might reasonably lead school authorities to forecast substantial disruption of school activities. That was the case, for example, where a school banned students from wearing a t-shirt with a photo of a deceased suspected gang member and the word "RIP." According to the court, the school district presented uncontroverted evidence at trial that when the ban was imposed they had information that reasonably led them to believe the t-shirts would cause a substantial disruption or interference with school activities because the t-shirts might elicit violence from gang members or others (*Kuhr v. Millard Pub. Sch. Dist.*, 2012 U.S. Dist. LEXIS 56189 (D. Neb. April 23, 2012)).

However, a broad ban on "gang-related" apparel such as rosaries or sports team logos, or the wearing of earrings by male students, would violate student First Amendment rights absent connection of such items or the student wearing them to any gang (see *Grzywna v. Schenectady City Sch. Dist.*, 489 F. Supp.2d 139 (N.D.N.Y. 2006); see *Chalifoux v. New Caney Indep. Sch. Dist.*, 976 F.Supp. 659 (S.D. Tex. 1997); *Jeglin v. San Jacinto Unified Sch. Dist.*, 827 F.Supp. 1459 (C.D. Cal. 1993); *Olesen v. Bd. of Educ. of Sch. Dist. No. 228*, 676 F.Supp. 820 (N.D. Ill. 1987)). So would a ban on clothing with messages that might create ill will, such as the "Top Ten Reasons You Might Be a Redneck Fan," but which are not related to gangs at a particular school (*Sypniewski v. Warren Hills Reg'l Bd. of Educ.*, 307 F.3d 243 (3d Cir. 2002), *cert. denied*, 538 US 1033 (2003)).

In addition, school rules banning gang-related clothing and accessories from school can violate student First Amendment rights also if they are vague. For example, it is not sufficient to merely state that "[g]ang related activities such as display of colors, symbols, signals, signs, etc., will not be tolerated on school grounds." Such a bare statement fails to provide adequate notice regarding unacceptable conduct, or offer clear guidance of its application (*Stephenson v. Davenport Cmty. Sch. Dist.*, 110 F.3d 1303 (8th Cir.), *reh'g, en banc, denied,* 1997 U.S. App. LEXIS 13019 (8th Cir. May 30, 1997); see also *Lopez v. Bay Shore UFSD*, 668 F.Supp.2d 406 (E.D.N.Y. 2009)). On the other hand, a school rule prohibiting specific activities, such as membership recruitment, and threatening or intimidating students to commit acts in furtherance of gang purposes would be sufficiently clear as to what activities are prohibited (*Fuller v. Decatur Pub. Sch. Bd. of Educ. Sch. Dist. No. 61,* 251 F.3d 662 (7th Cir. 2001)).

53:22. May school districts require that students wear a school uniform?

Not generally. The commissioner of education has ruled that under New York law, a school district lacks authority to compel students to wear a uniform or particular kind of clothing or force exclusion from school (*Appeal of Dalrymple*, 5 Ed Dept Rep 113 (1966)).

However a federal district court upheld a New York City School District policy mandating that students in prekindergarten through grade 8 wear a uniform, but which also allowed parents to secure an exception from that mandate. In addition, the policy provided that discipline for noncompliance could not include suspension from class or school, or affect an academic grade or participation in an extracurricular activity. Instead, the policy limited corrective measures to parent or student-teacher conferences and reprimands (*Lipsman v. N.Y. City Bd. of Educ.*, 1999 U.S. Dist. LEXIS 10591 (S.D.N.Y. July 14, 1999)).

Concerning the possibility that a school uniform policy might violate student First Amendment rights, one federal appellate court outside New York ruled that a mandatory school uniform policy implemented to reduce student behavior problems and improve the educational process did not violate such rights because the policy was viewpoint neutral, furthered an important governmental interest, and the restrictions placed on students' expressive rights were no greater than necessary to further the governmental interest (*Canady v. Bossier Parish Sch. Bd.*, 240 F.3d 437 (5th Cir. 2001); see also *Jacobs v. Clark Cnty. Sch. Dist.*, 526 F.3d 419 (9th Cir. 2008)). According to an Arizona state court, a mandatory uniform policy that allowed students who did not wish to wear a uniform to transfer to another district school without such a policy or to a school outside the district did not violate student First Amendment rights either (*Phoenix Elem. Sch. Dist. No. 1 v. Green*, 943 P.2d 836 (Ariz. App. Div. 2), *review denied,* (Ariz. App. Div. 2, Sept. 16, 1997)).

53:23. Can school districts ban fraternities, sororities or secret societies from their public schools?

Yes. New York's Education Law authorizes school boards to adopt rules and regulations that abolish and/or prohibit any fraternity, sorority, or secret society in any secondary school under their jurisdiction (§§ 1709-a(1), 2503-a(1), 2554-a(1)). Groups covered include those where the decision to accept new members is made by the group's membership rather than by the free choice of the student who wishes to enter. Certain organizations, such as the Boy Scouts and the Girl Scouts, are exempt from this definition (§§ 1709-a(2), 2503-a(3), 2554-a(3)).

Before taking action to abolish or prohibit any such group, a school board must determine that the group has, by virtue of its activities, caused or created a disruption of or interference with the academic processes of any secondary school, or caused or created such interference with the progress of any student or students in any secondary school within the district's jurisdiction (§§ 1709-a(1)(a), 2503-a(2), 2554-a(2)). Following adoption and dissemination of such a policy, a school district may discipline any student who promises to join, becomes a member of, remains a member of, or solicits any person to join the group in question (§§ 1709-a(3), 2503-a(4), 2554-a(4); for information on fraternity initiations, see §§ 120.16 and 120.17 of the Penal Law, which concern hazing).

Search and Seizure

53:24. Does the Fourth Amendment impose limitations on the ability of public school officials to search students and their belongings?

Yes. The Fourth Amendment to the U.S. Constitution prohibits government officials from conducting unreasonable searches and seizures (U.S. Const. Amend. IV). The U.S. Supreme Court has determined that the prohibition extends to searches by public school officials, including teachers and administrators (*New Jersey v. T.L.O.*, 469 U.S. 325 (1985)).

However, the Fourth Amendment rights of students in a public school setting and related school-sponsored activities are not as extensive as elsewhere (*New Jersey v. T.L.O.;* see also *Vernonia Sch. Dist. 47J v. Acton*, 515 U.S. 646 (1995); *Rhodes v. Guarricino*, 54 F.Supp.2d 186 (S.D.N.Y. 1999)). Generally, a search will violate the Fourth Amendment unless it is based on probable cause to believe that a violation of law has occurred and is conducted pursuant to a warrant. But the legality of a search by school officials is determined by balancing a school's need to maintain discipline in the classroom and on school grounds against a student's legitimate expectation of privacy. The legality of a search depends on the reasonableness of the search, under all the circumstances (*Id.*; see **53:25**).

A request by school officials for students to empty their pockets constitutes the equivalent of a search of the pockets themselves (*Appeal of a Student with a Disability*, 50 Ed Dept Rep, Dec. No. 16,168 (2010); *Appeal of J.R. and N.R.*, 48 Ed Dept Rep 239 (2008)). But asking a student to empty his pockets after reports that the student was high and acting differently was found to be, by a federal district court in New York, a minimally invasive search that was supported by reasonable suspicion the student was high and had drugs in his possession (*Faber v. Monticello CSD*, 2013 U.S. Dist. LEXIS 79869 (S.D.N.Y. 2013)).

School officials may conduct searches in the presence of witnesses. Such a practice provides corroboration of the findings and prevents or counteracts false claims of illegal items having been planted (*People v. Scott D.*, 34 N.Y.2d 483 (1974)).

53:25. Under what circumstances will a court deem a search of students and their belongings by public school officials to be valid?

In most cases, a search by public school officials will be valid if it passes two questions, commonly referred to as the *reasonable suspicion standard.* First, was the search justified at its inception? Second, was the scope of the search, as actually conducted, reasonably related to the circumstances that justified it? (*New Jersey v. T.L.O.*, 469 U.S. 325 (1985); see also *Binder v. Cold Spring Harbor CSD*, 2010 U.S. Dist. LEXIS 83493 (E.D.N.Y. July 19, 2010), *accepted by*, 2010 U.S. Dist. LEXIS 83485 (E.D.N.Y. Aug. 2010); *Appeal of a Student with a Disability*, 50 Ed Dept Rep, Dec. No. 16,168 (2010)).

A school search will be justified at its inception if the school officials had reasonable grounds to suspect it would turn up evidence that a student had violated or was violating law or school rules (*Id.*).

Under New York cases, the suspicion must be unequivocal, and the information that supports the suspicion must be reliable and precise (*People v. Scott D.*, 34 N.Y.2d 483 (1974); *People v. Singletary*, 37 N.Y.2d 310 (1975)).

The scope of a school search will be permissible if the measures used were related to the objectives of the search, and not excessively intrusive in light of the age and sex of the student and the nature of the infraction (*New Jersey v. T.L.O.*). Thus, its reasonableness may depend, for example, on the area searched in relation to the area where one could reasonably expect to find evidence of a violation of law or school rule; the time and place of the search in relation to when and where the alleged violation occurred; the duration of the search; and the intrusiveness of the search.

In cases involving a high degree of intrusiveness, such as the strip search of students, the U.S. Supreme Court has stated school officials must have a reasonable suspicion of danger or a reasonable suspicion that the student has hidden evidence beneath his or her underwear. There is a "quantum" difference between circumstances that justify the search of a student's backpack or outer clothing and those that warrant exposure of a student's private parts (*Safford Unified Sch. Dist. v. Redding,* 557 U.S. 364 (2009)).

Prior to the U.S. Supreme Court's ruling in *Safford Unified Sch. Dist.*, the U.S. Court of Appeals for the Second Circuit, with jurisdiction over New York, had determined that the reasonable suspicion standard requires a high level of suspicion to justify such a search at its inception (*Phaneuf v. Fraikin*, 448 F.3d 591 (2d Cir. 2006)). One New York federal district court had ruled that searching a student's shoes, socks, and sweatshirt and the exposure of his ankles and waistband did not constitute a strip search where the student was not asked to remove his shirt or pants (*Vasallo v. Lando*, 591 F.Supp.2d 172 (E.D.N.Y. 2008)). In comparison, a federal appellate court outside of New York facing a similar issue ruled, in a post-*Safford Unified Sch. Dist. v. Redding* decision, that a search requiring female students to lower their pants to their knees or thighs and unhook and shake their bras is "highly intrusive" (*Knisley v. Pike Cnty. Joint Vocational Sch. Dist.*, 604 F.3d 977 (6th Cir.), *cert. denied*, 131 S.Ct. 498 (2010)).

On the other hand, a New York federal district court has ruled that the actions of a school nurse requiring a female student to lower her pants to her ankles and lift her skirt over her bra in a closet in the school nurses office to determine whether the student was cutting herself did not constitute an unlawful search. According to the court, the search was conducted for medical reasons to determine if the student had injured herself, rather than to look for contraband or evidence of rule breaking. Thus, the search did not constitute a search under the Fourth Amendment (*Masciotta v. Clarkstown CSD,* 136 F.Supp.3d 527 (2015)).

53:26. Do different rules apply when police are involved in a school search?

There is no clear standard for assessing the validity of searches conducted by school officials in conjunction with or at the request of police authorities (see *New Jersey v. T.L.O.*, 469 U.S. 325 (1985); *Doyle v. Roundout Valley CSD*, 3 A.D.3d 669 (3d Dep't 2004)). Courts throughout the country have reached different conclusions.

One New York State appellate court declined to decide the issue when it dismissed a complaint on other grounds (*Doyle v. Roundout Valley CSD*). Since then, however, one federal district court in New York ruled that the reasonable suspicion standard (see **53:25**) applied to a search conducted by school officials with police assistance in a case where:

- School officials made the initial decision to conduct the search and call the police;
- The police did not use the actions by school officials as a pretext for circumventing probable cause and warrant requirements (see **53:24**); and
- The police merely assisted school officials in conducting the search together with and at the direction of the school officials (*Vassallo v. Lando*, 591 F.Supp.2d 172 (E.D.N.Y. 2008)).

Other federal courts outside New York also have applied the reasonable suspicion standard (see **53:25**) to combined police and school officials searches (see *Gray ex rel. Alexander v. Bostic,* 458 F.3d 1295 (11th Cir. 2006), *cert. denied,* 550 U.S. 956 (2007); *Cason v. Cook*, 810 F.2d 188 (8th Cir.), *cert. denied,* 482 U.S. 930 (1987); *Johnson v. City of Lincoln Park*, 434 F.Supp.2d 467 (E.D. Mich. 2006)).

However, at least one court has determined that the probable cause standard instead of the reasonable suspension standard would apply if the search is conducted solely at the behest of police, or police involvement is more than minimal (*M.D. v. Smith,* 504 F.Supp.2d 1238 (M.D. Ala. 2007)).

There also is no clear standard for assessing the validity of a school search conducted by police authorities with minimal involvement by public school officials. One New York appellate court applied the reasonable suspicion standard in a case where the search was conducted by a school safety officer assigned exclusively to school security (*Matter of Stephen A*., 308 A.D.2d 359 (1st Dep't 2003); see also *Shade v. City of Farmington*, 309 F.3d 1054 (8th Cir. 2002)). But other courts outside New York have determined that police officers involved in school searches with minimal school involvement require probable cause (*State v. Tywayne H*., 123 N.M. 42, *cert. denied*, 123 N.M. 83 (1997); *Picha v. Wielgos*, 410 F.Supp. 1214 (N.D. Ill. 1976); see also *M.D. v. Smith*).

53:27. Does New York provide students more protection than the Fourth Amendment?

Generally, the reasonable suspicion standard applied to school searches under the Fourth Amendment (see **53:25**) is also appropriate under the N.Y. Constitution (*In the Matter of Gregory M*., 82 N.Y.2d 588 (1993); see also *Appeal of a Student with a Disability*, 50 Ed Dept Rep, Dec. No. 16,168 (2010)).

However, New York's Education Law provides greater protection with respect to, for example, drug testing of students. Although the U.S. Supreme Court has upheld school policies requiring mandatory drug testing of student athletes (*Vernonia Sch. Dist. 47J v. Acton*, 515 U.S. 646 (1995)) and middle and high school students participating in extracurricular activities (*Bd. of Educ. of Indep. Sch. Dist. No. 92 of Pottawatomie Cnty. v. Earls*, 536 U.S. 822 (2002)), New York's Education Law prohibits such testing without parental consent (§ 912-a(2); *Appeal of Studley*, 38 Ed Dept Rep 258 (1998); see **53:31**).

A federal district court in New York upheld under the Fourth Amendment the administration of an initial saliva test by school officials who had reasonable suspicion to believe that a student was under the influence of illegal drugs (*Mac Ineirghe v. Bd. of Educ. of East Islip UFSD*, 2007 U.S. Dist. LEXIS 61841 (E.D.N.Y. Aug. 22, 2007)). However, regarding the student's claim of an illegal violation of New York's Education Law requirements, the court determined that the state's legislative scheme conferred upon the commissioner of education the duty to enforce those provisions (*Id*.).

53:28. Must public school officials have individualized suspicion of wrongdoing by a particular student before searching the student's person and/or belongings?

Not generally, but it is important to note that the level of suspicion and the scope of the search, as well as the specific school interest furthered by the search, can be relevant to assessing the overall reasonableness of a search (*Vernonia Sch. Dist. 47J v. Acton*, 515 U.S. 646 (1995); see also *Rhodes v. Guarricino*, 54 F.Supp.2d 186 (S.D.N.Y 1999); *Matter of Gregory M*., 82 N.Y.2d 588 (1993)).

Although individualized suspicion is not required, public school officials generally cannot conduct random causeless searches (*People v. Scott D*., 34 N.Y.2d 483 (1974); see also *Doe v. Little Rock Sch. Dist.,* 380 F.3d 349 (8th Cir. 2004)). Neither can they search students to merely remove materials that may cause distractions in order to foster a "calm focused learning environment" (*Hough v. Shakopee Pub. Schs*., 608 F.Supp.2d 1087 (D. Minn. 2009)).

53:29. May public school officials search students and/or their belongings based on an informant's tip?

It depends. In *New Jersey v. T.L.O.*, 469 U.S. 325 (1985), where the U.S. Supreme Court established the reasonable suspicion standard generally applicable to school searches (see **53:25**), a vice-principal searched a student's purse for cigarettes and found drug evidence based on a teacher's report that she found the student smoking in a lavatory. It should be noted, however, that although the student contested the legality of the search she never challenged the teacher's credibility or the validity of her information.

On the other hand, in a case pre-dating the *T.L.O.* decision, New York's Court of Appeals ruled unconstitutional a search based on a teacher's observation of "unusual behavior" by a student who entered a school bathroom twice during the same morning within one hour with another student, both exiting within seconds. There also was evidence that the student had been under observation for possible drug involvement based on information from confidential sources, and had been seen having lunch with another student also under suspicion. But both the bathroom visits and the student's lunch with another student were also susceptible of innocent explanation. In addition, there was no evidence of the informant's conclusion or reliability, who only indicated possible drug dealing (*People v. Scott D.*, 34 N.Y.2d 483 (1974)).

By comparison, the New York Court of Appeals upheld the validity of a search conducted based on a tip from a student-informant, where the student-informant had furnished information on the sale of narcotics on school premises on five prior occasions, each time leading school officials to the discovery of narcotics. School officials had acted based on concrete, articulable facts, provided by an informant with a proven reliable record (*People v. Singletary,* 37 N.Y.2d 310 (1975)).

Both New York cases establish that the reasonableness of a school search based on an informant's tip is predicated upon the proven reliability of the informant and unequivocal informant conclusions. Corroboration factors may help establish an informant's reliability and the validity of the tip provided.

School officials are not required to disclose the identity of an informant to a student subjected to a search (*People v. Singletary*).

53:30. Can public school officials "pat down" students and their belongings?

Yes, if the pat down is the least intrusive, most practical means of furthering a specific school objective and represents a reasonable balance between student privacy rights and school interests in maintaining order. That was the case where school officials patted the outer clothing of students as they arrived at school on Halloween to search for eggs and prevent a repeat of prior egg-throwing incidents. A student challenged the pat down after a gun was found in his waistband during the process (*Matter of Haseen N.*, 251 A.D.2d 505 (2d Dep't 1998)).

In a separate case, a court ruled that a less strict justification than reasonable suspicion supported the actions of a school security officer who ran his fingers over the outer surface of a student's book bag, and felt the outline of a gun. The bag made a metallic thud after the student tossed it on a metal shelf on his way to the Dean's office. A subsequent search of the bag revealed a gun. But in applying the graduated reasonableness standard, the court was careful to note the minimal nature of the search, and that it was conducted for school security needs rather than criminal investigative purposes (*In the Matter of Gregory M.*, 82 N.Y.2d 588 (1993)).

School officials must be careful not to consider the permissibility of the pat downs discussed above as authority to dispense with the reasonable suspicion standard applicable to the search of students actually suspected of violating a law or school rule and their belongings, or to engage in more intrusive searches of a student's person (see **53:25**).

53:31. Is it permissible to require that students submit to mandatory drug testing?

Not in New York State, unless the student's parent or legal guardian freely consent to such drug testing of his or her child (§ 912-a(2); *Appeal of Studley*, 38 Ed Dept Rep 258 (1998); see also **50:33**).

Drug testing involves a search under the Fourth Amendment. But the U.S. Supreme Court has upheld school policies requiring mandatory drug testing in two cases. One involved the testing of student athletes (*Vernonia Sch. Dist. 47J v. Acton*, 515 U.S. 646 (1995)). The other, middle and high school students participating in extracurricular activities (*Bd. of Educ. of Indep. Sch. Dist. No. 92 of Pottawatomie Cnty. v. Earls*, 536 U.S. 822 (2002)). In each case, the court weighed the severity of district concerns over illegal drug use, the limited privacy interest of students in a public school environment, and the relative unobtrusiveness of the process followed to conduct the tests.

However, according to the commissioner of education, New York school districts lack statutory authority to mandate that students submit to suspicionless drug testing, without parental consent. Moreover, since New York law only permits schools to drug test students upon the consent or request of a parent, the refusal of parents to give such consent cannot result in a student being prohibited from participating in sports (*Appeal of Studley*).

53:32. Can public school officials search student lockers?

Yes, unless they have relinquished control over the lockers assigned to students (*People v. Overton*, 20 N.Y.2d 360 (1967), *aff'd on reh'g*, 24 N.Y.2d 522 (1969); see also *Appeal of Chipman*, 10 Ed Dept Rep 224 (1971)). Otherwise, students have exclusive possession of their school locker over other students, but not against school authorities (*Id.*). School officials have not only a right to inspect student lockers, but also a duty to do so upon suspicion that illegal items are stored there (*People v. Overton*).

Accordingly, it is important that school authorities include in their policies and student handbooks a provision that states that lockers, desks, and other such storage spaces remain the exclusive property of the school, and that students have no expectation of privacy with respect to these areas.

School control of student lockers can be reinforced further by requiring that students give their lock combinations to school officials, and by school retention of a master key for accessing all lockers (*Id.*).

53:33. Can school districts use trained narcotics dogs to search for drugs in public school buildings?

School district use of trained narcotics dogs to detect the scent of drugs in public schools is still an open question in New York. But some federal appellate courts outside New York have upheld such use to sniff students' lockers and cars by ruling this type of action does not constitute a search under the Fourth Amendment (*Horton v. Goose Creek Indep. Sch. Dist.*, 690 F.2d 470 (5th Cir. 1982), *cert. denied*, 463 U.S. 1207 (1983); see also *Burlison v. Springfield Pub. Schools*, 708 F.3d 1034 (8th Cir.), *cert. denied*, 134 S.Ct. 151 (2013); *Doran v. Contoocook Valley Sch. Dist.*, 616 F.Supp.2d 184 (D.N.H. 2009); *Hill v. Sharber*, 544 F.Supp.2d 670 (M.D. Tenn. 2008)).

However, courts differ on the use of scent dogs to sniff a student's person. At least one court has determined dog sniffing of a student's person does not constitute a "search" under the Fourth Amendment that would otherwise require a suspicion the student possessed drugs (*Doe v. Renfrow*, 475 F.Supp. 1012 (D.C. Ind. 1979), *aff'd*, 631 F.2d 91 (7th Cir. 1980), *cert. denied*, 451 U.S. 1022 (1981)). But others have ruled otherwise, and subjected a district's use of scent dogs to sniff a student to the reasonable suspicion requirements applicable to other student searches (*B.C. v. Plumas Unified Sch. Dist.*, 192 F.3d 1260 (9th Cir. 1999); *Horton v. Goose Creek Indep. Sch. Dist.*).

53:34. Is the use of metal detectors and scanners to detect the presence of weapons in school permissible?

Yes, if students are given notice that scanning devices will be used and procedures are established to control the process. That was the case where a school using metal detectors posted signs outside the school building and informed students at the beginning of the school year that such devices would be used. In addition, guidelines established that all students entering the building had to go through the metal detector, but that if the lines became too long, it could be decided to require only every second or third student to go through. In addition, particular students could not be searched unless there was reasonable suspicion the student was in possession of a weapon (*People v. Dukes*, 151 Misc.2d 295 (Crim. Ct. N.Y. Cnty. 1992); see also *Appeal of Coleman*, 35 Ed Dept Rep 529 (1996)).

53:35. Are public school officials prohibited from conducting searches during off-campus school activities?

No. School officials may conduct searches related to a possible violation of law and/or school rules (see **53:24-25**) both on-campus and during off-campus school activities that are organized at school, and administered completely by school employees, including excursions or trips. The setting of the search is just a factor to consider in assessing the overall reasonableness of the search (*Rhodes v. Guarricino*, 54 F.Supp.2d 186 (S.D.N.Y. 1999)).

Thus, it was permissible for a school official who chaperoned a school-sponsored trip to Disney World to search student hotel rooms. Although the students might have had some expectation of privacy in their hotel rooms, the reasonableness of a search by school officials depends on the context within which the search takes place. Prior to the search, the school official had smelled a strong odor of marijuana outside one of the student's room. In addition, the students and their parents had been made aware prior to the trip that room checks would be conducted and that alcohol and drug use was absolutely forbidden during the trip (*Id.*).

53:36. What should school officials do when they discover illegal weapons and other contraband brought by a student to school or a school-sponsored activity?

School officials have the same responsibility as every other citizen to report violations of law. In addition to notifying police, they should take the item(s) away from the student, if possible, and notify the student's parents as well.

Furthermore, school officials should be aware that 14 and 15-year-olds who possess on school grounds a loaded firearm, as defined in the Penal Law, may be criminally prosecuted as adults (Crim. Proc. Law §§ 1.20(42), 190.71(a) and Penal Law §§ 10.00(18), 30.00(2), all as amended by L. 1998, c. 435; Penal Law § 220.00(14)).

53:37. May child welfare agency workers remove a student from school in cases of suspected child abuse?

Not without a court order, or parental notice or consent (*Tenenbaum v. Williams*, 193 F.3d 581 (2d Cir. 1999), *cert. denied,* 529 U.S. 1098 (2000)). The removal of a child from school in a case of suspected child abuse constitutes a "seizure" that generally is subject to the warrant and probable cause requirements of the Fourth Amendment.

An exception to the court order or parental consent requirement would exist if the information available warrants belief that a child is immediately threatened with harm and there is insufficient time to seek prior judicial authorization. The mere "possibility of danger" is insufficient (*Id.*; see also *Pacheco v. Hopmeier*, 770 F.Supp.2d 1174 (D.N.M. 2011) involving a child's removal from school by police).

53:38. May child protective services workers interview a student in school without parental consent?

Yes. Under appropriate circumstances, school districts are required to provide such assistance and data as will enable the local child protective services (CPS) to fulfill its responsibilities under the law. Such assistance can include access to records relevant to the investigation of suspected abuse or maltreatment. It also can include access to a student for interviewing the child without parental consent or a court order when circumstances warrant interviewing the child apart from family or other household members or at the home or household where child abuse or maltreatment allegedly occurred. (18 NYCRR §432.3(i)).

53:39. May police enter a school to remove or interrogate a student?

According to a 1959 Opinion of Counsel for the NYS Education Department, police officers may enter a school to remove a student only in the following circumstances. First, if they have a warrant for the arrest of the student, or other court order authorizing the student's removal. Second, if a crime has been committed on school premises (Opinion of Counsel, 1 Ed Dept Rep 800 (1959)).

Police may not remove students from school for questioning without parental consent. Neither may police interrogate students on school premises without parental permission, unless a crime has been committed on school premises. School officials are not authorized to provide the required consent. In every instance, they should immediately contact the student's parents or guardian and try to arrange for their presence if at all possible, or obtain their consent (*Id*).

However, a state appellate court upheld the refusal of a lower court to suppress statements made by a 16 year old student charged with criminal sexual conduct when questioned by State Police on school grounds (*Matter of Christopher QQ*, 40 A.D.3d 1183 (3d Dep't 2007)). The student argued in a juvenile delinquent proceeding that the statements needed to be suppressed because his parents were not present at the time of questioning. The court rejected the student's argument finding that the Family Court Act provisions that impose additional obligations on police when they take custody of a child, including parent notification, do not apply when the child is 16 years or older (*Id.*; see Family Court Act § 305.2). Other courts addressing the issue may decide differently. See also **53:40.**

In addition, the U.S. Supreme Court has ruled that police questioning minors without a *Miranda* warning must consider the effect of a minor's relative age in understanding whether he or she is being held in custody or not (*J.D.B. v. North Carolina*, 131 S. Ct. 2394 (2011); see also Family Court Act § 305.2). In a case where police interrogation of a 13-year-old child in relation to a number of neighborhood burglaries occurred on school grounds, the U.S. Supreme Court observed that the compulsory nature of a student's presence at school may have a coercive effect on the minor, who might believe he or she is not free to leave the interrogation, particularly when the minor has been removed from the classroom and brought into a room where school officials are also present (see *J.D.B. v. North Carolina*).

On the other hand, it is permissible for child protective services workers to interview students at school without parental consent or a court order under certain specified conditions set out in state regulations (18 NYCRR § 432.3(i)).

For information on how *Miranda* warning rights affect the ability of school officials to question students on school-related matters, see **53:40.**

Other

53:40. Must public school officials give students *Miranda* warnings before questioning them?

Generally, public school officials have no obligation to give students *Miranda*-type warnings prior to questioning them while investigating school-related misconduct or a breach of school security (*Pollnow v.*

Glennon, 594 F.Supp. 220 (S.D.N.Y. 1984), *aff'd,* 757 F.2d 496 (2d Cir. 1985); *In re Daquan M.*, 64 A.D.3d 713 (2d Dep't 2009); *People v. Butler,* 188 Misc.2d 48 (Sup. Ct. Kings Cnty. 2001); *In the Matter of Brendan H.*, 82 Misc.2d 1077 (N.Y. Fam. Ct. 1975)). But court decisions suggest there would be such an obligation if school officials act in concert with or as agents of the police when questioning one of their students (*In the Matter of Brendan H.*; *People v. Manley*, 26 A.D.3d 755 (4th Dep't 2006), *lv. to appeal denied*, 6 NY3d 836 (2006); *In re Angel S.*, 302 A.D.2d 303 (1st Dep't 2003); see also *S.E. v. Grant Cnty. Bd. of Educ.*, 544 F.3d 633 (6th Cir. 2008), *cert. denied,* 556 U.S. 1208 (2009)). That would be the case if police instigate or direct the interrogation, or give input or instructions to school officials questioning a student (*In re Angel S.*; *People v. Butler*).

However, the mere presence of police officers during the questioning does not require *Miranda* warnings (*In re Angel S.*), even when the school discipline matter on which school officials question a student would carry criminal sanctions (*People v. Butler*). The same would not be true if police instigate the questioning or the school officials' interview of the student was conducted in furtherance of a police objective (*In re Tateana R.*, 64 A.D.3d 459 (1st Dep't 2009), *lv. to appeal denied*, 13 N.Y.3d 709 (2009); see also **53:39**).

Similarly, when students enjoy *Miranda* rights pursuant to a school district's code of conduct, school officials would not violate those rights when questioning and searching a student in the presence of a school resource officer as part of a routine school discipline procedure, rather than as part of a formal police investigation or interrogation by police officials entering school property for that purpose (*Appeal of a Student with a Disability*, 48 Ed Dept Rep 98 (2008), *petition dismissed, Boblia v. Bd. of Educ., Hendrick Hudson CSD*, (Sup. Ct. Albany Cnty. 2009)). That would be the case where there is no evidence that school officials were acting under the direction, or eliciting evidence of criminality on behalf, of the police (*Id.*).

Statements obtained from a student during the course of a school-related misconduct investigation may be used as evidence for disciplinary purposes (*Appeal of M.F. & P.F.*, 43 Ed Dept Rep 174 (2003)). Communications between students and school personnel, including a student's admission of misconduct, are not protected by privilege (*Appeal of M.S.*, 44 Ed Dept Rep 478 (2005); *Appeal of Bd. of Educ. of the City Sch. Dist. of the City of N.Y.*, 31 Ed Dept Rep 378 (1992)).

53:41. Are parents entitled to prior notice before school officials question their children on a disciplinary matter?

No. Neither the Education Law nor the federal constitution require school officials to contact the parents of a student before questioning that student concerning an alleged infraction of a school rule (*Appeal of M.W. & K.W.*, 55 Ed Dept Rep, Dec. No. 16,903 (2016); *Appeal of D.H.*, 47 Ed Dept Rep 77 (2007); *Appeal of Pronti*, 31 Ed Dept Rep 259 (1992)). In addition, parent consent or presence is not necessary before school officials obtain a statement from a student (*Appeal of M.F. & P.F.*, 43 Ed Dept Rep 174 (2003); *Appeal of Lago*, 38 Ed Dept Rep 723 (1999)).

However, school officials should be mindful of the length of time and manner in which the questioning of a student takes place. In one case, a court refused to dismiss a false imprisonment claim brought by parents against a school district where the questioning occurred for several hours, during which time the student was brought to the nurse's office due to health concerns (*Zegarelli-Pecheone v. New Hartford CSD,* 132 A.D.3d 1258 (4th Dep't 2015)).

53:42. May school officials investigate off-campus conduct?

Yes. There is no prohibition against school officials questioning students or conducting an investigation regarding off-campus conduct in order to determine whether pursuing disciplinary action is warranted (*Appeal of L.D.*, 55 Ed Dept Rep, Dec. No. 16,864 (2016)).

53:43. Is it unconstitutional for a school district to require that students perform community service as a condition for graduation?

No. In *Immediato v. Rye Neck Sch. Dist.*, 73 F.3d 454 (2d Cir.), *cert. denied*, 519 U.S. 813 (1996), students challenged a school board graduation requirement that high school students complete 40 hours of community service for an organization of their choice and participate in a classroom discussion of their projects. The U.S. Court of Appeals for the Second Circuit, with jurisdiction over New York, ruled that the service mandated by the requirement did not violate federal constitutional rights with respect to either the prohibition against involuntary servitude secured by the Thirteenth Amendment, or any liberty, parental, or privacy rights protected by the Fourteenth Amendment.

53:44. Is it unconstitutional to preclude students from attending school on the basis of race, creed, color, or national origin?

Yes. In addition, the Education Law provides that no person may be refused admission to or be excluded from any public school in New York State because of race, creed, color, or national origin (§ 3201(1)).

Although the segregation of students by race is prohibited by the federal constitution (*Brown v. Bd. of Educ. of Topeka, Shawnee Cnty. Kan.*, 347 U.S. 483 (1954); *Lee v. Nyquist*, 318 F.Supp. 710 (W.D.N.Y. 1970), *aff'd*, 402 U.S. 935 (1971)), the mere existence of racially segregated schools does not constitute a federal constitutional or statutory violation (*United States v. Yonkers Bd. of Educ.*, 624 F.Supp. 1276 (S.D.N.Y. 1985), *aff'd*, 837 F.2d 1181 (2d Cir. 1987), *cert. denied,* 486 U.S. 1055 (1988)). That would be so in *de facto* segregation cases where segregation is inadvertent and without assistance of school authorities and not caused by any state action but rather by social, economic, and other factors (*Hart v. Cmty. Sch. Bd. of Educ. N.Y. Sch. Dist. No. 21*, 512 F.2d 37 (2d Cir. 1975)).

School officials can adopt voluntary plans to remedy the effects of *de facto* segregation (see *Balaban v. Rubin*, 14 N.Y.2d 193, *cert. denied*, 379 U.S. 881 (1964); *Van Blerkom v. Donovan*, 15 N.Y.2d 399 (1965); *Matter of Barnhart*, 21 Ed Dept Rep 126 (1981); see also *United States v. Yonkers Bd. of Educ.*; *Brewer v. West Irondequoit CSD*, 212 F.3d 738 (2d Cir. 2000)). In some circumstances, the commissioner of education has required districts to take action to counteract *de facto* racial imbalance (*Matter of Fishburne*, 12 Ed Dept Rep 5 (1972); *Appeal of Gray*, 6 Ed Dept Rep 92 (1967); but see *Appeal of Bennardo*, 33 Ed Dept Rep 178 (1993)).

But courts have determined the fact that a substantial number of students in a school district live below the federal poverty line does not deprive those students of their State Constitutional right to a sound basic education (*Paynter v. State of N.Y.*, 290 A.D.2d 95 (4th Dep't 2001), *aff'd,* 100 N.Y.2d 434 (2003)).

A school district attempting to counteract racial imbalance must be careful in how it attempts to do so. It may not make race a decisive factor of the admissions process, but can consider race among several factors (*Grutter v. Bollinger*, 539 U.S. 306 (2003); *Gratz v. Bollinger*, 539 U.S. 244 (2003); see also *Parents Involved in Cmty. Schs. v. Seattle Sch. Dist. No. 1*, 551 U.S. 701 (2007)). Nonetheless, redistricting plans that take race into consideration may be problematic even if they are not intended to, but have the effect of, assigning students to schools based on race (see *Doe v. Lower Merion Sch. Dist.*, 665 F.3d 524 (3d Cir. 2011), *cert. denied*, 132 S.Ct. 2773 (2012); *Lewis v. Ascension Parish Sch. Bd.*, 662 F.3d 343 (5th Cir. 2011)).

[illegible] constitutional [illegible] for a school district to require that students perform community service as a condition for graduation?

[illegible]

[illegible]

[illegible] federal [illegible]

[illegible]

[illegible]

Students

54. Student with Disabilities

Applicable Laws and Basic Definitions[1]

54:1. What laws govern the education of children with disabilities?

The following statutes and their accompanying regulations govern the education of children with disabilities:

- The federal Individuals with Disabilities Education Act (IDEA), which affords all eligible children with disabilities the right to a free appropriate public education in the least restrictive environment (20 USC §§ 1400–1482; 34 CFR Part 300).
- Section 504 of the Rehabilitation Act of 1973, which prohibits discrimination on the basis of disability (29 USC §§ 701, 705, 794; 34 CFR Part 104).
- Title II of the Americans with Disabilities Act of 1994, which prohibits discrimination on the basis of disability (42 USC §§ 12101–12213).
- Article 89 of the New York State Education Law and part 200 of the commissioner's regulations, which also serve as the primary vehicle for implementing IDEA requirements in New York State.

On occasion, there is a lag between changes in the federal statutes and regulations and the incorporation of those changes into state law and regulations. During such lags, school districts nonetheless are bound by the federal requirements, except with respect to those instances where New York State law and regulations confer greater rights on students with disabilities. For further information, see NYS Education Department, *New York State Law, Regulations and Policy Not Required by Federal Law/Regulation/Policy* (revised Feb. 2016), at: http://www.p12.nysed.gov/specialed/idea/part-b-app/608-Analysis-Chart-rev-Feb-2016.pdf.

54:2. What is the definition of a child with a disability?

Generally, *a child with a disability* is one who falls within one of the classifications set forth in the Individuals with Disabilities Education Act (IDEA) and section 200.1(zz) of the commissioner's regulations, and who, because of this, needs special education or related services (20 USC § 1401(3)(A); 34 CFR § 300.8; 8 NYCRR § 200.1(zz); see also § 4401(1)).

The classifications include children who suffer from: an intellectual disability; hearing impairments, including deafness; speech or language impairments; visual impairments, including blindness; emotional disturbance; orthopedic impairments; autism; traumatic brain injury; other health impairments; or specific learning disabilities (20 USC § 1401(3)(A)(i); 34 CFR § 300.8(a)(1); 8 NYCRR § 200.1(zz); see also § 4401(1)). The category of emotional disturbance does not apply to students who are just socially maladjusted (34 CFR § 300.8(c)(4); 8 NYCRR § 200.1(zz)(4); *P.C. & M.C. v. Oceanside UFSD*, 818 F.Supp.2d 516 (E.D.N.Y. 2011)).

Children who do not fall under any of those classifications, nonetheless, may be entitled to special education and related services pursuant to section 504 of the Rehabilitation Act of 1973 (section 504) and the Americans with Disabilities Act (ADA), both of which contain a broader definition as to who may

[1] This chapter addresses, primarily, a district's responsibilities under the IDEA and New York law and regulations.

be deemed an individual with a disability (*P.C. & M.C. v. Oceanside UFSD*; *Maus v. Wappingers CSD*, 688 F.Supp.2d 282 (S.D.N.Y. 2010)).

Under section 504, an individual with a disability includes any person who has a physical or mental impairment which substantially limits one or more of such person's major life activities, has a record of such an impairment, or is regarded as having such an impairment (29 USC § 705(20)(B); 42 USC § 12102; see also § 4401(1)). The ADA extends its benefits to disabled individuals "who, with or without reasonable modifications to rules, policies or practices, the removal of architectural, communication or transportation barriers, or the provision of auxiliary aids and services, meets the essential eligibility requirements for the receipt of services or the participation in programs or activities provided by a public entity" (42 USC § 12131(2)).

Federal regulations implementing section 504 expressly impose on school districts an obligation to provide a free appropriate public education in the least restrictive environment (see **54:3, 54:7**). Implementation of an individualized education program developed in accordance with the IDEA (see **54:6**) is only one means of meeting this obligation (34 CFR §§ 104.33(b)(1), (2), 104.34(a), (b)).

54:3. What is the definition of a "free appropriate public education"?

A *free appropriate public education* (FAPE) consists of special education and related services provided to an eligible child with a disability at public expense under public supervision and direction, and in conformity with an individualized education program that is tailored to meet the unique needs of that student (20 USC § 1401(9); 34 CFR § 300.17).

School districts must make a FAPE available to all eligible children with disabilities, regardless of the severity of their disability (20 USC § 1412(a)(1)(A), (3), (4), (5)(A); *Bd. of Educ. v. Rowley*, 458 U.S. 176 (1982); or their ability to benefit from special education (*Timothy W. v. Rochester, N.H. Sch. Dist.*, 875 F.2d 954 (1st Cir.), *cert. denied*, 493 U.S. 983 (1989)).

However, a school district is not obligated to provide an optional program or to match or surpass a program offered by a private school (*Matter of a Handicapped Child*, 26 Ed Dept Rep 70 (1986)). In addition, the fact that a student is not performing at the same level as his or her general education classmates does not constitute a denial of FAPE. Academic progress must be viewed in light of the limitations of the child's disability (*H.C. v. Katonah-Lewisboro UFSD*, 528 Fed. Appx. 64 (2d Cir. 2013) (unpublished)).

54:4. What is the definition of special education?

Special education means specially designed individualized or group instruction or special services or programs provided at no cost to the parent to meet the unique needs of an eligible student with a disability. It may include instruction conducted in the classroom, homes, hospital, and other settings, special classes and resource rooms, consultant teacher services, related services, and special transportation (20 USC § 1401(29); 34 CFR § 300.39; Educ. Law § 4401(2); 8 NYCRR § 200.1(ww)). *Specially designed instruction* refers to instruction adapted, as appropriate, to meet the needs of an eligible student with a disability (20 USC § 1401(29); 34 CFR § 300.39(b)(3); 8 NYCRR § 200.1(vv)).

54:5. What are related services?

Related services consist of transportation and such developmental, corrective, and other supportive services as may be required to assist a child with a disability, including the early identification and assessment of disabling conditions in students, speech-language pathology, and audiology services; interpreting services; psychological services; physical and occupational therapy; school social work services; counseling services (including rehabilitation counseling, orientation, and mobility services); medical services for diagnostic and evaluation purposes only; parent counseling and training; school health services and school nurse services; assistive technology services, other appropriate developmental or corrective support services; appropriate access to recreation (including therapeutic recreation), and other appropriate support services (20 USC § 1401(26); 34 CFR § 300.34; Educ. Law § 4401(2)(k); 8 NYCRR § 200.1(qq), (ss)).

Related services do not include a medical device that is surgically implanted, or the maintenance, programming, or replacement of such a device or an external component of the device (*Id.*; 34 CFR § 300.113(b)(2); 8 NYCRR § 200.1(qq)(1)). Neither do they include the optimization of that device's functioning (34 CFR § 300.34(b)(1); 8 NYCRR § 200.1(qq)(1)). However, a school district must routinely check an external component of a surgically-implanted device to make sure it is functioning properly (34 CFR §§ 300.34(b), 300.113(b); 8 NYCRR § 200.1(qq)(1)(iii)).

54:6. What is an individualized education program?

An *individualized education program* (IEP) is a written statement outlining the plan for providing an educational program for a disabled student based on the unique needs of that student. It must include, for example:

- The classification of the student's disability.
- The student's present levels of academic achievement and functional performance, and the individual needs of the student in the areas of academic achievement, functional performance and learning characteristics, social and physical development, and management needs.
- Measurable annual goals consistent with the student's needs and abilities to enable the student to be involved in and progress in the general education curriculum and meet the student's other educational needs related to his or her disability.
- How the student's progress toward meeting the annual goals will be measured and when the student's parents will be informed of that progress.
- Short-term instructional objectives and benchmarks for students who take a New York State alternate assessment and for preschool students with a disability.
- Recommended special education program and services that, to the extent practicable, are based on peer reviewed research.
- Any testing accommodations to be used consistently by the student in the recommended educational program and in the administration of districtwide and state assessments necessary to measure the student's academic achievement and functional performance.
- For a student participating in an alternate assessment, the reasons why the student cannot participate in the regular assessment and why the alternate assessment selected is appropriate.
- The extent to which the student will or will not participate in the regular education program or appropriate activities with age-appropriate nondisabled peers.
- Transition services to facilitate the student's movement from school to post-school activities, beginning no later than the first IEP to be in effect when the student is age 15 (or younger if appropriate).
- Information necessary for the provision of services during the months of July and August to a student eligible for a 12-month service and/or program.
- The projected date for an annual review of the student's IEP.
- The student's recommended placement (20 USC §§ 1401(14), 1414(d)(1)(A); 34 CFR §§ 300.22, 300.320–324; 8 NYCRR §§ 200.1(y), 200.4(d)(2)), which refers to the type of program a student will attend, rather than a specific school (*R.B. v. N.Y. City Dep't of Educ.*, 603 Fed. Appx. 36 (2d Cir. 2015); *T.Y. v. N.Y. City Dep't of Educ.*, 584 F.3d 412 (2d Cir. 2009)).

IEPs must be in a form prescribed by the commissioner of education (8 NYCRR § 200.4(d)(2); see NYS Education Department, *Questions and Answers on Individualized Education Program (IEP) Development, the State's Model IEP Form and Related Documents* (updated April 2011), at: http:www.p12.nysed.gov/specialed/formsnotices/IEP/training/questions.htm). Although they are not required to maximize a disabled child's potential (*Bd. of Educ. v. Rowley*, 458 U.S. 176 (1982)), IEPs must be likely to produce progress and provide for more than trivial advancement (*Doe v. East Lyme Bd. of Educ.*, 790 F.3d 440 (2d Cir. 2015); *T.P. ex. rel. S.P. v. Mamaroneck UFSD*, 554 F.3d 247 (2d Cir. 2009); see also *Cerra v. Pawling CSD* 427 F.3d 186 (2d Cir. 2005)).

School districts must ensure that each student with a disability has an IEP in place at the start of each school year (34 CFR § 300.323(a); 8 NYCRR § 200.4(e); *T.C. & A.C. v. N.Y. City Dep't of Educ.*, 2016 U.S. Dist. LEXIS 112977 (S.D.N.Y. 2016); *Tarlowe v. N.Y. City Dep't of Educ*., 2008 U.S. Dist. LEXIS 52704 (S.D.N.Y. July 3, 2008); *Application of the Bd. of Educ. of the [Redacted] Sch. Dist.*, SRO dec. no. 10-006 (2010)).

School districts also must ensure that personnel responsible for implementing or assisting in the implementation of an IEP understand their responsibilities and receive a copy of the IEP or be able to access it electronically (34 CFR § 300.323(d); Educ. Law § 4402(7); 8 NYCRR §§ 200.2(b)(11), 200.4(e)(3), 200.16(f)(6)).

54:7. What is the meaning of the term "least restrictive environment"?

The term *least restrictive environment* (LRE) refers to the setting in which students with disabilities are educated and the obligation to ensure that, to the maximum extent appropriate, they are not placed in special classes, separate schools, or otherwise removed from the regular educational environment unless the "nature and severity of the disability is such that education in regular classes with the use of supplementary aids and services cannot be achieved satisfactorily" (20 USC § 1412(a)(5)(A); 34 CFR §§ 300.114–120; 8 NYCRR § 200.1(cc)). *Supplementary aids and services* refers to aids, services and other supports that are provided in regular education classes or other education-related settings and extracurricular and nonacademic settings to enable children with disabilities to be educated with nondisabled children to the maximum extent appropriate, in accordance with LRE requirements (20 USC § 1401(33); 34 CFR §§ 300.42, 300.107, 300.117; 8 NYCRR § 200.1(bbb)). LRE requirements apply in the same way to extended school year placements as they apply to school-year placements (*T.M. v. Cornwall CSD*, 752 F.3d 145 (2d Cir. 2014); see also **54:18**).

School districts may not remove a student with disabilities from education in an age-appropriate classroom solely because of needed modification in the general curriculum (see *Application of a Child with a Disability*, SRO dec. no. 93-35 (1993)). Neither may school districts remove a disabled child from the regular education environment on the basis that the child might make greater academic progress in a segregated special education class (see *Oberti v. Bd. of Educ. Borough of Clementon Sch. Dist.*, 995 F.2d 1204 (3d Cir. 1993)).

Students who must be removed from regular classroom instruction must be provided services within a continuum of services (see **54:8**) and a continuum of placement options (see **54:9**) that provide the individualized special education needed by the student, and for the education of the student, to the maximum extent appropriate to the needs of the student, with other students who do not have disabilities. It also must be as close as possible to the student's home (34 CFR §§ 300.114(a)(2)(i), 300.115, 300.116(b)(3); 8 NYCRR § 200.1(cc)).

In addition, LRE requirements must be balanced against the requirement that students with disabilities receive an appropriate education (*T.M. v. Cornwall CSD*, 752 F.3d 145 (2d Cir. 2014); *Briggs v. Bd. of Educ. of the State of Conn.*, 882 F.2d 688 (2d Cir. 1989); see also 34 CFR § 300.116(d); *P. v. Newington Bd. of Educ.*, 546 F.3d 111 (2d Cir. 2008)).

Placement of a student with a disability in an integrated co-taught classroom where there could be as many as 12 other students with disabilities alongside general education students does not violate LRE requirements. A student with a disability is not entitled to a regular education classroom in which he or she is the only student with an IEP (*M.W. v. N.Y. City Dep't of Educ.*, 725 F.3d 131 (2d Cir. 2013)).

54:8. What is the meaning of the term "continuum of services"?

The term *continuum of services* refers to an array of services designed to meet an individual student's needs. It includes direct and/or indirect consultant teacher services, resource room services, related services, integrated co-teaching services, and special classes. Students who must be removed from regular classroom instruction must be provided services within such continuum (8 NYCRR § 200.6). For additional information on the continuum of services, see NYS Education Department, *Continuum of Special Education Services for School-Age Students with Disabilities* (updated Nov. 2013), at: http://www.p12.nysed.gov/specialed/publications/policy/schoolagecontinuum-revNov13.htm).

54:9. What is the meaning of the term "continuum of placement options"?

The term *continuum of placement options*, distinct from the continuum of services (see **54:8**), refers to settings that include public schools, boards of cooperative educational services, private approved day and residential schools, and home and hospital instruction, as well as interim alternative educational setting options for students with disabilities who have been suspended or removed temporarily from their current placement for more than 10 school days because of disciplinary or other behavior related issues (NYS Education Department, *Continuum of Special Education Services for School-Age Students with Disabilities* (updated Nov. 2013), at: http://www.p12.nysed.gov/specialed/publications/policy/schoolagecontinuum-revNov13.htm).

School District Responsibilities

54:10. What are a school district's basic responsibilities in providing for the education of children with disabilities?

The most basic responsibility school districts have regarding the education of children with disabilities is to provide all those eligible with a free appropriate public education in the least restrictive environment appropriate to meet their individual needs in conformity with their individualized education program (20 USC §§ 1401(3), 1412(a)(1)(A), (3), (4), (5)(A); 34 CFR §§ 300.101–02; *Bd. of Educ. v. Rowley*, 458 U.S. 176 (1982); *Application of a Child with a Handicapping Condition*, 30 Ed Dept Rep 64 (1990)), and regardless of the severity of their disabilities or their ability to benefit from special education (*Timothy W. v. Rochester Sch. Dist.*, 875 F.2d 954 (1st Cir.), *cert. denied*, 493 U.S. 983 (1989)). This responsibility applies, as well, to disabled students incarcerated in county correctional facilities for 10 or more calendar days (Educ. Law § 3202(7); 8 NYCRR Part 118; see also NYS Education Department, *Special Education Responsibilities for Students Incarcerated in County Correctional Facilities* (Oct. 2010), at: http://www.p12.nysed.gov/specialed/publications/qa/LEA-incarcerated.htm).

Districts also must:

- Identify, locate and/or evaluate, and maintain information about all children with disabilities who reside or attend private school within their districts (20 USC § 1412(a)(3)(A), (10)(A)(ii); 34 CFR §§ 300.111, 300.131; Educ. Law §§ 3602-c(2-a), 4402(1)(a); 8 NYCRR § 200.2(a)(1); see **54:13-14**).

- Establish an individualized education program (IEP) team known in New York as the committee on special education (CSE), CSE subcommittees as appropriate, and a committee on preschool special education (CPSE) to assure the timely identification, evaluation and placement of eligible school age students with disabilities and preschool children with disabilities (20 USC § 1414(b)(4)(A), (d)(1)(B); 34 CFR § 300.321; Educ. Law §§ 4402(1)(b), 4410(3); 8 NYCRR § 200.3(a), (c)).
- Ensure that testing and evaluation materials and procedures for identifying and placing children with disabilities meet the requirements of federal and state law and regulations and are neither racially nor culturally discriminatory (20 USC §§ 1412(a)(7), 1414(a), (b), (c); 34 CFR §§ 300.304–305; 8 NYCRR § 200.4(b)(6)).
- Arrange for special education programs and services based upon completion of a student's IEP and the recommendation of the CSE or CPSE (8 NYCRR §§ 200.2(d), 200.16(f)).
- Keep on file and make available for public inspection and review by the commissioner of education, an acceptable plan of service as required by Education Law § 3602(8)(b) (8 NYCRR § 200.2(c)).
- Provide procedural safeguards for children with disabilities and their parents (20 USC § 1415; 34 CFR §§ 300.500–520; 8 NYCRR § 200.5) and notice of those procedural safeguards at various times specified in law and regulations (20 USC § 1415(d)(1)(A); 34 CFR §§ 300.504–05; 8 NYCRR § 200.5(f)(3); see **54:23-24**).
- Appoint impartial hearing officers to hear appeals over the school district's actions concerning the identification, evaluation, and placement of students with disabilities (20 USC § 1415(f)(1)(A), (3)(A); 34 CFR § 300.511; Educ. Law § 4404(1); 8 NYCRR §§ 200.2(b)(9), 200.2(e)(1), 200.5(j)(3)(i), (ii)) and report to the NYS Education Department information related to the impartial hearing process as required by the commissioner (8 NYCRR § 200.5(j)(3)(xvi); see also NYS Education Department, *Impartial Hearing Reporting System* (May 2014), at: http://www.p12.nysed.gov/specialed/dueprocess/IHRS.htm).
- Notify parents, upon their child's enrollment or attendance in a public school, of their rights regarding referral and evaluation of their child for purposes of special education services and programs under federal and state law (§ 4402(8)).

In addition, school districts must have in place certain written policies and/or administrative practices and procedures specified in law and regulations (see **54:11**).

54:11. Are school boards required to adopt any specific policies regarding the education of children with disabilities?

Yes. School boards must adopt written policies that establish administrative practices and procedures:

- To ensure that, to the maximum extent appropriate to their needs, all children with disabilities have the opportunity to participate in school district programs available to all other public school students and preschool children to participate in preschool programs (20 USC §§ 1412(a)(2), 1413(a)(1); 34 CFR §§ 300.109, 300.201; 8 NYCRR § 200.2(b)(1), (2)).
- For the continual allocation of appropriate amount of space to meet the special education program and service needs of all students with disabilities (8 NYCRR § 200.2(c)(2)(iv), (v); see also 8 NYCRR §§ 155.1(a), 155.2(b)(2), 155.12(b)(6), (d)(5)(i), 155.15(c), 200.2(g)).
- For appointing and training appropriately qualified personnel, including members and chairpersons of the committee on special education (see **54:25-31**) and committee on preschool special education (see **54:97**) (20 USC §§ 1412(a)(14), 1413(a)(3); 34 CFR §§ 300.156, 300.207; 8 NYCRR § 200.2(b)(3)).

- To ensure students with disabilities are served within a continuum of services established in commissioner's regulations, and receive programs and services, to the extent appropriate to their individual needs, to enable them to be involved in and progress in the general education curriculum (34 CFR § 300.115; 8 NYCRR § 200.2(b)(4)).
- For ensuring that parents receive and understand the request for consent for evaluation of a preschool student (8 NYCRR § 200.2(b)(5)).
- For ensuring the confidentiality of personally identifiable data, information or records pertaining to students with disabilities, including compliance with the Federal Family and Educational Rights and Privacy Act (20 USC § 1417(c); 34 CFR §§ 300.610–27; 8 NYCRR § 200.2(b)(6); see also *Disability Rights New York v. North Colonie Bd. of Educ.*, 2016 U.S. Dist. LEXIS 36509 (N.D.N.Y. 2016)).
- For implementing schoolwide approaches and pre-referral interventions to remediate a student's performance prior to referral for special education, which may include a response to intervention process consistent with requirements established in commissioner's regulations (20 USC § 1413(a)(2)(D), (4)(A), (f); 34 CFR §§ 300.208, 300.226; 8 NYCRR § 200.2(b)(7); see also NYS Education Department, *Response to Intervention, Guidance for New York State School Districts* (Oct. 2010), at: http://www.p12.nysed.gov/specialed/RTI/guidance/cover.htm)
- For the appropriate declassification of students with disabilities as required by applicable law and regulations (20 USC § 1414(c)(5); 34 CFR § 300.305(e); 8 NYCRR § 200.2(b)(8)).
- For the selection and school board appointment of impartial hearing officers in accordance with the procedures established in commissioner's regulations (8 NYCRR § 200.2(b)(9)).
- To establish a plan that ensures all instructional materials used in the district are available in a usable alternative format that meets the National Instructional Materials Accessibility Standard established in federal law, for each student with a disability in accordance with the student's educational needs and course selections at the same time that such materials are available to nondisabled students (20 USC §§ 1412(a)(23), 1474(e); 34 CFR § 300.172; 8 NYCRR § 200.2(b)(10); see NYS Education Department, *Accessible Instructional Materials (AIM)* (updated June 2016), at: http://www.p12.nysed.gov/specialed/aim).
- For ensuring that personnel responsible for implementing or assisting in the implementation of a student's individualized education program (IEP) (see **54:6**) receive a copy of the IEP or are able to access it electronically. If the policy provides for electronic access, then it must ensure that the persons responsible for the implementation of the IEP are notified and trained on how to access it electronically. The policy must also ensure that prior to the implementation of the IEP that personnel responsible for the implementation are informed of their responsibility relating to the implementation and the specific accommodations, modifications, and supports that must be provided to the student in accordance with the IEP (34 CFR § 300.323(d); Educ. Law § 4402(7); 8 NYCRR §§ 200.2(b)(11), 200.4(e)(3), 200.16(f)(6)).
- To describe guidelines for the provision of appropriate accommodations necessary to measure the academic achievement and functional performance of students in the administration of districtwide assessments (8 NYCRR § 200.2(b)(13)).
- To identify how the district, to the extent feasible, will use universal design principles in developing and administering any districtwide assessment programs (34 CFR § 300.44; 8 NYCRR § 200.2(b)(14)).
- To ensure the school district publicly reports on revisions to its policies, procedures and/or practices upon a finding by the NYS Education Department that the district has inappropriate policies, procedures and practices resulting in a significant disproportionality by race/ethnicity in the suspension, identification, classification and/or placement of students with disabilities (8 NYCRR § 200.2(b)(15)).

54:12. When do a school district's responsibilities towards students with disabilities end?

The general rule is that school districts must provide special education services to students with disabilities until they obtain a local high school or Regents diploma, or until the end of the school year in which the child turns 21, whichever occurs first (20 USC § 1412(a)(1)(A); 34 CFR §§ 300.101(a), 300.102(a)(3); Educ. Law § 4402(5); 8 NYCRR § 200.5(a)(5)(iii); *Application of Herman & Fanny M.*, 18 Ed Dept Rep 127 (1978)).

However, districts may be ordered to provide compensatory education to disabled students beyond the statutory age where there has been a gross violation of the Individuals with Disabilities Education Act that denied or excluded the student from educational services for a substantial period of time (*Garro v. State of Conn.*, 23 F.3d 734 (2d Cir. 1994); *Cosgrove v. Bd. of Educ.*, 175 F.Supp.2d 375 (N.D.N.Y. 2001); *Application of a Child with a Disability*, SRO dec. no. 02-097 (2003); see also *Application of the Bd. of Educ. of the Gowanda CSD*, SRO dec. no. 04-016 (2004)). Courts will not award compensatory education in cases where a prolonged deprivation of the opportunity for a free appropriate public education is the result of parental "obstructionist tactics" (*French v. NYS Dep't of Ed.*, 476 Fed. Appx. 468 (2d Cir. 2011)).

According to one federal appellate court outside New York State the provision of services by unlicensed, unqualified personnel warrants an award of compensatory education (*Evanston Cmty. Consol. Sch. Dist. No. 65 v. Michael M.*, 356 F.3d 798 (7th Cir. 2004)).

An award of compensatory education requires that the school district set aside and place in escrow the value of the prospective compensatory education, for use in paying up-front the associated expenses. Any money left in the escrow account at the end of the period of compensatory education is returned to the district (*Streck v. Bd of Educ. of the East Greenbush CSD*, 408 Fed. Appx. 411 (2d Cir. 2010)).

Editor's Note: Compensatory educational services, distinct from compensatory education, may be awarded to students who remain eligible to attend school but have been denied appropriate services in cases where the deprivation of instruction could be remedied through the provision of compensatory educational services before the student becomes ineligible for instruction because of age or graduation (Bd. of Educ. of City Sch. Dist. of City of Buffalo v. Munoz, 16 A.D.3d 1142 (4th Dep't 2005); *Application of a Student with a Disability*, SRO dec. no. 09-122 (2010); *see also P. v. Newington Bd. of Educ.* 546 F.3d 111 (2d Cir. 2008)).

54:13. What specific "child find" responsibilities does a school board have for identifying and maintaining data on children with disabilities?

Each school board must identify, locate, and evaluate all children with disabilities within its district (including homeless children and children who are wards of the state, highly mobile children including migrant children, children attending private schools including religious schools and home-instructed children), who are in need of special education, regardless of the severity of their disabilities and their advancement from grade to grade (20 USC § 1412(a)(3)(A), (10)(A)(ii); 34 CFR §§ 300.111(a), (c), 300.131; Educ. Law §§ 3602-c, 4402(1)(a); 8 NYCRR § 200.2(a)(1)). This includes identifying and locating nonresident students from another district or from out-of-state who have been parentally placed and are attending a private school in the district (20 USC § 1412(a)(10)(A); 34 CFR § 300.131; Educ. Law § 3602-c(2-a); 8 NYCRR § 200.2(a)(7)). The child find responsibilities of a child's school district-of-residence do not end simply because the child is placed in an out-of-district private school by his or her parents and the district where the private school is located shares a similar obligation (*J.S. v. Scarsdale UFSD*, 826 F.Supp.2d 635 (S.D.N.Y. 2011)).

In addition, a register of all such children must be maintained and revised annually (Educ. Law § 4402(1)(a); 8 NYCRR § 200.2(a)(1), (7)), including parentally placed private school students (20 USC § 1412(a)(10)(A)(i)(V); 34 CFR § 300.132(c); 8 NYCRR § 200.2(a)(7)(ii)). Procedures must be implemented to ensure the availability of statistical data to determine the status of each child with a disability in the identification, location, and evaluation, placement, and program review process (8 NYCRR § 200.2(a)(1), (7)). Furthermore, anyone who collects this data must receive training and written information on the procedures for collecting the data (8 NYCRR § 200.2(a)(3)).

54:14. What "child find" activities must school districts conduct to locate children with disabilities attending private schools?

School districts must undertake "child find" activities with respect to private school children with disabilities, which are similar to those undertaken for children with disabilities in public schools (20 USC § 1412(a)(10)(A)(ii)(I), (III); 34 CFR § 300.131(c), (e); 8 NYCRR § 200.2(a)(7)). Such activities may include, for example, the wide distribution of informational brochures, regular public service announcements, and staffing exhibits at community activities (OSEP Questions and Answers, May 4, 2000, 34 IDELR 263). It is not necessary to conduct an individualized mailing to all private school students and their parents as part of their child-find efforts (*Doe v. Metro. Nashville Pub. Schs.*, 9 Fed. Appx. 453 (6th Cir. 2001)).

The child find activities for locating private school students must be completed in a time period comparable to that for other students attending public school (20 USC § 1412(a)(10)(A)(ii)(V); 34 CFR § 300.134(e); 8 NYCRR § 200.2(a)(7)).

Districts must consult with appropriate representatives of private schools and of parents of parentally placed private school children with disabilities regarding the child find process (20 USC § 1412(a)(10)(A)(ii)(I); 34 CFR § 300.134(a); 8 NYCRR § 200.2(a)(7)).

School districts must include in their child find process parentally placed private school students who reside in another state but attend a private school within their district (34 CFR § 300.131(f)).

For students attending private school outside their district of residence, prior consent from the student's parents, or from the student if 18 years of age or older, is required before any personally identifiable information can be exchanged between school officials of the district where the student resides and the district where the private school the student attends is located (8 NYCRR § 200.2(a)(7)(i)).

54:15. What are a school district's responsibilities toward students with disabilities who leave the public school system but return after a break in public school attendance?

Whether due to home instruction or private school placement, when the child returns to public school he or she remains a child with a disability eligible for special education and related services. Once identified, a student's eligibility for services continues until the student is no longer age eligible, has graduated high school with a regular diploma, or is determined through an evaluation to no longer be a child with a disability (*Letter to Goldman*, OSEP Response to Inquiry, 53 IDELR 97 (Mar. 2009)).

When the student re-enrolls in public school, the school district must convene a meeting of the committee on special education (see **54:25-31**), conduct any necessary revaluations, and develop an appropriate individualized education program for the student (*Letter to Goldman*).

54:16. What responsibilities do school districts have with regard to students with disabilities transitioning from high school to post-secondary activities such as college or employment?

School districts must provide such students with a coordinated set of "transition services" (20 USC § 1401(34)). Developing appropriate transition services is a "results-oriented process" that is "focused on improving the academic and functional achievement of the child with a disability to facilitate the child's movement from school to post-school activities, including post-secondary education, vocational education, integrated employment (including supported employment), continuing and adult education, adult services, independent living, or community participation" (20 USC § 1401(34)(A); 34 CFR § 300.43(a)(1); 8 NYCRR § 200.1(fff)).

Transition service activities must be based on the student's individual needs, taking into account his or her strengths, preferences and interests (20 USC § 1401(34)(B); 34 CFR § 300.43(a)(2); 8 NYCRR § 200.1(fff)). Such activities must include, at least, instruction, related services, community experiences, the development of employment and post-school adult living objectives, and, where appropriate, helping the student develop daily living skills and functional vocational evaluations (20 USC § 1401(34)(C); 34 CFR § 300.43(a)(2); 8 NYCRR § 200.1(fff)).

For more information on transition service requirements, see NYS Education Department, *Transition Planning and Services for Students with Disabilities* (updated Nov. 2011), at: http://www.p12.nysed.gov/specialed/publications/transitionplanning-2011.htm, and NYS Education Department, *Transition Requirements and Guidelines* (updated June 2014), at: http://www.p12.nysed.gov/specialed/transition/randg.htm.

54:17. Must school districts implement an individualized education program that was in effect in another district when a student transfers after the start of the school year?

School districts must provide transfer students with disabilities a free appropriate public education, including services comparable to those in the previous individualized education program (IEP) (see **54:6**). When a student transfers from another district within the state, that obligation extends until the new district, in consultation with the student's parents, develops, adopts, and implements a new IEP. When a student transfers from another state, it extends until the new district conducts an evaluation, if determined necessary, and develops a new IEP, if appropriate. Any new IEP must be consistent with both federal and state law (20 USC § 1414(d)(2)(C)(i); 34 CFR § 300.323(e), (f); 8 NYCRR § 200.4(e)(8)(i), (ii)).

To facilitate a transferring student's transition, the student's new and previous school must take steps for the prompt transmittal of the student's records, including the IEP and supporting documents, and any other records relating to the provision of special education and related services to the student in accordance with federal regulations implementing the Family Educational Rights and Privacy Act (20 USC § 1414(d)(2)(C)(ii); 34 CFR § 300.323(g); 8 NYCRR § 200.4(e)(8)(iii); 8 NYCRR § 100.2(x)(4)(iv)).

In addition, evaluations of students who transfer from one district to another in the same academic year must be coordinated between the child's prior and subsequent schools, as necessary and expeditiously as possible to ensure prompt completion of full evaluations (20 USC § 1414(b)(3)(D); 34 CFR § 300.304(c)(5); 8 NYCRR § 200.4(b)(6)(xvii)).

With respect to highly mobile students, the U.S. Department of Education's Office of Special Education and Rehabilitative Services has issued guidance regarding that group of students' unique educational needs and school districts' responsibilities under the Individuals with Disabilities Education Act at: http://www2.ed.gov/policy/speced/guid/idea/memosdcltrs/12-0392dclhighlymobile.pdf.

54:18. Are school districts required to provide year-round services to disabled students?

Yes, to students whose disabilities require a structured learning environment of up to 12 months' duration to prevent substantial regression. *Substantial regression* refers to the inability to maintain developmental levels due to a loss of skill or knowledge, during the months of July and August, severe enough to require an inordinate period of review at the beginning of the school year to reestablish and maintain the individualized education program's (IEP) goals and objectives (see **54:6**) mastered at the end of the previous school year (34 CFR § 300.106; 8 NYCRR §§ 200.1(aaa), (eee), 200.6(k)(1), 200.16(i)(3)(v); *Application of a Student with a Disability*, SRO dec. no. 09-084 (2009); *Appeal of a Child with a Handicapping Condition*, 31 Ed Dept Rep 17 (1991)). This standard does not require that children with disabilities actually regress in their skills before they are eligible for summer programs and services; what is required is a "reasonable basis" for concluding that regression would occur without these services *(Application of a Child with a Disability*, SRO dec. no. 93-28 (1993)).

School districts may not unilaterally limit the type, amount, or duration of year-round services for students with disabilities, or limit such services to particular categories of disabilities (34 CFR § 300.106(a)(3)). Programs providing services during the months of July and August must operate at least 30 school days. However, programs providing only related services must be provided with the frequency and duration specified in the student's IEP (8 NYCRR § 200.1(eee)).

Least restrictive environment (LRE) requirements (see **54:7**) apply in the same way to extended school year placements as they apply to school-year placements (*T.M. v. Cornwall CSD*, 752 F.3d 145 (2d Cir. 2014)).

For further information on year-round services, see NYS Education Department, *Extended School Year Programs and Services: Questions and Answers* (updated June 2011), at: http://www.p12.nysed.gov/specialed/finance/2011QA.htm.

54:19. Are school districts responsible for providing medical services to students with disabilities?

School districts are not required to provide medical services except for diagnostic and evaluative purposes (20 USC § 1401(26)(A); 34 CFR § 300.34(a); 8 NYCRR § 200.1(ee)). However, districts must provide necessary school health services and school nurse services to students with disabilities (20 USC § 1401(26)(A); 34 CFR § 300.34(c)(13); 8 NYCRR § 200.1(qq), (ss)).

Medical services for evaluative and diagnostic purposes refers to services provided by a licensed physician or by another licensed or registered health professional in consultation with or under the supervision of a licensed physician to determine whether a student has a medically related disability which may result in the student's need for special education and related services (8 NYCRR § 200.1(ee)).

School health services and *school nurse services* refer to services provided by a qualified nurse or other qualified person to enable students with disabilities to receive a free appropriate public education as described in their individualized education program (34 CFR § 300.34(c)(13); 8 NYCRR § 200.1(ss); see **54:6**).

The U.S. Supreme Court has ruled that school districts must provide health services to students with disabilities as long as the services do not have to be performed by a licensed physician and are necessary for the student to attend school and benefit from special education *(Cedar Rapids Cmty. Sch. Dist. v. Garrett F.*, 526 U.S. 66 (1999); *Irving Indep. Sch. Dist. v. Tatro*, 468 U.S. 883 (1984)).

54:20. May school districts require that children with disabilities take medication in order to attend school?

No. Both federal and state law prohibit school districts from requiring that children obtain a prescription for a substance covered under specified provisions of the federal Controlled Substances Act (21 USC § 812(c)) as a condition of attending school, receiving an evaluation or reevaluation, or receiving special education programs or services. However, this prohibition does not prevent teachers and other school staff from consulting or sharing with parents classroom-based observations about a student's academic and functional performances or classroom and school behavior, or the need for an evaluation (20 USC § 1412(a)(25); 34 CFR § 300.174(a); Educ. Law § 3208(4-a); 8 NYCRR § 200.4(b)(9), (e)(9); *Letter to Inhofe*, OSEP Response to Inquiry, 49 IDELR 286 (Oct. 2007)).

54:21. Must school districts ensure that students with disabilities have an opportunity to participate in nonacademic and extracurricular activities?

Yes. School districts must adopt and implement procedures for ensuring that students with disabilities are provided with an equal opportunity to participate in and benefit from extracurricular and nonacademic activities. This applies to students with disabilities eligible under the Individuals with Disabilities Act or section 504 of the Rehabilitation Act (34 CFR §§ 104.37, 300.107, 300.117; 8 NYCRR §§ 100.2(k); 200.2(b)(1)); *Rose Tree Media (PA) Sch. Dist.*, OCR Decision, 40 IDELR 188 (2003)).

Providing an equal opportunity to participate does not mean that school districts are required to ensure that students with disabilities participate in all of the extracurricular activities which the parents or child chooses (*Application of the Bd. of Educ. of the Port Washington UFSD,* SRO dec. no. 06-033 (2006); *Application of the Bd. of Educ. of the East Syracuse-Minoa CSD*, SRO dec. no. 92-11 (1992)).

The Office of Civil Rights (OCR) has issued guidance regarding school districts' responsibilities and the process that should be followed with respect to extracurricular athletics (U.S. Department of Education, Office of Civil Rights, *Dear Colleague Letter* (Jan. 25, 2013), at: https://www2.ed.gov/about/offices/list/ocr/letters/colleague-201301-504.pdf; see also U.S. Department of Education, Office of Civil Rights, *Letter from DiPaolo* (Dec. 16, 2013), at: https://www.nsba.org/sites/default/files/reports/OCR%20Dec.%2016%20%20Letter%20-%20RE%20-%20NSBA%20May%202013%20Letter.pdf).

Where necessary, a student's individualized education program (IEP) (see **54:6**) must include a statement of supplementary aids and services to be provided to enable a child to participate in such activities (34 CFR § 300.320(a)(4)(ii)). However, a student's IEP does not have to include participation in non-academic and extracurricular activities unless the student's needs are such that a free appropriate public education (see **54:3**) cannot be provided without such participation (*Application of a Child with a Disability*, SRO dec. no. 04-041 (2004)).

Nonacademic and extracurricular activities include, for example, counseling services, athletics, transportation, health services, school-sponsored special interest groups or clubs, and employment of students (34 CFR § 300.107(b)).

Actual knowledge by the disabled students' parents of district extracurricular programs and activities does not relieve the district of its obligation to notify students with disabilities and their parents of these activities (*Application of a Child with a Handicapping Condition*, 30 Ed Dept Rep 293 (1991)).

In addition, districts may make an individual determination concerning the physical capacity of a student with a disability to participate in an extracurricular athletic activity. If refused participation, the student then may commence a special court proceeding to appeal the district's decision preventing the student from participating (§ 3208-a(1)). If the court mandates participation, the law absolves the district from liability for injuries sustained during participation in the activity if the injury is attributable to the physical impairment involved in the court order (§ 3208-a(4)).

54:22. Are school districts required to address bullying against disabled students that is based on their disability?

Yes. Furthermore, a school district's failure to address reasonable parental concerns about severe bullying endured by their disabled child may result in the denial of a free appropriate public education (see **54:3**) and entitle the parents to tuition reimbursement if they choose to place their child in a private school. That was the case where a district refused to discuss the bullying of a student during the development of the student's individualized education program (IEP) (see **54:6**) despite repeated parental requests. The record showed that although the student performed at or near grade level, the bullying was, nonetheless, affecting her academic and non-academic development. According to the court, the district's dismissal of the parents request impeded their right to participate in the development of the IEP, potentially affected the substance of the IEP, and prevented the parents from "meaningfully" evaluating the sufficiency of the student's IEP, in violation of the Individuals with Disability Education Act (*T.K. & S.K. v. N.Y. City Dep't of Educ.*, 810 F.3d 869 (2d Cir. 2016)).

In addition, a school's district failure to address disability-based bullying may result in a disability-based harassment violation under Section 504 and Title II of the Americans with Disabilities Act (see U.S. Department of Education, Office for Civil Rights, *Dear Colleague Letter: Responding to Bullying of Students with Disabilities* (Oct. 2014), at: http://www2.ed.gov/about/offices/list/ocr/letters/colleague-bullying-201410.pdf).

54:23. What procedural safeguards must a school district provide to students with disabilities and their parents?

The federal Individuals with Disabilities Education Act and state law and regulations require that a school district afford a student with disabilities and the student's parents, procedural safeguards that include, for example, the right to:

- Prior written notice a reasonable time before the district proposes or refuses to initiate or change the identification, evaluation, or educational placement of the student, or the provision of a free appropriate public education.
- Consent to evaluations and reevaluations, the initial provision of services, the release of the student's personally identifiable information, and district access to the parent's private or public insurance proceeds for the first time.
- Access and examine the student's educational records, and to protection regarding the confidentiality of such records and other personally identifiable information related to the student.
- Obtain an independent educational evaluation.
- An opportunity to present a complaint to the NYS Education Department, participate in mediation, and initiate due process hearings, appeal to the State Review Officer, and initiate civil actions in state or federal courts related to the identification, evaluation or placement of the student, or the provision of a free appropriate public education.
- Have the student "stay-put" in his or her current educational placement during the pendency of due process proceedings.
- Attorneys' fees (20 USC § 1415; 34 CFR §§ 300.500–520; 8 NYCRR § 200.5(b), (f); NYS Education Department, *New York State Procedural Safeguards Notice: Rights for Parents of Children with Disabilities, Ages 3-21* (updated July 2013), at: http://www.p12.nysed.gov/specialed/formsnotices/psgn/psgn713.htm).

Federal regulations implementing Section 504 of the Rehabilitation Act of 1973 also require that districts receiving federal education funds establish a system of procedural safeguards concerning the identification, evaluation, and/or educational placement of children believed to need special instruction or related services, and give parents notice of their rights under Section 504 (34 CFR § 104.36; *Plainfield (CT) Pub. Sch.*, OCR Decision, 40 IDELR 18 (2003)).

54:24. Must a school district provide written notice of the procedural safeguards?

Yes. A school district must give parents written notice of the procedural safeguards at least once a year and also upon:

- A child's initial referral or parental request for evaluation.
- Receipt of the first filing of a state complaint or a due process complaint in a school year.

- Parental request (20 USC § 1415(d)(1); 34 CFR § 300.504(a); 8 NYCRR § 200.5(f)(3)).
- The date a decision is made to suspend or remove a child with a disability for a violation of a student code of conduct and the suspension or removal constitutes a disciplinary change in placement (34 CFR §§ 300.504(a)(3), 300.530(h); 8 NYCRR § 200.5(f)(3)).

A school district must use the procedural safeguards notice prescribed by the commissioner of education (8 NYCRR § 200.5(f)(1)) and provide it in the native language of the parent or other mode of communication used by the parent, unless it is clearly not feasible to do so (20 USC § 1415(d)(2); § 300.504(d); 8 NYCRR § 200.5(f)(2)). If the parent has no written language, notice must be given orally or by other means or mode of communication, and the district must ensure the parent understands the content of the notice and maintain written evidence that these requirements have been met (34 CFR § 300.503(c)(2); 8 NYCRR § 200.5(f)(2)). A copy of the State mandated procedural safeguards notice is available at: http://www.p12.nysed.gov/specialed/publications/PSGN-fm-713.pdf (updated July 2013).

A district may place a current copy of the procedural safeguards notice on its website if it has one (20 USC § 1415(d)(1)(B); 34 CFR § 300.504(b); 8 NYCRR § 200.5(f)(4)). Parents may elect to receive the procedural safeguards notice by an electronic mail (e-mail) communication if their school district makes that option available (20 USC § 1415(n); 34 CFR § 300.505; 8 NYCRR § 200.5(f)(5)).

The procedural safeguards notice prescribed by the commissioner applies only to children with disabilities eligible to receive special education and related services under the federal Individuals with Disabilities Education Act. School districts must give parents separate notice of their rights under Section 504 of the Rehabilitation Act of 1973 (34 CFR § 104.36; *Plainfield (CT) Pub. Sch.*, OCR Decision, 40 IDELR 18 (2003)).

The Committee on Special Education

54:25. What is the function of a school district's committee on special education?

The primary function of the committee on special education (CSE) is to identify, evaluate, review the status of, and make recommendations concerning the appropriate educational placement of each school-age child with a disability, or thought to have a disability, who resides within the school district (20 USC § 1414(b)(4)(A), (d)(3), (4); 34 CFR §§ 300.306(a), 300.324; Educ. Law §§ 4402(3), 4410(3); 8 NYCRR §§ 200.3, 200.4).

The CSE must also make an annual report to the school board on the status of services and facilities made available by the district for children with disabilities (Educ. Law § 4402(1)(b)(3), (f)). The CSE is also responsible for maintaining and annually revising the register of children with disabilities who are entitled to attend public school during the next school year or those referred to the committee (8 NYCRR § 200.2(a)(1)).

54:26. Who may refer a student to the committee on special education (CSE) for identification, evaluation, and possible special education placement?

Actual referrals for an initial evaluation to determine a student's eligibility for classification, special education services, and placement as a student with a disability may be made only by:

- A student's parent;
- A designee of the student's school district of residence or the district the student legally attends or is eligible to attend;
- The commissioner of education or a designee of a public agency responsible for the student's education; and/or

- A designee of an education program affiliated with a child care institution with CSE responsibility (20 USC § 1414(a)(1)(B); 34 CFR § 300.301(b); 8 NYCRR § 200.4(a)(1)(i)-(iv)).

On the other hand, written requests for referrals for an initial evaluation may be made by:

- A professional staff member of the student's school district of residence or the public or private school the student legally attends or is eligible to attend;
- A licensed physician;
- A judicial officer;
- A professional staff member of a public agency responsible for the welfare, health or education of children; or
- The student, if 18 years of age or older, or an emancipated minor and eligible to attend the district's public schools (8 NYCRR § 200.4(a)(2)(i)(a)-(e)).

Commissioner regulations establish procedures and timelines applicable when a school district receives a request for referral, depending upon who has made the request (8 NYCRR § 200.4(a)(2)(ii)-(iv)).

Strict timelines apply with respect to evaluating a student and, where applicable, developing and implementing an individualized education program (see **54:6**) for a student (20 USC § 1414(a); 34 CFR §§ 300.301(c), 300.323(c); 8 NYCRR §§ 200.4(b)(1), 200.5(b); see also *Application of [Redacted] Sch. Dist.*, SRO dec. no. 09-136 (2010)).

School districts must ensure that their implementation of response to intervention strategies does not delay or deny the timely initial evaluation of children presumed to have a disability (U.S. Department of Education, OSEP Memo 11-07 to State Directors of Special Education (Jan. 21, 2011), at: http://www2.ed.gov/policy/speced/guid/idea/memosdcltrs/osep11-07rtimemo.pdf).

54:27. Who are the mandated members of a school district's committee on special education (CSE)?

A CSE must include the following members:

- The parent or person in parental relationship to the student.
- At least one regular education teacher of the student (if the child is, or may be, participating in the regular education environment). The regular education teacher must be someone who is certified to teach the student under consideration, and who teaches in one of the regular education programs which might be appropriate for the student (*Application of a Child with a Disability*, SRO dec. no. 06-051 (2006); *Application of a Child with a Disability*, SRO dec. no. 04-088 (2004)). For example, a kindergarten teacher would not be an appropriate CSE member for a student being considered for a regular middle school class (*Application of a Child with a Disability*, SRO dec. no. 02-080 (2003)).
- At least one special education teacher of the student or, where appropriate, at least one special education provider of such child.
- A school psychologist.
- A representative of the school district who is:
  (1) qualified to provide or supervise special education,
  (2) knowledgeable about the general curriculum, and
  (3) knowledgeable about the availability of resources of the district (this individual may also be the special education teacher/provider or school psychologist if they meet the above qualifications. The representative of the school district must serve as the chairperson of the committee.)
- An individual who can interpret the instructional implications of evaluation results (this individual may also be one of the above district team members or a person having knowledge or special expertise regarding the student so determined by the district).

- At the discretion of the parent or the district, other individuals who have knowledge or special expertise regarding the child, including related services personnel, as appropriate. A parent's right to invite such individuals does not include the right to reimbursement and compensation related to their attendance (*Application of a Child with a Disability*, SRO dec. no. 02-009 (2003)). However, a CSE that chooses to resolve an impasse in reaching consensus by taking a vote is required to count the vote of every participant at the CSE meeting, including those invited by parents as having knowledge or special expertise about their child (*Sackets Harbor CSD v. Munoz*, 283 A.D.2d 756 (3d Dep't 2001)).
- A school physician, if requested in writing by the parents or the school district 72 hours before a meeting.
- A parent of another child with a disability residing in the district or a neighboring district if requested in writing by the parents or the school district 72 hours before a meeting. The parent of a declassified student no longer eligible for special education or of a disabled child who has graduated may serve as the additional parent member for up to five years beyond their child's declassification or graduation.
- Where appropriate, or otherwise required by law and/or regulation, the student (20 USC § 1414(d)(1)(B); 34 CFR § 300.321; Educ. Law § 4402(1)(b)(1)(a); 8 NYCRR § 200.3(a)(1); see also 34 CFR § 300.308).

54:28. Are there any individuals who are mandated members of the committee on special education (CSE) but only on certain occasions?

Yes. In the case of a child previously receiving, and transitioning out of, early intervention services, a school district must invite the service coordinator or other representative to the initial CSE meeting upon parental request (20 USC § 1414(d)(1)(D); 34 CFR § 300.321(f); see also 8 NYCRR § 200.5(c)(2)(viii)).

Any participating agency likely to be responsible for providing or paying for transition services designed to assist the student reach postsecondary goals must be invited, as well, to the extent appropriate and with the consent of the parent or the student if the student has reached the age of 18 (34 CFR § 300.321(b); 8 NYCRR § 200.4(d)(4)(i)(c)).

In addition, where a school district is considering the placement of a student in a residential therapeutic school, the CSE meeting at which the possible placement is discussed must include the participation of a representative from that school, even when the student's parents have indicated their intent to visit the school (*Werner v. Clarkstown CSD*, 363 F.Supp.2d 656 (S.D.N.Y. 2005)).

According to the U.S. Department of Education, Office of Civil Rights Western Division, Seattle (WA), a CSE also should include staff familiar with the English language acquisition needs and English proficiency of a limited English proficient (LEP) student who is also a student with a disability whenever the CSE is discussing the student's placement. Their participation is necessary to determine an appropriate placement for students with dual needs of a learning disability and English language acquisition, and to ensure coordination between special education and English language acquisition services. The failure to include such individuals would constitute a violation of Title VI, which prohibits discrimination on the basis of natural origin, and Section 504 of the Rehabilitation Act, which prohibits discrimination on the basis of disability (*Mt. Vernon (WA) Sch. Dist.*, OCR Decision, 52 IDELR 300 (2008)).

54:29. May committee on special education (CSE) members be excused from attending a CSE meeting?

Yes. Under the conditions specified in statute and regulations, a parent and school district may agree in writing that the attendance at a CSE meeting of the regular education teacher, special education teacher or special education provider, school district representative, or the CSE member who can interpret the instructional implications of evaluation results is either unnecessary or may be excused (20 USC § 1414(d)(1)(C); 34 CFR § 300.321(e); Educ. Law §§ 4402(1)(b)(1)(b-1)-(b-3), 4402(1)(b)(1)(d); 8 NYCRR § 200.3(f)).

54:30. May a school district have more than one committee on special education (CSE)?

Yes. Buffalo, New York City, Rochester, Syracuse, and Yonkers must establish CSE subcommittees to the extent necessary to ensure the timely evaluation and placement of students with disabilities. Other school districts also may establish CSE subcommittees but are not required to do so (Educ. Law §§ 4402(1)(b)(1), 4402(1)(b)(1)(d); 8 NYCRR § 200.3(c)).

54:31. Is there any difference in function between a committee on special education (CSE) and a CSE subcommittee?

A CSE subcommittee performs the same functions as a CSE, except that the CSE remains responsible for deciding cases concerning the initial placement of a student in a special class, in a special class outside of the student's school of attendance or in a school primarily serving children with disabilities or a school outside the student's district (Educ. Law § 4402(1)(b)(1)(d); 8 NYCRR § 200.3(c)(4)).

In addition, a CSE subcommittee must report to the CSE annually on the status of each student with a disability under its jurisdiction (Educ. Law § 4402(1)(b)(1)(d); 8 NYCRR § 200.3(c)(6)). Upon written parental request, the CSE subcommittee also must refer to the CSE for review any of its recommendations not acceptable to the parent (Educ. Law § 4402(1)(b)(1)(d); 8 NYCRR § 200.3(c)(5)).

54:32. Who are the members of a CSE subcommittee?

A CSE subcommittee must include the following members:

- The parent of the child with a disability.
- One regular education teacher (if the child is, or may be, participating in the regular education environment).
- A special education teacher of the student, or where appropriate, a special education provider of such child.
- A school psychologist, whenever a new psychological evaluation is reviewed, or a change to a program option with a more intensive staff/student ratio, as set forth in part 200.6(h)(4) of the commissioner's regulations, is considered.
- A representative of the school district who is:
  (1) qualified to provide, administer or supervise special education,
  (2) knowledgeable about the general curriculum, and
  (3) knowledgeable about the availability of resources of the district (this individual may also be the special education teacher/provider or school psychologist if they meet the above qualifications. The school district representative must serve as the chairperson of the subcommittee.)
- At the discretion of the parent or the district, other individuals who have knowledge or special expertise regarding the child, including related services personnel.
- An individual who can interpret the instructional implications of evaluation results (this individual may also be one of the above district team members).
- Where appropriate, the child with a disability (20 USC § 1414(d)(1)(B); 34 CFR § 300.321; Educ. Law § 4402(1)(b)(1); 8 NYCRR § 200.3(c)(2)).

54:33. What is the role of the committee on special education (CSE) and CSE subcommittee chairperson?

The CSE or CSE subcommittee chairperson is responsible for presiding over committee or subcommittee meetings. That individual also must carry out certain specified functions relating to, for example, the referral of students for evaluation, parental consent, and notice to individuals responsible for implementing a student's individualized education program of their specific responsibilities (8 NYCRR § 200.3(e)).

54:34. Must a parent of a disabled student be present at the committee on special education (CSE) or CSE subcommittee meeting where his or her child is being discussed?

A parent of a child with a disability is a mandated member of the CSE or the CSE subcommittee and should be present at all meetings of the committee in which his or her child is being discussed (20 USC §§ 1414(b)(4)(A), (e), (f), 1415(b)(1); 34 CFR §§ 300.321(a)(1), 300.322, 300.327, 300.501(b), (c); Educ. Law § 4402(1)(b); 8 NYCRR §§ 200.3(a)(1)(i), (c)(2)(i), 200.5(d)(1)). Parents unable to be physically present at a CSE meeting regarding their child's educational placement may agree with a school district to use other methods to ensure their participation, including individual conference calls or video conferencing (20 USC § 1414(f); 34 CFR §§ 300.322(c), 300.328; 8 NYCRR § 200.5(d)(7)).

In addition, the school district must ensure the parent understands the proceedings at the meetings, including arranging for an interpreter for deaf parents and parents whose native language is other than English (34 CFR § 300.322(e); 8 NYCRR § 200.5(d)(5)).

However, a CSE or CSE subcommittee may meet without the parent if it cannot convince the parent to attend, and has a record of its attempt to do so at a mutually agreed upon time and place (34 CFR § 300.322(d); 8 NYCRR § 200.5(d)(3); *J.G. v. Briarcliff Manor UFSD,* 682 F.Supp.2d 387 (S.D.N.Y. 2010)). It also may make a placement decision without parental involvement if the school is unable to obtain the parents' participation and has records of its attempts to secure their involvement (34 CFR § 300.501(c)(4); 8 NYCRR § 200.5(d)(4)).

54:35. Are there any meetings concerning students with disabilities that are not considered committee on special education (CSE) meetings?

Yes. A CSE meeting does not include informal or unscheduled conversations among school personnel and conversations about teaching methodology, lesson plans, or coordination of services provision if those issues are not addressed in the student's individualized education program (IEP) (see **54:6**). A CSE meeting does not include either preparatory activities by school personnel to develop a proposal or response to a parental proposal that will be discussed at a later meeting (34 CFR § 300.501(b)(3); 8 NYCRR § 200.5(d)(2); *T.P. v. Mamaroneck UFSD*, 554 F.3d 247 (2d Cir. 2009)). However, any student progress reports and recommendations for goals and objectives for a student's IEP must be reviewed and discussed at a CSE meeting, not just at the building level (*Application of a Child with a Disability*, SRO dec. no. 04-104 (2005)).

54:36. May a parent tape-record his or her child's committee on special education (CSE) or CSE subcommittee meeting?

Yes. A parent may tape-record his or her own child's CSE or CSE subcommittee meeting without approval by the CSE, CSE subcommittee or school board. However, the parent may forfeit the right to tape-record future proceedings if there are circumstances that indicate this right is being abused. A school district also must be permitted to tape-record CSE or CSE subcommittee meetings (*Application of a Child with a Handicapping Condition*, 30 Ed Dept Rep 178 (1990)). An impartial hearing officer may admit into evidence at a due process hearing, a parent's tape recording and transcript of a CSE meeting (*Application of a Child with a Disability*, SRO dec. no. 05-051 (2005)).

54:37. May the school attorney attend the district's committee on special education (CSE) or CSE subcommittee meetings?

School attorneys should attend such meetings only on those rare occasions when the committee's ability to perform its functions depends on the immediate resolution of critical legal issues. The school attorney should not become a listening post for the school board, nor may he or she attend CSE or CSE subcommittee meetings to intimidate parents or undermine the decision-making process (*Application of a Child with a Handicapping Condition*, 30 Ed Dept Rep 286 (1991)).

54:38. How often must a school district's committee on special education (CSE) review a student's individualized education program (IEP)?

The CSE must review each student's IEP at least annually. The annual review has two purposes. First, to determine whether the student's annual goals are being achieved. Second, to revise the IEP as appropriate to address any lack of expected progress toward the annual goals and in the general curriculum where appropriate, any reevaluation results and information provided by the student's parents, and the student's anticipated needs or other matters (20 USC § 1414(d)(4); 34 CFR § 300.324(b)(1); 8 NYCRR § 200.4(f)).

Although a school district may not change a student's IEP while administrative or judicial proceedings are pending, it must nonetheless comply with its obligation to timely review all IEPs. A district reviewing a student's IEP while a due process dispute is ongoing must continue to implement the last agreed-upon IEP for the duration of the dispute, unless the parents agree otherwise (*Letter to Watson*, OSEP Response to Inquiry, 48 IDELR 284 (Apr. 2007); see also *Norma P. v. Pelham Sch. Dist.*, 19 IDELR 938 (1st Cir. 1993)).

54:39. How often must a school district committee on special education (CSE) reevaluate previously identified students with disabilities?

A CSE must arrange an appropriate reevaluation of each student with a disability, if conditions warrant a reevaluation or if the child's parent or teacher requests a reevaluation, but the CSE must not conduct reevaluations more than once a year unless the parent and school district agree otherwise (20 USC § 1414(a)(2)(A), (B); 34 CFR § 300.303; Educ. Law § 4402(1)(b)(3)(d); 8 NYCRR § 200.4(b)(4)).

The CSE also must reevaluate a student with a disability at least once every three years, unless the parent and district agree, in writing, that such three-year reevaluation is unnecessary (20 USC § 1414(a)(2)(B)(ii); 34 CFR § 300.303(b)(2); Educ. Law § 4402(1)(b)(3)(d); 8 NYCRR § 200.4(b)(4)).

54:40. Must a school district's committee on special education (CSE) evaluate a child with a disability prior to declassification?

Yes, unless the CSE determines that it does not require additional data to decide whether the child continues to be a child with a disability. In such an instance, the district must notify the child's parent of its determination and the reasons thereof, as well as the parent's right to request an assessment. The school district is not required to conduct the assessment unless requested by the child's parent (20 USC § 1414 (c)(4), (5)(A); 34 CFR § 300.305(d), (e); 8 NYCRR § 200.4(b)(5)(iv), (c)(3)).

A declassification evaluation is not required when a student's eligibility for special education programs and services ends as a result of the student's graduation with a local high school or Regents' diploma, or because the student ages out (20 USC § 1414(c)(5)(B)(i); 34 CFR § 300.305(e)(2);

8 NYCRR § 200.4(c)(4)). However, in such an instance, a district must provide a summary of the student's academic achievement and functional performance, including recommendations on how to assist the student to meet postsecondary goals (20 USC § 1414(c)(5)(B)(ii); 34 CFR § 300.305(e)(3); 8 NYCRR § 200.4(c)(4)).

School districts must expressly notify parents if an upcoming CSE meeting will include a discussion of their child's possible declassification (*Bd. of Educ. of the Southhold UFSD*, SRO dec. no. 04-081 (2004)).

54:41. Must the committee on special education provide declassification support services to students it no longer considers eligible for special education services?

Yes. *Declassification support services* help a student transition from special education to full-time regular education and are directed at both the student and his or her teacher(s). Such services may include, for the student, psychological support, social work, speech and language services, and counseling other than career counseling. With respect to teachers, declassification services may include assistance from supplementary school personnel and consultation with appropriate personnel (8 NYCRR § 200.1(ooo)).

Providers of such services must be certified pursuant to Part 80 of the regulations of the commissioner of education (*Id.*).

54:42. What happens if the school board disagrees with the recommendation of the committee on special education (CSE) or the CSE subcommittee?

If a school board disagrees with either committee's recommendation, it may follow one of the following procedures:

- Return the recommendation to the committee with a statement of the board's objections or concerns. The committee must then consider the board's objections or concerns, revise the individualized education program (IEP) (see **54:6**) where appropriate, and resubmit a recommendation to the board. If the board continues to disagree with the recommendation, it may either continue to return the recommendation to the original committee for additional review or establish a second committee to develop a new recommendation.
- Establish a second committee to develop a new recommendation. If the board disagrees with the recommendation of the second committee, it may return the recommendation to the second committee with a statement of its objections or concerns. The second committee then must consider the board's objections or concerns, revise the IEP where appropriate and resubmit a recommendation to the board. If the board continues to disagree with the revised recommendation, it may continue to return the recommendation to the second committee for additional review.

Once a school board establishes a second CSE, the board may not select the recommendation of the initial CSE (8 NYCRR § 200.4(e)(2)).

Under either procedure, the school board must arrange for the programs and services in accordance with an IEP within 60 school days of receiving the consent to evaluate a student not previously identified as a student with a disability, or within 60 school days of the referral for review of the child with a disability. In cases involving a student's placement in a state approved private school, the school has 30 days from the day it receives the CSE recommendation to make the necessary arrangements (8 NYCRR § 200.4(e)(1)).

Only a CSE may determine the content of a student's IEP and a student's placement (*Application of the Bd. of Educ. of the Gowanda CSD*, SRO dec. no. 04-016 (2004)).

54:43. Must the school board notify the parents of a student with a disability of its disagreement with the recommendations of the committee on special education (CSE) or CSE subcommittee?

Yes. In addition, the notice must be in writing and set forth the school board's reasons and indicate that the recommendations will be sent back to the committee on special education or CSE subcommittee with notice of the need to schedule a timely meeting to review the board's concerns and revise the student's individualized education program as appropriate (8 NYCRR § 200.5(a)(6)(ii)).

54:44. Is a school district required to notify parents of its proposal or refusal to initiate or change the identification, evaluation or placement of a child with a disability?

Yes. A school district is required to give parents written notice (also referred to as notice of recommendation) of its proposal or refusal to initiate or change the identification, evaluation or placement of a child with a disability, or the provision of a free appropriate public education along with:

- A description of the action being proposed or refused.
- An explanation of the decision.
- A description of other options considered and why they were rejected.
- A description of each evaluation procedure, test, record, or report used as a basis for its action, as well as other factors relevant to the district's decision.

The notice must also include a statement that parents of a student with a disability have procedural protections under the Individuals with Disabilities Education Act (IDEA). Additionally, if the notice is not about an initial referral for evaluation, it must also inform the parent how to obtain a copy of the procedural safeguards, and where to obtain assistance in understanding parental rights under the IDEA (20 USC § 1415(c); 34 CFR § 300.503; 8 NYCRR § 200.5(a)(1), (2), (3)).

Notice involving referral for initial evaluation or a re-evaluation must include a description of the proposed evaluation or reevaluation and the uses to be made of the information, and indicate that the parent may submit evaluation information for consideration by the committee on special education (34 CFR § 300.503(b); 8 NYCRR § 200.5(a)(5)(i)).

If the proposed action involves placement in an approved private school, the notice must also include a copy of the private school's policy on the use of psychotropic medication if the school uses it (8 NYCRR § 200.5(a)(6)(v)).

School districts must use the prior written notice prescribed by the commissioner of education, (revised July 2013), which is available at: http://www.p12.nysed.gov/specialed/formsnotices/PWN/memo-revPWN-713.htm (8 NYCRR § 200.5(a)).

Parental Consent

54:45. Is parental consent required before the committee on special education (CSE) conducts an initial evaluation of a child presumed to have a disability or for any reevaluation of a child with a disability?

Yes. The parent must provide written consent for both an initial evaluation of a child presumed to have a disability and for any reevaluation of a child with a disability before the initial evaluation or reevaluation is conducted (20 USC § 1414(a)(1)(D)(i)(I), (c)(3); 34 CFR § 300.300(a)(1)(i), (c)(1)(i); 8 NYCRR § 200.5(b)(1)(i)).

If a parent fails to either give consent for an initial evaluation, or respond to a request for such consent, a school district must give the parent an opportunity to attend an informal conference with the

CSE or other prescribed individuals and ask questions about the proposed evaluation. If the parent does not request to attend such a conference or continues to withhold consent for 30 days after receipt of a referral, the school board may commence an impartial hearing to pursue the initial evaluation without parental consent. However, such an option is not available in the case of a preschool child, a student who is home instructed, or a parentally placed private school student (20 USC § 1414(a)(1)(D)(ii)(I); 34 CFR § 300.300(a)(3)(i); 8 NYCRR § 200.5(b)(1)(i)(c)). A school district that chooses not to pursue such option does not violate its child find and evaluation responsibilities (34 CFR § 300.300(a)(3)(ii)).

Similarly, a district may, but does not have to commence an impartial hearing to override a parent's refusal to consent to a reevaluation. A decision to not commence such a hearing does not constitute a violation of the district's child find and reevaluation responsibilities (34 CFR § 300.300(c)(1)(ii), (iii)).

The override procedures are not available in the case of students who are either home-schooled or voluntarily enrolled in private school at parental expense. When the parent of such a child refuses to provide consent for an initial evaluation or reevaluation, or to respond to a request for such consent, a school district is not required to consider the child eligible for services as a parentally-placed private school child (34 CFR § 300.300(d)(4)).

In addition, school districts must obtain parental consent to access a student's or parent's public benefits or insurance, or private insurance proceeds to pay for services provided to a child with a disability (34 CFR § 300.154(d), (e); 8 NYCRR § 200.5(b)(8), (9)).

54:46. Are there any exceptions to the evaluation/reevaluation consent rule?

Yes. A school district does not have to obtain parental consent for the initial evaluation of a ward of the State who is not residing with his or her parent if:

- it is unable to discover the parent's whereabouts despite reasonable efforts to do so,
- the parent's rights have been terminated in accordance with State law, or
- the parent's right to make educational decisions has been subrogated by a judge in accordance with State law and the individual appointed by the judge to represent the child has given consent (20 USC § 1414(a)(1)(D)(iii); 34 CFR § 300.300(a)(2); 8 NYCRR § 200.5(b)(6)).

Parental consent for a reevaluation is not necessary if a school district can demonstrate it has taken reasonable measures to obtain such consent and the child's parents failed to respond (20 USC § 1414(c)(3); 34 CFR § 300.300(c)(2); 8 NYCRR § 200.5(b)(1)(i)(b)). The district must have a record of its attempts to obtain parental consent (34 CFR § 300.300(d)(5); 8 NYCRR § 200.5(b)(1)(i)(b)).

In addition, consent is not required before reviewing existing data as part of an evaluation or reevaluation, or before administering a test or other evaluation administered to all children that does not require parental consent (34 CFR § 300.300(d)(1); 8 NYCRR § 200.5(b)(1)(i)(a)).

54:47. Is parental consent necessary before a district can provide special education programs and services to a child with a disability for the first time?

Yes. Consent for initial evaluation does not constitute consent for initial provision of special education services (20 USC § 1414(a)(1)(D)(i)(I); 34 CFR § 300.300(a)(1)(ii); 8 NYCRR § 200.5(b)(1)(ii)). Therefore, a school district must obtain parental consent prior to initially providing special education and related services to a child who has not previously been identified as having a disability (20 USC § 1414(a)(1)(D)(i)(II); 34 CFR § 300.300(b)(1); 8 NYCRR § 200.5(b)(1)(ii)). Consent is not required for the initial provision of special education services in a 12-month special service and /or program. However, if a school district provides special education services to a student for the first time during the months of July and August and the student has not previously been identified as a having a disability, consent must be obtained prior to the initial provision of special education services to the student (8 NYCRR § 200.5(b)(1)(ii)).

Unlike when parents refuse to consent to the initial evaluation of a child (see **54:45**), a school district may not initiate due process to override a parent's refusal to consent to the initial provision of special education and related services (20 USC § 1414(a)(1)(D)(ii)(II); 34 CFR § 300.300(b)(3); 8 NYCRR § 200.5(b)(4)). Under such circumstances, a district will not be considered in violation of its obligation to make a free appropriate public education (see **54:3**), available to the child as a result of its failure to provide the child the services for which it requested consent (20 USC § 1414(a)(1)(D)(ii)(III); 34 CFR § 300.300(b)(4); 8 NYCRR § 200.5(b)(4)). Neither does a school district have to apply the disciplinary protections available to students eligible for services under the Individuals with Disabilities Education Act when a student is not receiving services because of a parent's refusal to provide consent for the initial provision of services, or to allow an evaluation of the child (20 USC § 1415(k)(5)(C); 34 CFR § 300.534(c)(1); see **54:93**).

54:48. Can parents revoke their consent to an initial evaluation, reevaluation or initial provision of special education programs and services?

Yes. Parental consent is voluntary and may be revoked at any time. However, revocation of the consent does not negate district actions undertaken after consent was given but before it was revoked (34 CFR § 300.9(c)(2); 8 NYCRR § 200.1(l)(3)).

54:49. Can parents revoke consent for the continued provision of special education and related services after initial services have been provided?

Yes. Consent for continued provision of services may be revoked at any time in writing (34 CFR §§ 300.9(c)(1), 300.300(b)(4); 8 NYCRR § 200.5(b)(5)). If this occurs, a school district may not continue to provide the services nor may it use due process procedures to force continuation of services (34 CFR § 300.300(b)(4)(i), (ii); 8 NYCRR § 200.5(b)(5)(i), (ii)). However, it must provide the parents prior written notice before actually ceasing the services (8 NYCRR § 200.5(b)(5)(i); see **54:44**).

Upon receipt of a written revocation of consent, the district is not required to convene the committee on special education or develop an individualized education program (see **54:6**), for further provision of services (34 CFR § 300.300(b)(4)(iv); 8 NYCRR § 200.5(b)(5)(iv)). Neither is it required to amend the student's education records to remove any references to the child's receipt of such services (34 CFR § 300.9(c)(3); 8 NYCRR § 200.5(b)(5)(v)).

A district will not be deemed to have violated its duty to provide a free and appropriate public education (see **54:3**) to the student because it ceased providing special education and related services following receipt of the parent's written revocation of consent (34 CFR § 300.300(b)(4)(iii); 8 NYCRR § 200.5(b)(5)(iii)).

Parental Challenges

54:50. May the parents of a disabled student challenge the actions taken by the committee on special education (CSE), CSE subcommittee or the school board regarding the classification, evaluation, or placement of the student?

Yes. Parents who disagree with the actions taken by the CSE, CSE subcommittee, and/or the school board concerning the classification, evaluation or placement of their child may submit a complaint and request, in writing, an impartial due process hearing (20 USC § 1415(b)(6)(A), (f); 34 CFR §§ 300.507–514; Educ. Law § 4404(1); 8 NYCRR § 200.5(j)).

The complaint must be submitted within two years of the date the parents knew or should have known about the alleged action that forms the basis of the complaint. However, this time limitation will not apply where the parents were prevented from requesting a hearing due to either specific misrepresentations by the school district that it had resolved the problem(s) complained of, or the district's withholding of information it was required to provide the parents (20 USC § 1415(b)(6)(B), (f)(3)(C), (D); 34 CFR §§ 300.507(a)(2), 300.511(e), (f); 8 NYCRR § 200.5(j)(1)(i)).

School districts must inform parents requesting an impartial due process hearing of the availability of mediation and of any free or low cost legal and other relevant services in the area (20 USC § 1415(e); 34 CFR § 300.507(b); 8 NYCRR § 200.5(j)(1)(iii)).

54:51. Can non-custodial parents of disabled students challenge the actions taken by the committee on special education (CSE), CSE subcommittee or school board regarding their child?

Only if the separation agreement, custody order, or divorce decree authorizes the non-custodial parent to make education decisions for the child. Otherwise, non-custodial parents may not initiate impartial due process hearing requests to challenge actions taken by the CSE, CSE subcommittee or school board (*Fuentes v. Bd. of Educ. of the City of N.Y.*, 569 F.3d 46 (2d Cir. 2009) and 12 N.Y.3d 309 (2009)). Similarly, a federal appellate court with jurisdiction over New York dismissed a lawsuit by a non-custodial parent that alleged the school district violated the Americans with Disabilities Act integration mandate when it removed her child from public school to a residential facility. The court found the father had custody of the child and consented to the placement and determined the student's mother was precluded from establishing that the district acted with deliberate indifference to the student's rights (*Frank v. Sachem Sch. Dist.*, 633 Fed. Appx. 14 (2d Cir. 2016)).

However, even if they have no decision-making authority, non-custodial parents may still participate in the child's education. Absent specific provisions in a separation agreement, custody order, or divorce decree to the contrary, non-custodial parents can request information about, keep apprised of, and otherwise remain interested in their child's educational progress (*Fuentes v. Bd. of Educ. of the City of N.Y.*, 12 N.Y.3d 309 (2009); *Taylor v. Vermont Dep't of Educ.*, 313 F.3d 768 (2d Cir. 2002)).

54:52. Are school districts in receipt of a parental complaint required to try to resolve the problem(s) identified in the complaint in a resolution meeting conducted before proceeding with a hearing?

Yes. Prior to the actual commencement of such a hearing, a school district must convene a meeting with the complaining parents and the relevant member(s) of the committee on special education who have specific knowledge of the facts identified in the complaint. The meeting must be attended also by a district representative with decisionmaking authority on behalf of the district. The purpose of the meeting is to discuss the complaint and provide the district an opportunity to resolve it. The meeting must be held within 15 days after the district's receipt of the parents' complaint unless the parents and the school district agree to use mediation or waive the meeting by mutual agreement in writing (20 USC § 1415(f)(1)(B)(i); 34 CFR § 300.510(a); 8 NYCRR § 200.5(j)(2)).

If the parents and the district are unable to resolve the complaint within 30 days of the district's receipt of the parents' complaint, a due process hearing may commence (20 USC § 1415(f)(1)(B)(ii); 34 CFR § 300.510(b), (c); 8 NYCRR § 200.5(j)(2)(v)). The subject matter of the hearing will be limited to the issues expressly raised in the parents' complaint, unless the district agrees otherwise (20 USC § 1415(f)(3)(B); 34 CFR § 300.511(d); 8 NYCRR § 200.5(j)(1)(ii)).

54:53. Who conducts a due process hearing on a parental complaint?

A due process hearing on a parental complaint regarding the education of a child with a disability is conducted by an impartial hearing officer (IHO) appointed by the school board (20 USC § 1415(f)(1)(A), (3); 34 CFR § 300.511(b), (c)(3); Educ. Law § 4404(1); 8 NYCRR §§ 200.2(b)(9), 200.5(j)(3)(i), (ii); see **54:54**).

The IHO may schedule a pre-hearing conference with the parties to simplify or clarify the issue, establish dates for the completion of the hearing, identify evidence and witnesses, and address any other administrative matters necessary to complete a timely hearing (8 NYCRR § 200.5(j)(3)(xi)). Each party will have up to one day to present its case unless the IHO determines that additional time is necessary for a full, fair disclosure of the facts to arrive at a decision (8 NYCRR § 200.5(j)(3)(xiii)).

54:54. How are impartial hearing officers selected?

School districts appoint impartial hearing officers (IHO) on a rotation basis, from a list provided by the NYS Education Department and maintained in alphabetical order, beginning with the first name after the IHO who last served, or the first name on the list if no IHO on the list has served (Educ. Law § 4404(1); 8 NYCRR §§ 200.2(e)(1), 200.5(j)(3)(i); NYS Education Department, *Selection and Appointment of Special Education Impartial Hearing Officers* (April 2015), at: http://www.p12.nysed.gov/specialed/publications/2015-memos/impartial-hearing-officers-memo-april-2015.pdf).

The appointment process must be commenced immediately but no later than two business days after the district receives a due process complaint notice (8 NYCRR § 200.5(j)(3)(i)(a)). A school board may designate one or more of its members to appoint an IHO (8 NYCRR § 200.5(j)(3)(ii)). The commissioner's regulations set forth the process for consolidating multiple pending due process complaint notices involving the same parties and the same student with a disability (8 NYCRR § 200.5(j)(3)(ii)(a)).

An IHO may not accept appointment if unable to:

- make a determination regarding the sufficiency of a parental complaint notice within five days of receiving such a request, and
- start the hearing within the first 14 days after either receiving a written waiver of the resolution meeting or notice of the parties' inability to resolve their problems at the resolution meeting (see **54:52**), or the expiration of the 30-day period that started with the district's receipt of the parents' complaint, whichever occurs first (8 NYCRR § 200.5(j)(3)(i)(b), (iii)).

There are restrictions on who can serve as an impartial hearing officer. For example, individuals employed by a school district, school, or program serving students with disabilities placed there by a committee on special education, may not serve as an impartial hearing officer while so employed and for individuals employed by such schools or programs, for two years following the termination of such employment. An IHO who is serving as attorney in a due process complaint within the district or has served as the attorney in a due process complaint in the district within the two-year period preceding the offer of appointment may not accept appointment. An IHO with special knowledge or training with respect to students with disabilities who has accompanied and advised a party from the same school district regarding a due process complaint within a two year period may not accept appointment. In addition, impartial hearing officers may not have a personal or professional interest that conflicts with their objectivity in the hearing (20 USC § 1415(f)(3)(A)(i); 34 CFR § 300.511(c)(1)(i); 8 NYCRR § 200.1(x)(3)). An impartial hearing officer who also practices as a school district attorney must disclose this information at the outset of the hearing as a potentially conflicting interest and allow the parties an opportunity to question his or her impartiality (*Application of a Child with a Disability*, SRO dec. no. 06-051 (2006)).

54:55. What happens if an impartial hearing officer is unavailable or becomes unable to continue with a hearing already in progress?

A district must offer appointment to each successive impartial hearing officer (IHO) on the list (see **54:54**) whenever an IHO declines appointment or fails to respond or is unreachable within 24 hours after documented, independently verifiable, reasonable efforts by the district (8 NYCRR § 200.2(e)(1)(ii)).

A board must rescind an IHO appointment and appoint a new IHO if after a hearing commences the parents and the district agree that the IHO has become incapacitated or otherwise unavailable or unwilling to continue the hearing or issue a decision (8 NYCRR § 200.5(j)(3)(xv)).

54:56. Are there any limitations on the authority of an impartial hearing officer?

Yes. An impartial hearing officer (IHO) may not "sua sponte" (on his or her own) raise and decide issues that were not identified in the due process complaint notice filed by the parents or issues not otherwise addressed during the impartial hearing (*Application of the [redacted] Dep't of Educ*, SRO dec. no. 09-024 (2009)). For example, it was improper for a hearing officer to award tuition reimbursement (see **54:70-74**) to the parents of a student with disabilities because the parents had asked the hearing officer to decide only the stay-put placement (see **54:59-61**) of the student until they and the district could agree on an appropriate placement (*Application of the [redacted] Dep't of Educ.*, SRO dec. no. 09-027 (2009)). An IHO may not issue a so-ordered decision on the terms of a settlement agreement reached by the parties in other matters not before the IHO in the due process complaint or amended due process complaint (8 NYCRR § 200.5(j)(4)(iii).

In addition, the U.S. Court of Appeals for the Second Circuit, with jurisdiction over New York, has determined that an impartial due process hearing is not the appropriate vehicle for enforcing a prior settlement agreement entered into between parents and a school district under the Individuals with Disabilities Education Act. A settlement agreement is a contract between the parties to the agreement. The authority of IHOs is limited to matters relating to the identification, evaluation, or educational placement of a child, or the provision of a free appropriate public education (see **54:3**) to such child (*H.C. v. Colton-Pierreport CSD*, 341 Fed. Appx. 687 (2d Cir. 2009) (unpublished)).

54:57. On what basis must an impartial hearing officer decide the merits of a parental complaint?

An impartial hearing officer (IHO) must render a decision on substantive grounds based on a determination as to whether the student received a free appropriate public education (FAPE) (see **54:3**). Procedural violations will be deemed to have deprived a student of FAPE only if they impeded the student's right to FAPE, significantly impeded the parents' opportunity to participate in the decision-making process regarding the provision of FAPE to the student, or if they caused a deprivation of educational benefit (20 USC § 1415(f)(3)(E)(i), (ii); 34 CFR § 300.513(a); 8 NYCRR § 200.5(j)(4); *L.O. v. N.Y. City Dep't of Educ.*, 822 F.3d 95 (2d Cir. 2016)). For example, a district's persistent refusal to discuss a student's bullying during the development of her individualized educational program (IEP) was a procedural violation that significantly impeded the parents' right to participate in the development of their daughter's IEP and constituted a denial of FAPE (*T.K. & S.K. v. N.Y. City Dep't of Educ.*, 810 F.3d 869 (2d Cir. 2016)).

Generally, a complaint alleging a failure to make a valid offer of FAPE based on an allegedly inappropriate individualized educational program (IEP) must be resolved on the terms of the written IEP. Statements made by school staff to parents during a site visit are not binding on the district (*B.P. & S.H. v. N.Y. City Dep't of Educ.*, 634 Fed. Appx. 845 (2d Cir. 2015)). A school district may not submit evidence that they would have provided the student with services not listed in the IEP. This evidence is referred to as "retrospective testimony." A federal appellate court with jurisdiction over New York has concluded that retrospective testimony is not permissible in tuition-reimbursement cases. A school district may, however, provide testimony that explains or justifies the services listed in the IEP (*R.E. v. N. Y. City Dep't of Educ.*, 694 F.3d 167 (2d Cir. 2012), *cert. denied*, 133 S. Ct. 2802 (2013)).

In addition, it is not appropriate to consider a change in placement in an IEP developed after commencement of an impartial due process hearing as evidence that the placement included in the prior IEP was inappropriate. Holding against a school district placement decisions made after an IEP is challenged is inconsistent with the requirements of the Individuals with Disabilities Education Act that districts continually reassess the needs of disabled students (*Jordan S. v. Hewlett Woodmere UFSD*, 2010 U.S. Dist. LEXIS 127781 (E.D.N.Y. Dec. 1, 2010)).

The IHO must mail a copy of the decision, or at the parents' option, provide electronic findings of fact and decision to the parents, the school board, and the Office of Special Education at the NYS Education Department in accordance with the timelines set forth in regulations (30 CFR § 515; 8 NYCRR § 200.5(j)(5)).

54:58. May an impartial hearing officer's decision be appealed?

Yes. The impartial hearing officer's decision may be appealed to the state review officer (SRO) at the NYS Education Department's Office of State Review in accordance with the provisions of Part 279 of the commissioner's regulations (20 USC § 1415(g); 34 CFR § 300.514(b); Educ. Law § 4404(2); 8 NYCRR § 200.5(k)). However, the SRO will dismiss any appeal by a school district that is not supported by official school board action authorizing the appeal (*Application of Bd. of Educ. of the Carmel CSD*, SRO dec. no. 00-004 (2001)).

The SRO's decision may, in turn, be appealed to the New York State Supreme Court or federal district court (20 USC § 1415(i)(2)(A); 34 CFR §§ 300.514(d); 300.516; Educ. Law § 4404(3); 8 NYCRR § 200.5(k)(3)). Under New York's two-tier administrative review scheme, parties wishing to appeal the hearing officer's decision may not proceed directly to state or federal court without first appealing to the SRO (*Cave v. E. Meadow UFSD*, 514 F.3d 240 (2d Cir. 2008)).

54:59. What is the status of a student with a disability while proceedings regarding his or her classification, evaluation, or academic placement take place?

With the exception of certain disciplinary proceedings, during the pendency of proceedings challenging the classification, evaluation and placement of a student with a disability, that student must remain in his or her current educational placement unless the school district and the parent agree otherwise (20 USC § 1415(j), (k)(4)(A); 34 CFR §§ 300.518, 300.533). This is often referred to as "stay-put." Generally, the stay-put placement must be a program in which the student has actually participated, rather than a proposed program (*Application of Bd. of Educ. of the City Sch. Dist. of the City of Buffalo*, SRO dec. no. 05-006 (2005)). However, as set forth below, a child's particular circumstances may affect the determination of his or her stay-put placement.

A school district can alter its stay-put obligations by providing additional services while the parent's complaint is pending. In one case, the district's compliance with an impartial hearing officer's order to provide in-home applied behavioral analysis (ABA) immediately pending appeal precluded them from terminating those additional services at a later date (*M.G. and V.M. v. N.Y. City Dep't of Educ.*, 982 F.Supp.2d 240 (S.D.N.Y. 2013)).

The stay-put placement for a student applying for initial admission to a public school would be, with parental consent, the public school program (20 USC § 1415(j); 34 CFR § 300.518(b); Educ. Law § 4404(4); 8 NYCRR § 200.5(m)). Similarly, during the pendency of any due process proceeding related to the evaluation and initial placement in special education, the student shall not be evaluated and shall remain in the then current educational placement, unless the district and the parent agree otherwise (8 NYCRR § 200.5(m)).

Furthermore, where parents challenging their child's placement enroll the child in a private school, the private school becomes the child's stay-put placement if, on appeal, New York's State Review Officer agrees with the parents that the child's placement should be changed. In such an instance, the school district becomes financially responsible for maintaining the child at the private school during the pendency of any further appeals (*Mackey v. Bd. of Educ. for the Arlington CSD*, 386 F.3d 158 (2d Cir. 2004); *Bd. of Educ. of the Pawling CSD v. Schutz*, 290 F.3d 476 (2d Cir. 2002), *cert. denied,* 537 U.S. 1227 (2003)). However, that would not be the case if the child's parents subsequently enroll the child in a new private school and there is no evidence that the educational programs of both private schools are substantially similar (*Application of a Child with a Disability,* SRO dec. no. 02-031 (2002)).

54:60. Are there any circumstances under which the "stay-put" provisions that require students to remain in their current educational placement while proceedings are pending do not apply?

According to one federal district court in New York, the stay-put provisions (see **54:59**) do not apply during the pendency of an appeal from an order of compensatory education for a student who has aged out (see **54:12**) and is no longer otherwise eligible to receive services under the Individuals with Disabilities Education Act (*Cosgrove v. Bd. of Educ. of the Niskayuna CSD*, 175 F.Supp.2d 375 (N.D.N.Y. 2001)). In another ruling, a federal appellate court with jurisdiction outside New York held that the stay-put provisions do not apply where a student relocates from one state to another, even if the student is forced to cope in regular education without supports while the parents resolve their differences with the district in the *new* state (*Michael C. v. Radnor Twp. Sch. Dist.*, 202 F.3d 642 (3d Cir.), *cert. denied,* 531 U.S. 813 (2000)).

In addition, the stay-put provisions have been found not to apply when a child's current educational placement is no longer functionally available. That was the case where a Lovaas service provider who had the only state approved program that would satisfy the requirements of the student's IEP became unavailable to provide the services. In such an instance, parents and their school district remain free to agree on a new placement. Absent an agreement, a court may award relief seeking a change in placement where such a change is shown to be warranted (*Wagner v. Bd. of Educ. of Montgomery Cnty.*, 335 F.3d 297 (4th Cir. 2003)).

54:61. What is the status of a student transitioning from early intervention services while proceedings are pending relating to that transition?

According to both federal and state regulations, when a child is first transitioning from early childhood intervention services and is no longer eligible for such services because the child has turned three, a district does not have to provide the early intervention services the child had been receiving. Once the child is found eligible for special education and related services and there is parental consent for the initial provision of such services, the district must provide only those services that are not in dispute (34 CFR § 300.518(c); *Letter to Zahorchack*, OSEP Response to Inquiry, 48 IDELR 135 (Feb. 2007)). A student transitioning from early intervention to school-age IDEA services is not entitled to continuation of early intervention services during the pendency of a due process proceeding challenging his preschool placement (*M.M. v. N.Y. City Dep't of Educ.*, 583 F.Supp.2d 498 (S.D.N.Y. 2008)).

54:62. Are school districts liable for money damages when parents challenge their determination regarding their child's classification, evaluation or placement?

Not in a lawsuit brought directly under the Individuals with Disabilities Education Act (IDEA). However, parents may recover money damages if they prevail in a lawsuit under Section 1983 of the Civil Rights Act of 1964 alleging a violation of the IDEA (*Polera v. Bd. of Educ. of the Newburgh City Sch. Dist.,* 288 F.3d 478 (2d Cir. 2002)).

54:63. Are school districts liable for the cost of attorneys' fees incurred by parents who challenge a district's determination regarding the classification, evaluation, or placement of their child?

Yes, if the parents are the prevailing party on an action or proceeding (20 USC § 1415(i)(3); 34 CFR § 300.517), and are the parents of a student who has been deemed to be a child with a disability (*Durkee v. Livonia CSD*, 487 F.Supp.2d 318 (W.D.N.Y. 2007); see also *D.S. v. Neptune Twp. Bd. of Educ.*, 264 Fed. Appx. 186 (3d Cir. 2008)).

However, parents are not deemed prevailing parties entitled to attorneys' fees when they enter into a voluntary settlement of their differences with their school district, unless the agreement provides for court enforcement of the settlement. A settlement agreement that is enforceable by a court through a consent decree order would entitle parents to attorneys' fees (*Roberson v. Giuliani*, 346 F.3d 75 (2d Cir. 2003); *J.C. v. Reg'l Sch. Dist. 10*, 278 F.3d 119 (2d Cir. 2002); see also *Student X v. N.Y. City Dep't of Educ.*, 2008 U.S. Dist. LEXIS 88163 (E.D.N.Y. Oct. 30, 2008)). So would a settlement incorporated into an order from an impartial hearing officer otherwise dismissing a hearing. That a hearing officer has no jurisdiction to enforce the terms of the settlement (see **54:56**) is irrelevant, as long as judicial enforcement is available (*A.R. v. N.Y. City Dep't of Educ.*, 407 F.3d 65 (2d Cir. 2005)).

Attorneys' fees may be awarded even if their amount exceeds the cost of the settlement of a parent's claim (*Elliott v. Bd. of Educ. of the Rochester City Sch. Dist.*, 295 F.Supp.2d 282 (W.D.N.Y. 2003)). They must be based on rates prevailing in the community where the action or proceeding arose for the kind and quality of services furnished. No bonus or multiplier may be used in calculating attorneys' fees (20 USC § 1415(i)(3)(C); 34 CFR § 300.517(c)(1); *I.B. v N.Y. City Dep't of Educ.*, 336 F.3d 79 (2d Cir. 2003)). *Prevailing rates* refer to the amount actually charged by the attorneys and not the rate a school board pays when it agrees to pay attorneys' fees (*R.E. v. N. Y. City Bd. of Educ.*, 38 IDELR 66 (S.D.N.Y. 2003)). Westlaw computer research charges are not recoverable (*B.D. v. DeBuono*, 177 F.Supp.2d 201 (S.D.N.Y. 2001)).

54:64. Are school districts liable for the cost of attorneys' fees incurred by parents who prevail as defendants at an impartial due process hearing?

Yes. According to the U.S. Court of Appeals for the Second Circuit, which has jurisdiction over New York, parents would be entitled to an award of attorneys' fees, as well, if they are a "prevailing defendant." However, the court did not identify any standard for determining whether a prevailing defendant parent should be awarded such fees (*Mr. L. v. Sloan,* 449 F.3d 405 (2d Cir. 2006)).

Appellate courts will not reverse a district court's award of attorneys' fees unless the district court abused its discretion in awarding such fees (*Green v. City of N.Y.*, 403 Fed. Appx. 626 (2d Cir. 2010)).

54:65. Are school districts liable for attorneys' fees even when parents are represented by a publicly-funded attorney?

Yes. Attorneys' fees may be awarded despite the fact that the parents were represented by a publicly-funded attorney (*Yankton Sch. Dist. v. Schramm*, 93 F.3d 1369 (8th Cir. 1996)). However, attorneys' fees are not available to a lay advocate (*Connors v. Mills*, 34 F.Supp.2d 795 (N.D.N.Y. 1998)).

54:66. Are there any limitations on the ability of parents to recover attorneys' fees?

Yes. Attorneys' fees may not be awarded for an attorney's attendance at a committee on special education (CSE) meeting unless it is convened as a result of an administrative proceeding or judicial action (20 USC § 1415(i)(3)(D)(ii), (iii); 34 CFR § 300.517(c)(2)(ii), (iii)), a request for an impartial due process hearing (*V.G. v. Auburn Enlarged CSD*, 349 Fed. Appx. 582 (2d Cir. 2009); *F.R. & K.R. v. Bd. of*

Educ., Plainedge Pub. Schs., 67 F.Supp.2d 142 (E.D.N.Y. 1999)), or attendance at a complaint resolution meeting (20 USC § 1415(i)(3)(D)(iii); 34 CFR § 517(c)(2)(ii), (iii); see **54:52**). Neither may attorneys' fees be awarded for mediation that is conducted prior to the filing of a complaint, at the discretion of the State (20 USC § 1415(i)(3)(D)(ii)), or under certain circumstances for services performed after a written offer of settlement is made to a parent unless the parent was substantially justified in rejecting the settlement offer (20 USC § 1415(i)(3)(D)(i), (E); 34 CFR § 517(c)(2)(i), (3)).

In addition, attorneys' fees may be reduced under certain circumstances, including when the relief finally obtained by the parents is less favorable than a district's previous offer of settlement (20 USC § 1415(i)(3)(D)(i)(III)). Attorney's fees may be reduced also when the parent or the parent's attorney unreasonably protracted final resolution of the controversy, or the amount authorized unreasonably exceeds the hourly prevailing rate in the community for similar services by attorneys of reasonably comparable skill, reputation and experience (see **54:63**). One exception would be when a school district unreasonably protracts final resolution (20 USC § 1415(i)(3)(F), (G); 34 CFR § 517(c)(4), (5)). Attorneys fees may be reduced, as well, when parents reject a district's proposed settlement but the basics of an eventual court decree already had been provided to the parents and the minor changes and adjustments do not warrant the amount of time expanded by the attorney (*V.G. v. Auburn Enlarged City Sch. Dist.* 2008 U.S. Dist. LEXIS 99743 (N.D.N.Y. Dec. 9, 2008), *aff'd*, 349 Fed. Appx. 582 (2d Cir. 2009)).

54:67. Are school districts liable for the cost of services rendered by experts that are incurred by parents who challenge a school district's determination regarding the classification, evaluation or placement of their child?

No. According to the U. S. Supreme Court, the Individuals with Disabilities Education Act (IDEA) does not authorize prevailing parents to recover fees for services rendered by experts in IDEA actions, including the services of an educational consultant (*Arlington CSD Bd. of Educ. v. Murphy*, 548 U.S. 291 (2006)).

54:68. Are school districts entitled to attorneys' fees?

Yes, against the attorney of a parent who files a complaint or subsequent action that is determined to have been "frivolous, unreasonable or without foundation," or who "continues to litigate after the litigation clearly becomes frivolous, unreasonable, or without foundation" (20 USC § 1415(i)(3)(B)(i)(II); 34 CFR § 300.517(a)(1)(ii)). School districts may recover attorneys' fees, as well, against a parent or a parent's attorney if the parent's complaint or subsequent action was presented for an improper purpose, such as to harass, cause unnecessary delay, or needlessly increase the cost of litigation (20 USC § 1415(i)(3)(B)(i)(III); 34 CFR § 300.517(a)(1)(iii)).

54:69. Are the parents of a child with a disability entitled to an independent educational evaluation of their child at public expense?

Yes, if they disagree with the evaluation obtained by the school district (20 USC § 1415(b)(1); 34 CFR § 300.502(a); 8 NYCRR § 200.5(g)(1); *Application of a Student with a Disability*, SRO dec. no. 09-144 (2010)).

An *independent educational evaluation* (IEE) consists of an individual evaluation of a student conducted by a qualified examiner who is not employed by the public agency responsible for the education of the student (8 NYCRR § 200.1(z)).

However, when parents request an IEE, the district may initiate a hearing to show that its evaluation is appropriate or that the evaluation obtained by the parent does not meet school district criteria. If the hearing officer agrees with the school district, the parents still have a right to an IEE, but not at public expense (20 USC § 1415(b)(1), (d)(2)(A); 34 CFR § 300.502(b); 8 NYCRR § 200.5(g)).

When IEEs are at public expense they are subject to the same criteria that the school district uses when it initiates an evaluation, including the location of the evaluation and the qualifications of the examiner (34 CFR § 300.502(a)(2), (e); 8 NYCRR §§ 200.1(z), 200.5(g)(1)(ii)). Upper limits on the costs of particular tests may not simply be an average of fees customarily charged by professionals in the area, but must permit parents to choose from among qualified individuals in the area (*Application of a Child with a Handicapping Condition*, SRO dec. no. 92-35 (1992); *Application of a Child with a* Disability, SRO dec. no. 93-26 (1993)). A school district policy may cap the cost of an IEE unless the parents can demonstrate that their child's unique circumstances justify payment beyond the standard limit (*M.V. v. Shenendehowa CSD*, 2013 U.S. Dist. LEXIS 32069 (N.D.N.Y. 2013)). In addition, a parent is entitled only to one IEE at public expense each time a school district conducts an evaluation with which the parent disagrees (*Application of a Student with a Disability*, SRO dec. no. 09-144 (2010)).

A school district may ask, but not require, that parents tell why they disagree with the district's evaluation (34 CFR § 300.502(b)(4); 8 NYCRR § 200.5(g)(1)(iii)).

Tuition Reimbursement

54:70. May parents place their child in a private school and seek reimbursement of tuition costs if they disagree with a school district's determination concerning their child?

Yes, subject to certain conditions. A parent who disagrees with a school district's placement and proceeds to enroll his or her child in a private school may be entitled to tuition reimbursement if a court or hearing officer determines that the school district did not make a free appropriate public education (FAPE) (see **54:3**), available to the child in a timely manner and that the private placement is appropriate (20 USC § 1412(a)(10)(C)(ii); 34 CFR § 300.148(c)).

According to the U.S. Court of Appeals for the Second Circuit, with jurisdiction over New York, the appropriateness of a parent's private placement must be determined based upon the same considerations and criteria applicable to determining the appropriateness of a district's placement (*Gagliardo v. Arlington CSD*, 489 F.3d 105 (2d Cir. 2007); see also *Green v. N.Y. City Dep't of Educ.*, 50 IDELR 40 (S.D.N.Y. 2008); but compare *G.R. v. N.Y. City Dep't of Educ.*, 2009 U.S. Dist. LEXIS 69348 (S.D.N.Y. Aug. 7, 2009)). That means it must provide "educational instruction specifically designed to meet the unique needs of a [disabled] child." The basic question to ask is whether the private placement is "reasonably calculated to enable the child to receive educational benefit." However, a student's progress in a private placement does not itself demonstrate the appropriateness of the placement (*Gagliardo v. Arlington CSD*; see also *Omidian v. Bd. of Educ. of New Hartford CSD*, 2009 U.S. Dist. LEXIS 29016 (N.D.N.Y. Mar. 31, 2009)). In addition, the instruction specifically designed to meet the student's unique needs must be supported by such services as are necessary to allow the student to benefit from instruction (*Davis v. Wappingers CSD*, 431 Fed. Appx. 12 (2d Cir. 2011)). Accordingly, a private placement program that is predicated on a 12-step substance abuse treatment would not be deemed appropriate for reimbursement purposes, particularly when the program fails to "address the emotional and behavioral needs" that affect a student's ability to make educational progress (*P.C. & M.C. v. Oceanside UFSD*, 818 F.Supp.2d 516 (E.D.N.Y. 2011)).

The least restrictive environment requirement (see **54:7**) is a factor in the parents' choice of private placement, but it is not dispositive. Parents are not subject to the same mainstreaming requirements as a school district. Restrictiveness may be relevant in choosing between two or more otherwise appropriate private placement alternatives, or when considering whether a private placement is more restrictive than necessary to meet the student's needs. However, where the school district denies a student a FAPE, the restrictiveness of the private placement cannot be measured against the restrictiveness of the district's proposed placement (*C.L. v. Scarsdale UFSD*, 744 F.3d 826 (2d Cir. 2014); M.*S. v. Yonkers Bd. of Educ.*, 231 F.3d 96 (2d Cir. 2000), *cert. denied,* 532 U.S. 942 (2001); *Application of the Bd. of Educ. of the Irvington UFSD*, SRO dec. no. 01-035 (2002); *Application of a Child with a Disability*, SRO dec. no. 00-056 (2001); *Application of the Bd. of Educ. of the [Redacted] Sch. Dist.*, SRO dec. no. 08-016 (2008)). The parent bears the burden of proving that the private placement is appropriate.

A child does not have to have previously received special education and related services through a public school system in order for the child's parents to be able to recover tuition reimbursement (*Forest Grove Sch. Dist. v. T.A.*, 557 U.S. 230 (2009)).

54:71. Are there any limitations on a parent's right to tuition reimbursement?

Yes. Subject to certain limited exceptions (20 USC § 1412(a)(10)(C)(iv); 34 CFR § 300.148(e)), a court or hearing officer may deny or reduce the reimbursement if the parents fail to give the school district notice at the most recent individualized education program (IEP) meeting that they reject the proposed placement, and state their concerns and their intent to enroll the child in a private school at public expense, or provide 10 business days (including any holidays that occur on a business day) written notice to the district prior to removing the child (20 USC § 1412(a)(10)(C)(iii)(I)(aa), (bb); 34 CFR § 300.148(d)(1); see *J.S. v. Scarsdale UFSD*, 826 F.Supp.2d 635 (S.D.N.Y. 2011); see also *Berger v. Medina City Sch. Dist.*, 348 F.3d 513 (6th Cir. 2003); *Rafferty v. Cranston Pub. Sch. Comm.*, 315 F.3d 21 (1st Cir. 2002); *Pollowitz v. Weast,* 90 Fed. Appx. 438 (4th Cir. 2001)).

Tuition reimbursement may be denied or reduced also if,

- The school district gives the parents written notice of its intent to evaluate the child and the reasons for the evaluation prior to the parents' removal of the child, but the parents fail to make the child available for the evaluation (20 USC § 1412(a)(10)(C)(iii)(II); 34 CFR § 300.148(d)(2); see *Carmel CSD v. V.P.*, 373 F.Supp.2d 402 (S.D.N.Y. 2005), *aff'd*, 192 Fed. Appx. 62 (2d Cir. 2006)).
- The parents fail to cooperate with a school district by not allowing the district a reasonable opportunity to evaluate their child (*Patricia P. v. Bd. of Educ. of Oak Park & River Forest High Sch. Dist. No. 200*, 203 F.3d 462 (7th Cir. 2000)), or not making the child available for intake interviews at a proposed out-of-district placement (*J.S. v. Scarsdale UFSD*).
- The parents fail in their obligation to cooperate with their school district in finding an appropriate placement, such as when they secure a private placement with a large non-refundable deposit before they refer their child to the committee on special education (*Bettinger v. N.Y. City Bd. of Educ.*, 2007 U.S. Dist. LEXIS 86116 (S.D.N.Y. 2007); but compare *A.R. ex. rel. F.P. v. N.Y. City Dep't. of Educ.*, 2013 U.S. Dist. LEXIS 135855 (S.D.N.Y. 2013)), or have an apparent predisposition to view skeptically any district-suggested placement other than their own choice (*J.S. v. Scarsdale UFSD*; but compare *N.R. v. Dep't of Educ. of the City Sch. Dist. of the City of N.Y.*, 2009 U.S. Dist. LEXIS 27273 (S.D.N.Y. 2009)).
- A child's poor performance in a public school program is due, largely in part, to a parental request that the child not receive specific services and modifications recommended by the committee on special education and the child's teachers (*Application of a Child with a Disability*, SRO dec. no. 04-093 (2004)).

54:72. May parents seek tuition reimbursement even if they place their child at a private school that is not approved by the state?

Yes. According to the U.S. Supreme Court, the parents of a student with a disability may be awarded reimbursement for private school placement (see **54:70-71**), even if the private school does not meet state educational agency standards. Courts, however, may consider whether the private school costs are reasonable (*Florence Cnty. Sch. Dist. Four v. Carter*, 510 U.S. 7 (1993)). Further ruling that parents are not required to place their children at state-approved schools, the U.S. Supreme Court in the *Carter* case explained, that parents cannot be held to the same standards as public school districts when arranging for the placement of their children.

In addition, the school selected by the parent need not have teachers who are certified in regular or special education as long as the placement is otherwise appropriate (*Omidian v. Bd. of Educ. of New Hartford CSD*, 2009 U.S. Dist. LEXIS 29016 (N.D.N.Y. Mar. 31, 2009); *Green v. N.Y. City Dep't of Educ.*, 2008 U.S. Dist. LEXIS 32118 (S.D.N.Y. Mar. 31, 2008)).

54:73. May parents unilaterally place their child with a disability in another public school district and be reimbursed for that placement, if they disagree with the school district's determination concerning their child?

Yes. Parents may be entitled to reimbursement for tuition paid to another public school district and for reasonable transportation costs after the parents remove their child from the school district of residence because they are dissatisfied with the special education services provided to their child. However, they must establish that the district of residence failed to make a free appropriate public education (see **54:3**) available to their child in a timely manner and that their choice of placement is appropriate (*Application of a Child with a Disability*, SRO dec. no. 07-070 (2007); see also *Northeast CSD v. Sobol*, 79 N.Y.2d 598 (1992)).

54:74. May parents seek reimbursement for the cost of providing related services rather than the full cost of tuition at a private school?

Yes, according to a federal appellate court with jurisdiction outside of New York (*M.M. v. School Bd. of Miami-Dade Cnty., Fla.*, 437 F.3d 1085 (11th Cir. 2006)). In that case, the parents did not pay tuition at the private school because the mother worked there. However, they sought reimbursement of the cost of providing their child a particular form of therapy for deaf children because they disagreed with the methodology used by the district. Although the parents ultimately failed in disproving the appropriateness of the district's therapy, the court disagreed with the district that parents can seek reimbursement of only tuition costs.

In another case, New York's State Review Officer (SRO) denied a parent reimbursement for the cost of a private tutor for a student with reading difficulties retained only because the district had discontinued previously provided services at the parent's insistence so that the student could take a technology class. According to the SRO, it would have been inequitable to reimburse the parent for private services that replaced adequate school services the parent requested not be provided (*Application of a Child with a Disability*, SRO dec. no. 05-020 (2005); see also *Application of a Child with a Disability*, SRO dec. no. 04-093 (2004)).

Disciplining Students with Disabilities

54:75. May a student with a disability be suspended or removed from school?

School districts may suspend or remove a disabled student from school in accordance with the procedures and safeguards set forth in both federal and state law and regulations (20 USC § 1415(k); 34 CFR §§ 300.530–37; Educ. Law § 3214(3)(g), 4404(1); 8 NYCRR Part 201).

Students with disabilities attending summer school are entitled to the same discipline safeguards applicable during the regular school year (*LIH v. N.Y. City Bd. of Educ.*, 103 F.Supp.2d 658 (E.D.N.Y. 2000)).

54:76. Who may suspend or remove from school a student with a disability?

It depends on the length of the suspension or removal. A school board, the superintendent of schools, or a building principal may order the placement of a student with a disability into an appropriate interim alternative educational setting (IAES), another setting, or suspension for a period not to exceed five consecutive school days and the amount of time that a nondisabled student would be subject to suspension for the same behavior (20 USC § 1415(k)(1)(B); 34 CFR § 300.530(b)(1); 8 NYCRR § 201.7(b)).

A superintendent of schools, either directly or upon recommendation of a hearing officer designated to conduct a student disciplinary hearing pursuant to Education Law section 3214(3)(c), (g) may order the placement of a student in an appropriate IAES, another setting or suspension for up to 10 consecutive school days, inclusive of any period of suspension imposed pursuant to the above paragraph. The duration of the superintendent's suspension may not exceed the time a nondisabled student would be subject to suspension or removal for the same behavior (20 USC § 1415(k)(1)(B); 34 CFR § 300.530(b)(1); 8 NYCRR § 201.7(c)). The superintendent may order additional suspensions of not more than 10 consecutive school days in the same school year for separate incidents of misconduct that do not constitute a disciplinary change of placement (*Id.*; see **54:78**).

Under New York law, the school district must conduct a disciplinary hearing to determine if the student is guilty of the misconduct before a suspension penalty beyond five school days can be imposed (Educ. Law § 3214(3)(g)). The same applies to students presumed to have a disability for discipline purposes and to declassified students (Educ. Law § 3214(g)(2); 8 NYCRR § 201.5; *Appeal of a Student Presumed to Have a Disability*, 35 Ed Dept Rep 492 (1996); see **54:93**).

54:77. Are there any limitations on the authority to suspend or remove a student with a disability?

Yes. A student with a disability may not be suspended or otherwise removed from school for either a five or 10-school-day period (see **54:76**) if the suspension or removal would result in a disciplinary change in placement based on a pattern of suspensions or removals (20 USC § 1415(k)(1)(B); 34 CFR § 300.530(b)(1); 8 NYCRR § 201.7(d); see **54:78**).

In addition, according to the U.S. Department of Education, Office of Civil Rights Midwestern Division, Kansas City (Mo.), an in-school suspension may constitute a significant change in placement or count towards a pattern of suspension or removals that violates Section 504 of the Rehabilitation Act, depending on the nature and quality of the education services provided to the student and their comparability to services provided prior to the in-school suspension (*Dunkin (Mo) R-V Sch. Dist.*, OCR Decision, 52 IDELR 138 (Jan. 2009)). Section 504 prohibits discrimination on the basis of disability. In one case, an in-school suspension passed scrutiny under that law because the student received assignments to work on, had visits from his regular education teacher, and also had visits from his special education teacher in order to receive special education services (*Id.*).

54:78. What constitutes a disciplinary change in placement?

Generally, a suspension or removal of a student with a disability constitutes a *disciplinary change in placement* if it is for:

- more than 10 consecutive school days (34 CFR § 300.536(a)(1)), or
- 10 consecutive school days or less, if the student is subjected to a series of suspensions or removals that constitutes a pattern because they add to more than 10 school days in a school year, the child's behavior is substantially similar to behavior in prior incidents that resulted in suspension or removal, and because of additional factors such as the length of each suspension or removal,

the total amount of time the child is removed, and the proximity of the suspensions or removals to one another (34 CFR § 300.536(a)(2); 8 NYCRR § 201.2(e)).

The determination whether a suspension constitutes a disciplinary change of placement based on a pattern of removals is made on a case by case basis, depending on the particular student and facts involved, and is subject to review through due process and judicial proceedings (34 CFR § 300.536(b); 8 NYCRR § 201.2(e)). A school superintendent may not offer options as part of a student disciplinary process that would change the placement of a student with disabilities. Any such change may only occur by recommendation of the district's committee on special education (*Appeal of a Student with a Disability*, 52 Ed Dept Rep, Dec. No. 16,371 (2012); see **54:25**).

A school district must inform parents of any decision to subject their child to a suspension or removal that constitutes a disciplinary change in placement based on the child's violation of the student code of conduct on the date such a decision is made. Along with such notice, the district also must provide the parents a copy of their procedural safeguards (34 CFR § 300.530(h); see **54:23-24**).

54:79. Are there any exceptions to the disciplinary change in placement rule?

Yes. A student with a disability may be suspended or removed from school for a period that otherwise would constitute a disciplinary change in placement (see **54:78**) if the manifestation team (see **54:86**) determines that the student's behavior was not a manifestation of the student's disability (see **54:85**), or it involves the placement of a student in an interim alternative educational setting (see **54:80-81**) for behavior relating to the infliction of serious bodily injury upon another, weapons, or illegal drugs or controlled substances, or conduct that poses a risk of harm to the student or others (20 USC § 1415(k)(1)(C); 34 CFR § 300.530(c), (g); 8 NYCRR §§ 201.7(d), (e), 201.8).

School personnel may consider any unique circumstances on a case-by-case basis when determining whether to order a change in placement for a student with a disability who violates a code of student conduct (20 USC § 1415(k)(1)(A); 34 CFR § 300.530(a); 8 NYCRR § 201.7(f)).

54:80. What is an interim alternative education setting?

An *interim alternative education setting* (IAES) is a temporary educational placement determined by the committee on special education, other than the student's current placement at the time the behavior precipitating the IAES placement occurred (20 USC § 1415(k)(2); 34 CFR § 300.531; 8 NYCRR § 201.2(k); see **54:81-83**).

54:81. Under what circumstances may a student with disabilities be placed in an interim alternative education setting?

A superintendent of schools may opt to place a student in an interim alternative educational setting (IAES) (see **54:80**) for the same amount of time that a child without a disability would be subject to discipline but not more than 45 school days for each separate instance where the child:

- has inflicted serious bodily injury upon another person while at school, on school premises or at a school function under the district's jurisdiction;
- carries to or possesses a weapon at school, on school premises, or to or at a school function under the district's jurisdiction; or
- knowingly possesses or uses illegal drugs or sells or solicits the sale of a controlled substance while at school, on school premises, or a school function under the district's jurisdiction (20 USC § 1415(k)(1)(G); 34 CFR § 300.530(g); 8 NYCRR § 201.7(e)).

In addition, an impartial hearing officer (IHO) may order the placement of a child in an IAES for up to 45 school days at a time if the school district shows by substantial evidence that maintaining the child in his or her current placement is substantially likely to result in injury to the child or others. The IHO also must consider the appropriateness of the student's current placement, whether the district has taken steps to minimize the risk of harm in the child's current placement, and determine whether the proposed IAES will provide the student the required level of services (20 USC § 1415(k)(3)(B); 34 CFR § 300.532(b)(2)(ii); Educ. Law § 3214(3)(g)(3), (vii); 8 NYCRR § 201.8). For a description of the level of services that must be provided in an IAES, see **54:83**.

A student may be placed in an IAES on grounds of dangerousness and for misconduct relating to the infliction of serious bodily injury, weapons, illegal drugs, or controlled substance even if the behavior triggering the placement was a manifestation of the student's disability (20 USC § 1415(k)(1)(G); 34 CFR § 300.530(g); 8 NYCRR §§ 201.9(c)(3); see **54:85, 87**).

54:82. Who determines the interim alternative educational setting (IAES) for a student with disabilities?

The committee on special education determines the IAES for a student with a disability placed in an interim alternative educational setting (20 USC § 1415(k)(2); 34 CFR § 300.531; 8 NYCRR §§ 201.2(k), 201.7(e)(1)).

54:83. What level of services must a school district provide to a student with a disability placed in an interim alternative educational (IAES) setting?

A student with a disability who is placed in an IAES must:

- continue to receive educational services that enable the student to continue to participate in the general curriculum, although in another setting, and to progress toward meeting the goals set out in the student's individualized education program (see **54:6**); and
- receive, as appropriate, a functional behavioral assessment (see **54:88**) and behavioral intervention services (see **54:91**) and modifications that are designed to address the behavior violation so that it does not recur (20 USC § 1415(k)(1)(D); 34 CFR § 300.530(d); 8 NYCRR §§ 201.2(k), 201.10(c), (d)).

54:84. What level of services must be offered to students with disabilities during suspensions or removals other than those involving placement in an interim alternative educational setting?

During suspensions or removals for periods of up to 10 school days in a school year that do not constitute a disciplinary change in placement (see **54:78**), a school district must provide students with disabilities of compulsory education age with alternative instruction on the same basis as nondisabled students. With respect to students who are not of compulsory education age, a district must provide services only to the extent they are provided to nondisabled students of the same age who have been similarly suspended (34 CFR § 300.530(d)(3); 8 NYCRR § 201.10(b)).

School personnel, in consultation with at least one of the student's teachers determines the services to be provided to a student with a disability during subsequent suspensions or removals for periods of 10 consecutive school days or less that in the aggregate total more than 10 school days in a school year but do not constitute a disciplinary change in placement (see **54:77-79**), regardless of the manifestation determination (see **54:85**). The services provided must enable the student to continue to participate in the general curriculum and to progress toward meeting the goals in the student's individualized education program (IEP) (see **54:6**), and to receive, as appropriate, a functional behavioral assessment (see **54:88**), behavioral intervention services (see **54:91**), and modifications that are designed to address the behavior violation so it does not recur (8 NYCRR § 201.10(c)). The same applies to suspensions or removals in excess of 10 school days in a school year that constitute a disciplinary change of placement, except it is the committee on special education that determines the services to be provided (8 NYCRR § 201.10(d); see also **54:78**).

54:85. What is a manifestation determination?

A *manifestation determination* consists of a review of the relationship between a student's disability and the behavior subject to disciplinary action (8 NYCRR § 201.4(a)). Its purpose is to determine whether the conduct in question was:

- caused by or had a direct and substantial relationship to the student's disability, or
- the direct result of the school district's failure to implement the student's individualized education program (20 USC § 1415(k)(1)(E); 34 CFR § 300.530(e); 8 NYCRR § 201.4(c)).

Such a determination must be based on a review of all relevant information in the student's file including the student's individualized education program (IEP) (see **54:6**), any teacher observations, and any relevant information provided by the student's parents (34 CFR § 300.530(e)(1); 8 NYCRR § 201.4(c)).

The manifestation determination must be made immediately, if possible, but no later than 10 school days after an authorized school authority (see **54:76**) makes a decision to either place the student in an interim alternative educational setting (see **54:80-81**) or impose a suspension that constitutes a disciplinary change of placement (34 CFR § 300.530(e)(1); 8 NYCRR § 201.4(a); see **54:77-79**). The remedy imposed by the commissioner of education for the failure to conduct a timely manifestation determination is expungement of the pre-manifestation determination suspension from the student's record (*Appeal of D.W.*, 52 Ed Dept Rep, Dec. No. 16,436 (2012)).

Immediate steps must be taken to remedy any deficiencies in the student's IEP or placement, or their implementation, identified during the manifestation determination review process (34 CFR § 300.530(e)(3); 8 NYCRR § 201.4(e)).

54:86. Who conducts a manifestation determination?

A *manifestation team* conducts a manifestation determination. That team must include:

- a representative of the school district knowledgeable about the student and the interpretation of information about child behavior,
- the student's parent, and
- relevant members of the CSE as determined by the parent and the school district.

Districts must provide parents written notification prior to any manifestation team meeting (20 USC § 1415(k)(1)(E)(ii); 34 CFR § 300.530(e)(1), (2); 8 NYCRR § 201.4(b)).

54:87. What happens if the student's behavior is deemed a manifestation of the student's disability?

If the behavior is a manifestation (see **54:85**) of the student's disability, the committee on special education must conduct a functional behavioral assessment (see **54:88**) and implement a behavioral intervention plan (BIP) (see **54:91**) for the student, or review and modify, as necessary, an already existing BIP. In addition, with the exception of students placed in an interim alternative educational setting (see **54:80-81**), students must be returned to the placement from which they were removed unless the parent and the school district agree to a change of placement as part of the modification of the student's BIP (20 USC § 1415(k)(1)(F); 34 CFR § 300.530(f); 8 NYCRR §§ 201.3, 201.4(d), 201.7(e)).

54:88. What is a functional behavioral assessment?

A *functional behavioral assessment* (FBA) involves the process of determining why a student engages in behaviors that impede learning and how the student's behavior relates to the environment (8 NYCRR § 200.1(r)). It must be conducted when a student's behavior impedes his or her learning or that of others (8 NYCRR § 200.4(b)(1)(v); *Danielle G. v. N.Y. City Dep't of Educ.*, 2008 U.S. Dist. LEXIS 60192 (E.D.N.Y. Aug. 7, 2008)).

An FBA includes, but is not limited to, the identification of the problem behavior, the definition of the behavior in concrete terms, the identification of the contextual factors that contribute to the behavior, and the formulation of a hypothesis regarding the general conditions under which a behavior usually occurs, and probable consequences that serve to maintain it (8 NYCRR § 200.1(r)). The FBA must be based on multiple sources of data and provide information in sufficient detail to form the basis for a behavior intervention plan (BIP) (see **54:91**). It may not be based solely on a student's history of presenting problem behavior (8 NYCRR § 200.22(a)(2), (3)).

On that basis, it would be premature and improper for a committee on special education to conduct an FBA and develop a BIP for a student transitioning from an early intervening program to preschool, before the student attends the recommended placement (*M.M. v. N.Y. City Dep't of Educ.*, 583 F.Supp.2d 498 (S.D.N.Y. 2008)).

Similarly, a school district's failure to conduct a FBA might not rise to the level of denying a free appropriate public education (see **54:3**) to a student whose individualized education program (see **54:6**) provides for the use of interventions, supports and strategies that address the student's behavior, if the effectiveness of such interventions, supports and strategies informed the decision to not conduct the FBA (*A.C ex. rel. M.C. v. Bd. of Educ. of the Chappaqua CSD*, 553 F.3d 165 (2d Cir. 2009); but see *L.O. v. N.Y. City Dep't of Educ.*, 822 F.3d 95 (2d Cir. 2016)).

54:89. When must a committee on special education (CSE) conduct a functional behavioral assessment (FBA) in connection with a student disciplinary matter?

The CSE must conduct an FBA and implement a behavior intervention plan (BIP) (see **54:91**) for a student with a disability related to a disciplinary matter whenever the student's suspension or removal constitutes a disciplinary change of placement (see **54:78**) and the conduct is a manifestation (see **54:85**) of the student's disability (8 NYCRR § 201.3(a)).

If the student already had a BIP, the CSE must review the plan and its implementation for any necessary modifications (8 NYCRR § 201.3(b)).

54:90. What type of professionals conduct a functional behavior assessment (FBA)?

Neither federal nor state law specifies who should conduct an FBA. However, the Office of Special Education Services (OSEP) at the U.S. Department of Education has indicated that school districts are responsible for ensuring that "properly trained professionals" are available to conduct FBAs (*Letter to Janssen*, OSEP Response to Inquiry, 51 IDELR 253 (June 5, 2008)).

54:91. What is a behavioral intervention plan?

A *behavioral intervention plan* (BIP) consists of a plan that is based on the results of a functional behavioral assessment (see **54:88**) and, at a minimum, includes a description of the problem behavior, global and specific hypotheses as to why the behavior occurs, and intervention strategies to address the behavior (8 NYCRR § 200.1(mmm)).

Intervention strategies, including the use of time out rooms and emergency interventions, must be used consistent with standards prescribed in commissioner regulations (8 NYCRR § 200.22).

In addition to specified instances related to student discipline (see **54:87**), the committee on special education also must consider the development of a BIP when:

- a student exhibits persistent behavior that impedes his or her learning or that of others, despite consistently implemented general schoolwide or classroomwide interventions;
- a student's behavior places the student or others at risk of harm or injury; and
- a student is being considered for a more restrictive program or placement as a result of his or her behavior (8 NYCRR § 200.22(b)).

A student's need for a BIP must be documented in the student's individualized education program (IEP) (see **54:6**) and revised at least annually. The IEP must indicate if a particular device or service, including an intervention, accommodation, or other program modification is needed to address the student's behavior that impedes his or her learning or that of others (8 NYCRR § 200.22(b)(2)). The IEP also must specify scheduled intervals for monitoring regular progress in the implementation of a student's BIP (8 NYCRR § 200.22(b)(5)).

54:92. May parents challenge the placement of their child in an interim alternative educational setting (IAES) and/or a determination that the child's behavior is not a manifestation of his or her disability?

Yes (20 USC § 1415(k)(3)(A); 34 CFR § 300.532(a); 8 NYCRR § 201.11(a)(3), (4)). In such an instance, the school district must conduct an expedited due process hearing. A resolution meeting must occur within seven days of the district receipt of the parental request for a hearing (8 NYCRR § 201.11(b)(3)(i)). The expedited due process hearing must occur within 20 school days of the date the district received the parental request for a hearing (20 USC § 1415(k)(4)(B); 34 CFR § 300.532(c); 8 NYCRR § 201.11(b)(3)(iii)).

During the pendency of the hearing or appeal, the child remains in the IAES pending the outcome of the decision or until expiration of the IAES, whichever occurs first, unless the parents and the district agree otherwise (20 USC § 1415(k)(4)(A); 34 CFR § 300.533; 8 NYCRR § 201.11(d); see also **54:80-84** for more information interim alternative educational settings).

54:93. Are the procedures that apply to the discipline of disabled students also applicable to students who have not been classified as students with disabilities?

Yes, if the student is a student presumed to have a disability for discipline purposes, i.e., the school district is deemed to have had knowledge, as defined by law and regulation, that the child was a child with a disability before the misconduct occurred (20 USC § 1415(k)(5); 34 CFR § 300.534(a); Educ. Law § 3214(g)(2); 8 NYCRR § 201.5).

A school district will be deemed to have the requisite knowledge if prior to the behavior:

- the student's parents expressed concern in writing, unless the parent cannot write, to district supervisory or administrative staff or to one of the student's teachers that the student is in need of special education; or
- the parent requested an evaluation of the student; or
- one of the student's teachers, or other district staff expressed specific concerns about a pattern of behavior by the student directly to the director of special education or to other supervisory personnel (20 USC § 1415(k)(5)(B); 34 CFR § 300.534(b); 8 NYCRR § 201.5(b); *Appeal of a Student Suspected of Having a Disability*, 55 Ed Dep't Rep, Dec. No. 16,912 (2016)).

If there was no basis for knowledge, school officials can subject the student to the same disciplinary measures applicable to nondisabled students who engaged in comparable behaviors. However, if the student's parents request an evaluation during the disciplinary removal, the district must conduct an expedited evaluation (34 CFR § 300.534(d)(1), (2)(i); 8 NYCRR § 201.5(e)). Until completion of the expedited evaluation, the student remains in the educational placement determined by the school district, which can include suspension (20 USC § 1415(k)(5)(D); 34 CFR § 300.534(d)(2)(ii); 8 NYCRR § 201.6(c)).

Even if a district can be deemed to have had knowledge that a student is a student with a disability, the student will not be presumed to have a disability for discipline purposes if the student's parent did not allow the student to be evaluated or refused services, or the committees on special education previously determined the student is not a student with a disability (20 USC § 1415(k)(5)(C); 34 CFR § 300.534(c); 8 NYCRR § 201.5(c); see also **54:95** for information on committees on special education).

Due process safeguards apply, as well, to students who have been declassified but later exhibit behavioral problems (*Appeal of a Student Presumed to Have a Disability (South Country CSD)*, 35 Ed Dept Rep 492 (1996)).

54:94. Are students with disabilities subject to a school district's attendance policy?

Yes. However, a school district may not apply its attendance policy to a student with disabilities in order to deny the student course credit where the absences are related to the student's disability or to a medical condition which would constitute a handicap under section 504 of the Rehabilitation Act (*Appeal of a Child with a Handicapping Condition*, 32 Ed Dept Rep 56 (1992)).

Preschool Students with Disabilities

54:95. What are the school districts' responsibilities in regard to preschool special education?

School boards must adopt a written policy that establishes administrative practices and procedures to ensure that each preschool child with a disability can participate in preschool programs approved by the commissioner of education (8 NYCRR § 200.2(b)(2)). School districts, for instance, must identify, evaluate, refer, place and review the placement of preschool children (ages three and four) with disabilities, including children enrolled in Head Start programs (20 USC § 1400 *et seq.*; Educ. Law § 4410; 8 NYCRR §§ 200.2(a)(1), 200.16).

Every school board also must appoint and train qualified personnel to a committee on preschool special education (CPSE) (see **54:97**), which makes recommendations on the identification, evaluation, and appropriate services for these children (20 USC § 1413(a)(3); Educ. Law § 4410(3); 8 NYCRR §§ 200.2(b)(3), 200.3(a)(2), 200.16(b)), and ensure the allocation of appropriate space within the district for special education programs that meet the needs of preschool students with disabilities (8 NYCRR § 200.2(c)(2)(v)).

54:96. What types of services and programs must school districts provide to preschool children with disabilities?

Preschool children with disabilities are entitled, for example, to special education itinerant services, special classes in a half or full-day preschool program, and related services available to school-age children with disabilities (Educ. Law § 4410(1)(j), (k); 8 NYCRR §§ 200.1(nn), 200.16(e)(3), (i)).

Prior to recommending any program, the committee on preschool special education should consider the appropriateness of providing related services or special education itinerant services only, related services in coordination with special education itinerant services, and a half-day or full-day program.

Special education services must be provided consistent with least restrictive environment requirements (Educ. Law § 4410(5)(b)(i); 8 NYCRR § 200.16(e)(3), (i); see also **54:7**).

54:97. What is the difference between a committee on special education (CSE) and a committee on preschool special education (CPSE)?

Generally, the CSE addresses the needs of school-age children with disabilities (see **54:25-32**), while the CPSE focuses on the needs of preschool children with disabilities. However, generally speaking, parental rights and district responsibilities governing the CSE also apply to the CPSE.

A CSE and a CPSE also are made up of different members. The CPSE must include the following members:

- The parent of the preschool child with a disability.
- A regular education teacher (if the child is, or may be, participating in the regular education environment).
- A special education teacher, or where appropriate, a special education provider of such child.
- A representative of the school district who
  (1) is qualified to provide or supervise special education;
  (2) is knowledgeable about the general curriculum; and
  (3) is knowledgeable about the availability of preschool special education programs and services and other resources of the district and the municipality. This individual serves as the chairperson of the committee.
- A parent of a child with disabilities who resides in the district or a neighboring district and whose child is enrolled in a preschool or elementary-level education program if specifically requested in writing by the parent of the student or by a member of the committee at least 72 hours prior to the meeting. The district must provide written notice to the parent of their right to have an additional parent attend any meeting along with a statement from the state education department explaining the role of having an additional parent member attend.
- An individual who can interpret the instructional implications of evaluation results. (This individual may also be one of the above district team members or the school psychologist.)
- At the discretion of the parent or the district, other individuals who have knowledge or special expertise regarding the child, including related services personnel.
- For a child in transition from early intervention programs and services (infant and toddler programs), the appropriate professional designated by the agency that has been charged with the responsibility for the preschool child.

An appropriately certified or licensed professional from the municipality where the child resides should also attend; however, attendance of the appointee of the municipality is not required for a quorum of the CPSE (Educ. Law § 4410(3)(a); 8 NYCRR § 200.3(a)(2); see **54:27-28**, **54:30**, **54:32** for the membership of the CSE). Specific responsibilities for each CSE and CPSE are set forth in the Education Law sections 4402 and 4410; and part 200 of the commissioner's regulations.

Private School Students with Disabilities

54:98. Must school districts provide special education and related services to private school students with disabilities?

Yes. Under both the Individuals with Disabilities Education Act and the dual-enrollment provisions of the state Education Law, districts must provide special education and related services to parentally placed private school students with disabilities (20 USC § 1412(a)(10)(A)(i); 34 CFR §§ 300.129–144; Educ. Law § 3602-c(2)).

A school district, however, is not responsible for the student's tuition at the private school unless the parents have placed the student at the private school because they disagree with the program or placement recommended by the district, and they meet certain other conditions (see **54:70-72**).

Services provided to private school students with disabilities, including materials and equipment, must be secular, neutral, and nonideological (20 USC § 1412(a)(10)(A)(vi)(II); 34 CFR § 300.138(c)(2)).

54:99. What school district is responsible for providing special education and related services to parentally placed private school students with disabilities?

The school district where a private school is located (*district of location*) is responsible for complying with the legal requirements related to the equitable provision of services to parentally placed private school students with disabilities, including students who are not New York State residents. Those legal requirements involve:

- Child find activities;
- Timely and meaningful consultation with representatives of private schools located in their district and representatives of parentally placed students with disabilities attending private school within their district;
- The evaluation and possible identification of private school students as a student with a disability;
- The development of an individualized education services program, or service program;
- The provision of services (20 USC § 1412(a)(10)(A); 34 CFR §§ 300.130–144; Educ. Law § 3602-c(2)(a), (2-a)); and
- Obtaining parental consent, or consent from a student 18 years of age or older, for the exchange of personally identifiable information about the student between school officials of the student's district of residence and the district of location (Educ. Law § 3602-c(2-a); 8 NYCRR § 200.2(a)(7)(i)).

Some of the topics school districts of location must consult about with private school representatives include the child find process, the consultation process and how it will work throughout the school year, and how, where, and by whom services will be provided (20 USC § 1412(a)(10)(A)(iii); 34 CFR § 300.134). School districts must obtain a written and signed affirmation from representatives of participating private schools that the required consultation has occurred. If they are unable to, they must forward documentation of the consultation process to the NYS Education Department (20 USC § 1412(a)(10)(A)(iv); 34 CFR § 300.135).

For additional information on school district responsibilities towards parentally-placed private school students with disabilities, see NYS Education Department, *Guidance on Parentally-Placed Nonpublic Elementary and Secondary School Students* (Sept. 2007), at: http://www.p12.nysed.gov/specialed/publications/policy/nonpublic907.htm.

54:100. What is the process for requesting special education services for a parentally placed private school student?

Parents of New York resident students who voluntarily place their child in a private school must submit a written request for services on or before June 1 of the preceding school year for when the request is made. However, parents of students who are first identified as a student with a disability or move into a district after the June 1 deadline have 30 days after such an occurrence to submit their request. But in either case April 1 is the last date by which a parent may request services for the current year. Furthermore, for students who are first identified or establish residence after March 1, requests for services in the current year submitted after April 1 are deemed a request for services commencing in the following school year (Educ. Law § 3602-c(2); 8 NYCRR § 177.1).

Services must be provided by the district where the private school is located (Educ. Law § 3602-c(2); see **54:99**). A school district may not insist on providing those services only at one of its own schools (*Application of a Child with a Disability*, SRO dec. no. 02-035 (2003); see **54:101**).

54:101. Who is responsible for reviewing a request for special education services for a parentally placed private school student?

A request for special education services for a parentally placed private school student is reviewed by the committee of special education (CSE) of the school district where the private school is located (Educ. Law § 3602-c(2)(b), (2-b); see also *Application of a Student with a Disability*, SRO dec. no. 09-133 (2009)).

If the private school student is a New York State resident, and deemed eligible for services, then the CSE will develop an *individualized education services program* (IESP) based on the student's individual needs in the same manner and with the same contents as an individualized education program (see **54:6**). Services will be made available to the student on an equitable basis, as compared to special education programs and services provided to other students with disabilities attending public or private schools within the district (Educ. Law § 3602-c(2)(b)).

If the student is not a New York State resident, the CSE will develop for the student a *services plan* in accordance with federal law and regulations. Services will be provided to the student to the extent required by federal law and regulations (Educ. Law § 3602-c(2-b)). This entails the expenditure of a proportionate amount of federal funds made available under the Individuals with Disabilities Education Act, and timely and meaningful consultation with private school representatives and representatives of parentally placed private school students with disabilities regarding the provision of services to such students (20 USC § 1412(a)(10)(A); 34 CFR §§ 300.130–300.144).

54:102. May school districts provide on-site special education and related services to students with disabilities who attend private schools, including parochial schools?

Yes. The federal Individuals with Disabilities Education Act allows school districts to provide special education services to students with disabilities on the premises of private schools, including parochial schools, to the extent consistent with law (20 USC § 1412(a)(10)(A)(i)(III); 34 CFR § 300.139(a)). Furthermore, the U. S. Supreme Court has ruled that the federal constitution does not prevent a school district from providing services to students on-site at the premises of their parochial school (*Agostini v. Felton*, 521 U.S. 203 (1997)).

New York's dual-enrollment law provides for the participation of nonpublic school students with disabilities in special education programs on an equitable basis (Educ. Law § 3602-c(2)(b)(1)). However, it does not mandate that school districts provide services at a nonpublic school for each student (*Bd. of Educ. of Bayshore UFSD v. Thomas K.*, 14 N.Y.3d 289 (2010)). Nonetheless, a district would have to provide on-site special education related services at a nonpublic school to students whose educational needs require on-site delivery of such services, including the provision of a one-to-one aide (*Id.*). For information on the roles and responsibilities of one-to-one aides and factors to consider when deciding to assign one, see NYS Education Department, *Guidelines for Determining a Student with a Disability's Need for a One-to-One Aide* (updated Jan. 2014), at: http://www.p12.nysed.gov/specialed/publications/1-1aide-jan2012.htm.

Prior to the *Bayshore* decision, New York's State Review Officer had indicated that services which must be provided in a classroom setting such as a consultant teacher and full-time aide services had to be provided on-site in the student's private school. Services such as counseling and occupational therapy, which do not require a classroom setting, do not have to be provided on-site (*Application of a Child with a Disability*, SRO dec. no. 02-024 (2003)). However, according to the New York Court of Appeals in *Bayshore*, "the pertinent question is what the educational needs of [a particular] student require" (*Bd. of Educ. of Bayshore UFSD v. Thomas K.*).

54:103. Is there a mechanism for districts where private schools are located to recover the costs associated with providing services to students with disabilities attending such schools?

Yes. School districts where private schools are located that provide services to non-resident students who are New York State residents may recover costs of services, evaluation and committee on special education administration directly from a student's school district of residence, if parental consent is obtained for the release of personally identifiable information about the student. Otherwise, they may submit a claim to the commissioner of education and, upon certification of the claim by the commissioner, the state comptroller will deduct the amount of the claim from any state funds due to the student's school district of residence (Educ. Law § 3602-c(7)(b); NYS Education Department, *Guidance on Reimbursement Claims for the Cost of Providing Special Education Services to Parentally Placed Nonresident Students Pursuant to Education Law Section 3602-c* (June 2008), at: http://www.p12.nysed.gov/specialed/publications/policy/reimbursement608.htm).

The amount charged by a district of location may not exceed the actual cost to that district after deducting any costs paid with federal or state funds (Educ. Law § 3602-c(7)(c); *Guidance on Reimbursement Claims for the Cost of Providing Special Education Services to Parentally Placed Nonresident Students Pursuant to Education Law Section 3602-c*). Disputes over the amount of tuition or costs charged by a district of location must be resolved through the resolution process established in commissioner's regulations (Educ. Law § 3602-c(7)(c); 8 NYCRR § 177.2).

For further information on this topic, see NYS Education Department, *Addition of Section 177.2 of the Regulations of the Commissioner of Education Relating to Disputes of Reimbursement Claims for Special Education Students Provided to Nonresident Parentally-Placed Nonpublic School Students with Disabilities* (Dec. 2008), at: http://www.p12.nysed.gov/specialed/publications/policy/section1772-nonpublic.htm.

54:104. Are due process hearings available to parentally placed private school students with disabilities?

Yes. Parents of private school students, including out-of-state residents, may present a due process complaint and request a due process hearing regarding the alleged failure of a school district of location (see **54:99**) to comply with its child find responsibilities, including evaluation and eligibility determination requirements (Educ. Law § 3602-c(2)(c), (2-b)).

54:105. Are students with disabilities who are home-instructed by their parents eligible to receive special education and related services?

Yes. Home-schooled students with disabilities are deemed to be nonpublic school students solely for the purpose of receiving special education and its computation of state aid for such education. To be eligible for such services, the student must be entitled to attend public school tuition free, and have an individualized home instruction plan that has been determined to be in compliance with commissioner regulations by the superintendent of schools of the district in which the home school is located (§ 3602-c(2-c); see also NYS Education Department, *New Requirements for the Provision of Special Education Services to Home-Instructed ("Home-Schooled") Students* (July 2008), at: http://www.p12.nysed.gov/specialed/publications/policy/homeinstructed708.htm).

Students

55. Instruction and Curricula

Instructional Time Requirements

55:1. Is there an official school year for instruction?

No. The Education Law defines the school year as the period commencing on the first day of July in each year and ending on June 30 of the next year (§ 2(15)). However, court decisions recognize that a normal instructional year extends from September through June (see *Schneps v. Nyquist*, 58 A.D.2d 151 (3d Dep't 1997), *appeal denied*, 42 N.Y.2d 808 (1977); see also *Appeal of Lease*, 39 Ed Dept Rep 215 (1999)). But it is the July 1 through June 30 time period that applies regarding compulsory school attendance rules requiring that children remain in school until the last day of the school year in which they reach the age of 16 (*In the Matter of Kiesha BB*, 30 A.D.3d 704 (3d Dep't 2006); see **48:1**).

55:2. Who determines the actual length of a school district's instructional school year?

Local school districts determine the number of days that their schools will be in session and when personnel must report for duty. The NYS Education Department does not determine the local school year.

Additionally, individual school boards may divide the school year into semesters and marking periods and, following negotiation with the appropriate bargaining units, expand the number of instructional days for their districts (*City Sch. Dist. v. Helsby*, 42 A.D.2d 262 (3d Dep't 1973); see also *Matter of North Colonie Teachers Ass'n*, 41 PERB ¶ 3028 (2008)).

55:3. Is there a minimum number of school days in a school year?

Yes. Schools must be in session 190 days each year for instructional purposes, inclusive of legal holidays that occur during the school term and exclusive of Saturdays (§ 3204(4)(a); see also *Appeal of Block*, 21 Ed Dept Rep 704 (1982)).

The law also requires 180 days of instruction for state aid purposes (§ 3604(7)). The financial apportionment from the state will be reduced by 1/180th for each day less than 180 days the school actually is in session. However, the commissioner of education may disregard this reduction for up to five days for certain reasons, such as adverse weather or a breakdown of school facilities, where it is demonstrated that the district cannot make up such lost days of instruction during the school year (§ 3604(7)).

Pursuant to the Education Law and commissioner's regulations, districts may conduct up to four superintendent's conference days throughout a school year (§ 3604(8); 8 NYCRR § 175.5(f)). Districts may count any such conference days conducted in the last two weeks of August (subject to collective bargaining), as part of the required 180 days of instruction (§ 3604(8)).

55:4. Is there a minimum number of hours in a school day for public schools in New York State?

Yes. Section 175.5 of the commissioner's regulations lists the minimum daily session lengths for students. To qualify for apportionment of state aid, schools must be in session as follows:

- The daily sessions for students in half-day kindergarten must be a minimum of two-and-one-half hours (8 NYCRR § 175.5(a)(1)).

- The daily sessions for students in full-day kindergarten and grades 1–6 must be a minimum of five hours, exclusive of the time allowed for lunch (8 NYCRR § 175.5(a)(2)).
- The daily sessions for students in grades 7–12 must be a minimum of five-and-one-half hours, exclusive of the time allowed for lunch (8 NYCRR § 175.5(a)(3)).

The minimum number of hours requirements do not apply when there is a school day with a session of less time due to one of the circumstances specified in commissioner's regulations such as the scheduling of Regents Examinations or extraordinary adverse weather conditions (8 NYCRR § 175.5(b)).

There is no maximum number of hours in a school day and there is no requirement in law concerning the time of day classes must be held.

55:5. Are there minimum school-day hours for schools that operate on double or overlapping (split) sessions?

To qualify for apportionment of state aid, schools that operate on double or overlapping (split) sessions, with prior written approval by the commissioner of education, must meet the following minimum-hours requirements:

- The daily sessions for students in half-day kindergarten must be a minimum of two hours.
- The daily sessions for students in full-day kindergarten and grades 1–6 must be a minimum of four hours, exclusive of the time allowed for lunch.
- The daily sessions for students in grades 7–12 must be a minimum of four-and-one-half hours, exclusive of the time allowed for lunch (8 NYCRR § 175.5(c)).

55:6. May schools be in session during a legal holiday?

In general, no school may be in session on a Saturday or a legal holiday, except Election Day and Washington's and Lincoln's birthdays. However, driver education classes may be held on Saturdays (§ 3604(8)). Also, school authorities in a district having fewer than 600 students may provide classes for the disadvantaged on any day of the week, including Saturday and Sunday. However, they may not require students or teachers to attend such classes if they observe any such day as a Sabbath or holy day (§ 3604(8-b)).

A graduation ceremony is not considered a session. Therefore, it does not have to be held during a regular school day (*Appeal of Block*, 21 Ed Dept Rep 704 (1982)).

55:7. What are the legal holidays in New York State?

Section 24 of the General Construction Law lists the following public holidays in New York:

- New Year's Day (January 1)
- Dr. Martin Luther King, Jr. Day (third Monday in January)
- Lincoln's Birthday (February 12)
- Washington's Birthday (third Monday in February)
- Memorial Day (last Monday in May)
- Flag Day (second Sunday in June)
- Independence Day (July 4)
- Labor Day (first Monday in September)
- Columbus Day (second Monday in October)
- Veterans Day (November 11)
- Thanksgiving Day (fourth Thursday in November)
- Christmas Day (December 25)

In addition, each general election day and any day appointed by the president of the United States or by the governor of New York State "as a day of general thanksgiving, general fasting and prayer, or for other general religious observances" may be declared public holidays (Gen. Constr. Law § 24; see *Bloom v. N.Y. City Transit Auth.*, 19 A.D.2d 521 (1st Dep't 1963)).

Students in the New York City boroughs of Brooklyn and Queens also enjoy Anniversary Day, generally the first Thursday in June, as a school holiday (§ 2586).

School districts may close one or all of their schools on days of religious or cultural observance if they determine that a considerable proportion of the student population is unlikely to attend school on that day, and therefore result in a waste of educational resources (§ 3210(1)(b)).

Instructional Program Requirements Prekindergarten – Grade 8

55:8. Are school districts required to offer a prekindergarten program?

No. It is up to each local school board to decide whether or not to offer a prekindergarten program. A school board may choose to establish such a program pursuant to the universal prekindergarten legislation (§ 3602-e). Children would be eligible to participate in a universal prekindergarten program if they reside within the district and will be four years of age on or before December 1 of the year in which they are enrolled, or will otherwise be first eligible to enter public school kindergarten the following year (*Id.*; 8 NYCRR Subpart 151-1; see **55:9**).

A school district may offer a "summer only" universal prekindergarten program during the months of July and August, if the commissioner of education finds the district is unable to operate the program during the regular school session because of a lack of available space in both district buildings and eligible agencies (§ 3602-e(12)(m); 8 NYCRR § 151-1.4(b); see **48:9** for information on student age eligibility requirements for summer only prekindergarten programs).

55:9. Are school districts required to offer a kindergarten program?

No. It is within the discretion of a school board to offer a kindergarten program to resident students between the ages of four and six. In addition, a school board may fix a higher minimum age for admission to kindergarten (§ 1712(1)), by requiring that children be five years of age by December 1st of the school year in which they begin kindergarten (*Appeal of S.H.*, 40 Ed Dept Rep 527 (2001); *Appeal of Benjamin*, 26 Ed Dept Rep 533 (1987); see also *Appeal of S.A.P.*, 45 Ed Dept Rep 527 (2006)). The Syracuse, Utica, Rochester and Buffalo city school districts, are authorized to require minors who are five by December 1 to attend kindergarten unless parents choose not to enroll such child until the following September (§ 3205(2)(c)).

Children over the age of five may attend school regardless of whether or not the district maintains a kindergarten program, and are entitled to attend first grade (§ 3202(1); *Appeal of Carney*, 15 Ed Dept Rep 325 (1976); *Formal Opn. of Counsel No. 75*, 1 Ed Dept Rep 775 (1952); see also **48:5**).

55:10. What requirements must school districts comply with if they offer a prekindergarten and/or kindergarten program?

Schools operating prekindergarten and kindergarten programs must implement a curricula, aligned with the State learning standards, that ensures continuity with instruction in the early elementary grades and is integrated with the instructional program in grades 1–12 (8 NYCRR § 100.3(a)(1)).

In addition, schools operating a prekindergarten and/or kindergarten program must establish and provide an early literacy and emergent reading program based on effective, evidence-based instructional practices that include at least those essential components set forth in the commissioner's regulations (8 NYCRR § 100.3(a)(2)).

The education program is to be based on the ages, interests, strengths, and needs of the children and must include, but is not limited to, indoor and outdoor play activities, instruction in English language arts, mathematics, science, social studies, and the arts, including dance, music, theatre and visual arts (8 NYCRR § 100.3(a)(3)).

School districts must also develop procedures that invite the active participation of each child's parents or guardians in these programs including support in the transition from such programs to the early elementary grades (8 NYCRR § 100.3(a)(4)).

Additional requirements would apply to school districts operating a full-day prekindergarten program under a state competitive grant awarded pursuant to L. 2016, c. 54 pt. A § 23.

55:11. What are the program requirements for grades 1–6?

School districts must provide all students in grades 1–6 with instruction in:

- Mathematics, including arithmetic, science, and technology.
- English/language arts, including but not limited to reading, writing, and literary response and expression.
- Social studies, including geography and United States history.
- Languages other than English.
- The arts, including visual arts, music, dance, and theatre.
- Career development and occupational studies.
- Health education, physical education, and family and consumer sciences.

If student need is established, bilingual education and/or English as a second language instruction must also be provided (8 NYCRR §§ 100.3(b)(1), 100.4(b)(1)).

55:12. What are the program requirements for grades 7 and 8?

By the end of the eighth grade, students must complete the following:

- Two units of study each in English language arts, social studies, science, and mathematics.
- One unit of study in technology education.
- Three-quarters of a unit in home and career skills.
- Physical education (not less than three times per week in one semester and two times per week in the other semester).
- One-half unit study each in health education, the visual arts, and music.
- The equivalent of one period a week in library and information skills.
- Instruction in career development and occupational studies (8 NYCRR § 100.4(c)(1); see **55:46** for foreign language requirements).

A *unit of study* consists of at least 180 minutes of instruction per week throughout the school year or its equivalent (8 NYCRR § 100.1(a)).

Students who have been determined to need academic intervention services may have the unit of study requirements for one or more subjects reduced by the principal, if certain conditions set out in commissioner's regulations are met (8 NYCRR § 100.4(c)(5); see **55:29-35** for a more detailed discussion of academic intervention services).

55:13. Are school districts required to follow a particular model to operate their middle-level education program?

Yes. School districts must conduct their middle-level education program in accordance with one of three models set forth in commissioner's regulations referred to as Models A, B, and C (8 NYCRR § 100.4(h)(1)(ii-iv), (2)).

Middle-level education program refers to instruction in grades 5–8 or any lesser combination of such grades, as determined by a school district. However, any such combination must include instruction in grade 7 (8 NYCRR § 100.4(h)(1)(i)).

Model A refers to a middle-level education program that meets the instructional requirements applicable to middle-level grades and all other applicable sections of commissioner's regulations (8 NYCRR § 100.4(h)(1)(ii)).

Model B refers to a middle-level education program approved by the commissioner of education that strengthens the attainment of the State intermediate learning standards measured by required State assessments, provides effective academic intervention services, and ensures all students receive instruction in those standard areas where there are no required State assessments (8 NYCRR § 100.4(h)(1)(iii)).

Model C refers to a middle-level education program approved by the commissioner that either restructures the delivery of instruction designed to facilitate the attainment of the State intermediate learning standards; or enhances instruction related to one or more of the State intermediate standards for which there are no required State assessments (8 NYCRR § 100.4(h)(1)(iv)). Within Model C there may be either a restructuring of the full educational program (*Model C#1*) or specific program refinements (*Model C#2*) (*Id.*).

All districts are eligible to operate their middle-level education program under Model A (8 NYCRR § 100.4(h)(2)(i)(a)). Model B is available only to districts proposing programs for schools that are underperforming, or for newly formed or existing schools to be redesigned or restructured for school accountability purposes (8 NYCRR § 100.4(h)(2)(ii)(a)). Model C is available to school districts proposing a program for a newly formed school or an existing school other than as part of a school accountability redesign or restructuring (8 NYCRR § 100.4(h)(2)(iii)(a)).

Districts wishing to operate under Models B or C must get prior approval from the commissioner (8 NYCRR § 100.4(h)(2)(ii)(b)(1), (ii)(e), (iii)(b)(1), (iii)(e)). Districts that do not get approval to operate under Models B or C must operate under Model A (8 NYCRR § 100.4(h)(2)(i)(b)).

Irrespective of the model used, all middle-level education programs must be aligned with the Regents Policy Statement on Middle-Level Education and the NYS Education Department's Essential Elements of Standards-Focused Middle Level Schools and Programs (8 NYCRR § 100.4(h)(2)(i)(d)(3), (ii)(d)(3), (iii)(d)(3)).

55:14. Must school districts offer an accelerated program that allows grade 8 students to take, and earn credit in, high school-level courses?

Yes. Eighth-grade students must be given the opportunity to take high school courses in mathematics and in at least one of the following subjects: English, social studies, languages other than English, art, music, career and technical education, or science (8 NYCRR § 100.4(d)(1)). But first, they must demonstrate to the superintendent of schools, or his or her designee, their readiness in each subject in which they ask to begin high school courses in the eighth grade leading to a diploma (8 NYCRR § 100.4(d)(3)(i)).

Eighth-grade students may be awarded credit for such a course only if they meet one of the following conditions:

- Attend the class in a high school with high school students and pass the course on the same basis as the high school students, and credit is awarded by the high school.

- Pass the course and the associated State proficiency examination or Regents examination, credit for which must be accepted as transfer credit by all registered New York State high schools.
- If no appropriate State assessment is available, pass a course that has been approved for high school credit by the district superintendent or his or her designee, or the district where the middle, junior, or intermediate school, and high school is located (8 NYCRR § 100.4(d)(2)).

To receive high school credit for the course, the student must pass the applicable Regents or State proficiency examination, or if no such examination is available for the course, the student must pass a locally developed examination, which establishes student performance at a high school level, as determined by the principal (8 NYCRR § 100.4(d)(3)(ii)).

Instructional Program/Diploma Requirements Grades 9 – 12

55:15. What are the program requirements in grades 9–12 that students must complete to receive a high school diploma?

The program requirements for a high school diploma vary depending on whether a student is earning a Regents diploma or a Regents diploma with advanced designation (see **55:18-19**).

In addition to fulfilling program requirements, students must pass the various Regents examinations required for graduation as set forth in commissioner's regulations (8 NYCRR § 100.5(a)(5), (b)(5); see **56:11-13**).

55:16. Are Regent-level diplomas the only type of high school diploma available to students in New York State?

Yes, as a general rule (see 8 NYCRR § 100.5(b)(7)).

However, subject to the conditions set out in commissioner's regulations, local high school diplomas are available to:

- Students with disabilities (8 NYCRR § 100.5(b)(7)(vi)(b), (c), (viii), (d)(12); see also **56:12**).
- Students who fail to attain a passing score on two of the Regents examinations required for graduation, appeal those scores and their appeal is accepted (8 NYCRR § 100.5(d)(7)(v)(b)-(d); see also **56:14**).

These students must still take the Regents examinations required for graduation (see **56:12, 56:14**).

In addition, students may qualify for a *career development and occupational studies commencement* (CDOS) credential, or a skills and achievement commencement credential. The CDOS recognizes a student's work readiness skills and may be awarded either as a supplement to a high school diploma (Regents or local), or as a sole exiting credential for students unable to earn a high school diploma (8 NYCRR § 100.6(b)). The *skills and achievement commencement credential* is available to students with severe disabilities who are eligible to take the New York State alternate assessment. This credential replaces the previous individualized education program diploma and is accompanied by documentation of the student's skills and strengths and levels of independence in academic, career development and foundation skills needed for post-school living (8 NYCRR § 100.6(a)). Only students who are not eligible for the skills and achievement credential can obtain a CDOS credential (8 NYCRR § 100.6(b)).

School districts should be aware that veterans of World War II, Korea and Vietnam who do not have a high school diploma may be eligible for a local diploma upon application to the district in which they reside, if they meet the requirements set forth in commissioner's regulations (§ 100.5(b)(7)(xi)).

55:17. Does New York State offer a high school equivalency diploma?

Yes. Moreover, effective January 2, 2014, a new Test Assessing Secondary Completion (TASC) replaced the prior General Educational Development (GED) test (NYS Education Department, *The New High School Equivalency (HSE) Test for New York State Brochure* at: http://www.acces.nysed.gov/common/acces/files/hse/tascbrochure.pdf).

The TASC has five sections: Language Arts – Reading, Language Arts – Writing, Mathematics, Science and Social Studies, with the English language arts and mathematics components based on the national common core learning standards. It is available to any state resident, 19 years of age or older, who does not have a high school diploma (8 NYCRR § 100.7(a)(1)(i); see also **48:11**). However, individuals under age 19 may also take the TASC subject to the conditions set out in commissioner's regulations (8 NYCRR § 100.7(a)(1)).

Effective September 1, 2016, students who successfully complete the National External Diploma Program may also receive an equivalency diploma (8 NYCRR § 100.7(a)(2)(i)(d)), provided they are 18 years of age or older (8 NYCRR § 100.7(a)(1)(i)).

For additional information visit the NYS Education Department's High School Equivalency Office at: http://www.acces.nysed.gov/ged.

55:18. What are the program requirements for a Regents diploma?

To obtain a Regents diploma, students must earn 22 units of credit as follows:

- Four units of credit in English.
- Four units of social studies (including one unit of American history, one half unit of participation in government, and one-half unit of economics or their equivalent).
- Three units of science (at least one unit must be life sciences, at least one in physical sciences, and the third may be in either life or physical sciences).
- Three units of mathematics.
- One unit of visual arts and/or music, dance, or theatre.
- One-half unit of health education (8 NYCRR § 100.5(a)(3)).
- Two units of physical education, which count toward the required total units of credits (8 NYCRR § 100.5(a)(4)).

In addition, all students must attain State learning standards in parenting skills through either the health or family and consumer sciences programs or a separate course (8 NYCRR § 100.5(a)(3)(vi); see **55:39**). They also must earn one unit of commencement-level credit in a language other than English (LOTE), which can be earned by passing a state or locally developed second language proficiency examination and additional units to total 22 units of credit (8 NYCRR §§ 100.2(d), 100.5(b)(7)(iv)(g), (iv)(i); see also **55:46**). To earn the state seal of biliteracy on their diplomas, students must attain a high level of proficiency in one or more languages in addition to English (§ 815; 8 NYCRR § 100.5(h)).

Students who satisfy the credit requirements for a Regents diploma may also earn a career development and occupational studies credential in accordance with commissioner's regulations (8 NYCRR § 100.5(d)(11); see also 8 NYCRR § 100.6(b); NYS Education Department, Office of Instructional Support, *Career Development Occupational Studies Graduation Pathway Option* (updated June 2016), at: http://www.p12.nysed.gov/ciai/multiple-pathways/docs/cdos-field-memo-june-2016.pdf.

55:19. How are the program requirements for a Regents diploma with advanced designation different?

To obtain a Regents diploma with an advanced designation students must successfully complete not only the program requirements for a Regents diploma (see **55:18**), but also:

- Two additional foreign language units for a total of three (8 NYCRR § 100.5(b)(7)(v)(c));

- One additional Regents examination in science for a total of two, with at least one in life science and at least one in physical science (8 NYCRR § 100.5(b)(7)(v)(b)); and
- Additional Regents math examinations as determined by the commissioner of education, except that students must pass two or three commencement level examinations through one of the following combinations:

Two exam combinations	Three exam combinations
Mathematics A and B	**Mathematics A, Geometry, and either Mathematics B, Algebra2/Trigonometry, or Algebra II (common core)**
Mathematics A and Algebra2/Trigonometry	**Integrated Algebra, Geometry and either Mathematics B, Algebra2/Trigonometry, or Algebra II (common core)**
Mathematics B and Integrated Algebra	**Algebra1, Geometry and either Mathematics B, Algebra2 /Trigonometry, or Algebra II (common core)**

(8 NYCRR § 100.5(b)(7)(v)(a)).

Students with a disability that adversely affects their ability to learn a language may be excused from the additional foreign language requirement if their individualized education program indicates they are not appropriate for the student (8 NYCRR § 100.5(b)(7)(v)(c); see also 8 NYCRR § 100.5(b)(7)(iv)(g); see also **55:46**).

Students who complete a five unit sequence in career and technical education or the arts (visual arts, dance and theater) also are exempt from the additional foreign language requirement (8 NYCRR § 100.5(b)(7)(v)(c)).

55:20. May school districts establish program requirements for a high school diploma other than those required by the State?

It depends. School districts may not supplant the units of credit required for graduation (see **55:18-19**). However, they may impose reasonable diploma requirements that exceed the state minimum requirements (*Appeal of O'Neill*, 29 Ed Dept Rep 297 (1990); *Matter of Yanson*, 22 Ed Dept Rep 319 (1982)).

For example, school districts may require that students complete a prescribed number of hours of school/community service to earn a high school diploma as part of a course of study above and beyond the minimum state requirements (*Immediato v. Rye Neck CSD*, 73 F.3d 454 (2d Cir.), *cert. denied*, 519 U.S. 813 (1996); *Appeal of O'Neill*). But the extent, nature, and conditions of service, and the more exploitive purpose of such a program might warrant a finding of involuntary servitude in violation of the 13th Amendment of the U.S. Constitution. That might be the case if students are required to wash their teachers' cars, paint their houses or weed their gardens, for instance (*Immediato v. Rye Neck CSD*).

55:21. What program requirements apply to students who take more than four years to graduate high school?

Students who take more than four years to earn a high school diploma are subject to the same requirements that apply to the year they first entered grade 9 (8 NYCRR § 100.5(a)).

55:22. What program requirements apply to students who take less than four years to graduate?

Students who complete the diploma requirements in less than four years are subject to the diploma requirements applicable to students who entered grade 9 four years prior to the school year in which the accelerated diploma will be awarded. However, accelerated diploma students who graduate at the end of the fall semester are subject to the diploma requirements in effect for the preceding school year (8 NYCRR § 100.5(a), (e)). In each case, however, students who complete their diploma requirements in less than four years and are otherwise eligible to receive a diploma are not required to continue enrollment in high school for the sole purpose of completing the physical education requirements (8 NYCRR § 100.5(a)(4); see **55:45**).

The diploma may be awarded only at the end of the semester in which all requirements are completed, and not before in anticipation that requirements will be met (8 NYCRR § 100.5(e)).

55:23. May students earn units of credit toward graduation in a particular subject just by passing the applicable Regents exam without taking the required course for that subject?

It depends. Generally, a unit of credit is earned by mastery of the learning outcomes for a given subject after completing a unit of study that consists of at least 180 minutes of instruction per week throughout a school year (8 NYCRR § 100.1(b)(1)). Passing a Regents exam in any given subject will not be construed as having earned a unit of credit in that subject unless the student also passes the course as offered in a registered high school (8 NYCRR § 100.5(a)(5)(v)).

However, a student may earn up to six and one half units of credit toward a Regents or local diploma without taking a course if the student scores at least 85 or its equivalent on a Regents exam or state-approved examination, and successfully completes either an oral exam or a special project that shows proficiency in such knowledge, skills, and abilities normally developed in the course but not measured by the relevant Regents exam or state-approved test, as determined by the principal (8 NYCRR § 100.5(a)(5)(v), (d)(1)(ii), (iii); see also 8 NYCRR § 100.1(b)(2)). A student is eligible to earn credit by examination only if the superintendent of schools or the chief administrative officer of a registered nonpublic school determines that, based on the student's past academic performance, the student will benefit academically from this alternative (8 NYCRR § 100.5(d)(1)(i)). In addition, the student must attend school, or receive substantially equivalent instruction elsewhere until age 16 as required by the compulsory education law (8 NYCRR § 100.5(d)(1)(iv)).

For more information on Regents examinations and other state assessments, see **56:1-17**.

55:24. May students who fail to demonstrate mastery in a particular subject earn "make-up" units of credit toward a high school diploma?

Yes. A student who fails to demonstrate mastery in a unit of study in a subject may make-up credit toward either a Regents or local diploma (8 NYCRR § 100.5(d)(8)). To receive credit, the student must successfully complete a make-up credit program and demonstrate mastery of the subject's learning outcomes, including passing the Regents exam or other assessment required for graduation (8 NYCRR § 100.5(d)(8)(i)). The make-up credit program must meet the requirements set forth in the commissioner's regulations, including being aligned with the State learning standards for the subject (8 NYCRR § 100.5(d)(8)(ii)). The program may include repeating an entire course, taking the course in summer school, receiving intensive instruction in the areas of deficiency in the course, or completing online study (8 NYCRR § 100.5(d)(8)(iv)).

Student participation in make-up credit programs must first be approved by a school-based panel consisting at least of the principal, a teacher in the subject area, and a guidance director or other administrator (8 NYCRR § 100.5(d)(8)(iii)).

State Learning Standards

55:25. Are there state-mandated learning standards?

Yes. The term *learning standards* refers to the level of "knowledge, skills, and understandings that individuals can and do habitually demonstrate over time as a consequence of instruction and experience" adopted by the Board of Regents and set forth in commissioner's regulations (8 NYCRR § 100.1(t)).

At the time this publication went to press, New York State was in the process of reviewing, and revising as necessary, previously adopted common core learning standards for English language arts and mathematics in response to recommendations issued in December 2015 by a gubernatorial Common Core Task Force (see NYS Education Department, *Revision and Implementation of the New ELA and Mathematics Standards* (Feb. 2016), at: http://www.regents.nysed.gov/common/regents/files/P-12%20-%20Revision%20and%20Implementation%20of%20the%20New%20ELA%20and%20Mathematics%20Standards_0.pdf).

New state learning standards for science are expected to be adopted in fall 2016 (NYS Education Department, Office of Curriculum, Assessment and Education Technology, *New NYS P-12 Science Learning Standards* at: http://www.p12.nysed.gov/ciai/mst/sci/nyssls.html).

The state learning standards for social studies are subject to future revision. Meanwhile, the NYS Education Department recommends that school districts infuse the current standards for social studies with the common core Literacy Standards for History/Social Studies (see NYS Education Department, *Common Core Learning Standards, Frequently Asked Questions* (Feb. 2012), at: http://www.p12.nysed.gov/ciai/common_core_standards/faq.html). In addition, the *New York State K-12 Social Studies Framework*, intended to help school districts develop their own social studies curriculum, incorporates the New York State learning standards, identifies social studies practices, key ideas, conceptual understandings and content specifications (NYS Education Department, *New York State K-12 Social Studies Framework* (updated Mar. 2016), at: https://www.engageny.org/resource/new-york-state-k-12-social-studies-framework).

Consistent with the federal Every Student Succeeds Act, the learning standards must apply to all public elementary and secondary school students (§ 1111 (b)(1)(B)(i), (ii); see **56:25**).

55:26. To what areas of the curriculum do the State learning standards apply?

The learning standards are organized into and apply to seven general curriculum areas. Those curriculum areas include:

- English/language arts (8 NYCRR § 100.1(t)(1)(i)),
- mathematics, science and technology (8 NYCRR § 100.1(t)(1)(ii)),
- social studies (8 NYCRR § 100.1(t)(1)(iii)),
- languages other than English (8 NYCRR § 100.1(t)(1)(iv)),
- the arts (8 NYCRR § 100.1(t)(1)(v)),
- health and physical education, and family and consumer sciences (8 NYCRR § 100.1(t)(1)(vi)), and
- career development and occupational studies (8 NYCRR § 100.1(t)(1)(vii)).

55:27. Are the learning standards organized according to grade level?

Yes. The learning standards in each of seven general curriculum areas (see **55:26**) are organized into four instructional levels. These include:

- the elementary or elementary-level State learning standards, which encompass the knowledge, skills, and understandings all students are expected to know and be able to do by the end of grade 4;

- the intermediate or intermediate-level learning standards applicable through the end of grade 8;
- the commencement or commencement-level standards for a high school diploma; and
- the alternate performance level for students with severe disabilities who have limited cognitive abilities combined with behavioral and/or physical limitations, and who require highly specialized education and services (8 NYCRR § 100.1(t)(2)).

55:28. Do the learning standards apply to students with disabilities?

Yes. Students with disabilities entering the ninth grade after the 2001–02 school year are held to the same learning standards as nondisabled students. Students with disabilities and nondisabled students alike must pass the required courses based on the state's commencement level standards and take the required Regents examinations (see **55:15-16, 55:18-22, 56:11-12**).

However, a student with a disability that adversely affects the ability to learn a language may be excused from the foreign language requirements if the student's individualized education program indicates that such instruction would not be appropriate to the student's special educational needs. The student must still meet the requirements for the total number of credits required for a high school diploma (8 NYCRR § 100.5(b)(2)(ii)(b), (7)(iv)(g)).

For more information on how New York's learning standards affect the instruction of students with disabilities, see NYS Education Department, *Curriculum Instruction Toward the Common Core Learning Standards Special Education Advisory* (June 2014), at: http://www.p12.nysed.gov/specialed/commoncore/Parent-CCLS-June2014.pdf and *The Role of the Committee on Special Education in Relation to the Common Core Learning Standards Special Education Field Advisory* (June 2014), at: http://www.p12.nysed.gov/specialed/commoncore/roleofCSE-614.htm with an accompanying attachment at: http://www.p12.nysed.gov/specialed/commoncore/instructionCCLS-parents-614.htm#att1.

Academic Intervention Services

55:29. Must school districts provide academic intervention services to help students meet the learning standards?

Yes. School districts must provide academic intervention services (AIS) (see **55:30**) designed to assist students who lack reading readiness (in grades kindergarten through three), who are at risk of not achieving the learning standards in English language arts, mathematics, social studies, and/or science, or who are at risk of not gaining the knowledge and skills needed to meet or exceed designated performance levels on state required assessments (8 NYCRR §§ 100.1(g), 100.2(ee)(1), (2), (3)).

Furthermore, each district must develop, and each school board must approve, a description of the AIS it will provide including, for example, the procedures used to determine the need for AIS (see **55:32**), whether services will be offered during or outside the regular school day or year, and the criteria for ending services. Each district must review and revise its AIS program description every two years based on student performance results (8 NYCRR § 100.2(ee)(4)(i), (ii)). Based on performance criteria developed by the commissioner of education, certain districts may be required to submit their description of their AIS program to the NYS Education Department for review and approval (8 NYCRR § 100.2(ee)(4)(iv)).

School districts may provide a response to intervention (RTI) program in lieu of providing AIS to eligible students in a manner consistent with the requirements for RTI programs set out in the commissioner's regulations. Districts exercising this option must make available the RTI program at the grade levels and subject areas for which students are identified as eligible for AIS. They also must provide AIS to students eligible for such services who are not enrolled in the RTI program. In addition, districts providing an RTI program in lieu of AIS must submit a signed statement of assurance to the NYS Education Department that the RTI program meets regulatory requirements (8 NYCRR § 100.2(ee)(7); see also 8 NYCRR § 100.2(ii)).

55:30. What are the components of an academic intervention services program?

Academic intervention services (AIS) consist of:

- instruction that supplements the general curriculum instruction and assists students in meeting the learning standards (see **55:25-28**), and/or
- student support services which may include guidance, counseling, attendance, and study skills needed to support improved academic performance (8 NYCRR § 100.1(g)).

An AIS program may not replace services provided to students with limited English proficiency pursuant to part 154 of the commissioner's regulations, or special education services and programs as defined in Education Law section 4401(1) and (2) (*Id.*).

School districts may opt to provide a response to intervention model program in lieu of providing AIS (8 NYCRR § 100.2(ee)(7); see **55:29**).

55:31. Who may provide academic intervention services?

Academic intervention services must be provided by qualified staff certified pursuant to part 80 of the commissioner's regulations (8 NYCRR § 100.2(ee)(5)(iii)).

55:32. How do school districts identify students in need of academic intervention services?

The criteria and steps school districts must apply for identifying students in need of academic intervention services are set forth in commissioner's regulations at 8 NYCRR § 100.2(ee).

55:33. How soon after identification must school districts provide eligible students with academic intervention services?

Academic intervention services must start no later than the beginning of the semester following a determination that a student needs such services. The services must continue until the student's performance meets or exceeds the state-designated performance level on the next state assessment, or the student's achievement on district-selected assessment demonstrates the student is likely to meet or exceed state-designated performance levels on the next state assessment (8 NYCRR § 100.2(ee)(5)(iv)).

55:34. Must school districts make available academic intervention services to students with disabilities?

Yes. Academic intervention services must be made available to students with disabilities on the same basis as nondisabled students, provided that the services are consistent with the student's individualized education program pursuant to Education Law section 4402 (8 NYCRR § 100.1(g)).

55:35. What role do parents play in academic intervention services?

Once a student has been determined to need academic intervention services (AIS), the principal must notify the parent or person in parental relation to the student in writing, in the native language of the parent. The notice must include a summary of the AIS to be provided to the student, the reason the student needs such services, and the consequences of not achieving expected performance levels (8 NYCRR § 100.2(ee)(6)(i)).

The student's parent must be provided with an opportunity at least once per semester during the regular school year to consult with the student's regular classroom teacher(s) and other professional staff providing AIS. At least once each quarter during the regular school year, reports on the student's progress must be sent to the student's parent(s) by mail, telephone, or other means in a language or other mode of communication understood by the parents. In addition, parents must be provided with information on ways to work with their child and educators to improve the child's achievement, and ways to monitor their child's progress (8 NYCRR § 100.2(ee)(6)(iii)).

Districts must notify parents in writing when AIS services are no longer needed and, when appropriate, in the parents' native language or mode of communication (8 NYCRR § 100.2(ee)(6)(ii)).

Curriculum

55:36. Is there a state-prescribed curriculum that school districts must follow?

Not as such. Generally, school boards have the authority to prescribe the course of study in the schools of their districts (§§ 1709(3), 1804(1); *Bd. of Educ., Island Trees UFSD No. 26 v. Pico*, 457 U.S. 853 (1982); *Appeal of D. and N.G.*, 52 Ed Dept Rep, Dec. No. 16,381 (2012)).

However, there are seven general curriculum areas school districts must provide instruction in. These include English language arts, mathematics, science and technology, social studies, languages other than English, the arts, health, physical education, family and consumer sciences, and career development and occupational studies (8 NYCRR §§ 100.2(t), 100.3, 100.4, 100.5; see also **55:26**).

In addition, districts must provide to all students in kindergarten through 12th grade instruction in the following areas:

- Acquired immune deficiency syndrome (AIDS) (8 NYCRR § 135.3(b)(2), (c)(2)). Recommended guidelines for instruction are available from the NYS Education Department (SED).
- Human rights issues, including the study of the inhumanity of genocide and slavery (§ 801).
- Civility, citizenship, patriotism and character education (§ 801-a; 8 NYCRR § 100.2(c)(1)), including instruction that supports the development of a school environment free of harassment, bullying (including cyber bullying) and discrimination, as well as raise awareness and sensitivity to such conduct (8 NYCRR § 100.2(c)(2)).
- Respect for the American flag, its display and use, and certain holidays such as Lincoln's and Washington's birthday, Memorial Day and Flag Day (§ 802; 8 NYCRR §§ 100.2(c)(8), 108.4, 108.6, 108.7).
- Child abduction prevention (§ 803-a).
- Highway safety and traffic regulation (§ 806; 8 NYCRR § 100.2(c)(5)).
- Drug, alcohol, and tobacco misuse and abuse (§§ 804, 806-a(1)(a); 8 NYCRR §§ 100.2(c)(4), 135.3(a)). Junior and senior high school students must show their knowledge of this subject area through testing, a graded project or report, or other means prescribed by school authorities (§ 804(3)). An integrated K-12 health education curriculum that includes instruction in these areas is available from SED.
- Fire drills and safety drills on school buses (§§ 807, 3623(1)(c); 8 NYCRR §§ 100.2(c)(6), 156.3(f)).
- Fire and arson prevention, injury prevention and life safety, including the dangers of falsely reporting a criminal incident, an impending explosion or fire emergency involving danger

to life or property, an impending catastrophe, or a life safety emergency (§ 808; 8 NYCRR § 100.2(c)(6)).

- Conservation of natural resources (§ 810; 8 NYCRR § 100.2(c)(10)).

Elementary school students also must receive instruction in the humane treatment and protection of animals and birds (§ 809(1); 8 NYCRR § 100.2(c)(9)).

High school students also must receive instruction on methods of preventing and detecting certain cancers (§ 804(3-a)), and parenting skills, including the consequences and prevention of shaken baby syndrome (§ 804-b; 8 NYCRR § 100.5(a)(3)(vi)). They must receive, as well, instruction in cardiopulmonary resuscitation (CPR) and the use of an automated external defibrillator (AED) in accordance with standards outlined in regulation (8 NYCRR § 100.2(c)(11)(i)). A student with a disability that physically or cognitively renders the student unable to perform the tasks required for CPR and the use of an AED may be excused from such instruction as provided in the student's individualized education program or accommodation plan (8 NYCRR § 100.2(c)(11)(iv)).

Districts may provide instruction on Internet safety (§ 814). Suggested curricula and resources are available on SED's website at: http://www.p12.nysed.gov/technology/internet_safety/.

55:37. What is the role of the NYS Education Department regarding a school district's curriculum?

The Rules of the Board of Regents provide that school districts may not receive any state-aid apportionment unless they maintain an approved course of study that conforms with the Education Law, the commissioner's regulations and the Regents' rules, and meets all other legal requirements (8 NYCRR § 3.35(a)). Before a school district is entitled to receive state aid, the commissioner of education must be satisfied that proper instruction is given by qualified teachers for not less than 180 days (§ 3604(7)).

55:38. Is a school district's curriculum subject to voter approval?

No. What courses of study are offered in a school district's public schools is a matter of educational policy within the discretion of the district's school board (§§ 1709(3), 1804(1); *Appeal of Bash*, 38 Ed Dept Rep 688 (1999)). That includes the authority to establish reasonable instructional requirements above and beyond state mandated minimums (*Appeal of O'Neill*, 29 Ed Dept Rep 297 (1990); see **55:20**), and to terminate existing programs for budgetary reasons (*Appeal of Brush*, 34 Ed Dept Rep 273 (1994)). Such decisions are not within the powers of the voters (*Id.*).

55:39. Must school districts follow state syllabi when delivering instruction in required curriculum areas?

Not generally, although commissioner's regulations recommend their use where available (8 NYCRR § 100.2(b)). The *syllabi* set forth the expected learning outcomes, including the goals, objectives, concepts, skills and understanding in a given subject (8 NYCRR § 100.1(c)).

For further information on state syllabi, contact the NYS Education Department's Office of Curriculum and Instruction, 89 Washington Avenue, Rm. 318EB, Albany, N.Y., 12234, 518-474-5922, or visit that office's website at: http://www.p12.nysed.gov/ciai/.

However, the NYS Education Department has made available curriculum modules, examplars and related instructional materials as a resource for implementation of the state learning standards (see **55:25**) in English language arts and mathematics at: http://engageny.org/.

55:40. Are there any state requirements concerning homework?

No. There are no state requirements regarding the assignment or completion of homework by students. However, school boards may adopt policy providing that homework be assigned to students for the purpose of reinforcing, preparing, supplementing, and reviewing concepts that have been or will be taught (see, e.g., *Appeal of Human*, 36 Ed Dept Rep 351 (1997)).

55:41. Can school officials preclude a student from taking a course they believe the student won't pass?

Not when the student has maintained passing grades in any earlier courses that may be viewed as prerequisites.

However, districts may establish and apply reasonable criteria for the selection and retention of students in honors classes which may include, for example, teacher recommendations, standardized test scores, IQ scores and course grades (*Appeal of D.M. & M.M.*, 41 Ed Dept Rep 302 (2002); *Appeal of Dawn H.*, 39 Ed Dept Rep 635 (2000); *Appeal of Julio I*, 39 Ed Dept Rep 509 (2000); but compare *Appeal of C.C.*, 49 Ed Dept Rep 110 (2009) where the commissioner of education ruled that a school district may not preclude students from honors classes based on their failure to complete summer assignments as a result of insufficient teacher direction and supervision).

In addition, school districts may require that students complete certain reasonable prerequisites before admission to a board of cooperative educational services program (*Appeal of a Student with a Disability (North Colonie CSD)*, 42 Ed Dept Rep 163 (2002); *Matter of Tripi*, 21 Ed Dept Rep 349 (1981)).

Otherwise, school boards enjoy authority to place students in particular classes, absent evidence that it acted in an illegal, arbitrary or capricious manner. Furthermore, in making student placement decisions, school boards may consider a broad range of factors including the composition of the class, student academic levels and special needs, and teacher and confidential parental input (*Appeal of J.A.*, 49 Ed Dept Rep 167 (2009)).

55:42. May school officials limit a student's participation in curriculum courses and other program activities solely on the basis of sex or sexual orientation?

No. School districts may not deny students membership or participation in any school curricular or extracurricular program or activity on the basis of sex, race, marital status, color, religion, national origin, disability (§§ 313, 3201, 3201-a; Exec. Law § 291 *et seq.*; 8 NYCRR § 100.2(k)), or sexual orientation (§ 313; Exec. Law § 291 *et seq.*).

Similarly, Title IX of the Federal Educational Amendments of 1972 (20 USC § 1681 *et seq.*) and related regulations prohibit sexual discrimination in any activity or program receiving federal funds, including all of the operations of a local educational agency, vocational school system, or any other type of school system that receives federal aid (see 20 USC § 1687).

Special rules apply to male and female participation in extra class athletic activities (see 8 NYCRR §§ 100.2(k)(2), 135.4(c)(7)(ii)(c)(4); *Lantz v. Ambach*, 620 F.Supp. 663 (S.D.N.Y. 1985); *Appeal of Martin*, 38 Ed Dept Rep 130 (1998); *Appeal of Wilson*, 30 Ed Dept Rep 60 (1990)). The special rules accommodate both the interests and abilities of both sexes. However, scheduling a sport off-season for one of the sexes may constitute a violation of Title IX if the sport's participants are deprived of the opportunity to compete in other competition, and there is no adequate non-discriminatory reason for the off-season scheduling (*McCormick v. Sch. Dist. of Mamaroneck*, 370 F.3d 275 (2d Cir. 2004)).

55:43. Can students be excused from curriculum courses or lessons for religious reasons?

It depends. Parents do not have a right to tell a school what their children "will and will not be taught" (*Leebaert v. Harrington,* 332 F.3d 134 (2d Cir. 2003); see **48:3**; see also **65:3**), or to prevent their children's mere exposure to ideas or a point of view with which they disagree or find offensive (*Matter of Alfonso v. Fernandez*, 195 A.D.2d 46 (2d Dep't 1993), *lv. to appeal dismissed*, 83 N.Y.2d 906 (1994)). Indeed, mere exposure to courses and lessons with which someone disagrees does not burden a person's right to the free exercise of religion (see **65:3**) and, therefore, does not constitute a violation of the Free Exercise Clause of the First Amendment of the U.S. Constitution (*Mozert v. Hawkins County Bd. of Educ.*, 827 F.2d 1058 (6th Cir. 1987), *cert. denied*, 484 U.S. 1066 (1988)).

However, New York law and commissioner's regulations permit school officials to excuse students from any study of health and hygiene that conflicts with the religion of the student's parents (§ 3204(5); 8 NYCRR § 16.2). The conflict must be certified by a proper religious representative (*Id.*; *Application of Ernst*, 39 Ed Dept Rep 781 (2000)), even though a similar requirement in another context was deemed unconstitutional (see *Sherr v. Northport-East Northport UFSD*, 672 F.Supp. 81 (E.D.N.Y. 1987); *Lewis v. Sobol*, 710 F.Supp. 506 (S.D.N.Y. 1989); see **50:15**).

In addition, school officials must allow students who express a religious or moral objection to the performance or witnessing of animal dissections to complete an alternative project approved by their teacher instead, without penalty. Parents must substantiate, in writing, their children's religious or moral objection to participation in the dissection of animals. School districts are required to maintain a policy that provides for "reasonable notice" of the right to be excused from performing or witnessing animal dissections on religious or moral grounds. The notice must be made available at the school, upon request. It also must be distributed to parents and students enrolled in a course that includes animal dissection at least once at the beginning of the school year (§ 809(4)).

55:44. Can students be excused from instruction regarding acquired immune deficiency syndrome (AIDS)?

Yes, but only as to the prevention of AIDS. Commissioner's regulations allow school officials to excuse students from instruction on AIDS prevention upon the filing of a parental written request with the school principal, that also incorporates a parental agreement that the student will receive AIDS instruction at home (8 NYCRR § 135.3(b)(2), (c)(2); see also *Ware v. Valley Stream High Sch. Dist.*, 75 N.Y.2d 114 (1989)).

Students who are exempted from instruction in AIDS prevention must still receive instruction at school regarding the nature of the disease and methods of transmission (see *Appeal of Kerry*, 35 Ed Dept Rep 337 (1996); *Appeal of O'Shaughnessy*, 35 Ed Dept Rep 57 (1995)).

55:45. Can students be excused from the physical education curriculum?

It depends. Generally, all students must receive physical training as part of the required course of study each year they attend school, from kindergarten through grade 12 (§§ 803, 3204(3)(a)(1); 8 NYCRR § 135.4), and to obtain a high school diploma (8 NYCRR § 100.5(a)(3), (4)), with the frequency of their classes varying based on their grade level (8 NYCRR § 135.4(c)(2)).

However, a student who graduates high school in less than eight semesters and has successfully fulfilled the physical education requirements each semester up to then, does not have to continue enrollment solely to complete the physical education requirement (8 NYCRR § 100.5(a)(4)).

In addition, students who are temporarily or permanently unable to participate in the regular physical education program must be provided with adapted activities that meet their particular needs from a certified physical education teacher (8 NYCRR § 135.4(c)(1)(iv)), or a teaching assistant under the general supervision of a certified teacher (*Appeal of Branschback*, 38 Ed Dept Rep 493 (1999)). This includes students classified by a committee on special education who are unable to participate safely or successfully in the activities of the regular physical education program. In their case, their individualized education program must include a prescriptive physical education program (8 NYCRR § 200.4(d)(2)(viii)(d)).

Furthermore, districts may offer students in grades 7–12 alternatives to regularly scheduled physical education classes. Students in grades 10–12, for example, may be permitted to use an "extra-class" program for physical education credit if they show they have achieved acceptable levels of physical fitness and physical skills, and acquired knowledge of physical education activities (8 NYCRR § 135.4(c)(2)(ii)(c)).

Other equivalent program options must be approved by the commissioner of education (8 NYCRR § 135.4(c)(2)(i)(c), (ii)(e)).

55:46. What are the requirements for providing instruction in a language other than English?

Public school students are required to complete two units of study in a language other than English (LOTE) by the end of ninth grade (8 NYCRR § 100.2(d)(1); see also 8 NYCRR § 100.4(b)(1)(iv), (c)(1)(xi)). The units of study may be in more than one language, but at least one unit of study must be in the same language (8 NYCRR § 100.2(d)(1)(i)). School districts may start LOTE instruction at any grade level but must do so no later than the beginning of eighth grade so that students are provided the required two units of study by the end of ninth grade (8 NYCRR § 100.2(d)(2)).

A student with a disability that adversely affects the ability to learn a language may be exempted from these requirements by his or her individualized education program (8 NYCRR §§ 100.2 (d)(1)(iii), 100.5(b)(7)(iv)(g), (v)(c)).

55:47. What are the requirements for providing bilingual instruction and English as a new language (ENL) programs?

School districts are responsible for providing bilingual education programs if they have 20 or more English language learners (ELL) of the same grade level who share the same home language. In such an instance, a district must provide a sufficient number of bilingual education programs so that such programs are available for at least 70 percent of those students. However, if those students are assigned to the same school, the district must provide a bilingual education program at that school (8 NYCRR § 154-2.3(d)(2), (4)).

The term *English language learner* refers to a student who, by reason of foreign birth or ancestry, speaks or understands a language other than English and speaks or understands little or no English and requires support in order to become proficient in English, and is identified as ELL in accordance with commissioner's regulations (8 NYCRR § 154-2.2(f)).

A *bilingual education program* must include:

- A language arts instruction component, including home language arts and English language arts,
- An English as a new language component, and
- A bilingual content area instructional component (including all bilingual content areas, i.e., math, science, and social studies, depending on the bilingual education program model and the student's level of English language development, but must at a minimum include at least two bilingual core content areas, i.e., match, science and social studies) (8 NYCRR § 154-2.2(b)).

School districts must provide an ENL program to all ELL students who are not served by a bilingual program (8 NYCRR § 154-2.3(d)(9)).

An English as a new language program must include:

- A content area instructional component in English (including all core content, i.e., English language arts, math, science, or social studies) with home language supports and appropriate scaffolds, and
- An English language development component (stand-alone and/or integrated English as a new language) (8 NYCRR § 154-2.2(h); see also 8 NYCRR § 154-2.2(m) for a definition of integrated English as a new language).

In addition, school districts must take steps to identify ELL students upon their initial enrollment or reentry in a New York State public school in accordance with the process established in commissioner's regulations (8 NYCRR § 154-2.3(a), (b)), and provide parents notices and information specified in regulation (8 NYCRR § 154-2.3(f), (g)(2)).

55:48. Are school districts required to offer a gifted and talented instruction curriculum?

No. It is within the discretion of a school board to determine whether or not to provide instruction to meet the special needs of gifted students (§ 3204(2-b); *Matter of Bennett v. City Sch. Dist. of New Rochelle*, 114 A.D.2d 58 (2d Dep't 1985)). Article 90 of the Education Law, which authorizes the NYS Education Department to assist districts in meeting the educational needs of gifted students, does not establish an affirmative duty to provide such instruction (*Matter of Bennett v. City Sch. Dist. of New Rochelle*). Moreover, a school district's decision to not offer a gifted and talented program does not violate state constitutional requirements mandating the provision of a sound basic education, or equal protection guarantees *(Id.*).

Nonetheless, commissioner's regulations provide, in relevant part, for the screening of students entering the public schools for gifted abilities. Students so identified as possibly gifted must be reported to the superintendent and to the parent no later than 15 calendar days after completion of the screening (8 NYCRR §§ 117.1, 117.2(f), 117.3(g); Part 142).

In districts that do offer a gifted and talented program, students may be referred for participation in the program by a parent, a teacher, or an administrator (§ 4452(1)(d)). Districts may evaluate students to determine their eligibility only upon parental consent. Absent parental consent, a student may not be evaluated nor participate in the program (§ 4452(1)(e)).

Furthermore, districts that offer a gifted and talented program must accept into the program nonresident students attending a private school located within its boundaries. However, such a student must be a resident of the state and the student's parents must have submitted a request for participation by June 1 of the preceding school year. In addition, all legal, regulatory and district screening requirements must have been met (*Appeal of Goodman*, 38 Ed Dept Rep 824 (1999); *Appeal of Pfeffer*, 38 Ed Dept Rep 514 (1999)).

55:49. May school districts require that students participate in a summer reading program?

Yes. School boards may adopt a policy that requires students participate in a summer reading program (*Appeal of Lease*, 39 Ed Dept Rep 215 (1999)). Also, that they read books for such program from a school designated list. However, the books used as part of the mandatory assignment must be reasonably available to all students (*Appeal of Lahm*, 41 Ed Dept Rep 193 (2002)), at no cost (see *Appeal of Ciotti*, 44 Ed Ed Dept Rep 247 (2005)).

In addition, districts may require that students show their understanding of books they read over the summer during the first weeks of school. But they may not ask that students submit written assignments upon their return to school (*Appeal of Lahm*). In addition, mandatory written assignments for a grade without the benefit of a teacher's direction and supervision are unreasonable (*Appeal of Ciotti*, *Appeal of Lease*).

Districts without a mandatory summer reading program may, nonetheless, encourage students to get involved in summer reading. The New York State Library's Statewide Summer Reading Program is an example of an effective voluntary summer reading program, and is free to students and their families. More information on the program can be accessed at: http://www.nysl.nysed.gov/libdev/summer.

55:50. Can school districts distribute condoms to students as part of the acquired immune deficiency (AIDS) instruction curriculum?

Not without parental consent. Absent such consent, the distribution of condoms in public schools would both violate Public Health Law section 2504, and deny parents their constitutional rights "to influence and guide the sexual activity of their children without state interference" (*Alfonso v. Fernandez*, 195 A.D.2d 46 (2d Dep't 1993), *lv. to appeal dismissed*, 83 N.Y.2d 906 (1994)).

However, school districts may conduct demonstrations on the use of condoms as part of the AIDS instruction curriculum. But parents who enter into an opt-out agreement with their school district to have their children receive AIDS instruction at home instead of at school do not have to do the same (*Appeal of O'Shaughnessy*, 35 Ed Dept Rep 57 (1995); see **55:44**).

55:51. May school districts teach about religion?

Yes. Although the federal and state constitutions forbid the teaching of religion in the public schools, they do not prevent teaching about religion. Moreover, schools have a responsibility to teach about religion and its place in civilization, which may be a positive force in the inculcation of moral values in youths and in the development of a respect for religion and for religious beliefs (*Matter of Rubinstein,* 2 Ed Dept Rep 299 (1962); see **65:16-17**).

However, school districts may not require that creation science be taught as a counterbalance to the teaching of evolution (*Edwards v. Aguillard*, 482 U.S. 578 (1987)). Evolution science may not be taught as a religion either, to counterbalance the religious doctrine of creationism (*Peloza v. Capistrano Unified Sch. Dist.*, 37 F.3d 517 (9th Cir. 1994), *cert. denied*, 515 U.S. 1173 (1995); see **65:16-18**).

55:52. May school districts offer military instruction to their students?

Yes, but only as part of a junior reserve officer training program in conjunction with the U.S. Department of Defense to students in grades 9–12 who are at least 14 years of age. Enrollment and participation in such a program must be voluntary on the part of the student, and each student must obtain written consent of a parent or guardian. However, instruction in, or the presence within any school of, any type of current or future weaponry as part of such a program is prohibited (§ 802(3)).

55:53. May school districts teach about the use of firearms?

Yes. School boards may authorize instruction within their schools on the safe and proper use of firearms that are allowed by law to be used in hunting wild game, and on the study of game laws and proper hunting and conservation practices. However, both the NYS Education Department and the NYS Department of Environmental Conservation must approve this course (§ 809-a).

Although the federal Gun-Free Schools Act (20 USC § 7961) and state law (§ 3214(3)) prohibit firearms on school grounds, neither applies to activities that are school approved and authorized where a district has adopted appropriate safeguards to ensure student safety (20 USC § 7961(g); see **52:65**).

55:54. May school districts offer automobile driver education and training courses?

Yes. Authority for this is granted under section 507(1) of the Vehicle and Traffic Law (see also NYS Education Department, *Driver and Traffic Safety Education Guidelines; Program Description and Requirements* (Aug. 2015), at: http://www.p12.nysed.gov/cte/docs/NYS-DTSEGuidelinesAugust2015.pdf).

The courses must include a driver safety component, based on curriculum established by the commissioner of education (§ 806-a). Any vehicle used for driver training must bear identification indicating that the car is being driven by a student driver (see also Veh. & Traf. Law § 375(44)).

In addition, class time spent actually driving under the supervision of the instructor may be counted towards the supervised hours the holder of a learner's permit needs before taking a driving test. The instructor is required to issue a certificate detailing the time the student spent driving under instructor supervision upon request (§ 806-a(2); Veh. & Traf. Law § 502(2)(d); 8 NYCRR § 107.2).

55:55. May school districts create a student credit union to teach students about saving money?

Yes. School districts can authorize a credit union to open and maintain a student branch within elementary and secondary schools. The credit unions may only be open to students (Banking Law § 450-b).

55:56. May school districts use and have possession of hypodermic syringes and needles for instructional purposes?

Yes, provided school authorities file a certificate of need for such equipment with the commissioner of education and the NYS Department of Health, and their use is limited to actual educational demonstrations or other educational purposes designated in the certificate of need. Any other use is unauthorized and prohibited (§ 811; 8 NYCRR § 137.1; see also 10 NYCRR § 80.133).

A record of all hypodermic syringes and needles purchased, lost, stolen, or destroyed must be maintained and kept for a period of two years, and an annual physical inventory must be completed each June 30 (8 NYCRR § 137.3).

Instructional Materials and Resources

55:57. What is a textbook?

A *textbook* is defined as "any book, or a book substitute, which shall include hard covered or paperback books, work books, or manuals" and "any courseware or other content-based instructional materials in an electronic format, as such terms are defined in commissioner's regulations, which a pupil is required to use as a text, or a text-substitute, in a particular class or program in the school he or she legally attends" (§ 701(2)).

55:58. Does a school district have a duty to provide free textbooks to students?

Yes. School boards have the power and duty to purchase and to loan, upon individual requests, textbooks to all children residing in the district enrolled in kindergarten through 12th grade. These textbooks are to be loaned free to such students, subject to rules and regulations that are or may be prescribed by the Board of Regents and the school board (§ 701(3); *Appeal of Lease*, 39 Ed Dept Rep 215 (1999)).

For information on the purchase and loan of textbooks for nonpublic school students, see **4:15-20**.

55:59. Does a school district have a duty to provide alternative instructional materials to students with disabilities?

Yes. Each school board and board of cooperative educational services (BOCES) must establish a plan to ensure that every student with a disability who needs instructional materials in an alternative format not only will receive those materials, but also at the same time instructional materials are made available to nondisabled students. *Alternative format* is defined to mean any medium or format other than a traditional print textbook that is needed as an accommodation for a disabled student, including but not limited to, Braille, large print, open and closed caption, audio, or electronic files.

The plan must specify:

- a procurement policy giving a preference to vendors who agree to provide such alternative formats;
- how students will access electronic files, if needed, and how electronic files will be converted if necessary;
- the process to be used when ordering materials to identify the needs of students with disabilities residing in the district who will need alternative instructional materials;
- ordering timelines to ensure such materials are available at the same time as regular format materials;
- procedures to avoid delay in ordering such materials when students with disabilities move into the district or enroll in a BOCES program (§§ 1604(29-a), 1709(4-a), 1950(4-a), 2503(7-a), 2554(7-a), 3602(8)(b); 8 NYCRR § 200.2(b)(10)).

School districts must also have a plan to supply textbooks in alternative formats to preschool children with disabilities (8 NYCRR § 200.2(c)(2)(vi)).

55:60. Can the state dictate the use of certain textbooks in the public schools?

No. The school board, or whatever body or officer that performs the function of the board, designates the textbooks to be used (§ 701(1); Opn. Att'y Gen., 18 St. Dep't Rep. 456 (1919)).

55:61. Is there any limitation on how frequently textbooks may be changed in a school system?

Yes. After a textbook has been designated for use, the district is prohibited from replacing it with any other book within a five-year period from the time of its designation, unless three-fourths of the school board or whatever body or officer that performs the function votes to do otherwise (§ 702).

55:62. Do parents have a right to inspect classroom materials?

Under the Hatch Amendment (20 USC § 1232h), parents have the right "to inspect, upon request, any instructional material used as part of the educational curriculum for the student" (20 USC § 1232h(c)(1)(C)(i)). However, the Hatch Amendment does not give parents the right to inspect course materials because they find such materials offensive or just because the school receives federal aid.

In addition, parents have the right to inspect, upon request, any instrument used in the collection, disclosure, or use of personal information before the instrument is administered or distributed to a student (20 USC § 1232h(c)(1)(E), (F)). An exception applies for personal information collected from students for the exclusive purpose of developing, evaluating, or providing educational products or services for students or educational institutions, such as college or military recruitment, book clubs or magazines providing low-cost literary products or curriculum, tests and/or other instructional materials used by schools (20 USC § 1232h(c)(4)(A)).

Parents also have the right to inspect survey[s] created by a third party before the survey is administered or distributed by a school to a student, except a survey administered to a student in accordance with the Individuals with Disabilities Education Act (20 USC § 1232h(c)(1)(A)(i), (5)(A)).

Students may not be required to submit to a survey, analysis, or evaluation that reveals information regarding the following: political affiliation; mental or psychological problems of the student or his or her family; sex behavior and attitudes; illegal, anti-social, self-incriminating and demeaning behavior; critical appraisals of other individuals with close family relationship, legally recognized or analogous privileged relationship; religious practices, affiliations, or beliefs of the student or student's parent; or income. Participation in survey instruments soliciting such information requires the consent of the student, or his or her parent, if the student is a minor (20 USC § 1232h(b)). School districts must give parents and students annual notice of this right (20 USC § 1232h(c)(2)).

55:63. Do parents have the right to require that certain alleged controversial books or other curricular materials not be used or given to their child?

No. The school board has broad authority to determine what books will be used in its courses, and parents of a student cannot compel a board to use a particular textbook or to discontinue the use of one (*Appeal of Dimasio*, 39 Ed Dept Rep 827 (2000); *Appeal of Carney*, 39 Ed Dept Rep 255 (1999); *Appeal of Smith,* 34 Ed Dept Rep 346 (1994)). The only exceptions are for students who may be excused from that part of the study of health that conflicts with their religious beliefs, and from instruction about AIDS (§ 3204(5); 8 NYCRR §§ 16.2, 135.3(b)(2), (c)(2); see also **55:43-44**). Parents may not compel a school district to assign an alternate curriculum to their child either, based on their disapproval of classroom assignments (*Appeal of Carney*).

The courts have also upheld the broad discretion of school boards in selecting instructional materials against parental challenges that the use of particular materials violates the First Amendment rights of both them and their children. For example, despite the claim by parents in two separate cases that the use of the "Impressions" reading series fostered a pagan belief in the occult, in direct opposition to their Christian beliefs, two federal appellate courts with jurisdiction outside New York have ruled that the school districts' use of the book did not violate either the Establishment or Free Exercise Clause of the First Amendment (*Brown v. Woodland Joint Unified Sch. Dist.*, 27 F.3d 1373 (9th Cir. 1994); *Fleischfresser v. Dir. of Sch. Dist. 200*, 15 F.3d 680 (7th Cir. 1994)). Similarly, one court rejected a claim that curriculum materials which encourage respect for gay persons and couples violate the First Amendment rights of parents to raise their children as they wish (*Parker v. Hurley,* 474 F.Supp.2d 261 (D. Mass. 2007), *aff'd*, 514 F.3d 87 (1st Cir.), *cert. denied*, 555 U.S. 815 (2008)).

55:64. May a school board remove a previously approved textbook because of objections to the material contained in it, without violating the First Amendment?

Yes. However, according to a federal appellate court with jurisdiction outside New York, the removal and the methods used must be "reasonably related to legitimate pedagogical concerns." In *Virgil v. School Bd.*, 862 F.2d 1517 (11th Cir. 1989), the court reviewed the removal of a textbook used in an elective humanities course designed for 11th- and 12th-grade students because of the explicit sexuality and excessively vulgar language and subject matter contained in selections within the textbook of Aristophane's "Lysistrata" and Chaucer's "The Miller's Tale." Neither of these selections was required or assigned during the course. The book remained available in the school library for students' use, along with other adaptations and translations of "Lysistrata" and "The Miller's Tale."

In upholding the removal, the court applied the standard set by the U.S. Supreme Court in *Hazelwood Sch. Dist. v. Kuhlmeier*, 484 U.S. 260 (1988), which focused on a permissible school board regulation of expression that "may fairly be characterized as part of the school curriculum," provided such regulation is "reasonably related to legitimate pedagogical concerns." (The *Hazelwood* case had involved school censorship of a school-sponsored student newspaper.) In *Virgil*, the court found that the selections were part of the school curriculum because it was reasonable to think that the public may perceive them to bear the school's imprimatur, and that the motivation for the removal presented a legitimate concern regarding the appropriateness of the selections for the student audience in question.

Another federal appellate court with jurisdiction outside New York held that a parent could not proceed on a civil rights liability action claiming a First Amendment violation based on a school district's refusal to remove from a required reading list Mark Twain's *The Adventures of Huckleberry Finn* and William Faulkner's *A Rose for Emily*. The student and her parent found the books offensive because of their repeated use of racially derogatory terms (*Montiero v. Tempe Union High Sch. Dist.*, 158 F.3d 1022 (9th Cir. 1998)).

Although New York is under the jurisdiction of the Second Circuit, these cases may have some persuasive value in this state.

55:65. Are schools required to have a library?

Yes. The commissioner's regulations require each school to maintain a library that meets the needs of students and serves as an adequate complement to the instructional program in the various areas of the curriculum (8 NYCRR § 91.1).

The commissioner's regulations also provide the following direction as to the number of holdings that junior and senior high schools of different sizes must maintain:

- The library of a junior high school or high school with fewer than 200 students must contain at least 1,000 titles.
- The library of a junior-senior high school with fewer than 200 students must contain at least 2,000 titles.
- The library of a secondary school in which the average daily attendance is between 200 and 500 students must contain at least 3,000 titles.
- The library of a secondary school in which the average daily attendance is between 500 and 1,000 students must contain at least 5,000 titles.
- The library of a secondary school in which the average daily attendance is more than 1,000 students must contain at least 8,000 titles (8 NYCRR § 91.1).

55:66. Are schools required to have a school librarian?

Yes. Each district with a secondary school must employ a certified school library-media specialist, unless equivalent service is provided by an alternative arrangement approved by the commissioner of education, in accordance with specified standards contained in the commissioner's regulations (8 NYCRR § 91.2; *Appeal of Walker,* 43 Ed Dept Rep 528 (2004)).

55:67. May a school board remove books from the school library without violating the First Amendment?

The constitutional issues in the removal of books from a school library are focused on the school board's motivations in taking such action. In *Bd. of Educ. v. Pico*, 457 U.S. 853 (1982), the U.S. Supreme Court held that although a school board has the authority to remove certain books it deems inappropriate from the school library, the board may not remove such books to restrict access to certain social, political, and moral ideas which the board simply disapproves. In its decision, the court said that the school board would have been within its rights to remove the books if they contained vulgar language or if the school board had established a policy setting forth criteria, such as "educational suitability," for keeping books in the district's libraries.

Prior to the *Pico case*, a federal appellate court with jurisdiction outside New York had ruled that a district's removal of a film version of "The Lottery" by Shirley Jackson from the school library violated the First Amendment rights of students because the decision to remove the film was based on the fact that a majority of the board and some parents found the film's ideological and religious themes offensive (*Pratt v. Independent Sch. Dist. No. 831*, 670 F.2d 771 (8th Cir. 1982)).

Following *Pico*, the U.S. Court of Appeals for the Second Circuit, with jurisdiction over New York, dismissed a student's complaint that the school board had violated the First Amendment by removing certain library books because of their vulgar and obscene language (*Bicknell v. Vergennes Union High Sch. Bd. of Directors*, 638 F.2d 438 (2d Cir. 1980)). There was no dispute that the board had not removed the books in question simply because of the ideas they contained or that there was any political motivation on the part of the board. The school board had the right to remove those books because of their vulgar and sexually explicit content.

55:68. May teachers duplicate copyrighted material in books or musical compositions for their classes or student groups without prior permission?

With certain restrictions, yes. Federal law prohibits any "infringing use" of copyrighted works, that is, the use of copyrighted works without the consent of the author or owner of the copyright (see 17 USC §§ 101, 106, 107, 117).

The law specifically states, however, that the "fair use" of such works for teaching purposes, including making "multiple copies for classroom use," as well as for criticism, comment, scholarship or research, is not an infringing use. Fair use is not a rigidly defined term, but rather is based on a number of factors, including the purpose and character of the use, whether such use is of a commercial nature or is for nonprofit educational purposes, the nature of the original work, the size of the portion used, and the effect on the value or market of the original work (see *Basic Books, Inc., v. Kinko's Graphics Corp.*, 758 F.Supp. 1522 (S.D.N.Y. 1991); *Notes of Committee on the Judiciary*, House Report No. 94–1476, in note following 17 USC § 107).

Based on guidelines for classroom copying by the House Judiciary Subcommittee, teachers may reproduce materials if four tests are passed: brevity (a single short poem, story, essay or illustration, or a short excerpt of a larger work); spontaneity (a decision made by the teacher making the copy close to the time the material is to be used); cumulative use (generally no more than nine occasions per teacher per term); and notice (each copy must include the name of the copyright owner, year of publication and a (c) or © symbol).

Copyrighted, or "proprietary," computer software and documentation may not be reproduced other than to make archival back-ups or because the copy is an essential step to use the computer program in conjunction with a machine (see 17 USC § 117). "Shareware," which is software in the public domain, is not subject to this restriction (37 CFR § 201.26).

It is important to note that classroom and instructional fair use for plays and musical numbers does not include public performances, especially if an admission fee is charged (17 USC § 110).

Violation of copyright may result in fines and injunctive actions against a school district. Particularly in the case of computer software, violation of a license agreement may void any applicable warranty or continued service arrangement, even if the copyright laws have not been violated (17 USC §§ 501–505).

56. Student Performance Accountability

Student Participation in State Assessments

56:1. Are public school students required to participate in state assessments?

Yes. All public school students at the elementary, intermediate, and high school level must participate in state assessments that reflect the knowledge, skills, and understandings that all students are expected to know and be able to do at certain specified grade levels, and for receiving a high school diploma. This requirement applies, as well, to students with severe disabilities and the knowledge, skills, and understandings they are expected to know and be able to do as indicated in their individualized education program (8 NYCRR §§ 100.3(b)(2), 100.4(b)(2)(e), 100.5(a)(5), (b)(5), (c)(5), (d), (g); see **56:8-9**)).

The federal Every Student Succeeds Act (ESSA) requires yearly assessments in mathematics and reading or language arts in grades 3–8, and at least once in grades 9–12. It also requires assessments in science at least once during grades 3–5, 6–9, and 10–12 (§ 1111(b)(2)(B)). These assessments are the primary means for determining the yearly performance of the State and each of its school districts and public schools, and the academic achievement and growth of its students.

56:2. Must school districts administer all state required assessments?

Yes, unless the commissioner of education has approved the use of an alternative equivalent assessment (8 NYCRR § 100.5(a)(5)(i), (ii); see also 8 NYCRR § 100.2(f)).

Furthermore, Rules of the Board of Regents pertaining to apportionment specifically provide that secondary schools receiving state aid must use Regents examinations or approved equivalent examinations in the senior high school grades (8 NYCRR § 3.35).

56:3. Are there any exceptions to student participation in the regularly required state assessments?

Yes. The commissioner of education may approve the use of alternative assessments, which measure an equivalent level of knowledge and skill (8 NYCRR § 100.2(f)). The commissioner may also approve alternative testing procedures for students with severe disabilities and whose native language is other than English, subject to conditions set forth in the commissioner's regulations (8 NYCRR § 100.2(g)).

In addition, students with severe disabilities who cannot participate in regular state assessments, even with accommodations, may participate in a state alternate assessment recommended by their school district's committee on special education for use by disabled students who have limited cognitive abilities combined with behavioral and/or physical limitations and who require highly specialized education and services (8 NYCRR § 100.1(t)(2)(iv); see also 8 NYCRR § 100.2(p)(1)(vii)). In accordance with their individualized education program, students with severe disabilities instructed in the alternate achievement standards must be administered a state alternate assessment to measure their achievement (8 NYCRR § 100.4(g)).

56:4. Are home schooled students required to participate in state assessments?

No. Home schooled students (see **48:38-55**) may, but are not required to take, the state assessments required of public school students (8 NYCRR §§ 100.3(b)(2)(ii), 100.4(b)(2)(iv), (f)).

State Assessments and Other Standardized Tests – In General

56:5. Are there any limitations on the amount of time that can be devoted to state assessments and other standardized tests?

Yes. The amount of time devoted to state administered required assessments for each grade cannot exceed, in the aggregate, one percent of the minimum required annual instructional hours for such grade (§ 305(49)(a); 8 NYCRR § 8.4(b)). For information on how to calculate the one percent cap, see NYS Education Department, *Guidance on New York State's Annual Professional Performance Review For Teachers and Principals To Implement Education Law § 3012-d and the Commissioner's Regulations* (updated May 31, 2016), q. C31, at: https://www.engageny.org/resource/appr-3012-d.

Similarly, the amount of time school districts devote to standardized assessments that are not specifically required by state or federal law for each grade also cannot exceed, in the aggregate, one percent of the minimum required annual instructional hours for such grade (§ 305(49)(b); 8 NYCRR § 30-3.3(a)(3)(i)). For information on the calculation of the amount of time devoted to standardized assessments that are not specifically required by state or federal law, see *Guidance on New York State's Annual Professional Performance Review For Teachers and Principals To Implement Education Law § 3012-d and the Commissioner's Regulations*, q. C30; see also q. C34.

These limitations do not supersede the requirements of a section 504 plan or an individualized education program for a disabled student, or federal law relating to English language learners (§ 305(49)(c); 8 NYCRR §§ 8.4(b), 30-3.3(a)(3)(ii)).

56:6. Are there limitations on the amount of time school districts can devote to prepare students for standardized tests?

Yes. The amount of time school districts devote to test preparation under standardized testing conditions for each grade cannot exceed, in the aggregate two percent of the minimum required annual instructional hours for such grade (§ 305(49)(c); 8 NYCRR § 30-3.3(a)(3)(ii)). *Time devoted to test preparation under standardized testing conditions* refers to any traditional standardized assessment or historical version of a State or Regents assessment that students are required to take for purposes of preparing for end of the course assessments, and are administered under the same or similar standardized testing conditions required when taking a State or Regents examination (NYS Education Department, *Guidance on New York State's Annual Professional Performance Review For Teachers and Principals To Implement Education Law § 3012-d and the Commissioner's Regulations* (updated May 31, 2016), q. C31, at: https://www.engageny.org/resource/appr-3012-d). For information on how to calculate the two percent cap, see *Guidance on New York State's Annual Professional Performance Review For Teachers and Principals to Implement Education Law § 3012-d and the Commissioner's Regulations*, q. C33.

Not included in this limitation is time devoted to teacher administered classroom quizzes or exams, portfolio reviews, or performance assessments (§ 305(49)(b); 8 NYCRR § 30-3.3(a)(3)(ii)).

Furthermore, this limitation does not supersede the requirements of a section 504 plan or an individualized education program for a disabled student, or federal law relating to English language learners (*Id.*).

56:7. Can school districts and boards of cooperative educational services administer traditional standardized assessments that are not required by federal or state law?

Yes. However, they have an obligation to avoid over-testing their students by reducing or eliminating the use of such *traditional standardized assessments*, (L. 2014, c. 56 pt. AA, subpart F § 1), which refer to tests that require students to directly use a "bubble" answer sheet and choose one or more given options or choices as a response. Examples include multiple choice, true-false, and matching items assessments (8 NYCRR §§ 30-3.2(aa), 100.3(a)(5), (b)(2)(v)(a), 151-1.2(e)). Such tests do not include:

- Performance assessments or tests in which students perform real-world tasks that show application or knowledge of skills.
- Assessments otherwise required by federal law.
- Assessments used for diagnostic or formative purposes including, but not limited to, those administered under Education Law § 3208(5) to determine what new entrants to school may, for example, be gifted, have a disabling condition, or score below level two on either of the state's third grade reading or math tests (*Id.*).

State Assessment Requirements Prekindergarten – Grade 8

56:8. What state assessments must public school students regularly take through the eighth grade?

The state assessments public school students must take through the eighth grade vary according to a student's grade level.

Grades 3 and 4 — All students in grades 3 and 4 must take the English language arts elementary assessments and the mathematics elementary assessment. Students in grade 4 also must take the elementary science assessment (8 NYCRR § 100.3(b)(2)(i)(a), (b)).

Grades 5 and 6 — All students in grades 5 and 6 must take the English language arts and mathematics assessments (8 NYCRR § 100.4(b)(2)(ii)).

Grades 7 and 8 — All students in grades seven and eight must take the English language arts and mathematics assessments. Students in grade 8 also must take the science intermediate assessment (8 NYCRR § 100.4(e)(2), (4)).

Students in grades 7 and 8 may take a Regents examination in mathematics in place of or in addition to the mathematics assessment for those grades (8 NYCRR § 100.4(e)(2)). Students in grade 8 may take a Regents examination in science in place of or in addition to the grade 8 science intermediate assessment (8 NYCRR § 100.4(e)(4)).

56:9. Are students in prekindergarten through grade 2 subject to traditional standardized assessments?

No. New York's Education Law prohibits the participation of students in prekindergarten programs and in grades k-2 in traditional standardized tests (§§ 305(44), 3602-e(15); see 8 NYCRR §§ 30-3.2(b)(1), 100.3(a)(5)(ii)).

This prohibition, however, does not extend to assessments in which students perform real-world tasks that show application of knowledge and skills, or assessments that are otherwise required by federal law (§§ 305(44), 3602-e(15); 8 NYCRR §§ 30-3.2(b), 100.3(a)(5)(ii), (b)(2)(v)(b), 151-1.3(b)(4)).

56:10. How do state assessment results affect the promotion or placement of students in grades 3-8?

Pursuant to the Education Law, school districts are precluded from making student promotion or placement decisions based solely or primarily on student performance on the state-administered standardized English language arts or mathematics assessments for grades 3–8. Nonetheless, school districts may consider student performance on such assessments as part of multiple measures, provided the assessments do not constitute the major factor in such determinations (§ 305(47); 8 NYCRR §§ 100.3(b)(2)(iv), 100.4(b)(2)(vii), (e)(6)).

In this regard, school districts must annually notify parents of students attending their school of their grade promotion and placement policy with an explanation of how the policy was developed, either through the district's website or as part of an existing informational document provided to parents (§ 305(47); 8 NYCRR § 100.2(ll)).

Furthermore, through December 31, 2018, school districts and boards of cooperative educational services are precluded from including on a student's official transcript or permanent record any individual student score on a state administered standardized English language arts or math assessment for grades 3–8 (§ 305(45); 8 NYCRR § 104.3(a)). However, this prohibition does not interfere with required federal and state reporting, or excuse school districts from maintaining or transferring records of such test scores separately from a student's permanent record, including for purposes of required federal or state reporting (*Id.*).

In addition, when sending any such test results to parents, school districts must clearly and conspicuously notify them of this requirement and that the test results are being shared with them for diagnostic purposes (§ 305(46); 8 NYCRR § 104.3(b)).

State Assessment Requirements Grades 9 – 12

56:11. What state assessments must public school students take to obtain a high school diploma?

Generally, to obtain a high school diploma, public school students must take and pass Regents examinations in:

- English.
- Math.
- Global History and Geography.
- U.S. History and Government.
- Science (8 NYCRR § 100.5(a)(5)(i)).

However, the commissioner of education may approve the use of alternative assessments in place of the above (8 NYCRR § 100.5(a)(5)(ii); see also 8 NYCRR § 100.2(f)).

56:12. Are there any minimum scores students must achieve on required state assessments to obtain a high school diploma?

Yes. All students entering grade nine in September 2008 and thereafter must attain a score of 65 or above on all the Regents examinations required to earn a Regents diploma, or a Regents diploma with advanced designation (8 NYCRR § 100.5(a)(7)(ix); see **56:11**).

However, it may be possible for a student who fails to attain a passing score of 65 on one of the Regents exams to still earn a Regents diploma if that student is eligible to appeal his or her score, and the appeal is accepted (8 NYCRR § 100.5(d)(7)(i), (v); see **56:14**).

Minimum scores apply as well for students with disabilities earning a local diploma. In their case, a score of 55 – 64 is considered a passing score on any of the Regents examinations required for graduation for purposes of awarding such students a local high school diploma (8 NYCRR § 100.5(b)(7)(vi)(b); see also 8 NYCRR § 100.5(a)(5)(i)(a)(3), (b)(3), (c)(4), (d)(3), (e)(5)). However, students with disabilities may, for purposes of earning a local diploma, compensate a score of 45-54 on a Regents examination required for graduation, other than English or math, with a score of 65 or higher on one of the other required Regents examinations, subject to conditions set out in commissioner regulations (8 NYCRR § 100.5(b)(7)(vi)(c)).

The previous *safety net option* that allowed students with disabilities to earn a local high school diploma by passing one or more Regents competency tests was available only to students who entered grade nine prior to September 2011 (8 NYCRR § 100.5(a)(5)(i)(a)(3), (b)(3), (c)(4), (d)(3), (e)(5)), until they graduate with a regular diploma (Regents or local) or the end of the school year in which they turn 21 (see **54:12**).

56:13. May students retake Regents exams to improve their score and meet the requirements for a Regents diploma?

Yes. School districts must provide unlimited opportunities for all students to retake required Regents examinations to improve their scores (8 NYCRR § 100.5(d)(7)(i)).

56:14. May students appeal their score on a required Regents exam?

Yes, in some cases. Such an appeal may be initiated by a student, or the student's parent(s) or teacher (8 NYCRR § 100.5(d)(7)(ii)), but only if the student is eligible to proceed with such an appeal. At the outset, the student must have failed to attain a score of 65 or above after at least two attempts. Moreover, appeals are limited to scores on no more than two of the five Regents examinations required for graduation (8 NYCRR § 100.5(d)(7)(i); see **56:11**).

In addition, with respect to the subject area of the Regents examination under appeal, the student must have:

- Scored within five points of the 65 passing score and attained at least a 65 course average,
- Received academic intervention services,
- Attained a course average that meets or exceeds the school's required passing grade and is recorded on the student's official transcript with grades achieved by the student in each quarter of the school year, and
- Been recommended for an exemption to the passing score by his or her teacher or department chairperson (8 NYCRR § 100.5(d)(7)(i)(a)).

A similar opportunity to appeal a score between 55 and 61 on the required Regents English language arts for graduation is available to students who are identified as English language learners pursuant to Part 154 of commissioner's regulations, first entered school in the United States in either of grades 9 – 12 and are otherwise eligible to graduate (8 NYCRR § 100.5(d)(7)(i)(b)).

For purposes of obtaining a local diploma, students identified as having a disability defined in section 200.1(zz) of the commissioner's regulations may appeal a score below 55 on up to two of the required Regents examinations for graduation after at least two attempts. Such a student, however, must have scored within three points of a score of 55 on the required Regents examination under appeal and attained at least a 65 course average in the subject area of the Regents examination under appeal. In addition, a student with disabilities who elects to compensate a score of 45 – 54 on a Regents examination required for graduation, other than the English and mathematics examinations, by a score of 65 or higher on one of the other required Regents examinations may not appeal a score below 55 on the English language arts or mathematics Regents examination (8 NYCRR § 100.5(d)(7)(i)(c); see also 8 NYCRR § 100.5(b)(7)(vi)(c)).

The school superintendent, or in New York City the Chancellor or his or her designee, makes the final determination to accept or deny such an appeal (8 NYCRR § 100.5(d)(7)(iv)).

Students who successfully appeal their score on one required Regents exam and attain a passing scorc of at least 65 on the remaining four will earn a Regents diploma. But those who successfully appeal their score on two required Regents exams qualify to earn only a local diploma even if they score 65 or above on the remaining three (8 NYCRR § 100.5(d)(7)(v)).

56:15. Are there any restrictions as to who may take a Regents examination?

Generally, all students who have studied a subject at an approved school for at least a period of time not less than what has been prescribed by the commissioner of education have the right to take a Regents examination at such school (8 NYCRR § 8.2(a)). Others who may be entitled to be admitted to Regents examinations include those:

- Seeking to demonstrate academic proficiency acquired through independent, out-of-school or other study, at the discretion of the principal of the school administering the examination(s).
- Who are school district residents beyond the compulsory education age and are seeking to earn a degree in accordance with section 3.47(a)(2)(ii)(f) of the Rules of the Board of Regents (8 NYCRR § 8.2(b)), subject to other requirements set out in those Rules (*Id.*).

Anyone taking the Regents science exam must have satisfactorily met the laboratory requirements stated in the state syllabus for that science (8 NYCRR § 8.2(c)).

56:16. Can school districts preclude students who fail a local qualifying examination from taking a Regents exam?

No. While school boards may set requirements for admissions and for high school graduation that are more stringent than those prescribed by the state, they may not prohibit a student who has not met those requirements from taking a Regents examination, provided that student meets the requirements set by the Board of Regents (see 8 NYCRR § 8.2).

56:17. What can school districts do if students commit fraud in a Regents exam?

If a local administrator responsible for giving the examination concludes there is sufficient evidence of a student committing, or attempting to commit, fraud, he or she may cancel the examination, and exclude the student from further exams until that student has demonstrated by exemplary conduct and citizenship, to the administrator's satisfaction, that he or she is entitled to the restoration of this privilege.

Fraud includes the use of unfair means to pass an examination, giving aid to, or obtaining aid from, another person in any examination, alteration of any Regents pass card or other credential, and intentional misrepresentation in connection with examinations or credentials.

A student accused of fraud must be given an opportunity to make satisfactory explanations, including the right to appear before the school board or the board's designee with his or her parents and, if so desired by the parent(s), an attorney. All making such an appearance must be able to ask questions of the examiner(s) and others having direct personal knowledge of the facts.

In each instance where fraud is established, the administrator must promptly report to the commissioner of education the name of the student involved and a brief description of circumstances (8 NYCRR § 102.4; see also *Matter of Pellinger,* 20 Ed Dept Rep 53 (1980), regarding the level of evidence required in such cases).

School Report Cards

56:18. Must school districts report student results in state assessments?

Yes. As part of the district's school report card, each public school district must annually provide to the NYS Education Department the results of state assessments as part of the records required to be submitted to the commissioner of education (8 NYCRR § 100.2(bb)(2)).

In addition, Education Law § 3211-a requires that schools report the standardized reading test results of any student who scores at or below the 23rd percentile to his or her parents or guardian. School districts also must provide either a certified teacher of reading or other appropriate school district personnel to interpret the score of a child whose parents have requested an interpretation of such test results.

56:19. Must the state issue a school report card?

Yes. Under commissioner's regulations, the NYS Education Department (SED) issues an annual report card for each public school and school district to measure students' progress based on information it receives annually on educational programs and services, student performance and fiscal data from each public school district and each nonpublic school (8 NYCRR § 100.2(m) see **56:18**). In New York City, the chancellor produces a New York City School Report Card, as approved by the commissioner of education (8 NYCRR § 100.2(m)(1)).

The New York State School Report Card for each public school and school district (except the New York City School District) consists of three reports prepared by SED:

- the New York State report card,
- the New York State accountability report, and
- the fiscal supplement (8 NYCRR § 100.2(m)(1)).

In addition, the commissioner must issue a separate school progress report card that includes, in part, an assessment of a school's progress in achieving standards of excellence. The purpose of such a progress report card is to assist school boards, the state and the public in assessing the performance of school leaders, including school superintendents and building principals, and the schools that they lead. The school progress report card must be attached to the statement of estimated expenditures concerning a school district's budget. It also must be made available in the same manner as the school district report card (§ 305(39); see **56:20**).

56:20. Are school districts required to distribute their school report card?

Yes. Each school board must make available its report card by appending it to the proposed school budget that must be made available to the public at least 14 days before the budget vote, making it available for distribution at the annual meeting, transmitting it to local newspapers of general circulation, and making it available to parents (§§ 1716(6), 2554(24), 2590-e(8), 2601-a(7); 8 NYCRR § 100.2(m)(3); see **18:8**).

56:21. Are boards of cooperative educational services (BOCES) required to prepare a report card?

Yes. Each year, every BOCES must prepare a BOCES report card that includes the following components:

- Measures of the academic performance of the BOCES educational services – on a school-by-school or program-by-program basis, the academic performance indicators applicable for BOCES services, with a program evaluation based on academic performance for services provided by BOCES centers to component districts.
- Measures of the fiscal performance of the supervisory district – The per student expenditures that must be included in the annual report by the Board of Regents to the Governor and the Legislature,

a summary of BOCES expenditures for administration, program and capital, and a comparison of such measures of fiscal performance to statewide averages for all BOCES.

- Other measures that support the achievement of higher standards, such as curriculum and staff development activities, compared to statewide averages for all BOCES.
- Violent or disruptive incident report – summary of the BOCES' annual violent or disruptive incident report in a format prescribed by the commissioner of education (§ 1950(4)(kk); 8 NYCRR § 100.2(cc)).

BOCES must make available their report card by appending it to copies of the proposed administrative budget, making it available for distribution at the annual meeting, transmitting it to local newspapers of general circulation, making it available to parents, and otherwise disseminating it as required by the commissioner (§ 1950(4)(kk); 8 NYCRR § 100.2(cc)).

Student Report Cards and Progress Reports

56:22. Must school districts issue student progress reports, in the form of report cards, to parents or guardians?

Not generally, although most school districts provide parents or guardians with progress reports generally prepared by the students' teachers, which provide information on grades, attendance, conduct, and other relevant data. Report cards are issued each quarter in most districts. Districts also may send out additional information on student progress or lack of progress in the form of interim reports when a student is failing a course or has attained a noteworthy achievement.

However, for students who are receiving academic intervention services (see **55:29-35**), school districts are required to provide progress reports at least once each quarter during the regular school year. The reports must be sent to the student's parent(s) by mail, telephone, telecommunications, or other means in a language or other mode of communication understood by the parents. In addition, parents must be provided with information on ways to work with their child and educators to improve the child's achievement, and ways to monitor their child's progress (8 NYCRR § 100.2(ee)(6)(iii)(b), see **55:35**).

Similarly, school districts must issue student progress reports that provide parents or persons in parental relation with information on their child's performance on state assessments over multiple years of testing and explain the process by which they may obtain further information about their child's progress. Such reports must be written in plain English and in a form prescribed by the commissioner of education (§ 305(36)).

School Accountability

Editor's Note: At the time this publication went to press, the New York Board of Regents and State Education Department were involved in the process of determining how to implement in New York the federal Every Student Succeeds Act (ESSA) of 2015. The 2016-17 school year constitutes a year of transition during which school districts with priority and focus schools continue to implement the school improvement interventions that were in place during the 2015-16 school year.

Pending adoption of federal regulations and state statutory and regulatory changes, this section highlights the more basic school accountability aspects of ESSA. Citations references are to the statute itself.

56:23. How are underperforming schools identified under ESSA?

ESSA classifies underperforming schools into one of two accountability categories – comprehensive support and improvement schools and targeted support and improvement schools (§§ 1111(c)(4)(D)(i), (d)(1), (2)). In their discretion, states can establish additional statewide categories (§ 1111(c)(4)(D)(ii)).

Comprehensive support and improvement schools include, at least, the lowest performing five percent of all schools receiving Title I Part A funds, and all high schools failing to graduate one third or more of their students (§ 1111(c)(4), (d)(i)).

Targeted support and improvement schools are those with at least one consistently underperforming accountability group (§ 1111(d)(2)).

56:24. What are the accountability groups monitored under ESSA?

The *accountability groups* monitored under ESSA include:

- all students,
- economically disadvantaged students,
- students from major racial and ethnic background,
- children with disabilities, and
- English learners (§ 1111(c)(2)).

56:25. Does ESSA require states to adopt state academic standards?

Yes. ESSA requires that states receiving Title I Part I funds adopt *challenging state academic standards* that consist of challenging academic content standards and aligned academic achievement standards. The achievement standards must include at least three levels of achievement and the same knowledge, skills, and levels of achievement expected of all public school students in the state (§ 1111(b)(1)(A), (B)(ii)).

States must have challenging academic standards for mathematics, reading or language arts, and science (§ 1111(b)(1)(C)). The same challenging state academic standards must apply to all public schools and public school students across the state (§ 1111(b)(1)(B)(i)).

In addition, a state's challenging academic state standards must be aligned with entrance requirements for credit-bearing coursework in the State's system of public higher education, and relevant state career and technical education standards (§ 1111(b)(1)(D)(i)).

56:26. Does ESSA require states to administer student academic assessments?

Yes. ESSA requires that states implement a set of high quality student academic assessments in mathematics, reading or language arts, and science that must be administered at the various grade levels set out in the statute. For example, mathematics and reading or language arts assessments must be administered in each of grades 3 – 8 and at least once in grades 9 – 12. Science assessments must be administered not less than one time during grades 3 – 5, 6 – 9, and 10 – 12 (§ 1111(b)(2)(A), (B)(ii)).

56:27. What measures are used under ESSA to hold schools accountable for the performance of their students?

For such purpose, ESSA establishes four accountability indicators that include:

- Academic achievement as measure by state assessments,
- High school graduation rates,
- Progress of English learners in achieving English proficiency, and
- At least one indicator of school quality or student success.

The latter must allow for meaningful differentiation in school performance and be valid, reliable, comparable and of state-wide applicability. It may include student or educator engagement, student access to and completion of advanced coursework, postsecondary readiness, school climate and safety, and any other indicator that the state chooses (§ 1111(c)(4)(B)).

56:28. What happens after a school is identified as underperforming under ESSA?

Once identified as either a comprehensive support and improvement school or a targeted support and improvement school (see **56:23**), the school must develop a plan to improve student outcomes in partnership with the various stakeholders set out in the statute (§ 1111(d)(1)(B), (2)(B)).

In general, a comprehensive support and improvement plan must be based on a school level needs assessment and approved by the school, the school district, and the NYS Education Department (SED) as the state educational agency. SED monitors the implementation of the plan (§ 1111(d)(1)(B)). In comparison, a targeted support and improvement plan must be based on the needs of the underperforming accountability group(s). It is approved and monitored by the school district. (§ 1111(d)(2)(B)).

In addition, SED, as the state educational agency, may take action to initiate additional improvement in any school district with a significant number of schools that are either:

- Consistently identified for comprehensive support and improvement and not meeting the state-established criteria for exiting that designation (see **56:29**), or
- Implementing targeted support and improvement plans (§ 1111(d)(3)(B); see also § 1111(d)(3)(A)(i)).

A targeted support and improvement school with a subgroup that places the school in the lowest performing five percent and fails to meet the state-established exit criteria will be identified as a comprehensive support and improvement school (§ 1111(d)(3)(A)(iii)).

56:29. Can a school identified as underperforming under ESSA exit its accountability status?

Yes. The NYS Education Department, as the state educational agency, is required to establish statewide criteria for schools identified as either a comprehensive support and improvement school or a targeted support and improvement school (§ 1111(d)(3)(A)(i); see **56:23**). It also must provide technical assistance to school districts serving a significant number of such schools (§ 1111(d)(3)(A)(iii)).

Receivership

56:30. What constitutes receivership?

Receivership is basically the taking over and restructuring of struggling schools (L. 2015, c. 56 pt. EE, subpart H).

56:31. What types of struggling schools are deemed receivership schools?

Schools subject to receivership include:

- *Struggling schools*, which include those identified as a priority school for at least three consecutive school years and those falling among the lowest achieving five percent of public schools in the state, as set out in statute (§ 211-f (1)(a); 8 NYCRR § 100.19 (a)(1), (3)).
- *Persistently struggling schools*, which include those identified as a priority school for ten consecutive school years, as specified in the statute (§ 211-f (1)(b); 8 NYCRR § 100.19(a)(2)).
- *Schools newly designated as struggling*, which include those designated as a struggling school after the 2016-2017 school year (§ 211-f (1)(c)(ii)).

Struggling and persistently struggling schools do not include schools within a special act school district, or a charter school (§ 211-f (1)(a), (b); 8 NYCRR § 100.19(a)(1), (2)).

A school under receivership continues to operate in accordance with laws applicable to other public schools, unless such other laws conflict with the provisions of the receivership statute (§ 211-f (2)(c)).

56:32. Is there more than one type of receivership?

Yes. A *school district superintendent receivership* is applicable to struggling and persistently struggling schools as set out in law and regulation (§ 211-f (1)(c)(i), (ii); 8 NYCRR §100.19(a)(5)). *Independent receiverships* are applicable to schools newly designated as struggling after the 2016-2017 school year, and to struggling and persistently struggling schools that fail to make demonstrable improvement under a school district superintendent receivership (§ 211-f (1)(c)(i), (ii)).

56:33. Who can serve as a receiver?

A *school district superintendent receiver* is a school superintendent, or other chief school officer, of a district with one or more schools designated as struggling or persistently dangerous (see **56:31**) and in New York City the Chancellor or his/her designee, or an educational partnership organization that has assumed the powers and duties of the school superintendent for purposes of implementing the educational program of the school (8 NYCRR § 100.19 (a)(5), (9)).

An *independent receiver* can be a non-profit entity, an individual with a proven track record of improving school performance, or another school district in good standing appointed by a school district and approved by the commissioner of education. However, an individual serving as an independent receiver may not be an existing officer or employee of the school district at the time of such appointment (§ 211-f (2)(a); 8 NYCRR § 100.19(a)(6)).

56:34. What are the powers and duties of a receiver?

A school district superintendent receiver is vested with all the powers granted to an independent receiver, except that the superintendent or educational partnership organization, as applicable, (see **56:33**) may not override any decision of the school board regarding their employment (8 NYCRR § 100.19(a)(5); (d)(3), (g)(6)).

An independent receiver has the authority to manage and operate all aspects of the school (§ 211-f (2)(a), (c); 8 NYCRR § 100.19(a)(6), (d)(3), (g)(1)), and develop and implement a school intervention plan for the designated school that considers the recommendations of a statutorily established community engagement team (§ 211-f (2)(a); 8 NYCRR § 100.19(a)(6), (e)(4)(v)). In addition, the independent receiver can supersede any decision, policy or regulation of the superintendent or chief school officer, school board, another school officer, or the building principal that, in the receiver's sole judgment, conflicts with the school intervention plan. Such authority, however, does not apply to decisions that are not directly linked to the school intervention plan such as building usage plans, co-location, and student transportation to the extent that such decisions impact other schools in the district (§ 211-f (2)(b); 8 NYCRR § 100.19(g)(6)). Moreover, before exercising his or her supersession authority, an independent receiver must follow the process set out in the commissioner's regulations (8 NYCRR § 100.19(g)(7)).

Furthermore, an independent receiver has authority over:

- Instructional programs, including curriculum and program offerings (§ 211-f(7)(a)(i); 8 NYCRR § 100.19(g)(3)(i)), the length of school day and school year (§ 211-f(7)(a)(vi); 8 NYCRR § 100.19(g)(3)(vi)), and the addition of pre-kindergarten and full-day kindergarten classes as set forth in law and regulation (§ 211-f(7)(a)(vii); 8 NYCRR § 100.19(g)(3)(vii)).

- The school budget, including modification of the proposed budget in accordance with procedures set out in commissioner's regulations (§ 211-f(2)(b); 8 NYCRR § 100.19(g)(8)).
- Employment decisions, including replacement of teachers and administrators who are not properly certified, increasing salaries, and establishing steps (§ 211-f(7)(b)(ii), (iii), (iv); 8 NYCRR § 100.19(g)(3)(ii)-(iv)). Nonetheless, the school board remains the employer of record for the school (§ 211-f(2)(c)).
- Abolition of positions of all members of the teaching and administrative and supervisory staff assigned to the school, termination of the school building principal (§ 211-f(7)(a)(viii); 8 NYCRR § 100.19(g)(4)), and definition of new positions (§ 211-f(7)(c)).
- School conversions to community schools to provide expanded health, mental health and other services to students and their families (§ 211-f(7)(a); 8 NYCRR § 100.19(a)(6), (8), (g)(2)). In comparison, a school district superintendent receiver (see **56:33**) may but does not have to convert a receivership school (see **56:31**) into a community school (8 NYCRR § 100.19(a)(5), (d)(3), (g)(1)).
- Professional development, including job-embedded professional development for teachers (§ 211-f(7)(a)(ix)-(x), (d); 8 NYCRR § 100.19(g)(3)(vii), (ix)).

56:35. How do schools in receivership operate?

Persistently struggling and struggling schools under a school district superintendent receivership must operate under an intervention model or comprehensive education plan approved by the NYS Education Department, that includes rigorous performance metrics and goals, such as measures of student academic achievement and outcomes that include those set out in the receivership statute (§ 211-f (2)(c)(i), (ii), (6); 8 NYCRR § 100.19(a)(12)). Such schools do not have to create and implement a school intervention plan (8 NYCRR § 100.19(a)(5), (d)(3), (g)(1)).

On the other hand, independent receivers operating persistently struggling and struggling schools must develop and implement a school intervention plan within six months of appointment (§ 211-f (3)-(6); 8 NYCRR § 100.19(a)(13), (f), (g)(2)). The school intervention plan is subject to approval by the commissioner of education (§ 211-f (9)-(10); 8 NYCRR § 100.19(f)(9), (10)).

56:36. What happens after a receivership school starts operating under an intervention model or comprehensive education plan?

The commissioner of education will conduct a performance review of a receivership school operating under a school district superintendent receiver (see **56:32-33**) in consultation with the school district, the school's staff and the community engagement team:

- at the end of one school year for persistently struggling schools;
- at the end of two school years for struggling schools; and
- annually for any persistently struggling or struggling school that the commissioner determines made demonstrable progress and should continue under a school district superintendent receiver.

The purpose of the performance review is to determine whether the school will:

- be removed from its persistently struggling or struggling designation;
- remain under a school district superintendent receiver, in which case the school remains subject to annual review; or
- be placed under an independent receiver, subject to the annual evaluation provisions applicable to independent receiverships (8 NYCRR § 100.19(d)(5), (6)).

A receivership school operating under a school district superintendent receiver would be required to appoint an independent receiver if the commissioner revokes a prior approval of an intervention model or comprehensive education plan (8 NYCRR § 100.19(d)(7)).

56:37. What happens after a receivership school starts operating under a school intervention plan?

At least annually, the commissioner of education will evaluate each school with an independent receiver to determine whether the school has met the intervention plan's goals, and assess the plan's implementation (§ 211-f (12)(a); 8 NYCRR § 100.19(h)(1)). Based upon the evaluation findings, the commissioner may allow implementation of the school intervention plan to continue, or require that the plan be modified (§ 211-f (12)(b); 8 NYCRR § 100.19(h)(2)).

Upon the expiration of a school intervention plan, the commissioner will evaluate the school to determine whether the school has either improved sufficiently, requires further improvement, or failed to improve. Based on the findings, the commissioner may:

- Renew implementation of the intervention plan with the independent receiver for an additional period of not more than three years,
- Terminate the receiver and appoint a new one if the school remains struggling and the terms of the intervention plan were not substantially met, or
- Remove the school from its struggling or persistently struggling status if it has improved sufficiently for such purposes (§ 211-f (13); 8 NYCRR § 100.19(h)(2), (i)).

If the independent receiver is terminated, the commissioner may appoint an interim independent receiver. A newly appointed independent receiver must continue to implement the existing school intervention plan until a new one is developed and approved by the commissioner (8 NYCRR § 100.19(e)(3), (i)(1)(ii), (3)).

57. Transportation of Public School Students

Duty to Transport Students

57:1. Must a school district furnish school bus transportation for students residing within the district?

Yes. School districts, except city school districts, are required to transport all students in grades kindergarten through 12, in accordance with statutory or voter adopted distance limitations, including those attending nonpublic schools and charter schools (§§ 2853(4)(b), 3635; see **57:18, 58:1-8**). However, they have no authority to transport a child of less than school age, except where the child is accompanying a parent under age 21 to and from the parent's school (§ 3635(1)(f); *Appeal of a Pre-School Child with a Disability*, 43 Ed Dept Rep 343 (2004)). A district may transport prekindergarten children in only two instances. First, to those attending a state-approved, universal prekindergarten program sponsored by the district (§ 3602-e; 8 NYCRR § 151-1.2(a); *Appeal of McColgan*, 47 Ed Dept Rep 132, *aff'd, Bd. of Educ. of Lawrence UFSD Dist. No. 15 v. McColgan*, 18 Misc.3d 572 (Sup. Ct. Albany Cnty. 2007); see also *Appeal of Neubauer*, 32 Ed Dept Rep 320 (1992)). Second, to those attending another district-sponsored or district-run prekindergarten program subject to statutory conditions (§ 3635(1)(g)).

City school districts may, but are not required to, provide transportation (§ 3635(1)(c); *Appeal of Abeido*, 55 Ed Dept Rep, Dec. No. 16,859 (2016); *Appeal of D.G.*, 55 Ed Dept Rep, Dec. No. 16,833 (2015)). If it is provided, the transportation must be based on a reasonable and consistent policy that treats all children "in like circumstances" in a similar manner (*Ignizio v. City of N.Y.*, 85 A.D.3d 1171 (2d Dep't 2011)). However, students in different grade levels are not considered to be in "like circumstances" (*Appeal of Naranjo,* 51 Ed Dept Rep, Dec. No. 16,281 (2011); *Appeal of Kates,* 49 Ed Dept Rep 138 (2009); *Appeal of Cassin*, 32 Ed Dept Rep 373 (1992); *Matter of Cooper*, 5 Ed Dept Rep 31 (1965)). Therefore, a city school district may, for instance, provide transportation to students in certain grades and not others, based on its policy (*Ignizio v. City of N.Y.; Appeal of Cassin*). It also may choose to provide transportation based on both grade level and distance from school considerations (see *Appeal of Naranjo*).

In enlarged city school districts, transportation is required only for students residing outside the city limits, but it also may be provided to children living within the city limits (§ 2503(12)). An enlarged city school district may distinguish, in its transportation policy, between students residing within the city limits and those residing in areas of the enlarged city school district outside of the corporate boundaries of the city (*Matter of Collar*, 14 Ed Dept Rep 327 (1975)).

A district's mistake in providing transportation to students not eligible for such services cannot serve as a basis for continuing to provide inappropriate transportation. Instead, the solution to the mistake is to discontinue such transportation (*Appeal of Milliman-Estus*, 52 Ed Dept Rep, Dec. No. 16,394 (2012); *Appeal of McDermott,* 49 Ed Dept Rep 37 (2009); *Appeal of Keller*, 47 Ed Dept Rep 224 (2007)), even if there are empty seats on the bus (*Appeal of Ruescher,* 50 Ed Dept Rep, Dec. No. 16,245 (2011)).

57:2. Are all students entitled to the same transportation services?

No. Students receiving transportation services under section 3635 (see **57:1**) may be treated differently than children transported to and from school under other statutes (*Appeal of Neubauer*, 32 Ed Dept Rep 320 (1992)). For example, a school district that provides transportation to students with disabilities under the provisions of Article 89 of the Education Law is not required to transport students attending regular education beyond the distance limitations of section 3635 (see **57:18**), even if students with disabilities are transported a longer distance (*Appeal of Guiney*, 34 Ed Dept Rep 410 (1995)).

Similarly, students transported to a board of cooperative educational services pursuant to section 1950 of the Education Law may be transported for greater distances and are not considered to be in like circumstances to those transported under section 3635 (*Matter of Antonucci*, 21 Ed Dept Rep 93 (1981); *Matter of Frandsen*, 11 Ed Dept Rep 203 (1972); *Matter of Kling*, 10 Ed Dept Rep 8 (1970)).

In addition, homeless students who have designated their district of origin or a school district participating in a regional placement plan for attendance may be transported for distances beyond the limitations applicable to students transported under section 3635. However, such transportation may not exceed 50 miles one way, unless the commissioner of education determines it is in the best interest of the student (§ 3209(4)(c); 8 NYCRR § 100.2(x)(6)(ii); see **49:42**).

Furthermore, pursuant to the federal Every Student Succeeds Act (ESSA), by December 10, 2016, school districts and BOCES are required to develop and implement procedures regarding cost-effective transportation for children in foster care for the duration of the time they are in foster care (§ 1112(c)(5)).

57:3. Must a school district provide transportation to students who move to the district after the district budget has been passed and bus routes approved?

Yes, if the parents or guardians submit a written request within 30 days after establishing residency in the district. No late request may be denied if a reasonable explanation is provided for the delay. However, a statement by the parents that they were not aware of their obligation to submit a timely transportation request normally would not constitute a reasonable explanation for delay (§ 3635(2); *Appeal of Thomas*, 45 Ed Dept Rep 528 (2006)). Personal hardship is also not a basis for granting a late transportation request (*Appeal of Soler*, 51 Ed Dept Rep, Dec. No. 16,284 (2011)).

57:4. Must a school district furnish school bus transportation for resident students attending school outside their attendance zone?

Yes. Except as otherwise provided, the Education Law requires that school districts transport students to and from the school "they legally attend" (§ 3635(1); see **57:1-2**). According to the commissioner of education, if a district allows a child to attend a district school other than the one the child would normally be assigned to, the school outside the child's attendance zone becomes the school the child legally attends. As such, the district has a legal obligation to transport that child to and from school (*Appeal of Nicotri*, 38 Ed Dept Rep 80 (1998)).

However, when a child is permitted to attend a nonattendance zone school, the child's parent may agree to waive the provision of transportation that would otherwise be required (§ 3635(7)). The waiver must be voluntary (*Appeal of Jongebloed*, 16 Ed Dept Rep 385 (1977)) and the agreement to waive transportation must be renewed annually in writing (§ 3635(7)).

57:5. Must a school district provide transportation for resident students attending public school in another school district?

Not if the district of residence offers an instructional program for the student (*Appeal of C.C. and E.C.*, 48 Ed Dept Rep 528 (2009); *Appeal of M.G. and J.G.*, 40 Ed Dept Rep 336 (2000); *Appeal of Ortiz*, 34

Ed Dept Rep 341 (1995); *Appeal of Franzenburg*, 33 Ed Dept Rep 284 (1993)). This means, for example, that if a school district offers a middle school program, it does not have to provide transportation to a resident student attending a middle school program in another school district (*Appeal of C.C. and E.C.*).

57:6. Must a district provide transportation for a student attending summer school?

No. In *Appeal of Stamler*, 38 Ed Dept Rep 292 (1998), the commissioner of education ruled that a school district did not have to transport a district resident attending summer school in a neighboring district, even when the district had voluntarily agreed to pay the summer school tuition. The commissioner also noted that a school board is not obligated to provide transportation to and from any summer school program, except for students with disabilities in accordance with state law.

Nonetheless, a school district may elect to provide transportation to and from a district-operated summer school program (see NYS Education Department, *Handbook for Summer School Administrators and Principals* (Apr. 2015), at: http://www.p12.nysed.gov/sss/documents/2015_Summer_School_Handbook.pdf).

Transportation to and from approved summer school programs operated by a school district is eligible for state aid, subject to a prorated share of a state-wide cap of $5 million (§ 3622-a(6)).

57:7. Must a school district transport children of divorced parents to different locations on different days of the week?

No. According to the commissioner of education, a student can only have a single residence for school purposes even when that student's parents are divorced (see **49:9**). There is no statutory or regulatory requirement that a district transport a student whose parents share joint custody to one parent's home on some days of the week and to the other parent's home on different days of the week (*Appeal of Dickinson*, 39 Ed Dept Rep 41 (1999); *Appeal of Van Der Jagt*, 33 Ed Dept Rep 517 (1994)).

57:8. May a school district provide transportation between school and child care centers?

Yes. A school board may provide, at its discretion, transportation to any child attending kindergarten through eighth grade between a child's school and before and/or after-school child care locations in accordance with the district's general transportation mileage limitations. The Education Law defines a child care location as a place within the district, other than the child's home, where care for less than 24 hours a day is provided on a regular basis (§ 3635(1)(e)). "A regular basis" does not necessarily mean on a daily basis and a district may not deny transportation to a child care location just because a student is not to be transported there every day.

Once a board determines the district will provide transportation to child care locations, the transportation must be provided in accordance with the requirements of section 3635(1)(e) of the Education Law. Moreover, a child may be eligible for transportation between school and a child care location if it is within the district's mileage limitation even though the child would not otherwise be eligible for transportation between home and school (*Appeal of Berkins*, 39 Ed Dept Rep 620 (2000)).

However, a board may limit transportation to child care locations located within the attendance zone of the school the child attends and anywhere within the district for child care locations licensed pursuant to section 390 of the Social Services Law (§ 3635(1)(e); *Appeal of Tighe*, 47 Ed Dept Rep 206 (2007); *Appeal of Grove*, 33 Ed Dept Rep 176 (1993)). There is no statutory authority for a school district to provide transportation to a child care location outside of the district (*Appeal of Krevoy*, 48 Ed Dept Rep 103 (2008); *Appeal of a Student Suspected of Having a Disability*, 38 Ed Dept Rep 507 (1999)).

Upon request, a district providing transportation to a child care location would have to transport a student to his or her child care location on some days and his or her home on other days where both locations are within the district's mileage limitations (*Appeal of Seibt*, 40 Ed Dept Rep 186 (2002)).

The child's parents must request child care transportation in writing no later than April 1 preceeding the next school year, except where the family moves into the district later than April 1. In that case, the request must be made within 30 days of establishing residency in the district (§ 3635(1)(e)).

The cost of providing transportation between school and child care centers is state-aidable.

57:9. Must a school district transport back to school all students attending a field trip or extracurricular activity?

When a school district or board of cooperative education services provides students with transportation to a school-sponsored field trip, extracurricular activity, or any other similar event, it must transport those students back to either the point of departure, or an appropriate school, unless the student's parent or guardian has provided the school district with written notice, consistent with district policy, authorizing an alternative form of return transportation for the student. If the parent has not authorized alternative return transportation and intervening circumstances make such return transportation by the school district impractical, a district representative must contact the student(s)' parents and inform them of such intervening circumstances, and remain with the student(s) until each has been delivered to his or her parent (§§ 1604(41), 1709(41), 1804(11), 1903(2), 1950(19), 2503(20), 2554(27), 2590-e(10)).

57:10. What type of arrangements can school districts make to transport students?

School boards have broad discretion in determining the manner in which they will provide transportation to their students, after balancing safety, convenience, efficiency and cost. Moreover, a school board has both the responsibility and the authority to decide difficult questions in balancing the overall efficiency and economy of a transportation system against the convenience of individual students (*Appeal of Yavno*, 55 Ed Dept Rep, Dec. No. 16,884 (2016); *Appeal of D.G.*, 55 Ed Dept Rep, Dec. No. 16,833 (2015); *Appeal of Kyle*, 53 Ed Dept Rep, Dec. No. 16,626 (2014)). A district may provide transportation through any of the following means:

- Purchase or lease and maintain their own fleet of buses (§§ 1709(25), 1804(1), 1903(1), 2503(12), 3623).
- Contract with others including a person, corporation, another school district, a county, municipality, state office of children and family services, or boards of cooperative educational services (BOCES) (§§ 1604(21-b), 1709(25)(g), (h), (27), 1804(1), 1903(1), 1950(4)(q), 2503(12), 3625).
- Participate in regional transportation services jointly with other school districts or BOCES (§§ 1604(21-b), 1709(25)(g), (h), 1950(4)(q), 3621(8), (9); see **57:13**).
- Contract with parents for transporting their own children (*Matter of Antonette*, 18 Ed Dept Rep 413 (1979), subject to certain limitations (see **57:14**).
- Use private carriers and/or public transportation (*Appeal of Countryman*, 51 Ed Dept Rep, Dec. No 16,267 (2011); *Appeal of A.P.*, 48 Ed Dept Rep 380 (2009); *Appeal of Clancy*, 37 Ed Dept Rep 280 (1998); *Appeal of Bruner*, 32 Ed Dept Rep 276 (1992); *Appeal of Lavin*, 32 Ed Dept Rep 249 (1992); see **57:12**).

Until June 30, 2019, school boards may, in their discretion, provide student transportation based on patterns of actual ridership determined in accordance with criteria set forth in law, or approved by the commissioner of education (§ 3635(8)). This option does not relieve school districts of their responsibility to provide transportation to all students who are eligible, nor are districts authorized to permit standing passengers on school buses (§§ 3635(8)(a), 3635-c).

Districts electing to provide transportation based on patterns of actual ridership must post their plan on their website, if one exists, by August 15 of the school year in which the plan will be implemented. In addition, they must have a back-up plan as part of the district's emergency management practices for student transportation in the event a bus is filled to capacity (§ 3635(8)(a)).

Additional information is available from the NYS Education Department at: http://www.p12.nysed.gov/schoolbus/TransDirector/htm/better_use_of_school_buses.html.

57:11. May school districts use more than one type of transportation arrangement to transport their students?

Yes. School districts may use a combination of transportation methods. They may, for example, transport some students through a private carrier, and others through the use of a public transportation system. The mere fact that some students are transported on private buses does not mean that all must be (*Appeal of Countryman,* 51 Ed Dept Rep, Dec. No. 16,276 (2011); *Appeal of Clancy*, 37 Ed Dept Rep 280 (1998); *Appeal of Tomasso*, 23 Ed Dept Rep 120 (1983)). Similarly, they may transport some students in a 66-passenger bus and others in a 15-passenger van (*Appeal of McCarthy and Bacher*, 42 Ed Dept Rep 329 (2003)).

57:12. May a school district use a public carrier for student transportation?

Yes. The commissioner of education has ruled that a district's use of an existing public transportation system to transport students from school is neither illegal nor unreasonable (*Appeal of Casciano,* 52 Ed Dept Rep, Dec. No. 16,459 (2013); *Appeal of Clancy,* 37 Ed Dept Rep 280 (1998)). Occasionally, some districts do this by providing the students with bus tickets, a bus pass, or railroad tickets (*Ignizio v. City of N.Y.*, 85 A.D.3d 1171 (2d Dep't 2011); *Appeal of L.A.*, 55 Ed Dept Rep, Dec. No. 16,859 (2015); *Appeal of Countryman,* 51 Ed Dept Rep, Dec. No. 16,276 (2011); *Appeal of Schuler*, 43 Ed Dept Rep 490 (2004)). However, they may not advance cash for this purpose.

In addition, the mere fact that some students are transported on private buses does not mean that all must be (*Ignizio v. City of N.Y.; Appeal of Clancy; Appeal of Tomasso*, 23 Ed Dept Rep 120 (1983); see **57:11**).

57:13. May a school district provide regional transportation services?

Yes. A regional transportation system may include transportation:

- between home and school,
- during the day to and from school and a special education program or service, a board of cooperative educational services (BOCES) program, or an approved program at another school district,
- transportation for field trips or to and from extracurricular activities, and
- cooperative bus maintenance (§§ 1604(21-b), 1709(25)(g), (h)).

These regional services may be conducted jointly with other school districts or BOCES (§§ 1709(25)(g), 1950(4)(q), 3621(8), (9)). BOCES are authorized to provide transportation to and from BOCES classes at a district's request (§ 1950(4)(q)).

Additional information is available from the NYS Education Department at: http://www.p12.nysed.gov/schoolbus/regional.html.

57:14. Can a school district compensate parents for transporting their own children?

Yes, under certain circumstances. Although a district legally can contract with a parent for a student's transportation, this contract may not exceed the actual cost of the services provided (*Matter of Antonette*, 18 Ed Dept Rep 413 (1979)). In addition, such a contract is subject to competitive bidding. Unless an exemption is granted, the parent must satisfy the requirements of Article 19-A of the Vehicle and Traffic Law and part 156 of the regulations of the commissioner of education (NYS Education Department, *Contracted Transportation by Parents* (updated Sept. 2015), at: http://www.p12.nsed.gov/schoolbus/contracts/html/contracted_transportation_by_parentsd.html); NYS Education Department,

Transportation Contracts Preparation and Filing (updated Sept. 2015), at: https://stateaid.nysed.gov/trans/contract.htm).

According to the NYS Department of Transportation (DOT), parents' vehicles used in the transportation of their own children to and from school, and where the parents are being reimbursed accordingly, are not subject to a DOT inspection. However, if a parent's vehicle is used to transport his or her own children and other children to and from school, and the parent is being reimbursed for transporting other children, that vehicle is subject to a DOT inspection. On the other hand, under either scenario, the parental vehicles will be subject to the Department of Motor Vehicles' inspection program (see 17 NYCRR Part 720; 17 NYCRR § 720.1(w); Veh. & Traf. Law Articles 5 and 19-A; 8 NYCRR Part 156). For additional information contact the NYS Department of Transportation at 518-457-6195 or by visiting their website at: https://www.dot.ny.gov/divisions/operating/osss/bus/school.

57:15. Can a school district charge a fee to transport students?

There is no statute that specifically authorizes a school district to charge a fee for this purpose. However, a commissioner of education's decision that districts may not charge a fee or require a donation as a condition for participation in interscholastic athletic activities implies that such a charge is not permissible (*Matter of Ambrosio*, 30 Ed Dept Rep 387 (1991)).

57:16. Are there any restrictions on the length of time a student should ride to or from school?

No. Neither the Education Law nor the commissioner's regulations specify a maximum time limit for the transportation of students. The commissioner of education has ruled that, depending on the circumstances, one-way trips of up to one-and-one-half hours are not necessarily excessive (*Appeal of Hoffman*, 55 Ed Dept Rep, Dec. No. 16,831 (2015); *Appeal of McCarthy and Bacher*, 42 Ed Dept Rep 329 (2003); *Appeal of Devore*, 36 Ed Dept Rep 326 (1997); *Appeal of Polifka*, 31 Ed Dept Rep 61 (1991)).

Nonetheless, the time spent "en route" to and from school must be reasonable. Reasonableness will depend on factors such as a student's age, the distance between a student's home and school, safety, efficiency, cost, availability of buses, school opening and closing times, and the number of schools covered on a particular trip (NYS Education Department, *Maximum Time That a Pupil May Spend on a Bus* (Sept. 2009), at: http://www.p12.nysed.gov/schoolbus/Parents/htm/MaximumTimeThataPupilMaySpendonaBus.htm).

According to the commissioner, the school board is legally responsible for determining transportation routes and modes of transportation. A school board's transportation determination will be upheld unless the board's actions can be proven to be arbitrary or unreasonable (*Appeal of Devore; Appeal of Polifka; Matter of Rouis*, 20 Ed Dept Rep 493 (1981); *Matter of Lauth*, 2 Ed Dept Rep 484 (1963)).

On the same basis, the commissioner ruled against a parent who argued the school district should adopt a "first on, first off" policy to prevent students who are picked up early in the morning from being the last to be dropped off in the afternoon (*Appeal of Reich*, 38 Ed Dept Rep 565 (1999); *Appeal of Byrne*, 34 Ed Dept Rep 389 (1995)).

57:17. May a student's transportation privileges be suspended?

Yes. The school board and/or the superintendent of schools, not the bus driver, have the authority to suspend the transportation privileges of children who are disorderly and insubordinate. Students' rights to minimal due process applicable in classroom situations are not necessarily applicable to such student transportation cases (*Appeal of R.D.*, 42 Ed Dept Rep 237 (2003); *Appeal of Pennett,* 40 Ed Dept Rep

227 (2000); *Appeal of McGaw*, 28 Ed Dept Rep 84 (1988)). However, a student and his or her parents or guardian must be granted an opportunity to appear informally before the person or body authorized to impose discipline to discuss the factual situation underlying the threatened suspension from transportation (*Appeal of McGaw*; *Matter of Roach*, 19 Ed Dept Rep 377 (1980)). When a district suspends a student's transportation privileges, the parents or guardian of the child involved become responsible for seeing that the child gets to and from school. However, a district must consider the effect of a suspension of transportation on the student's attendance and must make appropriate arrangements for the student's education where the suspension of transportation is tantamount to a suspension from attendance because of the distance between the home and the school and the lack of alternate public or private means of transportation. According to the commissioner of education, a suspension of transportation privileges may not have the effect of depriving the student of education (*Matter of Stewart*, 21 Ed Dept Rep 654 (1982); *Matter of Roach*).

According to the U.S. Department of Education's Office of Civil Rights (OCR), where transportation is a related service, revocation of school bus transportation for an unruly student with disabilities is subject to the same due process protection that applies to the discipline of disabled students unless a school district provides transportation by other means (OCR Response to Inquiry, 20 IDELR 864 (1993)).

Distance Limitations

57:18. Are there any distance limitations for the transportation of students?

Yes. Although door-to-door transportation is not required (*Matter of Boyar*, 21 Ed Dept Rep 286 (1981); see **57:27**), eligibility for transportation is determined by the distance between a child's home and the school a child attends (§ 3635(1); *Studley v. Allen*, 24 A.D.2d 678 (3d Dep't 1965); *Appeal of Wenger*, 37 Ed Dept Rep 5 (1997); *Appeal of Neubauer*, 32 Ed Dept Rep 320 (1992); see **57:19-21**). A district may require children in grades K – 8 to walk a distance of up to two miles, and children in grades 9 – 12 to walk a distance of up to three miles, from their homes to their schools. The district must provide bus transportation up to a distance of 15 miles (§ 3635(1)(a), (c)).

However, transportation for distances less than two miles in the case of children in grade K – 8, or less than three miles in the case of students in grades 9 – 12, and for distances greater than 15 miles may be provided, if the voters approve (*Appeal of Poles*, 55 Ed Dept Rep, Dec. No. 16,800 (2015); *Appeal of Kyle*, 53 Ed Dept Rep, Dec. No. 16,626 (2014); *Appeal of Powell*, 46 Ed Dept Rep 565 (2007)). If transportation is provided, it must be offered equally to all children in like circumstances residing in the district (§ 3635(1)(a); see **57:1**).

The law does not require a district to provide transportation to or from a point other than a student's residence, child care location if such transportation is provided by the district, or pickup point established by school authorities along the route from a student's home to the school legally attended (§ 3635(1)(e); see *Matter of Wasserman*, 15 Ed Dept Rep 278 (1978)).

For information on distance limitations applicable to nonpublic school students, see **58:1-2**.

57:19. How are transportation distance limitations measured?

Distances to determine eligibility for transportation must be measured from home to school by the nearest available publicly maintained route from home to school (§ 3635(1)(a); *Appeal of Keller,* 47 Ed Dept Rep 114 (2007); *Matter of Kluge*, 31 Ed Dept Rep 107 (1991); *Matter of Nowak*, 22 Ed Dept Rep 91 (1982)). For example, a district's use of a footpath through a publicly owned and maintained park for purposes of determining the distance from home to school has been upheld by the commissioner of education and at least one court (*Arlyn Oaks Civic Ass'n v. Brucia*, 171 Misc.2d 634 (Sup. Ct. Nassau Cnty. 1997); *Appeal of Rosen*, 37 Ed Dept Rep 107 (1997)).

In measuring the distance between a child's home and school, a district may not deny a student transportation on the basis that the nearest available route is less safe, less direct and less efficient (*Appeal of Sanguine*, 48 Ed Dept Rep 179 (2008)).

The nearest available route is also the standard a school district must use when measuring the distance between the home and the nonpublic school attended by a student with disabilities to receive special education services similar to those recommended by the district's committee on special education (*Appeal of a Student with a Disability*, 48 Ed Dept Rep 223 (2008); see also § 4402(4)(d)). For more information on students with disabilities, see **chapter 54**.

57:20. How do school districts select the measuring points for calculating the distance between a student's home and school?

School boards have broad discretion in selecting measuring points on school property for purposes of determining eligibility for transportation (*Gundrum v. Ambach*, 83 A.D.2d 911 (3d Dep't 1981), *order rev'd*, 55 N.Y.2d 872 (1982); *B.D.H. v. Merrick UFSD*, 11 Misc.3d 1071(A) (Sup. Ct. Nassau Cnty. 2006) (unreported); *Appeal of Mogel*, 41 Ed Dept Rep 127 (2001), as long as it does so fairly and consistently (*Appeal of Kadukara*, 51 Ed Dept Rep, Dec. No. 16,345 (2012); *Appeal of Welch*, 48 Ed Dept Rep 176 (2008); *Appeal of Flemming*, 43 Ed Dept Rep 391 (2004)). For example, the commissioner of education has upheld a district policy of measuring distance limitations from "the nearest school exit to the beginning of a residential property line" (*Appeal of Mogel*). According to the commissioner, a district may measure transportation distance from any part of the school, including, for example:

- A corner of school property (*Appeal of Canossa*, 37 Ed Dept Rep 456 (1998)).
- The side rather than front entrance (*Appeal of Mermelstein*, 30 Ed Dept Rep 119 (1990)), even if the entrance may not be used by students to enter the school (*Appeal of Kadukara*).
- The midpoint of the school (*Appeal of Silbert*, 1 Ed Dept Rep 283 (1959)).
- A flagpole (*Appeal of McDermott*, 49 Ed Dept Rep 37 (2009)).
- Nearest pedestrian entrance to school property (*Appeal of Welch*).

What is required is that districts use the selected points fairly and consistently (*Appeal of McDermott,* 49 Ed Dept Rep 37 (2009); *Appeal of Welch*; *Appeal of Flemming*; *Appeal of Porzio*, 42 Ed Dept Rep 166 (2002)). That a district's policy may incorporate the use of multiple entrances to measure distances, or that some entrances may require students to walk farther than others, does not alone render the policy unreasonable or inconsistent (see *Appeal of Kadukara; Appeal of Welch*).

Similarly, a school district has broad discretion when selecting the measuring point on a student's property as long as it consistently uses the same measuring point (*Appeal of Flemming*; see also *B.D.H. v. Merrick UFSD*; *Appeal of Welch*).

57:21. Are school districts required to use any particular method for measuring the distance between a district's selected measuring points?

No. A school district's distance determination will be upheld so long as the means of measurement are reasonable (*Appeal of Adamitis*, 38 Ed Dept Rep 765 (1999); see also *Appeal of Kadukara*, 51 Ed Dept Rep, Dec. No. 16,345 (2012); see **57:20**). School districts do not have to spend an unreasonable amount of time, effort, or money when measuring distance to determine a student's eligibility for transportation. In addition, such measurements do not have to be made with the accuracy of a professional survey (*Appeal of Welch*, 48 Ed Dept Rep 176 (2008); *Appeal of Flemming*, 43 Ed Dept Rep 391 (2004)).

The use of a calibrated automobile odometer to measure distance is legally reasonable and sufficient (*Appeal of Adamitis*; *Appeal of Jagoda*, 34 Ed Dept Rep 154 (1994)). Proof of calibration is a reasonable response to a bona fide challenge to the accuracy of the odometer as a measuring device (*Appeal of Jagoda*).

In addition, a district's use of an aerial survey has also been viewed as reasonable by the commissioner of education (*Appeal of Canossa,* 37 Ed Dept Rep 456 (1998)), as well as a measuring wheel (*Appeal of Kadukara*).

57:22. Can a school district provide transportation to students who reside at a lesser distance from school than the minimum limitations solely on the basis of a hazard?

Yes. Eligibility for transportation in individual cases is not based on potential hazards (*Appeal of Ruescher*, 50 Ed Dept Rep, Dec. No. 16,245 (2011)). However, all districts except city school districts with more than 125,000 inhabitants (the Big 5) are authorized to adopt, without voter approval, a resolution to establish child safety zones and provide transportation to students who live less than two or three miles from school but must walk along hazardous zones (§ 3635-b). But, if such transportation will result in additional cost to the district, such expense must be approved by the voters in a separate proposition at the annual school district meeting (§ 3635-b(5)).

A child safety zone is determined based on regulations established by the commissioner of transportation and in consultation with local law enforcement officials (§ 3635-b(3); 17 NYCRR Part 191). Children living within this zone may be transported without regard for distance or the "like circumstances" requirement contained in section 3635(1)(a) of the Education Law (§ 3635-b(2); see **57:1-2**).

The cost of providing transportation within a child safety zone is state-aidable. It is also considered an ordinary contingent expense (§ 3635-b(10)).

In addition, within amounts appropriated therefor, the commissioner of transportation is required to establish and maintain a safe route to school program to eliminate or reduce physical impediments to students who walk or bicycle to school. Projects under such a program must provide, for example, for the construction, reconstruction, and other maintenance of crosswalks and bicycle lanes (Transp. Law § 14(35)).

Bus Routes and Pick-up Points

57:23. What is the statutory definition of a bus route?

A bus route consists of "a highway or highways over and upon which a school bus regularly travels in accordance with a schedule maintained for the transportation of pupils from their homes to school" (§ 3621(3)).

School districts are charged with planning and selecting bus routes that "promote maximum efficiency in the operation of a school bus on such route" (§ 3622).

Whenever practicable, routes should be planned to operate within the boundaries of the school district unless the pupils being transported receive instruction beyond the boundaries of the school district (*Id.*).

57:24. May a school bus be routed on private roads?

The commissioner of education has held that a school district is not required to provide transportation to students over privately maintained roads (see *Matter of Cohen*, 21 Ed Dept Rep 280 (1981)). However, a district may provide transportation to students over privately maintained roads with the landowner's consent (*Appeal of Taylor*, 26 Ed Dept Rep 255 (1986)).

57:25. Must a school bus travel roads that may be impassable or unsafe?

The commissioner of education has held that a school board may refuse to use a public road to provide transportation to students if the board can establish its use would involve an "unreasonably hazardous condition" (*Matter of Clark*, 15 Ed Dept Rep 260 (1976)).

In *Matter of McGibbon*, 14 Ed Dept Rep 271 (1975), for example, the district verified that a road where a parent wanted her child to be picked up by district transportation was so narrow that a school bus and another vehicle could not pass each other, the road did not have safe shoulders, and it included steep grades that buses had been unable to negotiate without skidding into trees. Based on this information, the commissioner held that it was not unreasonable or illegal for the student to walk a mile to a pick-up point rather than authorize the school bus to travel on an unsafe road.

In *Appeal of Warner*, 37 Ed Dept Rep 469 (1998), the commissioner upheld the district's decision to deny transportation along a particular roadway after district officials visited the site and hired an accident investigation expert to evaluate the roadway. The expert told the district that the sight distance and roadway width were inadequate and unsafe. An alternate pick-up point on another road was more consistent with student safety than traveling along the requested roadway (see also *Appeal of Gulla*, 39 Ed Dept Rep 716 (2000)).

57:26. Does a school district have a duty to act with reasonable care to other motorists when routing its buses and designating pick-up points for school buses?

Yes, according to one state supreme court that refused to dismiss a case alleging that an accident occurred because a school district was negligent in placing a bus stop in an area with hilly terrain and obscured visibility for drivers. In the court's view, "it would be unreasonable to hold that a school district owes absolutely no duty whatsoever to other motorists, when determining where to place a bus stop" (*Black v. Homer CSD,* 190 Misc.2d 17 (Sup. Ct. Cortland Cnty. 2001)).

In a subsequent decision involving the same case, however, the court also determined that the availability of alternative bus stop locations is only one factor and not enough alone to impose liability on a district. Instead, it must be shown that "the location chosen was unreasonably dangerous, given the entirety of the relevant circumstances" (*Black v. Homer CSD,* 7 Misc.3d 1029 (Sup. Ct. Cortland Cnty. 2005)).

57:27. May a school board designate pick-up points for school buses?

Yes. School districts are not required to provide transportation to students directly to and from home (§ 3635(1)(d); *Ossant v. Millard*, 72 Misc.2d 384 (Fam. Ct. Yates Cnty. 1972); see *Appeal of Petrella*, 48 Ed Dept Rep 45 (2008); see **57:18**). They may require students to walk to transportation pick-up points (*Appeal of Cook*, 51 Ed Dept Rep, Dec. No. 16,367 (2012); *Appeal of Fliss*, 51 Ed Dept Rep, Dec. No. 16,280 (2011); *Appeal of Girsdansky*, 46 Ed Dept Rep 105 (2006)). A school board is authorized to exercise discretion with reasonable care in designating pick-up points after considering and balancing issues of student safety, convenience, routing efficiency, and cost (*Appeal of Kyle*, 53 Ed Dept Rep, Dec. No. 16,626 (2014); *Appeal of Cook*; *Appeal of K.G. and A.G.*, 51 Ed Dept Rep, Dec. No. 16,269 (2011)).

To afford the greatest possible protection to school children, the school board or superintendent may designate drive-off places on public highways for school buses to drive off the highway to receive or discharge students. The state or municipality having jurisdiction over a highway so designated is authorized to provide construction and maintenance of drive-offs (§ 3635(5)). However, the fact that a pick-up point is located on a heavily traveled road or may require students to wait or travel on unlit narrow roadways with no sidewalks or walkways, or that the student's home is in a remote location, is insufficient to prove that the pick-up point is unsafe (*Appeal of K.G. and A.G.; Appeal of Weinschenk,* 47 Ed Dept Rep 518 (2008); *Appeal of Price*, 38 Ed Dept Rep 745 (1999); *Appeal of DiNapoli*, 38 Ed Dept Rep 269 (1998)).

It is the responsibility of the parent, not the school district, to see that his or her child reaches the pick-up point safely (*Pratt v. Robinson*, 39 N.Y.2d 554 (1976); *Appeal of Kyle*; *Appeal of K.G. and A.G.*; *Appeal of Brizell,* 48 Ed Dept Rep 128 (2008)). However, a district may not require parents to transport their child to a pick-up point, which is farther away than the distance limitations for pick-up points set by the district policy (*Appeal of Zwickel*, 42 Ed Dept Rep 346 (2003)).

57:28. What is the maximum distance a student can be made to walk to a pick-up point?

The school board may establish, through adoption of a policy, the maximum distance a student may be required to walk to a pick-up point. This policy may be applied to side roads as well as to the distance from the student's home to the school itself. For example, if a school policy provides that a student who lives more than 4/10ths of a mile will be transported to school, then students can be required to walk up to 4/10ths of a mile to reach the pick-up point (*Appeal of Marsh*, 36 Ed Dept Rep 134 (1996); see **57:18**).

57:29. May a school district establish and maintain shelters for students who take school buses at various places along its bus routes?

There is nothing in the law that prevents school districts from doing this. A district may be ordered to provide additional transportation for children who live off a main route in cases where it is unwilling to provide these children with suitable shelter to wait for the bus and where the district provides transportation for all other children at a point near their homes (*Matter of Spicer*, 73 St. Dep't Rep. 167 (1952)).

State Aid for Transportation

57:30. How is student transportation aid calculated?

Transportation aid is paid on general operations and on bus purchases. All school districts are entitled to transportation aid, between 6.5 percent and 90 percent of their approved transportation expense (§§ 3602(7), 3622-a, 3623-a).

If the voters approve transportation beyond the state-mandated mileage limitations, the transportation for the distance beyond one and one-half and two or three miles and over 15 miles is eligible for transportation aid (§§ 3621(2)(a), 3635(1)(a); 8 NYCRR § 156.2(a)).

The amount of state aid payable on the purchase of a school bus is limited to the actual cost of the bus or the state contract price for a similar bus, whichever is less, or, if no similar bus is available under a state contract, to the state-wide median cost of similar buses. Aid on bus purchases may be reduced based on calculations made by the NYS Education Department (§ 3602(7)(c)).

Sections 3602(7)(b) and 3623-a(1)(e) of the Education Law make the following additional expenses eligible for transportation aid, which include but are not limited to: certain salaries and retirement benefits related to transportation; health, life, and other insurance premiums for transportation personnel for whom salaries are approved; premiums for collision and other insurance coverage; uniforms; fuel, oil, tires, chains, maintenance and repairs for school buses; bridge tolls; and other expenses approved by the commissioner's regulations.

57:31. Can a school district count students enrolled in nonpublic schools in the formula to determine state transportation aid for the district?

Yes. Except for cities with populations of more than 1 million, the resident nonpublic school district enrollment must be included in the district's computation of the wealth per pupil formula used to determine state aid for transportation (§ 3602(7)(a)).

57:32. Is state aid available for the transportation of students above grade 6 to another school district when the district does not furnish instruction for these grades?

Yes. Districts that do not maintain a secondary school must provide transportation, when necessary, for their students who have completed the work in the sixth grade and are receiving instruction in another district. These districts are eligible for transportation aid under the same rules that apply to other transportation (§ 3622-a(2)).

57:33. Is state aid available for the transportation of students with disabilities?

Yes. The Education Law provides that school districts transporting students with disabilities to and from school are eligible for state aid reimbursement of between 6.5 percent and 90 percent of the approved cost of such transportation provided (see **57:30**).

However, it also provides that this transportation may not be in excess of 50 miles from the home of such a student to the appropriate special service or program, unless the commissioner of education certifies that no appropriate nonresidential special service or program is available within 50 miles. In this case, the commissioner may establish, by regulation, a maximum number of trips between a student's home and the private residential school that provides special services or programs (§§ 4401(4), 4402(4)(d); see also 8 NYCRR § 200.12).

57:34. Do school districts receive state aid for out-of-district transportation of students to nonpublic schools?

Yes. State aid for transportation of students to nonpublic schools is based on the same criteria as that of aid to public schools (§ 3622-a(4); see **57:30**).

58. Transportation of Nonpublic School Students

58:1. Are school districts required to provide transportation to nonpublic school students?

Yes. The Education Law requires that school districts must provide transportation to nonpublic school students within the same mileage limits established for resident students attending public schools (§ 3635; see **57:18**). If a district transports public school students beyond what is legally required, it must do the same for nonpublic school students (§ 3635(1); *Appeal of Poles*, 55 Ed Dept Rep, Dec. No. 16,800 (2015); *Appeal of Defeis*, 34 Ed Dept Rep 408 (1995); *Appeal of Whitaker*, 33 Ed Dept Rep 59 (1993)).

A school district is not required to transport students to a nonpublic school by private carrier rather than public transportation (*Appeal of Casciano,* 52 Ed Dept Rep, Dec. No. 16,459 (2013); *Appeal of Clancy*, 37 Ed Dept Rep 280 (1998); *Appeal of Lavin*, 32 Ed Dept Rep 249 (1992)).

Once children are transported to the nonpublic school, responsibility for their supervision belongs to the nonpublic school even if the children arrive before the start of the school day (*Appeal of Hamilton*, 21 Ed Dept Rep 30 (1981)).

58:2. How is eligibility for transportation to a nonpublic school determined?

To determine eligibility, the distance to be measured is from the student's home to the nonpublic school (see **57:19-21**). Generally, if a student lives within the mileage limitations, then the school district must provide direct transportation for the child to the nonpublic school (*Appeal of Ruescher*, 50 Ed Dept Rep, Dec. No. 16,245 (2011); *Appeal of Hurd*, 41 Ed Dept Rep 473 (2002); see also *Appeal of Markarian*, 47 Ed Dept Rep 114 (2007); *Appeal of Keller*, 47 Ed Dept Rep 224 (2007)).

If a nonpublic school operates multiple campuses in different locations, a student will only be entitled to transportation if the campus where the student actually attends classes is within the district's mileage limitations from the student's home. A student cannot qualify for transportation because a different campus of the nonpublic school is within the mileage limitations from the student's home (*Appeal of Sastow,* 47 Ed Dept Rep 486 (2008)).

The distance between home and school of a student with disabilities receiving transportation under section 4402 of the Education Law must be measured along the nearest available route (*Appeal of a Student with a Disability,* 48 Ed Dept Rep 223 (2008)).

58:3. Are nonpublic school students entitled to door to door transportation?

No. Similar to public school students, nonpublic school students may be required to walk to a pick-up point consistent with school district policy (§ 3635(1)(d); see **57:27**). Additionally, a school district may elect to transport nonpublic school students who live within the mileage limitations to a centralized "transfer" point at which they change buses and continue from there to their nonpublic school as part of a synchronized transportation plan for its public schools (*Appeal of Kyle*, 53 Ed Dept Rep, Dec. No. 16,626 (2014); *Appeal of Gorsky*, 47 Ed Dept Rep 162 (2007)). In such an instance, affected nonpublic schools that can reasonably adjust their starting time to accommodate a district's otherwise reasonable transportation plan must do so (*Appeal of Gorsky*).

58:4. May a student who lives outside the mileage limitations receive transportation to a nonpublic school?

Under certain circumstances, children who do not qualify for transportation from home to a nonpublic school may receive transportation. If a student lives outside the mileage limitations but the district provides transportation to others who attend that student's nonpublic school and live within the mileage limits, the district must designate one or more public schools as a centralized pick-up point to transport nonpublic school students who live outside the mileage limits (§ 3635(1)(b)(i); *Appeal of Marrone*, 50 Ed Dept Rep, Dec. No. 16,118 (2010); *Appeal of Del Prete*, 40 Ed Dept Rep 141 (2000); *Appeal of Defeis,* 34 Ed Dept Rep 408 (1995); see also *Appeal of Keller,* 47 Ed Dept Rep 224 (2007)). Those students then must be transported from the centralized pick-up point to their respective nonpublic schools (see **58:7**).

In addition, a school district may elect to provide transportation from a centralized pick-up point to a nonpublic school student whose school is located more than 15 miles from the student's residence if the district has provided transportation to that school in at least one of the three prior years, and the distance between the pick-up point and the nonpublic school is not more than 15 miles (§ 3635(1)(b)(ii); *Appeal of Poles*, 55 Ed Dept Rep, Dec. No. 16,800 (2015); *Appeal of Marrone*; *Appeal of Porzio*, 42 Ed Dept Rep 166 (2002)). A school district may stop providing transportation under these circumstances at any time (*Appeal of Ruescher*, 50 Ed Dept Rep, Dec. No. 16,245 (2011); *Appeal of Hughes*, 48 Ed Dept Rep 299 (2009)).

Districts do not have to provide transportation from centralized pick-up points to any nonpublic school to which regular home-to-school transportation is not already being provided (*Appeal of Hughes; Appeal of Porzio*; *Appeal of Lucente*, 40 Ed Dept Rep 455 (2000)).

Nonpublic school students, who are not otherwise eligible, cannot qualify for transportation on the basis that a district transports students to another nonpublic school near the one they attend (*Appeal of Keller*; *Appeal of Capeling*, 46 Ed Dept Rep 400 (2007)). Furthermore, when a district erroneously provides transportation to students who are not entitled to such services, the solution is to discontinue transportation (*Appeal of Poles*; *Appeal of Keller*).

The cost of providing transportation between centralized pick-up points and nonpublic schools is an ordinary contingent expense (§ 3635(1)(b)(ii)).

58:5. Are school districts required to provide transportation to charter school students?

Yes. A charter school is deemed a nonpublic school for transportation purposes. Therefore, a school district must provide transportation to charter school students who reside in the district to the same extent transportation is provided to resident students who attend nonpublic schools (§§ 2853(4)(b), 3635; *Appeal of New Covenant Charter Sch.,* 39 Ed Dept Rep 610 (2000)). Requests for transportation must be submitted by April 1 of the preceding school year, even if parents have not yet enrolled their child in the charter school (*Appeal of New Covenant Charter Sch.*, 41 Ed Dept Rep 358 (2002)).

58:6. If a student's parents are divorced and live in different districts but have joint custody may both districts provide transportation to the student's nonpublic school?

No. If the parents of a child who attends a nonpublic school live in two different districts and request transportation from both districts on different days of the week, only one district is obligated to provide transportation since the child can have only one legal residence (*Appeal of Pyskadlo,* 47 Ed Dept Rep 56 (2007); see **57:7**).

58:7. Are school districts responsible for providing transportation to nonpublic school students between their home and a centralized pick-up point?

No. A district is not obligated to provide transportation to nonpublic school students to and from the centralized pick-up point. A district may provide a nonpublic school student with transportation to the centralized pick-up point if the student lives on an established school bus route to the centralized pick-up point, and from there on to the nonpublic school, provided such transportation does not result in additional costs to the district (§ 3635(1)(b)(i)).

58:8. May a school district deny transportation to otherwise eligible nonpublic school students?

Yes. A parent must submit a request in writing for transportation to a nonpublic school no later than April 1, unless the family moves into the district after April 1, in which case the request must be made within 30 days of establishing residency (§ 3635(2); *Appeal of Giorno-Tocco*, 55 Ed Dept Rep, Dec. No. 16,877 (2016); see also NYS Education Department, *Transportation for Students Enrolled in Nonpublic Schools* (updated Feb. 2012), at: http://www.p12.nysed.gov/nonpub/handbookonservices/transportation.html). Personal hardship is not a basis for granting a late transportation request (*Appeal of Fakhoury*, 55 Ed Dept Rep, Dec. No. 16,880 (2016)).

A transportation request that is mailed prior to the April 1 deadline but is not received until later may still be a valid timely request even if the postmark is dated after April 1 (*Reopening of the Appeal of Calabrese,* 43 Ed Dept Rep 237 (2003)). In addition, the commissioner of education has suggested that a request that is never actually received by the district may be considered timely with clear and detailed proof that the request was properly addressed, stamped and mailed prior to the deadline (*Appeal of Giorno-Tocco*, 55 Ed Dept Rep, Dec. No. 16,877 (2016)).

The filing of a late request may result in a denial of transportation, even where the district has previously accepted late requests (*Appeal of Beer*, 33 Ed Dept Rep 620 (1994)). No late request may be denied, however, if a reasonable explanation is provided for the delay (§ 3635(2)). The school board has discretion to determine the reasonableness of the excuse, and its decision will not be set aside unless it constitutes an abuse of discretion (*Appeal of Fakhoury*; *Appeal of Guarneri*, 50 Ed Dept Rep, Dec. No. 16,108 (2010); *Appeal of Aguanno*, 41 Ed Dept Rep 326 (2002)).

Even in the absence of a reasonable explanation for the delay, a late request must be granted if it can be provided under existing transportation arrangements at no additional cost to the district (*Appeal of Giorno-Tocco*; *Appeal of Fakhoury*; *Appeal of Besson*, 50 Ed Dept Rep, Dec. No. 16,111 (2010)). For example, a school district did not abuse its discretion when it denied a late request for private school transportation to a student who had three siblings already receiving transportation to that school. The district contracted for transportation on a per-seat basis and it would have cost the district an additional $513.95 per month to grant the late transportation request (*Appeal of Aguanno*).

58:9. What are some examples of reasonable excuses for a late transportation request?

A change in designation of a nonpublic school different than the nonpublic school originally specified after the April 1 deadline constitutes a separate request that can be denied (*Appeal of Capeling*, 46 Ed Dept Rep 400 (2007); *Appeal of Galvani*, 34 Ed Dept Rep 370 (1995); *Appeal of McNair*, 33 Ed Dept Rep 418 (1994)). However, there would be a reasonable excuse for failing to meet the April 1 deadline where a student is admitted to a private boarding school but is subsequently denied enrollment by the private school after April 1 because the delay in making the request is not attributable to a belated parental decision but rather to the actions of the nonpublic school (*Appeal of Lamba*, 32 Ed Dept Rep 473 (1993)). That also would be the case where a parental decision to place a child in a private school is not made until after the annual review conducted for a student with a disability, and the review does not take place until after April 1 (*Appeal of a Student with a Disability,* 48 Ed Dept Rep 207 (2008); *Appeal of Student with a Disability*, 47 Ed Dept Rep 363 (2008)).

Similarly, the commissioner of education found a reasonable excuse for a transportation request to a charter school submitted after the April 1 deadline where the charter school did not receive formal approval to operate until after the deadline. However, parents of the charter school students would not be exempted from making timely requests in future years (*Appeal of New Covenant Charter Sch.,* 39 Ed Dept Rep 610 (2000)).

58:10. What are some examples of unreasonable excuses for late transportation requests?

A board need not accept ignorance or forgetfulness of the April 1 deadline as a reasonable excuse (*Appeal of Fakhoury*, 55 Ed Dept Rep, Dec. No. 16,880 (2016); *Appeal of Soler*, 51 Ed Dept Rep, Dec. No. 16,284 (2011); *Appeal of Mendiolaza,* 48 Ed Dept Rep 346 (2009)). A school district does not have to accept ignorance of the requirement that parents moving into a district after April 1 must submit a transportation request within 30 days of establishing residency (*Appeal of Thomas*, 45 Ed Dept Rep 528 (2006); see **58:8**). Similarly, a belated parental decision to enroll a child in a nonpublic school is not a reasonable excuse (*Appeal of L.J.*, 53 Ed Dept. Rep, Dec. No. 16,603 (2014); *Appeal of Levens-Freeman,* 48 Ed Dept Rep 163 (2008); *Appeal of Aguanno*, 41 Ed Dept Rep 326 (2002)). The same principle applies when a parent withdraws a timely request for transportation and renews the request after the April 1 deadline (*Appeal of Lippolt,* 48 Ed Dept Rep 457 (2009)). In addition, the fact that a charter school was subject to an enrollment cap at the time of the April 1 deadline that was subsequently lifted after April 1 is not a reasonable excuse (*Appeal of New Covenant Charter Sch.*, 41 Ed Dept Rep 358 (2002)).

Reliance on a nonpublic school to submit a list of students requiring transportation is not a reasonable excuse for filing a late request either (*Matter of Hendricks*, 21 Ed Dept Rep 302 (1981); see **58:11**). Neither is a parent's mistaken belief that a school district would automatically renew a nonpublic school student's transportation upon the nonpublic school's request for books to the district (*Appeal of Besson*, 50 Ed Dept Rep, Dec. No. 16,111 (2010)). A parent's reliance on transportation request forms supplied by a nonpublic school that contains the wrong address for submitting the request is also an insufficient excuse (*Appeal of Guarneri*, 50 Ed Dept Rep, Dec. No. 16,108 (2010)).

58:11. May a nonpublic school submit a list of students who require transportation?

Yes. However, while the nonpublic school may submit a list of nonpublic students requiring transportation, it is the responsibility of the parent or guardian of a nonpublic school student to ensure a written request is filed on time, or transportation may be denied (see *Matter of Hendricks*, 21 Ed Dept Rep 302 (1981); see **58:8–10**).

This list should contain the name, address, age, and grade of each child, and a signed affidavit that states that the school has been authorized by the parents or guardian of each child to act as his or her representative. This affidavit also should indicate that a copy of this authorization duly signed by the parents is on file in the school office.

58:12. Must public school districts provide transportation to nonpublic schools on days when public schools are not in session?

No (*Appeal of Brautigam,* 47 Ed Dept Rep 524 (2008)). However, when public schools are not in session, the New York City school district must provide transportation to nonpublic schools for a maximum of five days, or a maximum of 10 days in any year in which the last day of Passover and Easter Sunday are separated by more than seven days. Such five or 10 additional days are limited to the Tuesday, Wednesday, Thursday and Friday after Labor Day; Rosh Hashanah; Yom Kippur; the week in which public schools are closed for spring recess; December 24th; and the week between Christmas Day and New Year's Day; the Tuesday, Wednesday, Thursday and Friday after the observance of Washington's birthday; and, in the boroughs of Brooklyn and Queens only, Anniversary Day (§ 3635(2-a)).

58:13. Are school districts required to alter their schedule to accommodate the transportation needs of nonpublic school students?

No. However, the commissioner of education has noted repeatedly that public and nonpublic schools have an obligation to cooperate in a reasonable manner in the scheduling of classes and transportation (*Appeal of Student with a Disability*, 55 Ed Dept Rep, Dec. No. 16,858 (2016); *Appeal of Donn*, 49 Ed Dept Rep 187 (2009); *Appeal of Reilly*, 46 Ed Dept Rep 184 (2006)). Generally public school authorities may not dictate the opening or closing hours for a nonpublic school (*Id.*). However, they are not required to alter their own schedules in order to provide transportation to nonpublic school students. On the other hand, a nonpublic school may be required to accommodate a reasonable request that it modify its school day to be consistent with the starting and ending times of other nonpublic schools and a district's own synchronized transportation plan (*Appeal of Gorsky*, 47 Ed Dept Rep 162 (2007)).

According to the commissioner, a transportation scheme that delivers nonpublic school students to their school just 20 minutes before the start of the school day does not impose an unreasonable burden on the nonpublic school (*Matter of Stickley*, 27 Ed Dept Rep 328 (1988)). However, a transportation scheme that consistently delivers students late to nonpublic schools and on time to public schools is not reasonable (*Appeal of Gorsky*, 47 Ed Dept Rep 162 (2007); *Appeal of Pallos,* 39 Ed Dept Rep 650 (2000); *Matter of Hacker*, 28 Ed Dept Rep 141 (1988)).

The adoption of an "unreasonable" or erratic schedule by a nonpublic school will relieve a school district of its obligation to arrange for transportation services to meet that school's schedule (*Appeal of Donn; Appeal of Reilly*; *Appeal of Berger*, 22 Ed Dept Rep 443 (1983)). That was the case, for example, where a nonpublic school dismissed its elementary and middle school students at 3:20 p.m., but classes for high school students didn't end until 5:00 p.m. (*Appeal of Berger*). Another example of an unreasonable/erratic schedule was where a nonpublic school with regularly scheduled hours of 8:15 a.m. to 2:15 p.m. decided to offer a math course at 7:15 a.m. rather than during the normal school day (*Appeal of Reilly*).

58:14. Must school districts provide late-dismissal transportation for nonpublic school students?

It depends on the reasonableness of the request, taking into account the dismissal time, the reason for the dismissal time, the cost, and the additional arrangements that must be made (*Appeal of Donn*, 49 Ed Dept Rep 187 (2009)). Even when nonpublic school students are required to remain late for academic reasons, a district does not have to provide transportation beyond what is reasonable (*Appeal of Donn*; *Appeal of Reilly*, 46 Ed Dept Rep 184 (2006)).

A nonpublic school dismissal time that is only a half hour later than public school or the last scheduled late bus is not, in and of itself, reasonable. Accordingly, the commissioner of education upheld a district's denial of late dismissal transportation where a nonpublic school's dismissal time was 5:00 p.m. but the district's transportation contract provided for transportation pick-ups until 4:30 p.m. Pick-ups after that time involved an additional minimum cost of $5,500 per year (*Appeal of Donn*).

58:15. May a school district transport students who attend release-time religious instruction from the public school to a church or parochial school?

No. School districts have no legal authority to provide this service (*Appeal of Fitch*, 2 Ed Dept Rep 394 (1963); see also *Appeal of Santicola*, 37 Ed Dept Rep 79 (1997)).

Transportation

59. School Buses

General Requirements

59:1. What is the statutory definition of a school bus?

Pursuant to the Vehicle and Traffic Law, a *school bus* may be any "motor vehicle owned by a public or governmental agency or private school and operated for the transportation of pupils, children of pupils, teachers, and other persons acting in a supervisory capacity, to or from school or school activities, or privately owned and operated for compensation for the transportation of pupils, children of pupils, teachers and other persons acting in a supervisory capacity to or from school or school activities" (Veh. & Traf. Law § 142).

Under the regulations of the commissioner of education applicable to school bus drivers, monitors, attendants, and pupils, a school bus includes every vehicle owned, leased, or contracted for by a public school, board of cooperative educational services, or a nonpublic school and operated for the transportation of pupils, children of pupils, teachers, and other persons acting in a supervisory capacity to or from school or school activities (8 NYCRR § 156.3(a)(2)).

Pursuant to NYS Department of Transportation regulations, a vehicle is a school bus if it is "a bus. . . used to transport children to or from school or school activities" (17 NYCRR § 720.1(u)).

59:2. May a school district standardize its fleet with certain makes of school buses?

Yes. A school board may adopt a resolution, by a vote of at least three-fifths of all board members, which states that for reasons of efficiency or economy, it will standardize the bus fleet. This resolution must include the reasons for its adoption (Gen. Mun. Law § 103(5)).

A need for standardization does not permit a school district to dispense with competitive bidding. (*Id.*). It merely authorizes the district to specify a particular type or brand. For further information, see *Competitive Bidding under General Municipal Law Section 103* (NYS Comptroller, Research Paper, Opn. St. Comp., 2010, pp. 36-37).

59:3. Must all school buses be painted the same color?

Yes. All school buses, regardless of ownership, having a seating capacity of more than seven passengers, must be painted the yellow color known as "national school bus chrome" (Veh. & Traf. Law § 375(21)).

59:4. Must school buses be equipped with exterior reflective material?

Yes, every school bus manufactured for use in New York on or after April 1, 2000, and used to transport 10 or more passengers on or after September 1, 2002, must be equipped with exterior reflective markings that comply with rules and regulations promulgated by the NYS Department of Motor Vehicles.

State aid is available for the purchase of buses with exterior reflective markings and for the purchase and installation of exterior reflective markings on older school buses (Veh. & Traf. Law §§ 375(21-h), 3623-a(2)(c); 15 NYCRR § 46.12(a)).

To further enhance highway safety, strobe lights may be affixed on school buses for use when students are being picked up, discharged, or transported to and from school or school functions and conditions impair the visibility of the school bus. Installation and operation of school bus strobe lights must comply with regulations issued by the NYS Department of Motor Vehicles (15 NYCRR § 56.12).

59:5. Must a school bus be identified by a sign?

Yes. Buses having a seating capacity greater than seven passengers must have the designation "School Bus" displayed conspicuously on two signs located on the exterior of the bus. The black letters must be at least eight inches high, and each stroke of each letter must be at least one-inch wide. The background of the signs must be a yellow color known as "national school bus chrome" (Veh. & Traf. Law § 375(20)(b)(1); see **59:3**). These signs must be mounted securely on top of the bus. One must face forward and one must face backward, and each sign must be visible and readable from a distance of at least 200 feet. While the bus is being operated at night, the signs must be illuminated to be visible from a distance of at least 500 feet (Veh. & Traf. Law § 375(20)(c)).

In addition, the flashing red signal lamps with which school buses must be equipped must be attached securely in the proper position (15 NYCRR § 46.2(g)). This law applies to vehicles with a seating capacity of seven or more passengers used exclusively to transport pupils, teachers, and other persons acting in a supervisory capacity to and from school or school activities (15 NYCRR § 46.2(a)).

Every school bus equipped with a wheelchair lift that transports children with disabilities must conspicuously display on its exterior the universal handicapped symbol, blue against a white background illustrating a person seated on a wheelchair. The sign must meet size and other specifications set out in law and regulation (Veh. & Traf. Law § 375(20)(b)(2); 17 NYCRR §§ 720.3(a)(7), 720.8(b)(6)).

59:6. Must a school bus identify the owner and/or operator of the vehicle?

All school buses purchased, leased, or acquired on or after September 1, 1997, must have the area code and telephone number of the owner and/or operator printed in three-inch bold type on the left rear of the bus (Veh. & Traf. Law § 1223-a).

Buses used to transport students that are not owned or leased by a school district must show the telephone numbers and area codes of the owner/operator (17 NYCRR § 720.3(a)(2)).

59:7. Must school buses be equipped with first aid kits and fire extinguishers?

Yes. All school buses must be equipped with a first aid kit constructed of durable material. The bus operator, including a school district, may determine the appropriate contents for the first aid kit depending on the particular needs of the students riding on the bus, and supply the kit appropriately. The fire extinguisher should be located in driver's compartment in full view and easily accessible (17 NYCRR §§ 720.7(b)(1), (2)).

59:8. Must school buses be equipped with special safety glass and mirrors?

Yes. Under section 375(20)(e) of the Vehicle and Traffic Law, each school bus with a seating capacity of more than 12 and with the engine located ahead of the driver must be equipped with a convex mirror mounted in front of the bus. In this way, the seated driver can observe the road directly in front of the bus. This is for the protection of students passing in front of the bus after they leave the bus.

School buses must also be equipped with safety glass, and those manufactured after April 1, 1990 must have backup beepers to alert others when the bus is put in reverse, in addition to other safety equipment (Veh. & Traf. Law § 375(11), (21-g); 15 NYCRR § 46.8).

With certain exceptions, school buses used by contractors that provide transportation to a school district must meet the same safety specifications and requirements as district-owned buses (§ 3623(1)(b)).

59:9. Must school buses be equipped with automatic fire suppression systems?

Some. All school buses used to transport students who use wheelchairs or other assistive mobility devices that are fueled with a substance other than diesel fuel manufactured for use in New York State after January 1, 1990, and those fueled with diesel fuel manufactured for use in New York State on or after September 1, 2007, must be equipped with an engine fire suppression system that conforms to standards established by the commissioner of transportation (§ 3621(15); Veh. & Traf. Law § 375(21-i)). The purchase of such a system is state aidable (§ 3623-a(2)(c)).

59:10. Must other vehicles owned by a school district and used to transport students meet the same requirements that apply to regular school buses?

Only vehicles used "exclusively" or "primarily" to transport pupils to and from school must meet the school vehicle requirements of the Vehicle and Traffic Law (Veh. & Traf. Law § 375(20), (21); see *Smith v. Sherwood*, 16 N.Y.3d 130 (2011); *Wisoff v. Cnty. of Westchester*, 296 A.D.2d 402 (2002); *Sigmond v. Liberty Lines Transit, Inc.*, 261 A.D.2d 385 (2d Dep't 1999)).

There are additional requirements for vehicles having seating capacities in excess of seven passengers and other requirements for those with seating capacities in excess of 12 and/or 15 passengers. In addition, special requirements exist for mirrors for vehicles with engines located in front of the driver (see **59:8**). However, the commissioner of transportation is authorized to grant exemptions from the requirements (see Veh. & Traf. Law § 375(20), (21)).

59:11. Who has ultimate authority for regulating safety and certification of school buses?

The commissioner of transportation, in consultation with the commissioner of education, is responsible for the adoption, promulgation, and the enforcement of rules, standards, and specifications regulating and controlling the efficiency and equipment of school buses used to transport students. Particular attention is made toward the safety and convenience of students and adaptability of such school buses to the requirements of the school district. No school bus shall be purchased by a school district or used to transport students unless and until it has been approved by the commissioner of transportation as complying with the rules, standards, and specifications (§ 3623(1)(a)).

59:12. Must school buses in New York State be inspected regularly?

Yes. School buses in New York must be inspected every six months. NYS Department of Transportation regulations provide that school buses cannot be operated unless they carry a certificate of inspection for the preceding six months, prominently displayed in the lower right-hand corner on the interior surface of the windshield (17 NYCRR § 720.2; see NYS Department of Transportation, *Bus Inspection Program* at: https://www.dot.ny.gov/divisions/operating/osss/bus/inspection).

Permissible Uses

59:13. In addition to transporting students, what else may district-owned school buses be used for?

In addition to the transportation of students to and from school and/or school activities, district owned buses and conveyances may be used legitimately for the following:

- Transportation for students and teachers to school-related events such as field trips and athletic events (*Cook v. Griffin*, 47 A.D.2d 23 (4th Dep't 1975); *Matter of O'Donnell*, 18 Ed Dept Rep 259 (1978); see also § 2023(1)).
- Lease to another school district or Native American tribe for certain recreation projects or youth service projects (§ 1709(25)(c)).
- Lease to another school district, to a board of cooperative educational services (BOCES), to a county vocational education and extension board, or to a Native American tribe for educational purposes (§ 1709(25)(b)).
- Rent or lease to any senior citizens' center that is recognized and funded by the office for the aging (§ 1501-b(1)(a)).
- Rent or lease to any nonprofit incorporated organization serving senior citizens (§ 1501-b(1)(b)).
- Rent or lease to any nonprofit incorporated organization serving the physically or mentally disabled (§ 1501-b(1)(c)).
- Rent or lease to any nonprofit organization that provides recreation youth services or runs neighborhood playgrounds or recreation centers (§§ 1501-b(1)(d), 1604(21)).
- Rent or lease to any municipal corporation, as defined in the General Construction Law (§ 1501-b(1)(e)).
- Rent or lease to a fire company as defined in the Volunteer Firefighters' Benefit Law, or an ambulance company as defined in the Volunteer Ambulance Workers' Benefit Law (§ 1501-b(1)(i)).
- Rent or lease to a nonprofit organization providing transportation in rural counties for children participating in the agricultural child care program authorized by the Agriculture and Markets Law (§ 1501-b(1)(f); Transportation Law § 73-c(8)).
- Rent or lease to operators of a coordinated public transportation service as authorized by article 2-F of the Transportation Law (§ 1501-b(1)(g)).
- Rent or lease to a nonprofit, community organization, or educational or employment and training agency that provides education or employment training for youths and adults in a rural county, as defined by under section 73-c of the Transportation Law (§ 1501-b(1)(h)).
- Transportation for certain infants and toddlers of students enrolled in school district or BOCES programs. This is eligible for state aid (§ 3635(1)(f)).
- For districts wholly or partially located in rural areas, transportation to district residents enrolled in educational, job-training or other programs; children under age five traveling between home and day-care or preschool programs; and employees of school districts or other educational institutions (§ 1502(1)).

59:14. What rules apply when a school district leases its school buses to others?

Whenever a bus is leased or rented, the consideration paid by the lessee may not be less than the full amount of the costs and expenses incurred as a result thereof. In addition, the lessee must maintain insurance on each bus so leased, protecting the lessor district from all claims by reason of personal injury to persons and property damage. The lessee also is required to carry fire insurance as well as compensation insurance on the driver of the leased bus. To protect the lessor district against further loss, the lessee also is required to carry collision insurance in the amount of the value of the bus. The cost of this insurance must be paid by the entity that leases the bus (§§ 1501-b(4), 1604(21), 1709(25)(f)).

59:15. What are some examples of impermissible uses of school buses?

There is no authority for a district to use school buses to transport residents to parent-teacher meetings or on shopping trips. Also, a district may not use its school buses to transport senior citizens from a senior citizens housing facility to a polling place for a school election (*Appeal of Jordan*, 39 Ed Dept Rep 551 (2000)).

59:16. Can advertisements or public service messages be displayed on school buses?

No. It is unlawful for any motor vehicle having a seating capacity of more than seven passengers, that is used primarily to transport students and teachers to and from school, to have any sign, placard, or other display mounted, placed, or installed on the vehicle, other than signs required by law, such as indicating that the vehicle is a school bus, and the ownership of the school bus. This provision does not apply to cities with a population of 1 million or more (Veh. & Traf. Law § 375(21-h); see also **59:5-6**).

School Bus Safety

59:17. Must school bus engines be turned off while waiting for passengers to load or off load on school grounds?

Yes. Through June 30, 2019, every school district must ensure that each bus driver of a school bus or other vehicle owned, leased, or contracted for by the district turns off the engine while:

- Waiting for passengers to load or off load on school grounds.
- Parked or standing on school grounds.
- In front of or adjacent to any school (§ 3637(1); 8 NYCRR § 156.3(h)(1)(i)).

Idling may be allowed to the extent necessary only when needed for heating, mechanical, or emergency circumstances as set forth in the commissioner's regulations (§ 3637(2); 8 NYCRR § 156.3(h)(2); see also NYS Education Department, *Idling School Buses on School Grounds* (Aug. 2008), at: http://www.p12.nysed.gov/schoolbus/anti-idling/htm/letter_to_school_districts.htm).

School districts may adopt policies that provide for the prompt loading and unloading of individual school buses, rather than waiting for all buses to arrive before loading or unloading (8 NYCRR § 156.3(h)(1)(ii)).

Furthermore, school bus drivers must instruct students on the necessity of boarding the bus promptly to reduce loading time and park the buses diagonally in loading areas to minimize the amount of exhaust from adjacent buses that may enter the school bus and buildings (8 NYCRR § 156.3(h)(3)(i), (ii)).

Drivers transporting students and staff to school events or athletic contests must turn off the bus or vehicle while waiting for the event to be completed (8 NYCRR § 156.3(h)(3)(iii)).

59:18. Must school districts give notice of the prohibition against bus idling and monitor compliance with anti-idling requirements?

Yes. School districts must provide school personnel notice of the requirements for minimizing bus idling annually, no later than five days after the start of school (§ 3637(3); 8 NYCRR § 156.3(h)(4)). Instead of providing a copy of those requirements, school districts may inform their staff that the materials have been posted on all employee bulletin boards and the district's website (NYS Education Department,

Idling School Buses on School Grounds (Aug. 2008), at: http://www.p12.nysed.gov/schoolbus/anti-idling/htm/letter_to_school_districts.htm).

Periodically, school districts must monitor driver compliance with the bus idling requirements, including drivers of vehicles owned, leased or contracted for by the district (8 NYCRR § 156.3(h)(5)).

59:19. Is there an established speed limit for school buses?

Yes. Although the Vehicle and Traffic Law specifies a maximum speed limit of 55 miles per hour, and 65 miles per hour on certain stretches of specified state highways located in rural areas, the Education Law specifies that the maximum speed at which school vehicles engaged in student transportation may be operated shall be 55 miles per hour (§ 3624).

Other restrictions on speed in populated areas and elsewhere, as conditions warrant, are imposed by cities, villages, and the NYS Department of Transportation. School bus drivers should observe these regulations conscientiously at all times, and also should operate at speeds that are reasonable in terms of prevailing road, traffic and weather conditions. Speed should be reduced at curves, blind crossings, crests of hills, in fog, or wherever the view is curtailed so the bus will be able to stop within the distance of clear vision.

59:20. Must a school bus keep its headlights illuminated at all times?

Yes. School buses must keep their lights on at all times they are operated, even when they are not transporting students (Veh. & Traf. Law § 375(20)(i)).

59:21. How many stop arms must a school bus have?

Every school bus manufactured for use in New York on or after January 1, 2002, with a capacity of 45 persons or more, must be equipped with a second stop arm that has to be located on the driver's side as close as practical to the rear corner of the bus (Veh. & Traf. Law § 375(21-c); 15 NYCRR § 46.7).

59:22. Are two-way radios and strobe lights required equipment on school buses?

No. However, these devices are authorized as allowable transportation expenses (§ 3623-a(2)(c); 15 NYCRR §§ 46.6, 56.12; see **59:4**).

In addition, two-way radios may be installed and used on school buses only if the school district or contractor operating the buses has applied for and received a license from the Federal Communications Commission (15 NYCRR § 46.6).

59:23. Is a school bus permitted to turn right at a red traffic signal?

If the school bus is transporting students, the driver cannot turn right for any purpose if the bus is facing a steady red signal (Veh. & Traf. Law § 1111(d)(5)).

59:24. Must school buses stop at all railroad crossings?

Yes. Publicly and privately owned school buses must stop at all railroad crossings, whether or not they carry students, and proceed only when the driver can do so safely. While crossing the tracks, the driver must not shift gears (Veh. & Traf. Law § 1171(a)).

Section 3636 of the Education Law provides a school district may not use an unguarded railroad crossing when transporting students to and from school or other places unless a public hearing has been held and a resolution has been adopted by the school board determining that the use of another route would be impractical. This resolution must be filed with the NYS Education Department and the NYS Department of Transportation. Additionally, the district must prepare and maintain a map indicating the bus route used and must make it available for inspection by any resident of the district at a place designated by the school board.

59:25. Are seat belts for students required equipment on all school buses?

All school buses manufactured after July 1, 1987, must be designed to include seat belts and increased seat padding on the passenger seats. In addition, all motor vehicles weighing 10,000 pounds or less and used to transport students must have seat belts, regardless of the date of first use. The seat belts must be approved by the commissioner of transportation (15 NYCRR § 49.6; Veh. & Traf. Law § 383(5)(a)). Drivers' seat belts are required on all school bus vehicles owned or leased by the district (Veh. & Traf. Law § 383(4-a)).

59:26. Must students wear seat belts while on the school bus?

It depends. The state's Vehicle and Traffic Law requires the use of seat belts on school buses that are exempt from applicable federal school bus safety standards (Veh. & Traf. Law § 1229-c(13)). Those include vehicles with a seating capacity of less than 10 occupants that are not subject to federal safety standards such as the use of high backed, padded seats, compartmentalized passenger areas, and higher structural standards for crash worthiness (Veh. & Traf. Law § 1229-c(13)). That same law further requires the use of car seats for children ages 4–7 who are transported in vehicles exempt from applicable federal school bus safety standards (Veh. & Traf. Law §§ 1229-c(1), (2), (13)). Violations of these provisions are punishable by a civil fine of up to $100 (Veh. & Traf. Law § 1229-c(5)). See **59:28** regarding the use of car seats.

Otherwise, under the Education Law, no liability may be imposed against a school district, a school bus operator under contract with a district, or an operator of a school bus (including a driver, matron, or teacher serving as a chaperon) solely because the injured party was not wearing a seat belt (§ 3813(4); see *O'Connor v. Mahopac CSD*, 259 A.D.2d 530 (2d Dep't 1999)).

The Education Law further provides that following a public hearing, a school board may choose to adopt a resolution that provides for the use of seat belts on all school buses (§ 3635-a). In such an instance, however, a school district may become subject to liability that would not be possible otherwise.

59:27. Are school districts required to provide students with instruction on the use of seat belts?

Districts that transport students on school buses equipped with seat belts must ensure that all students who are transported on any school bus owned, leased, or contracted for by the district or board of cooperative educational services receive instruction on the use of seat belts. Instruction must be provided to both public and nonpublic school students at least three times a year (8 NYCRR § 156.3(g)). Instruction must include, at least, proper fastening and release of belts, acceptable placement of seat belts on students, times when seat belts should be fastened and released, and acceptable placement when not in use (8 NYCRR § 156.3(g)(1)–(4)).

59:28. Are car seats required on school buses?

All children under the age of four who are passengers on a school bus must be restrained in a federally-approved child restraint system appropriate for their height and weight approved by the commissioner of motor vehicles (Veh. & Traf. Law § 1229-c(1), (11)). This statutory requirement applies to all school buses that are owned and operated by public or private schools or privately owned and operated for compensation. In addition, children between the ages of 4–7 who are transported, not in a regular school bus, but in a vehicle for which there are no federal school bus safety standards (see **59:26**), must be restrained in car seats that meet federal safety standards (Veh. & Traf. Law § 1229-c(13)).

59:29. What is the law regarding standees on a school bus?

Generally, there may be no standing passengers on school buses owned or contracted to a school district when used exclusively to transport students, teachers, and other persons acting in a supervisory capacity to and from school or school activities. However, this prohibition does not apply during the first 10 days of session in each school year, nor in the event of a bus breakdown, accident, or other unforeseen occurrence that necessitates the transportation of standing passengers. City school districts with a population of one million or more may adopt and enforce local laws that comply with these provisions (§ 3635-c; Veh. & Traf. Law § 1229-b(2)). In addition, section 1229-b of the Vehicle and Traffic Law makes unlawful the operation of a camp or charter omnibus for 10 miles or more with any passenger standing.

59:30. Must students cross in front of the school bus when they are being picked up or discharged from it?

Yes. The driver of the school bus must instruct those students who must cross the highway or street to cross 10 feet in front of the bus (8 NYCRR § 156.3(d)(4)). Prior to stopping to receive or discharge passengers, the driver must activate the amber colored "pre warning" flashers to warn motorists the bus will soon stop (Veh. & Traf. Law § 375(20)(a)). The bus driver must keep the bus stopped with red signal lights flashing and stop arm employed until passengers are at least 15 feet from the bus and either off the highway, street, or private road or on a sidewalk (Veh. & Traf. Law § 1174(b); 8 NYCRR § 156.3(d)(4); 17 NYCRR § 721.4(g)).

59:31. May the school district employ a school crossing guard to direct traffic for school buses on a public highway?

No. However, section 208-a of the General Municipal Law gives any city, town, village, or county police department or police district the authority to appoint school crossing guards for these purposes (see *Ernest v. Red Creek CSD,* 93 N.Y.2d 664 (1999); Opn. Att'y Gen. I. 84-30; see also § 806(3); *Matter of Glasner*, 7 Ed Dept Rep 15 (1967); see generally Opn. Att'y Gen. I. 2013-3).

59:32. Are emergency drills required on school buses?

Yes. The commissioner's regulations (8 NYCRR § 156.3(f)) require emergency drills on school buses. These drills must include practice and instruction in the location, use, and operation of the emergency door, fire extinguisher, first-aid equipment, and windows as a means of escape in case of fire or accident (§ 3623(1)(c); 8 NYCRR § 156.3(f)(1)).

Drills also must include instruction in safe boarding and exiting procedures with specific emphasis on when and how to approach, board, disembark, and move away from the bus after disembarking. They must include specific instructions for students to advance at least 10 feet in front of the bus before crossing the highway after disembarking. They must address specific hazards encountered by students during snow, ice, rain, and other inclement weather, including, but not necessarily limited to, poor driver visibility, reduced vehicular control, and reduced hearing. They must include instruction in the importance of orderly conduct by all school bus passengers, with emphasis on student discipline (§ 3623(1)(c); 8 NYCRR § 156.3(f)(1)). This instruction and the conduct of the drills must be given by a member or members of the teaching or student transportation staff (8 NYCRR § 156.3(f)(1)).

Students attending public and nonpublic schools who do not participate in these drills must be provided with drills on school buses, or, as an alternative, must be provided with classroom instruction covering their content. A minimum of three drills must be held during the school year, the first to be conducted during the first seven days of school, the second between November 1 and December 31, and the third between March 1 and April 30 (§ 3623(1)(c); 8 NYCRR § 156.3(f)(2)). No drills may be conducted when buses are on routes (8 NYCRR § 156.3(f)(3)).

School authorities must certify in their annual report to the NYS Education Department that their district has complied with this requirement (8 NYCRR § 156.3(f)(4)).

59:33. What actions may a school district take to protect students from terrorist attacks on school buses?

The NYS Education Department Office of Pupil Transportation Services has issued *Terrorism Preparedness Guidelines* that urge school districts to consider school buses as actual targets of terrorism and evaluate their emergency management plan and daily operating procedure to avert any such incident. The Guidelines include a checklist to help address any deficiencies with respect to guarding against terrorist attacks on school buses.

Some questions to examine include, for example, whether the district requires bus drivers to examine the interior and exterior of buses for unknown objects or tampering as part of a driver's pre- and post-trip inspections. Schools districts should also examine whether they have developed a standardized radio transmission code with disguising conversation to notify the garage of trouble without alerting the potential wrongdoers.

A copy of the guidelines, dated June 2009, is found at: http://www.p12.nysed.gov/schoolbus/School_Bus_Terrorism/htm/terrorism_preparedness_guidelines.htm.

For more information on emergency management plans see **chapter 62**.

59:34. Are school bus drivers required to carry emergency information concerning children with disabilities?

Yes. Every school bus which is used to transport children with disabilities on a regularly scheduled route must maintain on the bus certain information about the children with the written consent of the parent, guardian, or person in loco parentis. This information, which must be kept confidential and used only for emergency purposes, includes the child's name, nature of the disability, and the name and telephone number of the person who can be contacted in case of an emergency. In this context, disability refers to a physical or mental impairment that substantially limits a student's major life activities on either a permanent or temporary basis (Veh. & Traf. Law § 375(20)(l)).

59:35. What is the state law in relation to vehicles overtaking or meeting buses transporting children to or from school?

Section 1174 of the Vehicle and Traffic Law prohibits motorists from passing stopped school buses while they are boarding or discharging school children. A vehicle overtaking or meeting a bus transporting children to and from school that is stopped to receive or discharge passengers on a public highway must come to a complete stop and remain stationary until the bus resumes motion or until signaled by the driver or a police officer to proceed, provided the bus carries flashing red signal lights and signs designating it as a school bus that are displayed as required by law (Veh. & Traf. Law § 1174; *Smith v. Sherwood*,

16 N.Y.3d 130 (2011)). Notably, motorists must stop when a bus is loading or unloading passengers even when the bus is on a divided highway (Veh. & Traf. Law § 1174(a)). Failure to obey this traffic rule can result in either a fine of between $250 and $400 or 30 days imprisonment, or both for a first offense. Penalties increase with repeat offenses (Veh. & Traf. Law § 1174(c)).

59:36. Is it unlawful to loiter on a school bus?

Yes. To loiter has been interpreted to mean to be slow in moving, to delay, to be dilatory, to saunter, or to lag behind. The Penal Law states that any person not having any reason or relationship involving custody of or responsibility for a student who loiters, remains in, or enters a school bus not having written permission or a specific, legitimate, purpose for being there, is guilty of loitering, a violation of law (Penal Law §§ 240.00, 240.35(5)).

59:37. What is the law regarding eating and drinking by school staff on school buses?

Bus drivers, monitors, and attendants are not allowed to eat or drink on a school bus while the vehicle is transporting students. Moreover, they may not perform any act or conduct themselves in a manner that may impair the safe operation of the bus, including smoking while within a school bus (8 NYCRR § 156.3(e)(5)).

59:38. May a school district restrict the type of objects students may bring onto a school bus?

Yes. NYS Department of Transportation regulations provide that the main aisle and the aisle to the door of a school bus may not be obstructed (17 NYCRR § 721.4(a)(11)). The commissioner of education upheld a district policy which prohibited students from carrying items on the bus which could not fit on their laps, including all musical instruments other than flutes or clarinets, hockey sticks, lacrosse sticks, baseball bats, ski equipment, large equipment bags, large art displays, and any other item of similar size and shape (*Appeal of Moyer*, 37 Ed Dept Rep 335 (1998)).

59:39. Who is responsible for the supervision and safety of students taking the school bus?

School districts are liable for the supervision and safety of students who are within their physical custody or authority (*Pratt v. Robinson*, 39 N.Y.2d 554 (1976)). Thus, when students are riding a school bus operated by a district, the district will generally be responsible for the safety of students. However, this does not mean a district will be liable for all injuries a student may incur while riding a school bus. Districts are not liable for all the "spontaneous acts which take place among students daily" (*Andrew T.B. v. Brewster CSD,* 67 A.D.3d 837 (2d Dep't 2009)).

Similarly, in one case, a district was found not liable for a wrist fracture a student sustained when a school bus was forced to stop short to avoid colliding with a car that suddenly cut in front of the bus. The bus driver acted reasonably in an emergency situation not of his own making (*Miloscia v. N.Y. City Dep't of Educ.,* 70 A.D.3d 904 (2d Dep't 2010)).

59:40. Who is responsible for the supervision and safety of students prior to boarding or after disembarking from a school bus?

Generally, school districts are not liable for the supervision and safety of students prior to boarding or after disembarking from a school bus. Custodial control and responsibility at those times rest with the parents (*Pratt v. Robinson*, 39 N.Y.2d 554 (1976); *Williams v. Weatherstone*, 2014 N.Y. LEXIS 1048 (2014); see **57:27**).

In one case, a state appellate court initially refused to dismiss a lawsuit against a district where a parent alleged that a district representative had promised to ensure that the student rode the school bus home rather than travel in another student's car. The court held that while a school district does not have a duty to compel students to ride the school bus home, if the district representative had made the promise, the district may have undertaken a special duty to the student (*Wenger v. Goodell*, 220 A.D.2d 937 (3d Dep't 1995)). However, after the facts were presented in the *Wenger* case, the district again moved to dismiss the case because the parent had not established that the district had in fact undertaken a special duty to the student. The appellate court agreed, and dismissed the action against the district (*Wenger v. Goodell*, 288 A.D.2d 815 (3d Dep't 2001); see also *Pistolese v. William Floyd UFSD*, 69 A.D.3d 825 (2d Dep't 2010); *Cerni v. Zambrana*, 271 A.D.2d 566 (2d Dep't 2000)).

In another case, a district was found liable when a student was hit by a pickup truck when walking home after school and crossing the road in front of the school while school buses were still departing. The driver's view was obstructed by a moving school bus. Normally, the district waited to release students who walked home until all the school buses were gone, but did not on the day of the accident. According to the New York Court of Appeals, while a district's duty of care toward a student generally ends when it relinquishes custody of the student, the duty of care continues when the student is released without further supervision into a foreseeably hazardous situation the district played a role in creating (*Ernest v. Red Creek CSD*, 93 N.Y.2d 664, *reargument denied* 93 N.Y.2d 1042 (1999)).

59:41. Who is responsible for the supervision and safety of students when a district hires an independent contractor for the transportation of students?

A school district ordinarily is not liable where it hires an independent contractor to provide transportation services and a student is injured in connection therewith (*Chainani v. Bd. of Educ. of the City of N.Y.*, 87 N.Y.2d 370 (1995); *Mallik v. Youngblood*, 274 A.D.2d 456 (2d Dept. 2000)). In *Chainani*, a district was sued by the parent of a student who suffered severe injuries when struck by her school bus after she had disembarked. The school bus was driven by the employee of a bus company serving as an independent contractor. The New York Court of Appeals ruled that the district was not directly liable for the student's injuries because the student was not within the custody of the school district at the time of the accident but rather was in the custody of the independent contractor. The court also refused to hold the school district vicariously liable for the student's injuries because the activity of transporting students is not inherently dangerous and the district was not aware that the independent contractor had created a peculiar unreasonable risk (but see *David XX v. St. Catherine's Ctr. for Children,* 267 A.D.2d 813 (3d Dep't 1999)).

Similarly, a school district was not liable for injuries sustained by a student when he tried to cross the road in front of a vehicle operated by an independent contractor that was not a yellow school bus. The vehicle did not have to meet safety features required of yellow school buses because it was not exclusively used to transport students. As a result, the bus driver and the bus company were only obligated to drop the student in a safe location. Their duty ended once the student safely disembarked, even if the student had to cross the street in front of the bus (*Smith v. Sherwood*, 16 N.Y.3d 130 (2011)).

59:42. Does a district's code of conduct apply to students transported to and from school by an independent contractor?

Yes. A school district remains responsible for enforcing its code of conduct while students are traveling on school buses whether or not the transportation is independently contracted for (*Appeal of M.H.*, 43 Ed Dept Rep 210 (2003); see **52:1–9** for further discussion on the code of conduct).

59:43. Who is responsible for ensuring no children are left behind on a school bus at the completion of a bus run?

School bus drivers, monitors, and attendants all share in this responsibility. They must check the vehicle at the conclusion of the bus route to ensure that no child is left on board unattended (8 NYCRR § 156.3(e)(4)).

59:44. May a school district use video cameras on school buses to ensure the safety of the driver and passengers?

Yes, video cameras may be used on school buses that transport students (8 NYCRR § 156.9(d)(1)). These cameras may be used to record the students' conduct to ensure their safety and to serve as evidence of their conduct for disciplinary purposes, if necessary (see *Appeal of Burrows*, 39 Ed Dept Rep 212 (1999)). Video cameras and other safety equipment may be eligible for state aid (see 8 NYCRR §§ 156.1(f), 156.9(d)(1)).

Purchases and Lease of School Buses

59:45. Must a school district competitively bid the purchase of a school bus?

In general, yes, if the purchase involves a reasonably expected aggregate expenditure of more than $20,000 (Gen. Mun. Law § 103; see **28:11–19** for more information on the bidding process). Financing must be approved by the school board and may be by a bond, note, or authorized as a specific item in the budget. Moreover, the purchase and maintenance of school buses must be authorized by a vote of the district's qualified voters (§ 1709(25)).

However, through July 31, 2017, an exception to the competitive bidding provisions is permissible when certain prerequisites are met (Gen. Mun. Law § 103(16); Office of the State Comptroller, *New "Piggybacking" Law – Exception to Competitive Bidding* (July 2016), at: https://www.osc.state.ny.us/localgov/pubs/piggybackinglaw.pdf; see also **chapter 28**).

In addition, a school board may replace a school bus because of damage or loss without voter approval, using any unencumbered funds or by using budget notes (§ 1709(25)(a); Loc. Fin. Law § 29.00).

59:46. May school districts participate in cooperative purchasing of school buses?

Yes. School districts may purchase school buses and other items cooperatively (Gen. Mun. Law Article 5-G, §§ 119-m–119-oo). This method requires the adoption of specifications that will be agreeable to all in the group. The voters of each district must grant the necessary appropriation or authorization to borrow money. The major benefit is the possibility of securing lower prices through quantity buying. Each district must award its own contract for purchase.

59:47. Must a school bus purchase be approved by the commissioner of education?

Yes. Any school bus purchase by a district must be approved by the commissioner of education. Transportation aid will not be apportioned for the purchase cost of the bus unless the district has obtained the required purchase approval (see 8 NYCRR § 156.4).

59:48. May school districts lease school buses or other motor vehicle for transportation of students?

Yes. Until September 1, 2017, a school board may lease a motor vehicle to transport students for a one school year term. However, when authorized by the voters, the lease may be for up to a five-year term.

Once the initial lease expires, any additional lease for the same or equivalent replacement vehicle(s) requires voter approval (§§ 1604(21-a), 1709(25)(i), 2503(12-a); see *Appeal of Shafer*, 43 Ed Dept Rep 9 (2003)). No voter approval is required in the Big 5 school districts (§ 2554(19-a)).

In addition, subject to approval by the commissioner of education, school buses may be leased under emergency conditions for up to 90 days (unless the emergency continues). Emergency conditions include, but are not limited to, strikes, delay in delivery date, theft, vandalism, fire and accident (§ 1709(25)(e); 8 NYCRR § 156.6).

59:49. What transportation-related items may districts purchase through state contracts?

School districts may purchase certain transportation-related items through state contracts with the NYS Office of General Services' Procurement Services Group or any other department or agency of the state subject to article 11 of the State Finance Law. The contracts can be for items such as school buses, gasoline, tires, spark plugs and motor oil, all at a considerable savings (Gen. Mun. Law §104(1)). The purchase or series of purchases of a specific item must exceed $500 (*Id.*). Nonpublic schools may purchase such state contract items through local school districts (Gen. Mun. Law § 109-a).

For information on state contracts, contact the Customer Services Unit of the Procurement Services Group at 518-474-6717 or visit the website at: http://www.ogs.ny.gov/BU/PC/.

59:50. What insurance must be carried on a school bus?

Minimum and maximum levels for public liability and property damage insurance for school buses are contained in section 370 of the Vehicle and Traffic Law. The law establishes a minimum amount of indemnity for damages and injuries to persons and for property damage.

Each school board must determine whether the statutory minimum sufficiently protects the district. If a board desires insurance in excess of the minimum, the amount of coverage must be specified in the district's advertisement for transportation contract bids. No-fault automobile insurance applies to school vehicles, although this law does not apply to losses incurred through property damage.

59:51. May a school district contract for the maintenance of school buses?

Yes. The process for entering into and extending any such contract is the same process applicable to contracts for the transportation of students (§ 305(14)(a); see 8 NYCRR § 156.12; see also **59:52-59**).

Pursuant to regulations of the NYS Department of Transportation, school districts that own or lease school buses must have in place an effective preventative maintenance program and examine and service their buses at regular intervals as established by the school board (17 NYCRR § 721.1(a)).

Transportation Contracts

59:52. May a school district contract for the transportation of students?

Yes. Contracts for the transportation of students that annually run more than $20,000 may be either competitively bid or secured through a request for proposals process (§ 305(14)(a), (e); 8 NYCRR § 156.12; Gen. Mun. Law § 103(1); see NYS Education Department, *When is it Necessary to Competitively Bid a Transportation Contract* (updated Oct. 2010), at: http://www.p12.nysed.gov/schoolbus/BusinessOfficial/htm/when_competitive_bid.htm; see Opn. St. Comp. 91-64; see **28:11-19** for more information on the bidding process).

At the time this publication went to press, a bill passed by both houses of the Legislature, but awaiting action by the governor, would amend Education Law section 305(14) to require the New York City school district to include employee protection provisions related to the retention or preference in hiring, wages, benefits and seniority of school bus workers in connection with such contracts (2016 Assembly Bill A.8019C).

For more information on pupil transportation contracts, visit the NYS Education Department's Office of Pupil Transportation Services website at: http://www.p12.nysed.gov/schoolbus/contracts.html.

59:53. May a school district engage in cooperative bidding or requests for proposals for contracts for pupil transportation?

Yes. School districts and boards of cooperative educational services (BOCES) have the ability to enter into cooperation agreements under section 119-o of the General Municipal Law for the performance of their respective functions and duties. Therefore, similar to cooperative bidding for purchasing school buses, school districts and BOCES can procure services by cooperatively preparing specifications and advertising for bids or proposals. Contracts awarded in this fashion should specifically refer to the underlying cooperative bid/proposal and specifically incorporate by reference the substantive terms of the bid request/request for proposal unless already set forth in the contract. For more information see NYS Education Department, *Cooperative Transportation Bids* (Feb. 2010), at: http://www.p12.nysed.gov/schoolbus/contracts/html/cooperative_trans_bids.html.

59:54. Must transportation contracts be approved by the commissioner of education?

Yes. A transportation contract does not become valid and binding upon either party until it has been approved by the commissioner of education (§§ 3625(4), 305(14)(a), (e); 8 NYCRR § 156.12(d)).

Transportation contracts may be made for a period not exceeding five years if the terms are approved by the district voters (§§ 1604(23), 1709(27)). These must be in writing, approved by the school superintendent, and signed by the superintendent and the school board president (§ 3625(1), (2)).

A contract extension may exceed the maximum amount specified, referenced by the consumer price index, to compensate for the criminal history and driver licensing testing fees attributable to special requirements for school bus drivers pursuant to articles 19 and 19-a of the Vehicle and Traffic Law. These costs must be approved by the commissioner (§ 305(14)(c)).

The state comptroller also is authorized to audit the financial records relating to contracts of school bus contractors that provide school transportation to districts (§ 3625(2)).

The contract must state the contractor agrees to come to a full stop before crossing any railroad track or state highway (§ 3625(1), (2); see **59:24**).

At the time this publication went to press, a bill passed by both houses of the Legislature, but awaiting action by the governor, would amend Education Law section 305(14) to authorize the commissioner of education to reject any extension of a contract for transportation, or new contract, if the amount to be paid by the district to the contractor in any year of such proposed contract fails to reflect the savings realized from the sales tax exemption on school buses, parts, equipment, lubricants, and fuel used for school purposes that would be afforded to the contractor under the same bill (2016 Assembly Bill A.8019C).

59:55. What procedures must a school district follow to award a transportation contract through the competitive bidding process?

When a school board awards a transportation contract through competitive bidding, the transportation contract must be advertised in the same manner as purchase contracts under section 103 of the General Municipal Law. All advertisements for bids must be published in a newspaper or newspapers, designated by the school board or trustees, with general circulation within the district. The advertisement must state when and where bids will be publicly opened and read, either by school authorities or their designee. At least five days must elapse between the first publication of the advertisement and the opening of bids (Educ. Law § 305(14)(a)).

A school board may solicit bids in alternative categories, such as soliciting bids for contracts for individual school bus routes and alternative bids for contracts for all of the district's school bus routes in the aggregate. The district may then select the lowest responsible bidder in either category (*Acme Bus Corp. v. Bd. of Educ. of the Roosevelt UFSD,* 91 N.Y.2d 51 (1999); *Appeal of Mitchell*, 40 Ed Dept Rep 88 (2000)). However, overly restrictive or atypical specifications for transportation contracts contained within bid specifications may violate the General Municipal Law due to their anti-competitive effect on bidding (*Matter of L & M Bus Corp. v. N.Y. City Dep't of Educ.*, 17 N.Y.3d 149 (2011)). Until July 31, 2017, exceptions to the competitive bidding provisions are permissible when certain prerequisites are met (see Office of the State Comptroller, *New "Piggybacking" Law – Exception to Competitive Bidding* (July 2016), at: https://www.osc.state.ny.us/localgov/pubs/piggybackinglaw.pdf; see also **28:2**).

If a district is faced with an emergency affecting student transportation services and must take immediate action, the school board may negotiate interim transportation contracts for a period not to exceed one month. During this time, the board or a district trustee must advertise for bids and award a contract as required by the law. The approved costs of the interim contracts will be eligible for transportation aid (§ 305(14)(b)).

59:56. What procedures must a school district follow to award a transportation contract through a request for proposals process?

When a school board awards a transportation contract through a request for proposals process, it must specify in its public notice soliciting proposals all the criteria it will use in evaluating the proposals and the weightings assigned to each criterion (8 NYCRR § 156.12(c)). The board must evaluate each proposal based upon the following criteria:

- previous experience of the contractor in transporting pupils;
- name of each transportation company of which the contractor has been an owner or manager;
- a description of any safety programs implemented by the contractor;
- record of accidents in motor vehicles under control of the contractor;
- the driving history of the contractor's employees;
- inspection records and model year of each of the motor vehicles under the control of the contractor;
- maintenance schedules of the motor vehicles under the control of the contractor;
- a financial analysis of the contractor;
- documentation of compliance with motor vehicle insurance requirements; and
- total cost of the proposal (8 NYCRR § 156.12(b)).

Proposals for contracts to meet anticipated needs during the following school year must be requested by June 1, except for contract proposals for the transportation of students with disabilities, which must be requested by July 1. If an emergency or other unforeseen situation prevents compliance with these deadlines, the proposals must be requested at least 30 days prior to the beginning date of service (8 NYCRR § 156.12(e), (g)).

59:57. Are there any exceptions to the competitive bidding or request for proposal process for awarding transportation service contracts?

Yes, within certain specified restrictions. When an emergency arises, or there is an unforeseen occurrence or condition affecting student transportation services that requires immediate action and cannot await competitive bidding or responses to request for proposals, a district may enter into an "interim contract." However, an interim contract may not exceed one month in duration, pending the award of a contract in compliance with the competitive bidding or request for proposal process (§ 305(14)(b); 8 NYCRR § 156.12(f)).

Furthermore, until July 31, 2017, exceptions to the competitive bidding provisions are permissible when certain prerequisites are met (see Office of the State Comptroller, *New "Piggybacking" Law – Exception to Competitive Bidding* (July 2016), at: https://www.osc.state.ny.us/localgov/pubs/piggybackinglaw.pdf; see also **28:2**).

59:58. May a school board extend an existing transportation contract?

Yes. Moreover, a school board choosing to extend an existing transportation contract is not required to undergo competitive bidding or a request for proposals process if it chooses to extend such a contract for up to five years.

A board electing to extend a transportation contract may, in its discretion, increase the amount to be paid in each year of the contract extension by an amount not to exceed the regional consumer price index increase for the New York, N.Y.-Northeastern New Jersey area, based upon the index for all urban consumers (CPI-U) during the preceding 12-month period, provided it has been satisfactorily established by the contractor that there has been at least an equivalent increase in its costs of operation during the period of the contract (§ 305(14)(a); *A.C. Transp., Inc. v. Bd. of Educ. of the City of N.Y.*, 253 A.D.2d 330 (1st Dep't 1999)).

The commissioner of education has the authority to reject any contract extension if he or she finds the amount in the proposed extension fails to reflect any decrease in the regional consumer price index for the New York, N.Y.-Northeastern New Jersey area, based upon the CPI-U during the preceding 12-month period, or, if in his or her opinion, the extension is not in the district's best interests. If the commissioner does reject a proposed extension, he or she may order the board to seek, obtain and consider other bids (§ 305(14)(a)).

At the time this publication went to press, a bill passed by both houses of the Legislature, but awaiting action by the governor, would expand the basis upon which the commissioner can reject a contract extension that involves a decision by a school board to increase the amount to be paid in each year of the contract extension (2016 Assembly Bill A.8019C).

59:59. May a school board amend an existing transportation contract?

Yes, in certain cases. Until January 1, 2020, school boards have the authority to amend existing student transportation contracts when necessary to comply with federal, state, or local laws, rules or regulations imposed after execution of the contract, or to enhance the safety of pupil transportation. Any such amendments are subject to approval by the commissioner of education and require demonstrable enhancements in pupil safety and/or increased savings consistent with maintaining student safety. In addition, any such amendment may not cause additional cost to the state, locality, or school district, circumvent competitive bidding requirements or other provisions of law, or fail to increase or maintain student transportation safety (§ 305(14)(d)).

60. School Bus Drivers, Monitors and Attendants

Bus Drivers

60:1. What is the definition of a school bus driver?

A *school bus driver* is any person who drives a school bus owned, leased, or contracted for by a public school district, board of cooperative educational services, or nonpublic school for the purpose of transporting students. However, a driver of a passenger or suburban type of vehicle is not considered a school bus driver if he or she is a school district employee who does not ordinarily transport students and is operating that vehicle to transport one or more students to a hospital or other medical facility, a physician's office, or home for medical treatment or because of illness. Likewise, a driver of a suburban intercity coach or transit bus who transports students on trips other than between home and school, such as field trips and athletic trips, is not considered to be a school bus driver. A parent who transports only his or her own children is also excluded from this definition. In addition, a volunteer driver for a nonpublic school who transports students on other than a regularly established route on an occasional basis is also excluded from this definition (8 NYCRR § 156.3(a)(1)).

60:2. What are the qualifications for a school bus driver?

The qualifications of school bus drivers are determined by regulations of the commissioner of education and the commissioner of motor vehicles (Educ. Law§ 3624; 8 NYCRR § 156.3(b); 15 NYCRR Part 6).

For an individual to be qualified as a school bus driver, he or she must:

- Be at least 21 years of age (8 NYCRR § 156.3(b)(2)).
- Have a currently valid driver's license or permit that is valid for the operation of a bus in New York State (8 NYCRR § 156.3(b)(4)).
- Pass a physical examination established by the commissioners of education and motor vehicles (8 NYCRR § 156.3(b)(3); see also Veh. & Traf. Law §§ 509-b(3), 509-d(1)(i), 509-g; 15 NYCRR §§ 6.3(c)(3), 6.10).
- Pass a physical performance test established by the commissioner of education (8 NYCRR § 156.3(b)(3)(iii)).
- Furnish to the superintendent at least three statements from three different persons not related to the applicant assessing his or her moral character and reliability (8 NYCRR § 156.3(b)(6)).
- Have no conviction, violation, or infraction listed in section 509-c or section 509-cc of the Vehicle and Traffic Law, or under any other provision of article 19-A of that law. In order to determine if an applicant has no such convictions, the applicant must submit fingerprints for a state criminal history check. The fingerprints may also be submitted to the FBI for a national check (Veh. & Traf. Law § 509-cc(5); see **60:18**).
- Meet all other licensing and training requirements for driving a school bus (Veh. & Traf. Law §§ 501, 509-b, 509-c; 8 NYCRR § 156.3).

In addition, any driver who received their initial license after July 18, 1999, with a passenger endorsement to operate on an intra-state basis only will be considered qualified if that person has no loss of a foot, leg, hand, or arm, impairment of a hand or finger which interferes with prehension or power grasping, or impairment of an arm, foot, or leg or any other significant limb impairment which interferes with the ability to perform normal tasks associated with operating a motor vehicle (49 CFR § 391.41(b)(1), (2); 17 NYCRR § 721.3(f)).

Persons with such impairments may qualify to drive a commercial vehicle if they have been granted a skill performance evaluation certificate based on their proven ability to operate knobs and switches, hold and maneuver a steering wheel, etc. (49 CFR § 391.41(b)), or meet alternative physical qualification standards for the loss or impairment of limbs (49 CFR § 391.49).

60:3. What are the licensure requirements for school bus drivers?

Licensure requirements for all school bus drivers currently are covered by article 19-A of the Vehicle and Traffic Law (Veh. & Traf. Law §§ 501, 501-a(1), 509-a to 509-o), part 6 of the rules and regulations of the commissioner of motor vehicles, and part 156 of the regulations of the commissioner of education.

Federal and state laws and regulations require all school bus drivers to be issued a commercial driver's license (CDL) (49 USC § 31308; 49 CFR § 383.23; Veh. & Traf. Law §§ 501-a(1), 509-b; 8 NYCRR § 156.3(b)(4)). This CDL is required of all commercial drivers, including school bus drivers, and makes them subject to the Federal Motor Carrier Safety Administration regulations related to commercial driver's licenses (49 CFR §§ 383.3, 390.3(b)).

The regulations of the commissioner of education require each driver of a motor vehicle conveying school children to have the appropriate operator's or commercial driver's license (8 NYCRR § 156.3(b)(4)).

The Education Law allows schools to receive transportation aid for certain approved costs associated with the licensing regulations such as the training of drivers for the CDL and the expenses incurred in fingerprinting drivers for background checks (Educ. Law §§ 3602(7)(b), 3623-a(1)(e)(6); see also **60:18**).

60:4. Are there any circumstances where an individual with a commercial drivers license can be disqualified from operating a school bus?

Yes. Pursuant to federal regulations, each person operating a school bus who is convicted of violating any type of state or local law relating to motor vehicle traffic control (other than a parking violation) must notify, in writing, his or her employer or the official designated by the state if the conviction occurs out of state within 30 days of conviction (49 CFR § 383.31). Certain convictions may result in a period of disqualification from driving (see 49 CFR §§ 383.51, 384.213). State law also requires school bus drivers to be disqualified from driving a commercial motor vehicle for different periods of time based upon convictions for both criminal and traffic offenses (see Veh. & Traf. Law § 509-cc; 15 NYCRR § 6.28).

In addition, a driver convicted twice of using a hand held mobile telephone while driving a school bus in separate incidents during any three-year period will be disqualified for 60 days, and a third or subsequent violation in any three-year period will result in disqualification for 120 days (Veh. & Traf. Law § 510-a (3)(a), (b), (4); see also 49 CFR §§ 383.51, 391.15(f), 390.3(f)(1)).

60:5. Are school bus drivers required to meet any physical requirements?

Yes. Each school bus driver must meet the requirements of section 6.10 of the regulations of the commissioner of motor vehicles, and the basic minimum physical requirements specified in the regulations of the commissioner of education, concerning, for example, vision and hearing. The superintendent must consider a physician's or nurse practitioner's written report in determining the driver's fitness to operate or continue to operate any transportation vehicle used by students (Educ. Law § 3624; 15 NYCRR § 6.10).

Restricting a colorblind person from driving a school bus does not constitute disability discrimination under the American with Disabilities Act. Moreover, such a person would not be entitled to an accommodation under that act that would not otherwise enable him to perform the essential function of distinguishing traffic signals (see *Shannon v. N.Y. City Transit Auth.*, 332 F.3d 95 (2d Cir. 2003)).

60:6. Are school bus drivers required to pass a physical performance test?

Yes. All bus drivers employed by a district, board of cooperative educational services, or contractor must pass a physical performance test approved by the commissioner of education at least once every two years. In no case shall the interval between physical performance tests exceed 24 months (8 NYCRR § 156.3(b)(3)(iii)). The test shall also be re-administered to each driver after an absence of 60 consecutive days or more from the employee's scheduled work duties (8 NYCRR § 156.3(b)(3)(iii)).

The test must be conducted by a certified school bus driver instructor. To pass the test, a bus driver must be able to perform the following functions:

- Repeatedly open and close a manually operated bus entrance door;
- Climb and descend bus steps;
- Operate hand controls simultaneously and quickly;
- Have quick reaction time from throttle to brake;
- Carry or drag individuals in a bus emergency evacuation;
- Repeatedly depress clutch and/or brake pedals; and
- Exit quickly oneself and students from an emergency door (8 NYCRR § 156.3(b)(3)(iii)(a)).

A bus driver who fails any part of the test may not operate a school bus until he or she passes a re-examination test. The re-examination must be taken no sooner than three days from the prior test. The employer will be responsible for paying for the re-examination if the bus driver passes; the bus driver is responsible for the cost if he or she fails the re-examination (8 NYCRR § 156.3(b)(3)(iii)(b); see also NYS Education Department, *School Bus Driver Physical Performance Test Form* (Feb. 2004), at: http://emsc32.nysed.gov/schoolbus/Drivers/pdf/PT900.pdf).

All nonpublic school drivers hired after January 1, 2005, must pass the driver performance test before they may transport students (8 NYCRR § 156.3(b)(3)(iii)(c)(2)).

60:7. Are school bus drivers required to undergo physical examinations?

Yes. Each regular or substitute driver of a school bus owned, leased, or contracted for by a school district, board of cooperative educational services, or a nonpublic school must be examined every year by a physician or nurse practitioner. In no case may the interval between exams exceed 13 months. When a driver is initially hired, he or she must be examined within four weeks prior to the beginning of service. The results of these physical examinations must be reported immediately to the superintendent on forms prescribed by the commissioner of education (§ 3624; 8 NYCRR § 156.3(b)(3)(ii); see **60:2**).

60:8. Are school bus drivers required to have school bus safety training?

Yes. Each school bus driver initially employed by a school board or transportation contractor after July 1, 1973, or by a nonpublic school after July 1, 2004, must complete instruction on school bus safety practices prior to beginning service.

In addition, during his or her first year of employment, each driver must complete a basic course of instruction in school bus safety practices approved by the commissioner of education. All school bus drivers must receive refresher instruction in school bus safety at least two times a year, at sessions conducted between July 1 and October 31 and between December 1 and May 1 of each school year (§ 3650; see 8 NYCRR § 156.3(b)(5)(i-iii)).

There are additional requirements with respect to training and instruction concerning the special needs of students with disabilities (§ 3650(2); 8 NYCRR § 156.3(b)(5), see **60:10**).

All training must be provided by or under the direct supervision of a school bus driver instructor certified by the commissioner of education, with the exception of pre-service training (8 NYCRR § 156.3(b)(5)(v)). An approved school bus driver instructor's physical presence is not required during training conducted on the initial employment of a school bus driver by the board or transportation contractor, provided such training is conducted under the general supervision of such an instructor (8 NYCRR § 156.3(b)(5)(v)(a)).

Each driver's compliance with the training requirements described above should be verified through the district's record-keeping system. Every school district must annually certify to the commissioner that its bus drivers have completed the required safety training. Such certification must also include a report on the implementation and effectiveness of the safety training program (§ 3650-b(3)).

Drivers who operate transportation vehicles owned, leased, or contracted for by nonpublic schools also must receive safety training (§ 305(34); 8 NYCRR § 156.3(b)(5)(ii), (v)).

60:9. Must occasional drivers receive the training specified in Question 60:8?

No. Under the commissioner's regulations, an occasional driver is defined as a certified teacher employed by a school district or board of cooperative educational services who is not primarily employed as a school bus driver or substitute school bus driver on either a full-time or part-time basis. Occasional drivers used for other than regular routes are not required to fulfill the training described in **60:8** (8 NYCRR § 156.3(b)(5)(iv)).

60:10. Are school bus drivers required to have training on the special needs of students with disabilities?

Yes, if they are or will be transporting students with disabilities. Such individuals must undergo training and instruction related to the understanding of and attention to the special needs of such students, at least once per year, in accordance with commissioner's regulations (§ 3650(2); see 8 NYCRR § 156.3(5)(i-iii)). Similar requirements apply to school bus attendants (Veh. & Traf. Law § 1229-d(4); see **60:29**).

60:11. Are school bus drivers subject to alcohol and drug testing?

Yes. School bus drivers who operate a commercial motor vehicle and are required to have commercial driver's licenses (CDLs) are subject to alcohol and drug testing, according to federal regulations (see 49 CFR Parts 40, 382, 391; US Department of Transportation, *Employees* (updated Nov. 2015), at: https://www.transportation.gov/odapc/employee). A school bus driver is subject to this requirement only when driving a vehicle that is designed to transport 16 or more passengers, including the driver (49 CFR §§ 382.103, 382.107).

A school district may terminate a bus driver who fails an alcohol test even if it is an isolated incident because a district has "a special obligation to safeguard the well-being of its students" and a bus driver's alcohol-related conduct jeopardizes "public safety and the safety of school children" in the driver's charge (*Will v. Frontier CSD Bd. of Educ.*, 97 N.Y.2d 690 (2002)). District policy and collective bargaining provisions may limit the ability to automatically terminate a bus driver with a positive test result. That was the case where a district was obligated to consider a less severe disciplinary penalty before proceeding to terminate (*Shenendehowa CSD v. Civil Serv. Employees Ass'n, Inc.*, 90 A.D.3d 1114 (3d Dep't 2011), *aff'd,* 20 N.Y. 3d. 1026 (2013)).

In addition, operating a school bus while under the influence of alcohol or drugs is a crime under state law, punishable by fines, imprisonment or both, as well as license suspension and/or license revocation. If a school bus driver is convicted of operating any vehicle while under the influence of alcohol or drugs, his or her license will be suspended or revoked and he or she will also be disqualified as a school bus driver for the period of that revocation or suspension. Such disqualification will be no less than six months (Veh. & Traf. Law §§ 509-cc(1)(g), 1193(1)(d)(1-a), (4-a), (2)(b)(4-a)).

60:12. When must bus drivers submit to alcohol and drug testing?

The regulations require school districts to have programs in place that will test school bus drivers for alcohol and drugs under the following circumstances:

- Before they are employed as bus drivers (49 CFR § 382.301(a); except that an employer is not required to administer pre-employment alcohol testing (49 CFR § 382.301(d)). Those that choose to can conduct the alcohol test only after making a contingent offer of employment or transfer subject to the employee passing the pre-employment alcohol test administered pursuant to the procedures of 49 CFR Part 40 (49 CFR § 382.301(d)(3), (4)).
- After a bus accident has occurred, if there was a fatality, or if the driver was cited for a moving violation in connection with the accident and there is an injury treated away from the scene of the accident or a disabled vehicle is towed away from the scene (49 CFR § 382.303(a)(1), (2); see **60:22**).
- If there is reasonable suspicion based on specific articulable observations of the driver's appearance, behavior, speech, or body odors that the driver has used drugs or alcohol (49 CFR § 382.307(a), (b)).
- Randomly, a minimum percentage of a district's average number of bus drivers per year — 10 percent for alcohol and 50 percent for drugs. These percentages may vary, according to the Federal Highway Authority. Random tests must be unannounced and spread reasonably throughout the year using a scientifically valid selection method such that each driver will have an equal chance of being selected each time random tests are conducted (49 CFR § 382.305).
- Drivers who have previously tested positive for alcohol and/or substance abuse must submit to a "return to duty" test for before returning to work (49 CFR §§ 40.305, 382.309).
- Unannounced follow-up tests on drivers referred by substance abuse professionals for alcohol or drug counseling and who have returned to work at a minimum of six times in the twelve month period following the return (49 CFR §§ 40.307, 40.309, 382.311).

Prior to implementing the testing programs, school districts must provide school bus drivers with information regarding the policy and regulation requirements, as well as information on alcohol and drug treatment programs and resources (49 CFR §§ 382.113, 382.601; see also U.S. Department of Transportation, *What Employers Need to Know About DOT Drug and Alcohol Testing [Guidance and Best Practices]* (June 2015), at: https://www.transportation.gov/sites/dot.gov/files/docs/ODAPC_Employer_Guidelines_%20June_1_2015_0.pdf).

60:13. Are bus driver alcohol and drug testing results confidential?

The general rule is that alcohol and drug testing records are confidential and may not be revealed to anyone other than the employer without the driver's consent. However, under federal regulations, employers must make these records available to an authorized representative of the U.S. Department of

Transportation, when requested, or any local or state official with regulatory authority over the employer or drivers. In addition, an employer may disclose the test results in criminal or civil actions in accordance with the regulations and in proceedings related to benefits sought by the employee, such as workers' compensation or unemployment insurance compensation. Post-accident records may also be disclosed to the National Transportation Safety Board in the course of an accident investigation, or as required by state law (49 CFR § 382.405).

Additionally, employers may release information regarding a driver's records or make records available upon written request from a driver authorizing such access to a subsequent employer or specified individual (49 CFR § 382.405(f)).

60:14. May a school bus driver be precluded from driving a school bus based upon alcohol and/or drug consumption?

Yes. In accordance with federal and state law, a school bus driver must not drive a school bus if he or she:

- Possesses, consumes, or is reasonably believed to possess or have consumed alcohol or a controlled substance while on duty (Veh. & Traf. Law § 509-l(1); 15 NYCRR § 6.24(a)); or
- Uses alcohol within four hours of going on duty (49 CFR § 382.207) or is under the influence of alcohol or a controlled substance within six hours or less before duty (Veh. & Traf. Law § 509-l(1)(a); 15 NYCRR § 6.24(a)(1)); or
- Has an alcohol concentration of 0.02 or higher (49 CFR § 40.23(c)); or
- Tests positive for a controlled substance (49 CFR §§ 382.307(e)(2), 382.213); or
- Has adulterated or substituted a test specimen (49 CFR § 382.215); or
- Refuses to take a required alcohol or controlled substance test (49 CFR § 382.211).

Any employee who is tested and found to have an alcohol concentration of at least 0.02, but less than 0.04, will be removed from the position until his or her next regularly scheduled duty period, but not less than 24 hours following the test (49 CFR § 382.505).

If the driver has an alcohol concentration of 0.04 or greater, has engaged in prohibited alcohol or controlled substance use, or has tests results that are verified as adulterated or substituted, he or she must be removed from driving duties and referred to a substance abuse professional (49 CFR § 40.23; see also 49 CFR §§ 40.285, 40.287, 382.201). No driver who has abused controlled substances or alcohol may return to duty unless he or she has successfully passed a required return-to-duty test (49 CFR § 382.309).

60:15. May a bus company be held liable if a bus driver operates a school bus while intoxicated?

Yes. No motor carrier shall permit a driver to be on duty or operate a bus, if by the driver's general appearance or conduct, he or she appears to have consumed an intoxicating liquor within the past six hours (Veh. & Traf. Law § 509-l(2)(b); 15 NYCRR § 6.24). In *In re Northland Transp., Inc. v. Jackson*, 271 A.D.2d 846 (3d Dep't 2000)), a school bus driver was on route to pick up children when her bus broke down. A state trooper who came to the aid of the disabled bus observed the driver was glassy-eyed and smelled strongly of alcohol. The driver failed four field sobriety tests, was placed under arrest for driving while intoxicated, and a later breathalyzer test revealed a blood alcohol content of 0.07 percent. The driver was later convicted of the charge.

The driver's employer was convicted of permitting the driver to drive that day, in violation of section 509-l of the Vehicle and Traffic Law, and was fined $2,500. On appeal, a state appellate court held that a motor carrier may be found guilty of violating the statute if it knew or through reasonable diligence or simple observation, should have known that one of its drivers appeared to have consumed alcohol in the preceding six-hour period. In this case, the court concluded the company had no procedure in place to address the clear mandates of the statute. If it had, the driver's "obvious intoxicated appearance and conduct would have been observed and she would not have been permitted to drive the bus that morning (*Id.*)."

60:16. Are school districts required to pay for the rehabilitation of bus drivers who fail an alcohol or drug test?

No. Any treatment or rehabilitation program must be provided in accordance with the employer's policy or labor/management contracts. Applicable regulations do not require the employer to provide rehabilitation, pay for treatment, or reinstate the employee (49 CFR §§ 40.289, 382.605).

60:17. May school bus drivers be terminated after a positive drug or alcohol test?

Yes. Applicable federal regulations do not require the employer to reinstate the employee after a positive drug or alcohol test (49 CFR § 40.289). Therefore, a school district may terminate a bus driver for a positive test result provided the school district follows any disciplinary procedures imposed by law or a collective bargaining agreement (*Shenendehowa CSD v. Civil Serv. Employees Ass'n, Inc.*, 90 A.D.3d 1114 (3d Dep't 2011), *aff'd*, 20 N.Y.3d. 1026 (2013)).

60:18. Must school bus drivers be fingerprinted?

Yes. The Vehicle and Traffic Law and NYS Department of Motor Vehicles regulations require all school bus drivers to be fingerprinted so a school district may obtain any criminal record from state and federal authorities (Veh. & Traf. Law §§ 509-d(2), 509-cc(5); 15 NYCRR § 6.4(b)). In addition, driving and employment records must be obtained (see **60:19-21**).

Districts can obtain reimbursement for most costs associated with fingerprinting school bus drivers (§§ 3602(7), 3623-a(1)(e)(6); see **60:3**).

60:19. Is a school district required to check a person's employment record before employing that person as a school bus driver?

Yes. The school district must conduct an investigation of the driver's employment record during the preceding three years, in a manner prescribed by the commissioner of motor vehicles (Veh. & Traf. Law § 509-d(1)(iii); 15 NYCRR § 6.3(c)(2)). For school bus drivers with passenger endorsement limited to intrastate travel initially licensed after July 18, 1999, employers must receive a list of an applicant's previous employers during the preceding 10 years (see U.S. Department of Transportation- Federal Motor Carrier Safety Administration, *Commercial Driver's License Program* (updated May 2014), at: https://www.fmcsa.dot.gov/registration/commercial-drivers-license/states). However, the employer is only required to investigate the employment record for the preceding three years (49 CFR §§ 391.21(b)(10), 391.23(d); 17 NYCRR § 721.3(f)).

60:20. Is a school district required to check a person's driving record before employing that person as a school bus driver?

Yes. A school district must obtain the driving record of each bus driver it employs from the appropriate agency in every state in which that driver resided or worked and/or held a driver's license or learner's permit during the preceding three years, in a manner prescribed by the commissioner of motor vehicles (Veh. & Traf. Law § 509-d(1)(ii)). A copy of the response by each state, showing the driving record or certifying that no driving record exists for that driver, must be forwarded to the NYS Department of Motor Vehicles, Bus Driver Certification Unit, within 10 days of receipt by the district and must be kept on file by the school district for three years (Veh. & Traf. Law § 509-d(3), (4); 15 NYCRR § 6.3(c)(8), (9)). The driving record must be updated annually by the bus driver, and such information must be kept in the employer's record (Veh. & Traf. Law § 509-f).

60:21. Is a school bus driver required to report his or her convictions for violations of the Vehicle and Traffic Law to his or her employer?

Yes. A school bus driver who is convicted of a misdemeanor or felony under the Vehicle and Traffic Law, or who has his or her driver's license revoked, suspended, or withdrawn, must notify his or her employer by the end of the business day following the date when the driver received notice of such action. Failure to provide this notice will subject the driver to a suspension of five working days or a suspension equivalent to the number of working days that the driver was not in compliance with this requirement, whichever is longer (Veh. & Traf. Law § 509-i(1); 15 NYCRR § 6.21(a)).

A school bus driver convicted of a traffic infraction in any jurisdiction must notify his or her employer within five working days of such a conviction. Failure to provide such notice within the required time period will subject the driver to a suspension of five working days (Veh. & Traf. Law § 509-i(1-a); see *In re Smith v. Bd. of Educ. of Taconic Hills CSD*, 235 A.D.2d 912 (3d Dep't 1997)).

School bus drivers convicted of an offense listed in section 509-c and/or 509-cc of the Vehicle and Traffic Law that would disqualify them from operating a bus must provide notice of such conviction in writing by the following business day. Any driver who fails to provide such notice may not be permitted to drive a bus (Veh. & Traf. Law § 509-i(2); see also 15 NYCRR § 6.28(a)(5)).

60:22. Is a school bus driver required to report his or her involvement in an accident to his or her employer?

Yes. A driver who is involved in an accident as defined in section 509-a of the Vehicle and Traffic Law, in any jurisdiction, must notify his or her employer within five working days from the date of the accident. Failure to so notify within the required time period will subject the driver to a suspension of five working days (Veh. & Traf. Law § 509-i(1-b); 15 NYCRR § 6.21(b); see also **60:12**).

60:23. Are school bus drivers subject to periodic tests or reviews of their driving skills and knowledge?

Yes. School districts are required to carry out a number of ongoing reviews of its bus drivers including:

- Annual review of a bus driver's driving record and a personal interview (including the driver's accident record, and tickets for speeding, reckless driving or driving under the influence) (Veh. & Traf. Law § 509-e; 15 NYCRR § 6.8(a), (b)).
- Regular observations of a driver's defensive driving performance while operating a bus with passengers (Veh. & Traf Law § 509-g(3); 15 NYCRR § 6.8(c)).
- A biennial behind the wheel driving test conducted by an individual certified by the NYS Department of Motor Vehicles (Veh. & Traf. § 509-g(4); 15 NYCRR § 6.11(a)).
- A biennial written or oral examination testing the driver's knowledge of the rules of the road, defensive driving practices, and the law regulating driving a bus in New York (Veh. & Traf. Law § 509-g(5); 15 NYCRR § 6.12).
- If a driver has had three accidents as defined in Vehicle and Traffic Law § 509-a within an 18-month period he or she will be subject to re-examination including a road test (Veh. & Traf. Law § 509-bb(1)).

60:24. Does a school bus driver have a responsibility to maintain order on the bus?

Yes. School bus drivers, monitors and attendants are all responsible for reasonable behavior of students in transit (8 NYCRR § 156.3(d)). However, drivers have no authority to suspend students for disorderly conduct. They should report those students who violate established rules to the school principal who should take appropriate action (see **57:17**).

Monitors and Attendants

60:25. What is the definition of a school bus monitor?

A *school bus monitor* is any person employed to assist children to safely enter and exit from a school bus owned, leased, or contracted for by a school district or board of cooperative educational services, and to assist the school bus driver in maintaining proper student behavior on the school bus (8 NYCRR § 156.3(a)(3)).

60:26. What is the definition of a school bus attendant?

A *school bus attendant* is any person employed to assist students with a disabling condition on a school bus owned, leased, or contracted for by a school district or board of cooperative educational services (8 NYCRR § 156.3(a)(4)).

60:27. What are the qualifications for a school bus monitor or attendant?

All school bus monitors and attendants must:

- Be at least 19 years of age.
- Have the physical and mental ability to satisfactorily carry out their duties.

Each monitor or attendant may be examined by a physician upon the order of the school superintendent within two weeks prior to the beginning of the monitor's or attendant's service in each school year. The school superintendent will consider the physician's report to determine the fitness of the monitor or attendant to carry out his or her functions (8 NYCRR § 156.3(c)(1)–(3)).

60:28. Are school bus monitors and attendants required to pass a physical performance test?

Yes. All school bus monitors and attendants are required to pass a physical performance test at least once every two years. Those hired after July 1, 2003, must take and pass the test before they may assume their duties. Additionally, the test must be administered to any monitor or attendant following an absence from service of 60 or more consecutive days from his or her scheduled work duties (8 NYCRR § 156.3(c)(3)(iii)).

The physical performance test must be administered by a certified school bus driver instructor who shall assess the ability of the school bus monitor or attendant to, for example, climb and descend bus steps, carry or drag students in a bus emergency evacuation, and exit quickly from an emergency door (8 NYCRR § 156.3(c)(3)(iii)(a)).

There are three standards a monitor or attendant must meet as part of the physical performance test. They are: climb and descend the bus steps three times within 30 seconds; starting in a seated position, quickly exit from an emergency door in 20 seconds; and carry or drag a 125-pound bag 30 feet in 30 seconds (NYS Education Department, *Monitors and Attendants Qualifications and Training Requirements Questions and Answers* (June 2009), at: http://www.p12.nysed.gov/schoolbus/TransDirector/htm/qualifications_monitors.htm).

School districts, boards of cooperative educational services, or transportation contractors that do not have enough school bus driver instructors or staff to administer the physical performance tests may apply for a waiver to have NYS Department of Motor Vehicles certified examiners administer the tests, provided they are conducted under the general supervision of a certified school bus driver instructor (8 NYCRR § 156.3(c)(3)(iii)(b)).

A monitor or attendant who fails a test may request a retest. The costs of the re-examination must be borne by the employer if the employee passes. Otherwise the employee bears the cost (8 NYCRR § 156.3(c)(3)(iii)(c)).

60:29. Are school bus monitors and attendants required to have safety training?

Yes. Specifically, all school bus monitors and attendants must receive three hours of pre-service instruction that includes, but is not limited to, school bus safety practices, child management techniques, and the proper techniques for assisting children to safely enter and exit a school bus. Monitors and attendants hired must complete the required training prior to beginning service (8 NYCRR § 156.3(c)(5)(i)).

Furthermore, within their first year of employment they must complete a basic course of instruction for monitors and attendants that provides at least 10 hours of instruction on topics prescribed by the commissioner of education (8 NYCRR § 156.3(c)(5)(iii)).

In addition, school bus monitors and attendants serving students with a disabling condition must receive instruction relating to special needs transportation including proper techniques for assisting disabled students in entering and exiting the school bus. School bus monitors and attendants must complete the special needs training prior to assuming their duties (Veh. & Traf Law § 1229-d; 8 NYCRR § 156.3(c)(5)(i)).

Moreover, school bus attendants serving one or more students with a disability must receive training and instruction relating to the understanding of and attention to the special needs of such students at least once per year, in accordance with commissioner's regulations. Those hired after January 1, 2009, must complete this training prior to assuming their duties (Veh. & Traf. Law § 1229-d; see **60:10** regarding similar requirements for bus drivers).

All monitors and attendants must receive a two-hour refresher training annually at sessions conducted between July 1 and the first day of school, and between December 1 and March 1 of each school year (8 NYCRR § 156.3(c)(5)(iv)).

60:30. Must school bus monitors and attendants be certified in cardiopulmonary resuscitation?

Only school bus attendants who serve students with a disabling condition are required to have and maintain certification in cardiopulmonary resuscitation (CPR), when such skills are required as part of a student's individualized education program (IEP). Those hired after January 1, 2004, must be CPR certified prior to assuming their duties (Veh. & Traf. Law § 1229-d(3); 8 NYCRR § 156.3(c)(4)).

Schools districts, boards of cooperative educational services, or contractors may also require both school bus monitors and attendants to maintain certification in first aid (8 NYCRR § 156.3(c)(4)).

60:31. Are school bus monitors and attendants permitted to leave a school bus when children are inside?

Yes, but only to help children enter or exit the school bus and to safely cross the street. Otherwise, when children are inside the bus, monitors and attendants must remain on the bus with them, except in an emergency. In such a case, the bus driver must stop the motor, remove the ignition key, and set the parking brake before the monitor or attendant leaves the bus (8 NYCRR § 156.3(e)(4)).

60:32. Can school districts require that school bus monitors and attendants be fingerprinted?

Yes. School bus monitors and attendants must be fingerprinted and cleared in a background check if such prospective employee has not been cleared using the Vehicle and Traffic Law fingerprint and criminal history check procedures (§ 1709(39); 8 NYCRR § 87.2(k)(3)(i)). Section 1229-d of the Vehicle and Traffic Law authorizes school districts to require that applicants for a position as school bus attendant submit fingerprints for a criminal history check (Veh. & Traf. Law § 1229-d(2)(a); see also NYS Education Department, *Who Must Be Fingerprinted Charts* (updated Jan. 2013), at: http:// www. highered.nysed.gov/tsei/ospra/fingerprintingcharts.html).

Transportation

Q. Can school districts require that [illegible]?

[illegible]

61. Buildings and Grounds

61:1. Are school districts required to prepare long-range plans on educational facilities?

Yes. Section 155.1 of the commissioner's regulations requires each school district to prepare and keep on file a comprehensive long-range plan pertaining to educational facilities.

The plan must be reevaluated and updated at least annually. It must include an appraisal of the following: the educational philosophy of the district with resulting administrative organization and program requirements; current and projected student enrollments; use of space and state-rated student capacity of existing facilities; the allocation of instructional space to meet the current and future special education program and service needs, and to serve students with disabilities in settings with nondisabled peers; priority of need of maintenance, repair or modernization of existing facilities, including consideration of the obsolescence and retirement of certain facilities; and the provision of additional facilities.

The numbers, types, space requirements and pupil capacities of facilities must relate to the present and projected needs of the school district programs, including mandated educational requirements and the current and future special education program and service space needed to serve all students with disabilities.

In addition, each school district must prepare a five-year capital facilities plan, as prescribed by the commissioner of education. The plan, which must be updated annually, must include the information required in commissioner's regulations and identify critical maintenance needs based upon consideration of the safety rating of each occupied building (§ 409-d(2)(d); 8 NYCRR §§ 155.1(a)(4), 155.3(c); see **62:21**).

61:2. Must the voters approve the designation of a site for a new school building?

Sometimes. Voter approval is required in a common school district and in any other school district that has a population of less than 5,000 (§§ 401(2), 2512(1), 2556(2)). However, although certain districts are not required to get voter approval for site selection, the board may still submit the issue of site selection to the voters (*Matter of Albanese*, 11 Ed Dept Rep 166 (1972)).

In addition, small city school districts must nonetheless submit for approval to the city planning commission any site it proposes to purchase and designate as a school site prior to such designation (§ 2512(6); *City of Glens Falls v. Bd. of Educ. of Glens Falls City Sch. Dist.*, 88 A.D.2d 233 (3d Dep't 1982); see also *Appeal of O'Brien,* 51 Ed Dept Rep, Dec. No. 16,316 (2011)). The city planning commission approval requirement applies only to the initial designation of a new location for any school building. It does not apply to subsequent determinations as to the specific use of a location previously designated and already in use as a school (*Id.*).

61:3. Must the commissioner of education approve the site for construction and enlargement of school district facilities?

Yes. Pursuant to section 408 of the Education Law, section 155.1(c) of the commissioner's regulations requires that sites for the construction or enlargement of facilities be approved by the commissioner of education. This regulation also requires the district to consider the following when selecting a site:

- The size and location of a site must be consistent with the long-term building plans of the district (8 NYCRR § 155.1(c)(1)).

- The educational adaptability of the site with consideration for the placement of the building and development of the grounds for outdoor educational programs and related activities, without excessive initial or development costs. Sites must also include the following minimum usable acres, unless otherwise approved by the commissioner: elementary school (K–6) — a three-acre base plus one acre for each 100 students, or fraction thereof; and secondary schools (7–12) — a 10-acre base plus one acre for each 100 students, or fraction thereof (8 NYCRR § 155.1(c)(2)).
- Sites must be developed to conserve natural resources and avoid environmental problems within the limits of the educational program. Care must be taken to ensure that the site and facilities are consistent with and contribute to the school and community environment and provide for the health and safety of occupants (8 NYCRR § 155.1(c)(3)).

The New York State School Boards Association recommends that a district considering a site contact the New York State Education Department's Office of Facilities Planning prior to purchase.

Acquisition and Disposal of School Property

61:4. How may a school district acquire real property for school purposes?

A school district may acquire real property for school purposes by gift, grant, devise (a clause in a will disposing of real property) or purchase; and by involuntary acquisition under some circumstances if an agreement cannot be made with the owner for the purchase (§ 404).

The school board as a corporate body holds title to real property (§§ 406, 1603, 1709(9)). In city school districts with fewer than 125,000 inhabitants, the school board holds title to real property purchased by it in the name of the school district (§ 2511(1)). In a Big 5 city school district, the school board takes title to real property in the name of the city, which holds the property in trust for use by the school district (§ 2557).

Special provisions regarding purchase and sale of real and personal property apply to large city school districts, as indicated in section 2556 of the Education Law.

61:5. Once a site has been properly selected, must the voters approve the purchase of real property?

Yes, except in city school districts with a population over 125,000 inhabitants, the purchase of real property is subject to the approval of the voters (§§ 416(1), 2511(1), 2556(1)).

61:6. Can a school board enter into an option agreement for the purchase of a school site without the voters' authorization or consent?

Yes, provided that the amount paid for the option is reasonable (*Opinion of Counsel No. 65*, 1 Ed Dept Rep 764 (1952)). In such instances, the district is purchasing the option to buy the site at a later date, and not the site itself.

61:7. If a school district is given a site as a gift, must the district still get the voters' approval to accept it?

No. Voter approval is not necessary to accept the property as a gift (§ 404). However, except in large city school districts, voter approval is necessary before a school building can be erected on the property (§§ 416(1), 2512(1), 2556(1)).

61:8. Can a school district enter into a lease for a school building?

Yes. The school board in any union free, central or city school district, and the chancellor of the New York City school district, may authorize the lease of a school building from either another school district or from any person, partnership or corporation (§§ 403-b(1), 1726, 2503(8), 2554(6), 2590-h(17)).

If the lease is between two school districts, the leased building must be within a reasonable distance of the leasing district, as determined by the commissioner of education (§ 403-b(1)). If the lease is between a school district and a non-school entity, the leased building or facility must be located within the school district (§ 403-b(1)).

All leases and leased facilities must meet the following requirements:

- No lease shall become effective until approved by the commissioner of education (§ 403-b(1)(c)).
- The lease may not exceed five years unless the district voters have approved a longer term. The initial term of lease, however, cannot exceed the period of probable usefulness as prescribed by law (§ 403-b(1)(a); Local Fin. Law § 11.00(a)(11), (12), (84), (97)).
- The voters in the lessee district must approve any renewal of the lease, except for those leases made by a large city school district (§§ 403-b(1)(d), 2503(8), 2554(6)).
- The voters in the lessee district must approve any capital project to be undertaken in a leased building or facility during the term of the lease subject to prior approval by the commissioner after the need for such project has been established, except for those leases made by a large city school district (§§ 403-b(1)(b), 2503(8), 2554(6)).
- The leased facility must meet all applicable standards for the health, safety and comfort of its occupants (§ 403-b(1)(c)(i)).
- The leased facility must be educationally adequate (§ 403-b(1)(c)(ii)).
- The school district must have a current five-year facilities plan or other applicable long-range facilities plan that includes such lease (§§ 403-b(1)(c)(iii), 2503(8), 2554(6)).

To be eligible for state aid, any leased facility must:

- Meet the requirements for access by individuals with disabilities.
- Be used to house programs for students in nursery, prekindergarten through 12th grade and students up to age 21 who have not received a high school diploma (other than preschool students with disabilities) with minimal associated administrative and support space.
- In New York City only, when the purpose of the leased space includes special education programs and services, the leased space must be consistent with the district's comprehensive long-range plan for the allocation of instructional space to meet the current and future special education program and service needs and to serve students with disabilities in settings with nondisabled peers (§§ 403-b(1)(e), 2503(8), 2554(6); 8 NYCRR § 155.12(b)(6), (d)(5)(i)).

61:9. May a school board enter into a lease-purchase agreement for the purchase of school buildings?

Yes. A school board may enter into agreements for the lease-purchase of buildings for school purposes, either to be placed or erected on a district-owned site. Such an agreement is subject to the requirements in section 1726 of the Education Law. Approval by the district voters and the commissioner of education is also required. However, no lease-purchase agreement may be made for a period exceeding the applicable period of probable usefulness for the property. Also any agreement made is subject to the competitive bidding requirements of the General Municipal Law including the Wick's Law provisions (§§ 1726, 2503(8); Local Fin. Law § 11.00(a)(11), (12), (84), (97); Gen. Mun. Law § 101; *Appeal of Brousseau*, 37 Ed Dept Rep 295 (1998)). In addition, a school district may not sell a school building currently in use for school purposes and then re-acquire it by installment or lease-purchase agreement (Opn. St. Comp. 2005-3).

61:10. May a school district sell its property?

Yes. A school board may, as prescribed by law, sell the real and personal property owned by the school district (§§ 1604(36), 1709(11), 1804(6)(a), (c), 2511, 2557; see **61:12** for lease or rental of school property).

When selling or disposing of school district property, school boards have a fiduciary responsibility to obtain the best price possible for any lawful use of the premises (*Matter of Ross v. Wilson*, 308 N.Y. 605 (1955); *Matter of New City Jewish Ctr. v. Flagg*, 111 A.D.2d 814 (2d Dep't 1985); *Appeal of Anderson*, 52 Ed Dept Rep, Dec. No. 16,438 (2012); *Appeal of White,* 50 Ed Dept Rep, Dec. No. 16,239 (2011); *Matter of Baker*, 14 Ed Dept Rep 5 (1974)). However, the board may exercise its judgment and discretion in good faith concerning the method of sale that will bring the best price (*Id.*), including consideration of future tax consequences (*Berkey v. Downing*, 68 Misc.2d 595 (Sup. Ct. Tompkins Cnty. 1972); Opn. St. Comp. 78-262). If a school board abuses its discretion or acts in an arbitrary or capricious manner with respect to the sale of a piece of school district property, the sale may be set aside (see *Matter of Yeshiva of Spring Valley v. Bd. of Educ. of East Ramapo CSD*, 132 A.D.2d 27 (2d Dep't 1988); *Appeal of White)*. That was the case where a school board received two contemporaneous varying appraisals of a building, but failed to adequately reconcile the difference in value. Moreover, both appraisals recommended aggressively marketing the property on a wide basis for at least nine months, but the school board approved the sale of the building after advertising strictly locally for only one month (*Appeal of White*). There is no requirement to use a real estate broker when selling real property (*Appeal of Anderson*).

Sale of real property

A school district may only sell real property that is no longer in use (§§ 402; 1709(11); Opn. St. Comp. 2005-3). It may not sell a building currently in use for school district purposes and then re-acquire it by installment or lease-purchase agreement (Opn. St. Comp. 2005-3).

In union free and small city school districts, voter approval is required to sell real property (§§ 1709(11), 2511). In central school districts that have been centralized for at least seven years, voter approval is not necessary unless a petition requesting a vote is submitted to the board, signed by at least 10 percent of the voters (§ 1804(6)(c); see *Appeal of White*). Large city school districts do not need voter approval to sell real property (§ 2557). A school board may, in its discretion, use the proceeds from the sale of real property to set up a reserve fund to reduce real property taxes in the district for a period of up to 10 school years (§ 1709(37); see also **26:2** and **26:5**).

Sale of personal property

With respect to the sale of unneeded personal property, such as a used station wagon, the sale must be bona fide and for adequate consideration. Bids at a public auction are not required (Opn. St. Comp. 58-120).

Private sale of surplus equipment to a school board member or other school official or employee who is involved in the purchasing function is generally prohibited (Gen. Mun. Law Art. 18; Opn. St. Comp. 58-120).

School districts and boards of cooperative educational services must adopt a resolution by two-thirds vote of their school board members to authorize a change in the status of a military monument or military memorial site located on their property including, for example, the lease, transfer, move or sale of such structures or sites (Gen. Mun. Law § 99-w; see **61:13**).

61:11. May a school district donate its property as a gift?

The Education Law authorizes a school district to donate unused school buildings and sites, but only to a *public corporation* for its use. The gift may be made on terms and conditions determined by the school board, and may or may not involve a money transaction. Except in large city school districts, voter approval is required (§ 405).

The term *public corporation* includes counties, cities, towns, villages, school districts, district corporations (territorial divisions of the state with the power to issue obligations and levy taxes or require the levy of taxes) and public-benefit corporations. This last category includes such units as the various bridge and housing authorities (Gen. Constr. Law § 66).

61:12. Can a school board lease or rent out a school building or other school property?

Yes. A school board may adopt a resolution which states that the real property to be leased is not currently needed for school district purposes and that the leasing of such real property is in the best interest of the school district (§ 403-a(1); see also *Camillus v. West Side Gymnastics Sch., Inc.*, 109 Misc.2d 609 (Sup. Ct. Onondaga Cnty. 1981); *Appeal of Brousseau*, 37 Ed Dept Rep 295 (1998)).

The terms of the lease must reflect a fair market rental value as determined by the school board; must not exceed a 10-year term; and require the lessee to restore the real property to its original condition, less ordinary depreciation, upon termination of the lease. The lease may be renewed for a period up to 10 years, upon approval of the commissioner of education (§ 403-a; *Matter of Hollister*, 39 Ed Dept Rep 109 (1999)).

There is no requirement that school boards seek competitive bids or market the property to be leased in a particular way. A school board may use its discretion to achieve the best lease price (*Appeal of Luciano*, 51 Ed Dept Rep, Dec. No. 16,308 (2011)). However, a board must take reasonable steps to ensure its decision is informed, and that it is receiving the best possible deal, which includes ascertaining the fair market value of the property and leasing the property competitively (*Appeal of Forrest*, 53 Ed Dept Rep, Dec. No. 16,501 (2013); see also *Yeshiva of Spring Valley, Inc. v. Bd. of Educ. of East Ramapo CSD*, 132 A.D.2d 27 (2d Dep't 1987)). The mere act of negotiating is not sufficient to determine fair market value (*Appeal of Forrest*).

There is no requirement either for voter approval of lease terms once the district has properly complied with the requirements of section 403-a of the Education Law (*Matter of Hollister*, 33 Ed Dept Rep 294 (1993)). However, voter approval must be sought for any proposed lease agreement that will exceed 10 years in length (§ 403-a(5)).

In addition, school boards and boards of cooperative educational services, without voter approval, may convey a right-of-way over school property for public utilities services to any municipality, municipal district, authority, or public utility. This is known as granting an easement (§ 405). However, although a school district may acquire, operate, and maintain parking facilities related to authorized uses of school facilities, it may not construct or enter into a lease for the construction of a parking garage to be used primarily by the public at large for commercial purposes unrelated to school activities (Opn. St. Comp. 2005-3).

61:13. What are districts' obligations regarding military monuments and memorials on district property?

A military monument is any structure, or part thereof, including a tablet, plaque, wall, or building, which honors a current or former armed forces member(s), or commemorates a military action. A military memorial is a park, field, grove, land or artwork surrounding a military monument (Gen. Mun. Law § 99-w(1)).

Any "change in status" (i.e., move, transfer, discontinue, discard, sale or lease) of a military monument or memorial on school district or board of cooperative educational services property is subject to a two-thirds vote of the board. Ninety days prior to the vote, the district must hold a public hearing. Notice of the hearing must be posted in at least five public places; and published in at least one newspaper of general circulation for three consecutive days, within 15 days of the hearing. Notice must also be published on the district's website for at least 15 days prior to the hearing. (Gen. Mun. Law § 99-w(2)).

Construction and Renovation of Facilities

61:14. Must the district voters approve the construction of new facilities?

Yes. Except in large city school districts, a majority of the voters in a school district must authorize and approve taxes for the addition, alteration, repair or improvement to the sites or buildings belonging to the district (§ 416(1), (7)).

In addition, the Education Law prohibits resubmission of propositions for construction of new school buildings (or additions at the same site) more than twice in a one-year period and prohibits the resubmission of the same or similar proposition within 90 days. However, this restriction does not apply if the proposition is to approve an additional amount necessary to carry out an already approved building project and it is determined that the bids for the project are in excess of the approved amount (§ 416(6)).

61:15. Can a school board print and distribute to the voters an informational brochure relating to a bond issue for a new school building to be approved at a district election?

Yes. However, the New York State of Appeals held that although a school board may use public funds to pay for an advertisement or newsletter to explain a proposed district budget or bond issue, it may not include subjective statements in such publications that, for example, urge district residents to vote "yes" because the board believes that particular budget or bond issue to be in the best interest of the school district (*Phillips v. Maurer*, 67 N.Y.2d 672 (1986); see also **15:33-47**).

In order to avoid any appearance of impropriety, any informational materials sent to district voters should be kept strictly factual and impartial (*Appeal of Sotirovich,* 51 Ed Dept Rep, Dec. No. 16,360 (2012); *Appeal of Hubbard,* 39 Ed Dept Rep 363 (1999); *Appeal of Meyer*, 38 Ed Dept Rep 285 (1998); *Appeal of Friedman*, 37 Ed Dept Rep 363 (1998); *Appeal of Moessinger*, 33 Ed Dept Rep 487 (1994)). Further, individual board members should exercise caution when using private funds to make a partisan statement about a vote, and should identify their views as their own. Any links on the district website to partisan viewpoints should contain a disclaimer (*Appeal of Koehler*, 52 Ed Dept Rep, Dec. No. 16,373 (2012); see **15:33-47**).

61:16. May a school board contract with an architect for the preparation of preliminary plans and specifications for a school building construction project before submitting the building project to the voters?

Yes. The school board may so contract with an architect, whose fee may legitimately be paid by the district. However, before an architect prepares final plans, voter approval must be obtained at a school district meeting, except in large city school districts (*Formal Opn. of Counsel No. 1*, 1 Ed Dept Rep 701 (1951)).

61:17. Can the cost of construction of a new public school building exceed the amount authorized by the school district's voters?

No. Where the voters of a school district have approved a maximum expenditure for the construction of a school, the district may not exceed the maximum amount authorized (Local Fin. Law § 37.00; 12 Opn. St. Comp. 4 (1956)).

Additional funds may be authorized only with the voters' approval either in a regular budget vote or by special referendum (see § 416). If the school board deems it an emergency situation, then, within certain restrictions, a budget note can be issued to cover the excess cost (Local Fin. Law § 29.00). For information on the issuance of bonds in a construction project, see **27:1-6**.

61:18. Are there required specifications on the construction of school buildings in New York State?

Yes. Details on construction of public school buildings may be found in Part 155 of the commissioner's regulations and in the NYS Education Department's *Manual of Planning Standards* and *Instruction Guide for Public School Districts and BOCES Obtaining Building Permits for Capital Construction Projects*. Both of these publications are available from the Department's Office of Facilities Planning in Albany. Construction information is also available from the Office of Facilities Planning website at: http://www.p12.nysed.gov/facplan/.

In developing plans and specifications for the construction, enlargement, or remodeling of school facilities, school districts are encouraged to review the energy conservation and saving best practices available from the New York State Education Department and the New York State Energy Research and Development Authority (§ 408(3)).

61:19. Are there any specific standards that apply to the design and construction of sustainable environmentally-friendly high performance schools?

Yes. Such schools optimize resources over the life of the facility, are less expensive to operate than standard buildings, and help to ensure healthy, safe, and high quality learning environments. Requirements in seven major categories are set forth in guidelines issued jointly by the New York State Education Department and the New York State Energy Research and Development Authority. The guidelines can be accessed at: http://www.p12.nysed.gov/facplan/news.html.

61:20. Must plans and specifications for school buildings be approved by the commissioner of education?

Yes. Plans and specifications for the construction, enlargement, repair or remodeling of school facilities of a school district (other than in a city school district having at least one million residents), and a board of cooperative educational services district, must be submitted for the commissioner's approval when the cost of the work is anticipated to be at least $10,000, and for all projects that affect the health and safety of students (§ 408; 8 NYCRR § 155.2(b)).

Plans and specifications must show detailed requirements of design and construction, space layout, circulation and exits, smoke and fire control, accident protection, visual and thermal environment and related electrical and mechanical work, sanitation features and related plumbing work (8 NYCRR § 155.2(b)(1)(i)). All plans and specifications for new instructional space must be consistent with the needs of participating students with disabilities (8 NYCRR § 155.2(b)(2); see 8 NYCRR 200.2(g)). They must conform to the State Uniform Fire Prevention and Building Code (19 NYCRR Parts 1220-1227) and Part 155 of the commissioner's regulations including, but not limited to, the uniform safety standards for school construction and maintenance projects (see 8 NYCRR §§ 155.2, 155.5). In addition, any construction or remodeling project also must comply with the state Uniform Fire Prevention and Building Code (8 NYCRR § 155.2(c), (d)).

In developing such plans and specifications, districts should review energy conservation and saving best practices (§ 408(3); see **61:19**).

The commissioner's approval of school building plans signifies only that the plans and specifications meet the minimum requirements of sections 408 and 409 of the Education Law, the commissioner's regulations, and policies of the Office of Facilities Planning relating to educational requirements, heating, ventilation, lighting, sanitation and health, and fire and accident protection. It does not signify approval of architectural or structural design, choice of building materials, any contracts that may be awarded or executed, or any features that will go beyond the minimum requirements. Additionally, this approval gives no assurance that this project qualifies for state aid for education in accordance with the provisions of section 3602 of the Education Law.

Upon approval of plans and specifications, the commissioner will issue a building permit, provided that a licensed architect or engineer properly supervise the project during construction (8 NYCRR § 155.2(b)(5)).

61:21. What is the process for a school district to obtain approval and a building permit for a school construction project?

Approval of building projects is the responsibility of the New York State Education Department (SED). Receipt of a building permit from SED is evidence of official approval of a building project and is obtained according to the following procedure:

- A district sends one of four letter of intent (LOI) forms depending upon the project:
  - New buildings, additions to existing buildings, or reconstruction work to be done in or on an existing building;
  - Leasing building space off district property or buildings that have been constructed or placed on district property without first obtaining a Building Permit from SED;
  - Placing manufactured buildings on district property; or
  - Setting up district-wide projects.

The Office of Facilities Planning sends a letter to the district acknowledging receipt of the letter of intent and informing the district of their assigned 15-digit control number and the name of the project manager assigned to their project. The project manager coordinates all aspects of the project and serves as the district's contact with SED.

The district must then:

- Submit a State Smart Growth Public Infrastructure Impact Statement explaining how the project meets the state smart growth public infrastructure criteria or, alternatively, that the project does not meet the criteria because compliance is impractical. The district must determine if the project minimizes unnecessary costs of sprawl development, such as environmental degradation and loss of open space (Envtl. Consv. Law §§ 6-0101–6-0111; NYS Education Department, Office of Facilities Planning *Newsletter #106* (May 2011), at: http://www.p12.nysed.gov/facplan/documents/final106Newsletter.pdf).
- Complete the State Environment Quality Review (SEQR) process. Under the SEQR process the district must determine if the building project will have an effect on the environment such that an environmental impact statement (EIS) should be completed. Once the SEQR is completed, the district will submit copies of all SEQR documents used by the district to make the final determination as to the type of action for each capital project proposed by the district.
- Consult with the State Historic Preservation Office (SHPO) as to whether historic or archaeological resources will be impacted and, if so, how any substantial adverse impacts can be avoided or mitigated. If adverse environmental impact cannot be avoided or adequately mitigated, an agreement must be reached between SHPO and the district, if possible. SED and the Office of Parks, Recreation and Historic Preservation (OPRHP) have agreed to exempt from SHPO review projects that may have an impact upon buildings, structures, objects, or sites listed or eligible for listing on the State Register of Historic Places, if the building itself or the nature of the project meet certain specified criteria. Projects that are subject to the National

Historic Preservation Law must still be fully reviewed by SHPO on behalf of the federal government (see *Letter of Resolution between the New York State Office of Parks, Recreation and Historic Preservation and the New York State Education Department* (June 2010), at: http://www.p12.nysed.gov/facplan/documents/SHPOLtrOfResolution_062010.pdf; see also PRHP Law § 14.09; 34 CFR Part 800).

- Final plans are submitted to a district's project manager. Only if a project involves the construction of a new instructional facility or the addition to an existing instructional facility, will the district need to make a preliminary submission prior to the final submission. The project manager has the authority to waive a preliminary submission. Final plans are reviewed by bureau staff, architects, and engineers.
- Upon approval, the district will be sent a set of final approval documents, including the building permit for each approved project, a bond certificate when required, a certificate of approval plans and specifications, a certification of substantial completion form and any other documents necessary for final inspection and certification (see 8 NYCRR § 155.9; see also 6 NYCRR Part 617; NYS Education Department, *Instruction Guide for Public School Districts and BOCES Obtaining Building Permits for Capital Construction Projects* (July 2002), at: http://www.p12.nysed.gov/facplan/publicat/BP_instruction_guide.PDF).

61:22. Can the commissioner revoke a building permit for a school construction project?

Yes, in the event of violations of the State Uniform Fire Prevention and Building Code, Part 155 of the commissioner's regulations or other safety standards imposed by law or regulation (8 NYCRR § 155.2(b)(5)(ii)).

61:23. Must school districts advertise for bids for construction projects?

Yes. In addition, section 101 of the General Municipal Law, more commonly referred to as the Wicks Law, requires that school districts bid out separate specifications for plumbing and gas fitting; steam heating, hot water, ventilating and air conditioning apparatus; and electrical wiring and standard illuminating fixtures on any construction project exceeding $3 million in the counties of Bronx, Kings, Queens, New York, and Richmond, $1.5 million in the counties of Nassau, Suffolk, and Westchester and $500,000 in all other counties. Separate contracts must be awarded in these areas in accordance with the competitive bidding requirements of the General Municipal Law. Contracts not subject to the separate specification requirements are subject to other procedures under the General Municipal Law including a requirement for bidders to include a sealed list of any subcontractors they intend to use with their bid (Gen. Mun. Law § 101(5); see **28:11-19**).

However, districts may not advertise bids for school building construction projects that exceed $100,000 until the plans and specifications have been submitted to and approved by the commissioner of education. There is an exception for city districts with populations of one million or more (§ 408(1); 8 NYCRR § 155.2(b)). Furthermore, the uniform standards for school construction and maintenance projects require that bid specifications and contract documents must address the issue of safety during construction before contract documents are advertised for bid (8 NYCRR § 155.5(c)).

61:24. Are there legal restrictions in determining wages for workers on school construction projects?

Yes. The state Labor Law requires that the "prevailing rate of wages" be paid to all workers on public school building projects in the state. This includes construction, alterations and repairs (Lab. Law

§ 220(3)), even when the work is performed by staff from a board of cooperative educational services (BOCES) (*Cayuga-Onondaga Counties BOCES v. Sweeney*, 89 N.Y.2d 395 (1996)). However, BOCES students who participated in the construction of an office building as part of their educational experience were not employees of a contractor and therefore were not entitled to payment of prevailing wages for public work (*Onondaga-Cortland-Madison BOCES v. McGowan,* 285 A.D.2d 36 (3d Dep't 2001)). Similarly, since independent contractors are neither expressly included nor excluded from Labor Law § 220, the facts of the actual employment determine whether an independent contractor is an "employee" entitled to prevailing wages (*Jackson v. U.S. Specialty Ins. Co.,* 2014 N.Y. Misc. LEXIS 369; see NYS Dept. of Labor, *Frequently Asked Questions Regarding Public Work – Article 8, Section 220, NYS Labor Law* (*05.10*) Question VI. C., at: http://www.labor.state.ny.us/workerprotection/publicwork/PDFs/Article8FAQS.pdf).

The determination of prevailing wages must be made in accordance with the rates of wages paid pursuant to collective bargaining agreements in the locality in which the work is done (Lab. Law § 220(5)(a)). Parties cannot eliminate prevailing wage requirements through collective bargaining (*RI, Inc. v. Gardner*, 889 F. Supp.2d 408 (E.D.N.Y. 2012)).

As a method of ensuring compliance with the prevailing wage requirements, contractors and subcontractors on a public work project must file with the project's owner sworn to or affirmed as true payroll records. Toward this end, school districts must designate who among their employees is responsible for receiving, collecting, and reviewing the facial validity of such records. In addition, they must post the name of their designee in a conspicuous location at the project site (Lab. Law § 220(3-a)(a)(iii), (iv)). Also, every contract for a school construction project must state that the filing of payrolls in the manner required by law is a condition precedent to the payment of any sums due and owing to any person for work done on the project (Lab. Law § 220(3)(d)(iv)).

61:25. May new school buildings be occupied before they are completely finished?

Yes, but be aware that conditions may exist that could compromise the health and safety of students when new schools are occupied before they are completed.

At the time of substantial completion of the project (when the work is sufficiently complete for occupancy of the building for its intended use), the architect or engineer must submit a certification of substantial completion form to the commissioner of education and certify that the project was completed in conformance with the State Uniform Fire and Prevention and Building Code, part 155 of the commissioner's regulations, and the project plans and specifications previously approved by the commissioner (8 NYCRR § 155.2(b)(6)). Following receipt and posting of the certificate of occupancy, the building can be fully used. In addition, the district's health and safety committee must have the opportunity for a walk through to confirm the area is ready to be opened for use (see 8 NYCRR § 155.5(n)).

61:26. Must school buildings be accessible to persons with disabilities?

Yes. Under the federal Americans with Disabilities Act, school districts must ensure that all new construction or alterations to existing facilities are accessible to persons with disabilities. However, districts are not required to make structural changes to existing facilities if other methods would make their programs accessible to individuals with disabilities (42 USC § 12101 *et seq.*).

61:27. Is a school district subject to zoning regulations or the jurisdiction of local historic preservation agencies with regard to its buildings or proposed buildings?

No. School districts are not subject to town, city or village zoning provisions regulating setback, selection of a school building site, school building construction and the size of the open areas surrounding school buildings. A district is not required to obtain a municipal building permit (Opn. St. Comp. 68-426). Similarly, a school district is not subject to a municipal noise ordinance that requires application for a building permit to engage in construction activities after 5:30 p.m. and on weekends (Opn. Att'y Gen. 99-20). It also does not have to comply with the provisions of a town building code (*Bd. of Educ. v. Buffalo*, 32 A.D.2d 98 (4th Dep't 1969); *Camillus v. West Side Gymnastics Sch., Inc.*, 109 Misc.2d 609 (Sup. Ct. Onondaga Cnty. 1981); see also **61:21**).

In addition, according to one appellate court, school districts that own historic buildings are subject to oversight and regulation by only state agencies such as the Office of Parks, Recreation and Historic Preservation. Therefore, a local historic preservation agency has no authority to prevent the demolition of a historic building owned by a school district (*Matter of Ithaca City Sch. Dist. v. City of Ithaca*, 82 A.D.3d 1316 (3d Dep't 2011)).

61:28. May a public school rent highway equipment from a county highway department to construct or repair school roads or for snow removal?

Yes, as provided in section 133-a of the Highway Law. The state comptroller has indicated that loaning an operator for the equipment is also an implied authorization (Opn. St. Comp. 58-328).

61:29. Can a school district receive building aid for a leased building?

Yes. A district can receive building aid if the leased school or facility meets requirements for access by individuals with disabilities to both facilities and programs, by complying with commissioner's regulations (§ 403-b(1)(e); 8 NYCRR §§ 155.12(b)(6)(i), 200.2). The leased space must be used to house programs for students in grades prekindergarten through 12, including kindergarten, nursery school, night school, but not for preschool students with disabilities, with minimal associated administrative and support services space, as approved by the commissioner of education (§§ 3602(6), 2503(8), 2554(6)).

In addition, for New York City only, space leased for special education programs and services is eligible for building aid if the space is consistent with the district's comprehensive long-range plan for the allocation of instructional space to meet the current and future special education program and services needs and to serve students with disabilities in settings with nondisabled peers (8 NYCRR § 155.12(d)(5)(i)).

Closing of School Buildings

61:30. Can the commissioner of education declare certain areas of a school building unsafe and unusable?

Yes. If the commissioner judges the general condition of a school building, or any part or area, would be detrimental to the health and safety of its occupants, he may designate an area or areas of the building as unusable or may limit the number of occupants allowed in that area (8 NYCRR § 155.7(j)).

In New York City, both the city board and the chancellor may take emergency action and close a school on a temporary basis to preserve student health, safety or general welfare (§§ 2590-g(9); 2590-h(2-a)(f)). The emergency closure of a school building may not exceed the period of duration specified in law (*Id.*). During that time period, an educational impact statement must be prepared and hearings conducted before the city board may extend or make permanent the school's closure (§§ 2590-g(9); 2590-h(2-a)(f)).

61:31. Does a school board have the right to close school buildings and create new attendance zones without voter approval?

Yes. Decisions about the assignment of students and the establishment of reasonable methods of zoning for the purpose of school attendance rest with the school board under section 1709 of the Education Law (see *Appeal of Strade*, 48 Ed Dept Rep 73 (2008); *Matter of Lanfear*, 31 Ed Dept Rep 340 (1992); *Matter of Furman*, 15 Ed Dept Rep 70 (1975)).

In New York City, that authority rests with the city board following consideration of an educational impact statement prepared by the chancellor and public hearings on the proposal (§§ 2590-g(1)(h), (8), (9), 2590-h(2-a)).

61:32. Are there any specific procedures a school board must follow before closing down a school building?

Not outside New York City. Decisions regarding the closure and discontinuance of use of school buildings rest exclusively within a school board's discretion (*Appeal of Ransom*, 54 Ed Dept Rep, Dec. No. 16,647 (2014); *Appeal of Herrala,* 51 Ed Dept Rep, Dec. No. 16,264 (2011); *Appeal of Tzach,* 49 Ed Dept Rep 247 (2010); *Appeal of Hatton,* 49 Ed Dept Rep 47 (2009); *Appeal of Hamblin,* 48 Ed Dept Rep 421 (2009)). Furthermore, any such decision will not be set aside unless it is arbitrary, capricious, lacking a rational basis, or contrary to sound educational policy (*Id.*).

Factors a school board may consider in exercising its discretion to close a school building include, for example, cost, capacity, transportation, program impacts, declining enrollment and/or enrollment trends (*Appeal of Fuller*, 54 Ed Dept Rep, Dec. No. 16,758 (2015); *Appeal of Ad Hoc Comm. to Save Kings Elementary Sch.* 53 Ed Dept Rep, Dec. No. 16,530 (2013); *Appeal of Bailey,* 45 Ed Dept Rep 270 (2005)), changes in state and federal funding, increases in operating costs and budget projections (*Appeal of Hamblin),* class size caps, accessibility, classroom lavatories (*Appeal of Baum,* 49 Ed Dept Rep 260 (2010)), and the need to reduce the district's budget while minimizing educational impact (*Appeal of People Against the Consolidation of Elementary. Schs*., 47 Ed Dept Rep 4 (2007)).

Nonetheless, section 402-a of the Education Law authorizes and recommends, but does not require, that a district establish an advisory committee on school building utilization to investigate the educational impact of a closing six months prior to the scheduled closing. The decision to establish such an advisory committee rests with the board (§ 402-a(1); *Appeal of Hockswender*, 52 Ed Dept Rep, Dec. No. 16,400 (2012); *Appeal of Andrews*, 45 Ed Dept Rep 248 (2005); *Appeal of Patashnick & Waters*, 39 Ed Dept Rep 236 (1999); *Appeal of Seligman*, 31 Ed Dept Rep 131 (1991)). However, the final responsibility regarding closure rests with the board, even if an advisory committee is established (*Appeal of Tzach; Appeal of Hatton; Appeal of Andrews; Appeal of Seligman*).

If a committee is established, it must review, at least, the following factors:

- The current and projected pupil enrollment, the prospective need for such a building, the ramifications of such closing upon the community, initial costs and savings resulting from such closing, and the potential disposability of the closed school.
- The possible use of the school building for other educational programs or administrative services.
- The effect of the closing on personnel needs, and on the costs of instruction, administration, transportation and other support services.
- The type, age and physical condition of the building, outstanding indebtedness, maintenance and energy costs, recent or planned improvements for the building, and the building's special features.
- The ability of the other schools in the affected district to accommodate students if the building closes.
- The possible shared utilization of space in the building during or after regular school hours, pursuant to the Education Law (§ 402-a(2)).

The committee's educational impact statement findings must be filed with the school board, followed by notice of the proposed closing and a public hearing. Thereafter, the school board must make its final decision at a board meeting (§ 402-a(3)). The procedures in section 402-a apply only where a school board elects to establish an advisory committee concerning a school closing (*Appeal of Bailey*). They do not apply when a district simply wants to convert a building to a different use (*Appeal of Patashnick & Waters; Appeal of Malone & Trombley*, 39 Ed Dept Rep 135 (1999)).

By comparison, in New York City the Chancellor must prepare and disseminate an educational impact statement regarding any proposed school closing or significant change in school utilization, including the phase-out, re-siting, or co-location of schools. The educational impact statement must address the ramifications of such school closing or change in building use, initial costs and savings, the impact of the proposed action on the affected students and personnel, and the ability of other surrounding schools to accommodate the pupils, among other items (§ 2590-h(2-a); see also § 2853(3)(a-3) regarding co-location of charter schools). In addition, public hearings must be held before the city board approves the school closure or other school utilization proposal (§§ 2590-g(1)(h), (8), 2590-h(2-a)). Noncompliance with the required statutory procedures invalidates any school closing or change in school utilization adopted in violation of those procedures (*Mulgrew v. Bd. of Educ. of the City Sch. Dist. of the City of N.Y.*, 28 Misc.3d 204 (Sup. Ct. New York Cnty. 2010); see also *Appeal of Espinet,* 50 Ed Dept Rep, Dec. No. 16,212 (2011); *Appeal of Battis*, 50 Ed Dept Rep, Dec. No. 16,115 (2010); *Appeal of Santos*, 50 Ed Dept Rep, Dec. No. 16,116 (2010)).

Public School Facilities

Display of the Flag on School Grounds

61:33. Must school districts display the American flag?

Yes. The Education and Executive Laws require that districts purchase and display the American flag in, on or near the public school building during school hours every school day (§ 418; Exec. Law § 403(5)). However, the flag may not be displayed in inclement weather, in which case it is to be displayed in the "principal room in the schoolhouse" (§ 420; Exec. Law § 403(3)). Outside display, except on special occasions for patriotic effects, is limited to the hours from sunrise to sunset (Exec. Law § 403(1)).

In addition, the flag must be displayed in the main assembly room of every school (i.e., the auditorium). The willful failure to do so is a misdemeanor (§ 419; 8 NYCRR Part 108). If a school is used as a polling place, the flag must be displayed in or near the building on election days (Exec. Law § 403(4)).

61:34. When must school districts display the American flag?

The Executive Law requires that the flag be displayed, weather permitting, every day the district is open to the public (Exec. Law § 403(2)). In addition, it must be displayed on holidays, including:

- New Year's Day (January 1)
- Dr. Martin Luther King, Jr. Day (third Monday in January)
- Lincoln's Birthday (February 12)
- Washington's Birthday (third Monday in February)
- Memorial Day (last Monday in May)
- Flag Day (second Sunday in June)
- Independence Day (July 4)
- Labor Day (first Monday in September)
- September 11th Remembrance Day (September 11): at half-staff (see **61:35**)
- POW/MIA Recognition Day (third Friday in September, or if this is in conflict with a religious observance, the second Friday in September): at half-staff (see **61:35**)

- Columbus Day (second Monday in October)
- Veterans Day (November 11)
- Thanksgiving Day (fourth Thursday in November)
- Pearl Harbor Day (December 7)
- Christmas Day (December 25)

If any of these holidays fall on a Sunday (except for Flag Day), the flag should be displayed the next day. In addition, the flag must be displayed on any general election day and on any day designated by the president of the United States or the governor of New York State as a day of general thanksgiving or for displaying the flag (Exec. Law § 403(2)).

61:35. May school districts display the American flag at half-staff?

Yes, on certain occasions. The flag is to be displayed at full staff except that it must be flown at half-staff on September 11th Remembrance Day and December 7 (Pearl Harbor Day); on days commemorating the death of a personage of national or state standing, of a local serviceman, or of an official or public servant who, in the opinion of the school district, contributed to the community; and it may be flown at half-staff on days designated by the president of the United States or the governor of New York State as special periods of mourning (Exec. Law § 403(21)).

Additionally, school districts may enact regulations to display the flag at half-staff to commemorate the death of a present or former board member, or present employee, teacher, student, clerk or custodian (Exec. Law § 402). One court has held, however, that it is improper for a district to fly its flag at half-staff as an expression of political dissent (*Lapolla v. Dullaghan*, 63 Misc.2d 157 (Sup. Ct. Westchester Cnty. 1970)).

61:36. Must school districts establish rules for the proper care of the American flag?

Yes. The Education Law requires that school authorities establish rules and regulations governing the proper care, custody and display of the flag (§ 420). Both the United States Code and the Executive Law provide guidance regarding the proper display and care of the flag (4 USC §§ 5–10; Exec. Law § 403). In addition, the commissioner's regulations provide the requirements for the material and size of the flag, care of the flag, and for its display in assembly rooms (8 NYCRR Part 108).

61:37. Must the salute to the flag and the pledge of allegiance to the flag be recited daily in school?

Yes. Section 802 of the Education Law requires that the commissioner of education prepare a program for public schools that provides for the salute to the flag and a daily pledge of allegiance to the flag, and for instruction in its correct use and display (§ 802; 8 NYCRR Part 108).

The official text of the pledge and the manner in which it must be recited is contained in the commissioner's regulations. The text is: "I pledge allegiance to the Flag of the United States of America and to the Republic for which it stands, one Nation, under God, indivisible, with liberty and justice for all" (8 NYCRR § 108.5).

61:38. Can students and teachers abstain from reciting the pledge of allegiance?

Yes. Students have the right to abstain from reciting the pledge and teachers have the right to stand silently during the daily recitation of the pledge. In *West Virginia State Bd. of Educ. v. Barnette*, 319 U.S. 624 (1943), the U.S. Supreme Court ruled that requiring teachers and students to stand in salute of the flag and recite the pledge of allegiance against their religious beliefs constituted a violation of their rights under the Free Exercise Clause of the First Amendment to the U.S. Constitution (see also *Russo v. CSD No. 1*, 469 F.2d 623 (2d Cir. 1972), *cert. denied, CSD No. 1 v. Russo*, 411 U.S. 932 (1973)).

In addition, those refusing to salute the flag may not be required to either stand or leave the room, according to the U.S. Court of Appeals for the Second Circuit, which has jurisdiction over New York State. According to the court, the act of standing itself is a "gesture of acceptance;" the option of leaving the room, "punishment [for] nonparticipation" (*Goetz v. Ansell*, 477 F.2d 636 (2d Cir. 1973)).

The U.S. Supreme Court dismissed, on procedural grounds, a lawsuit claiming that it violates the Establishment Clause of the federal constitution to require students to listen daily to the recitation of the Pledge of Allegiance, because the Pledge contains the words "One Nation, Under God" within its text (*Elk Grove Unified Sch. Dist. v. Newdow*, 542 U.S. 1 (2004)). By declining to rule on the merits of the claim, the court left the substantive constitutional question for another day. See also **65:8**.

Parking and Traffic Rules

61:39. May a school district establish its own traffic and parking regulations on school property?

Yes. School districts may regulate, restrict or prohibit parking or standing, the direction and speed of traffic, and movement of motor traffic on any parking fields, driveways or public ways accessory to any school, playground or facility under their jurisdiction (Veh. & Traf. Law § 1670). Any violation of district traffic regulations will be considered a traffic infraction (Opn. St. Comp. 79-26).

61:40. Are there any New York State traffic rules pertaining to schools zones and school buses?

Yes. Section 1174 of the Vehicle and Traffic Law prohibits motorists from passing stopped school buses while they are boarding or discharging school children on public highways and school property. In addition, motorists may not exceed maximum school speed limits established on a highway adjacent to a school during school days at the times indicated on the school zone speed limit sign, or when beacons attached to the school zone speed limit sign are flashing and indicate the speed limit is in effect. Beacons may only flash during student activities at the school and up to 30 minutes immediately before and up to 30 minutes immediately after such student activity. Motorists also may not make U-turns within school zones during posted hours. (Veh. & Traf. Law §§ 1161(b); 1180(c)(2)).

61:41. What rules apply to the idling of vehicles on school property?

School districts must ensure that bus drivers turn off engines while waiting for passengers to load, or off load or while such vehicle is parked or standing on school grounds or in front of any school (8 NYCRR § 156.3(h)(1)(i)). Idling is permitted for mechanical work, to maintain temperatures for passenger comfort and during emergency evacuations where necessary to operate wheelchair lifts (8 NYCRR § 156.3(h)(2)). School districts must periodically monitor compliance with this requirement (8 NYCRR § 156.3(h)(5); see also **59:17-18**).

62. Building Safety

Emergency Management

Editor's Note: Chapter 54 of the Laws of 2016 enacted amendments to Education Law § 2801-a regarding school safety plans.

62:1. Must school districts have school safety plans?

Yes. The Education Law requires that public school districts and boards of cooperative educational services (BOCES) adopt a comprehensive district-wide school safety plan and building-level emergency response plans on crisis intervention, and emergency response and management (§ 2801-a(1); 8 NYCRR § 155.17(a)). Districts having only one school building may appeal from duplicative requirements if the commissioner in consultation with the superintendent of state police, develops an appeals process (§2801-a(1)).

These plans must be designed to prevent or minimize the effects of serious violent incidents and emergencies and to facilitate the coordination of schools and school districts with local and county resources in the event of such incidents or emergencies (8 NYCRR § 155.17(c)).

An *emergency* comprises a situation, including but not limited to a disaster that requires immediate action, occurs unpredictably, and poses a threat of injury or loss of life to students or school personnel or of severe damage to school property (8 NYCRR § 155.17(b)(4)).

A *disaster* refers to an occurrence or imminent threat of widespread or severe damage, injury, or loss of life or property resulting from any natural or manmade causes such as fire, flood, drought, windstorms, hurricane, tornado, wave action, earthquake, high water, chemical accident, explosion, epidemic, air and water contamination, landslide, mudslide, war or civil disturbance (8 NYCRR § 155.17(b)(3)).

A serious violent incident refers to an incident of violent criminal conduct that is, or appears to be, life threatening and warrants the evacuation of students and/or staff because of an imminent threat to their safety or health. Examples include a riot, hostage-taking, kidnapping and/or the use or threatened use of a firearm, explosive, bomb, incendiary device, chemical or biological weapon, knife, or other dangerous instrument capable of causing death or serious injury (8 NYCRR § 155.17(b)(18)).

62:2. Who is responsible for developing and updating school safety plans?

The district-wide school safety plan and building-level emergency response plan must be developed respectively by a district-wide school safety team and building-level emergency response team in accordance with a form prescribed by the commissioner of education (§ 2801-a(1); 8 NYCRR § 155.17(a)).

Each building-level emergency response team must be appointed by the building principal, or the chancellor of education in New York City, in accordance with board-established guidelines or regulations and must include at least representatives of teacher, administrator and parent organizations; school safety personnel and other school personnel; community members; law enforcement officials; fire officials or other emergency response agencies; and any other representatives the school board or chancellor deem appropriate (§ 2801-a(4); 8 NYCRR § 155.17(b)(12)).

The district-wide school safety team must be appointed by the school board, or the chancellor of education in New York City, and include board representatives, representatives of student, teacher, administrator and parent organizations; school safety personnel; and other school personnel (§ 2801-a(4); 8 NYCRR § 155.17(b)(14)). At the discretion of the board, or the chancellor in the city of New York, a student may be allowed to participate on the district-wide team, provided no details regarding the confidential building level emergency response plan may be shared with the student nor may the student be present during any discussions concerning the building level emergency response plan (*Id.*).

Each team also is responsible for reviewing their respective plan at least annually and updating it as needed by September 1 each year (§ 2801-a(5); 8 NYCRR § 155.17(a)).

The state has established School Safety Improvement Teams which will, upon request, review the safety plans of school districts (with a population under 125,000 inhabitants) and BOCES, and make recommendations for improvement. These teams are composed of representatives from the NYS Division of Homeland and Security and Emergency Services, the NYS Division of the State Police, the NYS Division of Criminal Justice Services and the NYS Education Department (§ 2801-b).

62:3. What is the process for adopting school safety plans?

A school board or the chancellor of education in New York City must adopt the district wide school safety plan after a public comment period of at least 30 days and at least one public hearing. Current copies of the district-wide plan and any amendments thereto are to be filed with the commissioner within 30 days of adoption. Building-level emergency response plans and any amendments thereto must be filed with the state police and local law enforcement within 30 days of adoption (§ 2801-a(6), (7)).

Building-level plans are confidential and are not subject to release under the Freedom of Information Law or any other provision of law. This includes floor plans, blue prints, schematics or other maps of the school's interior, school grounds, road maps of the immediate surrounding area and other similar documents that may be incorporated into the building level emergency response plan (§ 2801-a(3); 8 NYCRR § 155.17(c)(2)).

Each safety plan must be reviewed at least annually and updated as needed by September 1 each year (§ 2801-a(5); 8 NYCRR § 155.17(a)). In addition, the school safety plan must be updated to reflect any changes necessary to accommodate school construction projects, including an updated emergency exit plan indicating temporary exits required due to construction, and provisions for the emergency evacuation and relocation or release of students and staff in the event of a construction incident. The district must familiarize students and staff with any temporary exits and emergency procedures established as a result of the construction project (8 NYCRR § 155.5(c)(3), (4); see also **62:23**).

Superintendents and building principals are required to provide written information to all students and staff regarding emergency procedures by October 1 of each year (8 NYCRR § 155.17(g)).

Except in the case of routine snow emergency days, districts must notify the commissioner of education whenever the emergency plan or building-level emergency response plan is activated and results in the closing of a school building as prescribed by commissioner's regulations (8 NYCRR § 155.17(f)).

62:4. What must be included in a district-wide school safety plan?

A district-wide school safety plan, which consists of a comprehensive, multi-hazard school safety plan that covers all school buildings and addresses crisis intervention, emergency response and management at the district level (8 NYCRR § 155.17(b)(13)), must:

- Include appropriate prevention and intervention strategies as specified in law and commissioner's regulations.
- Identify appropriate responses to emergencies, including protocols for responding to bomb threats, hostage-takings, intrusions, and kidnappings.

- Include strategies for improving communications among students and between students and staff and reporting of potentially violent incidents.
- Describe the duties of hall monitors and any other safety personnel, the training required of all personnel acting in a school security capacity, and the hiring and screening process for all personnel acting in a school security capacity (§ 2801-a(2); 8 NYCRR § 155.17(c)(1)(iii), (xv)–(xvii)).

In addition, a district-wide school safety plan must include policies and procedures for:

- Responding to implied or direct threats of violence including threats of self-harm and suicide by students, as well as actual acts of violence, by students, teachers, other school personnel, and visitors to the school.
- Contacting appropriate law enforcement officials in the event of a violent incident.
- Contacting parents, guardians or persons in parental relation to district students in the event of a violent incident or an early dismissal, as well as when a student makes an implied or direct threat of self-harm or suicide.
- School building security including, where appropriate, the use of school safety officers and/or security devices or procedures.
- Disseminating informative materials regarding the early detection of potentially violent behaviors as specified in commissioner's regulations.
- Annual multi-hazard school safety training for staff and students.
- Review and the conduct of drills and other exercises to test components of the emergency response plan (§ 2801-a(2); 8 NYCRR § 155.17(c)(1)(i), (ii), (iv), (ix)–(xiv)).

Furthermore, except in the case of New York City, district-wide school safety plans must also:

- Describe arrangements for obtaining assistance during emergencies from emergency services organizations and local governmental agencies.
- Include procedures for obtaining advice and assistance from local government officials.
- Identify district resources that may be available for use during an emergency.
- Describe procedures for coordinating the use of school district resources and manpower during emergencies (8 NYCRR § 155.17(c)(1)(ii), (v)–(viii)).

School districts, other than New York City, must also include in their district-wide school safety plan a system for informing all educational agencies within the district of a disaster (8 NYCRR § 155.17(c)(1)(xvii)). *Educational agencies* include public and nonpublic elementary and secondary schools, public and private nursery schools, approved private schools for the education of students with disabilities, and public and private schools for the education of preschool children with disabilities (8 NYCRR § 155.17(b)(1)).

The plan must name the superintendent or the superintendent's designee as the district chief emergency officer (§ 2801-a(2)(l); 8 NYCRR § 155.17(c)(1)(xix)). The chief emergency officer is responsible for: coordinating communication between school staff, law enforcement and other first responders, ensuring staff understand the district level safety plan and coordinating appropriate staff training. The chief emergency officer must also ensure the yearly review and any necessary updates of the district wide safety plan and building level emergency response plans are undertaken, required safety drills are conducted as well as assist in the selection of security related technology (*Id.*).

The plan also must be updated to reflect any changes necessary to accommodate school construction projects, including an updated emergency exit plan indicating temporary exits required due to construction; and provisions for the emergency evacuation and relocation or release of students and staff in the event of a construction incident. The district must familiarize students and staff with any temporary exits and emergency procedures established as a result of the construction project (8 NYCRR § 155.5(c)(3), (4); see also **62:23**).

Districts providing transportation based on patterns of actual ridership (see **57:10**), also must include a backup plan as part of their emergency management practices in the event a bus is filled beyond capacity (§ 3635(8)).

62:5. What must be included in a building-level emergency response plan?

A building-level emergency response plan, which consists of a building-specific school emergency response plan that addresses crisis intervention, emergency response, and management at the building level (8 NYCRR § 155.17(b)(11)), must:

- Designate an emergency response team, other appropriate incident response teams, and a post-incident response team.
- Include floor plans, blue prints, schematics or other maps of school interior, school grounds and road maps of the immediate surrounding area.
- Establish internal and external communication systems in emergencies.
- Define the chain of command consistent with the National Incident Management System (NIMS) Incident Command System (ICS).
- Coordinate the building level emergency response plan with the statewide plan for disaster mental health services to assure access to federal, state, and local mental health resources in the event of a violent incident (8 NYCRR § 155.17(c)(2)(ii), (iv)–(vi)). For more information on incident command systems, see **62:7**.

The building-specific emergency response plan must include policies and procedures for response to emergency situations, such as those requiring evacuation, sheltering and lockdown. At a minimum such policies must detail evacuation routes, shelter sites, procedures for addressing medical needs, transportation and emergency notification of parents and guardians (§ 2801-a(3); 8 NYCRR § 155.17(c)(2)(i)). Additionally, plans must address the required annual review as well as the conduct of drills and other exercises to test components of the plan (§ 2801-a(3); 8 NYCRR § 155.17(c)(2)(vii)). The plan must also detail information on school population, number of staff, transportation needs and the business and home telephone numbers of key officials (8 NYCRR § 155.17(c)(2)(ix)).

62:6. Must the district ensure all staff are trained on the emergency response plan?

Yes. Each school district must annually certify by September 15th to the commissioner that all staff have undergone annual training on the emergency response plan including training on violence prevention and mental health (§ 2801-a(2)(h); 8 NYCRR § 155.17(c)(1)(xiii)). Such training may be provided as part of existing professional development. Additionally, new employees hired after the start of the school year must be trained within 30 days of hire or as part of the district's new hire training program, whichever is sooner (*Id.*).

62:7. What is the role of an incident command system (ICS) in school safety plans?

An incident command system (ICS) establishes protocols with emergency responders to ensure everyone understands their respective roles and responsibilities during an emergency, disaster, or serious violent incident (see NYS Education Department, NYS Police, NYS Office of Homeland Security and the NYS Emergency Management Office, *New York State School Safety Guide* (Revised 2013), at: http://nebula.wsimg.com/33dfa5aea88bcc32b48e5dcfcbdcbbed?AccessKeyId=E4407BC842376B77B1CC&disposition=0&alloworigin=1; see also **62:1**).

ICS training for school officials is available through the NYS Office of Emergency Management as part of a curriculum for training in the National Incident Management System (NIMS) Incident Command System. Information on this course is available online at: http://www.dhses.ny.gov/oem/training/ics.cfm#resources. School officials also should complete ICS training collaboratively developed by the Federal Emergency Management Agency and the U.S. Department of Education. That course is available online at: http://training.fema.gov/is/courseoverview.aspx?code=IS-100.SCa.

62:8. Who makes the decision to close schools because of an emergency?

Schools may be closed in response to an emergency in accordance with the district-wide school safety plan (see **23:21** for the impact closing schools may have on state aid payments). While schools are not allowed to operate without utilities such as electricity, water, or sanitation systems, in emergencies it is up to local school officials to determine whether an utility outage will result in school closings pursuant to the district-wide school safety plan (8 NYCRR § 155.7(e), (g); NYS Education Department Office of Facilities Planning *Newsletter #46* (Dec. 2003), at: http://www.p12.nysed.gov/facplan/Newsletter/Newsletter_46.html).

62:9. Who is responsible for notifying educational agencies of local or state emergencies?

During the occurrence of a local or state emergency, the district (BOCES) superintendent serves as the chief communications liaison to notify all educational agencies within his or her geographic jurisdiction. The superintendent of schools in the cities of Buffalo, Rochester, Syracuse, and Yonkers perform this function for all educational agencies within their respective city district (8 NYCRR § 155.17(e)).

Both public and nonpublic schools must inform students and staff about emergency procedures in writing by October 1 of each school year (8 NYCRR § 155.17(g)). Except in New York City, all educational agencies must provide the school superintendent of the public school district within which they are located with information about their school population, number of staff, transportation needs, and the business and home telephone number of their key officials (8 NYCRR § 155.17(i); see **62:5**).

62:10. What is an emergency response team?

An *emergency response team* is a building-specific team designated by the building-level emergency response team to assist the school community in responding to a serious violent incident or emergency and providing the initial response to all emergency situations. It must include appropriate school personnel, law enforcement officials, fire officials, and representatives from local, regional and/or state emergency response agencies (§ 2801-a(3)(b); 8 NYCRR § 155.17(b)(15)).

Outside New York City there should be an emergency response team for each school building. In New York City, a unique team for each school building is not required; emergency response teams can be developed at the district level with participation from building-level personnel (8 NYCRR § 155.17(b) (15); see also NYS Education Department, *School Safety Plans Guidance* (June 2010), at: http://www.p12.nysed.gov/sss/ssae/schoolsafety/save/documents/SchoolSafetyPlansDoc_NEW_June9_10_Prot.pdf.

62:11. What is a post-incident response team?

A *post-incident response team* is a building-specific team designated by the building-level emergency response team to assist the school community in coping with the aftermath of an emergency or serious violent incident. This team is comprised of appropriate school personnel, medical personnel, mental health counselors, and others who can assist the school community in coping during the aftermath. Each school building is required to have its own team. In New York City, however, there may be a district-wide post-incident response team with building-level participation instead of a unique team for each school (§ 2801-a(3)(b); 8 NYCRR § 155.17(b)(16)).

The post-incident response team has both short and long-term responsibilities. Its short-term responsibilities include developing procedures for mental health counseling of students and staff, building security, facility restoration, and it must perform a post-incident response critique. Long-term, the team must monitor for post-traumatic stress, ensure building security and perform mitigation (reduce the likelihood of occurrence and impact if the situation does occur again) (NYS Education Department, *School Safety Plans Guidance* (June 2010), at: http://www.emsc.nysed.gov/ssae/schoolsafety/save/documents/SchoolSafetyPlansDoc_NEW_June9_10_Prot.pdf).

62:12. Are school districts required to conduct emergency drills?

Yes. School districts must conduct fire drills at least 12 times each school year (eight between September 1 and December 31) to ensure that, in the event of an emergency, students will be able to respond appropriately in the shortest possible time and without confusion or panic (§ 807(1)).

Eight of the drills must be evacuation drills, of which at least four must use fire escapes or identified secondary means of egress (§ 807(1)). Four of the drills must be lock down drills (*Id.*). All drills must be conducted at different times of the school day. Students must be instructed on the procedure to follow in the event of a fire during a lunch period or assembly but such instruction may be waived if a drill is conducted at those times (*Id.*). Moreover, fire drills must be conducted during construction projects to familiarize students and staff with temporary exits and revised emergency procedures whenever temporary exits and revised emergency procedures exist (8 NYCRR § 155.5(c)(4)).

In addition, at least once every school year, each school district and BOCES must conduct a test of its emergency plan or its emergency response procedures under each of its building-level emergency response plans (at a time no earlier than 15 minutes before normal dismissal), in cooperation with local county emergency-preparedness-plan officials if possible. The drill also must test the usefulness of the communications and transportation systems during emergencies. Parents or guardians must be notified of the drill at least one week in advance (8 NYCRR § 155.17(h)).

62:13. Are school districts required to hold emergency drills for after-school programs?

No. However, a principal or other person in charge of the school building during an after-school program, event, or performance must notify the participants who are not regular occupants of the building of the procedures to be followed, should an emergency occur (§ 807(1-a)).

62:14. What should a school district do if it receives a bomb threat?

A school district should respond to a bomb threat in accordance with the response protocols set forth in its school safety plan.

In accordance with commissioner's regulations (8 NYCRR § 155.17) and the *New York State School Safety Guide* (Revised 2013), available at: http://nebula.wsimg.com/33dfa5aea88bcc32b48e5dcfcbdcbbed?AccessKeyId=E4407BC842376B77B1CC&disposition=0&alloworigin=1 issued jointly by the NYS Education Department, the NYS Office of Homeland Security and the NYS Office of Emergency Management, the district should keep in mind the following:

- All bomb threats must be taken seriously and no bomb threat may be treated as a hoax.
- Schools must have a consistent, unified plan of action to deal with bomb threats. Bomb threat plans must be included in the district's school safety plan as required by commissioner's regulations.
- Anyone receiving information about a bomb threat must immediately call 911 and notify the school building administrator or his or her designee who, in turn, will activate the school building's emergency response plan (see **62:5**).
- A school's specific response to a bomb threat depends upon information received in the threat including but not limited to, the location of the bomb, the time left to reach a place of safety, and how credible that information is. Evacuating a building may not be the safest response. The school district administration makes the decision regarding evacuation, continuation or dismissal of school. Potential shelter sites must be pre-established and stated in the school building emergency

response plan in case a decision is made to evacuate a school building. Sheltering sites and routes of egress and evacuation must be thoroughly searched for suspicious objects before or during an evacuation in accordance with the process set forth in the district's emergency management plan. The search for something unusual does not involve touching or handling the suspect object.

- A bomb threat is a criminal act and must be treated as one. Appropriate state, county, and/or local law enforcement authorities must be notified immediately upon receiving a bomb threat. Law enforcement officers will contact fire and/or county emergency coordinators as the situation requires, and, upon finding suspicious objects, will call for appropriate bomb technicians. Any person caught reporting a bomb threat will be prosecuted to the fullest extent of the law (see **62:15**).
- Staff should be trained on how to handle telephone and written bomb threats and how to handle mail bombs and suspicious packages.

School officials must inform parents and guardians as soon as possible of any incident that activates the school emergency management plan, along with actions taken to protect students, staff and property. They also must report all incidents involving bomb threats or false alarms on the Individual Violent and Disruptive Incident Report (NYS Education Department, *School Safety and the Educational Climate Incident Data Collection Questions & Answers Regarding Reporting Violent and Disruptive Incidents* (Apr. 2016), at: http://www.p12.nysed.gov/sss/documents/VADIRFAQ_April2016.pdf).

Questions regarding school emergency planning may be directed the NYSED Office of Student Support Services at 518-486-6090 or StudentSupportServices@nysed.gov, or the NYS Center for School Safety at 844-509-7161.

62:15. What penalties can be imposed on persons who falsely report a bomb threat or place a false bomb or hazardous substance on school grounds?

Any person who knowingly reports false information or initiates or circulates a false warning of an impending occurrence of a fire or explosion as well as the release of a hazardous substance to an official organization that deals with emergencies is guilty of a class E felony for a first offense and a class D felony for two or more offenses (Penal Law §§ 240.55, 240.60).

Any person who places upon school grounds a device or object that appears to be or to contain a bomb, destructive device, explosive, or hazardous substance but is actually inoperative is guilty of a class D felony (Penal Law § 240.62). A person convicted of falsely reporting an incident pursuant to Penal Law § 240.60 or placing a false bomb or hazardous substance in the first degree on school grounds will have his or her driving license suspended for one year (Veh. & Traf. Law § 510(2)(b)(xii)).

62:16. Must school districts report any activation of their school safety plans?

Yes. Except in the case of routine snow emergency days, each superintendent must notify the commissioner of education as soon as possible whenever the district-wide school safety plan or a building level emergency response plan is activated and results in a school building closing. Districts within a supervisory district must notify the BOCES superintendent who is responsible for passing on the information to the commissioner (8 NYCRR § 155.17(f)).

62:17. May the commissioner of education order school districts to take emergency response actions?

Yes. The commissioner may order individual school districts to take emergency response actions if local officials are unable or unwilling to take action deemed appropriate under county or state emergency preparedness plans or directions (8 NYCRR § 155.17(k)).

62:18. May school districts share resources with other municipalities during an emergency?

Yes. Under the Intrastate Mutual Aid Program, school districts and BOCES may participate in offering aid to, or requesting aid from, other municipalities, upon a formal declaration of a disaster by a local government. School districts and BOCES are limited to sharing facilities management and administrative personnel and equipment (Exec. Law § 29-h(1); see also 8 NYCRR § 155.17(d)). The cost of any aid provided by a school district or BOCES will be reimbursed by the requesting municipality (Exec. Law § 29-h(8)(b)). Participation in this program does not preclude districts and BOCES from entering into other mutual aid agreements (Exec. Law § 29-h(4)(c)).

Building Structure Safety

Editor's Note: The Office of Facilities Planning at the New York State Education Department oversees building structure, safety and construction. Information is available from that office at: http://www.p12.nysed.gov/facplan or by calling 518-474-3906.

62:19. Who promulgates health and safety regulations for public school buildings in New York State?

The commissioner of education is authorized to promulgate health and safety regulations for all educational facilities (§ 409; see 8 NYCRR Part 155). The commissioner also is authorized to establish, develop, and monitor a comprehensive public school building safety program (§ 409-d; see 8 NYCRR § 155.3; see also **62:21**) and a uniform code of public school building inspections, safety rating, and monitoring (§ 409-e; see 8 NYCRR § 155.4; see also **62:22**).

Furthermore, for districts other than the Big 5, the commissioner has the power to designate a school building or a particular area within a school building as unusable for pupil occupancy when, based on these regulations, the general conditions of the building indicate it would be detrimental to the health and safety of its occupants (8 NYCRR § 155.7(j)).

When approving new lease agreements by union free or central school districts, the commissioner must determine whether the leased facility meets all applicable standards for the health, safety, and comfort of occupants, is educationally adequate and has a five-year capital facilities plan (§ 403-b(1)(c); see also **62:21**).

62:20. What school building health and safety subjects are covered by the commissioner's regulations?

The commissioner's regulations detail safety requirements for a broad range of subjects such as building exits (8 NYCRR § 155.7(a)); fire and smoke control (8 NYCRR § 155.7(b)); accident protection (8 NYCRR § 155.7(c)); mechanical equipment, including heating, ventilation and air conditioning (HVAC) systems (8 NYCRR § 155.7(d)); water and sanitation systems (8 NYCRR § 155.7(e)); natural gas (8 NYCRR § 155.7(f)); and electrical systems (8 NYCRR § 155.7(g)). For example, the regulations forbid the obstruction of emergency exits and mandate that safety glass be used in certain areas of school buildings (8 NYCRR § 155.7(a), (c)(1)).

The regulations also cover fire and building safety inspections (8 NYCRR § 155.8) and school safety plans (8 NYCRR § 155.17; see **62:1**). Additionally, they establish a comprehensive public school safety program (8 NYCRR § 155.3); a uniform code of public school building inspections, safety rating and monitoring (8 NYCRR § 155.4); and, uniform safety standards for school construction and maintenance projects (8 NYCRR § 155.5).

62:21. What is the comprehensive public school safety program?

The comprehensive public school safety program serves to ensure that all occupied school facilities, whether owned, operated or leased by a district, are properly maintained and preserved and provide suitable educational settings. Waivers from the requirements of the comprehensive public school safety program may be granted to districts with a preexisting inspection program substantially similar to the one required by the commissioner's regulations (§ 409-d; 8 NYCRR § 155.3).

The comprehensive public school safety program has four basic components:

1. *Building condition surveys* that must be conducted every five years on structures occupied by students and/or staff. The surveys must include every major building system or component. A team that includes at least a licensed architect or engineer must conduct physical inspections in order to complete a survey (8 NYCRR §§ 155.3(a), 155.4(b)(1)).
2. *Annual visual inspections.* The requirement for annual visual inspections has been suspended through June 30, 2019 pursuant to Chapter 437 of the Laws of 2014. (See NYS Education Department, Office of Facilities Planning, *Newsletter #118* (Jan. 2015), at: http://www.p12.nysed.gov/facplan/documents/118_Jan2015.pdf).
3. *Five-year capital facilities plans* that must be updated annually, using the safety rating of each occupied building. The plan, to be prepared in a manner and format prescribed by the commissioner, must identify critical maintenance needs and information designed to evaluate the safety and health conditions in school facilities. The goal of the five-year plan is to collect, coordinate, analyze, and prioritize facility infrastructure and building program needs on a district-wide basis. It must be submitted to the commissioner upon request (8 NYCRR §§ 155.1(a)(4), 155.3(c)).
4. *Monitoring systems* comprised of procedures to monitor the safety and condition of all occupied public school buildings (8 NYCRR §§ 155.3(d), 155.4(d)). As part of these procedures, districts must establish a health and safety committee made up of representatives from district officials, staff, bargaining units, and parents, and, during a construction project, the architect, construction manager, and project contractors, as well. Districts also must establish a comprehensive maintenance plan for all major building systems to ensure the building is maintained in a state of good repair, provide for the least toxic approach to integrated pest management, and maintenance procedures and guidelines concerning acceptable indoor air quality. School boards must annually review and approve the five-year building condition surveys (8 NYCRR § 155.4(d)).

In addition, monitoring systems procedures must ensure that annual fire safety inspections are conducted for each school building, and that a current and valid certificate of occupancy is maintained and posted conspicuously. The procedures must ensure a process that allows for a health and safety committee to participate in the investigation and disposition of complaints related to health and safety, and that the district takes and reports to the commissioner immediate action to remedy serious conditions affecting health and safety. They must ensure that all construction and maintenance activities comply with the uniform safety standards for school and maintenance projects set forth in the commissioner's regulations (8 NYCRR §§ 155.4(d), 155.5(c)(2)).

62:22. What is the uniform code of public school buildings, inspections, safety rating, and monitoring?

The uniform code of public school buildings, inspections, safety rating, and monitoring provides standardized procedures for periodic inspections and the monitoring system required by the comprehensive public school safety program (§ 409-e; 8 NYCRR § 155.4; see § 409-d(2)(e); 8 NYCRR

§ 155.3(d), **62:21**). Under the program, school districts provide an annual safety rating of occupied school buildings keyed to the structural integrity and overall safety of the building. Each district must establish a safety rating in consultation with the district's health and safety committee and in accordance with the commissioner's regulations (8 NYCRR § 155.4(c)(1)).

Each building's safety rating must identify and assess the condition of every major building component by assigning it to one of the following categories: excellent, satisfactory, unsatisfactory, unsafe/unhealthful, or indeterminate (8 NYCRR § 155.4(c)(2)). Building system deficiencies must be categorized as health and safety, structural, comfort, or aesthetic (8 NYCRR § 155.4(c)(3)).

The overall rating of a building is determined by a weighted system developed by the commissioner that results in identifying each building in one of the following categories: excellent, good, satisfactory, and unsafe/unhealthful. A rating of unsafe/unhealthful will cause the revocation of the building certificate of occupancy (8 NYCRR § 155.4(c)(4)).

62:23. What are the uniform safety standards for school construction and maintenance projects?

The uniform safety standards for school construction and maintenance projects establish standardized procedures for ensuring the safety of school buildings and their occupants during construction and maintenance projects (see **61:18**). They address the following issues:

- The monitoring of construction and maintenance activities.
- The investigation and disposition of complaints.
- Pre-construction testing, planning, and notification of construction projects.
- General safety and security standards.
- Separation of construction from occupied spaces.
- Maintenance of exits and ventilation.
- Fire and hazard prevention.
- Noise abatement during construction and maintenance.
- Control of chemical fumes, gases, and other contaminants.
- Asbestos abatement and lead paint protocols (see **63:19-34**).
- School radon responsibilities (see **63:16**).
- Post-construction inspections (§ 409-e(4)(b); 8 NYCRR § 155.5).

62:24. What are some examples of the specific procedures school districts must follow under uniform safety standards for school construction and maintenance projects?

The uniform safety standards for school construction and maintenance projects provide that school boards must ensure, for example:

- Occupied portions of any school buildings undergoing construction comply with the minimum requirements to maintain a certificate of occupancy, and that school district personnel monitor the occupied areas during construction and maintenance activities for any safety violations (8 NYCRR § 155.5(a)).
- All bid specifications and contract documents address safety issues before contract documents are advertised for bid. All areas disturbed during renovation or demolition must be tested for lead and asbestos. District school safety plans must be updated as necessary, including emergency exit plans during construction, and provisions for emergency evacuations of students and staff during a construction incident (8 NYCRR § 155.5(c)).
- Establish procedures to notify parents, staff, and the community of a construction project costing $10,000 or more in an occupied building at least two months in advance of initial date of

construction or in the case of emergency construction, as far in advance of the start of construction as practicable (8 NYCRR § 155.5(d)).

- Construction materials are stored safely and securely; gates to construction areas must be locked; workers must wear photo-identification badges at all times while working at occupied sites (8 NYCRR § 155.5(e)).
- Construction areas are separated from occupied spaces including designation of separate stairways and elevators for construction workers during work hours. In addition, provisions must be made to prevent the passage of dust and contaminants into occupied parts of a building and for the removal of debris through enclosed chutes or a similar sealed system (8 NYCRR § 155.5(f)).
- Proper exiting and adequate ventilation are maintained (8 NYCRR § 155.5(g)).
- School district personnel conduct daily inspections of district occupied areas to ensure that fire exits and emergency egress windows are not blocked by construction materials, equipment or debris. Also, no smoking rules must be strictly enforced on school property, including construction areas (8 NYCRR § 155.5(h)).
- Noise in excess of 60 dBA (decibels adjusted) in occupied spaces occurs only when the building or affected building spaces are unoccupied or when acoustical abatement measures are taken (8 NYCRR § 155.5(i)).

62:25. Are there other safety standards that apply to school construction and maintenance projects?

Yes. Additional requirements are imposed by the state's Uniform Fire Prevention and Building Code. For more information on these requirements, contact the NYS Department of State at 518-474-4073 or visit its website at: http://www.dos.ny.gov/dcea/; see also **61:20**).

Furthermore, the NYS Education Department (SED) recommends that, in addition to complying with the required uniform safety standards, districts follow a protocol it developed in consultation with the NYS Department of Health regarding the management of caulk containing Polychlorinated Biphenyls (PCBs) during building renovations and maintenance (NYS Education Department, *Protocol for Addressing Polychlorinated Biphenyls (PCBs) in Caulking Materials in School Buildings* (May 2014), at: http://www.p12.nysed.gov/facplan/HealthSafety/PCBinCaulkProtocol-070615.html), see **63:39** for more on PCBs.

62:26. Are school districts required to maintain certain temperatures in schools?

Yes. The "Property Maintenance Code of New York State," part of the "New York State Uniform Fire Prevention and Building Code," requires that "indoor occupiable work spaces be supplied with heat during the period from September 15 to May 31 to maintain a minimum temperature of 65°F (18°C) during the period the spaces are occupied." However, there are exceptions for areas of vigorous physical activity (gymnasiums) and processing spaces (coolers or freezers) (19 NYCRR § 1226.1; Property Maintenance Code of New York State § 602.4 at: http://codes.iccsafe.org/app/book/content/2015-I-Codes/NY/2015_IPMC_HTML/Chapter%206.html; see also NYS Department of Education, Office of Facilities Planning, *Newsletter #119* (Feb. 2015), at: http://www.p12.nysed.gov/facplan/documents/119_Feb2015.pdf; 19 NYCRR §§ 1219-1227).

While there is no law or regulation which addresses maximum temperature in school buildings, the NYS Education Department recommends that common sense be exercised when determining whether the indoor temperature in a school building poses a health risk (see NYS Education Department, Office of Facilities Planning, Newsletter #111 (Sept. 2013), at: http://www.p12.nysed.gov/facplan/documents/111September2013.pdf).

62:27. Are electrically-operated partitions or doors covered by safety rules?

Yes. School districts that have electrically-operated doors or partitions must post conspicuous notices in the immediate vicinity of the operating mechanism concerning their safe and proper operation and supervision, must have established procedures concerning notification on their operation to employees and others who regularly use the area, and must inform those employees of the penalties for disabling safety devices on the doors or partitions. Any person who disables or directs another to disable such a safety device is subject to a fine and up to 15 days in jail or both. In addition, every electrically-operated partition or door must have safety devices to stop the motion of the partition or door if a body or other object is in its path (§ 409-f; 8 NYCRR § 155.25(c)(3)).

The commissioner's regulations further require every partition to be equipped with two key-operated control stations so that two people must simultaneously activate the controls and apply constant pressure to open or close the partition. The control stations must be located at opposite ends of and opposite sides of, and in view of, the partition. The partition must be capable of being reversed at any point while opening or closing, and must be installed such that the failure of any safety device renders the partition inoperable until such device is fixed (8 NYCRR § 155.25(c)(1), (2)).

Students are not permitted to operate such partitions, and all students present during partition operation must be directly supervised by trained staff, must keep away from the partition, and are not allowed to cross the path of the moving partition. Staff members who regularly use the partitions must be trained in the safe operation of the partition and its safety features. Training must include discussion of past accidents and the potential and possibility of serious injury or death. Records of such training must be maintained (8 NYCRR § 155.25(d)).

Any district with an electrically operated partition whose safety system is not operating properly may not use the partition until it is repaired. The electronically operated partition must be locked out, tagged out at the electrical panel and remain inoperative until all safety systems are in proper working order (NYS Education Department, Office of Facilities Planning, *Newsletter #106* (May 2011), at: http:// www.p12.nysed.gov/facplan/documents/final106Newsletter.pdf). Additionally, school districts which have passive infrared sensors to provide required safety coverage to cease operation of the stacking mechanism in the pocket (stacking area) must ensure the sensors cover the entire pocket in order to meet the standards required by the regulation. If a district determines its sensors do not meet regulatory requirements it must cease operation of the partition until the safety systems are corrected and verified as operating properly (NYS Education Department, Office of Facilities Planning, *Newsletter #123* (Aug. 2015), at: http:// www.p12.nysed.gov/facplan/documents/123_August2015.pdf).

62:28. Are fire safety inspections required for school buildings?

Yes. Annual inspections are required for fire and safety hazards that may endanger the lives of students and district employees. Boards of cooperative educational services (BOCES) and school districts, except for the Big 5, must have all their school buildings inspected by a qualified inspector under procedures established by the State Fire Administrator. This inspection report must be filed in the district offices and with the commissioner of education. The annual inspection must be conducted in accordance with a schedule established by the commissioner of education. That schedule breaks the state into regions, each with a fire inspection period during which the inspection must take place and a deadline for filing inspection reports. Each building, including any owned, leased or used in any manner by the district, must have a separate fire safety inspection (§ 807-a; see also 8 NYCRR § 155.8; 19 NYCRR Part 1225; NYS Education Department, *Manual for New York State Public School Facility Fire Safety Inspections* (May 2016), at: http://www.p12.nysed.gov/facplan/documents/PUBLICFireSafetyManual.pdf).

In addition, the commissioner may order a fire safety inspection at any reasonable time. School authorities may not refuse the inspector access to the school building. Further, any public school building may be inspected at any reasonable time by the local fire chief or a fire fighter assigned to do so by the fire chief. A school administrator has the right to be present during this inspection (§ 807-a(6), (7)).

In the event that an inspection reveals a violation that, if uncorrected, would cause the State Education Department to deny an annual certificate of occupancy, the commissioner will require additional re-inspections until the violation has been corrected (§ 807-a(6)).

For further information on fire inspection, see *Manual for New York State Public School Facility Fire Safety Inspections*.

62:29. Who is responsible for enforcing fire safety requirements in the public schools?

The commissioner of education has the responsibility to administer and enforce the New York State Uniform Fire Prevention and Building Code (see 19 NYCRR Parts 1219–1227) with respect to buildings, premises, and equipment in the custody of school districts and boards of cooperative educational services (BOCES) (8 NYCRR § 155.8(a)–(c)).

The commissioner has the authority to issue a certificate of occupancy to public school districts that indicates that a school building is in compliance with part 155 of the commissioner's regulations and with the state Uniform Fire Prevention and Building Code (8 NYCRR § 155.8(e)(1)). The commissioner also has the power to issue temporary certificates of occupancy, and to deny or revoke certificates of occupancy to school districts that fail to comply with these standards (8 NYCRR § 155.8(e)(2), (3)).

62:30. What happens if a public school building does not pass a fire inspection?

If a school building fails to pass a fire inspection, the school board must adopt a plan, approved by the commissioner of education, to correct all violations. The commissioner may issue a temporary certificate of occupancy pending these corrections and, particularly when the building is not suitable for occupancy or intended use, he may refuse to issue or he may revoke an existing certificate of occupancy (8 NYCRR § 155.8(c), (e)).

62:31. Must the school district inform the public of the results of fire-safety inspections?

Yes. Fire inspection reports must be filed in the school district and with the commissioner of education (see **62:28**). All such reports shall be retained as public record for at least three years. Within 20 days, school districts also must publish a notice in a local newspaper stating the report has been filed (§ 807-a(5)(a)–(c)).

62:32. Must a school's fire alarm system be connected with the community's fire departments?

Yes, wherever practical. The school's fire alarm system must be connected if the school building is located in a fire district that has an electrically-operated, general municipal fire alarm box system so that sounding the school-building fire alarm system automatically relays the alarm to the fire department (§ 807-c; 8 NYCRR § 155.7(g)(4)). Additionally, wherever practical, a fire alarm box compatible with the municipal system must be located and accessible on the site or in the school building (8 NYCRR § 155.7(g)(4)).

In a case where a fire district may not have an electrically-operated, general municipal fire alarm system, it is up to the board and the governing body of the local fire department to decide whether to connect the school building to the fire department (§ 807-c; see also 8 NYCRR § 155.7(g)(4)).

62:33. What authority does the local fire department have if a school building fire alarm is activated?

If a school building's fire alarm goes off, the fire department has the authority to enter the school building to determine whether the fire is out and whether the building is safe for occupancy, even in the event of a false alarm (Gen. Mun. Law § 204-d). School officials may not deny fire fighters access to the school building or order them to leave (Inf. Opn. Att'y Gen. 81-13).

If a school building's fire alarm sounds, students may not reenter the building until the fire department determines the building is safe for occupancy. Only the fire department, not the police department or school district, has the authority to order students back into the building (Inf. Opn. Att'y Gen. 81-13, 83-67).

62:34. Must a school district install carbon monoxide detectors?

Yes. All existing school building must have carbon monoxide alarms or detection systems installed (19 NYCRR §§ 1219.1, 1225.1; International Fire Code §§ 915.1-915.6, 1103.9 available at: http:// codes.iccsafe.org/app/book/toc/2015/I-Codes/NY/2015_IFC_HTML/index.html). Carbon monoxide detectors must be installed in buildings which contain devices that may emit products of combustion including fuel fired heating systems, emergency standby electric generators, and fuel burning appliances including certain lab and shop equipment. Detectors will also need to be installed if a school building includes a garage (*Id.*). The number and placement of alarms or detectors will be dictated by the carbon monoxide sources in each building.

In existing buildings where carbon monoxide alarms are installed the alarms may be wired directly into the building's power circuit with a battery back-up or they may be solely battery powered by a battery with a 10 year life (*Id.*; NYS Education Department, Office of Facilities Planning, *Technical Guideline for School Districts and BOCES to Comply with Regulations for Carbon Monoxide Detection in Commercial Buildings* (Sept. 2015), at: http://www.p12.nysed.gov/facplan/documents/CarbonMonoxideGuidelines.pdf and *Carbon Monoxide Regulations Presentation* (Dec. 2015) at: http://www.p12.nysed.gov/facplan/documents/carbonmonoxidepresentation-BOCES12-15-15.pdf). If a carbon monoxide detection system is installed into existing buildings it must not activate fire alarm notification devices (*Technical Guideline for School Districts and BOCES to Comply with Regulations for Carbon Monoxide Detection in Commercial Buildings*).

Newly constructed buildings must also have such detectors but may not use carbon monoxide alarms which are solely battery powered (International Fire Code § 915.4.1). A building qualifies as newly constructed if it did not have a building permit filed by December 31, 2015 (*Carbon Monoxide Regulations Presentation*).

If a school district or BOCES leases space from a private entity the building owner has an obligation to comply with the regulations and leases will not be approved in buildings without carbon monoxide detection system or alarms (*Technical Guideline for School Districts and BOCES to comply with Regulations for Carbon Monoxide Detection in Commercial Buildings;* see **61:8**).

Air Quality

62:35. What is indoor air quality?

Indoor air quality refers to the numerous environmental and physical elements that affect the purity of air or the perceived purity of air within enclosed structures. Factors that influence indoor air quality include temperature, humidity, air movement or lack thereof, and contaminants such as dust, tobacco smoke, fumes from paints, cleaning materials, fumes from copy or print machines, mold, and formaldehyde. Building exhausts, car exhausts, mowing equipment and dust, paving, roofing and other activities may cause pollution to come into school buildings and affect the quality of air within. Information about indoor air quality, including an action toolkit, is available electronically through the Environmental Protection Agency (EPA) at: http://www.epa.gov/iaq/schools.

Mold is a fungal growth that thrives in damp areas, and some molds can produce toxins. The NYS Education Department recommends that school districts take prompt action at first signs of excess moisture to prevent mold growth. Waiting for mold problems to develop can cost much more to correct, in terms of money, time, absenteeism, building closures, and poor morale (NYS Education Department, Office of Facilities Planning *Newsletter #37* (Mar. 2003), at: http://www.p12.nysed.gov/facplan/Newsletter/Newsletter_37.html and *Newsletter #58* (Dec. 2004), at: http://www.p12.nysed.gov/facplan/Newsletter/Newsletter_58.html). The EPA offers guidance, information, and recommendations. See, for example, *Mold Remediation in Schools and Commercial Buildings*, EPA, Office of Air and Radiation, Indoor Environments Division, (Sept. 2008), at: https://www.epa.gov/sites/production/files/2014-08/documents/moldremediation.pdf.

The heat, ventilation, and air-conditioning (HVAC) system in a school building may affect its indoor air quality under certain circumstances. School districts should periodically clean their ducts and filters. Districts also should pay special attention to changes in and around school buildings due to plant growth (trees and shrubs) and during construction and maintenance activities.

62:36. What laws apply to indoor air quality in the schools?

The comprehensive public school safety program and the uniform code of public school building inspection, safety and monitoring require that school districts establish a comprehensive maintenance plan that includes maintenance procedures and guidelines that will contribute to acceptable indoor air quality (8 NYCRR §§ 155.3, 155.4(d)(2)).

The uniform safety standards for school construction and maintenance projects require that all plans and specifications for construction projects in occupied facilities include a plan detailing, in part, how adequate ventilation will be maintained during construction (8 NYCRR § 155.5(g)). It also requires that districts make provisions to prevent the passage of dust and contaminants into occupied areas (8 NYCRR § 155.5(f)), and the control of chemical fumes, gases, and other contaminants during construction and maintenance projects (8 NYCRR § 155.5(f), (j)).

In the past, the commissioner of education has ordered a school district to monitor students' physical symptoms when the air quality of a school building allegedly caused health problems (*Appeal of Anibaldi*, 33 Ed Dept Rep 166 (1993)).

An appellate court has held that, while a teacher's allergic reaction to dust and mold in the work environment does not constitute an "occupational disease" when the condition does not result from some distinctive feature of employment, it may constitute an "accidental injury" compensable under Workers' Compensation Law (*Matter of Martin v. Fulton City Sch. Dist.*, 300 A.D.2d 901 (3d Dep't 2002)).

The NYS Energy Research and Development Authority (NYSERDA) offers technical assistance to help school districts address their indoor air-quality problems. For more information, contact NYSERDA at 518-862-1090 or 866-697-3732 (http://www.nyserda.ny.gov/).

62:37. Is smoking permitted in school buildings?

No. The federal Pro-Children Act of 1994 prohibits tobacco use in an indoor facility used for the routine provision of education or library services for students in schools receiving federal education aid. This prohibition extends to the entire school building, not just the classrooms used for instruction (20 USC §§ 6083(a); 7973(a)). For example, teachers' lounges located in school buildings must be smoke free (U.S. Dept. of Education, *Guidance Concerning State and Local Responsibilities Under the Pro-Children Act of 2001*, at: http://www2.ed.gov/policy/elsec/guid/prochildact01.pdf).

The Education Law further restricts smoking in schools by prohibiting smoking in school buildings and on school grounds (§ 409(2)). The Education Law defines school grounds as "any building, structure, and surrounding outdoor grounds including entrances or exits, contained within a public or private pre-school, nursery school, elementary or secondary school's legally-defined property boundaries as registered in a county clerk's office (*Id.*). The Public Health Law adds to that definition "and any vehicles used to transport children or school personnel" (Pub. Health Law § 1399-n(6); see also Pub. Health Law § 1399-o(3)).

Additionally, smoking is not allowed within 100 feet of any school entrance, exit, or outdoor area, except within a private residence or within the boundaries of that residential property, or on a playground between sunrise and sunset when a child under age 12 is present (Pub. Health Law §§ 1399-o(1), (3); 1399-o-1). The commissioner's regulations require strict enforcement of the no-smoking policy on public school property in construction areas (8 NYCRR § 155.5(h)(1)).

62:38. Does collective bargaining affect the rules concerning smoking in the workplace?

State law does not allow smoking on any school grounds or in any place of employment, including school districts (§ 409(2); Pub. Health Law §§ 1399-n, 1399-o). There is no longer an exception for designating smoking areas in non-instructional buildings during nonschool hours.

Workplace Safety

62:39. Are school districts required to provide a safe workplace for school employees?

Yes. However, while the employer is required to furnish a workplace that is free from recognized hazards to employees, employees also must comply with safety and health standards and other regulations that are applicable to their own actions and conduct (Lab. Law § 27-a(3)(a), (b); see also Lab. Law § 884-887 for information on workplace safety training and education programs).

62:40. Must school districts comply with workers' safety rules established by the federal Occupational Safety and Health Administration (OSHA)?

Yes. The Public Employees' Safety and Health (PESH) Bureau adopts all OSHA regulations through state rule-making procedures (Lab. Law § 27-a(4); 12 NYCRR § 800.3), even though OSHA itself has jurisdiction only over private employers. School districts must comply with PESH regulations; therefore, indirectly they are complying with OSHA regulations. Thus, PESH is responsible for enforcement and interpretation of these rules.

62:41. Who is responsible for enforcing workplace safety requirements?

Schools are governed by the Public Employees' Safety and Health (PESH) Bureau of the New York State Department of Labor, which was established by the State Occupational Safety and Health Act (Lab. Law § 27-a), to protect public employees from hazards in their workplaces. PESH's jurisdiction covers public employers and employees, including both instructional and non-instructional employees of school districts (Lab. Law § 27-a(1)(a), (d)).

62:42. What does the Public Employees' Safety and Health (PESH) Bureau require of school districts with regard to worker safety rules?

School districts must comply with worker safety rules adopted by PESH that range from very general to explicitly precise. In general, districts are required to maintain a safe workplace under what is known as the general duty clause (Lab. Law § 27-a(3)(a)(1)). Other PESH rules are more detailed and precise, such as the Hazard Communication Standard (see **63:1–3**) and the chemical laboratory safety rules (see **63:4**).

62:43. What happens if a school district violates a workers' safety rule established by the Public Employees' Safety and Health (PESH) Bureau?

PESH is authorized to issue stringent monetary penalties for safety violations committed by public employers. However, the procedures adopted by PESH permit school districts to correct their mistakes before fines are imposed (Lab. Law § 27-a(6)).

Initially, an employer is cited by a PESH safety inspector for a safety violation that is labeled at the time of the citation as either "serious" or "non-serious." Then the employer is given a certain period of time to correct the violation. If the employer fails to correct this problem by a set deadline, then PESH can assess a fine (Lab. Law § 27-a(6)).

The fine for a non-serious violation can be up to $50 per day beyond the deadline; for a serious violation, it could be as high as $200 per day. A state formula for calculating penalties also takes into account other mitigating factors, such as the district's good faith efforts to remediate (Lab. Law § 27-a(6); for penalty guidelines, see NYS Department of Labor, *Public Employee Safety and Health Field Operations Manual* (Revised Feb. 2014), at: http://www.labor.state.ny.us/workerprotection/safetyhealth/doc/PESH%20FOM%2021110.doc; see also *Matter of New York City Transit Auth. v. NYS Dep't of Labor*, 88 N.Y.2d 225 (1996)).

The seriousness of a violation is decided in part by a determination of the extent of injury or potential death that could occur to workers exposed to the hazard in question (Lab. Law § 27-a(6)). Because a majority of hazards could result in injury, many violations may be considered serious by PESH.

62:44. Is financial assistance available to comply with a citation from the Public Employees' Safety and Health (PESH) Bureau?

Yes. Section 27-a of the state Labor Law provides grants under certain circumstances in conjunction with the State Occupational Safety and Health Act (SOSHA) (see Lab. Law § 27-a(15)). Under this section, the state Department of Labor is authorized to provide school districts with 75 percent of the cost of capital abatement projects incurred in order to comply with a SOSHA citation (Lab. Law § 27-a(16)(A)).

62:45. Do worker safety rules apply to shop classes and other instructional locations?

Yes. Under the federal Occupational Safety and Health Administration (OSHA) rules adopted by PESH, school districts must ensure that teachers and other instructional employees in shop classes and other instructional locations are protected by fundamental safety measures. In machine technology or shop classes, these safety measures include, for example, adequate guards for radial-arm saws and grinders; disconnecting switches for power driven woodworking machines and safety guards for abrasive wheel machines (see 29 CFR §§ 1910.213, 1910.215).

School districts also must implement a chemical hygiene plan capable of protecting employees from health hazards in all chemical laboratories (29 CFR § 1910.1450(b), (e); see **63:4**).

In addition, school districts must determine if hazards that necessitate the use of personal protective equipment are present or likely to be present in the workplace, including asbestos (see **63:21–24**). The district must provide this information to its employees and must have a written certification of making this assessment (29 CFR § 1910.132(d), see also 29 CFR § 1910.1001(h)).

62:46. What is a school district's responsibility for protecting employees from exposure to the human immunodeficiency virus (HIV) and hepatitis infections?

The Public Employees' Safety and Health (PESH) Bureau has adopted federal Occupational Safety and Health Administration (OSHA) standards for workers' protection from blood-borne pathogens such as HIV and hepatitis B (see 29 CFR § 1910.1030). These require public employers, including school districts, to develop, implement, and evaluate exposure-control plans to eliminate or minimize employees' exposure to blood-borne diseases, and to use various methods of compliance to protect workers. Methods of compliance include requiring employees to wash their hands, handle needles properly, use plastic gloves made available by the employer in the workplace, and ensure work areas contaminated by blood or body fluids are properly decontaminated. Further information is available at: http://www.health.ny.gov/diseases/aids/index.htm.

Employers must provide additional protection to certain employees who encounter "occupational exposure" to blood-borne pathogens (29 CFR § 1910.1030(b)). These include participation in special training programs and free hepatitis B vaccinations for employees who choose to be vaccinated. In addition, employers having "occupationally exposed" employees must establish a written exposure control plan accessible to all employees and must review it annually.

Employers must also identify tasks associated with any job classification that occupationally exposes or may expose employees. Employees are "occupationally exposed" to blood-borne pathogens if "reasonably anticipated" skin, eye, mucous membrane, or parenteral contact with blood or body fluid "may result" from an employee's performance of his or her duties (*Id.*). Under these regulations, school nurses are probably occupationally exposed, and other school employees, such as special education teachers and coaches, may be exposed (see 29 CFR § 1910.1030(b), (c); see also NYS Department of Labor, FAQs for PESH Programs at: http://www.labor.state.ny.us/workerprotection/safetyhealth/Program%20FAQs.shtm#sec4; NYS Education Department, Office of Student Support Services, *Blood Borne Pathogens in Classrooms* (Mar. 2014), at: http://www.p12.nysed.gov/sss/documents/bloodbornepathogenlettereducatorskhfinal.pdf).

62:47. What can school districts do to prevent the spread of methicillin-resistant staphylococcus aureus (MRSA) infection in the school setting?

MRSA is a type of staph bacteria commonly carried on the skin or in the nose of healthy people that is resistant to a certain class of antiobiotics. MRSA is most frequently transmitted by skin-to-skin contact. The most effective method of preventing transmission is good hygiene.

The NYS Education Department and the NYS Department of Health recommend that school districts should take the following steps to help reduce the spread of MRSA:

- Provide ready access to sinks, soaps, and clean paper towels.
- Practice good hygiene and good skin care.
- Keep hands clean by washing thoroughly with soap (preferably not bar soap) and water. Use alcohol-based hand sanitizers when hands are not visibly dirty. Observe caution regarding the accessibility of alcohol-based hand sanitizers to children.
- Wash any cut or break in the skin with soap and water and apply a clean bandage until healed.
- Avoid contact with other people's wounds or bandages. Use standard barrier precautions when exposed to body fluids.
- Avoid sharing personal items such as cloth towels.
- Students or staff with symptoms of MRSA should contact a healthcare provider.
- Unless directed by a physician, students with MRSA infections should not be excluded from attending school. However, students with any open or draining wounds, should be excluded from swimming pools, whirlpools, hot tubs, etc., until the wound has healed.

It isn't necessary to inform the school community about a single MRSA infection. But when an outbreak or increase in MRSA infections occurs, or if transmission within a school is identified, districts should contact the local health department. Parent and staff notification should be based on consultation with the local health department and in accordance with established school board policy.

More information about MRSA and the schools is available from a guidance issued jointly by the NYS Education Department and the NYS Department of Health entitled *Health Advisory: Prevention of Methicillin-Resistant Staphylococcus Aureus (MRSA) Infections in the School Setting* (Dec. 2008), at: http://www.p12.nysed.gov/sss/schoolhealth/schoolhealthservices/MRSASchoolAdvisoryDec2008.pdf., or from the Centers for Disease Control and Prevention at: http://www.cdc.gov/mrsa/community/schools/index.html.

63. Hazardous Materials and Toxic Substances

General School District Responsibilities

63:1. What are a school district's responsibilities regarding the presence of hazardous materials and toxic substances on school premises?

Districts must comply with the federal Occupational and Safety Health Administration (OSHA) Hazard Communication Standard (29 CFR § 1910.1200), adopted by the Public Employees' Safety and Health (PESH) Bureau, concerning hazardous substances, and New York's Right-to-Know Law concerning toxic substances (Lab. Law §§ 875–883; Pub. Health Law §§ 4800–4808; see 12 NYCRR Part 820). Both laws require school districts to develop and maintain a written hazard-communication program that includes information and training about materials that pose potential health and/or safety hazards. Both also apply to materials commonly used by employees as part of a daily occupational routine, such as cleaning fluids, photocopier toner, glues, and photographic developing fluids.

The hazard-communication program must ensure containers that hold hazardous materials are properly labeled to identify their contents and warn of any hazards that may be related to their use. It also must provide for the maintenance of safety data sheets at the work site, as well as employee training at the work site. In addition, school districts must make available for inspection a list of all hazardous chemicals to which employees might be exposed and document employee training in hazardous materials management and protection, as well as any incident that involves an employee's exposure to hazardous materials (29 CFR § 1910.1200(e)(1)).

OSHA regulations further require school districts to adopt and implement a written respiratory protection program (29 CFR § 1910.134(a)(2), (c)), which includes effective engineering control methods to prevent employee breathing of contaminated air and provisions for employee use of respirators, if necessary, to protect health and safety.

63:2. Must school districts maintain material safety data sheets on hazardous materials?

Yes. The federal Hazard Communication Standard requires a safety data sheet (SDS) for each known hazardous material on school district property, which includes information such as the name of the chemical or compound, any possible ill effects a worker may experience from exposure to it, and instructions on how to handle a related hazard, should one occur.

The supplier or manufacturer of a chemical or compound usually provides an SDS. They also are available through the NYS Department of Health, the Environmental Protection Agency or the National Institute of Occupational Safety and Health. However, it is the district's responsibility to obtain an SDS for each chemical or compound, if one has not been automatically supplied (29 CFR § 1910.1200(g); Lab. Law § 876).

The state Right-to-Know Law requires that information about known hazardous materials in the workplace, such as an SDS, be provided to an employee requesting such information within 72 hours, excluding weekends and public holidays, of the district's receipt of the request. If the information is not provided, the employee may not be required to work with the toxic substance until the information is made available (Lab. Law § 876(7)).

63:3. What happens if a school district fails to comply with hazardous materials record maintenance and information dissemination laws?

Employers who violate the Hazard Communication Standard are subject to fines imposed by the Public Employees' Safety and Health (PESH) Bureau for violation of state regulations (Lab. Law § 27-a(6); *N.Y. City Transit Auth. v. N.Y. State Dep't of Labor*, 88 N.Y.2d 225 (1996); see **62:43**; see also NYS Department of Labor, *Public Employee Safety and Health Field Operations Manual* (Jan. 2007), at: https://labor.ny.gov/formsdocs/wp/FOM%203%20wp.pdf for the state penalty guidelines).

In addition, if a school district fails to provide timely information on known hazardous materials (see **63:1-2**), the employee is permitted under the state's Right-to-Know Law to refuse to work with the material until the information is furnished (Lab. Law § 876(7)). This provision is known as the right-to-strike provision.

63:4. What are a school district's responsibilities regarding the use of chemicals in school laboratories by district employees?

Districts must comply with federal Occupational Health and Safety Administration (OSHA) regulations governing the use of certain hazardous chemicals in school laboratories (29 CFR § 1910.1450). The state Public Employees' Safety and Health (PESH) Bureau has interpreted these regulations to be applicable only to chemicals used in science laboratories and not to the use of compounds in industrial arts and other school subjects (see 29 CFR § 1910.1450(a)(3)).

Under the regulations, school districts must adopt a chemical hygiene plan that includes practices, policies, and procedures to ensure that employees are protected from all potentially hazardous chemicals in their work areas, including keeping exposures below regulatory limits (29 CFR § 1910.1450(b), (e)). In addition, districts must:

- Monitor employees' exposure to chemicals (29 CFR § 1910.1450(d)).
- Provide permanent and temporary employees with training and information (29 CFR § 1910.1450(f)).
- Provide updated training when a new toxic substance is introduced into the workplace (29 CFR § 1910.1450(f)).
- Provide employees with medical consultations and examinations under certain circumstances (29 CFR § 1910.1450(e), (g)).
- Identify hazards of chemicals used in the workplace, including the maintenance of labels and safety data sheets (SDSs) of chemicals (29 CFR § 1910.1450(h)).
- Provide employees with respirators at no cost when required (29 CFR § 1910.1450(i)).
- Maintain certain records proving compliance with the regulations (29 CFR § 1910.1450(j)).

In addition, section 305(19) of the Education Law requires school districts to follow certain procedures to ensure safety in school science laboratories and directs the commissioner of education to adopt regulations on chemical laboratory safety. It requires that all schools store chemicals in locked, secured rooms and cabinets, and provides for the arrangement, ventilation, and fire protection of chemicals in accordance with guidelines issued by the commissioner (see NYS Education Department, *Chemical Storage Guidelines* at: http://www.p12.nysed.gov/ciai/mst/sci/chemstorguid.html).

School districts also must take an annual inventory of all chemicals used in their science laboratories, including specific information on each substance, and must retain the inventory and make it available to the commissioner for inspection (§ 305(19); 29 CFR § 1910.1200(e)(1)(i)).

63:5. What are a school district's responsibilities regarding the disposal of hazardous waste?

A school district is obligated to properly dispose of hazardous waste (42 USC § 9601 *et seq.*; Envtl. Conserv. Law § 27-0900 *et seq.*). A district's liability for the disposal of hazardous waste is far-reaching. Under federal "cradle-to-grave" liability policies, one who arranges for the disposal of hazardous wastes may be liable for the cost of cleaning up those substances forever, even though the person or entity lawfully disposed of the waste with a licensed waste hauler. Continuing liability stems from the interwoven obligations created by numerous federal hazardous waste laws and regulations, including the Resource Conservation and Recovery Act (RCRA) (42 USC § 6901 *et seq.*), and the Comprehensive Environmental Response, Compensation, and Liability Act (CERCLA) (42 USC § 9601 *et seq.*).

School districts do not have to pay special assessments for hazardous waste generated at elementary and secondary schools provided certain conditions are met related to the clean-up and remediation of such waste (Envtl. Conserv. Law § 27-0923(3)(f)).

63:6. What are a school district's responsibilities for underground storage tanks for petroleum?

The state Department of Environmental Conservation (DEC) has adopted regulations applicable to owners of both underground and above-ground storage tanks for petroleum to prevent and/or minimize damage from leaks and spills from tanks. The federal Resource Conservation and Recovery Act (RCRA) and the Environmental Protection Agency (EPA), the federal agency that enforces RCRA, impose additional requirements on owners of underground storage tanks. Local and county health departments may impose additional restrictions.

The regulations adopted by the DEC require school districts that own underground and above-ground storage tanks containing petroleum to register and pay a registration fee for storage tanks (6 NYCRR § 613-1.9). In addition, school district responsibilities include, but are not limited to:

- Employing practices for preventing spills and overfilling as well as operation and maintenance of corrosion protection (6 NYCRR §§ 613-2.2(a), (b), 613-4.2(a), (b)).
- Installing secondary containment systems and gauges for above-ground tanks (6 NYCRR § 613-4.1(b)(1)(v), (c)(1)).
- Testing underground and above-ground storage tanks for leaking (6 NYCRR §§ 613-2.3, 613-3.3, 613-4.3).
- Inspecting above-ground storage tanks for leakage and damage each month (6 NYCRR § 613-4.3(a)(1), (b)(1)).
- Preparing daily inventory records for underground storage tanks (6 NYCRR § 613-2.3(c)(1)).
- Conducting an extensive inspection of above-ground storage tanks when the tank is 10 years old (6 NYCRR § 613-4.3(a)(1)(ii), (b)(2)).
- Conducting an extensive reinspection of above-ground storage tanks every 10 years from the date of the last test (6 NYCRR § 613-4.3(a), (b)(2)).
- Ensuring district employee(s) are appropriately trained and pass DEC's requisite operator exam(s) (6 NYCRR § 613-2.5).

The regulations also contain provisions about record-keeping and reporting requirements in the event of a spill or leak from a tank (6 NYCRR §§ 613-2.3(e), 613-2.4, 613-4.3(e), 613-4.4). Finally, the regulations impose strict requirements for underground storage tanks, above-ground tanks, and for closing out-of-service tanks (6 NYCRR §§ 613-2.1, 613-2.6, 613-4.1, 613-4.5).

The federal law and regulations require owners of underground storage tanks to meet strict standards designed to prevent leaks and to ensure financial responsibility for clean-up costs and third-party damage claims (40 CFR Part 280). The financial responsibility requirement of the EPA regulation requires school districts and other owners of underground storage tanks to demonstrate their ability to pay for site clean-up and any liability to others for leak damage (40 CFR § 280.93). The regulations relieve a district of the obligation to carry special insurance policies for such coverage if it can meet one of two alternative requirements: a bond-rating test or a worksheet test. The bond-rating test requires the district to have at least $1 million of general obligation bonds of investment grade or better outstanding. The worksheet test involves the calculation of financial ratios (40 CFR §§ 280.104, 280.105).

Use of Deodorizers and Green Cleaning Products

Editor's Note: Guidelines on the procurement and use of green cleaning products for schools are available from the NYS Office of General Services and can be accessed electronically at: https://greencleaning.ny.gov/Entry.asp.

63:7. What laws apply to the use of deodorizers in school restrooms?

Urinal or toilet deodorizers containing paradichlorobenzene have been banned in public and nonpublic schools (§ 409-g; see also NYS Education Department, *Toilet/Urinal Deodorizer's Containing Paradichlorobenzene* (updated Apr. 2014), at: http://www.p12.nysed.gov/facplan/Deodorizers_with_paradichlorobenzene.htm). Paradichlorobenzene, which is also known as 1, 4-dichlorobenzene or as p-DCB, has been known to cause headaches, nausea and other detrimental health effects.

63:8. What laws apply to the procurement of cleaning and maintenance products?

All public and nonpublic elementary and secondary schools are required to purchase and use *environmentally sensitive cleaning and maintenance products* commonly referred to as "green cleaning products" (§ 409-i; State Fin. Law §§ 163(3)(b)(viii), 163-b). The term specifically refers to products that minimize adverse impacts on children's health and the environment (§ 409-i(1)(b)).

63:9. Are school districts required to use any particular type of green cleaning product?

The commissioner of general services is responsible for preparing and disseminating a sample list of products that meet his or her guidance and specifications for the use of such products in the schools (§ 409-i(2), (3); see also State Fin. Law § 163-b). The commissioner of general services is also responsible for providing assistance and guidance to the schools in carrying out the use of green cleaning products requirements (§ 409-i(3)).

Pesticides

Editor's Note: For more information concerning pesticides, refer to 6 NYCRR Part 325 and Environmental Conservation Law Article 33, contact the nearest regional DEC office, or visit its website at: http://www.dec.ny.gov. The Environmental Protection Agency's Office of Pesticide Programs offers the publication Pest Control in the School Environment: Adopting Integrated Pest Management *(Aug. 1993), at:*

https://www.epa.gov/sites/production/files/2014-10/documents/epa-735-f-93-012.pdf or by calling the pesticide hotline at: 1-800-858-7378.

63:10. What are a school district's responsibilities regarding the use of pesticides on school premises?

Generally, school districts and boards of cooperative educational services may not apply pesticides to any playground, turf, athletic, or playing fields. However, an emergency application of a pesticide is allowed. With some exceptions, the term pesticide includes any substance or mixture of substances intended for preventing, destroying, repelling, or mitigating any pest, or for use as a plant regulator, defoliant, or desiccant (§ 409-k; Envtl. Conserv. Law § 33-0101(35); see also NYS Department of Environmental Conservation, *Guidance on Chapter 85, Laws of 2010* (Dec. 2010), at: http://www.dec.ny.gov/docs/materials_minerals_pdf/guidancech85.pdf).

In addition, the comprehensive public school safety program and the uniform code of public school building inspection, safety, ratings, and monitoring require that school districts establish a comprehensive maintenance plan that includes provisions for a least toxic approach to integrated pest management (8 NYCRR §§ 155.3(d), 155.4(d)(2)).

63:11. What is integrated pest management?

Integrated pest management (IPM) is a systematic approach to managing pests that focuses on long-term prevention or suppression with minimal impact on human health, the environment, and non-targeted organisms (6 NYCRR § 325.1(al); see also NYS Education Department, Office of Facilities Planning, *Newsletter #112* (Nov. 2013), at: http://www.p12.nysed.gov/facplan/documents/112November2013.pdf).

IPM is offered as a state contract under the NYS Office of General Services. Information is available from the Office of General Services at: http://ogs.ny.gov/default.asp and by phone at 518-474-3899.

The NYS Department of Environmental Conservation (DEC) provides guidelines for integrated pest management for school districts in its book, *IPM Workbook for New York State Schools* (Cornell Cooperative Extension Community IPM Program with support from NYS Department of Environmental Conservation, Aug. 1998). Copies are available from DEC's Bureau of Pesticides Management at: http://www.nysipm.cornell.edu/publications/school_wkbk/files/schoolwkbk.pdf or by calling 518-402-8788.

The DEC also has issued regulations regarding the use of pesticides (6 NYCRR Part 325). Under these regulations, a contractor's responsibilities include, but are not limited to:

- Stating in the written contracts which chemicals are going to be used (6 NYCRR § 325.40).
- Posting on the grounds visible signs prior to and at least 24 hours after pesticide application, warning of the pesticide use. The signs must be made of rigid material with black letters at least 4 inches by 5 inches in size on a yellow background (6 NYCRR § 325.40(f), (h)).
- Ensuring that an apprentice may not apply pesticides on any school premises without the direct supervision of a certified applicator (6 NYCRR §§ 325.7, 325.10(a)).

Districts using a district employee to apply pesticides must register and file an annual report with the DEC, which includes the quantity of pesticide product used (6 NYCRR §§ 325.23, 325.25; see also Envtl. Conserv. Law § 33-0907).

In addition, Environmental Conservation Law section 33-0725 requires that a pesticide be used only in accordance with its labeling (exceptions provided are for agricultural purposes only).

63:12. Must school districts give notice of pesticide applications?

Yes. School districts must give prior written notice of pesticide applications to anyone who has asked to receive such notice, in accordance with notification provisions set forth in the Education Law and regulations of the commissioner of education (§ 409-h; 8 NYCRR § 155.24). For example, at the beginning of each school year or summer school session, the school district must provide written notification to all staff and parents that pesticides may be used periodically throughout the school year or summer school session, that the district is required to maintain a list of those people who wish to receive 48-hour notice prior to the application of pesticides, and how to register for the list and the name and phone number of the school pesticide representative (§ 409-h(2); 8 NYCRR § 155.24(b); see also NYS Department of Environmental Conservation, *Summary of NYS Requirements for Pesticide Neighbor Notification* at: http://www.dec.ny.gov/chemical/42920.html).

Further information and training is available through the Health and Safety Office of local boards of cooperative educational services, as well as the Integrated Pest Management Program at Cornell University at: https://nysipm.cornell.edu and the NYS Education Department Office of Facilities Planning at: http://www.p12.nysed.gov/facplan/ or at: 518-474-3906.

Treated Lumber and Debris

63:13. Are there any restrictions on the use of pressure treated lumber in public school facilities?

Yes. School districts and boards of cooperative educational services (BOCES) are prohibited from using lumber that has been pressure treated with chromated copper arsenate (CCA) in the construction of playground structures owned or operated by the district or BOCES (Envtl. Conserv. Law § 37-0109(1)). This is due to the possible risk of contamination and poisoning by arsenic and chrome, which are two known human carcinogens.

Moreover, school districts and BOCES must maintain and operate all existing playground structures previously constructed using CCA pressure treated lumber and any surrounding ground cover including gravel, wood chips, or rubber in a manner that minimizes the leaching of the CCA from such structures (Envtl. Conserv. Law § 37-0109(2)). This can be done by staining or painting the structures with certain penetrating coatings as advised by the NYS Department of Environmental Conservation (see NYS Education Department, *Chromated Copper Arsenate (CCA) Playgrounds Prohibition* (Nov. 2002), at: http://www.p12.nysed.gov/facplan/Laws_Regs/CCA_letter_2002.html).

63:14. Where can school districts obtain information on the hazards of pressure treated lumber?

The Department of Environmental Conservation (DEC) commissioner must compile and publish information on the dangers and hazards to public health and to the environment in connection with the use of chromated copper arsenate (CCA) treated lumber. The commissioner is also required to publish a list of less toxic materials that may be used as an alternative. Furthermore, the DEC must publish and widely disseminate to the public information about non-toxic methods and materials that are available to adequately maintain playground structures to minimize leaching of CCA from such structures (Envtl. Conserv. Law § 37-0109(3)).

The DEC has published some of this information on its website at: http://www.dec.ny.gov/ (search for "chromated"). Information may also be obtained at the DEC's Division of Materials Management, Bureau of Waste Reduction and Recycling at: 518-402-8706 or 625 Broadway, Albany, NY 12233.

There are several products that may be used in place of CCA treated lumber. The EPA has registered a number of alternate wood preservatives. In addition, untreated wood (e.g., cedar and redwood) and non-wood alternatives, such as plastics, metal, and composite materials, are available (see NYS Education Department, *Chromated Copper Arsenate (CCA) Playgrounds Prohibition* (Nov. 2002), at: www.p12.nysed.gov/facplan/Laws_Regs/CCA_letter_2002.html).

63:15. Are there any safety concerns with respect to using construction and demolition debris as fill for athletic fields?

Yes. Construction and demolition debris (C&D debris) generally includes uncontaminated solid waste resulting from construction, remodeling, repair, and demolition of structures or roads. However, if the debris has been mechanically processed it may be contaminated with lead or other harmful materials.

Problems with use of contaminated C&D debris at schools caused the NYS Education Department to mandate that in the case of a major field reconstruction where the elevation of the playing field surface is to be raised significantly, the project will require a full review by the Office of Facilities Planning. Previously, site work did not require review and issuance of a building permit (NYS Education Department, Office of Facilities Planning, *Letter to Superintendents* (Aug. 2003), at: http://www.p12.nysed.gov/facplan/documents/fill_for_fields_072903.pdf).

Radon

63:16. What are a school district's responsibilities over the presence of radon in schools?

Radon is a naturally occurring colorless, odorless, tasteless gas in the ground and atmosphere created by the natural breakdown (radioactive decay) of uranium deposits in the earth. When it is present in the air, it causes ionization (or splitting) of the molecules that make up the air. This ionization process results in the release of uranium, lead, and other substances in the environment, often called radon progeny. The radiation from radon and its progeny can affect cell development adversely in humans and exposure to high levels can lead to an increased risk of cancer.

The uniform safety standards for school construction and maintenance projects require that school districts take responsibility to be aware of the geological potential for high levels of radon and to test and mitigate as appropriate (8 NYCRR § 155.5(m); see also NYS Education Department, Office of Facilities Planning, *Newsletter #123* (Aug. 2015), at: http://www.p12.nysed.gov/facplan/documents/123_August2015.pdf).

63:17. Is there assistance available to school districts regarding radon detection and control?

Yes. The Office of Facilities Planning at the State Education Department provides assistance to school districts regarding detection and control. Staff at that office can be reached at: 518-474-3906.

Lead

63:18. What is lead?

Lead is a naturally occurring toxic metal that is harmful to one's health and can cause damage to the brain and nervous system resulting in reduced attention span, behavioral problems, impaired hearing, and a lowered IQ. Lead is especially dangerous to young children, pregnant women and fetuses. Lead enters the human body through inhalation (by breathing particles of lead-contaminated dust) and by ingestion (by drinking lead-contaminated water). Common sources of exposure to lead include paint chips, dust from paint that contains lead and lead leached in water from lead solder or pipes.

63:19. What are a school district's responsibilities over the presence of lead in the schools?

The uniform safety standards for school construction and maintenance projects require that school districts test all areas to be disturbed during renovation or demolition and areas of flaking and peeling paint for the presence of lead (8 NYCRR § 155.5(c), (l)). Any construction or maintenance operations that will disturb lead-based paint must be abated in accordance with federal *Guidelines for the Evaluation and Control of Lead-Based Paint Hazards in Housing*, U.S. Department of Housing and Urban Development, Washington D.C. (July 2012), at: http://portal.hud.gov/hudportal/HUD?src=/program_offices/healthy_homes/lbp/hudguidelines. Areas of flaking and peeling paint must be abated or encapsulated in accordance with the same guidelines (8 NYCRR § 155.5(l)). According to the regulations of the commissioner of education, abatement involves mitigation of the lead hazard in accordance with guidelines from the federal Housing and Urban Development (HUD) Department (8 NYCRR § 155.5(l)), which differ from the Environmental Protection Agency (EPA) at 40 CFR Part 745.

Copies of the guidelines and additional information are also available through the NYS Education Department, Office of Facilities Planning, EBA, Room 1060, Albany, N.Y. 12234 and at: http://www.p12.nysed.gov/facplan/.

63:20. What are a school district's responsibilities over the presence of lead in its water supply?

School districts and boards of cooperative educational services (BOCES) that supply their own water from wells they own must test for lead contamination under the federal Safe Drinking Water Act of 1974 (42 USC § 300f *et seq*.; 40 CFR Parts 141, 142). Pursuant to state law and regulations, however, all districts and BOCES, not just those that supply water from their own wells, must test their water supplies for lead contamination (see Pub. Health Law § 1110; 10 NYCRR Part 67-4).

The state law testing requirement does not apply to buildings that have been deemed to be lead free under the Safe Drinking Water Act on the basis that, for example, the lead content of plumbing fixtures in the building meets lead free standards (see 42 USC § 300g-6 (a), (d)). Districts and BOCES must publish a list of all their buildings deemed to be lead free on their website and report the same to the commissioner of public health (Pub. Health Law § 1110(3); 10 NYCRR §§ 67-4.5(a), 67-4.6(a)(3)).

In each school building that may be occupied by children or students, water samples from any potable water fixture currently or potentially used for drinking or cooking purposes must be taken (10 NYCRR §§ 67-4.2(e), 67-4.3), collected and tested in accordance with applicable regulations from the Department Health (10 NYCRR § 67-4.3(c),(e)). The required testing must be done in accordance with the following schedule:

- Schools serving pre-kindergarten through grade 5 had to collect samples by September 30, 2016 and schools serving grade levels 6 through 12 had to collect samples by October 31, 2016.
- For new buildings occupied after October 31, 2016 testing must be completed prior to occupancy (10 NYCRR § 67-4.3(c)(1), (2)).
- In 2020, and at least every five years thereafter (10 NYCRR § 67-4.3(d)).

If a school district conducted sampling after January 1, 2015 consistent with the requirements of Subpart 67-4 of the Department of Health regulations it may apply for a waiver from the testing requirement (10 NYCRR §§ 67-4.3(3), 67-4.8).

All test results must be reported to the commissioner of health, the local health department, and the State Education Department. Additionally, districts and BOCES must publish on their website all test results and any lead remediation plans that have been undertaken after a finding of lead contamination (Pub. Health Law § 1110(6); 10 NYCRR §§ 67-4.5(b)(1), 67-4.6).

When there is a finding of lead contamination greater than 15 parts per billion (ppb), districts and BOCES must take the following actions:

- Prohibit use of the particular water outlet until a lead remediation plan is implemented and test results indicate lead levels at or below 15 ppb;
- Provide building occupants with an adequate supply of potable water for drinking and cooking while remediation is performed;
- Report the test results to the local health department within in 1 business day of receipt of the laboratory report; and
- Notify all staff and persons in parental relation to students of the test results in writing as soon as practicable, but no later than 10 days after receipt of the laboratory report (Pub. Health Law § 1110(2), 10 NYCRR §§ 67-4.4, 67-4.5(b)).

Officers and employees of the State Department of Health and local health departments may enter school buildings with reasonable notice to determine compliance with the law (10 NYCRR § 67-4.9(a)). Civil penalties may be accessed for failure to comply (10 NYCRR § 67-4.9(b)).

Building aid is available for both testing and the installation of filters or other remedial measures provided the installation of remedial measures has been approved or reviewed by a professional with expertise in the field of water quality and remediation and the cost is incurred prior to July 1, 2019 (§ 3602(6-h); see also §§ 1950(5)(b), 3602(6-e)).

Asbestos

63:21. What is asbestos?

Asbestos is a group of naturally occurring minerals that can be processed into fibers, which may cause several medical problems, including cancer and lung damage. Its presence can be detected only through the use of laboratory analysis.

Asbestos-containing materials (ACM) were used widely in school building construction from the 1940s to the 1970s. They commonly included acoustical material, wall board, sprayed-on fireproofing, air cell pipe wrap, thermal insulation, and floor and ceiling tiles. ACM may be potentially harmful if it is sanded, sawed, or subjected to any action that would release asbestos fibers and render them airborne (Environmental Protection Agency, Office of Pollution Prevention and Toxics, *The ABCs of Asbestos in Schools* (Aug. 2003), at: http://www.epa.gov/sites/production/files/documents/abcsfinal.pdf).

According to a joint memorandum from the NYS Education Department (SED) and the NYS Department of Health, some art clays may contain talc that is contaminated with asbestos and may be the source of asbestos in the air in school art classrooms. Although there is limited information on the topic, school districts are advised to take measures to reduce possible exposures. These can include the use of talc-free clays, pre-mixed wet clays, and cleaning methods that reduce airborne dust, such as wet mops, sponges, and rags, and/or high efficiency particulate air (HEPA) filtration vacuums (NYS Education Department and NYS Department of Health, *Potential for Asbestos Contamination of Art Clays due to Talc* (Oct. 2007), at: www.p12.nysed.gov/facplan/documents/AsbestosinTalc-101507.doc). Additional information can be obtained from SED by calling 518-474-3906 and from the following SED publication: *New York State Elementary & Secondary Schools Asbestos Guidebook for the Schools and the Community* (Central Services Team 1, undated), a portion of which was updated by SED's Office of Facilities Planning, *Newsletter #90* (Aug. 2007), at: http://www.p12.nysed.gov/facplan/Newsletter/OfficeofFacilitiesPlanning-Newsletter90-August2007.htm.

Information and financial assistance is also available through the Environmental Protection Agency under the federal Asbestos School Hazard Abatement Act (20 USC §§ 4011–4022).

63:22. What is friable asbestos?

Under New York State law, *friable asbestos* is a "condition of crumbled, pulverized, powdered, crushed or exposed asbestos which is capable of being released into the air by hand pressure" (Lab. Law

§ 901(12); 12 NYCRR § 56-2.1(bh)). Friable asbestos could pose a danger by releasing toxic fibers into the air. This can occur during the demolition/renovation of a school building or removal of asbestos-containing material (ACM).

In its rule entitled "Damaged Friable Surfacing ACM," the federal Environmental Protection Agency (EPA) defines damaged friable surfacing ACM to include the following: deteriorated or physically injured material such that the internal structure of the material is inadequate; or the bond of the lamination to its substrate is inadequate; or a lack of fiber cohesion or adhesion qualities; flaking, blistering, or crumbling; water damage, significant water stain, scraped, gouged, marred or other signs of physical injury (see 40 CFR § 763.83).

63:23. What laws govern a school district's obligations regarding asbestos-containing material?

The federal Asbestos Hazard Emergency Response Act (AHERA) (see 15 USC §§ 2641–2656) and Article 30 of the New York State Labor Law govern requirements regarding asbestos management for school districts.

AHERA is administered by the federal Environmental Protection Agency (EPA). The EPA has adopted regulations concerning asbestos-containing material in schools (see 40 CFR §§ 763.80-763.99; see **63:24** for more information about AHERA). The NYS Education Department (SED) is the AHERA designee for New York schools and, thus, serves a role in providing information to schools and in collecting information, such as asbestos-management plans.

In addition, the NYS Department of Labor has adopted work rules concerning asbestos known as Industrial Code Rule 56 (see 12 NYCRR Part 56; see also **63:24** for more information about Industrial Code Rule 56).

AHERA and the EPA regulations describe requirements concerning inspection and management of asbestos-containing material in school buildings, while the state Labor Law and Industrial Code Rule 56 control work practices for interaction with asbestos-containing material. The asbestos laws and regulations seek to reduce or eliminate potential risks associated with asbestos fibers.

Furthermore, uniform safety standards for school construction and maintenance projects, which require that all school areas to be disturbed during renovation or demolition be treated for the presence of asbestos and that prohibit certain asbestos abatement projects while a building is occupied, are found in regulations of the commissioner of education (see 8 NYCRR § 155.5(c), (k); see also **62:23**).

More information on AHERA is available at SED's website at: http://www.p12.nysed.gov/facplan/HealthSafety.htm.

63:24. What are some of the specific requirements school districts must comply with regarding asbestos-containing materials (ACM)?

The federal Asbestos Hazard Emergency Response Act (AHERA) requires that school districts:

- Identify all friable and non-friable ACM in school buildings (40 CFR §§ 763.85–763.88).
- Appoint an individual as asbestos designee to ensure that AHERA requirements are implemented (40 CFR § 763.84(g)(1)).
- Conduct an initial inspection and subsequent reinspection once every three years (40 CFR § 763.85(a), (b)).
- Conduct periodic asbestos surveillance in each building at least once every six months (40 CFR § 763.92(b)).
- Prepare, administer, and maintain an asbestos-management plan (40 CFR § 763.93(a)).
- Adopt and execute appropriate response actions (40 CFR § 763.90).

- Notify workers and building occupants or their legal guardians about inspections, response actions, and post-response actions at least once each school year (40 CFR §§ 763.84(c), 763.93(e)(10)).
- Notify short-term workers such as telephone repair workers, electricians and exterminators of the specific location of asbestos-containing materials in a building (40 CFR § 763.84(d)).

AHERA also requires that districts clearly post warning labels on all materials containing asbestos fibers, post signs at and approaching each regulated area and in routine maintenance areas (29 CFR § 1910.1001(j)(4), (5); 40 CFR § 763.95) and properly train all custodial and maintenance employees annually (29 CFR § 1910.1001(j)(7); 40 CFR §§ 763.92(a)(1), 763.84(b)). Two hours of asbestos awareness training must be provided for new employees (29 CFR § 1910.1001(j)(7); 40 CFR § 763.92(a)(1)).

Districts also must provide personal protective equipment, including the use of respirators where necessary, for housekeeping and other employees who are exposed to dangerous levels of ACM (29 CFR § 1910.1001(g), (h), (j)).

Furthermore, districts must properly maintain and distribute the various records required under AHERA regulations, including a copy of the district's asbestos management plan in the district's administrative office. Each building also must have a copy of that building's asbestos management plan in its administrative office (40 CFR § 763.93(g)(2), (3)).

The management plan must be made available without cost for inspection by the Environmental Protection Agency and others as required by law (40 CFR § 763.93(g)(2), (3)). AHERA asbestos records must be kept for at least three years after the last required inspection (40 CFR § 763.94(a); see **63:25**).

New York State Industrial Code Rule 56, which conforms with AHERA, requires that persons employed in any aspect of an asbestos project, as well as those who supervise them, be trained appropriately and certified. In addition, Industrial Code Rule 56 sets standards and procedures for the removal, enclosure, application, encapsulation, or disturbance of friable asbestos and the handling of asbestos or ACM in a manner that prevents the release of asbestos fibers (see **63:26**). For example, school districts must conduct an asbestos survey and removal project of all asbestos identified when a school building is scheduled for demolition (12 NYCRR § 56-2.1(y); see also 12 NYCRR Subpart 56-5). This rule also establishes an inspection and enforcement program administered by the NYS Department of Labor and sets forth record-keeping, reporting, and retention requirements for asbestos contractors (12 NYCRR § 56-5.1).

63:25. Are school districts responsible for conducting ongoing asbestos reinspections?

Yes. The asbestos management plans required by the Asbestos Hazard Emergency Response Act (see **63:24**) must contain a time schedule for the triennial reinspection and periodic visual surveillance of school buildings. A certified inspector or management planner must physically and visually reinspect the buildings in all areas that contain either known or assumed asbestos-containing material (ACM). With each reinspection, a state-certified inspector must visually and physically inspect material that was previously considered non-friable and determine whether it has become friable since the last inspection (40 CFR § 763.85(b)(3)(ii)). The asbestos designee must be satisfied that the reported information is accurate and complete and must sign a statement to that effect (40 CFR § 763.93(i)).

The management plan's time schedule should outline surveillance of all friable and non-friable known or assumed ACM every six months (40 CFR § 763.92(b)). This surveillance need not be performed by a certified inspector, but the person who performs the surveillance must have undergone at least two hours of asbestos-awareness training. Since this is a visual inspection, no additional training is necessary (only required for handling ACM) (40 CFR § 763.92(a)(1)).

63:26. What actions may school districts take in response to the presence of asbestos in the schools?

There are five federally approved response actions or methods of responding to the presence of asbestos from which school officials may choose: removal, encapsulation, enclosure, repair, and operations and maintenance (40 CFR §§ 763.90, 763.91).

- *Removal* involves taking out or stripping of any asbestos-containing materials (ACM) from an area in a school building (40 CFR § 763.83; see 12 NYCRR § 56-2.1(da)).
- *Encapsulation* is the application of either a penetrating material that penetrates the ACM and binds the components together or a bridging agent that surrounds the asbestos fibers or embeds them in an adhesive matrix, creating a membrane over the surface of the ACM (40 CFR § 763.83; see 12 NYCRR §§ 56-2.1(bb), 56-8.7).
- *Enclosure* involves the construction of airtight walls, ceilings, and floors between the ACM and the facility's environment, or around surfaces coated with asbestos material or any other appropriate procedure that prevents the release of asbestos fiber (40 CFR § 763.83; 12 NYCRR §§ 56-2.1(bc), 56-8.8). The goal of enclosure is to create an airtight, impermeable, permanent barrier around the ACM to prevent release of asbestos fibers into the air (see 40 CFR § 763.83).
- *Repair* consists of returning damaged ACM to an undamaged condition or an intact state to prevent the release of asbestos fibers (40 CFR § 763.83). The NYS Department of Labor defines repair as corrective action using required work practices to control the release of asbestos fiber from damaged ACM (12 NYCRR § 56-2.1(dd)).
- *Operation and maintenance* is a program of work practices to maintain ACM in good condition, ensure cleanup of asbestos fibers previously released, and prevent further release by minimizing and controlling ACM disturbance or damage (40 CFR § 763.83).

The Environmental Protection Agency (EPA) requires school districts to select from these options a response action that protects human health and the environment and is the "least burdensome method" (40 CFR § 763.90(a)). Currently, the EPA suggests that the safest and most cost-effective response action is to manage the asbestos in place.

The state Labor Law and Industrial Code Rule 56 authorizes asbestos projects to be undertaken by a licensed contractor, which involves any aspect of the removal, encapsulation, enclosure, or disturbance of friable asbestos or any handling of asbestos material that may result in the release of asbestos fiber (Lab. Law § 901(7); 12 NYCRR § 56-1.2(a), (b)). The contractor's obligations may depend on the amount of square and/or linear feet of asbestos or ACM, and whether the asbestos project is defined as a large, small, or minor asbestos project (12 NYCRR § 56-2.1(w)(2); see **63:27**). In addition, certain asbestos projects may qualify as "emergency asbestos projects" or a "repair," resulting in slight variance from some of the general rules concerning asbestos projects (12 NYCRR §§ 56-2.1(ay), (az), (dc), 56-3.5).

63:27. Are school officials required by law to remove all asbestos-containing material to make a school safe?

No. In fact, an asbestos-removal project may, on occasion, increase the amount of airborne asbestos fibers in a building if it is not conducted and monitored properly. Therefore, removal should be considered only as a last resort.

In addition, the uniform safety standards for school construction and maintenance projects that require that all asbestos abatement work comply with all applicable federal and state laws, forbid large and small asbestos projects (see **63:31**) while a school building is being occupied. However, minor projects involving the removal, disturbance, repair, encapsulation, enclosure, or handling of 10 square feet or less, or 25 linear feet or less, of asbestos or asbestos material are permissible in unoccupied areas of an occupied building in accordance with applicable law and regulations (8 NYCRR § 155.5(k)).

63:28. Once asbestos has been removed from a school district, does all liability cease?

No. A school district still must concern itself with how the material is handled, where it is to be stored, how it is to be transported, and whether it is transported to an approved dumping site. If the abatement contractor violates any of the rules regarding these matters, the school district may share liability for an Environmental Protection Agency fine (see **63:5**).

Additionally, diseases attributed to exposure to asbestos have long periods of latency, perhaps as much as 40 years. Under the current statute of limitations on certain personal injury lawsuits, injured persons now have up to three years after they discover they have an asbestos-related disease to bring a lawsuit against a school district or other party that they allege has wrongfully exposed them to asbestos (C.P.L.R. § 214-c). However, the discovery of the mere presence of asbestos is not the same as the discovery of an asbestos-related disease for statute of limitation purposes (*Germantown CSD v. Clark*, 294 A.D.2d 93 (3d Dep't 2002), *aff'd*, 100 N.Y.2d 202 (2003)).

63:29. Who is responsible for ensuring a school district's compliance with the asbestos laws?

An asbestos designee appointed by the school district (see **63:24**) is responsible for coordinating the asbestos program in the district and for keeping the district in compliance with all asbestos mandates. The asbestos designee must receive adequate training on the federal, state, and local laws and regulations concerning asbestos (40 CFR § 763.84(g)). The asbestos designee need not be a separate position within the district, but may be added to the responsibilities of an existing position. The designee may be an outside consultant who does not have to be on-site and may be shared with other school districts (see Environmental Protection Agency, *Asbestos Frequently Asked Questions* at: http://www.epa.gov/sites/production/files/documents/asbestosfaqs_0.pdf).

63:30. Who may conduct asbestos inspections, develop asbestos management plans and effectuate response actions on behalf of a school district?

School district employees or a person or persons or company from outside the school district may conduct inspections, develop management plans, and effectuate response actions. If a district uses a member of its own staff to perform these duties, it must obtain a New York contractor's license, and the person who re-inspects a school building or performs a response action must obtain the appropriate certification from the NYS Department of Labor. This certification requires special training that may be available through a board of cooperative educational services health and safety office or through a private organization whose courses have been approved by the NYS Department of Health.

If a district employs outside personnel to perform these duties, school officials must take special care to be sure that the outside company's certification is valid in New York; that the laboratories used for testing purposes are certified and approved by the state Department of Health's Environmental Laboratory Approval Program; and that the company has adequate facilities and properly trained, certified personnel to fulfill the requirements of all laws and regulations pertaining to the potential disturbance of asbestos (Pub. Health Law § 502; see 12 NYCRR §§ 56-3.1, 56-4.2; 10 NYCRR Part 55-2).

63:31. Are there any notice requirements that must be met before an asbestos project begins?

Yes. In a large asbestos project, defined as one involving more than 260 linear feet or 160 square feet of material, the contractor must notify both the Environmental Protection Agency's (EPA) Hazardous Materials Division and the commissioner of the NYS Department of Labor's Asbestos Control Bureau at least 10 days before beginning the project (Lab. Law § 904(2); 12 NYCRR § 56-3.4(b)(1)). If an asbestos hazard is present that requires immediate attention, or if emergency conditions make it impossible to give 10 days notice, the owner, owners' agent, consultant, or contractor must notify the

Program Manager's office at the Asbestos Control Bureau in Albany by telephone at 518-457-1255, or in person (Bldg. 12, Room 157, State Campus, Albany, NY 12240), prior to beginning the project (12 NYCRR § 56-3.5).

In addition, the Labor Law and Industrial Code Rule 56 require all contractors engaged in the abatement portion of an asbestos project to provide "business occupants" written notice 10 days prior to beginning any work on any asbestos project in a building. With regard to projects being conducted in school buildings, the faculty, staff, and students attending such school are considered "business occupants" (Lab. Law § 904(4); 12 NYCRR § 56-3.6(a)). If the contract is signed less than 10 days prior to scheduled work, contractors are required to give three days' notice (Lab. Law § 904(4); 12 NYCRR § 56-3.6(b)). In an emergency, written notice to business occupants must be given as soon as practicable (Lab. Law § 904(4); 12 NYCRR § 56-3.6(c)).

63:32. Must air sampling be performed during an asbestos-abatement project?

Yes. *Air sampling* is the process of measuring the asbestos fiber content of a known volume of air collected during a specific period of time (12 NYCRR § 56-2.1(i)). Air sampling is performed in conjunction with an abatement project in order to determine the asbestos fiber content in the air in the vicinity of the project. The size of the abatement project, as defined under Industrial Code Rule 56, determines when air sampling must be performed (12 NYCRR § 56-4.9).

Under Industrial Code Rule 56, monitoring the same methodology for air sampling and analysis of asbestos must be used for all pre-abatement, abatement, and post-abatement (12 NYCRR § 56-4.6).

For information about all sampling requirements for asbestos abatement in dirt floored crawl spaces, see NYS Education Department, Office of Facilities Planning, *Newsletter #104* (July 2010), at: http://www.p12.nysed.gov/facplan/documents/Newsletter_104.pdf.

63:33. How is a containment area formed around an asbestos-abatement project?

There are extensive rules and regulations about the type and quantity of plastic to be used in an asbestos-abatement project and the number of layers of plastic to be placed on floors, walls, ceilings and other surfaces to prevent any possible release of asbestos fibers from the containment area. Negative air pressure helps to ensure that air from inside the containment area flows through high-efficiency particulate air filters before being discharged back into the air as clean air. In addition, workers leaving the work area must comply with detailed procedures to prevent contamination outside the project area (see 12 NYCRR subparts 56-7 through 56-11).

63:34. Must an asbestos contractor and its employees be licensed and certified?

Yes. The NYS Department of Labor issues that licenses to contractors who wish to conduct asbestos-abatement projects in this state. In addition, that Department issues a variety of certificates for workers who wish to work for asbestos-abatement contractors (see 12 NYCRR § 56-3.2), which are valid for one year and cost from $50 to $150 (see Lab. Law § 903; 12 NYCRR § 56-3.2).

All contractors who engage in an asbestos project, as well as any business that provides management planning, project design, monitoring, inspection and/or air-monitoring services, must have an asbestos-handling license. This license costs $500 initially and $300 at every annual renewal (Lab. Law §§ 902(1), 903(2), (3), (4); 12 NYCRR § 56-3.1(a)).

Although the Department of Labor actually issues the license or certification, the NYS Department of Health has the responsibility for approving training programs (12 NYCRR § 56-3.2(a)).

Mercury

63:35. What is mercury and where would it be found on school property?

Mercury is a metal that occurs naturally in the environment in several forms. The most common form, metallic or elemental, is a silvery, odorless liquid.

Instruments containing mercury can be found virtually anywhere on school property — in the nurse's office, science rooms, gymnasiums, art rooms, and boiler rooms. Liquid mercury is used in instruments that measure temperature (thermometers), pressure (barometers or sphygmo-manometers), humidity (hygrometers), vacuum (laboratory manometers), flow (water meters), and air speed (anemometers). Mercury can also be found in lights (particularly gymnasium and fluorescent lights), thermostats, heating/ventilation and air conditioning (HVAC) systems, plumbing systems, cafeteria equipment, medical devices, regulators, gauges, and science room equipment (see NYS Department of Health, *Mercury and Schools: A Risky Combination* (Feb. 2011), a series of brochures at: http://www.health.ny.gov/environmental/chemicals/hsees/mercury/).

Exposure to high levels of mercury can damage the nervous system and kidneys. Exposure to mercury is particularly a concern in children and unborn babies because their nervous systems are still developing, and the nervous system is a target organ for mercury. Health effects might include brain damage as well as behavioral and developmental problems (*Id.*).

63:36. Are there any restrictions regarding the use of mercury in public schools?

Yes. No primary or secondary school may use or purchase elemental mercury that consists of mercury as a silvery-white liquid at room temperature (Envtl. Conserv. Law § 27-2107(4); see also **63:37**).

63:37. Are schools required to stop using and dispose of mercury fever thermometers, mercury body thermometers, science thermometers, and other mercury added equipment?

No. Existing thermometers may continue to be used. However, if a mercury thermometer is replaced, it must be replaced with a non-mercury thermometer, unless a mercury fever thermometer is prescribed by a physician (NYS Education Department, *Mercury Q & A for Schools* (Sept. 2004), at: http://www.p12.nysed.gov/facplan/Emergency/mercury_law_QA_101904.html).

Broken mercury thermometers must be cleaned up and disposed of properly. Mercury-added products must be discarded and disposed of according to the NYS Department of Environmental Conservation (DEC) regulations. A DEC guidance document entitled, *How to Initiate a Mercury Clean Out in Your School*, provides information on the collection and disposal of mercury in the schools. It is available online at: http://www.dec.ny.gov/chemical/35381.html.

63:38. Are existing building mechanical systems that may contain mercury, such as switches and thermostats, permitted in schools?

Yes. Mercury-added consumer products, such as switches, thermostats, fluorescent bulbs, and electrical relays, may be left in place. If these products are replaced, they must be disposed of properly. Any replacement mercury added consumer products must be labeled by the manufacturer indicating the presence of any mercury (NYS Education Department, *Mercury Q & A for Schools* (Sept. 2004), at: http://www.p12.nysed.gov/facplan/Emergency/mercury_law_QA_101904.html).

Polychlorinated Biphenyls (PCBs)

63:39. What are PCBs, and how should schools handle their presence?

PCBs (Polychlorinated Biphenyls) are synthetic organic chemical compounds now classified as probable human carcinogens, but were used extensively as an ingredient in caulk and in fluorescent lighting ballasts through the late 1970s. Devices that contain PCBs can leak with age and become a source of exposure to PCBs.

Districts do not have to test for the presence of PCBs, but the federal Toxic Substances Control Act requires that when leaks are found, steps be taken to decrease any potential exposure and to remove and dispose of the PCBs in accordance with local, state, and federal laws (40 CFR Part 761; see NYS Education Department, Office of Facilities Planning, *Newsletter #106* (May 2011), at: http://www.p12.nysed.gov/facplan/documents/final106Newsletter.pdf).

School buildings constructed prior to 1979 may have caulking containing PCBs in electrical equipment, around masonry openings and windows, doors, louvers, and expansion joints both inside and outside the facility. The NYS Departments of Education and Health jointly developed a protocol to address concerns about properly managing PCB caulking during building renovations and maintenance available at: http://www.p12.nysed.gov/facplan/HealthSafety/PCBinCaulkProtocol-070615.html. Any required abatement must follow and comply with federal Environmental Protection Agency (EPA) regulations (see 40 CFR §§ 761.50, 761.60-761.62 see also **62:25**).

Possible PCBs in electrical equipment or fluorescent lighting pose a separate hazard. Because most PCB-containing lighting ballasts in schools have now exceeded their life span and are expected to begin to smoke and leak, the EPA and the NYS Education Department recommend that districts remove PCB-containing fluorescent lighting ballasts as part of lighting upgrades or as a stand-alone project (NYS Education Department, Office of Facilities Planning, *Newsletter #113* (Dec. 2013), at: http://www.p12.nysed.gov/facplan/documents/113December2013.pdf). An EPA guidance document on steps districts should take to reduce potential exposure to PCBs from older fluorescent lighting fixtures is available at: http://www.epa.gov/epawaste/hazard/tsd/pcbs/pubs/ballasts.htm.

64. School Facilities – Use and Conduct

Permissible Uses of School Buildings and Grounds

64:1. Who has the final authority in granting use of a public school building?

Section 414 of the Education Law gives a school board the authority to adopt reasonable regulations with regard to granting the use of school buildings to outside organizations.

No association or organization has the right to use a school building without the express permission of the board. For example, local teachers' associations or organizations are not entitled as a matter of right to use a school building for meetings (*Matter of Charlotte Valley*, 18 PERB ¶ 3010 (1985)).

The board has the authority to prescribe the terms of use of a school building, including a rental fee sufficient to cover expenses resulting from the prescribed use (with limited exceptions) (see **64:17**), and may also refuse to grant an organization's request for use. For example, if it can be proven that a "clear and present danger" of possible damage to the building exists, the board can deny access to the organization (*Matter of Ellis*, 77 St. Dep't Rep. 32 (1956)).

64:2. What uses of school buildings may be permitted by a school board under the Education Law?

Section 414(1) of the Education Law sets forth the permissible uses of school buildings. As long as the school board determines that the particular use will not disrupt normal school operations, school buildings and grounds and other property of the district may be used for the following:

- Instruction in any branch of education, learning or the arts (§ 414(1)(a)).
- Public libraries or stations of public libraries (§ 414(1)(b)).
- Social, civic and recreational meetings and entertainments, and other uses pertaining to the welfare of the community that are nonexclusive and open to the general public. A civic meeting includes but is not limited to meetings of parent and parent-teacher associations (§ 414(1)(c); *Appeal of Emilio*, 33 Ed Dept Rep 75 (1993)). Civic meetings also include a "meet the candidates" night (*Appeal of Barse*, 54 Ed Dept Rep, Dec. No. 16,753 (2015)).
- Meetings, entertainments and occasions where admission fees are charged, when the proceeds are to be expended for an educational or charitable purpose. However, these uses are not permitted if they are under exclusive control and the proceeds are to be applied for the benefit of a society, association or organization of a religious sect or denomination, or of a fraternal, secret or exclusive society or organization other than organizations of veterans of the military, naval and marine service of the United States and organizations of volunteer fire fighters or volunteer ambulance workers (§ 414(1)(d)).
- Polling places for holding primaries and elections, for the registration of voters and for holding political meetings. However, no meetings sponsored by political organizations are permitted unless authorized by the voters or, in cities, approved by the school board. Except in cities, it is the school board's duty to call a special meeting for these purposes upon the petition of at least 10 percent of the qualified electors of the district (see § 414(1)(e); Elec. Law § 4-104).
- Civic forums and community centers (see § 414(1)(f)).
- Classes of instruction for intellectually disabled minors operated by a private organization that is approved by the commissioner of education (§ 414(1)(g); see 8 NYCRR § 200.1(zz)(7)).

- Recreation, physical training and athletics, including competitive athletic contests of children attending a private, nonprofit school (§ 414(1)(h)).
- Child-care programs when school is not in session, or when school is in session for the children of students attending schools of the district and, if there is additional space available, for children of employees of the district, to be determined by the school board (§ 414(1)(i)).
- Graduation exercises held by not-for-profit elementary and secondary schools, provided that no religious service is performed (§ 414(1)(k)).

School districts and building principals need to be mindful of ensuring compliance with the State's Uniform Fire Prevention and Building Code during assembly events, which include any activities conducted in a school's large public places such as cafeterias, pools, gymnasiums, and auditoriums. At such events there should be no blocked exits and obstructions in corridors, and fire access lanes should be clear to ensure the ability of emergency responders to reach the scene (NYS Education Department, *Evening Assembly Event Alert* (Feb. 9, 2004), at: http://www.p12.nysed.gov/facplan/FireSafety/evening_event_safety_030104.html).

A district permitting community use of school property for after-school programs must ensure such programs are open to all children in the school district, regardless of whether they attend public or private school (see § 414(2)).

64:3. Can a school building be used as a polling place in a general election?

Yes. A school building can be designated as a registration and polling place if this use of the building will not interfere with its customary use, and if it is conveniently situated for the voters residing in the election district. Any expense incurred as a result of this use must be paid like the expenses of other registration and polling places (§ 414; Elec. Law § 4-104(3)).

If an election board selects a public school as a polling place, school officials are required to make available a room suitable for registration and voting as close as possible to the main entrance (Elec. Law § 4-104(3)).

64:4. Can a school building be used for a health clinic?

Yes. A licensed school-based health, dental, or mental health clinic may be located in a school building. The clinics provide services during school and nonschool hours to school age and pre-school students. Although located in school buildings, such clinics are operated by medically licensed entities other than the school district. The cost of providing services incurred by such clinics is not a charge upon the school district. Instead, it is paid from federal, state, or other local funds made available for such purpose (§ 414(1)(j)(i), (iii)).

64:5. May school property be used to provide child-care services?

Yes. Section 410-c(5) of the Social Services Law and section 414 of the Education Law authorize child-care programs for school-age children during hours school is not in session and permits school buildings to be used for this purpose. In addition, section 414(1)(i) of the Education Law authorizes the use of school facilities for child-care services during school hours for children of students attending school. These services may also be made available to school employees, depending on space availability and as determined by the school board (*Id.*).

64:6. Are games of chance such as bingo and raffles allowed in school district buildings?

Only in limited circumstances. Generally the organization conducting the game of chance must be domiciled in a municipality (including a city, town, or village) that has passed a local law allowing games of chance. In addition, the organization must apply for and obtain a games of chance identification number from the NYS Gaming Commission, Division of Charitable Gaming. A license does not need to be obtained if the organization conducting the raffle shall derive proceeds of less than $5,000 during the conduct of one raffle and less than $20,000 in one calendar year (Gen. Mun. Law § 190-a(1)). Lastly, the proceeds must be disbursed for one of the lawful purposes allowed in the General Municipal Law (Exec. Law Art. 19-B; Gen. Mun. Law Art. 9-a, 14-H).

Only bona fide religious, charitable, or nonprofit organizations are permitted to conduct these games, as long as the entire net proceeds are devoted to the lawful purposes of the organization. However, section 414 of the Education Law prohibits the use of a school building by exclusionary groups. Therefore, the only types of outside groups that could use a school building for this purpose would be charitable or nonprofit organizations, such as parent-teacher associations, veterans, volunteer firefighters or volunteer ambulance workers. Proceeds from the games would go to benefit these groups, and only after the city, town or village approved the games. Additionally, where an admission fee is charge, the proceeds must be used for an educational or charitable purpose (§ 414(1)(d)).

It should be noted that no person under the age of eighteen shall be permitted to play, operate or assist in any raffle or game of chance conducted pursuant to the licensing exceptions under section 190-a of the General Municipal Law (Gen. Mun. Law § 190-a(3)), and may only attend such games of chance at the discretion of the licensee (Gen. Mun. Law § 195-a).

More information on charitable gaming is available at: http://www.gaming.ny.gov/charitablegaming/.

64:7. Is it permissible for the military to use school district facilities to recruit students?

Yes. Section 2-a of the Education Law provides such authority. In addition, federal law requires that any district receiving financial assistance under the act provide military recruiters the same access to secondary school students it provides to post-secondary educational institutions and prospective employers (20 USC § 7908(a)(3)).

64:8. May a school building be used for religious instruction during school hours?

No. The use of a school building for religious instruction is prohibited by article 11 of the New York State Constitution (*see Illinois ex rel. McCollum v. Bd. of Educ.*, 333 U.S. 203 (1948); see also **65:1, 65:16-18, 65:36**). However, schools may offer comparative religion courses so long as such courses teach about religion as opposed to proselytizing religious messages.

64:9. May school districts permit the use of school facilities for religious worship services or religious instruction?

The use of school property for religious worship or instruction is not among the uses expressly authorized in the Education Law (§ 414). In addition, the U.S. Supreme Court has not directly addressed whether school facilities may be used solely for religious worship or instruction. Rather, when holding that a school district improperly barred a Bible study group from school facilities, it merely noted the group's activities were not "mere religious worship, divorced from any teaching of moral values" (*Good News Club v. Milford CSD*, 533 U.S. 98, 112 (2001)). Thus, it left open the question as to whether use of school facilities solely for worship services or religious instruction is permissible.

Based on that U.S. Supreme Court decision, the U.S. Court of Appeals for the Second Circuit, with jurisdiction over New York State, ruled against a school district that barred a church from using its school premises to conduct Sunday worship services because the services also involved activities related to teaching moral values (*The Bronx Household of Faith v. Bd. of Educ. of the City of N.Y. & Cmty. Sch.*

Dist. No. 10, 331 F.3d 342 (2d Cir. 2003)). The district had permitted access to outside groups such as the Boy Scouts, who provided a moral message to members of the community. Therefore, the church had to be given the same opportunity. The school district subsequently revised its policy to prohibit granting access for the purpose of "holding religious worship services, or otherwise using a school as a house of worship." The Second Circuit upheld the validity of the revised policy on the grounds that it does not exclude expressions of religious points of view, but rather includes a reasonable content-based restriction that bars only one type of activity—the conduct of worship services (*The Bronx Household of Faith v. Bd. of Educ. of the City of N.Y.,* 650 F.3d 30 (2d Cir.), *cert. denied,* 132 S.Ct. 816 (2011)).

A later challenge to the revised policy on both Free Exercise and Establishment clause grounds was similarly rejected by the Second Circuit. The court held that the policy did not prevent the church from the free exercise of religion because there is no requirement for government to provide subsidized facilities for religious worship. Furthermore, the district's action in disallowing use for worship services was not unconstitutional given that it runs a substantial risk of incurring a violation of the Establishment Clause by "hosting and subsidizing the conduct of religious worship services." (*The Bronx Household of Faith v. Bd. of Educ. of the City of N.Y.*, 750 F.3d 184 (2d Cir. 2014), *cert. denied*, 135 S.Ct. 1730 (2015)).

Right of Access to School Facilities

64:10. May a school district deny the Boy Scouts of America use of its facilities because of its discrimination practices?

No. Under federal law, a school district may not deny use of its facilities to any group affiliated with the Boy Scouts of America or any other youth group listed as a patriotic society in federal law, including, for example, the Girl Scouts and the Boys and Girls Club, based solely on the group's membership or leadership criteria or oath of allegiance to God and country (20 USC § 7905(b)(1)).

64:11. May a school building be used by an outside religious organization?

Yes. A school building may be used by an outside religious organization just like any other community group (§ 414(1)(d); *Good News Club v. Milford CSD*, 533 U.S. 98 (2001); *Lamb's Chapel v. Center Moriches UFSD*, 508 U.S. 384 (1993); see also **64:9**). However, it may not be used by such an organization if a meeting, entertainment or occasion sponsored by such an organization is under its exclusive control and any proceeds from its activity are to be applied for the benefit of the religious organization (§ 414(1)(d)).

The U.S. Supreme Court has ruled that school districts cannot deny access to religious organizations solely on the basis that they would present a religious perspective where the school would permit other groups to present their views on the same topic. To do so would constitute impermissible viewpoint discrimination (*Good News Club v. Milford CSD*; *Lamb's Chapel v. Center Moriches UFSD*).

A district may enact a policy that prohibits any organization from using school facilities for lectures, presentations, demonstrations, political events or seminars. The key requirement is that such a restriction be applied uniformly to all applicants, regardless of their viewpoints (*Saratoga Bible Institute, Inc. v. Schuylerville CSD*, 18 F.Supp.2d 178 (N.D.N.Y. 1998)).

For more information on this topic and religion in public schools, see **chapter 65**.

64:12. May student groups meet on school grounds?

Yes, under the federal Equal Access Act (20 USC § 4071 et seq.). Generally, the act requires that public secondary schools which receive federal financial assistance provide students equal access and may not deny them use of school facilities during non-instructional time on the basis of the religious, political, philosophical or other content of the speech that can be expected to take place at the meeting if it permits student groups to use school premises for any non-curriculum-related purpose (20 USC § 4071(a); see **65:36**). The U.S. Supreme Court held the act is constitutional in *Bd. of Educ. of Westside Cmty. Schs. v. Mergens*, 496 U.S. 226 (1990).

The act also requires that:

- Meetings be voluntary and initiated by the students.
- There be no sponsorship of the meeting by the school, the government, or its agents or employees.
- Employees or agents of the school or government attend only in a non-participatory capacity.
- Meetings do not interfere materially and substantially with the orderly conduct of educational activities within the school.
- Non-school people do not direct, conduct, control or regularly attend activities of student groups (20 USC § 4071(c)).

For more information on the use of school facilities by student groups for religious purposes, see **65:36-38**.

64:13. Can school districts bar reporters from school events?

It depends. Generally, school districts may not impermissibly limit or restrict anyone's freedom of speech or right to peaceful assembly. However, that was not the case where a federal district court for the Northern District of New York found that a school district which barred a reporter from school grounds did not violate the reporter's First Amendment rights to freedom of the press, speech or association. The reporter had attempted to initiate personal contact of a sexual nature with two female coaches and then failed to stop at the district's directive. The court found the district's order to bar the reporter from attending athletic events and restricting his contact with coaches to written and telephone contact through the main office or athletic office was a reasonably tailored time, place and manner regulation that did not restrict all forms of news gathering access (*Hone v. Cortland City Sch. Dist.*, 985 F.Supp. 262 (N.D.N.Y. 1998)).

Conversely, when a superintendent, in her capacity as school receiver, barred reporters from a public meeting discussing transformation plans a court found she violated a requirement in section 211-f of the education law that a public meeting be held for such purpose and a provision of section 414 which requires meetings for civic purposes be open to the general public (*News 12 Co. v. Hempstead Public Schools Bd. of Educ.,* 52 Misc. 3d 479 (Nassau Cnty 2016); see **64:2**).

64:14. Can school districts ban nonresidents from attending school events?

Yes, but not on a permanent basis. In addition, the potential for a ban from school facilities should be included within the code of conduct. In *Appeal of M.S.,* 47 Ed Dept Rep 396 (2008), a district sought to permanently ban a student from another district from its school property after the student, a spectator, engaged in rowdy conduct while at a basketball game. According to the commissioner of education, a permanent ban would have prevented the student from participating in any future school events or competitions even as a valid participant. Additionally, it would interfere with his rights as a parent and a registered voter to access school property if the student became a resident of the district as an adult.

64:15. May school districts bar from school events parents who engage in aggressive behavior?

Yes. The commissioner of education upheld a school district's decision to bar a parent from attending future athletic events and practices, because the parent persisted in engaging in threatening and aggressive behavior, even after the district's athletic director and superintendent met with him to discuss complaints about him and gave him written warning that his continued misbehavior would result in the district barring him from future events. The commissioner also held that the parent was not entitled to a full hearing and that he did not have a "right" of access to school property (*Appeal of Mayer*, 39 Ed Dept Rep 195 (1999)).

Similarly, a New York appellate court upheld a school district's decision to temporarily bar a parent from entering her child's school building following an incident where the parent twice entered the school building carrying a handgun (that she was licensed to carry in connection with her employment as a probation officer) in violation of district policy requiring prior written permission to bring a gun into the schoolhouse, and in violation of the building principal's directive communicated to her personally to remove her gun prior to entering the school building to attend a parent-teacher conference (*Cina v. Waters*, 9 A.D.3d 550 (3d Dep't 2004)).

It was also permissible for a district to bar a teacher with pending disciplinary charges against her for berating, harassing, and threatening behavior toward district employees, from attending her own children's home athletic events given that she might encounter the complainants against her in the unsupervised athletic venues (*Appeal of Anonymous II*, 48 Ed Dept Rep 503 (2009)).

64:16. May school boards bar sex offenders from school grounds?

State law governing sex offenders contains restrictions on certain sex offenders' ability to access school property. Persons convicted of sex offenses where the victim was under age 18 who are placed on probation or conditional discharge, and any person designated a level three sex offender, are barred from knowingly entering upon school grounds during such term of probation or conditional discharge. If such sentenced offender is a registered student or employee of such facility or has a family member enrolled in such facility, he or she may, with written authorization of his or her probation officer or the court *and* the superintendent of schools enter school grounds for limited purposes authorized by the aforementioned parties (Penal Law § 65.10(4-a); Exec. Law § 259-c(14); see *Williams v. Dep't of Corr. and Community Supervision*, 136 A.D.3d 147 (1st Dep't 2016); *Appeal of K.M.*, 55 Ed Dept Rep, Dec. No. 16,796 (2015)). School grounds is defined to include any building, structure, athletic field or land contained within the boundaries of a school and any area accessible to the public within 1000 feet of the boundary line, including any parked motor vehicle (Penal Law § 220.00(14); Exec. Law § 259-c(14)). The law has the effect of prohibiting sex offender parolees from living within 1000 feet of a school (*People v. Diack*, 24 N.Y.3d 674 (2015); *Williams v. Dep't of Corr. and Community Supervision*).

Separately, level two or level three sex offenders will be guilty of criminal trespass in the second degree if they enter or remain on school grounds knowing that the victim of the offense for which they received their designation either is required to attend or formerly attended that school. Exceptions apply if the sex offender is:

- a lawfully registered student at the school;
- a lawful student participant in a school-sponsored event;
- the parent or guardian of a lawfully registered student at the school and enters the school to attend his or her child's event or activity;
- entering the school strictly to vote, if the school is the sex offender's designated polling place; or
- entering the school for limited purposes authorized by the school superintendent (Penal Law § 140.15(2)).

The Court of Appeals has ruled that the state's comprehensive legislative scheme regulating registered sex offenders pre-empts the ability of local municipalities to adopt residency restrictions for sex offenders (*People v. Diack; see also Appeal of K.M.*, 55 Ed Dept Rep, Dec. No. 16,796 (2015)). As such, the ability of school boards to adopt policies which further limit the ability of registered sex offenders to enter school grounds beyond that established in law is doubtful. However, registered sex offenders who are not subject to any statutory restrictions regarding entering school grounds would still need to comply with school policies applicable to all visitors.

64:17. May a school district charge for the use of its facilities by outside organizations?

Yes. The Education Law provides that a school board may adopt reasonable regulations for the use of its buildings and grounds, including a schedule of fees as prescribed by such regulations (§ 414). For instance, a school district is authorized to charge for the cost of maintaining its facility or property (i.e., heat, electricity, custodian/maintenance costs). Although this issue has not yet come before the courts, failure to charge for such costs might be deemed to violate the state constitutional prohibition against gifts of public funds (N.Y. Const. art. 8, § 1; see **25:32**).

A school board may also charge a nonresident for the use of district property (e.g., jogging track), since the commissioner of education has interpreted the Education Law to require that any meeting, entertainment or other use for the benefit of the community be non-exclusive and open only to the general public of the school district, that is, to the residents of the school district (*Matter of Emilio*, 33 Ed Dept Rep 75 (1993)). According to the commissioner, it would be highly unusual to interpret the language of section 414(1)(c) as compelling school districts to open up the uses of its property intended to promote the welfare of the community served by the school district to those who did not reside in the community (*Id.*).

However, a school district may not charge churches higher fees than other nonprofit organizations for the use of school facilities. To do so would discriminate against religious speech and interfere with or burden the church's right to speak and practice religion as protected by the free exercise clause (*Fairfax Covenant Church v. Fairfax Cnty. Sch. Bd.*, 17 F.3d 703 (4th Cir.), *cert. denied*, 511 U.S. 1143 (1994)).

64:18. May a school district allow admission fees to be charged to school-sponsored athletic events held on school grounds and permit the broadcasting of such events?

Yes. A school board may allow admission fees to be charged to school-sponsored athletic events held on school grounds as long as the proceeds are expended for school purposes (§ 414(1)(d); Opn. St. Comp. 81-18). A board also may allow radio and television stations to broadcast reports on high school games and other events, even though the broadcasts may be commercially sponsored (Arts & Cult. Aff. Law § 61.09).

Conduct on School Property

64:19. May school boards regulate conduct on school district property?

Yes. School boards must adopt rules and regulations for the maintenance of public order on school property and ensure they are enforced (§ 2801(2)). These rules and regulations must govern the conduct of students, teachers and other staff, as well as visitors and other licensees and invitees. They must be filed with the Board of Regents and the commissioner of education. This requirement also applies to any amendments, which must be filed no later than 30 days after their adoption (§ 2801(5)(b)). If a board fails to follow these filing requirements, the district may not be eligible to receive any state aid or assistance until the regulations are filed (§ 2801-a(9)).

The code of conduct governs, as well, behavior on school buses operated by private companies under contract to the district and at school-authorized extracurricular activities or other school-sponsored events, which take place off campus (§ 2801(1); *Appeal of M.H.*, 43 Ed Dept Rep 210 (2003)). For more information on discipline of students for off-campus behavior see **52:8**.

The penalties for violations must be clearly set forth and must include provisions for banning or ejecting a person from school property, and, in the case of a student or teacher, his or her suspension, or other appropriate disciplinary action (§ 2801(2)(a); see *Appeal of M.S.*, 47 Ed Dept Rep 396 (2008); see also **64:13-16**).

64:20. Is it unlawful to loiter or trespass on school grounds?

Yes. To loiter has been interpreted to mean to be slow in moving, to delay, to be dilatory, to saunter or to lag behind. Section 240.35(5) of the Penal Law states that any person who is not a parent or legal guardian of a student in regular attendance, who loiters on or about any school building or grounds, public or private or a school bus, without written permission or a specific, legitimate purpose for being there, is guilty of violating the law. In addition, a person may be charged with criminal trespass if he or she enters or remains in a school building in violation of conspicuously posted rules regarding entry and use of the building (Penal Law § 140.10(b)).

"School grounds" are defined by the Penal Law (Penal Law § 240.00(3)).

64:21. Is it unlawful to draw graffiti upon school property?

Yes. Sections 145.60 and 145.65 of the state Penal Law establish the making of graffiti as a class A misdemeanor and the possession of graffiti instruments a class B misdemeanor. The Education Law states that school districts may offer monetary rewards of no more than $1,000 to individuals for information leading to the arrest and conviction of any person or persons for felonies or misdemeanors directly connected to vandalism of district property (§§ 1604(38), 1709(38)).

In addition, a school district can seek restitution from the parent or legal guardian of a minor child between the ages of 10 and 18 who willfully and maliciously damages school district real or personal property or who falsely reports a bomb threat or places a bomb for the expense of responding to such false report or incident. The total expense recoverable may not exceed $5,000 (Gen. Oblig. Law § 3-112).

64:22. Can a school district prohibit the sale of sweetened foods to students in school?

Yes. Section 915 of the Education Law prohibits the sale of certain sweetened foods, including, but not limited to, soda, chewing gum and candy, from the beginning of the school day until the end of the last scheduled meal period.

64:23. What are drug-free school zones?

A *drug-free school zone* is an area within 1,000 feet of a private or public school, including nursery, prekindergarten, kindergarten, elementary, intermediate, junior high, vocational, or high school, and child-care center facilities, as defined by law (Penal Law §§ 220.00(14), 220.44(5)).

Under the Penal Law it is a felony to sell drugs in any school building, structure, athletic playing field, playground or land contained within a drug-free zone school, or in any area accessible to the public or any parked vehicle located within such zone or is a school bus (Penal Law §§ 220.00, 220.34, 220.44).

According to New York's Court of Appeals, the state's highest court, drug free school zones are to be measured by a straight-line method radiating out from the boundaries of school district grounds to prevent drug dealers from avoiding felony prosecution by erecting barriers that make the distance from a school to a drug transaction follow a circuitous route that exceeds 1,000 feet (*People v. Robbins*, 5 N.Y.3d 556 (2005)).

Signs designating the drug-free school zone may be erected upon the request of a school district and in cooperation with those entities having jurisdiction over the highways (High. Law § 317).

64:24. Are there funds available to help school districts prevent violence and drug abuse within the community?

As part of the Student Support and Academic Achievement Grants authorized by the Every Student Succeeds Act, (Pub. Law 114-95) funding is available to local school districts to develop and implement programs and activities that are coordinated with other schools and community based services and programs to foster safe, healthy, supportive and drug free environments that support academic achievement (20 USC § 7118). For example, school districts are eligible to receive funds for:

- Evidence based drug and violence prevention programs that educate students against the use of alcohol, tobacco, marijuana, smokeless tobacco products and electronic cigarettes;
- School based mental health services including early identification of mental health symptoms, drug use and violence and appropriate referrals to counseling services;
- Professional development and training for staff and interested community members in early identification, mentoring and recovery support services related to drug and violence prevention;
- Improved instructional practices for recognition and prevention of coercion, violence or abuse including teen and dating violence, stalking, domestic abuse and sexual violence and harassment; and
- High quality training for school personnel related to suicide prevention, crisis management and conflict resolution techniques, school based violence prevention strategies, drug abuse, bullying and harassment prevention (20 USC § 7118(5)).

Programs must promote the involvement of parents in the activity or program and may be conducted in partnership with colleges and universities, businesses, nonprofit organizations, community based organizations or other public or private entities with a demonstrated record of success implementing such activities (20 USC § 7118(3), (4)).

64:25. May school districts regulate student possession of cell phones while on school property?

Yes. According to one state appellate court, a policy banning student possession of cell phones on school grounds is a permissible exercise of administrative authority over the general management, operation, control, maintenance, and discipline in schools. Furthermore, a ban on cell phone possession is reasonable particularly when merely banning cell phone use would not be sufficient to address school concerns over disciplinary incidents involving the use of cell phones to harass and intimidate others, and to cheat (*Price v. N.Y. City Bd. of Educ.*, 51 A.D.3d 277 (1st Dep't), *lv. to appeal denied*, 11 N.Y.3d 702 (2008); see also *Appeal of Rosten*, 49 Ed Dept Rep 237 (2010)).

Dismissing an argument that a cell phone ban interferes with parents' constitutional right to guide the care, custody, and control of their children, the court noted such a ban does not forbid communications between parents and children before or after school. Furthermore, a cell phone ban is rationally related to the legitimate goal of keeping discipline and order in the schools. In the case before it, the appellate court also found it noteworthy that the ban allowed exceptions for children with legitimate medical needs (*Price v. N.Y. City Bd. of Educ.*).

Commercialism in Public Schools

64:26. Can a school district allow the sale of student photographs by a private business firm on school grounds?

Ordinarily, no, because this action would violate the New York State Constitution (N.Y. Const. art. 8, § 1). However, where photographs are taken "for a valid school purpose," such as for the school yearbook, student records or identification cards, they may be taken on school premises during school hours. But school personnel may not solicit or collect money for this purpose (*Appeal of Tarolli*, 38 Ed Dept Rep 60 (1998); *Matter of Fusare*, 20 Ed Dept Rep 14 (1980); *Matter of Hoyt*, 17 Ed Dept Rep 173 (1977); *Matter of Albert*, 7 Ed Dept Rep 7 (1967); see also NYS Education Department, Office of Counsel *Sale of School Photographs Memo* (Aug. 1974)). Additionally, photographers cannot meet with students on school grounds for the purpose of taking personal photographs or to choose what proofs students would like printed for personal use as these activities lack a school purpose (*Appeal of Tarolli*).

Similarly, school rings may be sold on the school premises if certain specific conditions are met (*Matter of Gary Credit Corp.*, 26 Ed Dept Rep 414 (1987)).

64:27. Can a school district allow commercial television or radio programming in its schools?

No. Part 23 of the Rules of the Board of Regents prohibits a school district from entering into a contract that, in whole or in part, promises the district will permit commercial promotional activity on school premises through electronic media, such as the promotion or sale of products and services on television or radio (8 NYCRR § 23.2). However, the rules state that this should not be construed as prohibiting commercial sponsorship of school activities.

64:28. Can a school district enter into a contract that gives a specific beverage manufacturer the exclusive right to sell its beverages on campus in exchange for a fee?

Yes, with certain limitations. Commercialism on school property is generally prohibited. However, an agreement with a commercial vendor for the exclusive right to sell its beverage on campus, known as a "pouring rights" contract, may be permissible if the contract complies with all applicable New York laws, including but not limited to, the state constitution, the competitive bidding requirements of the General Municipal Law, the Freedom of Information Law, and provisions restricting the hours of operation of beverage vending machines (see *Appeal of American Quality Beverages LLC I & II*, 42 Ed Dept Rep 144 and 153 (2002) *petition dismissed*, J. O'Connor (Sup. Ct. Albany Cnty. Oct. 7, 2004), *appeal dismissed* (3d Dep't Aug. 17, 2006); *Appeal of Citizens for Responsible Fiscal & Educ. Policy,* 40 Ed Dept Rep 315 (2000); N.Y. Const. art. 8, § 1; Gen. Mun. Law Article 5-A; Pub. Off. Law Article 6; § 915).

Pouring rights contracts are not subject to approval by the commissioner of education because they do not involve private food service management companies. According to the commissioner, although the sale of pre-sweetened beverages does not violate a school district's obligation to provide physical and health education in an environment conducive to healthful living, districts should consider whether the installation of vending machines in school is in the best interest of student's health, particularly at the elementary level (*Appeal of American Quality Beverages LLC I & II*).

64:29. What must be included in a pouring rights contract?

The NYS Education Department's model pouring rights contract offers guidance on framing these type of contracts (NYS Education Department, Office of Counsel, *Contracts for Exclusive 'Pouring*

Rights,' Memorandum to District Superintendents and Superintendents of Schools, Kathy Ahearn, Deputy Commissioner for Legal Affairs, (July 10, 1998)). A copy of the model contract is available from SED's Office of Counsel. However, it should be noted the commissioner of education invalidated a provision in *Appeal of Citizens for Responsible Fiscal & Educ. Policy,* 40 Ed Dept Rep 315 (2000), that contained similar language to that of the model contract. The provision allowed the vendor to sell its products to fundraising groups "based on a presale of cases of products to students' family and friends." Individual buyers would redeem their orders at school by exchanging a receipt for the beverages. The commissioner found "no statutory authority for the use of school premises or school district staff to facilitate the sale of a vendor's products to fundraising groups."

In addition, the commissioner has cautioned that districts should not accept any advance payment on pouring rights that they would be required to pay back in the event of early termination (*Appeal of American Quality Beverages LLC I & II*, 42 Ed Dept Rep 144 and 153 (2002), *petition dismissed*, J. O'Connor (Sup. Ct. Albany Cnty. Oct. 7, 2004), *appeal dismissed* (3d Dep't Aug. 17, 2006)).

64:30. Do lighted panels on vending machines constitute unlawful advertising?

No. According to the commissioner of education, the advertising effect of lighted panels that simply illuminate static pictures is incidental. However, districts need to consider whether promotional statements on the panels are appropriate for school environments and whether plain panels should be used instead (*Appeal of American Quality Beverages LLC I & II*, 42 Ed Dept Rep 144 and 153 (2002), *petition dismissed*, J. O'Connor (Sup. Ct. Albany Cnty. Oct. 7, 2004), *appeal dismissed* (3d Dep't Aug. 17, 2006)).

64:31. Can a school district allow the collection of money from students for charitable donations in the schools?

No. Section 19.6 of the Rules of the Board of Regents prohibits the direct solicitation of charitable donations from children in the public schools during the school day. However, there are three types of activities that this section does not proscribe:

- Fundraising activities that take place off school premises or outside of the regular school day. Thus, recruiting children during the school day for participation in fundraising activities is permissible as long as the activities themselves occur off school premises or outside of the school day.
- Arms-length transactions where the contributor receives something for his or her donation. Thus, this rule does not prohibit the sale of goods or tickets for concerts or admission to social events where the proceeds go to charity, because the purchaser receives a consideration — the concert or admission to a social event for the funds expended.
- Indirect forms of charitable solicitation on school premises that do not involve coercion, such as having a bin or collection box in a hallway or other common area for the donation of food, clothing or money. In these instances, the collection activity is passive, and no pressure is exerted upon students to participate.

What the rule does prohibit is approaching students in their classrooms or homerooms and asking them directly to donate money or goods to charity (see *Appeal of Ponte*, 38 Ed Dept Rep 280 (1998); NYS Education Department, Office of Counsel, *Questions and Answers on Solicitation of Charitable Donations from School Children* (June 2009), at: http://www.counsel.nysed.gov/questions/ques.html).

64:32. Can school districts allow fundraising activities involving the participation of students during school hours?

No. The solicitation of charitable donations cannot become intertwined with a school's educational responsibilities. That happened in a case where students shot baskets to raise money for the American

Heart Association in a "Hoop for Hearts" program during physical education class. Although the students solicited and collected pledges from the community off school grounds, and parent volunteers collected the funds in the school's hallway, the commissioner of education determined that the funds raised accrued during class time on school grounds. In addition, students were awarded prizes during the school day for achieving the pledge goals. According to the commissioner, this level of activity belied the intent and purpose of section 19.6 of the Rules of the Board of Regents (see **64:31**). It was irrelevant that the activity was sponsored by the Parent-Teacher Association (*Appeal of Ponte*, 38 Ed Dept Rep 280 (1998)).

65. Religion in Public Schools

Overview

65:1. What constitutional provisions govern the role of religion in the public schools?

The Establishment and Free Exercise Clauses of the First Amendment of the U.S. Constitution primarily govern the role of religion in the public schools. New York's Blaine Amendment (N.Y. Const. art. 11, § 3), also imposes certain limitations on the relationship between government authorities (including school districts) and religious schools.

65:2. What is the Establishment Clause?

The Establishment Clause states: "Congress shall make no law respecting an establishment of religion." It has been interpreted to require the separation of church and state and is applicable to the states and their subdivisions, including school districts. It requires that government pursue a course of "complete neutrality toward religion," and not promote religion or entangle itself in religious matters (see *McCreary Cnty. v. ACLU*, 545 U.S. 844 (2005); *Bd. of Educ. of the Kiryas Joel Village Sch. Dist. v. Grumet*, 512 U.S. 687 (1994); *Lee v. Weisman*, 505 U.S. 577 (1992); *Wallace v. Jaffree*, 472 U.S. 38 (1985); *Larson v. Valente*, 456 U.S. 228, *reh'g denied*, 457 U.S. 1111 (1982)).

However, not all governmental conduct that confers a benefit on or gives special recognition to religion is automatically prohibited. It depends on all the circumstances surrounding the particular church-state relationship (*Lynch v. Donnelly*, 465 U.S. 668, *reh'g denied*, 466 U.S. 994 (1984); see **65:5**).

65:3. What is the Free Exercise Clause?

The Free Exercise Clause addresses the freedom of individual belief and religious expression. It states: "Congress shall make no law prohibiting the free exercise" of religion. This clause is also applicable to the states and their political subdivisions, and prohibits government from restricting the right of an individual to believe in whatever he or she may choose. This right, however, may not be read "to require the Government to conduct its own internal affairs in ways that comport with the religious beliefs of particular citizens" (*Bowen v. Roy*, 476 U.S. 693 (1986); *Lyng v. Northwest Indian Cemetery Protective Ass'n*, 485 U.S. 439 (1988)). Although "government may accommodate the free exercise of religion," it may not "supersede the fundamental limitations imposed by the Establishment Clause" (*Lee v. Weisman*, 505 U.S. 577 (1992); see also *Bd. of Educ. of the Kiryas Joel Village Sch. Dist. v. Grumet*, 512 U.S. 687 (1994)).

65:4. How does New York's Blaine Amendment affect religion and public education?

Article 11, section 3 of the New York State Constitution, also known as the Blaine Amendment, provides that neither the state nor any state subdivision, including school districts, may authorize the use of its property, credit or public funds, directly or indirectly, to assist any school under the control of any religious denomination or which teaches any denominational tenet or doctrine. The purpose of this article is to prevent state aid to religion, but the article has been interpreted as not prohibiting every state action that may provide some benefit to religious schools (*Bd. of Educ. of CSD No.1 v. Allen*, 392 U.S. 236 (1968)). For example, this article specifically exempts the *transportation* of students to and from nonpublic schools, and the district's examination or inspection of such schools.

The U.S. Supreme Court has not ruled directly on the validity of state constitutional provisions that are stricter than the Establishment Clause (see, e.g., *Locke v. Davey*, 540 U.S. 712 (2004); *Witters v. Washington Dep't of Servs*., 474 U.S. 481, *reh'g denied,* 475 U.S. 1091 (1986)).

65:5. Are there standards to determine whether a certain government action violates the Establishment Clause?

Yes. There are several standards which the U.S. Supreme Court and other courts apply when deciding cases alleging a violation of the Establishment Clause. The most commonly used standard is the *Lemon* test, a three-pronged test established by the U.S. Supreme Court and named after the lawsuit that gave rise to it, *Lemon v. Kurtzman*, 403 U.S. 602, *reh'g denied*, 404 U.S. 876 (1971), *on remand*, 348 F.Supp. 300 (E.D. Pa. 1972), *aff'd*, 411 U.S. 192 (1973); see also *Bronx Household of Faith v. Bd. of Educ. of the City of N.Y.*, 650 F.3d 30 (2d Cir.), *cert. denied*, 132 S. Ct. 816 (2011); *Bronx Household of Faith v. Bd. of Educ. of the City of N.Y.*, 750 F.3d 184 (2d Cir.), *cert. denied*, 135 S.Ct. 1730 (2015)). To be constitutional, an action must: (1) not have a religious purpose; (2) not have a principal or primary effect of advancing or inhibiting religion; and (3) not foster excessive government entanglement with religion (*Id.*).

Religion

While several justices have questioned the continued appropriateness of the *Lemon* test, the Supreme Court as a whole has not overruled *Lemon* and still makes use of its principles as necessary (see, e.g., *McCreary Cnty. v. ACLU*, 545 U.S. 844 (2005); see *Santa Fe Indep. Sch. Dist. v. Doe.*, 530 U.S. 290 (2000); *Agostini v. Felton*, 521 U.S. 203 (1997)).

As a result, the Supreme Court has decided Establishment Clause cases without reference to the *Lemon* test (see *Bd. of Educ. of the Kiryas Joel Village Sch. Dist. v. Grumet*, 512 U.S. 687 (1994); *Zobrest v. Catalina Foothills Sch. Dist*., 509 U.S. 1 (1993); *Lambs Chapel v. Center Moriches UFSD*, 508 U.S. 384 (1993), *remanded without op.,* 17 F.3d 1425 (2d Cir. 1994); *Lee v. Weisman*, 505 U.S. 577 (1992)).

For example, it has used an analysis that focuses on global principles of neutrality not linked to a specific test. Under these neutrality principles, the Establishment Clause is violated when government acts in a non-neutral manner toward religion by favoring (1) religion over nonreligion, (2) nonreligion over religion, or (3) a particular denomination over another (see, e.g., *Zelman v. Simmons-Harris*, 536 U.S. 639 (2002); *Bd. of Educ. of the Kiryas Joel Village Sch. Dist. Grumet; Wallace v. Jaffree*, 472 U.S. 38 (1985); *Larson v. Valente*, 456 U.S. 228, *reh'g denied*, 457 U.S. 1111 (1982)).

65:6. Are there standards to determine whether a certain government action violates the Free Exercise Clause?

Claims of violations of the Free Exercise Clause in an educational context traditionally have been measured by balancing the state's interest in providing public education against the right of the parent, student, or employee to freely exercise or practice his or her religion. However, the right to exercise one's religion freely is not burdened simply by mandating one to be exposed to ideas with which that person disagrees (*Leebaert v. Harrington*, 332 F.3d 134 (2d Cir. 2003); *Brown v. Hot, Sexy & Safer Prods*., 68 F.3d 525 (1st Cir. 1995), *cert. denied*, 516 U.S. 1159 (1996); *Mozert v. Hawkins Cnty. Bd. of Educ*., 827 F.2d 1058 (6th Cir. 1987), *cert. denied*, 484 U.S. 1066 (1988); *Parker v. Hurley*, 474 F. Supp.2d 261 (D. Mass. 2007), *aff'd*, 514 F.3d 87 (1st Cir.), *cert denied*, 555 U.S. 815 (2008)).

Prayer and Moments of Silence

Editor's Note: The federal Every Student Succeeds Act (ESSA) prohibits any school district policy or practice that denies participation in constitutionally protected prayer in the public schools (20 USC § 7904). A Guidance on Constitutionally Protected Prayer in Public Elementary and Secondary Schools *is available from the U.S. Department of Education at: http://www2.ed.gov/policy/gen/guid/religionandschools/prayer_guidance.html. Districts should review their policies periodically to ensure they are compliant with the Guidance and applicable court decisions.*

65:7. May school boards open their public meetings with a prayer?

Neither the U.S. Supreme Court nor the U.S. Court of Appeals for the Second Circuit, with jurisdiction over New York, has answered this question directly. However, the U.S. Supreme Court has reviewed a town board's practice of opening its meeting with prayer led by a local chaplain or community member and determined such practice did not violate the Establishment Clause. In its view, the practice was consistent with historic legislative prayer practices engaged in by Congress and other state legislative bodies (*Town of Greece, New York v. Galloway*, 134 S.Ct. 1811 (2014); *Marsh v. Chambers,* 463 U.S. 783 (1983); see also *Doe v. Tangipahoa Parish Sch. Bd.*, 631 F. Supp.2d 823 (E.D. La., 2009) but compare *Lund v. Rowan Couty, N.C.,* 103 F. Supp.3d 712 (M.D.N.C. 2015) (prayer led by member of county board of commissioners directed at board and public violates Establishment Clause)).

At least two other federal appellate courts outside New York have ruled such practice at school board meetings unconstitutional (*Doe v. Indian River Sch. Dist.*, 653 F.3d 256 (3d Cir.), *cert. denied,* 132 S. Ct. 1097 (2011); *Coles v. Cleveland Bd. of Educ.*, 171 F.3d 369, *reh'g denied*, 183 F.3d. 538 (6th Cir. 1999)). In *Coles v. Cleveland Bd. of Educ.*, the court rejected the argument that opening prayers at school board meetings are constitutionally permissible because prayers at sessions of the state legislature have been ruled constitutional (see *Marsh v. Chambers,* 463 U.S. 783 (1983)). According to the court, the school board is an integral part of the public school system. School board meetings can and are attended by students who may actively participate in the discussions. In addition, even though prayers at school board meetings differ from the graduation prayers ruled unconstitutional in *Lee v. Weisman*, 505 U.S. 577 (1992) (see **65:13**), because they are not said in front of the student body as a whole, "the school-board setting is arguably more coercive to participating students than the graduation ceremony at issue in *Lee*" (*Coles v. Cleveland Bd. of Educ.*).

In *Doe v. Indian River Sch. Dist*. the court emphasized that given a high degree of student participation at board meetings, offering prayers at school board meetings could coerce a student to choose between participating in the prayer, or appearing to participate to avoid a disturbance, or forfeiting intangible benefits gained by observing the meetings as part of student government (*Doe v. Indian River Sch. Dist.*).

65:8. May public school districts organize or require class participation in daily prayer?

No. Policies promoting school-sponsored prayer in public schools consistently have been struck down as unconstitutional acts of government. The U.S. Supreme Court has ruled repeatedly that the separation of church and state principles embodied in the Establishment Clause of the First Amendment prohibit school-sponsored prayers and religious exercises, even when the prayer is nondenominational and participation is voluntary.

For example, the high court ruled unconstitutional a prayer endorsed by the New York State Board of Regents for use in public schools (*Engle v. Vitale*, 370 U.S. 421 (1962)). It also struck down a state statute requiring readings from the Bible, even if students were not required to engage in such prayers (*School Dist. of Abington Tp., Pa. v. Schempp*, 374 U.S. 203 (1963)).

In another case, the U.S. Supreme Court dismissed, on procedural grounds, a lawsuit claiming that it violates the Establishment Clause of the federal constitution to require students to listen daily to the recitation of the Pledge of Allegiance, because the Pledge contains the words "One Nation, *Under God*" within its text (*Elk Grove Unified Sch. Dist. v. Newdow*, 542 U.S. 1 (2004)). By declining to rule on the merits of the claim, the court left the substantive constitutional question for another day. However, several federal appellate courts outside of New York have determined that neither the Pledge nor the phrase "under God" contained therein is a prayer. Instead, its recitation by virtue of state law has the effect of advancing patriotism, not religion, and does not convey a school's or state's endorsement of religion (*Freedom from Religion Foundation v. Hanover Sch. Dist.*, 626 F.3d 1 (1st Cir. 2010); *Croft v. Perry*, 624 F.3d 157 (5th Cir. 2010); *Newdow v. Rio Linda Union Sch. Dist.*, 597 F.3d 1007 (9th Cir. 2010)).

65:9. May school districts organize or require students to participate in moments of silent meditation?

In 1985, the U.S. Supreme Court struck down a state statute requiring a one-minute period of silence for "meditation or voluntary prayer during the school day" (*Wallace v. Jaffree*, 472 U.S. 38 (1985)). In *Jaffree,* the legislative history of the statute reviewed by the court made it clear that the purpose was to permit prayer. Therefore, the statute was found to be unconstitutional.

Since *Jaffree* several federal appellate courts have examined statutes enacting moments of silence for quiet contemplation or reflection (*Croft v. Governor of Texas*, 562 F.3d 735 (5th Cir. 2009); *Brown v. Gilmore*, 258 F.3d 265 (4th Cir.), *cert. denied*, 534 U.S. 996 (2001); *Bown v. Gwinnett Cnty. Sch. Dist.*, 112 F.3d 1464 (11th Cir. 1997); see also *May v. Cooperman*, 780 F.2d 240 (3d Cir. 1985), *appeal dismissed for lack of jurisdiction*, 484 U.S. 72 (1987)) or to calm students and ready them for the start of the school day (*Sherman v. Koch*, 623 F.3d 501 (7th Cir. 2010), *cert. denied*, 132 S. Ct. 92 (2011)). In four of the cases, the statutes were upheld as there was no evidence showing intent to promote prayer (*Brown v. Gilmore, Bown v. Gwinnett Cnty. Sch. Dist., Croft v. Governor of Texas; Sherman v. Koch*).

New York's Education Law allows for a moment of silence in the public schools at the opening of school every school day (§ 3029-a). It specifically provides: "The silent meditation authorized. . . is not intended to be, and shall not be conducted as, a religious service or exercise, but may be considered an opportunity for silent meditation on a religious theme by those who are so disposed, or a moment of silent reflection on the anticipated activities of the day." Students may remain seated and may not be required to stand.

New York's statute has not been challenged in the courts. According to a 1964 Formal Opinion of Counsel from the NYS Education Department, the application of the statute would be impermissible if the statutory moment of silence were prefaced with the statement: "We will now have a moment of silence to acknowledge our Supreme Being" (Opn. Educ. Dep't, 3 Ed Dept Rep 255 (1964)). Since the legislative history of that statute does not indicate that it was enacted to foster organized religious prayer, it may pass constitutional scrutiny.

65:10. May school districts permit students to lead others in organized prayer during school hours?

No. Although the U.S. Supreme Court has not ruled on this question, other courts have found this to violate the separation of church and state requirements of the Establishment Clause. For example, where a student club was allowed to broadcast inspirational readings from the Bible and sectarian prayers over the school intercom system after the school's morning announcements, and where student-initiated prayers were allowed in individual classrooms during classroom hours, the courts perceived the school district as endorsing such religious messages (*Herdahl v. Pontotoc Cnty. Sch. Dist.*, 887 F.Supp. 902 (N.D. Miss. 1995); see also *Ingebretsen v. Jackson Pub. Sch. Dist.*, 88 F.3d 274 (5th Cir.), *cert. denied*, 519 U.S. 965 (1996)).

Similarly, a federal district court in New York ruled that a school district properly halted broadcasting a Mohawk Indian "Thanksgiving Address" over the school intercom, at pep rallies and before lacrosse games. While not considered a prayer by Mohawks, the address contained speech reasonably interpreted as religious in nature. The district avoided an endorsement problem by halting the practice (*Jock v. Ransom*, 2007 U.S. Dist. LEXIS 47027 (N.D.N.Y June 28, 2007), *aff'd*, 2009 U.S. App. LEXIS 6043 (2d Cir. 2009)).

A federal appellate court outside New York upheld a school district policy that prohibited faculty participation in student initiated prayer in any school-sponsored setting including classes, practices, pep rallies, team meetings and athletic events (*Borden v. Sch. Dist. of Tp. of East Brunswick*, 523 F.3d 153 (3d Cir. 2008), *cert. denied*, 555 U.S. 1212 (2009)).

65:11. May a public school district permit students to deliver prayers before, during, or after school-sponsored extracurricular activities?

No. The U.S. Supreme Court, in *Santa Fe Indep. Sch. Dist. v. Doe*, 530 U.S. 290 (2000), ruled that a school policy that allowed student-initiated, student-delivered, nonsectarian, nonproselytizing prayer at high school football games violates the separation of church and state.

According to the high court, the policy involved "both perceived and actual endorsement of religion.... The degree of school involvement makes it clear that the pregame prayer bears the imprint of the State and thus put school-aged children who objected in an untenable position." In addition, "members of the listening audience must perceive the pre-game message as a public expression of the issues of the majority of the student body with the approval of school administrators." As such, the pre-game prayer would be inevitably perceived as being stamped with the school's seal of approval.

The court further determined that "adolescents will often submit to pressure from their peers towards conformity, and that the influence is strongest in matters of social connection. . . . The constitutional command will not permit the district to exact religious conformity from a student as the price of joining classmates at a varsity football game."

Similarly, the U.S. Court of Appeals for the Second Circuit, with jurisdiction over New York, has determined that school districts may prohibit religious organizations from conducting religious worship services in school buildings when not in use by students (*Bronx Household of Faith v. Bd. of Educ. of City of N.Y.*, 650 F.3d 30 (2d Cir.), *cert. denied*, 132 S. Ct. 816 (2011); see also *Bronx Household of Faith v. Bd. of Educ. of the City of N.Y.*, 750 F.3d 184 (2d Cir. 2014), *cert. denied,* 135 S. Ct. 1730 (2015) (a related case on this issue); see **64:2**, **64:9**, **64:11**).

65:12. May school districts permit students to deliver prayers at public school graduation ceremonies?

The U.S. Supreme Court has not addressed the factual issue of whether student-initiated prayer at graduation ceremonies is constitutional. Some believe that the high court would invalidate a school district policy that allows student-initiated prayers at graduation ceremonies based on its decision in *Santa Fe Indep. Sch. Dist. v. Doe*, 530 U.S. 290 (2000), where the court ruled against a school district that allowed students to deliver prayer at a football game (see **65:11**).

Nonetheless, one federal appellate court has distinguished the *Santa Fe* case to reach a different result. In *Adler v. Duval County Sch. Bd.*, 250 F.3d 1330 (11th Cir.), *cert. denied*, 534 U.S. 1065

(2001), the U.S. Court of Appeals for the 11th Circuit upheld a school board policy that allowed the graduating class the option of selecting one of its members to deliver a message of his or her choice at graduation, with the school having no control over the selection of the student, whether there would be a student graduation message, or the content of the student's message. According to that court even if the student elected to deliver a religious message, "the total absence of state involvement" prevented a violation of the Establishment Clause, unlike in the *Santa Fe* case (see also *American Humanist Ass'n v. Greenville County Sch. Dist.*, 108 F.Supp.3d 355 (D.S.C. 2015)).

In comparison, a federal district court in New York upheld the actions of a school district that refused to permit a middle school student to deliver a line from a speech she prepared for the district's "moving up" ceremony because it sounded too religious (*A.M. v. Taconic Hills Cent. Sch. Dist.*, 2012 U.S. Dist. LEXIS 7372 (N.D.N.Y. Jan. 23, 2012), *aff'd* 510 Fed. Appx. 3 (2d Cir.), *cert denied* 134 S.Ct. 196 (2013); see **53:2**). According to the court, the district did not unreasonably seek to remove the religious component of the speech given its fear of offending listeners of different religious backgrounds and of violating the Establishment Clause, and a recent history of complaints from parents about the district's treatment of religion in the schools (*Id.*).

Likewise, a federal district court outside New York ruled unconstitutional a school district's practice of letting the senior class vote on whether a member of the class would lead a non-denominational prayer at graduation. According to the court, the delivery of the prayer was the direct result of a school-mandated election where a religious message was the only option (*Workman v. Greenwood Cmty. Sch. Corp.*, 2010 U.S. Dist. LEXIS 42813 (S.D. Ind. Apr. 30, 2010)).

Prior to the *Santa Fe* decision federal appellate courts had been split on the issue. For example, in *Jones v. Clear Creek Indep. Sch. Dist.*, 977 F.2d 963 (5th Cir. 1992), *cert. denied*, 508 U.S. 967 (1993), the U.S. Court of Appeals for the Fifth Circuit ruled that student-initiated and student-led nonsectarian graduation prayers are permissible because they solemnize the occasion. The Third Circuit took an opposing view in *American Civil Liberties Union of New Jersey v. Black Horse Pike Reg'l Bd. of Educ.*, 84 F.3d 1471 (3d Cir. 1996).

65:13. May a school district allow religious leaders to deliver benedictions and invocations at public school graduation ceremonies?

No. The U.S. Supreme Court ruled that it is unconstitutional for public schools to permit invocations and benedictions delivered by religious leaders at graduation ceremonies because of a potential coercive effect on the impressionable students who attend these ceremonies (*Lee v. Weisman*, 505 U.S. 577 (1992)). In so ruling, the high court rejected the argument that attendance at graduation ceremonies is voluntary. According to the court, "high school graduation is one of life's most significant occasions [and] a student is not free to absent herself from the graduation exercise in any real sense of the term voluntary."

65:14. Does a school district violate the Establishment Clause if a school board member delivers a prayer at graduation ceremonies?

It depends. According to a federal appellate court outside of New York, a school district did not violate the Establishment Clause when a school board member recited the Lord's Prayer at a graduation ceremony. According to the court, at the time, the board member was engaged in private speech. There was no involvement by the district in determining that the board member would speak, and the autonomy afforded to him in determining the contents of his remarks deemed his speech private (*Doe v. Sch. Dist. of the City of Norfolk*, 340 F.3d 605, *reh'g and reh'g en banc denied*, 2003 U.S. App. LEXIS 20987 (8th Cir. Oct. 16, 2003)). Under different circumstances, a court might rule otherwise.

65:15. Does a school district violate the Establishment Clause if it holds a graduation ceremony at a religious house of worship?

It may, depending upon the circumstances. According to one federal appellate court outside of New York, a school district practice of renting a non-denominational Christian church for graduation ceremonies violated the Establishment Clause because religious items were visible throughout the church, school and religious banners hung side by side and church members handed out literature about the church during the event (*Doe ex rel Doe v. Elmbrook Sch. Dist.*, 687 F.3d 840 (7th Cir. 2012), *cert. denied*, 134 S.Ct. 2283 (2014)). The court found the particular facts in this case to represent "an unacceptable amount of religious endorsement and coercion" (*Id.*).

Teaching of Religion

65:16. May a school district allow the teaching of creationism in its schools?

No. In addition, the U.S. Supreme Court has established that a school district cannot prohibit the instruction of evolution or require that the instruction of evolution be balanced with instruction of creation science (*Epperson v. Arkansas*, 393 U.S. 97 (1968); *Edwards v. Aguillard*, 482 U.S. 578 (1987)).

Furthermore, according to one federal appellate court outside of New York, a school district may not require that a disclaimer regarding flaws in the theory of evolution be read before the teaching of evolution in its schools (*Freiler v. Tangipahoa Parish Bd. of Educ.*, 185 F.3d 337 (5th Cir. 1999), *cert. denied*, 530 U.S. 1251 (2000)).

65:17. May a school district allow the teaching of intelligent design?

Not according to the only court to address this question. In *Kitzmiller v. Dover Area Sch. Dist.*, 400 F.Supp.2d 707 (M.D. Pa. 2005), a federal district court in Pennsylvania ruled that a school board's policy requiring the teaching of intelligent design in science classes violated the Establishment Clause (see **65:2**). According to the court, intelligent design is predicated upon the theory that natural selection cannot account for all of life's evolution and that an "intelligent designer" must have guided the process. A reasonable observer would view it as just a new form of creationism, a theory that the U.S. Supreme Court has long held is nothing more than a religious belief.

65:18. May a school district allow the Bible to be taught as part of its curriculum?

It depends. Biblical instruction that is non-devotional and focuses on literature, history, or social customs would not violate the Establishment Clause. However, one federal appellate court outside New York found a school district's use of a Bible Education Ministry program to meet its character education requirement violated the Establishment Clause because the program taught the Bible as religious truth in addition to focusing on themes of responsibility and courage (*Doe v. Porter*, 370 F.3d 558 (6th Cir. 2004); see also *Wiley v. Franklin*, 497 F. Supp. 390 (E.D. Tenn. 1980)).

65:19. May a school district impose limitations on teacher references to religion in the classroom?

Yes. In *Marchi v. Bd. of Coop. Educ. Serv. of Albany, Schoharie, Schenectady & Saratoga Counties*, 173 F.3d 469 (2d Cir.), *cert. denied,* 528 U.S. 869 (1999), the U.S. Court of Appeals for the Second Circuit, with jurisdiction over New York State, upheld a board of cooperative educational services directive instructing one of its employees to stop using "references to religion in the delivery of [his] instructional program unless it is a required element of a course of instruction and . . . has prior approval by [his] supervisor."

The teacher, who had recently converted to Christianity, admitted modifying his instructional program to discuss such matters as "forgiveness, reconciliation, and God." He also played a religious music tape in class called "Wee 2 Sing the Bible," given to him by one of his student's parents.

According to the Second Circuit, a public school risks violating the separation of church and state "if any of its teachers' activities gives the impression that the school endorses religion." In order to avoid such a violation, a school may prohibit teacher religious expressions and teacher-parent interactions that "risk giving the impression" that the district endorses religion (*Id.*).

Similarly, in another case, the Second Circuit also found a school district lawfully terminated a substitute teacher for speaking with students about her religious views in class after hearing that a student had died. Even if her religious discussion had addressed an issue of "public concern," the school board's "'compelling interest in avoiding Establishment Clause violations' justified its actions" in terminating her (*Rosario v. Does 1–10*, 36 Fed. Appx. 25 (2d Cir. 2002)). In comparison, according to one federal appellate court outside New York, teachers are permitted some leeway to discuss controversial religious topics as part of a relevant curriculum in order to challenge students' critical thinking skills and analytic abilities (*C.F. v. Capistrano Unif. Sch. Dist.*, 654 F.3d 975 (9th Cir. 2011)).

65:20. May members of the clergy participate as volunteer staff in public school educational programs?

There is no specific case in New York that addresses this issue. However, one federal appellate court outside New York ruled that a school district violated the separation of church and state when it implemented a "Clergy in Schools" volunteer counseling program because it recruited volunteers exclusively from among the local clergy to provide counseling to students in school, during school hours (*Doe v. Beaumont Indep. Sch. Dist.*, 173 F.3d 274 (5th Cir. 1999), *on remand,* 224 F.Supp.2d 1099 (E.D. Tex. 2002)).

The district's failure to include lay professionals well qualified to mentor students concerning morals and virtue nullified the secular character of the program, even though the clergy were told to focus on civic values, refrain from discussing sex and abortion, and not to pray with students. The absence of lay volunteers indicated that the selection of volunteers was based on the fact that they were religious representatives rather than on their alleged listening and communications skills.

Similarly, a federal district court outside New York ruled a school district violated the Establishment Clause when it arranged a panel comprised exclusively of clergy members to discuss homosexuality and religion at a program held during its diversity week (*Hansen v. Ann Arbor Pub. Schs.*, 293 F.Supp.2d 780 (E.D. Mich. 2003)).

Religious Observances

65:21. May a school district close school for the observance of a religious holiday?

The education law gives school boards the authority to close one or all of their schools on a particular day of religious or cultural observance, based on a determination that keeping the schools open would result in a waste of educational resources because a considerable proportion of the student population is unlikely to attend school on that day (§ 3210(1)(b)(ii)).

65:22. May a school district acknowledge the observance of religious holidays through plays, pageants, and other programs containing religious themes?

School districts may acknowledge religious holidays in programs that have religious significance as long as these programs also contain some educational or cultural purpose (*Florey v. Sioux Falls Sch. Dist. 49-5*, 619 F.2d 1311 (8th Cir.), *cert. denied*, 449 U.S. 987 (1980)).

Thus, singing "God Bless America" at a general school assembly memorializing the tragic events of September 11, 2001, did not violate the Establishment Clause (*Appeal of Cayot*, 42 Ed Dept Rep 97 (2002)). However, a school board's resolution to change the name of its "Winter" concert to the "Christmas" concert did because it began: "We, being a Christian community. . .," which the commissioner of education found indicated an unconstitutional religious purpose (*Appeal of Sebouhian*, 31 Ed Dept Rep 397 (1992)). Similarly, a federal district court outside New York, found that a live nativity scene that lasted for 12 minutes as part of a district's Christmas Spectacular show impermissibly endorsed Christianity (*Freedom from Religion Foundation v. Concord Community Schools,* 148 F. Supp. 3d 727 (N.D.I.N. Dec. 2, 2015)).

According to one federal appellate court outside New York, a district policy prohibiting the performance of celebratory religious music at school-sponsored events did not convey hostility towards religion because it constituted the district's attempt to maintain neutrality toward religion. In contrast, the policy permitted religious music when presented objectively and appropriate for the curriculum (*Stratechuk v. Bd. of Educ., S. Orange-Maplewood Sch. Dist.*, 587 F.3d 597 (3d Cir. 2009), *cert. denied*, 131 S. Ct. 72 (2010); see also *Nurre v. Whitehead*, 580 F.3d 1087 (9th Cir. 2009), *cert. denied*, 130 S. Ct. 1937 (2010)).

The U.S. Court of Appeals for the Second Circuit, with jurisdiction over New York, ruled that Earth Day celebrations did not impermissibly endorse religion in a case where the record showed no one attending the ceremonies "worshipped" the earth or attached any significance of a religious nature to the celebration activities (*Altman v. Bedford CSD*, 245 F.3d 49 (2d Cir.), *cert. denied, Dibari v. Bedford CSD*, 534 U.S. 827 (2001)).

65:23. May school districts adopt guidelines regarding the observance and treatment of religious holidays?

Yes. A school district may adopt guidelines for the treatment of religious and cultural holidays in the instructional program (*Appeal of Pasquale*, 30 Ed Dept Rep 361 (1991)). According to the commissioner of education, the adoption of such guidelines falls within the broad statutory authority of school boards to adopt bylaws and rules for the governance of the schools (§ 1709)).

In this regard, a federal appellate court with jurisdiction outside of New York ruled that a district did not violate the free exercise of religion rights of an elementary school student when it denied the student permission to distribute gifts containing religious messages at an in-class holiday party. According to the court, because young impressionable students could easily misinterpret a fellow student's message, schools must be able to "restrict student expression that contradicts or distracts from a curricular activity." The court found significant that the student had not been asked to express his views about the personal significance of the holiday, in which case he would have been attempting to respond to a class assignment or activity (*Walz v. Egg Harbor Tp. Bd. of Educ.*, 342 F.3d 271 (3d Cir. 2003), *cert. denied*, 541 U.S. 936 (2004); but cf. *Morgan v. Swanson*, 659 F.3d 359 (5th Cir. 2011), *cert. denied*, 132 S. Ct. 2740 (2012)).

Similarly, in another case, a federal appellate court outside New York found it was permissible for a district to prevent a student from "selling" a Christmas holiday candy cane ornament with a religious message attached as part of a class marketplace project. According to that court, the class assignment did not invite the expression of personal views and the school exhibited a valid educational purpose in seeking to avoid offense to students or parents at a curricular event (*Curry v. Hensiner*, 513 F.3d 570 (6th Cir.), *cert. denied*, 555 U.S. 1069 (2008)).

For a discussion regarding the display of religious symbols in schools, see **65:30-35**.

65:24. May a school district include themes of religious significance in its educational program?

Yes, if the educational program is generally secular in nature. That was the case in *Matter of Rosenbaum*, 28 Ed Dept Rep 138 (1988), where the commissioner of education upheld a school district's policy permitting religious music and art in its curriculum. They were taught as part of a genuine secular program of education and the policy excused students from participating in those parts of the curriculum which conflicted with their religious beliefs.

65:25. May a school district excuse or release a student from school attendance for religious observance or religious instruction?

Yes. School absences for the observance of religious holidays outside of the official state holidays and for attendance at religious instruction are permitted by state law and regulation upon written request from a parent or guardian (§ 3210(1)(b)(i); 8 NYCRR § 109.2(a)). Students may be released to take such religious instruction in accordance with the commissioner's regulations (8 NYCRR § 109.2), as long as that instruction is not provided at the public school (*Zorach v. Clauson*, 343 U.S. 306 (1952); see also *Pierce v. Sullivan West CSD*, 379 F.3d 56 (2d Cir. 2004)), including a private trailer parked on school grounds for such purpose (see *H.S. v. Huntington Cnty. Cmty. Sch. Corp.*, 616 F. Supp.2d 863 (N.D. Ind. 2009)).

New York's regulation also allows a school district the discretion to establish an optional program for students in grades 9-12 that would permit students with parental permission to enroll in a course of religion in a nonpublic school. Enrollment is subject to prior approval of the public school principal with respect to course schedule, pupil attendance and reporting pupil's achievement (8 NYCRR § 109.2(f)). Similarly, according to one federal district court outside New York, it is permissible to award academic credit to students who are released from public school to take religious instruction offered through private schools to accommodate students who want to receive such instruction without risking the loss of academic credit required for graduation from public school (*Moss v. Spartanburg Cnty. Sch. Dist. No. 7*, 775 F. Supp.2d 858 (D.S.C. 2011), *cert. denied,* 133 S.Ct. 623 (2012)).

65:26. Must school districts accommodate employee religious observance needs?

Pursuant to Title VII of the Civil Rights Act of 1964, employers must make reasonable accommodations that allow employees to fulfill religious observance requirements, including all aspects of religious practice and belief, unless to do so would create an undue hardship (see *U.S. v. N.Y. City Transit Auth.*, 2010 U.S. Dist. LEXIS 102704 (E.D.N.Y. Sept. 24, 2010)). What constitutes a reasonable accommodation will depend on the facts of each case (see *Leifer v. N.Y. State Div. of Parole*, 391 Fed. Appx. 32 (2d Cir. 2010)). For example, an accommodation that allows an employee to attend morning religious services but requires him or her to work after religious services would not be reasonable for an employee who must abstain from work totally on the Sabbath (*Baker v. The Home Depot*, 445 F.3d 541 (2d Cir. 2006)). In contrast, an accommodation that eliminated an employee having to work on the Sabbath but required a weekend overnight shift was reasonable as the schedule provided eight hours off between shifts (*Marmulszteyn v. Napolitano*, 2012 LEXIS 3645776 (E.D.N.Y. 2012), *aff'd*, 523 Fed. Appx. 13 (2d Cir. 2013)).

Generally, courts have permitted teachers to take approximately five to ten days off for religious reasons, even where substitutes must be hired (see *Wangsness v. Watertown Sch. Dist.*, 541 F. Supp. 332 (D.S.D. 1982); *Niederhuber v. Camden Cnty. Vocational & Tech. Sch. Dist. Bd. of Educ.*, 495 F. Supp. 273 (D.N.J. 1980), *aff'd without op.*, 671 F.2d 496 (3d Cir. 1981)). Presumably, more than five or ten teacher absences for religious observances would be considered an undue hardship for a school district and outside the scope of an employee's Title VII protection.

As with Title VII, the New York State Human Rights Law (Exec. Law § 296(10)) also makes it unlawful for any employer to discriminate against an employee because the employee observes a particular Sabbath day or days in accordance with his or her religious beliefs. Moreover, except in emergencies, a district cannot require a teacher to work on a Sabbath or holy day and must allow the teacher time to travel to his or her home or to places of religious observance (Exec. Law § 296(10)(b)).

In *N.Y. City Transit Auth. v. State of N.Y. Div. of Human Rights*, 89 N.Y.2d 79 (1996), the New York Court of Appeals ruled that an employer unlawfully discriminated against an employee by firing her when she refused to work at any time from sundown on Friday to sundown on Saturday because of the tenets of her religion. Employers must make a "good-faith" effort to accommodate Sabbath-observing employees, even though an accommodation ultimately may not be available. The collective bargaining agreement required the employer to give senior employees preference in selecting days off. The court determined that the employer still had an obligation under the law to attempt to accommodate the employee's religious observance, and that the employer had not made any effort to do so.

65:27. Is an employee's leave for religious observance paid or unpaid?

According to the U.S. Supreme Court, public employees are entitled to unpaid leave for religious observances if they require days in excess of personal leave days already provided (*Ansonia Bd. of Educ. v. Philbrook*, 479 U.S. 60 (1986)). While dismissing a religious discrimination claim as time barred, a federal district court in New York stated a school board met its obligation to provide an accommodation when it allowed a teacher to take unpaid leave in excess of his paid leave to attend prayer services on Friday afternoons (*McLaughlin v. N.Y. City Bd. of Educ.*, 2008 U.S. Dist. LEXIS 4794 (S.D.N.Y. Jan. 22, 2008)).

65:28. May a school district offer paid leave specifically for religious observance?

There is a difference of opinion among New York state courts regarding the availability of paid leave for religious observance.

One state supreme court has ruled that paid leave for religious observance is a permissive subject of bargaining (*Binghamton City Sch. Dist. v. Andreatta*, 30 PERB ¶ 7504 (Sup. Ct. Broome Cnty. 1997)). But a state appellate court upheld a school district's unilateral decision to no longer comply with a collective bargaining contract provision that allowed teachers to take paid religious holidays determining, in part, that the provision was unconstitutional (*Matter of Port Washington UFSD v. Port Washington Teachers Ass'n*, 268 A.D.2d 523 (2d Dep't), *appeal dismissed,* 95 N.Y.2d 790, *lv. to appeal denied,* 95 N.Y.2d 761 (2000)).

In contrast, another state appellate court upheld a collectively bargained provision that authorized three days of paid leave for religious observance leave because it did not specify which holidays could be taken. According to that court, the provision merely provided a religious accommodation (*Maine Endwell Teachers Ass'n v. Bd. of Educ. of the Maine-Endwell CSD*, 3 A.D.3d 685 (3d Dep't

2004)). Similarly, a federal district court with jurisdiction in New York determined that a collectively bargained provision that allowed employees to utilize sick leave for religious observance provided a permissible religious accommodation (*Berkowitz v. East Ramapo Cent. Sch. Dist.*, 932 F.Supp.2d 513 (S.D.N.Y. 2013)).

65:29. Must school districts negotiate over paid leave for religious observance?

The Public Employment Relations Board (PERB) has ruled in two cases that a school district did not violate its duty to bargain in good faith by unilaterally rescinding a past practice of allowing employees to take extra paid leave for religious observances, finding that it was an unconstitutional practice and therefore not mandatorily negotiable (*Auburn Teachers Ass'n v. Auburn Enlarged City Sch. Dist.*, 29 PERB ¶ 4671 (1997); *CSEA v. Eastchester UFSD*, 29 PERB ¶ 3041 (1996)). Similarly, one state appellate court deemed unconstitutional a negotiated provision allowing for such leave (*Matter of Bd. of Educ. of the Mineola UFSD v. Mineola Teachers Assoc.*, 104 A.D.3d 939 (2d Dep't) *appeal withdrawn*, 22 N.Y.3d 995 (2013); *Matter of Port Washington UFSD v. Port Washington Teachers Ass'n*, 268 A.D.2d 523 (2d Dep't), *appeal dismissed,* 95 N.Y.2d 790, *lv. to appeal denied,* 95 N.Y.2d 761 (2000)). But according to another state appellate court the issue is negotiable (*Maine-Endwell Teachers Ass'n v. Bd. of Educ. of the Maine-Endwell CSD*, 3 A.D.3d 685 (3d Dep't 2004); see also **65:27**).

Religion

Religious Symbols

65:30. May school districts display religious symbols?

It depends. The U.S. Supreme Court has invalidated a statute requiring the posting of the Ten Commandments inside public classrooms under the Establishment Clause after determining that the statute's preeminent purpose was religious in nature (*Stone v. Graham*, 449 U.S. 39 (1980), *reh'g denied*, 449 U.S. 1104, *on remand*, 612 S.W.2d 133 (Ky. 1981); see also *Freedom From Religion Foundation v. Connellsville Area School Dist.*, 127 F. Supp.3d 283 (W.D.P.A. 2015) (monument of Ten Commandments on school grounds violated Establishment Clause); see **65:5**). However, it has allowed the display of religious symbols as part of displays that acknowledge cultural aspects of a holiday (*Lynch v. Donnelly*, 465 U.S. 668, *reh'g denied*, 466 U.S. 994 (1984); see also **65:24**).

A federal appellate court outside New York ruled that a school district violated the Establishment Clause when it displayed for 30 years a portrait of Jesus Christ in the hallway of a public school (*Washegesic v. Bloomingdale Pub. Sch.*, 33 F.3d 679 (6th Cir. 1994), *cert. denied*, 514 U.S. 1095 (1995)). However, the court indicated that its decision would have been different if the school had placed representative symbols of many of the world's religions on a common wall.

Similarly, a federal district court in New York ordered a school district to remove a mural depicting a crucifixion that was painted by a former student and displayed on a wall in the school auditorium (*Joki v. Bd. of Educ. of Schuylerville CSD*, 745 F. Supp. 823 (N.D.N.Y. 1990)). The court held that since the mural was patently religious, it violated the Establishment Clause because impressionable students might assume school sponsorship of religion. In comparison, that same federal district court in New York ruled that a school district that sold bricks to community members to be placed in a walkway in front of the high school had to allow the placement of bricks with religious messages. Disallowance of such bricks would constitute religious viewpoint discrimination (*Kiesinger v. Mexico Acad. & Cent. Sch.*, 427 F. Supp.2d 182 (N.D.N.Y. 2006)). See also *Weinbaum v. City of Las Cruces*, 541 F.3d 1017 (10th Cir. 2008), where a federal appellate court upheld use of the city's seal (three crosses against a mountain backdrop) in a sculpture outside a school district's athletic facility, and in a student-created mural.

65:31. What factors do courts consider when determining if a particular type of display violates the Establishment Clause?

Courts have considered a variety of factors when determining what types of displays pass scrutiny under the Establishment Clause. In *Cnty. of Allegheny v. American Civil Liberties Union, Greater Pittsburgh Chapter*, 492 U.S. 573 (1989), the U.S. Supreme Court noted several factors that included:

- The location of the display.
- Whether the display is part of a larger configuration that includes nonreligious items.
- The religious intensity of the display.
- Whether the display is shown in connection with a general secular holiday.
- The degree of public participation in the ownership and maintenance of the display.
- The existence of disclaimers of public sponsorship. Most notably, the court indicated that a greater level of sensitivity must be exercised with respect to the public schools.

Applying those factors, the high court found that a nativity scene inside a county courthouse by itself violated the separation of church and state. However, the display of a large Christmas tree and a Hanukkah menorah with the message "A Salute to Liberty" outside that same county courthouse did not (*Id.*).

65:32. May a school district display religious symbols as part of temporary displays commemorating religious holidays?

Yes. The U.S. Supreme Court has ruled that inclusion of a nativity scene in its Christmas display, along with a Santa Claus, a Christmas tree, a reindeer, a clown, a teddy bear, and other holiday items, does not to violate the Establishment Clause (*Lynch v. Donnelly*, 465 U.S. 668, *reh'g denied*, 466 U.S. 994 (1984); see also *Elewski v. City of Syracuse*, 123 F.3d 51 (2d Cir. 1997), *cert. denied*, 523 U.S. 1004 (1998)). However, it is not necessary for a school district to include a crèche in a display including recognized secular symbols of Christmas, even if the display includes a menorah representing Chanukah and a star and crescent representing Ramadan (*Skoros v. City of N.Y.*, 437 F.3d 1 (2d Cir. 2006), *cert. denied,* 549 U.S. 1205 (2007)).

According to a federal appellate court outside New York, a school district's temporary display of religious symbols associated with religious holidays does not violate the Establishment Clause if the display is not proselytizing in nature and merely acknowledges cultural and historical aspects of the holiday (*Florey v. Sioux Falls Sch. Dist. 49-5*, 619 F.2d 1311 (8th Cir.), *cert. denied*, 449 U.S. 987 (1980)). But according to a federal district court in New York a village display in a public park of a menorah next to a spot-lighted but unadorned evergreen tree violated the Establishment Clause as it appeared to endorse Judaism (*Ritell v. Village of Briarcliff Manor*, 466 F.Supp.2d 514 (S.D.N.Y. 2006)). And according to a state appellate court in New York, allowing the use of municipal funds, labor and equipment to light a menorah nightly would foster excessive government entanglement with religion in violation of the Establishment Clause, even when the menorah is part of a diverse holiday season display (*Chabad of Mid-Hudson Valley v. City of Poughkeepsie*, 76 A.D.3d 693 (2d Dep't 2010)).

65:33. May a school district display items associated with Halloween?

In a case that the U.S. Supreme Court declined to hear, a Florida state court ruled that the depiction of witches, cauldrons and brooms, and related costumes during a school Halloween celebration did not violate the Establishment Clause (*Guyer v. Sch. Bd. of Alachua Cnty.*, 634 So.2d 806 (Fla. App. 1 Dist.), *cert. denied*, 513 U.S. 1044 (1994)). The Florida court rejected the argument that use of the symbols and costumes endorsed and promoted "Wicca" (a religion based on witchcraft and religious principles), after finding that the symbols were not "singularly" or "distinctively" religious. Although the decision is not binding in New York, it might be persuasive to courts with jurisdiction over the state.

65:34. Can the use of certain symbols as school mascots be unconstitutional?

Litigation on the issue of school mascots and the religion clauses of the First Amendment of the U.S. Constitution has been scarce. However, the focus has been on whether the use of a particular symbol advances religion and violates the separation of church and state. For example, in *Kunselman v. Western Reserve Local Sch. Dist. Bd. of Educ.*, 70 F.3d 931 (6th Cir. 1995), parents unsuccessfully argued that use and display of a "blue devil" as the school's mascot violated the Establishment Clause by encouraging devil worship. In the court's opinion, "No reasonable person would think that the school authorities here are advocating Satanism . . . when they use the name and symbol."

Aside from the constitutionality issue, a determination as to the appropriateness of a school mascot rests with the local school board. Such a determination will be put aside only upon a showing that the board has abused its discretion (*Appeal of Tobin*, 25 Ed Dept Rep 301 (1986), 30 Ed Dept Rep 315 (1991)). However, school districts should examine whether district mascots that are based upon Native American themes are inappropriate or offensive (see *Appeal of D'Orazio*, 41 Ed Dept Rep 292 (2002); see also NYS Education Department, *Public School Use of Native American Names, Symbols and Mascots*, Memorandum from Education Commissioner Richard P. Mills (Feb. 5, 2001); *Appeal of Eurich*, 37 Ed Dept Rep 707 (1998)).

Religion

65:35. May school districts prevent a teacher from wearing religious garb while teaching?

In a decision from the turn of the last century, the New York State Court of Appeals upheld a prohibition against the wearing of religious clothing by teachers (*O'Connor v. Hendrick*, 184 N.Y. 421 (1906)). The court found that a teacher's religious attire might unduly influence impressionable students, and that this sectarian influence is unconstitutional.

Other states' statutes prohibiting wearing of religious garb by teachers have been upheld as advancing the compelling interest in maintaining the appearance of religious neutrality in public classrooms (*U.S. v. Bd. of Educ. for Sch. Dist. of Phila.*, 911 F.2d 882 (3d Cir. 1990); *Cooper v. Eugene Sch. Dist. No. 4J*, 723 P.2d 298 (1986), *app. dismissed*, 480 U.S. 942 (1987)).

More recently, the U.S. Supreme Court found a private employer violated Title VII's prohibition against employment discrimination on the basis of religion when it failed to hire a Muslim woman who wore a headscarf because the headscarf conflicted with the employer's dress policy (*E.E.O.C. v. Abercrombie & Fitch Stores, Inc.* 135 S.Ct. 2028 (2015)). In its decision the Supreme Court stated that Title VII gives religious practices favored treatment, requiring employers "not to fail or refuse to hire or discharge any individual because of such individual's religious observance and practice" (*Id.* at 2034). Consequently, in order to continue to ban religious garments, a school district may have to show that an accommodation of the teacher's wishes would cause undue hardship to the district. The U.S. Equal Employment Opportunity Commission has issued guidance addressing religious garb and grooming in the workplace that outlines examples of accommodations and undue hardship (see U.S. Equal Employment Opportunity Commission, *Religious Garb and Grooming in the Workplace: Rights and Responsibilities*, (Mar. 2014), at: http://www.eeoc.gov/eeoc/publications/qa_religious_garb_grooming.cfm).

Student Religious Groups

65:36. May student groups meet on school premises and openly pray or conduct Bible study activities?

Yes. The federal Equal Access Act (20 USC §§ 4071–74) requires that public schools allow such use of its facilities, but only during noninstructional time, if the students are high school students, if the meeting or activity is not school-sponsored, and if the school district already allows other student-run, noncurriculum-related student groups to meet on school premises during "noninstructional time" (see also *Youth Alive v. Hauppauge Sch. Dist.*, 2011 U.S. Dist. LEXIS 113628 (E.D.N.Y. Sept. 30, 2011), *partially dismissed*, 2012 U.S. Dist. LEXIS 148086 (E.D.N.Y. Oct. 15, 2012)).

Noninstructional time generally means before or after school. However, one federal appellate court has ruled that a public high school's lunch break was "noninstructional time," rejecting the district's position that only time set aside before and after school constituted "noninstructional time" (*Ceniceros v. Bd. of Trustees of San Diego Unified Sch. Dist.*, 106 F.3d 878 (9th Cir. 1997)). According to another federal appellate court, an activity period between homeroom and the first period of instruction is also noninstructional time (*Donovan v. Punxsutawney Area Sch. Bd.*, 336 F.3d 211 (3d Cir. 2003)).

A student group is noncurriculum-related unless the subject matter of that group is actually taught or concerns the body of courses as a whole, or participation in such a group is a course requirement or provides the participants with academic credit (*Bd. of Educ. of Westside Cmty. Schs. v. Mergens*, 496 U.S. 226 (1990)).

According to the U.S. Supreme Court, the Equal Access Act does not violate the Establishment Clause, because, under the act, schools are not endorsing religious speech; they are merely permitting such speech on a nondiscriminatory basis (*Id.*). For more information on the Equal Access Act see **64:12**.

65:37. May school districts deny use of their facilities to student religious groups that limit participation to those who share their religious beliefs?

Not in New York. In *Hsu v. Roslyn UFSD No. 3*, 85 F.3d 839 (2d Cir.), *cert. denied*, 519 U.S. 1040 (1996), the United States Court of Appeals for the Second Circuit, with jurisdiction over New York, ruled that the Equal Access Act precludes a school district from enforcing nondiscrimination policies that would prohibit a student Bible club from meeting on school property solely because the group allowed only Christians to serve as officers of the club.

In contrast, a federal appellate court outside New York found a district did not violate the Act when it denied a Bible club access because the club restricted membership to Christians in violation of district policies requiring student groups to be non-discriminatory (*Truth v. Kent Sch. Dist.*, 524 F.3d 957 (9th Cir.), *amended by* 542 F.3d 634 (9th Cir. 2008), *cert. denied*, 129 S. Ct. 2866 (2009)).

Compare also *Christian Legal Soc'y Chapter of the Univ. of Cal., Hastings Coll. of Law v. Martinez*, 561 U.S. 661 (2010), where the U.S. Supreme Court upheld a public law school's application of its nondiscrimination policy in student groups and clubs, and thus access to school funds, avenues of communication, and other benefits to a student group with bylaws that required its members share the group's beliefs on faith and relationships. While not an Equal Access Act case, some courts may consider its applicability in public schools with similar policies requiring that student club membership be open to all.

65:38. May school personnel attend student group meetings where students openly pray or conduct Bible study activities?

Yes. However, under the federal Equal Access Act (20 USC §§ 4071–74), school personnel may attend such meetings only as monitors, not as advisors or participants, and the meetings may not interfere materially or substantially with the orderly conduct of school activities. Furthermore, non-school persons or groups may not direct, control or regularly attend these student group meetings and activities.

Nonetheless, according to a federal appellate court outside New York, an elementary school teacher can participate in meetings of an after-school religious club for children, even if the meetings are held at the same school where she is assigned to teach. According to that court, the teacher's participation does not violate separation of church and state principles under the Establishment Clause because a reasonable observer would view her as any private citizen exercising the right to religious freedom and speech (see *Wigg v. Sioux Falls Sch. Dist.*, 382 F.3d 807 (8th Cir. 2004)).

In comparison, another federal appellate court upheld a school district policy that prohibited faculty participation in student initiated prayer in any school-sponsored setting including classes, practices, pep rallies, team meetings and athletic events (*Borden v. Sch. Dist. of Tp. of East Brunswick*, 523 F.3d 153 (3d Cir. 2008), *cert denied,* 555 U.S. 1212 (2009)).

Vouchers

65:39. Do publicly-funded voucher programs necessarily violate the Establishment Clause?

It depends. According to the U.S. Supreme Court,

> [A] government aid program is not readily subject to challenge under the Establishment Clause (see **65:2**), if it is neutral with respect to religion and provides assistance directly to a broad class of citizens who, in turn, direct government aid to religious schools wholly as a result of their own genuine and independent private choice. Under such a program, government aid reaches the religious institutions only by way of the deliberate choices of numerous individual recipients. The incidental advancement of a religious mission, or the perceived endorsement of a religious message, is reasonably attributable to the individual aid recipients not the government, whose role ends with the disbursement of benefits (*Zelman v. Simmons-Harris*, 536 U.S. 639 (2002)).

However, state courts have invalidated state voucher programs based on state constitutional grounds (see *Bush v. Holmes*, 919 So. 2d 392 (Fla. 2006); see **65:4**).

Similarly, a school district's loan of federally-funded educational materials to parochial schools has been deemed to not violate the Establishment Clause (*Mitchell v. Helms*, 530 U.S. 793 (2000)). Whether such a program would be constitutional in New York State, in conformity with the New York State Constitution's Blaine Amendment, remains to be seen. (see **65:1, 65:4**.)

66. General Rules and Sources of Liability

School District and Personal Liability

66:1. Are school districts exempt from lawsuits?

No. The concept of sovereign immunity, which prevented lawsuits against the state and other governmental entities, has been abolished in New York State by virtue of the Court of Claims Act (Court of Claims Act § 8).

66:2. What is the scope of a school district's potential liability as a result of a lawsuit?

Liability entails the financial responsibility to pay a person or entity, or to otherwise remedy a wrong, when there is injury or damage to such person or entity due to the wrongful action or inaction of the school district, school board members, or their employees.

School districts carrying liability insurance generally are protected to the limits of such insurance. Above these limits, and under any applicable deductible in the insurance policy, the responsibility to pay the claim rests with the school district.

66:3. Under what circumstances may a school district be liable as a result of a lawsuit?

A school district may be liable as a corporate entity for its own negligence and other improper actions such as breach of contract. It also may be liable for the wrongful actions of school board members, and the negligence of its employees in the performance of their official duties that results in injury to others (*Helbig v. City of N.Y. Bd. of Educ.*, 212 A.D.2d 506 (2d Dep't 1995)).

66:4. Are school board members exempt from lawsuits brought against them personally?

No. However, there is immunity for school board members when they carry out official functions within the context of a school board meeting. For such immunity to apply, these functions must involve the exercise of discretion or reasoned judgment that could produce different acceptable results, rather than be exclusively ministerial (*Metz v. State,* 20 N.Y.3d 175 (2012); *Valdez v. City of N.Y.*, 18 N.Y.3d 69 (2011); *McLean v. City. of N.Y.*, 12 N.Y.3d 194 (2009); *Haddock v. City of N.Y.*, 75 N.Y.2d 478 (1990)), which involves direct adherence to a rule or standard with a compulsory result (*McLean v. City of N.Y*; *Haddock v. City of N.Y.*).

Nonetheless, discretionary functions may result in liability if they produce consequences that result from a failure to adhere to internal procedures that affect the exercise of judgment (*Valdez v. City of N.Y.*; see also *Newsome v. Cnty. of Suffolk*, 109 A.D.3d 802 (2d Dep't 2013)). Similarly, ministerial actions may form the basis of liability if they are inconsistent with a special duty owed to a person injured as a result of those actions (*McLean v. City of N.Y.*; see also *Valdez v. City of N.Y.*).

Liability and Litigation

Notice of Claim Requirements

66:5. Are there any procedural requirements applicable to the commencement of a lawsuit against a school district?

Yes. The purpose of those requirements is to alert school districts to the pending claim and enable the district to conduct an efficient investigation (*Field v. Tonawanda City Sch. Dist.*, 604 F. Supp.2d 544 (W.D.N.Y. 2008)). Furthermore, the procedural requirements depend on the type of lawsuit involved.

Actions or special proceedings that relate to district property, or claims against the district, or involve the rights or interests of the district

This type of lawsuit cannot proceed unless the claimant files a written verified notice of claim with the governing body of the district as required under the Education Law (§ 3813(1); see also *Flaherty v. Massapequa Pub. Schs.*, 752 F. Supp.2d 286 (E.D.N.Y. 2010); *Averginos v. Palmyra-Macedon CSD*, 690 F. Supp.2d 115 (W.D.N.Y. 2008)). It is not sufficient to file the notice of claim with an employee (*Kingsley Arms, Inc. v. Copake-Taconic Hills CSD*, 9 A.D.3d 696 (3d Dep't), *lv. to appeal dismissed,* 3 N.Y.3d 767 (2004); see also *Clune v. Garden City UFSD*, 34 A.D.3d 618 (2d Dep't 2006), not even with the superintendent of schools (*Carter v. City of Syracuse*, 2012 U.S. Dist. LEXIS 36612 (N.D.N.Y. Mar. 19, 2012); *Newman v. LeRoy CSD*, 2008 U.S. Dist. LEXIS 28581 (W.D.N.Y. Apr. 8, 2008)). Unverified e-mails and letters to staff regarding a plaintiff's complaint do not satisfy the statutory notice requirements either (*Clune v. Garden City UFSD; Gastman v. Dep't of Educ. of City of N.Y.*, 60 A.D.3d 444 (1st Dep't), *lv. to appeal denied*, 12 N.Y.3d 711 (2009)).

The notice of claim in this type of lawsuit must be filed within three months after the accrual of the claim (§ 3813(1); *Carlson v. Geneva City Sch. Dist.*, 679 F. Supp.2d 355 (W.D.N.Y. 2010)).

Actions or special proceedings involving a claim for the payment of money owed arising out of a contract

This type of lawsuit is also subject to the notice of claim requirements under the Education Law § 3813(1). These claims are deemed to accrue as of the date on which payment for the amount claimed was denied (§ 3813(1); *Mitchell v. Bd. of Educ. of the City Sch. Dist. of the City of N.Y.*, 15 A.D. 3d 279 (1st Dep't 2005); *Zurich Am. Ins. Co. v. Ramapo CSD*, 63 A.D.3d 729 (2d Dep't 2009)). A denial of payment can be deemed to occur when a school district explicitly refuses to pay or when a claim for payment should be viewed as having been constructively rejected (*Sch. Aid Specialist, LLC v. Bd. of Educ. of Warwick Valley CSD*, 130 A.D.3d 1006 (2d Dep't 2015); *Granite Capital Holdings, Inc. v. Sherburne-Earlville CSD*, 84 A.D.3d 1607 (3d Dep't 2011)). A district's statement that it does not view itself as bound by a contract is insufficient to support a defense of constructive rejection when it is not possible to make a demand for payment until the end of the contract because the damages do not become certain and ascertainable until then (see *Granite Capital Holdings, Inc. v. Sherburne-Earlville CSD*).

Actions involving a tort claim for personal injury

This type of lawsuit against school officials, teachers, or other employees is subject to the procedural requirements of the General Municipal Law. In such cases, for example, the notice of claim must be made and served upon the district within 90 days after the claim arose (§ 3813(2); Gen. Mun. Law §§ 50-e, 50-i).

In addition, school districts should be aware that plaintiffs may file a notice of claim for personal injury actions by filing the notice of claim upon the secretary of state who then forwards the claim to the school district (Gen. Mun. Law §§ 50-e(3)(f), 53). School districts must file a certificate with the secretary of state that designates the secretary as the agent for service of a notice of claim, provides the name and address of an officer, person or designee for the transmittal of notices of claim served upon the secretary and contains the applicable time limit for filing a notice of claim upon a school district (Gen. Mun Law § 53(2)). It is recommended school districts consult with their school attorney about the contents of this designation.

66:6. What must the notice of claim include?

For personal injury claims (see **66:5**), the notice of claim must comply with General Muncipal Law § 50-e which requires, in part, a written sworn claim, a statement of the nature of the claim, the time when, the place where and the manner in which the claim arose, and the item of damage or injuries sustained (§ 3813(2); see Gen. Mun. § 50-e(2); *Carter v. City of Syracuse*, 2012 U.S. Dist. LEXIS 36612 (N.D.N.Y. Mar. 19, 2012)).

For claims covered by § 3813(1) (see **66:5**), the complaint or necessary moving papers must indicate that a verified claim was presented and the officer or body with authority to adjust or pay the claim neglected or refused to do so for 30 days after the claim was presented (§ 3813(1)). This 30-day waiting period between the filing of the notice of claim and the commencement of the action extends the four-month statute of limitations for bringing an Article 78 proceeding (*Gardner v. Coxsackie-Athens CSD*, 92 A.D.3d 1093 (3d Dep't 2012); *Perlin v. South Orangetown CSD*, 216 A.D.2d 397 (2d Dep't), *lv. to appeal dismissed*, 86 N.Y.2d 886 (1995)).

66:7. Can the late filing of a notice of claim be excused?

Sometimes. Upon application, a court, at its discretion, may extend the time to serve the notice of claim on the school district, provided the application to extend the time is made prior to the expiration of the relevant statute of limitations for bringing the lawsuit (§ 3813(2-a), (2-b); Gen. Mun. Law § 50-e(5); *Sainato v. Western Suffolk BOCES*, 242 A.D.2d 301 (2d Dep't 1997); *Babcock v. Walton CSD*, 119 A.D.3d 1061 (3d Dep't 2014); *Flaherty v. Massapequa Pub. Schs.*, 752 F. Supp. 2d 286 (E.D.N.Y. 2010)).

66:8. On what basis may court extend the time to serve a notice of claim on a school district?

In granting an extension to serve a late notice of claim, a court will consider a variety of factors, including whether:

- the district (or its attorney or insurer) acquired actual knowledge of the facts of the claim within three months of the incident or a reasonable time thereafter (*see Candino v. Starpoint CSD*, 115 A.D.3d 1170 (4th Dep't), *aff'd*, 24 N.Y.3d 925 (2014)),
- the claimant was an infant or physically or mentally incapacitated when the claim arose,
- the claimant died before the time limited for service of the notice of claim,
- the claimant justifiably relied upon settlement representations made by the district or the insurance carrier,
- the claimant made an excusable error concerning the identity of the district, and
- the delay substantially prejudiced the district in maintaining its defense on the merits (§ 3813(2-a); Gen. Mun. Law § 50-e(5); *Matter of Iglesias v. Brentwood UFSD*, 118 A.D.3d 785 (2d Dep't 2014); *Matter of Formisano v. Eastchester UFSD*, 59 A.D.3d 543 (2d Dep't 2009); *Matter of Felice v. Eastport/South Manor CSD*, 50 A.D.3d 138 (2d Dep't 2008); *Sica v. Bd. of Educ. of the City of N.Y.*, 226 A.D.2d 542 (2d Dep't 1996); see also *Matter of Newcomb v. Middle Country CSD*, 128 A.D.3d 701 (2d Dep't 2015)).

66:9. Are there any factors that weigh more in a court's decision to extend the time for the filing of a notice of claim?

No. While courts pay "particular" care to the first factor, none of the factors are determinative (§ 3813 (2-a); Gen. Mun. § 50-e(5); *Munro v. Ossining UFSD*, 55 A.D.3d 697 (2d Dep't 2008); *Matter of Felice v. Eastport/South Manor CSD*, 50 A.D.3d 138 (2d Dep't 2008); see also *Lavender v. Garden City UFSD*, 93 A.D.3d 670 (2d Dep't 2010)). The fact that a plaintiff is an infant does not compel the granting of a petition for leave to serve a late notice of claim (*Lamprecht v. Eastport-South Manor CSD*, 129 A.D.3d 1084 (2d Dep't 2015); *Sparrow v. Hewlett-Woodmere UFSD*, 110 A.D.3d 905 (2d Dep't 2013); *Harris v. City of N.Y.,* 297 A.D.2d 473 (1st Dep't 2002)). Courts will also look at whether there was a nexus between the claimant's infancy and the failure to serve a timely notice of claim (see *Horn v. Bellmore UFSD*, 139 AD 3d 1006 (2d Dep't 2016); *Saponara v. Lakeland CSD*, 138 A.D.3d 870 (2d Dep't 2016); *Lamprecht v. Eastport-South Manor CSD,* 129 A.D.3d 1084 (2d Dep't 2015)).

In one case a mother was able to file a late notice three years after her child was allegedly sexually abused on a school bus. The child did not show symptoms of the abuse until more than three years later. Not only was there a nexus between the delay and the child's infancy, but also the district was not prejudiced by the late filing because it had learned of the facts at the time of the incident and even offered counseling to the child (*Matter of Andrew T.B. v. Brewster CSD*, 18 A.D.3d 745 (2d Dep't 2005); see also *Doe v. North Tonawanda CSD*, 88 A.D.3d 1289 (4th Dep't 2011); *Place v. Beekmantown CSD*, 69 A.D.3d 1035 (3d Dep't 2010)). In comparison, a student who initially denied that any improper sexual relationship existed with one of his teachers and recanted one year later was denied leave to file a late notice of claim because the school district lacked actual knowledge of the facts within a reasonable time and the student failed to offer a persuasive explanation as to the nearly one year delay between the time he reached the age of majority and his application (*Babcock v. Walton CSD*, 119 A.D.3d 1061 (3d Dep't 2014); see also *Bazile v. City of N.Y.*, 94 A.D.3d 929 (2d Dep't 2012); *Matter of Diggs v. Bd. of Educ. of City of Yonkers*, 79 A.D.3d 869 (2d Dep't 2010)).

A claimant's unfamiliarity with the filing requirements typically will not constitute a reasonable excuse (*Matter of Werner v. Nyack UFSD*, 76 A.D.3d 1026 (2d Dep't 2010); *Troy v. Town of Hyde Park*, 63 A.D.3d 913 (2d Dep't 2009)). Neither will assertions, without supporting medical evidence, that the nature and severity of the injury were not immediately appreciated (*Matter of Werner v. Nyack UFSD*, 76 A.D.3d 1026 (2d Dep't 2010)).

66:10. Can the time to commence a lawsuit after filing a notice of claim be delayed?

Yes, in cases involving infants. Where the person entitled to commence an action is an infant at the time the cause of action accrues, the statute of limitations for filing a claim against a municipality, including a school district, is tolled (frozen in time) until the child turns 18 (C.P.L.R. § 208).

This is so even when a parent files a notice of claim pursuant to the General Municipal Law during the period of infancy (*Henry v. City of N.Y.*, 94 N.Y.2d 275 (1999)). However, the infancy toll applies exclusively to the minor and does not toll the statute of limitations for any claims parents may raise on their own behalf (see *Bazile v. City of N.Y.*, 94 A.D.3d 929 (2d Dep't 2012); *Kim L. v. Port Jervis City Sch. Dist.*, 77 A.D.3d 627 (2d Dep't 2010)).

66:11. Can a lawsuit against a school district proceed without the filing of a notice of claim at all?

Sometimes. Under certain limited exceptions, the notice of claim requirement does not apply, such as when the action or proceeding against the district "seeks to vindicate a public interest" rather than a private right (*Bd. of Educ. of Union-Endicott CSD v. PERB*, 197 A.D.2d 276 (3d Dep't), *lv. to appeal denied*, 84 N.Y.2d 803 (1994); *UFSD No. 6 v. N.Y. State Human Rights Appeal Bd.*, 35 N.Y.2d 371 (1974), *rehearing denied*, 36 N.Y.2d 806 (1975)). That was the case when a social worker brought a petition in state supreme court seeking reinstatement only, and no monetary damages (*Kahn v. Dep't of Educ. of City of N.Y.*, 26 Misc.3d 366 (Sup. Ct. N.Y. Cnty. 2009), *rev'd on other grounds,* 79 A.D.3d 521 (1st Dep't 2010), *aff'd*, 18 N.Y.3d 457 (2012)). Similarly, no notice of claim is required in an action against school district officers pursuant to Civil Service Law § 102(2), to recover sums paid to an employee illegally appointed to a position (*Eldridge v. Carmel CSD Bd. of Educ.*, 82 A.D.3d 1147 (2d Dep't 2011)).

Moreover, the notice of claim requirements are inapplicable to employment discrimination complaints filed with the New York State Division of Human Rights for that agency's administrative review (*Freudenthal v. Cnty. of Nassau*, 99 N.Y.2d 285 (2003)). The same is not true with respect to a lawsuit filed in court against a school district as opposed to a complaint filed with the Division of Human Rights. In the case of a lawsuit, a plaintiff must first file a notice of claim with the district (*Pinder v. City of N.Y.*, 49 A.D.3d 280 (1st Dep't 2008); see also *Moore v. City of N.Y.*, 2010 U.S. Dist. LEXIS 19183 (S.D.N.Y. Mar. 2, 2010); see **66:5**).

Likewise, the notice of claim provisions of the Education Law do not apply to actions seeking declaratory judgments (*Levert v. CSD No. 6, Town of Huntington,* 24 Misc.2d 832 (Sup. Ct. Suffolk Cnty. 1960)) or to New York C.P.L.R. Article 78 special proceedings in the nature of mandamus, seeking judicial enforcement of a legal right derived from positive law (*Piaggone v. Bd. of Educ., Floral Park-Bellrose UFSD,* 92 A.D.2d 106 (2d Dep't 1983); *Matter of Thomas v. N.Y. City. Dep't of Educ.*, 28 Misc.3d 1201(A) (Sup. Ct. N.Y. City. 2010)).

The Public Employment Relations Board has questioned whether the notice of claim requirement applies to improper practice charges filed under the Taylor Law (*Manhasset Educ. Support Pers. Ass'n, NYSUT*, 41 PERB ¶ 3005 (2008)), notwithstanding its acknowledgment of state appellate court decisions to the contrary (see *Matter of Manhasset UFSD v. PERB*, 61 A.D.3d 1231 (3d Dep't 2009); see **46:32**).

66:12. Can the commencement of other types of proceedings substitute for service of a notice of claim upon a school district?

Sometimes. For example, a notice of issuance of a right-to-sue letter sent by the Equal Employment Opportunity Commission (EEOC) will constitute effective service of a notice of claim (*Kushner v. Valenti*, 285 F. Supp.2d 314 (E.D.N.Y. 2003)). However, federal district courts addressing the issue in New York are split on whether timely service of an EEOC discrimination charge upon the school board may constitute effective service of a notice of claim. Some have concluded that the service of an EEOC complaint may, under certain circumstance, satisfy the notice requirement (*Brtalik v. South Huntington UFSD*, 2010 U.S. Dist. LEXIS 107373 (E.D.N.Y. Oct. 6, 2010); *Field v. Tonawanda City Sch. Dist.*, 604 F. Supp.2d 544 (W.D.N.Y. 2009); *Fischer v. N.Y. City Dep't of Educ.*, 666 F.Supp.2d 309 (E.D.N.Y. 2009)). Other courts have suggested that the filing of an EEOC complaint cannot satisfy the notice requirement (*Santiago v. Newburgh Enlarged City Sch. Dist.*, 434 F. Supp.2d 193 (S.D.N.Y. 2006); *Biggers v. Brookhaven-Comsewogue UFSD*, 127 F. Supp.2d 452 (S.D.N.Y. 2001)). According to one of them, a complaint filed with the EEOC can serve as a substitute for § 3813 notice of claim requirements only when the EEOC charge puts the district on notice of the precise claims, is served on the school board, and is served within the statutory time period (*Brtalik v. South Huntington UFSD*).

In addition, two separate state appellate courts have determined that a petition to the commissioner of education also can serve as the "functional equivalent" of a notice of claim (*Menella v. Uniondale UFSD*, 287 A.D.2d 636 (2d Dep't 2001); see also *Matter of Bd. of Educ. of Westbury UFSD v. Ambach*, 81 A.D.2d 691 (3d Dep't 1981)). A paper that is not denominated a notice of claim may satisfy the notice requirement if it gives notice of the nature of the claim, and the "'essential facts underlying the claim'" (*Menella v. Uniondale UFSD*).

However, when a notice of claim is properly filed and a lawsuit commenced for an ongoing contractual payment issue, the original lawsuit does not suffice as subsequent notices of claim for continuing contractual payment issues during the course of the lawsuit. The claimant must file a new notice of claim every three months (*Varsity Transit Inc. v. Bd. of Educ. of the City of N.Y.*, 5 N.Y.3d 532 (2005)).

66:13. Is a notice of claim required for commencing an appeal before the commissioner of education?

No. The notice of claim provisions of the Education Law (see **66:5**) do not apply to appeals filed with the commissioner of education (*Appeal of the Bd. of Educ. of the Canastota CSD,* 48 Ed Dept Rep 235 (2008); *Appeal of Hollister*, 39 Ed Dept Rep 109 (1999); *Appeal of Sole Trustee of Hickory South Mountain*, 38 Ed Dept Rep 577 (1999); *Appeal of Shusterman*, 18 Ed Dept Rep 516 (1979)).

However, a copy of the petition for appeal filed with the commissioner must be personally served upon each respondent. When a school district itself is named as a respondent, personal service upon the district is made by delivering a copy of the petition to the district clerk, any school board member, the school superintendent, or a person in the school superintendent's office designated by the board to accept service (8 NYCRR § 275.8(a); *Appeal of Peppaceno*, 55 Ed Dept Rep, Dec. No. 16,807 (2015); *Appeal of Kalnitz,* 53 Ed Dept Rep, Dec. No. 16,600 (2014); *Appeal of Green*, 48 Ed Dept Rep 294 (2009)). If the person accepting service on behalf of the district is not authorized to do so, service is improper and the appeal must be dismissed (*Id.*). That was the case, for example, where a copy of the appeal petition challenging a district's denial of transportation services was served on the transportation supervisor who had not been designated to accept service on behalf of the district (*Appeal of Green*).

Negligence

Liability and Litigation

66:14. What is negligence?

Negligence is a legal principle that imposes liability on entities and individuals who breach a duty they owe to others, thereby causing them reasonably foreseeable injury (see *Prosser & Keaton on the Law of Torts* § 30 (5th ed. 1984)).

66:15. What is the scope of a school district's duty for the supervision and care of students?

In general, school districts have a duty to supervise students in their care and to maintain the school premises and any equipment in a safe working condition, and will be held liable for foreseeable student injuries that are proximately caused by a lack of adequate supervision. However, a school district has only the duty to exercise the same degree of care toward its students as would a reasonable, prudent parent under comparable circumstances (*Mirand v. City of N.Y.*, 84 N.Y.2d 44 (1994); *Shante D. by Ada D. v. City of N.Y.*, 190 A.D.2d 356 (1st Dep't 1993), *aff'd*, 83 N.Y.2d 948 (1994); *Lawes v. Bd. of Educ.*, 16 N.Y.2d 302 (1965); see also *Rinaldo v. Williamsville CSD*, 35 Misc.3d 1232(A) (Sup. Ct. Erie Cnty. 2012)). Should a breach of this duty by either the school system, board members or their employees result in an injury to a student, the school district may be held liable in negligence. That was the case, for example, where a district released a student into a reasonably foreseeable hazard of crossing a street while school buses were pulling out (*Ernest v. Red Creek CSD*, 93 N.Y.2d 664 (1999); see **66:25**). A school district was also found liable when a student drowned in a wave pool at a water park during a school field trip (*Maracallo v. Bd. of Educ. of the City of N.Y.*, 2 Misc.3d 703 (Sup. Ct. Bronx Cnty. 2003)).

66:16. Are there any instances in which a school district will not be found to have violated its duty of care toward students?

Yes. For example, school districts will not be held liable for injuries that occur as a result of spontaneous and unintentional accidents, where no amount of supervision could have prevented the injury (*Mirand v. City of N.Y.; Emmanuel B., v. City of N.Y.*, 131 A.D.3d 831 (2d Dep't 2015); *Staten v. City of N.Y.*, 127 A.D.3d 1066 (2d Dep't 2015); *Nash v. Port Washington UFSD*, 83 A.D.3d 136 (2d Dep't 2011); *Bellinger v. Ballston Spa CSD*, 57 A.D.3d 1296 (3d Dep't 2008), *lv. to appeal denied*, 12 N.Y.3d 704 (2009); *Paragas v. Comsewogue UFSD*, 65 A.D.3d 1111 (2d Dep't 2009)). However, even when an incident occurs quickly and spontaneously, a school district could be held liable for student injuries in cases where the school's disciplinary record establishes a pattern of undisciplined and disruptive behavior such that it is foreseeable that a student would engage in assaultive conduct (*Hodge v. Town of Hempstead Bd. of Educ.*, 2010 N.Y. Misc. LEXIS 1347 (Sup. Ct. Nassau Cnty. Jan. 15, 2010); see also *Hofmann v. Coxsackie-Athens CSD*, 70 A.D.3d 1116 (3d Dep't 2010)).

In addition, a school district generally is not liable for the intentional acts of others but it could be found liable for negligent supervision if the injuries caused by the intentional acts of others could have been anticipated or were foreseeable (*Sacino v. Warwick Valley CSD*, 138 A.D.3d 717 (2d Dept. 2016); *Timothy Mc. v. Beacon City Sch. Dist.*, 127 A.D.3d 826 (2d Dept. 2015)).

Furthermore, a school district's duty of supervision and care is co-extensive with its physical custody and control over the student. Thus, generally a school district will not be liable for injuries that occur once a student has left school property or activities (*Diaz v. Brentwood UFSD*, 141 A.D.3d 556 (2d Dep't 2016); *Davis v. Marzo*, 55 A.D.3d 1404 (4th Dep't 2008); *Chalen v. Glen Cove Sch. Dist.*, 29 A.D.3d 508 (2d Dep't), *lv. to appeal denied,* 7 N.Y.3d 709 (2006); *Martinez v. City of N.Y.*, 90 A.D.3d 718 (2d Dep't 2011), *lv. to appeal denied.* 19 N.Y.3d 802 (2012)). This includes injuries sustained by students attending a program provided by a board of cooperative services (BOCES) pursuant to a contract between a school district and a BOCES (*Ferraro v. North Babylon UFSD*, 69 A.D.3d 559 (2d Dep't 2010)).

66:17. Can a school district be held liable for negligently failing to protect students from criminal acts committed by third parties?

Yes, when the crime is a "reasonably foreseeable" consequence of circumstances created by the school district, and the school had sufficiently specific knowledge or notice of the dangerous condition which caused the injury. That was the case where a school district failed to protect two students notwithstanding the district's knowledge of threats against them and the potential for harm (*Mirand v. City of N.Y.*, 84 N.Y.2d 44 (1994); see also *LaValley v. Northeastern Clinton CSD*, 130 A.D.3d 1276 (3d Dep't 2015); *Mathis v. Bd. of Educ. of City of N.Y.*, 126 A.D.3d 951 (2d Dep't 2015); *Hofmann v. Coxsackie-Athens CSD*, 70 A.D.3d 1116 (3d Dep't 2010); *Walley v. Bivins & Onondaga CSD*, 81 A.D.3d 1286 (4th Dep't 2011); compare *Brandy B. v. Eden CSD*, 15 N.Y.3d 297 (2010); *Moffatt v. North Colonie CSD*, 82 A.D.3d 1311 (3d Dep't 2011)). But not where a school failed to notify the parent of the victim of an assault by another student off school grounds of a prior fight between them at school, because the district had suspended both students for their prior fight. In addition, the victim's mother was unable to prove that with notice of the prior fight, she could have prevented the second assault (*Stephenson v. City of N.Y.*, 85 A.D.3d 523 (1st Dep't 2011), *aff'd* 19 N.Y.3d 1031 (2012)). Similarly, a state appellate court dismissed a case against a district that took pro-active steps such as mediation and counseling to avoid a rumored fight between two students given the subsequent fight was not foreseeable based on the students' disciplinary histories (*Conklin v. Saugerties,* 106 A.D.3d 1424 (3d Dep't 2013)).

Another district was found liable for the sexual assault of a kindergartner by an older student in the school bathroom when the kindergartner was allowed by his teacher to go to the bathroom unaccompanied despite two memoranda instructing staff to the contrary (*Garcia v. City of N.Y.*, 222 A.D.2d 192 (1st Dep't 1996), *lv. to appeal denied*, 89 N.Y.2d 808 (1997); see also *Shante D. by Ada D. v. City of N.Y.,* 190 A.D.2d 356 (1st Dep't 1993), *aff'd*, 83 N.Y.2d 948 (1994); compare *Geywits ex rel Geywits v. Carlotte Valley CSD*, 98 A.D.3d 804 (3d Dep't 2012)). Similarly, a case of alleged sexual abuse by a sixth grader of a kindergartener was allowed to proceed where the abuse was alleged to have occurred over several weeks on both the school bus and in a school bathroom and reports of suspicious activities were made by both a teacher aide and the bus driver (*Doe v. Bd. of Educ. of Morris Cent. Sch.*, 9 A.D.3d 588 (3d Dep't 2004)).

In still another case, the New York Court of Appeals upheld a jury verdict based on negligent supervision against a school district for injuries sustained by a student who was raped off school premises while on a school field trip *(Bell v. Bd. of Educ. of City of N.Y.*, 90 N.Y.2d 944 (1997)). By comparison, a district was not deemed liable for the sexual assault of a female student by two male students on school grounds during the school day because the male students' actions were so "extraordinary and intervening" that they were not "foreseeable" by the district (*Schrader v. Bd. of Educ. of Taconic Hills CSD*, 249 A.D.2d 741 (3d Dep't), *appeal denied*, 92 N.Y.2d 806 (1998); see also *Marshall v. Cortland Enlarged City Sch. Dist.*, 265 A.D.2d 782 (3d Dep't 1999)). Likewise, another district was deemed not liable for the alleged sexual abuse on a school bus of a kindergartener by a fifth grade student with prior history of severe behavioral issues because the behaviors had not manifested for more than two years, the student's behavior had improved, there was no history of sexual aggression and the victim's mother, who had requested the victim not be seated with the alleged abuser, failed to identify the abuser by name (*Brandy B. v. Eden CSD*).

66:18. Can a school district be held liable in negligence for criminal acts against students by district employees?

Yes. A school district has a duty to supervise its employees to the extent that those employees may potentially harm students, as when the school district has knowledge or notice of an employee's propensity or likelihood to engage in conduct harmful to students, such that the employee's actions could have been anticipated or were foreseeable (*Doe v. N.Y. City Dept. of Educ.,* 126 A.D.3d 612 (1st Dep't 2015); *Kelly G. v. Bd. of Educ. of the City of Yonkers,* 99 A.D.3d 756 (2d Dep't 2012); *Bliss v. Putnam Valley CSD*, 2011 U.S. Dist. LEXIS 35485 (S.D.N.Y. Mar. 24, 2011); *Tesoriero v. Syosset CSD*, 382 F. Supp.2d 387 (E.D.N.Y. 2005); *Doe v. Whitney*, 8 A.D.3d 610 (2d Dep't 2004); *Dia CC. v. Ithaca City Sch. Dist.*, 304 A.D.2d 955 (3d Dep't), *appeal denied,* 100 N.Y.2d 506 (2003)).

According to one federal district court in New York, to the extent that teachers may potentially abuse students, districts have a duty to supervise teachers and exercise such care for students as a parent of ordinary prudence would in comparable circumstances (*Bliss v. Putnam Valley CSD*). Similarly, a state appellate court refused to dismiss a case against a school where the student claimed she was sexually abused over a period of several years by her first grade teacher. The teacher had continually removed the child from her second and third grade classrooms without explanation and kept the child with him during recess. The court held a reasonable fact finder could conclude the continual removal of a student from classes and recess without explanation constituted a breach of duty of a parent of ordinary prudence (*Doe v. Whitney*). The same appellate court also refused to dismiss a case against a school district where a teacher found guilty, pursuant to a § 3020-a hearing, of sexual misconduct relating to students was subsequently accused of similar behavior. The court reasoned that a triable issue of fact was raised as to whether the teacher's propensity to engage in such misconduct was known or should have been known by the district (*Kelly G. v. Bd. of Educ. of the City of Yonkers*).

While school districts may be liable in negligence for employee criminal acts against students, they cannot be held "vicariously liable" for intentional acts, such as the sexual assault of a student, not within their scope of employment (see *Kelly G. v. Bd. of Educ. of the City of Yonkers; Dia CC. v. Ithaca City Sch. Dist.,; Doe v. N.Y. City Dept. of Educ.*).

66:19. Can a school district be held liable in negligence if one of its teachers sexually molests students off school grounds, at a nonschool event?

Each case will depend upon its own facts. But in one notable case, a New York State appellate court dismissed a lawsuit against a school district that claimed district officials negligently hired and supervised a teacher who allegedly sexually molested two students at their home after being invited to a holiday party at the students' home by their parents. According to the court, any connection between the teacher's employment with the district and his alleged sexual molestation of the students at their home "was severed by time, distance, and the intervening independent acts of their parents" (*Anonymous v. Dobbs Ferry UFSD*, 290 A.D.2d 464 (2d Dep't), *lv. to appeal denied,* 98 N.Y.2d 616 (2002); see also *Doe v. N.Y. City Dept. of Educ.*. 126 A.D.3d 612 (1st Dep't 2015); *Doe 1 v. Bd. of Educ. of Greenport UFSD,* 100 A.D.3d 703 (2d Dep't 2012); *K.I. v. N.Y. City Bd. of Educ.*, 256 A.D.2d 189 (1st Dep't 1998)).

66:20. Can a school district be held liable in negligence for educational malpractice?

No. The New York Court of Appeals has held that actions for educational malpractice are barred by public policy considerations because the courts will not second-guess the professional judgments of school officials and educators in selecting and implementing educational programs and evaluating students (*Torres v. Little Flower Children's Servs.*, 64 N.Y.2d 119 (1984), *cert. denied*, 474 U.S. 864 (1985); *Hoffman v. Bd. of Educ. of the City of N.Y.*, 49 N.Y.2d 121 (1979); *Donohue v. Copiague UFSD*, 47 N.Y.2d 440 (1979)).

For example, where a high school graduate, who could not read or write sufficiently to complete a job application, sued the district for its failure to provide him with adequate teachers, administrators, and psychologists in order to evaluate his progress, the Court of Appeals explained it is not for the courts to make a judgment on the validity of school board policies or to review day-to-day implementation of these policies (*Donahue v. Copiague UFSD*; see also *McGovern v. Nassau Cnty. Dep't of Soc. Servs.*, 60 A.D.3d 1016 (2d Dep't 2009)).

On the other hand, where a principal willfully and intentionally falsified test scores as a result of which a student was denied remedial and special education, a state appellate court dismissed the educational malpractice claim against the school district, but gave permission to the student's parent to proceed against the principal on the basis of intentional wrongdoing, as well as against the school district, under the doctrine of respondent superior, in the event the principal's actions were reasonably foreseeable (*Helbig v. City of N.Y.*, 212 A.D.2d 506 (2d Dep't 1995)).

66:21. Can a school district be held liable for negligence in its hiring or retention of staff?

Yes, if it fails to follow its own established procedures for making employment decisions, such as those which might require investigating the criminal history of new employees (*Haddock v. New York*, 75 N.Y.2d 478 (1990)). However, where there is no violation of internal procedures and policies, a school district enjoys immunity with respect to the exercise of discretion in deciding whether to hire a particular employee (*Mon v. New York*, 78 N.Y.2d 309 (1991)).

A school district also may be held liable for negligent hiring and supervision if it knew of an employee's propensity to engage in injurious conduct, or should have known of such propensity had it conducted an adequate hiring procedure (*Ernest L. v. Charlton Sch.*, 30 A.D.3d 649 (3d Dep't 2006)).

Regarding negligent retention, one court refused to dismiss such a case against a school district where, prior to a bus driver's alleged sexual assault of two students during a field trip, the parent had complained to the transportation supervisor that the driver had previously lowered his pants and exposed his adult diaper to students on the bus, and the district failed to conduct an investigation (*Doe v. Chenango Valley CSD*, 92 A.D.3d 1016 (3d Dep't 2012)).

66:22. Can a school district that provides a false or misleading recommendation about a former employee be held liable in negligence if the employee injures students in another district?

No. In one case, a school district recommended a former employee to another public school district for a position as a grammar school teacher, without disclosing that the teacher had been charged with sexual misconduct. Years later, the teacher injured a student and the student sued the district that recommended the teacher, claiming it was negligent in its failure to warn the new district of the teacher's past history. Dismissing the case, a state appellate court explained that there is no general duty "to control the conduct of another or to warn those endangered by such conduct, in the absence of a special relationship between either the person who threatens harmful conduct or the foreseeable victim. . . . The mere recommendation of a person for potential employment is not a proper basis for asserting a claim of negligence where another party is responsible for the actual hiring. . . . Nor are there sound policy reasons warranting the expansion of the common-law duty of the schools since the plaintiffs have an adequate remedy at law as against the school district which had custody of the infant at the time of the injury and also against the wrongdoer." (*Cohen v. Wales*, 133 A.D.2d 94 (2d Dep't), *appeal denied*, 70 N.Y.2d 612 (1987); see also *K.I. v. N.Y. City Bd. of Educ.*, 256 A.D.2d 189 (1st Dep't 1998)).

66:23. Can school districts be held liable for negligently failing to protect teachers from students or other third parties?

Not generally. The courts have not found school districts liable for injury to teachers who are assaulted by students at school, ruling that districts do not owe a duty to teachers to protect them from harm by third parties (*Brumer v. City of N.Y.*, 132 A.D.3d 795 (2d Dep't 2015); *Guerrieri v. N.Y. City Dep't/Bd. of Educ.*, 132 A.D.3d 949 (2d Dep't 2015); *Zimmerman v. City of N.Y.*, 74 A.D.3d 439 (1st Dep't 2010); *lv. to appeal denied*, 16 N.Y.3d 707 (2011); *Krakower v. City of N.Y.*, 217 A.D.2d 441 (1st Dep't), *appeal denied*, 87 N.Y.2d 804 (1995)). Furthermore, a district does not assume such a duty merely because it implements security measures (*Bonner v. City of N.Y.*, 73 N.Y.2d 930 (1989); *Bain v. N.Y. City Bd. of Educ.*, 268 A.D.2d 451 (2d Dep't 2000); *Johnson v. N.Y. City Bd. of Educ.*, 270 A.D.2d 310 (2d Dep't 2000)).

However, a district may be held liable for injuries to a teacher by a student, if the district has entered into a "special relationship" with the teacher through, for example, affirmative promises to act on behalf of the teacher, knowledge that inaction could lead to harm, and justifiable reliance by the teacher on the district's promises (see *Pascuccui v. Bd. of Educ. of the City of N.Y.*, 305 A.D.2d 103 (1st Dep't 2003)).

A special relationship was not established, for instance, where a teacher was told "things were being worked on" and urged to "hang in there because something was being done" after she expressed concerns to her supervisor about her safety in the classroom because of a student's ongoing aggressive behavior. When subsequently she was injured trying to restrain the student from attacking another, she argued that her supervisor's assurances evidenced the school board's assumption of an affirmative duty to remove the student and that she justifiably relied on those assurances. New York's Court of Appeals disagreed explaining that assurances giving rise to a special relationship must be definitive enough to generate justifiable reliance. The assurances given to the teacher were vaguely worded and did not constitute action that would lull someone into a false sense of security or generate justifiable reliance (*Dinardo v. City of N.Y.*, 13 N.Y.3d 872 (2009); see also *Rivera v. Bd. of Educ. of the City of N.Y.*, 82 A.D.3d 614 (1st Dep't 2011)). That also was not the case when a parent followed and attacked a teacher in a stairwell, after a school safety agent who witnessed the initial confrontation and separated the teacher and the parent advised the teacher to walk away. There was no evidence that the teacher relied on the safety agent for protection, or that the agent was aware the parent posed a threat of violence (*France v. N.Y. City Bd. of Educ.*, 40 A.D.3d 268 (1st Dep't 2007); see also *Zimmerman v. City of N.Y.*).

Additionally, a school district's continued failure to exercise disciplinary authority over student harassment of teachers might serve as the basis for liability in a civil rights lawsuit alleging the existence of a hostile work environment (*Peries v. N.Y. City Bd. of Educ.*, 2001 U.S. Dist. LEXIS 23393 (E.D.N.Y. Aug. 6, 2001)).

66:24. Can a school district be held liable for the negligence of its independent contractors?

It depends. The general rule is that employers are not liable for the negligence of independent contractors because they have no control over how independent contractors perform their work. Instead, independent contractors are liable for their own improper actions. Accordingly, a school district was not liable when a bus driver employed by a bus company the district contracted with for the transportation of students drove over a student after dropping her off at her bus stop (*Chainani v. Bd. of Educ. of the City of N.Y.*, 87 N.Y.2d 370 (1995); see also *Merges v. Aramark Corp.*, 2012 U.S. Dist. LEXIS 46261 (W.D.N.Y. Mar. 30, 2012)). Similarly, a school district that placed a student with a disability in a private school in New Jersey through an individualized education program was not liable for any alleged negligence that occurred at the private school causing the student's death. According to the court, the district could not be an insurer against acts of negligence conducted by private school employees over whom the district had no control (*Begley v. City of N.Y.*, 111 A.D.3d 5 (2d Dep't 2013)).

There are exceptions, however, such as when an employer owes a non-delegable duty to the individual harmed by an independent contractor, or when such individual would be left without a remedy if the general rule was applied strictly (*Feliberty v. Damon*, 72 N.Y.2d 112 (1988); *Prosser & Keaton on the Law of Torts* § 71 (5th ed. 1984)). Thus, a state appellate court refused to dismiss a lawsuit against a school district that failed to comply with a contractual provision in its agreement with a bus company that required the presence of an aide on the bus. As a result, a student was repeatedly sexually abused while on the school bus by another student with a documented history of aggressive sexual behavior. In the court's view, the general rule exempting employers from liability for the negligence of independent contractors does not apply where students are released to an independent contractor into circumstances that pose a foreseeable risk of harm without the taking of steps to minimize the risk (*David "XX" v. St. Catherine's Ctr. for Children*, 267 A.D.2d 813 (3d Dep't 1999)).

Distinct from negligence, a school district will not be held liable for the intentional torts of an employee of an independent contractor (see *Doe v. Rohan*, 17 A.D.3d 509 (2d Dep't), *lv. to appeal denied*, 6 N.Y.3d 701 (2005)).

66:25. On what basis can a school district be found negligent when there is an accident involving children on their way to and from school?

As a general rule, school districts have no legal responsibility for children before they arrive on school grounds at the start of the school day and after they leave school grounds at the end of the school day (*Chainani v. Bd. of Educ. of the City of N.Y.*, 87 N.Y.2d 370 (1995)). Therefore, districts cannot be found negligent for any injuries sustained by students on their way to and from school when they have no physical custody or control over the students (*Pratt v. Robinson*, 39 N.Y.2d 554 (1976); *Chainani v. Bd. of Educ. of the City of N.Y.*; *Williams v. Weatherstone,* 2014 N.Y. LEXIS 1048 (2014); *Williams v. Gonzalez,* 113 A.D.3d 757 (2d Dep't 2014); *Molina v. Conklin*, 57 A.D.3d 860 (2d Dep't 2008)).

That would not be the case when a district releases students into a foreseeable hazardous situation the district itself played a role in creating. This happened where a district deviated from its normal practice of not releasing students who walk home from school until after all the school buses were gone. As a result, one of those students was hit by a pickup truck when crossing the road in front of the school while school buses were still departing. The pickup driver's view was obstructed by a moving school bus (*Ernest v. Red Creek CSD*, 93 N.Y.2d 664 (1999)).

Likewise, school districts that transport students to and from school may be liable for their own negligence in failing to provide a "reasonably safe mode of conveyance" (*Williams v. Bd. of Trustee Dist. No. 1, Town of Eaton*, 210 A.D. 161 (4th Dep't 1924); see also *Blair v. Bd. of Educ. of Sherburne-Earlville CSD*, 86 A.D.2d 933 (3d Dep't 1982)). That is the case even though, generally, districts would not be liable for the negligence of a bus company hired as an independent contractor to provide student transportation services, or for the negligence of that company's employees (*Chainani v. Bd. of Educ. of the City of N.Y.*; but see *David "XX" v. St. Catherine's Ctr. for Children*, 267 A.D.2d 813 (3d Dept 1999)).

The legal responsibilities of a district that transports students to and from school begin when a child is picked up and ends when he or she has been properly discharged from the bus (see *Pratt v. Robinson*; *Hanley v. East Moriches UFSD II*, 275 A.D.2d 389 (2d Dep't 2000); *Fornaro v. Kerry*, 139 A.D.2d 561 (2d Dep't 1988); Veh. & Traf. Law § 1174(b); 8 NYCRR § 156.3(d)). In this regard, it has been ruled that a school district is not liable for injuries sustained by a student who leaves the custody of the district by exiting from a school bus prior to reaching school, or getting off before his or her regular bus stop at the end of the school day even if that student's conduct violates school policy (*Bushnell v. Berne-Knox-Westerlo Sch. Dist.*, 125 A.D.2d 859 (3d Dep't 1986), *appeal denied*, 69 N.Y.2d 609 (1987); *Hurlburt v. Noxon*, 149 Misc.2d 374 (Sup. Ct. Chenango Cnty. 1990)). Neither was a district liable when a student was injured attempting to cross the road after a bus driver unintentionally drove past her and turned around but planned to turn again to pick her up on her side of the street (*Williams v. Weatherstone*).

66:26. Can a school district be found negligent when a student gets injured after failing to get on a school bus?

It depends. There is no general duty to assure that students get on the school bus. Therefore, a school district would generally not be found negligent where a student, who fails to get on the school bus, gets injured (see *Wenger v. Goodell*, 288 A.D.2d 815 (3d Dep't 2001), *lv. to appeal denied,* 98 N.Y.2d 605 (2002); *Pistolese v. William Floyd CSD*, 69 A.D.3d 825 (2d Dep't 2010); *Briggs v. Rhinebeck CSD*, 2 A.D.3d 383 (2d Dep't 2003), *lv. to appeal denied*, 2 N.Y.3d 706 (2004)).

However, a district that promises to ensure a child gets on a school bus would be liable in negligence for injuries a child sustains as a result of its failure to keep the promise. That would be so because the district would be deemed to have assumed a special duty to protect the student through the making of the promise (see *Wenger v. Goodell*).

In addition, a district could be subject to liability if a student gets injured after leaving school in the car of a fellow student with a valid driver's license, if it was foreseeable that allowing the student to do so would have resulted in the student being injured in a collision accident (see *Briggs v. Rhinebeck CSD*; *Davis v. Marzo*, 55 A.D.3d 1404 (4th Dep't 2008)).

66:27. On what basis can school districts be found negligent when there is an accident involving students who leave school grounds without permission?

Generally, school districts have no duty to supervise a student who leaves school grounds without permission, although the courts will examine all the circumstances, such as the student's age and whether school authorities provided or should have provided supervision.

For example, a court refused to find a school district negligent where a 14-year-old student was involved in a car accident at 5:00 p.m. the same day he had left school without permission. The court rejected the parents' argument that the district had breached its duty of supervision, finding that "once a student is beyond its lawful control, the school district owes no legal duty to supervise the activities of a student." In addition, the court refused to rule that a school district must impose security measures to prevent students from leaving the premises (*Palella v. Ulmer*, 136 Misc.2d 34 (Sup. Ct. Rensselaer Cnty. 1987), *rev'd on other grounds*, *Palella v. State*, 141 A.D.2d 999 (3d Dep't 1988)).

Neither was a school district liable for the death of a 13-year-old student who left school without being signed out. There was no basis for school officials to reasonably foresee she would leave school and commit suicide. Under such circumstances, a school district is not responsible for the protection of students who remove themselves from school grounds (*Chalen v. Glen Cove Sch. Dist.*, 29 A.D.3d 508 (2d Dep't 2006), *lv. to appeal denied,* 7 N.Y.3d 709 (2006)).

In another case, a state appellate court found a school district was not negligent for injuries to third parties caused by a 10th-grade student who drove his own car from his home district to a BOCES in violation of school policy, which required that he take the school bus. The court refused to find that the school district assumed a legal duty to prevent injury to the public by the mere adoption of its no-driving policy (*Thompson v. Ange*, 83 A.D.2d 193 (4th Dep't 1981); see also *Davis v. Marzo*, 55 A.D.3d 1404 (4th Dep't 2008), where that same court found a district was not negligent in a case where senior students died in a car accident on the way back to school from their lunch break under a school program that allowed eligible seniors to leave the school campus during their lunch period).

66:28. On what basis can school districts be found negligent when student participants in school-sponsored athletic events are injured?

School districts must exercise "reasonable care" to protect student athletes from injuries that may result from unassumed, concealed or unreasonably increased risks (see *Benitez v. N.Y. City Bd. of Educ.*, 73 N.Y.2d 650 (1989); *Reed v. Pawling*, 245 A.D.2d 281 (2d Dep't), *lv. to appeal denied*, 91 N.Y.2d 809 (1997)). However, they are not liable for the assumed risks of competition, including "injury and fatigue. . . inherent in team competitive sports" particularly when students are properly equipped, well trained, and play voluntarily (*Benitez v. N.Y. City Bd. of Educ.*).

The *assumption of risk* defense is available to shield districts from liability only with respect to voluntary athletic activities (*Trupia v. Lake George CSD*, 14 N.Y.3d 392 (2010)), including elective sport classes (*Navarro v. City of N.Y.*, 87 A.D.3d 877 (1st Dep't 2011) and voluntary sporting activities during recess when the risk of injury is inherent in the activity (*Altagracia v. Harrison CSD*, 136 A.D.3d 848 (2d Dep't 2016)). It is not an available defense when students are injured while participating in compulsory physical education class activities (*Stoughtenger v. Hannibal CSD*, 90 A.D.3d 1696 (4th Dep't 2011); see also *Mills v. Dep't of Educ. of the City of N.Y.,* 109 A.D.3d 643 (2d Dep't 2013)).

66:29. What are some examples of cases where a student has been deemed to assume the risk of injury for participation in school sponsored athletic events?

Cases in which students have been deemed to have reasonably assumed the risk of injury, and a district found not negligent, have involved:

- An experienced lacrosse player injured executing a body check he executed using "excellent technique" approximately 20 to 30 times a game (*Ciccone v. Bedford CSD*, 21 A.D.3d 437 (2d Dep't), *lv. to appeal denied,* 6 N.Y.3d 702 (2005)).
- A varsity wrestler who was struck in the jaw by an opponent in a weight classification one category higher (*Edelson v. Uniondale UFSD*, 219 A.D.2d 614 (2d Dep't 1995)).
- An experienced football player who was injured during a tackling drill (*Hagon v. Northport-East Northport UFSD No. 4*, 273 A.D.2d 441 (2d Dep't 2000)).
- A wrestler's contracting herpes simplex I during a match, when the district specifically warned students of the risk of contracting this and other diseases through skin-to-skin contact (*Farrell v. Hochhauser*, 65 A.D.3d 663 (2d Dep't 2009)).
- An experienced high school cheerleader injured while performing a straddling jump during practice (*Weber v. William Floyd Sch. Dist.*, 272 A.D.2d 396 (2d Dep't 2000)), and while practicing on a hardwood gym floor (*Williams v. Clinton CSD*, 59 A.D.3d 938 (4th Dep't 2009); see also *Stach v. Warwick Valley CSD,* 106 A.D.3d 720 (2d Dep't 2013); *Lomonico v. Massapequa Pub. Schs*., 84 A.D.3d 1033 (2d Dep't 2011)).
- A cheerleader injured while practicing stunts with an injured teammate who the cheerleader knew was not cleared to practice (*Jurgensen v. Webster CSD*, 126 A.D.3d 1423 (4th Dep't 2015)).
- A hockey player injured by a teammate's skate after practice, while walking barefoot in the locker room toward the shower area (*Litz v. Clinton CSD*, 126 A.D.3d 1306 (4th Dep't 2015)).

66:30. What are some examples of cases where a district was found liable because a student did not assume a risk of injury?

Cases in which students have not been deemed to have reasonably assumed the risk of injury, and a district found negligent, have involved:

- An inexperienced student pole-vaulter who injured his knee when he landed on a concealed seam in the mat, and the pole had been placed six inches higher than he ever had cleared (*Laboy v. Wallkill CSD*, 201 A.D.2d 780 (3d Dep't 1994)).
- A softball player injured by a hidden spike in the base path of a softball field (*Simmons v. Smithtown CSD*, 272 A.D.2d 391 (2d Dep't 2000); see also *Simmons v. Saugerties CSD*, 82 A.D.3d 1407 (3d Dep't 2011)).
- A high school wrestler who was paired during practice with a teammate who weighed 30–35 pounds more, where the coach testified he was unsure if such weight difference was safe and State safety guidelines advised against such mismatches in weight (*DeLucas v. City of Lockport Sch. Dist.*, 26 Misc.3d 1227(A) (Sup. Ct. Niagara Cnty. 2009), *aff'd,* 70 A.D.3d 1382 (4th Dep't 2010)).
- A junior varsity football player injured before practice when catapulted by a teammate using a blocking sled (*Duffy v. Long Beach City Sch. Dist.*, 134 A.D.3d 761 (2d Dep't 2015)).

In addition, courts have refused to dismiss lawsuits against school districts by students who were injured during an athletic activity where the district may have failed to provide adequate supervision for the activity, or take reasonable steps to ensure that the equipment used by the student did not unreasonably increase the risk of injury (*Phillipou v. Baldwin UFSD,* 105 A.D.3d 928 (2d Dep't 2013); *Weinberger v. Solomon Schechter Sch. of Westchester,* 102 A.D.3d 675 (2d Dep't 2013); *Robinson v. N.Y. City Dep't of Educ*., 94 A.D.3d 428 (1st Dep't 2012); *McGrath v. Shenendehowa CSD*, 76 A.D.3d 755 (3d Dep't 2010); *Fithian v. Sag Harbor UFSD*, 54 A.D.3d 719 (2d Dep't 2008); *Kane v. North Colonie CSD*, 273 A.D.2d 526 (3d Dep't 2000)). Similary, the assumption of the risk defense is not available when the injury results from the reckless or intentional conduct of others (see *Dimisa v. Oceanside UFSD*, 140 A.D.3d 692 (2d Dep't 2016)).

66:31. On what basis can school districts be found negligent when nonstudent participants at school-sponsored events are injured?

Assumption of risk principles applicable to student athletes (see **66:28**) apply also to non-student participants in school-sponsored athletic events. For example, in *Arbegast v. Bd. of Educ. of S. New Berlin Cent. Sch.*, 65 N.Y.2d 161 (1985), a student teacher was injured when the donkey she was riding in a donkey basketball game put its head down and she fell off. The participants had been told they might fall off and that they were participating at their own risk. The court held that the teacher had assumed the risk and found the school district not liable.

66:32. Are school districts liable for spectator injuries at school-sponsored events?

Generally, spectators are deemed to have assumed the normal risks associated with attendance at a game. For instance, in *Akins v. Glens Falls City Sch. Dist.*, 53 N.Y.2d 325, *rehearing denied,* 54 N.Y.2d 831 (1981), a spectator sitting and watching a school's baseball game was injured. The court held the district was not liable, explaining that the owner of a baseball field is only required to exercise reasonable care and need only provide screening for the area of the field behind home plate, where the danger of getting hit by a ball is the greatest (see also *Streichler v. Plainview/Old Bethpage CSD*, 82 A.D.3d 1082 (2d Dep't 2011)). In another case, a school district was not liable for injuries that resulted from a fight which took place after a football game. Even though the district supplied security at the school, it did not give rise to a special duty of protection (*Jerideau v. Huntington UFSD*, 21 A.D.3d 992 (2d Dep't 2005)).

66:33. Can a school district be held liable for injuries occurring during the use of school facilities by an outside organization?

Yes, if it has been found that the school district was negligent in some manner. A school district was not liable for injuries a basketball referee sustained when a student punched him in the eye because the basketball tournament was run solely by an outside organization and the attacker was not there representing the district (*Curcio v. Watervliet City Sch. Dist.*, 21 A.D.3d 666 (3d Dep't), *lv. to appeal denied,* 5 N.Y.3d 715 (2005)). In comparison, a court refused to dismiss a case against a school district where a student was injured at a parent teacher association sponsored family fun night because questions existed as to whether the district had sufficient control over the event so that it could have taken steps to prevent the accident that caused injury (*Butler v. Germantown CSD Parent Teacher Student Ass'n,* 101 A.D.3d 1415 (3d Dep't 2012)).

The requirement of some school boards that outside organizations carry liability insurance when they use school property may relieve the school district from liability in the event of an accident to either a participant or a spectator (see *Ambrosio v. Newburgh Enlarged City Sch. Dist.*, 5 A.D.3d 410 (2d Dep't 2004)). In the alternative, the district's own liability insurance policy may cover this type of situation.

Civil Rights Liability

66:34. What is Section 1983 liability and how do school districts become exposed to it?

Section 1983 liability, also referred to as federal civil rights liability, arises under section 1983 of the Civil Rights Act of 1876 which provides a mechanism for addressing violations of federal constitutional and statutory rights (42 USC § 1983; see also *D.D. v. N.Y. City Bd. of Educ.*, 465 F.3d 503 (2d Cir. 2006); *Bracey v. Bd. of Educ. of City of Bridgeport*, 368 F.3d 108 (2d Cir. 2004); *Sykes v. James*, 13 F.3d 515 (2d Cir.), *cert. denied,* 512 U.S. 1240 (1993)).

Liability can attach to a school district itself or to school officials who:

- "acting under color of state law" (be it pursuant to a statute, regulation, custom, policy or practice),
- deprive a person of his or her federal constitutional and/or statutory rights, (42 USC § 1983; *Monnell v. Dep't of Soc. Servs.*, 436 U.S. 658 (1978); *Roe v. City of Waterbury*, 542 F.3d 31 (2d Cir. 2008)).

To act "under color of state law" means to "exercis[e] power 'possessed by virtue of state law... made possible only because [one] is clothed with the authority of state law'" (*Polk Cnty. v. Dodson*, 454 U.S. 312 (1981); see *Back v. Hastings on Hudson UFSD*, 365 F.3d 107 (2d Cir. 2004)).

"Policy" includes policies and decisions officially adopted and promulgated by the school board; regulations and decisions adopted and promulgated by school officials to whom the board has delegated final policy-making authority in the particular area in question; and widespread practices of officials and employees which, although not authorized by adopted policy, are so common and well settled as to constitute a custom that fairly represents district policy (*City of St. Louis v. Praprotnik*, 485 U.S. 112 (1988)).

Under certain circumstances, the existence of a policy can be established by the failure to properly train or supervise employees or the failure to discipline employees whose actions violate an individual's federally protected rights (*Oliveras v. Saranac Lake CSD,* 2014 U.S. Dist. LEXIS 44603 (N.D.N.Y. 2014); *Biswas v. City of N.Y.* 973 F.Supp.2d 504 (S.D.N.Y. 2013); *Delrosario v. City of N.Y.*, 2010 U.S. Dist. LEXIS 20923 (S.D.N.Y. Mar. 4, 2010)).

66:35. Are all federal statutory rights enforceable through a section 1983 lawsuit?

No. Some statutes have enforcement mechanisms that do not allow for the use of section 1983 to address alleged violations of their provisions. The reasons vary including, for example, whether a statute provides for private lawsuits to enforce its provisions, or whether a statute provides its own exclusive enforcement mechanism. Accordingly, courts have determined that section 1983 may not be used to enforce:

- Federal regulations implementing Title VI of the Civil Rights Act of 1964 prohibiting "disparate impact" discrimination because Congress did not intend to authorize private enforcement of those regulations (*Alexander v. Sandoval*, 532 U.S. 275 (2001)).
- The Family Education Rights and Privacy Act because the statute does not authorize private lawsuits for violations of its provisions (*Gonzaga v. Doe*, 536 U.S. 273 (2002); *Simpson v. Uniondale UFSD*, 702 F. Supp.2d 122 (E.D.N.Y. 2010)).
- The Uniformed Services Employment and Re-Employment Rights Act because it has an exclusive remedy scheme that bars enforcement through a § 1983 lawsuit (*Morris-Hayes v. Bd. of Educ. of the Chester UFSD*, 423 F.3d 153 (2d Cir. 2005)).
- Section 722 the Rehabilitation Act of 1973 (vocational rehabilitation services), because it provides a comprehensive scheme to challenge benefit determinations (*Wasser v. N.Y. State Office of Voc. & Educ. Servs. for Individuals with Disabilities*, 683 F. Supp.2d 201 (E.D.N.Y. 2008), *aff'd*, 602 F.3d 476 (2d Cir. 2010) and 373 Fed. Appx. 120 (2d Cir. 2010)).

66:36. On what basis may a school district itself be held liable in a section 1983 lawsuit?

For a school district to be held liable under Section 1983, it must be shown that one or more of its policies and/or customs caused the deprivation of a federal constitutional or statutory right (*Monell v. Dep't of Soc. Servs.*, 436 U.S. 658 (1978); see also *Connick v. Thompson,* 131 S. Ct. 1350 (2011); *Back v.*

Hastings-on-Hudson UFSD, 365 F.3d 107 (2d Cir. 2004); *DeFabio v. E. Hampton UFSD*, 658 F. Supp.2d 461 (E.D.N.Y. 2009), *aff'd*, 623 F.3d 71 (2d Cir. 2010), *cert. denied*, 131 S. Ct. 1578 (2011); *Geras v. Hempstead UFSD*, 149 F. Supp. 3d 300 (E.D.N.Y. 2015). A school district cannot be liable under section 1983 solely on a theory of *respondeat superior,* which holds an employer responsible for employee wrongdoings (*Monell v. Dep't of Soc. Servs.*; *Roe v. City of Waterbury*, 542 F.3d 31 (2d Cir. 2008); see also *Burns v. City of Utica,* 2014 LEXIS 21029 (N.D.N.Y. 2014); *Gerardi v. Huntington UFSD*, 124 F. Supp.3d 206 (E.D.N.Y. 2015); *T.E. v. Pine Bush CSD*, 58 F. Supp.3d 332 (S.D.N.Y. 2014); *K.D. ex rel Duncan v. White Plains Sch. Dist.*, 921 F. Supp.2d 197 (S.D.N.Y. 2013); *Dzugas-Smith v. Southold UFSD*, 2012 U.S. Dist. LEXIS 70773 (E.D.N.Y. May 9, 2012)).

66:37. On what basis can the existence of a policy or custom that might expose a school district to section 1983 liability be established?

Such policy or custom can be proven in one of two ways. First, if the school official(s) who allegedly deprived a plaintiff of a federal constitutional or statutory right acted pursuant to an official district policy or longstanding practice or custom (*Monell v. Dep't of Soc. Servs.; Jeffes v. Barnes*, 208 F.3d 49 (2d Cir. 2000); see *Hurdle v. Bd. of Educ. of the City of N.Y.*, 113 Fed.Appx. 423 (2d Cir. 2004); *Gerardi v. Huntington UFSD; Shapiro v. NYC Dep't of Educ.*, 561 F. Supp.2d 413 (S.D.N.Y. 2008)). Second, if the conduct underlying the alleged unlawful deprivation was undertaken or caused by an official whose actions represent official policy (see *Jett v. Dallas Indep. Sch. Dist.*, 491 U.S. 701 (1989); see also *Jeffes v. Barnes; Shapiro v. N.Y. City Dep't of Educ.*; *Eldridge v. Rochester City Sch. Dist.*, 968 F. Supp.2d 546 (W.D.N.Y. 2013); *Lopez v. Bay Shore UFSD*, 668 F. Supp. 2d 406 (E.D.N.Y. 2009)). It is not enough that the official has been granted discretion in the performance of his or her official duties. The official has to have had "final policymaking authority" in the particular area, or on the particular issue involved in order for the school district to be held liable (*City of St. Louis v. Praprotnik*, 485 U.S. 112 (1988); see also *Nagle v. Marron*, 663 F.3d 100 (2d Cir. 2011); *Jeffes v. Barnes; Roe v. City of Waterbury*; *Hurdle v. Bd. of Educ. of the City of N.Y.*)).

66:38. On what basis may school officials be held liable in an individual capacity in a section 1983 lawsuit?

School officials, including school board members and district employees, may be held liable as individuals under section 1983 if they act under color of state law and their actions cause the deprivation of a federal constitutional or statutory right (see *Monroe v. Pape*, 365 U.S. 167 (1961); see also *Lilly v. Lewiston-Porter CSD*, 853 F. Supp.2d 346 (W.D.N.Y. 2011); *Burgess v. Fairport CSD*, 2008 U.S. Dist. LEXIS 48142 (W.D.N.Y. June 20, 2008), *aff'd,* 371 Fed.Appx. 140 (2d Cir. 2010); *Ragin v. Newburgh Enlarged City Sch. Dist.*, 2009 U.S. Dist. LEXIS 118704 (S.D.N.Y. Dec. 17, 2009)).

Governmental officials will not be liable for damages under section 1983 solely because they hold a high position of authority. They have to have been personally involved in the alleged deprivation (*Ashcroft v. Iqbal*, 556 U.S. 662 (2009); *Black v. Coughlin*, 76 F.3d 72 (2d Cir. 1996); see also *Rosenberg v. City of N.Y.*, 2011 U.S. Dist. LEXIS 112818 (E.D.N.Y. Sept. 30, 2011); *Young v. State of N.Y.*, 649 F. Supp.2d 282 (S.D.N.Y. 2009)).

Evidence of personal involvement may consist of:

(1) the school official's direct participation in the unlawful act(s),

(2) his or her failure to take remedial action following receipt of information concerning unlawful conduct,

(3) actions creating or allowing the continuance of a policy or practice under which unconstitutional practices occur,

(4) his or her gross negligence in the supervision of alleged violators, or

(5) his or her deliberate indifference evidenced by a failure to act on information indicating unlawful acts (*Colon v. Coughlin*, 58 F.3d 865 (2d Cir. 1995); see also *Littlejohn v. City of N.Y.*, 795 F.3d 297 (2d Cir. 2015); *Sash v. United States*, 674 F.Supp.2d 531 (S.D.N.Y. 2009)).

There is a split among federal district courts in New York as to which of those five factors should be used to establish personal liability (*Raspardo v. Carlone*, 770 F.3d 97 (2d Cir. 2014); *LaMagna v. Brown*, 474 Fed. Appx. 788 (2d Cir. 2012)). Some courts have determined that only the first and third factors are viable (see *Firestone v. Berrios,* 2013 U.S. Dist. LEXIS 8535 (E.D.N.Y. 2013); *Bouche v. City of Mt. Vernon*, 2012 U.S. Dist. LEXIS 40246 (S.D.N.Y. Mar. 23, 2012)), while others have held that the viability of the second, fourth and fifth factors depends on the underlying constitutional claim (see *Carris v. First Student, Inc.*, 132 F. Supp. 3d 321 (N.D.N.Y. 2015); *Henrius v. Cnty. of Nassau*, 2016 U.S. Dist. LEXIS 43795 (E.D.N.Y. 2016); *McLennon v. The City of N.Y.*, 2016 U.S. Dist. LEXIS 35380 (E.D.N.Y. 2016)).

66:39. Are there any circumstances in which school officials have *absolute immunity* from section 1983 liability?

Yes. School officials, including board members have *absolute immunity* in connection with lawsuits arising out of their performance of legislative activities (*Bogan v. Scott-Harris*, 523 U.S. 44 (1998); see also *Schubert v. City of Rye*, 775 F.Supp.2d 689 (S.D.N.Y. 2011)). An example of a legislative activity undertaken by school boards concerns the abolishment of positions. The actual hiring or firing of a particular employee, however, does not entitle school officials to such immunity (*Bogan v. Scott-Harris*; see also *Harhay v. Town of Ellington Bd. of Educ.*, 323 F.3d 206 (2d Cir. 2003); *Ramirez v. Hempstead UFSD,* 2014 U.S. Dist. LEXIS 97391 (E.D.N.Y. 2014); *Ross v. Lichtenfeld*, 755 F.Supp.2d 467 (S.D.N.Y. 2010), *rev. on other grounds, Ross v. Breslin,* 693 F.3d 300 (2d. Cir. 2012)).

66:40. Are there any circumstances in which school officials have *qualified immunity* from being held individually liable under section 1983?

Yes. School board members and district employees enjoy *qualified immunity* that protects them from liability when their actions or their performance of "'discretionary functions'... do not violate a clearly established constitutional or statutory right of which a reasonable person would have known" (*Harlow v. Fitzgerald*, 457 U.S. 800 (1982); see also *Filarsky v. Delia*, 132 S. Ct. 1657 (2012), *reh'g denied,* 132 S. Ct. 1657; *Pearson v. Callahan*, 555 U.S. 223 (2009); *Davis v. Scherer*, 468 U.S. 183 (1984), *reh'g denied,* 468 U.S. 1226 (1984); *Coollick v. Hughes,* 699 F.3d 211 (2d Cir. 2012); *DT v. Somers CSD*, 588 F.Supp.2d 485 (S.D.N.Y. 2008), *aff'd,* 348 Fed. Appx. 697 (2d Cir. 2009); *Jackson v. Peekskill City Sch. Dist.,* 106 F. Supp.3d 420 (S.D.N.Y. 2015)).

When determining whether a constitutional right was "clearly established" at the time the alleged violation occurred, the U.S. Court of Appeals for the Second Circuit, with jurisdiction over New York, employs the following analysis:

- has the rule of law been defined with reasonable clarity,
- has the U.S. Supreme Court or the U.S. Court of Appeals for the Second Circuit affirmed the rule,
- would a reasonable defendant have understood that the conduct was unlawful (*Distiso v. Town of Wolcott*, 352 Fed. Appx. 478 (2d Cir. 2009); see also *Doninger v. Niehoff*, 642 F.3d 334 (2d Cir. 2011), *cert. denied*, 132 S.Ct. 499 (2011); *Young v. Cnty. of Fulton*, 160 F.3d 899 (2d Cir. 1998); *K.D. ex rel Duncan v. White Plains Sch. Dist.*, 921 F. Supp.2d 197 (S.D.N.Y. 2013)).

Private individuals performing work for governmental entities on a temporary or less than full-time basis may be entitled to qualified immunity in connection with their work for that entity, including a private attorney hired to investigate a governmental employee's potential wrongdoing (*Filarsky v. Delia)*.

66:41. How is it determined whether a school official is entitled to qualified immunity from section 1983 liability?

Whether or not a person is entitled to qualified immunity in a particular case depends on the answers to the following two-step inquiry:

First, has the plaintiff alleged a violation of a constitutional right?

Second, if yes, was that right "clearly established" at the time of the alleged violation of that right? (*Pearson v. Callahan*, 555 U.S. 223 (2009); *Taravella v. Town of Wolcott*, 599 F.3d 129 (2d Cir. 2010); see **66:40**).

A sequential order of the inquiry is usually appropriate, but is not mandatory. The order can depend on the particular circumstances of the case (*Pearson v. Callahan; Rathbun v. DiLorenzo*, 438 Fed. Appx. 48 (2d Cir. 2011); *Taravella v. Town of Wolcott*; *Distiso v. Town of Wolcott*, 352 Fed. Appx. 478 (2d Cir. 2009)).

Nonetheless, in cases where a right was clearly established, the Second Circuit conducts a third inquiry into whether it was objectively reasonable for the defendant to believe that his or her actions were lawful (*Nagel v. Marron*, 663 F.3d 100 (2d Cir. 2011); *Distiso v. Town of Wolcott*; *Higazy v. Templeton*, 505 F.3d 161 (2d Cir. 2007)).

66:42. Are there any specific theories of liability courts use to impose liability in a section 1983 lawsuit?

Yes. Courts use several separate and distinct theories of liability when adjudicating section 1983 lawsuits. As further discussed below, these include:

- Deliberate indifference to the federal constitutional and statutory rights of others (see **66:43**).
- The existence of a special relationship that imposes an affirmative duty of care and protection (see **66:45**).
- Violation of substantive due process rights (see **66:46**).
- The existence of a state-created danger (see **66:47**).

66:43. What are the basic elements of the deliberate indifference theory of liability in a section 1983 lawsuit?

Generally, *deliberate indifference* will be found both when governmental response to known discrimination is unreasonable in light of the known circumstances and when remedial action only follows after a lengthy and unjustified delay (*Hayut v. SUNY,* 352 F.3d 733 (2d Cir. 2003)). The viability of such claims will depend on the specific facts of each case (*Connick v. Thompson*, 131 S.Ct. 1350 (2011)).

Deliberate indifference can be established by the showing of:

- a continuing, widespread, persistent pattern of unconstitutional misconduct by government officials and employees;
- deliberate indifference to or tacit authorization of such conduct by policy-making officials following notice of the misconduct; and

- injury to the complaining party as a result of conduct undertaken pursuant to official policy or custom (*Johnson v. Newburgh Enlarged Sch. Dist*., 239 F.3d 246 (2d Cir. 2001); *Sauerhaft v. Bd. of Educ. of Hastings-on-Hudson UFSD*, 2009 U.S. Dist. LEXIS 46196 (S.D.N.Y. June 1, 2009) *aff'd*, 371 Fed. Appx. 231 (2d Cir. 2010)).

66:44. What are some examples of deliberate indifference cases?

Deliberate indifference cases have involved, for example, the failure to properly train staff (*City of Canton v. Harris*, 489 U.S. 378 (1989); *Mays v. City of Middletown*, 70 A.D.3d 900 (2d Dep't 2010); *Okin v. Village of Cornwall-on-Hudson*, 577 F.3d 415 (2d Cir. 2009); see also *T.E. v. Pine Bush CSD*, 58 F. Supp.3d 332 (2014)), in disregard of the rights of those with whom untrained employees come into contact (*Connick v. Thompson,* 131 S.Ct. 1350 (2011)). That would be the case, for example, where a governmental employer has actual or constructive notice that a particular omission in its training causes its employees to violate the rights of others, but continues to use the same training program (*Bd. of Comm'rs of Bryan Cnty. v. Brown*, 520 U.S. 397 (1997)).

Deliberate indifference cases also have included the failure to promptly investigate claims of harassment and institute corrective measures (*Sauerhaft v. Bd. of Educ. of Hastings-on-Hudson UFSD*, 2009 U.S. Dist. LEXIS 46196 (S.D.N.Y. June 1, 2009), *aff'd*, 371 Fed. Appx. 231 (2d Cir. 2010)), and to effectively address a hostile environment created by repeated incidents of harassment (*Zeno v. Pine Plains CSD*, 2009 U.S. Dist. LEXIS 42848 (S.D.N.Y. May 19, 2009), *aff'd,* 702 F.3d 655 (2d Cir. 2012); see also *DiStiso v. Cook,* 691 F.3d 226 (2d Cir. 2012); compare *Oliveras v. Saranac Lake CSD,* 2014 LEXIS 44603 (N.D.N.Y. 2014)). Deliberate indifference can be found, as well, in cases where school personnel fail to take reasonable steps to prevent bullying, and such inaction substantially restricts educational opportunities as a result of which a student with a disability is denied the right to a free appropriate public education under the Individuals with Disabilities Education Act (*T.K. v. N.Y. City Dep't of Educ*., 779 F. Supp.2d 289 (E.D.N.Y. 2011); see **54:22**).

Liability and Litigation

66:45. What are the basic elements of the special relationship theory of liability in a section 1983 lawsuit?

The *special relationship* theory of liability has been narrowly circumscribed to cases where the government has deprived individuals of their liberty and ability to defend themselves as in the case of prisoners and involuntarily institutionalized patients (*DeShaney v. Winnebago Cnty. Dep't of Soc. Servs*., 489 U.S. 189 (1989); *Stoneking v. Bradford Area Sch. Dist*., 856 F.2d 594 (3d Cir. 1988), *vacated sub nom. Smith v. Stoneking*, 489 U.S. 1062 (1989), *on remand*, 882 F.2d 720 (3d Cir. 1989), *cert. denied*, 493 U.S. 1044 (1990)). Thus, a special relationship is deemed to exist when a government entity does not normally have a duty to protect an individual, but its words, actions, or policies give rise to an affirmative duty to act (*DeShaney v. Winnebago Cnty. Dep't of Soc. Servs*.).

Federal circuit courts outside New York have refused to consider state compulsory education laws as placing students in the "functional custody" of school authorities with a concurrent affirmative duty to protect students from injury (*Armijo v. Wagon Mound Pub. Sch*., 159 F.3d 1253 (10th Cir. 1998); *Wright v. Lovin*, 32 F.3d 538 (11th Cir. 1994); *Walton v. Alexander*, 44 F.3d 1297 (5th Cir. 1995); *Doe v. Covington Cnty. Sch. Dist*., 675 F.3d 849 (5th Cir. 2012); *Stoneking v. Bradford Area Sch. Dist*.; see also *Davis v. Carter*, 555 F.3d 979 (11th Cir. 2009)).

Although the U.S. Court of Appeals for the Second Circuit, with jurisdiction over New York, has not addressed the issue, some federal district courts in New York have found a special relationship with students based on the state's compulsory education law (see, e.g., *Lichtler v. Cnty. of Orange*, 813 F. Supp. 1054 (S.D.N.Y. 1993); *Robert G. v. Newburgh City Sch. Dist*., 1990 U.S. Dist. LEXIS 91 (S.D.N.Y. Jan. 8, 1990); see also *Pagano v. Massapequa Pub. Schs*., 714 F. Supp. 641 (E.D.N.Y. 1989)).

Others have held that compulsory school attendance laws do not establish a special relationship giving rise to a constitutional duty to protect students against violence from other students (see *Drain v. Freeport UFSD*, 2015 U.S. Dist. LEXIS 28346 (E.D.N.Y. 2015); *P.W. v. Fairport CSD,* 927 F. Supp.2d 76 (W.D.N.Y. 2013); *Faccio v. Eggleston*, 2011 U.S. Dist. LEXIS 93649 (N.D.N.Y. Aug. 22, 2011); *Santucci v. Newark Valley Sch. Dist.*, 2005 U.S. Dist. LEXIS 26202 (N.D.N.Y. Oct. 24, 2005) and *Robertson v. Arlington CSD*, 31 IDELR 236 (S.D.N.Y. 2000), *aff'd,* 229 F.3d 1136 (2d Cir. 2000)).

66:46. What are the basic elements of the violation of substantive due process rights theory of liability in a section 1983 lawsuit?

Substantive due process protects individuals from arbitrary government action that deprives individuals of fundamental constitutional rights (*Washington v. Glucksberg*, 521 U.S. 702 (1997); *Wolff v. McDonnell*, 418 U.S. 539 (1974); see also *Smith v. Guilford Bd. of Educ.*, 226 Fed. Appx. 58 (2d Cir. 2007); *DeFabio v. East Hampton UFSD*, 658 F. Supp.2d 461 (E.D.N.Y. 2009)).

Courts have established a very high legal standard for establishing a violation of the right to substantive due process. Generally, it requires a showing of "egregious conduct which goes beyond merely 'offend[ing] some fastidious squeamishness or private sentimentalism' and can fairly be viewed as so 'brutal' and 'offensive to human dignity' as to shock the conscience" (*Smith v. Half Hollow Hills CSD*, 298 F.3d 168 (2d Cir. 2002); see also *Spring v. Allegany-Limestone CSD*, 138 F. Supp.3d 282 (W.D.N.Y. 2015); *P.W. v. Fairport CSD*, 927 F. Supp.2d 76 (W.D.N.Y. 2013); *Chambers v. North Rockland CSD*, 815 F. Supp.2d 753 (S.D.N.Y. 2011)). According to the U.S. Supreme Court this heightened standard "screens out" all but the most significant due process violations so that the Constitution is not "demoted to... a font of tort law" (*Cnty. of Sacramento v. Lewis*, 523 U.S. 847 n.8 (1998); see also *Perrin v. Canandaigua City Sch. Dist.*, 2008 U.S. Dist. LEXIS 95280 (W.D.N.Y. Nov. 21, 2008)).

66:47. What are the basic elements of the state created danger theory of liability in a section 1983 lawsuit?

Under the *state-created danger* theory, a school district could be held liable for injuries inflicted by a private individual if the district or its agents assisted in creating or increasing the danger to the victim (*Matican v. City of N.Y.*, 524 F.3d 151 (2d Cir.), *cert. denied*, 129 S. Ct. 636 (2008); see also *Spring v. Allegany-Limestone CSD*, 138 F. Supp.3d 282*; Campbell v. Brentwood UFSD,* 904 F. Supp.2d 275 (E.D.N.Y. 2012)). It also would apply in cases where a governmental employee's non-responsiveness to a situation communicates, even implicitly, that a private individual's actions causing injury to others is acceptable (see *Chambers v. North Rockland CSD*, 815 F. Supp.2d 753 (S.D.N.Y. 2011); see also *Pena v. DePrisco*, 432 F.3d 98 (2d Cir. 2005); *Spring v. Allegany-Limestone CSD; P.W. v. Fairport CSD,* 927 F.Supp. 2d 76 (W.D.N.Y. 2013)).

The state-created danger theory of liability would apply in cases where, for example, state actors:

- created a substantially dangerous environment,
- knew of the danger, and
- used state authority to create an opportunity that would not have otherwise existed for the injury to occur (*Armijo v. Wagon Mound Pub. Sch.*, 159 F.3d 1253 (10th Cir. 1998); *Johnson v. Dallas*, 38 F.3d 198 (5th Cir. 1994), *cert. denied*, 514 U.S. 1017 (1995); *Reed v. Gardner*, 986 F.2d 1122 (7th Cir.), *cert. denied*, 510 U.S. 947 (1993); but see *Shrum v. Kluk*, 249 F.3d 773 (8th Cir. 2001); *Doe v. Covington Cnty. Sch. Dist.*, 675 F.3d 849 (5th Cir. 2012)).

Applying this standard, a federal appellate court outside New York refused to dismiss a lawsuit against school officials who suspended and sent home alone, without notifying his parents, a special education student who had, to the officials' knowledge, voiced suicidal thoughts that same day and displayed depression in prior months (*Armijo v. Wagon Mound Pub. Sch.*; but see *Martin v. Shawano-Gresham Sch. Dist.*, 295 F.3d 701 (7th Cir.), *cert. denied,* 537 U.S. 1047 (2002)).

Even where there is no section 1983 liability, a student may have a claim against a school district if the district's negligence is the proximate cause of the student's injuries (see **66:14-21, 66:24-27**).

66:48. Can a school district be required to pay a prevailing party's attorneys' fees in a civil rights lawsuit?

Yes. A prevailing party in a civil rights lawsuit is entitled to have his or her attorneys' fees paid by the district (42 USC § 1988). According to the U.S Supreme Court, when a court enters a judgment on the merits in favor of a plaintiff or orders a consent decree (i.e., a court ordered settlement) that favors the plaintiff, the plaintiff is deemed a prevailing party (*Buckhannon Bd. & Care Home, Inc. v. W. Va. Dep't of Health & Human Res.*, 532 U.S. 598 (2001)). It is sufficient for the party to have obtained "at least some relief on the merits of [the] claim" (*Farrar v. Hobby*, 506 U.S. 103 (1992); see also *Spencer v. City of N.Y.*, 2013 U.S. Dist. LEXIS 161693 (S.D.N.Y. 2013)).

In contrast, a private settlement between parties, even if on terms favorable to the plaintiff, generally will not confer prevailing party status on the plaintiff, because such settlements are not judicially sanctioned (*Buckhannon Bd. & Care Home, Inc. v. W. Va. Dep't of Health & Human Res.*). Even so ordered stipulations of dismissal will be insufficient to confer prevailing party status if they do not require ongoing judicial monitoring to ensure compliance with the order (*Hugee v. Kimso Apartments, LLC*, 852 F. Supp.2d 281 (E.D.N.Y. 2012)). Similarly, attorneys' fees will not be awarded where a party achieves his or her desired outcome during the course of litigation because the lawsuit brought about a voluntarily change in the defendant's conduct (*Garcia v. Yonkers Sch. Dist.*, 561 F.3d 97 (2d Cir. 2009); *Buckhannon Bd. & Care Home, Inc. v. W. Va. Dep't of Health & Human Res.*), or when a party wins only the moral satisfaction of having a court conclude his or her rights were violated, with no award of either compensatory or punitive damages (*Degregorio v. Richmond Italian Pavilion, Inc.*, 90 A.D.3d 807 (2d Dep't 2011)).

According to the U.S. Court of Appeals for the Second Circuit, with jurisdiction over New York, a judgment on the merits or court-ordered consent decree are only examples of judicial action that convey prevailing party status. Other types of judicial action can support an award of attorneys' fees, "so long as the action carries with it sufficient judicial imprimatur." That would be the case where a trial court retains jurisdiction over a private settlement by including the terms of the settlement agreement in its dismissal order because the trial court's retention of jurisdiction would mean that a breach of the settlement agreement also would constitute a breach of the dismissal order (*Roberson v. Guiliani*, 346 F.3d 75 (2d Cir. 2003); see also *Perez v. Westchester Cnty. Dep't of Corr.*, 587 F.3d 143 (2d Cir. 2009)).

67. Defense and Indemnification

The School Attorney

67:1. Must school districts retain an attorney?

No. Although most school districts and boards of cooperative educational services (BOCES) retain counsel to provide legal advice to the school board and represent it in matters pending before the courts or administrative tribunals (*Yorktown CSD v. Yorktown Congress of Teachers*, 42 A.D.2d 422 (2d Dep't 1973)), there is no requirement that every district or BOCES retain counsel. Such a decision is within the discretion of the school board.

Some districts retain outside counsel for specific purposes, such as labor negotiations or disciplinary proceedings against tenured teachers; others appoint attorneys to handle any legal matters that arise. Some districts have attorneys on staff serving in this capacity. The specific function performed by school attorneys for a particular school district will vary depending on the needs of the district.

Outside attorneys are independent contractors who may be employed pursuant to a retainer agreement that is terminable at any time, or pursuant to a contract at a fixed salary, except that a school board cannot bind successor boards to a contract with an attorney (see *Harrison CSD v. Nyquist*, 59 A.D.2d 434 (3d Dep't 1977), *appeal denied*, 44 N.Y.2d 645 (1978)).

A school attorney may not simultaneously be an independent contractor and a school district or BOCES employee for the purpose of providing legal services to those entities. Whether a school attorney is deemed an independent contractor or employee depends on the factors set forth in the regulations of the New York State and Local Employee Retirement System (2 NYCRR Part 315). School attorneys who are not district or BOCES employees cannot be treated as such for purposes of compensation, remuneration, health insurance, pension, and other benefits and emoluments associated with employee status.

Districts and BOCES must file with the NYS Education Department (SED), the Office of the Comptroller, and the Attorney General a report that specifies:

- All the lawyers who provide legal services to them;
- Whether those lawyers were hired as employees; and
- All remuneration and compensation paid for legal services.

The report must be filed on or before the forty-fifth day after the commencement of their fiscal year (§§ 2050-54). For additional information and answers to frequently asked questions regarding school attorney reporting, see NYS Education Department, *Education Law Section 2053 Reporting* (updated Jan. 2012), at: http://www.p12.nysed.gov/mgtserv/2053/memo083110.html, or contact the Office of the New York State Attorney General at 212-416-8090.

Liability and Litigation

67:2. Is the employment of a school attorney subject to the competitive bidding process?

No. The appointment of a school attorney falls within the "professional services exception" to the competitive bidding requirements of the General Municipal Law (see **28:17**). Therefore, districts need not subject the selection of their attorney(s) to a bidding process (*People ex rel. Smith v. Flagg*, 17 N.Y. 584 (1858); *Appeal of Gootzeit*, 51 Ed Dept Rep, Dec. No. 16,338 (2012)). However, districts are required to adopt and follow internal policies and procedures governing procurement of professional services, such as those provided by a school attorney, "so as to assure the prudent and economical use of public moneys in the best interests of the taxpayers" (Gen. Mun. Law § 104-b; *Appeal of Gootzeit*; see also **28:17–18**).

Duty to Defend and Indemnify

67:3. Are school districts responsible for defending and indemnifying school board members and employees who are sued for negligence and other improper actions?

Yes. Section 3811 of the Education Law requires school districts (other than New York City) and boards of cooperative educational services (BOCES) to defend and indemnify any superintendent, principal, teacher, other member of the teaching and supervisory staff, non-instructional employee, any school board member, any member of the committee on special education (CSE) or subcommittee thereof, or any person appointed to serve as a surrogate parent on local CSEs, for all reasonable costs and expenses, including awards resulting from any action or proceeding against him or her arising out of the exercise of his or her powers or the performance of his or her duties (other than one brought by a school district or a criminal action brought against the individual) (*Matyas v. Bd. of Educ., Chenango Forks CSD*, 63 A.D.3d 1273 (3d Dep't 2009); *James v. Bd. of Educ., Marathon CSD,* 42 Misc.3d 1202(A) (Sup. Ct. Cortland Cnty. 2013); *Appeal of Carmand*, 54 Ed Dept Rep, Dec. No. 16,689 (2014); see also **67:8**).

A school board member who initiates litigation against individual fellow board members should not participate in the board's discussion and vote regarding whether to grant the sued board members' request for defense and indemnification (*Appeal of Laub*, 48 Ed Dept Rep 481 (2009)).

Any such costs and expenses must be approved pursuant to board resolution, which also authorizes the levying of a tax for such purpose (§ 3811). Section 3812 provides for inclusion of these costs in the next annual budget so that they may be assessed against the school district.

With respect to New York City, in general, section 2560 of the Education Law requires the New York City school district to provide legal representation and indemnification against claims to school board members, employees, members of CSEs, and authorized participants in school volunteer programs in the city, pursuant to section 50-k of the General Municipal Law (§ 2560; see **67:4** for exception).

In addition, section 3023 of the Education Law requires school boards and BOCES boards to indemnify and provide legal representation to teachers, practice or cadet teachers, members of the supervisory and administrative staff, other employees and authorized participants in volunteer programs against lawsuits for negligence, accidental bodily injury or property damage, provided those persons were performing their duties within the scope of employment or their authorized volunteer duties and under the direction of the board. Section 3023 also permits school boards to arrange for and maintain appropriate insurance with any appropriate insurance company or to self-insure to protect the district against the risk of claims under this section of law.

67:4. Are school districts responsible for defending and indemnifying teachers, supervisors and administrators who are sued for taking disciplinary action against students?

Yes, and also volunteers. Section 3028 of the Education Law requires all school boards and boards of cooperative educational services (BOCES) to provide an attorney and to pay the attorneys' fees and expenses incurred in the defense of teachers supervisors and administrators as well as authorized volunteers who are sued either in a civil or criminal action arising out of disciplinary action taken against any student of the district.

As with most indemnification provisions, the protection applies only if the individual was discharging his or her duties within the scope of employment or authorized volunteer duties when the disciplinary action took place (see, *e.g., Inglis v. Dundee CSD Bd. of Educ.*, 180 Misc.2d 156 (Sup. Ct. Yates Cnty. 1999); see also *Cromer v. City Sch. Dist. of Albany Bd. of Educ.*, 2002 N.Y. Misc. LEXIS 580 (N.Y. App. Term Apr. 5, 2002)). One state supreme court ruled a physical education teacher was acting within the scope of employment when he grabbed a student by his sweatshirt and led him to a doorway after he refused to follow the teacher's directions, and used his feet and legs to move the student after the student fell through the gym doorway. According to the court, the teacher was "disciplining a student while engaged in his employment as a physical education teacher and his actions were generally foreseeable" (*Cromer v. City Sch. Dist. of Albany Bd. of Educ.*).

A district's obligation extends only to charges arising out of disciplinary action by a teacher as determined by the actual facts underlying the incident giving rise to the allegations of teacher misconduct, (*Timmerman v. Bd. of Educ. of City Sch. Dist. of City of N.Y.*, 50 A.D.3d 592 (1st Dep't 2008); *Lamb v. Westmoreland CSD*, 143 A.D.2d 535 (4th Dep't 1988), *appeal denied*, 73 N.Y.2d 704 (1989); *Cutler v. Poughkeepsie City Sch. Dist.*, 73 A.D.2d 967 (2d Dep't 1980)).

The New York Court of Appeals has held that these same rights apply to employees' in New York City pursuant to section 3028 of the Education Law and are thus unaffected by section 2560 of the Education Law and section 50-k of the General Municipal Law's requirement that the actions not be "in violation of any rule or regulation" (*Sagel-Cotler v. Bd. of Educ. of the City of N.Y.*, 20 N.Y.3d 671 (2013)).

67:5. Are school districts responsible for defending teachers who use unauthorized corporal punishment?

Yes. The Board of Regents has strictly limited the circumstances under which teachers may legally use physical force against students (see **32:17, 52:17**). Therefore, the NYS Department of Financial Services (formerly the NYS Insurance Department) has indicated that insurance carriers may limit their coverage to damages arising out of the use of physical force as permitted by the Regents while not providing coverage for unauthorized corporal punishment. However, a school district's duty to provide a legal defense and/or pay attorneys' fees is not affected by the availability of liability insurance.

For additional information, contact the NYS Department of Financial Services, Office of General Counsel, at (800) 342-3736, or by e-mail at counsel@dfs.ny.gov.

Procedural Requirements

67:6. Are there any procedures that school board members and employees must comply with before a school district can defend and indemnify them?

Pursuant to section 3811 of the Education Law, the board member or employee must notify the board in writing of the commencement of the proceeding against him or her within five days after service of process. Failure to provide the required five days' notice would not necessarily result in the dismissal of a lawsuit by a school board member or employee seeking defense and indemnification from a school district if the district itself is otherwise aware of the board member's or employee's wish to have the district provide defense and indemnification (*Sharpe v. Strom*, 28 A.D.3d 777 (2d Dep't 2006)). Upon the timely receipt of notice of the commencement of a legal action or proceeding, the school board has 10 days within which to designate and appoint legal counsel to represent the individual. In the absence of such a designation and appointment, the individual may select his or her own counsel (§ 3811(1)).

In accordance with sections 3023 and 3028 (see **67:3–4**), the teacher or other employee or volunteer must deliver the original or a copy of the summons, complaint, process, notice or pleading to the board within 10 days of the time he or she was served with the summons, complaint, process, notice or pleading.

In addition, for these protections to apply, the individual must obtain a "certificate of good faith" either from an appropriate court or from the commissioner of education, which certifies that the individual appeared to have acted in good faith with respect to the exercise of his or her powers or the performance of duties (§ 3811(1); see *Appeal of Rivera*, 54 Ed Dept Rep, Dec. No. 16,768 (2015); *Appeal of Paladino,* 53 Ed Dept Rep, Dec. No. 16,594 (2014); *Appeal of Reis and Argus*, 51 Ed Dept Rep, Dec. No. 16,335 (2012); *Appeal of Nett*, 45 Ed Dept Rep 259 (2005)). Board members, for example, would not be entitled to a certificate of good faith to obtain reimbursement of legal expenses incurred in defending removal proceedings initiated against them by their school district. This is so because there is no authority or obligation under the law to defend and indemnify a board member or district employee in an action or proceeding brought against them by the district (§ 3811; see also *Reopening of the Application of the Bd. of Educ. of the Elmont UFSD*, 48 Ed Dept Rep 135 (2008)).

If a school board disputes the amount of costs claimed by an individual, it may be adjusted by the county judge in the county in which the district or any part of it is located (§ 3811(2)).

67:7. Are there any alternative provisions affecting a school district's responsibilities regarding indemnification and defense of school board members and district employees?

Yes. If a school board or board of cooperative educational services (BOCES) adopts a resolution as prescribed by section 18 of the Public Officers Law, board members, officers, and employees acting within the scope of their employment or duties may be covered by this statute. This coverage may supplant or supplement the protection provided under the Education Law, depending on the language of the resolution passed by the board (see *Scimeca v. Brentwood UFSD*, 140 A.D.3d 1174 (2d Dep't 2016); *Appeal of Carmand*, 54 Ed Dept Rep, Dec. No. 16,689 (2014); *Matter of Percy*, 31 Ed Dept Rep 199 (1991)). In order to supplement the Education Law protection, the resolution must do so explicitly (*Id.*).

Section 18 also requires the district or BOCES to pay for employees' legal defense costs and damages if the case is of the type covered by the statute, provided that the employee was acting within the scope of his or her duties when the allegedly wrongful act occurred (Pub. Off. Law § 18(3)(a); see also *Larson v. Cnty. of Seneca*, 22 Misc.3d 1118(A) (Sup. Ct. Ontario Cnty 2009)). Legal defense costs can include private counsel service (*Scimeca v. Brentwood UFSD*).

The employee must forward a copy of any summons or other court papers to the superintendent of schools or school attorney within 10 days after he or she is served in order to obtain protection under the statute, and must fully cooperate in his or her defense and in the defense of any action or proceeding against the district based upon the same act or omission (Pub. Off. Law § 18(5)).

Unlike the Education Law (see **67:6**), the Public Officers Law does not require the employee to obtain a good faith certificate to be protected under the statute. But like the Education Law (see **67:6**), a school official will not be entitled to defense and indemnification under section 18 of the Public Officers Law if the case was brought against him or her by the school board (*Matter of Barkan v. Roslyn UFSD*, 67 A.D.3d 61 (2d Dep't 2009)).

67:8. On what basis can a school district's decision to deny a request for defense and indemnification be set aside?

A school board's decision to deny defense and indemnification will be set aside only if it lacks a rational basis and is arbitrary and capricious (*Matyas v. Bd. of Educ., Chenango Forks CSD*, 63 A.D.3d 1273 (3d Dep't 2009)). According to one state appellate court, it was unreasonable for a school district to deny defense and indemnification to a teacher who was sued for assault by another teacher following an altercation between them during the grading of Regents exams. The "teacher in charge" placed the co-worker in a headlock when the co-worker threw water at him after being asked to sit down and continue grading exams. The district denied the request for defense and indemnification by the teacher in charge, on the basis that his participation in the altercation did not arise out of the exercise of his powers or the performance of his duties. The appellate court determined the district's denial of the request was unreasonable because the altercation occurred on school grounds while both teachers were grading Regents exams. Therefore, the altercation was not "wholly personal" (*Cotter v. Bd. of Educ. of Garden City UFSD*, 63 A.D.3d 1060 (2d Dep't 2009)). In comparison, another state appellate court sent back for a hearing a board's decision to deny a request for defense and indemnification. In that case, a teacher/coach was sued for malicious prosecution by a parent who was acquitted of criminal charges filed by the teacher following an altercation during a baseball game. There was a dispute between the district and the teacher as to whether the teacher initiated the charges without the district's support, which brought into question whether the district had a factual basis for denying the request (*Matyas*).

67:9. May an insurance carrier refuse to defend or indemnify a school district sued for "intentional" acts committed by its employees?

It depends on the nature of the claim, the type of insurance policy in effect, and the court that hears the claim. For example, in a case where a teacher allegedly engaged in sexual misconduct with students, an insurance company was still responsible for defending and indemnifying the district. The district's insurance policy contained an errors and omission provision that excluded from coverage "assault and battery" and "bodily injury and emotional distress." However, a state appellate court explained that although the teacher allegedly engaged in intentional sexual assaults on students, the district was sued based on its own allegedly negligent conduct in hiring the teacher and in failing to aggressively investigate complaints of sexual misconduct by the teacher (*Watkins Glen CSD v. Nat'l Union Fire Ins. Co.*, 286 A.D.2d 48 (2d Dep't 2001); see also *American Auto. Ins. Co. v. Security Income Planners & Co.*, 847 F. Supp.2d 454 (E.D.N.Y. 2012)).

In contrast, another state appellate court in a separate case ruled that "it is the nature of the underlying acts, not the theory of liability" that determines whether the insurance policy at issue requires the insurer to defend and indemnify the insured. Therefore, the insurance company was not responsible for defending and indemnifying a school district sued for negligent hiring, retention, and supervision of a teacher accused of assaulting and sexually abusing students. The allegations against the district stemmed from the underlying intentional acts of the teacher (*Sweet Home CSD v. Aetna Commercial Ins. Co.*, 263 A.D.2d 949 (4th Dep't 1999), *appeal withdrawn*, 94 N.Y.2d 915 (2000)).

For more information on school insurance, see **chapter 69**.

[illegible] defense and indemnification [illegible] who was sued for assault by another teacher following [illegible] between them [illegible] grading of [illegible] exams. The [illegible] placed the [illegible] after being asked to [illegible] and [illegible]. The [illegible] the request for defense and indemnification [illegible] the [illegible] of his [illegible] the [illegible] determined the [illegible] of the [illegible] was [illegible] school grounds while both teachers were [illegible] exams. Therefore, the [illegible] was not wholly personal [illegible] (N.Y. App. Div. [illegible] 2000). In [illegible] apologize immediately [illegible] defense and indemnification. In this case [illegible] was [illegible] of criminal [illegible] by the [illegible]. There was a dispute between the district and the [illegible] whether the [illegible] the district's support, which it ought into [illegible] for denying the request [illegible].

9. May an [illegible] district sued [illegible]

[illegible] the court [illegible] conduct [illegible] The [illegible] excluded from [illegible] However, [illegible] the district was [illegible] investigate [illegible] (N.Y. App. Div. [illegible])

[illegible] the nature of the [illegible] whether the [illegible] the insurance company was not responsible for [illegible] the [illegible] (N.Y. [illegible])

[illegible] see chapter 60.

Liability and Litigation

68. Employment Discrimination

Legal Framework

68:1. What constitutes employment discrimination?

Generally, employment discrimination consists of practices that impair employment opportunities and benefits for individuals who meet certain protected characteristics such as race, sex, or disability, in violation of federal and/or state law (see **68:2–5**), or are otherwise entitled to employment protection under specific laws (see **68:4**).

State law affords protection against employment discrimination not only to employees, but also to interns who perform work for the purpose of training under circumstances set out in law (N.Y. Exec. Law § 296-c).

68:2. What federal laws prohibit employment discrimination?

At the federal level several laws prohibit employment discrimination including, for example:

- *Title VII* of the Civil Rights Act of 1964 (42 USC § 2000e-2) prohibits all employers with 15 or more employees from discriminating in the hiring, firing, demotion or promotion of employees on the basis of race, color, sex, religion and national origin.

  It also forbids employers from retaliating against an employee or job applicant who makes a charge or who testifies, assists, or participates in a Title VII proceeding or investigation (42 USC § 2000e-2; 42 USC § 2000e-3; *Crawford v. Metropolitan Gov't of Nashville and Davidson Cnty.*, 555 U.S. 271 (2009); *McDonnell Douglas Corp. v. Green*, 411 U.S. 792 (1973); see also *Vega v. Hempstead UFSD*, 801 F.3d 72 (2d Cir. 2015); *Gordon v. N.Y. City Dep't of Educ.*, 232 F.3d 111 (2d Cir. 2000)).

  As amended by the *Pregnancy Discrimination Act* of 1978 (PDA) (42 USC § 2000e(k)), Title VII further prohibits discrimination in employment against pregnant women and requires that pregnant women be treated no differently than any other temporarily disabled employee (see *AT&T Corp. v. Hulteen*, 556 U.S. 701 (2009)). It protects, as well, the right of reinstatement of women on leave for reasons related to pregnancy (42 USC § 2000e(k)) and the right to accommodation of pregnancy-related conditions (*Young v. United Parcel Service, Inc.*, 135 S.Ct. 1338 (2015)). For more information on pregnancy discrimination, see Equal Employment Opportunity Commission, *Enforcement Guidance: Pregnancy Discrimination and Related Issues* (June 2015), at: https://www.eeoc.gov/laws/guidance/pregnancy_guidance.cfm.
- The *Age Discrimination in Employment Act* (ADEA) (29 USC § 621 *et seq.*) prohibits age discrimination in employment with respect to employees 40 years old or older. It applies also to former employees, even when they have signed a release of all claims against the employer if the release does not meet the specific requirements of the Older Workers Benefit Protection Act (OWBPA) (29 USC § 626(f); 29 CFR § 1625.23; *Oubre v. Entergy Operations, Inc.*, 522 U.S. 422 (1998); see also *Ridinger v. Dow Jones & Co., Inc.*, 651 F.3d 309 (2d Cir. 2011); *Hodge v. N.Y. College of Podiatric Med.*, 157 F.3d 164 (2d Cir. 1998); *Tung v. Texaco, Inc.*, 150 F.3d 206 (2d Cir. 1998)).

- *Section 504 of the Rehabilitation Act of 1973* (29 USC § 794 *et seq.*) prohibits the exclusion of otherwise qualified individuals with a disability from participation in or the benefits of, as well as discrimination under, any program or activity receiving federal financial assistance.
- The *Americans with Disabilities Act* (ADA) (42 USC § 12101 *et seq.*) prohibits discrimination on the basis of disability against qualified disabled individuals who can perform the essential functions of a position with or without reasonable accommodation in both private and public employment, public services, public accommodations, and telecommunications (*Thompson v. N.Y. City Dep't of Probation*, 348 Fed. Appx. 643 (2d Cir. 2009); see also *Noll v. Int'l Business Machines Corp.*, 787 F.3d 89 (2d Cir. 2015); *Scalera v. Electrograph Sys. Inc.*, 848 F.Supp.2d 352 (E.D.N.Y. 2012)). Employers must engage in an interactive process to determine whether the employee's disability can be reasonably accommodated (*Thompson v. N.Y. City Dep't of Probation; McBride v. Bic Consumer Prod. Mfg. Co., Inc.,* 583 F.3d 92 (2d Cir. 2009); *Brady v. Wal-Mart Stores Inc.*, 531 F.3d 127 (2d Cir. 2008); see also *Scalera v. Electrograph Sys. Inc.*), and employers are required to provide reasonable accommodations that do not impose an undue hardship on the employer (42 USC § 12111(9), (10)), because they require significant difficulty and expense (*Reilly v. Revlon, Inc.*, 620 F.Supp.2d 524 (S.D.N.Y. 2009)). While an accommodation must be effective, it does not have to be perfect or the accommodation strongly preferred by the employee (*Noll v. Int'l Business Machines Corp.*). See also U.S. Department of Justice, *ADA Update: A Primer for State and Local Governments* (June 2015), at: http://www.ada.gov/regs2010/titleII_2010/title_ii_primer.html; see also **30:11-12**).

In addition, both *Title VII* and the *ADA* prohibit "family responsibility discrimination" and hold employers liable for the disparate treatment of employees with caregiver responsibilities. According to a federal Equal Employment Opportunity Commission guidance document, characteristics such as sex, race, color or disability protected by Title VII and the ADA preclude discrimination against employees with caregiver responsibilities that include not only child care, but also caring for elder family members and relatives with disabilities (Equal Employment Opportunity Commission, *Enforcement Guidance: Unlawful Disparate Treatment of Workers with Caregiving Responsibilities,* (modified Feb. 2011), at: http://www.eeoc.gov/policy/docs/caregiving.html and *Employer Best Practices for Workers with Caregiving Responsibilities,* (modified Jan. 2011), at: http://www.eeoc.gov/policy/docs/caregiver-best-practices.html); see also *Back v. Hastings on Hudson UFSD*, 365 F.3d 107 (2d Cir. 2004); *Bell v. Prefix, Inc.,* 321 Fed. Appx. 423 (6th Cir. 2009)).

68:3. Can the denial of tenure be considered an "adverse employment action" under Title VII and other discrimination statutes?

Yes. This may be even in cases where the employee is offered an additional year of probationary employment in place of termination that normally accompanies a denial of tenure. According to a federal appellate court with jurisdiction over New York, "Extending an employment relationship by one year by itself may not qualify as an adverse employment action. But when coupled with the denial of tenure, it is assuredly an adverse employment action" (*Tolbert v. Smith*, 790 F.3d 427 (2d Cir. 2015); see also *Donnelly v. Greenburgh CSD No. 7*, 691 F.3d 134 (2d Cir. 2012); *Leibowitz v. Cornell Univ.*, 445 F.3d 586 (2d Cir. 2006)).

68:4. What state laws prohibit employment discrimination?

At the state level, several laws prohibit employment discrimination including, for example:

- The *Human Rights Law,* which prohibits discrimination in employment, and in compensation or in terms, conditions, or privileges of employment against individuals who meet characteristics similar to those in federal discrimination laws including race, sex, disability, and age, in addition to others such as predisposing genetic characteristics (Exec. Law § 296; see *Brentwood v. Kirkland*, 126 A.D.3d 898 (2d Dept. 2015)). It expands the federal discrimination laws in some ways, such as by extending protection to victims of domestic violence and prohibiting discrimination on the basis of sexual orientation (Exec. Law § 296). This prohibition requires, as well, that public employers afford spousal healthcare benefits to same sex spouses in a marriage lawfully entered into outside New York State (*Martinez v. Cnty. of Monroe*, 50 A.D.3d 189 (4th Dep't 2008), *lv. to appeal dismissed*, 10 N.Y.3d 856 (2008); see also *Lewis v. N.Y. State Dep't of Civ. Serv.*, 60 A.D.3d 216 (3d Dep't 2009), *aff'd, Godfrey v. Spano*, 13 N.Y.3d 358 (2009)). Similarly, the *Marriage-Equality Act* requires that marriages of same-sex and different sex couples be treated equally in all respects (Dom. Rel. §§ 10-a, 10-b). Pursuant to regulation, *unlawful discriminatory practices* include discrimination based on an individual's known relationship or association with a member of a protected category (9 NYCRR § 466.14). Claims alleging a violation of New York's Human Rights Law are resolved using the same legal principles applicable to federal discrimination claims under Title VII of the Civil Rights Act of 1964 (see *Mittl v. Rivera-Maldonado*, 100 N.Y.2d 326 (2003); see also *Torres v. Pisano*, 116 F.3d 625 (2d Cir. 1997), *cert. denied*, 522 U.S. 997 (1997); *Bell v. N.Y. State Div. of Human Rights*, 36 A.D.3d 1129 (3d Dep't 2007); *Curcio v. Roosevelt UFSD*, 283 F.R.D. 102 (E.D.N.Y 2012); *Desir v. Bd. of Co-op. Educ. Srvs., Nassau Cnty.*, 803 F.Supp.2d 168 (E.D.N.Y. 2011)).

- The *Corrections Law* makes it illegal to refuse to license or hire someone with a criminal record, absent a direct relationship between the criminal offense and the license or employment sought, or an unreasonable risk to property or the safety or welfare of specific individuals or the public (Corrections Law § 752). Whether such an unreasonable risk is posed depends on factors such as the time elapsed since the crime was committed, the seriousness of the offense and the duties and responsibilities of the position sought. But, there is a rebuttable presumption of rehabilitation for applicants with a certificate of relief from civil disabilities (Corrections Law § 753; *Matter of Arrocha v. Bd. of Educ. of the City of N.Y.*, 93 N.Y.2d 361 (1999); *Matter of Boatman v. N.Y. State Dep't of Educ.*, 72 A.D.3d 1467 (3d Dep't 2010); *Matter of Acosta v. N.Y. City Dep't of Educ.*, 62 A.D.3d 455 (1st Dep't 2009), *aff'd as modified*, 16 N.Y.3d 309 (2011); *Matter of El v. N.Y. City Dep't of Educ.*, 23 Misc.3d 1121(A) (Sup.Ct. New York Cnty. 2009); see **31:38**). That presumption does not establish a *prima facie* entitlement to a license or employment (*Dempsey v. N.Y. City Dept. of Educ.*, 25 N.Y.3d 291 (2015)).
- The *Whistle-blower Law* prohibits retaliation against employees who disclose to a governmental body information regarding a violation of a law, rule, or regulation that "creates and presents a substantial and specific danger to the public health or safety" or information "which the employee reasonably believes to be true and reasonably believes constitutes an improper governmental action" (Civ. Serv. Law § 75-b(1)(a)(iii), (2)(a)). By comparison, private sector employees may be fired for reporting possible violations of law, because the statute protecting them (Lab. Law § 740) applies only to reports of actual violations of law (*Bordell v. General Elec. Co.*, 88 N.Y.2d 869 (1996); see also **39:43**).
- The *Legal Activities Law* protects employees who engage in certain legal activities after work hours, such as consuming legal substances, recreational activities that do not involve compensation, and political activities (Lab. Law § 201-d), including membership in a union (*Muhitch v. St. Gregory the Great Roman Catholic Church & Sch.*, 239 A.D.2d 901 (4th Dep't 1997)), and off-duty political activity (*Fishman v. County of Nassau*, 2013 LEXIS 1339466 (E.D.N.Y. Apr. 2013); *Baker v. City of Elmira*, 271 A.D.2d 906 (3d Dep't 2000); *Richardson v. City of Saratoga Springs*, 246 A.D.2d 900 (3d Dep't 1998)). On the other hand, this law does not protect picketing after work hours in

front of a public agency's building to protest alleged waste of taxpayer money (*Kolb v. Camilleri*, 2008 U.S. Dist. LEXIS 59549 (W.D.N.Y. Aug. 1, 2008)). Dating and romantic relationships, including extramarital affairs between co-workers, do not fall within the protection of this law either (see *State v. Wal-Mart Stores*, 207 A.D.2d 150 (3d Dep't 1995); see also *Hudson v. Goldman*, 283 A.D.2d 246 (1st Dep't 2001); *Bilquin v. Roman Catholic Church*, 286 A.D.2d 409 (2d Dep't 2001); see also *McCavitt v. Swiss Reinsurance Am. Corp.*, 237 F.3d 166 (2d Cir. 2001)).

68:5. Does the State Human Rights Law prohibit discrimination on the basis of gender identity or the status of being transgender?

Yes. Prohibitions in the Human Rights Law against discrimination on the basis of sex also prohibit discrimination on the basis of gender identity or the status of being transgender (Exec. Law § 296). Pursuant to implementing regulations, *gender identity* refers to "having or being perceived as having a gender identity, self-image, appearance, behavior or expression whether or not that gender identity, self-image, appearance, behavior or expression is different from that traditionally associated with the sex assigned to that person at birth" (9 NYCRR § 466.13).

Similarly, the prohibition in the Human Rights Law against discrimination on the basis of disability extends to prohibit discrimination on the basis of *gender dysphoria* which is a recognized medical condition related to a person having a gender identity different from the sex assigned at birth (*Id.*).

68:6. Can employers be held liable for retaliating against employees who report discrimination in the workplace?

Yes. Title VII of the federal Civil Rights Act of 1964, for example, prohibits employers from discriminating or retaliating against any employee who (1) opposes an unlawful, discriminatory employment practice or (2) filed a charge, testified, assisted, or participated in any manner in an investigation, proceeding, or hearing under Title VII (42 U.S.C. § 2000e-3(a); *Crawford v. Metro. Gov't of Nashville and Davidson Cnty.*, 555 U.S. 271 (2009); *Hicks v. Baines*, 593 F.3d 159 (2d Cir. 2010)). That includes both employees who initiate or instigate a complaint, and those who answer questions relating to an employer's internal investigation and express their belief a fellow employee has engaged or is engaging in discriminatory behavior (*Crawford v. Metro. Gov't of Nashville and Davidson Cnty.*).

However, according to the U.S. Court of Appeals for the Second Circuit, with jurisdiction over New York, an employee who participated in an internal investigation that is not connected with a formal proceeding of the Equal Employment Opportunity Commission (EEOC) was not entitled to protection against retaliation under Title VII (*Townsend v. Benjamin Enterprises, Inc.*, 679 F.3d 41 (2d Cir. 2012); *see also, Littlejohn v. City of N.Y.*, 795 F.3d 297 (2d. Cir. 2015)). In so ruling, the Second Circuit expressly left open the question as to whether participation in an internal investigation begun after the filing of a formal charge with the EEOC would be protected (*Id.*)

State law also forbids employer retaliation against employees who oppose practices made unlawful by the New York State Human Rights Law (N.Y. Exec. Law § 296(7); *Torres v. Pisano*, 116 F.3d 625 (2d Cir. 1997), *cert. denied*, 522 U.S. 997 (1997); *VanDeWater v. Canandaigua Nat'l Bank*, 70 A.D.3d 1434 (4th Dep't 2010)).

68:7. What constitutes impermissible retaliation?

Impermissible retaliation includes adverse employment actions that affect the terms and conditions of employment (such as hiring, firing, failing to promote, reassignment with significantly different responsibilities, or a decision resulting in a significant change in benefits), or that is disadvantageous to the employee and could dissuade a reasonable worker from making or supporting a charge of employment discrimination including, but not limited to, harassment (*Burlington Indus., Inc. v. Ellerth*, 524 U.S. 742 (1998); *Crawford v. Metro. Gov't of Nashville and Davidson Cnty.*, 555 U.S. 271 (2009); *Kercado-Clymer v. City of Amsterdam*, 370 Fed. Appx. 238 (2d Cir. 2010); *Tepperwien v. Entergy Nuclear Operations, Inc.*, 606 F.Supp.2d 427 (S.D.N.Y. 2009), *aff'd*, 663 F.3d 556 (2d Cir. 2011); *Graham v. Elmira City Sch. Dist.*, 2011 U.S. Dist. LEXIS 76160 (W.D.N.Y. Jul. 14, 2011)). That was the case where a supervisor denied desk duty to an employee who made an allegation of sexual harassment, caused her to receive a counseling memorandum, and initiated disciplinary charges against her that led to loss of accrued vacation time (*Kercado-Clymer v. City of Amsterdam*). It also can be the case where a schedule change has a significant impact on a young mother with school-age children (*Burlington N. and Santa Fe Ry. Co. v. White*, 548 U.S. 53 (2006)). Retaliation against a third party could be actionable, depending upon the facts of the situation, such as when an employee was fired after a co-worker he was engaged to filed a sex-discrimination charge with the EEOC (*Thompson v. North American Stainless, LP*, 131 S. Ct. 863 (2011)).

To prove retaliation, an employee must show (1) they engaged in a protected activity known to the employer, (2) an adverse employment action (*Hicks v. Baines*, 593 F.3d 159 (2d Cir. 2010); *Richardson v. Comm'n on Human Rights and Opportunities*, 532 F.3d 114 (2d Cir. 2008); *McIntyre v. Longwood CSD*, 658 F.Supp.2d 400 (E.D.N.Y. 2009), *aff'd*, 380 Fed. Appx. 44 (2d Cir. 2010) and (3) was subjected to the adverse employment action because of his/her participation in the protected activity (but-for causation) (*Univ. of Texas Southwestern Med. Ctr. v. Nassar*, 133 S. Ct. 2517 (2013); *Cox v. Onondaga County Sheriff's Dept.*, 760 F.3d 139 (2d Cir. 2014); *Russo v. NYS Div. of Human Rights*, 137 A.D.3d 1600 (4th Dept. 2016); *Geras v. Hempstead UFSD*, 149 F. Supp. 3d 300 (E.D.N.Y. 2015); *Lotocky v. Elmira City Sch. Dist.*, 149 F. Supp. 3d 429 (W.D.N.Y 2015)).

68:8. What constitutes workplace harassment/hostile work environment?

Title VII prohibits conduct that has the purpose or effect of creating an intimidating, hostile, or offensive working environment. In order to establish a hostile work environment pursuant to Title VII, a plaintiff must produce evidence that the conduct (1) is objectively severe or pervasive; that it creates an environment that a reasonable person would find hostile or abusive; (2) creates an environment that the plaintiff perceives as hostile or abusive; and (3) creates such an environment due to the plaintiff's protected characteristics (*Robinson v. Harvard Prot. Servs.*, 495 F.App'x 140 (2d Cir. 2012); *Geras v. Hempstead UFSD*, 149 F. Supp. 3d 300 (E.D.N.Y. 2015); see also, *Rodriguez v. Westbury Public Schools*, 2015 U.S. Dist. LEXIS 95023 (E.D.N.Y 2015)).

In determining whether an environment is hostile or abusive, courts will review the totality of circumstances including the following factors: "(1) the frequency of the discriminatory conduct; (2) its severity; (3) whether the conduct was physically threatening or humiliating, or a mere offensive utterance; (4) whether the conduct unreasonably interfered with plaintiff's work; and (5) what psychological harm, if any, resulted." (*Richardson v. N.Y. State Dep't of Correction Serv.*, 180 F.3d 426 (2d. Cir. 1999).

68:9. Under what circumstances can a school district be held liable for workplace harassment?

A school district may be liable under Title VII of the Civil Rights Act for workplace harassment depending on the circumstances and in particular the status of the harasser. If the harasser is the victim's co-worker, the school district would be held liable only if it was negligent in controlling working conditions. However, if the harasser is a supervisor who is empowered to take tangible employment actions against the victim, the district will be vicariously liable. In this context, the U.S. Supreme Court has defined *supervisor* as an individual who can take actions against the victim that effect a significant change in employment status, such as hiring, firing, failing to promote, reassignment with significantly different responsibilities, or a decision causing a significant change in benefits (*Vance v. Ball State University*, 133 S. Ct. 2434 (2013)).

The U.S. Court of Appeals for the Second Circuit, which has jurisdiction over New York, has determined that the standard described above regarding harassment by a co-worker applies to workplace harassment by non-employees, depending on the nature and extent of control the employer may have over the conduct of the non-employees (*Summa v. Hofstra Univ.*, 708 F.3d 115 (2d Cir. 2013)).

68:10. Can individual employees be held personally liable for employment discrimination?

Sometimes. The United States Court of Appeals for the Second Circuit ruled, for example, that two employees could be held personally liable for their use of gender stereotypes in discriminating against a female employee who had young children in violation of the federal constitutional Equal Protection Clause (*Back v. Hastings on Hudson UFSD*, 365 F.3d 107 (2d Cir. 2004)).

On the other hand, the Second Circuit also has ruled that employees may not be held individually liable for acts of discrimination under Title VII of the Civil Rights Act of 1964 (*Kercado-Clymer v. City of Amsterdam*, 370 Fed. Appx. 238 (2d Cir. 2010); *Patterson v. Cnty. of Oneida*, 375 F.3d 206 (2d Cir. 2004); see *Tomka v. Seiler Corp.*, 66 F.3d 1295 (2d Cir. 1995); *abrogated on other grounds by Burlington Indus. Inc. v. Ellerth*, 524 U.S. 742 (1998); see also *Guerra v. James*, 421 Fed. Appx. 15 (2d Cir. 2011)).

Similarly, the Second Circuit has ruled that employees may not be held individually liable under the Americans with Disabilities Act (ADA) (42 USC § 12101 *et seq.*) including the ADA's retaliation provisions (see *Spiegel v. Schulman*, 604 F.3d 72 (2d Cir. 2010)) or the Age Discrimination in Employment Act (29 USC § 621 *et seq.*) because both laws preclude individual liability (*Darcy v. Lippman*, 356 Fed. Appx. 434 (2d Cir. 2009); see also *Davis v. N.Y.C. Dep't of Educ.*, 2012 U.S. Dist. LEXIS 5633 (E.D.N.Y. Jan. 18, 2012); *Quattrone v. Erie 2-Chautauqua-Cattaraugus BOCES*, 2011 U.S. Dist. LEXIS 118250 (W.D.N.Y. Oct. 13, 2011)).

In comparison, individual liability may be possible under the New York State Human Rights Law. Generally, employment discrimination and retaliation under that law are resolved the same as similar claims under Title VII (*Mittl v. Rivera-Maldonado*, 100 N.Y.2d 326 (2003); see also **68:4**). However, New York's Human Rights Law allows for the imposition of liability on individual employees if they also can be deemed an "employer" under that law (Exec. Law §§ 292(5), 296(1); see *Patrowich v. Chem. Bank*, 63 N.Y.2d 541 (1984); see also *Townsend v. Benjamin Enter., Inc.*, 679 F.3d 41 (2d Cir. 2012); *Alexander v. Westbury UFSD*, 829 F.Supp.2d 89 (E.D.N.Y. 2011), or if they aid-or-abet discriminatory practices (Exec. Law § 296(6); see *Feingold v. New York*, 366 F.3d 138 (2d Cir. 2004); see also *Geras v. Hempstead UFSD*, 149 F. Supp. 3d 300 (E.D.N.Y. 2015); *Frank v. Lawrence UFSD*, 688 F.Supp.2d 160 (E.D.N.Y. 2010)).

68:11. Can an employee waive the right to sue for employment discrimination in exchange for a severance package?

Yes. An employee can agree to waive the legal right to file a discrimination lawsuit in exchange for a severance package, but the waiver must be made knowingly and voluntarily.

Moreover, any time a current or former employee signs a release agreeing to waive the right to sue an employer for discrimination, the release must comply with applicable laws. For example, a release of claims against an employer for age discrimination must comply with the specific requirements of a federal law known as the Older Workers Benefit Protection Act (OWBPA) (29 USC § 626(f); 29 CFR

§ 1625.23; *Oubre v. Entergy Operations, Inc.*, 522 U.S. 422 (1998); see also *Aylaian v. Town of Huntington*, 459 Fed. Appx. 25 (2d Cir. 2012)). If a release under the OWBPA does not comply with specific requirements set forth in that law, then it may be invalid, and the employee may be able to sue the employer anyway.

One federal district court in New York ruled, in a case commenced under Title VII, that an employer may require an employee to execute a binding undertaking that requires the employee to pay back the employer (including possible interest) if the release is later ruled invalid (*Kristoferson v. Spunkmeyer, Inc.*, 965 F.Supp. 545 (S.D.N.Y. 1997)).

For more information on legal right waivers, see Equal Employment Opportunity Commission, *Understanding Waivers of Discrimination Claims in Employee Severance Agreements* (July 2009), at: http://www.eeoc.gov/policy/docs/qanda_severance-agreements.html.

Sexual Harassment

68:12. What is sexual harassment?

Sexual harassment is a form of sex discrimination or gender-based employment discrimination. It violates the following:

- Title VII of the federal Civil Rights Act of 1964, which prohibits employment discrimination on the basis of sex (42 USC § 2000e-2; *Meritor Sav. Bank, FSB v. Vinson*, 477 U.S. 57 (1986)).
- Title IX of the 1972 Educational Amendments (20 USC § 1681), which prohibits discrimination in educational programs and activities that receive federal funds (*Fitzgerald v. Barnstable Sch. Comm.*, 555 U.S. 246 (2009); *Davis v. Monroe Cnty. Bd. of Educ.*, 526 U.S. 629 (1999); *Franklin v. Gwinnett Cnty. Pub. Sch.*, 503 U.S. 60 (1992); *Bruneau v. South Kortright CSD*, 163 F.3d 749 (2d Cir. 1998), *cert. denied*, 526 U.S. 1145 (1999); see also *Romero v. City of N.Y.*, 839 F.Supp. 2d 588 (E.D.N.Y. 2012); *Pratt v. Indian River CSD*, 803 F.Supp.2d 135 (N.D.N.Y. 2011)). See also U.S. Department of Education, Office of Civil Rights, *Title IX Resource Guide* (April 2015), at: http://www2.ed.gov/about/offices/list/ocr/docs/dcl-title-ix-coordinators-guide-201504.pdf.
- New York's Human Rights Law, which prohibits discrimination in employment on the basis of certain immutable characteristics such as sex and sexual orientation (Exec. Law § 296; see **68:4**).

If the sexual harassment is so pervasive that it is calculated to drive someone out of the workplace, it also may be a constitutional violation (*Annis v. Cnty. of Westchester*, 36 F.3d 251 (2d Cir. 1994), *aff'd in part, vacated on other grounds*, 136 F.3d 239 (2d Cir. 1998)).

Men can be victims of sexual harassment by female supervisors (*Forte v. East Harlem Block Schs.*, 1994 U.S. Dist. LEXIS 7944, 65 Fair Empl. Prac. Case (BNA) 383 (S.D.N.Y. 1994); *Goering v. NYNEX Info. Resources Co.*, 209 A.D.2d 834 (3d Dep't 1994)). Sexual harassment directed at members of the same sex is also actionable (*Oncale v. Sundowner Offshore Servs., Inc.*, 523 U.S. 75 (1998); *Redd v. N.Y.S. Div. of Parole*, 678 F.3d 166 (2d Cir. 2012); see also *Eastport Assocs. Inc. v. N.Y. State Div. of Human Rights*, 71 A.D.3d 890 (2d Dep't 2010)).

Damages may be awarded under both state and federal law if the complainant produces testimony concerning hurt and humiliation derived from the acts of sex discrimination (*N.Y. State Dep't of Corr. Servs. v. State Div. of Human Rights*, 215 A.D.2d 908 (3d Dep't 1995); *Cornwell v. Robinson*, 23 F.3d 694 (2d Cir. 1994)). New York's Human Rights Law limits such awards to compensatory damages based on actual pecuniary loss and emotional injury. It does not allow damages that are punitive in nature (*NYS Div. of Human Rights v. Young Legends, Inc.*, 90 A.D.3d 1265 (3d Dep't 2011)).

Additional information concerning sexual harassment and discrimination in an educational setting is available from the U.S. Department of Education, Office for Civil Rights, at: http://www.ed.gov/about/offices/list/ocr/frontpage/faq/readingroom.html.

68:13. What are the characteristics of sexual harassment?

Sexual harassment consists of "unwelcome sexual advances, requests for sexual favors, and other verbal or physical conduct of a sexual nature" when submission to such conduct is explicitly or implicitly a term and condition of an individual's employment, submission to or rejection of the conduct by an individual is used as the basis for an employment decision affecting such individual, or the conduct unreasonably interferes with an individual's work performance by creating a hostile, intimidating, or offensive work environment (29 CFR § 1604.11(a)). The conduct need not be motivated by sexual desire to constitute sexual harassment, but it must be motivated by gender (*Kaytor v. Electric Boat Corp.*, 609 F.3d 537 (2d Cir. 2010)).

There are two types of sexual harassment: "quid pro quo" and "hostile environment" (*Meritor Sav. Bank, FSB v. Vinson*, 477 U.S. 57 (1986)).

Quid pro quo sexual harassment involves situations where an employee's submission to or rejection of unwelcome sexual conduct by a supervisor is used to determine that person's terms or conditions of employment (*Karibian v. Columbia Univ.*, 14 F.3d 773 (2d Cir. 1994), *cert. denied*, 512 U.S. 1213 (1994); see also *Alexander v. Westbury UFSD*, 829 F.Supp.2d 89 (E.D.N.Y. 2011); see also *Cajamarca v. Regal Entertainment Group*, 863 F.Supp.2d 237 (E.D.N.Y. (2012)), including a school board member (*Ragin v. Newburgh Enlarged City Sch. Dist.*, 2009 U.S. Dist. LEXIS 118704 (S.D.N.Y. Dec. 17, 2009)). Examples of this kind of sexual harassment would include being given or denied a raise, transfer, or being disciplined for refusing to accede to the sexual advances of a supervisor.

Hostile environment sexual harassment, on the other hand, can take many forms. Usually, it is a pattern of unwelcome sexual conduct sufficiently severe to interfere with an individual's performance or to create an intimidating, hostile, or offensive working environment. Examples of this would include repeated sexual remarks aimed at an individual who finds the remarks offensive, and "physical assault and sexual intimidation" such as unwelcome sexual touching and contact (see *Maher v. Alliance Mortg. Banking Corp.*, 650 F.Supp.2d 249 (E.D.N.Y. 2009)). As a general rule a few isolated incidents would not be sufficient to support a hostile environment sexual harassment claim. However, a single incident would be sufficient if it was extraordinarily severe, and so would separate incidents if they were sufficiently continuous and concerted so as to alter the work environment (*Clark Cnty. Sch. Dist. v. Breeden*, 532 U.S. 268 (2001); *Terry v. Ashcroft*, 336 F.3d 128 (2d Cir. 2003)). Courts will look at the totality of the circumstances, including the frequency and severity of the objectionable conduct, whether it is physically threatening or humiliating or merely an offensive utterance, and whether it unreasonably interferes with an employee's work performance (*Harris v. Forklift Sys. Inc.*, 510 U.S. 17 (1993); *Cristofaro v. Lake Shore CSD*, 473 Fed. Appx. 28 (2d Cir. 2012); *Redd v. New York Div. of Parole*, 678 F.3d 166 (2d Cir. 2012)).

To succeed in a sexual harassment lawsuit, it is not necessary for an employee to prove serious psychological harm, although it is relevant to whether the plaintiff actually found the environment abusive (*Harris v. Forklift Sys. Inc.*; see also *McRedmond v. Sutton Place Restaurant and Bar*, 95 A.D.3d 671 (1st Dep't 2012)).

68:14. Can employers be liable for failing to protect employees against sexual harassment in the workplace?

Yes. An employer, including a school district, may be held liable for the harassment of an employee by a supervisor with authority over the employee even if the employer did not know that the harassment was taking place (*Vance v. Ball State Univ.*, 133 S. Ct. 2434 (2013); *Burlington Indus. v. Ellerth*, 524 U.S. 742 (1998); *Faragher v. City of Boca Raton*, 524 U.S. 775 (1998); see also *Crawford v. Metro. Gov't of Nashville and Davidson Cnty.*, 555 U.S. 271 (2009)) including a school board member (*Ragin v. Newburgh Enlarged City Sch. Dist.*, 2009 U.S. Dist. LEXIS 118704 (S.D.N.Y. Dec. 17, 2009)).

However, an employer that has not taken any "tangible employment action" against the person complaining of the harassment can successfully defend itself by proving that it exercised reasonable care to prevent and promptly correct sexually harassing behavior and that the employee "unreasonably failed to take advantage of preventive or corrective opportunities provided by the employer or to otherwise avoid harm" (*Faragher v. City of Boca Raton*; see also *Crawford v. Metro. Gov't of Nashville and Davidson Cnty.; Gorzynski v. JetBlue Airways Corp.*, 596 F.3d 93 (2d Cir. 2010); *Alexander v. Westbury UFSD*, 829 F. Supp.2d 89 (E.D.N.Y. 2011); compare *Edwards v. City of Kingston*, 2010 U.S. Dist. LEXIS 98047 (N.D.N.Y. Sept. 20, 2010)). This defense is available also in "constructive discharge" cases, where an employee alleges that as a result of sexual harassment the workplace has become a hostile environment and is so intolerable that it is reasonable for the employee to involuntarily resign. The defense would not be available, however, if the supervisor precipitated the resignation by taking deliberate, formal, employer-sanctioned, adverse employment action against the employee (such as demoting the employee or drastically reducing her pay) (*Pennsylvania State Police v. Suders*, 542 U.S. 129 (2004)). It is not available either under the New York City Human Rights Law (*Zakrzewska v. New School*, 14 N.Y.3d 469 (2010)), or when a supervisor who engages in unlawful sexual harassment can be considered the employer's proxy or alter ego (*Townsend v. Benjamin Enters. Inc.*, 679 F.3d 41 (2d Cir. 2012)).

68:15. Can employers be held liable for failing to protect from sexual harassment employees who insist on keeping their complaint confidential?

It depends on whether the employer's decision to honor a request for confidentiality is reasonable under the circumstances. There may be a point at which harassing conduct could become so severe that a reasonable employer would be required to take action, despite an employee's request to the contrary (*Torres v. Pisano*, 116 F.3d 625 (2d Cir. 1997), *cert. denied*, 522 U.S. 997 (1997)).

68:16. What should a school district do to protect itself against claims of sexual harassment?

School districts should adopt comprehensive sexual harassment prevention programs that include the following elements:

- policies that condemn sexual harassment and which contain procedures for clearly and regularly communicating the district's strong disapproval of sexual misconduct;
- procedures for resolving complaints which encourage victims to come forward, and ensure their confidentiality and protect them against retaliation; and
- provisions for immediate and effective remedies.

Districts also should take appropriate disciplinary action against offenders, and provide ongoing and comprehensive training for district employees and students (see *Alexander v. Westbury UFSD*, 829 F.Supp.2d 89 (E.D.N.Y. 2011)).

In addition, school districts should be aware that Title IX of the 1972 Educational Amendments (20 USC § 1681) requires federal fund recipients not only to adopt a policy that condemns actions prohibited by the act, but also to appoint an employee responsible for ensuring compliance with Title IX (34 CFR § 106.8). This policy must be posted and disseminated to all students and employees, as well as to the parents of students (34 CFR § 106.9; *Gebser v. Lago Vista Indep. Sch. Dist.*, 524 U.S. 274 (1989)). Prior to adopting or revising a sexual harassment policy and procedures, school districts may have an obligation to negotiate certain aspects of the policy and procedures relating to employee discipline with employee organizations (unions), such as mandatory employee participation in investigatory interviews and the potential for disciplinary action against those who might admit harassing behavior (*Patchogue Medford UFSD*, 30 PERB ¶ 3041 (1997)).

Additional information on a school district's responsibility to provide students an educational environment free of sexual harassment is available from the U.S. Department of Education at: http://www2.ed.gov/about/offices/list/ocr/letters/colleague-201104.html (Apr. 4, 2011) and http://www2.ed.gov/about/offices/list/ocr/letters/colleague-201010.html (Oct. 26, 2010).

69. Insurance Protection

In General

69:1. Must a school board have insurance or other protection against damage to school property?

Yes. Section 1709(8) of the Education Law states that a school board must "insure the schoolhouses and their furniture, apparatus and appurtenances, and the school library. . . ." School districts may establish a liability and casualty reserve fund for self-insurance purposes (§ 1709(8-c); Gen. Mun. Law § 6-n; see **26:2, 26:5-6**).

69:2. What other types of insurance are commonly purchased by school boards to protect their districts?

Many school districts purchase what is known as special multi-peril insurance policies. These are package policies designed to provide a combination of property and general liability coverage. Other coverage often purchased by districts are floater policies to protect district property that is taken off school grounds; automobile coverage, which protects against vehicular accidents; and school board members' errors and omissions coverage, also known as school board legal liability coverage.

School districts also may purchase catastrophe-umbrella or excess policies to protect the district against large losses. The school district's administrative staff and insurance professionals can help the school board determine an adequate amount of coverage for the types of insurance they choose to purchase.

69:3. How much insurance should a school board maintain for its district?

There is no simple answer to this question that would be appropriate for all school districts given that the risks of liability differ among school districts depending on issues such as the number of students and employees, programs operated and other factors. A district may go many years without being sued, or face several lawsuits in a short span of time. In addition, the possible cost to a district of a lawsuit varies greatly, in part, depending upon the type of lawsuit and the damages the plaintiff is seeking. Predicting the outcome of multiple lawsuits is even more difficult. Therefore, school boards should examine closely the risks faced by their district and consult with their school attorney and professionals in the insurance field to determine appropriate coverage.

69:4. Do the legal requirements on competitive bidding apply to the purchase of school insurance?

No. It has been determined that insurance contracts are not "purchase contracts" within the meaning of Section 103 of the General Municipal Law and are exempt as professional services (*Lynd v. Heffernan*, 286 A.D. 597 (3d Dep't 1955); *Surdell v. Oswego*, 91 Misc.2d 1041 (Sup. Ct. Oswego Cnty. 1977); Opn. St. Comp. 61-233; see **28:17**).

However, the General Municipal Law requires that school districts adopt internal policies and procedures governing the procurement of professional services, such as insurance, so they are procured "in a manner so as to assure the prudent and economical use of public moneys in the best interests of the taxpayers" (Gen. Mun. Law § 104-b; see also Office of the State Comptroller, Division of Local Government and School

Liability and Litigation

Accountability, *Local Government Management Guide, Seeking Competition in Procurement* (July 2014), at: http://www.osc.state.ny.us/localgov/pubs/lgmg/seekingcompetition.pdf; see **28:18**).

69:5. How may a school board secure information on the reliability or financial status of an insurance company with whom it wishes to do business?

A school board can receive information that would be helpful in evaluating an insurance company by consulting an insurance reference such as Best's Key Rating Guide, or the NYS Department of Financial Services, Insurance Division, at 800-342-3736 or by mail One State Street, New York, N.Y. 10004-1511; or 1399 Franklin Avenue, Suite 203, Garden City, N.Y. 11530; or One Commerce Plaza, Albany, N.Y. 12257; or Walter Mahoney Office Building, 65 Court Street Room 7, Buffalo, N.Y. 14202; or 333 East Washington Street, Syracuse N.Y. 13202; or 28 Hill Street, Room 210, Oneonta, N.Y. 13820; or the website at http://www.dfs.ny.gov/insurance/dfs_insurance.htm.

69:6. May a school district act as a self-insurer for protection against claims?

Yes. A self-insurance fund may be established by any school district or board of cooperative educational services (BOCES) except one in a city with a population of 125,000 or more. This fund may be used to pay for almost any loss, claim, action or judgment for which the district is authorized or required to purchase or maintain insurance (Gen. Mun. Law § 6-n(1), (2)). The amount paid into such fund may not exceed the greater of $33,000, or 5 percent of the total district budget for the fiscal year (Gen. Mun. Law § 6-n(4); see **26:6**).

The law provides for oversight and regulation of municipal cooperative health insurance plans and self-funded health insurance consortia by the NYS Department of Financial Services (formerly the NYS Insurance Department) and provides legal and regulatory requirements, safeguards, and other conditions for the plans (Ins. Law Art. 47).

69:7. Are school districts permitted to arrange group insurance programs for district employees?

Yes. Sections 1604(31-a), 1709(34-a), and 2503(10-a) of the Education Law permit the establishment of group insurance programs applying to teachers and other employees on life insurance, accident and health insurance, medical and surgical benefits, and hospital benefits (see also Gen. Mun. Law § 92-a). These sections of the law make it permissible, at the discretion of the board, to pay all or part of the cost of group insurance for school employees.

For unionized employees, depending on the language of the collective bargaining agreement, most benefits cannot be changed without collective negotiations (*Genesee-Livingston-Steuben-Wyoming BOCES*, 29 PERB ¶ 3065 (1996), *conf'd*, 30 PERB ¶ 7009 (Sup. Ct. Livingston Cnty. 1997)).

69:8. Can school boards legally withhold funds for the payment of various group insurance programs from employees' salaries?

Yes. School boards have the legal right to withhold, at the written request of individual employees, a portion of their salaries to pay group insurance premiums (§§ 1604(31-a), 1709(34-a), 2503(10-a)).

69:9. Are school board members permitted to participate in school employee hospitalization and medical service plans?

Yes. Section 92-a(4) of the General Municipal Law permits school board members to participate in hospitalization and medical service plans, but they must pay the total cost for both themselves and their family members.

Retired school board members with at least 20 years of service in such a position are also eligible for these plans, as long as they pay the total cost (Gen. Mun. Law § 92-a(1-a)).

69:10. May a school board insure its students against personal accidents regardless of whether or not the district is responsible for the accident?

Yes. School boards may, at their discretion, purchase insurance against accidents to students occurring in school; on school grounds; during physical education classes; during intramural and interscholastic sports activities; while being transported between home and school in a school bus; and during school-sponsored trips. The premiums may be paid from district funds (§§ 1604(7-a), (7-b), 1709(8-a), (8-b)).

69:11. May a school require students to purchase insurance as a pre-requisite for participation in a school program?

No. Although school boards are authorized to insure students against injuries sustained while participating in school programs, they may not lawfully pass on to their students the cost of such insurance or require the students to purchase it themselves. In addition, a school board may not use its staff to solicit the purchase of insurance, because this is considered an unconstitutional use of public moneys, property, and services in aid of a private corporation (*Matter of Shapnek*, 3 Ed Dept Rep 99 (1963); *Matter of Countryman*, 1 Ed Dept Rep 538 (1960)).

69:12. Can a bidder on a school construction job be required to secure surety bonds from a particular insurance company or broker?

No. This would be a violation of section 2504(a)(1) of the New York State Insurance Law.

Workers' Compensation Insurance

69:13. Are school districts required to carry workers' compensation insurance?

Yes. School districts must provide workers' compensation coverage for all teachers and other employees for injuries incurred in the performance of their duties and must post notifications of said insurance or be subject to a fine (§§ 1604(31), 1709(34), 2503(10); Work. Comp. Law § 51). As a general matter, employees are entitled to compensation for their disability or death from injury "arising out of and in the course of the employment" (Work. Comp. Law § 10). However, they may not sue their employer for accidental injuries that arise out of and occur in the course of employment, including claims for damages caused by negligent supervision or hiring, negligent failure to institute and follow anti-discrimination policies, or negligently carrying out disciplinary action (see *Maas v. Cornell Univ.*, 253 A.D.2d 1 (3d Dep't), *aff'd*, 94 N.Y.2d 87 (1999)).

School districts may purchase workers' compensation policies as they would other types of insurance, self-insure by establishing a workers compensation reserve fund or participate in a group self-insurance plan (Gen. Mun. Law §§ 6-j, 119-o; see **26:6, 69:4**).

School districts may elect to cover employees unable to work because of an injury unrelated to their employment under the Disability Benefits Law (Work. Comp. Law § 212(2)).

School districts may not discharge employees for claiming or attempting to claim workers' compensation benefits. An employee who establishes he or she was terminated for such a reason would be entitled to reinstatement with lost compensation and the recovery of attorneys' fees. The employee may also be awarded predecision interest on the lost compensation (*Greenberg v. N.Y. City Trans. Auth. Workers' Compensation Bd.*, 7 N.Y.3d 139 (2006)).

69:14. Under what circumstances will an employee be entitled to workers' compensation benefits?

As a general matter, employees are entitled to workers' compensation benefits if they suffer an injury that arises out of and in the course of their employment (Work. Comp. Law § 10).

Some circumstances where employees have been deemed entitled to workers' compensation benefits have involved:

- Injuries sustained by an elementary school teacher volunteering as a stage hand in a high school play (*Walker v. Greene CSD*, 6 A.D.3d 965 (3d Dep't 2004)).
- Altercation between co-workers resulting in the death of an employee on a stairwell not part of the employer's premises, but where said altercation was "rooted in events . . . started at or about the premises of the employer" that were found to arise in the course of employment (*Rosen v. First Manhattan Bank*, 84 N.Y.2d 856 (1994)).
- Injuries that occur while the employee is on a "special errand" while traveling to or from work and home, and the employer encouraged the errand and obtained a benefit as a result of its performance (*Neacosia v. N.Y. Power Auth.*, 85 N.Y.2d 471 (1995); *Matter of Borgeat v. C & A Bakery*, 89 A.D.3d 1296 (3d Dep't 2011); *Dziedzic v. Orchard Park CSD*, 283 A.D.2d 878 (3d Dep't 2001)).
- Injuries sustained by an employee, who does not have a fixed worksite, in the course of travel between assigned work locations (*Bednarek v. Caring Professionals, Inc.*, 111 A.D.3d 997 (3d Dep't 2013)).

In contrast, a temporarily disabled employee was not entitled to workers' compensation benefits for lost or reduced benefits following his resignation and acceptance of another position at a reduced salary, where the employee resigned in response to denial of tenure rather than as a result of his disability (*Tawil v. Fallsburg CSD*, 106 A.D.3d 1314 (3d Dep't 2013)).

Unemployment Insurance

69:15. Are school districts required to provide unemployment insurance coverage?

Yes. All school districts must provide unemployment insurance coverage. The federal government requires that unemployment insurance be provided to all employees of state and local governments, including public school employees, in order for states to be in conformity with federal law (see 26 USC § 3304; *Cnty. of Los Angeles v. Marshall*, 442 F. Supp. 1186 (D.D.C. 1977), *aff'd*, 631 F.2d 767 (D.C. Cir.), *cert. denied*, 449 U.S. 837 (1980); Lab. Law §§ 512, 565).

Section 565(7) of the Labor Law indicates that any two or more school districts may form a joint account to pay unemployment insurance benefits, pursuant to the rules and regulations of the commissioner of labor. In addition, school districts and boards of cooperative educational services (BOCES), along with other municipal corporations, are specifically authorized to establish reserve funds for unemployment insurance payments (Gen. Mun. Law § 6-m; see **26:6**).

Additionally, there are other special rules related to state and local governments regarding their responsibilities under the Federal Unemployment Tax Act. For example, state and local governments are specifically granted the option to pay on the reimbursement method instead of being subject to federal unemployment payroll tax (26 USC § 3309(a)(2); see Lab. Law § 565(4), (5)). Thus, districts only pay for the actual benefits sent to former employees, rather than the administrative costs of the program.

69:16. Are there circumstances under which school district employees are not eligible for unemployment benefits?

Yes. For instance, school district employees generally are not entitled to unemployment insurance benefits if they voluntarily resign from employment without good cause. That was the case where a teacher who was advised her program was being discontinued resigned in anticipation of discharge. The teacher had enough seniority to "bump" (see **36:10**) another employee and had been told she would be transferred to a new position. According to a state appellate court, her failure to make an effort to remain employed disqualified her from receiving unemployment benefits (*In the Matter of Ruggiero v. Comm'r of Labor*, 63 A.D.3d 1477 (3d Dep't 2009)).

In addition, school district employees generally are not entitled to unemployment benefits for periods between academic years or terms if they have a contract or a "reasonable assurance" that they will perform services in such capacity for both such academic years or terms. (Lab. Law § 590(10), (11); *Matter of Bicjan (N.Y. City Bd. of Educ.—Comm'r of Labor)*, 219 A.D.2d 751 (3d Dep't 1995); see also *Matter of Ganster* (*Comm'r of Labor*), 111 A.D.3d 1014 (3d Dep't 2013); *Matter of Breton* (*Comm'r of Labor*), 30 A.D.3d 661 (3d Dep't 2006); *Matter of Hammond* (*Comm'r of Labor*), 252 A.D.2d 638 (3d Dep't 1998)). Similarly, a school district employee is generally not entitled to unemployment benefits for any vacation period or holiday recess periods provided that he/she performed services for the district immediately before such vacation or holiday recess period and there is a reasonable assurance that the employee will perform services in the period immediately following the vacation or holiday recess period (*Scott v. South Colonie CSD*, 25 A.D.3d 939 (3d Dep't 2006)). Individual notices in combination with a collective bargaining agreement have been deemed to constitute such a contract (*Matter of La Mountain* (*Westport CSD—Ross*), 51 N.Y.2d 318 (1980)). Monetarily speaking, a reasonable assurance means an employee will earn at least 90 percent of the prior year's earnings (*Matter of Moss* (*Greece CSD—Comm'r of Labor*), 9 A.D.3d 753 (3d Dep't 2004)).

Similarly, school employees who work 10 months but are paid over 12 months and who are laid off after the end of the school year do not qualify for unemployment benefits until the expiration of the twelfth month, as they are not totally unemployed over the summer months (*Matter of Summers* (*N.Y. City Dept. of Educ.—Comm'r of Labor*), 21 A.D.3d 669 (3d Dep't 2005)).

69:17. Can misconduct disqualify a school district employee from unemployment benefits?

Yes. The unemployment insurance law expressly disqualifies from unemployment insurance benefits those individuals who find themselves unemployed because of "misconduct in connection with [their] employment" (Lab. Law § 593 (3)). Accordingly, employees dismissed for "unprofessional and discourteous conduct, which is detrimental to the interest of an employer" engage in misconduct that disqualifies them from receiving unemployment insurance benefits. That was the case where a computer technology teacher was deemed to have acted rudely and unprofessionally at a meeting with her mentor and a student's parents, after having been warned about similar behavior on a prior occasion and its consequences (*Matter of Moore* (*Comm'r of Labor*), 49 A.D.3d 1124 (3d Dep't 2008)).

Furthermore, in a case involving a teacher who was suspended without pay after a section 3020-a proceeding (see **chapter 38**), a state appellate court ruled that the teacher's behavior underlying the suspension rose to the level of disqualifying misconduct. In that case, the teacher made inappropriate demeaning and sarcastic comments to students, and sent unprofessional emails to staff and parents. He also showed a violent movie to his class without obtaining parental consent, and confiscated a student's cell phone and impersonated her to learn what others thought of him (*Brown v. Erie 2 Chautauqua-Cattaraugus BOCES*, 133 A.D.3d 1146 (3d Dep't 2015).

69:18. Are substitute teachers entitled to unemployment benefits?

They may be. Courts have found certain substitute teachers qualify for unemployment benefits.

For example, a substitute teacher who continued to receive periodic employment from a district but still applied for unemployment benefits on the days of the week she did not work was entitled to unemployment payments because she had the requisite number of "effective days" of total unemployment (see *Matter of Taylor* (*Naples CSD—Comm'r of Labor*)*,* 25 A.D.3d 892 (3d Dep't 2006)). A substitute teacher who had been unable to work due to an injury until the week before the winter break was entitled to unemployment benefits for that period as she did not work immediately before the vacation period and thus was not disqualified from receiving benefits under Labor Law section 590(10) (see *Matter of Scott* (*Comm'r of Labor*)*,* 25 A.D.3d 939 (3d Dep't 2006)).

However, a per-diem substitute teacher who received a letter indicating that her employment for the upcoming school year would be similar to that of the school year just ending when she worked for 127 days was not entitled to unemployment insurance. According to a state appellate court, the district letter provided her with a reasonable assurance of continued employment (*Matter of Cortorreal* (*N.Y. City Dept. of Educ.*), 32 A.D.3d 1126 (2006); see also *Matter of Murphy* (*Comm'r of Labor*), 85 A.D.3d 1478 (3d Dep't 2011); *Matter of Schwartz* (*N.Y. City Dept of Educ.—Comm'r of Labor*), 68 A.D.3d 1323 (3d Dep't 2009)). In comparison, a substitute teacher claiming he did not receive a letter advising him the district was retaining his services and requesting his response was granted unemployment benefits. The district sent the letter to his parents' house where he had not lived for some time, his parents never forwarded the letter, and the district did not register him with the substitute service (*Matter of Lincoln* (*Holley CSD—Comm'r of Labor*)*,* 66 A.D.3d 1259 (3d Dep't 2009)).

69:19. Are employees who resign entitled to unemployment benefits?

It depends on whether the employee had good cause for resigning. That did not happen, for example, where a teacher resigned after allegedly being verbally harassed and physically threatened by students. According to a state appellate court, fear for one's safety does not constitute good cause for resigning absent evidence that remaining on the job would place the employee in actual jeopardy. In addition, school officials in that case had been responsive to the teacher's concerns and taken disciplinary action against the students involved in the incidents the teacher actually reported (*Matter of Viera* (*City Sch. Dist. of the City of N.Y.—Comm'r of Labor*), 48 A.D.3d 870 (3d Dep't 2008)).

Individuals who resign for compelling family reasons also are eligible for unemployment insurance benefits. A compelling family reason includes, for example:

- Verified domestic violence that causes the individual to reasonably believe their continued employment would jeopardize his or her safety or that of an immediate family member.
- Illness or disability of an immediate family member requiring care for a period longer than the employer is willing to grant leave.
- Relocation due to a change in a spouse's employment to a location from which it is impractical to commute (Lab. Law § 593(1)).

69:20. Are part-time workers entitled to unemployment benefits?

It depends. Part-time workers are eligible for unemployment benefits if they worked part-time for the majority of the time during their base period and are available to work a corresponding number of hours in new employment. They may not be denied unemployment benefits solely because they are seeking part-time work (Lab. Law § 596(5)).

69:21. If a district employee who was terminated and received unemployment benefits is subsequently reinstated with back pay by order of the commissioner of education or a court, can a district deduct unemployment payments from the employee's paycheck?

No. A district may not recoup monies paid by deducting unemployment payments from an employee's paycheck even where the district has paid the unemployment tax directly to the state Labor Department's Unemployment Insurance Division on behalf of the employee (*Appeal of Lessing*, 35 Ed Dept Rep 116 (1995)). Any repayment obligation that the employee may have is to the State Labor Department (*Id.*; Lab. Law § 597(4)).

Index

Index

Index

Index

E

Index

Index

Index

Index